ISBN 978-0-428-78291-7
PIBN 10782173

This book is a reproduction of an important historical work. Forgotten Books uses
state-of-the-art technology to digitally reconstruct the work, preserving the original format
whilst repairing imperfections present in the aged copy. In rare cases, an imperfection in
the original, such as a blemish or missing page, may be replicated in our edition. We do,
however, repair the vast majority of imperfections successfully; any imperfections that
remain are intentionally left to preserve the state of such historical works.

THE
Gentleman's Magazine:
OR,
Monthly Intelligencer.

For the YEAR 1733.

CONTAINING,

I. Proceedings and Debates in PARLIAMENT.

II. ESSAYS *Controverfial, Humorous,* and *Satirical; Religious, Moral,* and *Political:* Collected chiefly from the *Public Papers.*

III. Select Pieces of POETRY.

IV. A fuccinct Account of the moft *remarkable Tranfactions* Foreign and Domeftick.

V. *Births, Marriages, Deaths, Promotions,* and *Bankrupts.*

VI. The Prices of *Goods* and Stocks, and Bill of *Mortality.*

VII. A Regifter of Books.

With proper INDEXES.

VOL. III.

By SYLVANUS URBAN, Gent.

Prodeffe & delectare.   *E Pluribus Unum.*

LONDON:
Printed, and fold at St *John's Gate,* by *F. Jefferies* in *Ludgate-ftreet,* and moft Bookfellers.

TO

Sylvanus Urban, *Author of the* Gentleman's Magazine.

Urban, accept this tribute of my lays;
Which to thy worth a stranger poet pays,
Pleas'd and improv'd, 'tis grateful to confess
Thy high desert, and hail thy known success.
Still may'st thou triumph foremost in re-
    nown!
May added laurels still thy temples crown!
There shall they flourish, ever fresh and
    green,
Snatch'd at by rivals, and with envy seen.
  Malice in vain her monthly venom spits;
And weekly pedants club their frothy wits:
Vainly in different forms they hope success,
And fruitless schemes their feeble force con-
    fess.
So when the angry viper bit the file,
It broke his teeth, and mock'd his foolish toil.
  · * E'en that preposť'rous candidate for fame
As well in merit female as in name;
Of size prodigious, of discernment small;
Who for an author's sense transcrib'd him all;
Soon disappearing gave this lesson forth,
That bulk is not the certain test of worth.
So * * *'s work we strive in vain to find,
While * * * * lives historian of mankind.
  Urban, Go on; thy honest task pursue;
With pleasing wonder we the labour view,
Thy painful steps thro' ev'ry month we trace;
A just abridgment, not a common-place.
Sense rises thick in ev'ry crouded page,
And various subjects various tastes engage.
  When Caleb mingles eloquence and zeal,
And seems in travail for the common-weal;
Whether his own, or publick good's his aim,
Whether a patriot or seditious flame
Works his high blood, or forms his deep de-
    signs,
His labours live in thy judicious lines.
  When Fog deals out for arguments his
    jeers,
Still baffling reason with ill-natur'd sheers,

We see his meaning thro' his dark disguise;
Thy work presents him perfect to our eyes.
  These are the daring heroes, who engage
With courts and pow'r, and war eternal wage.
With these as warm antagonists contend;
Each to his country as profess'd a friend.
  Arm'd cap-a-pee, see! Osborne leads the
    van;
His lofty air distinguishes the man!
In mood and figure, lo! he lays about,
Advances slowly, but is always stout.
  There little Walsingham the centre keeps,
Or to the right or left he nimbly leaps;
Active to shift, and parry off the blow,
He pours out keen invectives on the foe. ·
  Behind steps careful on the Courantier,
Defends the baggage, and brings up the rear.
Marodes in parties, lies in ambuscade,
And all that straggles is his plunder made.
Their various arts of war, and weapons
    keen,
Are well recorded in thy Magazine,
  But all have not for politicks a taste;
(For every genius has a diff'rent cast)
Heedless of courts and camps, some gravely
    say,
Shew us to heav'n the nearest, plainest way;
Point out distinctly all the rocks and shelves,
On which mankind are apt to wreck them-
    selves;
To these the Miscellany lends his hand,
A willing pilot to the promis'd land.
  Others confess a more scholastick turn,
And sterling sense from drossy would discern.
Lo! Bavius tells what will the standard bear,
What Authors frothy and pedantic are:
Candid by intervals, his rules are good;
But rivals put him into furious mood:
Then he roars out of pirates! Magazines!
Heav'ns! no Law 'gainst such pestif'rous
    fiends!

The *Auditor* old *Bickerstaff* revives
Good his design, and honestly he strives
To yield his readers rational delight.
May they his modest industry requite !
The young *Spectator* too, with studious
   care,
Weekly provides, and dishes out his fare:
Tales, humour, morals, modes, intrigues,
   and wit,
To suit all tempers, and both sexes fit.
Here might I say the catalogue pursue ;
And give the *Weekly Register* its due ;
The *Corn-cutter*, and *What d'ye call it*, names
To cripple verse, and quench a poet's flames:
But by thy choice their merit will appear:
Perhaps they fill a column in a year.
Now we behold how senators debate ;
And from their freedom learn our happy
   state.

If country Wits in narrow districts shine,
Their labours charm the world, transfus'd in
   thine.
Nor can the prints monopolize thy page,
The correspondent muse exerts her rage:
Beauties original augment thy store ;
And copied thence shall honour thee the
   more :
These thy materials, *Urban*, and with these
Thy furnish'd MAGAZINE shall ever please,
Their choicest thoughts in comely dress ar-
   ray'd,
By thousands read, to other realms convey'd,
(The richest merchandize for foreign climes)
And safely handed down to future times,
Wherever learning spreads shall yield de-
   light ;
And grateful Worlds in thy just praise unite.
              M. B.

On seeing the following *Caveat* written by an *Irish* Father Inquisitor on the first
  Leaf of some Volumes of Mr *Addison's Guardians* and the *Gentleman's Magazine*,
  which had been seized among the Books of an *English* Merchant, and detained
  six Months in the *Spanish* Inquisition.

N. B. *This whole work is to be cautiously read, being written* (in the latter
    compiled) *by a condemned Author.*

PRinces and priests, by int'rest join'd,
   To raise themselves, enslave mankind:
One shakes the sword, and t'other spreads
'Thro' all the soul a thousand dreads.
The church confirms the monarch's right ;
And for their mother monarchs fight.
   This once in *Britain* was the scene ;
And dulness made those days serene ;
Dulness, ordain'd the strong support
Of her two seats, the church and court !
In solemn *Spain* who dares oppose
Or pope or king, in verse, or prose ?
   But *Britain* now rejects the chains ;
And reason here securely reigns.
'Twixt truth and falshood taught the odds
No more we worship mortal Gods.
'Tis ours, religion to divide
From bugbear schemes, and priestly pride;
To bound the sov'reigns rightful sway ;
Assert our freedom, yet obey.
Shall we confine to names or blood
An office rais'd for publick good ?
Or close our eyes against the light,
And hire a guide to lead us right ?

How feeble seems the Jesuit's rage,
Who thus condemns this free-born page ;
Where *English* sentiments are drest,
Warm as they flow from ev'ry breast !
How low the race ! how dull the beast
Rid by this grave *Bœotian* priest !
Each genuin *Briton* smiles disdain,
Blesses himself, and pities *Spain*.
   There live, unworthy of thy clime !
Thy country's scandal and her crime !
Nor ever taste that freedom more,
Which gilds *Hibernia's* happy shore !
O never feel, thou lost to thought !
What godlike *Addison* has taught.
Exil'd, enslav'd, despis'd, asham'd,
Live long a priest, then die unnam'd ?
   URBAN, thy labours shall proceed,
Till servile *Spaniards* dare to read.
To grov'lling minds shalt thou dispense
True patriot warmth, and manly sense.
On bigot realms shall reason smile ;
And souls unfetter'd bless this isle :
E'en distant climes shall, with delight,
Behold how *Britons* think and write.

*We are too sensible of imperfections, to assume to ourselves what is so largely advanced
in the above pieces to our praise, but as we could not leave out those poetical heightenings,
which otherwise we ought not in modesty to have let pass, without spoiling the lines ; so
we can most truely affirm, that our endeavours have been received in such a favourable
manner, as to produce a great many letters of acknowledgment, in which our good-natur'd
correspondents have express'd themselves in a manner little short of the real meaning of these
poems ; and we may add, that they have also inform'd us of certain practices made use of
to our prejudice, which they condemn with the utmost indignation.*

The Gentleman's Magazine:

St John's Gate.

Lond.Gazette
Londo Jour.
Fog's Journ.
Applebee's ::
Read's : : : :
Craftsman
U: Spectator
Grubstreet J
W. lp Register
Free: Briton
Hyp: Doctor
Daily Court
Daily:: Post
Dai. Journal
Da. Post-boy
D. Advertiser
St James' Ev.
Whitehall Ev
Lond. Ev. Es
Weekly Mif:
Corn cutter's J.
Gen. Ev. Post

York 2 News
Dublin 6 :::
Edinburgh 2
Bristol :::
Norwich 2::
Exeter 2 :::
Worcester :
Northampton
Gloucester::
Stamford :::
Nottingham
Bury Poun.
Chester ditto
Derby ditto
Ipswich do.
Reading do.
Leeds Merc
Newcastle2
Canterbury
Boston :::: ¶
Jamaica, &c.
Barbados ::

Or, MONTHLY INTELLIGENCER

For JANUARY 1733.

CONTAINING,

/more in Quantity, and greater Variety, than any Book of the Kind and Price./

I. A VIEW of the WEEKLY ESSAYS; *viz.* Origin of the *Grubs*, Scheme &c. of the *Auditor*, and the *Weekly Miscellany*: Of Beauty, Action, being Toasts, and Profusion; Petition for and against *Sunday*; of a new Opera, Man, Pride, Jealousy, Religion, Morality, Antiquity, Pyrrhonism, the *Dutch* Spectator, &c.

II. POLITICAL POINTS. Mr P---y against The *Salt* Tax; on standing Armies, Sir R. W.'s Genuine Speech. Of Tyranny, Free-Governments, Navy and Militia; the *Craftsman* a Prophet; of Tests, Civil Power in Religion; Excises, Necessity and Corruption; Sugar Trade, and Taxes; Frauds in Wine and Tobacco; Public Wisdom and Improvements.

III. POETRY. Verses to Dean *Swift*; the Laureat's Ode, with Criticisms; Ode on Sickness and Death; Advice to *Sally*, her Answer; an Excise Ballad; on a late Duel; Epigrams, &c.

IV. OCCURRENCES FOREIGN and DOMESTIC. King's Speech, Deaths, Promotions, Sheriffs, Prices of Goods, &c.

V. Instructions to a Member of Parliamt.

VI. REGISTER of Books.

VII. Table of CONTENTS.

The SECOND EDITION.

By *SYLVANUS URBAN*, Gent.

LONDON: Printed, and sold at St *John's* Gate: By F. ....., in *Lud.... ....reet*, all othe

CONTENTS.

THE
Gentleman's Magazine:
JANUARY, 1733.

A View of the Weekly DISPUTES *and* ESSAYS *in this Month.*

London Journal Dec. 30. No. 705.
[Omitted in our laſt]

An Anſwer to a Pamphlet call'd, No Time proper to repeal the Teſt Act, continued from p. 1115.

T HE Author of this Pamphlet proceeds to object againſt the Repeal of the Teſt, that it would divide the King's Friends, ſince ſeveral of the Whig-Churchmen are againſt it.] If there be any ſuch Churchmen, they muſt be weak indeed, not to know, that the King's Intereſt and the Intereſt of Liberty conſiſt in a firm Union of all the Whigs in the Kingdom. The Whig Intereſt brought the Royal Family to the Throne, and preſerved them in it, againſt all the Efforts of the Jacobites and Tories; and if united, will preſerve them 'till Time ſhall be no more. Shall we then enrage ſome, and cool others, of the King's Friends? Or, ſhall we repeal this Act, and heal all Wounds on Account of Religion and Politicks? Do this and live. Repealing this Act will ſtrengthen the Whig Intereſt, as it will render Thouſands capable of ſerving their King and Country who now, thro' religious Scruples, are abſolutely incapable.

The Church will be the ſafer by this Repeal; for, the Diſſenters being put, in all Civil Affairs, upon an equal Foot with Churchmen, will have nothing further to aſk; and looking on the Church as their faſt Friends, they will inſenſibly abate of their Prejudices, and grow into a Liking of them. There were Ten Diſſenters 40 Years ago, to one now, who counted Communion with the Church ſinful: And if this Act be repealed, there may not be one 20 years hence; unleſs a Quaker; for Good Senſe, the Daughter of Liberty, will leſſen them every Day.

The Whig-Churchmen and Diſſenters are grown wiſer; they ſee that theſe Differences about Rites and Ceremonies, are Trifles, and beneath the Conſideration of a Man of Senſe; But if Churchmen will revive the old monſtrous Doctrines of no Biſhop no King, and that the Church is the State, the Conſequence is, a Man may be made a State Criminal for reaſoning againſt any Doctrine contained in eſtabliſh'd Articles or Creeds; which is the very Eſſence of Popery, and we ſhall be Slaves by Law eſtabliſh'd. But we will not be brought again under the Yoke.'

Another Argument againſt the Repeal,

B

Peal, is, The *States* of *Holland* employ no Perfon in *Civil Trufts* but thofe of the *Eftablifhed Church*.] What then? The States of *Holland* are againft *Trials by Juries*, and the *Liberty of the People* in chufing Magiftrates. But the Fact is not fairly ftated; there never was a *Law* in *Holland* to incapacitate the *Arminians*, or any *Proteftant* Diffenters, for *Civil* Trufts. 'Tis true, indeed, the *Arminians* have not been employ'd fince they were in the *Barnevelt Facton* againft the *Houfe of Orange.* So that they are laid by, not on a *Religious*, but *Civil* Account, as the *Papifts* are both here and in *Holland.*

It is faid by the Friends of the Miniftry, that tho' it may be reafonable in itfelf *to repeal the Teft Act*, yet a Government is not always in a Condition to do what is reafonable; that Minifters are not to confult what is beft for one *particular Man* or *Body* of Men, but the *whole Community*; that *all Parties* ought to be confider'd, and the *beft Ballance* poffible fettled amongft them; that as the *Prejudices of the Diffenters* fhould be regarded, fo fhould *thofe of Churchmen*, who would be alarm'd by this Bill, and roar out the *Danger of the Church*; and that all good Subjects will fubmit to *Neceffity*, and wait *proper Junctures.*

The beft Advice to the *Diffenters* is, if the *Teft Act* fhould not be repeal'd, not to refent it fo far as to join with the *Tories*, and fo break the *Whig Intereft*, render themfelves *odious* among the *Whigs*, *contemptible* amongft the *Tories*, *obnoxious* at Court, and terribly *affect themfelves* as well as the *Interefts* of Liberty. Let them confider that if the *Whigs* don't do them *all the Good* they defire, the *Tories* will do them *all the Ill* they are able. They will remember, that in the latter End of Q. *Anne's* Reign there was a Defign to deprive them of their Right of voting, as well as a Law made to deprive them of their Right of *educating* their Children. The *Quakers*

were actually tried to give up their Right of Voting: For when they apply'd to Parliament to have their *Affirmation Act lengthened*, the *October Club* at the *Bell* Tavern in *Weftminfter*, fent for fome of their *Leaders*, and told them, they would pafs their *Affirmation Act*, on Condition they would confent to have a Claufe in it *to take away their Right of Voting for Members of Parliament*; which they rejected with Indignation, refigned themfelves to Providence, and waited a more convenient Seafon, which happen'd at the Acceffion of the prefent Royal Ramily.

I wifh from my Soul, the *Whigs in the Houfe* would confider, and not force Gentlemen into Meafures in their *own Defence* againft their *Principles*, and the *true Intereft* of their Country.   Socrates.

The *Free Briton*, Jan. 4. No. 162.

Of a Standing Army.

MY prefent Defign, fays *Walfingham*, is to obferve the Miftakes of the *Craftfman*. He treats the two Papers which I publifhed on the Subject of the Army (See p. 645,651. Vol. II.) as drawn from what was fpoken in the *Houfe of Commons* by the Hon. *Gentleman in the Adminiftration*; but I affure the Publick I had not the Honour of fo great an Authority. The *Difpofition of Forces*, which the *Craftfman* remarks on (fee p. 1120 C) were drawn from the Obfervation of a *noble martial Duke* in the other Houfe. But to prevent any future Miftakes, the *genuine Speech* which the *Chancellor of the Exchequer* fpoke in the Committee on the Debate of the Army, is as follows;

" I have obferved that Gentlemen, through the whole Courfe of this Debate have well exercifed their Parts, and declaimed very juftly againft the Wickednefs and Danger of Standing Armies. It is a very large Field of Debate, it is one of the greateft Arguments that

ever

ever was diſcuſſed. I am ſenſible of the Danger of Standing Armies, and the great Miſchiefs which they have always brought upon the Countries where they were eſtabliſhed, and I ſhall always oppoſe them with as much Zeal as any Gentleman whatever: But this is not now the Queſtion; the Queſtion is, *Whether for the Service of the preſent Year* 17,000 Soldiers ſhould be maintain'd, or 12,000; This is the Point, and I could heartily wiſh, that Gentlemen would confine themſelves to it, and weigh impartially the Arguments on both Sides. Gentlemen talk much in Generals, and throw many Reflections. I have not only on this Account, but on many others, borne much Reproach, and I hope I ſhall always bear it with Patience, without making uſe of the ſame Weapons. Gentlemen call the Thing in Debate what it is not, in order to ſuppoſe what it really is; whereas,if they called it what it is, they would want Arguments to object againſt it. I wiſh Gentlemen would conſider that the Queſtion is not about Standing-Armies, but only for allowing his Majeſty 17,000 Forces or this Year, and for this Year only. Gentlemen talk as if what they granted now was to be perpetual, and their Vote this Seſſion muſt bind them in the next; but this cannot be the Caſe; ſurely, Sir, every Body will be as much at Liberty to vote againſt them next Year, as they are now. It will never be ſaid to any Gentleman, Sir, *you voted for them laſt Year, therefore you muſt this:* No, Sir, every Gentleman knows he ſhall be as much at Liberty to vote according to his Opinion and Conſcience then as he is now. Let us then conſider what is now asked of us; it is 17,000 Men, and theſe for one Year; they are the Soldiers of the People, kept for their Safety only, for the Support of the Nation againſt foreign Invaſions; What is it then that Gentlemen are afraid of? Do they think theſe Soldiers are deſigned to be made uſe of againſt our Liberties? Do they think their Arms are to be turned againſt their Country? I will not make uſe of the Name of the KING,

I think it ought to have no Awe on our Debates, nor will I ever attempt it. I am in that Way of thinking, and do hold the Maxim juſt, that *the* KING *can do no Wrong,* neither by LAW nor FORCE, and *his Miniſters are reſponſible for every Thing;* therefore I will with all my Soul put the Fate of the Queſtion, and the whole Debate upon this Iſſue. I deſire every Gentleman to look into his own Breaſt, and to appeal to his own Conſcience: Let him ask himſelf if he does ſeriouſly think that the Miniſtry, who ask theſe Forces, have any Intention to employ them againſt our Liberties, or to turn them againſt our Rights? And let every Gentleman ſpeak as his Conſcience dictates in this Affair; I ſhall very gladly ſubmit the Queſtion to this Diciſion, and do ſincerely make this Appeal to the Heart of every Gentleman.

But Gentlemen ſay, in Oppoſition to the preſent Motion, Where is the Advantage of this honourable Peace, this profound Tranquillity that is ſo much boaſted of? His Majeſty, they ſay, has told us in his Speech, that it was obtained upon ſuch Terms as can give no juſt Reaſon of Provocation to any of the Powers of *Europe,* and that it hath taken nothing from any Power; Where then is the Danger now? Whom have we to fear? And what are the Motives from whence theſe Troops are asked? If we are to keep up the ſame Force in Peace where is the Benefit of it? Gentlemen, who talk in this Strain now were of another Opinion the firſt Day of the Seſſion; they could not then ſee that we had an advantageous Peace, that we had this profound Tranquillity; 'twas then only a Wound skinned over that had Gangrenes and Mortifications underneath it, which would ſoon break out again; 'twas then only a popular Covering to perſuade the Parliament into good Humour on the firſt Day of the Seſſion. Have theſe Gentlemen then really changed their Opinion? Did they think it a bad Peace on the firſt Day of the Seſſion, and do they now think it a laſt-
ing

Eng honoruable one? Or do they only ufe thefe Expreffions for a prefent
Purpofe? And will their good Opinion
of the publick Tranquillity laft longer
than a few Hours? As I believe this
is really the Cafe with thefe Gentlemen, I think they can upon no Pretence, with no Colour of Argument,
oppofe the Maintainance of thefe Soldiers; for if Affairs be as they apprehend, if the Wound is only skinned
over, if we are in as much Danger as
before we, ought by no Means to dif-
band our Forces: They, Sir, furely can
neverrecommend to his Majefty to leave
his Kingdom naked and defencelefs in
fuch a Situation; and therefore thefe
Gentlemen fhould never be againft the
prefent Queftion. Nor can I think it
proper to leffen our Forces at this Juncture, though the Peace be eftablifhed
on the moft juft, moft folid Foundations. It is an Infant juft born, a hopeful Child it is, and I hope it will grow
up to Manhood: But fhall we defert it
in its Infancy? Shall the firft grateful
Return, which we make to his Majefty,
be Diftruft, and depriving him of his
Forces?

All the *Courts of Europe* now look
upon the Diffatisfaction among us, to
arife from the Enemies of the *Proteftant
Succeffion.* The Cafe of Difaffeftion
is now reduced quite to *Jacobitifm*; I
know that fome Gentlemen would gladly have this looked on only as a *Bugbear,* and they would rejoice to fee the
Time, when any Alarms, any Infinuations of Danger from that Quarter,
fhould be received with Ridicule, and
turned into Joke. I had like to have
faid that I was forry there was no *Jacobite* in this Houfe. No, Sir, I am
heartily glad of it; but if I was in an
Affembly of Jacobites, I would ask them
If they had not very lately, in fome
Corners, in fome private Meetings, in
fome fecret Cabals, flattered themfelves,
and given one another great Expectation,
that a favourable Time was not far off, to
advance the Intereft of the *Pretender?* If
this be true, thefe Gentlemen would be

very glad to fee our Forces reduced, our
Kingdom in fuch a Situation, as might
afford our Enemies little Difficulty to
make an Invafion. If it be all Chimæra, if there be no Danger of this Kind,
I fhould be very glad to know it. This
I am fure of, that our Forces never have
been leffened, but it gave Occafion to foreign Powers to form Defigns upon us,
and attempt Invafions; and yet it never
hath been done but with great Pretences, great fhew of Zeal for the Safety
of the People. The Pill muft be gilded with Popularity; it was fo in the
Queen's Time, and I believe no Gentleman doubts with what View our Forces were then reduced.

I believe Gentlemen imagine, that
the Reduction which they propofe of
5000 Men, will be a greater Saving to
the Publick than it really will; for, of
thefe 5000 to be disbanded 2000 will be
Invalids, that muft return to *Chelfea College;* fo that the Saving from them will
be but a *Farthing a Day,* which will make
the whole not fo confiderable as may be
apprehended. Gentlemen feem to me to
have let flip out of their Memory, what
was dropt in the Opening of the Debate;
that if there fhould be any Power in
Europe, that can be induced to form any
Defigns againft us, this muft be the favourable Juncture, when their Arms
have no Call any other Way. While
Affairs in Europe, were unfettled, and
Danger was threatned from every
Quarter, and on every Hand, there
was no Temptation to embroil themfelves in new Difficulties; but now,
Sir, there is Leifure for Ambition to
look round.

I am the more convinced of the
Hopes of the Enemies of the *Proteftant
Succeffion,* and that it would give them
great Pleafure to fee our Forces reduced,
and our Kingdom defencelefs from an
Accident that happened laft Night,
which I will beg leave to relate to the
Houfe. I had the Honour to be prefent at a Committee of Council, where
no lefs than *five Bills* were laid before
us from *Ireland,* to pevent the *Growth*
and

and Encouragement *of* Popery, which prevailed and flourished so much in that Kingdom, as was very alarming. There was a Council * who pleaded on their behalf; a Gentleman of great Learning, and who made the best of a bad Cause. In the Course of his Pleading, he cited the *Articles* of *Limerick*, which being called for by the *Lords of the Council*, a *Popish Solicitor*, who attended on this Affair, produced it in a little Book, which he took out of his Pocket. I had the Curiosity to look into this Book, which I supposed might be his *Vade Mecum*, and I found it to be a Collection of *five Pamphlets*, the first was the *Articles* of *Limerick*, the second was the *French King's Declaration*, and the *three others* were THREE ARGUMENTS AGAINST A STANDING ARMY.

* Mr *V----rney*

Fog's Journal, Jan. 6. No. 218,

THIS Writer having already published two Journals censuring Mr *Osborne's* Letters in the *London Journal* (see p. 974, 1021) in this continues his Remarks to the same Purpose.

Uniformity, especially in a voluminous Writer, has ever been esteemed a great Perfection; and no-body can more justly claim the Merit of it than Mr *Osborne*; for, whatever happens to be the Subject of Debate, he has continually Recourse to his *legerdemain abstract Principles* of *Right* and *Wrong*.

In *moral Science* his Method is the same; and if the Conclusiveness of any Part of his Argument be questioned, he only changes the *Position* or *Postulatum*, with which, in the first Instance, he supported the Proof, for another, which he applies in the same manner; and at last draws so boisterous a Conclusion, that he usually puts his Adversary to Flight.

He has the *Vanity* to stile himself a *Politician*, altho' he is not instructed even in the first Principles of *Policy*.

The Question concerning *Excises* is too *abstruse* and *knotty* for him to have

any Share in it, and therefore he prudently declines it; tho' just before it began, he gave us a *general* Testimony, how well he stood disposed towards the *Scheme* (see p. 813.).

By a peculiar Talent of Reasoning, Mr *Osborne* can prove a Treaty calculated for the *wisest Ends*, or that all Treaties are *useless*, *ridiculous Ceremonies*, and consequently, that there is no *Wisdom* in any Treaty.

He would be esteemed a Judge of History both *antient* and *modern*; altho' he has no Acquaintance with any but his *Mother Tongue*, nor does he seem to understand *one half* of the Words in the *English* Language. He lately complimented *Rapin* as an Historian, at the Expence of all the *Greek* and *Latin* Historians Characters (see p. 1023) tho' about 12 Months ago, this *Great Historian* was the Object of Mr *Osborne's* Contempt.

Concludes with a Remark on a Paper of his, intitled, *A Discourse on Infidelity*, sign'd SOCRATES (see p. 1071.) Whatever *imaginary Deity* he would bestow on *Virtue* and *Morality*, in Opposition to the Principle of *Self Love*, he is actually espousing the Cause of *Immorality*, by destroying the *natural* and *genuine* Principle by which alone it can subsist.---If the Pleasure which each Individual proposes to himself, in the doing a *virtuous and friendly Action*, be not the Motive upon which he acts, it's impossible any Principle should be found in human Nature, upon which *Morality* can be supported. It will therefore be incumbent on him to prove, that " the Concern which a friendly Man feels at the Misfortunes of one he has a Regard for, proceeds from any other Motive, than the Pleasure he proposes to himself of being freed from the Uneasiness he feels on Account of his Friend; and that the Relief he gives him is not acting upon the Principles of *Self Love*: Since, if the Misfortunes of his Friend gave him no Uneasiness, he could have no Motive to relieve him."

To say, that a *benevolent Man* and a *selfish Man* are *distinct* Characters, is saying nothing. They are indeed distinct in the *Estimation* of Mankind, and in *Nature* too, while the *benevolent* Man's Uneasiness is *produced* by the *Regard* he has for his *Friends*, and the *selfish* Man's by the Regard he has for *himself*; but does this prove *Self-Love* is not the *immediate Motive* of both their Actions? Are they not both *prompted* to Action from some Uneasiness, in the removing of which a *Good* is proposed to each Individual? The Cause of this Uneasiness is not material. *Socrates* can't distinguish between the immediate Spring of *moral Actions*, which is the Design of *God* founded upon *Uneasiness*, and that which produces this *Uneasiness*. When he has thought of this, he will hardly *hurt* his Head again in a Controversy, which, in the Manner he conducts it, *may be very injurious to his* Patron, *by weakening that Principle upon which alone he seems to have any Credit with any Part of Mankind*, and even with *Socrates* himself.

London Journal, Jan. 6. No. 706.

Of Tyranny, Anarchy, and Free Governments.

I Dolizers of Power have so debauch'd the Minds of Men with false Notions of *human Nature, Morals,* and *Politicks,* that some celebrated Writers have supposed Mankind so *ill made,* that they could not subsist without *Subjection to Power. Anarchy,* or the State of Man without Government, they have represented as Chaos and Confusion; and a *State of Nature,* as a continual War of every Man against every Man. Thus human Nature, Truth, Justice, and the Honour of God, are *prostituted* to the Support of *arbitrary Power;* altho' a State of Nature is infinitely preferable to *Tyranny* and *arbitrary Power.*

A State *of Nature* is, where every Man's allowed to do what he will with his own Person and Property, consistent with other Men's; and those *common Rights* are so easily discerned, that the *Indians* live much better than Men under any *Tyranny* and arbitary Government. Their *Virtue* and *Happiness* are owing to their being untaught by those whose *highest Interest* it is to *deceive* them.

The *great Inequality of Property is* the Source of almost all Murders, Robberies, and other Vices among ourselves; which the *wiser* and *happier* Savages knowing nothing of, are blessed with *Security* and *Ease:* For, they *naturally* assent to that divine Truth, *Sufficient unto the Day is the Evil, and the Good thereof too:* every Man provides for himself and his Offspring, and, invading no Man's Property, is invaded by no Man; and they are content to die as they live, not worth a Groat; when they have *no Occasion* for it, they have *no Occasion* for Government: For all Government owes its Necessity to the Inequality of Property.

They who have learnt to admire the Power of *Tyranny* as Sacred and Divine, are debauch'd as much in their *Religion* as *Morals: Publick Good,* in their Apprehension, is as little the Measure of Government in the *Universe,* as in the *State. Omnipotence,* they think would hardly be itself, was it not at liberty to *dispence* with the Laws of Equity, and change at Pleasure the *Standard* of moral Rectitude.

That Government only is *just* and *Perfectly free,* where there are no Laws but what relate to the Security of Person and Property; where the Subject may do what he pleases with his Person and Property, consistently with the Rights of others; and where there is no Power but the Civil; where there are no Laws but of a Civil Nature, and those Laws the *standing Measure* of Government and Obedience; and where there is also a *dernier Resort,* or *real Power* left in the *Community* to defend

defend themselves against any Attack on their Liberties.

The Government of *England* comes the nearest to this Plan of any in the World. We have our Defects indeed ; and one is, a Spiritual Power extending to Men's Persons and Properties, issuing out Writs and Processes in its *own Name*, by virtue of an Authority which seemed *distinct* from Civil. There should be no Power Spiritual, but what relates to Spirits or Minds, such as *turning out* disorderly Members ; and that should be without any consequent Penalties relating to Body or Estate.

We have other Defects, such as being *unequally* represented, the *Uselessness* of some Laws, the *Unreasonableness* of others, &c. But with all our Defects, our Government is so good, that it deserves to be well guarded. We should guard against the *Growth of Prerogative*, and the *least Exercise* of Ecclesiastical Power ; but above all, against Corruption in ourselves, by living *within our own Fortunes*.

Universal Spectator. Jan. 6. No. 222.

Of ACTION.

ACTION is the Art of proper Gesture, expressing our Ideas and Conceptions in the most graceful and intelligible Manner ; and deserves the closest Application of a Performer. By this the Powers and Faculties of Nature are taught to exert themselves in a proper and becoming Manner. Suppose, for instance, an Actor, by the poetical Justice of an Author is in the same Person and Play, obliged to personate the different Parts of a King and a Beggar. Before he can be Master of the Action proper for each Personage, he must lay down certain Principles by which he is to govern himself in the Representation: As thus : He considers that the Person of a King is attended with Magnificence, Grandeur, and Majesty ; his Speech wise, grave, and solemn ; his Deportment

stately and majestick ; and his Actions great and heroic : But the same Man reduced to the calamitous Circumstances of a Beggar, speaks, acts, and behaves in a Manner suitable to such a Condition. Thus, by a Propriety of Gesture, the Actor will possess the very Souls as well as the Eyes and Ears of an Audience, and communicate to them the same Fury and Passion by which he himself is agitated. The intelligent Actor considers the Gestures that are proper to express that particular Species of Humour allotted him by the Poet, enters upon it with a becoming Assurance, and performs it with that Life and Energy, that our Eyes are apt to give our Knowledge the Lie, and almost to persuade us, that that is real which we know to be Fiction. Representation, and Nature at second hand.

Weekly Miscellany. Jan. 6 No. 4.

On the TEST ACT.

THE following Letter was written before the Dissenters Resolved to desist from their Attempt to get the Corporation and Test Acts repealed ; but as they have only *postpon'd* their Designs, the Author thinks proper to give it a Place.

THE common Question in all Companies is, *Do the Dissenters go on with their Design of petitioning the Parliament for a Repeal of the Corporation and Test Act?*] For my Part, says this Writer, I could never think they had any such Design. The *Style* of their *Resolutions* and *Writings* shew the contrary. For a *Petition* is always used in the Nature of a *Prayer*, and the Subject Matter of *a Prayer* is some *Favour*. But the Dissenters openly declare, that what they mean to *apply* for, is not Matter of *Favour*, but of *strict Justice*.

What Methods they intend to use *they* best know (tho' *History* is not silent in this Point) but with respect to the Ministry they speak plainly that unless they will to them Justice, they will op-

B　　pose

pose them at the next *Election* for Members of Parliament. This is declared by way of *Menace*; as thinking their Interest of such Consequence, that the *Ministry dares* not disoblige them. By these *moderate* Measures the Constitution was over-turned in the Reign of K. *Charles* I.

They would be thought to have a particular Regard for his Majesty's *Person*, and Affection for his *Government.* But they manifestly slight his Majesty's *Person* and shew more Attachment to their *own* Interest than *his*. In all their late Meetings, and Pamphlets, no Notice is taken of the *King*; no Talk of *addressing his Majesty*, tho' this is a Point which immediately affects his Majesty's Safety, as well as the Interest of the Nation; especially in matters of *Religion*, where the *Supremacy* of the *King* is more peculiarly concerned; and highly fitting it was, in Reason and Decency, they should first have resolved upon *addressing* his Majesty concerning the Qualification of his *own Servants*, on whose Integrity and Abilities so much depends. But their Conduct is agreeable to that Principle advanced in a Paper *pretended* to be written by a *Friend* of his Majesty, *viz.* That the People are the Fountain of all Power and Authority; (See p. 950.) and then the Parliament being the *Representatives* of the People, all Applications ought to be made to *them*.

An *uncommon* Zeal for the Honour of *Religion* is as another of their Pretences. For some Time they have been all silent about the Repeal, and *now* many of them think it an *improper Time*. Why? Their Pamphlets assign Reasons of *Policy*. If, as they affirm, the making the Sacrament a *Test*, is *profaning* and *perverting* the most solemn Act of Christian Worship, the Repeal of it ought not to be deferred upon any Consideration, because sinful in itself. It has been justly observed by the Author of the *Dispute adjusted, That they offer'd a Clause a little after the Revolution, that the receiving the Sacrament*

in their *own Meetings should be a Qualification*; as if the *Place* occasion'd any Alteration in the *Action.*

We have lived with them inoffensively for many Years; they have enjoyed their Opinions, and the Profession of them uninterrupted and unenvied; even the Liberty of *voting* in Elections for our Preachers; which is a greater Instance of *our Moderation* than of *their Modesty*. From *His Majesty* they have met with as much Grace and Favour as is consistent with our Constitution; from our *Constitution* as much Indulgence as the Legislature thought safe to grant them: Yet so far are they from being *thankful*, that they accuse the Legislature of *Oppression*; the Bishops and Clergy of *Tyrannical Pride* and *Ambition*; the whole Communion with the Want of the *Spirit* of *Religion, Honour*, and *Liberty*; the whole World who think *Establishments* and *Disqualifications* lawful, of *Bigotry* and *Self-Interest.* If by sober Argument they can shew the Unlawfulness of all *Disqualifications*, or this *particular Test*, let them do it; they have tried heretofore and were foil'd. However, 'tis great Chance but the Legislature will agree with the judicious Author of the *Dispute adjusted*, 'That whenever the Tolera-
'tion breaks in upon the Establish-
'ment, or the Establishment upon the
'Toleration, the Peace of this King-
'dom will be at an End.'

Craftsman Jan. 6 No. 340.
Of the Navy *and* Militia.

ON these two Bulwarks our Ancestors have safely relied for many Generations; even during the long and bloody Wars between the Houses of *York* and *Lancaster*, the Party that prevail'd disbanded their Army, as soon as the Action was over, and scorn'd to secure themselves by a *military Government.*

I suppose, says *Danvers*, it will not be denied that we have at present the finest Navy, and the bravest Seamen in the World; and I hope the former will not be suffered to decline, nor the latter by being discourag'd or ill Usage be forc'd into foreign Service. But the common Method of Manning our Fleets by *Impressing*, I am persuaded, is inconsistent with *Magna Charta*, the Rights of *Englishmen*, and of pernicious Consequence to Trade.

Whilst we are able to keep up such a *naval Power*, we shall easily maintain the *Sovereignty of the Seas*, and safely despise any Attempts from Abroad.

But Mr *Walsingham* says *there can be no absolute Dependance on a* naval Force, *to oppose or defeat an Invasion*; see p. 652. Vol. II.] Nobody can be ignorant that the necessary Preparations for such an Enterprize take up a great deal of Time, and require such a Number of Ships, that all *Europe* must be asleep, if it should pass unobserved. The *Spanish Armada* consisted but of 18,000 Men; and K. *William* brought but 14,000 in 6 or 700 Ships; so that nothing but the most egregious Indolence can expose us to such an Attempt, without some Warning and Time for Defence. This was the Case of the late K. *James*, who paid no Regard to the repeated Advices from *France*, concerning the Pr. of *Orange's* Designs, till the Prince declared it himself, and was ready to set Sail.

As to K. *James's* Fleet lying Windbound in the Mouth of the *Thames*, *when the Pr. of* Orange *sail'd by*, it's doubted whether our Deliverer was not as much obliged to the Affections of the Officers and Seamen, who compos'd *that Fleet*, as to the *Winds*.

But granting that some *foreign Power* in the Interest of the *Pretender*, should conjure up a great *naval Armament* on a Sudden, and steal it into *England* in a dark *Night*, or by a favourable Wind, what are they to do?

" The Case then is thus, says Mr *Trenchard*, that 20,000 Men, of which few can be Horse, are landed in *England*, without any human Probability of being supply'd from Abroad. This Army shall never march 20 Miles into the Country; for they cannot put themselves in a marching Posture in less than a *Fortnight or 3 Weeks*, by which Time we may have 100,000 Militia drawn down upon them; whereof 10,000 shall be *Horse*, and as many *Dragoons* as we please; and if *this Militia* does nothing but *drive the Country*, cut off their *Foragers*, and intercept Provisions, their Army must be destroy'd in a short Time."

If then our *Militia* is back'd only with 5 or 6000 regular Troops, what Danger can we apprehend from an Invasion? --- This was the Opinion of the late D. of *Marlborough*, who declared he would undertake to defeat any Body of Men, which could be possibly landed on us by Surprize, with only his own Regiment of *Guards*, two or three of *Dragoons*, and such a Train of Artillery as he could easily draw out; whereas they they could not bring any with them of Consequence; nor stand long, having no *fortify'd Towns* to secure themselves.

The Success of the *Revolution* was entirely owing to the *Disaffection* spread amongst all Ranks and Degrees of People.

Militia are the natural, strongest and most proper Defence of *free Countries*; and were always rely'd upon in *England*, till the Reign of K. *Charles* II.

Sir *Robert Cotton*, in his Advice to K. *Charles* I. lets him know how the People resented his *keeping up an Army in the Winter*; tho' we were then in War both with *France* and *Spain*.

When the D. of *Alençon* came to the Court of Q. *Elizabeth*, and for some Time had admir'd the Riches of the *City*, the Conduct of her *Government*, and the Magnificence of her *Court*, he ask'd her, amidst so much Splendour, where were her Guards? Pointing to the People, (who received her in Crouds with repeated Acclamations) *These* said she, *my Lord, are my Guards*. These have their *Hands, Hearts*, and *Purses* always at my Command,

To this it has been objected by the Hon. Gentleman and his Advocates, that the Circumstances of Affairs in *Europe* are entirely alter'd in this Respect.

This Alteration took Place when most of the *free States* of *Europe* were converted into *absolute Monarchies.* Yet still in *Holland* and other free States the inland Towns are defended by their Militia and Burghers only.

I would not be thought to mean, adds *D'anvers,* that our Militia are fit to defend our Country, or indeed for any Thing, besides furnishing the Town with a ridiculous Diversion, and cramming their Guts at the Expence of their industrious Fellow-Subjects. For this Reason they are laid aside every where but in *Middlesex.* See p. 208. Vol. I.

But it's absurd to suppose that the Militia cannot be made useful.——From whence is our *present Army* rais'd but from the *Body of the People?* Do's clapping a red Coat upon a Man's Back make him a Soldier? May not a great Part of the present Army, when disbanded, be incorporated into the *Militia?*'

The Difficulty is in getting them disbanded, as Mr *Gay* observes:

Soldiers are perfect Devils in their Way, [fay. When once they're rais'd, they're curs'd hard to

Daily Courant. Jan. 9.
Remarks on the Craftsman.

THE Inconsistency of the *Craftsman* may be easily evinced, if we only compare his *Journal* of the 15th of *April* last (see p. 701) with the foregoing of the 6th Instant.

Supposing, as he affirms, that the Militia were the only *Forces* made use of in the Wars between the Houses of *York* and *Lancaster;* how does this prove, that our Ancestors relied wholly on the *Militia* against an Invasion of foreign regular Troops? Or supposing the *Militia* in those Days, or even in the Reign of Q. *Elizabeth,* were to be relied on against a foreign

Invasion, will the *Craftsman* assert, that the *Militia* of *these Days,* who, he acknowledges are good for nothing but cramming their Guts) equals in Bravery the *Militia* in those *Reigns?*

But, says he, nothing can be more absurd than to suppose that the *Militia* can't be made useful; yet complains, that it's in vain to propose any Scheme of this Kind, whilst no Pains are spared to make the *Militia* contemptible; tho' in the Paragraph just before, he had himself called them "Men fit for no Service, besides cramming their Guts at the Expence of their industrious Fellow Subjects."

Mr *Trenchard* is his great *Oracle.* In the Quotation which Mr *D'anvers* takes from him, *two* Things are to be observed; ——one, that Mr *Trenchard* supposes 20,000 regular Forces may be landed upon us *in a dark Night;* the other, that the 100,000 *Militia* are not supposed to have been *made useful,* but Men fit for no Service but *cramming their Guts:* With which, no doubt, the Nation would be better pleased than 18,000 regular Forces. For, suppose these 20,000 regular Forces landed in *Scotland,* what is to be *done?* Draw down, says he, 100,000 *Militia* immediately upon them, whereof 10,000 to be Horse, and as many Dragoons as you please; march them to the Northern Parts of *England;* drive the Country of all Provisions; burn, destroy all Villages, Towns, Houses, and their Army must be destroy'd in a short time.'———This was the great Mr *Trenchard's* Scheme! and let all the *Northern Counties* declare how they *approve* of it.

This Reasoning, *D'anvers* tells us, was never yet *answered.* But (see p. 701) and we shall find he has answer'd it himself, where he asks, "Whether it would have been an easy Matter to drive an Army of 10,000 *Swedes* out of this Kingdom?" Now he modestly demands, What Danger we can possibly apprehend, if 20,000 Men were to land upon us?

Grubstreet Journal. Jan 9. N° 159.
Of the Original of the GRUBEANS.

SIR,

AS we have two worshipful Societies now flourishing *viz.* the FREE-MASONS and GRUBEANS, it may not be an improper Entertainment to give a Sketch of the Nature of these antient Companies. First of the GRUBEANS, otherwise called the *Grubstreet Society.*

Mævius, in his Epistle to the present Lord Mayor, observ'd, that the Street, in which the PEGASUS is situated, gave Name to the Society. But, I think, our very venerable Society gave Name to the Street, as *Newgate* to *Newgate-street*, *Lud's* Castle or Gate, to *Ludgate-street*, &c. as Brother *Stow's Survey of London* manifestly shews.

But 'twill be ask'd, how came we to be called GRUBS. This is answer'd by an inveterate Enemy to our Society, in his Epistle to Brother *Moore of Abchurch Lane*, that in general.

——All human kind are WORMS.

Man is a very WORM by Birth,
Vile Reptile, weak, and vain;
A while he crawls upon the Earth,
Then shrinks to Earth again.

Now, if all Men are of the Worm kind, or so represented, it was natural for the Wits of yore to divide the whole Species into several Classes. Not only Worms, but all Insects and Beasts have served to distinguish the several Capacities and Inclinations of the rational World.

——SIMONIDES with lighter Air
In Beasts, and Apes, and Vermin paints the Fair:
The good SCRIBLERUS in like forms displays
The reptile Rhimesters of these latter Days.
                    HARTE's *Ep. on Satire.*

Another Enemy to our Society represents modern Authors by Six Hieroglyphics,

The Flood, Flame, Swine, the Lion, and the Snake.
Those five fold monsters modern Authors make.
The Snakes reign most; Snakes PLINY, says, are bred,
When the Brain's perish'd in a human Head.

Ye groveling, trodden, whipt stript turn-coat Things,   [Stings, &c.
Made up of Venom, Volumes, Stains, and
    Dr YOUNG's *Ep. to Mr* POPE.

Upon reading these Lines, some may think the Pegasian Members justly intitled to the Appellation of Snakes: But I shall prove the Propriety of our antient Title GRUBS.

And first, a Snake is *made up of Venom and Stings*; whereas we have neither *Venom* nor *Stings*. Like GRUBS indeed, we leave behind us a kind of shining slimy Trail, disagreeable, 'tis true, but not destructive.——Secondly, Snakes are swift in their Motions; whereas the contrary is the Property of GRUBS, and therefore some call them Slugs.——Lastly, Snakes cast their Slouths or Coats, and put on new ones every Year; but we are forced to make our old ones serve several Years.

GRUBS, and not Snakes, are therefore our proper Emblems, which may be further prov'd. These Insects are more frequently bred in human Heads than Snakes; especially if GRUBS are, as BAILEY affirms, a *Sort of Maggots.*

E'en BUTTON's Wits to WORMS shall turn,
Who MAGGOTS were before

These Insects are very fond of Cabbage, an Herb sacred to the Poets of former Ages; as appears by a Canticle in your 46th *Journal.*

All hail arch-poet, without Peer,
Vine, Laurel, CABBAGE fit to wear,
And worthy of thy Prince's Ear.

Nor was this Herb more grateful to the antient Poets than to the modern; as it was the Crown of the former, it is the Food of the latter.——The obscure Crawling, in opposition to Soaring, makes GRUBS the more proper Insects to denote Writers of our Rank.——I can't think our Name deriv'd from a GRUB, signifying a *Dwarf* or *short Fellow*, intimating we are low Writers; much less from *grubbing* up Characters; (See p. 12. Vol. I.) but rather from the maggotty Grubs, so well known to our beloved Kinsmen the Gardiners, As to our.

our being called GRUBEANS, it's a Corruption of our true Name; the Free Masons may as properly be called MASONIANS.

To conclude; CRANE-Court may possibly take its Name from the learned Society there, famous for diving into secret Things; which the extraordinary Length of the Neck and Beak of the *Crane* makes that Fowl capable of doing. And 'tis probable the antient Name of *Old-street*, was Owl-street, and chang'd in the Reign of *Edw.* V. in whose Time was constantly held there a Chapter or Society of Antiquaries, in Honour of whom it took the Appellation of *Old*-street.   *Yours A.H.*

Free Briton, Jan. 11. Nº 163.

OF NATURE.

THE Study of human Nature affords the most useful Knowledge; and therefore History is instructive beyond all other Works of Learning, as it shews the secret Springs and Motives of Actions, and the Passions that work in Mankind and produce the most important and surprising Events.

The whole Series of History, indeed, appears but a melancholy Detail of Crimes and Calamities, and Struggles of Oppression and Liberty.

There is a Principle which prevails thro' all the animal as well as rational World; the Strong oppress the Weak, unless the oppressing Power can be balanced by Art or Force. We talk of social Virtues and Benevolence in many living Creatures; but in Fact there are but few, who do not devour, if they can. — nor is the human Species more beneficent than the Animals they set so much below them.

The noblest Passion in every Creature is Gratitude. The most Savage Beasts have a Sense of Kindness; and the proudest, fiercest, Animal is tame and humble to him that does it friendly Offices. To renounce this meritorious Virtue seems the most unnatural Part which any Creature can perform; and

the Man who is guilty of it, is unworthy of a Being even among the Beasts, for they disown the Vice. How the ungenerous Man can excuse himself to his own Mind, is hard to say; but an honest Man delights to return the most equal Acts of Kindness.

To say that the present Age is without this Virtue, would be the severest Reproach to our Times and Country; yet it is our Misfortune to see the same Spirit prevail that has cursed and blacken'd every Period in History, and every Nation upon Earth. Scarce a Government or an Administration can be found which has not been charged with deserting its best Friends and deceiving those who relied upon Promises. This is the present Case with us to charge not a few with deserting and deceiving the Government, whilst those, who are thus guilty of Ingratitude, have no other Refuge, than to tax it with excessive Bounty, and abuse the Men whom they hate, for the Favours they have received. It should be observ'd, that this is the first Instance that a Government has been quarrelled with for being too good to those who deserve its Encouragement. The ingenious Mr *Rowe* spent much Time and Pains, at the late E. of *Oxford*'s Command, to qualify himself with Languages, in View to a publick Employment; yet received no better Return, than to be told *He had the much envied Pleasure of reading some celebrated Authors in their Originals.* All the World will agree, such Usage would have justified even a *Craftsman* against that Minister.

But whatever Attempts some Persons may make to asperse an Administration, or whatever their Motives may be, 'tis infinitely less criminal, than for the Friends of those Ministers to betray and deceive them. Not that a Man is obliged to run any Length, or concur with unreasonable Measures: But when a designing, mercenary Creature, unsteady in every Attachment, has no Motives of Gratitude and Generosity, but sacrifices every Thing to

But

his own Interest, what Abhorrence does he not deserve ? This Character is compleatly infamous ; is distinguished by mean Parts, and low Cunning, a slavish obsequious Temper, and a vain Conceit of great Abilities. Whenever you discover such a Man, suspect him for a Shuffler, and when you detect his Deceit, Common Sense will teach you to despise him.

The Craftsman, Jan. 13. N° 341.
D'anvers *a Prophet.*

THIS Journal is one continued Compliment, from some supposed Correspondent, to the *Craftsman,* on the lucky Event of several Predictions he gave out in some former Papers.

You have often explain'd, says this Writer to *D'anvers,* the evil Consequences of Power given to *Directors* to *coin* Money in the Shape of Bonds ; to enter into chimerical Projects of Trade ; to permit, and be themselves concern'd with the Companies Servants in Frauds and Embezzlements.

You was early in explaining some Frauds in the *E. India Company* ; and have not some late Discoveries demonstrated the Truth of what you then charged them with ?—Is not the present Decline of their Trade (notwithstanding an *Excise* to support it) a Proof of some bad Management ?—Hath it not already obliged them to reduce their *Dividend ?* and brought them under the present critical Dilemma, as to their Bonds ? See p. 1079 E.

With Regard to the *S. Sea Company,* you very early observed, that the *Assiento* Trade was a losing Contract ; and that the Annual Ship granted as an Equivalent for it, besides the Disadvantage it brought upon our *African* and *American* Trade by their *Tenders* &c. it occasion'd frequents Differences betwen the two Crowns, exposed our Merchants to Depredations and Insults, and made the *Spaniards* secure from any Reprisals. And tho' for these seasonable Notices you have been insulted

and reproached as an Enemy to pub-lick Credit, have not all you said of *this Company* proved true ?—Have not the *Directors* own'd, they have sustained great Losses in Trade, and that great Frauds have been committed in the Management of it ? See p. 583.

Did not the *worthy Sub-Governor* himself tell us that the Company was not one Farthing in Disburse on Account of TRADE ? Tho' he had just before confessed, the Company had sustained insupportable Losses in Trade, which obliged them to reduce their Dividend from 6 to 4 *per Cent.* in order to account for the immense Load of *Bond Debts,* and to annihilate a considerable Part of their *Capital,* for the Payment only of half of it ? See p. 721. —Have they not acknowledg'd their Losses in the *Greenland Trade,* and given it up ? See p. 1081. Have not some Persons shewn an Inclination to give up Part of the *American* Trade ; even the most profitable Part of it ?

Thus stands the Case of the two great Companies. *One* of them made Application to Parliament last Session, which will probably bring them there again ; and the *other,* 'tis said, have Thoughts of applying there for some Indulgence, without which they find it impossible to continue their Trade with Advantage.

The Case of the *Charitable Corporation* is still depending before that august Assembly, and the Gentlemen of the *York Buildings* Company seem resolv'd to seek Relief, or Justice, in the same Place ; so that our *Representatives* would have Business enough this Session, tho' they had no *Standing Armies* nor *Excises* to encounter.

I shall conclude with an Observation you have often made, *viz.* That such Corporations *are not only destructive of* Trade, *dangerous to* Liberty *in general ; but, by Fraud and Mismanagement, are commonly attended with great Losses to the* Proprietors *themselves.*

London

London Journal. Jan. 13. N° 707.
On the Army.

IN Answer to the *Craftsman* (See p. 1119, Vol. II. 8, Vol. III.) we shall first shew, says *Osborne*, the Necessity and Reasonableness of having some Regular Troops; and then consider the Weight of the Objections against it.

An Age ago *Europe* had nothing but *Militias*; but ever since Card. *Richlieu* shewed the Way, all this Part of the World is got into the dreadful Custom of keeping up a mighty Force, and the most powerful of all these Kingdoms and States is our next Neighbour, our constant Rival in Trade, and between whom and us there can be no common Interest. This neighb'ring Kingdom keeps up great Armies; and we may appear too inviting, if we lie in such an open and unguarded Condition, that the Success of the Attempt may appear not only *probable*, but certain.—To this 'tis said, What is our Fleet for? *The Answer is*, To do us all the Good a Fleet is able to do: But a Fleet is neither *Omnipotent* nor *Omnipresent*; an Enemy may be so *secret* in their Design, and bring over so many Thousand Regular Forces in a few Vessels, that we may be absolutely unprepared. A strong Proof of this is, that the *French* in Q. *Anne*'s Time shipp'd, 7000 Soldiers in Eleven Fregates, of which we knew nothing till three Weeks before they put to Sea; and had they been good Runners, they might have landed them, and fetch'd 7000 more, without hindrance from us; so that we ought not to be without this double Security of Fleet and Army.

Some Army then is necessary against Foreign Invasions, tho' not against popular Insurrections; the natural Strength of the Kingdom, the *Militia* and *Civil Magistrates*, beside the Influence which the Disposition of Employments, gives the King over the Nobility and Gentry In every Country, would be sufficient against all popular Insurrections; especially, if it be true, that there is no Disaffection among us but *Jacobitism*, and that the Church is converted.

But Mr *Trenchard* says, "That Army which can do *no* Hurt can do *no* Good; and if it be sufficient to oppose a foreign Power, it is sufficient to suppress the Subjects at Home. The first part of this Assertion is only a trifling Jingle or Turn of Words: For it holds as strong against all Power upon Earth, as against an Army.——The Truth is this: If it appears that a Body of Regular Troops ought to be kept up against Foreign Invasions, it's our Duty to keep 'em up, tho' they may possibly do Hurt: But that they can conquer the Parliament and Nation is a ridiculous Supposition.

Our Representatives are our *Dernier Resort* from Opposition; so that while they continue uncorrupt, 'will be impossible for a King of *England*, with such and Army, to subdue the Nation, or make himself absolute; but if ever *they* should grow so corrupt, as to give into Arbitrary Power, our *Dernier Resort* will be, *ourselves* Sword in Hand.

When the *Craftsman* asserts, "That during the Wars between the Houses of *York* and *Lancaster*, they disbanded their Armies as soon as the Action was over, and scorn'd to secure themselves, by subjecting the Kingdom to a Military Government, " he does not consider, that their Armies were then the *Vassals* of their several Lords, who, after the Battle was over, went home to their several *Huts* and *Vassalage*. The Kingdom was then a Military Government; and all *Lands* held by Military Service.

What is said that Q. *Elizabeth* had none but Train-Bands against the mighty Force of the *Spaniards*, is nothing to the Purpose; for who can tell the Event, if the *Spaniards* had landed 20,000 Regular Forces? The Queen indeed seemed not to fear; but wise and brave Men feared, and one of the *Veres* declared, he trembled for the Event; and twas believed that had the *Spaniards* joined the Prince of *Parma*'s Forces and landed, we had been conquer'd; but God preserved us.

Weekly Miscellany, Jan. 13. No. 5.
Of Civil Power in Matters of Religion.
[*Continued from* Vol. II. p. 1115.]

THE Question now to be discuss'd is, Whether the *supream Legiflative Power, has a Right to limit the publick Encouragements, allotted to those who shall be appointed to teach the People, to the Ministry so subscribing.*

Let it be granted, that in settling the publick Revenues upon the Clergy, the Legiflature confider'd the *Church of England* as conftituted according to the Order and Appointment of Chrift. It follows; fo far as the *Diffenters* differ from us in Doctrine and Worfhip, fo far they muft be fuppofed by the Legiflature to have departed from the Doctrine and Will of Chrift. In this Cafe the Legiflature may permit Men to differ from them; but have no Right to compel any to join in a Worfhip they don't approve. But—Are they bound to encourage an Oppofition to what they apprehend to be the Doctrine of Chrift? Little will it avail to fay, there is no Infalliblity in the Legiflature; for, fallible as it is, it's the Judgment, according to which they muft act. Will a Father, in chufing a Tutor for his Children, take one that agrees with, or one that differs from him in Judgment? When the *Schifm Bill* was offer'd in a late Reign, did not the *Diffenters* complain of it as a great Hardfhip, that they fhould be denied the Liberty of educating their Children their own Way? Yet *this* they now think it reafonable the Magiftrate fhould fubmit to!

TheLegiflature encourages one Method of Religion, in Diftinction from all others. You think it reafonable they fhould encourage all alike. What is the Difference? Why this; that in the one Way the Magiftrate propagates one Syftem of Doctrines, which in fome Points may poffibly be erroneous: In the other he would propagate many Syftems, which he may be morally certain will be erroneous. The *Diffenters* would have the *Church of England* open wide her Gates to many who differ from her in Doctrine, to all forts of Sectaries and Hereticks, who pafs for Chriftians, and interpret Scripture as they are able. Let Mr *Chandler* anfwer to this Point, and then tell us why Mr *Woolfton* has not as good a Title to a Benefice as he? But why does Mr *Chandler* plead, that all,

but profeffed *Deifts*, fhould be admitted to Ecclefiaftical Preferments? The only good Reafon why *Deifts* fhould be excluded, is, that the Magiftrates, as *Chriftians*, ought not to encourage an Oppofition to *Chriftianity*. And is there not as much Senfe in faying, that the Magiftrate, as perfuaded of the Soundnefs of the *Church of England*, ought not to encourage *any* Sect which fhall oppofe her Doctrines?

The next Queftion is———*Ought the Corporation and Teft Acts to be repealed or not?* To determine this Point, two Things muft be confidered: 1ft. Whether thefe Laws propofe a juft End? 2. Whether they purfue the End by juft Means?

The ultimate End of thefe Laws, is the *Security of the Church of England as by Law eftablifhed.* (Stat. 10 *Anna* cap. 2.) The immediate End, fubfervient to the other, is to keep Nonconformifts of all Sorts out of Offices Civil and Military, and out of the Government and Direction of Corporations; to the End that " the Succeffion may moft probably be perpetuated in the Hands of Perfons well affected to his Majefty and the eftablifhed Government." The Reafon why the Eftablifhed Government would not be fecure, if Power was put into the Hands of Diffenters, is becaufe they are difaffected to one Part of the Conftitution, as the Papifts are to both? And our Laws know of no Friends to the Eftablifhed Government, who are not well affected to the Conftitution in Church and State.

The Diffenters infift much on their Zeal for his Majefty's Government, as a Reafon for their being admitted to Offices of Truft in common with other Subjects. But where does their Zeal end? Why, for his Majefty's Government, confider'd only as oppos'd to the Claims of the *Pretender*, and a *Popifh Adminiftration*; and furely the Clergy and People of the Church of *England* are as little inclin'd to either of thefe as themfelves. One of the Reafons for excluding K. *James* II. and the *Popifh Line*, was the Security of the *Church of England*; for which Security his Majefty and his Proteftant Succeffors ftand Guarantees. How then can Affection to his Majefty's Government confift with Difaffection to the *Church of England?*

To the Second Queftion, do thefe Laws purfue the End propofed by *proper Means?* The Author fays but little:

The

Basis, my future Animadversions upon all Degrees shall turn, and be interspers'd with Instruction and Pleasure, Improvement and Diversion; their chief Scope being to fill the Heart with an indelible Tincture of *True Philosophy*; maintaining Tenderness for Persons and Things.

I foresee it will be objected to the Title of this Paper, that the discursive and theoretick part of Life only, comes under my Consideration. But the Example of the *Spectator*, will justify my entering into the Scenes of active Life.

Nº II. The *Auditor* introduces this Paper with some Reflections on the Follies current when the *Tatlers* and *Spectators* were written; that there was not then that Stagnation of Taste, nor Want of Desire in People to improve themselves as now; that Works of Genius were more frequent than at this Time; professes his Design is to awaken both Sexes out of their different Kinds of Lethargy; and then proceeds to give an Account of himself to the following Purport:

I was born about the middle of the Year 1689, ever memorable for the glorious Dawn of restor'd Liberty; my Father a Gentleman, esteem'd for his Virtue, had one *Foiblesse*, a Prepossession in Favour of *Astrological Predictions*. Accordingly he consulted an Adept, who having drawn my Horoscope, assur'd my Father, that from the combin'd Influence of the Planets reigning at my Birth, the Seeds of Benevolence and Humanity were implanted strongly in my Nature, for which I should be distinguish'd. He intrusted me therefore to the Tuition of an ingenious Gentlemen to my 15th Year, then sent me to the University.

The first four Years of my Academical Institution I spent in improving myself in the Poetic and Oratorian Taste; and having inscribed a Copy of *Latin* Verses to a certain illustrious Professor, he thank'd me, but gave me to understand, that the Advantage arising from such Studies was but light, if compared to the useful Knowledge from which they diverted me. Such, added he, is the Study of the Mathematicks, and of Nature, which enlarges the Mind, and capacitates it to receive the most exalted Notions of the Deity and Religion.

Pursuant to his Advice, the Mathematicks and Nature became my Study; in which I continu'd to my 23d Year, when on Examination, I found I had acted the

Part of a self-interested, useless Portion of Existence. This Reflection raised in me a Desire of Improvement in that part of Knowledge which restores the distemper'd *Microcosm* to its pristine State. Accordingly I apply'd myself to the Lecture of the antient Physicians, who best delineate the History of Diseases, and enumerate their distinguishing Symptoms. Here I had an Opportunity of exercising that Benevolence, the Seeds of which had been implanted in me.

A long Attendance on the Sick gave room to a narrower Inspection of Man; which led me into an Acquaintance of a Distemper unmention'd in *Hippocrates*, out of the Reach of *Galen* or *Hermes*, viz. *an universal Corruption of the Heart, a general Disregard of our first Duties.* A serious Reflection turn'd all my future Attention to the Cure of this universal Malady. Accordingly, I left the University, and came to Town, where I have liv'd several Years, personally known to many, really to few, free and independent of all, my Father having at his Death, left me Master of a very easy Fortune; wherefore I shall dedicate most of my leisure Hours to the Use of the Publick.

Nº III. *Quales esse decet.*

The Auditor's *Account of his Club.*

The first Person is Sir *Charles Freeman*, Son of the late Sir *Robert*, of *Gloucestershire*; whose Lot of younger Brother has been instrumental in attaining the many valuable Qualities he possesses. The Study of History and Mathematicks at the University, led him to the Army, where he made so quick an Advancement, that the late D. of *Marlborough* honour'd him with Marks of peculiar Esteem. At the Conclusion of the Peace at *Utrecht*, he retired to his Estate. His long Continuance in the Army has qualified him to be a perfect Judge of Men. In his Conversation he is open and unconfined; in his Behaviour free and disengaged. He has the Courage and Impartiality of *Manly* in the *Plain Dealer*, without his Spleen or Bitterness.

Frank Easy is what they call a *Woman's Man*: He dances excellently, is a Proficient in Musick, and has a Smattering of Architecture and Painting: His Dress is rich, but not tawdry; and his Conversation *light*, yet agreeable enough. *Frank* has made the Tour of *France* and

Easy

Italy, and speaks the Language of each fluently. He is perfectly versed in that sort Conversation in which Men of Sense make the least Figure. Tho' his grand Foible is an amorous Disposition, yet it is blended with Sentiments of Probity and Goodnature. He thinks it inconsistent with the Character of a Man of Honour, after seducing, to abandon the unhappy Wretch; and takes pleasure in declaring he has expended above 3000 *l.* in voluntary Settlements.

The third Member of this Society is an *Italian* by Birth, of the Family and Name with the celebrated Author of *Advices from Parnassus.* His Aversion to Bigotry and Superstition obliged him to quit his own Country. He has a competent Knowledge of the Power, Riches, and Trade of all the flourishing States in *Europe.* He is a constant Check upon that Prevention and Redundancy of Zeal, so natural to an *Englishman*, in Favour of ourselves. He is free from the deceitful Knavery of his own Countrymen, the Levity of the *French*, the Gravity of the *Spaniard*, and the Ferocity of a certain Northern Island mention'd by *Horace.*

The last is *Tom Cynick*, a Fellow of an odd, splenetick Frame of Mind. From a thoro' Knowledge of the Beauties of the Antients, he is become an unfit Companion for the modern Virtuosi. He is a bitter Enemy to all those brilliant Excursions into the modish Sublime of the present Dramatists. But his Knowledge is not confined to the Stage; for he is not only Master of that Branch of Learning which we owe to *Greece* and *Rome*, but of that which we borrow from *Egypt* and *Arabia.* *Frank* looks upon him as a *Magazine* of Learning, and often asks him about the *Grecian* Ladies, and the *French* Temples dedicated to *Venus*; whether they went to Church in them, as they do in our World? He is of great Use in our Club when *Frank* is too talkative. In short, we owe a good deal of our Mirth to the Spleen of the one, and the extravagant Flights of the other.

We meet at a Tavern near the *Temple*, almost every Evening at 9, but never fail on *Wednesday* and *Saturday*. Over our Chimney is the Figure of a *Mole*, with this Motto, IN AUDITU SALUS. The venerable *Nestor Ironside* often alarm'd the World with the roaring of his Lion; We have chose an Animal of a more pacifick Nature, and juster Emblem of ourselves.

By the Benefit of each his little Engine to his Ear, we converse in a Manner imperceptible to the nearest Stander-by. A new Drawer coming to attend us just as we were in a Fit of Laughter, and seeing our Lips move without hearing us, was so confounded and frightned as to run away and leave the House.

N° IV. *O Dea certe*——

As I was intently studying the other Morning in my Elbow-Chair, I was surprized with the Appearance of the most beautiful Woman I had ever beheld. Grave as I am, I felt more than a common Warmth; and jumping up, to give her my Hand, I overset the Table: I made the best Apology I could, and in leading her to her Seat, tript against a large Folio that had fallen with the Table, and in the Endeavour to save myself, pull'd her down. I was so confounded at this Series of Misfortunes, that I had not a Word to say, and should have stood staring till now, had not the charming *Florimel* told me, she excused me, and desired I would recover myself, because she had Matters of Importance to consult me upon. She staid a Quarter of an Hour, and then told me she could not prevail upon herself to speak, but would write; and, upon taking her Leave, with a malicious Smile, bid me beware how I strove to make myself agreeable again. I handed her to her Coach with great Success, and, with a profound Reverence, retired. These various Incidents produced a Speculation upon the wonderful Force of Beauty.

No Objects so effectually move our Admiration as the Sight of a young and beautiful Woman. When I see *Angelina* dance with all the Graces imaginable, and afterward behold the awkward Endeavours of her ungenteel Admirer *Rusticus*, I am no longer at a loss to know why he exposes himself to the Raillery of Every-body. He sees what Advantage a regular Motion is to a fine Shape, and thinks it will have the same Effects on a bad one, not considering, that it serves only to multiply his Deformity, and that what is graceful in one, is not always so in another.

Amongst the many Follies this way of thinking causes, the Extravagancies of Dress is not the most inconsiderable. Old *Calvus* thinks he cannot appear too airy in the Eyes of the wild *Harriet*; whilst *Calvisus* consults the Taste of the staid

Sophrosynia

Sophrosunia in the moſt trifling Points of Dreſs. *Irus*, whoſe Eſtate amounts to but 20*l.* a Year, will play for twice as much, tho' he knows no more how to raiſe it than how to refuſe *Omnamante*, who tells him ſhe can't abide a *near Man*.

Juſt as I was finiſhing this Paper, the A following Letter was brought me:

" *Sir*, When I acquaint you that *Helena* is a top Toaſt, I need not tell you, that *Beauty* ought to be compleat in her; but I aſſure you, for I have bribed her Maid, who has told me—ſhe has—and B is——. This you ought to publiſh, to prevent the *Beau Monde* being impoſed upon. I think myſelf, for I have been told ſo a thouſand Times, perfectly qualified for a Toaſt, and to ſucceed *Helena*; which if by your Means I can obtain, I ſhall thank you after what Manner you pleaſe.   *Tours*, &c. LINDAMIRA."

Anſ. You are miſtaken in your Man, *Lindamira.* —— As to your Beauty, I take your Word for it; but then give me Leave to ſay, you are equally conceited. Beauty, not tempered with Humility, is its own greateſt Enemy. D If you are ambitious of being admired under the inſignificant Character of a Toaſt, conſider how precarious your Empire is; a Fit of Sickneſs, or a few Years will infallibly put an End to it. Is there any real Pleaſure in this tranſitory Reign that can equal the ſolid Felicity E in making one Man of Senſe happy, or giving Life to a Race of Children, in whom you will ſee *revived* the ſame Form that charm'd your Huſband ? — Obſerve the Boxes round, and view the Diſcontent that appears in the Faces of the *Lindamira's* of the laſt Age : Like *you*, theſe F were the Toaſts of the Gay and Young; like *you* they *were*, like *them* you *will be.*   *The* AUDITOR.

Free Briton, Jan. 18. No. 164.

Neceſſity and Corruption.

OFfices of State are acknowledged to be in the Power and Diſpoſal of the Adminiſtration; but all Men who can ſerve or hurt them, think they have a Right to influence that Power: Hence Miniſters are often neceſſitated to advance worthleſs Perſons, being ſeldom left to their own Choice: For ſhould they H act otherwiſe, it would be worſe; half the Courtiers would oppoſe their Meaſures.

Governors muſt indulge the Humours of the Times, they muſt preſerve every uſeful Friendſhip, and prevent every formidable Enmity; few good Offices are done to Governments but what they dearly pay for. Can Miniſters then be complained of, who purchaſe Friends for the Publick ? The noble Virtues are long ſince loſt, that engaged thoſe Patriot Volunteers whoſe Names do Honour to Humanity.

The common People are more prone to Corruption than Men of ſuperior Fortunes and liberal Educations. *Cæſar*, who bribed the Multitude, could never buy the *Roman* Senate and *Cato*.

When the Genius of the Times becomes depraved, thoſe who wiſh well to Mankind, if they cannot entirely ſuppreſs Corruption, will turn it to the beſt Advantage. When *Cæſar* ſtood for the Conſulſhip, even *Cato* thought it lawful to bribe the Populace, in order to bridle that aſpiring Man; and accordingly, the Nobility raiſed an immenſe Sum to carry the Election of a powerful Colleague.

Wiſe Governors always recurred to the readieſt Means of ſaving their Country. Even Q. *Elizabeth* had Penſioners in the Courts of *France* and *Rome*; and if ſhe had few at Home, it was becauſe the Horrors of Popery were ſo ſtrong in her People, that they readily came into any Meaſures againſt it.

The Reign of K. *Charles* II. was ſcandalous, on Account of thoſe Miniſters who became Penſioners to foreign Courts. The Times are alter'd ſince, and we have allowed large Subſidies and Penſions to our Neighbours; which, however juſt, have been greatly clamour'd at. In Q. *Anne's* Time, 'twas done to ſupport a War; ſince, to ſave one; and a Prevention is better than a Remedy.

Would our popular Patriots recommend the Virtues of publick Frugality and Œconomy, let them purge their own Characters from all Suſpicion of Guilt, and prove that they never adminiſtred the Publick for corrupt Expectations; that G they never bribed Voices, and bought Elections, nor in any wiſe defiled themſelves with this Sin of Uncleanneſs.

I believe, concludes *Walſingham*, there are ſome alive, who remember particular Gentlemen who generally voted againſt a Court, and expreſſed an extraordinary Vehemence on moſt Occaſions; yet at certain Times would come into healing Meaſures, if their Aſſiſtance was

wanted,

waxed: Which shews, that some Men only make Virtue a Pretence, and sell their Country when they have a fair Opportunity.

The Daily Courant, *Jan.* 18.

THE Writer in this Courant questions the Fairness and Honesty of their Proceedings who endeavour to inflame the People against the Administration, upon the bare Supposition of an Excise. They have painted the Figure of a horrible Monster like those in the Ballad published on this Occasion; which indeed gives us a lively Idea of their own Writings upon this Subject, but which never had any Foundation in Truth.

The whole Weight of their Arguments has been turned against a General Excise, as if that was the Scheme which the Administration had in View. Was this indeed the Thing proposed, it would deserve to be rejected with the utmost Indignation against the Projectors of it; and a Minister would find it as dangerous to make such a Proposition to his Majesty, as he would find it difficult to thrust it down upon the People.

But supposing a real Design to extend the Excise Laws to Wine and Tobacco; what Tendency has this to a General Excise? A General Excise, is an Excise upon all the Commodities of our own Produce, as well as of those imported, upon the common Necessaries of Life, as well as upon those Things that administer to Luxury. But no body will say, that he cannot live without he drinks Wine, or smoaks Tobacco; he may as well aver, that unless he wears Velvet, he cannot keep himself warm.

I have heard, says this Writer, that *Daniel De Foe* would write an Answer to Books before they were published; and that once he wrote an Answer to a Book that was never published; but I never thought Mr *D'anvers* would have follow'd the Example of so mercenary a Writer, for whom he takes every Occasion to express so great a Contempt.

Daily Courant, *Jan.* 19.

Excise no new Thing.

THE World knows, that the common Topicks in the *Craftsman* are Complaints of the Load of Taxes, particularly those that lie heaviest upon the Poor, viz. 1st, the Taxes upon *Soap* and *Candles*; 2dly, the Method of levying

Taxes by the Laws of *Excise.*——Now whoever looks into the Statute-book will find, that — in the 9th Year of Q. *Anne's* Reign, and first of *Oxford's* Ministry, Stat. 6. a Tax is laid on *Candles* for 32 Years, to be levied by the Officers of the *Excise.*—That by Stat. 21. in the same Year, the said Tax is made perpetual.— That by Stat. 36, in the next Year, Duties are laid on Starch, Leather, Coffee, Tea, Druggs, *&c.* and Gold and Silver Wire,—all to be collected by the Officers of *Excise.* — That by Stat. 19. in the 10th of Q. *Anne,* the Tax is laid on *Soap,* to be collected by, and subject to the Laws of *Excise.* — That by Stat. 9. in the 12th of Q. *Anne* (during the blessed Peace of *Utrecht*) an additional Tax is laid on *Soap,*—still by the Way of *Excise.*

Now I appeal to any impartial Man, whether I can be justly suspected of caballing with Mr *D'anvers,* in crying out on the Grievances of these Taxes on the Poor.   *Yours,* HARRY GAMBOL.

The Craftsman, *Jan.* 20. No. 342.

Extracts from a Pamphlet, entitl'd, Remarks on the horrible Oppressions, Insolencies, and unjustifiable Partialities, *of the* Commissioners of Excise, *publish'd in the Reign of* Q. Anne.

THE *Preface* is address'd to the *Commons of England,* in Parliament assembled, as the only sovereign Expositors of the Laws made by them.

When, by a long-since dormant Law, You ordered, that the *Brewers* and *Distillers,* in case of a small Penalty of 5 *l.* as to the *Excise,* upon certain Miscarriages, should be decisively heard by *Commissioners,* &c. it cannot be imagin'd *you* ever designed to condemn the *Brewers* and *Distillers* to the Loss of their native Privileges, as *Englishmen*; and that *they* alone should be thought unworthy of *their* Share in the *Magna Charta of England,* viz. to be try'd by their *Peers.* This Consideration it is hoped will move you to redress their intolerable Pressures, under the present Tyranny of the *Commissioners* of *Excise*; especially when you reflect, that the said Penalties being risen by sundry subsequent Acts, a *Brewer* or *Distiller* is now liable to forfeit 2 or 300 *l. per Diem.*

After some general Reflections on the oppressive Management of the *Commissioners of Excise,* the Author goes on to examine. 1. Whether there is not an *exorbitant*

bitant Power, arbitrary, and in its Nature *illegal,* tho' literally otherwife, accidentally and perhaps unwarily put in their Hands ? 2. Whether they have not made ufe of that Power to different Purpofes, from the true Intent of the *Law* from whence they derive it ?

The firft Point will be beft enquired into by confidering the *Laws* of *England,* in their general Defign, the *Nature* and *Reafon* of them.

Among other of the native Branches of *Juftice,* for which *Englifh Laws* are famous, thefe are fome; 1. That every *Englifhman,* offending or trefpaffing, fhall have a fair Trial by his Peers, and not otherwife. 2. That *indifferent Judges* fhall try the Caufe between the *Prince* and the *Subject,* and not *Parties concerned.* 3. That no Man fhall be admitted an Evidence in a Cafe, where he fhall be a *Gainer* by the Condemnation of the Perfon he witneffeth againft.

Now, if thefe *three known Maxims of the Law* are invaded in the prefent Cafe, let all indifferent People judge, whether the *Commiffioners of Excife* are not vefted with an *exorbitant Power, illegal,* and contrary to the Rights and Priviledges of the *Englifh* Nation; and whether it is not too much to be committed to any *Sett of Men* lefs than a *Parliamentary Affembly.*

It follows to enquire, Whether *thefe Commiffioners* have not applied *this Power,* vefted in them by the Law, contrary to the true Intent, *&c.* This will beft appear in the *five Heads of Articles,* exhibited to the *Parliament,* by the *Diftillers, viz.* 1. *Informations* being exhibited unknown to the Perfons inform'd againft, tho' pretended Summons have been fent, are frequently fuffered to lye feveral Years unpurfued, 'till the *Servants* and *Witneffes,* by which the Perfons *accufed* might defend themfelves, are gone from them, or dead, or have forgot the Particulars. 2. Complaints made by the *Diftillers,* for the Injuries and Outrages of their *Officers,* have been left unheard, 'till they have not been able to make out the particulars. 3. They arbitrarily determine *Property,* and refufing the *Duty,* when lawfully tender'd by *Perfons* from whom it is legally and only due, demand it of others wholly unconcerned, and pretend to *Forfeitures* for the Default. 4. When they have been fummoned to *Trials,* either on Informations, or Complaints, and have duly attended with *Council* and *Witneffes,* they

have been put off, without Reafon given, from Time to Time; on purpofe to tire them out with the Charge and *Expence of Attendance.* 5. That fundry Perfons have been *condemned* and *fined* by the arbitrary Sentence of the *Commiffioners;* and at other Times, *acquitted* for the fame *Kind of Facts,* which *To-day* is, and *To-morrow* is not, or in *this Perfon* is, and in *another* is not, a Crime, according to the Pleafure of the *Commiffioners;* fo that no Man can know when he acts fafely, and when not.

Fog's Journal, Jan. 20. No. 220.

Calculations on Trade and Taxes.

NExt to the avoiding chargeable Undertakings, the beft Expedient is to defray them by Taxes rais'd within the Year. This was poffible for *England* in the two late Wars with *France,* for the Land-Tax of 4*s.* the Malt-Tax, and what is raifed at prefent by all the Funds, amount to 6 *Millions;* which with the Charges of Collection and Poor's Tax, is a greater Sum than *England* ought ever to have rais'd, or what was fairly expended. It is true, the War in the late Queen's Time, (by carrying it into *Spain)* coft Yearly at an Average 4,800,00*l.* but the firft and laft War, at an Average, not above 4,000,000*l.* a Year.

This Maxim of defraying our yearly Expences by Taxes raifed within the Year, is more neceffary now, than it was in the Beginning of the firft War, fince our Trade, by being already much burthened, is the lefs fufceptible of any further Burden.

Since the Peace of *Utrecht* there has been rais'd upon the People of *Great-Britain* for fome Years 9 Millions Yearly, and for fome Years to come there may be rais'd 8 Millions yearly, arifing from the following Particulars; *viz.* Yearly Expence; Civil Lift; Intereft and Sinking Fund; Charges of collecting and disburfing; Poor's Tax; Highways, *&c.*

Eight Millions is 20*s.* per Head on every Individual in *Great-Britain,* fuppofing the Number of the People 8 Millions.

All the Effects of any Nation are Land and Water, or the Products of them manufactur'd, which may be valued at above 19 Parts in 20: Therefore the Riches of *Great-Britain* and the Manufactures of the People may pafs for convertible Terms.

In a Mafs of People not above one half labour, fuppofe the Limits of the Age of

Labour

Labour to be between 13 and 63; there are 2 Thirds or 8 Twelfths between these Ages; and from these 8 you must subduct at least a Fourth or two Eighths under the following Classes: Females sequestrated from Labour by the Condition of their Sex; the Idle by Rank or Choice; Men of Professions who vend the Manufacture of others; the Sick and Impotent; so that there only remain 6 of 12 labouring or manufacturing; therefore by the present Rate of Taxes there is raised 20s. per Head upon every Invidual, which makes 40s. upon the Labour, and perhaps 30s. upon the annual Labour of every Individual.

If the Yearly Expences of every Individual be 5l. then 1l. paid in Taxes increaseth the Expences of Living 20 *per Ct.*

The Price of Labour is rais'd in Proportion to the Scarcity of Labourers. Suppose of 3 Millions of labouring People 30,000, carrying Arms, or levying Taxes, 30,000 is one *per Cent.* on 3 Millions, by which the Price of Labour will be increased one *per Cent.* and these living upon the Labour of the rest make another one *per Cent.* or double of the Proportion; but the Proportion is much higher in *Britain*; for the 30,000 cost above 30l. per Head. Therefore great Armies and numerous Collectors increase greatly the Price of a Manufacture of a Country.

All Taxes upon Commodities of universal Consumption raise at least 10, perhaps 15 *per Cent.* more than their Rate on the People; because the Dealers in those Commodities exact that Interest for the Money advanced for the Tax.

There can be no Security for foreign Trade, except the Monopoly or Cheapness of Commodities. The Course of Trade is changeable by the Difference of one or two *per Cent.*

Suppose the Ballance of our Trade two Millions *per Annum*, there is a Duty upon this of 20 *per Cent.* by the Interest due to Foreigners upon publick Funds, which may be put at 400,000l. *per Ann.*

From the Premisses it is apparent that our exportable Commodities have a Duty of 30 *per Cent.* upon them, which operates in Abatement of our Exportation; therefore it would be imprudent to increase the Price of our Commodities, by laying further Duties on our Consumption.

Excises upon Commodities of universal Consumption are Poll-Taxes raised without Distinction of Ranks or Abilities. Supposing the Expence of every Individual be increased 9d. yearly by the Tax upon Salt; it were better for the Master of a Family to have it collected by a Poll-Tax by the Parish Officers, than by Excise; by which Means the Expence, and the 10 *per Cent.* upon the Advance of the Tax would be saved, (See p. 604, 605, Vol. II.)

Excises upon the Necessaries of Life encrease the Expence of the manufacturing People more, in Proportion, than that of others in a higher Rank; for Example, Day-light — infinite *per Cent.* Salt Tax, at 300 *per Cent.* Candle-Light, Coals, Soap, Leather, at a Medium of 25 *per Cent.* Money received by Apprentices 2 and a half *per Cent.*

As it is pernicious to burden Trade, so it's prudent to ease it of those Taxes which seem more immediately to affect it, even by abating the Income of the Sinking Fund.

Suppose the Annuity payable by the Sinking-Fund to be one Million, and the National Debt 49 Millions. Such Annuity will pay such Debt in about 28 Years, at Half yearly Payments, and 4 *per Cent.* Interest. An Annuity of 800,000l. will clear the same Debt in 32 Years. Suppose that the Abatement of some Taxes may extend your Exportation to the amount of an equivalent Sum of 200,000l. *per Ann.* at the End of 32 Years the Nation will be richer by above 12 Millions upon that single Account of postponing the Payment of their Debts only 4 Years.

This Piece of OEconomy proposed, is reduc'd to a single Point, *viz. B* owes a great Debt, he allots a certain annual Sum to clear it, which Sum operates in sinking his Debt at the Rate of 4 *per Ct. per Ann.* but some Part of this Sum kept in his own Hands may produce perhaps 10 *per Cent.* Which is more eligible, the continuing, or abating of his Sinking-Fund?

Applebee's Journal, Jan. 20.

THE *Polemical Writer* in this Journ. having dropp'd his Correspondence, the former Author resumes his Character of a *Friend* to *Mankind,* tho' attach'd to no *Party.* As the Town is now growing full, Men by *displaying* their *Follies* will afford him *Means* and Opportunity to *amend* them.

Is sorry, at the Entrance of his *Weekly Course* he cannot compliment the Publick with a *Panegyrick* on any extraordinary Performance with which they have been lately entertained. However, ventures to inform them, that the Expectation of the Town is raised in Favour of a *new Piece*, by a celebrated Author, quickly to be play'd. The Title of it, according to some Advices, is *Achilles*, others, the *Thracian Maid*. It is assured, it is an excellent *Dramatick* Performance ; its Characters *just* ; the Songs *lively* and *agreeable* ; the Moral *wonderfully instructive*. These are strange Things to be said of a *Ballad Opera* ?

It having been objected to his Writings, that they are *too grave*, he declares he will write nothing for the future but what shall carry the *Mark of Politeness*.

With Regard to the Ladies, hopes it will never be a part of his Duty to *reprove them*. He has been told, indeed, that some indecent Fashions have crept in amongst them ; that Women who have not given up *all* Pretences to *Virtue*, stray out 'till *Midnight* with a *Male Acquaintance*, and then are extremely *out of Humour*, if their *inquisitive* Husbands express any Uneasiness, as to *where* they have been, and *what* they have been *doing*. But takes these for *malicious Aspersions* of the Enemies of the Sex, and therefore will not offer a *Word of Caution*.

Universal Spectator, Jan. 20. Nº 224.

On the Observation of Sunday.

ON a Time several Ladies of Quality presented a Petition to Parliament, setting forth the many and great Inconveniencies that accrue to the Publick from the *Observation* of *Sunday*, as it is now by Law established. That the Petitioners were in the utmost Distress how to render that Day tolerable to them, they being then, (as if predestin'd by the Stars) inevitably either asleep or in the Vapours ; that the Dutchess of *Maydew* had been constantly indisposed every *Sunday* for upwards of 40 *Years*, and that tho' she had been attended by the most eminent Physicians, and was herself the most dexterous Artist at improving a bad Face, yet her Constitution by such frequent Relapses, was entirely destroy'd, and her Face irreparably decay'd ; that the Countess of *Hazardall* had every *Sunday* for several Years condescended to an Action beneath her Quality, and set apart that Day for inspecting and settling the Accounts of her Family ; yet was continually tortur'd with the Head-ach, and plagu'd with *Betty*'s Awkwardness in dressing her, which once especially affect-

(Gent. Mag. Vol. III. Nº xiv.)

ed her Spirits so violently, that she could not recover them 'till the *Thursday* following, when upon an agreeable Visit from Mr *Spadille*, and five or six of his younger Brothers, her Spirits were restored to their wonted Harmony: But, that notwithstanding the strict Friendship, and the frequent good Offices of this Kind from the Family of the *Mattadores*, those Grievances had risen so intolerably, that her Ladyship had been forced to change her Woman 19 Times, and have 23 Cooks in one Year. It likewise represented that the Lady *Primly* had for 10 Years frequented the Church on *Sundays*, but that she had no sooner paid her Compliments to her Acquaintance, and made a few slight Remarks on the awkward Dresses of the People, but she was frequently seized with a Fit of Drowsiness, which she knew not how to attribute to any Thing but her own Silence, and a continual Murmur in the Place ; that she could not recollect above two Instances of her being able to keep awake throughout *Divine Service* ; one was, when the Lady *Talkative* entertain'd her with a true and impartial History of *Miss Wanton's* Tympany, and the other, when the young Lord *Amorous* in the next Pew, made Love to her. That by sleeping so frequently in such open Places she was never free from *Cricks*, *Coughs*, *Spleen*, *Cholick*, *Hystericks*, &c. For these and other good Causes the Petitioners pray'd, that for the future all the Days in the Week might be reputed upon an *equal* footing.

Against this Petition a Remonstrance was immediately drawn up by the *Tradesmen's Wives* and *Apprentices*, importing that if the Petition was granted, no Time would be allow'd them for Diversion ; whereas on *Sundays* they had the Pleasure of shewing their fine Cloaths, Visiting, going to Church, where they could see good Company, learn the Fashions, ogle the Men, and reap all the Advantages of a Play without the Expence of it. The Apprentices urg'd they were as much confined as their Mistresses, and consequently that *Sunday* was the only Day in which they were at Liberty to *Whore* and *Drink*. That considering the constant *Vigils* which the Ladies of Quality kept at Cards, Masquerades, &c. the Sleep which they met with at Church, was so far from being an Inconvenience, as pretended, that it was hardly sufficient to compensate for the Deficiencies of the Week past ; and that as frequent *Physick* is neceſſary to preſerve the Conſtitution of a fine Lady, they might take it on that Day without Loſs of Time.

This Remonſtrance was back'd by another from the *Clergy*. The Topicks they went upon were, that the *Seventh Day* had been appointed by Divine Command; that it had ever been ſtrictly obſerved by the *Apoſtles* and *Primitive Chriſtians*; that the *Soul* was much more valuable than the *Body*, and *Eternity* infinitely preferrable to *Time*; with 20 ſuch old-faſhion'd Arguments, which had nothing in the World but downright *Grace* and *Godlineſs* to recommend them.

The Female Remonſtrants, upon hearing this Defence of the *Clergy*, were quite dejected and confounded; fearing ſuch Advocates would prove worſe than none. On the contrary, the Ladies of Quality doubted not but the Gentlemen of the Houſe of Commons were of too Genteel a Turn of Thought to be moved by ſuch *weak* Pretences: But it happen'd that the Members did not prove to be ſuch *fine Gentlemen* as expected, but unanimouſly voted in favour of *Sundays* and the *Clergy*.

London Journal, Jan. 20. No. 701.

Of publick Wiſdom.

PUblick *Wiſdom*, or the Wiſdom of Men at the Head of Affairs, conſiſts in having the *Good of the Publick* conſtantly before their Eyes, and purſuing that Good by *juſt* and *worthy* Means; for there is ſuch a cloſe Connection between *Honeſty* and *publick Happineſs*, that nothing can be for the Proſperity of a Nation, which is *unjuſt* in itſelf, or oppreſſive to any part of the Subjects.

Gentlemen in *Power*, ſhould not for any *partial* or *private* Conſideration, employ it to the *Detriment of the People*; they ſhould conſider not only what is for the *real Benefit* of the Nation, but ſhould pay ſome Regard to the *Humours, Inclinations* and *Prejudices* of the People, yet, not ſo as to *depart from what is Right*, or lay by a Scheme apparently for the Good of the Nation, becauſe the People are againſt it, this would ſhew Puſillanimity, and Want of *Abilities* and *Reſolution*. But then it ſhould be conſidered, whether the Scheme is Right upon the whole; whether it is *got* one Way is not *loſt* another; whether it is not better to *bear with ſome Frauds* in Duties, than *oppreſs* or *grieve* the Sub-

ject by a *new Manner* of Collecting, terrible in Apprehenſion, and perhaps *burthenſome* to themſelves and Poſterity.

Gentlemen *out of Power* ought to employ all their Abilities for the Benefit of the Nation, and never *oppoſe*, but *for the Sake of the Publick*. Kingdoms happy and flouriſhing have been deſtroy'd by *Oppoſition*; and many Miniſters of State, *good in themſelves*, have been driven to do Things againſt their Natures, from the Difficulties created by the turbulent Paſſions of *Men out of Power*. 'Tis but laſt Week, that the *Craftſman* quoted *Shakeſpeare* to ſhew, that we are on the *Brink of Ruin*; that we were leas'd out, and had made a *Conqueſt of ourſelves*; and his Correſpondent ſays, the Quotation *deſerved* a Place in his Journal *at this Juncture*, becauſe it is a Speech of *John of Gaunt's*, repreſenting *the Grievances of the Nation*, under one of our *moſt unhappy Princes*. Is this *Wiſdom* or *Madneſs*? *Virtue*, or *Malice*? *Patriotiſm*, or *Faction*?

Is it *Wiſdom* to ſet the People *all in a Roar*, about what *they know nothing of*? To make them meet in Bodies all over the Kingdom, and reſolve ſtrenuouſly to *oppoſe* an *imaginary Monſter* in any Form or Shape? Would not *Wiſdom* have taught them Patience, 'till the Scheme was laid before the Publick, and then, if any Part of it appears againſt the Intereſts of Trade, they will have full Liberty to make their Objections; and if they can't get it laid aſide, may obtain ſuch *Alteration* as will give them Satisfaction.

It ſeems very improbable, that the Miniſtry ſhould engage in a Scheme *detrimental* to the *Publick*, and which muſt neceſſarily affect their *own Intereſt*; by ſetting all the Trading Part of the Nation againſt them.

It is ſaid by the Friends of the Miniſtry, that *this Scheme* is highly advantageous to the Intereſt of the *fair and honeſt* Traders; that it will not ſubject them to *the Power of Officers*, and will bring in near 400,000 *l.* a Year upon the *preſent Duties*, all which is now *fraudulently* loſt.

It is ſaid, when Taxes are laid they ought to be *paid*; that it is very unreaſonable ſome Tradeſmen ſhould pay *Duties*, and others get Eſtates by *paying none*; and, that if ever the Miniſters were right in any Thing for the Good of the Nation, they are *right in this*. They ought not to be *condemned before* they are *tried*. Their *Reasons* will short-ly be laid before the House; and, 'till then, I suspend my Judgment.

Weekly Miscellany. Jan. 20. No. 8.

Of MAN.

THE Philosophers have given us several Definitions of *Man*; *Animal Religiosum*; *Animal Risibile*; *Animal Rationale*; *religious, laughing, and reasoning*. But these Definitions are imperfect. The only way of judging of the Power and Capacities of a Being, is, by *Experience*. If a Man has all Opportunities of acquiring a Sense of Religion, and Occasions of shewing it, and yet does not appear to have any; it is presumed, that *all* Men are not *religious* Animals, not *capable* of being such. Whether this be not the Case of *many* Men let the Reader determine from his *own* Knowledge. There is in great Numbers (who pass under the Denominations of Men) not only an *Inaptitude* to Religion, but a strong *Antipathy* to it. To give a Case *in Point*, as the Lawyers term it: A Gentleman, in seeming good Health, upon Sight of the Word *Religion* in this Paper, turned pale, and grew sick, and left the Table. I myself, says this Writer, have seen Gentlemen, who call themselves *Free-Thinkers*, in the Height of a Fit of Merriment fall into the greatest Disorder at the Sight of a *Clergyman*.

The next Definition is, that Man is a *risible Animal*, or *capable of laughing*. But this does not belong to *every* Man: There are some Tempers that have an Aversion to every Thing *jocular* or *chearful*. It is not certain whether this Aversion be natural, or the Effect of a settled Persuasion, that *Banter* and *Ridicule* are inconsistent with the *Dignity* of our *Nature*, or the *Gravity* of a *serious Design*: Let such know, that Wit is no such *wicked* Thing as they imagine. Some Arguments, tho' the Subject be grave, are too *absurd* to be exposed so effectually as by *Raillery*. These *ludicrous* Batteries have been often played against *Religion*, and have been turned as successfully upon the *Enemy*. An Author, who has a great Share of it observes, 'That *Wit* is one of the noblest Faculties of the Mind. And in the *Sacred* Writings, we have Instances of the strongest and most elegant *Raillery*. Shall we succeed better, if we define Man a *rational Animal*? Much worse; What Multitudes are there, who assume

the Name of *Men*, yet are irreconcileable Enemies to *Reason*, and incapable of understanding its Dictates? either through some Defect in the *intellectual Faculties*, or an *Incapacity* of *Attention*: They live without *Consideration*, and read, as they all, for the Employment of their *Senses*.

The Author having thus expatiated on the different Capacities and Tempers of Men, and declared his Willingness to gratify the Taste of his Readers in general observes, that his Design being various and extensive, the *Manner* must be diversified as the Occasion requires, hopes he shall meet with as much Candour from the Publick as 'Squire *D'anvers*, or the *profound* Mr *Osborne*; and doubts not of Encouragement, since his Design is to promote *Religion, Morality, Learning, Good Sense, and Ingenuity*, without abusing either *Persons* or *Parties*.

Next follows in the Literary Articles,

Account of a Book, entitled, An Examination of Pyrrhonism, antient and modern, by Mr *de Crousaz*, of the Royal Academy of Sciences, &c. Printed at the *Hagua*, in Folio.

THE Author's Design in this Work is to combat the Principles of Pyrrhonism; which he thinks the more necessary in this Age, as this Sect has met with a powerful Assistant in Mr *Bayle*, one of the greatest Genius's of his Time. He defines the Pyrrhonians to be a Sect, who ' will not allow that a Man can be ' certain of any Truth whatever, either ' General or Particular.'

The Idea which Mr *Crousaz* gives of the Pyrrhonians amounts to this: They are a Sett of Men, who speak and think like the rest of the World, except in two Particulars: 1. When a Question is proposed, they are always of the opposite Sentiment to that of others. Their Aim, in raising Difficulties, is not so clear but darkens the Subject, and nothing is more shameful with them, than to yield the Point in Question. 2. The Spirit of Contradiction shews itself most in these Men, when you talk to them of Religion and Morality: Whatever they don't like in either they are sure to doubt the Truth of.

Mr *Crousaz* then goes on to assign the Causes of Pyrrhonism, or extreme Scepticism, (for they are the same.)

The 1st is, A Fondness for Conjectures. This the Author illustrates by several Examples

amples borrow'd from Opticks and Morality. This Inclination puts us sometimes upon pronouncing peremptorily in a Matter, of which we are totally ignorant; sometimes upon concluding, that we ought not to believe any Thing because we can't prove every Thing.

The 2d is, An Itch at Disputation, which was much in Vogue among the *Greeks*, and contributes greatly to the Establishment of Pyrrhonism. The Study of Divinity, among the Moderns, has furnish'd out a great Number of disputable Questions unknown to the Antients.

A Third Occasion of Universal Scepticism, is, When a Man in examining the Articles of his Belief fancies he discovers one Proposition to be false; and is thereby led to doubt of them all.

A superficial Mind, an insatiable desire of Knowledge, a Disregard of Religion, and the great Variety of Opinion to be met with among Mankind, are other Causes of Pyrrhonism assigned by this Author.

From Pointing out the Nature and Causes of this Distemper, he goes on to prescribe the Remedies for it, the Principal of which is a prevailing Love of Truth. This will inspire a Fear of falling into Error; it will put us upon Diligence in our Enquiries; and instead of the ill-natur'd Pleasure of detecting the Weakness of other Mens Sentiments, will teach us to relish the noble Satisfaction of laying hold on something certain.

Other Remedies against Pyrrhonism are, Not to be in haste to build Systems, to embrace or reject no Sentiment upon Motives of Party, To settle distinctly, and pursue exactly, the State of the Question, &c.

As to Authority, in Matters of Opinion which some are fond of, as being the shortest Way of putting an End to all Controversies, our Author gives it as his Judgment, ' That in Countries, where ' Authority in Matters of Opinion is the ' most respected, there is as great a Di- ' versity of Opinions, as any where; be- ' sides, that the Decisions of Authority ' in different Countries is different, nor ' can we be sure, that the Tribunal, esta- ' blish'd in our own Country, is effectu- ' ally in lawful Possession of all the Pri- ' vileges it pretends to.'

Afterwards the Journalist informs us of a *Dutch Spectator* in 3 vols, printed at *Amsterdam*, in Imitation of the *English Spectator*, which tho' the Author

does not pretend to equal, yet as every People has its peculiar Manners, Customs, Virtues and Vices, he thought it but just that *Holland* should have her *Spectator*, as well as *England* and *France*. A Specimen, in the Character of a Coquet is given from it, with this Encomium, That the *Dutch Spectator* wants neither Sense nor Genius: So that we may expect the Whole in our Language, as they have long had our *Spectators* in theirs.

The Auditor Jan. 23. No. 5.

I Was reading *Epictetus* last Night, where he compares the Universe to a Drama, contrived by a divine Poet. The Notion dwelt so strong upon me, that I was no sooner asleep, but I fancied myself in a Place whose Extent was beyond the Reach of human Eyes. I saw an infinite Multitude, and prodigious Variety of Creatures in every Element, all employed suitably to their different Natures.

Whilst I was contemplating their different Pleasures, Oh! why, must that Creature alone, said I, for whose Ease and Support all these were formed, be more unhappy than they? I was interrupted by the Appearance of an ancient Man, who ask'd me, If that was the only Reflection such a Scene was capable of raising in me? And leading me to a large Plain, bid me tell him what I saw, I see, said I, a Herd of Men and Women; some stretch'd on the Grass, others upon the Banks of Rivers; some gather the Fruits of the bending Trees, some slake their Thirst at the clear Springs; others sleep, they seem to love Society and live together. " This (said my divine Guide), was the Life Mankind at first led; how full of Innocence and Happiness!" And observing my Inclination to become one of them;

" The Gods, continued he, when they formed the Universe, endowed each Creature with a Capacity for Knowledge, and Faculties answerable to that Capacity: To the human Creature they gave a greater Degree in Capacity, a quicker Apprehension, and an Intenseness of Thought, above other Animals. From the lowest Degree of Being to the highest, in the visible Part of the Creation, there is a reigning Principle, a Law of Life of divine Establishment; to keep to which, is the Perfection and Happiness of each Creature; to be false to it, its Defect and Misery. The highest Principle of the animal World is Sense, to which it keeps. *But*

But to the human Principle the Gods have given a higher Principle, a divine Power. It has a Capacity to know itself and Original; and partakes more amply of the divine Nature. The human Nature has *x* in it, which the animal has ———— This is its reigning Principle and Intelligent Life. He is a good Actor, and answers the End of the divine Former of the Drama, that enters chearfully into the Part allotted him, and does ———— think himself superior to his Roll; this is Wisdom, Happiness, Virtue."

I was going to ask some Questions, when casting my Eyes upon the Plain, I observed the Herd of Human Creatures, forming Parties, arming and advancing against each other, seemingly all animated with a Desire of Superiority. The old Men, who had not forgot their former Simplicity, interposed, endeavouring to restore Tranquillity, but finding their Efforts vain, retired together, prepared for their Defence, and formed Laws against any Disturbance within.

My Guide, guessing at my Thoughts, relieved my Admiration, as follows.

" You see, says he, the Bonds of Union that kept this Herd together are dissolved, and they are obliged to maintain by Art, what they before supported by Nature only. All this is owing to their being false to their reigning Principle, and Law of Life. From hence may be deduced the Origin of Government, Civil and Military. Whilst the first Simplicity of Manners and Innocence remained among the Herd; while they continued true to those Principles the divine Former and Director of the Universe gave them, there was no Occasion either for Arms or Laws. So soon as they became false to their reigning Principle, and listened to their lower Faculties, Distrusts and Jealousies, Greediness of Power, extravagant Love of Self, and all the Evils that proceed from being false to Truth crowded in upon them. To prevent the Disorders consequent hereon, wise Men established Laws,and made use of Arms."

Striving to make a Reply, I awoke.

The Daily Courant. Jan. 23.

The Craftsman *on the Army answer'd*,

IT is no Security, says D'*anvers*, to the Publick, that our Troops are commanded *by Men of Family and Fortune*; for the Troops of other Nations are commanded by the *Nobility*, and yet the *People are Slaves*.] By this he would suppose our *Nobility* to be in *Vaſſalage*, and as dependent on the Crown as the *French* and *Germans*, tho' no two Bodies of Men are more unlike.

After this Insinuation on their Honesty, he says, *Suppoſing our Officers of Quality ſhould continue Friends to their Country in ſpite of Bribes,*———they are liable to *be removed*, and a Sett of Desparadoes *put in their Room*; and ſo the Business is done, and we are made *Bond Slaves* for ever.] But can any one imagine that these brave Officers, who had Spirit enough to refuſe to enſlave their Country, would tamely ſit down, and ſee it done by others?

Mr D'*anvers* takes it for granted, that the Militia are able to ſtarve 20,000 Foreigners.—Will it not be as eaſy for them, especially when headed by the above diſbanded Officers, to do the like by 18,000 of their own Countrymen? How the ſage Mr D'*anvers* blunders into Abſurdities!

His next Objection to the preſent *Military Eſtabliſhment* is, that it is giving too much Power into the Hands of the Sovereign, whoſe perſonal Virtues, tho' never ſo great, are no Security from the Abuſe of it.] This Aſſertion is abſolutely falſe; for it has ever been obſerv'd, that could a Line of virtuous Princes continue uninterrupted, even an arbitrary Government would be moſt eligible. A Prince's Virtues therefore are his People's Security; and I know of no Action of his *preſent Majeſty*, that can lead us to miſtruſt his.

If a *Land Force* was neceſſary, his Majeſty could not give greater Proof of his ſincere Attachment to the general Good, than by giving the Command of it to Gentlemen who had Eſtates to preſerve, and Families to continue free. This Circumſtance, no doubt, was intended to quiet the Fears of the moſt Doubtful, and prevent the Calumnies of the moſt Malicious; tho' it has proved a fruitleſs Expedient; as the Conduct of the *Craftſman* and his *Adherents* has evinc'd.

Grubſtreet Journal. Jan. 25. No. 161.

State of the Nation, by John Gabriel. *Continued from* p. 997, 1067, Vol. II.

No Country's Safety *Britain*'s can ſurpaſs, If walled round with Iron, and with Braſs.

BRASS and Iron, tho' inferior in Value to Gold and Silver, yet are more uſeful Metals; for which Reaſon, no doub doubt, they are kept at Home, when the two latter are sent Abroad to please Foreigners. Without the Help of Iron, the numerous Malefactors, and more numerous Debtors, could not be secured; nor City, and Country, by 20,000 Standing Forces. But when the Contest between *Tomkins* and *Wood* is decided, it is hoped, we shall have Swords and Musket Barrels, Bolts, Bars, and Fetters, at more reasonable Rates. How the latter's Project came to miscarry in a neighbouring Island is Matter of Wonder. Some imagine, that the Natives, having large Quantities of *Copper*, but little Gold or Silver, would not suffer any more of the first to pass among them. Others, that they rejected it because alloy'd with too much *English* Lead. However, a certain Dean, a professed Enemy to all Mixture of that heavy Metal, was the chief Occasion of a swift Re-exportation.

But Copper, or Brass, which may be called Copper *hibernized*, meets with a better Reception among the *English*; and both Sexes are extremely fond of that which is foreign, especially if instrumental in concluding amorous Treaties: Thus the Foreigner with the frightful Face is grown immensely rich.

Mr *Woolston's* allegorical Explication of the Axiom above, is, that By *Iron* and *Brass* are denoted two Armies; one of military, the other of nominally civil Persons, *viz.* Officers of the *Customs*, *Excise*, &c.

Here end the Axioms; then follows Chap. XI. *De arte legatoria*, or *the Art of Embassy.*

Mercurius dulcis, was one of the archest Wags that ever was sent of an Errant, but a notorious Filcher; and had certainly lost his Place, had not some of his Superiors gone halves with him. If ever he got a Finger into a Pie, he generally scoop'd out the Meat and under-crust, leaving it fair to the Eye as before.

Some may object, that the Kingdom of *Utopia* was never baked in an Oven, and therefore the Simile fails. Granted —Suppose then it be compared to a Hodge-pot, as *Lord Coke* has it, consisting of Meat, Pudding, &c. Suppose this stirred with a long Pole, the Plumbs would sink to the Bottom, where the experienc'd Pole-man would secure the greatest Share to himself allowing his Companions a few now and then to please them. There was one, a short, squat Man, he would not suffer to come near, who in great Indignation, would every

now and then hold up his Ladle; but the political Stirrer, knowing his Adversary's Ladle too short to reach him, laugh'd heartily. I don't condemn HORACE's *Risum teneatis*, or *dulce ridentem*, as being false *Latin*.

But we forget Ambassador *Mercury*, who was a Pimp as well as a Plenipo. But, had *Amphytrion* been able to detect *Jupiter*, and bring him *coram nobis* into *Westminster-hall*, so that a *Middlesex* Jury might have given Verdict against him, *Olympus* must have been mortgaged, or his Godship have scampered away incog. as did Card. *Coscia*, the Duke *Ri. perda*, &c.

It requires great Address to manage State Affairs dexterously in foreign Nations; the Tempers of the Court Ladies, as well as the Gentlemen, are to be diligently studied. Some Politicians will cut one's Throat with a Feather. Every Traveller who has been at *Rome* has not studied in the Vatican Library. And tho' Pope *Adrian* was choaked with a Gnat, yet several of his Predecessors and Successors could easily swallow Camels.

There were excellent Politicians Embassadors, Ministers of State, in the *Augustan* Age. Tho' *Mecænas* was much inferior to Sir *James Baker*, late Knight of the Spur. A very little learning in a great Man, is still magnified by his Parasites. The little Pains such a one now and then takes, (of which the greatest is the telling of Money;) are rewarded with pompous Affluence; and the Fatigue soon washed away with Burgundy and Champagne. Whilst all the immense Labour I have undergone in compiling this Treatise can scarce secure me a Bottle of muddled Port. But how will our great, great, great Grand Children's great, great Grand Children, in the Year 3000, lift up their Hands in Amazement, that I, *John Gabriel* was not made Prime Minister to the stiff, starch'd Potentate of *Greenland*! —I'll proceed no farther. I don't speak or write for every body. What! shall the Town pretend to see thro' a Man's Words and Writings; since the chief End of both is rather to conceal than explain one's Meaning; were that the Case, a Man would hate every Letter in the Alphabet, as cordially, as some Patriots do an R and a W. Some whimsical Persons, indeed imagine the Nation would be happy, if every Man had a Window (as the Dissenters said) to his Conscience, and every Woman a Padlock on her——Mind, as *Pryor* has it. But I am of a different Opinion, since this would make the Ladies sole Managers of foreign, as well as domestick Affairs, which are at present chiefly under their Direction.

Free Briton. Jan. 25. No. 175.

Considerations occasion'd by the Craftsman on Excises.

THE Pamphlet under this Title being the most worthy Notice of any yet publish'd, *Walsingham* gives us the following Extracts from it.

The nearer the Duty upon any Commodity is paid to the Time of Consumption, the Consumer may be afforded that Commodity the cheaper; and as the Consumer pays all Taxes, in that Respect the Tax itself is lessened by being collected as an Excise; the Inconveniencies of which however are so great, that the Design of a General Excise could never be entertain'd by any Man.

But the Tobacco Trade has been found liable to so great Frauds in the Discounts and Drawbacks, that 'tis impossible to remedy them, but by some Alteration in collecting the Duty; the fair Trader suffers, the fraudulent is enriched The Duty upon the Importation of Tobacco at the Port, which must be immediately paid, or bonded, all Discounts deducted, is 5 d. and a Fraction per lb. The Merchant gives Credit to the Retailer, both for the Duty, and the clear Cost of the Commodity. How many Merchants and their Bondsmen have been ruin'd by this Credit which they are obliged to give, the clear Coast of the Commodity being but two sevenths of it. Tobacco is one of our chief Commodities, and should be encourag'd. The *French* have large Plantations of it in *Orange*, and prohibit the Importation of it from hence. The *Dutch* have planted it in *Guelderland*. About 9 Years since the Parliament allowed the whole Duty to be drawn back upon Exportation; but this does not answer the End.

We have lately had Accounts of the sad Distress of the Tobacco Planters in *Maryland*. This was partly brought on them by their Factors being oblig'd to advance Money for the Duties at the Importation; of which grievous Charge they will be eas'd, when the Method of collecting the Duty is chang'd to *Excise*, and our Ports will then be as Free Ports for that Commodity.

How melancholy is the State of the Sugar Trade! we first gain'd it, by the *Portuguese* being obliged to relinquish it. The *French* have extended their Plantations so as almost to put us in the same Condition with the *Portuguese.* The least Encouragement that should be given to this Trade, is to allow also all the Duty to be drawn back upon Exportation.

As to Wine, there is a Composition so called, and sold for such, which has not in it one Drop of the Juice of the Grape, with what Art and Dexterity do they work it up to *Strong, Deep, Fresh, and fit for Bottling?* The Duty of Wine being paid at the Port upon Importation, this Liquid, which was never perhaps out of the Cellar where it was sold, escapes Duty-free; and the Vender saves the Duty, as a kind of Bounty, for dispensing Wine of his own making. When a Vintner fails, his Wine is often sold for less than the Duty, tho' as found and good as ever. By the proposed Method, nothing will be drank as Wine, but what is Wine; it must pass through the Merchant's Hands, and he will find a Benefit in being eased of the Payment of the Duties, which must now be paid perhaps a Year or two before the Wine is fit for Sale. The Alteration of the Duty on *Coffee, Tea,* and *Chocolate,* has been attended with a Gain to the Publick of near 100,000 l. per Ann. What might be farther sav'd by this means would be a vast Ease to the *Nation.*

With Regard to Liberty, if a Government is free, and the Laws are suffer'd to take their Course, Taxes will be rais'd according to Law, and without Oppression or Favour. In *Holland* Excises are paid, and the People are free. Would *France* be free, were there no Excises? Are we less free now Excises are paid, than in the Reign of K. *Charles* I. when there were no Excises?

The Auditor, Jan. 26. No. 6.

Nulla venenato est litera mista joco.
                                        Ovid.

SINCE my Appearance in the World, I have received several Letters recommending different Subjects to my Consideration. One advises me to be very satyrical; another acquaints me, that one valuable Quality of my Writings is, that they reflect on Nobody; a third is mightily pleas'd with my Paper mark'd No. IV. *Hillaria* writes me word she

she is in Love with *Frank Eafy*; *Melissa* hopes the *Auditor* will give her a *Hearing* in Things relating to the *Beau Monde*. Mrs *Cicely*, who keeps her Father's Books, having thrown away a little Money, defires I would *audit her Accompts*, fo as to blind the old Gentleman.

Mr *Auditor*,

§ I am a plain Man, and have to my Wife a handfome young Woman, who fings, dances, talks *French*, and is perfectly well bred. But there's an impodent young Dog, who frequents my Houfe (as he frankly tells me) only becaufe I have a pretty Wife; and indeed, the Liberties he takes with her makes me believe him. Now, Sir, ought I not to forbid him my Houfe?

Yours, *Jacob Meanwell*

I advife him not, till he fees how Mrs *Meanwell* will relifh the Publication of this; if fhe has any Love for honeft *Jacob*, or Regard for her own Reputation, fhe will fave him the Trouble; in the mean time, whenever Mrs *Meanwell* goes beyond the Bounds of a *Cheapfide* Wife, let him repeat to himfelf the following Speech of *Othello*.

——*'Tis not to make me jealous,
To fay my Wife is fair, feeds well, loves Company,
Is free of Speech, fings, plays, and dances well,
Where Virtue is, thefe are moft virtuous.*

Friend AUDITOR,

§ For as much as thou fetteft up for a Reformer of Manners, I advife thee, that thou derideft not the Brethren, neither holdeft the meek in Scorn; and if thou intehdeft to be fatyrical, to chufe proper Objects, and ridicule them with Difcretion, Good-nature, and Humanity. Be not vain when thou art commended, neither angry when reproved; for one deftroyeth itfelf, the other fheweth, thou deferveft Reproof, but haft not Senfe to bear it. If thou art as thou feemeft to be, thou wilt animadvert on the Scorn Men of thy Perfuafion make of the Habit of the Friends: Thou knoweft the Corn of the Fields is not fo beautiful as the Butter-flower, neither the Pomegranate fo alluring to the Eye as other Fruits: neverthelefs, the Corn of the Fields is more ufeful than the Butter flower, and the Infide of the Pomegranate more delicious than that of other Fruits. I reft thy loving Friend, *Ephraim Plain*.

§ There is nothing more ftupid than to make a Jeft of the Habit of this fet of People. Would they turn the Raillery upon us, they might do it with much more Reafon; the Variety of Fafhions that annually fucceed each other, being a plain Indication of a Levity of Mind we can't charge them with.

§ Next is the Petition of *Heliogabalus*, fetting forth, that the Petitioner has a downright *Englifh* Stomach, but can never appeafe his Hunger, without becoming the manifeft Ridicule of his Mefs-mates. Prayshim therefore to acquaint hisFriends that there is as much *Gormondize* in fatisfying their little Appetites, as there is in complying with his that is larger.

§ The laft is a Letter from *William Bar*, Keeper of *Button's* Coffee-houfe, inviting the *Auditor* to fettle his Club there, promifing, if he will tranfport his Mole thither, he will be at the Charge of a new Drawer to receive Letters, whereby the *Auditor* may be the Inftrument of making *Bar*'s Fortune, and *Button's* once more the Seat of Wits, and the Glory of Coffee-houfes.

The *Auditor* promifes to mention it to the Club.

THE *Hyp-Doctor* obferves upon the *Craftfman's* Saying " K. *Wm* was as much obliged to the *Affections of the Officers* of the Fleet, as to the *Winds*." (See p. 8.) that then the Navy and Militia are not the only Security of our Liberties, as he afferts, but the Affections of the People; therefore *D'anvers* in endeavouring to leffen their Affections, endeavours to leffen the natural Strength and Security of the Kingdom.

ARGUMENT *againft the* SALT-BILL:

(See p. 1087 to 1093. Vol. II.)

MR P——y, ' Sir, From what his Majefty was gracioufly pleafed to tell us from the Throne, I believe the whole People of *England* did expect fome Eafe as to our Taxes. How are thefe Expectations to be anfwer'd? By the Propofition now made, the greateft Part of them are to be fubjected to a new Tax, the reft are to be indeed free of a Part of an old Tax, but in place thereof are to pay a new Tax which will be equally grievous to moft of them, and to every other Perfon in the Nation. This, Sir, is the Relief the People of *England* are, by the Propofition now made, to meet with from the Eftablifhment

ment of a profound Tranquillity both A-broad and at Home.

Two Years ago, his Majesty was pleased to open the Session with a most gracious Speech, in which he expressed a Concern for the Hardships of the poor Artificers and Manufacturers. From whence we must conclude, that his Majesty's Opinion then was, that they labour'd under the greatest Hardships, and were the first who ought to be relieved. The Landed Gentlemen are not, I hope, grown less able to bear Burthens, the poor Artificers and Manufacturers are not, I am sure grown richer; and therefore I must think that his Majesty has not altered his Opinion, whatever some Gentlemen may have done: It is certain some of them have, because at that Time there was not so much as one Man in this House that differ'd in Opinion from His Majesty. This Tax upon Salt was then thought so grievous upon the Poor, that it was given up even by the Rt Hon. Gentleman who has now made the Motion for Reviving it. I wish he had given us some Reason for his being now of a different Opinion; for it must proceed from some Fact that has either happen'd since that Time, or is soon to happen. If he foresees any extraordinary Event, I wish he had been so good as to communicate it; for my part, I can see none that can possibly induce me to change my Opinion; but many for confirming me in it, and which I think ought to confirm every Man who has a stronger Regard for the Liberties of his Country, and the Happiness of Posterity, than he has for his own immediate Interest.

I am very willing to believe that every Man acts from the justest Motives, and from a sincere Regard for the Interest of his Country. But let us not believe that the Question now before us, is, Whether or no Relief ought to be granted to the Landed Interest. By the Resolutions of this House upon the Supply, there is 500,000 *l.* to be raised for the current Service of the Year; and the only Question before us, is, whether we are to raise this Sum by laying a Shilling upon Land, or by reviving the Duty upon Salt. Neither of them can be a Relief to the Landed Gentlemen; both must be burthensome to them. But the one or the other we have made necessary. We are to consider therefore which of these Methods will be most convenient for the Nation in general. The Thoughts of raising a

General Excise have been disclaim'd by every Gentleman who has spoke on this Head: I hope this Nation will never be in such slavish Circumstances, as that any Man dare openly avow such a Design, but I wish that every Gentleman that has talk'd upon this Subject had explain'd to us what he meant by a General Excise; for if any Gentleman thereby means, that the People are to pay Excises upon every thing they use either for Food or Raiment he will find that there is no such General Excise in the most slavish Country upon Earth. The proper Meaning of a General Excise relates not to the Things upon which it is raised, but to the Persons from whom; and every Excise is a General Excise, if the whole Body of the People, the Poor, the Needy, the most Wretched are obliged to contribute thereto. The Excise new proposed to be raised upon the People of this Nation, is as General as any one that ever was invented under the most absolute Tyranny. And if this be granted, and tamely submitted to by the People, it may be an Encouragement to ambitious and wicked Ministers in future Times to lay another Excise upon some other Commodity used by the Generality of the People; That again will give Encouragement to a third Attempt, and so on, till at last the People of this Country be subjected, as well as some of our Neighbours, to a General Excise in the most extensive Sense; that is, an Excise upon every Person, and upon almost every Thing that can be converted to the Use of Man.

When we were involved in a heavy and expensive War, and fighting for every thing that was dear to us, when our Land-Tax was at 4 *s.* in the Pound, and every thing we could think on was loaded with Duties and Customs, it was then a Sort of Necessity upon us to submit to such an Excise; but if we agree to it now during a Time of profound Peace, will it not then be a Precedent for every Excise that in future Times may or can be invented? And a few more Excises would, I fear, render our Liberties precarious, and entirely dependent upon the Good-will and Pleasure of those who shall happen to be entrusted with the chief Power of collecting the publick Revenue. I hope no Project will ever be set on Foot for converting any of our present Taxes or Customs into Excises; but if ever such a Project be set on foot, I shall then, I believe, be able to shew, that no *Dutch* Cus-

Cuftom can in that refpect be a good Rule for us. The Nature of their Government, the Situation and Condition of their Country, and the Nature of the Commerce carried on by them, is fo vaftly different from ours, that what may be fafe and eafy in one Country, may be grievous to the People, and inconfiftent with the Liberties of the other.

The Character of thofe great Patriots, who firft contrived this Duty, was no Argument for the Continuance of it, much lefs is it an Argument for the Reviving of it. They were conftrained by a fatal Neceffity to lay it upon the Nation at that Time. They made no bad Ufe of it, but we are not from thence to infer, that no bad Ufe will ever be made of it. Whenever there is any Danger to be feared, we ought not willingly to expofe ourfelves thereunto. Evils may be eafily avoided, but are not eafily removed. One of the chief Reafons urged for abolifhing of this Duty, was the Number of Officers employ'd in the collecting thereof; fuch a Number of Officers was then faid to be inconfiftent with the Liberties of a free People. This Argument was then admitted to be a good Argument; how it comes now to be fuch a trifling one, I cannot comprehend. But if it is not now admitted as a fufficientArgument against the Reviving of this Duty for 3 Years, I much fufpect, that at the End of this Term, neither this Argument, nor any other, will have Weight enough to prevent the continuing of it for a much longer Term.

I am aftonifh'd to hear any Man who has ever read the Articles of Union, pretend that the People of *Scotland* are any way entitled to an Exemption from the Salt Duty, or from any Part of it, when it is to be laid on for the current Service of the Year. It was laid down by the Commiffioners of both Kingdoms, as the Bafis and Foundation of the Union, that there fhall be an Equality of Excifes, Cuftoms, and all other Taxes throughout the United Kingdoms. The only Queftion then is, Whether we ought out of Compaffion to indulge them with fuch an Exemption, becaufe the poor People of that Country are not able to pay it. I really think we ought to have fo much Compaffion for the People of that Country; but then I hope it will be allow'd me, that we ought to have an equal Compaffion for the poor People of *England*, Journeymen, and Day-Labourers, who

have no Stock, no Property, are equally poor in all Countries; they have nothing but what they work for from Day to Day; and if it be faid, that the poor People in *England* are able to pay this Duty, becaufe they have high Wages, it is an unanfwerable Argument against the Tax in general. It is now an univerfal Complaint in this Country, that the high Wages given to Workmen is the chief Caufe of the Decay of our Trade and Manufactures; our Bufinefs then is, to take all the Meafures we can think of, to enable our Workmen to work for lefs Wages than they do at prefent, and therefore it muft be contrary to good Policy, to lay on a Tax, which it is granted would be infupportable to the Poor, if it were not for the high Wages they have; for the laying on of fuch a Tax, muft make the Continuance of fuch high Wages abfolutely neceffary, and the Continuance of them will certainly bring the Nation to Poverty and Diftrefs.

The Diftinction that has been made between the grofs Charge, and the grofs Produce of this Duty, feems to be fomething new. But fuppofing it to be reafonable, yet if we examine the Particulars of the Account that has been given us, we fhall find that feveral Articles have been put to the grofs Charge, which really ought to be put to the grofs Produce, becaufe they are actually raifed upon the People, though they come not to the Ufe of the Publick, but to the Ufe of the Merchants and Dealers in Salt. I am furprized to hear it pretended, that the Allowance for prompt Payment ought not to be reckoned as a Part of the grofs Produce, or that the Sum allow'd by Parliament for that Difcount is not raifed upon the People. Does any Man fuppofe, that the wealthy Dealer pays his ready Money for the Benefit of his Cuftomers, or that the Confumer pays the lefs for his Salt, becaufe the Merchant from whom he purchafes paid the Duties in ready Money? Does not every Man know, that thefe prompt Payments are made by the rich Dealers, only for their own Account; and that notwithftanding their being allow'd a Difcount of 10 *per Cent.* yet they fell as dear as if they had paid the full Duties? The Article then of 20,000 *l.* for prompt Payment, is not to be deducted, but is to be look'd on as a Part of the grofs Produce.

The 11,000 *l.* allow'd for Wafte on Salt carried Coaftwife, is likewife an Advan-

tag.

rage only to the Dealer: For every Farthing of that Sum is raised upon the People. This Allowance arose from a Presumption that there was a Waste on Salt carried Coastwise; and therefore 3 *d. per* Bushel on all White Salt, and 3 Half-pence *per* bushel on all Rock Salt carried Coastwise, was allowed to the Dealer in Salt. But it is certain, that in such Case there can be no Waste, there is always rather an Increase, because of its being very dry when put on board, and afterwards made to swell and become more weighty by the Moisture of the Air, to which it is exposed in the removing of it from Place to Place: Since there can be no Waste, we must presume, that the Whole is bought and consumed by the People; and we know that they always paid for it the same Price as if the full Duty had been paid by the Dealer. This Allowance did not even so much as induce the Dealer to sell cheaper; for the Consumer always paid for the Carriage, as well as for the Duty and first Cost; and the longer the Carriage was, the Consumer always paid the higher Price. This 11,000 *l.* is therefore to be considered as a Part of the gross Produce.

The Allowance for Rock Salt melted, is of the same Nature. This arose from a Supposition, that in the Melting of Rock Salt, and Refining it into White Salt, there was a great Waste, and therefore 10 Pound Weight in 65 was allowed Duty free. But I have been informed, that Rock Salt dissolved in fresh Water, will produce its own Weight in White Salt; and when dissolved in Sea Water, it will produce one Fourth part more. Therefore we must conclude, that though this allowance of ten Pound Weight out of sixty five, be a Deduction from the Revenue, yet the Duty upon every Grain of it is raised upon the People; and consequently this Article, which is 36,000 *l. per Ann.* must likewise be added to the gross Produce. These three Sums therefore of 20,000 *l.* 11,000 *l.* and 36,000 *l.* being added to the gross Produce, as stated by the Gentleman who was pleased to enter particularly into this Account, will make it amount to 297,350 *l.* which is the lowest Computation we can make of the Sum that is to be yearly raised upon the People of *England* only, by the Revival of this Tax.

But, Sir, if we consider the many Frauds that have always been committed as to Salt pretended to have been exported, and as to the Salt pretended to have been used in the Curing of Fish, we must presume, that a great deal more Salt is every Year used by the People, than what pays Duty to the Publick; and as the Consumer always pays the full Price, as if the Duty had been regularly paid upon the Whole, though these Frauds occasion a Deduction from the Revenue, yet the Duty upon the Whole is paid by the People; and therefore we must presume, that a much larger Sum than what I have mentioned must be yearly raised upon the People. This Presumption is brought almost to a Demonstration, by the Number of the People in this Nation, even as computed by those who have spoke in Favour of this Duty: According to their own Account, the Number of the Inhabitants in *England* amounts to 8,000,000; if then we suppose that every one of them uses, one with another, but a Peck of Salt in a Year, we must reckon that 1 *s.* at least is raised upon every Person by the Means of this Duty, because the laying on of this Duty makes the Salt at least 1 *s.* a Peck dearer than it would otherwise be; and therefore we must compute, that by the Reviving of this Duty, there will be at least 8,000,000 of Shillings, or 400,000 *l.* raised Yearly upon the People of *England* only.

We are to raise 500,000 *l.* for the current Service of the Year; this we certainly ought to do in that Method, which will be least burthensome to the Nation in general; and if we chuse to raise this Sum by Reviving the Salt Duty for three Years, we make the People really pay 1,200,000 *l.* out of which there is but 500,000 *l.* brought clear into the Publick Revenue. If this be a Relief or an Ease to the People of *England*, I leave the World to judge. We have by our former Resolution made the raising of 500,000 *l.* necessary, but do not let us charge the People with the Payment of 1,200,000, in order to raise this 500,000 *l.*

From what I have said, it plainly appears how much more Expensive it will be to the Nation, to raise 500,000 *l.* by Reviving the Salt Duty, than to raise it by 1 *s.* in the Pound Land Tax; and yet it has been pretended, that there will be but a small Difference as to the Expence. In order to bring this Difference as low as possible, it has been pretended, that the raising of the Salt Duty will cost but 22,000 *l. per Ann.* but I always reckon that it cost full 25,000 *l.* and I must ——
re

reckon fo, till I fee it contradicted by the Commiffioners Accounts; for the Raifing of, or, Paying the 19,000 *l. Annually* for Bounties, was never any additional Expence to the Publick. It has likewife been pretended, that the Raifing 1 *s.* in the Pound Land Tax, cofts near 18,000*l per Ann.* by reafon of the Office kept in Commiffion for that Purpofe; but thefe Gentlemen forget, that this Office is kept up, and cofts as much when there is but 1 *s.* in the Pound, as when there is 4 *s* in the Pound Land Tax, and therefore I ftill infift upon it, that the Raifing of 500,000 *l.* by 1 *s.* in the Pound Additional Land Tax, will really coft the Nation but 13,500 *l. per Ann.* Extraordinary Expence, and confequently the Difference as to this Article in *England* only, is at leaft 11,500 *l. per Ann.* But muft not we add to this, the 2,600 *l* extraordinary Charge in the Victualling Office, occafioned by this Duty; for this is certainly a Charge brought upon the Nation by reviving this Duty, which we fhould not be liable to, if we fhould raife what Money we want by a Land Tax. Muft not we likewife add the 20,000 *l. per Ann.* allow'd for prompt Payment? for as this is no Benefit to the Confumer, it is a real Expence to the People, as much as the 25,000 *l.* is which is paid for Management. Thefe three Sums added together, makes the real Difference of the yearly Expence between the Salt-Tax and 1 *s.* in the Pound Land Tax, amount yearly to the 34,100 *l.* I hope no Man that confiders it, will pretend that this, or even three Times the Sum, is the whole Difference of the Expence the Nation is to be at in raifing 500,000 *l.* by a Salt Duty in three Years in place of raifing 500,000 *l.* by 1 *s.* in the Pound Land-Tax in one Year; for the Difference will then be a great deal more than three Times this Sum. We muft then reckon the whole Expence of the Salt Duty for three Years, and from that deduct the Expence of raifing 1 *s.* in the Pound Land Tax for one Year only: The Salt-Tax will then coft us 3 Times 25,000 *l.* or 75,000 *l.* for Management? three Times 2,600 *l.* or 7,800 *l.* for extraordinary Expence in the Navy; and 3 Times 20,000 *l.* or 60,000 *l.* for prompt Payment; which three Sums added together, amount to 142,800 *l.* And from this we are only to deduct 13,500 *l.* to wit, one Year's Expence of raifing 1 *s.* in the Pound Land, the remaining Sum will then be 129,300 *l.* This is the real

Difference of the Expence which the Nation is to pay for the raifing of this 500,000 *l.* in three Years by a Salt Duty, in place of raifing it in one Year by a Land Tax. This is near 26 *per Cent.* and if we add the additional Expence in *Scotland*; and the Intereft which the Publick muft pay upon borrowing this 500,000 *l.* for the Current Service of the Year, it will, I am fure, amount to above 30 *per Cent.* which, I muft fay, is a pretty confiderable Premium for three Years Forbearance of Payment, even if the Nation were not to pay 1 *s* of the Money till the full End of the Term. This is the moft favourable Light that the Affair before us can with any tolerable Reafon be put in; but if we confider it in the Light I have before put it in, and fuppofe that 400,000 *l.* is to be raifed Yearly upon the People by the Means of this Duty, it will then appear much more odious; for upon that Suppofition which, I am afraid, will prove too true, the Nation is to pay 700,000 *l* for three Years Forbearance of the Payment of 500,000 *l.* which is a Premium very near 150 *per Cent.*

To pretend, that this Duty cannot give Occafion to any great Frauds or Perjuries, becaufe there is little or no Money advanced by the Subject, and repaid by the Government upon any Event, is to me a little odd. It is not the Repayment of Money by the Government that is the Caufe of Frauds and Perjuries; it is the great Advantage that a private Dealer may make and the little Risk he runs by fuch Frauds and Perjuries, that tempts him to the committing of fuch. He does not confider from whom, but how much Money he may make by fuch a Fraud; and therefore in all manner of Taxes, where the Tax or Luty amount to much more than the Prime Coft, there have always been great Frauds; if the Dealer can by any Fraud avoid paying the Duty, he makes his Advantage by felling at a high Price. Confidering then that this Duty to be laid upon Salt is no lefs then ten Times the Price it may be bought for at the Pits, what a fruitful Fund do we eftablifh for Frauds and Perjuries? It may not perhaps be eafy to fmuggle Salt away from the Pits without paying the Duty; but how eafy will it be for the Dealer, after he has given Bond to pay the Duty, and taken the Salt away from the Pits, to put it aboard of a Ship, and re-land it again at fome Bye Creek

Creek or Corner, or by some other Way to get a Certificate of its having been exported? By this Fraud he gets up the Bond which he gave for the Duty and tho' he gets no Money back from the Government, yet when he sells to the Consumer, Salt for four or five Shillings a Bushel, which cost him but a Groat a Bushel, does he not make a delicious, a tempting Profit? and the more tempting it must be, because of the little Risk he runs; for he risks only the Loss of a Groat for the Venture of making 4 *s.* clear Profit. If he can but cheat the Publick, he drives the Trade, I may say, of an Apothecary, and makes 1 *s.* of every Penny he lays out. Again, as to the Salt delivered Duty-free for the Fishery, there is still a greater Temptation, since it depends entirely upon the Honesty of the Curers; none but themselves can tell what Quantities they have made Use of; if they can but sell their Salt privately to Dealers or Consumers, they may get free of the Duty by swearing that the Whole was employed in Curing of Fish; and considering what little Regard is had to what is now by way of Proverb called a *Custom house Oath,* I am afraid this Sort of Perjury will be too frequent; Nor is the Loss sustained by the Revenue the only Disadvantage; these Baits and Temptations that are thrown in the People's way for perjuring themselves, may at last destroy all Sort of common Honesty among them, and may so much diminish that Regard which every Man ought to have for an Oath, that no Man's Life or Property can be secure, against the Plots and Perjuries of his Neighbours.

As to our Manufacturers and poor Labourers, this Tax certainly will be a Charge upon every one of them. It will be 1 *s.* at least to every single Man or Woman that is fit for Labour; and if we suppose a poor Man to have a Wife and three small Children, we can hardly suppose him to make use of less than a Bushel of Salt a Year for his Family; to such a Man this Tax will amount to at least 4 *s. 6 d. per Annum.*

This Tax must be a Charge upon all our Manufactures in general, for if it be a Charge upon the Manufactures, they must lay it upon the Manufacturers they deal in; and if we consider how narrowly the Foreign Merchant goes to work in the Bargains he makes, we must see what a Disadvantage this Tax may be to our

Export of Manufactures. If any of our Neighbours can sell but one tenth Part of a Farthing in a Yard cheaper than we can do, they will at last turn us entirely out of the Business. This holds as to all our Manufactures in general, but as to some particular Manufactures, such as Glass Leather, Earthen Ware, &*c.* It is still more grievous, because Salt is one of the Materials made Use of in their very Composition, and therefore I am hopeful, if this Duty be revived, there will be an Exception as to them.

It is granted by all, that the making Use of Salt is an Improvement to Land; but it is said, that this Tax cannot injure such Improvements, because every Man may have as much foul Salt Duty-free at the Pits, as he pleases, if he has an Officer along with him. But does not every Man see, that this can only be of Advantage to those, whose Lands lie near the Salt Pits? even as to them this Duty will be an additional Charge, for they cannot get an Officer to attend for nothing; we all know, that when a Man is once got into an Office, he has many Ways of squeezing a Perquisite from those who are obliged to apply to him; and as to all Lands that lie at a Distance from Salt Pits it must be allowed, that the Reviving of this Tax will be a full Bar to any future Improvements of them by Salt, which is an Improvement that has been successfully made Use of, through all Parts of *England* ever since the Duty was taken off.

[*To be continued.*]

The *Craftsman,* Jan. 27. No. 343.

Proceedings of the Merchants defended.

NOtwithstanding what *Osborne,* and other Ministerial Writers have said backward and forward in behalf of the *Excise* Project, he can't be ignorant of *Principiis obsta, venienti occurrite Morbo,* the old School Maxim. Instead of this He advises us to trust entirely to a *good Constitution,* and let the Distemper run on to a *Crisis* before we apply any Remedy.

It is the undoubted Privilege of *Englishmen* to petition the *Parliament,* and apply to, and even instruct their *Representatives,* when they apprehend their *Interests,* or *Liberties* are concern'd.

As therefore the *mercantile* Part of the Kingdom are thus warranted in their Conduct, I think, they have distinguish'd their Prudence in the Course of *this* Opposition;

position; which they began at the *most proper Time*, and have carried on in the most *dutiful* and *peaceable Manner*, tho' with *great Vigour*, and without any Regard to *Party-Considerations*.

They had an Eye to the Example of the *Druggists*, who waited 'till the *Scheme of the Tea Act was made publick*, and then made their Objections, but neither got it *laid aside*, nor obtain'd *such Alterations* as gave them Satisfaction. (See last *Lond. Journ.* p 24.)

Neither ought this to be deem'd *encountring an imaginary Monster*; it is a *real Beast of Prey*, which they oppose. In plain Terms, the Nature of *this Project* is to alter the present Course of the Law with Regard to the *Customs*, which the Merchants are desirous should remain in its antient Channel; and is built on a Supposition, that *some extraordinary, additional Powers* are requisite to prevent Frauds in the Revenue; and tho' the *Projectors* may qualify them with *some Restrictions*, These will soon be removed, if found to be a Clog upon it.

A GENERAL EXCISE is a TROJAN HORSE, and has an *Army* in its Belly. Let us therefore keep a constant Guard at our Gates; and if *another impudent Sinon* should endeavour to introduce *such a Monster*, under any *specious Pretences* whatsoever, let us reject his Offers with the utmost Indignation.

Fog's Journal, Jan 27. No. 221.

Multitudes of Civil Officers a Grievance.

IN the Reign of *Henry* IV. of *France*, when a Sum was wanted to carry on the War, some of the Counsellors of Parliament proposed, That all the Taxes which affected the middling and lower People should be quite taken off, and none be taxed but themselves, and others of equal Estates. Others proposed, That all Persons in Civil Employments should be obliged to serve without Perquisites or Salaries; saying, They ought to be content with the Honour. But the Plunderers of the preceding Reign hinder'd this Proposal from taking Effect, knowing it would reflect on them as Beasts of Prey.

In *Holland* and *Venice* no Man ever made a Fortune by a Civil Employment; in the latter a Fine is laid by Law on those who refuse to take one; and in the former the Revenues are collected with scarce any Expence to the State: But if they had had a Swarm of Civil Vermin

continually exhausting the Strength and Spirit of the Commonwealth, they would never have been able, as they did, to bear the immense Charge of repairing their Dykes, and at the same Time maintain a War 40 Years against the whole Power of *Spain*.

In Countries where the Charge of Civil Offices lay heavy on the People, it has been customary, for a Publick Supply, to purge the Men of Business as Physicians do Leeches; that is—by making them refund But Card. *Richelieu*, thought this look'd like *compounding Felony*; therefore advised to *hang them*.

In a certain Country, the Men in Office were so insolent as to tell the People, that they should be able, by holding their Employments a considerable Time, to purchase all the Lands in the Kingdom.—What a deplorable State of Servitude must that Nation be in. *See* p. 713.

Applebee's Journal, Jan. 27.

Pride of all others the most dangerous Fault, Proceeds from want of Sense, or want of Thought.

ONE of the *rankest Weeds*, and the most *common among* us is *Pride*; not that Sort of *Pride* which is tinctur'd with Ambition, and which thro' Care and Application may be reformed and made useful; but modern *Pride* is rather a *Swelling Sufficiency*, than an Appetite towards acquiring Glory; 'tis a strutting Indolence of Mind, awake only to receive Respect, and asleep to any Method which might deserve it. Mr *Pope* has drawn this *Vice* in the following Picture.

Of all the Causes which conspire to blind
Man's erring *Judgment* and mislead the *Mind*;
What the weak Head with strongest Bias rules,
Is *Pride*, the never failing *Vice of Fools*,
Whatever Nature has in worth deny'd,
She gives in large recruits of *needful Pride*;
For as in *Bodies* thus in *Souls* we find,
What wants in Blood and Spirits swell'd with Wind.
Pride, where Wit fails, steps into our Defence,
And fills up all the mighty *Void of Sense*;
If once right Reason puff that cloud away,
Truth breaks upon us with resistless *Day*,

Let those who are infected with this Vice, *weigh* well what Qualities they have to be *proud* of. A *smart Coat*, powder'd *Wigg*, and *laced Linnen*, may give a Man Preference in the Street, but the *Man of Mode* should be inform'd that these Ornaments will be a Prejudice to him, if not supported by real Merit. A

Man

Man who might have escaped Censure in a *plain Suit*, becomes a *Jest* in his *Embroidery*.

A Relation of an Intrigue, the History of a Night's Ramble, or a Run of Self-Raillery on a battered Constitution, may force a Company to laugh while they are repeated, but can never give a Man a Place in our *Esteem*, or make him pass for any thing better than a *Debauchee*, void alike of *Virtue* and *Discretion*.

London Journal. Jan. 27. No. 709.

THE Enemies of the present Administration *create* Evils, and by false Representations, base Insinuations, and wrong Calculations fill the Minds of the People with Spite and Malice against the Ministry; and then gravely say, *Was there ever a Ministry* so hated? Thus came we by a Noise of a *General Excise*, and Calculations of Government-Expences at about *Nine Millions* a Year; when they might as well have reckoned up what it cost the Nation in *Meat, Drink,* and *Cloaths*, and so have made the Sum about 40 Millions more.

The Government of *England* pursues the Good of the Publick, when it takes Care to *keep off War*, and preserve the Peace of *Europe*.

Our Foreign Affairs are perfectly right; and our *Domestick* Affairs are carried on, at least as well, as we have Reason to apprehend *any other Sett of Men* would carry them on. Our Liberties are untouch'd, our Properties secured; we have no Taxes but what the *Necessities* of the Government, and the *Circumstances* of the Kingdom demand; we make our own *Laws*; so that if Things are not right, we have none to blame but ourselves. There are no *invidious* or *partial* Things done to any Party; and, excepting *one*, there is not a Law in being, to exclude any of his Majesty's good Subjects from the *Privileges* of the most *favour'd*.

The *Daily Courant,* Jan. 27.

The Occasional Financer, No. I.

THE Drift of this Essay is to shew the *Expediency* of an *Inland Duty on Wines*. This the Writer endeavours to maintain from what has been argued by the Opposers of the Ministry; *viz.* That Taxes should be laid not on Manufactures and Necessaries of Life, but on Things tending to Luxury only. He farther enforces this Argument by observing,

that Wine itself is not only an Article of Luxury; but the Composition fraudulently brewed by the Dealers, and so called, is a great deal worse, even an Imposition on the Purses, and a Poyson to the Constitutions of the Drinkers. On which last Consideration alone, Inspectors ought to be appointed (as well as for the Apothecary's Shops) were the Revenue not to be increased by it. Whereas it is probable the Increase may amount to 2 or 300,000 *l. per Ann.* which Sum would operate to the speedy reducing the National Debt, or the taking off the Duties on Soap, Candles, Leather, and other real Necessaries of Life. And this would be a great Ease to our Manufacturers, and not in the least prejudice Trade, unless a Brewer of Wines can be called a Branch of our Trade, and a Manufacturer.

Concludes, that such a Tax in its Consequences would preserve our Health, increase our Exports, is perfectly agreeable to the Justice and Wisdom of Parliament, and seems to have all the *good Qualities* so lately recommended from the Throne.

Weekly Miscellany. Jan. 27. No. 7.

Mr Osborne censur'd.

THERE is a Method of *Argumentation* much in Use among our *great Reasoners*, which saves the Writer a great deal of Trouble, and secures him from being confuted. They assume a *positive, overbearing Style*; assert *strongly* and *passionately*; and declare that none but *Knaves* and *Bigots* will contradict them. *We are* obliged to *prove* every Thing, as often as they deny it, and to confute their Assertions, tho' they assign no Reasons, nor take any Notice of what has been written against them.

Wilfully mistaking Facts, and mistaking the same Fact after it has been contradicted, is likewise notoriously practised by Mr *Osborne* and his Confederates. To give an Instance: Mr *Osborne* says (See p. 1115, Vol. II.) 'True Religion can only be preserved by making no Laws about it, because if one believes the establish'd Doctrines, because enjoined by the Civil Power, his Belief is in *Man*, not in *God.*' Does the Church of *England require* any Man to believe a Doctrine against his Judgment, or to conform against his Conscience?

It is as impossible to fix any *determinate* Opinion upon his Letters of *Government*, or *Religion*, as it is to *misunderstand*

ſtand his *real* Meaning. In *Politicks* he is for a *State of Nature* (See p. 5. Vol. III.) tho' there never was ſuch a State ſince Mankind was in being.

In reſpect to *Religion*, his Reaſoning always takes its *Riſe* from *Deiſm*, or *terminates* in it. He aſſerts there can be no Religion in obſerving *poſitive Duties*, or in believing any *ſpeculative Doctrines*; which Opinion is abſolutely inconſiſtent with the Belief of Chriſtianity that requireth *both*. He ſeems to make our natural Appetites and Inclinations the Rule of our Actions, under no other Reſtrictions than *preſent Conveniency*, and *worldly Prudence*, without any uneaſy Reflections upon our *paſt* Conduct, or Apprehenſions concerning our *future* Condition.

Univerſal Spectator. Jan. 27. No. 225.

Of Antiquity.

THERE's ſomething in *Antiquity* which ſtrikes the Mind with a kind of *awful Reverence*. One cannot behold an antient *Ruin*, *Monument*, or even the *Place* where a *memorable Action* has been perform'd, without an *internal Satisfaction* not eaſy to be deſcrib'd. Akin to this is that exquiſite Delight which reſults from the Study of the *moſt ancient Writings*. 'Tis a Pleaſure like what one finds amongſt the Tombs of the *renowned Dead* in *Weſtminſter Cathedral*. As every *Epitaph* there affords a *Piece of Hiſtory*, ſo in the Writings of the *Antients*, every *Leaf* is as it were the *Epitaph* of ſome great Man, whom neither *Virtue*, Strength, *Wiſdom*, nor Courage could exempt from Death.

The oldeſt *Writings* in the World are thoſe of *Moſes*, the nobleſt Treaſure of *Antiquity*, containing the beſt Account of the *Creation*, and of the *firſt Age*; they are written in a manner ſo plain, yet with ſo much *Force*, that even in the Tranſlation, they retain a *Grandeur and Sublimity*, that pierces the Soul; as we experience in the Hiſtory of *Joſeph*.

The next moſt ancient valuable Writer is *Homer*, in whom we find the noble Sentiments of *Antiquity*. " They (ſays Mr *Pope*) loſe much of the Pleaſure of *Homer*, who read him only as a *Poet*; He gives us an exact Image of *ancient Life*, their *Manners*, *Cuſtoms*, *Laws*, and *Politicks*." In him we behold *Monarchs* without their Guards, *Princes* tending their Flocks, and *Princeſſes* drawing Water from the Springs.—This is the

ſame *authentick Picture* we find in *Scripture*, which in many Particulars he nearly reſembles.

But what deſerves our preſent Regard are his *Piety*, his *Beneficence*, and ſtrict *Morality*, peculiarly neceſſary at this Time, when not only the *Authority of Scripture*, but even the Diſtinction of *Good* and *Evil* is denied by ſome.

In this, and ſome ſucceeding Papers, which this Writer promiſes, he takes Notice of ſuch *Paſſages* in *Homer* as expreſs the *Omnipotence*, *Juſtice*, *Power*, and other Attributes of the *Deity*; a *Belief of*, a *Dependance* on, or a *Veneration* for him; ſuch as recommend *Benevolence* and *Humanity*, or regard the *Happineſs* of ourſelves.

'Tis true, his *Theology* in many Caſes is *groſs* and *imperfect*, yet he ever recommends our Duty to the Gods by *Prayers*, *Sacrifices*, and all the *Rites* in that *Age* eſteemed religious, and ſcarce ever makes thoſe ſucceſsful who omit them.

Can any thing expreſs a greater Submiſſion, Acknowledgment, and Veneration than the Lines following:

> O Father of Mankind! Superior Lord!
> On lofty *Ida*'s Holy Hill ador'd; [Throne,
> Who in the higheſt Heav'n haſt fix'd thy
> Supreme of Gods! Unbounded, and alone.

Again; where he repreſents him as ſeated on the Throne of his Majeſty.

> ———————— a rolling Cloud
> Involv'd the Mount: The T under roar'd aloud;
> Th' affrighted Hills from their Foundations nod,
> And blaze beneath the Lightnings of the God.

This bears a near Reſemblance to *Moſes*'s Deſcription of the Lord *Jehovah* deſcending upon Mount *Sinai*, Exod. xix. 16.

> The Sire of Gods his awful Silence broke;
> The Heav'ns attentive as trembled he ſpoke.
> He ſpoke, and aweful bends his ſable Brows;
> ————————— He gives the Nod;
> The Stamp of Fate, and Sanct on o' th' God,
> High Heav'n with trembling th' dread Signal
> And all *Olympus* to the Cent r ſhook. [took

Nothing but the Sacred Writings can exceed the Grandeur of theſe Deſcriptions.

His Majeſty's Speech to the Parliament, January 16, 1732-3.

My Lords and Gentlemen,

IT is a great Satisfaction to Me, that the preſent Situation of Affairs, both at Home and Abroad, make it unneceſſary fary for Me to lay before you any other Reasons for my calling you together at this Time, but the ordinary Dispatch of the Publick Business, and that I may have an Opportunity of receiving your Advice upon such Affairs, as may occur to you, and shall require the Care and Consideration of Parliament.

Gentlemen of the House of Commons.

I will order the proper Officers to lay before you the Estimates for the Service of the current Year, and I make no doubt, but that you will, with the same Chearfulness, as I have always experienced in you, effectually raise such Supplies, as you shall judge necessary for the Honour, Safety, and Defence of the Kingdom; and I cannot but recommend it to you, as a Consideration worthy the Commons of *Great Britain*, that in all your Deliberations, as well upon raising the annual Supplies, as the Distribution of the Publick Revenues, you pursue such Measures, as will most conduce to the present and future Ease of those you represent.

My Lords and Gentlemen,

You must be sensible, that it is very desirable to give all possible Dispatch to the Publick Business, and that nothing can give more Weight and Credit to all your Resolutions, than to avoid unreasonable Heats and Animosities, and not to suffer your selves to be diverted, by any specious Pretences, from stedfastly pursuing the true Interest of your Country; Let that be your first and principal Care, and the People will be sensible of the Benefits they shall receive, from your Wisdom and Resolution, in preferring their Ease and the Publick Good to all other Considerations.

Agreeable to this Speech, both Houses of Parliament made most Loyal ADDRESSES to His Majesty, (*See* p. 391.)and received the following most Gracious Answers.

To the LORDS.

My LORDS,

I Thank you for this Dutiful and Loyal Address. As the Ease of my People and the Publick Good have always been my chief Care and Concern, the Zeal that you shew for the promoting of them cannot but be very acceptable to me, and will most effectually recommend you to my Favour and Protection.

To the COMMONS.

Gentlemen,

I Return you my Thanks for these Dutiful Assurances of your Zeal and Affection for Me: And I make no doubt, but that your Resolutions to pursue such Measures as will most conduce to the Ease and true Interest of all my Subjects,

(*Gent Mag.* Vol. III. No. xxv.)

will as effectually recommend you to the Good Opinion and Esteem of my People, as they are acceptable to Me.

N. B. *The* ODE *on the* Poet Laureat, *and the Letter from* Phil-Urbanus *came too late to be inserted. We are oblig'd to our Correspondent in the North ; he will perceive by* p. 40. *how far his Fears are ill-grounded. We will oblige our other Poetical Friends as soon as we have Room.*

ODE

ODE *on* NEW-YEARS-DAY, 1733.   *By* Colly Cibber, *Esq;* Poet-Laureat.

RECITATIVO.

Sicilian sisters, tuneful nine,
　Assist our lays with sounds divine,
Melodious, soft, and sweetly gay,
Sweet as the soul oblig'd would pay,
　To glorious *George* and *Caroline*. 　5

AIR.

Awake the grateful song,
Inspire the warbling string,
Let with the heart the tongue
To *Albion's* monarch sing.
Sing, sing m *George's* gentle sway, 　10
And joy for joys receiv'd repay.

RECITATIVO.

May every morn that gilds the skies,
Like this, be thankful for the past;

And suns on annual suns arise,
　As greatly glorious as the last. 　1J

AIR.

Europe now of bleeding wounds,
　Sadly shall no more complain;
George the jars of jealous crowns
　Heals with halcyon days again.
Faction, fear, and false surmise, 　a6
　Suddenly shall sink to rest,
Loth howe'er to join our joys,
　Undeserving shall be blest.

RECITATIVO.

Where, *Britons*, shall thy froward sons have ease, 　25
If days, like thine, are scant of happiness?
If not enjoy'd in godlike *George's* reign,
The hand of heaven were bountiful in vain.

ANNOTATIONS, *from the* GRUBSTREET JOURNAL.

VER. 1. *Sicilian Sisters, tuneful nine*.] The Antients applied the Appellation of *Sicilian* only to the Muses of the Pastoral Kind. The Invocation of these pastoral Muses, at the composing an *Ode*, and the giving to the whole *nine* the Title of *Sicilian Sisters*, is a double Improvement; and the *Laureat* has dignify'd the *tuneful nine*, in honour of his Imperial Majesty, with a Title they never had before.

Ver. 2. *Assist our Lays with Sounds divine*.] The Antients were wont to desire the Muses to furnish the Matter, as well as the Music of their Songs: But our *Laureat* is more modest, his Request is very reasonable: When he has provided the Sense, they cannot surely refuse the Sound, he asks it so prettily, *Sicilian Sisters af-sist*.

Ver. 3. *Melodious, soft and sweetly gay*.] Since *soft* and *sweet*, when applied to Musical *Sounds*, signify the same Thing with melodious, the Qualities desired in these Sounds are, that they should be *divine*, and *Soft*, and *Soft* and *gayly Soft*. So that, in this and the preceding Verse, two beautiful Figures, are happily exemplified, the Anti-climax, and the Tautology.

Ver. 5. *To glorious George and Caroline*.] This is borrow'd from the 27th Verse of the *Birth-Day Ode* last *October*.

Ver. 6. *Awake the grateful Song*.] 'Twas disputed in the Society, whether this whole *Air* be a Continuation of the Poet's Address to the *Sicilian Sisters*, or a new one to the *British Songsters*. Tho' the next Verse *Inspire*, &c. seemed to favour the former Opinion; yet the 8th and 11th determined for the latter. Which was likewise confirmed by the first Verse of the last *New-Tear's Ode*. (See p. 586. Vol. II.)— The Propriety of the Word *awake*, as applied to *Songs*, was much question'd. A musical Instrument, when silent, might be elegantly said asleep; and consequently *awakened* when played upon. But a Song, *Sung* to a Tune is never in a silent State, for then it would cease to be a *Song*.

Ver. 7. *Inspire the warbling String*.] It was objected to the Word *Inspire*, that it could not be properly used in Relation to any Instruments but those of Wind Musick, as a Flute or Trumpet; but how a *String* can be *inspir'd* is incomprehensible.

Ver. 8. *Let with the Heart the Tongue*.] The surprizing Sublimity of this Verse needs no Explanation to make it admir'd.

Ver. 9. *To Albion's Monarch Sing, Sing, Sing*, &c.] In his *Birth Day Ode*. *Oct.* 1731. ver. 53. Sing, Sing the Morn &c. In *October* last ver. 42. *Sing, joyous Britons, Sing*. A most happy Use of the Figure Epizeuxis!

Ver. 10. *Sing, Sing* to George's *gentle Sway*.] The Second *Sing* should be changed into *drink*; as it is more natural to *Englishmen* to *drink* than to *Sing*.

Ver. 11. *And Joy for Joys receiv'd repay*.] 'Tis odd he should advise the *Repayment of Joys* in the Plural by *Joy* in the Singular.

Ver. 14. *And Suns*, &c. [Tho' this is new and very Sublime, yet it flags by the Addition of *as greatly glorious as the last*: Which is much exceeded by the *Chorus* in the *New Tear's Ode*, 1731. See p. 20. Vol. I.

　Like this, may every annual Sun
　　Add brighter Glories to thy Crown.

N. B. By *Annual Suns* are meant the *Suns*, which appear only once a Year upon New-Year's Day.

Ver. 20. *Faction*, &c.] The best way of explaining this poetical Prophecy, is from a parallel place in the *New-Tear's Ode*, 1732. ver. 43. (See p. 580.) *Faction shall be pleas'd, or die.* And then the meaning will be, *Faction*, &c. *shall die* by a sudden Death, properly described by *suddenly sinking to Rest*. And tho' this may seem a Contradiction to Ver. 23. *Undeserving shall be blest*; yet is consistent with it, because a sudden Death is a *Blessing*, if compar'd with a lingering, tormenting Death; and such a *Blessing* as *Faction*, &c. do not at all deserve, because they do not *join our Joys*.

Ver. 95. *Scant of Happiness*.] An Expression how poetical and happy!

Ver. 26. *If not enjoy'd*, &c.] This religious Thought is borrowed from the last *Birth-Day Ode*. ver. 16. &c.

　The Word that form'd the World
　　In vain had made Mankind;
　Unless his Passions to restrain,
　Almighty Wisdom had design'd　[*reign.*
　Sometimes a WILLIAM *or a* GEORGE *should*

AIR.

As freedom the jewel of life is,
'Twas bought by old battle array;
But now with our monarch the strife is,   30
Who beſt ſhall protect or obey,
While hinds for their plenty ſhow ſadneſs,
They praiſe in reproaching their ſtate.
Ye murmurers, tell us, what madneſs,
Would want out of plenty create?   35

RECITATIVO.

Ah! ſwains, with grateful eyes regard the throne,
That builds on your proſperity its own:
In vocal joy your golden days confeſs,
Nor ſlight, becauſe ſecure, your happineſs.

CHORUS.

May every morn that gilds the skies,   40
Like this be thankful for the paſt;
And ſuns on annual ſuns ariſe,
As greatly glorious as the laſt.

ANNOTATIONS.

V. 28. As Freedom, &c.] A Member in a threadbare Coat, wonder'd ſo precious a Jewel could be bought *by old battle array*; and was for reading *held* inſtead of *old*. If I tell you, ſaid he, that this Coat was *bought by an old* Morning Gown, you may think I meant, that it was *bought of old by a* Morning Gown; tho' I *bought* it perhaps but yeſterday. The ſame Perſon ask'd whether *Battle* was a Subſtantive, or an Adjective; and was anſwer'd by a Diſciple of Mr *Orator*, it was *a Subſtantive put by Appoſition to* Array; but in the Judgment of the Society, 'tis an Adjective.
Ver. 34. Te Murmurers, tell as, &c.] To create

ſomething out of Nothing, was the Work of Omnipotence: But to *create* Nothing out of Something, ſeems beyond the Power of Omnipotence itſelf.
Ver 38. In vocal Joy your golden Days confeſs] If the *Swains* are the *Hinds*, who in *ver,* 32. are ſaid to *ſhew Sadneſs for their Plenty,* they will ſcarce follow his Advice.
§ The WEEKLY REGISTER remarks on this ODE, That *Melpomene*'s Chamber-Maid had *inſpired* the Poet with a *falſe* Spark of Fire in the *Abſence* of her *Miſtreſs,* and had often *abuſed* him in the ſame Manner.

To SILVANUS URBAN, on the Death of the *Weekly Magazine.*

WHilſt in bright order rang'd by * princely hand
Thy choice collections high diſtinguiſh'd ſtand,
Seven *wiſe* projectors, *on pyratic* Watch,
A *weekly groveling imitation hatch*;
On thy *foundation built their mighty ſchemes,*
And big *with fame and wealth the bubble ſeems*;
Mankind, indignant, impoſitions ſhun;
The thought *was thine, and ſhould be thine alone.*
To ſtand *this ſickly month, it ſtrove for* Breath,
But fainting *drop'd, and ſhar'd the common death.*
So juſt a fate *may all pretenſions meet,*
Where ſordid Views defile *the ſpotleſs ſheet.*

* Alluding to the *Gentleman's Magazine,* Royal Paper, Gilt and Letter'd, being in the Libraries of the Pr. of *Wales,* and D. of *Cumberland.*

To the Rev. Dr *Swift,* with a *Preſent of a Paper Book finely bound.* By the E. of O——y.

TO thee, dear SWIFT, theſe ſpotleſs leaves
I ſend;
Small is the preſent, but ſincere the Friend:
Think not ſo poor a book below thy care:
Who knows the price that thou canſt make it bear
Tho' tawdry now, and like *Tyrilla's* face,
The ſpecious front ſhines out with borrow'd grace
Tho' paſt-boards glittering, like a tinſel'd coat,
A *Raſa Tabula* within denote;
Yet, if a venal and corrupted age,
And modern v ices, ſhould provoke thy rage;
If, warn'd once more by their impending fate,
A ſinking Country, and an injur'd ſtate *
Thy great aſſiſtance ſhould again demand,
And call forth *reaſon* to defend the land; [prize
Then ſhall we view theſe ſheets, with glad ſur-
Inſpir'd with thought, and ſpeaking to our eyes:

Each vacant ſpace ſhall then, enrich'd, diſpenſe
True force of eloquence, and nervous ſenſe;
Inform the judgment, animate the Heart,
And ſacred rules of policy impart:
The ſpangled covering, bright with ſplendid ore,
Shall cheat the ſight with empty ſhew no more:
But lead us inward to thoſe golden mines,
Where all thy ſoul in native luſtre ſhines.
So when the eye ſurveys ſome lovely fair,
With bloom of beauty grac'd, with ſhape and air;
How is the rapture heighten'd when we find
Her form excell'd by her celeſtial mind?

† Alluding to his writing againſt WOOD's half-pence.

VERSES *left with a Silver Standiſh on Dean* Swift's *Deſk, by Dr* D——y.

HIther from *Mexico* I came
To ſerve a proud *Iernian* dame;
Was long ſubmitted to her will;
At length ſhe loſt me at *quadrille.*
Thro' various ſhapes I often paſs'd,
Still hoping to have reſt at laſt;
And ſtill ambitious to obtain
Admittance to the *Patriot Dean:*
And ſometimes got within his door,
But ſtill turn'd out to ſerve the poor, *
Not ſtroling idleneſs to aid,
But honeſt Induſtry decay'd.
At length an artiſt purchas'd me,
And brought me to the ſhape you ſee,
This done, to *Hermes* I apply'd;
Oh *Hermes,* gratify my Pride:
Be it my fate to ſerve a ſage
The greateſt genius of his age:
That matchleſs pen let me ſupply,
Whoſe living lines will never die.
I grant your Suit, the god reply'd,
And here he left me to reſide.

* Alluding to 500 l. a Tear lent by the DEAN without intereſt, to poor tradeſmen.

Sally's *Answer to*—Dear *Sally* Emblem of thy, &c. p. 1121. N° 24.

From the Grubstreet Journal.

Rejoice with me, ye fisters of the trade,
My name's in print, and verfes on me made.
In vain I have not os'd my tongs, and bellows,
Since notic'd by the fmarteft, prettieft fellows:
My art in dreffing brought me from the dark;
My kitchen fire has kindled many a fpark:
That fire, pernicious to complexions fair,
Has mine improv'd, and giv'n a brighter air.
My beard's defcription garnifhes our meat,
Yet makes our guefts to gaze, not drink and eat:
The tankard froths with fmiles fo fit,
And on the liquor fquirts the zeft of wit.
His purpofe good, yet fee the bad effect:
I mimick him in rhime, my chops neglect,
Sour as my pickles, I on others look;
When he's away, the de'il may be the cook.

   Then prithee, Damon, Sally don't forfake,
But leave vain bufinefs for a tender ftake,
Hot, full of gravy flowing round the plate;
Which wants no fauce, but what it can create.
Tho' 'tis not large, 'twill prove beyond your wifh
More than enough, a found, fubftantial difh.
With linen clean you'll find the table fpread,
And the deck'd board an emblem of my bed.

On the QUEEN's GROTTO.

From the Weekly Miscellany.

This indigefted pile appears
   The relict of a thoufand years;
As if the rock, in favage dance,
Amphion hither brought by chance;
Which, crowding round the tuneful tongue,
In regular confufion hung,
Fixt by attention, while he fung.
See! fragments on rough fragments hurl'd!
Like atoms, joftled to a world.
Their fall you dread approaching nigh,
Yet they, for ages, ftorms defy:
With that fuperiour fkill conjoin'd
As cheats the fenfe, but harms the mind.
With inward graces more polite,
The vaulted dome attracts the fight.
Where, as in difputation, ftand
Four Worthies, from the fculptor's hand;
Who, with unwearied ftretch of thought,
The richeft ftores of knowledge fought;
Trac'd nature to her dark recefs,
Then fhew'd her in the lovelieft Drefs.
The chiffel has fuch juftice done,
They reafon, and confute, in ftone.
Thus curious medals often grace
The infide of a fhagreen cafe:
Thus fiction ftern *Minerva* dreft
With Gorgon's head, and martial creft,
While underneath the threatning arms
Of wifdom, fhe conceals the charms.
Hither, ye mufes, incenfe bring,
Now, *Stephen*, touch the founding ftring;
To praife this fabrick be thy part,
In ftrains as innocent of art:
Pure native wit will copy beft,
A rural beauty, when undreft.

While Caroline condefcends to raife
This lafting monument to *learning's* praife,
With grateful homage let the tuneful nine,
To celebrate her gifts, in concert join;
This grotto, then, o'er pyramids fhall rife,
And lift her matchlefs glories to the fkies.
Beyond where *Newton* view'd with *Galileo's* eyes.}

The *Conftitution Clapp'd, an* Excise BALLAD.

From the Grubstreet Journal.

Come liften to me, of excifes I fing,
   Which, like a difeafe, you all know firs,
The body politic to achings muft bring:
   And this is now what we will fhow, firs,
      For excife, like a clap,
      Deem'd a trivial mifhap,
   Firft caught by old Noll's revolution;
      When general grown,
      Like a pox in the bone,
   Muft ruin the conftitution.
                        Fal a-lal, &c.

And firft, tho' a clap with tickling begins,
   Soon piffing with pain it will caufe, firs:
Your brandies excis'd, and excifed your wines,
   To piffing this alfo gives laws, firs.
         For excife, like, &c.

Your piffing now painful, will make you with care
   Abftain from all things that inflame, firs:
Your ginger, and pepper, and fuch fpicery ware
   Reduc'd to excife, do the fame firs.
         For excife, like &c.

Like needles and pins, intolerable grown,
   Of nothing that's falt you muft eat, firs:
The excife upon falt, laft feffions laid on,
   Prevents too confumption of meat, firs.
         For excife, like, &c.

But if the diftemper the blood fhall have feiz'd,
   All vifcids and acids forbear, firs:
An acid you'll find your tobacco excis'd,
   And your fugars too vifcid, I fear, firs.
         For excife, like, &c.

The difeafe allarming, to doctor you run,
   His pills and his potions to take, firs:
By excife extended you're no lefs undone,
   If your doctor of ftate's a quack, firs.
         For excife, like, &c.

At length the whole frame by th' infection o'er-
      run,
   Of achings all o'er you complain, firs:
Thus in every country, and city, and town,
   A general excife will give pain, firs.
         For excife, like, &c.

To fome regular doctors apply; fpare no coft,
   Their advice your fate may prevent, firs:
If falivated well, or fluxed at moft,
   Recover you may and repent, firs,
         For excife, like, &c.

But if lift'ning to quacks, you choofe for your lot
   With bolus and pills to be cramm'd, firs:
Circumcifed, incis'd, excifed you'll rot.
   And piece-meal will die, and be damn, firs
         For excife like, &c.

SICKNESS. *An* ODE.

From the GRUBSTREET JOURNAL.

AT midnight when the fever rag'd,
 By phyfic's art ftill unaffwag'd,
 And tortur'd me with pain:
When moft it fcorch'd my aching head,
Like fulph'rous fire, or liquid lead,
 And hifs'd through every vein:
With filent fteps approaching nigh,
Pale death ftood trembling in my eye,
 And fhook th' up-lifted dart.
My mind did various thoughts debate
Of this, and of an after ftate,
 Which terrify'd my heart:

I thought 'twas hard, in youthful age,
To quit this fine delightful ftage,
 No more to view the day;
Nor e'er again the night to fpend
In focial converfe with a friend,
 Ingenious, learn'd, and gay.

No more in curious books to read
The wifdom of th' illuftrious dead;
 All that is dear to leave;
Relations friends, and MIRA too,
Without one kifs, one dear adieu,
 To moulder in the grave.

Incircled with congenial clay,
To worms and creeping things a prey,
 To wafte, diffolve, and rot:
To lie wrapp'd cold within a fhroud,
Mingled amongft the vileft crowd,
 Unnoted, and forgot.

Oh horror! by this train of thought
My mind was to diftraction brought,
 Impoffible to tell:
The fever rag'd ftill more without,
Whilft dark difpair, or difmal doubt,
 Made all within me hell.

At length, with grave, yet cheerful air.
Repentance came, ferenely fair,
 As fummer's evening fun;
At fight of whom extatic joy
Did all that horrid fcene deftroy,
 And every fear was gone.

If join'd in confort, with one voice,
Angels at fuch a change rejoice;
 I heard their joy expreft.
If there be mufic in the fpheres,
That mufic ftruck my ravifh'd ears,
 And charm'd my foul to reft.

A true DREAM.

I Dreamt,—my dear; (quoth *Ralph* to *Joan*,
 One morning as they lay alone)
I can't help laughing, faith!---I dreamt.
Our Neighbour *Charles* was impotent,---
There is no truth in dreams (fays *Joan*;)
And whilft I live I'll credit none.——
But afterward (quoth *Ralph*) I dreamt.
For all that he was impotent,
He got in bed, my dear, to thee!
And made a fhift to cuckold me.—
Good luck! (cry'd *Joan*) I never knew
A dream before that happen'd true.

On a late DUEL.

THE prating, playful, little pleader flain!·
 O, no! lord Teague and Dicky did but feign
Doubting twelve months, if 'twould be wrong
 or right:
At laft they did, as 'twere, agree---to fight.
And, 'tis a wonderful account, if true,
They met, they talk'd, they drew, and then
 ---withdrew.

Advice to SALLY, *at the Chop-houfe.*

From the GRUBSTREET JOURNAL.

AH SALLY! unrelenting maid!
 Think how time pofts away:
Think, that thofe rofes foon muft fade,
 Pale victims to decay.

Think, that five years (an age in love!)
 Is fcarce a point in time---
Ah, SALLY! this advice approve;
 And ufe thy prefent prime.

See at thy feet a motly train,
 Glad captives to thofe eyes;
See, how they figh, and hug the chain---
 Ah, SALLY! hear their cries.

Let not thy looks bely thy heart,
 (Thofe pitiful appear;)
Let mercy exercife her part;)
 Be kind as you are fair.

See, how the prentice leaves unfwept
 His fhop, and baftes to dine:
See, how the merchant leaves unkept
 His books---to get in thine.

E'en trade fufpends; for fee, e'er two
 The crowd to thee repairs.
Boaft, SALLY, boaft, fince only you
 Can ftop the world's affairs.

But time thou can'ft not ftop---he flies
 Without the leaft delay;
Bears youth and beauty, both his prize,
 Unheeded, far away.

What tho' the trimm'd up numbers fhine
 In rival gaiety;
Tho' pudding they forfake, and wine,
 To dine on chops and thee!

Yet foon, alas! they'll quit the flage,
 When thy frail charms are gone;
When thy eyes twinkle in dull age,
 They'll let thee---dine alone.

You'll fay, perhaps---I vainly preach,
 My precepts you defpife---
O then, let an example teach,
 And warm you to be wife.

See that frefh loin, that hangs up there,
 How lovely is the meat!
How kindly is its grain! how fair!
 How picturefque! how fweet!

But caft your eyes fome three days hence,
 And view the felf-fame loin;
How dry'd! how alter'd! what offence!
 The fight enough to dine!

Ah, SALLY! fpeak, is it not juft?
 Runs this not *Par* with you?
I will not fay that thou art duft---
 But thou art mutton too.

THE
Monthly Intelligencer.
JANUARY, 1733.

Tuesday, 2.

ONE *William Wright*, a Youth about 18 Years old, was found at *Faldingworth Gate* near *Market-Rising* in *Lincolnshire*, lying in a Chaise, with his Head almost sever'd from his Body, and cover'd with the Seat-cloth. *Two Men suspected to be the Murtherers, being described in the Gazette, and a Reward, &c. offered, were taken about the End of the Month; they had committed 65 Robberies, which they confest, with this and another Murder.* (See p. 99, 154.)

Saturday 6.

A Messenger arrived from *Spain* with Advice that his Catholick Majesty had enlarged the Term for the Commissaries appointed to adjust the Differences between the two Nations, with respect to the Depredations of the *Spaniards* upon the Ships and Effects of the *British* Merchants, three Years longer.

Wednesday, 10.

About this Time Coughs and Colds began to grow so rife that scarce a Family escaped them, which carried off a great many both Old and Young. The Distemper discover'd itself by a Shivering in the Limbs, a Pain in the Head, and a Difficulty in Breathing. The Remedies prescribed by the Physicians were various, but especially Bleeding, drinking cold Water, small Broths, and such thin Liquids as dilute the Blood.

Friday 12.

Was held a General Court of the *York Buildings* Company, when it was resolved to apply to Parliament for Relief: and the Seal of the Company was affixed in Court to the Petition for that Purpose, after it had been carried by a Ballot taken the same Day 168 against 25.

A Committee appointed by the Merchants and Traders of this City waited on the Speaker of the House of Commons, concerning the Affair of a General Excise.

Not only the Merchants, &c. of this City, but likewise those of *Bristol*, and most other Cities, Towns, and Corporations, have been alarmed at the Rumour of a General Excise, and resolved to oppose it to the utmost of their Power, by all dutiful and lawful Means.

Monday, 15.

The Sessions ended at the *Old-Bailey*, when 6 Criminals received Sentence of Death, viz. *Thomas Banks* for Burglary, *Samuel Thomas* for the Murder of his Wife; *Alexander Emerton*, alias *Mears*, alias *Cromwit*, for robbing Mr *Holder* of several Goods; *John Akers, John Weston*, and *Wm Booth*, for robbing Mr *Harvey* in the Street; 33 were cast for Transportation, and 2 burnt in the Hand, viz. *John Bennett* Waterman try'd for killing his Apprentice, and *John Turner*, for stealing Lead.

Tuesday, 16.

The Parliament met at *Westminster*, when the King made a Speech to both Houses. (See p. 38)

Thursday 18.

Monf. *Fontenelle*, the famous *French* Poet, was admitted a Fellow of the Royal Society.

Friday, 19.

Was held a General Court of the South-Sea Company, which Sir *John Eyles* open'd by acquainting them, that the Matters before them were, the Consideration of the Attorney General's Opinion on the Case, whether the Company could properly treat with *Spain* for the Surrender of the Assiento Contract, or have Power to let out the Tonnage of their Annual Ship without the Consent of *this Crown*; the agreeing upon the Dividend for last Half-year; and addressing his Majesty to continue Governor.—The Address was agreed upon; and the Court resolved, That the Dividend should be 2 per Cent. and deferr'd the Consideration of the Case to the next General Court.——Then the Sub-Governor, in a pathetick Speech, thank'd the Company for the Honours they had done him in chusing him four Times succeffively into that Post; that his close Application to the Company's Affairs had impair'd his Health to that Degree, as to determine him not to stand Candidate at the next Election for the Station he was in; and therefore desir'd them to think of another.

Wednesday, 24.

John Merril, Esq; was elected Representative in Parliament for *St Albans*, when the Corporation gave him the following Instructions under their Common Seal; *viz.*

SIR,

WE *have chose you to be our Reprefentative in Parliament, which is the higheft Truft we can repose in you; and in return for so great a Confidence, we expect you will have a conftant Regard for the Interest of your Country, and especially of this Borough; but as this is a very critical Conjuncture, we think it necessary to give you more particular Inftructions. In the firft Place, Sir, as we are in profound Peace, we are furprized to find no Reduction of the Land Forces, which we conceive to be dangerous to our Conftitution, and we feel to be very burthenfome and oppressive to us. In the next Place, we are alarm'd with an Attempt to be made this Session of Parliament, for extending the Excise Laws to Commodities not yet excised. We hope, however, that these Reports are false, and raised by the Enemies to our Conftitution, and to his Majesty's Government. But if any one who calls himself an Englishman, should be so much an Enemy to his Majesty and us, as to propose such a Scheme, we expect, Sir, from you, the most vigorous Opposition to it; for we fhall look upon the Continuance of so great a Body of Land Forces, and an Increase of Excise Officers, under our present Circumstances, as a fure Prefage of an entire Subverfion of our antient Conftitution, and all the valuable Privileges belonging to it, which have so long diftinguifh'd us from our neighbouring Nations.*

A Conftitution, Sir, that our Fore-fathers have, at the Expence of their Lives and Fortunes, deliver'd down fafe to us, and which, we hope, We fhall have the Virtue and Courage to deliver to lateft Pofterity, under a Succession of Princes issuing from his present moft facred Majefty, whofe Fa-

mily came in on the Principles of Liberty, and who can be maintained on no other; whoever, therefore, tries to fap the Foundations of Liberty, is at the fame Time undermining his Majefty's Title to the Crown, which Thoughts give us the utmost Abhorrence, and we expect from you, Sir, a conftant and fteady Purfuit of fuch Measures as will keep our Conftitution, as near as may be in the fame Situation under which it has long flourifh'd; and we don't doubt but in fuch Conduct you will have the Assistance of our other worthy Member, and of all honeft Englishmen.

The Mayor, Aldermen, and Burgesses of *Newbury, Berks* Petitioned Sir *John Stonehouse*, Bt, and *Winchcomb Howard Packer*, Efq; Members, for that County they would to the utmost oppose any Attempt towards a new Excise, or any ways extending the present Excise. Likewise the Corporations of *Briftol, York, Hull, Worcester, Exeter, Norwich, Reading,* and many others, wrote to their respective Members to the fame Purpose.

Tuesday, 23.

At a Court-Martial held at *Portsmouth* on board his Majesty's Ship the *Dreadnought* (Vice-Admiral *Cavendish* Prefident) Capt. *Cotterel* of the *Rose*, was mulcted 3 Month's Pay, for his ill Treatment of his Ship's Company, who were permitted to be difcharged from their Captain's Service.

Friday 26.

Capt. *Cotterel*, late of the *Rose*, was appointed Captain of the *Lowestoffe*; and Capt. *Wyndham* Commander of the *Rose*.

Monday 29.

Was a Rehearfal of the Mufick to be perform'd on the Feaft-day of the Sons of the Clergy, and 240*l.* 5*s.* 9*d.* collected.

Twelve Malefactors, condemn'd in the three preceding Seffions, at the *Old-Batley*, were executed at *Tyburn*.

Tuesday, 30.

Being the Anniverfary of the Martyrdom of K. *Charles* I. their Majesties and Royal Family appeared in Mourning. Dr *Peploe* Bp of *Chefter* preach'd before the House of Lords at *Weftminfter-Abbey*; the Rev. Dr *Mawfon* before the House of Commons, at *St Margarets Weftminfter*; and the Rev. Dr *Berriman* before the Lord-Mayor at *St Paul's*.

MEMBERS chofe this Month.
Matthew Norris, Efq; for *Rye*.
Tho. Walker, Efq; for *Weftlow, Cornwal*.
John Merril, Efq; for *St Albans*.
John White, Efq; for *Retford*.

BIRTHS.

THE Wife of *Henry Bromley* Efq; one of the Knights of the Shire for *Cambridge*, deliver'd of a Son, and died.

The Lady of the Ld Vifc. *Glenorcky*, Kt of the Bath, deliver'd of a Son and Heir.

MARRIAGES.

MR *Luther*, formerly Steward to Baron *Bothmar*, married to the Daughter of Mr *Crew*, Stay-maker to her Majefty.

Philip Broke, Efq; Member for *Ipfwich* : : to Mifs *Bowes*, of *Bury St Edmonds*, with 15,000 *l*.

John Shelton, of *Canterbury*, Efq; : : to Mifs *Holmes*, a 5000 *l*. Fortune.

The Son of the late Dr *Cade* : : to a Sifter of Mr Alderman *Perry*, with a Fortune of 12,000*l*.

Jerwoife, Efq; of *Hampfhire* : : to the Daughter and Heirefs of Mr *Huddlefton*, Mercer of *Bedford-ftreet*, *Covent-Garden*, with a Fortune of 13,009 *l*.

The Hon. *Wm Finch*, Efq; : : to the Lady *Anne Douglas*, Sifter to the D. of *Queensberry* and *Dover*, a 15,000 Fortune,

Sir *John Wilton*, of *Buckinghamfhire*, Bar. : : to the Daughter of *John Edwin*, Efq; with a Fortune of 10,000 *l*.

Thomas Bramfton Efq; Member of Parliament for *Malden* in *Effex* : : to the Daughter of *Rich. Berney* of *Norwich* Efq;

DEATHS.

Jan. 1. DIED, the Countefs of *Clanriccard*, in *Pall-mall*.

2. The Rev. Mr *Betts* Reader to *Chrift's Hofpital*.

3. Ballard Efq; Brother to Mr *Halfpenny* of the *Six Clerks Office*. He took the firft Name for a large Eftate left him by a Relation.

Sir *Samuel Woodham*, an *Eaft-India* Merchant, reputed worth 30,000*l*.

The Ld *Coningsby*, new born Son of Sir *Michael Newton*, Knight of the Bath.

John Henley of the *Red Lodge* Efq; at *Briftol*.

John Hampton of *Whitby*, *Torkfh*. Efq;

Mrs *Sarah Houblon*, only furviving Daughter of Sir *James Houblon*, Kt.

The Widow of Col. *Francis Charteris*, remarkable for her Charity to the Poor.

Mrs *Larocque* in *St Mary Ax*, in the 98th Year of her Age, Widow of a *Spanifh* Merchant, reputed worth 30,000*l*.

4. Sir *Geofry Palmer*, Bart. at *Carlton* in *Northamptonfhire* ; and dying without Iffue, the Dignity and Eftate defcend to his Nephew (now) Sir *Tho. Palmer* Bart.

5. Col. *Hawker* Lieut. Governor of the Town and Garrifon of *Portfmouth*.

8. *Prattle* Efq; in the Commiffion of the Peace for *Middlefex*.

Mr *Leonard Woodiffon*, Clerk to the Commiffioners of his Majefty's Works.

Chriftopher Rawlinfon of *Lancafh*. Efq; defcended from the *Monks*, Dukes of *Albemarle* by the Mother's Side. He ordered his Wood Coffin to be Heart of Oak and cover'd with red Leather.

Mr *Bendall*, an eminent *Quaker* in the *Minories*, reputed worth 20,000 *l*.

9. The Wife of *Henry Seymour* Efq; eldeft Daughter of the Abp of *Canterbury*.

Col. *Wm Lee* of the 2d Reg. of Guards.

Edmund-Bacon Dickenfon of *Newark* upon *Trent* Efq;

The Relict of Sir *Peter Myer* Kt.

Mr *Charles Snell*, an eminent Writing-mafter in *Fofter-lane*.

11. The Rev. Mr *Huxley*, Curate of *St Mary Whitechapel*, Lecturer of *St Geo. in the Eaft*, and Senior Fellow of *Brazen-Nofe* College, *Oxon*.

The Lady *Katharine Hay*, in *Scotland*, aged 93.

Sir *William Bennet* of *Grubet*, Bart.

Baynbrig Buckridge, Efq; formerly in the *Eaft-India* Company's Service at *Fort St George*.

Dr *Rich. Danelly*, Fellow of the Royal College of Phyficians.

14. *Chefhire* Efq; Nephew of Sir *John Chefhire*.

The Rev. Mr *Robt Orme*, a Nonjuring Clergyman, in *Jewen ftreet*.

15. Mr *Walker*, formerly Hall-keeper at *Guildhall*.

Mr *Sexton*, Page of the Back Stairs to the King.

The Vifcountefs Dowager of *Hatton*, at *Kenfington*.

Mr *Pettit*, Woollen-Draper, by *Aldgate*.

16. Dr *Ja. Campbell* in *Covent-garden*.

The Lady of Sir *Robert Clarke* Bar. late Knight of the Shire for *Cambridgefhire*.

17. *George Byng*, Vifc. *Torrington*, Baron *Byng* of *Southill*, Knight of the Privy Council, Firft Commiffioner of the Admiralty, Admiral of the Red, Rear Admiral of *England*, Commander in Chief of his Majefty's Fleet, and one of the Governors of *Greenwich* Hofpital. He commanded the Fleet off *Scotland* in 1708, and was prefented by the Magiftracy of *Edinburgh* with the Freedom of that City; the fame Year he conducted the prefent Q. of *Portugal* to *Lisbon*

Lisbon; and the next was appointed a Lord of the Admiralty; in 1715 he was created a Baronet; in 1718, he commanded the *British* Fleet in the *Mediterranean*, was Plenipotentiary to all the Princes and States in *Italy*, and to the Emperor of *Morocco*; and upon his Return, in Confideration of his having crush'd the labour'd Efforts of *Spain* to fet up a Power at Sea, by which the Arms of *Britain* were advanced to fuch a Pitch of Reputation that her Flag gave Laws to the contending Parties, and her Crown enabled to refettle the Tranquillity of *Europe*, he was created a Peer. He married the Daughter of *James Masters*, of *East Langdon*, Efq; and has left feven Sons and one Daughter theLady *Osborne*; and is fucceeded in Honour and Estate by the Hon. *Pattee Byng* Efq; Knight of the Shire for *Bedford*, Privy Counfellor, and Treafurer of the Navy; who married, in 1724, the youngeft Sifter to the D. of *Manchester*.

17. Sir *Sam. Jackson*, at his Lodgings in *Cornhill*.

Wm Lewis le Grand, Efq; Gentleman of the Bed-chamber to his Majefty.

James Scot of *Logie*, Efq; Member of Parliament for the Shire of *Forfar*.

Mr *John Arnold*, an Apothecary in *Salisbury Court*, Common-Council-man in the Ward of *Farringdon Without*.

18. *John Hastings*, Efq; Verdurer of *Whittlewood* Forest in *Northamptonshire*, Senior Fellow of *Grays-Inn*, and a Juftice of the Peace. He left the Bulk of his Eftate to his Niece, the Wife of the fecond Son of the E. of *Abercorn*.

19. Mr *Charles Smith*, Clerk of the *Spanish Hall* in *Blackwell-Hall*.

20. *William Sharpe*, Efq; Clerk of the Cheque to the King's Meffengers.

Maj. *Richard Handy*, at *Chelfea*.

Mrs *Anne*, Daughter of Sir *Fifher Tench*, Bart.

Dr *Fortescue*, who left 100 *l. per Ann.* to his Nephew a Journeyman Shoemaker at *Northampton*.

Mrs *Adams*, Matron of *Chrift's Hofpital*.

21. Dr *Mandeville*, Author of *The Fable of the Bees* and other Pieces.

Lieut. Col. *Gore*, of the Train-bands, formerly an Apothecary in *Fleet-ftreet*.

The Hon. *Montague Blundel*, Efq; only Son of the Ld Vifc. *Blundell*.

Sir *Chriftopher Defbouverie*, Kt.

Dr *Moze*, a learned Antiquarian and Botanift, aged 95.

Mr *Brown*, an eminent Merchant, in *Monument-yard*, worth 40,000 *l.*

22. *Tho. Herbert*, E. of *Pembroke* and

Montgomery, Baron *Herbert* of *Cardiff*, Baron *Rofs* of *Kendall*, *Parr*, *Fitzbugh*, *Marmion*, *St Quintin*, and *Herbert* of *Shurland*, Knight of the Garter, Fellow of the Royal Society; one of the Governors of the *Charter-houfe*, Ld Lieut. of the County of *Wilts*, one of the Privy Council, and one of the Society for propagating the Gofpel in Foreign Parts. In the Beginning of K. *Wm's* Reign, Ambaffador Extraordinary to the States General, afterwards of the Privy Council, Col. of a Reg. of Marines, Firft Commiffioner of the Admiralty, Ld Privy Seal, Firft Plenipotentiary at the Treaty of *Ryfwick*, Ld High Admiral of *England* and *Ireland*, and Prefident of the Council. In 1707, appointed a Commiffioner to treat of a Union between *England* and *Scotland*; and alfo Ld Lieut. of *Ireland*. His firft Wife was *Margaret*, fole Daughter and Heirefs of Sir *Robert Sawyer*, Attorney General in the Reign of K. *Char.* II. and by her had five Sons and five Daughters: By his fecond Wife *Barbara*, Daughter to Sir *Henry Slingfby* of *Yorkfhire* Bar. he had one Daughter. In 1725, he married Mifs *Mary How*, Sifter to *Scroop* Ld Vifc. *How*, by whom he had no Iffue. Is fucceeded in Honour and Eftate by his eldeft Son the Ld *Herbert*, Capt. of the Firft Troop of Horfe Guards, and one of the Lords of the Bed-chamber to the King.

His Lordfhip's Coachman, aged 80, 50 of which he paffed in the Earl's Service, died the fame Day.

Thomas Foley, Baron of *Kidderminfter* in the County of *Worcefter*, fo created in 1711. He married the Daughter of Serjeant *Strode*; by whom he has left Iffue, *Thomas*, who fucceeds him in Honour and Eftate, and *Elizabeth*, both unmarried.

The Relict of *Alexander Morrifon*, a *Scots* Vifcount.

Mrs *Vanbutchefon*, only Child of Mr *Delmo* (Uncle of Sir *Peter*) who gave her at feveral Times upwards of 100,000 *l.*

Mr *Hals*, Broker, in *Exchange Alley*.

Mr *Daude*, who had formerly a Place in the Exchequer, who has left 8000 *l.* to a Nephew, and 400 *l.* to a *French* Hofpital, call'd the *Peft-houfe*.

23. The Relict of the late Sir *John Thorold*, Bart.

Edward Grofe, Efq; a Juftice of Peace for *Middlefex*; and one of the Dep. Lieuts.

Sir *John Blunt*, Bat. at *Bath*, one of the S. Sea Directors in 1720. He has left five Sons and two Daughters, and is fucceeded in Honour and Eftate by his eldeft Son, now Sir *Charles Blunt*, Bart.

Capt.

Capt. *Atkins* of the 3d Reg. of Guards.
Thomas Manly, Efq; at *Clapham*.

24. Mr *Brook*,Meſſenger to the Commiſſioners for Q. *Anne*'s Bounty.

Mr *Joſeph Atkins*, Man-Midwife.

The Dutcheſs Dowager of *Rutland*, A
Grandmother to the preſent Duke.

Joſeph Taylor, Efq; late High Sheriff of
Oxfordſhire, Maſter of the Coopers Com-
pany, and a Common-Council-man for
Tower-Ward, reputed worth 40,000 *l.*

Mr *Ball*, a *W. India* Mercht, at *Hoxton*.

25. Sir *Gilbert Heathcote*, Kt and Bart, B
Father of the City, Alderman of *Bridge
Ward Without*, Col. of the Blue Reg. of
Train'd-Bands, a Director of the Bank,
and Member for *St Germains* in *Cornwal*;
reputed the richeſt Commoner in *Great
Britain*,aged 82. He was reckon'd worth C
700,000 *l.* which together with the Dignity of Baronet, lately conferred on him,
deſcend to his only Son, now Sir *John
Heathcote*, Bart. Sir *Gilbert* will'd a handſome Legacy to the Rev. Dr *Johnſon*,
who about 4 Years ago cur'd him of an
Ulcer in his Leg, after he had been given
over by ſeveral eminent Surgeons as in- D
curable; 500 *l.* to *St Thomas*'s *Hoſpital*;
500 *l.* to the Poor of *Cheſterfield*, where
he was born; and ordered that hisTenants
ſhould not have their Rents raiſed, whatever Improvements they make.

The Wife of Mr *Theophilus Cibber*, a
celebrated actreſs.

Robert *Booth*, Efq; Member for *Bodmin* E
&c. in *Cornwall*.

The Ld *Binning*, Son of the E. of *Haddington*, at *Naples*.

Gen. *Syburg*, Governor of *Fort William*
in *Scotland*, reputed worth 80,000 *l.*

Sir *Philip Ryley*, Kt, at *Norwich*, ma-
ny Years Surveyor General of the Woods,
Ranger of *Dane Foreſt*, Commiſſioner of F
Excife, and Serj. at Arms to the Treaſury.

26. Mr *Debonar*, a *French* Merchant, in
Laurence Lane.

Thomas Sweethall, Efq; in the Commiſſion of the Peace for *Berkſhire*.

Jacob-Delamot Blagney, Efq; in the G
Commiſſion of the Peace reputed worth
20,000 *l.* There was found in an Iron
Cheſt in his Cloſet upwards of 10,000*l.*
in Gold and Silver.

The Rev. Mr *Pocock*, Reader of *St Saviour*'s, *Southwark*; likewiſe his Wife.

Mr *Woolſton*, Author of *Diſcourſes on
our Saviour*'s *Miracles*, aged 66. About H
4 or 5 Minutes before he died, he
utter'd theſe Words, *This is a hard Struggle which all Men muſt go thro'*, *and*

which I bear not only *with Patience*, *but
Willingneſs*.

Mr *Colebland Anamet*, an eminent
Sugar-baker in *Hounſditch*.

Mr *Edward Collings*, a Carpenter in St
James's. He left 100 *l.* to the Girls of
the Charity School of St *Giles in the
Fields*; his Freehold Eſtate to his Maid
Servant during her Life, after that to the
Girls of the Charity School of St *James*'s
at *Weſtminſter*.

Lieut. *Hay*, who had been in the Army
upwards of 60 Years; Aged 92.

28. The Rev. Dr *Richardſon*, aged 86
Rector of *Alhallows on the Wall* 40 Years.

29. Mr *Rider*, formerly a Mercer ta
the Indian Queen by St *Bartholomew*'s
Hoſpital.

The Rev. Dr *Godolphin*, aged 90, Pro-
voſt of *Eaton* Col. and formerly Dean of
St *Pauls*: He was Uncle to the E. of
Godolphin, and left 2 Sons and a Daughter.

PROMOTIONS.

HIS Majeſty preſented the Gold Staff
of Deputy Earl Marſhal of *England* to *Francis* Earl of *Effingham*.

Col. *Bragge*, appointed Governor of the
Royal Hoſpital at *Dublin*, in the Room
of Maj. Gen. *Stearne* deceaſed; and Lieut.
Col. in Lieut. Gen. *Pearſe*'s Reg of Horſe.

Col. *Blakeney*, made Lieut. Col. of the
Ld *Moleſworth*'s Reg. of Dragoons, in *Ireland*, in the Room of

Col. *Dalway*, appointed Lieut. Col. of
Col. *Legonier*'s Reg. of Horſe.

Cap. *Eaton*, appointed Col. of a Company in Third Reg. of Foot Guards, in
the Room of Col. *Bragge*.

Sir *Rich. Hopkins*,elected Sub-Governor
of the *South Sea* Company, and

John Briſtow, Efq, Deputy Governour.

The Hon. *Wm Finch*, Efq; appointed
Plenipotentiary to the States General.

Sir *Charles Wager*, Kt. Admiral of the
Blue, appointed Firſt Commiſſioner of the
Admiralty, in the Room of the Ld *Tor-
rington*, and one of the Privy Council.

The other Admirals are as follow:
James Earl, of *Berkley*, Admiral and
Commander in Chief and Vice Admiral of
Great Britain, Sir *John Jennings*, Adm.
of the Red and Rear-Admiral of *England*;
Sir *John Norris*, Admiral of the White;
Sir *George Walton*,Vice. Adm. of the Red;
Adm. *Morris* Vice of the White; *Philip
Cavendiſh*, Efq; Vice Adm. of the Blue;
Adm. *Balchin*,Rear of the Red; *Cha. Stu-
art*, Efq; Rear Admiral of the White; and
Sir *George Saunders*, Rear of the Blue.

Cap.

Cap. *James Winter*, elected an Elder Brother of the *Trinity House*.

John Belcher, of the *Middle Temple*, Esq; Son to the Governor, created Master of Arts, in a full Senate at *Cambridge*.

Henry Fox and *Rich. Bateman*, Esqs; appointed Receivers General of the Revenues in the Counties of *Glamorgan*, *Monmouth*, *Radnor*, *Brecknock*, *Carmarthen*, *Cardigan* and *Pembroke*, and in the Town of *Haverford-Weſt* in *South-Wales*.

Mr Hawkins, Footman to the Prince of *Wales*, appointed Houſekeeper to his R. Highneſs, at his Houſe in *Pall-mall*.

Mr *Thomas Kynaſton*, appointed Clerk to *Hugh Howard*, Esq; Paymaſter to the Board of Works, in the room of *Leonard Woodeſſon*, Esq; deceaſed.

Eccleſiaſtical PREFERMENTS.

MR *John Ingram*, preſented to the Living of *Stoneham*, in *Hants*.

Mr *Jenkins*,—to the Rectory of *Wandſworth* in *Surry*.

Mr *James Richardſon*, of *Blackheath*, appointed Reading Chaplain at *Whitehall*.

Mr *Fairfax*, Rector of *Enſbury* in *Huntingdonſhire*, appointed one of the Prebendaries of *Lincoln*.

Mr *Hargrove*, preſented to the Rectory of *Luckin* near *Minehead*, *Somerſetſhire*.

Dr *Robert Butts*, Dean of *Norwich*, made Dean of *Norwich*, in the Room of Dr *Baker* deceas'd.

Dr *Charles Cecil*,—Rector of *Hatfield*, in *Hertfordſhire*, (a near Relation of the E. of *Saliſbury*,) made Bp of *Briſtol*, in the room of Bp *Bradſhaw*, decd.

Dr *Coneybeare*, made Dean of *Chriſt-Church*, in the Room of the ſaid Biſhop.

Mr *John Wilkinſon*, preſented to the Rectory of *Milborn Port*, in *Somerſetſhire*.

A Diſpenſation is granted to enable Mr *Edmund Marten*, L. L. D. of *New College*, *Oxon*, to hold the Rectory of *Angmering*, in *Suſſex*, together with the Rectory of *Wolbeding* in the ſaid County.

Mr *Waters* goes Chaplain to Ld *Forbes*, Embaſſador to the Empreſs of *Ruſſia*.

Mr *Atwell*, who was Tutor to the preſent E. *Cowper*, whom he accompanied in his Travels, had the Degree of Doctor of Divinity confer'd on him by the Univerſity of *Oxford*, and was appointed Rector of *Exeter College*, in the Room of Dr *Coneybeare*.

Mr *John Guiſe*, a diſſenting Miniſter, made a Doctor of Divinity by the Univerſity of *Aberdeen*.

Mr *Morſe*, Chaplain to the D. of *Kent*, made a Prebendary of *Hereford*.

Mr *Billio*, inducted to the Living of *High Roding* in *Eſſex*.

Baptiſt Noel Barton, D. D. preſented to the Rectory of *Wing*, in the County of *Durham*.

John Freak, M. A. to the Vicarage of *Clanbury*, in *Devonſhire*.

The Rev. Mr *Lancaſter*, Rector of St *Martins* in the City of *Cheſter*, appointed a Chaplain to the Pr. of *Wales*.

Wm Hunt, M. A. preſented to the Rectory of *St Peter* in *Norfolk*.

Richard White, D. D.—to the Rectory of *Abbotſham* in *Devonſhire*.

John Ball, D. D.—to the Rectory of *Thoreſway* in *Lincolnſhire*.

BANKRUPTS.

CHarles Grant, of St *Clements Danes*, Haberdaſher.

John Collier of *Briſtol*, Merchant.

Peter Shenton, of *Wallingford, Berks*, Draper.

John Conran, of St *Giles's Cripplegate*, Diſtiller.

James Mourguez, of the *Old Baily*, *London*, Wine Merchant.

Daniel Bedell, of *Biſhopſgate ſtreet*, *London*, Plumber.

Robert Green, of *Biſhopſgate-ſtr. Lond*. Diſtiller.

Tho. Phillips, of the *Devizes*, *Wilts*, Seedſman.

Peter Ingham, of *Theberton Suffolk*, Maltſter.

Henry Cruſh, of *Eaſtbergholt*, *Suff*. Corn Mercht.

John Sedding, of *St Mary La Bone*, *Middleſex* Chapman.

Wm Brown, of *St Clements Dane*, Victualler.

John & Dempſter, of *Hampton Road*, *Glou-*
Thomas } *—ceſterſhire*, Chapmen.

Stonier Parret of *Coventry*, Coal Merchant.

Joſeph Richardſon, of *Cirenceſter*, *Glouceſter*, &c. Chapman.

John Hobbs of *Buttolph Lane*, Orange Mercht.

James Brown, of *Wapping*, *Middleſex*, Baker.

Amos Avery, of *Devizes Wilts*. Drugget maker

Dan. Wall, of *Manningtree*, *Eſſex*, Shopkeeper.

Henry Hunter, of *Newcaſtle upon Tyne*, Butcher.

Tho. Seaton, of *Mitre Co. Fleet ſtr*. Coffeeman.

Wm Penſeld, of *Newport Market*, *Weſtm* Vintner and Draper.

Ellis Gamble, of *Leiceſterfields*, Goldſmith.

Thomas Gould of *Cornhill*, *London*, Banker.

William Farrow, of *Southwark*, Carrier.

John Young, of St *James's Weſtminſter*, Hatter and Woollendraper.

Wm Sherborne, of *Finch Lane*, *London*, Broker.

Thomas Taylor, Sen. of St *Pauls Shadwel*, Lighterman.

John Bann, of *Chicklane*, *London*, Saleſman.

Abraham Boulton, of *Glouceſterſh*. Waggoner.

Tho. Bond, of St *Pancras*, *Middx*. Coachmaker.

Jonathan Brookes, of St *Giles* in the *Fields*, Chapman.

Geo. Collingwood, of *Wapping*, *Midd*. Lighterman

Alex. Daniel, of *Penzance Cornwal*. Mercer.

Richard Moot, of *Brew Warwickſhire*, Hoſier.

Course of Exchange.	*S T O C K S.*
Amsterdam — 31 1	S. Sea 105 1/8
Ditto at Sight 34 10	—— Annu. 110 1/4
Hamburgh — 34 2 4 1	Bank 150 1/4 a 1/8
Rotterdam - - 35 2	India 159 1/2
Antwerp —— 35 9	3 *per C. Ann.* 100 1/4
Madrid —— 42 1/2 a 5/8	Mil. Bank 115
Bilboa —— 42 1/8	African 35
Cadiz —— 42 5/8 a 3/4	York Build. 2 1/4
Venice —— 48 7/8	Royal Aff. 104 1/2
Leghorn —— 50 5/8 a 3/4	Lon. ditto 13 3/8
Genoa —— 53 1/8	Eng. Copp. 1 *l.* 18 *s.*
Paris —— 32 1/8	Welsh ditto 1 *l.* 13 *s.*
Bourdeaux — 31 7/8 a 1/2	Bank Cir. 5 *l.* 5 *s.*
Oporto —— 5 4 1/4	India Bonds 5 *l.* 6 *s.*
Lisbon - - - 5 5 1/2	3 *p. Cent.* ditto 1 *l.* 19
Dublin - - - 11 3/8	S. Sea ditto 2 *l.* 8 *s.*

Monthly BILL of Mortality, from Dec. 26. *to Jan.* 23.

Christned { Males 834, Females 746 } 1579

Buried { Males 1015, Females 1175 } 2190

Died under 2 Years old	804
Between 2 and 5	161
Between 5 and 10	76
Between 10 and 20	54
Between 20 and 30	147
Between 30 and 40	206
Between 40 and 50	240
Between 50 and 60	61
Between 60 and 70	186
Between 70 and 80	128
Between 80 and 90	110
Between 90 and 100	23
	2190

Price of Grain at *Bear-Key, per* Qr.

Wheat 21 *s.* to 25 *s.* od.	P. Malt 17 *s.* to 22 *s.*
Rye 14 *s.* to 16 *s.* od	B. Malt 17 *s.* to 19 *s.*
Barley 11 *s.* to 13 *s.* 6 *d*	Tares 16 *s.* to 20 *s.* od
Oats 10 *s.* to 12 *s.* od.	H. Pease 14 *s.* to 16 *s.*
Pease 16 *s.* to 18 *s.*	H. Beans 14 *s.* to 17 *s.*

Weekly	Burials
Nov. 21	484
28	603
Dec. 5	680
12	734
19	700
Jan 30	1588

Weekly	Burials
Dec. 26	421
Jan. 2	412
9	430
16	445
23	482
	2190

Prices of Goods, &c. in *London.* Hay 1 *l.* 16 *s.* to 2 *l.* 2 *s.* a Load.

Coals per Chaldron 27 *s.* to 29 *s.*
Old Hops per Hun. 4 *l.* to 7 *l.*
New Hops 9 *l.* to 10 *l.*
Rape Seed 10 *l.* to 11 *l.* 00 *s.*
Lead the Fodder 19 *Hun.* & *half on board,* 15 *l.* 10 *s.*
Tin in Blocks 4 *l.* 00 *s.*
Ditto in Bars 4 *l.* 02 *s. exclusive of* 3 *s. per Hun. Duty.*
Copper Eng. best 5 *l.* 5 *s. per C.*
Ditto ordinary 4 *l.* 16 *s. per C.*
Ditto Barbary 3 *l.* 10 *s.*
Iron of Bilboa 15 *l.* 10 *s. per Ton.*
Dit. of Sweden 16 *l.* 10 *s. per Ton*
Town Tallow 40 *to* 36 *s. pr C.*
Country Tallow 1 *l.* 17 *s.* 0 *d.*
Cochineal 17 *s.* 3 *d. per lb.*

Grocery Wares.

Raisins of the Sun 25 *s. new per C.*
Ditto Malaga
Ditto Smirna new 17 *s.*
Ditto Alicant 15 *s.*
Ditto Lipra new 16 *s.*
Ditto Belvedera 18 *s.*
Currants none
Ditto new 42
Prunes French 17 *s.*
Figs 18 *s.*

Sugar Powder best 59 *s. per C.*
Ditto second sort 49 *per C.*
Loaf Sugar double refine 09 *d. per lb.*
Ditto single refin. 60 *s.* to 70 *s. per C.*
Cinamon 7 *s.* 9 *d.*
Cloves 9 *s.* 1 *d.*
Mace 16 *s.* 6 *d. per lb.*
Nutmegs 8 *s.* 7 *d. per lb.*
Sugar Candy white 12 *d.* to 17 *d.*
Ditto brown 6 *d. Half penny per lb.*
Pepper for Home consump. 14 *d.*
Ditto for exportation 10 *d. farthing*
Tea Bohea fine 12 *s.* to 14 *s. per lb.*
Ditto ordinary 10 *s. per lb.*
Ditto Congo 12 *s.* to 16 *s. per lb.*
ditto Pekoe 18 *s. per lb.*
ditto Green fine 12 *s.* to 15 *s. per lb.*
ditto Imperial 14 *per lb.*
ditto Hyson 35 *s.* to 00 *s.*

Drugs by the lb.

Balsam Peru 16 *s.*
Cardamoms 3 *s.* 4 *d.*
Camphire refin'd 24 *s.*
Crabs Eyes 22 *s.* 8 *d*
Jallop 3 *s.* 9 *d.*
Manna 1 *s.* 6 *d.* to 2 *s.*

Mastick white 4 *s.* 6 *d.*
Opium 10 *s.* 0 *d.*
Quicksilver 4 *s.* 4 *d.'*
Rhubarb 18 *s.* a 20 *s.*
Sarsaparilla 3 *s.* 0 *d.*
Saffron Eng. 36 *s.* 00 *d.*
Wormseeds 4 *s.* 6 *d.*
Balsam Capiva 2 *s.* 10 *d.*
Balsam of Gillead 14 *s.* 00 *d.*
Hypocacuana 5 *s.* 6 *d.*
Ambergreece per oz. 14 *s.* 00

Wine, Brandy, and Rum.

Oporto red, per T. 36 *l.*
ditto white 24 *l.*
Lisbon red 30 *l.*
ditto white 26 *l.*
Sherry 26 *l.*
Canary new 30
ditto old 36 *l.*
Florence 3 *l. per chest*
French red 30 *l.* a 40 *l.*
ditto white 20 *l.*
Mountain malaga old 24 *l.*
ditto new 20 *l.* to 21 *l.*
Brandy Fr. per Gal. 6 *s.* to 6 *s.* 6 *d*
Rum of Jam. 6 *s.* to 7 *s.* 0 *d.*
ditto Lew. Islands 6 *s.* 4 *d*
Spirits Eng. 20 *l. per Ton.*

GOLD in Bars, 3 *l.* 18 *s.* 1 *d.* to 2 *d.*—Ditto in Coin 3 *l.* 18 *s.* 3 *d.*—SILVER in Bars, Standard 5 *s.* 4 *d.* Half-penny—Pillar Pieces of Eight 5 *s.* to 5 *s.* 5 *d.* 3 Farth. ditto Mexico 5 *s.* 5 *d.* Farth.

FROM *Virginia*, That the Assembly had advanced 2200*l.* to *Jn Randolph*, Efq; their Agent at *London*, to get Tobacco Excifed, and the Law for fecuring the Payment of Debts in the Plantations, to the Merchants of *England*, repealed.

From *Barcelona*, That two *Spanish* Cruizers had brought in the *Seafare* of *Plymouth* with Sugar from *Legborn*, having 3 *Moorish* Paffengers on board, on whofe account they pretend to make her a Prize; becaufe the *Moors* do the fame to fuch *British* Ships as have *Spaniards* on board.

From *Vienna*, That the burning Mountains in the Neighbourhood of *Prague*, had continued to flame out in a terrible manner.

From *Paris*, That an Alliance was much talk'd of between their Chriftian and Catholic Majefties.

From *Vienna*, That Mr *Robinfon*, the *British* Minifter, had propofed to the Imperial Court an Expedient for terminating the Differences touching the Titles which the Infant *Don Carlos* has affumed fince his Arrival in *Italy*.

From *Poland*, That the frequent Ruptures of the Dyets of that Kingdom without doing any Bufinefs, had involved it in great Confufion.

From *Spain*, That the *Jefuits* had been expell'd the Country of *Paraguay* in *South America*, for affuming a defpotick Power over the Lives, Eftates, Bodies and Souls of the Inhabitants.

From *Perfia*, That *Thamas Kouli-Kam*, who depofed his Mafter, is for purfuing War with the *Turks*, but has fignify'd his Willingnefs to live in Peace with the *Mufcovites*.

From *Oran*, That the *Moors* were affembling again near that Place; notwithftanding the Defeat they received by the *Spaniards*, whofe Victory, if it may be called fo, coft them very dear, having loft 3,000 Soldiers and 200 Officers; among them the Marquis *de Santa Cruz*, and *Valde Cannas*, who were faid to be taken Prifoners, but the Truth of it is fince very much doubted.

The *Spaniards* in the faid Action were on the Point of being entirely routed, 3 Regiments having thrown down their Arms fled before the Enemy; and the Day was turning in favour of the *Moors*, when at that Inftant fome Troops landed from on board a Convoy, march'd under their Commander, an *Irifhman*, repuls'd the purfuing *Moors*, and gave the difconcerted *Spaniards* a Time to rally, (See p. 8. D)

From *Rome*, That the Pope has complimented the eldeft Son of the Chevalier *St. George* with a Brief, capacitating him to enjoy any Abby, or other Ecclefiaftical Benefice; and had affur'd the Chevalier, that his Recommendation of Sig. *Riviera* to the Purple fhall take Place, notwithftanding the Intereft made by the Emperor for Sig. *Stampe* the Apoftolick Nuncio at *Venice*.

From *Turin*, That one *Nolo*, who had been in Prifon 7 Years on an Accufation of having poifoned his Wife, was admitted to Bail: When, fearing the Fact might afterwards come out, he procur'd about 40 Perfons to be affaffinated, who had either aided him in the Murder, or were acquainted with it. Complaints being made of frefh Murders, *Nolo* was again taken up and threatned with the Queftion; upon which he confefs'd he had been concern'd in more than 120 Murders, of having poyfon'd his Wife, and deftroy'd a Child about 4 Years old by fplitting it in two, of having buried a Prieft alive, poyfon'd a Footboy who was the Confident of his Crimes, and once to avoid paying a poor Gardener his Debt, order'd him to carry a Sack full of Stones to throw in a River, which being by *Nolo* faften'd on his Back, drew the poor Fellow along with it.

From *Carthagena*, That 2 *Maltefe* Men of War, having attack'd the Capitana and three more Algerine Men of War, after a bloody Fight, funk two of them, but took their Companies on board, and fo fhatter'd the Capitana and the remaining Algerine, that they fheer'd off.

A REGISTER of BOOKS publish'd in JANUARY, 1733.

The Gardiners Dictionary: Containing, The Methods of cultivating and improving the Kitchen, Fruit and Flower Garden, as also the Phyfick Garden, Wildernefs, Confervatory, and Vineyard; according to the Practice of the moft experienc'd Gardiners of the prefent Age. Interfpers'd with the Hiftory of the Plants, the Characters of each Genus, and the Names of all the particular Species, in Latin and Englifh; and an Explanation of all the Terms ufed in Botany and Gardening,

Together with Accounts of the Nature and Ufe of Barometers, Thermometers and Hygrometers, proper for Gardeners; And of the Origin, Caufes, and Nature of Meteors, and the particular Influences of Air, Earth, Fire and Water upon Vegetation, according to the beft Natural Philofophers. Adorned with Copper Plates.

By PHILIP MILLER, Gardener to the Worfhipful Company of Apothecaries, at their Botannick Garden at Chelfea, and F. R. S. The Second Edition, with his Majefty's Royal Licence. Printed for the Author. Pr. 1l. 1cs. Bound.

2. The Gardener's Kallender, directing what Works are neceffary to be done every Month in the Year. By the fame Author. The Second Edition. To which is added, a Compleat Index. Price 4s.

Both fold by C. Rivington at the Bible and Crown in St Pauls Church Yard.

3. Art of Teaching French without the Help of any Grammar. By Claudius Arnaux. Printed for the Author, Pr. 1s.

4. A Brief Enquiry concerning the Dignity of the Ordinance of the Lord's Supper, and the Care that all, efpecially Magiftrates and Minifters, ought to take to prevent and remove the Occafions of its being leffened. Printed for J. Peele. pr. 6d.

5. Declarations and Pleadings, in Englifh, in the moft ufual Actions brought in the feveral Courts of King's-Bench and Common-Pleas at Weftminfter. By W. Bohun, Efq; Printed for D. Brown.

6. Of the Ufe of Riches. An Epiftle to the Right Hon. Allen Lord Bathurft. By Mr Pope. Printed for Lawton Gulliver, pr. 1s.

7. The Theory of Vifion, or vifual Language; fhewing the immediate Prefence and Providence of a Deity, vindicated and explained. By the Author of Alciphron, or the Minute Philofopher. Printed for J. Tonfon. Price 1s.

8. A View of the Prefent State of Scotland, in regard to the Tenures and Slavifh Dependencies of the Subjects of that Part of North Britain. In a Memorial drawn by William Lygon, Efq; a Scotifh Gentleman. Printed for J. Wilford. pr. 4d.

9. The Female Gloffary: Being a particular Defcription of the principal Commodities of this Ifland; wherein the various Names, Qualities and Properties of each are handfomely handled. Collected for the Benefit of the Inquifitive, and the Help of Weak Memories. By an old Trader. Printed for W. Shaw, pr. 6d.

10. A Prefervation againft the Wiles, of Popery: Or, Modern Deifm, Real Jefuitifm. Wherein Deifm is try'd, unmask'd and condemn'd. In a Letter to a Gentleman at Oxford. Occafioned by a late Jefuit—1 Treatife, entitled, Chriftianity as old as the Creation. Printed for J. Wilford, pr. 1s.

11. The Conduct of the Miniftry compared with its Confequence: Or An impartial View of the prefent State of Affairs. Printed for J. Crichly, pr. 1s.

12. A Paraphrafe and Notes on St Paul's Epiftle to Timothy, in Imitation of Mr Locke's Manner, with an Appendix concerning Infpiration; occafion'd by St Paul's Advice to Timothy, 1 Tim. v. 25. Printed for R. Ford, price 6d.

13. Anfwer to a late Pamphlet intitled, Burnt Children dread the Fire.

14. The humble Remonftrance of the Five-Foot-Highians againft the Antichriftian Practice of ufing a Standard in enlifting Soldiers To which is added, The Wounds o' th' Kirk of Scotland, &c.

15. A brief and diftinct Account of the Mineral Waters of Pyrmont, &c. By George Turner, M. D. Printed for A. Miller pr. 2s

16. A Treatife of the natural Grounds and Principles of Harmony. By Wm. Holder, D.D. F. R. S. Printed by W. Peirfon, pr. 3s. 6d.

17. An honeft Mind the beft Security againft Error in Matters of Religion. A Sermon on John vii. 17. By Geo. Wishart, A. M. Printed for A. Miller, pr. 6d.

18. Six New Sonata's for two German Flutes or two Violins; with a thorough Bafs for the Harpficord. By Sig. Quantz.

19. The young Clerk's Affiftant; or Penmanfhip made eafy, inftructive, and entertaining. Being a compleat Copy-book, with felect Poems, and a curious Drawing-book, defign'd by Mr Picart, and engraved on 73 Copper-plates by G. Bickham jun. Printed for R. Ware, pr. 3s. 6d

20. A Letter from Rome; fhewing an exact Conformity between Popery and Paganifm: Or the Religion of the prefent Roman derived from that of their Heathen Anceftors. By Conyers Middleton, D. D. The 3d Edition Printed for W. Innys.

21. Memoirs of John Gordon of Glencat in the County of Aberdeen in Scotland, who wa

13

13 Years in the *Scots* College at *Paris* amongst the secular Clergy. Wherein the Absurdities and Delusions of Popery was laid open; the Balanism, Jansenism, and the Constitution U-nigenitus, impartially related, and the Infalli-bility of the *Romish* Church confuted. With an Appendix, &c. By *John Gordon*, A. M. Printed for *J. Oswald*, pr. 2s.

22. An Abstract of an Essay of the Im-provement of Husbandry, and working of Mines. Printed for *J. Roberts*, pr. 1s.

23. A compleat List of the Stewards, Pre-sidents Vice Presidents, and Treasurers, be-longing to the Royal Corporation for the Re-lief of the poor Widows and Children of Clergymen, from the Time their Charter was granted by K. *Charles* II. 1678. Together with the Names of all the Preachers, &c. Printed for *W. Mears*, pr. 1s.

24. A Treatise on Mercury: Shewing the Danger of taking it crude for all Manner of Disorders, after the present Fashion; from its Nature; its manner of operating in the human Body, and Facts. With Remarks on the an-nent Physician's Legacy. Printed for *J. Ro-berts*, pr. 1s.

25. The *Norfolk* Miscellany: Or, a Hue and Cry after Sir *Blue String*. Printed for *T. Reynolds*, pr. 6d.

26. The Proceedings at the *Old-Baily*, on the 11th, 13th, and 15th of *January*, Printed for *J. Wilford*, pr. 6d.

27. An Account of the Bank of Loan at *Amsterdam*, commonly called the *Lombard*. By *Philopolis*. Printed for *J. Roberts*, pr. 4d.

28. The happy Life: An Epistle to the Hon Lieut. Gen. *Wade*. Printed for *The. Goffe*, pr. 6d.

29. The Argument from Prophecy, in Proof that Jesus is the Messiah, vindicated: Or, some Considerations on the Prophecies of the Old Testament as the Grounds and Rea-sons of the Christian Religion. Printed for *John Gray*, pr 1s. 6d.

30. the Boarding School: Or, The Sham Captain. An Opera. By Mr *Coffee*. Printed for *J. Watts*.

31. The History of the Test Act; in which the Mistakes in some late Writings are rectify'd and the Importance of it to the Church ex-plained. Printed for *J. Roberts*, pr. 6d.

32. The Church in Peril among false Bre-thren: Or the Danger of the Church from her pretended Friends, but secret Enemies, review'd. In which Objections against the Repeal of the Sacramental-Test, and the Arguments for it, are consider'd in their re-ligious and political Aspect. Printed for *J. Roberts*, pr. 6d

33. Reflexions on the 11th Query contain'd in a Paper, intitled, Reasons offered against Pushing for the Repeal of the Corporation and Test Acts. And on the Animadversions on the Answer to it. In a Letter to a Friend. In which a particular Answer is given to the further Calumnies contained in the Animad-

versions against a certain Lord, relating to his Conversation and Conduct in *London*, and *Bristol*, about the Repeal of the Corporation and Test Acts, at the Time when the Occasi-onal and Schism Bills were repealed, and at the Time of the Union. Printed for *J. Ro-berts*, pr. 6d.

34. *Britannia Excisa*: Britain Excis'd. A New Ballad: To be sung in Time, and to some Tune. pr. 6d. printed for *T. R.*

35. A Sequel to Britannia Excisa. A New Political Ballad. Printed for *T. Cooper*, pr. 6d.

36. An Argument against Excises. In se-veral Essays first published in the *Craftsman* and now Collected together. By *Caleb Dan-vers*, Esq; pr. 1s.

37. The second Part of an Argument a-gainst Excises, in Answer to several Writers; especially with Regard to that Part of the Subject relating to the Power and Conduct of the Commissioners and Officers of Excise. With some Remarks on the present State of Affairs. By Caleb *D'anvers*, Esq;

38. An Answer to the Considerations oc-casioned by the Craftsman upon Excise, so far as it relates to the Tobacco Trade. Printed for *E. Nutt*.

39. Observations upon the Laws of Excise. Printed for *J. Wilford*.

40. Some reasonable Animadversions on Excises; occasioned by a Pamphlet lately pub-lished, intitled, Considerations occasion'd by the Craftsman. Printed for *J. Wilford*, pr. 6d

41. Reflections upon a Pamphlet, intitled, Observations on the Laws of Excise. Printed for *J. Roberts*, pr. 6d.

42. Some General Considerations concern-ing the Alterations and Improvement of Pub-lick Revenues. Printed for *J. Roberts*, pr. 6d.

43. *Moliere's* Plays, *French* and *English*, in 8 Vol. pr. 1l.

44. Miscellaneous Observations on Authors, 2 Vols, 8vo. with compleat Indexes.

45. Political State for *Dec.* pr. 1s. 6d.

46. Historical Register.

47. Modern History.

48. *Bayle's* Historical and Critical Dictiona-ry, translated. 8 Sheets a Fortnight, at 1s.

49. The practising Scrivener, or modern Conveyancer. 8 Sheets for 1s. Weekly.

50. History of the Popes, No. 3.

Books publish'd Weekly by Numbers, at 6d. each,
Baker's Chronicle. 5 Sheets.
Act Regia. ditto.
Rapin's Hist. of *England*, by *Tindal* ditto.
Josephus by Sir *R. L'Estrange*.
Sir *Walt. Raleigh's* Hist. of the World. 4to.
Dr *Colbatch's* Legacy, or Family Physician.
The Magazine of Architecture, by *Oakley*.
Keating's Hist. of *Ireland*.
Hist. of the Bible, printed by *T. Edlin*.
Universal Traveller. 2 Sheets, at 3d.
Book of Martyrs ditto.

*62. The RIGHT USE of LENT: Or, a Help to PENITENTS. Containing, a Pre-
paratory

paratory Meditations on the Defign of LENT, the Nature of Sin, &c. 2, the Reason, Inftitution and Benefits of Fafting, 3. Some RULES and Advices concerning it. 4. What we are to Repent of. 5. The *Way* and *Method* of Repentance, with some Forms of Penitential Devotions. The 3d Edition. To which is added, Bp KENN's Paftoral Letter to his Clergy; concerning the keeping of LENT. Printed for *C. Rivington*, pr. 1 s 6 d.

63. Spiramina, or Refpiration Review'd. Being the Arguments of that great Philofopher by Fire *Johannes Baptifta Van Helmont*, Difcovering certain Ufes of the Lungs not commonly obferved; and afferting, that they have not that Alternate Motion, generally afcribed to them, but that in a found Man, they are porous, pervious to the Air, and conftantly at Reft. Humbly offer'd, with some Additions interfperfed to the Confideration of the Curious and Inquifitive. By *M. Jaxon*. Sold by the Author at *Tamworth* and by *T. Warren* Bookfeller in *Birmingham*.

Juft Publifh'd

Printed on good Paper, in 2 Vols. 8vo. Price bound 10 s. *and fold at St* John's Gate.

THIRTY-NINE SERMONS, by (a late very Celebrated PREACHER) *John Cook*, A. M. Rector of the United Parifhes of St *George* the Martyr and St *Mary Magdalen* in *Canterbury*, and of *Merfham* in *Kent*, and one of the fix Preachers of the Cathedral Church of *Canterbury*: From the Manufcript Copy, prepar'd by him for the Prefs: (there being feveral Copies of some of the Sermons abroad in Writing, firft granted at the Requeft of the Countefs of *Coventry* and other Perfons of Diftinction) On the following Heads and Occafions; viz Of *Faith. Happinefs. Coming to Chrift. Vanity. Righteoufnefs, Temperance, and Judgment to come. Cleannefs miftaken. God's Omnifcience. On Prayer. Of Friendfhip with God. The Enmity of the Devil. Refolution in Faith and Practice. Of Proving and Perfevering. The Nature of Cleannefs. Naaman's Cure. Of Vifion, Revelation, and Repentance. Of Zeal. The Crown of Glory. The Righteous Man's Reward. The Wicked Man's Lot. Bleffed are the Meek. Mercy to the Merciful. Purity in Heart. Holding faft the Faith. Godly Fear and Obedience. Covetoufnefs. The Sabbath. Sion preferred. Of Superftition. The Difficulty of Salvation. On St Peter's Denial. Upon the Fifth of November,* Preach'd before the Lower Houfe of Convocation, who requefted this Sermon to be Printed.

The Gentleman's *Magazine:*

LondGazette
Londs Jour.
Fog's Journ.
Applebce's : :
Read's : : : :
Craftsman :
P. Spctato2
Grubftreet J
W.ly Regifter
Free = Briton
Hpp = Doctor
Daily Court
Daily = Post
Dai. Journal
Da. Post-boy
D. Abbertifer
Evening Post
St James's Eb
Whitehall Eb
Lōdon Ebīg
Flying = Post
Weekly Mif-
cellany.
The Auditor

St John's Gate.

Posk = Pews
Dublin 6 : : :
Edinburgh :
Briftol : : : :
Po2wich : :
Exeter : : : :
Wo2ceffer : :
Northampton
Gloucefter : :
Stamfo2d : :
Nottingham
Burp Journ
Chefter ditt
erby ditto
Ipfwich do.
Reading do,
Leeds ditter
Newcastle E
Canterbury
Birmingham
Manchefter
Oston : : : c
Jamaica, &c
Barbados : :

Or, MONTHLY INTELLIGENCER.

For FEBRUARY, 1733.

CONTAINING,

/more in Quantity, and greater Variety, than any Book of the kind and Price/

By *SYLVANUS URBAN*, Gent.

LONDON: Printed, for the AUTHOR, and sold at St *John's* Gate: By F. *Jefferies* in *Ludgatestreet*; at the Pamphlet Shops; and by most Booksellers. Where may be had the former Numbers, or compleat Setts bound; a few on Royal Paper.

N. B. *This Book shall be forwarded Monthly as soon as publish'd to any Part, on sending proper Directions to the Printer at* St John's-Gate.

CONTENTS.

N. B. The Variety of Schemes that have been built on that of the Gentleman's Magazine, and the small Success the Generality of them have met with, is a Confession both of its Usefulness, and the Candour of the Publick in encouraging That which was primarily calculated for their Entertainment. The most assiduous Endeavours shall be used to deserve a Continuance of their Favour.

Notwithstanding the Weekly Productions multiply so fast, we trust we shall be able, by a new Letter that is casting for us, to give a Satisfactory Account of the whole Month's. We shall always preserve our Impartiality, and publish our Book as early as any other, tho' it should not happen to be advertis'd so soon in the News-Papers, in some of which our Advertisement has been more than once postponed several Days.

THE
Gentleman's Magazine:
FEBRUARY, 1733.

A View of the Weekly Disputes *and* Essays *in this Month.*

Free Briton, Feb. 1. No. 166.
The Malecontent and Incendiary.

THE beloved End of a Malecontent is to diftrefs the Government, and divide the Multitude by inftilling Jealoufies of Men in Power.

The unaccountable Appetite of the People for Scandal and fecret Hiftory is of prodigious Benefit to an Incendiary. Hence he is encouraged to vilify the Great and Powerful in Fables, Shades, and Allegories; and to bring the beft Charafters into Difrepute by Queries, Innuendoes, and bafe Infinuations. The common People love to be counted important; and to think the High exalted are brought before their Tribunal, and levelled with themfelves, is a favourite Chimæra with the Vulgar, who embrace the dear Incendiary who feeds and flatters this Vanity.

But if, in the Courfe of this defamatory Work, Minifters fenfibly injured fhould apply for Redrefs, our Malecontent muft loudly infift on the Liberty of the Prefs, clamour againft the Laws, appeal to the raging Paffions of the Rabble; and declaim againft the Government as cruel and infolent. He muft be careful to proclaim himfelf a Gentleman, allowing that Charafter to no other Perfoa; hence he has a Privilege for all the fcurrilities he defires to ufe.

Walfingham concludes with a few Words to his dear Countrymen—Such Men as thefe are among you; and the Point chiefly refts with you, what they deferve, or how they fhall be dealt with.

Grubftreet Journal, Feb. 1. No. 162.
Little Mafter's Letter from Cambridge.
Midonius to Sophronia.

Hon. and deareft Auntee,

WELL: I'm refolved I won't ftay in this ftrange place, and fo I would have you tell Mamma: I am fure you two can perfuade Papa to any thing—Here indeed they put me on a fine Gown; but L—d, I can't laugh when I will, and fay what I pleafe. Here the Wretches call me an infigniificant Creature, a Thing, a pert Coxcomb, a Fop, a Fool; I won't bear it: I didn't come here to be laugh'd at, that I didn't: I am fure I cry'd bitterly, when Papa threw the pretty Baby into the Fire, which I drefs'd up fo fine, and out did you know who, when I was at —— School. Tho' Papa frowns, I won't bear the Flears of thefe bookifh unmannerly Fellows that don't put on a clean Shirt above once a Week; and as for Bungundy and Champaign, good Gads! 'tis all Arabic to them. I vow you'd fplit your Sides at a great greafy Animal, that thinks himfelf a Philofopher,

pher, with a Pifs-burnt Wig, and thread-bare Coat. Here's a Wretch too had the Impudence to tell me, my Face wasn't my own, when you know, dear Auntee, I never us'd any thing but your Wafh, to cure Pimples, and Dr ——'s Cofmetic.—Well; I long to fee you, I muft fee you, and will fee you; and fo with Duty to Papa and Mamma, I am, deareft Auntee, your moft obedient Nephew,   MIDONIUS.

P. S. Tell Mamma I can't eat Mutton, and have juft forgot my Dancing.

The Tubítot, Feb. 2. No. 8.

—*Retinent—Commiffa fideliter Aures.*
                                    Hor.

NOT long fince *Frank Eafy* and I dined at an Ordinary not far from St *James's*. After Dinner moft of the Company feem'd defirous of fitting an Hour or two, *Florio* excepted, who faid he had an important Appointment. *Curio* prefs'd him to ftay; humoroufly adding, *She would not fure be uneafy to wait an Hour or two.* *Florio* fwore he would not omit going for any Confideration whatfoever. *Curio* then begg'd to go along with him. *Florio*, to get rid of him, took him afide, and whifper'd to him, " That he muft inftantly go to *White's*, and wait there for a Letter, which he fhould have by fix, at fartheft. Oh! the delicious Creature! fcarce 14! a Virgin too! Be eafy, and this Day Month fhe fhall be yours. " *Curio* defifted. This was unheard by all the Company but *Curio*, and myfelf by means of my *Eccho*; *Frank* being engaged at another Part of the Table. I call'd him afide, and begg'd his Affiftance in difappointing the Execution of this abominable Defign; which he readily granted, when he underftood that the poor Creature was to be abandon'd to Proftitution and Infamy; and immediately went to the *Chocolate-Houfe* to have an Eye on *Florio*, whilft I ftaid to write the following Letter.

To the Honourable—Efq; at *Whites's*.
Sir,

THE Son of a Nobleman fhould be more diftinguifh'd by the Merit of his Actions than his Birth. Confider then, the innocent Creature, the intended Victim of your brutal Appetite, is equally dear to a virtuous Mother and induftrious Father, as your Sifter is to her noble Parents and to you. If thefe Reafons are not fufficient to prevent your Defign, let Intereft prevail. A Letter with a full Account of it, is fent to your Father. Make haft and prevent its falling into his Hands; and believe me, you will rejoice hereafter at this providential Difappointment, and acknowledge the Friendfhip of *Your's*, &c.

I fent the Letter to the Chocolate-Houfe, and following it foon after, I found *Florio* fo deeply affected, that he went directly Home. He was not gone many Minutes, when a Porter came in with a Letter directed to *Florio*, which I, not regarding Ceremony where a real Evil can be prevented, made no fcruple to open and read as follows.

Honourable Sir,

THE dear little Creature is come: fure, nothing was ever fo handfome and innocent! Well! your Honour may boldly fay, you will be this Night Mafter of the fineft Morfel in *England*: But fhe cannot be too pretty for your Honour. I long to fee you together, and am, &c.   LUPA.

By the Direction of the Porter who brought the Letter, we foon got to the Place, where we found the deteftable Engine of Lewdnefs at Tea with the lovlieft Creature I ever beheld, whom therefore I fhall call *Hebe*. *Frank* told the old Procurefs I was a Juftice of Peace, and that *Bridewel* and a Cart muft be her Portion. *Hebe* burft into Tears, but I bid her be of good Heart, and hearing her Story, wrote a Letter to her Miftrefs, a Habit-maker in *Covent-Garden*, reproving her for trufting fo much Beauty to fo vile a Wretch; I wrote alfo to her Mother; then called a Coach, and charg'd the Coachman to deliver her into her Miftrefs's Hands. However this may create me Enemies in my own Sex, it will prove me a true Lover of the other.

                                    The

The Craftsman, Feb. 3. No. 344.

Of the JURY ACT.

THis Act being near expiring, and a just Exception having been taken to a Clause in it concerning *Special Juries*, 'tis hoped our Representatives will secure us from any Danger therefrom, should they think fit to continue *this Law*. The Clause is to the Purport following : *viz.* " That it shall and may be lawful for the Court of *King's Bench, Common Pleas*, and *Exchequer*, upon Motion made in Behalf of His Majesty, or of any Prosecutor, or Defendant, in any Indictment or Information, for any Misdemeanour, &c. or on the Motion of any Plaintiff or Defendant, in any Action, Cause or Suit whatsoever; and the said Courts are authoriz'd and requir'd to appoint a *Jury* to be struck before the Officer of the respective Court, for the Trial of any Issue tryable by a *Jury of Twelve Men*, in such a manner as *special Juries* have been and are usually struck in Trials at Bar in the said Courts. "

The chief Provision of *this Act* is, in a great Measure, defeated by this *Clause*; and no Man can depend on being tried by a Jury chosen by *Ballot*.— It is therefore hoped, that in the Renewal of This Act the said Clause will be left out, or so limited as to prevent the bad Effects of it ; by excepting all Cases where the *Crown* is concern'd ; or restraining the Judges from granting a *special Jury*, unless *both Parties* consent to it. ANGLICUS.

Applebee's Journal, Febr. 3.

Of LIFE and DEATH.

BEsides the Variety of Conditions and Callings in Life, there is a *common* one which all are obliged to profess; that of *Being* and *Living* like Men ; which ought to regulate all the rest.

Life is a Journey toward Death, and Death an Entrance upon a New and Everlasting Life : But as this Entrance hath *double Doors*, one of which leads to eternal Misery, the other to eternal

Happiness, so, to live well, is to tread the Path which leads to this, and to live ill, is to walk in that which brings to the other. The Way to everlasting Misery is unfortunate, tho' strew'd with Flowers ; that ending in eternal Happiness, fortunate and good, tho' beset with Thorns and Briars.

All things are upon a kind of *Balance*. The good or bad Fortune of several *Conditions* is so even poised, that almost Equal Proportions of both are to be found in all ; so that Mens Error consists in imagining that each is happier, or more miserable, than his Neighbour. However that be, nothing can destroy the Inequality deriv'd from the Ends of these two Ways. And it being so very dreadful, is also so visible, that did Men act but as rational Creatures, they would mind the Way that leads to endless Happiness, and carefully shun the other. Yet the Consideration of this *double* End has scarce any Influence on the Choice they make of a Way to walk in during Life. The Reason of it seems to be this : They follow their Inclinations and Passions, and take up with Maxims the Tendency of which they will not give themselves the trouble to examine.

The Weekly Miscellany, Feb. 3. N° 8.

The World is obliged to this Paper for the first *Publication of this Remarkable* WILL *of* RICH. NORTON, *Esq;*

IN the Name of God, Amen. I RICHARD NORTON, of *Southwick*, in the County of *Southampton*, having no Child to inherit after me, and my paternal Kindred, for whom I have a true Respect as such, being in suitable and easy Circumstances of their own, do make this my last Will and Testament, being in perfect Health and sound of Mind, hereby revoking all and every Will and Wills by me before made.

My Estate, at present, being incumbred with a Jointure Settlement, some Payments, and with some Debts, I must leave the Issue of the first to God ; and as to the other, I shall do my best Endeavour to clear them, and shall, to that End, most willingly undergo any Self-Denial that may manifest my true Intent of having all I have (except as is herein after excepted) as free to those I shall make my Heirs, as I can, and in the mean Time

I

sha.

shall lay hold of any Opportunity can be had of selling and giving all to them; but in case that cannot be done in my Life-time, I must look to Futurity; and therefore, after mature and serious Consideration, I do, with a true Intent and Meaning, and with the utmost of my Power, to the Glory of God, make my last Will and Testament.

And first I do resign, commit, and offer my Soul and Body to God in the most Holy Trinity, most humbly beseeching him to give me Light, Rest, and Mercy, both now and for ever, for the Sake and Satisfaction of my most adored Saviour *Jesus Christ.* Amen.

I Will, that my Body be put into a Leaden Coffin, and laid and buried ten Feet deep in the Earth, on the South-Side of the Altar in *Southwick* Church, being freest, I think, from disturbing any Bodies of my dead Ancestors; or in the Church-Yard, with Expedition and Quiet. And I Will, that *Thomas Bird* my Tenant, and *Edward Wynn* my Servant, both or either of them, together with what other Men only they, or either of them shall appoint, do lay me forth, and put me into my Coffin; and that the said *Thomas Bird* and *Edward Wynn*, both, or either of them, do pay to the Poor of the Parish of *Southwick,* such as use to receive the Sacrament Money, 20 l. to be equally distributed amongst them on the Day of my Burial; and that they, or either of them do put all my Servants into Mourning, proper for them on the same Day, and that they or either of them do pay the Expences thereof, at or presently after the same. And I Will, that the whole Charge, with the several Particulars above-mentioned, do not exceed 100 l. for the which there shall be a Bill, or Note, sealed up with this my Will, together with the other Papers.

I do give to all my Servants that I may have, one Years Wages, over and above what is owing to each at my Death, to be paid to them by my Executors or their Order, within one Year after.

I do Will and Give the several Sums herein after-mentioned, to all and several the Parishes under-named, and do charge my Farm called Post Down Farm, with the Yearly Payment of all and several the said Sums under written, to be paid by my Heirs Yearly on *Passion Sunday;* to be distributed by the Rector, Vicar, or Curate, together with some of the chief Inhabitants of the said Parishes, immediately after Divine Service in the Morning, to the poorest Inhabitants of such said Parish; that is to say,

To the Parish of *Southwick* 20 s. *Barnham* 30 s. *Wickham* 5 s. *Hambleton* 5 s. *Havant* 10 s. *Bedhampton* 5 s. *Emsworth* and *Warblington* 5 s. *Farlington* 5 s. *Widley* 5 s. *Wimering* 5 s. *Portchester* 15 s. *Farnham* 10 s.

I do Will, that the said Poor be desired to say the Lord's Prayer at the Receipt of the same Yearly.

I do give to all my Kindred, either by Father's or Mother's Side, 10 l. to each; that

shall out-live me, to be paid by my Executors, or their Order.

I do charge all my Real and Personal Estates whatsoever except what Legacies I shall give in a Paper sealed up, or in Parchment with this my Will, with the full Payment, Satisfaction and Discharge of all and singular my Debts; and after my Funeral Expences, my Legacies and Debts shall be fully and punctually discharged, and paid, I do Devise, Will, and Give all my Real and Personal Estate whatsoever (except as aforesaid) in the County of Southampton, with every thing that I hold, possess and enjoy, or in any manner whatsoever it be belonging to the same Real and Personal Estates, to the Poor; that is to say, to the Poor Hungry, and Thirsty, Naked, and Strangers, Sick and; Wounded, and Prisoners, and to and for no other Use, or Uses whatsoever; and I do hereby make, constitute and appoint the Poor aforesaid to be my general and absolute Heir, and Heirs, to the End of the World.

I do presume to make, constitute, and appoint all and every Person and Persons, that do, shall, or may make or compose, or are to be the supream Legislature of *Great-Britain* in Parliament assembled, to be my Executor, or Executors, of this my last Will and Testament; and if I have presumed too high, and it be refused, then, and in that Case only, I Will and Beseech the most Reverend the Archbishops, together with the Right Reverend the Bishops of *Great-Britain,* or of *England,* for the Time being, and all and every of their Successors, Archbishops and Bishops as aforesaid; And I do hereby constitute and appoint all and every of them, all and every of their Successors, as aforesaid, to be my Executor, and Executors of this my said last Will and Testament. And I do Will, that any Five of them, whereof the Archbishop of *Canterbury* to be one, shall and may, by any Order in Writing under their Hands and Seals, act, order, do, and fully perform and execute my true Meaning and Intent herein declared and mentioned to be performed, to the End of the World. And I do most humbly beg of them all, to be zealous Advocates for the Poor, as aforesaid, to the Legislature of *Great-Britain.* And if it shall happen, that at the Time of my Decease the supream Legislature aforesaid shall not be held or sitting, then I Will, That the most Reverend and the Right Reverend Fathers in God, they and every of them, their and every of their Successors, as aforesaid, or any Five of them, whereof the Lord Archbishop of Canterbury to be one, may immediately be pleased to take Care provisionally, of all Matters and Things herein contained, and may and shall act, order, do, and fully perform, by Order in Writing, as aforesaid, all and every such Act or Acts as shall by them, as aforesaid, be judged necessary to be done, acted, or performed, according to this my last Will and Testament, until such Time as the supream Legislature aforesaid shall

shall next meet, fit, or be held; and I humbly implore Almighty God to guide and direct every Person or Persons concerned, or to be concerned, in the true and just Execution and Performance of this my last Will and Testament, according to my true Intent and Meaning, and that he would be pleased to bless and prosper all and every of them in and for their so doing, through our Lord Jesus Christ, Amen. To this my last Will and Testament I have set my Hand and Seal, it being all written with my own Hand, this 24th Day of June, being the Nativity of St *John Baptist*, in the Year of our Lord God 1714.

RICHARD NORTON.

Signed, sealed, and published by the within written Testator, as and for his last Will and Testament, in the Presence of us whose Names are here under-written, who have, in the Presence of the said Testator, subscribed our Names as Witnesses hereunto,

Arthur Goodrich,
Thomas Sutton,
Arthur Goodrich, jun.

When, by the Goodness of God, I came first to my Estate, I suffered a Recovery thereof, which will be found among my Writings, as well as elsewhere, so that my Estate is in my free Gift, as I have formerly been advised, having no Child, and this is the third Will I have made with this very Intent, in Case I had no Child: My Wife's Jointure takes Place if she survives, for 700 *l.* per Ann.

Memorandum, That for, and as a Codicil or Supplement, to be added to, and taken as Part of the last Will and Testament of Mr *Richard Norton*, of *Southwick*, in the County of *Southampton*, bearing Date the 24th of June, in the Year of our Lord 1714. I do further declare my Will to be, and I do hereby give and devise, bequeath, and appoint all that Messuage or Tenement, Farm, Lands, and Premises called Cullens, situate, lying, and being at *Beckford*, in the Parish of *Southwick* aforesaid, which I lately purchased of *Thomas Maidlow, William Walderon,* and *John Upsdale,* and their several Wives, unto my universal Heir or Heirs, as it is constituted and appointed in my last Will and Testament aforesaid.

And I do declare this to be Part of my last Will and Testament, and appoint it to be taken and accepted as such accordingly. In witness whereof I have hereunto set my Hand and Seal, hereby in all other Things ratifying and confirming my last Will, all written with my own Hand this 24th Day of *April*, in the Year of our Lord 1725.

RICHARD NORTON.

Signed, sealed, and published, and declared in the Presence of,

Ed. Wynn, Tho. Sutton, Art. Goodrich.

I do herein and hereby give and devise the afternamed particular Things, as a Gift or Legacy to each Person and Persons herein afternamed by me; but if any of my herein named Legatees should die before me, not express'd as general Legatees, then I do give and devise

all and every such particular limited Legacies to my Heir or Heirs, appointed by my last Will and Testament, dated the 24th Day of June 1714.

And first of all I do most humbly give and devise to the King's most excellent Majesty, his Heirs and Successors, to the End of the World, all my fine Pictures, Drawings in Frames with Glasses over them, and the famous Printof St Cecilia, by Raphael D'Urbino, in a Frame with a Glass over it, where-ever they may be, and not otherwise herein and by Deed excepted, or by me disposed of otherwise in my Life-time, and all and every Pictures by me bought hereafter.

I do give and devise to my Heir or Heirs, appointed by me by my last Will and Testament dated as abovesaid, the true Hair of my dearly beloved Sovereign King *William* III. which is now in a Japan Box, together with the small Jewels, &c. therein, designed for Ornaments to a Crown, to be placed over a Gold Case, in the Figure or Form of a Monument, in which shall be put the said Hair, and inclosed with the proper Inscription as is now written on the Outside; and my earnest Desire is, that it may be kept and preserved in the same Manner in *Southwick* House to the End of the World.

I do also give and devise to my said Heir or Heirs, my Picture of Our Lord upon the Cross, with the Blessed Virgin and St *John* on each Side, in Chiaro Oscuro; and also my Picture of Our Lord on the Cross, with Angels, in Oil Colours; together with my Crucifix of Ivory on a black Cross; and my Father, Mother, and my own Pictures, in half Length; mine is by Sir *Godfrey Kneller*, the other Copies by Mr *Tilson*, and a Head of my Father by Sir *Peter Lilly*, with the Pictures of King *William* and Queen *Mary*.

I do humbly give and devise to his Grace the Archbishop of *Canterbury* for the Time to come, to his and their Successors, Archbishops of *Canterbury*, my large Saphire Ring, to be by him, and all and every of them, daily and successively worn to the End of the World.

I do humbly give and devise to his Grace the Archbishop of *York*, a large Saphire Ring, to be bought out of my Personal Estate, by my Executors, or their Order, to and for the very same Use, Intent, and Purpose only as aforesaid, to the End of the World.

I do give and devise to all and every Bishop and Bishops of *Great Britain* or *England*, a Ring to each, whereon is to be enamelled a Holy Lamb, set round with Diamonds, to be bought by my Executors, or their Order, to and for the very same Use, Intent, and Purpose only as aforesaid, to the End of the World.

To my Cousin *Richard Whithed*, and his Heirs, I do give and devise all my Pictures of the *White's* Family, and the Head in Painting by Sir *Peter Lilly*, of his Grandmother *Whithed*, and 10 *l.* for what he please.

I do give and devise to my Cousin *Thomas Norton*, and his Heirs, all my Family Pictures
of

of the *Norton* Line, and *Frimurffes*, and 10 *l.* for what he please.

I did, at the Birth of his Son, give him my Consent to renew his own and Son's Lives after me, of *Old Aletford*, with the Bishop of *Winton*, which would be a considerable Gift to them, at my Years.

I do give and devise to my Brother *John Chichley*, my Gold Chain and Medal thereto belonging, which was left to me by our Grandfather Sir *John Lawson*, Admiral, and also my Brilliant Diamond Ring, which was left me by our Mother, since set round by me with 17 small Brilliants.

I do likewise give and devise to him all my Jewels of precious Stones, which I may have by me at my Death; excepted out of this Gift, those which are before or hereafter excepted.

I do give and devise to my Sister *Elizabeth Hughes*, her own Picture, a half Length, with all my Silver Plate whatsoever, except my Shaving Bason, and Ewer thereto belonging with all my Linen and China Ware, except my Wearing-Linen; likewise I do give and devise to her all the Goods and Furniture in the Green Damask Bed-Chamber in *Southwick* House, with my large *Tunguin* Chest, and all Things in it; hereby is excepted the Church Plate which I gave to the Parish Church of *Southwick*, and the small gilt Chalice and Paten used in my Chapel.

I do give and devise to my Brother, *Richard* and *William Chichley*, 10 *l.* each, for what they please.

I do give and devise to my Cousin, Mrs *Henrietta-Maria Maynard*, of *Wed'ry*, near *Reading* in *Berkshire*, 200 *l.* after the Death of her Husband, Mr *Maynard*, but if she dies before her said Husband, then I do give and devise the said 200 *l.* to her Children, Share and Share alike.

I do give and devise to my God-daughter and Cousin, Mrs *Susan Meredith*, my Half-length Picture of Sir *John Lawson*, with her Grand-mother, St *George's* Picture, Half-length, and my least Diamond Buckle, and a Gold Coronation Medal of K. *William* and Q. *Mary*, I having two of them.

I have given my God-son *Robert Philips*, his Life in a Copyhold.

I do give and devise to my God-daughter Mrs *Elizabeth Bignell*, Daughter to Mr *John Bignell*, of *Suffolk-street*, Sadler, deceased, 20 *l.*

I do give and devise to *Andrew* and *James Philips*, Brothers, of *Southwick* Parish born, 20 *l.* to each of them.

I do give and devise to my God-son *Thomas Brandon*, Son to *William Brandon*, late of *Portsmouth*, Alderman, 10 *l.*

I do give and devise to *Edward Buckland*, who I bound Apprentice to Mr *Townsend*, a Stone Mason, 20 *l.*

I do give and devise to Mr *John Mills*, my long Acquaintance, living now in *Drury-Lane*, my Pulling Clock in my Bed Chamber.

I do give and devise to *James Missing*, who

I bound Apprentice to Mr *John Cook* at the *Pine-Apple* in *New-street*, *Covent-Garden*, a Cook, 20 *l.*

I do give and devise to *Richard Hirst*, my Servant, 5 *l.*

I do give and devise to *Isaac Friend*, my own Apprentice, 50 *l.*

I do give and devise to *Edward Wynn*, my Servant, 500 *l.* one of my Gold Coronation Medals of K. *Wm* and Q. *Mary*, my Gold Watch with the Gold Chain and Seals thereto belonging.

I do give and devise to the said *Edward Wynn*, my two Parlour Clocks, my Mortgage on one *Pye's* House at *Fareham*, to make the best of it, unless I should sell or dispose of it before I die, together with my Coach, Chariot, Chaise, and Chair, and all my Horses, Mares, and Colts, and Harness, Bridles, Saddles. &c. whatsoever, upon this Condition nevertheless, that if he the said *Edward Wynn* shall faithfully and punctually do and perform all and every Thing and Things that are required of him in my said last Will and Testament, or by any other Direction I shall or may give him to be observed at or after my Death, either Verbally or in Writing, or else these Gifts shall be, and are totally void, and of none Effect.

I do give and devise to my Tenant *Tho. Bird*, upon the very same Condition only as abovesaid, all my Cows, Hogs, or Pigs, and also 50 *l.* in Money.

I do give and devise to the Servant who dresses me at or about the Time of my Decease, my Silver Shaving Bason and Ewer belonging, my Gold Buttons at my Hand-wrist Bands, and all my Wearing Linen and Apparel whatsoever.

I give and devise to the Inhabitants of *Southwick*, in the County of *Southampton*, the two Silver Flaggons, Chalice, Paten, Bason, and Spoon, all gilt, and engraven with my poor Name, &c. for the Use only of the most Holy Sacrament for ever.

I do give and devise the smaller Silver gilt Chalice and Paten for the Use of the most Holy Sacrament, to *Southwick* House for ever.

I do give and devise to *Jn. Hall* of *Havant* 10 *l.*

I do give and devise to *Tho. Knight*, Organ-builder, formerly Apprentice to the famous Father *Smith*, in *Suffolk-street*, *London*, 5 *l.*

All my aforesaid Legacies and Gifts and Devises, are to be paid by my most Noble Executors, out of my Personal Estate, if it may arise to so much, as I trust it will without Charge on the Real.

To all before by me written in eight Pages, witness my Hand, the 5th Day of *December*, in the Year of our Lord 1721.

RICHARD NORTON.

I do give and devise to my Noble Friend Count *Bothmar*, all the Goods and Furniture whatsoever, which are in the King's Apartment in *Southwick* House, except that in the Great Dining Room. Witness my Hand, the 20th Day of *March*, in the Year of our Lord God 1724.

RICHARD NORTON.

I do give and devise to Colonel *Peter Hawker*, now

now Deputy Governor of *Portsmouth*, 50*l.* If he should die before me, I give and devise the same to his Son Mr *Peter Hawker*. Witness my Hand this 3d Day of *March*, 1725.

RICHARD NORTON.

I do give and devise to my former Servant *William Ware*, 10*l.* Witness my Hand the 12th Day of *August*, 1725.

RICHARD NORTON.

Whereas I have added in these Papers of my Legacies 200*l.* more to my Legacy to *Edward Wynn* my Servant, which makes 500*l.* to *Edward Wynn* aforesaid, with all my Mare or Mares, Colt or Colts added also. Witness my Hand, the 30th Day of *August*, 1725.

Item, I do give, devise and bequeath unto the said *Edward Wynn*, my Walnut-tree Cabinet, with the Drawers under it, with all that is in them, not the Glass Cabinet, except such Papers as may belong to my Estate. Witness my Hand, this 8th Day of *September*, 1725.

RICHARD NORTON.

Whereas I have given unto my Sister *Elizabeth Chichley*, the Wife of Mr *Edward Hughes*, all my Plate, Linen, China, and all my Furniture in my Green Damask Bed-Chamber, I do hereby declare my Intent of the Devise to be, and do appoint that the said *Elizabeth Hughes* shall have and enjoy the Use and Usage of all the aforesaid Effects, for and during the Term of her natural Life only, and that immediately from and after her Decease, all the said Effects shall be divided in equal Value, among such Children of the said *Elizabeth Hughes*, as shall be living at the Time of her Decease, to whom I give and bequeath the said Effects accordingly: witness my Hand, this 8th Day of *September*, 1725. RICHARD NORTON.

My Directions to my Servant Edward Wynn, *concerning my Death and Burial.*

I would be embowelled by a good Surgeon, with all Privateness possible, as soon as may be, at least within 24 Hours after my Decease: my Bowels to be put into a square leaden Case, and laid at my Feet in my Grave. You must lay forth my Body decently with the help only of Men Servants, placing it into a Lead Coffin as soon as you can; both the Case and the Coffin to be sodered up immediately as finished. But before my Coffin is sodered up, I would have you lay a plain Plate of Lead upon my Breast, cut deep with the Sign of the Cross,

✠ and the Words following, as the Day Year and of my Death shall happen.

RICHARD NORTON, of *Southwich*, was Born the 4th Day of *May* 1666, and Died the and the very same only to be cut on the Lid of my Coffin outside.

I have in my Will directed that my Body be put into a leaden Coffin, and buried ten Feet deep on the South Side of the Altar, in *Southwich* Church; but you are to see that the Grave be vaulted with Brick Work, rammed with Earth above, and the Pavement laid down as before. You are to bury me as soon as possible: I will have no Pomp, therefore no Escutcheons: but out of the 100*l.* I have allowed by my Will for Funeral Charges and Servants Mourning only, you are to buy a new black Velvet Pall, to be carried over my Coffin to my Grave, and then and there to be thrown over me; and presently the Grave is to be arched over with Brickwork: The said Pall to remain over me in the Grave. You to see this done; you and my Tenant *Tho. Bird* are appointed by my Will to direct my Funeral, and I have given to you both Legacies, worth your Pains for so doing, or else you are to have nothing. And in my Will I have ordered 100*l.* and no more, to be laid out upon my Funeral, in which Mourning for my Servants, and 20*l.* to be distributed to the Poor of *Southwick*, on the Day of my Burial it must be, are all included; and to those that shall carry me to my Grave, give 20*s.* a-piece, rather than Drink, to buy them a Gold Ring; or do you buy them for them. I have said I would have no Pomp nor Escutcheons, so no Pall-Bearers have I thought of at all. I would have all Candles lighted in the Church that time, as usual, to be at any Time you have seen, excepting where it cannot be, because of the Grave; and I earnestly wish that our Anthem out of the 106th Psalm, with every Verse and Chorus, might be sung or read during the Burial Office; the very same Verses as are in that Anthem, and no other, or more of the Psalm: And I will have no other Part of the Service to be performed, remember this, but only the Burial Office. You need fear no Threats from any Pretenders to my Estate. If any should be so barbarous to endeavour to hinder you, or either of you, to perform this last good Office to me, you are both named and authorized by my Will for so doing, which will shew who I appoint to be my Heirs. I intend to lodge one in the Hands of the Arch Bishop of *Canterbury*, having two in the same Words; and the other I shall keep by me, which you are to open and read before three Witnesses, as soon as I am dead. *Tho. Bird* will see, I trust him; so, good and faithful *Ned*, use my Body with all Decency, and see me laid easily, quietly and speedily in my Grave, according to these my Directions. What Money I have by me, or due to me any ways, are by my Will charged with my said Funeral Expences; and this shall be sufficient Authority and Power to you *Edw. Wynn*, and to you *Tho. Bird*, both and either of you to act and do according to these Directions afore-written. Witness my Hand, this 7th Day of *Novemb.* 1731. RICHARD NORTON.

Ned,

Mr *Moody*, of *Havant*, hath a Deed of mine in his keeping, by which I have given you *Stony Dean*, and many other valuable Things; I have given you by Legacy; take care of that Writing sealed up, concerning my Legacies, therefore written upon and called so.

Southwich-House, Aug. 20, 1725.

I do hereby give and devise to *Edward Wynn*, my Servant, 150 Guineas, sealed with my Seal, in a little Bag, upon this Condition only; That he do pay and defray all and every my Funeral Charges

Charges and Expences, and 20l. to the Poor of the Parish of *Southwick*, on the Day of my Funeral, with the said Sum which he hath in his keeping. Witness my Hand the Day and Year above written.   RICHARD NORTON.

Indorsed on the Inner Cover, in which the **A**
Will and Codicils were first sealed up.

My last Will and Testament to be opened and read before three Witnesses, immediately after my Death, together with my Paper of Legacies herein.   RICHARD NORTON.

Edward Wynn, and
Thomas Bird,

Or either of them, I charge to do as aforesaid, **B** keep this and the Cover of my Will.

Indorsed on the outer Case, in which the
Will and Codicils were Sealed up.

My Last Will and Testament, which I do hereby charge (as they will answer it to God) my Servant *Edward Wynn*, and my Tenant *Tho. Bird*, or either of them, to break open and read, as soon as I am dead, before three Witnesses, **C** therein being Directions necessary and presently to be known for my Funeral ; therefore no Relation of mine need be present, but keeping this Paper will be a sufficient Security to them, or either of them, against all Men ; and I do charge them not to suffer this Will to go out of their Hands, neither for Flattery or Fear.
   RICHARD NORTON. **D**

Wrote on a Paper in which Sir John Lawson's
Gold Chain and Medal was sealed up.

My Brother-in-Law, Mr *John Chichley*, being dead, I do give the inclosed Gold Medal and Chain, which the Parliament gave to Sir *John Lawson*, our Grandfather, and I bequeath them to my Brother Mr *Richard Chichley*. Witness my Hand this 16th Day of *December*, 1717.   RICHARD NORTON. **E**

Conclusion of Mr. P---y's ARGUMENT
against the SALT-BILL. *see* p. 34.

It has in this Debate been admitted by all, that the Duty upon the Salt made use of in Curing the Salt Provisions necessary for a **F** Ship of 150 Tons for a Six Month's Voyage will amount to 40 s. and yet it has been asserted by some, that the Reviving of this Duty will be no Burthen upon the Navigation of *Great Britain*. Those who reason in this Manner, do not surely consider the Frugality and Sparingness that must be observed in Trade. I am sure there is not a Merchant in *Europe*, that has Occasion to freight a Ship, but will think 40 s. a very great Difference in the Freight between two Ships of 150 Tons each, if they be of equal Goodness in every other respect, and he will always employ that which he can have 40 s. cheaper than the other. This Tax must therefore be not only a Burthen upon our Navigation, but we must **H** consider, that it would soon be the entire Destruction of our Navigation, and consequently of our Navy, if it were not for the Navigation Act, and some naturall Advantages

which we have over the rest of the World.

I come now, *Sir*, to consider this Tax with respect to the Farmers of *England*. I hope no Farmer in *England* is as yet obliged to make his Family dine upon Bread and Cheese, or upon boil'd Cabbage, with a Bit of pickled Pork, Salt Beef, or Bacon, to give them a Savour. I do not know indeed what they may be brought to ; but I must look upon them and their Servants as making Use of some Salt Provisions now almost every Day in the week for the whole Year round. In such View, a Family of 16 working Persons will consume in Salt, after this Duty is laid on, above 2 s. worth apiece ; it has been computed by Men who understood thoroughly the OEconomy of their Family, that a Family of ten Persons would for all Uses generally cost the Master at least 6d. a Week for Salt, according to the Price it sold at formerly, when this Duty was subsisting. At this rate there is scarcely a Farmer in *England* but must pay above 20 s. a Year towards this Tax, and if he pays a Rack Rent, I do not know where he is to get this 20 s. unless he runs in Arrear to his Landlord, in order to answer what he must pay to the Tax-Gatherer. In such a Case, I believe, our Landed Gentlemen will not get much by the Relief that is now pretended to be given them. I believe no man will pretend that any Gentleman of a Free Estate of 500 l. a Year in Land or upwards, is in the present Case an Object of Compassion, or that the Relieving of such Men from the Payment of 1 s. in the Pound Land Tax, can have any Weight in the present Debate ; and as for those Gentlemen who have large Estates in Land, but heavily charg'd with Mortgages, if they will, for the sake of Grandeur, and the Name of having a great Estate, continue to pay the Land Tax and the Interest upon the Mortgages, it is certainly their own Fault, and therefore they do not deserve the Consideration of this House. The Landed Gentlemen then, whose Estates are under 500l. a Year, are the only Persons whose Condition and Circumstances can in the present Case be of any Consequence ; and as to such, let us examine whether, what is now proposed, will prove to be any Relief to 'em. It's well known there are many Landed Gentlemen in *England*, whose Estates are valued so low, that they do not pay above a Groat of a 1 s. in the Pound Land Tax ; it may **G** therefore be reasonable to suppose, that all the Land Estates in *England* are one with another rated for the Land Tax at one half of the real Value. It has been admitted that a Farmer of 300 l. a Year, has generally 16 Persons in Family ; I think we may then reasonably suppose, that the Landed Gentlemen in *England* of 400 l. a Year, keep one with another, 20 Persons in Family ; and upon these Suppositions let us see what Relief the Gentleman of 400 l. a Year is to receive from the fine Scheme now before us. Such a Man's Estate is supposed to be valued at 200l.

a

a Year as to the Land Tax, consequently at 1 s. in the Pound he saves only 10 l. in the whole, by the taking off this 1 s. Now let us consider what he must pay towards the Duty upon the Salt consumed in his Family; a common Farmer with 10 Persons in his Family, is supposed to pay 6 d. a Week for the Salt consumed in his Family, and therefore a common Farmer with 20 Persons in his Family must be supposed to pay 1 s. a Week, one with another, for the Salt consumed in his Family; and if we consider the great Waste that is made of that Commodity about a Gentleman's Family, and the many Visitors and their Servants, and the poor necessitous Neighbours that will always be hanging in or about a Gentleman's Family who has an Estate of 400 l. a Year, we cannot allow less than Eighteen Pennyworth of Salt consumed weekly about such a Gentleman's Family; we must therefore suppose that every Gentleman of such an Estate pays yearly for the Salt consumed in his Family 3 l. 18 s. and since by the laying on of this Duty, we raise Salt to above ten times the Price it formerly sold at, therefore we must conclude that nine Tenths of 3 l. 18 s. that is, about 3 l. 10 s. is yearly drawn from every Gentleman of 400 l. a Year by Means of this Duty upon Salt; and as he is to pay this Sum yearly for three Years, in place of the 10 l. Land Tax which he is by this Means to be made free of, is it not plain and evident, that he pays Ten Guineas in three Years for the sake of getting free of the Payment of 10 l. in one Year? The utmost then, that can be pretended, is, that he saves by this fine Scheme about half a Year's Interest on 10 l.

As to all the Landed Gentlemen of smaller Fortunes, they will be Losers by this Measure that is proposed for their Relief. Their Families cannot be a great deal less numerous than the others; their Servants will be as wasteful, and they must entertain their Visitors as well as the other; therefore we cannot suppose that any Gentleman's Family in the Country will cost him less than 1 s. a Week for Salt, at this rate he must pay yearly towards the Duty now to be laid on, very near 2 l. 7 s. that amounts in three Years to 7 l. so that a Gentleman of 200 l. a Year will be 2 l. out of Pocket, and a Gentleman of 100 l. a Year will be 4 l. 10 s. out of Pocket by reviving the Salt Duty for three Years, in place of laying on 1 s. in the Pound Land Tax for one Year.

Having thus shewed to what sort of People this Salt Duty will be a Disadvantage, I think it would not be just in me, not to take some Notice of those to whom it will be an immediate Advantage. As to all the Gentlemen in England of very large Estates, it will be an immediate Advantage: But this immediate Advantage accruing to the rich Landed Men will be soon overbalanced by the Ruin that it will bring upon their Country, and upon their own particular Estates; and I am glad to find, that most of the Rich landed Gentlemen in England are upon the same Side of the Questi-on with me, but those who will reap the greatest Advantage from the Measure now proposed are those who are in good Places, and have handsome Salaries coming in. It is true, that their Salaries are rated at the full Value to the Land Tax: The taking off 1 s. in the Pound Land Tax is really putting 5 per Cent into their Pockets, which cannot be drawn out again by the Salt Duty, because they either keep no Families, or they keep their Families in Town, where most of their Servants are at Board-wages. To such Gentlemen the Measure now proposed will certainly be advantageous, and to such only that Compassion which we have heard so much of, is properly to be apply'd. Since then it appears plain, that what is now proposed can be no manner of Relief, but will certainly be an Additional Charge upon the Landed Gentlemen of small Estates; and since they are the only Landed Gentlemen in England who stand in Need of, and deserve Compassion, I think all the Arguments that can be drawn from Pity and Compassion, come full against our agreeing to the Revival of this Duty; therefore I may in my Turn plead with all those who bear me, to have Pity and Compassion upon the Landed Gentlemen in England. How hard will it be to make a poor Landed Gentleman of 100 l. a Year, pay 7 l. in place of 50 s. Why should the poor Landed Gentlemen be so much overcharged for the sake of a small Ease to those who have plentiful Estates in Land, or considerable Salaries coming in from a Post of little or no Trouble? This is really, if I may be allowed, to make use of the Words, *Giving to the Rich, and sending the Poor empty away.* But in the present Case, our Compassion pleads not only for the poor Landed Gentlemen, but for all the Poor of the Nation. Let us but consider how many poor Families are maintained upon 8 d. or 1 s. a Day, which the Father earns by hard Labour and Toil. A Bushel of Salt is the least that can be consumed in a Year by a poor Man, his Wife and three or four small Children: How cruel is it to take 4 or 5 s. a Year away from the Support of such a poor Family, more especially when one half of that Money at least is to be made a Compliment of to wealthy or fraudulent Dealers, or to idle and profligate Tax-Gatherers? I hope every Man that hears me, will allow his Pity and Compassion to exert itself to its utmost height. I hope every Man will consider on which Side of the present Question are the Cries of the Poor and the Wretched, and the Blessings of those that are yet unborn. The Happiness or Misery of Posterity, the Flourishing or Decay of our Trade and Commerce, the Preservation, or Loss of our Liberties, in my Opinion, depend in a great Measure on the Question now before us; and therefore I am persuaded that every Gentleman will consider it thoroughly before he determines what he is to do?

[To be continued largely in our next.]

Weekly Miscellany, Jan. 27. and Feb. 3. On Morality *and* Religion.

In a Letter to the Author.

THE Notion of a reasonable Creature implies, that he proposes to himself some End. This End can be no other than the Perfection of his Being; nothing relates to him but what relates to his Happiness; and if he has *Liberty* of Will, 'tis impossible any thing else should move or affect him.

The Means of attaining this End, must be to recommend himself to the Favour of those Beings on whom he depends. But as himself and all other Beings depend absolutely on the Deity, 'tis plain the Favour of God will be the only adequate and effectual Means to attain his End, *i. e.* Happiness upon the Whole: And therefore whatever tends to obtain the Divine Favour, will be of perpetual Obligation. And though certain Actions will recommend us to the Favour of those other Beings to whom we stand related, and so may become Duties; yet, since all the Reason for pursuing them can only be their Fitness to bring Happiness, which they are not always fit and likely to do, the Will of God must intervene to enforce these Duties.

'Tis not then any *Relations* of Things, which in themselves consider'd, oblige us to the Practice of moral Virtue, but the Will of God which enjoins it, and which alone affords an *eternal and immutable* Reason for the Practice of it. Therefore to set aside the Deity, and to teach that Virtue is to be practised for its *native Loveliness and intrinsick Worth*, is to mistake the Means for the End. Virtue is lovely for its good Effects; and they who follow it for the immediate *Pleasure* which attends the Exercise of it, must either allow, we have some innate Instinct or Affection which infallibly directs and forcibly inclines us to what is right; (which is false) or else they practise Virtue for a Reason common to any other Practice, and will equally lead them to any. To do what our Judgment approves, or we have set our Hearts upon, will give us this immediate Pleasure in any Course of Life.

To describe Virtue to be *following Nature*, amounts to this, Do what you like best, or follow your present Humour.

They who practise Virtue for present *Convenience, Interest or Reputation*, stand upon mere solid Ground, which nevertheless will often fail them.

§. To prove that the Will of God is our only adequate Rule of Action, and includes perpetual Obligation, he proceeds (*Feb.* 3.) to shew the Necessity of such a Rule, and what Kind of Conformity to it will secure the End proposed, *i. e.* our Happiness.

AS the Deity had no other Design in framing the World, nor can have any End in preserving, and governing it, but our Happiness, his Will and our Happiness become co-incident, and may be substituted one for the other. He makes the Good of his Creatures the Rule and Reason of all he enjoins: An absolute implicit Compliance with His Will may therefore be call'd our ultimate End, and ought to be esteem'd and acted on as such, in all particular Cases. Our Knowledge of ourselves and all about us is short and imperfect, and we are apt to deviate into Error and Absurdity; we need therefore some *Rule* on which we may constantly depend: and this can only be the Will of that Being in whose Hands we are, and who is able to reward us to the uttermost. We must next enquire how we shall secure this Reward, or what will obtain his Favour; and that is *Obedience*, or having a Regard to his Will in all our Actions.

'Tis not the *Matter*, but the *Intention* of the *Act* that makes Guilt or Merit imputable to the Agent. As far as any particular Action is intended to obey the Will of God, and advance the End of his Government, in preference to any other Interest or Inclination, so far it is meritorious or acceptable to him. As far as it is done in compliance with any particular Interest or Inclination, in opposition to, or in disregard of the Will of God, so far is it offensive and injurious to him. As far as it is done without any distinct End, or Consideration of the Will of God in that End, so far it is at best purely indifferent, and of no Moral or Religious Account at all. If the End terminate in ourselves *immediately*, the Action can be but innocent at best; we serve not God herein, but ourselves: and if we attain the natural good Effects thereof in this Life, we have our Reward. And tho', for several Reasons, we cannot properly be said to *merit* any thing of God, yet by *Covenant* and *Promise* we may certainly be entitled to his Favour, so far as we comply with those Terms of Salvation which he has proposed, and perform such Duties as he hath commanded, purely in *Obedience* to him, which is the only Principle that can make any thing Rewardable by him.

Not

Not that it's neceſſary to have this Principle always in View; it is ſufficient to recommend and juſtify an Action, if it have ſome Connection or other with what is manifeſtly our Duty. Nay, ſome Actions are directed to no diſtinct End at all, may become rewardable by virtue of certain *Habits*, whereof they are Conſequences, and for which we are accountable. Thus a Servant ſufficiently deſerves both the Title and Reward of being Faithful and Obedient, if he have acquir'd ſuch Labour and Diligence in his Maſter's Buſineſs, as will carry him regularly thro' it, tho' he ſeldom conſider the End of all his Labour, or think of his Maſter in it.

Univerſal Spectator, Feb. 3. No. 226.

Of Engliſhing the Laws.

THE Time is at Hand, when the Laws of our Country, and the Proceedings thereupon, are to be in our own Tongue. We are perhaps the only free and civiliz'd Nation under Heaven, whoſe Natives have been govern'd by a *Law* in the Language of Foreigners. The *Romans* carried both their *Laws* and their *Language* into all the Countries they ſubdued. Other Conquerors took the ſame method; whence our mixture of *Roman* and *Saxon Laws*, *Daniſh* and *Norman*, who being the laſt Conqueror, the *Law-French*, introduced by him, continued the longer among us. The Introduction of Foreign Laws and Languages was a notorious Mark of our Dependence and Vaſſalage, and therefore to be aboliſh'd with the firſt Opportunity. The unconquer'd *Welch* were in the mean Time free from this Reproach; the Laws of their King *Arthur*, and of *Howel the Good*, were in their native Tongue; as were probably the Laws of *Kent*, ſo far as related to the Rights and Tenures of a People, whom the *Conqueror* did not care to diſoblige.

The retaining ſo many ſtrange and undefin'd *Terms* and *technical* Expreſſions in our *Laws*, is not owing to Gentlemen of the *long Robe*, as imagin'd, but to the *Client*, whoſe Avarice, and eager Deſire of Conqueſt; together with the Artifices, Ignorance, and Knavery of his *Under-Agents*, multiply Caſes, and add to the Increaſe and bulky Burden of our Laws, and the Dilatorineſs of the Proceedings of our Courts. (See Vol. I. p. 106.)

As Things now ſtand, every *Attorney* or Solicitor is not only an *Interpreter of the Laws*, but likewiſe *Reader* to his Client, otherwiſe he may continue a Stranger to his own *Bill:* And tho' ſome

Attorneys, in Condeſcenſion to the Capacities of their *Client*, may poſſibly read *Navidavy* for *Affidavit*, Form of Paper for *Formâ Pauperis*, *Hizy Prizy* for *Niſi Prius*----and *Zezzerero* for *Certiorari*---- Yet as theſe Alterations do not obſtruct the Hearer's *implicit* Faith or *explicit* Payment, ſo in thoſe Parts of the *Bill*, which are in Danger of being underſtood, Care may be taken to mumble over the *Items* ſo as nothing ſhall dwell upon the *Auditor* but the *Sum total*; juſt as they adminiſter Oaths, in which nothing is ſpoke to be underſtood but the Concluſion---- "Give me a Shilling."

That which has obſtructed the rendring our Laws into *plain Engliſh* was the unſucceſsful Attempt made by *Cromwel's Parliament*, under their Speaker *Barebones:* But theſe Fellows being *Tranſlators* only in the *Roman Cobler's* Senſe of the Word, could give no better Account of the Law, than they had done of the Goſpel; they left their mark on the Bible as well as Statute Book. For the *Book of Kings* they read *the Book of Parliaments;* they ſcratch'd *Finis* out of the laſt *Page*, and inſerted *Foreſpeech* inſtead of *Preface*. Some Advice may be ſeaſonable to thoſe engag'd in the preſent Undertaking. ---

Our *Statutes*, tho' generally worded in intelligible Terms, have ſome Expreſſions which may be render'd in more ſignificative *Engliſh*; ſuch as—*Special Matter—Reprizes—Eſſoigne—Pledge or Wager at Law—Imparlance*—which has really given Offence to ſome honeſt well-meaning Juſtices in the Country.

Since there appears ſuch an Averſion to our Laws being in the learned Languages, of which we have an Inſtance in the famous *Neck Verſe*, ſo long laid aſide; and ſince theſe other Expreſſions *Totos meos Barnos, Stabulos & Outhouſas* are capable of ſo eaſy a Tranſlation, the Verſion therefore may be as pure and terſe as poſſible.

Whether the *Law-French* is wholly laid aſide, or how the following Expreſſions are render'd, *Feme Coverte—Ouſter le main—Sans aſſault de meſme*, may be worth examining into.

The Book *De Naturâ Brevium* will give our *Law-Tranſlators* a good deal of Trouble; and when thoſe noble Terms— *Qui tam—Quare clauſum fregit—Simul cum—Niſi Prius—Non Aſſumpſit—Quindena Paſch'—* come to be truly render'd, how will the People be ſurpriz'd at the amazing Diſcoveries conceal'd under thoſe *oracular Expreſſions !*

K   If

If our *Wits* and *Writers* should happen to be at Leisure from the present Glut of *Translations*, they may Join the *Lawyers*, and the one be a Cheque upon the other, The Lawyers should be employ'd who A have already given us *Specimens* of their Skill in *translating*, witness those noble *Versions* in the *Declaration Form Una Chariotta cum quatuor equis,* Anglice, *A Chariot and Four— Centum Bundelli Lignorum minorum,* Anglice, *A Hundred of Faggots—* and the *Wits* and *Criticks* B should confine the Lawyers to such an accurate Tuanslation, as to exclude all future Attempts to correct and amend their Works. Like the inimitable Product of the Lawyer in the Play — *Commensabo actionem contra omnes & singulos : Et habebo pinguia damagia : Et trounsabo* C *vos ut homo nunquam fuit trounsatus in toto mundo—Debet enim surgete per tempus qui me decipit.*

Too close a *Translation* may be attended with Inconveniencies ; thus, instead of an *O-yez ! O-yez !* should the Cryer baul out, *Hear ye ! Hear ye ! All man-* D *ner of Persons who have any thing more to do before my Lords the King's Justices of Unless before, Hearing and Determining, and General Goal-Delivery,* &c. This new Form, after the first Surprize, would attract no more Auditors and Attendants than the old one. And too loose E and rambling a Translation may occasion strange Alterations in the Mouths and Muscles of our best Pleaders.

Daily Courant, Feb. 5.
Of Excises.

ONE conspicuous Characteristick of the *Craftsman's Consistency,* and of F which he so much vaunts (See p. 12) is, that whenever it serves his Purpose of Clamour and Sedition, he thunders heroically against *Luxury :* But when any Judicious Step is taken by the *Administration* to teach us *Parsimony* and *Frugality,* then our consistent Author tacks G about, and sooths the *Upholders* of what he has so often exclaimed against. This upon Examination of his late Principles, will appear to be exactly his Case.

'Tis an allowed Maxim, that the Consumption of foreign Commodities of mere *Luxury,* is so much Loss to the Nation as they amount to. The *Dutch* make use H of *Excises,* to obviate too great a Consumption of Foreign Goods amongst them. The *French* study to prevent it by Duties of *Importation,* of *Consumption, Tolls, Restraints, Visitations,* and *Prohibitions,*

wearing their own Manufactures, and living chiefly upon the Produce of their own Country.

From the same Motives we have been induced to lay high Duties and Impositions upon all sorts of foreign Commodities for Consumption and Luxury. But hitherto the Measures taken by Parliament, in the Article of *Wine,* have been ineffectual. If therefore an *Excise* upon *Wine* will diminish the Consumption, and render the *Balance* of that Branch of *Trade* more in our Favour, 'tis worthy a *British Parliament.* In the Case of *Wines,* the whole Import is consumed among ourselves, and no Prospect of future Gains, by Re-exportation, as in other imported foreign Commodities, is open'd to us. What is still more sensibly grievous, is, that this Quantity is doubled upon us by destructive Mixtures, and the People deprived of the only Good that can result from such Importations, *viz.* The Duties laid on them by Parliament.

But should the *Land Tax* be taken off ; if the *Wine* and *Tobacco* Duties be only transformed into *Excises* ; 'twill follow, that our *Wool* will become cheaper, and our Manufactures so of course.

'Tis the common Plea for Adulteration of *Wines,* that without it they would not fit the *English* Palate. This is reported by the chief Managers of the Art, the *Wine-Coopers,* who, within these few Years have almost engrossed the *Wine-Trade.* But as the foreign Luxuries make *Gouts, Epilepsies, Apoplexies,* and *Palsies* more frequent among us than in any other Part of *Europe,* 'tis Time to think of less pernicious Liquors. Our native Produce is healthful ; and had it once the Sanction of Mode and made the Fashion, the value of *Lands* would be enhanced, and the *Balance* of Trade augmented. Since *Portugal* supply'd us with Wines, their *Lands,* being before waste, are greatly improved and cultivated.

The Tobacco Merchants are likewise aggrieved at the Thoughts of an *Excise* upon *Tobacco* ; tho' thereby our *Plantations* may be saved from Ruin, and that Trade preserved from the Jaws of our *Rivals,* the *French.* Commission upon the high Duties, *Sales* and *Returns,* &c. are heavy Burthens upon the poor *Planters,* and call for the Relief of *Parliament.* The Profits are so small after the several *Deductions* of their *Factors,* that they must unavoidably run in Debt ; which will oblige them to take Refuge in the *French* Plantations, where they will find more
Encou-

Encouragement for their Industry. Nor have the *Tobacco Merchants* such Reason to complain; for the large Sums which they are now obliged to expend for Duties, they may employ another way. And if the Planters once work themselves out of Debt, the *Factors* will receive larger *Commissions* from them.

The common Cry has been, that a Deprivation of *Trials* by *Juries* under the *Excise* will endanger our *Liberties.* But this is no more than a Pretext. For, let the *Revenue* be ever so much augmented by an *Excise*, the *Crown* has not the least Advantage by it. Tho' particular Sums are appropriated for the Payment of the *Civil-List Revenue*, yet if these Sums exceed the Sum fixed by Parliament, the *Surplusses* will be applied to ease the *Land.* As to other Parts of the Revenue, the King is no more than a *Steward*, or *Trustee* for the People, who constantly renders an account how every Sum raised has been applied for their Benefit and Safeguard. Whatever is deficient in one Fund must be raised by another; therefore the *Prince* can be no way interested in the Determinations of the *Commissioners* of *Excise*; nor the *Commissioners* advantaged by oppressing the *Subject*; so that every Contest of this Nature is not a Dispute between the *Prince* and his *Subject*, but between the whole *collective Body of the People* and an *Individual* of the Community; and therefore that *Barrier* to our *Liberties* between the *Prerogative* and the People, a Trial by Juries, is not affected by any Point relating to the Collection of the publick Revenue.

T' *Daily Courant*, Feb 7.
Benefits of Excising Wines.

THE *Occasional Financer* argues that a Law for *Excising* Wines will be of great Advantage

1. To the fair Trader, as then there will be no *Sophisticators* to under-sell him.
2. To the *Merchant*, by increasing his Imports, when Brewing of Wines ceases.
3. To all Makers and Dealers in Manufactures, by augmenting their Export.
4. To Shipwrights, Seamen, and Owners by doubling of Freight.
5. To Numbers of Workmen, and to the Nation in general, by increasing our Navigation.
6. To Land-Owners, and Farmers, by taking off the Land-Tax.
7. To the whole Body of Traders, Manufacturers, and our Foreign Commerce; by enabling the Government to abolish the Taxes on Necessaries of Life, and make Labour and Commodities cheaper.

. How beneficial then, *says he,* would our Luxury in Wine prove ! It would be an additional Pleasure to every *benevolent Man*, who, while he drank his Bottle much securer of his own Health, might then reflect that his Expences were, by the wisdom of the Legislature, directed to the Benefit of a thousand industrious Hands, then labouring to furnish him with some other Conveniency of Life, instead of being lavish'd away, as in great part they now are, on a dishonest *Handful*, whose utmost Skill and Industry is to deceive his Palate, to the tricking him of his Health and Money. (See p. 72)

The *Auditor*, Feb. 6. No. 9.
Cur in Theatrum Cato severe venisti ?

TOM *Cynick* prevail'd on me last Week to go to *Drury-Lane* with him to see *Hamlet.* After the first Act was over, I would not, says *Tom*, take away from Mr *Mills* the Merit of being a good Actor; but those who have seen him act *Horatio*, can never relish him in *Hamlet.* 'Tis as impossible for Mr *Mills* to take *Hamlet*'s supposed Figure, as for the Spectator to lose that of Mr *Mills.* But I suppose, adds he, the top Parts are given to those who have the best Interest, but not the best Pretension to act them. What an *Horatio* have we here ? Could any Person so mistake himself ?

. The second Act being over, a Gentleman addressed himself to *Tom*, and told him, that tho' in the main his Remarks might be right, yet he thought the great Loss the Stage had suffer'd, might in some Measure apologize for any irregular Distribution of Parts. *Tom* replied, he would make as many allowances on that score as he pleased: But, sure, that can be no Reason for giving Parts to Actors who can never be what they ought to be: While these very Actors have happily appeared in Parts naturally adapted to them, and while others in the House want nothing but Encouragement and Practice, to make them endeavour to compensate for the Loss of their Predecessors, in those Parts from which some of 'em are by Nature excluded. There's a young Fellow to-night that acts *Laertes*: I have seen him act *Charles* in the *Fop's Fortune*, in such a manner, that I did not miss Mr *Wilks*; nay, I think him inferior to Mr *Mills* in many respects. All I would insinuate is, that it's an additional Pleasure to an Audience, and Advantage to an Actor,

Actor, when he not only speaks the Sentiments of the Person he represents, but is in Figure, as like as can be, what we conceive of him. But this is no more a Merit in young *Hallam*, than it is a Fault in Mr *Mills*. Mr *Wilks*, under all the Disadvantages of Age, had the luck to hit this conceived Figure of *Hamlet* so justly, that his very Sight moved Compassion before he opened his Mouth. *Hallam* succeeds him in the Melancholy of his Looks in this Character; and indeed in his Action, Tone of Voice, and Method of Speaking. I think he comes nearest Mr *Wilks* of any Actor in the House.

After the Play was over I prevail'd on *Tom* with much Difficulty to stay to see the new *Entertainment* of the *Boarding-School Romps*, or *Sham Captain*. For what? says he? you know the Author; what can be expected from him? I told him, 'twas but putting on his Eccho's, and if he did not like it, he might turn the Pin downwards, and his Ears would be impenetrable. *Tom* took my Advice. He sat patiently, till *Harper* (in the Character of Lady *Termagant*) coming in, dress'd in Woman's Cloaths, *Tom* rose up in a Passion, What is it come to this? To please an Audience, must the Stage of *Great-Britain* dress a fat Man in Woman's Cloaths? If I stay a Moment longer, I'll give you leave to---- and immediately made his way thro' a crouded Pitt; and amidst the Ralleries of some, and the Imprecations of others, got safe to the Door. I impatiently waited for the End of this shameless *Entertainment*; and in going out saw *Frank Easy* handing a pretty Lady to her Coach. After he had done his Office I joined him. We call'd for a Coach, and drove to the Club. *Tom* was before us, and had been venting his Spleen to Sir *Charles* and *Boccalini*. *Frank*, to whom I had related *Tom's* precipitate Flight, had a Mind to laugh a little. Really Mr *Cynick*, says he, it's a Misfortune to have so nice a Taste, as you have. Must the Town be deprived the

Pleasure of seeing Mrs *Charke* devour a Pound of Bread and Butter with as much Grace as ever *Pinkethman* did a Chicken, because it does not suit your antiquated Notions? Must we lose Miss *Raftor's* Minuet, because you don't love Dancing? Mr *Easy*, said *Tom*, you may be as witty as you please; I cannot look on this monstrous Corruption in the ludicrous manner you do. What a Figure must we make (I refer it to Signior *Boccalini*) with respect to Foreigners, when such Rapsodies of Nonsense are admitted on the *Theatre-Royal* of *England*; and that a Patent from his Majesty, intended to encourage Virtue, and expose Vice, is prostituted to the vilest and lowest Degree of Buffoonery? Be witty on some other Topick; and when you speak of this, speak of it with a Seriousness equally becoming the Speaker and the Subject.

As *Frank* is one of those happy Tempers which nothing ruffles, *Tom's* Reprimand did not put him out of Humour, and (the Subject of Conversation changing) the Evening went off as agreeably as usual.

Grubstreet Journal, Feb. 8. No. 163.

Of the FREE MASONS.

Mr *Bavius*,

FIRST, I suppose this Fraternity might as well be called a Society of Carpenters, or Rat-catchers, as Masons. For, tho' they assume the real Art, as well as Name of Masonry; and join with themselves all the antient Architects, Masons, Geometricians, &c. since *Adam*; and amuse the World with their Squares, Angles, &c. yet we may attribute this Gallimawfry to the Restorer of the Society; of whom may be said,

> —He could coin or counterfeit
> New words, with little or no Wit;
> Words so debas'd and hard, no Stone
> Was hard enough to touch them on. Hudib.

And his Reason for propagating this Jargon might be, that the great *Arcanum* should be thought congruous to the Title of the Club, as in his Days it ftood corrupted; for fo it will appear by my Argument to prove, That the Mafons are no Mafons.

A learned Brother in a late *prologue*, addreffing himfelf to this myfterious Science, fays,

The Ufe of Accents from thy Aid is thrown,
Thou form'ft a filent Language of thy own;
Difdain'ft that Records fhou'd contain thy Art,
And only liv'ft within the faithful Heart.

This Doctrine is alfo regifter'd in their *Conftitution Books*: But Mafonry hath been often publickly handled, explained, and commented upon by Antients and Moderns. If fo, how can this be the Art, that is thus fecret in the Breafts of the Members of the modern Lodges?

In the Next Place, There are in the Mafon's Society, a great Number of Brethren not quite *Euclidical* enough to comprehend an intricate mathematical Demonftration, or even a Geometrical Definition. Neither does it appear, that they are taught in the Lodge to *Hew, Square, Mouldftone, lay a Level*, or *raife a Perpendicular*: How then are they Mafons?

Laftly, If the Art of Mafonry be really and truly vefted among them, why then do the *Brethren*, like fome of the *Grubs*, build nothing but Caftles in the Air?

Let us now confider, whence the Word *Mafon*, as applied to this Club, may be corrupted. They will fcarce thank me for acknowledging, that fuch a ftrange Society may be as old as *Chaucer*, in whofe Days the word *Mafe* was ufed to fignify a Whim, or Fancy; as fay that laborious Antiquary Mr *Thomas Herne*, and that as laborious Philologos *N. Bailey*. What then could be more natural, than to diftinguifh a Society by the Name of a Whim, or, in *Chaucer*'s Language, a *Mafe*, which hath fo many peculiar Whimfical Oddities! *Mafon* muft therefore be a Corruption of this *Mafe*. In Devonfhire they ftill call a Perfon whom they imagine to be mad, a *Mafe* or *Maze* Man or Woman. Some wicked Perfons, indeed, would derive this

Name from the Popifh *Mafs*: but this I difallow, becaufe fo many Zealous Proteftants, nay even Jews, the conftant Enemies to Tranfubftantiation, are accepted Brethren.

Your affectionate Brother *A. H.*

Free Briton, Feb. 8. No. 167.

HUman Nature was undoubtedly created for Happinefs; and Happinefs in general muft depend upon the Knowledge of Means moft effectual to procure it. This can only be derived from the Underftanding, which is properly adapted to inveftigate Truth and Happinefs. What one Man may call Truth, may be fuch to him, but not to another; however, every Man ought to act by, and adhere to, what appears to be Truth in his Apprehenfion. For it is abfurd to think that any Man can or ought to purfue Happinefs, by other Means than that of his own Underftanding. But as fome Years pafs before Mankind have common Difcernment, and the Happinefs of Life, nay, the Joys of an endlefs Futurity, depend upon our Knowledge of Truth, how vaftly defirable muft any Aid be, which we can procure from fuch of our Fellow Creatures, whom Inftruction or Experience has made wifer than ourfelves?

Admit, that Men are often deceived, is this any Objection againft Advice offer'd with an honeft Intention? Is there a better Quality than a fincere Difpofition to improve the Underftandings of others? Honours and Emoluments are therefore moft juftly due to to the Men who reafon beft, and inftruct us moft. If all were heard with equal Advantage, the Opinion moft enforced by Reafon would moft powerfully prevail.

The Tatler, Feb. 9. N° 10.
Of HOPE.

Mr Auditor,

THere is fcarce a Man who does not hope for, and really expect, more Honour, Affluence of Fortune, or Eafe, than he at prefent enjoys. The great Man for greater Preferment, the Trader for larger Returns of Gain. Even in Men of the most despicable Circumstances we find a Hope and an Expectation of some Rise, which, tho' without any probable Foundation, bears them up against the most calamitous Sufferings: so that the Effects of such *Hope* is of great *Benefit* to Mankind. I was led into these Reflections by a Letter I received not long ago from one *Hopefull Stately*, Fore-man to a Taylor near the *Strand*, who, on Account of a Conjurer's saying he should arrive to great Honours, had waited 40 Years in full Expectation of his promised Greatness, adjusting his Notions, Behaviour, and Conduct conformably to such a State, and wanted to have my Opinion, and to be informed from what Quarter his Preferment might come. *W. A.*

I advise Mr *Stately* to lay aside all Thoughts of Grandeur, betake himself to his own Occupation with Assiduity, and let his Ambition be an Incentive to him to become eminent therein.

The *Hope* mention'd by my Correspondent is so far from being *beneficial*, that it is one of the most hurtful Notions the meaner sort of People can imbibe. It has been objected, with Reason, to *Charity-schools*, that they give those unhappy Foundlings Ideas too exalted for their future Condition: Nay, some have attributed the Number of Beggars and Robbers to a Love of Idleness and Extravagance contracted by this elevated way of Thinking in the Vulgar. How many are there whom the Hope of something better so intoxicates, that they neglect, and despise, a State of Life in which they might get an honest Livelihood? A Man that can live moderately and easily, yet amuses himself with imaginary Schemes of Greatness, is a just Object of Ridicule and Satire. It was a noble Saying of *Epictetus*, ' That in what Place and ' Condition soever a Man should find ' himself, he might still be happy."

But I must defer this Subject, to give Hearing to a Correspondent, who may otherwise slip out of my Hands.

Are you then now Auditor, my Dear? Here is a Letter for you, Dear Joy.

MASTER AUDIT,

DO you know, my Dear, that I am just come from *Tipperary* ? and I do intend to furnish you with some Speculation ; for I have two Ears on both sides my Head, and am qualified to be your Cronie. Shall I tell you I am of a great Family ? My Father was a great Man, and so was my Mother too ; and they have a great Estate upon the Bog in my Country; and they did want to put the Drain upon their Bog, but had no Money : Moreover I did borrow some upon the Road, and did leave my Estate to save my Neck ; for they would hang me for trying to drain the Bog, and then my Family would expire, for it is very numerous, *viz.* the *Tiptops, Tipfies, Tippets, Tiplings*, and *Tipfasts* ; then the next Generation did put the Change upon it, and did call themselves any Thing but *Tip* ; so that no body having that Name, my Family might preserve it to themselves. You see now I am qualified to write when I can find a Subject. Arrah, my Dear, now what is my Subject? Shall I tell you I only send this Letter to show you an *Irish* Man can write, and not make *Bulls* ? I am, *Dear Master* Audit,

Your Servant always, TIP.

Tipperary, Jan. 25. 1733.

London Journal, Feb. 10. No. 711.
The Conduct *of the People, the Case of* Opposition.

THE Happiness or Misery of Mankind depend so much on *good* or *bad* Government, that as reasonable Opposition to Bad is the highest Virtue, so *unreasonable Opposition* to *good* Government is the greatest Vice. Tho' some *slavish Writers* do recommend *Tyranny* as the only Remedy against *Faction*, yet is the Remedy infinitely worse than the Disease. Not that all Opposition is Faction ; that only is so, which is made against a *good* Government, and *just* Measures

But

But we have seen the People run into Frenzies, meeting in great Bodies, swearing to oppose, with their Lives and Fortunes, a *huge Monster* to be brought into the Nation by King, Lords and Commons, on purpose to devour us and our Children; and we have seen their Petitions from all Parts of the Kingdom, beseeching their Representatives not to suffer this Monster to invade us: The *Substance* and *Sense* of which Petitions is this; "*Gentlemen*, We are informed by some, who have a *mortal Aversion* to the Government, and by others who have an *implacable Hatred* to the Ministry, that there's a Design to enact a Law which will make *Beggars* and *Slaves* of us and our Posterity for ever. We believe you are V - - - s enough to do this, only because your *Enemies* say it, and for *no other Reason* in the World. But for God's sake, consider; you will not only make Beggers and Slaves of us, but of *your Selves* and *Children* too: Therefore, tho' you have no Regard to the Interest of Liberty, and the Happiness of Mankind, have Mercy upon us for *your own Sakes*. If you comply with our Request, God *Save you*; if not, G———"

Let every *unprejudiced* Man judge, whether this is not the *genuine Sense* of all the late Petitions? And whether this be a Conduct worthy of a *wise* and *free* People under the best Government, and administred so well, that had not some *out of Power* set up *Incendiary Journals to deceive and inflame*, not one Man in a Thousand would have said a Word against the Administration. But *ambitious* and *crafty* Men have put Words into their Mouths; like *Parrots*, they repeat, and then, like *Sheep*, follow their Leaders. What else could have produced those Instructions from *St Albans ?* We ought, however to do Justice to the *Inhabitants* of that Borough, who have clear'd themselves of the base and villainous Insinuations contained in those Instructions, which they have shewn, are

neither the Sense of the *Inhabitants*, or of the *Corporation* ; for no *Court* was call'd, but the *Instructions* were sign'd in a clandestine Manner, by the Mayor and a few of his Brethren, after they had been drawn up by one of *the Agents* for the *Craftsman*, who insinuates among others Things, that our *Poor*, tho' *Work* was never more plenty, nor *Provisions* cheaper, are starving; Work so plenty, and Provisions so cheap, that in *Bradford*, a Cloath-working Town near the *Bath*, there was drank by the labouring People, from *June* 1731, to *June* 1732 above 7000 Pounds worth of strong Beer,

The **Craftsman**, Feb. 10 Num 343.

WHen the People are generally aggrieved they shew their Resentments in Satyrical Ballads, Allegories, By-Sayings, and Ironical Points of *low Wit*, and in hieroglyphical Expressions of their Anger, against the *Projector* of any Injury done or intended them; and these a prudent Minister ought not for his own Safety to despise.

The general Aversion to an Excise hath discover'd itself in the same manner. Mr *D'Anvers* gives Instances of this *gibing Wit* from some emblematical Cuts on Ballads and *Tobacco* Papers, representing the Excise as a Monster, by a *Dragon* with many Heads; as tending to Slavery, by a Coat of Arms with 3 *wooden* Shoes, Supporters an *Exciseman* and a *Grenadier* ; not omitting to signify the Downfal of the *Projector*, by a Man pictured as tumbling out of a *Chariot*, and beheaded, or *Excised* ; which Word, adds *D'anvers*, is now applied by all sorts of People to what seems most grievous to them. Thus Robbing on the Highway is term'd *Collecting* or *Excising* ; being *Beested* at Quadrille, *Excised* ; Spadille is the *Projector*, the other, Mattadores *Commissioners* : the *Test* Act is an *Excise* upon Conscience; the late Epidemical Distemper, which cut off so many, an *Excise Plague* ; and an old Lady is introduced saying, It is no more than we might expect *this Year* according to the Proverb

When

When my Lord falls in my Lady's Lap,
England, beware of a great Clap.

These odd Ideas of *Dragons*, *Chariots*, *Excises*, &c. caused *D'anvers* to dream he was in a magnificent Anti-Chamber; at the upper End of which, he says, sat a *goodly fat Personage*, not unlike the Figure I had observed in the *hieroglyphical Chariot*. Several shabby looking Fellows, crowded his Levee. I perceiv'd they were Projectors of various Schemes for *raising Money*. Upon the Labels of their Projects were written *perpetual Mortgages*, *Capitations*, *Poll Taxes*, &c. which the Man in the Chair receiv'd but told them with a smile *Not Yet*. Next a whimsical plump Creature came bustling thro' the Room with the Term *Excisor* in Capitals on his Breast, and the Words *Coffee*, *Tea* and *Chocolate* inscrib'd on his Forehead. He deliver'd a Paper, which the *Person in Authority* read with a visible Satisfaction, then call'd for *Wine* and *Tobacco*; and addressing himself to his *Clients*—*Gentlemen*, said he, *I have a particular Esteem for you all, and out of meer Regard for your Health, I will take Care for the future that your Wine and Tobacco shall be unadulterated.*—This *Specious* Declaration, however, gave Offence to several grave-looking Persons, who remonstrated against the Project, but he replied, *It is resolved.*——

I was immediatley waked by loud Conclamations of *No Excises*, &c. and fell into the following Considerations on the Subject:

The *Occasional Financer* (see p. 66.) insists chiefly on two Points in behalf of the Scheme, *viz.* that it will prevent the *Adulteration of Wine*, and *increase the Public Revenue*. Tho' I am far from being an Advocate for these *Wine-coiners*, *Wizzards* and *Anti-chymists*, as he calls them, yet I do not take them to be such *barbarous, bloody, and inhumane* Murtherers as he represents them. I'm afraid there is too much Reason for the common Complaints of *Wine-brewing*; yet do not apprehend the Ingre-

dients to be of such a *pernicious* and *deadly Nature*; tho' they are certainly *Impositions* on the Publick. There is no great Harm in Water, Cyder, and other home-made Liquors, with which they are supposed to lengthen out their *foreign Wines*, and Profit seems the only Inducement to such Mixtures, since the arrantest Wine-brewer can have no Interest in *poysoning* his Customer.

I do not conceive how this Practice can be prevented by the *present Scheme*; however, 'tis presumed the *Vintners* will not be restrained from mixing *bad* Wines with *good*; (which perhaps is the most *pernicious Mixture* of all) or prohibited the Use of *such Ingredients*, as are necessary to fine the *neatest Wines*, and fit 'em for Sale.

Neither do I think *this Scheme* will *improve the Revenue*; as the *Price* of Wines would be advanced, the *Consumption* will be diminished, which will lessen the *Revenue*; or the *Importation* be enlarged, which will affect the *Balance of our Trade*.

But granting the *Financer* all these Points, the two principal Objections to his Scheme, with Regard to our *Liberties*, still remain in full Force; as it will deprive particular Persons of the Privilege of being try'd by a *Jury*, and endanger the Constitution, by an *Increase of Crown Officers*.

Fog's Journal Feb. 10. No. 223.

Of the Revolution in Portugal, 1640.

MR *Fog* makes an Extract from the *Abbe Vertot*, to prove that a few Gentlemen of Courage, and publick Spirit, may rescue their Country from Slavery.

Portugal was at that Time subject to the King of *Spain*, and was govern'd by a Vice-Queen; but the whole Authority was lodged in the Hands of *Vasconcellos*, her Prime Minister, a *Portuguese* by Birth, by Inclination a *Spaniard*. What recommended him to the *Spanish* Government, was his Care to encrease the Royal Revenue. For this purpose he was continually invent-

ing

ing new Ways of extorting Money from the People, yet made as little scruple to defraud his Master as to rob his Country. He treated the Nobility with the greatest Indignity; and Ecclesiastical Preferments were disposed of without Regard to Merit or Learning; their extensive and flourishing Trade was now decay'd; yet the Citizens and Merchants of *Lisbon* were daily laid under new Hardships and Imposts.

Tho' the People loudly complained, yet were they so aw'd by the Army, that for some Years they patiently submitted to these Oppressions. At length *Pinto Ribeiro*, a private Person, then Comptroller to the Duke of *Braganza*, set on Foot a Conspiracy which took Effect, deliver'd his Country from Slavery, and rais'd his Master to the Crown of *Portugal.* Having concerted proper Measures with the Nobility, Gentry, and Tradesmen, the Death of *Vasconcellos* was unanimously resolv'd on. The first of *December*, 1640, Pinto at the Head of the Conspirators, having surpriz'd the Guard, forced his way into the Palace, and enter'd *Vasconcellos'* Apartment, where they found him hid under a heap of Papers in a Press. They shot him thro' the Head, and threw him out of the Window, crying out *Liberty! Liberty! The Tyrant is dead! Long live Don John King of Portugal.* The People rush'd upon the Carcass, each being eager to give it a Stab, as if they would prevent Tyranny from ever rising again.

From the History of this Revolution arise the following Reflections.

1. That the *Portuguese* endured their Oppressions much longer than they need have done, for want of a proper Concert among themselves.

2. Tho' some of the Nobility might engage in this Enterprize out of Revenge, Disappointment, or other Views; yet the Love of Liberty, and the Hopes of securing the Remainder of their Properties was the Cement of this glorious Undertaking. The Citizens of *Lisbon*, who were the greater Number

of Conspirators, by the new Method of Taxation, foresaw the total Ruin of their Commerce, and chose to die Sword in Hand, rather than to live Beggars and Slaves.

3. The Inflexibility of *Vasconcellos'* Behaviour, when the strongest Remonstrances were made to him, caused many of his Enemies, as well as his Friends, to repute him a Man of great Fortitude of Mind, they were undeceiv'd by his Conduct at his Death; for when he saw his real Danger, he had not the Presence of Mind to utter one Word. — A late Accident at the Opera of *Julius Cæsar*, will explain this Part of *Vasconcellos'* Character. A Piece of the Machinery tumbled down from the Roof of the Theatre upon the Stage just as *Senesino* had chanted forth

Cæsare non seppe mai, che sia Timore,
Cæsar does not know what Fear is,

the poor Hero was so frighten'd, that he trembled, lost his Voice, and fell a-crying. Just such is every Tyrant.

Universal Spectator, Feb. 10. No. 218.

Of HOMER's THEOLOGY.

IN a former Paper (See p. 37.) were collected those grand Descriptions of the *Almighty* and *Supreme Being* which *Homer* gives us. In this the same Writer shews that the Attributes *Homer* assigns him, and the *Submission* and *Obedience* he requires *Mankind* to pay him, are exactly suitable to such magnificent and sublime Ideas; and must certainly be some Entertainment to the Curious, to see at one View what Mankind thought of these Matters above 3000 Years ago, and which are so strongly declar'd in the following beautiful Passages.

ODYS. 14. v. 494.
From *God's* own Hand descend our *Joys* and Woes;
These he *decrees*, and he but suffers *those*;
All *Pow'r* is his, and whatsoe'er he *wills*,
The *Will* it self, omnipotent *fulfils*.
IL. 9. v. 31.
So JOVE decrees, Almighty Lord of all!
Jove, at whose Nod whole Empires *rise* and *fall*;
Who *shakes* the *feeble* Props of human *Trust*,
And *Tow'rs* and *Armies* tumble to the Dust.
IL.

IL. 17. v. 197.
So JOVE's high *Will* is ever uncontroul'd,
The *Strong* he *withers*, and *confounds* the *Bold:*
Now *crowns* with *Fame* the *mighty Man*, and
    now
Strikes the fresh *Garland* from the *Victor's* Brow.
    Again: IL. 9. v. 150.
That *happy Man* whom JOVE still honours most
Is more than *Armies*, and himself an *Host.*
    Again: IL. 20. v. 503.
I know thy *Force* to mine superior far ;
But *Heav's* alone confers *Success* in *War* :
Mean as I am, the *Gods* may *guide* my *Dart*,
And *give* it *Entrance* in a braver Heart.
    Again: IL. 1. v. 228.
If thou hast *Strength*, 'twas *Heav'n* that *Strength*
    bestow'd :
For know, *vain Man!* thy *Valour* is from *God.*
        IL. 17. v. 674.
At one *Regard* of his *All-seeing Eye*,
The *Vanquish'd* triumph, and the *Victors* fly.
        ODYS. 23. v. 13
The *righteous Pow'rs* who tread the starry Skies
The *Weak* enlighten, and confound the *Wise*,
And *human Thoughts*, with unresisted Sway,
Depress, or *raise*; *enlarge*, or *take away.*
    So likewise, ODYS. 16. v. 232.
The *Gods* with Ease frail Man *depress* or *raise*,
Exalt the *Lowly*, and the *Proud* debase.
        IL. 12. v. 9.
Without the *Gods*, how short a Period stands,
The proudest *Monument* of mortal Hands!
    Which last is exactly what the *Psalmist* says,
*Except the Lord build the House, their Labour
is but lost that build it.*

    The *Subtor*, Feb. 13. No. 11.

DEAR SIR,

A New Character, I suppose, will make
    you prick up your Ears as briskly
as a new Lover would mine. Open 'em
wide then, while I draw a Picture half
the young Fellows in Town may sit to.

A FLAP (alluding to that Part of
the Male Garment, which is more for
Shew than Use) is a Creature with as
little Sense as can be conceived in a
human Being. He is in every Respect
the Reverse of the sensible Part of Mankind. As to his Dress, he generally
wears a *Pig-tail*, or *Bag* and *Solitaire*,
with a *Tupee* well plaister'd ; but never
appears in a *Tye Wig*. His Cloaths are
commonly better than he can afford,
with some particular in the Cut, either
to hide a Defect or to set off some fancied Beauty. His Sphere of Action
seldom stretches beyond the Boxes at
the Playhouses, Assemblies, or the *Mall*
when there's no Wind. In any other

Company he is a ridiculous Figure.
As a Levity of Temper makes him easily acquainted with one, so a great Flow
of Spirits render him very noisy and
troublesome ; not having Sense enough
to entertain you in a rational way, his
natural Fire spends itself in Gesticula-
tions and Monkey Tricks. Thus a
FLAP will struggle an hour with a Lady to get her Fan, and be admirably
entertain'd with it. But, if a FLAP
happens to be a handsome Fellow, he
is agreeable enough. He will fly from
one Room to another after a Lady,
and perhaps bruise an Eye with *great
Satisfaction*. A FLAP is perfect Master of the *Scotch* Step, and knows
Country Dances, as another does Authors, and generally carries a Book in
his Pocket with the Names and Tunes
of them, in case the Fidler should be
ignorant. I shall defer several other
Circumstances relating to him, particularly the Method of Address a FLAP
uses with our Sex, when he would
make himself agreeable.   Your Admirer   COQUETILLA.
    P. S. The *Scotch* Step is vastly pret-
ty ; so pretty, that without it Country
Dances are good for nothing.

    Dear Sir,

S Ince you express your great Con-
    cern for the whole Sex in general,
pray don't forget the *Petticoat* in particular. The Fashion of *little* Men
wearing *great* Sticks is so intolerable,
that if you will not suppress it, I know
not what we shall do. What can be
more provoking than to see a little short
Figure with a stick longer than himself,
which he trails thro' the Dirt, till he
spies something like a pretty Woman,
when with the utmost of his Strength,
he raises it from the ground, and carries
it in a Poise ? By which Practice I have
not got home with a clean Petticoat
this Season, tho' I seldom walk more
than a Street's length to visit my Grand-
Mama. Pray why must the little Men
only affect these long Sticks ? and the
tall comely Men never use them ? If
you will regulate this, and state the Size
    of

·of the Stick according to that of the Wearer, you'll remove a publick Nusance, and oblige your attentive

ELENESSA.

This Grievance I can say nothing to, till I have consulted *Frank Easy*. In the mean time I shall be obliged to my Correspondent, if she will tell me Why *fair* Women like Men of dark Complexions, and *black* Men *fair* Women, and of what Complexion she herself is.

Grubstreet Journal, Feb. 15. No. 164.

THE humble REMONSTRANCE of the Ladies of the Cities of London and Westminster, in behalf of themselves, and all the female Bodies Corporat in Great Britain, laying open the greeat Inconveniencies, to which their Boroughs in particular will be Subject, from any extension of the Laws of Excise.

1. It will oblige us to make an Entry of the House and Place, where our Commodities are kept; so that our Chambers will be subject to the Visits of Officers, whenever they think fit to make a Rummage.

2. To keep Books of Account of all Transactions is Impracticable, particularly to those who cannot write.

3. If we are obliged to take out Permits, whenever we have Occasion to remove our Commodities, it will be very troublesome, and hinder the Dispatch of Business, by Reason, that Chapmen must often go away unserved, Permits not being at all Times to be obtained.

4. That if our Vessels are to be gauged, and in a proper manner, it's presumed, there would not be found a sufficient Number of Persons equal to so great a Work, unless the Standing Army were disbanded.

5. We conceive that the Instruments now used in Gauging, would by no means be suitable to our Vessels; so that the Government would be put to great Expence for new Tools.

6. We have good Reason to believe, that the Instruments of the Officers

would be often so much damaged, if not entirely spoiled, that the Government's Expence in repairing them, would amount to as much as the Money arising from this new Imposition.

7. We apprehend with great Terror, that it may be in the Power of wicked Officers wilfully to ruin us, by having at the End of their dipping Rods, something that may very much hurt, if not entirely spoil our Vessels, and occasion continual Leakage, a Case that has happen'd to others, and may to us, as we cannot refuse an Entry.

8. The Statutes now in force against adulterating these Commodities, lay such heavy Penalties on the Adulterer, that scarce any will be found hardy enough to break thro' such wholesome Laws; especially when they consider the terrible Examples that have happen'd of late years.

9. We conceive, the chief Design of the intended Extension of Excise, is to prevent the Running of the Commodities aforesaid; which may be done by suppressing the Hawkers, who infest the Streets Night and Day, impudently offering their damag'd Ware to every one, to the great Detriment of the fair Trader.

Therefore we humbly hope, as the Honour, Dignity, and Interest of the Nation, depends on the Use of our Commodities, that every Member will vigorously and strongly oppose any thing that may tend to our Disadvantage.

Free Briton, Feb. 15. No 168.

Of Publick MONEY *ill laid out.*

IT hath been observed these two Years past of an *illustrious Patriot*, that he opens the Sessions with some Declaration of War against this unfortunate Paper. Such a Distinction might gratify any Man's Pride. But when this is done by a Person who hath no other Way left to gratify the Bitterness of a base Resentment, and who hath fled from the Argument of that Writer whom he rails at, it must raise

the

the higheſt Contempt and Indignation to ſee him *Sculk* and *Scold* in the H——ſe *of* C——*ns*, the only Place where his Adverſary cannot anſwer him. It is however ſome Conſolation that *his* Reproach is ſome Degree of Praiſe, ſince it comes from a Tongue ſo *flippant of Abuſe* againſt the moſt honourable Characters. Had I, ſays *Walſingham*, been one of the Audience in the laſt and preſent Seſſion when he diſtinguiſh'd me by his *little ridiculous Malice*, I ſhould have had no Concern on hearing myſelf aſperſed *by him*. I had indeed the Satisfaction laſt Year to hear, that an *Honourable Gentleman* eſpouſed the Cauſe of the Abſent and the Injured. For the ſake of having one ſuch Advocate, I ſhould be content with having a thouſand Defamers: And I ſhould be eaſy under any Deſamation, if at the ſame Time it might happen as it did *laſt Week*, that the Perſon abuſing me ſhould, in the Wantonneſs of his Scurrility, fall upon a Gentleman of the *greateſt Honour* and *Worth*, with the *baſeſt*, *falſeſt*, and moſt *cruel Reflections*, to the utmoſt Indignation of every Man that heard him.

I know there is an awful Regard due to the great Aſſembly, wherein the Scene of this Abuſe was laid: But as *perſonal Invective* can never come under the Privilege of Parliament, neither can it be ſuppoſed to deſerve, or to meet with Protection from a H——ſe *of* C——*ns*: If therefore a Gentleman will take the poor Advantage of miſrepreſenting a Writer, where he cannot anſwer for himſelf, the Gentleman muſt be content with ſuch Reply as is in the Power of that Writer to give him.

The *Honourable Gentleman* was pleaſed to ſay, that *if the Author of this Paper hath had any Money from the Government, he was ſure it was very ill laid out.*] An Account Stated between *him* and his *little Implements*, would not ſhew much *Generoſity*, or more *Wiſdom*. The loweſt *Slaves* have had his Audience, and the *baſeſt Inſtruments* his Countenance; nor ſhould we

forget, that the *Craftſman* was honour'd with his Recommendation, as a Writer of the firſt Rank and Credit, after having been declared a *Profligate* and an *infamous Perſon* by the *Vote* of this preſent *Houſe of Commons*: Neither the *Honourable Perſon* himſelf, nor his Friends, nor any Man elſe, contradicting.

Since *Money ill laid out* is charged upon the Government, let this Gentleman ſay how much has been laid out on his own Account. He ſays, *be got as little by his Employment as any Man.* I fear he is not willing the Truth ſhould be known. He coſt the Government for every *Shilling* he put in his Pocket more than *half a Crown*; and never ſpent a *Farthing* for the Honour of the Government. To make this appear *Walſingham* ſtates the Account between this *Hon. Gentleman* and the Government, See p. 278, 380, Vol. I.

The Sum total receiv'd of the Government to his own Uſe, on Account of his being employ'd in the Service of the Crown	13,775 13 0
Charge occaſion'd to the Publick, by procuring Employments and Advantages for him in the Service of the Crown	23,700 00 0
	37,475 13 0

Asks, *whether all this Money was not ill laid out?* And whether he did not get as much Money by his Employments as any Man who ever enjoy'd them?

The **Auditor**, Feb. 16, N° 12.

Oauſque ſuit baculum Silveſtre Siniſtra. Ovid.

HAving conſulted *Frank Eaſy* on the Complaint of *Eleneſſa* (See p. 75-6) I ſhall communicate what I have gather'd from his Converſation.

The *Romiſh* Countries abound with idle Fellows under the Appellation of *Pilgrims*, who are equipp'd with ſham Reliques, and religious Trinkets; and in their Hands generally bear a long Staff,

Stuff. *Frank*, by a ludicrous Allusion, has given the Name of *Pilgrim* to our *Oak-plant-Bearers*, and distinguish'd them into three Classes; *viz.* those of *Bacchus, Venus*, and *Hercules*, and says, a shrewd Guess of the Humour and Temper of the Man may be given from the Representation on the upper Part of his Stick, or from the Size of it. Those among the Bacchanalians who love a copious Glass prefer a Head with a chearful Countenance; while the more devoted Sons of *Bacchus* delight in Figures of *Cranes* or *Herons* to denote their plentiful Swallow, or their Resolution to dive to the Bottom of the Glass.

The Votaries of *Venus* every Month change their walking Implement with as much *Circumspection* as a Lady the Mount of her Fan. Admirers of black Women chuse the Sculpture of a beautiful Æthiopian; the *Ivory Profile* shews a *Liking of the Fair*; the round polish'd Head-piece is us'd to preserve the Softness of a plump Palm. Those who prey on the Property of others are distinguish'd by the Device of a Husband, whose Head receives a supernumerary Embellishment from the Kindness of his Spouse.

The *Herculean* Body is the most formidable, as they seem to have retain'd the old Gothick way of arguing, called *Argumentum Baculinum*, or *Cudgel Law*. He distinguishes them by the Name of *Fustigers*. These *Bear-garden* Heroes are arm'd with an Oaken Cudgel, of a monstrous Thickness and Length, with a massy Head of the same Wood; tho' all their Courage is commonly contain'd in the enormous Bulk of their Weapon.

As to *Eleneffa's* Question, "Why the shortest Men affect the longest and heaviest Sticks," *Frank* says, it may be in Imitation of inferior Hunters in the Country, who carry a Long Pole wherewith to leap a Ditch in Pursuit of their Game; thus the long Saplings are equally useful to our Diminutives in crossing a Kennel after a Rain. Heavy

Sticks are worn by these undergrown Gentlemen, as Bees, in windy Weather, balance their Bodies with a Pebble carried in their Legs.

As to the other Part of *Eleneffa's* Question, "Why tall personable Men, make use of the smallest, and least offensive Sticks?" *Frank* believes it is either out of Contradiction to the Practice of *Short Men*, or to shew that Nature has supplied them with Faculties sufficient to perform all Actions becoming a Man, without any borrow'd Help.

Order'd, That a Man from five Foot to five Foot and a half may carry a Stick 3 Foot long, the upper part of it to be at most one Inch and a half, and to decrease in a taper Manner to the Ferril. A Man from Five foot and a half to six foot high to wear a Stick not exceeding 3 foot and a half, in Thickness towards the Head at most 2 Inches, to decrease gradually as the former. Whoever transgresses these Rules to be obliged to wear their Hands in their Pockets. No Stick or Cane to be rais'd above half a foot from the Ground, nor trail'd in the Dirt, nor carried under the Arm; but to be borne in the Hand most remote from the Wall which is always given to the fair *Sex*.

Mr Auditor,

MAke me happy, and say, It was not you; for I'm told an *Auditor* was near being demolish'd at the *Opera* of *Achilles*, last *Saturday* Night: And hearing he had an *Eccho* with him, my Fears for you increased. Yours, as much as possible Dol Common.

Dear Madam,

I Received no other Damage at *Gay's* new *Opera* last *Saturday* Night, than was common to every *Auditor* there; *viz.* A very disagreeable Noise in my *Ears*, very little to amuse my *Eyes*, and nothing to please my *Understanding*. I thank you for your Concern, but can make you no Return but what becomes

The Auditor,

Daily

Daily Courant, Feb. 16.

Remarks on the Opera of Achilles.

ACbilles could not confide so much in his invulnerable Quality, but there appeared, at the first opening of the Doors, a considerable Number of Hon. and Right Hon. Patrons to support him. This gave no great Opinion of the Performance to impartial Judges.—He appear'd, but how alter'd from the Character old *Homer* gave him! Where is the Humour of his being in Petticoats? He is tenacious of his Virtue when *Lycomedes* addresses him as a Woman; and the most dull Gallant to *Deidamia*, (tho' he debauches her) when in the Person of *Achilles*. Where is the

Impiger, iracundus, inexorabilis, acer, the Life, the Vivacity of an amorous young Warrior? All lost in the whining, virtuous, yet debauched Modern.—*Lycomedes* and *Theaspe*, the King and Queen, are introduced only for a few marriage Bickerings and low Jokes. The Scenes are long and tedious; the Satyr (said to contain secret History) unintelligible; the Wit low, and the Moral—past finding out. The Songs are so far from equalling the *Beggar's Opera*, that had they not been made publick under Mr. *Gay's* Name they might have pass'd for the Productions of some of those dull Imitators he ridicules in the Prologue.—In the first Scene, *Achilles*, with a surprizing Poignancy, assures his Mamma, he thirsts for Fame and Glory,

as   —the Glutton
         Does after Mutton.—

The Description of a Coquet is not a less happy Comparison; where the *Coquet Cat* having got a Mouse,

Now pawing, Now toying;
—Mouse gets loose and bilks her Chace.

The Quaintness of the Turn in

Reputation back'd and cut,
Can ne'er be mended again.

: cannot but raise *Admiration* in the Audience; and for the *Sharpness* of the *Sting,* is admirably equal'd in another Catch on a Jealous Woman; who

—*herself deceives*   -
Raising Fears, which she believes.

Quotations are not so easy, as it has not yet appeared in print; but the humorous Description of

Hercules's *Shirt*
Which burnt him to — Dirt,
And set him all on Fire — a,

has so peculiar a Quaintness of Expression, it could not pass unheeded. If Reason was not reckon'd absurd in modern Poetry, it

might be ask'd how, after he was *burnt* to *Dirt*, he could be set on *Fire?*—As the Simile of the Cat was introduc'd in the Beginning of the Opera, it is likewise made to conclude it. The Dignity of *Achilles,* when leaving the Toys of Love at the Sight of the Armour, is pompously describ'd by *Puss's* leaving her *Caterwauling* at the Sight of a *Mouse.*

Mr *Gay* could not *deviate* into so much *Dulness.* He had the Plan given him, but unhappily died, the Play unfinish'd, and the Songs not wrote: But rather than the Scheme should fail, the Patriot became the Poet.—Sir *W.* the Esquire, the Satyrist, and his Grace, held their Consultations: Nor could it be unpleasant to hear a *discarded Courtier* humming out—Joan's *Placket is rent and tore* — then

Reputation back'd and cut
Can never be mended again. .

While a noble Lady, with a *natural Simplicity of Thought,* recollects ——

My a Dilding, my a Dolding, ..
Lilly bright and shinee.

The *Scot* insists in eternizing the Memory of his *Cat;* while the *little Satyrist* tags the Verse, and *points* the Song.

Mr *Gay* was often obliged to own what he never wrote, when the Success did not answer; and others took the Reputation of what was approved of, and he willingly resigned Fame to Interest or Friendship: But his good Friends have wounded his Reputation more by *writing for him,* than his most inveterate Enemies by writing against him. The Songs in general are spurious, yet establish Mr *Gay's* Character, who was said to have receiv'd considerable Assistance in those of the *Beggar's Opera;* since those supposed Assistants have *now,* not only wrote beneath the *Beggar's Opera,* but even the Imitations of it.

Fog's Journal, Feb. 17. No. 224.

A Writer in this *Journal* says, he has read with Pleasure, *The Genuine Thoughts of a Merchant, shewing, that in all the Libels, Remonstrances, and pretended Letters, against the new Method of Levying the Duties on Tobacco and Wine, there is not so much as one Word worth answering.* This Piece, he is inform'd, is the genuine Production of that great Genius, whose Speech was lately published in the *Free Briton.* (See p. 2.)

The

The Author ushers in his Work by telling us, that he was made a Convert from the popular Notion about an Excise, by some Arguments, sent him by an eminent Merchant, which, turn'd into plain *English*, says the Journalist, will run thus.——The Bent of the whole Nation is against an Excise; so that if the Excise goes on, it will become a Party Word like *Sacheverel*, &c. throw the Nation into Convulsions, and be of great Detriment to the Publick; *ergo*, Every reasonable Man ought to be for an Excise. Again: In *Holland, Hamburgh*, &c. where the People have no other way of raising Taxes, but by an Excise, an Excise is found most convenient; *ergo*, an Excise is the most convenient way of Taxing in *England*. Again: If all the Evils feared from Excisemen and an Excise could be prevented, *i. e.* if there was no Excise at all, then an Excise would be a great Blessing to the Nation. Again: Tho' many Evils are apprehended from an Excise, yet there's but one Objection, *viz.* that about Excisemen, worth answering; but as Excisemen are only wooden Figures, *ergo*, that Objection is not worth answering. Lastly, The very Jacobites and Tories cry out *Liberty, no Excise*; *ergo*, Liberty must needs be a very bad Thing, and Excise a very good one.

He goes on to some other Passages which he says must be understood thus,——" There are some Whigs and Dissenters (about 99 in 100) who join with the Tories and Jacobites, in crying out Liberty; *ergo*, these Whigs and Dissenters are deluded Men; and because they don't as yet know every Part of this Excise-Scheme, as not being in the Projector's Secrets, *ergo*, 'tis preposterous to think such ignorant People are in their right Senses, or indeed, that they have any Senses at all.

It being intended to excise Wine and Tobacco imported from *Portugal* and *Virginia*, we can't imagine what Reasons the *Portugal* and *Virginia* Merchants have to oppose this Excise, they being the Persons chiefly affected by it.

If an Excise can be imposed without calling it an Excise, surely they'll have no Reason to complain. And if the Manner of levying the Duty is not prejudicial to the Subject, either in his Liberty or Property, then the Subject has no Reason to complain, that it is prejudicial to him in his Liberty and Property. *Ergo*, The Subject has no Reason to complain that an Excise is prejudicial to him in his Liberty and Property.——

Quotes several other Passages from the said Piece, and ridicules them in the same satyrical way; but the above-recited may be sufficient for a Specimen.

The *Craftsman*, Feb. 17. No. 346.
An Address to the Land-holders.
Gentlemen.

I Must observe that it hath always been the Method of ill-designing Men to *divide the People*; whom they would enslave; therefore is reviv'd the invidious Distinction of the *landed* and *trading Interest*, which are really united. For this Reason I shall lay before you some Considerations on the *present Scheme, for collecting the Duties on Wine and Tobacco.*

The immediate Advantage proposed by this Scheme is, that a Surplus, beyond what is now produced by *Wine* and *Tobacco*, will be raised, sufficient to answer *one Shilling in the Pound upon Land*. To this it may be answer'd, that the whole Duties upon *these Commodities* do not amount to near such a Sum; and it's very improbable that this Method should more than double it.

But if it should be design'd to give *these Duties for a number of Years to come*, as in the *Salt Tax*, to answer the *Land Tax of one Shilling in the Pound for one Year*; you should consider whether it be for your Advantage to run in Debt, and mortgage your Estates to the Publick, on that Account. Consider, if there should be a Deficiency, it may, in a year or two, occasion *one Shilling in the Pound extraordinary upon Land*, to make it good.

Con-

Compute your Savings by the *Salt Duty.* A Gentleman of 500*l. per Ann.* hath this year paid 25*l.* less to the Government; but hath paid 3*s.* 4*d.* per Bushel on *Salt* consumed in his Family.

Another Reason urg'd for *this Alteration,* is the Care of our *Health,* by preventing *Mixtures* in *Wine.* 'Tis fear'd this End will not be answer'd; for *these Mixtures* may be afforded cheaper than Wine can be imported, even tho' they should *pay the Duty on Wines.* But it should be well weigh'd whether *good Wine* may not do more Harm to the Publick than *bad,* as it will tempt People to *Excess,* and occasion a larger Importation of *that Commodity,* consequently a larger Ballance in Favour of Foreigners, and less Consumption of *Malt Spirits, Cyder, &c.* 'Tis urg'd likewise that *many Duties* are collected this Way already! But it's a very insolent way of Reasoning, that because *a great Number of People are already oppress'd,* therefore 'twill be no Grievance *to increase the Numbers.*

We have been at the Expence of above 200 Millions, in support of our common Liberties, since the Revolution; I hope you will not consent to lessen them, for the Sum of 3 or 400 thousand Pounds a Year.

Your Consent to *such a Scheme* may hereafter be made an Argument with the *Burgesses of England* to consent to the Abridgement, or Invasion of *your Liberties;* an Handle which I hope you will never give them.

The *Projector's* Concern for your Interest may be collected from the vast Quantities of *French Brandy,* permitted to be imported from *Dunkirk* at the *Flemish* Duty; by which a considerable Part of the Produce of your Estates sells at so low a Price.

But I hope a generous Concern for the Liberties of Mankind will animate you above any mean Considerations of *private Interest.* I am Yours, &c. S. S.

In the next place Mr *D'anvers,* in his own Name, treats Mr *Osborne* very ludicrously, calls him a *male old Wo-*

man; says, his Admirers are only a *few old Quidnuncs,* like himself; and that his brightest Productions are what the Chymists call *Anima Saturni; the Soul, or Quintessence of* LEAD.

He goes on to answer *Osborne's* Cavil about *the Instructions* from St. *Albans,* (See p. 71 A) which alludes only to an obscure Advertisement.—That Corporation (says *D'anvers*) consists of a Mayor and 12 Aldermen, the Seal was put to *these Instructions* by the *Mayor and ten Aldermen,* all who were then in Town; and *one of the two absent* wrote a Letter to the *new elected Member,* in much stronger Terms than the *Instructions.* But the most effectual way to convince the World that *these Instructions do not contain the Sense of the Corporation* will be, to procure a Petition from St *Albans* in Favour of *Excises.*

As to the Account *Osborne* gives of the extravagant Living of the People of *Bradford,* they must have been considerable Benefactors to the *Revenue;* and 'twould be kind if he would oblige us with the same good News from all the manufacturing Towns in the Kingdom, but he should remember, that, according to Logick, no *general Conclusion* can be drawn from *particular Premises.*

Mr *Osborne* is likewise angry at a Report, *that as soon as the* present Scheme *is finished, we shall have no more* Parliaments, *or that the* present *will perpetuate themselves.* To this *D'anvers* replies, by assuring Mr *Osborne* that he is so far from spreading or encouraging such a Report, that he constantly endeavours to suppress it; for the People are sufficiently dissatisfied with a *Septennial Parliament;* and a farther Extension of *that Term* would certainly throw them into a Flame.

Universal Spectator, Feb. 17. No. 228.
A Guardian's Advice to a young Gentleman at the University.

'TIS no small Part of Wisdom to guard against Folly, and it may be a better Way of telling a young
Man

Man what he *should not do*, than what he *should*. There are so many *Temptations*, and *Promoters* of them, that you cannot be too much upon your Guard. Not that you should look *coldly* upon every one that speaks to you, or shew an *aukward Shiness* in your Behaviour: You may converse with *Easiness* and *Familiarity*, and not run into too much *Openness* or *Intimacy*. An extraordinary Fondness for your *Person*, and Zeal for your *Interest*, are suspicious in a Stranger to you.—There are a Sort of *Land Pyrates*, who live upon *plundering* without Distinction; they hang out false Colours, like their *Brethren at Sea*, and are sure of their *Prey*, if they can but bring them to *board*. Of these you must be exceeding careful, since they appear in all Shapes. Beware likewise of the *Money Jobber*, a plausible, and consequently a more dangerous Creature than the former.

Too much *Confidence in yourself* is always dangerous; your own *natural good Sense* is not sufficient without the Assistance of *Experience* to apply it.

As soon as you return into the Country, your Neighbours will offer you their Assistance to bring you into Parliament. By no means jump at such *Proposals*, if it were only for Fear of *bad Company*, and the Danger of being drown'd in such *wet Popularity*. The great Struggles to get into the *House of Commons*, and the odd Reasons some assign for them, have made a Seat there scarce creditable enough to make amends for the *prodigious Expence* of it. If a *Family Interest* is to be kept up at the Expence of a *Family Estate*, there's no great Difficulty of making your Choice.—The *Service of your Country* is another Argument; but if put in Ballance against the *Harm* you will do yourself, the Odds will be against you.—Yet I would not exclude you from a *Post* your *Ancestors* have enjoy'd, and your Estate entitles you to. First read the History of other *Countries*, and get acquainted with your own, before you set up.

Another Attempt will be made upon you by your *Female Kindred*, by proposing *Wives* to you: For, however it happens, *Matrimony* is the first Thing that gets into a *Woman's Head*, and the last that goes out of it. As you should not absolutely reject their *Proposals*, so it will be improper to give a *serious Answer* to any thing of that sort too soon. To have an Estate parcell'd out into *Jointures* and *Provision*, and, as it were, cut into *Sippets*; to be but a better Sort of *Steward* of your own Fortune— You had need be well assured your *Trammels* will sit easy, before you suffer them to be *so fast put on*.

Read *good Books*. 'Tis the *Good* of that *sort* of *Company*, that you may have it, when you will, and change it, without Scandal or Offence. Without it, you must be perpetually in a *Crowd*, or fall into a *Solitude*, which will end in downright *Stupidity*.

There are but few *general Rules* to be laid down for your Carriage.

Nothing *sits well* upon a Man that is not in some sort *natural* to him; what we admire in *One* may appear absurd in *Another*. There are *two Things* very common, yet become no one, those are *Affectation* and *Ill-nature*. The first indeed, only makes a Man *ridiculous*; but the other *obnoxious* to his *Company*.

By *Ill-nature* I mean, setting up for a *Wit* at the Expence of others; a Character the most unamiable that can be imagin'd. *Fine Raillery* requires a delicate Turn of Thought, as well as Accuracy of Judgment; yet even this I should not desire in a Person I wished well to.—A good Understanding, improv'd by reading the *best Books*, and keeping the *best Company*, will make you welcome, without the mean Helps of *Railing* and *Scandal*. An ingenious and sprightly Conversation upon the most indifferent Subjects, distinguishes a *Man of fine Parts* from the *meer Men of the Town*.

You should not endeavour too much to *shine* in Company. There is a *Jealousy*

M

Iousy in Mankind, which you should take Care not to raise, for instead of applauding, they will be looking for something to *censure*. 'Tis a common Error among *young People*, to judge of their *Wit* by the *Mirth* it occasions. *Laughter* is not always a sign of being pleased; or if it were, it is what the least knowing are most remarkable for. The lower the Diversion, the louder the Laugh; therefore a *Harlequin*, or *Merry Andrew*, is, by some, preferr'd to all other *Dramatick Performances*.

Examine into the Nature of Things, for fear of being deceiv'd. Downright *Impudence*, is frequently cover'd under the Notion of a *good Assurance*; the one is necessary, but the other intolerable. A Man may as well set a *value* upon his *Money*, as upon his own *Merits*, since neither will pass in *Dealing* but at the common Rate.

Some People are so afraid of being thought *Ceremonious*, that they are scarce *commonly civil*: But *Decency* and *good Sense* are so near a-kin, that whoever lays aside the one, will forfeit his Title to the other. To treat all alike is a *senseless Affectation*.

To conclude, *Be not interested. Keep your Temper. Run not into Extremes.*

Weekly Miscellany. Feb. 17.

Of Morality and Religion, from *p.* 65.

THE Author proceeds to examine the *material* Part of Virtue, and to obviate some Mistakes about it. The most common one, is to put the *Matter* of any Duty for the whole Duty. Thus some have defined moral Goodness to be nothing more than chusing, willing, or procuring *Natural Good*, private and publick: Others make it consist in producing the greatest Degree of *Pleasure*, *i. e.* in the Agent himself; or in pursuing *private Happiness*: But these being only the *material parts of* Virtue, their Descriptions are partial and defective. Moral Goodness, or moral Virtue, is the chusing Natural Good without View to present Reward, and in Prospect of a future Recompence only.

The greatest Natural Good is so provided for by God, by the strong Appetites he has implanted in Men, or the Necessities he has laid them under, that there is no Virtue in chusing it. The greatest natural Good is what concerns the Being of the Moral World; and the second greatest, what concerns their *Well-being*. Now God has taken Care to preserve the World in Being, to continue both the Species and Individual, By implanting a strong Love of Life in every Man; by the Appetites of Hunger and Thirst; by warm Desires for propagating the Species; by the Στοργη of Parents towards their Offspring; by necessitating Men to unite in Society, &c. insomuch that the Virtue lies not in chusing those Actions, but in regulating or moderating them.

The Case is the same in Acts of the most beneficial Tendency, whether directed to the Publick in general, to inferior Society, or particular Persons. To defend, relieve, assist a Friend, if it proceed from selfish Views, or no distinct View at all, or from the present Pleasure of performing it, 'tis nothing. To preserve the Rights, Laws and Liberties of our Country, &c. Actions tho' never so good in their Effects, and right as to the *Matter* of them, if there is no Regard had to the Deity in them, they cannot be reckon'd strictly virtuous, nor claim a Place in Morals or Religion. Moral Goodness, therefore, is not barely the willing, or producing, *natural Good*, whether publick or private; but is the doing Good to Mankind in Obedience to the Will of God, and for the sake of eternal Happiness.

IN the Foreign Literary Articles the Author mentions two remarkable Books; one is the History of the Empire, containing its Origin, Form of Government, &c. By Mr *Heiss*. The other, An History of the Low Countries by *Fr. van Micris*, in which the Author gives us the Rise of wearing Perukes. *Philip*, Duke of *Burgundy*, set
the

the Example, tho' involuntarily. A tedious Diftemper had made his Hair fall off; upon which, by the Advice of his Phyficians, he cover'd himfelf with an artificial Head of Hair. His Courtiers, upon this, were fo complaifant, that 500 Gentlemen in the fingle Town of *Bruffels*, follow'd his Example. From that time, Convenience, and an Air of Grandeur, contributed to make it a Fafhion. •

London Journal, Feb. 17. No. 712.
Seafonable Advice *to the People.*
Faithful are the Wounds of a Friend; but the Kiffes of an Enemy are deceitful.

LOOK back upon yourfelves a little; confider *what* you have been doing, and *who* made you do it: You have fuffer'd yourfelves to be wrought into Phrenzies: You have run about, curfing the Miniftry and Government; muttering out Slavery and Beggery, and fullenly threatning Sedition, Tumults and Arms; wifhing the Revolution revers'd, and the Royal Family at *Hanover.*—This you have done; and pray who moved and inflamed you? Why, *two Writers*, of very different Principles, but joining in the fame Defign, *i. e.* to work up your Paffions againft the Government; and then, rather than not carry their Point, throw all Things into Confufion. Thefe Writers are the *Craftfman* and *Fog*: The *firft*, indeed, is only an *Anti-minifterial* Writer; but *Fog* hath publifhed feveral Papers againft the *Revolution*, and prefent Settlement of the Crown. They both write from the deepeft Malice, Rage, and Difappointment; yet, meerly on the Report of the moft *imbitter'd Enemies*, you have affembled in Bodies, made dreadful Remonftrances, and fent *dire Petitions* from all Parts of the Kingdom, fometimes threatning, and fometimes praying, " That you may not be d—d by thofe whom you fent to *fave* you. " What is this but abfolute Madnefs? That you have a *Right* to petition the Houfe of Commons, and to fend *Inftructions* to your Reprefentatives, is

undeniable; but you have no Right to calumniate, or charge the Houfe with a Defign of deftroying your Liberties, as in a Petition from *Rochefter!* meerly becaufe Mr *D'anvers* and Mr *Fog* tell you fo. *They* rais'd the Clamour; and if it be true, what Mr *D'anvers* fays in his laft Journal, " That *Epidemical Clamour* is a Spirit not eafily laid, or fatisfied without taking *Revenge on the Perfons* who rais'd it, " their Deftruction is near at Hand; for they have been the *Conjurors* up of this *Spirit.* Mr *Fog* goes fo far in his laft Journal (See p. 72-3) as to call upon you to *arm*; to *ftrike home*, and *revenge your Country's Wrongs.* He gives you indeed a fhort Account of the Revolution in *Portugal*, but 'tis on purpofe to incite you to *murder the Minifter*, and *revolt from the Prince*: Tells you that one can't be done without the other; and that you might have done it long ago, had you not wanted a *proper Concert* among yourfelves; for the *Wifhes and Inclinations* of the People are as one Man.—What a *Tale* is here to believe upon the Credit of a Couple of Writers, who fubfift, by *defaming* the very Men whom you are taught to fear! We fhould never believe improbable Relations, tho' told by indifferent Perfons; but when a moft *improbable Story* is told by *mortal Enemies*, it's below Notice, and rejected with Contempt by all Men of Senfe. Juft fo fhould we reject thefe Stories about a *General Excife* and *Slavery.*

The Scheme, tho' *myfterious* at prefent, will fhortly come into the Houfe, where you will find it fo ufeful to the Publick, and fo harmlefs with Regard to you, That, inftead of hating the Miniftry for their *Oppreffion*, you will laugh at yourfelves for your *Credulity.*
F. OSBORNE.

The Daily Courant, Feb. 17.
CArus, in a long Letter, wrote in a good Stile, informs us of the various Methods made ufe of by the *Difcontented* to difturb the common Peace which he concludes in this manner.
—Q[f]

— Of all the licentious Difcour fes publifhed of late to exafperate the Nation againft thofe to whom they owe Obedience, the Letter in *Fog's Journal* of laft *Saturday*, (See p. 72-3.) is penned with the greateft Malice and the moft wicked Intention. The Con dition we are in, is there compared to that of the *Portuguefe* under the Oppref fion of the *Spaniards*; the Taxes raifed by Parliament, to the Sums extorted by Conquerors from a vanquifhed, enflaved People. The Charafter of *Vafconcellos* is added to the many which have been heretofore expofed to make an *Honour able Perfon* odious. The Drift of all this is to exhort the *Mob* of *Faction* to attempt fomething, in order to bring about a *Revolution*, the *Death* of a Mi *nifter*, &c. For he tells us, he prefents the Publick with this Extraft to fhew, *That a few Gentlemen of Courage may refcue their Country from Slavery.*

The Auditor, *Feb.* 20.

Hic (rogo) non furor eft, ne moriare, mori?

THE Topick which the *Auditor* makes the Entertainment of this Day, is the Vanity and evil Confequence of appearing above what our Circum ftances will allow. This he illuftrates from the Examples of *Probus* and *Inda mora*, who defired his Advice. The firft had almoft ruined himfelf by living beyond the Poft he was in, to make a Figure, in compliance with the Mode and Expeftation of the Publick. The latter was reduced to want by the fame Folly and Extravagance in her Mother, and is now daily expofed to the Adref fes of the gay and gaudy *Rapax*, who would take Advantage of her Neceffi ties to feduce her.

The Auditor tells *Probus*, he may yet retrieve his Fortune, if he will take up a firm Refolution to prefer his own good Senfe to this vain Opinion of the Pub lick : and moft pathetically expatiates on *Indamora's* hard Dilemma, finely de fcribing the ftrong fluftuating Trial be tween Virtue and Want! Lofs of Ho nour and Plenty ! *but adds*, fhe knows, as well as he, where the Viftory *fhould* fall.

Grubftreet Journal, *Feb.* 22. No. 165.
Of Impoftures.

THE News Papers of this Month have an Article from *France*, im porting, that a Girl born with a Latin Infcription round the Sight of her Eye, refembling that upon a Crown Piece, *i.e.* LUD. XV. D. G. FR. ET NAV. REX. was lately, being then 9 Years old, prefented to their Majefties ; they add, nor is this without a *Precedent*.] We had indeed, about 30 Years ago, one of *Henry Kens*, a *Dutch* Child: In one of his Eyes, round about the Iris, was the Word ELOHIM ; and in the fame part of the other Eye DEUS MEUS. This was looked upon as the Effeft of the immediate Finger of God; and the *Jews* were in Hopes of his being the *Meffiah*; but 'twas found to be a Cheat, managed by two Pieces of painted Glafs, fitted to the Eye. — The fame may be judg'd of this Cafe; the rather, as no Reafon is affign'd, why fo extraor dinary a Phænomenon fhould not be ta ken notice of till the Child was 9 Years old; fince it was the Intereft of the Pa rents to have fhow'd it much fooner.

The Story of the Rabbit-breeder of *Godalmin* is frefh in every Body's Me mory. And a-kin to this is the Hifto ry of the Golden Tooth in 1593, faid to grow among the Molares in a Child's Mouth. The Learned were divided about the Caufe of fuch an extraordina ry Appearance, and what it prognofti cated. JACOBUS HORSTIUS immedi ately publifhed his Book *De Dente au reo*; in which he gave it as his Opini on, that it was partly natural, and part ly miraculous; being defigned to keep up the Courage of the Chriftians, then at War with the Turks. Others like wife publifhed Treatifes upon the fame Subjeft. At length a Journey-man Sil verfmith unexpeftedly furprized the Mouth of the Child, and difcover'd the Tooth to be nothing but an ordinary Tooth, to which fome Gold-leaves were applied. CALLIOPIUS.

§ One, who fubfcribes himfelf SOME BODY, animadverts on the Remarks made

made on the new Opera of Achilles, (See p. 78) calls the Remarker a young Man, and his Criticisms childish. Says, the Author of this Opera, did not intend to draw *Achilles* at full Length, as in the Iliad. There is no Necessity to draw him *impetuous, wrathful, inexorable, and severe,* unless he be plac'd in such a Situation, as where he demands Reparation to his Honour, for the Injuries and Affronts heaped on him by Agamemnon; then

'—*Honoratum si fortè reponis* Achillem, he should be

Impiger, iracundus, inexorabilis, acer.

N.B. The *Craftsman,* who seems to favour this *Opera,* says, It is written on the same Model with the *Beggar's Opera,* only that the Persons of the *Drama* are of a superior Rank, turned into *Travesty;* the Plot being founded on *Achilles's* being concealed in the Court of King *Lycomedes,* under Women's Apparel, to prevent his going to the Siege of *Troy,* where it was prophesy'd he should be slain ; That as this Story furnish'd the Poet with several humorous Incidents, so He hath enliven'd it with a great many agreeable Airs, in the modern Ballad Way; which met with a general Applause the 1st Night, when there was a noble and crouded Audience, and that it continued to run with the same Success.

Free Briton. Feb. 22. No. 169.

MR *Walsingham* having laid down this Maxim, That publick Divisions and personal Differences are inseparable ; and observ'd how difficult it is for Men to quarrel with each others Actions, yet love each others Persons ; proceeds thus : If Men begin to enquire into other Mens Characters and Conduct, they must not expect that their own should pass unexamin'd. I have seen a bitter and vindictive Enemy misrepresenting the Administration, raging against, and with the worst of ill Language treating their Persons, and threatning them with Destruction : I have seen this Person within Doors and

without reply'd to in as high a Strain : but intimates that this is the only Member of —— a certain Body, that is likely to receive the same Indignities, none else being likely to commit the same Injuries. Nay, he has seen another Adversary of the Ministers, whose Dislike has been as strong, and Enmity as irreconcileable, yet carrying on his Opposition in such a well-govern'd manner, that no Man thought himself at liberty, as receiving no Provocation, to treat his Person with Reproach, or to attack his publick or private Character.

It is to be wish'd, adds he, that such Reprizals might always have been spared ; a good Man and a generous Adversary regrets that they ever proceeded from him, even against his worst Enemy ; yet ought he to be excused, when receiving an outrageous Provocation, in the Person of himself and his Friend.

Concludes :—I have not an Enemy but whom I can forgive and spare ; but cannot so easily forgive the Enemies of my Friends. Where a long continued Scene of Injuries, done to my Friends, hath engaged me to unmask the Views of any Man, however proud, imperious, or vindictive, no *Power,* or *Vengeance,* shall deter my Hand : whilst the one is just, I have no Cause to fear it, and whilst the other *works by Day-light,* I shall scorn to fly it.

The Auditor, Feb. 23. Nº 14.

—— Ridiculum acri, fortius, & melius.

Mr Auditor,

I Stole the other morning, by the help of my invisible Faculty, into the Bed-chamber of a Flap. Upon his Dressing-table lay the Auditor upon that Sect. He desir'd his Barber just come in, to read it, who pronounc'd it so emphatically, that the *Flap* might have discover'd his own Picture, but the only curs'd the Author for an old Prig, and order'd his Hair to be curl'd with that very part of *Coquetilla's* Letter wherein he was most fully describ'd. *see* p. 74.

Your faithful Friend, Pacolet.

I am not surprized at his Behaviour, nor

nor the Lady's who twisted my Advice to *Lindamira* up like a Fan, and gave it a little Miss to play with.

Dear Sir,

I Live in a Family, where the eldest Son is a most notorious Flap; to shew him his Folly, my Master has converted me into *one*; I mean, as to Dress, for he cannot curtail my Understanding to the Pitch of a Flap's. I now wear a *short Wigg*, to which my *Eye-brows* are comb'd up, and *pasted down* over it, by way of *Tupee*. I wear my Cloaths so very genteel, I have no shape, but am all Flap; my Waste beginning at my *Shoulders*: and my *Oaken Stick* is so long, that I don't know what to do with it. This Habit is a greater Bondage to me than wearing my Chain. I beg you'll order my Release, and I shall be infinitely yours   PUG.

I pity Pug's Misfortune, and think 'twould be a reciprocal Piece of Justice, as Pug is converted into a *Flap*, to convert the *Flap* into a *Monkey*. *Ovid* mentions a whole People changed for their Behaviour into Monkeys; his Description of 'em is suitable to the *Flaps*.

Th' abandon'd Race transform'd to Beasts be-
To mimick the Impertinence of Man: (gan
—— with Grimace they grin,
And look, to what they were, too near a kin.
Merry in Make, and busy to no end,
This Moment they *divert*, the next *offend*.
So much this Species of their past remains,
Tho' lost the *Language*, yet the *Noise* remains.

Dear Mr Auditor,

I Apply'd to several *Flaps* to explain the *Latin* Lines in your Paper, No. XI. ——*Pol mi occidistis Amici.* &c. Indeed one of them told me *Pol* was *Latin* for *Parrot*; but that not clearing the point, I asked a good plain Man, who informed   Yours Favonia.

I advise my fair Readers to seek out some plain Man to interpret all my future Mottoes, which they may then explain to the *Flaps*.

Fog's Journal, Feb. 24. No. 225.

Of Pensioners *and* Place-men.

MEzeray tells us, that an Edict for raising Money being presented to the Parliament of *Paris*, in the reign

of *Henry* 3. M. *de Thou*, or *Thuanus*, observed, that the last Edict for Money was no sooner verify'd, than Assignments were made out upon it to a worthless Crew of *Place-men* and *Pensioners*, at once the Plague and Disgrace of the Kingdom; however he would not oppose the verifying this Edict, provided they would extirpate those Harpies, who had been the occasion of the present Wants of the Public.

If I'm ask'd, says *Fog*, Is it not necessary some Persons should be appointed to do the public Business? I answer, In Countries, where the Revenues are over loaded with Salaries, I would not desire that more than 19 in 20 of the Great, and 9 in 10 of the inferiour, should be disbanded, because I would allow even more than are absolutely necessary for Service; nor would I vote for reducing the Salaries of those that are left above two Thirds; by which Regulation, if out of every 100 Crowns drawn from the People for this Use, 96 were left in their Hands, to employ in Industry; or was appropriated to discharge the public Debts, if any, I conceive they would be as well laid out, as in purchasing gay Equipages, Harlots, Operas, &c. for those whose Merit generally consists in a slavish Dependance on their corrupt Leaders.

At a certain Time in *Florence* when a Tax of an extraordinary Nature was proposed in the Senate, by the Men in Employments, *Gulielmo Poggio* made a Speech to the Effect following.

Most Magnificent Lords, Some noble *Florentines* have given me to understand, that our whole Business of Meeting here is to drain the People by Taxes and Imposts, in order to swell the Pride, and fill the Coffers of some private Families amongst ourselves. But consider, with regard to the present Proposal, how many insignificant Offices have already been created for the most insignificant of Men. 'Tis true, some of these Offices have the Appearance of Use, yet one Man with common Sense, might do the Business
which

which five or six Drones have large Appointments to execute. What an Alteration have thefe things occafioñ'd ? The Spirit of the People feems fled with their Money, and they meanly wait at the Doors of thefe Upftarts to be directed in the Choice of Magiftrates, only to have a Scrap of that Bread thrown back to them, which is fqueez'd from them in Taxes.

Should I be ask'd, if I would let the State fink for want of a prefent Supply, I anfwer, No—Let it be rais'd on thofe who are able to fpare it, on the Men in publick Offices ; if their Vices have not left them fufficient, let us make Sale of their Lands, Palaces, Jewels, &c. that were bought with the publick Money, and fhould be applied to the publick Wants.

I prefer this Method to the continuing them in their Offices, and accepting a Donative of their Salaries for a certain Time ; becaufe the latter would be a kind of Acknowledgment that their Services were of fome Ufe, which would be againft my Confcience.

The **Craftfman**, Feb. 24. No. 347.

THE *Craftfman* prefents the Publick with a Letter from *Chefter*, wherein the Writer fets in a true Light, againft the Mifreprefentations of the **Daily Courant**, and other Court Papers, fome Tranfactions at the late Elections of a Mayor and Reprefentative in that City.

The Riots and Outrages there committed, the *Letter Writer* obferves, had their Beginning from the private Views of Mr *Manley*, in his negotiating the Bufinefs of making the River *Dee* navigable, That from that Time Numbers of *Vagrants* and *diforderly People* were taken into regular Pay, who infulted and abufed the Magiftrates, and the *Grofvenor* Family ; that Mr *Manley* appear'd feveral Times in the Streets at the Head of the Mob, arm'd with *broad Swords* and *other Weapons*; that at the Election of a *Mayor*, great Numbers of *Officers* in different

Branches of the *Revenue*, as well as *common Soldiers* were detach'd from every Quarter of the Kingdom to vote in favour of Mr *Manley*. This *D'anvers* obferves is fuch an Inftance of Danger to our Liberties from the prefent Number of *Crown Officers*, as ftrongly pleads againft any Increafe of them.

At the Election for a *Member* the Mob difcover'd the fame Inclination to Riots ; but by the Refolution of the Conftables, who were then increas'd the better to preferve the Peace, than it had been at the Election of a *Mayor*, the *Rioters* were difarm'd and difpers'd, to the great Satisfaction of the Inhabitants ; who, having the Freedom of polling without Danger, Mr *Grofvenor* (now Sir *Robert*,) had a Majority of *Refiants* 166, and of Votes in general 361. The Particulars of thefe Proceedings the Writer fays, can be juftified by undeniable Vouchers and Affidavits.

Note. The *Courant* Mr *D'anvers* means is of *Octob.* 25, laft, which afferts that the Mobbing at *Chefter* was begun in Mr *Manley's* abfence, and even before he declar'd himfelf a Candidate; that an Attempt to make 300 Honorary Freemen to deprive the Citizens of their Rights, highly - exafperated them, and was the Caufe of their Violent Proceedings ; which Mr *Manley* did not promote, but reftrain ; fome Gentlemen in Mr *Grofvenor's* Intereft coming into *Chefter* with their Swords drawn at the Head of 500 Welchmen, the Citizens ftood on their Defence ; and that 20 or 30 Guineas was given for a Vote, at the Election of a Mayor, by the *Grofvenor* Party : the Truth of which Facts, would be made appear on legal and full Evidence.

As to the Election of a Reprefentative —the *Courant* of *Feb.* 5. fays, that of the pretended Majority for Mr *Grofvenor* (againft whom Mr *Manley* has petition'd) there are a confiderable Number of Paupers ; and feveral entered on the Poll-Books as Inhabitants, who were properly Foreigners, and were polled as fuch at the Mayor's laft Election ;

Election: befides Minors, and Honorary Freemen: So that 'tis apprehended, upon a Scrutiny, the Number of Free-men-Inhabitants (paying Scot and Lot) for Mr *Manley* will be near equal, if not fuperior, befides the Conftables,— That the Appointment of thefe Conftables is a Proceeding of a very extraordinary Nature in the Magiftrates; who, inftead of making an equal Number man.ed by each Candidate, as has been ufually practifed on the like Occafions, have turned out fuch of the 36 Standing Conftables of the City as were in Mr *Manley's* intereft; and not only made others in their room in Mr *Grofvenor's* Side, they being paid Half a Crown a Day, under Pretence of acting as Conftables; and at the fame time effectually difcharged Mr *Manley's* Friends, many of them being threatened, obftructed, beaten, and terrified by thefe Conftables, under the Pretence of Authority, from voting for him.

The ***Weekly Mifcellany***. Feb. 24. Nº 11

OF MURDER.

S I R,

THE Account of fome barbarous *Murders* lately committed, has rais'd in me many ferious Reflections.—Without the *Poor* we cannot live. In proportion as they grow *ufelefs*, every Station of Life is uncomfortable. But what muft be the Confequence, if inftead of being *ufeful* to Society, they fhall be employ'd to the Deftruction of their Fellow Creatures! It's evident that nothing can curb the *brutal Appetites* of Men, and reftrain them from Acts of *Violence*, but either a *Senfe of Religion*, or the Dread of *humane Laws*. But what can *Laws* avail, when all Senfe of *Religion* is gone? The Fear of *Death* may reftrain thofe who may think it *worth their while to live*; but if a Man has nothing to hope for *here* nor to fear *hereafter*, he will be under ftrong Temptations to *Steal*, and take his *Chance*, rather than *Work* or *Starve*.

That this is the Condition and practice of Thoufands, the *Prifons* and *Gal-*

lows's are now more than ever, an undeniable Evidence. To what, then, can fuch an Increafe of *Wickednefs* be imputed, but to the *Decay of Religion*, and a Neglect in obferving *the Lord's Day*? A Day which has been treated with Reverence; and there are Laws now in Force which oblige all Perfons, if not reafonably hinder'd, to refort every Lord's Day to fome publick Place of Worfhip. But if *Churchwardens* fhould offer to *prefent* Abfenters, an Outcry would be rais'd, as if the *Inquifition* was breaking in upon us. And how is it poffible *Religion* fhould ftand, when *atheiftical* and *irreligious* Books and Pamphlets are fo liberally fcatter'd thro' the Kingdom? and the People left at Liberty to neglect all proper Means to bring them to *Thought*, and guard them againft the *fpreading Contagion*?

That fome Remedy is wanting for this Evil the Thing itfelf fpeaks. The Bulk of Mankind are guided and influenc'd both in refpect to *Virtue* and *Vice*, by the Judgment and Behaviour of their Betters. If Men of *fenfe* and *Reputation* would make a Confcience of profaning the Lord's Day, the reft of the World would be afhamed of it. Tho' this is a Debt which all Perfons owe to the *Publick*, yet it fhould be confider'd how it affects every Man in his *private Intereft*. Whoever takes a Servant gives him a *Power* over his Property and Life. And is it of no Confequence whether he ferves him faithfully or not? 'Tis therefore thofe who have no Religion themfelves are defirous their *Servants* fhould have fome. But what avails it to fend *Servants* to Church, while the Mafter ftays at home? In better Days, the *Heads* of Families reforted regularly to their *Parifh Church*, attended by their *Servants* and *Children*; now the Refort of a *Sunday* is to *Cake-houfes*, and *Taverns*, and the *Fields*. I am far from thinking *Religion* forbids innocent *Recreations*. If a Man, who can afford it, retires at proper Seafons, with his Family to his Houfe in the Country,

for

for *Refreshment* or *Health,* who will find fault with it? But when *Tradesmen,* on a Saturday crowd out of Town, as if the Plague was coming on *Sunday,* what can be expected from the Children and Servants that are left behind? Is it not reasonable, that *God* should receive the Testimony of their Gratitude in *the very Place* where they have received the Tokens of his Blessing?

Another Cause of this Corruption of Manners, is, the great Increase of *Drunkenness.* The Remedy for this, is to restrain the Number of *Ale-houses* and *Strong-Water Shops,* which are so increas'd that one half of the Town seems set up to furnish *Poyson* to destroy the other Half. What can the publick gain by the Increase of the *Revenues,* when it robs us of those Hands that are our chief support?

THEOPHILUS.

London Journal. Feb. 24. No. 713.

A Letter from St. Albans.

THE *Instructions* pretended to be given, under the common Seal of this Corporation, to their new Representative (See our last p. 44.) were obtained in the following Manner:

As soon as the Election was over, (which was not without Opposition) Mr *M——* entertained a large Number of the Inhabitants at the House of *Wm C—* Mayor of St *Albans.* After Dinner, the Mayor, (who is also Post-master) and two or three of the Aldermen were called out by Mr *M—,* and going into his Chamber, sign'd a Paper of Instructions, which was ready ingross'd, but not by the Town-Clerk, nor any Person in Town, and which, we have *Reason* to believe, was brought down by the Secretary of a *certain* Gentleman, *once* honourable, but *now* not so much as a Justice of Peace. The same Paper was afterwards presented to others of the Aldermen to sign, and to some at their own Houses. After the Signing, the Mayor fixed the Corporation Seal to it; for doing which he is challenged to produce the *Consent* and

A *Approbation* of his Brethren, and 'tis expresly charged on him, that he did it without a *Court being called,* and without the *previous Knowledge* of his Brethren.

It is very surprizing to see so great a Profession of Zeal for the *Constitution,* and *Liberty* of the Subject, made by a *Body* of *Men,* who, in Defiance of their *Oaths,* and the *Rights* and B *Privileges* of the Inhabitants of St. *Albans,* have *arbitrarily* made great Numbers of *Non-resident Freemen,* not warranted by their Charter or Constitutions. About 200 have been made by this Mayor and his Brethren, of Gentlemen, Servants, and near 30 Clergymen, collected out of *London* and 5 or 6 Counties, who are all inrolled in the Company of Mercers or Innholders; and, when summon'd to serve a Party, come to over-power the *Inhabitants* and *legal Freemen;* a Proceeding agreeable to the Model set by the late K. *James,* under whose *arbitrary* Reign the first *non-resident* Freemen and Aldermen were made. Yours *&c.*

MUCH after the same Manner, says *Osborne,* were the *Rochester Instructions* obtain'd: A hot-headed *Jacobite* of the Bench, *turn'd out* of his Places, got a virulent Libel drawn up, brought it to the Mayor, when sick; and told him they wanted a Seal to *another Paper,* which they read to him, and then fix'd it to their *Instructions.*

By these *detestable* Arts of *Jacobites* and *Malecontents* on one Hand, and *unfair Traders* working upon the Simplicity of the Ignorant on the other, have the *Petitions* and *Representations* been obtain'd; Petitions about they know not what. Which puts me in Mind, says he, of an Indictment drawn up in *Henry* VI's Reign, by a *wise* Common Council of *London,* against a Man suspected of Heresy, in these Words, *For writing Books which they did not understand; and saying Things which they could not tell what to make of.* Whatever has been reported against this

N

this Scheme, has been said thro' *gross Ignorance*, or consummate *Malice*; for by the *Scheme*, Appeals and *Juries* too will be allowed; and no Officers permitted to enter *private Houses*, but upon an *Affidavit* of prohibited Goods. Nor will the *Ministry* bring in a Bill *prejudicial* to Trade, or *injurious* to Tradesmen, because 'tis against their own *immediate highest* and *greatest* Interest; nor will the Parliament come into such a Bill for the same Reason.

'Tis said, the Ministry *dare* not bring in the Bill; or, if they do, we shall never see *another Parliament*; but they are not to be *bullied* out of their Reason, I say they *dare* bring it in, and yet we shall see another Parliament. If they are *frighten'd*, they are *gone*; for, after such *Cowardice*, their Enemies will never suffer them to pass any Act they han't a Mind to.

Univerſal Spectator, Feb. 24. No. 229.

Of Jealouſy.

OF all the Plagues that imbitter a married Life none is greater than Jealouſy: This will appear from the following Story,

Belmour is about Forty, and has been married ten Years to *Angelica* a beautiful young Lady. After three Years he grew jealous of *Townly*, his Wife's Couſin. But *Belmour* was miſtaken in the Man. *Angelica*'s Heart was indeed engaged, but she affected a free Way with *Townly* to divert her Husband's Suſpiçions, whilſt she carried on an Intrigue with her dear *Ranger*, which commenc'd by an accidental Interview at a Maſquerade. This was wholly a Secret to *Belmour*, who, however, perſuaded himſelf there was something more than he could diſcover betwixt *Townly* and his Wife; to prove it he broke off all nuptial Commerce with her for three Months, and then told her she muſt prepare herſelf to ſet out in 4 Days for a fine Seat in the *North*.

Ranger being made acquainted therewith, put on a Livery, and Matters were ſo order'd, that *Belmour* took him

into his Service, where he enjoy'd thoſe Pleaſures his Maſter continu'd to deprive himſelf off.

At length *Angelica* perceived herſelf with Child. This extremely perplex'd her. They return'd to *London*, and an unforeſeen Affair obliging *Belmour* to ſet out for *Ireland*, where he ſtaid ſix Months, in that Interval, *Angelica* was privately deliver'd of a Son. After great Conſultations 'twas reſolv'd to baptize it under a ſtrange Name, and intruſt the Care of it's Education to a noted Midwife. It was ſent dreſs'd up in fine ſwaddling Cloaths, therein a Purſe of 300 Guineas, with half an old *Roman* Piece of Gold, and the following Note:

This Child is deſir'd to be brought up with Diſtinction, and ſhall be fetch'd away by one who will bring the Counterpart of this Piece.

The Husband return'd, but diſcover'd nothing; yet kept his Reſolution of not bedding with his Wife. They had a Son the firſt year of their Marriage, and he contented himſelf with this Heir.

But Fortune is fickle. *Angelica* went often to one of her Relations, whither *Townly* went likewiſe, which was enough to revive *Belmour*'s Jealouſy. Hereupon he doubled his Vigilance, and at laſt diſcover'd that *Angelica* had lain in; who receiv'd the Infant; and where it was baptiz'd. *Angelica* own'd it, but conceal'd the Father. Wherefore he commenced a Suit with *Townly*, who could not conceive why he was brought into a Scrape, in which he had no Share. In the mean Time *Belmour* loſt his only Son; and this Foundling, had not his Mother declar'd him illegitimate, all the Law in *England* would have allow'd to be Heir. 'Tis probable alſo ſhe had not wrong'd him, but for his Jealouſy.

PHILO-CAMAENES.

As the Sun will ſoon become Scorching, the Auditor of Feb. 27. recommends to the Ladies the wearing of Straw Hats, as they will employ our own Poor, and ſett off their Beauty better than Bermudas Hats.

The

The Subſtance of An Account of the reputed Writers in the News-Papers, *publiſh'd by an Anonymous Author, whom we ſhall call Mr* B.

THat the CRAFTSMAN is written by Mr P....y and his Friends, is no Secret; but the Care of publiſhing lies on Mr N. Am--ſt, of St John's College, Oxon, till expelled for having, ſome ſay, too much Wit. His Writings in Verſe and Proſe, on different Subjects, have been well receiv'd.

FOG's Journal is a Tranſition from MIST's Journal, which was a favourite Paper with the Public; but the Printers were ſo proſecuted and diſturb'd on the Account of a Letter inſerted, which was ſent from France by the late D. of Wharton, containing ſome preſumptuous Reflections, that Mr Miſt's Friends conſulting together thought it expedient to change the Title. From that time it has been writ with more Caution, and the chief Director of it (Miſt and his late Supervilor of the Preſs Wolf, being fled to France) known but to few. Mr Fg ſeems, ſays Mr B, reſolved to keep D'anvers's back Hand.

The Letters in the DAILY COURANT (the beſt Pieces on the ſide of the Miniſtry) are thought to be written by Dr Bl—d, Dr H—n, H—t W—e, Mr Conc—n, and Mr G—d.

The LONDON Journal by Mr P—t, under the Name of Oſborne. He had a Place in the Cuſtoms given him about 2 years ago, by Sir R. W. was a Country School-maſter (at Norwich), appears to be a Deiſt and zealous Admirer of the late Lord Shaftsbury. Some of his Papers on Moral Subjects, ſign'd Socrates, have been well wrote. Adds, as Hear-ſay, that this Paper gave the Government ſo much Uneaſineſs in 1720. about the S. Sea Scheme, that they thought fit to buy it into their own Hands.

The FREE-BRITON, by Mr A—d, a young Man, lately a Clerk to an Attorney; ſeveral Paſſages in his Papers ſhew that he enjoys the Confidence of a certain Great Man.

For the HYP DOCTOR Mr B. names no Author, but thinks it will ſuffice to ſay, he has more than reſtored the elegance of the Antients, and, that it is as impoſſible to imitate (or abridge) him as not to admire him.

The GRUBSTREET Journal, ſays Mr B. ſeems to claim the firſt Place among the Papers deſigned for the Amuſement and Diverſion of the Town. Mr R—l, a nonjuring Clergyman, is ſuſpected to be at the head of it, and Mr P—e, and other Gentlemen, to have wrote ſome Pieces in it. Whoever the Authors be, they have ſhewn, on ſeveral Occaſions, they want neither Wit nor Learning. [It is writ as by a Society, and in ſeveral Characters, ſo that it often contains more Letters or Eſſays than one, at the ſame time Verſes on different Subjects, and humourous Remarks on the Articles of News quoted from other Papers. —— Out of ſo much Variety we can only (with others) pretend to pick the moſt remarkable Pieces.

To the WEEKLY REGISTER, is aſcribed no Author, it has had ſome good Things in it, ſays Mr B. but little taken notice of, perhaps leſs than it deſerved.

The UNIVERSAL SPECTATOR Mr B. thinks an ill choſen Title, as it is a ſort of prophaning the Word Spectator to prefix it to any thing Mean or Dull; not but that he has ſeen ſome pretty Eſſays in this preſent Spectator. The Bookſellers, who are Proprietors of it, have got ſeveral Gentlemen to write for them, among whom Mr K—y, Mr C—l, Mr Ch—n. We could add ſome of our own Knowledge.

The AUDITOR, he does not know who is the Author of, but can tell who is not, i. e. meaning himſelf. He allows it to be a commendable Deſign, but difficult to execute, yet will not judge too haſtily. [Our Readers will obſerve we have diſtinguiſh'd this Paper from the beginning, but as it comes out twice a Week, we are oblig'd to confine it in too narrow a Compaſs to preſerve the Beauty of this manner of Writing. We doubt not to have given a ſufficient Taſte to incite a good many of our Readers to peruſe him unabridg'd, as one Correſpondent hints he has done ſome Papers thrice over, and liked them better every time.

The WEEKLY MISCELLANY, he ſays, is, newly ſet up on an extenſive and fine Plan (See No. 24. p. 1117.) the Author the Rev. Dr We—r, a Clergyman, who has given us ſeveral Diſcourſes againſt, taking off the Taſt. [If this means his Writing them, it is a Miſtake.

The LONDON CRIER firſt appear'd Jan. 29. the Author (meaning Mr K—y,) propoſes to publiſh it daily, in Oppoſition to the Bookſellers, who having all the News Papers in their Hands (he excepts the Craftſman) ſhut out of the ſaid Papers the advertiſing of every thing that does not go thro' their Hands, to the great diſcouragement of Learning, and Prejudice of the Public; intimating that they will not allow an Author who writes under them ſufficient Encouragement to do it with Credit enough to bear his Name; and that they endeavour to ſuppreſs, by all the ways in their Power, whatever they have not a Concern in. —— Mr B. allows, there are juſt Reaſons to complain of theſe Proceedings.

As to APPLEBEE's Original Journal, Mr B. tells us it was really the firſt that appeared, but that a Pack of modern Wits and Upſtarts had almoſt kick'd him out of Doors; ſo that the Memoirs of dying Criminals are become the moſt peculiar Entertainment of his Paper.

READ's Journal is taken up with relating piece-meal Voltaire's Life of the K. of Sweden, and the Sufferings of Iſaac Martin in the Inquiſition. Mr B. remarks, humourouſly enough, that this Procedure might give occaſion to the firſt Hint of Printing Weekly Rapin, Joſephus, Rawleigh, Bayle, &c. and that it might not be amiſs to print the Bible this way, that ſo People who are frighten'd at a large Volume might be drawn in to read the Scriptures.

The CONVERT *to* TOBACCO.
A TALE.   (From a MS.)

Disce Tobo genitos haurire et reddere Fumos.

HAIL RALEIGH ! Venerable Shade,
   Accept this Tribute humbly paid,
Great Patron of the Sailing Crew,
Who gav'st us Weed to smoke and chew,
Kindly accept these Honours due.
To Thee we owe our Country's Wealth,
And smirking Glee, and lusty Health.
From Ashes white as driven Snow,
Tobacco Clouds, 'tis what we owe,
In Fragrant Wreaths ascend the Sky
To Thee, the Smoaker's Deity.

Immortal Weed! all-healing Plant !
Possessing Thee we nothing want.
Assistant Chief to Country Vicar,
Next to his Concordance and Liquor ;
If Text obscure perplex his Brain,
He scratches, thinks, but all in vain,
Till lighted Pipe's prevailing Ray,
Like Phœbus, drives the Fog away.
Concomitant of Cambro Briton,
(If I a Rhime, for that cou'd hit on)
Content with thee, he'll bare-foot trudge it,
His Hose and Shoes fast bound in Budget
Bleak blow the Winds, thick fall the Snow,
With thee he warms his dripping Nose,
And scrubs, and puffs, and on he goes.
With Thee, dear Partner of his Ale,
The Justice grave prolongs his Tale,
And fast asleep does wisely prate us,
Whilst sober Whiff fills each HIATUS.
With thee—but hark'ee, says a Friend,
TOM, will thy Preface never end ?
We want the Tale, you promis'd us;
The Tale d'ye want ?—then take it thus:

BUXOMA was a Banker's Widow,
Frolick and free as good Queen Dido;
For now twelve Months were past and gone;
Since Spouse lay cover'd with a Stone.
At first, indeed, for Fashion Sake,
She must not rest a-sleep, or wake;
The wretched'st Woman sure alive,
The best of Husbands to survive.
O had she dy'd (but 'twas too late !)
To save her Dearee from his Fate.
Poor ten per Cent ! his Hour was come,
E'er he had half made up his Plumb.
You'd swear she'd learnt to mourn at School;
She sigh'd by Note, and wept by Rule.
The Neighbours saw't; and who but she
For Conjugal Sincerity !
But now the Farce was o'er, she saw
'Twas time the Vizard to withdraw.
The Sable Weeds, are thrown aside,
No more she wrung her Hands and cry'd ;
But gay at all Assemblies shone,
And — who was blest that lay alone ?
The Charms of Forty Thousand Pound
Drew from each Quarter all around;
The Templer spruce, and formal Cit,
The Man of War, and Man of Wit.
The last indeed despair'd to win her,
Yet still pursu'd her for a Dinner.
For Madam's Gate, or she's belie'd,
Stood ever hospitably wide.

Good Beef and Mutton grac'd her Table,
And who eat most she judg'd most able.
The Cloth remov'd, the Board was spread,
With Choice of Wine, both White and Red.
Pipes and Tobacco next appear,
And Tapers bright bring up the Rear.
Now by the by, Sir, you must know,
Our Widow whilom made a Vow,
Tho' Age and Ugliness o'ertook her,
Never to wed with filthy Smoaker :
And therefore slyly laid a Plot
To try who smoakt, and who did not.
   Unhappy State of human kind!
To future Evils ever blind !
The gilded Pill we rashly swallow,
Nor heed what Bitterness may follow,
This to make out and eke my Tale,
Our Lovers smoak'd it one and all,
Unthinking of th' impending Doom,
And spicy Whiffs perfum'd the Room :
When strait the Widow, SANS excuse,
Their Offers bluntly did refuse.
   Thus had she packt off Lovers plenty,
Some say a Dozen, others Twenty;
And now began to fear, I trow,
Lest she were bamper'd in her Vow.
When lo ! a Swain of Irish Race
With Back of Steel, and Front of Brass,
Resolv'd SUXOMA to assail,
And wisely, that he might not fail,
Struck in with Mistress ABIGAIL.
Now ABIGAILS, the learned say,
To Lady's Hearts can pave the way ;
The Jade, unable to resist
Five Pieces clapt in Lilly Fist,
Betray'd (a Mercenary Whore!)
The Vow I told you of before,
And MAC succeeds in his Amour.
He wou'd not smoke, to save his Life,
Prais'd the good Taste of PAULO's Wife;
" Tobacco, Fogh ! he cou'd not bear it,
" Filthy Concomitant of Claret.
   Our Widow chuckled here to find
At last a Lover to her Mind ;
And strait an honest Parson got
To tye the Matrimonial Knot.
Here, to be short, the Wedding-day
Was eat, and drank, and danc'd away;
The wishing Guests the Stocking threw,
Jested a while, and then withdrew.
When loud the Groom began to roar,
And bang his Slipper 'gainst the Floor,
—Here bring a Pipe—A Pipe ! she cry'd !—
' Nay, do not fret, good angry Bride,
' For I must smoak, or else—my Dear,
(Then whisper'd something in her Ear)
' Tis true by Heaven ! My former Spouse
' Lov'd to see Pipes come into th' House.
With wistful Eye, poor Madam view'd
Her Dear Deceiver, thought him rude ;
Yet Silent lay, in sad Suspence,
Waiting the happy Consequence,
Which, Authors say, she did not miss;
The Pipe was out, an eager Kiss
Peluded to th' ensuing Bliss.
He smoak'd a Second, and a Third,
Nay, and a Fourth too ('tis aver'd,)

And still the well experienc'd Dame
Found the yet wish'd Effect the Same.
Some have affirm'd, he was so stout
To take a Fifth e'er he gave out.
What yet again, the Devil's in thee.
NAY! Fetch the Pound of SLY's Virginia,
All the new Pipes, and a fresh Light,
Your Master says he'll smoak all Night.

An ODE or Ballad *supposed to be written by* C—C— *Esq; Poet Laureat.*

ASsist, O *Sicelides Muse,*
 Whom VIRGIL has render'd so famous:
Tho' whether you hear, or refuse me,
Vix paulo majora canamus.

Old OVID relates, *inter alia,*
 How DAPHNE stript off her apparel,
Clapt on her green *paraphanalia,*
 And was turn'd in a trice to a laurel.

Without the poetical madness
 With which your old bards are elate,
Who bot L. in down-right sober sadness,
 Could laurel from nothing *create?*

Like a cricket each winter I *sing,*
 Sing, sing, in the same tuneful strain;
Nor touch on excise; jarring string;
 But leave that to the jacobite train:

Who cry, prefer freedom to gold,
 Ne'er fall to corruption a prey;
Nor let what was gotten by *old*
 Be lost by *new battle array.*

When your ministers all are so true t' ye,
 To murmurers, cease to repine:
Don't grudge them so trifling a duty,
 As that on tobacco, or wine.

How foolish the man that presumes,
 On folks in high stations to joke!
Since wine raises nothing but fumes,
 And tobacco expires in a smoke.

Ah! learn then, each British wine-bibber,
 Of me, to be merry and wise;
The same mirth and wit from your C—
 You'll find, tho' his sack pay excise.   Grub.

BELINDA's *Canary-Bird.*

DElightful, airy, skipping thing,
 To charm by Nature taught;
how canst thou thus imprison'd sing,
 And swell thy downy Throat?

Divine would be the Poet's Lays
 Breath'd with thit melting Air,
With which thy warbling Voice repays
 Thy beauteous Feeder's Care.

Perhaps the Favours of her Hand
 These happy Strains infuse,
And I might Notes as sweet command,
 Rais'd by so fair a Muse.

The Influence of her radiant Eye,
 And her reviving Smiles,
The Absence of That Sun supply,
 Which chears thy native Isles.

Blest Isles! where with such kind'y Rays
 On Birds and Trees he shines,
We thence enjoy seraphick Lays,
 And thence celestial Wines!

See the enliven'd Liquor rise,
 As dancing to her Song!
And Virtue with the Musick vies,
 As sweet, as clear, as strong.

Had but those Forests *Orpheus* drew,
 Clos'd in their Shades a Bird
Of equal Harmony with You,
 No Tree of Taste had stirr'd.

The Groves had listen'd to the Tongue
 Of their own feather'd Choir,
Nor on the vocal Strings had hung,
 But on their Boughs the Lyre.   Miso.

The TOWN LADY's *Answer to—What tho' I am a Country Lass*

WHAT tho' I am a London dame,
 And lofty looks I bear, a?
I carry, sure, as good a name,
 As those who ruffet wear, a.
What, tho' my cloaths are rich brocades?
 My skin it is more white, a,
Than any of the country maids
 That in the fields delight, a.

What, tho' I to assemblies go,
 And at the Operas shine, a?
It is a thing all girls must do,
 That will be ladies fine, a:
And while I hear FAUSTINA sing
 Before the king and queen, a,
My eyes they are upon the wing,
 To see, if I am seen, a.

My Pekn and imperial tea
 Are brought me in the morn, a,
At noon, Champaign, and rich Tokay
 My table do adorn, a.
The evening then does me invite
 To play at dear Quadrille, a:
And sure in this there's more delight,
 Than in a purling rill, a.

Then since my fortune does allow
 Me to live as I please, a;
I'll never milk my father's cow,
 Nor press his coming cheese, a.
But take my swing both night and day,
 I'm sure it is no sin, a:
And as for what the grave ones say,
 I value not a pin, a.   Grub.

EPIGRAM.

IN our Forefather's stupid Days, the Name
 Of MISS, at Twenty, was exchang'd for
DAME.
But these wise Times to Compliment exhort ye,
Our modern MISSES are full Nine and Forty.

The true Sportsman's *Prayer to* Cupid.

CUpid, make your Virgins tender,
 Make them easy to be won;
Let them presently surrender,
 When the Siege is once begun:
Such as like a tedious Wooing,
 Let them cruel Damsels find;
Give me such as would be doing,
 Prithee, CUPID, make them kind.

An ODE, *on Occasion of Mr* Handel's *Great* Te
Deum, *at the Feast of the Sons of the Clergy.*

SO *David*, to the God, who touch'd his Lyre,
The God, who did, at once, inspire
The *Poet's* Numbers, and the *Prophet's* Fire,
Taught the wing'd Anthems to aspire!
The Thoughts of Men, in Godlike Sounds, he
sung,
And *voic'd* Devotion, for an Angel's Tongue.
At once, with pow'rful *Words*, and skilful *Air*,
The Priestly King, who knew the Weight of
Prayer,
To his high Purpose, match'd his Cares
To deathless Concords, tun'd his mortal Lays,
And, with a Sound, *like* Heav'ns, gave Heav'n
its Praise.

Where has thy Soul, O Musick! *slept*, since then?
Or, through what Lengths of deep Creation led;
Has Heav'n indulg'd th' All-daring Pow'r to tread?
On other Globes, to other Forms of Men,
Hast thou been sent, their Maker's Name to spread?
Or, o'er some dying Orb, in tuneful Dread,
Proclaiming *Judgment*, wak'd th' unwilling Dead!
Or, have *new* Worlds, from wand'ring Comets,
rais'd,
Heard, and leapt forth, and into *Being* blaz'd?

Say, sacred Origin of Song!
Where hast thou bid thyself so long?
Thou *Soul* of Handel!—through what shining
Way,
Lost, to our Earth, since *David's* long past Day,
Didst thou, for all this Length of Ages, stray!
What wond'ring Angels hast thou breath'd among,
By none, of all th' immortal Choirs, outsung?

But, 'tis enough—since thou art *here again*;
Where thou hast wand'er'd, gives no Pain :
We *hear*—we *feel*, thou art return'd, once more,
With Musick, *mightier* than before;
As if in ev'ry Orb,
From every *Note*, of *God's*, which thou wert
shown,
Thy Spirit did th' Harmonious Pow'r absorb,
And made the moving Airs of Heav'n thy *own!*

Ah! give *thy Passport*, to the Nation's Prayer,
Ne'er did Religion's languid Fire,
Burn fainter—never more require
The Aid of such a fam'd Enliv'ners Care :
Thy Pow'r can *force* the stubborn Heart to feel,
And rouse the Lukewarm Doubter into Zeal.

Teach us to pray, as *David* pray'd before;
Lift our Thanksgiving to th' Almighty's Throne,
In Numbers, like his own :
Teach us yet more,
Teach us, undying Charmer, to compose
Our inbred Storms, and 'scape impending Woes :
Lull our wanton Hearts to Ease,
Teach Happiness to *please*;
And, since thy Notes can ne'er, in vain, implore!
Bid 'em becalm unresting Faction o'er :
Inspire Content, and Peace, in each proud Breast,
Bid th' unwilling Land be blest.
If Aught we wish for seems too long to stay,
Bid us believe, that Heav'n best knows it's Day :
Bid us, securely, reap the Good we may,
Nor, Tools to other's *haughty Hopes*, throw our
own Peace away, *&c.*

GEORGIA *and* CAROLINA.

WHile, yet, Unripe, the glowing *Purpose* lay,
And conscious Silence *plann'd* its *opening*
Way;
Kind, o'er the rising Scheme, an Angel hung,
And breath'd this Council, from a friendly
Tongue.

To *Britain's Queen*, unfold the dear Design :
Build *Carolina's* Hopes on *Caroline.*
Her Breast by Nature warm'd with Pity's Flame,
Shall draw new Motives, from the Kindred Name.
Hence, the charm'd Vowels, into Musick bound!
For, Prophets hid this Meaning, in their Sound!
The Guardian Angel heard—that lives, Her
Guest,
And holds his Heav'n, in *Carolina's* Breast :
' Learn'd, in the Heart I watch, (He cry'd)—
forbear,———— [Prayer,
' The rash Mistake wou'd blast your fruitless
' By Her own Honour, Ever, least inclin'd,
' To *Carolina*, be a Georgia join'd!
' Then shall Both Colonies sure Progress make ;
' Endear'd to Either, for the Other's Sake :
' Georgia shall *Caroline's* Protection move :
' And Carolina bloom, by *George's* Love.

Epilogue *to the* Eunuch *of* Terence *acted
by the King's Scholars at* Westmr, Feb. 6.

OF old the Romans acted comic plays,
Alike on funeral, and on festal days.
And here, tho' mirth should all our souls employ,
And our glad genius give a loose to joy ;
Grief still intrudes, since he must disappear,
Whose mourn'd departure claims a duteous tear.
Beneath whose care these walls compleatly rose ;
Whose art each secret grace of Terence shows :
A glory Latin Ædiles never knew,
To build their theatres, and actors too.
How ancient bards and orators could soar,
Much taught his precepts, his example more.
Oft as th' Election's yearly pomp displays
His weight of sense, and elegance of phrase ;
Rapid, yet pure, the torrent pour'd along,
Smooth as the Roman, as the Grecian strong.
Let neighb'ring tombs his matchless style declare,
More worth than all the neighb'ring sculptures
there ;
That hids the buried live by skill resin'd,
In each distinguish'd feature of the mind :
From whence e'en South still brighter finds his
name
And his own Busby deigns to borrow fame.
What scholar, great, and grateful, as thou *Freind*,
Thy worth to future ages shall commend ?
Not Busby's self in equal height maintain'd
The school, where half a century he reign'd.
Daily through *Freind*, her swelling numbers rose,
The hate—but more the envy of her foes.
Forgive the last respect to him we show :
To him in virtue train'd ourselves we owe,
If ought too much his nicer judgment sees,
'Tis thus, thus only, that we would displease.
But all besides our duty must approve,
The sons, and patrons of the place they love :
And tho' small praise our mean performance
draws,
Will crown our master's *exit* with applause.

On Dean S——T's *asserting the Superiority of the Antients over the Moderns.* *

While the D——n, with more Wit than Man
  ever wanted,
Or at least more than Heaven to Man ever granted,
Endeavours to prove how the Antients in Know-
  ledge,
Have excell'd our Adepts of each modern College;
How by Heroes of old our Chiefs are surpass'd,
In each useful Science, true Learning, and Taste:
While thus he behaves with more Courage than
  Manners,
And fights for the Foe, deserting our Banners:
While *Bentley*, and *Wotton*, our Champions, he foils,
And wants neither *Temple*'s Assistance, nor *Boyle*'s;
In Spite of his Learning, fine Reasons, and Stile,
(Wou'd ye think it?) He favours our Cause all the
  While;
We raise by his Conquest our Glory the higher,
And from a Defeat to a Triumph aspire!
Our great Brother Modern, the Boast of our Day,
Unconscious, has gain'd for our Party the Bays:
St *James*'s old Authors, so fam'd on each Shelf,
Are vanquish'd by what he has written himself.

*Vide Battle of the Books in St James's Library.

An Irish Miller, *to Mr.* Stephen Duck.

O *Stephen, Stephen,* if thy gentler Ear
  Can yet a rustick Verse unruffled hear,
Receive these Lines, but look not for much Skill,
Nor yet for Smoothness, from a Water-mill.
I near the Hopper stand with dusty Coat,
And, if my Mouth be open, dusty Throat.
The Stones, the Wheels, the Water make a Din;
Hogs grunt without, or squeeks a Rat within.
To meditate sweet Verse, is this a Place?
Or will the Muses such a Mansion grace?
Think when thy Flail rebounded from the Floor,
Was't then you made the Shunamite?——no sure.
And can I write? ah! make my Case your own,
A Miller Poet let a Thresher own.
Smooth gliding *Thames* now bids thy Notes refine,
And Royal *Richmond*'s Shades, and *Caroline*.
The wond'rous Grotto may thy Song inspire,
And Foundress influence like Celestial Fire.
Were I awhile from Noise and Dust releas'd,
And Sacks, and Horses, and the mooter Chest;
And could I see that Hermitage, even I,
As well as you, my little Skill might try,
The splendid Scene attempting to recite,
Princes can build——and shall not Poets write?
As the good Queen, as Fame acquaints us here,
Does ev'ry way so excellent appear,
Around her such diffusive Bounty sheds,
So constant in the path of Glory treads,
That they who know her Nobleness of Mind,
Not much t' admire in works of Art can find.
Shou'd she build Palaces that charm the sight,
Her Godlike Virtues would give more delight.
Shou'd she command high Pyramids to frame,
Her fair Perfections would more wonder claim.
The Grotto, *Stephen,* no bard Task has been,
Its where's an equal Pen to such a Queen?
Carrey's Mill   *John* Frizzle.
near Banishillon.

Of two tainted Limbs of the LAW.

NAT is an arch and artful knave;
  JOHN full as artful is, but grave.
NAT, with a tongue as smooth as oyl,
Wou'd even the elect beguile.
JOHN's half-shut eyes and formal face,
Evince him a true babe of grace.
NAT ne'er pretends religious merit;
JOHN has the form, but not the spirit;
Whose inward man contrives to starve you,
Whilst th' outward hopes in God to serve you.
NAT will by no means e'er come nigh
The direct paths of honesty;
But through long, dark, and crooked ways,
His clients leads into a maze.
JOHN does the like; a different road
Brings all his to the same abode.
One's way the right-hand, one's the left is,
'Till client soon of all bereft is.
For, when bewilder'd and astray,
They both devour their proper prey.
Good BAVIUS, tell us, if you can,
Is NAT, or JOHN, the juster man?

ANSWER.

SInce none is just, neither is juster:
  And therefore neither can pass muster.
Both knaves alike: tho' he's the worse,
Whose hand sunk deepest in your purse. *Grub.*

The EPITAPH of MARGERY SCOTT *who died at* DUNKELD *in* SCOTLAND, *Feb.* 26, 1728.

STop, Passenger, untill my Life you read;
  The Living may get knowledge from the dead.
Five times five years I led a Virgin Life;
Ten times five years I was a virtuous Wife;
Ten times five years I liv'd a Widow chaste;
— Now tired of this mortal Life I rest.
Between my Cradle and my Grave hath been,
Eight mighty Kings of *Scotland,* and a Queen;
Four times five years a Common-wealth I saw;
Ten times the Subject rose against the Law.
Twice did I see old Prelacy pull'd down,
And twice the Cloak was humbled by the Gown;
An end of *Stuart*'s Race,—I say no more,—
I saw my Country sold for *English* Oar.
Such Desolation in my time hath been,
I have an End of all Perfection seen.

On the Old Bust, *with a four Air, on Mr* DRYDEN'*s Monument, in* Westminster-Abbey.

AT *Dryden*'s Tomb, inscrib'd with Sh——m's
  Name,
That Mite, slow offer'd, to establish'd Fame!
Fill'd with Raw Wonder, *Tyro* stopt, to gaze;
And bless'd *His* bounteous Grace,—in kind A m ae.
The Guardian Genius, from the sacred Dust,
Re-kindling upward, wak'd, the quick'ning Bust:
Glowing, from every aweful Feature,—broke
Disdainful Life—and, thus, the Marble spoke.
Teach thy blind Love of H onesty to see;—
'Tis not my Monument—tho' built on me.
Great Piers, 'tis known, can in Oblivion, lie:
But no Great Poet has the Power, to die.
At cheap Expence, behold thy 'scap'd Fame:
The task'd Advocate of a tyrant Name.

The pompous Craft one Lucky Lord shall *save* :
And *Sh—d* borrow Life, from *Dryden's* Grave.
'Twas said—and, e'er the short Sensation dy'd,
The stiff'ning Marble *wrish'd* it's Form *aside* :
Back, from the *Titled* Waste of mould'ring State,
He turn'd—neglectful of the Court, too late !
And, sadly conscious of mis-pointed Praise,
Frowns, thro' the Stone, and *shrinks*, beneath his
Bays.

The PATRIOT *no* POET.

P--*t*--y, in vain, to make thy Poet live,
Thou mak'st him *borrow* Fame, he us'd to *give*.
Vain would *thy* Muse, in Numbers sweet yet strong,
Turn the smart Epigram, or point the Song:
But, striving *Gay's unfinish'd* Scenes to save,
You *blast* the Poet's Laurels o'er his *Grave*.
Too dang'rous Friend; if thus by Friendship led,
To shew you lov'd him *living*, wound him *dead*.
By this one Act thy *matchless Worth* we see:
For P--*t*--y, who with him compar'd can be ?
Who with his *Love* a *pois'nous Taint* instills ?
Whose *Hate* is *harmless*, but whose *Friendship* kills.

Bavius in the *Grubstreet Journal*, is desir'd to
refer the Author of the foregoing Verses to the
Decree pronounced against him in the Dunciad.

Silence, ye Wolves ! while RALPH to CYN-
THIA howls,
And makes *Night* hideous—Anlwer him ye Owls.

Of the QUEEN's Hermitage.

NOT more by Ensigns than select Abodes,
Distinguish'd are the Goddesses and Gods.
In PAPHOS Isle fair CYTHAREA dwells;
NEPTUNE and THETIS in their wat'ry Cells;
High on OLYMPUS Top sits Scepter'd JOVE,
And BRITAIN'S PALLAS in her green Alcove.

MARTIAE CALENDAE.

WALLIA quem celebrat, DAVIDESque insignūt
olim,
Nascentem vidit Te, CAROLINA, Dies.
O Lux ! bis fœlix ! O Luce sacratior omni,
Cui DIVUS præfit, DIVAque Laude pari.

The first of MARCH.

WElchmen thee honour, DAVID did adorn ;
Thy Light saw first fair CAROLINA born.
O twice auspicious Day ! To thee we owe
A SAINT above, a matchless QUEEN below.

Verses on PROVIDENCE, *extracted* from the ESSAY on MAN.

WHo finds not Providence all-good and wise,
Alike in what it gives, and what denies?
See, thro' this Air, this Ocean, and this Earth,
All Nature quick, and bursting into birth.
Above, how high progressive Life may go?
Around, how wide? how deep, extend below?
Vast Chain of Being! which from God began,
Ethereal Essence, Spirit, Substance, Man,
Beast, Bird, Fish, Insect! what no Eye can see,
No Glass can reach! from Infinite to Thee!
From Thee to Nothing !----On superior Pow'rs
Were we to press, inferior might on ours;

Or in the full Creation leave a Void,
Where one step broken, the great Scale's destroy'd:
From Nature's Chain whatever Link you strike,
Tenth, or ten thousandth, breaks the chain alike.
And if each System in Gradation roll,
Alike essential to th' amazing Whole ;
The least Confusion but in one, not all
That System only, but the whole must fall.
And this dread Order, shall it break ? For thee?
Vile Worm! ---- O Madness! Pride! Impiety!
What if the Foot, ordain'd the dust to tread,
Or Hand to toil, aspir'd to be the Head?
What if the Head, the Eye or Ear, repin'd
To serve mere Engines to the ruling Mind?
Just as absurd, for any Part to claim
To be another, in this gen'ral Frame:
Just as absurd, to mourn the tasks or pains,
The great directing MIND of all ordains.
All are but Parts of one stupendous Whole:
Whose Body *Nature* is, and *God* the Soul.
That, chang'd thro' all and yet in all the same,
Great in the Earth as in the Æthereal frame,
Warms in the Sun, refreshes in the Breeze,
Glows in the Stars, and blossoms in the Trees,
Lives thro' all Life, extends thro' all extent,
Spreads undivided, operates unspent,
Breathes in our soul, informs our mortal part,
As full, as perfect, in a hair, as heart;
As full, as perfect, in vile Man that mourns,
As the rapt Seraphim, that sings and burns;
To Him no high, no low, no great, no small;
He fills, he bounds, connects, and equals all.
Cease then, nor ORDER *Imperfection* name:
Our proper bliss depends on what we blame.
Know thy own *Point*. This just, this kind degree
Of Blindness, Weakness, Heav'n bestows on thee.
Submit ---- in this, or any other Sphere,
Secure to be as blest as thou canst bear.
All Nature is but Art, unknown to thee;
All Chance, Direction which thou canst not see;
All Discord, Harmony not understood;
All partial Evil, universal Good:
And spight of Pride, and in thy Reason's spight,
One truth is clear; " Whatever Is, is RIGHT."

*We acknowledge several Favours from our
poetical Friends, but can't oblige all.
Local Pieces, and such as are long, least
suit our Design.
The Account we have receiv'd of a Schoolmaster rudely correcting the Palm of a
little Miss, and the too severe Revenge
taken of him for it by her Relation, a
Magistrate, after a Submission to ask
the Child's Pardon on his Knees, shall,
together with the Cases of the Vaulting
Doctor, the young Widow ; and the barbarous Guardian, be communicated to
the Auditor, under whose Province they
more properly fall ; and if he thinks
fit to give these Rural Incidents a Hearing, our Correspondents shall have the
Substance of his Observations in our u-
sual Manner. P.S. We should be more
particularly informed of the Girl's Crime,
and the Doctor's Age.*

THE
Monthly Intelligencer.
FEBRUARY, 1733.

Thursday, Feb. 1.

MR Handel's *Te Deum* and *Jubilate*, with two Anthems, were perform'd before the Corporation of Clergymens Sons, at St Paul's Cathedral, by a much greater Number of Voices and Instruments than usual, about 50 Gentlemen performing *gratis*. Dr *Stebbing* preach'd the Sermon; after which they dined at *Merchant Taylor's Hall*. The Collection came to 954 *l*. 10*s*. 3*d*. (*see* p. 624. No. 14.)

Saturday, 3.

A Cause was try'd at *Guild-hall* between *William Snelling*, Esq; Plaintiff, and the Gentlemen of the Select Vestry of the Parish of St *Botolph Bishopsgate*, Defendants, on the Legality of their holding a Select Vestry, their Authority in assessing the Parishioners, and electing Parish Officers; a Verdict was given to the Plaintiff of 8*l*. Damages, with Costs of Suit.

Sunday, 4.

Mrs *Lydia Duncomb*, aged 80, and *Eliz. Harrison*, her Companion, aged 60, were found strangled, and *Ann Price* her Maid, aged 17, with her Throat cut, in their Beds, at the said Mrs *Duncombe's* Apartments in *Tanfield Court* in the *Temple*: *Sarah Malcolm*, a Chairwoman, was apprehended the same Evening on the Information of Mr *Kerrel*, who had Chambers in the same Staircase, and had found some bloody Linnen under his Bed, and a Silver Tankard in his Close Stool, which she had hid there. She made a pretended Confession, and gave Information against *Thomas Alexander*, *James Alexander*, and *Mary Tracey*, that they committed the Murder and Robbery, and she only stood on the Stairs as a Watch; that they took away 300*l*. and some valuable Goods of which she had not more than her share, but the Coroner's Inquest gave

their Verdict *Wilful Murder* against *Malcolm* only. However the other 3 being easily taken were committed to *Newgate*, (See 23d Day)

Monday, 5.

At a General Court of the *S. Sea Company*, the following Gentlemen, nominated by the Proprietors, at the Swan Tavern, were declared duly elected, on the Ballot by a great Majority, against the House List, for Directors of the said Comp. *viz.* Mr Thomas Thomas, George Jennings, Esq; Samuel Bosanquet, Esq; Michael Impey, Esq; Mr Jonathan Collyer, Roger Mainwaring, Esq; Mr Robert Henley, Mr Richard Coope, Mr John Edwards, Henry Gaultier, Esq; John Girardot de Tillieux, Esq; Richard Howard, Esq; Sr James Lowther, Bar. Richard Jackson, Esq; Henry Muilman, Esq; Thomas Cowslad, Esq; Sir John Lade, Bar. John Phillipson, Esq; Mr Joshua Baker, James Lambe, Esq; Mr Jospeh Beachcroft, Joseph Fawthrop, Esq; Francis Wilks, Esq; Lewis Way, Esq; Mr Robert Lovick, John Fullerton, Esq; John Hamilton, Esq; Edward Haistwell, Esq; Mr Pinckey Wilkinson, Mr John South.

N. B. Sir *Richard Hopkins*, was chosen Governor, and *John Bristow*, Esq; Deputy-Governor a few Days before.

Monday, 12.

William Rayner, who had been under Prosecution for publishing a Pamphlet, call'd *Robin's Game*, or *Seven's the Main*, not surrendering himself, was taken by a Writ of Execution from the Crown, and carried to the King's Bench Prison, and will next Term receive Judgment.

Tuesday, 13.

Count *Kinski*, the Imperial Ambassador, arrived at his House in *Hanover Square*, and brought with him a good Parcel of rich Needle-work Handkerchiefs, as a Present from the Empress to her Majesty.

O   Came

Thurſday, 15.

Came on the Ballot at the *Eaſt India* Houſe, Whether the Company ſhould proceed in the Law Suit commenc'd againſt Mr *Naiſ*, their Supercargo, for miſmanaging their Affairs when abroad in their Service, or leave it to the Arbitration of a Committee of the Court of Directors: The firſt was carried by 147 to 94.

A Court of Common Council was held at *Guild-Hall*, when, upon a Motion of Sir *Francis Child*, a Repreſentation was drawn up, and preſented to the four Members of this City, who were then preſent as Aldermen, and is as follows,

THis Court doth apprehend, from the Experience of the *Laws of Exciſe* now in being, that *extending thoſe Laws* to any Commodities, not yet exciſed, muſt neceſſarily be very prejudicial to TRADE, both as it will probably diminiſh the Conſumption of the Commodity to be exciſed; and ſubject the fair Trader to the frequent and arbitrary Viſitation of *Officers*, and the judicial Determination of *Commiſſioners*, removeable at Pleaſure, from whom there is no Appeal.

That the *Extenſion of ſuch Laws* muſt neceſſarily increaſe the Number and Power of *Officers*, which will be inconſiſtent with thoſe Principles of *Liberty*, on which our happy Conſtitution is founded, and will further deprive the Subjects of *England* of ſome of thoſe valuable Privileges, which have hitherto diſtinguiſhed them from the neighbouring Nations.

Wherefore *this Court* doth earneſtly recommend it to You, their Repreſentatives, to uſe your utmoſt Diligence in oppoſing a *Scheme of this Nature*, ſhould any ſuch be offered in Parliament, *in any Shape, or however limited, in its firſt Appearance*, being fully convinced, that an *Inland Duty* on Goods, now rated at the *Cuſtom-houſe*, cannot be effectually collected, even with an *Extenſion of the Powers*, or the *ſevereſt Exerciſe of all the Rigours of the preſent Laws of Exciſe*.

Friday, 16.

Was a Rehearing of the following Cauſe in Doctor's Commons, *viz.* one Mrs *Lewis* being a Widow, made her Will, and married again; her ſecond Huſband died and ſhe ſurvived. The Will made in her firſt Widowhood ſtill remaining, and being found after her Death, the Queſtion was, Whether the ſame was a good Will or not? The Council againſt the Will argued, that upon the ſecond Marriage the Will became void, and could not be revived

without ſome new Act of the Deceaſed's to give it Life.—The Council for the Will ſhew'd, that the *Romans*, who made their Wills and were afterwards taken Captives, ſuch Wills became in Force by the Teſtators repoſſeſſing their Liberty; thence inferring, that as Matrimony was a State of Captivity, Wills made by unmarried Perſons, who by ſurviving their Huſbands became again free, the ſame ought to revive with their Freedoms. But a Diſtinction being made between Matrimony and Captivity, the one being the Effect of Compulſion, and the other a voluntary Act, the Judges declared the Will to be void.

Monday, 19.

Copy of a Letter from the Borough of Sudbury, *in the County of* Suffolk, *to* John Knight *and* Carteret Leathes, *Eſquires their Repreſentatives in Parliament*.

Gentlemen, Feb. 19, 1732.

THE many gradual Advances that the Laws of Exciſe have made upon us, proves burthenſome and diſcouraging to Trade; and the preſent Deſign, which we hear is on Foot, to extend them further, gives us too much Reaſon to fear, that they will increaſe to ſo great a Number as will prove fatal to Trade and the Liberty of the Subject.

And therefore, as you are our Repreſentatives in Parliament, we earneſtly requeſt, nay, let us conjure you, by all the Obligations which the important Truſt repoſed in you, and your high Station lays you under, that if a Motion for extending the ſaid Law, ſhould be made in Parliament, you would ſtrenuouſly oppoſe it, and thereby demonſtrate you are acting becoming the Repreſentatives of a Trading Borough, in the Honourable Houſe of Commons of Great Britain, which will much oblige many of the Electors of the Borough of *Sudbury*, and, *Your Humble Servants.*

The Anſwer of a Member of Parliament, to a Letter lately ſent him from the Borough of————.

Gentlemen,

I Have received the Letter you have lately been pleaſed to honour me with, wherein you ſeem to be under great Apprehenſions, that ſomething will ſhortly be offered to the Houſe, injurious to Trade, and dangerous to the very Being of Parliaments, and our excellent Conſtitution—— Should that be the Caſe, I flatter

/ *ter*

ter myself you will never entertain so disadvantageous an Opinion of me as to think I can be regardless of the Trust which you have reposed in me, or of that Duty which I owe my Country.

As to Trade, I have ever thought it a Matter of such Consequence, as to deserve the more immediate Care of the Representatives of a Trading People, almost preferable to every other Consideration, as the surest Basis of the Riches, Strength and Prosperity of these Kingdoms.

You are pleased however to own, that your Apprehensions on this Occasion proceed from Surmises which you can scarce give Credit to; and I hope you will very soon be convinced, that they are without any real Foundation.

But as I am not acquainted with what is intended to be proposed, I think it would very ill become me, to be so far guided by implicit Faith, as either to approve or condemn what at present I am a Stranger to.

Should it tend to what Jealousy may possibly suggest; should it appear detrimental to Trade; dangerous to the Constitution of Parliament, or the Liberties of my Fellow-Subjects, I hope it is not in my Nature to forget that I am an Englishman.

But, If, contrary to the Sentiments which are at present entertained by many Persons who wish well to their Country, it should prove a Benefit to Trade, by pointing out a Remedy for the Frauds which are so universally practis'd, to the great Discouragement and Prejudice of the fair Trader; if without creating any new Duties, or increasing those which are already establish'd, it should so considerably improve the Revenues, as upon any Emergency to supply the Necessities of the Publick; if the Government should be thereby enabled to lessen the National Debt, or give Ease to those Branches of Trade, which are most burthensome to our poor Manufacturers; if this should be the Tendency of the Scheme, I am sure my Assent to it cannot fail of your Approbation.

In Confidence of which, acting upon these Principles, and upon this Foundation, I can have no Reason to doubt the Continuance of your Favour, which it will always be my Endeavour to deserve.

I am,   *Gentlemen,*
Feb. 16.   *Tour most faithful,*
1732-3.   *and obedient humble Servant,*

* * * * *

*To the Mayor, Aldermen, Common-
Council, and Burgesses of* * * * *

Tuesday, 20.

Were brought to *Lincoln* Goal the two Rogues who murder'd the young Man in the Chaise, (See p. 43.) They are named *Hallam,* being Brothers; on entering *Lincoln* they were treated with the utmost Ignominy and Reproach; one of them was for murdering all they attacked, and when taken upbraided the other with hindering him from doing it, as the chief cause of their being apprehended.

They forc'd a Postboy on the Road, to blow his Horn, then told him it was his *Death-Peal,* and immediately cut his Throat, and that of his Horse. The Postboys greeted them as they pass'd through *Lincoln,* in the same manner, sounding their Horns; on which one of 'em wept.

A Cause was tried in the Court of King's Bench, *Westminster,* between one *Thomas,* Plaintiff, and a Pawn-broker, Defendant, for Goods pawn'd, which he refus'd to deliver up at the Interest of 5 *per Cent.* A Verdict was given for the Plaintiff, and 200 *l.* Damages.

Thursday, 22.

His Majesty went to the House of Peers, and gave the Royal Assent to the the Malt Bill, to a Bill for granting further Time to *John Thompson* to appear and discover the Effects of the Charitable Corporation, (See No. XXIII. p. 1078) and to one private Bill.

A Proclamation was published to forbid any Persons to receive or utter in Payment by Tale, any of the Gold Coins of 25 or 23 Shillings, or Halves or Quarters thereof, and to direct the Collectors of the Revenues, and the Officers of the Mint to receive the same by weight for the Space of one Year, at the Rate of 4*l.* 1*s.* per Ounce, Troy Weight. *These Pieces being now to pass by weight, the following Observations may be of use to some of our Readers, viz. at* 4 l. 1 s. per Ounce, *the* three and Twenty Piece *should weigh* 5 Pennyweights 16 Grains *and a Half;* Each *five and* Twenty Piece 6 Pennyweight 4 Grains *and a Half. Every Pennyweight less decreases the Value* 4 s. *and about a Halfpenny; and every Grain being the* 24th *of a* Pennyweight, 2 Pence.

Friday, 23.

Came on at the *Old Bailey,* the Trial of *Sarah Malcolm,* for Murder, &c. (See 4th Day,) when it appear'd that Mrs *Duncombe* had but 54*l.* in her Box, and 53*l.* 11*s.* 6*d.* of it were found upon *Malcolm* betwixt her Cap and Hair. She own'd her being concern'd in the Robbery, but deny'd she knew any thing of the Murder ders, till she went in with other Company to see the Deceased. The Jury found her Guilty of both. She was strongly suspected to have been concern'd in the Murder of Mr *Nisbet* in 1729, near *Drury lane*, for which one *Kelly* alias *Owen* was hang'd; the Grounds for his Conviction being, only a bloody Razor found under the murder'd Man's Head that was known to be his. But he deny'd to the last his being concern'd in the Murder, and said, in his Defence, he lent the Razor to a Woman he did not know.

Saturday, 24.

Was a Trial at *Hicks's Hall* upon an Indictment against one *Laye*, a Barber and Solicitor, for making out a Bill of *Middlesex* at the Suit of *Robert Davis* against one *Griffith Payn* for 174*l.* 3*s.* who was serv'd with it and carried to *Newgate*, but being without Authority, the Bailiff, tho' ignorant of the Fraud, was committed to the *King's Bench*, where, and in finding out and prosecuting this Piece of Villany, he was at near 60 *l.* Expence; *Laye* was found Guilty and committed to *Newgate* for 6 Months.

The Sessions ended at the *Old Bailey*, when the following Malefactors receiv'd Sentence of Death, viz. *Joseph Fretwel*, *Rowland Turner*, and *Edward Dilley*, for the Highway; *George Dawson*, *Wm Atterbury*, and *Rd Norman*, for Shoplifting; *Wm West*, and *And. Curd*, for Burglary; *Wm Chamberlain*, for a Street Robbery; and *Sarah Malcolm*, for Murder; 44 were order'd for Transportation, 1 burnt in the Hand, and 4 to be whipt. *James* and *Thomas Alexander*, are to remain in *Newgate* till the next Sessions.

Monday, 26.

The Sheriffs of *London* and *Middlesex* waited on the House of Commons with a Petition from the Lord Mayor, Court of Aldermen, and Common Council, for the Filling up of that Part of Fleet Ditch next *Holborn*, in order to make a Market.

Tuesday, 27.

Orders were dispatched to the Sheriffs of the several Counties in Great Britain, to summon the absent Members to attend the House of Commons by the 13th of next Month, when 'tis expected the Bill for the alteration of Collecting some Duties on Wine and Tobacco will be brought into the House.

At the same time a Pamphlet was published to explain the Scheme; and asserting that by it there will not be an Increase of above 150 Excise Officers thro' the whole Kingdom.

BIRTHS.

THE Lady of the E. of *Litchfield*, deliver'd of a Son.

27. The Lady of the Hon. *Thomas Townsend*, Esq; second Son of the Ld Visc. *Townsend*, deliver'd of a Son.

MARRIAGES.

GEorge *Trevelyan*, Esq; only Son of Sir *John Trevelyan*, of *Nettlecomb* in *Somersetshire*, Bart. Married to the only Daughter of Sir *Walter Calverley*, in *Yorkshire*, Bart with 12,000 *l.* Fortune.

The Son of *Wm Rawlinson* of *Graithwait*, in *Lancashire*, to a Niece of the late Sir *Rd Oldner*, of the same County.

Sir *Robert Laurie*, of *Maxeltown* in *Scotland*, to the Daughter of Mr *Charles Areskine*, his Majesty's Advocate.

William Penton, of *Winchester*, Esq; to Miss *Symonds*, Daughter to the Wife of *John Goddard*, Esq; Representative for *Tregony*, in *Cornwal*, and one of the Commissaries for accommodating the Differences with *Spain*.

Lieut. *Price*, of the Guards, to Miss *Mackenzie*, Dresser to the Princesses *Mary* and *Louisa*.

Stephen Poyntz, Esq; to Mrs *Anna-Maria Mordaunt*, and receiv'd 3000 *l.* as of Royal Bounty, she having been Maid of Honour to her Majesty.

Dr *Leybourn*, Rector of *Stepney*, to Miss *Towne*, of *Bow*, a Fortune of 6000 *l.*

Henry Fox, Esq; Brother of *Stephen Fox* Esq; Representative for *Shaftsbury*, :: to Miss *Dives* late Maid of Honour to the Q.

DEATHS.

Jan. 12. WIlliam *Levinston*, late Visc. of *Kilsyth*. He was in the Rebellion in 1715, and his Estate is now in the Hands of the *York Building's* Company.

23. Dr *James Gadderar*, a Nonjuring Bishop, in *Scotland*.

Feb. 1. The Hon. *Robert Price*, Esq; made a Baron of the Exchequer in 1702, afterward one of the Justices of the Court of Common Pleas, in which Station he died. He was descended of the antient Family of *Prices* of *Geeler* in *Denbighshire*. In the House of Commons, and on the Bench, he approved himself an unbiass'd Senator and impartial Judge. In private Life, a Person endu'd with the most amiable Qualities and a general Benevolence to Mankind; for the Truth of this, the whole Kingdom may be appeal'd to, where, in the Circuits he went thro' as a Judge for above 30 Years, he was ever receiv'd with the highest Complacency and Satisfaction.

The Relict of *Henry Audley* of *Dear Church* in *Essex*, Esq; and Daughter of Ld *Strangford* of *Ireland*.

3. The Ld *Harold*, only Son and Heir to the D. of *Kent*, aged about 6 Months.

Samuel Goodyard, Esq; at *Wendover* in *Buckinghamshire*.

4. Mr *Richard Woodward*, late Banker in *Exchange Alley*.

George Aylmer, M.D. and Fellow of *Corpus Christi* College in *Oxford*.

Westby, Esq; formerly one of the Governors of St *Thomas's* Hospital.

William Smith, Esq; and Alderman of *Portsmouth*, also Doctor of Physick, and reputed worth upwards of 20,000 l. He left his Dwelling House to be a Charity School for Grammatical Learning; and 100 l. *per Ann.* to endow it.

James Hustler, Esq; a Yorkshire Gent.

The Relict of Sir *Richard Sandford*, formerly an Officer in the *Mint*.

Sir *Thomas Grosvenor*, Bar. one of the Representatives for *Chester*, at *Naples*.

5. Lieut. General *Dillon*, in the Castle of St *Germains* in *France*, Uncle to the present Ld *Dillon* in *Ireland*. He commanded a Regiment before he was 20 Years of age, in the Service of *France*, and gain'd great Reputation in the last Wars.

William Weld, Esq; formerly a Captain in the *East India* Service.

James Wilkinson, Esq; a Justice of the Peace for *Surry*. and late a Director of the York-Building's Company.

Capt. *Swall*, an old Officer who signaliz'd himself at the Battle of *Almanza*.

Mr *Francis Beuzelin*, a *Spanish* Merchant in *Leadenhall-street*.

Mr *Thomas Barclay*, of *Foster Lane*, a *Scots* Gentleman, and left 20 l. to the Poor of old *Aberdeen*; 20 l. to the Beadhouse Hospital there; 5 l. to the Poor of St *Leonard Foster Lane*; and several other Charities.

6. *Hender Molesworth*, Esq; at *Newington*, Brother to Sir *John Molesworth*, of *Pencarrow* in *Cornwal*.

William Ravenhill, Esq; at *Southgate*.

Mr *John Darby*, an eminent Printer.

The Rev. Mr *William Wade*, at *Bath*, Prebendary of *Windsor*, and Brother to the General.

Mr *Charles Nevil*, formerly Master of Child's Coffee-house in St *Paul's* Churchyard.

Francis Stoyte, Esq; Recorder of *Dublin*.

Capt *Armstrong*, of the Red Regiment of *Westminster* Militia.

8. The Rev. Mr *Abbots*, Minister of St *John's*, and the Rev. Mr *Church*, of St *Michael's* in *Gloucester*.

Capt *Slow*, Adjutant of the first Regiment of Foot Guards.

Richard Turnor, Esq; formerly a Turkey Merchant, reckon'd worth upwards of 100,000 l. (and therefore nick-nam'd Plumb Turner) the Bulk of which he settled on Sir *Edward Turnor*, of *Bicester*, in *Oxfordshire*, Bar.

9. *John Fitz-Gerald*, Ld *Villiers*, Son and Heir to the Ld Visc. *Villiers*, aged 9 Months and 17 Days.

Francis Cannings, Esq; at *Foxcot* in the County of *Warwickshire*.

Dr *Mempson*, Prebendary of *Southwell*.

Wm *Lethievillier*, Esq;

John Seawell, of *Newgate-street*, Common-council Man.

10. *Benjamin Rokeby* of *Stratford* in *Essex* one of the Governors of *Christ's* Hospital, and Brother to Judge *Rokeby*, who dy'd many Years ago.

Mr *Thomas Port*, Goldsmith, and Common Council-Man for *Cheap* Ward.

11. The Rev. Mr *Samuel Heskins*, Rector of *Tudworth*, and Vicar of *Husborne Tenant*, in *Wiltshire*.

The Rev and learned Mr *Rymer* Lecturer of St *Nicholas* Church, and late Master of the Grammar School at *Durham*. which Place he had resign'd about 2 months.

Capt. *Perry*, the Engineer, fam'd for several great Works in *Muscovy*, and for stopping *Daggenham* Breach.

13. Mr *Hugh Hopley*, Clerk of St *Andrews Holbourn*, worth several thousand Pounds. The place was given him by Dr *Sacheverel*, whose Servant he was.

14. Col. *Ed. Warder*, of the foot Guards.

The Lady of Sir *Francis Vincent*, Bar.

15. *Thomas-James Maitland*, Esq;

William Megg, Esq; Quarter Master in the D. of *Bolton's* Regiment.

Edw. Cook, Esq; Barrister at Law.

Mr *Joseph Lowe*, Merchant, in *Sherbourne* Lane.

16. The Rev. Mr *Mullins*, Chaplain to the *Dock Yard* at *Deptford*.

17. The Lady *Eleanor Hedges*, Mother of *John Hedges*, Esq; Treasurer to the Pr. of *Wales*, and Relict of Sir *Charles Hedges*, formerly Secretary of State.

Sir *Richard Everard*, Bar. in *Red-Lyonstreet*, *Holbourn*, late Governor of *North Carolina* in *America*.

18.

18. *John Winer*, Efq; at *Rochefter* in *Kent*, an old Commander in the Navy.

19. Sir *Henry Bunbury*, of *Bunbury* in *Chefhire*, Bart. Member for *Chefter* in feveral Parliaments.

The Rev. Mr *Simms*, at *Cambridge*.

Edw. Reynolds, Efq; of *Warwickfhire*, *William Lamb*, M. D. at *York*.

20. *Wm. Hafeling* the oldeft Penfioner in *Chelfea* College, aged 112 Years, and 6 Months, He was in the Parliament Army at *Edgehill*; ferv'd under K. *William* in *Ireland*, and the D. of *Marlborough* in *Flanders*. He married and buried 2 Wives fince he was 100, and the 3d, who furvives him, he married about 2 Years ago. Befides his Allowance from the College, he had a Crown a week from the D. of *Richmond*, and another from Sir *Robert Walpole*.

At *Dublin*, Sir *Ralph Gore* Bt one of the Lords Juftices, and Speaker of the Houfe of Commons in *Ireland*.

21. The Rev. Mr *John James*, Rector of *Stratfield Turges* in *Hampfhire*.

Mr *Prefton*, Farrier to the Pr. of *Wales*.

John Jekyl, Efq; Nephew to Sr *Jofeph Jekyl*, Mafter of the Rolls, *Dec.* 30. at *Bofton* in *New England*, Collector of the Cuftoms.

Abraham Borden, Efq; General Treafurer of *Rhode Ifland*, the fame Day.

Mr *Henry Shrubfole*, Batchelor of Laws, and Proctor in the Commons.

At *Edinburgh* Mr *James Penman*, aged 97, Effay Mafter of his Majefty's Mint, and oldeft Freeman of that Burgh.

22. *Robert Chefter*, Efq; one of the late Directors of the S. Sea Company.

Jones, Efq; Counfellor at Law.

John Stone, Efq; at *Baldwin's Brightwel* in *Oxfordfhire*.

23. The Wife of *John Sawbridge*, Efq; in Childbed, at *Afhford* in *Kent*.

The Ld *William Beauclerk*, Brother to the D. of St *Albans*, at *Bath*, and Reprefentative for *Chichefter*.

Mr *Francis Sturges*, Stable-keeper to his Majefty at *Hampton Court*.

Mrs *Anne Kerney*, a maiden Gentlewoman, in *Red-Lyon ftreet* aged 110.

Thomas Wright, Efq; of *Carey Lane*, of a Mortification in his Toe.

Sir *Jofeph Spence*, at *Colebrook*, formerly a *Hamburgh* Merchant, reputed worth 70,000 l.

24. Mr *Twifden*, Uncle to Sir *Thomas*.

25. The Lady *Fleetwood Belafyfe*, Relict of Sir *Henry Belafyfe* of *Durham*.

PROMOTIONS.

CAPT. *Jackfon*, made Deputy Governor of *Portfmouth*, in the room of Col. *Hawker*, deceas'd.

John Sharp, Efq; Clerk of the Cheque to the King's Meffengers.

Robert Reeves, Efq; one of the King's Council, a Judge in the Court of Common Pleas, in the room of Judge *Price*, decd.

Robert Lindfay, made a Judge in the Court of Common Pleas in *Ireland*.

George Crowle, Efq; Reprefentative for *Kingfton upon Hull*, appointed one of the Commiffioners of the Victualling Office.

The Son of Sir *Richard Lane*, Member for *Worcefter* Commiffioner for Licenfing Hawkers and Pedlars.

Capt. *Leg*, of the 2d. Regiment of Foot Guards, appointed Lieutenant of the faid Regiment, in the room of Capt. *Eaton*, appointed to the Command of Col. *Lee's* Company in the faid Regiment.

John Ld *Hinton*, Eldeft Son to E. *Paulet*, one of the Gentlemen of his Majefty's Bedchamber.

Henry Talbot, Efq; Commiffioner of the Salt Office, in the room of *Thomas Woodcock*, Efq; decd.

Samuel Sandys, Efq; Member of Parliament for *Worcefter*, chofen Chairman of the Committee appointed to infpect into the Affairs of the Char. Corporation.

General *Wade* made Governor of Fort *William* in *Scotland*, in the room of General *Syburg* decd.

Mr *Andrew White* of *Cambridge*, and Mr *Robinfon* of *Newmarket*, elected Coroners for the County of *Cambridge*.

Robert Kendal, Efq; Alderman of *Cheap* Ward, in the room of

Sir *Wm Humphreys*, Bar. who accepted of *Bridge* Ward.

Mr *George Arnold*, appointed Deputy to Alderman *Kendal*.

Mr *Hall*, made Treafurer and Receiver of the Land Tax Revenue for the City and Liberty of *Weftminfter*.

Mifs *Sarah Dives*, Daughter to Col. *Dives*, now beyond Sea, appointed Dreffer to the Princeffes *Mary* and *Louifa*.

Hugh Clopton, Efq; of *Stratford upon Avon*, *Warwickfhire*, Knighted.

Richard Fitz William, Efq; appointed Captain General and Governor in Chief of the *Bahama* Iflands in *America*.

Sir *Robert Walpole*, elected High Steward of *Great Tarmouth*, in the room of the Earl of *Tarmouth*, deceafed.

Mr *Randolph Webb*, chofen Town Clerk of *Bath*.

M3

Mr *Martin* of *Cambridge*, elected Professor of Botany in that University, in the room of Mr *Bradley*, deceased.

Mr *Charles Jones*, late under Marshal, made Head Marshal of the City of *London*.

Sir *Thomas Allin*, Bar. made Serjeant at Arms to the Treasury.

Sir *John Jennings*, made Rear Admiral of *Great Britain*.

Mr *Darling* made Farrier to the Pr. of *Wales*, in the room of Mr *Preston*, decd.

Mr *Thomas Hatchett*, of *Guildford*, appointed Surveyor for Houses for the County of *Surry*.

The Ld *Harrington*, made Governor of the Charterhouse, in the room of the E. of *Pembroke* decd.

Mr *John Ree*, Butler to the Bp. of *London*, appointed Messenger to Q. *Anne's* Bounty for Augmentation of Poor Clergymen's Livings.

Sir *Gerard Conyers*, Knt and Ald. chosen Governor of St *Thomas's Hospital* in the room of Sir *Gilbert Heathcote* Bar. decd.

Sir *Charles Wager*, chosen President of the Corporation for the Relief of poor Sea Officers Widows, in the room of the Ld *Torrington*.

Mr *John Murphew*, appointed Yeoman Farrier to his Majesty.

New Members of Parliament elected.
Charles Fitzroy, Esq; Master of the King's Tennis Courts, for *Thetford* in *Norfolk*.

Sir *John Heathcote*, Bar. for *Bodmin, Cornw*.
Richard Elliot, Esq; for St *Germans*, ditto.
George Lee, L. L. D. Esq; for *Brackley*
William Wollaston, Esq; for *Ipswich*.
John Monro, Esq; for *Ross-shire, Scotland*.

Ecclesiastical PREFERMENTS

MR *Steward*, presented to the Living of *Sudbury*, *Suffolk*

Mr *William Hunt*, to the Rectories of St *Peter* and *Neatspeard*, *Norfolk*.

Dr *Tyrwhit*, appointed Canon Residentiary of the Cathedral Church of St *Paul*, in the room of Dr *Goldolphin*, decd.

Mr *Woodford*, presented to the Living of *Alhallows London-Wall*.

Dr *Newland*, to the Rectory of *Fitz* in *Shropshire*.

Mr *Thomas*, to the Rectory of *Wandsworth*, in *Surry*.

Mr *Lloyd*, Curate of St *George* in the East, chosen Lecturer of the said Church.

Dr *Lewis*, Minister of *Kew*, appointed Residentiary Canon of *Windsor*

Mr *Lovet*, Chaplain to the A.bp of *York*, presented to the Prebend of *Southwel*.

Dr *Webster* presented to the Rectory of *Depden* in *Suffolk*.

Mr *Lancaster*, Chaplain to the Prince of *Wales*, made a Doctor of Civil Law, by the A.bp. of *Canterbury*.

The Rev. Mr *Cheyne*, of *Oxford*, to the Living of *Ipplepen* & *Woodlands* in *Devon*.

Dr *Castleman*, to the Vicarage of *Elverton* in *Gloucestershire*.

Mr *Griffith Jones*, to the Vicarage of *Llandewer-Willsnry*, in *Pembrokeshire*.

Mr *Williams*, to the Rectory of *Wedbleys* in the County of *Radnor*.

Mr *Wilson*, chosen Chaplain to the *Lock*.

Mr *Norman Mead*, appointed one of the Readers of *Christ's Church, London*.

Mr *James Sheppbanks*, elected Vicar of *Little Wakering*, in *Essex*.

The following Dispensations have been granted, viz. to enable

Mr *Samuel Horne*, Chaplain to the Earl of *Sussex*, to hold the Rectory of *Ottham* in *Kent*, with that of *Brede* in *Sussex*.

Mr *James Tait*, Chaplain to the E. of *Suffolk*, to hold the Rectory of *Chesterford Parva* in *Essex*, with that of *Chesterford Magna*; and

Mr *Cumberland*, Chaplain to the Bishop of *Gloucester*, to hold the Rectory of St *Andrew* and St *Mary Bredman* in *Canterbury*, with that of *Hastinly*, in *Kent*.

The Rev. and Hon. Ld *James Beauclerc*, Brother to the D. of St *Albans*, made Prebendary of *Windsor*, in the room of the Rev. Mr *Wm Wade* decea'd.

John Baron, M. A. made Dean of *Norwich*, in the room of Dr *Butts*.

The Rev. Mr *Nichols*, second, was appointed Head Master of *Westminster* School, in the room of Dr *Freind*, who resign'd; and the Revd Mr *Johnson*, Secretary to the Bp of *Rochester*, succeeds Mr *Nichols*.

Mr *Thomas Woore*, presented to the Rectory of St *Michaels* in *Gloucester*, and Mr *Elliot* to the Rectory of St *John* in the said City.

BANKRUPTS.

ISaac Panchond, of *Cannon-st. Lond.* Merch.
Wm Woolley, of *Thames-street* Seedsman.
George Masters, of *Packington, Warwickshi.* Merchant.

Jn Marshal of St *Albans*, Stage Coachman.
Edw. Farmer, of St *Mary Magdalen Bermondsey Southwark*, Trotterman.
Samuel Phillips of *Westminster*, Carpenter.
Wm. Andrews, of *Bread-street*, Tobacconist.
Ja. Hasell, Sent of *Sudbury Suffolk*, Staymaker.
Wm Newman, of St *Brides Lond.* Carpenter.
Robt Gaty, of *Bromham, Wilts*, Drugget-maker.
Henry Moore, of *Westminster*, Marchant.
Robt Bishop, of *Cornhill, Lond.* Woollen Draper.
Mich. Kevan, of *Rochester, Kent*, Mercer.

Towards the End of the Month.

Course of Exchange.		STOCKS
Amsterdam—	35,3411	S. Sea 102 3/8
Ditto at Sight	34 10	—Annu. 110 1/4
Hamburgh—	34	Bank 151 3/4
Rotterdam—	35 1	India 159 3/4
Antwerp —	35 6	3 *per C. Ann.* 100 1/4
Madrid ——	42 1/8 *a* 1/3	M. Bank 115
Bilboa ——	42 1/8 *a* 1/4	African 35
Cadiz ——	42 1/4	York Buil. no Transf.
Venice ——	48 7/8 *a* 49	Royal Aff. 105 1/4 1/2
Leghorn —	50 1/8 *a* 1/2	Lon. ditto 13 1/4
Genoa ——	53 1/8	Eng. Copp. 1*l.* 18*s.*
Paris ——	32 1	Welsh ditto 1*l.* 10*s.*
Bourdeaux –	31 7/8	Bank Cir. 5*l.* 12*s.* 6*d.*
Oporto——	5 4 1/4 *a* 3 7/8	India Bonds 5*l.* 6*s.* 7*s.*
Lisbon——	5 5 1/4 *a* 4 1/4	3 *p. Cent* ditto 2*l.* 10
Dublin——	11 1/4 *a* 1/8	S. Sea ditto 2*l.* 7*s.*

Monthly BILL *of Mortality, from* Dec. 26. *to* Jan. 23.

Christned	Males	990	1979
	Females	989	
Buried	Males	1848	3973
	Femal.	2125	

Died under 2 Years old	1120
Between 2 and 5	249
Between 5 and 10	83
Between 10 and 20	100
Between 20 and 30	263
Between 30 and 40	379
Between 40 and 50	418
Between 50 and 60	363
Between 60 and 70	397
Between 70 and 80	290
Between 80 and 90	232
Between 90 and 103	79
	3973

Price of Grain at *Bear-Key, per* Qr.

Wheat 20*s.* to 25*s.*	P. Malt 14*s.* to 19*s.*	Salt per Bushel 4*s.*	Weekly Burials
Rye 13*s.* to 15*s.*	B. Malt 14*s.* to 18*s.*	Houf. fine 18*s.* to 21*s.*	*Jan.* 30 --- 1588
Barley 11*s.* to 14*s.* 0*d.*	Tares 15*s.* to 17*s.*	dit. second 17*s.* to 19.	*Feb.* 6 --- 166
Oats 09*s.* to 12*s.*	H. Pease 13*s.* to 15*s.*	Peckloaf Wheaten 18*d.*	13 --- 628
Pease 17*s.* to 18*s.*	H. Beans 14*s.* to 19*s.*	—Houf. 13*d.* half pen.	20 --- 591

Prices of Goods, *&c.* in *London.* Hay 1*l.* 14*s.* to 2*l.* 0*s.* a Load.

Coals per Chaldron 25*s.* *to* 26*s.*
Old Hops per Hun. 3*l.* *to* 6*l.*
New Hops 9*l.* *to* 10*l.*
Rape Seed 10*l.* *to* 11*l.* *per Last*
Lead the Fodder 14 *Hun.* 1 *half on board,* 14*l.* *to* 16*l.* 00*s.*
Tin in Blocks 4*l.* 00*s*
Ditto in Bars 4*l.* 02*s.* *exclusive of* 3*s.* *per Hun. Duty.*
Copper Eng. best 5*l.* 05*s.* *per C.*
Ditto ord. 4*l.* 16*s.* *to* 5*l.* *per C.*
Ditto Barbary 70*s.* *to* 80*s.*
Iron of Bilboa 14*l.* 10*s.* *per Tun*
Dit. of Sweden 15*l.* 10*s.* *per Tun*
Town Tallow 31*s.* 35*s.* *per C.*
Country Tallow 30*s.* *to* 34*s.*

Grocery Wares.

Raisins of the Sun 28*s.* 0*d.* *per C.*
Ditto Malaga Frailes 18*s.*
Ditto Smirna new 20*s.*
Ditto Alicant, 18*s.*
Ditto Lipra new 19*s.*
Ditto Belvedera 20*s.*
Currants old none
Ditto new 45*s.* *to* 00*s.*
Prunes French 17*s.*
Figs 20*s.*
Sugar Powd. best 54*s.* *a* 59*s.* *per C.*
Ditto second sort 46*s.* *to* 50*s.* *per C.*
Loaf Sugar double refine 8*d.* *Half-penny a* 9*d.* *per lb.*
Ditto single refin. 56*s.* *to* 64*s.* *per C.*
Cinamon 7*s.* 8*d.* *per lb.*
Cloves 9*s.* 1*d.*
Mace 15*s.* 0*d.* *per lb.*
Nutmegs 8*s.* 7*d.* *per lb.*
Sugar Candy white 14*d.* *to* 18*d.*
Ditto brown 7*d.* *per lb.*
Pepper for Home cons. 16*d.* *Farth.*
Ditto for exportation 12*d.* *half-p.*
Tea Bohea fine 9*s.* *to* 11*s.* *per lb.*
Ditto ordinary 7*s.* 6*s.* *per lb.*
Ditto Congo 10*s.* *to* 14*s.* *per lb.*
ditto Pekoe 8*s.* *a* 14*s.* *per lb.*
ditto Green fine 8*s.* *to* 12*s.* *per lb.*
ditto Imperial 10*s.* *to* 16*s.* *per lb.*
ditto Hyson 24*s.* *to* 28*s.*

Drugs *by the lb.*

Balsom Peru 14*s.* *to* 15*s.*
Cardamoms 3*s.* 3*d.*
Camphire refin'd 18*s.*
Crabs Eyes 2*s.* 8*d.*
Jallop 2*s.* 8*d.* *to* 3*s.* 1*d.*
Manna 1*s.* 8*d.* *a* 2*s.* 9*d.*
Mastick white 3*s.* 6*d.* *to* 4*s.*
Opium 11*s.* 00*d.*
Quicksilver 4*s.* 3*d.*
Rhubarb fine 25*s.* *a* 30*s.*
Sarsaparilla 3*s.* 0*d.*
Saffron Eng. 28*s.* 00*d.*
Wormseeds 3*s.* *a* 5*s.*
Balsam Capaiva 2*s.* 10*d.*
Balsam of Gillead 18*s.* 00*d.*
Hipecacuana 6*s.* *to* 7*s.*
Ambergreece per oz. 9*s.* *to* 12*s.*
Cochineal 18*s.* 6*d.* *per lb.*

Wine, Brandy, *and* Rum.

Oporto red, per Pipe 36*l.*
ditto white 24*l.*
Lisbon red 30*l.*
ditto white, 26*l.*
Sherry 26*l.*
Canary new 30*l.*
ditto old 36*l.*
Florence 3*l.* *per Chest*
French red 30*l.* *a* 40*l.*
ditto white 20*l.*
Mountain malaga old 24*l.*
ditto new 20 *to* 21*l.*
Brandy Fr. per Gal. 6*s.* *to* 6*s.* 6*d.*
Rum of Jamaica 7*s.* *to* 0*s.*
ditto Lew. Islands 6*s.* 4*d.*
Spirits Eng. 30*l.* *per Ton.*

GOLD in Bars, 3*l.* 18*s.* 4*d.*---Ditto in Coin 3*l.* 18*s.* 3*d.* *to* 4*l.* 1*s.*---SILVER in Bars, Standard, 5*s.* 4*d.* half-penny.—Pillar Pieces of Eight 5*s.* to 5*s.* 5*d.* 3 farth. ditto Mexico 5*s.* 5*d.* 3 farth.

FROM *Warſaw, Feb.* 1. That the King of *Poland* in going from his Coach to his Apartment, ſtruck the Toe of his diſtemper'd Foot ſuch a Blow as ſet it a bleeding, upon which he ſwooned, being very ill before; this being follow'd by a Fever, and the Sore mortifying, he died in a few Hours; having juſt arrived to his Grand Climacterick, the 63*d* Year of his Age. He has left one only Son, now Elector of *Saxony*. A Report was ſpread, grounded upon a Prediction made to his Majeſty when in the *Ukraine*, that the *Polanders* had maſſacred him. When he was only Prince of *Saxony*, he was ſhewn himſelf in a Glaſs, with the Electoral Coronet upon his Head, then with a Royal Crown, and laſtly drowned in his own Blood, ſurrounded with Sabres; all which has exactly happen'd as they make it out, thus: He firſt ſucceeded his Brother in the Electorate; was afterwards elected King of *Poland*; and died by the Loſs of a great deal of Blood by his Foot, whilſt the Dyet was aſſembled, and had drawn their Sabres upon the Nuncio *Hurka.* The firſt of *May* is fixed for the Election of a new King.

From *Verſailles, Feb.* 4. That Madame *de France,* their Majeſties third Daughter, died, aged 4 Years, 6 Months, and 21 Days. Great Preparations are making for War all over the Kingdom, and a Squadron of 13 Men of War is fitting out at *Toulon.*

From *Naples, Feb.* 9. The Shocks of an Earthquake was felt almoſt throughout the Kingdom; particularly at *Benevente.*—That about the ſame Time Mount *Etna* had thrown out a prodigious Number of large Stones, ſome being carried as far as *Catanea.*

From the *Hague,* That the *States General* had appointed a Day for ſolemn Thankſgiving, with Faſting and Prayers to be kept the 11*th* of next Month; alledging, among other Cauſes, the new Scourge brought upon that State by Sea Worms, which had eaten the Piles and wooden Works deſigned to preſerve and ſecure the Dykes againſt the Violence of the Sea; (tho' that Scourge was neither ſo great nor ſo dangerous, as the Publick were made to believe, by groundleſs Reports maliciouſly ſpread) whence it happens, that the State, already groaning under the heavy Taxes of former Wars, cannot yet recover itſelf. Three *Pruſſian* Officers having been ſeiz'd at *Maeſtricht* for endeavouring to corrupt ſome Soldiers of that Gariſon, and inviegle them into the Service of the King their Maſter, had been condemn'd by the States General; two of them were beheaded; their Guide (being a Subject of the State) was hanged; and the Serjeant, having ſeen the Execution, was ſent away, as guilty of no Crime but of obeying the Orders of his Superiors. The King of *Pruſſia,* enraged at theſe reſolute Proceedings, threatned the States with the Effect of his Diſpleaſure, and actually made Reprizals, by ſeizing ſome of their Officers in the Dutchy of *Cleves.*

From *Bruſſels, Feb.* 3. The Pariſh Prieſt of *Haaren,* imagining that ſomewhat amiſs in the Air was the Occaſion of the then Epidemical Colds, ſtuck a white Loaf upon a high Pole in his Garden, and let it remain 24 Hours; after which he gave a Piece of the Bread to his own Dog, and a Piece to his Neighbour's, of which they both burſt.

From *Seville,* That the Marquis of *Santa Cruz,* of whoſe Fate there had been various Reports, was alive at *Algiers,* but not entirely recover'd of the Wounds which he receiv'd when taken Priſoner in the Engagement with the *Moors* before *Oran;* that he had been ſpoken to by the *Spaniſh* Agent for Redemption at *Algiers;* and that the King had offer'd 400,000 Pieces of Eight to the Marchioneſs towards the Redemption of her Husband.

From *Barcelona,* that a Veſſel, carrying the *Engliſh* Flag, had been attack'd off that Place by a *Spaniſh* Privateer, but defended herſelf with great Bravery, tho' ſhe loſt all her Men except three, who carried her ſafe into *Cagliari.*

P   *A*

A REGISTER of BOOKS publish'd in FEBRUARY, 1733.

THE Attorney's Pocket Companion: Or a Guide to the Practisers of the Law; being a Translation of Law Proceedings in the Courts of King's Bench and Common Pleas; containing a Collection of the common Forms, beginning with the Original, and ending with the Jodicial Procels. Together with an Historical as well as Practical Treatise on Ejectments. By a Student of the Inner Temple. In Two Parts. Printed for R. Gosling, pr. 5s.6d.

2. The Beau's Adventures: A Farce, by B. Bennet. Printed for T. Astley. pr. 1s.

3. Johannis Freind. M. D. Serenissimæ Reginæ Carolinæ Archiatti Opera omnia Medica. Printed for W. Innys, R. Manby and L. Gilliver, pr. 1 l. 6 s.

4. Excise Anatomized: Declaring an unequal Imposition of Excise to be the only Cause of the Ruin of Trade, a universal Impoverishment, and destructive to the Liberty of the whole Nation. By A. Z. a Well-wisher of the common Good. Printed for M. Smith, pr. 6 d.

5. The Jew Decoy'd: Or, The Progress of a Harlot; a New Ballad Opera of three Acts. With a curious Frontispiece. Printed for E. Nutt, &c. pr. 1s.

6. The Present State of the Republick of Letters for January, 1733. Printed for W. Innys, pr. 1 s.

7. Medical Essays and Observations revised and published. By a Society at Edinburgh. Sold by J. Osborne and T. Longman.

8. Observations upon the Prophecies of Daniel and the Apocalypse of St John. In Two Parts. By Sir Isaac Newton, pr. 8 s. in Boards.

9. The Argument from Prophesy, in Proof that Jesus is the Messiah, Vindicated: Or, Some Considerations on the Prophesies of the Old Testament, as the Grounds and Reasons of the Christian Religion. Printed for J. Gray, pr. 1 s. 6 d.

10. Killing no Murder: Briefly Discoursed in three Questions. By Col. Titus, alias William Allen. Printed for T. Bowman, pr. 6 d.

11. Hortus Elthamensis, seu Plantarum Rariarum quas in Horto suo Elthami in Cantio coluit Vir Ornatissimus & Præstantissimus Jacobus Sherard, M. D. Soc. Reg. & Col. Med. Lond. Soc. Galielmi. P. M. Frater, Delineationes & Descriptiones quarum Historia vel plane non vel imperfectè à rei Herbariæ Scriptoribus tradita fuit. Auctore Johanne Jacobo Dilienio, M. D. Sold by J. Nourse.

12. The Life of Mr Woolston: With an Impartial Account of his Writings. Printed for J. Roberts, pr. 6 d.

13. A full and true Account of a curious Dialogue between one Mr D'Anvers and one Mr Cat, a great Tobacco Merchant, and one Mr Dash a rich Vintner, which happened on Sunday, at the Sign of the Swan and Hoop in Cornhill. With Remarks thereupon by a Fair Trader. Printed for J. Roberts, pr. 4 d.

14. Good Goose don't Bite: Or the City in a Hubbub. A New Ballad; to the Tune of, Joan sleep'd, &c. Printed for W. Shaw, pr. 6 d.

15. The Scholar's Manual: Being a Collection of Meditations, Reflections, and Reasonings, designed for establishing and promoting Christian Principles and Practice, in Irreligious and Sceptical Times. With suitable Devotions, extracted from some of the best ancient and modern Authors, chiefly in their Original Languages. By a Gentleman of Oxford. Printed for C. Rivington.

16. A Sermon preached before the Lords, by Samuel Lord Bishop of Chester, Jan. 30. 1732-3. Printed for C. King in Westminster-Hall. pr. 6 d.

17. A Sermon preach'd before the Commons, by Dr Mawson. Printed for J. Roberts, pr. 6 d.

18. An Essay upon the Usefulness of Revelation, notwithstanding the great Excellence of Human Reason. In Eight Discourses. By Christopher Robinson, M. A. Printed for J. Pemberton, pr. 2 s.

19 A Sermon before the Sons of the Clergy, by Dr Stebbing, Feb. 1. Printed for J. Pemberton.

20. The Life of Achilles, extracted from various Authors. Printed for J. Roberts, pr. 6 d.

21. The Conjectural Scheme. Being the Contents of the Speech of —— Esq; and Alderman, before the Principal Tradesmen of the Corporation of —— in Opposition to the common Notion of a General Excise. Printed for J. Roberts, pr. 2 d.

22. The Genuine Thoughts of a Merchant, concerning a new Method of levying the Duties on Tobacco and Wine; shewing, that in all the Libels, Remonstrances, and pretended Letters against it, there is not so much as one Word worth answering. Printed for J. Roberts, pr. 6 d.

23. The Congress of Excise Asses: Or, Sir B——ue S——g's Overthrow. Dedicated to the Hon. —Pulteney, Esq; Printed for Mr Nicholas, pr. 6 d.

24. La Zayre, de M. de Voltaire. Representée a Paris aux Mois d'Aoust, Novembre & Decembre, &c. 1732. Augmentée de l'Epitre Dedicatoire, à Paris 1732. Sold by John Nourse.

25. A Memorial concerning the Origin and Authority of the Parliament of France, call'd Judicium Francorum, the Judgment or Tribunal of the Franks. With an Account of the Council of State. Printed for J. Roberts, pr. 6 d.

26. The first Satyr of the second Book of Horace imitated, in a Dialogue between, Alexander

lexander Pope of *Twickenham* in Com' *Middle-son.* Efq; on the one Part, and his learned Council on the other.

27. A Collection of Poems, By the Author of a Poem on the *Cambridge* Ladies, printed by *W. Fenner,* pr. 6 d.

28. The Main Argument of a late Book, intitled, Chriftianity as Old as the Creation, fairly ftated and examin'd: Or a fhort view of that whole Controverfy. Printed for *S. Lobb.* at *Bath,* pr. 1 s. 6 d.

29. He, who worft. may ftill hold the Candle: Or, the Country Gentleman's Addrefs to the Grumbling Traders in London. A new Ballad. To the Tune of, But we'll be as merry with our Comrades, *&c.* Printed for *T. Towers,* pr. 4 d.

30. Modern Amours: Or, a fecret Hiftory of the Adventures of fome Perfons of the Firft Rank. With a Key prefixed. Dedicated to her Grace the Duchefs of *Bolton.* Printed for Mefs. *Parker, Jackfon, Jolliffe,* pr. 2 s. ftitch'd.

31. Free Parliaments: Or, an Argument on their Conftitution, proving fome of thofe Powers to be independent. Printed for *D. Browne.*

32. Orlando, an Opera. Compofed by Mr *Handel.* Engraven on a fair Character. Printed for *J. Welfh.*

33. The Life, Amours, and Adventures of Mr *John Gay.* Author of the Beggar's Opera, *&c.* With a particular Account of his Writings, and alfo explaining feveral Literary paffages therein, hitherto unknown. Printed for *E. Curl,* pr. 1 s. 6 d.

34. A Penitential Office: Or, a Form of Prayers and Interceffions on Behalf of the Church. Recommended to the Ufe of all fuch who mourn for the Iniquities of the prefent Times, and tremble at the Profpect of Impending Judgments. Printed for *C. Rivington,* pr. 6 d.

35. A Brief Effay on the Chronology of fome Paffages contained in the Holy Scriptures, *viz.* Of the Seventy Weeks in the Prophecy of *Daniel.* 2. Of the Time of Chrift's Birth. 3. Of the Time when *John Baptift* began to preach, *&c.* 4. Of the Time of, Chrift's Baptifm. 5. Of the Time when our bleffed Saviour began his Sacred Miniftry, of Preaching, and working Miracles, *&c.* 6. Of the Time of *John Baptift's* Imprifonment, Printed for *J. Roberts,* pr. 2 s.

36. The Law of Pledges and Pawns, as it was in ufe among the *Romans,* and as it is now practifed in moft Foreign Nations. Written on Occafion of the prefent Enquiry into the State of the Charitable Corporation. By *John Ayliffe,* Doctor of Laws. Printed for *F. Clay,* pr. 1 s.

37. The Game Law: Or, the Laws relating to the Game, Containing all the Laws and Statutes for preferving thereof to the Gentry to whom it belongs. With Variety of Law Cafes, *&c.* In Two Parts. Printed for *W. Mears,* pr. 3 s.

38. Authentick Memoirs of that exquifite Villainous Jefuit Father *Richard Wolpole,* lay-

ing open his abominable Practices, and bafe Dealings with that wicked Traytor *Edward Squire,* pr. 1 s.

39. The Oxford Methodifts: Being fome Account of a Society of young Gentlemen, in that City, fo denominated; fetting forth their Rife, Views, and Defigns. With fome occafional Remarks on a Letter inferted in *Fog's* Journal of *December* 9, relating thereto. In a Letter from a Gent. near *Oxford* to his Friend in *London.* Printed for *J. Roberts,* pr. 6 d.

40. The Wanton Countefs: Or, 10.000 l. for a Pregnancy. A new Ballad Opera. Founded on True fecret Hiftory. Dedicated to Sir *Timothy Gaudy,* of *Gaudy Hall, N—h,* pr. 1 s.

41. Propofals offer'd for the Sugar Planter's Redrefs, and for reviving the Sugar Commerce. In a further Letter from a Gentleman of *Barbadoes* to his Friend in *London.* Printed for *J. Wilford.*

42. A Sermon preached before the Learned Society of *Lincoln's Inn,* on *Jan.* 30. from *Job* 34. 30. By a Layman. Printed for *J. Peele,* pr. 1 s.

43. Obfervations on the Sea- or Pile-Worms which have been lately difcover'd to have made great Ravages in the Pile- or Wood-Works on the Coaft of *Holland, &c.* By Mr *Rouffet,* of the Royal Academy of Sciences at *Berlin.* Done from the Original Low-Dutch, and Illuftrated with Copper-Plates. Printed for *J. Roberts,* pr. 6 d.

44. Memoria Technica: Or, a new Method of Artificial Memory, applied to and exemplified in Chronology, Hiftory, Geography, Aftronomy, alfo Jewifh, Grecian, and Roman Coins, Weights and Meafures, *&c.* 2d Edition. Printed for *C. King.*

45. Travels of the Chevalier *D'Arvieux* in *Arabia* the *Defart* Written by himfelf, and publifh'd by Mr *De la Roque*: Giving a very accurate and entertaining Account of the Religion, Rights, Cuftoms, Diverfions, *&c.* of the Bedouins, or Arabian Scenites. Undertaken by Order of the late French King; to which is added, a General Defcription of Arabia, by *Sultan Ifhmael Abulfeda,* tranflated from the beft M S. with Notes, 2d Edition.

46. The Happinefs of Retirement. In an Epiftle from *Lancafhire,* to a Friend at Court. To which is added, An Encomium on the Town of *Prefton.* Printed for *J. Ofwald.* pr. 6 d.

47. An Antidote: Or, fome Remarks upon a Treatife on Mercury; endeavouring to fhrew that the Danger therein afferted of taking it crude is not fupported by Facts, or by Reafon; and that in treating promifcuoufly of Mercury crude, and its various Preparations, all the evil Confequences which often attend it when prepared are affigned to the crude, in Order to alarm People's Fears, and deter them from this innocent and very efficacious Practice. Printed for *J. Roberts,* pr. 6 d.

48. Memoirs of Affairs of State. Containing Letters written by Minifters employ'd in Foreign Negotiations, from the year 1697 to the latter End of 1728. With Treaties, Memorials

moriab, and Tranfactions mentioned in the faid Letters. Publifhed by *Chriftian Cole*, Efq; Printed by *H. Woodfall.*

49. Anacreontis Teii Carmina, accurate edita (græcè) cum notis perpetuis & Verfione Latina Numeris Elegiacis paraphraftice expreffa Accedunt ejusdem, ut perhibentur, Fragmenta; ac Poetriæ Sapphus quæ fuperfunt. Impenfis *L. Gulliver.*

50. An Effay on Man. Addrefs'd to a Friend. Part I. Printed for *J. Wilford,* pr. 1s.

51. A Letter from a Member of Parliament to his Friends in the Country, concerning the Duties on *Wine* and *Tobacco.* Printed for *T. Cooper,* pr. 6d.

52. The Nature of the prefent Excife, and the Confeqnences of its farther Extenfion, examin'd. In a Letter to a Member of Parliament. Printed for *J. Roberts,* pr. 6d.

53. The Court Regifter, and Statefman's Remembrancer. Containing a Series of all the Great Offices, Prime Minifters of State, *&c.* Printed for *R. Gofling,* pr. 2s.

54. Literæ de Re Nummaria, in Oppofition to the common Opinion, that the *Denarii Romani* were never larger than 7 in an Ounce. With fome Remarks on Dr *Arbuthnot's* Book and Tables. And fome other Mifcellanies relating to the fame Subject. Sold by *C. Rivington.*

55. The Englifh Malady; Or a Treatife of Nervous Difeafes of all Kinds, as Spleen, Vapours, Lownefs of Spirits, Hypocondriacal and Hyfterical Diftempers, &c. by *George Cheyne,* M. D.

56. Philofophical Effays on various Subjects *viz.* Space, Subftance, Body, Spirit, the Operation of the Soul in Union with the Body, Perpetual Confcioufnefs, Place and Motion of Spirits, the Departing Soul, the Refurrection of the Body, the Production and Operation of Plants and Animals, with fome Remarks on Mr Locke's Effay on Human Underftanding. To which is fubjoined, a Brief Scheme of Ontology, or the Science of Being in general with its Affections. By *J. W.* printed for *R. Ford.*

57. A Defcription of *Bath*; a Poem. printed for *J. Roberts,* pr. 1s.

58. Free Thoughts on Religion, the Church, and National Happinefs. By *Bernard Mandeville,* M.D. Author of the Fable of the Bees. Printed for *J. Brotherton.*

59. A Compleat Key to the Political Characters in the Ballad Opera of Achilles. Written by Mr *Gay.* With the exact plan upon which it is founded. With critical Remarks upon the whole. Printed for *W. Mears,* pr. 6d

60. A full and particular Account of the barbarous Murders of Mrs *Lydia Dancomb,* Mrs *Elizabeth Harrifon,* and *Anne Price,* that were committed on Sunday Morning, Feb. 4. 1732-3. at N° 3 in Tanfield Court, in the Temple. With a Narrative of the infamous Actions of *Sarah Malcolm,* now in Newgate for the faid Murders. price 6d.

61. The School of Miniature, erected for the Inftruction of the Ignorant, the Improve-

ment of Proficients, and the general Information of fuch as are pleafed with Pictures in Small. Herein are contained the moft expeditious and infallible Ways of Drawing without being taught; and all the Methods of Colouring, Stippling. &c. printed for *S. Harding,* pr. 1s.

62. A Review of the Text of Milton's Paradife Loft: In which the Chief of Dr *Bentley's* Emendations are confider'd; and feveral other Emendations and Obfervations are offer'd to the Publick. To which is added an Appendix Part III. Printed for *J. Shuckburgh.*

63. The Upper Gallery. A Poem. Sold by *J. Roberts,* pr. 6d.

64. Ancient Accounts of *India* and *China,* by two Mohammedan Travellers, tranflated from an Arabian Manufcript, by the learned *Eufebius Renaudot,* Doctor of the Sorbonne, and one of the *French* Academy. for *S. Harding,* pr. 5s.

65. Rofalinda, A Novel. Intermix'd with a Variety of the moft affecting Scenes, both of Diftrefs and Happinefs. By a Man of Quality. Tranflated from the *French.* Printed for *C. Davis,* pr. 4s. 6d.

66. Political State for *Dec.* pr. 1s. 6d.

68. Modern Hiftory.

69. *Bayle's* Hiftorical and Critical Dictionary, tranflated. 8 Sheets a Fortnight, at 1s.

70. The practifing Scrivener, or modern Conveyancer. 8 Sheets for 1s. Weekly.

71. Hiftory of the Popes, No. 3.

Books publifh'd Weekly by Numbers, at 6d. each.
Baker's Chronicle. 5 Sheets.
Acta Regia. ditto.
Rapin's Hift. of *England,* by *Tindal.* ditto.
Jofephus, by Sir *R. L'Eftrange.* ditto.
Sir *Walt. Raleigh's* Hift. of the World. 4 fh.
Dr *Colbatch's* Legacy, or Family Phyfician.
The Magazine of Architecture, by *Oakley.*
Keating's Hift. of *Ireland.*
Hift. of the Bible, printed for *T. Edlin.*
Ditto by Mr *Stackhoufe*
Univerfal Traveller. 2 Sheets, at 3d.
Book of Martyrs. ditto.

85. PHYSICAL and PHILOSOPHICAL REMARKS on Dr DOVER's late Pamphlet, entitled, the Ancient Phyfician's *Legacy* to his *Country,* together with fome Animadverfions on his fcurrilous Treatment of the Profeffors of *Phyfick* in general. With a Word or two on the Ufefulnefs of his *Legacy* to all Private Families. Wherein is likewife fhewn, that the *Enthufiaft* and the *Empirick* is not upon fo good a foot as the *Scholar* and the *Phyfician*; that the former acts upon Uncertainties, and the latter upon fure Rules and Obfervations.
To which is Added
An Account of the Remarkable Cafes of Two Patients, who late Fell under a certain Doctor's Care.
With a Particular Cafe of the Author's on the ufe of the Bark in ftopping Mortifications.
Addrefs'd to the Company of Apothecaries,   By H. BRADLEY, Surgeon
Printed for *C. Rivington,* pr. 2s.

The Gentleman's Magazine:

Lond.Gazette
Londō Jour.
Fog's Journ.
Applebee's ::
Read's :: ::
Craftsman :
D. Spectato;
Grubstreet J
W. ly Register
Free Briton
Hyp Doctor
Daily Court
Daily Post
Dai. Journal
Da. Post boy
D. Advertiser
Evening Post
S. James's Eb.
Whitehall Eb.
Lōdon Eb. fig
Flying Post
Weekly Miscellany
The Auditor

St John's Gate.

York News
Dublin 6 ::
Edinburgh ::
Bristol ::::
Norwich ::
Exeter a :::
Worcester ::
Northampton
Gloucester::
Stamford ::
Nottingham
Bury Journ
Chester ditto
Derby ditto
Ipswich do.
Reading do.
Leeds Mere.
Newcastle
Canterbury :
Birmingham
Manchester
Boston ::: a
Jamaica, &c.
Barbadoes ::

Or, MONTHLY INTELLIGENCER.

For MARCH, 1733.

CONTAINING,
(more in Quantity, and greater Variety, than any Book of the Kind and Price)

I. A View of the WEEKLY ESSAYS, *viz.* Advice to *Indamora* and *Rapax*, Provisions for young Gentlewomen; *Homer's* Notions of Fate, Destiny, &c. Of Lord *Clarendon's* History; Fidelity without Matrimony; New Plays critic'd; *Cromwel's* honest Advice; of Window Blinds, Flap-Fans; a Map of Happiness; Augmentation of poor Livings; Powder and Plaistering, Hoops; High-heels, &c.
II. POLITICAL POINTS, *viz.* Of the *Roman* Senate and Parliament of *Paris*; Excises in *Venice, Holland,* and *England*; Member of Parliament'sLetter; Dulness

excis'd; *Hercules* and *D'amvers*; of State Murmurs; Trade of Taxes; *Chester* Election; *Rochester* Instructions; Tobacco Planters Case with their Factors; Debates on the Pension and Mutiny Bills.
III. SARAHMALCOLM's Paper; Behaviour of the *Hallams* and *Alcock*, Murderers.
IV. POETICAL PIECES. A large Collection; several not printed before.
V. OCCURRENCES FOREIGN and DOMESTIC; Deaths, Marriages, Promotions Prices of Goods, Monthly Bill, &c.
VI. REGISTER of Books.
VII. Table of CONTENTS.

By SYLVANUS URBAN, Gent.

LONDON: Printed, for the AUTHOR, and sold at St *John's Gate*: By F. *Jefferies* in *Ludgatestreet*; at the Pamphlet Shops; and by most Booksellers. Where may be had the former Numbers, or compleat Setts bound; a few on Royal Paper.
N. B. *This Book shall be forwarded Monthly as soon as publish'd to any Part, on sending proper Directions to the Printer at St John's-Gate.*

CONTENTS.

N. B. *The Variety of Schemes that have been built on that of the* Gentleman's Magazine, *and the small Success the Generality of them have met with, is a Confession both of its Usefulness, and the Candour of the Publick in encouraging That which was primarily calculated for their Entertainment. The most assiduous Endeavours shall be used to deserve a Continuance of their Favour, wi hout augmenting the Charge.*

Notwithstanding the Weekly Productions multiply so fast, we trust we shall be able, by a new Letter that is casting for us, to give a Satisfactory Account of the whole Month's. We shall always preserve our Impartiality, and publish our Book as early as any other, tho' it should not happen to be advertis'd so soon in the News-Papers, in some of which our Advertisement has been more than once postponed several Days.

THE
Gentleman's Magazine:
MARCH, 1733.

A View of the Weekly DISPUTES *and* ESSAYS *in this Month.*

No. 167, 168.

M R *Bavius,* after a Differtation on the ufefulnefs of Modern News Papers, condefcends to make fome Remarks on the *Gentleman's Magazine,* and on thofe fet on foot by feveral Bookfellers in imitation of it. He allows us the *firſt* Place, and informs the World, (for which we are oblig'd to him) that we have undertaken to abridge for 6*d.* a Month as many Papers, it ſeems, as would coſt our Country Readers 6*s.* befides Carriage. What further glances from him in our Favour, we ſhall not repeat, fince our Readers have feen the Piecces, (the Originals of which we affure him are not by the fame Perfon) from whence he picks what he judges for his Purpofe. We ought not however to omit that he cenfures our Vanity in publifhing thofe Pieces; but as they were no more than two (out of a great Number fent us in Praife of our Undertaking) we might be allowed to flatter ourfelves they were fincerely meant, and if, we may judge by our Succefs, not wide of Truth; we can produce more Inftances of felf Praife and puffing in the *Grubſtreet* Journal itfelf, whofe Author is pleafed to attack us on this head. His

greateſt Charge upon us is *downright* or *upright* Piracy, as he waggifhly calls it, in printing the works of others fo within the Letter of the Law, that the Injured can procure no Reparation for the Damage, and in this he compares us to the late Mr *Hills,* who *charitably printed* for the fake of the Poor, and fold *ſix penny* Sermons at *one penny* each. Mr *Bavius,* who cenfures the Simile in an Epigram to our Praife; as too wide from the Purpofe, allowing nothing for *poetica Licentia,* does not himfelf bring here even in Profe a Parallel Cafe; for Mr *Hills* printed whole Sermons, ours is only an Abridgement; and in this Point Mr *B.* allows us to have proceeded on the great *Model* of the Bookfellers in Mr *Hills's* Days; we can make appear, that tho' we have had our Property invaded divers Times, yet we are far from being on an equal footing. Several Bookfellers of this Day, who have declared, and their Practice fhews that they will have no Regard at all to what has been called Property. We are from hence perfuaded Mr *Bavius* will, upon a little Recollection, leave us Room to juſtify ourfelves; efpecially, fince he muſt perceive that we proceed in a more defenfible way than fome that have followed us. As to Merit, we fhall only fay, that we have avoided feveral Articles flagrantly Falfe, which other Compilers have incautiouſly tranfcribed, and have earlier Intelligence.

In No 168, Mr No one, gives Mr *Bavius* A List of *proper Names, properly so called,* some of which are as follows, *viz.*

Barrel, a Tapster. Dr Blow, an Organist. Mr Byyard, a Mercer. Mr Cant, a Presbyterian Teacher at *Edinburgh.* Mr Cheatham, Attorney. Mr Cumberfoot, Goaler at *Canterbury.* ——Driver, a Coachman. Peregrine Fury, Esq; of the War-Office. Ginn, a Rat-catcher. Mr Godly, Clergyman. Mr Holyday, a Schoolmaster. Mr Hyde, a Tanner. Hunt, a Bailiff. Keen, a Barber. Mr Latin, a Schoolmaster. Mr Medicine, Apothecary. ——Oats, an Hostler. —Trim, a Barber. —Trowel, a Mason. — Waters, a Waterman. Mr Pen, a Writing Master. Mr Quilton, Upholster. Mr Rodd, a Schoolmaster. Miss Yard, at Coney-hatch, &c. &c. To which we could add a Hundred more Mr Somebody has communicated to us; such as, Mr Post, a Timber Merchant. Mrs Brokenbrow, an old Maid. —Hardy, a Sea Captain. —Raike, ditto. Scrivener, Cerk to an Attorney. The Rev. Mr Church at Cambridge. Mr Coalpits, Agent to the Colliers at Newcastle. Wicket, a Nobleman's Porter. Miss Bright, a Yorkshire Toast. Allsop, a Fellow covetous of Liquor. Cheatham, a Wine Merchant. Mr Majoribanks, of the Bank at *Edinburg.*

We shall break off here, believing we have given some of our Readers too large a Specimen of this Kind of Wit; and having a little room left, will crowd into it the known Story of the Old Man and his Ass, with which one of our Brothers has fill'd two Pages.

THE old Man observing these Truths come
  to pass,
That neither his leading, nor mounting his Ass,
Or his Son's Walking, or Riding, *could please;*
Nor the Ass carrying both; much concern'd,
  be agrees   [Strength,
His Son and himself should join their whole
And carry the Beast; concluding at length
He would satisfy all, and prevent any Jest,
But this last occasion'd more Sneers than the rest.
   M O R A L.
So he who the Praises of all would obtain,
Shews a deal of good Nature, but *labours in vain.*

The Chinese *Gentleman.*

WRiting is the only Test by which a Man of Sense desires to be try'd, and which a Coxcomb dreads and avoids. All Authors agree, that the *Chinese* excell all other Nations in the Art of Government. This is acknowledged by the *French,* who admire those political Maxims collected, methodized, and commented upon by the Great *Confucius.* On these Principles the *Chinese* Government has subsisted 4500 Years; the *Chinese* say much longer. Their *Honours* or *Titles* are not *Hereditary;* a worthless Fellow is so far from being valu'd for the Merit of his Ancestors, that he is more contemptible than the *meanest Mechanick.* No Man cou'd be made a *Mandarine,* i. e. a *Gentleman,* or be capable of any *Post* in the *Government,* who was not a Man of *Parts* and *Learning.*

The *Mandarines* are chosen once a Year at the Metropolis of *China.* Candidates for this *Order* are examin'd in this Manner; Each of them is put into a separate Cell, which is guarded, to prevent any Assistance in the Pieces given him to compose, by which he is to prove himself Master of the *Mandarine* Language, the *Chinese* History, and of the Writings of *Confucius;* and capable of drawing up any Instrument or Act of State; in the *Writing* and *Wording* of which the *Chinese* are very *correct.* These Pieces, when compos'd, are impartially examin'd by a select Number of *Mandarines,* at the Head of whom the Emperor himself always presides. *Excepting the Sovereign's Presence, the Examinations which our Gentlemen at the University pass thro', to prove their Abilities for Future Employments, we conceive, would seem to the* Chinese *as regular and effectual as their own.*

The Address to the Freeholders is received, but we chuse not to be the first to publish any Reflections on so large a Body of the Nation and our Readers, since what has happen'd to the Daily Courant and London Journal. We can't suppose the Freeholders either ignorant of their Interest or Duty.

. The *Hyp.* Feb. 27. and March 2.

Improbe Amor, quid non mortalia pectora cogis?

EVER fince I receiv'd INDAMORA's Letter, (*See* p. 84) my Fears for her made fo powerful an Impreffion on my Mind, that I imagin'd fhe was prefent, and fpoke to her in the following Manner :—Yes, *Indamora*, you are as dear to me as the charming *Hebe*, and with the fame Pleafure · would I refcue you from Danger. (*See p.* 56, G) The Dread of ftarving affords a difmal Profpect ; but

If there's a Power above us, ·
(And that there is, all Nature cries aloud
Thro' all her Works) he muft delight in Virtue,
And, that which he delights in, muft be happy.

This *Sovereign Being*, who feeds the whole Creation, will never let the *Virtuous* perifh : 'Tis he can foften the flinty Heart, and mould into Virtue the moft profligate. An invincible Refiftance in you may work fuch a Change in the diffolute *Rapax* : Perfift in your virtuous Refolution ; your Virtue will fhew him the Bafenefs of his Defign in a Light which ought to give him an Abhorrence of it ; and incite him to behave as becomes a Man of Honour, to the Woman he profeffes to love.

You are born a *Gentlewoman*, and would · fupport the Dignity of your Birth : But ftill the Bitternefs of Want and Poverty furrounds you. Shall a Gentlewoman ftoop to Servitude? How much lefs ought a Gentlewoman to think of fubmitting to what is below the moft abject Degree of Slavery? The meaneft Servant Maid, decked with fimple Virtue, is more a Gentlewoman, than the moft fumptuous Miftrefs. Numbers of the latter Sort have been in Circumftances like yours, who, had they kept true to the firft Impulfe of their *Virtue*, would not have had fo juft a Right to fay, with the Poet,

Drive me, o drive me, from that Traitor, MAN,
So I might 'fcape that Monfter, let me dwell
In Lyon's Haunts, or in fome Tyger's Den !
Can there be found fo terrible a Ruin
As MAN, falfe MAN, fmiling deftructive MAN?
You may judge from hence, on which Side I would have *Victory* incline.—

As to *Rapax* ; methinks I fee him wantonly gazing on the beauteous *Indamora* : I know his eager Wifhes to poffefs the lovely Maid. Hold, ungenerous *Rapax* ! Cannot ·fuch amiable Innocence, ftop the Impetuofity of your Defires ? Can you be a Gentleman, and turn the Neceffity of a Woman to her Ruin? Prefer a Method that will make your Pleafure and Honour agree. Indulge your Love, and act the Man of Honour, by marrying her. But fhe has no Fortune ! What then? Your Honour will not fuffer from her Family; and her Beauty and her Virtue are fufficient to compenfate her want of Fortune. Confider, the Wife that brings a Fortune proportionable to your Eftate, will expect her *Equipage*, *Drefs*, &c. fuitable to the Portion fhe brings you ; whereas *Indamora*, grateful as *virtuous, frugal* as *handfome*, will not look after fuch Pageantry ; but by a Juftnefs of OEconomy, be more valuable to you than the haughty, richportion'd Wife. You would be glad to have your Name perpetuated, and your Eftate tranfmitted to ·your Children ; if fo, what Iffue may you not hope from the deferving *Indamora* ? Is it not natural to believe they will inherit the Mother's Virtue and Beauty, together with the Grandfather's Honour and Integrity !——

The Subject of this Paper reminds me of the noble Foundation of St *Cyr* by the celebrated *Madam de Maintenon*, for the Education and Provifion of Gentlemen's Daughters ; and an Infcription, on a Monument in *Weftminfter Abbey*, for *Charles Godolphin*, Efq; which commemorates an Inftitution of his to educate in a fuitable Manner, eight young Gentlewomen *born fuch* ; and I would recommend this elevated Beneficence to our Quality. ·

MARCH 2.
—— fragili quærens illidere dentem
Offendet folido. . *Hor.*

I Am accufed, in the following Letter, of the *very thing*, I had condemn'd in *Rapax*.

Q

Mr

Mr. Auditor,   *Feb. 25.*—

EVer since I told you my lamentable Story I have impatiently expected some Comfort at your Hands; but I find even the Auditor is a Man. I was this Morning reflecting on the Pleasure a good Parent must have, when he can leave his Children free from the Temptations Want may expose them to; and that such a Condition might have been mine, had not Providence otherwise decreed. At the same Instant I happen'd to lay my Hand on a Pistol, the only thing I have that belong'd to my poor Father; and began to think he left it me as a Legacy, with which to free my self from the Danger I was in. At the same Time Rapax enter'd my Apartment, and accosted me much to this Purpose: "Sure, Miss, you could not imagine I should mistake you under the Name of Indamora; I have long known the Auditor, and knew what he would say, before I read his Animadversions on your Letter; and to shew you how much he thought your Refusal your Disadvantage, he has painted your Distress, and forbore declaring an Opinion you may conjecture from his Conclusion: Let me add his Weight to my earnest Solicitations."—I stopp'd him, and shew'd him my Father's Legacy: Rapax, said I, do you think Heaven gave you much, and me nothing, without making me otherwise amends? Know, I have Virtue and Honesty proportion'd to your Riches. If you will make me your Honest Wife, I'll endeavour to forget the Destruction you intended me; but I will never be your abandon'd Mistress: the Moment you renew your Attempts I know how to free my self, and rid the World of a Villain. He made me a reverend Bow, and withdrew. Upon reading your Paper of the 20th, I too plainly perceiv'd your Friendship for Rapax. You have painted my Distress in more lively Colours, than my real Sufferings would permit me to do, in order to make me taste the Thought of a different Life. If it be any Pleasure to you to hear my last

Resolution, remember, Life and Virtue have the same Duration with

INDAMORA. —

Whoever this fair Volunteer is, (for she is not the same who wrote the first Letter,) I dare say, were she in the Case of the true Indamora, she would have little Occasion for my Advice.

There are some People who are very ingenious in giving a good natur'd Sentiment an evil Tendency. Severity, and Haughtiness of Virtue, has undone more Persons than a little Relaxation has harmed.

The Auditor proceeds to shew the Unreasonableness of those who would banish from Society one who, pressed by hard, hard Misery, strays a little from the Strictness of Virtue's Rules; yet shew Respect to such in Affluence, and even to those luxurious Wives, who uncompelled, and of Choice, do the same Thing. He adds, If a Man thro' Good-Nature, pities the former, he is immediately a Favourer of Vice, a Corrupter of Morals. Let me look kindly on the Unfortunate, as long as I see Vice is not their Inclination; let me be just, but not severe.

Shakespeare has found room for Pity, where he would have been excusable had he shewn the greatest Hardness of Heart. This appears in the Words he puts into the Mouth of the Ghost of Hamlet's Father, when he bids him revenge his Murder:

But howsoever thou pursu'st this Act,
Taint not thy Mind, nor let thy Soul contrive
Against thy Mother, ought.—
Oh! step between her and her fighting Soul.

Yet Hamlet's Mother committed Adultery, and murder'd her Husband.

Mr Auditor,

WE hear in the Country that you have cry'd down long Sticks.—I have a Brother, whose Life depends on his being humour'd; nothing will please him but a long Stick.— Now he has over his big Belly, a short Waistcoat, and a Coat without a Waist, and thinks a long Stick would make him a complete Gentleman.—Therefore, dear

Mr *Auditor*, let not a hopeful Youth be loft for one long Stick, for he will pine toDeath, if you don't allow it him; and you fhall hear farther from

Country Chloe.

Fog's Journal. March 5. N° 226.

Of Corruption in the Roman Senate.

I Sometimes make myfelf merry, fays *Fog*, with thofe Parts of Hiftory, which difcover the impudent and flagitious Conduct of a Corrupt *Roman Senate*.—The whole Proceeding carried on in that Senate againft *Jugurtha* was a meer Farce; for though at firft, their Refentment ran high againft him, he fent Ambaffadors to *Rome*, with fuch large Sums of Money, for the Senators, that inftead of one 3d Part of the Kingdom, it was agreed he fhould have Half. He afterwards kills his Partner in the Kingdom; for which an Army was fent againft him; but he found Means to corrupt both Senate and Generals with *Numidian* Gold; on which *Fog* demands Where is the Wonder that fo infamous a People fhould lofe their Liberties?

Some Time after, *Cicero* propofed, that the Law for punifhing Governors of Provinces who fhould plunder the People, and Officers for imbezzling the publick Money, fhould be repeal'd; becaufe, fays he, when once a Man is guilty, he can't be fatisfied with enough for himfelf, unlefs he has fufficient to bribe the corrupt Part of the Senate, to protect him from the Penalties of this Law, and therefore it would be a Benefit to the People to have it repeal'd.

When *Olivarez* and *Vafconcellos* were Minifters for *Spain*, Complaints were made againft a Perfon in a high Station at *Mexico*, that he had made an immenfe Fortune by indirect Means. Upon this a Friend of his wrote to him in this Manner; " I have heard you have fill'd your Coffers by various Extortions, and I hope it is true, for then you may depend upon the Protection of our Minifter, who does what he pleafes; — if you have taken but

little, you are undone; therefore mend your Hand, if it be not too late."

Thus it is that every thing goes under a corrupt Adminiftration. How happy are the People where no fuch Scenes are acted!

The Craftfman. March 3. No, 348,

Excifes in Venice, Holland, *and* England *compar'd.*

IN *Venice* and *Holland*, the *Officers of Excife* are empower'd only to collect thofe Duties, not to harrafs the People; whereas *our Excifemen* may put the fair Trader to infinite Trouble, after the Crown is fully fatisfy'd.—The *Dutch Excifemen* have no Power of entring and fearching Houfes as the *Englifh* have.— In *Holland* they are not appointed by the *Stadtholder*, nor in *Venice* by the *Doge*; as in *England* they are by the King, and removeable at his Pleafure.—In *Holland* and *Venice*, thefe Duties are entirely apply'd to the Publick Service; but in *England* great Part of the *Fines* and *Forfeitures* comes into the Pockets of the *Crown Officers*, and tempts 'em to opprefs the Subject.

Another Circumftance with Regard to *Excife* in *Holland*, and which makes it impracticable here, is, The *Provincial States of Holland* meet four Times a Year. During the Interval of their Seffions a *Committee* fits continually, and calls them together as they feeCaufe. With their *Summons*, they fend a *Particular of the Heads* to be debated by the *Affembly*, that every City may give fuch Orders to their *refpective* Deputies as they judge proper. But our *worthy Advocates for Excifes* contend that the Cities and Boroughs of *Great Britain*, are guilty of Sedition, in giving their *Proxies* Inftructions to oppofe an Extenfion of *Excife Laws*, tho' unanimous in their Opinion of its bad Confequences. Nay the old Court Party of *Abhorrers*, fo juftly branded by Parliament in the Reign of K. *Charles* II. begins to revive and menace us, with the profound Mr. *Ofborne* at their Head.

As

As to the Government of *Venice*, the *Doge* is little more than a *Pageant of State*, is no Gainer by that *Dignity*, his Income not being equal to his Expence; he pays a larger Share of the Taxes than any other Perſon and is liable to be called to an Account. - But the King of *Great Britain* hath not only a *civil Liſt* of near one Million *per Ann.* for the Support of his Royal Houſhold, but is alſo intruſted with the Diſpoſition of the *publick Revenues*. All Officers, civil and military, are in his Nomination, and moſt of them removable at his Pleaſure. He appoints and tranſlates the *Biſhops*. In ſhort, nothing can reſtrain the Power of the Crown from being *abſolute*, but the perſonal Virtues of the *Prince*, and the Continuance of a free and *uncorrupt Parliament*.— The *Exciſes* in *France* are under much the ſame Regulations with Regard to *Officers*, as thoſe in *Venice* and *Holland*.

But, ſay theſe *Advocates for Power*, the Merchants ſhall have greater Encouragement by an *Exciſe* than they now enjoy; and the Fetters will be ſo nicely fitted that the Wearers will be in Love with them, and verify the Prediction of our *excellent Laureat*, in his *Birth Day* Ode.

And haughty Britons *hug their Chains*.

But ſurely the *Merchants* are the beſt Judges in Caſes of this Nature. It is downright *Popery in Politicks*, to call Chains and Incumbrances on Trade, *Liberty* and *Encouragement*.

If it could be ſo managed that the Burthen ſhould not fall directly on the *Importers*, would not the Oppreſſion of the *Retailers* ultimately affect them?

The modeſt Author of the *genuine Thoughts* tells us, that *the Loſs in the Duties on* Wine *and* Tobacco *does not fall far ſhort of* 12 d. *in the Pound upon* Land *; and that all* Frauds *will be prevented, if the* Retailer *pays the Duty*,] Were this true, near 500,000 *l. per Ann.* would be advanced by an *Exciſe* on *Wine* and *Tobacco*; but a great Part of theſe Duties being appropriated to

the Uſe of the *Crown*; the Publick will have only a Part of *this Advance*. If the *Civil Liſt* therefore be conſiderably augmented, and the Number of Officers increaſed, may not it prove dangerous to the Conſtitution? The Safety of *Europe* is preſerved only by a *due Balance of Power*. The Safety of all *free Governments* is founded on the ſame *Equilibrium*.—Is not the Power of the *Crown* greater, and the *Civil Liſt Revenues* larger than in former Ages?—Let it be conſider'd whether the People have too much Power. They have concurred, almoſt univerſally, in their Declarations againſt *this Project*, without Regard to *Party Diſtinctions*, or *Differences in Religion;* yet the *Scheme* is ſtill purſued; and the, *Projector* hath declared his Reſolution to make an Attempt on their *Repreſentatives*, to put them under this *Yoke*.— Doth not this ſhew that the united Strength of the *whole People* is inconſiderable in his Eyes? And if he ſhould ſucceed, will it not be a Demonſtration, that the People do not abound with too much Power, even at this Time? or rather, that the *Balance* is already too much againſt them?

The Author of the *genuine Thoughts*, tells us, that *in a Revolution Government, the* Crown *ſignifies no more than the* Conſtitution, *or the executive Power of the Laws*.] This is admitted; but how will it ſerve his Purpoſe? For the *Revolution* was founded on Principles of *Liberty*, and with a Deſign of abridging the Power of the *Crown;* whereas the *Crown* is already poſſeſt of more Power than it enjoy'd under any of the *Stuarts*.

Univerſal Spectator: March 3. No. 230.

Homer's Notions of Fate, Deſtiny, &c.

HOMER imagines all *Events* proceed from the ſole *Will* and *Pleaſure*, of *Almighty* JUPITER, whoſe *Appointment* of the *Means* or *ſecond Cauſes* of their being *brought about* is what he means

means by *Fate*, which operates so as to leave a *Free Will* to Man.

We shall find, says Mr *Pope* in his Notes, *Homer* assigns three Causes of all the *Good* and *Evil* that happens in the World.. 1. *The Will of God*, superior to all. 2. *Destiny* or *Fate*, meaning the Laws and Order of Nature, affecting the Constitutions of Men, and disposing them to Good or Evil, Prosperity or Misfortune; which the *supreme Being* may over-rule, but which he generally suffers to take Effect. 3. Our own *Free Will*, which either by *Prudence* overcomes those *Influences* and *Passions*, or by *Folly* suffers us to fall under 'em. All these Particulars are illustrated from the Speech of *Jupiter*, and other the following Passages.

Celestial States, immortal *Gods* give ear.
Hear our *Decree*, and rev'rence what ye hear:
The fix'd *Decree*, which not all Heav'n can move,
Thou *Fate!* fulfill it———— IL. 8. v. 7.

Ourself will sit and see the Hand of *Fate*
Work out our *Will*——— IL. 20. v. 34.

Against what *Fate* and pow'rful *Jove* ordain,
Vain was thy Friend's *Comands*, thy *Courage* vain.

For he, the *God*, whose *Counsels* uncontroll'd,
Dismay the Mighty, and *confound* the *Bold*;
The *God* who *gives*, *resumes*, and *orders* all,
He *urg'd* thee on, and *urg'd* thee on to *fall*.
————v. 841.

This is not unlike what we meet with, 2 *Chron. Chap.* 16. where *God* makes use of an *extraordinary* Method to incline *Ahab* to go to *Ramoth Gilead*, whither he *went*, and was *kill'd*, notwithstanding the Prophet's Warning:

For *wicked Ears* are deaf to *Wisdom*'s Call,
And *Vengeance* strikes whom *Heav'n* has doom'd to *fall*. ODYS. 16. v. 300.

JUPITER's Speech, *Odys.* I. v.
Perverse Mankind, whose *Will*'s created *free*,
Charge all their *Woes* on *absolute Decrees*
All to the dooming *Gods* their *Guilt* translate,
And *Follies* are miscall'd the *Crimes* of *Fate*.
When to his Lust, ÆGYSTHUS gave the Rein,
Did *Fate*, or *We*, th' adult'rous Act *constrain*?
Did *Fate*, or *We*, when great ATRIDES dy'd,
Urge the bold *Traitor* to the *Regicide*?
HERMES I sent, while yet his *Soul* remain'd
Sincere from *Royal Blood*, and *Faith prophan'd*?
To *warn* the *Wretch*, that young ORESTES grown
To manly Years should re-assert the Throne,
Yet *impotent* of *Mind*, and *uncontroll'd*,
He plung'd into the *Gulf* which Heav'n *foretold*.

By this *Messenger* (*Hermes* or *Mercury* we are to understand *Reason*, or the *Light* of *Nature*, which Heaven implants in the Breast of every Man, and continually dictates to him, *This is good*, or *this is evil*.

That a certain *fatal Moment* was decreed by *Destiny*, which could not be *retarded*, but might be *hastened*, HOMER and VIRGIL both agree. See IL. 20. v. 41.
————*Ilion's* sacred Wall
May *fall* this Day, tho' *Fate* forbids the *Fall*.
IL. 20. v. 41.

And VIRGIL writes, speaking of the Death of *Dido*; *Lib.* 4.
————*nec* Fato, *merita nec morte peribat*,
Sed misera ante diem.————

They likewise extended *Destiny* (or the *Care of Providence*) to the very *Beasts*.

As when the Force of *Men* and *Dogs* combin'd,
Invade the Mountain *Goat*, or branching *Hind*,
Far from the *Hunter*'s Rage secure they lie,
Close in the Rock——*not fated yet to die*.
IL. 15. v. 308.

In the Book of *Jonah* Gods Compassion towards the *brute Beasts*, is one of the Reasons himself gives against destroying *Nineveh*. *Shall I not spare the great City, in which there are more than Six score thousand Persons, and also much Cattle?* Matt. Chap. 13. Ver. 29. *Are not two Sparrows sold for a Farthing? and yet one of them shall not fall to the Ground without your Father.* God had even fix'd the time for the Destruction of *Nineveh*; yet forty Days and Nineveh *shall be overthrown*: Notwithstanding, when the People *lamented* their *Transgressions*, and cried mightily unto God, *he repented of the Evil that he had said he would do unto them, and* he did it not. So. HOMER, IL. 17. v. 380.

There have been *Hero's*, who by virtuous Care, By Valour, Numbers, and by Arts of War, Have *forc'd* the *Pow'rs* to save a *sinking State*, And gain'd at length the glorious Odds of Fate.

Weekly Miscellany, March 3. N° 12.
Of Ld Clarendon's *History.*

A Gentleman, who signs himself *Oxoniensis*, endeavours to prove the Genuineness of Ld *Clarendon*'s History, a new Edition of which is now ready for Publication at *Oxford*.

This Writer does not examine the Charge of Mr *Oldmixon* (see p. 514.) and Mr *Clark* of *Hull*, but considers the Proofs which the *Work itself* brought into the World with it.

The Evidence he brings is *external* and *internal*; such as arises from the *Testimony of others*, or from the *Work itself*; both which concur in Proof that

that this History was the genuine Work of the Ld *Clarendon.* The Uniformity of Style, and the Congruity of the Whole with the Sentiments, Conduct, and Character of *the reputed* Author, is an *internal* Proof of its Genuineness.

The *external* Evidence, is the Testimony of the Editors, who were the Sons of the noble Author, *viz.* Henry Earl of *Clarendon,* and *Lawrence* Earl of *Rochester,* under whose joint Authority the Preface was addreſs'd to the World, tho' the E. of *Rochester's* Pen is only to be distinguiſh'd. It came to the Preſs in his Hand, and was printed as it came to the Preſs; and both Brothers jointly declare their Fidelity in executing the Truſt their Father repoſed in them by his Laſt Will, of publiſhing this Work, juſt as it was deliver'd to them.

That theſe noble Editors could not be capable of *interpolating* or *forging* any part of the Hiſtory, will be allow'd from the Teſtimony of Bp *Burnet,* who gives a great Character of their Honour, Sincerity, and Worth.

London Journal. March 3. N° 714.
Hercules *and* D'anvers *compar'd.*

IN the *Craftſman* of *Jan.* 13. one of Mr *D'anvers's* Correſpondents had compared him to *Hercules.* After a little Banter, *Philo-mythologus* gives ſome Particulars where the Reſemblance holds good, between 'Squire *Hercules* the Elder, and 'Squire *D'anvers.*

Hercules was called up to *Olympus* by *Jupiter,* as an Auxiliary in the War with the Giants, in Conſequence of a Rumour that thoſe Rebels could not be over-come unleſs ſome *Mortal* ſhould aſſiſt in the War; all which figure the monſtrous *High Church Rebellion* in the late Reign; and the Sovereign's Grace and Condeſcenſion in calling ſuch a *Mortal* to his *Councils* and *Adminiſtration;* and that to a *Rumour* he owed his Riſe.

Hercules is ſaid to have marry'd *Hebe* the Goddeſs of Youth, who chancing

to make a Slip had ſuffer'd Diſgrace ; but *Osborne* does not inſiſt much on this *Circumstance.*

It's ſaid, that the Travels and Labours of *Hercules* were owing to the ill Fate he was born under, whereby he was oblig'd to ſubmit to whatever Labours *Euriſtheus* ſhould impoſe upon him to deſtroy him. This typifies the *ſervile Obſequiouſneſs* of the *Craftſman,* who hath every Topick of Calumny dictated to him by *Fog,* in *order to bring him to Deſtruction.*

The firſt Labour impoſed on *Hercules* was, to deſtroy the *Nemæan Lyon* that fell from the Circle of the Moon, and had a Skin invulnerable. He attack'd it in vain with his *Arrows;* but bruiſing it with his Club he tore it to pieces with his Hands, and made a Garment of the Skin. By the *Lion* is meant the *Britiſh State,* the *Lion* being its *Arms, Creſt* and *chief Supporter;* that it had fallen from the *Moon,* ſignifies from a *Changeableneſs* in its Councils, to a *ſteady Management* and Purſuit of its true Intereſt. By his *Arrows* are meant the *malicious Aſperſions* thrown at thoſe in Authority to no purpoſe. His bruiſing with his *Club* denotes the *ſavage* Spirit of the 'Squire, and the *barbarous* Manner in which he lays about him. By the *Lion's Skin* muſt be meant, the *Large Grants* obtained from the *Crown,* which, as a *Garment,* may be ſaid to inveſt, and defend him from thoſe Laſhes of the Law, which *Pauper Scribblers* are expoſed to.

Hercules being ſtruck with Madneſs ſlew his *own Children,* imagining them to be *Enemies;* a glaring *Type* of the Male-treatment the 'Squire has beſtow'd upon his *beſt Friends.*

Hercules was adviſ'd to go to *Atlas,* and hold up the *Heavens* in his ſtead; a *Type* of our 'Squire's Ambition to ſupplant one of the ableſt Stateſman of the Age.

Hercules's Wife ſuſpecting his *Fidelity* ſent him an invenom'd Coat, which threw him into ſuch a *burning Fever* and raging *Torments,* that, not able to
endure

endure it, he made a Pile of burning Wood on Mount *Ætna*, and flung him-self into it. This intimates, that the Fury which revels in the 'Squire's Blood, tears his Breast, distracts his Head, and misguides his Pen, may be the *Effect* of some *fatal.Present* made him by one of the *fair Sex*; that his *unreasonable Torments within* cause him to fall thus furiously upon all *without*, and may lead him to end his Course in a Blaze, for which he need not *pile up* much wood, since his *own Papers* may prove sufficient to singe him.

The Auditor, March 6. No. 17.

Felices ter & amplius
Quos irrupta tenet Copula; nec malis
Divulfus queremoniis
Supremâ citius solvet Amor die. *Hor.*

THE *Auditor* makes some Difficul-ty in publishing the following Letter, as it encourages, tho' indirectly, a Method of Life. not suitable to the Laws of Society now in force, and to glance at one founded on those very Laws; but as the Writer's Design is to make a proper Distinction between such Women as *Constantia* is supposed to be, and the common Prostitutes of the Town; and to shew how commenda-ble Fidelity is in any Shape; that tho' Marriage could secure Reputation, it was no Fence against the evil Courses of a Mind wickedly bent. These Rea-sons prevail'd on him to publish it, how-ever with a Caution to his fair Readers to suspend their Judgment, till he gives them a Clue to lead them thro' *Fidelio's* pleasing Maze.

Mr Auditor,

I Never saw a fine Woman, but I con-ceived an Idea of Constancy to her Individual: But I found my Ideas of Constancy so constantly interrupted, that I began to imagine there was no Dependance upon my self; therefore I determin'd against Marriage; but ha-ving entertain'd some pleasing Concep-tions of that sort of Life, I resolv'd to make a Trial, tho' in a peculiar way.

It was not long before I found an Object that drew my whole Attention; I soon perceived my Addresses in the honourable Way were not disagreeable. to the fair *Constantia.* The more I convers'd with her, the more I was con-vinc'd she deserv'd my sincerest Regard.

Constantia was her own Mistress, and in Possession of a plentiful Fortune; and was only unhappy in loving a Person, who from his natural Inconstancy was little capable of making a just Return. What could I do? I loved her, she me. In short I told her plainly, I loved her too well to marry her. It is impossible to paint the Passion, Rage, Love, and Despair, in the Colours she then shew-ed them—Much she said, and when she had done, I told her how much she wronged me; that if she thought me so much a Man of Honour from the Experience she had of me, as to be-lieve me incapable of Baseness, we might live together as Man and Wife; her Fortune would be her own, and if I should prove a Villain, she might re-tire with the same Income she brought. Many Difficulties were started on her side; but at last I laid them all; and we have lived together these ten Years without the least *Matrimonial Jarr.* Nor have I had the least Inclination to change: Her Interest has been mine, and mine hers; and I believe the know-ing ourselves free, has united us more strongly than all the Ties of Art can invent.

So far we are compleatly happy, and there are three or four Ladies in the Town nearest us, of no great Reputa-tion for Constancy to their Husbands, who, over their Tea-Table, speak of *Constantia* as one who had prostituted her Chastity. You may tell me, the Remedy for this is in my own Power, by marrying the Person I have been so long happy with. But why should I, to obviate the Impertinence of a few, run the Risque of altering the Scene of my Happiness? And how am I certain that the Thoughts of being irrevoca-bly tied, may not revive my old incon-stant Temper? All I expect from your

printing

printing my Cafe is, to ftop the Scandal of the Ladies before mentioned; to let them know how commendable Fidelity is in any Shape; and to affure them *Matrimony is no Screen for Vice.*

FIDELIO.

Mr AUDITOR,

I Am a young Woman about 25, unmarried (to my great Misfortune) and fhall remain fo, unlefs you can correct the Men from perfuading us to take their Words. Shew them how much a married State will conduce to *their* Happinefs as well as *ours*; and that no Station of Life can equal *that*, where two Perfons come together with Friendfhip, Love, Honour and Generofity; as for Fortune, if it be on one Side it's fufficient; as to Beauty.

—*Its Blaze, tho' fierce, is quickly paft,
While Love, Good Senfe, and Virtue, always laft.*

As to thofe who are drawn into the Snare of coming together upon Honour, what a miferable Life muft they undergo? A Woman in thefe unhappy Circumftances can never love the Author of her Ruin; fhe only fcars him, and like the *Indians*, worfhips the Devil. And what Satisfaction can accrue to the Man? On the contrary, what a Pleafure muft a Man feel when he comes from the Fatigue of Bufinefs, to be welcom'd by a kind, virtuous Wife, and to fee what he gets, improved by her both to his Credit and Comfort!

Harriot Loveworth.

Grubftreet Journal. March 8. No. 167.
The Tragedy of Cælia *criticis'd.*

Mr BAVIUS,

MY chief Intent, in corresponding with you, is to fhew how infufficient the prefent Managers of *Drury-Lane* Play-houfe are to difcharge their Truft, as Directors of our Entertainments.

The Fable of *Cælia* is this: A modeft young Lady is deluded from her Father's Houfe by a Gentleman who had been hofpitably entertained there; he is with Child; and he provides her Lodging with a notorious Bawd. She had not been long there, before fhe was hurried among common Proftitutes to *Bridewell.* Mean while, the Spoiler of Beauty and Virtue boafts his Succefs, and this falfe Gallantry; but is feverely reprehended by an Acquaintance, formerly an honourable Suitor to *Cælia.* The Father comes to *Bridewell,* and finds his Daughter in a moft forlorn Condition, with a heavy Heart takes her in his Arms, and promifes the Continuance of his paternal Affection. A Meffenger enters, and relates a Duel betwixt the Ruiner of *Cælia,* and her former Lover, in which the guilty fell; foon after *Cælia* expires in her Father's Arms.

This Fable, in the Hands of a Genius, might have been improved into a Play that would have fcourg'd fome of thofe Vices that ruin Thoufands. But the Author followed Nature, without cloathing her in that poetical Drefs which allures the Fancy; the Diction is fuch, as cannot move much more than an accurate Relation of the Tale by a fingle Perfon; yet the late Mrs *Cibber* went thro' the part of *Cælia* fo pathetically, as to draw Tears from *Eyes unufed to the melting Mood*; and was the laft Character that agreeable Actrefs perform'd on the Stage.

This Tragedy is a Proof that fomething more is neceffary in dramatick Poetry, than barely the purfuit of Nature. The Story itfelf is moving, and had the Diction been truly poetical, feveral Paffages would make fuch an Impreffion on the Readers, that on particular Occafions they would recollect and apply them often. For Example, I don't remember that I have been difcompos'd with Liquor for feveral Years paft, but the next Morning I recollected thofe Words of *Shakefpear's Othello,* "O that Men fhould put an Enemy in their Mouths to fteal away their Brains!" This Paffage, ftript of its metaphor, is not worth Obfervation. The Efficacy of Poetry is fuch that it forces itfelf on the Mind, whether any ufeful Doctrine is conveyed in it or not. The following

Lines

Lines, in *Lee's Maſſacre of Paris,* always leave a ſtrong Impreſſion upon me, whenever I recollect them:

Ceaſe, Marmoutier, *the Torrent of thy Tears; Which, when I ſtrive to climb the Hill of Honour, Waſhes my bold away,*

The Beauty of this Paſſage is, the charming Aſſemblage of Ideas made to convey a common Sentiment.

Men of Taſte may judge of what I advance. I dare ſay none of the Managers of Drury-Lane Play-houſe except one, (not the Laureat,) know any more of what I have been ſaying about Taſte, than if I had written in Latin.

As to *Cælia,* the Managers denied it a ſecond appearance on the Stage, tho' it had more merit than the *Boarding School Romps,* or the *Devil to pay.*

The Author intituled it *The Deluded Maid;* but the Laureat propoſed to call it *Maidens beware;* which Mr *Booth* rejected, as more proper for Bartholomew-Fair; at laſt they called it *Cælia, or, The Perjur'd Lover.*

The **Free-Briton,** March 8, *and* 15.

Extract of a Letter from a Member of Parliament to his Friends in the Country, concerning the Duties *on* Wines *and* Tobacco.

YOU deſire me to oppoſe any Propoſition for a *General Excise, or any Extenſion of Excise Laws, or any Alteration in the preſent Method of collecting the publick Revenues.*

It was neceſſary to blend theſe ſeveral Things together in order to raiſe a Propoſal, which, if conſider'd ſingly, might appear both *juſt* and *neceſſary.*

With this View a *General Excise* has been eccho'd thro' the Nation as an *intended Project.* But, who ever formed, ſupported, or defended ſuch a Project?

The next Thing you warn me againſt is, any *Extenſion* of the *Excise Laws.* This is an ambiguous Expreſſion, but may be brought under the *third Head* of your Advice, To oppoſe *any Alteration* in the *preſent Method* of *collecting the Revenues.* To which let

it ſuffice to anſwer, that *Taxes* are abſolutely neceſſary to the *Being of all Governments;* and the chief Care of the Legiſlature is to impoſe ſuch as are *eaſiⁱeſt borne.*

The late Wars have occaſioned many Taxes, but they have been ſo prudently manag'd, with an inviolable Regard to the *Publick Debts,* that they are more than ſufficient to anſwer the annual Intereſt, and to diſcharge *one Million* yearly of the Principal; to Thoſe who then moſt contributed to ſupport the publick Expences. This being the Caſe, and the Tax on Land being already reduc'd from 4 *s.* to 1 *s.* in the Pound; and if it ſhall be found practicable to continue this ſeaſonable *Eaſe to the landed Intereſt;* if the *Annual Exigences of the Government* can be ſupplied; if the growing Intereſt may be duly paid to the Creditors of the Publick; if a *Million per Ann.* may be applied to the Diſcharge of *publick Debts,* without burthening the Land, or laying any *new* or *additional* Duty on any Commodity; is not ſuch a Propoſition worthy the mature Deliberation of Parliament?

The *Frauds* committed in the Importation and Exportation of *Wine* and *Tobacco* are ſo great, that no *Duty* is paid for at leaſt *one Half* of them conſumed at Home. How the propoſed Alteration will prevent theſe Frauds will appear thus:

There is but one Opportunity at preſent of detecting an *unfair Trader:* if he gets his Goods landed without the Inſpection of a *Cuſtom-houſe Officer,* there's no farther Check; (without an Information) But if he won't run the Hazard of a Seizure, 'tis worth his while to blind the Officer with a large Bribe, and then he is, and muſt be, his Slave for ever. Thus the Publick has been doubly defrauded by falſe Weights and falſe Meaſures; ſmall Weights at Importation, by which the Duty is paid; large Weights on Exportation, by which the Duty is drawn back.

Tobacco is exported in groſs and with the Stalks. Now, if the Exporter's Correſpondent

R

respondent abroad will get it cut and stript, and contrive some Method *to run it in again*, he sells it to the *Consumer*, and makes a *double Profit*, by receiving a second Time the *whole* Duty of the Tobacco, so re-imported, from the *Consumer*, which he had before receiv'd from the *Publick*, and which he *never* once paid.

As to the *Frauds* in the *Wine Trade*, they are allow'd to be *equally notorious*; a great deal is *clandestinely run*, the *greatest Part* of what is sold in publick Houses is a *poysonous Composition*; and the *poor Consumer* is again saddled with a Price, as if the Duty was *really paid*.

Since therefore the *Frauds* in both these *Branches* of Trade are *uncontroverted*, the only Question remains, *Whether the Method proposed will not be an effectual Remedy? and if so, Whether, the Remedy be worse than the Disease*; But these Questions are both answer'd by the Effect of the Alteration in collecting the Duties on Tea, Coffee, and Chocolate, to Excise, which in 8 Years last past, has produc'd above a Million of Money more to the Publick, than in the former 8 Years, and without any Inconvenience.

Universal Spectator, March 10. No. 212.

A Project of Projects.

INstead of an Excise on *Wine* and *Tobacco*, Mr *Stonecastle*, proposes to have it laid on a *Staple* Nusance of this Kingdom, call'd *Dullness*. The Tax, says he, would be almost *general*, but then it would conduce to the *Good* of the People, and prove a large Increase of the publick Revenues.

Every one may observe the publick Spirit of the *Projector*, in proposing an Excise, of which himself must bear a large Proportion. He might, indeed, doubt the success of the Scheme, as it is not calculated to serve any *Party*; but the Novelty of Self-denial only, may gain over some to his Design: Yet he can scarce imagine he shall make Proselytes of the *learned* Mayors, &c. of Corporations, who have already

shewn their Resentment to *Excises under any Denomination.*

'Tis a Maxim in Politicks, that all Taxes or Excises be equally laid on the Body of the People. What then can be more justly calculated than this? Where there can be no peculiar Indulgence either to the *landed* or the *money'd Man*, to the Commonalty or Nobility?

It's to be apprehended some Corporations will send their Instructions to oppose it, and that several *Bodies Politick*, and *Sagacious Societies* may think their *Charters* infring'd; and the Major Part of the Senior Fellows of *Colleges* may be disgusted at this Project, as abrogating the Privileges they have enjoy'd Time out of Mind; however among those learned Bodies it is pretty sure of some *Patrons*; such will be the Undergraduates of each University, in hopes of seeing Pecuniary Mulcts set on their *Tutors* and *Deans*, who had often set many on them.

As the *Sages of the long Robe* may *themselves* incur the Penalties of the *Act*, by resolving Knotty Points, in settling the Degrees of *Dullness*, it will be proper to distinguish those which shall be *cognizable* by Law.

Political Dullness, seems the first Degree to be *Excised*: But as several *eloquent Orators* in the *Senate* may look on it as a Design on their *Freedom of Speech*, there must be allow'd some Exemptions: However it should reach to every Coffee-House Orator, who upon lawful Conviction of *dully defending* or *accusing* Affairs of State, should forfeit *Six Pence for each Offence*. The annual Amount of this Branch only within the Cities of *London* and *Westminster*, wou'd at least equal the Duties expected from the Excise on Wine.

Every one under the Degree of an Esquire, who shall be found guilty of making Treaties, forming Alliances, or proclaiming War, shall forfeit *One Shilling*. But as *Jews, Stockjobbers, Infidels* and *Exchange Brokers*, may be entirely impoverish'd by this Clause, they might be allow'd once *per* Month to make Peace or War, &c. *Chelsea* and *Greenwich* Penfioners, Half-pay Officers, Foot Soldiers, Foremaft and Lettermen, Staff-Officers, and Cabbin-Boys, may be allowed the fame Liberty.

Likewife no Excife fhould be laid on any *Papers*, *Tracts*, or *Journals*, that relate to *political Affairs*, not only as it would be a Hardfhip on the learned and voluminous Authors of *Grubftreet*, but as it would be an evident Attempt on the *Liberty of the Prefs*.

Should *Ecclefiaftical Dullnefs* be excis'd : fome perhaps will think the *Church in Danger*. But to obviate any fuch Apprehenfions, let only an Excife of *One Shilling* be laid on every *Sermon* or *Pamphlet* wrote directly or indirectly againft our eftablifh'd Religion, or any fundamental Maxim thereof ; the Authors, if in *Holy Orders*, to be amerc'd double the Sum. This Excife fhould alfo extend to every *Exercife, Declamation, Difputation, &c.* held or deliver'd within the Jurifdiction of either *Univerfity*. This Branch only would raife 4000 *l.* a Term, not including Philofophical or W—d—n Lectures.

Every *known* and *ordain'd Clergyman* who fhall *willingly* and *attentively* hear *irreligious Tenets* advanc'd, and the *holy Scriptures* ridiculed, fhall forfeit *One Shilling*. Provided this do not extend to thofe who have not *Capacity* to confute a Schifmatick, yet have Prudence to fhun him : Provided alfo there is an Exemption to all *young Curates*, and *unbenefic'd Clergymen*, while in Company of their Patrons, otherwife they might lofe all Hope of Preferment.

Fog's Journal. March 10. N° 227.
Mr FOG,

WHen I fent you an Extract from *Vertot's Hiftory of the Revolutions of Portugal*, (See p. 72.) I little thought that harmlefs inoffenfive Letter would have been wire-drawn into Sedition and Defamation. But the Sagacious Mr *Ofborne* has difcover'd a Meaning which neither the Author nor Tranflator of this Hiftory ever intended. It feems as if this Journalift was betraying the Caufe he pretends to defend ; how elfe fhall we account for his applying the Characters of *Sejanus, Woolfey, Vafconcellos, &c.* to his Patron, whenever they are occafionally mention'd by You, or the *Craftfman.*

What induc'd Mr *Ofborne* to expofe his *Patron* by a moft ridiculous Defence (See p. 83.) I will not fay ; but according to his Manner of Reafoning, and by the Aid of his new Doctrine of Parallels, it would not be difficult to extract Blafphemy out of the Bible, and Treafon out of the Hiftory of *Tom Thumb*. As Sir *Walter Rawleigh* was one Day fmoaking his Pipe in his Clofet, a Servant going with a Bafon of Water was fo furprized to find the Clofet full of *Smoak*, and a Cloud iffuing out of his Mafter's Mouth, that he imagin'd the good Man was on fire, and caft the Water in his Face to quench it. How eafily might *Ofborne* adapt this Story to his own Purpofe ? By a fmall Inverfion Sir *W. R.* might be made to ftand for Sir *R. W.* and then by fome ftrong Innuendoes, the Relator of this comical Paffage might be charg'd with Calumny and Sedition, with a Defign to explode the new Scheme for exciting *Tobacco*, and with a moft wicked Intention to excite the the Domefticks of a certain *Hon. Perfon* to drown their Mafter. By the fame Rule many Hiftorical Relations, even in the Old Teftament, might be interpreted fo as to caft the moft odious Colours on the prefent glorious A———. The *Craftfman* and you ought efpecially to beware, whilft Mr *Ofborne* is in this Mood, that you make no mention of *Naboth's* Vineyard, left this old Story be trumpt up to calumniate the new Project of Taxing *Wines*, and to expofe the Iniquity of the *Projector*.

To treat this Matter ferioufly ; whenever Things, or Characters are applied in the Manner of *Ofborne*, there muft be a Confcioufnefs of Guilt.—When I was a Boy, I heard my Grandfather tell
the

the following Story. During the U-
surpation of *Cromwel*, Sir *John* ----
of *Surrey*, one of *Cromwel's* Knights, and
attach'd to his Party, was sued by the
Minister of the Parish for Tythes.
While the dispute was pending, Sir
John fancied the Parson preach'd at him
every *Sunday*. Whereupon he complain'd to the *Protector*, who having
heard the Parson's Defence, and that
he only preach'd in general Terms a-
gainst Whoremongers, Drunkards, Liars, Thieves, and Robbers, he dismiss'd
the Knight with this Reprimand, ‘ Sir
‘ *John*, go Home, and hereafter live in
‘ good Friendship with your Minister.
‘ The Word of the Lord is a searching
‘ Word, and I am afraid it has now
‘ found you out. W. LILLY.

London Journal, March. 10. No. 715.

On State Murmurs.

NO Wickedness is equal to *that of
defaming a good* Government by
Murmurs and *Seditions* unjustly scatter'd among the People. These *State-
Murmurs*, are elegantly describ'd in the
following Lines; and if we put the
Words *General Excise*, &c. in the room
of *young Arthur*, the Description will
exactly suit our Times.

Old Men and Beldames in the Streets
Do *prophesy* upon it dangerously;
General Excise is common in their Mouths,
And when they talk of *That* they shake their
Heads'----
Taylors and mean Artificers, their Work laid by,
Tell of Thousands of devouring Dragons
Landed on *Norfolk* Coast, of Aspect dire;
Then madly roar out GENERAL EXCISE.

This is the *Engine* which the *Jacobites* and *Male-content Whigs* play off
against the Government, tho' they are
assured, that the sole Invention of the
proposed Bill is *more effectually to secure
the Payment of the Duties already laid.*
But this is not the *Voice of the People*,
but of *Fools* led on by *Knaves*, who impose on their Understanding by *Calumny* and *Misrepresentation*; several Instances of which are in the last *Craftsman* (See p. 115) where among other
Falsities, 'tis said, *that the Old Court-
Party of* Abhorrers, *branded in K. Cha.*

*II Reign, begins to revive and menace
us, with the profound* Mr Osborne *at
their Head.* Which is false. The *Abhorrers* he refers to ought to be *abhorred*
indeed; for they made Addresses of.
Abhorrence to the King against those
brave Men who *petitioned* for the sitting
of the Parliament, which was prorogued
about 1679, from Time to Time, on
purpose to put off any further Enquiry
into the Popish Plot, and prevent the
glorious Acts design'd to secure our Liberties and Properties, against the growing Power of Popery and Tyranny.
But the *Abhorrers now*, (of whom *Osborne* owns himself one) abhor Men,
who in their very *Petitions* and *Instructions*, abuse a Parliament which
have always appeared in the *true Interest* of Liberty, charging them with a
Design of passing an Act to destroy the
very being of Parliaments, and totally
subvert the Constitution.

The *Folly* of these Writers and Petitioners is equal to their Wickedness;
for, can any thing be more *ridiculous*
than to affirm, that *Excising Wine* will
destroy Trade, and *subvert our Liberties*? Is the Trade of *Malting* and
Brewing destroy'd by Excise? Or, are
our Liberties *less secure* for a few paul-
try Excisemen, without Family, Interest, or Influence, but over *Knaves*,
who design to cheat the Government?
Nor is there above 150 of this begger-
ly Troop to be added by the *new Scheme*.

Mr. *D'anvers* says, in *Holland* and
Venice, the Officers never harrass the
People after the Duties are paid ;] nor
is any Man harrass'd here who trades
honestly.

Again; the Officers of Excise in
Holland are not appointed by the *Stads-
holder*, nor in *Venice* by the *Doge*; but
in *England* are nominated by the King.]
What a wise Remark is here ! In *Holland*, *Stadtholders* are abolish'd; and if
in *Venice*, they are not chosen by the
Doge, they are by the Government.

The *Craftsman* likewise says, in *Holland* and *Venice*, the Duties by Excise
are applied to *publick Service*? whereas
in

in *England*, great Part of the *Fines and Forfeitures* come into the Pockets of the Crown Officers.] But he should not have oppos'd *Fines and Forfeitures* in *England*, to *Duties* in *Holland*, but have prov'd that the *Duties* in *England* were not applied to the publick Service, and that Appointers of the Officers in those Countries have not the least Gain from *Fines and Forfeitures.*

In *Holland* the People have no Power; they make no Laws, chuse no Officers; nor are tried by their Peers, or *Juries.* The *Senate of Amsterdam,* composed of 36 Persons, chuse all Officers, from one of the States General, to the *Burgo-masters, Eschevins,* and *Scouts.* Sr *Wm Temple* says, when the Burghers, about 150 Years ago, yielded this *absolute Power* to the *Senate of Amsterdam,* it was follow'd by general *Consent,* in all the Towns of the Provinces; therefore the *English* Government is infinitely preferable to that in *Holland.* 'Tis not true, as the *Craftsman* affirms, that great Part of the Duties will be appropriated to the *Civil List;* for a very small Part belongs to it; and even *that,* will remain where it is, in the Customs.

The **Craftsman,** March. 10. No. 349.

THe Author of *The genuine Thoughts* having enrich'd his Performance with Quotations from a Treatise, among the State Tracts, entitled *Taxes no Charge,* published soon after the *Revolution,* with a Design to reconcile the People to the Methods of Taxation then thought necessary, *D'anvers* cites some other Passages from the same Tract, against the *ministerial Writers,* bantering the Arguments they use to recommend, saying they may as well be employ'd to explode, an *Excise, viz.*

We are told, says *D'anvers,* that the *Venetians* pay Excise for every Bit of Bread and Meat, nay for the very Salt they eat] To what Purpose this is quoted, says *D'anvers,* I can't conceive. Don't we pay Excise for every Grain of Salt ten times above the original Va-

lue. Is it not an Excise so grievous as to have occasion'd Insurrections in divers Nations? Nay, the first Introducer of it among the *Romans* was branded to Posterity with the Name of *Salinator,* or what we may call in *English, The Dry Salter.*

The Author of the Tract above-mentioned having condemned all Taxes which tend to debauch and impoverish a Nation, by, *lessening* its *publick Stock,* or *carrying away* its *People,* proceeds thus, ' In both These the *Trade of Taxes* hath the Advantage, it carries nothing out of the Kingdom, on the contrary employs the *Poor,* and many reduced to ask *Charity* are taken into the *Hospital of the Revenue.*] The *Trade of Taxes* (certainly a proper Expression, says *D'anvers,*) has been lately the most *flourishing Trade* in the Kingdom; for, in the *Index to Keeble's Statutes* there's no less than ten or a dozen large Columns in Folio, fill'd up with the single Article of *Taxes.*

What a *noble Hospital* is that of the Revenue, how amply endow'd within these few Years? I dare say, it contains at present above three Times as many *Pensioners* as *Chelsea* and *Greenwich* put together.

The *Trade of Taxes* (adds the Author) employs the *poor Artizans* and *Mechanicks* more than our *Virginia* and *Plantation Trade*;] It's surprizing, says *D'anvers,* none of the *Advocates for Excises* have yet insisted on these Arguments. How might they have expatiated on the Advantages of a *General Excise,* by enlarging the *Hospital of the Revenue,* and making a parcel of idle Fellows useful to the State, by enabling them to spend Money, without any Stock of their own? They might likewise from hence have taken Occasion of removing those popular Prejudices, in Favour of our *Virginia and Plantation Trade,* which have possess'd a great many silly People, and recommending the *Trade of Taxes,* in the Room of it, as the only desirable and beneficial Commerce in the Kingdom.

free

Free Briton Extraordinary, March 11.
On the Chester Election, in Answer to
the Craftsman of Feb. 24. (See p. 87.)

THIS being a long Defence of Mr
Manley, a particular Justification
of his and his Friends Conduct at the
late Elections for Mayor and Representative for Chester, throws the Charge
of beginning the Riots on the other
Party, and asserts, That the Livery Servants of WATKIN WILLIAMS WYNN,
Esq; armed with Pistols, on Horseback,
march'd into Chester the 11th of October, at the Head of 8 or 900 Welchmen
with Clubs, Staves, and other dangerous Weapons, crying Down with the
Rumps, knocking down and wounding
several Persons; they were welcom'd
by Mr Wynn and other Gentlemen with
their Swords drawn, with loud Huzza's,
and entertained at the Expence of the
Grosvenor-Party, they being brought in
to protect the Magistrates in their illegal Design to make 300 honorary Freemen. This extraordinary Proceeding
oblig'd the Citizens to arm in their
own Defence, and they drove the
Welchmen out of the City.

Mr Manley was never at the Head
of any Mob in Chester, excepting on
the Night of this Memorable Day, after the Welch had been defeated; and
this for no other Reason, but the Protection of Mr W. W. Wynn. Mr Manley accidentally met his Friends in the
Street, after they had drove out the
Welch, and finding they resolved to see
the Welch General out of the Town,
with some Indignity to his Person, Mr
Manley rather chose to be conducted
Home by a Multitude, than that this
Multitude should insult a Gentleman
of Mr W. W. Wynn's Rank.

The Citizens of Chester have petitioned the House of Commons, complaining of the Violence offer'd to their Persons, and of the Invasion of their Rights
by the Magistrates, in their illegal Exercise of Power, and in their creating
200 Party Constables in the Face of this
Election, when the City was in per-

fect Tranquillity: But Mr Manley had
too much Regard for the Welfare of
the Citizens to mix his private Interests
with their publick Concerns, or to embroil them with any Contentions, at Westminster, meerly personal to himself. He
rather desired to preserve the Peace of
the City, without disputing the late
Election, or lodging any Petition a-
gainst the Return.

The Auditor, March 13. No. 19.

DIning the other Day at a Great
Man's Table, I observ'd, to my
Surprize, four Wax Tapers brought
in, when only the removing two thick
Blinds from the Windows wou'd have
answer'd the End better; I ask'd his
Lordship, Why he chang'd a natural
Light for an artificial one? He reply'd,
How can one eat with any tolerable Sa-
tisfaction, when one is over-looked by a
Set of Dirty Hungry Rascals, who are
bawling perpetually at the Windows as
long as they can see thro' them, and ready
to eat the Victuals out of one's Mouth.

On returning to my Chamber; his
Lordship's Answer to my Question,
dwelt so strongly upon my Mind as to
cause the following Reflections.

Nature, kind and indulgent to all its
Creatures, has amply furnished the
Earth with more than sufficient for
the Necessity and Pleasure of each Individual: Could Man have been contented, Want would never have appeared
in the World: The inordinate Desire
of more first induc'd one Man to take
both his and his Neighbour's Share;
and as this stolen Wealth necessarily
drew on Dependents, it shewed the Indolent a way of getting more, and toiling
less. Thus it has happen'd that many
are oblig'd to rack their Invention for
Methods of squandering their useless Superfluities, whilst there are too many
Objects, who have not wherewithal to
supply the Necessaries of Life.

How truly great would a Great Man
be, was he to keep up his Grandeur
by relieving the Wretched out of his
Over abundance? Would not a well-
turned

turned Mind receive more Pleasure from the Blessings of poor Objects relieved, through *open Windows*, than his Lordship can have from any *Invention to prevent his seeing the Poor?*

There are many to whom this *should* prove an *useful* Lesson. If Interest is their *Point of View*, let them consider, that every poor Neighbour relieved, is an Acquisition of an humble *Friend*, and a faithful *Dependant*, ready to *assist* upon the least *Summons*. If this can be done only by carefully disposing of the *superfluous* Superfluities of their Tables, Who would not rather see Crowds of Poor blessing one at one's Door, than be oblig'd to *blind* one's Windows to avoid seeing them?

There's a certain great Man, whose Example I would recommend, and whose Name it's needless to mention, when I say he is remarkable for his *extended Charity*; one Instance of which is, his daily giving at his Door, to the Poor and Hungry, the large Remains of a well cover'd Table.

The *Auditor* next inserts a Letter of Encouragement brought him by *Pacolet* from his old Master *Isaac Bickerstaff*. After that 2 others, containing Queries printed against himself, to the following Effect;

QUERE I.

When you at your Club, Sir, with Eccho's chat,
" No Stander-by is the wiser for that. "
And when you discourse without 'em, I pray,
" Is any the wiser for what you then say? "

QUERE 2.

The Breeches to wear no Women insist,
You suppose'—You're not married I wist?

Fog's Journal. March 17. No. 218.

The first Part of this Journal being in Substance the same with what the Reader may find *p.* 35, we shall proceed to the latter Part of it, which contains a Speech, *Fog* relates, was made by *Furfante*, a Senator of *Florence*, to his Faction.

Most Magnificent Lords, *and worthy* Companions,

YOU heard with what Insolence *Poggio* (*See* p. 86 H) inveigh'd the other Day against those excellent Customs which we have introduc'd, in order to establish our selves in Wealth and Greatness. His Invectives against Bribery and Corruption, I take as levell'd against me, all which I receive as Complements to my superior Genius; for I glory in being counted the Man who first brought the Art of fleecing the People into such Credit and Reputation. I may say, without Vanity, that those Persons whom the Disaffected through Envy stigmatise with the Names of Knaves and Plunderers, owe their Establishment and Security to my indefatigable Labours; by which the ingenious Art of *Legerdemain* is so improv'd in this City, that if ten Persons were set a-shore in an uninhabited Island with only one of our Society, if in a Month's Time he did not cheat the other nine of all they had, I would not own him to be one of us.---- Let the Disaffected reproach us with the Conduct of *Camillus*, *Regulus*, and *Cincinnatus*, who from Conquest return'd to the Plough. Had any of them so much Money as some here present? No; I have my self got more by one Jobb in a Morning than all those musty Patriots got by all their Victories put together. Let the Wisdom of the Head be theirs, but ours the Wisdom of the Fingers.---- Our Enemies have found Means to engage the Affections of the giddy Multitude, which might have prov'd fatal to us, had I not took Care to sink the Trade of this City.----*Meum* and *Tuum* disturb the World; we should take this Bone of Contention from the Multitude; by what is already done, you see they are much quieter for it---Stick together; upon that depends our common Safety,--- never admit any Thing advanced by the Disaffected, tho' never so evident; but if I should think it necessary to assert that 3 and 2 make 150, you must swear to it. Hear no Reasons, but face 'em down.---Lastly, I exhort you to breed your Sons up in Virtue; let them learn betimes to play at Cups and Balls; to slip a Card, and cog a Die; tho' I never practic'd much the last Science

ence mention'd, yet I have liv'd in great Familiarity with such, and found them Men fit to be incorporated with us.—Let us fleece on, the Wool will grow again; for the Flocks are made for the Use of the Shepherds.

Furfants ended here, and the Company agreed he spoke like an Angel.

The **Daily Courant,** March 7.

CArus says, he has more than once expressed his Astonishment at the erecting this *new Tribunal* (the People) to which none that he can meet with in History ever desired to refer themselves, but when their *Causes* were so bad as to be incapable of Defence before proper Judges.

He next proceeds to shew, that the *Craftsman* endeavours, (See p. 115.) to prove the Expediency of reducing the Prerogative of the *Crown* within as narrow Bounds as that of the Duke of *Venice*. However he admits, that the Governments of *Holland* and *Venice* are rightly stated in the *Craftsman*; but says, Inconveniencies have sometimes attended the consulting every particular Town, on every Matter that is debated in the *Provincial Assembly*, and can produce Instances of it. In order to have given a perfect Draught of the *Venetian* Government, *D'anvers* should have told us, that their *Nobles* were *Rich*, and the *People Slaves*. He should have painted an arbitrary Inquisition, call'd the *Council of Ten*, who sit at *Midnight*, hear *Accusations* of the highest Nature on the *Spot*, give *Sentence*, and award *Execution* before *Morning;* that it's the *Policy* of that *State* to depopulate their *Provinces* on the *Terra-firma* to prevent *Rebellion*, and that their *Subjects* on the opposite Coast always put themselves under the Protection of the *Turk*, whenever they can change their *Masters*. But he takes no Notice of the *Power* of the *People* of *England* to impeach any *Minister* acting against the *Statutes* of the *Realm*, tho' by the Direction of the *Monarch;* does not mention the Judges being re-

movable, as well on the *Address* of either House, as at the King's *Pleasure;* nor on what Ground his Million Calculation is founded. But it seems the *Faction* intends to keep no Measures, and *Wooden Shoes* have been sent for from *France* to furbish up a scandalous *Entry* at the *Custom-House*, and a seditious *Paragraph* in the *Craftsman*.

Craftsman, March 17. N° 350.

Remarks on the Craftsman's *Adversaries*.

Mr *D'anvers*,

THE *occasional Financer* having answer'd my Address to the *Landholders*, (See p. 7p.) I shall first appeal to Mankind, who first revived the invidious Distinction of the *landed* and *trading Interest;* which I shall be glad to hear of no more; the Trader being no more interested than the *Land-holder*, since all Taxes must be paid by the *Consumer*.

The *Financer* insinuates, the Number of Purchases made since the *Revolution*, is owing to the large *Land-Tax*, which has obliged the *Land-holder* to sell, and to the Exemption from Taxes, which has enabled Traders to buy.] Have *Purchasers* of late years been principally People, who have got their Money by Trade, or such as have raised large Fortunes by the *publick Funds*? or have not such Gentlemen who have *sold* been obliged to it, by their living expensively in Town, in Hopes of getting Places or Pensions?

Once more, *Gentlemen*, consider, how large a Number of the Burgesses and Freeholders of this Kingdom are already aw'd and influenc'd by the *Commissioners of Excise;* that every new Article of *Trade* subjected to Excise, is one step nearer to a *General Excise;* that the Majority of the *House of Commons* are sent from *Boroughs*, and that a large Proportion of *Burgesses* and *Free-holders* will be Dealers in *Exciseable* Commodities; whose Houses and Shops will be open to *Excise Officers*, appointed by the *Crown*, and themselves liable to severe Penalties for the Faults of their Servants. *Tour's* S. S.

In answer to *Carus* in the *Courant* (See above) *Phileleutherus Britannicus* replies, that *Carus* has but small reason to be surpriz'd at the erecting this *new Tribunal* (of the People) or that a Reference to them is a sign of a bad Cause, since he intitules his own Paper of *Feb.* 2. *A Review of the Dispute concerning* Excise; *addressed to the* People *of Great Britain,*
and

and began it thus, FRIENDS and COUNTRYMEN. But because the People will not regard the Address of such an Author, he calls them a *Mob*, and says, *Reasonings are out of the way of the Multitude.* Now if all Causes are *bad*, which are referred to the *Tribunal of the People*, does not this prove that the Cause of *Excise* which *Carus* refers to them, must be *bad*?

The *Craftsman* never mentioned the Governments of *Holland* or *Venice*, as Examples for our Imitation, but insists, that the Government of *Great Britain* ought to be preserved by a due Balance of Power between *King* and *People*; neither did he assert that the People of *Holland*, or *Venice*, had greater Liberty than the People of *England*, by their Constitution.

Carus says, there are Inconveniences in *Holland*. in consulting every particular Town on every Matter debated in the *provincial Assembly*.] Allowing this, it does not follow, that Consultations are in no respect necessary; and that no Regard is to be had to the *unanimous Instructions of all the seven Provinces*; or that the Deputies ought to be at Liberty of acting contrary to such *united Instructions*. To apply this to the Constitution of *Great Britain*; tho' the Instructions of a *particular County, City, or Town*, ought not to prevail against the *Instructions of all the rest of the Kingdom*; yet, when the Nation in general concur in the same Thing, as they have done against any farther *Extension of the Excise Laws*, this Voice of the whole People ought to be consider'd as of great Weight.

At a Parliament holden 9 *Edward* III. when a Motion was made for a *Subsidy* of a *new Kind*, the rest of the Commons answer'd, that they would have a Conference with Those of their several *Counties and Places*, who had put them in Trust, before they treated of any such Matter. And this Practice ought, says D'*anvers*, still to be observed.

Weekly Miscellany. March 17.

Of Ld Clarendon's *History; from p.* 117.

OXonienſis pursues his Arguments to prove the Genuineness of Ld *Clarendon's* History, by considering the Reception it met with when published. It is true, there were many clamorous Opposers, who disputed meerly the Truth of his *Assertions*, or the Justness of his Characters, but never question'd the *Genuine-ness* of the Work, nor suspected any *Forgery*. All Mr *Oldmixon's* Charges of its being interpolated are no more than Suspicions, grounded on the *Gallicisms* that often occur in the Work, which he conjectur'd were too modern to be us'd by the Earl; but on this he lays no great Stress, as indeed he ought not, the Earl's Misfortunes having made the *French* familiar to him.

Nothing of this Kind is mention'd among the defamatory Falshoods published by Dr *Ayliff*; nor in that famous Collection of University Scandal, *Terræ Filius*. The most plausible Reasons for questioning the Genuineness of this History were founded on the following Circumstances, *viz*. That the Right of the Copy was vested in the University of *Oxford*, and which Dr *Ayliff* says, the Earl bequeathed to them, who were also entrusted with the Copy of the Manuscript. Accordingly, many imagining it was kept in the publick Library, desir'd a Sight of it, but being dissatisfied with the Answer they receiv'd, suspected there were some private Reasons for not producing it; and I, says *Oxonienſis*, was led into the same Mistake, of which I am thoroughly convinc'd.

To these Suppositions, and uncertain Presumptions, are added the Remarks of Mr *Clark* of *Hull*, who, in his Essay upon Study, says, that Ld *Clarendon's* History is so interpolated, as not to be depended upon; and adds, that that famous University has been fully convicted of corrupting the Faith of History.] But surely a charitable Man would suspend his Assent upon such a tender Point, and not have aggravated a heinous Charge against Persons of high Character, and triumph in the imagin'd Success of a malicious Imputation.

In the Preface to the History of the *Stuarts* we are inform'd, that those who directed the pretended Alterations, were zealous for the *Laudean* Hierarchy; and in particular were Dean *Aldrich*, *Atterbury*, *Smalridge*; Persons so unlikely to be confederate in such a scandalous Fraud, that their Names will be sufficient to confute the Calumny; and it's still more improbable they should employ another Person in the Execution of the Design: Yet these Persons were pitch'd upon, as being supposed incapable of vindicating themselves: Dean *Aldrich* has been dead above 29 Years; *Smalridge* above 11; and *Atterbury* thought as good as dead; the last however has disappointed their Expectations, and publish'd a Vindication of himself and the other Parties,

S Tone

London Journal, March 17. No. 716.

A Letter from Rochester.

MR *Osborne*, having charg'd a *Jacobite* of the *Bench* at *Rochester* with getting some of his Brethren to *trick the Mayor* out of the Seal (See p. 89 E) and this having been since contradicted in the *Daily Post*, *Osborne* publishes a Letter from thence to justify his Charge.

SIR,

ON the 3d of *February*, there was an usual Meeting of a Deputy-Mayor (the Mayor being sick) the Aldermen and Common Council, some among them (who hate both Ministry and Government) perswaded the Deputy to put it to the Vote, Whether the Members should be wrote to about the *Excise?* They had procured Strength to carry it in the Affirmative; and a Committee was appointed for that Purpose. Two Letters were drawn up, which should have been *reported* in order for Approbation, but were not. The Committee, with some others, met on the *Monday* following, and contriv'd to obtain the *City* Seal, under a *Pretence* of sealing a publick Lease, and against the Consent of the Deputy-Mayor, and without the least Knowledge of the Mayor, fixed the Seal to the two Letters. They gave no publick Notice to the rest of the Bench to meet and consult, or call a Common-Hall, as was done in the Case of Sir *Stafford Fairbone.* So that these *Instructions* appear to be only the Sense, or rather *Nonsense* and *Malice* of 8 or 9 Persons, but not the Sense of the Inhabitants of the City, who wish those insolent and seditious *Letters of Instructions* were burnt by the Hands of the Common Hangman,

Tours, &c.

Universal Spectator, March 17. No. 230.

Homer's *Notion's of Fore-knowledge,* &c. *continu'd from p.* 116.

MR *Stonecastle* collects some *Passages* from *Homer*, which reprove, as impertinent, vain and impious, a *too curious Inquiry* into the *secret Purposes* of the *Almighty;* and likewise such as recommend a *firm Reliance,* on him, and a chearful *Submission* to whatever *Lot* God is pleased to assign us,

That *God* supreme, to whose eternal Eye,
The *Registers* of *Fate* expanded lie.

ODYS. 20. v. 90.

------ To *Heav*'n alone
Th' *Event* of *Actions* and our *Fates* are known. ODYS. 22. v. 320.

------ Then seek thou not to find
The sacred *Counsels* of th' *Almighty Mind :*
Involv'd in *Darkness* lies the great *Decree :*
Nor can the *Depths* of *Fate* be pierc'd by *Thee.*
IL. 1. v. 704.

------ Oh restless *Fate* of *Pride,* [bides
That strives to *learn* what *Heav*'n resolves to
Vain is the search, *presumptuous* and *abhor'd.*

Let this suffice : Th' *immutable Decree*
No Force can shake : What *is*, that *ought* to be.
JUPITER to JUNO.--- IL. 1. v. 726.

Whatever be thy *Condition,* whatever thou mayst have to *fear* or *hope for,*

OD. 13. v. 486. ------ be thy Soul at rest,
And know, whatever *Heav*'n ordains is *best.*

Homer is every where inculcating the *Goodness* and *Justice*, as well as the *Omnipotence* of the DEITY, and from thence inferring, that we ought to place an intire *Confidence* in him, and so doing make ourselves entirely easy.

Oh Impotence of Faith! MINERVA cries,
If *Man* on frail *unknowing Man* relies.
Doubt you the *Gods ?* ------
In me *affianc'd,* fortify thy Breast, [test ;
Tho' Myriads leagu'd thy rightful *Claim* con-
My sure *Divinity* shall bear the *Shield,*
And edge thy *Sword* to reap the glorious Field.
ODYS. 20. v. 56.

The latter Part of this *Speech* is likewise consonant to *sacred Verity, viz.*
Psalm 3. v. 6. *I will not be afraid of* ten thousands *of the People, that have set themselves against me round about.*------

Like to which is what HOMER puts in the Mouth of *Ulysses, Odys.* 13. v. 445.

Tho' leagu'd against me hundred *Heroes* stand,
Hundreds shall fall, if *Pallas* aid my Hand.
Whate'er the *Gods* shall destine me to bear,--
'Tis mine to *master,* with a constant *Mind :*
Inur'd to Perils, to the worst resign'd.

By Seas, by Wars, so many Dangers run,
Still I can suffer : -- *their high Will be done.*

He reads us another noble *Lecture* to the same purpose, *Odys.* 18. v. 155. We often see the *Righteous* suffer, and the *Ungodly* flourishing and prosperous. HOMER resolves this into the Sovereign *Will* of JUPITER, and therefore it is our Duty to submit with Patience.

JOVE weighs Affairs of Earth in dubious Scales,
And the *Good* suffers, while the *Bad* prevails ;
Bear

Bear with a Soul refign'd, the *Will* of JOVE ;
Who breathe, muft mourn ; thy Woes are
  from *above.*   ODYS. 6. v. 229.
. Thus Pfalm 75. v. 9. *In the Hand of the*
Lord there is a Cup ; it is full mix'd, and he
poureth out of the fame.
O thou, *great Father*, Lord of Earth andSkies,
Above the Thought of Man, fupremely wife !
If from thy Hand the *Fate* of *Mortals* flow,
From whence this *Favour* to an *impious Foe* ?
A *Godlefs Crew, abandon'd* and *unjuft,*
Still breathing *Rapine, Violence* and *Luft.*
               IL. 13. v. 789.
. This is not unlike the *Expoftulation* of the
Prophet *Jeremiah*, Chap. 12. v. 1. *Righteous*
art Thou, O Lord, *when I plead with Thee :*
yet let me talk with Thee of thy Judgments :
Wherefore doth the Way of the Wicked *prof-*
per? Wherefore are all they happy that deal
very treacheroufly ? But *Homer* afferts, that
Heaven is juft and will punifh at laft,
—When Heaven's Revenge is flow,
JOVE *but prepares to* ftrike the *fiercer Blow.*
               IL. 4. v. 194.

From the **Auditor**, March 16. No. 20.

        Nugis addere Pondus,

THE following Letter is inferted to
    recommend an honeft Tradefman to
the Notice of the Publick ; in the fame Manner as *Charles Lilly*, the Perfumer, was wrote
into Reputation by the *Tatler.*

    Mr AUDITOR,

YOur facetious Correfpondent PUG (See
    p. 86, A) having lately fat for his Pic-
ture at my Houfe, I have converted it into a
FAN ; which I call the *Flap-Fan.* I have
feveral of thefe FANS by me, and humbly
hope you will recommend them to the World,
that I may have it to fay, The AUDITOR'S
Hints are *profitable* as well as *inftructive.*

Caftle-ftreet,   Yours, &*c.*
Leicefter-fields.   RICH. DUTTON, F

    The AUDITOR makes feveral fine Obfer-
vations on this Occafion, which we have not
room to ftore up in our *Magazine*, therefore muft refer our Readers of Tafte to the
Original ; and fhall only add, that he enjoins
his Fair Difciples to buy at leaft one a piece
of thefe FANS, under the Penalty of being
call'd FEMALE FLAPS.   M *a*

    We hope the *Auditor* will excufe the Li-
berty we have taken to put into Rhime fome
Hints at the latter End of this and another
Paper.

    On HOOPS and HIGH-HEELS.

THE Petticoat's *of modeft Ufe ;*
   · But fhould a Lady chance to full,
The Hoop forbidden Secrets fhews,
And lo ! our Eyes difcover all.
Then Breeches *with* High Heels, *I trow,*
All hooped modeft Ladies wear ;
For it is plain, thefe Modes we owe
To Cupid and the willing Fair.

    The **Auditor**, March 20. No. 21.

ALLegory, in all Ages, has been look'd
    upon as the beft Method of conveying
Inftruction : The Wifdom of the Ancients
never appeared to a greater Advantage, than
in the Choice of their Allegories, The Hea-
then *Mythology* is one continued *Allegory*,
and the moft beautiful that ever was framed.
Who, even now, is not charmed to fee eternal
Power, Wifdom and *Beauty*, fhadowed out in
the Characters of JUPITER, MINERVA,
VENUS ? Every *Grove*, every *Tree*, every
Spring, had its attendant *Deity* : The DRY-
ADS, FAUNS, and NAYADS, &c. were fo
many *Allegorical Beings*, by which the wife
Founders of their Religion would exprefs how
Sacred every Part of the *Univerfe* ought to
be held.

    So far in the *Auditor's* own Words : Af-
ter which he introduces a very Inftructive
Letter from a Correfpondent, who figns AN-
TIQUÆ, and in the allegorical Manner by the
Defcription of a Voyage fhews, nay he demon-
ftrates by a Map, that the way to the *King-*
dom of *Happinefs*, and *Land* of *Felicity*, ad-
joining to which is the Ifthmus of *Pleafure*, is
by the Ifles of *Arts* and *Sciences*, and the
Principality of Peace, only touching at the
Ifland of *Love.* Being thus arrived by the
Port of *Learning*, at the City of *Virtue*, in
the *Kingdom* of *Happinefs*, he fhews, how we
may fafely and agreeably travel, if we have
Defire for our Guide, to the Ifles of *Plenty,*
Frugality, and *Contentment*, and vifit with
Delight from the Ifthmus of *Pleafure*, at one
End of the *Kingdom* of *Happinefs*, to the High
Land of *Felicity*, at the other.

    The Writer gives a regular Journal, but
we can only mention the Names of the feveral Places in his Map, *viz.*

    ARTS and SCIENCES, Iflands of, divided
into feveral Countries, as *Painting, Sculpture,*
Mufic, Geometry, Aftronomy, &c. each of
which has a Prefident.

    LOVE, Ifland of, Leaders, natural *Innocence,*
and *Simplicity* ; chief Port, *Sincerity.*

    PEACE, a Principality in the way to
HAPPINESS, Kingdom of, chief Place,
the Delightful City of *Virtue*, Governour
Wifdom ; his Favourites, *Honour, Circumfpec-*
tion and *Affability* ; Chief Port, *Learning*,
but thinly inhabited.

    PLENTY, Ifland of, Governour's Name,
Temperance.

    PLEASURE, Ifthmus of, Rulers *Gravity*
and *Moderation.*

    FRUGALITY, Ifland, Directors *Care* and
Diligence.

    CONTENTMENT, Ifland, Governour's
Name *Philofophy*, Dep. Gov. *Morality.*

    DISCONTENTMENT, a Rock, Danger-
ous in fudden Gales,

    FELICITY, Land of, Governour, *Pru-*
dence ; chief Port *Friendfhip.*   *a* Q

Grubstreet Journal, March 22. N° 161.

Mr BAVIUS,

BIshop *Parker* tells us, in the *History of his own Times*, what he had heard from Arch Bp *Sheldon's* own Mouth, that after the Treaty of the *Isle of Wight*, in the last Despair of K. *Charles's* Affairs, his Friends and Servants driven from him, he obtained leave for *Sheldon*, to be left alone with him one Day. The King took this Opportunity to unbosom to him the Instructions which he would have him deliver to his Son; the greatest of which was, That he would redeem the Sin of Sacrilege, in restoring the Revenues plunder'd from the Church; a Thing he had vowed to God, if ever he were restored to the Throne.

The Son instead of making Restitution, sold off all the Fee-farm Rents, about 60,000 *l. per Ann.* and how the remaining firstFruits, and Tenths were employed, we may guess by one 30,000.*l.* Grant out of them to the D—ss of P—.

But the Grand-Daughter, our late good Queen, began her Reign by restoring to the Church the First Fruits and Tenths, being a Revenue of about 17,000 *l. per Ann.* which was more almost by the whole Sum, than had been done for the Church by all her Predecessors since the Reformation.

By the wise Method which directs this Benefaction, it is as extensive as it will be lasting. About 4000 poor Livings immediately tasted the Benefit of it, by being discharged from Payment of First Fruits and Tenths, and if there be, as Mr *Eston* affirms, about 2000 more capable of Augmentation, the whole Number of poor Livings may be counted upwards of 6000. The present Revenue of the Corporation, since the Discharge of those Livings, is reckon'd at about 13,000 *l. per Ann.* which is sufficient to augment better than 60 Livings a Year; and consequently may take in the whole 6000 in 100 Years. The first Augmentation began in 1714.

To make this Charity the greater, every private Benefactor, who will lay down 200 *l.* in Money, or the Value in Tythes

or Lands, shall have it joined with the like Sum out of the Royal Bounty, for the Augmentation of any Living within the Rules prescribed.

In an Estate acquir'd by the private Fraud of the Father, the Children know not, perhaps, to whom to make Restitution; but in this Case, Tythes in their own Nature, carry upon them the indelable Badges of LEVI.

If by way of Defence it be pleaded, that there are very few Ecclesiastical Estates in the same Families to which they were at first alienated; yet receiving and keeping of things to which the Goodness of the Title is at best dubious, comes nearest to the original Injustice of actually taking them away.

As to the legal Validity of the Title, it should be consider'd, that all the Tythes and Glebe-Lands, have been frequently, and with great Execration, dedicated to God, exclusively of all other Persons. And what Authority has he given to any one to surrender them back again? Has he confirmed, or acknowledged the Right of the Present Possessors? Has he suffered Possession to continue long peaceable and interrupted? See Instances to the contrary in Sir *Henry Spelman's History of Sacrilege*; and Mr. *Lesly's Essay upon* Tythes.

What is here said is not design'd to affect the Abbey Lands, but only Glebe-Lands and Tythes; concerning which, if, any Impropriator should be asked, How he came to be paid, and why the former were annexed to the Cure of Souls, what Answer can he return which will not condemn himself? What doth he with these Glebe-Lands, or for them?

In a Word, to see so many Persons of Learning and Piety, who are excluded from all other Methods of getting a Livelihood, compell'd to hackney about from Church to Church, and to officiate in two or three incompatible Cures by Halves, just enough to keep them from starving while the plentiful Revenues of the Church are swallow'd up by Persons who cannot perform any Ecclesiastical Offices themselves, and will not contribute to
those

thofe who do, is a melancholy Confideration.   *Ihurs* PHILOCLERUS.

Extract of the Cafe of the Planters in *Virginia*, with fome Account of the Scheme for relieving them, and fecuring the Duties on Tobacco.

AFter reprefenting the intolerable Hardfhips they lie under in an authentick Manner, figned in the Name of the Council, by the Prefident and Speaker, &c. all they defire of the *Britifh* Parliament is.——" *That the Merchants be no longer folely trufted with the keiping of Tobacco, but that it be depofited in Warehoufes under the Lock and Key of the King and Merchant ; That all the Duties be reduced to four pence three farthings the Pound, which is the Net Duty at prefent, after difcounting the 25 per Cent. That Tobacco be weighed when it is landed, and weigh'd again when fold and deliver'd out to the Retailer or Exporter ; That fuch Retailer pay down the Duty according to the laft weight, aud only remain anfwerable to the Merchant for the Remainder of the Price ; That all Tobacco be exported Duty free, and the fame Time allowed for Exportation as is now ; and That fome feverer Penalties be annexed to the Relanding of Tobacco deliver'd out for Exportation or felling it at Home. By this Method no Alteration will be made in Refpect to the Duty, that will be better fecured, and cannot fail of being encreafed, by fuppreffing the Multitude of Frauds which muft needs arife from the Merchants having the Tobacco in his Power, and bonding the Duties : many Perjuries will be prevented, the Merchant then will have no Intereft in leffening the Weights ; but for the Sake of his Commiffions will fee that Juftice be done to the King and the Planter, and the Cuftom-boufe Books will be a Check upon him, if he does any Wrong, and the Planters will be able to chufe their Factors for their Probity and kind Treatment, and not for their Riches or Credit.*"

This Defire of the Planters being fo reafonable, and the Reprefentation of their Cafe having convinced the Miniftry of the great Frauds committed with Relation to the Duties on Tobacco ; they have fo far favoured them as to encourage a Scheme agreeable to what they propofe, for remedying both thefe Evils ; accordingly it was moved in the Houfe *Wednefday* the 14th, and reported the *Friday* following ; the Majority for it being about 60.

What Alterations the faid Scheme may receive in its Progrefs thro' the Houfe, from the Confiderations of fo wife a Body, we can't pretend to guefs, but believe our Readers in the Country will be pleafed to have fome (tho' imperfect) Information of it : As it lately ftood, we gather'd from the *Conjectural Schemift*, publifh'd a Month ago, that as this Commodity was to be laid under an Excife, it was hinted there fhould be an Appeal from the Commiffioners of Excife ; we fince learn, this Appeal, as propofed, is to be determin'd by three Judges of *Weftminfter-ball*, one of each Court ; that is to fay for *London* or the Bills of Mortality ; for the Country, the Appeal to be from the Juftices to the Judges of Affize : And thefe Appeals to extend to every Branch under the Management of the Excife. That the Excife Officers are to be increafed only 126. That the impofing an Oath tending to make Perfons accufe themfelves, which was to be taken or forfeit 20 *l.* be laid afide. That all the Duty (except one Penny *per* Pound to the Civil Lift be paid on landing) and all Forfeitures and Penalties go to the Ufe of the Publick. That 15 *per Cent.* be allowed for wafte, and 10 *per Cent.* on prompt payment of the faid Penny, which Penny to be wholly drawn back on Exportation. The remaining Duty of four Pence *per* Pound, to be paid on removing the Tobacco from the King's Ware-houfes by the Buyer, whofe Ware-houfe to be enter'd at the Excife Office, &c. as in other excifable Commodities.

It is propofed by this Scheme, befides relieving the Planters, to improve the Revenue on Tobacco from 160,000 *l.* (which is the Produce on a Medium for 7 Years paft) to 299,000 *l. per Ann.* the Difference between thefe Sums being now loft or funk in Frauds. It is thus calculated ; fuppofe 163,000 Hogfheads fent in a Year from the Plantations at 720 *l* weight each (which is within the Truth) and allowing two thirds for Exportation, the Duty will be 239,000 *l.* above the prefent Produce.

This Reprefentation of the Planters is in Print, accompanied with a Vindication of it, fhewing feveral Accounts ftated between the Planters and their Factors, whereby the former are brought in Debt 11 *s.* on the Sale of a Hogfh. of Tobacco, while the Merchants make 50 *per Cent.* of their Money in this Trade ; but we fhall not go into particulars, as the Book may be feen every where.

     Being

Being come to a Conclusion of the most remarkable Speeches made in the H—of C—ns on the Salt Bill; we shall not at present pursue that Debate in the other House, but pass to those on the Pension and Mutiny Bills, and the rather, as from the Arguments which were then used the Reader may conceive the Reasons their Lordships went upon in this Sessions for passing the latter, 101 to 49, and rejecting the former a third Time, 82 to 39.

ON *Feb.* 17. the PENSION BILL (See Vol. II. p. 990 G.) was read in the House of Lords, after which

D—y spoke as follows:—My Lords, which has been now read, is to the same Purpose, and almost in the same with that Bill with that which has already been twice refused by your Lordships; and therefore I cannot but look upon the sending up of such a Bill as an Indignity offered to this House; for which Reason I am of Opinion this Bill ought to be rejected.

The E—l of Str—d said: It is true, My Lords, a Bill of the same Purport, and almost in the same Words, has been twice sent up, and as often refused by this House: But we must remember, that the Bill never came the Length of a Committee. If your Lordships had last Year thought fit to take the Bill under your Consideration in a Committee, the several Clauses thereof would have been particularly examined, and it would have been known what Clauses or Words your Lordships would except against; but as no such Thing was done, the Gentlemen of the other House could not know how to amend the Bill; for which Reason I must think that the sending up of this Bill in the same Words with the former, is shewing the utmost Respect to this House, by leaving it to your Lordships to alter and amend it as you shall judge proper.—Corruption, My Lords, has been always thought of most pernicious Consequence, and therefore many Acts of Parliament have been pass'd for preventing it: Particularly in the Reign of Qeen *Anne*; in the first Parliament of his late Majesty; and the very Act of Settlement, This shews that the bringing in of such Bill was never thought any Injury to the Crown; on the contrary, the Honour and Safety of the Crown depend on the Honour and Integrity of the Members of Parliament. One Design of this Bill in the other House, was to wipe off any Suspicion of Corruption that there might be against them: Do not let us, My Lords, deprive them of the only Means of convincing the World, there is no such Thing among them. An Objection against any particular Clause, may be a Reason for altering or amending the Bill, but it never can be a Reason for throwing it out altogether; I shall therefore be, for ordering it to be read a second Time.

V—t F—sh. My Lords, This Bill bears a very specious Preamble; from the first View of it one would be apt to conclude, something very beneficial to the Nation was intended; but on a more serious Perusal, we find, there is really nothing intended, that can in the least contribute to the Publick Good. We all know, My Lords, how some Motions come to be made, in the other House. Such Bills as this now before us, are often brought in by would-be Ministers, Gentlemen who affect Popularity, and set themselves up as Protectors of the Liberties of the People, and under the Pretence encourage and promote Faction and Discontent, in order thereby to raise themselves to be the chief Men in the Administration. I shall always be for insuring the Liberties and Privileges of the People; and if any Attempts were making against them, as ready as any Man to concert Measures for shortning the Arms of the Crown: But, My Lords, when I find no Attempts are made by the Crown, against the Liberties of the People; and when popular Cries for Liberty are spirited up only by the Factious and Discontented, I shall never be for diminishing the Power of the Crown, especially when it has but just enough to support itself against the Factious and Disaffected. I remember, a noble Lord put the Question last Session of Parliament, when this very Affair was before us, How the Pretender would desire one to vote in this Case? I believe the proper Answer would still be, that he would desire us to vote for the Bill: I doubt not, but he would be for diminishing his Majesty's Power of rewarding those who merit well of their Country, by a zealous Opposition to him and his Faction. I hope, My Lords, there will always be Men of Honour and Integrity in this Country to defend us against that or any Faction, without the Hopes of a Reward; but if it should be found necessary for our Defence, I would rather chuse that the Government should have it in its Power to give Rewards to those that contributed to the preserving of us, than that the Factious should have it in their Power to give Rewards to those that assisted them in the destroying of us. The Methods proposed by this Bill, are so far from being proper for preventing Bribery and Corruption, that I am afraid they will give such an Encouragement to Faction, as may lead us into Confusion; and therefore I should be for rejecting the Bill.

L—d C—t. My Lords, I am for receiving this Bill in the most respectful Manner; because of the Dignity of the Subject, and for the Respect due to the other House; as well as ourselves. The Subject of this Bill is of the utmost Consequence to the Liberties of this Nation; the Preamble is in my Opinion very proper for such a Subject; but if not, why may it not be altered? One Thing, My Lords, I am sure of, that if we treat the Bill with so much Contempt, as to reject it upon the first Reading, the whole Nation will make a Preamble for us. I do not know whether this Bill was brought into the other House by would-be Ministers or no; but I am very certain,

tain, that as good Minifters as ever were in *England*, have laid the Foundation for fuch Bills; and if Men Act for the publick Good, it fignifies nothing to us, or the People, what were their Motives. I hope fuch Motives will be always a Check to ambitious Minifters.

It is no Argument againft this Bill, that it is in the fame Words with the laft; I hope there is no Man in this Nation pretends to be infallible. Some Arguments may now be brought for paffing it, which were not then thought of. The Publick Tranquility was not then fo firmly eftablifhed as at prefent, and therefore it might now be thought a more proper Time for us to take Precautions for preferving our Liberties againft Domeftick Enemies. If your Lordfhips fhould fend down a good Bill and the fame fhould be returned by the Commons, would that be any Argument againft ever fending that Bill down to them again? Or, would their having once refufed it, be an Argument for their rejecting it at the firft reading, upon its being brought a fecond time before them? No, *My Lords*, if your Lordfhips were convinced the Bill was neceffary, and drawn up in proper Terms, you would fend it down in the very fame Words again and again, till its own Weight carried it through.

I am, *My Lords*, far from fufpecting any Attempts during his prefent Majefty's Reign, againft the Liberties of this Nation: His Majefty has too much Goodnefs to encourage or admitt any fuch being made; but for this Reafon we ought now to bring in fuch Bills as may be conducive to the Prefervation of our Liberties: His Majefty never will oppofe what is neceffary for fecuring the Liberties and the Properties of his People; whereas, if we never think of taking any Precautions againft Arbitrary Power, till we have a Prince on the Throne, that is aiming at Arbitrary Power, it will then be too late; there is certainly at prefent nothing to be feared from Bribery and Corruption: His Majefty reigns in the Affections of the People; his Defigns are all for the Publick Good, and therefore he has no Occafion for making ufe of any illegal and corrupt fort of Influence; but to pretend, that our prefent Happinefs is a Reafon for our not taking proper Precautions againft the Evils that may come upon this Nation in future Times, is the fame thing as to fay, You are not to bring in any Bills againft Bribery and Corruption, till a Majority of both Houfes of Parliament are corrupted.

The D--ke of *N--le. My Lords*, If this Bill defign'd only to prevent Bribery and Corruption, I fhould be for it with all my Heart; but we can eafily fee that the Intention of this Bill is to give the other Houfe an Opportunity of affuming a Power they never yet pretended to, and their affuming thereof would be the Overthrow of our prefent happy Conftitution. By this Bill, *My Lords*, the Commons may affume a Power of judging what Gratuities are proper to be given by the Crown to any Member of that Houfe; for tho' the Bill fays only, that the Members of that Houfe are to declare what Gratuities or Rewards they receive from the Crown, within fourteen Days after the Receipt thereof, yet, *My Lords*, we might eafily forefee that the Houfe will enter into the Confideration of the Declaration, and will take upon them to determine whether or no fuch Gratuity was given by way of Bribe; fo that thereby the Crown will be difabled from giving any Reward to a Gentleman that has merited well of his Country, at leaft as long as he continues to be a Member of Parliament. This would put fo much Power into the Hands of the Commons, that it would entirely overturn that Balance on which our Conftitution depends; and therefore I have been always againft this Bill, and fhall now be for rejecting it.—— After thefe and feveral other Speeches, the Queftion was put and carried againft the Bill 96 to 40.

Whereupon a Proteft was enter'd (which fee p. 215. Vol. I.)

On *Feb.* 24. the Bill to prevent Mutiny and Defertion, &c. which pafs'd the H--of C--ns without any remarkable Debate, was read the firft Time in the Houfe of Lords, and the D--ke of *N--le* mov'd that it might be order'd to be read a fecond Time on the Tuefday following.

The E--l of *A--n* fpoke to this Effect, *My Lords*, confidering his Majefty has in his Speech affured us, that the publick Tranquillity is fully eftablifhed, I can't think there is now any Ufe for a Standing Army; therefore, muft be againft this Bill; for I am fure if we have no Ufe for a Standing Army we have no Ufe for a Bill againft Mutiny and Defertion. Being therefore againft the very Bill itfelf, I muft be againft giving it a fecond Reading. I have, *My Lords*, been an Eye-Witnefs to one Revolution, I hope I fhall never fee another, and therefore I fhall always be againft any Meafure which, in my Opinion, has the leaft Tendency towards it. Out of the Refpect I have for the illuftrious Family now upon the Throne, I muft always be againft fuch Meafures as I obferved to be the chief Caufes of the laft Revolution; and it is well known, that the chief Caufe of the laft, was the keeping up of a Standing Army in Time of Peace: by this Means the King firft lofes the Hearts of the People, and he is then in great Danger of lofing the Hearts even of that Army in which he puts his Truft. It was, *My Lords*, a wife and glorious Saying of our great Queen *Elizabeth*, when the *Spanifh* Ambaffador ask'd her, where her Guards were; that great Princefs pointed to the People in the Streets, *Thefe* fays fhe, *are my Guards, my People are all my Friends.* She, *My Lords*, put her whole Truft in her People; fhe always continu'd to do fo, and therefore the People always continu'd her Friends, and fupported her againft as powerful Enemies, as ever any King or Queen of *England* had. The difmal Effects of the contrary Maxims,

Maxim, I was an Eye-witness to, and therefore I am, and always shall be, against keeping up a Standing Army in Time of Peace.

L—d D——r said, That any Objection against the Bill, might be properly offer'd upon the Second Reading; till then it could not be supposed, that their Lordships had fully consider'd the Contents thereof, and therefore he was for ordering it to be read a second Time.

The E—l of *Ay—rd. My Lords,* I cannot but be against even giving this Bill a second Reading, because at first View it appears to be for supporting a numerous Standing Army in Time of Peace, and this, *My Lords,* is against the very Words of the Petition of Right, and alters the very Nature of our Constitution. All the Confusion brought upon this Kingdom for many Years, hath been by Means of Standing Armies: It was *My Lords,* a Standing Army, that took off K. *Charles* I*st*'s Head, and turn'd that very Parliament out of Doors which had establish'd them; and the same Army that had murdered the Father, restor'd the Son: It was by K. *James* IId's keeping up a Standing Army, that the Affections of the People were alienated from him; and by that very Army in whom he had put his only Trust he was turn'd out; for by their joining the other Side, the Scales were turned against him, and he found himself at last obliged to succumb under the just Resentments of an injur'd People.

E—l of *I—y, My Lords,* I am persuaded there is not one of your Lordships, but thinks it is necessary to keep up some Troops; if the Number necessary, did not exceed 500, the Bill now brought in is necessary; for without such a Bill it would be impossible to keep even that Number in proper Order or Discipline; I cannot therefore think, that any of your Lordships will be against this Bill entirely. The Number of Troops proposed to be kept up by this Bill, may perhaps by some be thought too large; but that cannot properly come in to be debated, till we go into a Committee upon the Bill.—The keeping up of a Standing Army in Time of Peace, without Consent of Parliament, is indeed against the express Words of the Petition of Right: But, *My Lords,* the very Design of this Bill, is to procure that Consent, without which no Standing Army can be legally kept up in this Kingdom. This Bill cannot therefore be contrary to the Petition of Right, since it is brought in, in Compliance therewith: Nor can the Passing of this Bill make any Alteration in our Constitution: For the Laws of the Kingdom are certainly a Part of our Constitution, and if this Bill were once passed into a Law, it will be as much a Part of our Constitution, as any other Law that ever was made; even *Magna Charta* itself was once a new Law; yet that and all Laws as soon as they were enacted, became a Part of our Constitution, and still continue so, or did continue so, till they were alter'd or repeal'd.

E—l of *Str—d. My Lords,* It is certainly necessary for us upon Occasion of this Bill, to take the Army under our Consideration, and to determine what Number of Troops ought to be kept up; because this is the only Opportunity we can have of reducing the Number allowed of, if we think it too great; and if this Bill goes the Length of a Committee, I shall then declare my Sentiments upon that Head. But, *My Lords,* I now rise up to declare, that I am entirely against this Bill, or any Mutiny Bill; because I always look'd on it, as setting up a Constitution within a Constitution, or rather indeed, it is turning of our Civil Government into a Military one. This, 'tis true, we may do by a Law, and that Law when passed will be a Part of our Constitution, yet I hope it will not be said, that such an extraordinary Law would make no Alteration in our Constitution. I cannot think the keeping up of any regular Troops in this Kingdom is absolutely necessary; but granting it were, I am certain, that in order to keep such Troops under proper Discipline, it is not absolutely necessary to have a Law against Mutiny and Desertion. I had, *My Lords,* the Honour to command a Regiment of Dragoons in the Reign of K. *William,* which was given me at the Time of the Siege of *Namur;* and there was not at that Time in *England* any such Law, as what is now by this Bill to be enacted: We had then no such Thing as Mutiny Bills yearly brought in, yet we found Means to keep our Regiment in good enough Order, and I believe there was as exact Discipline observ'd in the Regiments then quarter'd in *England,* as has been observ'd at any Time since. If any of the Soldiers committed any Crime, they were sure to be punished, but then they were punished according to the ancient Laws of the Kingdom: The Officers took Care to deliver them up to the Civil Power, and to see them convicted and punished, as severely as the Laws of their Country would admit of, which we always found was sufficient.—I could make strong Objections against several Clauses of this Bill; I shall only mention that of Desertion; how unnecessary, how cruel is it in Time of Peace, to punish that Crime with Death; In Time of War, such a severe Punishment was necessary, because the Deserters generally ran to the Enemy, and turned their Arms against their Country; if a poor Fellow deserts, he runs but from one of our own Regiments to another; and the cruel Treatment he meets with from some of the Officers, may often afford him an Excuse. How many poor Country Fellows, out of a Frolick go and list themselves for Soldiers! when such a poor Fellow begins to cool, he perhaps repents of what he has done, and deserts without any other View but that of returning Home, and following some industrious Way of Living in his own Country. Is it not hard, that such a poor Fellow should be shot for such a trifling Crime? The Law perhaps may not be executed with Rigour; that may

be

be an Excuse for the Judge, but none for the Lawgiver; considering that the Officers are the Sufferers by Desertion, and also the Judges in all Trials of that Crime, I think, *My Lords*, that their not executing the Law with Rigour, is a convincing Argument, that the Pains are too severe; but, as I am against the Bill itself, I am therefore against giving it a second Reading, or entering into the Consideration of the several Clauses thereof.

The Question was however carried, for ordering this Bill to be read a second Time; after which it was ordered to be committed, and an Instruction being thereupon moved for and refused, a Protest was entered, (See p. 815. Vol. II.)

The Bill was at last carried thro' the Committee, and on *March* 10 was read the 3d Time, and passed, on a Division 69 to 19.

The Substance of the Paper deliver'd by Sarah Malcolm to Mr Piddington.

(See p. 97, and Occurr. *March* 7.)

THere is a just God, before whom we must give an exact Account of all our Actions; and as I must appear before the all-seeing Judge of Heaven and Earth, to give an Account of mine; so I take that great Judge to witness, what I declare is true.

Sunday *Jan.* the 28th, *Mary Tracy* came to me, and drank Tea, and then I did consent to that unhappy Act of robbing Mrs *Duncomb*; but I do declare before the Almighty God, that I did not know of the Murder. On Saturday the 3d of *Feb.* was the Time appointed; and accordingly about Ten o'Clock at Night, *Mary Tracy* came to Mr *Kerrol's* Chambers, and I went to Mrs *Duncomb's*, and on the Stairs I met the Maid, and she ask'd me, whether I was going to *Eliz. Harrison*; and I answer'd, Yes; and as soon as I thought she had got down Stairs, I would have gone in, but fearing Suspicion, I ask'd Who would go in? and *James Alexander* replied, He would; and the Door being left open for the Maid, against her Return, I gave *James Alexander* Directions to lye under the Maid's Bed, and desired *Tracey* and *Thomas Alexander* to go and stay for me at my Master's Door until my Return, and accordingly they did; and when I came, I desired they would go and stay for me at Mrs *Duncomb's* Stairs; and I went and lighted a Candle, and stirr'd my Master's Fire, and went again to *Tracey* and *T. Alexander*, who were on Mrs *Duncomb's* Stairs, and there we waited till about Two of the Clock on Sunday the 4th of *Feb.* when I would have gone in; but then *Thomas Alexander* and *Mary Tracey* interrupted me, and said if you go in and they awake, they will know you, and if you stay on the Stairs, it may be that some one will come up and see you; I made answer, that no one lived up so high but Mrs *Duncomb*; and at length it was concluded that *Mary Tracey* and *T. Alexander* should go in, and shut the Door, and accordingly they did; and there I

remained till between Four and Five o'Clock, when they came out and said, Hip; and I came higher up; they asked, which Way they should shut the Door; and I told them to run the Bolt back, and it would spring into its Place, which they did, and came down: They asked, where they should divide what they had got? I asked, how much it was? they said, about 300*l.* in Goods and Money; but said they, we were forced to gag them all. I desired to know where they had found it; they said, that Fifty Guineas of it was in the old Maid's Pocket, in a Leathern Purse, besides Silver? and above 150*l.* in a Drawer, besides the Money they had out of a Box, the Tankard, one Silver Spoon, a Ring which was looped with Thread, one square Piece of Plate; one Pair of Sheets, two Pillow beers, and five Shifts. We did divide all this near Figtree-Court, as also near Pump Court, and they said, Before that you bury the Cole and Plate under Ground, untill the Robbery is all over, &c.

I being apprehended on Sunday Night, on the Monday Morning, when I was in the Compter, I saw *Bridgwater*, and he ask'd whether I had sent for any Friends; I told him I had. Soon after he called to me, and said there was a Friend come to me; I ask'd whether it was *Will Gibbs*, he reply'd, yes; upon which I enquir'd of *Gibbs* how the *Alexanders* were, he said they were well; he ask'd how I came to be taken; and I told him my Master having found the Tankard and some Linnen, and he having seen 90*l.* 16*s.* on Sunday the 4th of *Feb.* which perhaps through Surprize he forgot, but I had it all. He said if I would give him Money he would get People that would swear that the Tankard was my Mother's; but said I, you must get some to swear that I was at their House; he said it must be a Woman, and she would not go without Four Guineas, and the Four Men two Guineas a-piece; so I gave him Twelve Guineas, and he and his Friends were to be at the Bull's Head in *Bread-street*; but when I ask'd for them they were not there, and when I came before the worshipful Alderman *Brocas* I was committed to Newgate. When I was brought up to the Common-Side, I was order'd to pull off my Riding-hood, and *Peter Back* observed a Bulk in my Hair to hang down behind, and told *Roger Johnson* that I certainly had Money in my Hair; then *Johnson* brought me down in a Cellar, and told me that *Peter Back* said I had Money in my Hair, and he laid his Hand on my Head and bid me rake it out, which I did and he counted 36 Moidores, 18 Guineas, 6 Broad Pieces (two of them 25*s.* and four 23*s.* Pieces) half a 23*s.* five Crowns, two Half Crowns, and one Shilling: He then said he would be clear'd and get out of Goal on that Account. (N. B. *The Money was restor'd to Mrs* Duncomb's *Executrix.*)

☞ She gave the same account of the Fact at her Trial, in a long and fluent Speech; yet the Expectation for this Paper was so great, that the Copy was sold by Mr P. for 20*l.*

T The

The 𝕯𝖆𝖎𝖑𝖞 𝕮𝖔𝖚𝖗𝖆𝖓𝖙, March 14.

We should not have reprinted the Reflections in this Paper, but to shew our Readers why the Merchants had it burnt. See Occurr. *20th Day.*

THERE are a Set of People whose Interest it is to oppose any Change in Collecting the Duties on Tobacco; these are Commission Men and Brokers, Agents and Factors, who, out of the Labour of the poor Planter, vye with the greatest of the Nobility in Opulence and Splendour; tho' at the same Time they will hardly allow the unhappy Wretch, by whose Drudgery they support their Luxury, such a small Proportion out of their exorbitant Gains, as is sufficient to buy Bread for himself and Family : It's no wonder they should be alarmed at any Proposal to relieve those miserable People from their *Egyptian* Bondage; because the Slavery of the Planter, and Grandeur of the Broker must end together.

It is certainly reasonable, that every one be allowed a competent Profit in that Business he was bred up to. But why must the Publick be cheated ? Why must whole Families be Starved to aggrandize and enrich a few Men, who perhaps originally sprung from the Dregs of the People ? Who, may be, were placed out upon Charity, and who ought not therefore to contend for the Superfluities and Luxuries of Life ; especially if they cannot obtain them without the vilest Frauds and most scandalous Abuses. If such a Man a-mass Riches by these Means, if he swagger about in his Chariot, and resides in a Palace, when his Father drove the Plough and lay in a Barn ; where is the dangerous Consequence? How is it an Invasion upon the Liberties of the Subject, if an easy Remedy be found out to prevent the Growth of such Monsters for the future ? *See* p. 144.

Would any Writer but the *Craftsman* have asserted, (see p. 116. G.) that *the Crown is already possessed of more Power than it enjoyed under any* of *the* Stuarts ? What does he think of the Power of the Crown in the Reign of *James* I. when several Members of Parliament were imprison'd by the King's Sole Authority, for Speeches they made in the House ; in which Confinement some of them died? What were the oppressive Laws, the Ship Money, the cruel arbitrary Punishments in the Time of *Charles* I? What does he call the depriving the City of *London* of its Charter by *Ch.* II? and the restraining them from chusing their Magistrates without his Approbation ? What the Power of the Crown was under *James* II. is in the Memory of many now alive ; therefore the Writer that can assert so barefaced a Falshood deserves no Credit for the future.

The *Auditor*, March 23. No. 22.

Ah! MISER! Quantâ laboris in CHARYBDI!

THE MISER, a Comedy, having been taken, as the Author confesses, from *Plautus* and *Moliere*, Mr CYNICK bestows some Remarks on it.

In *Poetry*, as in Painting, there are Pieces for the *Judges*, and Pieces for the *Many*. The *first* are satisfied with one *Figure drawn to the Life*, and *of a Piece with itself*. The other require gay Colourings, and Variety of Figures; no matter whether there be any Relation to each other. *Plautus* has drawn the Character of a *Miser*, naturally, as he is; *Moliere* has a little left the Character of a *Miser*, by giving him Thoughts of marrying one in *mean Circumstances*.   Our *English* Poet, the Impetuosity of whose Genius allows him not time to consider *Nature*, has given his *Miser* not only Thoughts of Marriage with one whose Wealth he has but an indifferent Account of, but makes him very much *in Love*, and contrary to his Interest; an Absurdity *Moliere* avoided.

The Character of *Mariana* (which in *Moliere* is most beautiful) is no more of a Piece than that of *Lovegold* the Miser. In the first Act *She is a most intolerable Coquette*, and eternally at

Cards;

Cards;—This, it seems, is the Reverse of the Medal; *the right side contains Beauty, Wit, Genteelness, Politeness.*] But, where is the Difference between the *Right* and the *Reverse?* Beauty, Wit, Genteelness, Politeness, are all. Ingredients of a Coquette. In the second Act she declares Love for *Frederick.* In the third she disclaims it, and consents to marry the Miser. In the fourth the Contract is signed, and *Frederick* dismiss'd and laugh'd at. In the fifth she enters as Mistress of *Lovegold's* Family; and a wonderous Discovery is made, *viz.* the Forfeiture of the Bond is to be bestowed on *Frederick* whom *Mariana* marries. If she really loved *Frederick,* why did she consent to marry the Miser? If not, why bestow on him the 8000l. and herself?

The principal Plot of the Play is as ridiculous as the rest. A *true Miser,* if he had been foolish enough to have signed a Bond of 10,000l. as he did, to marry *Mariana,* would have married, rather than pay the Forfeiture. When she was once his Wife; he might have govern'd her as he pleas'd.

A young Girl that really loves, would not have ventur'd so far, tho' she was a Coquette. But it's to be question'd, whether a Coquette can *really love;* and, if she *can,* whether she would so easily give up her *Love* to her *Coquetry,* when nothing obliges her to do it; which is the Case of *Mariana.*

These are the two principal Characters in the *English* Miser, and are contrary to the Maxims laid down by the best Criticks, as well as Poets,

Servetur ad imum
Qualis ab incepto, processerit, & sibi constet.

Notwithstanding, the *Auditor* allows it to be the only Play deserving the Name of Comedy, this long while, except the *married Philosopher.*

Craftsman, March 24, No. 351.

Of Excise.

WE have been charg'd with dressing up an imaginary scare-crow to frighten the People, but upon com-

paring the *present Scheme,* says *D'anvers,* as far as it hath been open'd to us, with the *Project,* which we have encounter'd for several Months past, I can find no material Difference between them. The *Laws of Excise,* are to be extended by it; the *Officers* are to have Power to *enter Houses;* and vast Numbers are to be abridg'd of *Trials by Juries.*

Appeals indeed will be allowed to THREE JUDGES, instead of the *Commissioners;* this, tho' an alteration for the better, is not to be compar'd to the antient *Method of Tryal,* establish'd by *Magna Charta;* and, tho' the *Judges* are not so much under the Influence of the *Crown,* yet considering the Infirmities of human Nature and the Temptations of Power, no sensible Man would willingly see his Property made absolutely dependent on their Virtues.

Supposing *Frauds* will be prevented (which is very improbable) no Improvement of the Revenue ought to be put in Competition with those two great Privileges, *Trials per Pares,* and the *Freedom of our own Houses.*

Considering that most of our native Commodities and Manufactures are already excis'd, as well as several imported Goods, and that *Wine* and *Tobacco* are the two principal Commodities now remaining unexcis'd; what Scheme can have a more immediate Tendency to a *general Excise* than the present?

We are told that only about 150 Officers, besides Warehousemen, Clerks, &c. will be necessary; and how can these endanger our Liberties? This Argument was made use of last Year on Account of 600 *Salt Officers;* and may be repeated every Year *ad infinitum.*

We do not, says *D'anvers,* argue against the Existence of such Men as Officers; but they have commonly prov'd the Pests of Society; and in Scripture, *Publicans* (or *Tax-gatherers*) and *Sinners* are joined; and tho' they are necessary Evils, like *Bayliffs* and *Hangmen,* it's a sure sign of a bad Government, to be over-run with 'em.

Is there no difference between opposing.

fing *all Taxes*, and a particular Method of *collecting them* ? If fo, why was the Chimney Money abolifh'd, after the Revolution, and branded by Parliament, as " *a Badge of Slavery*, expofing every Man's Houfe to be enter'd into, and fearch'd at Pleafure, by *Perfons unknown to him* ".

When we have argu'd, that an *Excife* cannot prevent an *Adulteration* of *Wine* and *Tobacco*, we are anfwer'd, that the Duties on thefe Commodities are only Taxes upon *Luxury*, and that it would be happy for the Nation if all our Luxuries were taxed.] *Tobacco* is grown fo habitual to vaft Multitudes of People, efpecially the Poor, that they can hardly fubfift without it ; and *Wine* is become equally natural to higher Ranks of Men ; therefore it can't properly be call'd *Luxury*, any more than *Sugar*, *Spice*, &c. It might have been more to the purpofe to have laid a Tax upon Gold and Silver Lace, foreign Thread-Lace, and fine Linnens, fumptuous Equipage, coftly Pictures, &c.

But how are the *Landed Gentlemen* to be eas'd by an *Improvement of the Revenue* ? or what will become of the *Government* itfelf, which is principally fupported by this kind of *Luxury* ?

We are informed that the old Subfidy upon *Wine* and *Tobacco*, which belongs to the *Civil Lift*, will be continu'd at the *Cuftom-houfe*; and therefore the Crown will be no confiderable Gainer by the *Scheme*.] This is fo far from anfwering the Objection, that it's a new Argument againft the *Project* itfelf, not only as it prevents any Reduction of *Cuftom-houfe Officers*, but as it will fubject Dealers to the Vexation of *two Officers* at once.

The *Advocates* for it are therefore reduced to the laft Shift of calling Names, and reprefenting thofe who oppofe it as *Sturdy Beggers*; which feems a little unhappily apply'd ; for *Sturdy Beggers* and *Robertfmen* are ufed as fynonimous Terms in our old Statutes. This brings to my Mind the Fellow, whofe Method was to ftep to a Coach fide with

a *Rabbit* in one Hand, and a *Piftol* in the other. *Gentlemem*, faid he, will *you pleafe to buy my Rabbit* ? They anfwer'd, *We don't love Rabbits.* To which he return'd ; By G—, *Gentlemen*, *you muft and fhall buy this Rabbit.*

D'anvers asks, Who were the *Sturdy Beggers* in this Cafe ?

Weekly Mifcellany, March 24. No. 15.
Remarks on Ld Clarendon's *Hiftory.*

OXONIENSIS proceeds to examine the Charge againft Lord *Clarendon's* Hiftory. In order to this he enquires what is brought to fupport it.

Firft with Regard to the *Time when* the fuppos'd Difcovery was made. This was in *June* 1710, about 7 Years after the Commiffion of the Fact, That fuch a Fraud fhould fo long lie conceal'd, is hardly Credible : But it will ftill appear more improbable, when we confider the Perfon fuppofed to have made the Difcovery, or the Perfon *to whom* it was made, Mr *Edmund Smith* of *Oxford, Author of* Phædra *and* Hippolitus, *a Tragedy*—And *George Ducket*, Efq;

They who knew Mr *Smith* beft, believe it was fcarce poffible for him to be concern'd in the Affair; or that he fhould be employ'd by Dean *Aldrich.* No ; his repeated Irregularities provok'd the Cenfures of his mild Governor. He was continually difcountenanced, punifhed, and perfecuted—denied the Cenforfhip, and finally expell'd. In Return, Mr *Smith* made Reprifals upon the Dean, by ufing his Wit to vilify and ridicule him. Could the Dean make a Confident of a Man diftinguifh'd by the Marks of his Difpleafure? Or could *Smith*, thus exafperated, conceal this important Secret fo long, under the ftrongeft Temptations to difcover it ? being too of a different *Party* ?

As to *George Ducket*, Efq; he was late one of the Commiffioners of Excife, and now deceas'd. Whatever this Gentleman's Character might be with Regard to *Party*, it's certain, that He, who communicated to Mr *Oldmixon* the Difcovery, was never ready to atteft

teſt the Truth of his Letters. Neither Bp *Atterbury's* Vindication,—neither private Application of Friends,—nor Mr *Oldmixon's* Importunity could provoke or perſwade him to do this Act of Juſtice. The Imputation of *Diſingenuity* and *Cowardice* will reſt on his Memory, for miſrepreſenting the Dead, and impoſing upon the Living, without either avowing or retracting his Aſſertion.

Further, the *ſingular Manner* in which the Gentleman was ſo ſuddenly convicted of the Truth of a Story ſo improbable, deſerves our Notice. The bare Aſſertion of Mr *Smith*, and the Sight of a Printed Copy *ſcored* and *underlined* produced this ſtrange Effect. To receive Conviction upon ſuch Evidence there muſt be a Turn of *Prejudice* and *Credulity* in the Mind. And where there is ſuch weakneſs of Judgment, who would expect that an important Secret ſhould be conceal'd 20 Years?

Moreover the *Manner*, in which this Diſcovery was *publiſhed*, renders the whole Story queſtionable. It came into the World with the Air of *Secrecy* and *Guilt*, communicated in a Letter pretended to be occaſionally written by an *Anonymous* Correſpondent, to the *Publiſher* of it, who is the Author of the *Medley*, the ſecret Hiſtory of *Europe*, the *Critical Hiſtory*, of *Whitlock* and *Clarendon* Compared, the Hiſtory of the *Stuarts*, the undaunted Mr *Oldmixon*. From the Recital of theſe Titles let the Reader judge of the Veracity and Candour of this Critick.

The *Oxford* Editors are accuſed of *interpolating*, making Additions, and Alterations in Ld *Clarendon's* Hiſtory; and the Fact proved by an Hearſay, *from a Perſon ſuperior to all Suſpicions, and too illuſtrious to be named without Leave*; by an Appeal to a *very honourable Perſon*; by an Appeal to a *Revd Doctor then living*; by an Appeal to a *Gentleman of Diſtinction both for Merit and Quality*.] What does all this amount to, more than that certain Perſons, not proper to be named, inform-

ed Mr *Oldmixon* of theſe Frauds in the *Oxford* Edition; But there is a Revd Doctor now living, *T. Terry*, Canon of *Chriſt Church*, who was Corrector to the Preſs of that Edition, who can atteſt the Contrary.

London Journal. March 24. No. 717.

WHile others are loading all Gentlemen in Power, and all who *vote* with, or *write* or *ſpeak* for them, with the odious Names of *Placemen* and *Penſioners*, *Hirelings* and *Proſtitutes*, I, ſays *Osborne*, will not oppoſe Rage to Rage; for I had much rather be † *abuſed* than *abuſe*, and *ſuffer* ill than *do* ill; I am content to do my *Duty*, and take the *Event*.

He then proceeds to defend and explain the *new Scheme* for an *Exciſe*, by expatiating on the great national Benefits which will ariſe from it: But as we have already given an Account of it (See p. 133.) we ſhall only take Notice of a few Things not there mentioned, *viz*. That after the 25 *per Cent* Diſcount, there will be only 3 farthings *per* Pound on Tobacco for the King, and that to be paid only when the Tobacco is ſold for Home Conſumption; ſo that as nothing will be paid on Tobacco ſold for Exportation; there can't be any *Drawback* whatever. The Tobacco will be kept in Warehouſes, and the Merchant relieved from giving Bond, or paying any Money till he ſells it; ſo no Room will be left for the Factors to abuſe the poor Planters.

The Smuglers of Wine and Tobacco ſupply not only Places on the *Coaſt*, but many *Inland Towns*, which the *Fair Traders* of *London* formerly furniſh'd. Is it not then ſurprizing, they ſhould object to this Method of collecting the Duties, which will, by prevent-

† *Osborne ſpeaks this in Relation to his being hiſs'd off the* Royal Exchange; *the* CRAFTSMAN *has it, in an Ironical way, by the* STURDY BEGGERS *aſſembled there, on whi.h, adds he, the old Gentlewoman fled to the oppoſite Alley, and was received with open Arms by the honeſt* Traders *who ſupport the Credit of the Nation by the flouriſhing Commeyce of that Place.*

ing

ing Smuggling, return their loſt Trade into their own Hands again ? But the Author of *The Budget open'd* ſays, he can't ſee the Difference to the People between a new Tax and a new Method of collecting an old Tax. I'll tell this antiminiſterial Buffoon, ſays *Osborne,—* A *new Tax* will bring *new* Money out of the People's Pockets, but a *new Method* of collecting the old Tax is *only* taking Money from the *fraudulent* Dealers, which they ought to pay in Law and Conſcience.

Univerſal Spectator; March 24. No. 233.
The Project continu'd from p. 123.

IN order to promote *Literature* and the *Liberal Sciences,* this Writer propoſes to *excise* thoſe Branches of Learning which neither conduce to the Improvement of the Mind, nor yield any Benefit to the Publick. Here he includes all *Virtuoſo Philoſophers,* and *Nick-nackatory Antiquarians,* not ſo as to oppoſe the learned Members of the R - - l S - - - y ; but to make their Studies and Lucubrations uſeful : For that purpoſe a Tax of 1 *s.* ſhould be laid on every *dry'd Fly, Hornet, Ladybird, Moth, Caterpillar,* &c. likewiſe on all *Foſſils, Shells,* &c. to be doubled on thoſe of Foreign Importation. In like manner, for every 20 *s.* laid out in *ruſted* Coins, maimed Buſtoes, and broken Vaſes, above double their intrinſic Value, one Third to be deducted for increaſing the Revenue ; that ſo theſe *ſportive* Productions of Nature, and inſignificant *Gimcracks* may be render'd beneficial.

As to Profeſſors of the *Law,* there is a Figure of Speech call'd *Tautology,* frequently uſed at the Bar, which muſt come under this Tax. By a moderate Computation there will not be leſs than 10,000 Sentences a day during Term-Time, liable to the Penalty, which, at 1 *s.* for each Offence, would annually amount to 60,000*l.* But Junior Barriſters may, during their firſt three Terms, be allow'd theſe uſeful Expletives, *Pleaſe you my Lord; with humble Submiſſion to your Lordſhip, &c.*

Likewiſe Phyſicians ſhould come under this Law, by which they will be made in ſome meaſure to compenſate the Miſchief they Yearly do the Publick. Profeſſed Poets may be allow'd the Claim of Exemption ; but the vaſt Benefit that will accrue from all affected Rhymeſters, will plead ſtrongly for their being Exciſed.

In Men and Women of Modern *Wit, Taſte,* and *Pleaſure,* he is for Taxing but two Things, as downright Dulneſs, viz. *Blaſphemy* and *Bawdry,* and thoſe at half a Crown each Offence. The Military men will probably inſinuate that ſuch a Tax will tend to their entire Ruin, but he can't excuſe 'em in time of Peace, and by no means Country 'Squires, Students of the Law, Players, Dancing-maſters ; and Singers, this being the only Method to keep them within good manners.

As this Scheme would produce more than that for exciſing *Wine* and *Tobacco,* and call for more Officers, Collectors, &c. to be made, therefore he hopes it will be received, and he, the Projector, made a *Commiſſioner.*

Fog's Journal, March 24. No. 229.
The Parliament of Paris, *and the* Roman *Senate under the* Cæſars *compar'd.*

AFter giving ſome high Encomiums on the Honour, Integrity, and Moderation of the Parliament of *Paris,* from *Mezaray's* Life of that excellent Prince *Charles* VIII. *Fog* proceeds

The Parliament of *Paris* never met but for the Comfort of the People; the *Senate* ſcarce ever aſſembled, but to their Terror and Deſtruction: Which occaſion'd a ſatyrical Expreſſion of a Man of Wit, who being told, that the Senate would be aſſembled in a ſhort Time, anſwer'd, He hoped they would firſt perform Quarentine, leſt they ſhould bring a Plague upon the People. Foreign Princes have referr'd their Diſputes to the Parliament of *Paris;* but no *Roman* wou'd have referr'd a Diſpute of half a Talent Value to a *Roman* Senate.

Edicts

Edicts, tho' recommended by the King and Ministers, have been often rejected by the Parliament of *Paris.* *Tiberius* being present in his Senate, said he would give his Opinion in the Affair **A** then to be debated, to encourage others to do the like.—*C. Piso* perceived that the corrupt Majority had not been inftructed which way to vote, wherefore he said, In what Order, oh *Tiberius !* do you intend to give your Opinion ? **B** If you do it laft, many will speak as they think, and so their Opinions may differ from yours; but if you speak firft, your Opinion will be theirs, tho' it shou'd tend to the Deftruction of *Rome.*

The Parliament of *Paris* by an Arret, **C** declared Card. *Mazarine,* with all his Accomplices and Adherents, Traitors to the State, and order'd all his Eftates, to be confifcated to the Publick Ufe. In the Senate of *Rome* no Oppreffor was fo much as cenfur'd while in Po- **D** wer, but if he loft the Favour of the Court, he was fometimes lopp'd the Head fhorter.

A penfionary Senate is as blindly o- bedient to the Command of the fcanda- lous Knave who directs them, as a Bo- dy of Men, under Military Difcipline, **E** are to their fuperior Officer. It has of- ten happen'd in the Senate of *Rome,* that a Senator coming into the Senate Houfe when they have been ready to divide about fome Affair, having Saga- city enough to follow his Paymafter, **F** has been heard to fay, I am glad we have carried the Queftion, but, *Pray what was it ?*

When any Oppreffion was intended, no doubt but the Mercenaries were fummon'd, and had their Inftructions when to interrupt the oppofite Side, **G** when to call Names, and when to flat- ter the Paymafter; and if fome of them fhou'd be a little fhy, then Bribes muft rife; for their Scruples muft be removed. *A rich, low-born, vain Plebeian muft be introduced into the Order of Patrici-* **H** *ani;* fuch a one has feveral Sons, one muft be made a Centurion;—this de- mands an Addition to his Penfion;—that

wou'd be a Prætor;—and a fourth muft have his Debts paid; all muft be com- plied with upon a Pinch.—Yet were there never greater Boafts of Liberty than at the Time when that State was in this moft miferable Servitude.

It was certainly but Mockery, to talk of the Regard Men in Power had to the Laws, while the Majority of the Se- nate were as fubfervient to a vile *Seja- nus,* as the Negroes in the *Weft-Indies* now are to the Planter that buys them. But examine the Conduct of the Parlia- ment of *Paris,* from its Inftitution to this Day, and you will meet with no Inftances of fuch flavifh Submiffions.

Tho' the *French* do not poffefs all the Privileges they formerly enjoy'd, yet Property is fafe there, nor *do the Taxes bend the People to the Earth with their Weight*; and Things againft the general Inclination of the People are not infifted on.

The late D. of *Orleans* could not prevail on the Parliament of *Paris* to give a Sanction to *Laws*'s Scheme. That Projector at laft was glad to efcape in the D. of *Bourbon*'s Chaife.

From the **Auditor,** March 27. Nᵒ 23.

Dear Mr Auditor,

A S I and two more Ladies were ta- king a ferious Walk in the Mall, a Flap took that Opportunity of talk- ing fuch ridiculous Stuff to me, that I was fick to Death.—At laft being tired with his apifh Chattering, I walk'd a little fafter ; but he like, a Scaramouch, ran after me, till all his plaifter'd Brains fell on my Manteel, and have utterly fpoiled it. I wonder Mr Auditor you don't fupprefs this *plaiftering.*
                                    Cleomena.

My pretty Correfpondent's Letter had almoft perfuaded me to come into her way of Thinking, but finding by the following, that this Profufion of Powder is no fmall Guard on the Sex's Chaftity, I exprefly defire all my Rea- ders, Male and Female, to wear it in greater Quantities.
                                    Mr

Mr AUDITOR,   *March* 23.

I Drefs fashionably, and therefore wear a great deal of Powder. Yesterday I visited a young Lady, whom I found without her Mother at home, you may be sure I was neither *tongue-ty'd* nor *motionlefs*: nor did she expect I shou'd; but as *Milton* fays,

——From my *Mouth*,
Not *Words* alone pleafed her.

In comes Mama: and before she could get up Stairs, we had the whole Room between us. After she had fat a while, looking accidentally on her Daughter, she found her black Silk Gown (Curfe on the Mourning) whiter than ordinary, and gueffing we had been *clofer* than we then were, she civilly defir'd me to walk down, and told me, her Daughter was never after to be feen by me, but in *her Company*. I had not a word to fay, but went off at once. Pray tell thefe young Cox-combs from whom our Fafhions take their Rife, there is fomething more than *powdering* and *Plaiftering*, requifite to recommend them to the other Sex.

O   INFORTUNATUS.

He next mentions a Story of the Be-haviour of a D——r in a Country Town Weftward, jumping into a Tub in the Prefence of fome Ladies and ufing other ridiculous Airs, which Mr *Auditor* obferves, fo refembles that of a FLAP, in jumping and skipping a-bout, that he cannot but look on him as an awkward Mimick of that Species: However, is not a little pleafed to fee it does not take fo much in the Country as in Town.

Free Briton. March 29.

G Ives a State of the Cafe between the Tobacco Planters and their Factors, to enable People to judge of the Merit of the Difpute between them.

He shews by an Account of Charges on a Hogfhead of Tobacco fold for Home Confumption at *L.* 24 10 10, as the Practice now is, the neat Pro-ceed is but *L.* 4 11 11. A Hogfhead fold for Exportation but *L.* 3 3 3.

From this manner of charging, a Factor who pays prompt Payment, may without defrauding the Revenue, gain *L.* 2 7 9 *per* Hogfhead confumed at home; and 11 *s.* 7 *d.* on a Hogfhead exported on Bond; but by the Regula-tions propofed, allowing the fame Char-ges, the neat Proceed will be, at the fame Price, for Home Confumption *L.* 2 11 6 more; for Exportation 7 *s.* 5 *d.* Hence the Reafon appears how much the Factors are concern'd to oppofe fuch Bill as would fo far re-duce their Gains; which however, when fo reduced, will be much more than our Factors had formerly, and a-bove double what the Factors in *Hol-land* have now.

The Writer of this Calculation adds, the many Tradefmen who feem to be fo much alarm'd at the propofed Re-gulation, will thereby have 70,000 *l.* more in a Year laid out amongft them in the Purchafe of Goods and Manu-factures for the Ufe of the Planters, than at prefent; all which is now fpent by the Factors in luxurious living. See p. 138.

Grubftreet Journal. March 29. No. 179.

A true Copy of an Anfwer from a Mem-ber of Parliament, to a Letter from his Borough concerning the Excife.

Gentlemen,

'YOurs I received, and am very
' much furprized at your Info-
' lence in troubling me about the *Ex-*
' *cife.* You know what I know very
' well; that I bought you. I know
' what perhaps you think I don't know,
' that you are about felling yourfelves
' to fomebody elfe; and I know what
' perhaps you don't know; that I am
' about buying another Borough.——
' And now may the curfe of God light
' upon you all; and may your Houfes
' be as common to *Excifemen*, as your
' Wives and Daughters were to me,
' when I ftood Candidate for your
' Corporation.   a. h!

Two other Pieces in this Journal we refer to our next; one being unfinished, the other to be anfwer'd·

The **Auditor**, March 30. No. 24.

THIS Paper confifts of feveral Letters from Correfpondents, with the *Auditor's* Reflections upon each; particularly one about the falfe wit of certain maritime Gentlemen who teach Parrots obfcene Words, on purpofe to divert themfelves with the Blufhes of the fair Sex unexpectedly raifed by the innocent Bird. If this polite Diverfion continues, the *Auditor* will fend a Detachment of FLAPS to twift off the necks of their Parrots.

Another from a Tradefman's Widow worth 5,000*l.* who would be married again, but the Man not to be a Day older than herfelf. She likes the *Auditor* for his Writings, but is afraid he is too old. The *Auditor* perceiving a particular drift in her, fays fhe knows what fhe's about, and does not offer himfelf, nor recommend any other; tho' a little further in the Paper he is for venturing on a young Lady of 30,000*l.* Fortune, to fave her from falling into bad Hands, fhe being run from her Father.

At laft is an Account of a Country Magiftrate who had unmercifully beat a Schoolmafter for having ferula'd his Niece. Upon which the *Auditor* obferves, That the Fondnefs of Parents has been the Ruin of many a Child: *Mafter* and *Mifs* muft not be corrected; yet muft the School-mafter be anfwerable for the Improvement they make, and be cenfur'd in cafe it does not come up to the Parent's Satisfaction. However, it is unufual to ferula young Ladies of great Fortunes.

The **Craftfman**, March 31.

WE have been told *that the Parliament don't fit to pleafe the Merchants;* and indeed, if they are really a Band of *Sturdy Beggers,* they ought not only not to be gratify'd, but the Laws againft *Vagrants* fhould be put in Force againft them: Nay, if all the Foreign Commodities, which they import for the *Conveniency of Life,* in Return for our *fuperfluous* Manufactures, are to be rank'd under the Denomination of *Luxury,* as we are likewife told, Trade itfelf ought to be fupprefs'd, as well as the *Merchants.* Thefe Doctrines favour more of *Republican Principles* than any I ever advanced. Thofe therefore who argue againft Luxury, are guilty of the moft ridiculous Sophiftry, as regarding only the *Neceffaries* and *Superfluities* of Life, whereas, in all civiliz'd Countries, *Conveniences* ought to have a Place, if thefe feeming *Levellers* would have any Diftinction made between different Ranks of Men. To obviate thefe Notions, by Authority; D'*anvers* tranfcribes an excellent Effay on TRADE and MERCHANTS from a *Spectator* of Mr *Addifon's,* which concludes thus:

There are not more ufeful Members in a Commonwealth than *Merchants.* They knit Mankind together in a mutual Intercourfe of good Offices; diftribute the Gifts of Nature; and Work for the *Poor;* add Wealth to the *Rich;* and Magnificence to the *Great.* Our *Englifh Merchant* converts the Tin of his own Country into Gold, and exchanges his Wool for Rubies. The *Mahometans* are cloath'd in our *Britifh* Manufacture, and the Inhabitants of the *Frozen Zone* warm'd with our Fleeces. When I have been upon the *Change,* I have often fancied one of our *old Kings* ftanding in Perfon, where he is reprefented in Effigy, and looking down upon the wealthy Concourfe of People, with which that Place is every Day fill'd. In this Cafe, how would he be furpriz'd to hear all the Languages of *Europe* fpoken in this little Spot of his former Dominions; and to fee fo many *private Men,* who in his Time would have been the *Vaffals of fome powerful Baron,* negotiating like *Princes* for greater Sums of Money than were formerly to be met with in the royal Treafury! *Trade,* without enlarging the *Britifh* Territories, has given us a kind of additional Empire. It has multiplied the Number of the *Rich,* made our *Landed Eftates* infinitely more valuable than they were formerly, and added to them an Acceffion of *other Eftates* as valuable as the *Lands* themfelves.

Mr D'*anvers* next inferts a long Letter from *Rochefter* fign'd *Philo Anglicus,* in Anfwer to that publifh'd by *Ofborne* in the *London Journal* (See p. 130.) *Philo Anglicus* accufes *Ofborne,* or his Correfpondent, of making a very falfe and partial Reprefentation of the Affair, and maintaining, that the Letter to their Members was regularly voted, with the ufual Freedom, and by 16 out of 18 of the Court prefent, the whole Number being but 23. That the Letter when drawn up was reported on a *Court Day,* approved by all prefent without Amendment, and the City Seal order'd to be affix'd. All this was as much a *Corporate Act,* and with as much *Unanimity,* as any of their Proceedings ever were. A common Hall indeed was not call'd, as in the Cafe of Sir *Staff. Fairbon,* becaufe that was entirely in the breaft of the Mayor, who was known to be under Influence another way.

U

Fog's Journal, March 31. No. 230.

THIS Paper is written in Answer to a Pamphlet entitled *Remarks on Fog's Journal of Feb.* 19, *exciting the People to an Assassination*, of which *Fog* supposes Mr *Walsingham* the Author, at least the Designer. This admirable Piece, adds he, consists of a Short *Introduction*, four choice *Arguments*, some fine *Strokes* of *Panegyrick*, and many *Sarcastical Descriptions* or *Definitions* of *Fog* and his *Journal*. These *Fog* exposeth each in its Order, and puts the Arguments into such a ludicrous Light as at once to ridicule both the Author and his Performance.

One Instance take as follows; The Author, says *Fog*, tell us, That in the Reign of K. *James* II. after *Monmouth's* Rebellion, a Medal was struck by *some body* with the King's Head in Profile on one Side, and on the Reverse *Justice* standing on a Pedestal with her *Sword* in one Hand and her *Balance* in the other; below, a *headless body* neither *stabbed* nor *mangled*, nor deliver'd to an *incensed Multitude*. From hence it may be demonstrated, that *Fog* or his *Principals* intend the Murder of Sir — which if they should atchieve, they will strike a Medal in Honour of the Assassination, but much larger, and with more terrifying Circumstances than the other.] Some think, *Justice* with her *Sword*, *Balance*, and the *Executioner's Block*, should not have been introduc'd on his Occasion.—'Tis an ugly Hint—I wish, says *Fog*, She does not take the Work out of my Hands, and so spoil the Parallel. *Justice* is *blind*, or if she should open her Eyes, Sir——can deal with her.

Some may wonder how a Medal, struck in the Reign of K. *James* II. cou'd be introduc'd to explain a Political or Historical Paper, published about 47 Years after. But a skilful Medallist chuses to illustrate his Argument by an antique Image, or Inscription, rather than by Logick or Demonstration. If any *Vintner* or *Tobacconist* shou'd want a quaint Device or Symbol suitable to the present Times, let him go to the *Oxford Museum*, where the Keeper will shew him a Silver *Medallion*, struck in 1659. On one Side is the Image of a *goodly fat* Man, and *Britannia* astride his Shoulders with this Motto, *Quid Valeant Humeri*. Over her Head *Stuprum Passa Tyr*—The last Letters are defaced, but the ingenious Mess. *Osborne* and *Walsingham* can supply that Defect. On the Reverse of the Medal you see a *Groupe* of Figures, *Lords* and *Citizens*, *Cavaliers* and *Round Heads*, *Churchmen* and *Dissenters*, *Vagrants* and *Sturdy Beggers*, standing on a Pedestal embracing one another; at the Bottom of it this Motto, *Quos Ego*. Some part of the Crowd point at a *Vine* growing out of a *Rock*, which *Vine* an ill-favour'd Fellow is cutting down; near him this Motto, *Excisa renascitur*. Another part is observing an *Indian* in a fine Coat, sitting on an *Hogshead* of *Tobacco*, counting a Heap of Money; on the Hogshead read *Ex Re qualibet*. Hard by stands a *bulky Figure*, throwing Handfuls of *Sugar Plumbs* to the Crowd; near it this Motto, *Utile dulci*.

This Writer says *Fog*, by the foregoing Argument, would insinuate, that *certain Things*, which happen'd in the Reign of K. *James* II. are like *certain other Things* which have *not* happened in the Reign of K. *George* II. and that *something* and *nothing* may be made to resemble each other, *provided* they *both* belong to a Jacobite, *i. e.* to any Person disaffected to Sir ————.

Weekly Miscellany, March 31. No. 16.

THIS No. compleats the Defence of Ld *Clarendon's* History, not only by further refuting the Improbability of the Charge, but by referring to the controverted Clause) concerning Mr *Hampden*, viz. *that he had a Head to contrive, a Heart to conceive, and a Hand to execute any Villany*) in the Original written by the Earl's own Hand, at Mr *Ratcliffe's*, in *Bartlet Buildings Holbourn*, who as an Executor, has the seven first Books of the Manuscript Histo-

History in his Keeping.   The Paſſage
has been read by the Ld Chancellor,
the Speaker of the Houſe of Commons,
Dr *G. Clarke*, and ſeveral other Perſons
of Diſtinction.   It is alſo in another
M. S. of the Earl's, call'd *the Hiſtory of
his Life*, to be ſeen at the *Bodleian* Library,
by ſuch as require ocular Demonſtration.

The learned are obliged to this Journal for
Accounts of and Extracts from Foreign Books
(too long for us) alſo for ſeveral pretty Poems,
among which the two following.

The INVITATION
To a Poetical Friend in *Devonſhire*.

IF you can leave, for *Books*, the rural *Sport*,
  And Bowls of Bourdeaux for a Pint of Port;
*And three Hours Meals, and tedious Bills of Fare,
To taſte the Luxury of Hunger, here;
To theſe ſweet Solitudes, without Delay,
Break, from the World's Impertinence, away.*

*Here, we a thouſand Secrets ſhall explore,
That ſtept, conceal'd in Nature's Womb, before.
Soon as the Sun ſtreams from the ethereal Way,
And breaks triumphant thro' the Gates of Day;
Through every Scene of Nature will we run,
And all the vaſt Creation is our own.*

*But when his golden Globe, with faded Light,
Yields to the ſolemn Empire of the Night;
And in her clouded Majeſty, the Moon,
With milder Glories, mounts her Silver Throne,
Amidſt ten thouſand Orbs, with Splendors crown'd,
That pour their tributary Beams around;
Thro' the long levell'd Tube, our ſtretching Sight,
Shall mark diſtinct the Spangles of the Night:
From World to World ſhall rove the boundleſs Eye,
And dart from Star to Star, from Sky to Sky.*

*The buzzing Inſect Families appear,
When Suns unbind the Rigors of the Year;
In the cool Evening Air they friſk and play,
Hoſts of an Hour! and Nations of a Day!
With pleaſing Wonder will we ſee them paſs,
Stretcht out in Bulk, within the poliſh'd Glaſs;
Thro' whoſe ſmall Convex, a new World we ſpy,
Ne'er ſeen before, but by a Seraph's Eye.
So long in Darkneſs, ſhut from Human-kind,
Lay half God's Wonders, to a Point confin'd:
But in one peopled Drop we now ſurvey,
In Pride of Pow'r, ſome little Monſter play;
O'er Tribes inviſible, He reigns alone,
And ſtruts, the Tyrant of a World his own.*

*Now, will we ſtudy Homer's awful Page;
Now, warm per Souls with Pindar's God-like
    Rage;
To Engliſh Lays ſhall Flaccus' Lyre be ſtrung,
And Heavenly Virgil ſpeak the Britiſh Tongue.
Immortal Virgil! —at thy ſacred Name,
I tremble now, and now I pant for Fame;
With eager Hopes this Moment I aſpire
To catch, or emulate thy glorious Fire;
The next, purſue the vaſh Attempt no more,
But drop the Quill, bow, tremble, and adore.
By thy ſtrong Genius overcome and aw'd;
That Fire from Heav'n! the Spirit of a God!
Pleaſ'd and tranſported with thy Name, I tend
Beyond my Theme, forgetful of my Friend;*

*And from my firſt Deſign, by Rapture led,
Neglect the Living Poet, for the Dead.*

After a Recovery from the SMALL-POX.

WHen languid Heat, in e'ery Vein,
  Swell'd with high Tyde the Crimſon
And wild Ideas to the Brain   [Flood,
Did in fantaſtic Viſions crowd;
When all within, inflam'd with Pains,
Was melted, like the flowing Stream;
And all without, deform'd with Stains,
Was curdled, like the turning Cream;
With Boils and putrifying Sores
When this frail Frame was ſtudded o'er,
And tainted Blood, thro' all the Pores;
Made me my very ſelf abhor?
I, in that gloomy Hour, my Truſt
In his Almighty Arm repoſ'd,
That can reſtore the moulder'd Duſt,
Which Urns, for Ages, have encloſ'd.
Nor was my Truſt repoſ'd in vain,
His Providence was then my Stay;
He rais'd me from the Bed of Pain,
And bleſt me, with the chearful Day.
O! may my Life, by Him reſtor'd,
In Honour to his Name be ſpent!
In Duty to. my gracious Lord,
May I return the Bleſſings lent!
May the Reſentments in my Breaſt
Inſpir'd by this Salvation laſt,
Till on my Skin the Marks, impreſt
By the Diſtemper, are eraz'd.*

London Journal. March. 31. Nº 718.
To the Merchants and Tradeſmen.

Gentlemen,

YOU know I am your Friend, and a Friend
of the People, and that I think *every Act*
of Government ſhould tend to their *Happineſs.*
Your preſent *Opinion,* at leaſt *Diſcourſe,* is,
That the *Scheme* relating to *Tobacco* and *Wine,*
tends to deſtroy *Trade* and *Liberty;* therefore
you attribute to *ill Motives* my appearing for
it: But, to undeceive you, I ſhall give you the
true Reaſons, (*We omit the particulars which
have been enlarged on before*) On the whole, I
believe it to be a good one, as it will not cauſe
any *new Viſitation* of Officers, but a *Continuation* of the old, and thoſe on an eaſier footing;
for above half the Retailers of Tobacco are
viſited already for *other exciſeable* Commodities; and the *Vintners* are all viſited for Arrack,
Brandy and Rum; and as it is calculated for the
Benefit of all fair Traders; and of the Nation
in general, as you'll find in a year's time.

Let me entreat you therefore, *reſtrain* your
Paſſions, and run not into the wild Extravagancies of Bigots and Enthuſiaſts, *burning Books
and Papers* which you don't like.   Is this like
ſober Citizens of *London?*   Is this like Proteſtants, Whigs, and Free-thinkers?   How ſevere-
ly have you cenſur'd ſuch a Conduct on other
Occaſions?   How are you *departed* from. your
Principles?—— But I leave you to your own
Reflections, and am *&c.*   F. OSBORNE.

The *Univerſal Spectator.* March 31. contains only ſome more Quotations from *Homer,*
as before.

HOR. *ODE* ix. LIB. iii.

Ad LYDIAM.

H. Donec gratus eram tibi,
Nec quisquam potior brachia candida
Cervici juvenis dabat,
Perfarum vigui rege beatior.

L. Donec non alia magis
Arfifti, neque erat Lydia post Chloen:
Multi Lydia nominis
Romana vigui clarior Ilia.

H. Me nunc Thressa Chloë regit
Dulces docta modos, & cithara sciens:
Pro qua non metuam mori,
Si parcent animæ fata superstiti.

L. Me torret face mutua
Thurini Calais filius Ornithi;
Pro quo bis patiar mori,
Si parcent puero fata superstiti.

H. Quid si prisca redit Venus,
Diductosque jugo cogit ahenco?
Si flava excutitur Chloë,
Rejectaque patet janua Lydiæ?

L. Quanquam sydere pulchrior
Ille est, tu levior cortice, & improba
Iracundior Adria:
Tecum vivere amem, tecum obeam libens.

HORACE *ODE* ix. BOOK iii.

Wrote long since by Bp ATTERBURY.

H. WHilst I was fond, and you were kind,
  Nor any dearer Youth, reclin'd
On your soft Bosom, sought to rest,
PHRAATES was not half so blest.

L. Whilst you ador'd no other Face,
Nor Lov'd me in the second place,
My happy celebrated Fame
Out-shone ev'n ILIA's envy'd Flame.

H. Me CHLOE now possesses whole,
Her Voice and Lyre command my Soul,
Nor would I Death itself decline,
Could her Life ransom'd be with mine.

L. For me young Lovely Calais burns,
And Warmth for Warmth my Heart returns,
Twice would I Life with ease resign,
Could his be ransom'd once with mine.

H. What if sweet Love, whose bands we broke,
Again should tame us to the yoke,
Should banish'd CHLOE cease to reign,
And LYDIA her lost power regain?

L. Tho' HESP'RUS be less fair than he,
Thou wilder than the raging Sea,
Lighter than Down, yet gladly I
With thee would live, with thee would dye.

An awkward Stage-Monarch.

LO! here in majesty a monarch comes,
  Usher'd by trumpets, and the beat of
    drums;
The plumes around his head, with martial pride,
Wave, as he sallies on from side to side:
Bold in the stage's front he claims a place,
And into posture screws his dismal face.
As from a distant cart, a pond'rous load
Of stones, prepar'd to mend a rugged road,
With inarticulate and dreadful sound,
Our ears invading---rumble to the ground;
So from his Lips a charge important breaks,
And the scar'd Audience tremble as he speaks.

On the CREATION.

WE to JEHOVAH's Altar bring,
  The Incense of these pious Lays,
May he inspire us, while we sing
His Goodness, and his Greatness praise.

But how shall we exalt his Name,
Whose wond'rous Energy of Thought,
The Substance of this mighty Frame
From the void Womb of Nothing brought?

Who, when in Realms of silent Night
The blended Elements lay hurl'd,
By his bare FIAT form'd the Light,
And into Beauty call'd a World.

Cœlestial Hosts of Cherubs say,
Attendants on his awful Nod,
How issued forth the dawning Ray,
Refulgent Shadow of the GOD?

Rais'd with stupendous Arch, the Skies
Widely their azure Mantle spread,
On sable Wings the Tempest flies,
New-risen from the liquid Bed.

The marshall'd Waves, with eager Course,
Retreat from the aspiring Land,
And rally their divided Force,
Obsequious to the Great Command.

Nocturnal Lamps, their measur'd Round
Now leading, kindly Blessings shed,
The Sun, with matchless Beauty crown'd,
Just lighted, rears his radiant Head.

Unbrooded Flocks in Æther rise,
Bright shoals enliven all the Deep;
There Infant Eagles brave the Skies,
Here Whales in madding Tempests sleep.

But Oh! what Numbers shall we find,
  Expressing how ourselves began?
When the ador'd Almighty Mind
His Scheme epitomiz'd in MAN!

Resemblance of Himself imprest
In Reason, Sanctity, Command,
With Wisdom fill'd his stately Breast,
With Sceptre of the Globe, his Hand.

Ye Glorious Works of Heav'n and Earth,
Chiefly thou last, HOSANNAHS raise
To Him, whose Goodness gave you Birth,
The Great CREATOR ever praise.

EPIGRAM.

SIR PRIM, a doughty man of war,
  Who likes to see the foe from far,
Once being in a lonely place,
Shew'd signs of fear in limbs and face.
His friend perceiving him look pale,
Cries, Captain——what! does courage fail?
The heroe stiffly does deny
The charge, and makes this bold reply;
I dread nor man, nor sword, nor gun;
But z——! I'm lame, and cannot run.

Advice to a YOUNG LADY.

From the *Universal Spectator.*

THE Counsel of a Friend, *Belinda* hear,
  Too roughly kind, to please a Lady's Ear;
Unlike the Flatteries of a Lover's Pen,
Such Truths as Women seldom learn from Men;
Nor think I praise you ill, when thus I show,
What Female Vanity might fear to know:
Some Merit's mine, to dare to be sincere,
But greater Yours Sincerity to bear.
Hard is the Fortune that your Sex attends,
Women, like Princes, find no real Friends;
All who approach them their own Ends pursue,
Lovers, and Ministers, are never true!
Hence oft from Reason heedless Beauty strays,
And the most trusted Guide the most betrays.
Hence by fond Dreams of fancied Power amus'd,
When most you tyrannize, you're most abus'd.
  What is your Sex's latest earliest, Care,
Your Heart's supreme Ambition?---to be fair.
For this the Toilet ev'ry Hour employs,
Hence all the Toils of Dress, and all the Joys!
For this, Hands, Lips, and Eyes, are put to School,
And each instructed Feature has its Rule;
And yet, how few have learnt, when this is given,
Not to disgrace the partial Boon of Heaven;
How few with all their Pride of Form can move,
How few are lovely, Nature form'd to Love?
  Do you, my Fair, endeavour to possess,
An Elegance of Mind, as well as Dress;
Be that your Ornament, and know to please,
By graceful Nature's unaffected Ease.
Nor make to dang'rous Wit a vain Pretence,
But wisely rest content with modest Sense;
For Wit, like Wine, intoxicates the Brain,
Too strong for feeble Woman to sustain:
Of those who claim it, more than half have none,
And half of those who have it are undone.
  Be still superiour to your Sex's Arts,
Nor think Dishonesty a Proof of Parts.
For you the plainest, is the wisest Rule,
A Cunning Woman is a Knavish Fool:
Be good yourself, nor think another's Shame,
Can raise your Merit, or adorn your Fame.
Prudes rail at Whores, as Statesmen in Disgrace
At Ministers, because they wish their Place.
Virtue is Amiable, Mild, Serene,
Without, all Beauty, and all Peace within.
The Honour of a Prude is Rage and Scorn,
'Tis Ugliness, in its most frightful Form.
Fiercely it stands, defying Gods and Men,
As fiery Monsters guard a Giant's Den.
Seek to be good, but aim not to be great,
A Woman's noblest Station is Retreat;
Her fairest Virtues fly from publick Sight,
Domestick Worth, that shuns too great a Light.
  To rougher Man, Ambition's Task resign,
'Tis ours in Senates, or in Courts to shine:
To labour for a sunk corrupted State,
Or dare the Rage of Envy, and be Great;
One only Care, your gentle Breasts should move,
Th' important Business of your Life is Love.
To this great Point, direct your constant Aim,
This makes your Happiness, and this your Fame.
  Be never Temperance with Passion join'd,
Love not at all, or else be fondly kind.

In this, Extream alone can truly bless,
The Virtue of a Lover, is Excess.
Contemn the little Pride of giving Pain,
Nor think that Conquest justifies Disdain;
Short is the Period of insulting Pow'r,
Offended CUPID finds his vengeful Hour;
Soon he'll resume the Empire that he gave,
And soon the Tyrant shall become the Slave.
  Bless'd is the Maid, and worthy to be bless'd,
Whose Soul, entire by him she loves possess'd,
Feels ev'ry Vanity in Fondness lost,
And asks no Power, but that of pleasing most;
Hers is the Bliss, in sweet Returns to prove
The honest Warmth of undissembled Love.
For her, inconstant Man might cease to range,
And Gratitude forbid Desire to change.
  Thus I, *Belinda*, would your Charms improve,
And form your Heart to all the Arts of Love.
The Task were harder, to secure my own
Against the Power of those already known.
For well you twist the secret Chains that bind,
With gentle Force, the captivated Mind;
Skill'd ev'ry soft Attraction to employ,
Each flatt'ring Hope, and each alluring Joy.
I own your Genius, and from you receive
The Rules of pleasing which to you I give.

The RETIRED PATRIOT.

ENough to glory and his country giv'n,
  The pious hero now aspires to heav'n;
Quits the eternal round of noise and care,
And bids his soul for calmer joys prepare.
A second SCIPIO he from state retires;
His breast the love of simple nature fires:
Triumphant greatness! more illustrious far,
Than all the glories of victorious war.
There the proud madman boasts in hostile blood;
But here the peaceful victor seeks his God;
Asserts imperial reason's noble sway,
And teaches rebel passions to obey;
Lord of himself each night the sage can say,
Repose my soul, for I have liv'd to-day.
Serene and calm amidst the storms of fate,
He bids his thoughts on God and nature wait;
The beauteous face of smiling earth surveys,
And wrapt in wonder, sings his maker's praise.
  "Each verdant plant, each fragrant herb that
     grows,
The great JEHOVA's forming wisdom shows:
How each bright stem its species will produce,
Each vein, each fibre has its proper use;
How the male plant impregns the softer kind,
And their joint beauties in the sons we find.
JEHOVA hung the radiant orbs on high,
Pois'd the brute earth in air, and arch'd the sky.
JEHOVA gave the sun his piercing ray,
To glad dull mortals, and to rule the day;
To call each secret seed from nature's womb,
Mature the birth, and swell the fragrant bloom.
JEHOVA lent the moon her paler light,
To cheer the darkling horrors of the night:
The magick queen asserts her sway below,
And makes reluctant waters ebb and flow.
JEHOVA paints the plains with various hue,
Scoops the low vale, exalts the hills to view,
And bids the purling stream its winding course
     pursue."   *Gr. J.*

The following EPIGRAMS, by an unknown Hand, being all refer'd to page 17 of
Mr P—e's Dialogue in Imitation of the first
Satire of the second Book of HORACE, we chuse
to give the whole Passage, then the *Epigrams*.

Could pension'd *Boileau* lash in honest Strain
  Flatt'rers and Bigots ev'n in LOUIS Reign?
Could Laureate *Dryden* Pimp and Fry'er engage,
Yet neither CHARLES nor JAMES be in a Rage?
And I not strip the Gilding off a Knave,
Unplac'd, unpes.sion'd, no man's Heir, or Slave?
—Dash the proud Gamester in his gilded Car?
Bare the mean Heart that lurks beneath a Star?
I will, or perish in the Gen'rous Cause,
Hear this, and tremble, you who 'scape the Laws.
To VIRTUE only, and HER FRIENDS, a FRIEND,
The World beside may murmur, or commend.
Know, all the distant Din that World can keep,
Rolls o'er my Grotto, and but sooths my Sleep.
There my Retreat the best Companions grace,
Chiefs, out of War, and Statesmen out of Place.
There ST JOHN mingles with my friendly Bowl,
The Feast of Reason, and the Flow of Soul:
And He, whose Lightning pierc'd th' Iberian
    Lines,
Now, forms my Quincunx, and now ranks my,
Or tames the Genius of the stubborn Plain,
Almost as quickly as he conquer'd *Spain*.

Envy must own, I live among the Great,
No Pimp of Pleasure, and no Spy of State,
With Eyes that pry not, Tongue that ne'er repeats,
Fond to spread Friendships, but to cover Heats;
To help who want, to forward who excel;
This, all who know me, know; who love me, tell;
And who unknown defame me, let them be,
Scriblers or Peers, alike are MOB to me.

EPIGRAM I.

S—J—N, a quondam Statesman out of Place,
  Makes Punch for P—e, nor thinks it a Disgrace.
In mingling Punch S—J—N must needs have
  Merit;
He never us'd one Drop of BRITISH Spirit.

EPIGRAM II.

CHiefs out of War, and Statesmen out of Place,
  It seems, the *Twick'nham* Poet's Mansion grace:
Some *Stories tell*, others form *his* Quincunx;
He sneers, then prints, and sells them for *Quidams*.

EPIGRAM III.

PHÆBUS turn'd Mason, as old Poets sing,
  Built Walls, but then the GOD work'd for a
    KING.
Iberian MARS, it seems, much humbler grown,
Turns GARD'NER to a SQUIRE of Twick'nam
  Town.

The Passages referr'd to in the following ADVICE
to Mr P. are so many, that we have not room,
agreeably to our professed Impartiality, to insert
them; but the Reader will find an Answer to
it at the End of the Lines of his above quoted.

ADVICE to Mr P—E.

Sent us from the same unknown Hand.

THe Muse quite jaded, P—r rhimes on in Prose,
  Writes worse and worse, and lashes Friends
  and Foes.

Can CH—os, B——N, or B—ST 'scape
The Grins and Paws of this unlucky Ape?
All the three Patrons has he satiris'd,
The first * *here fac'd*, the other † two disguis'd;
WREN praises, to the Peer that copies JONES,
WREN! Gallo-Gothic Heaper up of Stones!
Makes † B—ST think, what his good Heart denies
" That Men were made for Heav'n the Standing
    Jests."

Thought! that cou'd only rise in his low Mind,
Who to himself wou'd level all Mankind;
Who talks of ETHICS † with a forc'd Grimace,
And scarce refrains from laughing in your Face;
Who † puts among the daily Wants of Life,
" Equal to Want of *Bread*, his Neighbour's Wife;
Whose Sentiments, stript of their Tinsel-Dress,
Prove *mean*, or *false*, or the *bad Heart* confess.

Let the declining Bard at length grow wise,
Nor take a LAWYER's, but a FRIEND's Advice
His flagging Muse why will he not release?
Why whip and spur her on? she pants for Ease!
The * RIDICULE why bears he not in Mind
Of the *quick-hearing Flanks*, and *broken Wind*?
WHAT e're it was, his Talent NOW is CHAT,
Then let him quit the PEN and stick to THAT.

  * See the *Epistle upon Taste,* † *See the Epistle of*
on the Use of Riches, ‡ *See all* P—e's *Epistle*
and his new Satyrical Dialogue *with his Learn'd*
Council, *in Imitation of* Horace.

  * *Solve* Senescentem, *maturè Sannus, Equum, ne*
Peccet *ad extremum* ridendus, *et ilia Ducat.* Hor.

From Mr POPE's *Poem on* RICHES.

ASK we what makes one keep, and one bestow?
  That Power which bids the Ocean ebb and flow,
Bids Seed-time, Harvest, equal Course maintain;
Thro' reconcil'd Extremes of Drought and Rain
Builds Life on Death; on Change Duration founds
And gives th' eternal Wheels to know their Rounds
Riches, like Insects, when conceal'd, they lie,
Wait but for Wings, and in their Season fly.

  On a profuse DUKE *and Sir* J. CUTLER. *ib.*

HIS Grace's Fate sage *Cutler* could foresee (me.
  And well, he thought, advis'd him, " Live like
As well his Grace reply'd, " Like you, Sir J.
" That I can do, when all I have is gone."
Resolve me, Reason, which of these is worse?
Want with a full, or with an empty Purse?

EPIGRAM. *From the* Gr. Journ.

WHen patriots strike at palace or at sleep,
  They beg the help of all good Christian
  people;
Whose virtue, sense, and pow'r are highly prais'd
For, and by them, all kings to thrones are rais'd
By them depos'd, when, slaves to their own will,
They break their sacred oaths, and govern ill.
When thus cajol'd, they've done their leaders
Pow'r, sense and virtue gone, they're chang'd
  mob:
Like beasts of burthen now once more regard,
And with a double load their backs rewarded.
Thus GENERAL NOLL espous'd the People
The cause of liberty, religion, laws: [can
Dear, ancient rights secur'd by *Magna Charta*!
But NOLL PROTECTOR call'd it *Magna F—*

PART of PSALM CXIV. proper for EASTER.

WHen, from proud *Egypt's* hard and cruel Hand,
  High-fummon'd *Ifrael* fought the Promis'd
The Op'ning *Sea* divided, at her Call: (Land,
And refluent *Jordan* rofe, a wat'ry Wall!
Light, as met Lambs, the ftarting Hills leapt, wide:
And the flow Mountains roll'd themfelves afide.
Why, O Thou Sea! did thy vaft Depth *divide?*
And, *wherefore, Jordan!* fled thy back'ning Tide?
Why leapt your Lines, Ye frighted Hills, aftray?
And *what,* O Mountains, rent your Roots away?
Hark! I will *tell.*—Proud Earth confefs'd Her
  GOD:
And mark'd His Footfteps; trembling, as He trod,
While, bent to *blefs,* He chear'd His thirfty Flock?
And, into Floods, of liquid Length, diffolv'd the
  loos'ning Rock.   PHILOTHEUS.

Occafion'd by reading the ESSAY *on* MAN.
(See our laft Book, p. 96.)

GO on, great Genius, with thy bold Defign,
  And Profe's Strength with Verfe's Softnefs
Teach us the wife, the neceffary Skill, (join:
To fearch the Heart, and curb the headftrong Will.
No more let Pride's delufive Arts prevail,
And Prejudice decide, where Reas'nings fail.
Of Reafon's Self affign the juft Extent,
Nor let her aim beyond what Nature meant:
Eternal Laws have fix'd her bounded Sway,
Nor can fhe from her ftated Limits ftray.
Shall Mortals ftrive to know what Heav'n denies?
Or view Immenfity with purblind Eyes?
Inftruct eternal Wifdom how to reign,
And count each Link of the Almighty Chain,
Vain Creatures, own your vain dependant State,
Nor hope to pry into th' Abyfs of Fate.
Content with the fmall Share of Good poffeft,
Act well your Parts, and leave to Heav'n the reft.

The Ord——*y of* N——e *to* Sarah Malcolm.

TO *Malcolm* G——y cries, confefs the Murther;
  The Truth difclofe, and trouble me no further:
Think on both Worlds; the Pain which thou muft
In that, and what a Load of Scandal here. (bear
Confefs, confefs, and you'll avoid it all;
You fha'n't be then cut up at Surgeons Hall;
No *Grubftreet* Hack fhall dare to ufe your Ghoft ill;
H——ß fhall read upon your Poft a *Poftil;*
Ha——th tranfmit your Charms to future Times;
And C——t record your Life in Profe and Rhimes.

An ACROSTICK *by a* NAKEDAMIAN, *prefented
to the* Naked-Society, *at a* Nocturnal Meeting,
held at the Tavern *near the* Hay-market.

NAture thus naked has full Pow'r to charm;
  And Luft, like Buff preferves the Body warm.
Keep on your Raggs, ye Cuftom-cover'd Fools;
Ever abafh'd, and Slaves to modeft Rules:
Inftead to the Pleafures of our modern Schools.
All Hail dread *Lucifer!* great Mafter, Hail!
As ake us but Bold, thy Tenet cannot Fail,
In this Ingenious Age:—— We thus refin'd,
And free'd from Shame, defie all Human kind:
Naked we came, then Naked let us Live,
So Nature gave us, fo let her receive.

The Hibernian POETESS's Addrefs and Recommendation of her Son, to her dear Coufin
    Efq; L   M   *of London.*

TO the late King of *Britain* a Savage was brought,
  Which wild in the Woods of *Germania* was
  caught.
This Prefent fo princely, was train'd up with care;
And knew how to eat, and to jump, and to ftare:
The Beaus and the Belles beheld it with joy,
And, at court, the high mode was, to fee the wild
Reflecting on this, with a politick view, (boy.
I determin'd to fend fuch a Prefent to you:
In the wilds of *Hibernia,* this Boy was befet,
And caught, (as the Natives are there) in a Net.
The Creature has Senfe, and in my Eye, is pretty:
And has Talents to make a good-man—in the City.
Is induftrious and orderly, prudent and fmart;
Has not too much of Confcience, or too little Art;
Nor fcrup'oufly honeft; a Heart fet on Gain;
Whofe higheft Ambition is fix'd on the Chain.
From you he may learn a fondnefs for reading,
And how to improve in fine Senfe and good breed-
To fill well the ftation to which he afpires, [ing
And well to become the wealth he acquires.

The following Lines to the Earl of O---Y, were
wrote laft Year at BATH by the fame Gentlewoman; who is about to publish her POEMS.

Sent to the E. *of* O--y *half an hour paft* 9.

'TIS faid, for every common Grief,
    The Mufes can infpire Relief;
And furely, on that heavenly Train,
A BOYLE can never call in Vain:
Then ftrait invoke the facred Nine,
Nor, impious, flight their Gifts Divine.
Difpell thofe Clouds that damp your Fire,
Shew BATH like TUNBRIDGE can infpire.

Receiv'd for Anfwer, the fame Hour.

Nor BATH nor TUNBRIDGE can my Lays infpire,
Nor radiant Beauty make me ftrike the Lyre;
Far from the bufy Crowd I fit forlorn,
I figh in Secret, and in Silence mourn;
Nor can my Anguifh ever find an End,
I weep a FATHER, and have loft a FRIEND.

Mrs B——*t's Reply.*

Your Anguifh is infectious, I confefs,
I try'd to cure, and I have caught Diftrefs.
Reftrain your Sighs, and dry your Tears, 'tis time;
Excefs of Virtue may become a Crime.
You've loft a FRIEND, you fay, and FATHER too,
But know, Mankind will lofe a FRIEND in you.

As it will be very difficult for us to do Juftice to
a moft exalted Act of Benevolence and Generofity in a truly noble PEER, which was
communicated to us with fome of the foregoing Verfes, we fhall be glad if our unknown
Correfpondent will fend it us ready drawn up
in a Manner that will moft effectually perpetuate fo rare an Inftance of Greatnefs
and Goodnefs happily united. We have fomething partly to this Purpofe, at the Clofe of
page 126; and no doubt, the Author of thofe
Obfervations, did he know all the Circumftances would delightfully expatiate on fo
pleafing a Theme, as this would be to him-

On the Return of the SUN.

Inserted at the Desire of Mr. S. P.

BEhold, the Sun returning from afar,   [Isle,
  Sheds his soft Influence o'er our wretched
Which long to direful Storms of Hail and Wind,
Devoted, lay in Ruin ; long had the Frost,
In icey Fetters, bound her teeming Womb ;
Till thy all-chearing Ray, exhaustless Light !
With boundless Majesty, dispensing Day,
Dispel'd the Winter, sullenly severe.
  'Tis now, for thee, all Harmony awakes,
And Nature, joyful, smiles at thy Return :
With thee the tuneful Larks waking arise,
Studious to usher in thy gladsome Beams ;
When in the Mid-way Sky, on steady Wings
Up-rear'd, they sing their Mattins in thy Praise;
The humbler Quires, harmonious on the Boughs
Of blooming Trees, in Consort join their Notes.
While, by their restless Motion, glitt'ring Pearls,
That Pendant hung, from every trembling Leaf,
Fall unregarded. Now the early Swains,
Wakeful, quick starting from their wholesome Beds
Gladsome to all their rural Labours haste ;
But now the Rich and Great (shameful to tell)
Luxuriously immers'd in Beds of Down,
In slumbers drown'd, unknowing true Delight.
Miss the gay Prospect of the early Morn ;
Where Nature lies in all her Charms display'd,
When the Sun's milder Heat o're all the World
In soft Effusion pours his genial Rays :
The verdant Meads and Mountains ting'd with Dew
O'er spangled, glitter in the rising Sun.
The humbler Vales, o'er spread with various
Profusely gay, inimitably dress'd,   [Flow'rs,
Send grateful Odours through the scented Air,
Amid a Stream of living Waters flow,   [Sound
Here gliding smoothly, there with murm'ring
Chides interrupting Pebbles ; from each Hill
The neighbouring Trees and vaulted Roof of
   Heaven
Inverted, tremble in the restless Stream.

Two Freeholders, on the Candidates for Kent.

1st.

WHose Interest, pray Neighbour, shall you appear in ?
For Sir Thomas D'AETH, or Sir Edw. DERING?

2d.

Thy impertinent Question my right'ous Soul vexes,
Who would not appear against Death and Taxes?

1st.

Your passionate Warmth, Friend, has exhausted
  your Breath ;   [Death ?
When loaded with Taxes, who would not chuse
For Dearing you may pay Dear all your Days ;
In electing of D'AETH you'll find certain Ease.

Wrote extempore by a Member after the Debate in the House, March 14. 1733.

SOme Duties of Customs turn'd into Excise
  Flagrant Thefts will prevent and sad Perjuries.
Who says, it will tend to make *Free Britons* Slaves,
Says, *Britons* to be *Free*, must needs be Knaves.

To the Rev. Dr FREIND, on his quitting West minster-School. By STEPHEN DUCK.

IF void of Art my languid Verse appears,
  Forgive, O FREIND, the Bard that sings in Tears
Rude are the Lays which only Grief adorns,
And dull the Muses when *Apollo* mourns.
When Science trembles o'er *Minerva's* Shrine,
To see her fav'rite Priest his Charge resign.——
Yet why should Grief debase his glorious Name
Or blast the Bays his Merits justly claim ?
No venal View his noble Temper sways ;
He quits with Honour what he kept with Praise
As some wise Leader in successful Wars,
Worn out with Age, and cover'd o'er with Scars
Resigns the Post he bravely hath sustain'd,
Crown'd with the Palm his former Valour gain'd
So thou, paternal Sage, may'st now repose,
Nor seek new Laurels to adorn thy Brows.
Review thy Toils, and see what polish'd Peers
Honour thy forming Hand, and studious Care
Let learned CARTERET, Elegant of Taste,
Confess the Mould in which his Mind was cast.
Let HARVEY's Muse her Tutor's Worth proclaim
And TALBOT's Royal Trust declare thy Fame,
PELHAM, in whose capacious Soul we find
The Scholar, Statesman, and the Patriot join'd.
Nor shall the tender Plants that round thee stand
E'er prove ungrateful to the Planter's Hand:
Water'd by thee, their well-fix'd Roots extend
Their Branches flourish, and the Fruits ascend,
While pleasing Hope with Expectation smiles,
To reap the future Product of thy Toils :
Intent to see thy Pupils shining forth,
Whose Actions soon shall better speak thy Worth
When in the Train of Senators they come
Refin'd with all the Arts of *Greece* and *Rome*
Whilst in each Act their prudent Counsels shew
Their Master's Loyalty and Learning too.
Thus have thy Precepts made thy Province shine
And ev'n *Minerva's Athens* yield to thine.

To a Beautiful Young LADY who Painted fine ly, but drew a DISADVANTAGEOUS likeness of all the TOASTS in her Neighbourhood.

SAY, *Myra* ! why with cruel Skill
  You call the Pencil to your Aid;
In Effigy defame the Fair,
  And triumph o'er the vanquish'd Shade?

Be just, fond Nymph, and ask thy Heart,
  How That such Injuries could brook,
Should e'er thy beauteous Self be shewn
  Less killing by a single Look.

Fear not,—tho' Thou each Rival's Face
  With more than native Charms shou'd'st croud
Thy utmost Skill can ne'er pourtray
  A Form more Lovely than thy own.

* *The Birth Day Verses shall be inserted in our next just as desired.*
Those spoke at the Tripod at Cambridge would be disagreeable to many of our Readers, besides, Ladies, were they not Personal.
The Dialogue by H. de Canette is too long.
The Subject of Belinda's Letter is under Consideration In the mean while she will do well to keep the on his good Behaviour.

THE
Monthly Intelligencer.
MARCH, 1733.

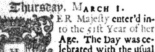

Thursday, March 1.

HER Majesty enter'd into the 51st Year of her Age. The Day was celebrated with the usual Solemnity. The antient *Britons* had an elegant Feast at Merchant Taylors-hall, at which 30 l. was collected for placing out *Welch* Children.

At *Rippon*, was the greatest Flood ever known there; about 4 Miles from thence the Waters came down so suddenly to a Mill, that the Miller was obliged to fly with 3 of his Children to the uppermost Room, where he broke out, and carried his Children singly ashore in a large Tub, which was overset with his last Cargoe, but Assistance being ready, they got safe to Land. Presently after Part of the House was carried away.

Saturday, 3.

Mr *John Thompson*, late Warehousekeeper to the Charitable Corporation, (See p. 1078, Vol. II. p. 99, No XXVI.) was several Hours under Examination, before the Committee of the House of Commons.

Monday, 5.

Eight Malefactors, condemn'd the preceeding Sessions at the *Old-Baily* (See p. 100) were executed. *Dawson* repriev'd.

Wednesday, 7.

Sarah Malcolm, (See p. 97 D 99 H) was executed on a Gibbet opposite Mitre Court in Fleet-street. She was attended by the Revd Mr *Piddington*, Curate of St *Bartholomew the Great*; seem'd penitent, and intimated she had deliver'd to him a genuine Account sealed up the Night before, which contained her whole Confession. (See p. 137.) She desired to see her Master *Kerrol*, but as she did not, protested that all Accusations concerning

We have endeavoured to gratify our Readers with as near a Resemblance of the Face of this Woman, who has made so much Noise, as this manner of printing will allow. She went to Execution neatly dressed in a Crape mourning Gown, holding up her Head in the Cart with an Air, and looking as if she was painted, which some did not scruple to affirm.

Her Corpse was carried to an Undertakers upon Snow-Hill where Multitudes of People resorted, and gave Money to see it; among the rest a Gentleman in deep new Mourning, who kiss'd her; and gave the People Half a Crown. She was about 25 Years of Age.

X

him were falſe. She was buried in St Sepbulcber's Church-Yard. During her Impriſonment ſhe received a Letter from her Father at *Dublin*, who was in too bad Circumſtances to ſend her ſuch a Sum as 17*l.* which ſhe had pretended he did.

Was held a High Court of Chivalry in *Doctors Commons*, when the Earl of *Effingham*, Deputy Earl Marſhal of of *England*, took the Oaths, and his Seat, as Judge, on his being re-appointed by the preſent Duke of *Norfolk* ; ſeveral Perſons were called upon to anſwer to their Pretenſions of Arms, and order'd to attend the Court on the 19th of *May* next.

Friday, 9.

Was executed at *Northampton William Alcock*, for the Murder of his Wife (See p. 981) He never own'd the Fact, nor was at all concern'd at his approaching Death; refuſing the Prayers and Aſſiſtance of any Perſons. In the Morning he drank more than was ſufficient, yet ſent and paid for a Pint of Wine, which being deny'd him, he would not enter the Cart before he had his Money return'd. On his way to the Gallows he ſung part of an old Song of *Robin Hood*, with the Chorus, *Derry, derry, down*, &c. and ſwore, kick'd, and ſpurn'd at every Perſon that laid hold of the Cart ; and before he was turn'd off, took off his Shoes, to avoid a well known Proverb ; and being told by a Perſon in the Cart with him, it was more proper for him to read, or hear ſomebody read to him, than ſo vilely to ſwear and ſing, he ſtruck the Book out of the Perſon's Hands, and went on damning the Spectators and calling for Wine. Whilſt Pſalms and Prayers were performing at the Tree he did little but talk to one or other, deſiring ſome to remember him, others to drink to his good Journey, and to the laſt Moment declared the Injuſtice of his Caſe.

Tueſday, 13.

Mr *John*, Reſident from the King of *Denmark* had his firſt Audience of his Majeſty.

Wedneſday 14.

The Houſe of Commons being to enter upon the Propoſal for altering the Method of collecting the Duties on Wine and Tobacco, a very great Appearance of Merchants and Traders attended to make their Applications to the Members againſt it.

The Aſſizes ended at *Hereford*, when 4 Perſons receiv'd Sentence of Death, *viz.* *Thomas Rapar*, for Houſe . breaking ; *Richard Wiſmer*, for Horſe ſtealing; and

Wm Wilſon and *Wm Robinſon* for Forgery and Perjury, in giving Evidence at the laſt Aſſizes to prove certain Writings, which they ſwore to be the Hand-writing of a Gentleman deceaſed ; whereby the next Heir would have been (had their Evidence prevail'd) diſpoſſeſſed of 150*l. per Annum.*

Thurſday, 15.

Was held a General Court of the S. Sea Company, wherein it was agreed to apply to Parliament to divide their preſent Capital, *viz.* Three Parts into Annuities, and the remaining Fourth into a Trading Capital, agreeable to a former Reſolution; (See p. 675) and reſolved, That from and after *Michaelmas* next, no more than 3 and a half *per Cent.* Intereſt be allowed on their Bonds, which if any refuſed to accept, ſuch Bonds ſhould be paid off.

Friday, 16.

At the Aſſizes at *Taunton, Somerſetſh.* 5 Perſons receiv'd Sentence of Death, *viz.* two for Horſeſtealing, one for a Rape on a Girl 9 Years old, and a Woman for the Murder of a Baſtard Child.

Monday, 19.

The Place of Accomptant-General of the S. Sea Company, lately poſſeſs'd by *Charles Lockyer*, Eſq; was by the Directors voted uſeleſs ; and ſeveral Clerks, for the ſame Reaſon, were diſcharged.

Friday, 23.

Were executed at *Lincoln Iſaac* and *Thomas Hallam*, for the Murders and Robberies of Mr *William Wright* of *Market-Raſen*, and *Thomas Gardner* the *Lincoln* Poſt Boy in *Jan.* laſt (ſee p. 41) While in Gaol they confeſs'd they had committed upwards of 50 Robberies ; and after Condemnation, attempted to break out off Priſon by ſawing of their Fetters with a Caſe Knife notch'd like a Saw, and digging thro' the Wall with a large Nail ; but being diſcover'd, they then, and not before begun to think ſeriouſly of their approaching End. In paſſing to Execution, near the Place where they murder'd the Poſt Boy, *Iſaac* fell into violent Agonies and Pertrbation of Mind ; at the Tree having no Clergyman to aſſiſt him, he beckon'd to one who was there as a Spectator, who readily comply'd with his Requeſt, and pray'd with him fervently. After which being turn'd off, and his Brother *Thomas* ſeeing him hanging in the Air ſtruggling for Life, ſhriek'd out dreadfully at the ſhocking Sight ; and was then led to Execution nigh

nigh the Place where they had murder'd Mr *Wright*. He, as well as his Brother, acknowledg'd the juftice of his Sentence and calling upon God was turn'd off.

Thurfday, 21.

His Majefty went to the Houfe of Peers and gave the Royal Affent to the following Bills, *viz. That for punifhing Mutiny and Defertion; to allow Time for taking the Oaths to thofe who had omitted to qualify themfelves for Employments; for importing Diamonds Cuftom free; the* Englifh *Law Bill; for Rebuilding St George's Church,* Southwark*; for making the River* Dun *navigable; to allow further Time for the Inrollment of Deeds and Wills made by Papifts and for Relief of Proteftant Purchafers and Leffees; and* to four private Acts. The Commons adjourn'd to *Monday* the 2d, and the Lords to *Tuefday* the 3d, of *April*.

Monday, 26.

The Act for qualifying Juftices of the Peace; and *Englifh* Law Act took place.

Thurfday, 29.

A Scandalous and fictitious Letter having been difperfed in Writing and Print, highly reflecting on the Town of *Southampton* (See p. 144) that Corporation, in an Advertifement publifhed this Day, figned by *John Godfrey* Town Clerk, declare it to be forged, and that the following is the real Letter.

GENTLEMEN— *I received your Commands with the Greateft Pleafure, and fhall obey them. I hope if any other thing fhould be fet on foot to your Prejudice, you'll give me your Inftructions; which fhall always be obferv'd by*
SIRS,
Your Obliged Hum. Ser.
Lond. Jan. 25, 1732   Ant. *Henley*.

The *Charles* and *Mary* Sloop, Captain *Curtis*, bound to *Holland*, with 25,000 *l.* in Gold Coin on board, was loft off *Ald. borough* in *Suffolk*, and all the Crew, with 30 Paffengers, were drowned.

A Mayor of a Corporation's Anfwer to a Member's Letter. (See p. 98.)

SIR,

I Had the Favour of yours, and communicated the Contents to thofe who lately troubled you with their Sentiments on the important Subject of Excife Laws; and I have Authority to affure you, that nothing in your Anfwer has in the leaft alter'd our Thoughts; and if you vote for a Bill of that Nature, even in the

Shape you feem to be pleas'd with, or in any other, you can't reafonably expect our Approbation, fince we are fully convinced that all Excife Laws are deftruc-
A tive to Trade, Innovations on our antient Rights, and altogether inconfiftent with the true Intereft of a free People.

The fpecious Pretence of ferving the fair Trader can no longer amufe us, when we too often fee thofe very Laws, which were calculated for their Protection, u-
B fed againft them, nor can it be otherwife expected, whilft the Execution of thofe Laws is under the Management of fuch as by their ill Conduct have render'd themfelves juftly odious in all Parts of the Kingdom, by often making it a Part of their Duty to be troublefome, in Hopes of meriting by Their Activity and
C Vigilance.

If you would act agreeable to our Wifhes and Inclination, befote you think of improving or extending the Revenues, make it a Preliminary, that the Laws of Excife be firft regulated, and Trade and the poor Manufacturer eafed; and when
D this is done, affure yourfelf nothing will be more grateful to us than to fee the Neceffities of the Government fully fupply'd, as well as proper Provifion made to anfwer all National Engagements, fo as they are annual, and repeated no oftner than Occafion requires, and the Manner
E of Collection be made eafy to the Subject. Acting on thefe Principles, you cannot fail of having the Approbation and Thanks of us, and all true Lovers of their Country. *Colchefter*, Feb.   I am, Sir, 28. 1732-3.   Your moft Hum. Serv.
The MAYOR.

To *Sam. Tufnel*, Efq;

Friday, 30.

The Cafhire of the Cuftoms paid into the Exchequer 13,000 *l.* the Cafhire of the Excife 28,000 *l.* for one Week.

Saturday, 31.

A Volcano, or burning Mountain, has
G been obferv'd on the Sea Coaft of *Ireland*, which we are promis'd a particular Account of for our next Magazine.

A Charter is paffed the Great Seal of *Ireland*, for the erecting and maintaining of Schools for teaching the Natives the *Englifh* Tongue, and inftructing them in the Proteftant Religion.

H Lieut. *George Crowe*, having a Competency in the Country to fubfift on, has refigned his Half Pay, amounting to 45 *l.* 12s. 6d. *per Ann.* to the Lords of the Admiralty

miralty for the Use of the Corporation for the Relief of the poor Widows of Sea Officers.

The Parish of St *Botolph Aldgate* have contributed very handsomely, by a Collection made this Month, towards the noble Design of settling the Colony of *Georgia*.

The Earl of *Burlington* has projected a Plan for building two new Houses of Parliament, and a Public Library between them, to be finish'd against next Session, and to cost the Public about 30,000 *l.*

On *Tuesday* 13, there were present in the House of Commons at the Call, 490 Members. On *Wednesday* 14, sitting very late, but 469, *viz.* 265 and 204. On the 16th but 345, *viz.* 256 and 189.

The Epidemick Colds, lately so mortal here, have been felt in most Parts of *Europe*; 60,000 were blooded on that Occasion in and about *Paris*, and 18,000 died notwithstanding.

BIRTHS.

THE Lady of the Ld *Anne Hamilton*, deliver'd of a Son.

The Lady of Sir *William Tonge*, Knt of the *Bath*, deliver'd of a Son, at their House in *Pall-mall*.

The Lady of Sir *Henry Blunt*, lately burnt out on *Laurence Pountney* Hill, delivered of a Son.

The Wife of *George Chamberlayne*, Esq; Representative for *Buckingham*, delivered of a Daughter.

The Wife of *David Papillion*, Esq; of a Son.

MARRIAGES.

EDward *Cape Hopton*, Esq; (Son of *Richard Hopton*, Esq; formerly Kt. of the Shire for the County of *Hereford*.) married to Miss *Briggenshaw*, a Fortune of 30,000 *l.*

John Simpson, Esq; of *Rochester*, : : to a Daughter of Capt. *Farmer*, of *Maidstone* in *Kent*.

—— *Winstanly*, of *Leicestershire*, Esq; : : to a Daughter of the late Sir *Edmund Prideaux*.

George Venables of *Staines*, Esq; : : to the Daughter and Heiress of *John Edworth* of *Kingston upon Thames*, Esq; a Lady of 6000 *l.* and 200 *l. per Ann.* Fortune.

Mr *Richard Blunt*, Distiller in *Bread-street*, : : to a Daughter of Mr *Jn Smart*, of *Guildhall*.

Sir *George Blacket*, : : to the Daughter of — *Reynolds*, Esq; of *New-Bond-street*, a Fortune of 15,000 *l.*

Charles Palmer, Esq; of *Wiltshire*, : : to Miss *Blake* of *Hatton Garden*.

The Ld *Augustus Fitzroy*, second Son to the Duke of *Grafton*, now on his Travels, : : to the second Daughter of Col. *Cosby*, Governor of the *Leward Islands*; as advised from abroad.

Henry Pye, of *Farringdon*, in *Berkshire*, Esq; a Gentleman of 3000 *l. per Ann.* : : to Mrs *Warren*, Sister in-law to *Richard Aston*, of *Wadley*, Esq;

William Webb, of *Derbyshire*, Esq; : : to Miss *Baven* of St *Clements Danes*.

Thomas Hannier, Esq; : : to the Daughter of the Lord *Percival*.

—— *Waring*, Esq; Son to Brigadier *Waring*, : : to a Grand Daughter of Sir *Wm Humphreys*, Bar. a Fortune of 20,000 *l.*

Robert Chester, Esq; : : to Miss *Thornton*, of *Leicester-fields*, a Fortune of 18,000 *l.*

Sir *John Ellis*, : : to Miss *Barnes* of *Chelsea*, a Fortune of 12,000 *l.*

John Drake, Esq; : : to Miss *Jenny Long*, Sister to Cornet *Long*.

Sir *Edward Leighton*, of *Loton*, *Salop*, Bart : : to the Relict of Capt. *Thwaits*.

DEATHS.

Feb. 26. THE Relict of Sir *Thomas Wilson* of *Wilts*, Bart.

James Langham, Esq; of *Bloomsbury*.

28. *George Hearne*, Esq; of *Lancashire*.

March 1. *Thomas Brayfield*, Esq; Deputy Warden of the *Fleet* Prison.

Mr *James Pinfold*, an eminent Proctor in *Doctors Commons*, and Deputy Register of the Court of Delegates.

Thomas Wright, Esq; of *Cary-lane*, formerly a Water-Gilder. He left 500 *l. per Ann.* to a poor Relation, and to the Charity Schools of St *Anne's* within *Aldersgate*, and St *Michael's Foster-lane*, 100 *l.* each.

Samuel Bulkly, Esq; at *Hackney*.

John Warren, Esq; a *West India* Mercht

—— *Gundy*, Esq; aged 116, at *Hyde-Park* Corner; reputed worth 100,000 *l.*

Sir *William Smithson*, Bart formerly Representative for *Nottinghamshire*.

2. *Thomas Bloom*, Esq; at *Hoddesden*, *Hertfordshire*.

Mr *Clement*, Postmaster of *Durham*.

3. Capt. *Frome*, at *Chelsea*.

4. *John Jones*, of the *Inner Temple*, Esq;
John Glover, Esq; at *Cheshunt*, *Hertfdsh*.
John James, Esq; Barrister at Law, in
the *Inner Temple*.
The Relict of Sir *Theodore Lawson*.

5. *William Mason*, Esq; of *Somersetsh*.
The Sister of *John Medcalf*, Esq;
John Woodford, Esq; at *Dartford* in *Kent*.

6. The Relict of *William Prafer*, Esq;
Daughter to the Earl of *Buchan*.
Dame *Mary Lloyd*, Aunt to *William*
Gwyn Vaughan, Esq; Knight of the Shire
for the County of *Brecon*.

7. *Thomas Weston*, Esq; of *Norfolk-street*.
Stephen Adcock, Esq; in *Mincing-lane*.
Mr *Turner*, an eminent Clothier at
Trowbridge in *Wilts*, burnt to Death by a
Fall into the Fire; reputed worth 40,000 *l*.
James Young, Esq; near *Carnaby Market*, lately come of age, worth 1000 *l. p. An.*
Sir *Robert Furnese*, Bart Knight of the
Shire for the County of *Kent*; succeeded
by his Son Sir *Henry*, a Minor.
Edward Worth, M. D.

8. *James Bridges*, Esq; one of the Commissioners of his Majesty's Board of Works.
Capt *William Norman*, at *Isleworth*.
John Thornbury, Esq; at *Cheshunt* in
Hertfordshire, formerly a Merchant.

9. The Lady *Gore*, in *Greek-street*, *Soho*.
John Crawford, Esq; at *Uxbridge*.
Mr *Mecklam*, Fishmonger in *Thames-street*, reputed worth 20,000 *l*.
Charles Halstead, Esq; in *Pall-mall*.
Dr *Dawes*, M. D. F. R. S. of *Guernsey*.
Wm Bellamy, Esq; Bencher of the *Inner
Temple*, Master of the Crown Office, and Auditor General of the Dutchy of *Lancaster*.

10. *John Bouchier*, Esq; at *Endfield*.
Mr *William Carr*, Mayor and Post-Master of St *Albans*. (See p. 89.)
Mr *Hopkins*, a Merchant, at *Kensington Gravel-pits*, said to be worth 30,000 *l*.
Thomas Havers, Esq; Senior Alderman
of *Norwich*.
The Relict of Sir *Cæfar Childe*, of
Woodford Bridge, Bart.

13. Mr *Whitfield*, an eminent Attorney
of *New Inn*.
Joshua Sayer, Deputy Post-master at *Deal*.

14. — *Dennis*, Esq; in *Hatton Garden*.
Thomas Stuart, Esq; Nephew of Sir *Archibald Stuart*, a *Scots* Baronet.

15. Mr *Thomas Bride*, Clerk of his
Majesty's Works in the *Meuse*.
Mr *Tho. Page*, Stationer on *Tower-hill*.
John Sheldon, Esq; of *Worcestershire*.
Mr *James Lane*, Broker, *Exchange-alley*.
Mr *Sa. Palmer*, a *Blackwell-Lall* Factor.

16. *Henry Trent*, Esq; of *Westminster*.
John Goodgroom, Esq; at *Chelsea*.
Mr *Sam. Totton*, Warden of *Trinity College*, *Greenwich*.
Mrs *Jane Egerton*, a Lady of considerable Fortune and Family.

17. *Thomas Beake*, Esq; one of the
Clerks of the Council, and Manager of the
Charitable Corporation.
Sir *James Woodward*. at *Putney*, *Turkey* Merchant, worth 80,000 *l*.
Mr *Whadcock*, Surgeon in *Bread-street*.
The Revd Mr *Thomas Rudd*, Rector of
Washington in the County of *Durham*, and
Head Master of the Grammar School of
Durham, and afterwards of *Newcastle*.

18. *John Hanger*, Esq; one of the Directors of the *Bank*, worth 40,000 *l*.

19. *Thomas Salt*, Esq; Purveyor of the
King's Houshold.
Capt. *Bennet*, Commander of the *Flamborough* Man of War at *Jamaica*.
Sir *Robert Raymond*, Knt, Ld *Raymond*
of *Abbots-Langley* in the County of *Hertford*. In 1710 he was appointed Sollicitor
General to Q. *Anne*, elected Member for
Lymington in *Hants*, and so continu'd
during that Reign; but in 1714 his Patent
was revoked. In 1720, he was appointed
Attorney General to his late Majesty; and
in 1723-4, was made a Serjeant at Law,
and the next Day appointed one of the
Justices, and in *Feb.* 1724-5, Lord Chief
Justice of the *King's Bench*, in the room
of L. Ch. J. *Pratt*; in 1730 he was elected a Governor of the *Charter-house*, in
the room of L. *Trevor*; and in *Jan.* 1730-1,
created a Peer of *Great Britain*. He married a Daughter of the late Sir *Edward
Northey*, Attorney General to Q. *Anne*,
by whom he has left one Son aged 16.

20. The Ld Visc. *Blaney*; at *Dublin*.
Edward Beckham, Esq; formerly a Director of the *East-India Comp*. He left
900 *l*. per An. to the Hospital of *Bethlehem*.
Samuel Mead, Esq; Counsellor at Law,
Brother to Dr *Mead*.

21. Mrs *Mary Calcott*, a maiden Lady,
in St *Martin's*, reputed worth 40,000 *l*.
Mrs *Talman*, Relict of an ingenious
Virtuoso of that Name, at *Hinxford*, *Hert*.
Mr *Joseph Gilman*, Apothecary at *New-Windsor*, worth 10,000 *l*.

22. Mr *Coffart*, a *Hamburg* Merchant,
worth 50000 *l*.
The Wife of *Peter St Eloy*, Esq; one of
the Procurators-General of the Arches
Court of *Canterbury*.

23. The Wife of *Philip Southerd*, Esq;
at his Seat in *Essex*.

The Rev. Mr *Steadman*, Chaplain to the Bishop of *London*, Rector of *Bramshot* in *Hampshire*, and Prebendary of St *Paul's*.

Col. *Floyer*, Son of the late Sir *Peter Floyer*, the noted Refiner in *Fosler-lane*, and has left the Bulk of his Estate, of a-bout 6000 *l. per Ann.* to his Sister Mrs *Letitia Floyer*, of *Islington*.

—— *Hammond*, Esq; formerly a Wine Merchant in *Tower-flreet*.

24. Capt. *Pelltoukerfield*, in *Witch-flreet*, worth 70,000 *l.*

Mr *Dominick*, Head Porter and Ward-keeper of St *Thomas's* Hospital.

25. *John Roberts*, Esq; formerly Governor of St *Helena*.

The Wife of Sir *John Werden*, Bar.

26. Miss *Dive*, second Daughter of *John Dive*, Esq; one of the Under-Tellers of the *Exchequer*.

Mr *Humphreys*, a Master of Musick.

27. *Toby Chauncy*, Esq; of *Edgeot*, Representative for *Banbury*.

The Rev. Mr *Rees*, Reader, Lecturer, and Schoolmaster in the united Parishes of St *Laurence Jewry*, and St *Mary Magdalen*, *Milk-flreet*.

The Wife of *Rogers Holland*, Esq; Member of Parliament for *Chippenham*.

Richard Bowater, Esq; Common Council-man for *Cripplegate within* Ward.

Thomas Ramfay, Esq; Son of Sir *Alexander Ramfay*, of *Scotland*, Bar.

Mr *Blunt*, noted for supplying the Nobility and Gentry with Sets of Horses. His Father offer'd to furnish the late King, in the Time of the Rebellion, with 500 Horses in 3 Days time.

The Lady *Charlotte Whitfield*, reputed worth 130,000 *l.*

28. *Thomas Jobber*, Esq; Sollicitor to the Admiralty.

Hyde, Esq; formerly a Linnen Draper. He was Governor of several Hospitals of this City.

PROMOTIONS.

Miss *Sarah Pitt*, 3d Sister to *Thomas Pitt*, Esq; Member for *Oakhampton*, APPOINTED Maid of Honour to her Majesty, in the room of Mrs *Pointz*.

Mr *Smith*, Deputy Register of the Court of Delegates.

Capt. *Farringdon*, Auditor of the South Part of *Wales*, in the room of *Sidney Godolphin*, Esq;

Wm Horner, of *Alton* in *Hampshire*, Esq; a Master Extraordinary in Chancery.

Thomas Penrose, Esq; made Admiral of the *North* and *South* Parts of *Cornwal*.

Ld *Muskerry*, Commander of the *Romney*, a 4th Rate ; and

Mr *O. Hearne*, Lieutenant of the same.

Henry, Earl of *Pembroke* and *Montgomery* made Lord High Steward of the City of *Salisbury*, in room of his Father.

Promotions in the 3d Reg. of Foot Guards.

John Scott, Esq; appointed a Colonel in the room of Col *Bragge*.

Capt. *Fargent*, to succeed Col *Scott*.

Ensign *Nevett*, to succeed Capt. *Fargent*.

Thomas Hervey, Esq; second Son to the Earl of *Briflol*, and Equerry to her Majesty, appointed Vice-Chamberlain of her Majesty's Houshold, in the room of the Lord *William Beauclerk*, deceased.

Mr *Reynolds*, a Dry-Salter in *Bread-flreet*, chose Clerk of St *Mildred's* Parish.

George Woodward, Esq; appointed Envoy Extraordinary to the Kingdom and Republick of *Poland*.

William Maflerman, Esq; Master of the Crown Office, in the Room of *William Bellamy*, Esq; deceased.

Mr *Samuel Torin*, Exchange Broker, chosen Common-Council-Man of *Cordwainers* Ward.

James Leak, of *Bath*, commissioned by the Trustees for the Colony of *Georgia*, to receive Benefactions for that Charity.

Mr *Ridge*, and Mr *Green*, declared High Burgesses of *Weflminster*, and

Mr *Rawlinson*, High Constable, for the Year ensuing.

Charles Shelley, Esq; Brother to Sir *John Shelley*, Bar. appointed Auditor of all his Majesty's Revenues in the Counties of *Lincoln*, *Nottingham*, *Derby*, and *Chefter*; also Auditor of the Alienation Office, in the room of *Sidney Godolphin*, Esq; dec.

Mr *John Ruffel*, admitted Veftry Clerk to the Parish of St *James's Weflminster*.

William Matthews, Esq; appointed Governor and Commander in Chief of the *Leeward Iflands*.

Mr *Puland*, Surgeon to the 2d Regiment of Foot Guard, appointed Ensign to Col *Johnson's* Company in the said Regiment.

Robert Mercer, Esq; Capt Lieut. in the Earl of *Albemarle's* Regiment of Foot at *Gibraltar*.

Mr *Bond*, made a Land Surveyor.

Mr *James Brodier*, a King's Waiter in the Port of *London*.

Mr *Chapple*, Master Bricklayer and Surveyor of *Woolwich* Yard. -

By the Death of Capt *Floyer, the following Promotions have been made in the 4th Troop of Life Guards, viz.*

Capt *Stevenson,* Exempt,

Capt *Miller,* Sub-Brigadier, and Mr *Abden,* Riding-Master.

Sir *Jacob Ackworth,* appointed Clerk of the Surveys at *Deptford.*

Richard Palmer, Esq; Brother to Sir *Thomas Palmer,* Bart made a Clerk in Chancery.

Thomas Lothbury, Esq; appointed Cornet in a Troop of Horse on the *Irish* Establishment.

The Ld *Muskerry,* Commadore of a Squadron, to be sent to *Newfoundland,* to protect our Fishery.

Sir *Thomas Saunderson,* High Steward of the Manor of *Kirton,* in *Lincolnsh.*

Mr *Clarke,* Author of *Writing improv'd,* or *Penmanship made easy,* by the Death of Mr *Snell,* has had the Golden Pen bestow'd upon him, as a Prize claimable by the best Master in the Art of Writing.

Members of Parliament elected.

Dudley Rider, Esq; for *St. Germans.*
Sir *Thomas Prendergast,* for *Chichester.*
Sir *Charles Bunbury,* for *Chester.*
Sir *Edward Dering,* for *Kent.*
Robert Scot, Esq; for the Shire of *Forfar.*

Ecclesiastical P R E F E R M E N T S.

MR *Jones,* Chaplain to the Ld Visc. *Lisburne,* PRESENTED to the Vicarage of *Tregaron* in *Cardiganshire.*

Mr *John Pember,* : : to the Cantership of *St Davies*

Mr *Thomas Tryce,* : : to the Vicarage of *Downton, Hertfordshire.*

Dr *Trapp,* : : to the Living of *Dawley Middlesex,* by the late Ld V. *Bolingbroke.*

Mr *Charles Huet,* : : to the Rectory of St *Mary's* in the Town of *Stafford.*

Mr *Thomas Aubrey,* : : to the Vicarage of *Hellington* in *Huntingtonshire,* worth 300l. *per Ann.*

Mr *Richard Roche,* : : to the Vicarage of *Locking* in *Somersetshire.*

Mr *Nathanael Troughton,* : : to the Rectory of *Bexterley* in *Warwickshire.*

Mr *John Baron,* made a Doctor of Divinity.

Dispensations have passed the Seals, to enable

John Freke, M. A. and Chaplain to the Bp of *Norwich,* to hold the Vicarage of *Spayton* in *Devonshire,* with the Rectory of *Cluncborough.*

Samuel Hill, M. A. Chaplain to the Ld *Falkland,* to hold the Rectory of *Little Somerford* in *Wilts,* with the Rectory of *Kilmington* in *Somersetshire.*

Stephen White, M. A. Chaplain to the E. of *Moreton,* to hold the Vicarage of *Swaffham Bulbeck* in *Cambridgeshire,* with the Rectory of *Helton* in *Suffolk.*

Mr *Church,* appointed Reader of the Morning and Evening Service at St *Ann's Westminster.*

Mr *Morse,* Chaplain to the D. of *Kent,* presented to the Rectory of *Horsley Magna* in *Essex,* worth 300l. *per Ann.*

Mr *Edward Turner,* to the Vicarage of *Worlington, Dorset.*

Mr *Michael Blackborne,* to the Vicarage of *Taunton, Somerset.*

Mr *Rollaston,* collated to the Arch-Deaconry of *Sarum.*

Mr *Sager,* to the Prebend of *Gillingham* in the said Church.

Mr *Richard Newcome,* to the Rectory of *Bishops-stoke* in *Southamptonshire.*

Mr *Tough,* Rector of St *Paul's, Covent Garden* appointed Chaplain to the Duke of *Bedford.*

Mr *Le Plage,* presented to the Vicarage of *Rockingham, Salop.*

Mr *John Straight,* of *Tindon in Suffex,* collated to the Prebend of *Warminster,* in the Church of *Sarum ;* and

Mr *William Lane,* to the Prebend of *Netherhaven,* in the said Church.

Mr *Edward Stephens Escourt,* elected Master of Sir *Thomas Rich's* Hospital at *Gloucester,* in the room of the Revd Mr *Abbotts,* deceased.

Mr *Jacob,* inducted to the Rectory of *Taynton* in *Gloucestershire.*

Dr *Thomas,* chosen Lecturer of St *Bennet, Paul's Wharf.*

B A N K R U P T S.

CHristopher Wetheral, of Lond. Merchant.
John Barnard, of Sudbury. Suff. Mercer.
Henry Gambier, of London, Broker.
Joseph Crosier, of Hendon Middlesex, Victualler.
Thomas Law, of Norwich, Butcher.
Tho. Powel, of St Giles's Middlesex, Mealman.
Lydia Peck, of St Paul's Church yard, Milliner.
Henry Sherman, of Witnesham Suff. Maltster.
John Duell, of St Clement Danes, Mid. Chapman.
Charles Kessing, of Watling-street, Lond. Merch.
James Morgan, jun. of Shafton Dorset, Tanner.
Christopher Roberts, } of London, Merchants
George Stainforth. } and Partners.
Mary Haskins, of Bristol, Upholster.
Robert Collington, of Stamford, Linc. Grocer.
Joseph Baker, of London, Merchant.
Thomas Row, of London, Tobacconist.

STOCKS

Courſe of Exchange.	STOCKS	*Monthly* BILL *of Mortality;* from Feb. 20. *to* March 27.

Courſe of Exchange.	STOCKS	*Monthly Bill of Mortality*
Amſterdam— 35	S. Sea 102 ⅛	Chriſtned { Males 885 / Females 876 } 1761
Ditto at Sight 34 10	—Annu. 110 ¼	
Hamburgh— 34	Bank 150 ¼	Buried { Males 1395 / Femal. 1424 } 2819
Rotterdam— 35 2 a 3	India 158 ⅝	
Antwerp — 35 5 a 6	3 *per C. Ann.* 100 ½	Died under 2 Years old --- 1081
Madrid — 42 ¼ a ¼	M. Bank 116	Between 2 and 5 ---- 210
Bilboa — 42	African 35	Between 5 and 10 ---- 106
Cadiz — 42 ½ a 2	YorkBuil. no Transf.	Between 10 and 20 ---- 83
Venice — 48 ¾	Royal Aſſ. 105 ¼ ½	Between 20 and 30 ---- 184
Leghorn — 50 ⅝	Lon. ditto 13 ¼	Between 30 and 40 ---- 255
Genoa — 53	Eng. Copp. 1*l.* 18*s.*	Between 40 and 50 ---- 256
Paris — 32	Welſh ditto 1*l.* 10*s.*	Between 50 and 60 ---- 198
Bourdeaux -- 31	BankCir. 6*l.* 12*s.* 6*d.*	Between 60 and 70 ---- 184
Oporto— 53 ½ a ⅞	India Bonds 5*l.* 7*s.*	Between 70 and 80 ---- 137
Lisbon— 5 5 ¼ a 4 ½	3 *p. Cent* ditto 2*l.* 10	Between 80 and 90 ---- 105
Dublin— 11 ¼ a 12	S. Sea ditto 2*l.* 12*s.*	Between 90 and 103 ---- 20

2819

Price of Grain at Bear-Key, *per* Qr.		N. B. The laſt Monthly Bill ſhould have been dated from Jan. 23 to Feb. 20.	*Weekly* Burials
Wheat 20*s.* to 25*s.*	P. Malt 17*s.* to 20*s.*		Feb. 27 — 613
Rye 12*s.* to 15*s.*	B. Malt 14*s.* to 18*s.*		March 6 — 507
Barley 12*s.* to 14*s.* 0*d.*	Tares 15*s.* to 17*s.*		13 — 542
Oats 09*s.* to 12*s.*	H. Peaſe 13*s.* to 15*s.*		20 — 567
Peaſe 16*s.* to 17*s.*	H. Beans 14*s.* to 19*s.*		27 — 590

Prices of Goods, &c. in London. Hay 1 *l.* 14*s.* to 2 *l.* 0*s.* a Load.

Coals per Chaldron 25*s.* to 26*s.*	Ditto ſecond ſort 46*s.* to 50*s.* per C.	Opium 11*s.* 00*d.*
Old Hops per Hun. 3*l.* to 6*l.*	Leaf Sugar double refine 8*d.* Half-penny a 9*d.* per lb.	Quickſilver 4*s.* 3*d.*
New Hops 9*l.* to 10*l.*		Rhubarb fine 25*s.* a 30*s.*
Rape Seed 10*l.* to 11*l.* per Laſt	Ditto ſingle refin. 5*6 s.* to 64*s.* per C.	Sarſaparilla 3*s.* 0*d.*
Lead the Fodder 14*Hun.* 1 half on board, 14*l.* to 16 *l.* 00 *s.*	Cinamon 7*s.* 8*d.* per lb.	Saffron Eng. 28*s.* 00*d.*
Tin in Blocks, 4*l.* 00*s.*	Cloves 9*s.* 1*d.*	Wormſeeds 3*s.* a 5*s.*
Ditto in Bars 4*l.* 02*s.* excluſive of 3*s.* per Hun. Duty.	Mace 15*s.* 0*d.* per lb.	Balſam Capaivæ 2*s.* 10*d.*
Copper Eng. beſt 5*l.* 05*s.* per C.	Nutmegs 8*s.* 7*d.* per lb.	Balſam of Gilead 18*s.* 00*d.*
Ditto ord. 4*l.* 16*s.* to 5*l.* per C.	Sugar Candy white 14*d.* to 18*d.*	Hipocacuana 6*s.* to 7*s.*
Ditto Barbary 70*l.* to 80*l.*	Ditto brown 7*d.* per lb.	Ambergreece per oz. 9*s.* to 12*s.*
Iron of Bilboa 14*l.* 10*s.* per Tun	Pepper for Home conſ. 16*d.* Farth.	Cochineal 18*s.* 3*d.* per lb.
Dit. of Sweden 15*l.* 10*s.* per Tun	Ditto for exportation 12*d.* half-p.	
Town Tallow 34*s.* 35*s.* per C.	Tea Bohea fine 9*s.* to 11*s.* per lb.	**Wine, Brandy, and Rum.**
Country Tallow 30*s.* to 34*s.*	Ditto ordinary 7*s.* 6*s.* per lb.	Oporto red, per Pipe 36*l.*
	Ditto Congo 10*s.* to 14*s.* per lb.	ditto white 24 *l.*
Grocery Wares.	ditto Pekoe 8*s.* a 14*s.* per lb.	Liſbon red 30*l.*
Raiſins of the Sun 31*s.* 0*d.* per C.	ditto Green fine 8*s.* to 12*s.* per lb.	ditto white, 26 *l.*
Ditto Malaga Frailes 19*s.*	ditto Imperial 10*s.* to 16*s.* per lb.	Sherry 26 *l.*
Ditto Smirna new 20*s.*	ditto Hyſon 24*s.* to 28*s.*	Canary new 30*l.*
Ditto Alicant. 18*s.*		Florence 3 *l.* per Cheſt
Ditto Lipra new 19*s.*	**Drugs** *by the lb.*	French red 30 *l.* a 40 *l.*
Ditto Belvedere 20*s.*	Balſom Peru 14*s.* to 15*s.*	ditto white 20 *l.*
Currants old none	Cardamoms 3*s.* 3*d.*	Mountain malaga old 24*l.*
Ditto new 45*s.* to 00*s.*	Camphire refin'd 19*s.*	ditto new 20 to 21*l.*
Prunes French 18*s.*	Crabs Eyes 2*s.* 8*d.*	Brandy Fr. per Gal. 6*s.* to 6*s.* 6*d.*
Figs 20*s.*	Jallop 2*s.* 3*d.* to 3*s.* 1*d.*	Rum of Jamaica 7*s.* to 8*s.*
Sugar Powd. beſt 54*s.* a 59*s.* per C.	Manna 1*s.* 8*d.* a 2*s.* 9*d.*	ditto Leew. Iſlands 6*s.* 4*d.*
	Maſtick white 3*s.* 6*d.* to 4*s.*	Spirits Eng. 30*s.* per Tun.

GOLD in Bars, 3*l.* 18*s.* 4*d.*---Ditto in Coin 3*l.* 18*s.* 3*d.* to 4*l.* 1*s.*—SILVER in Bars, Standard, 5*s.* 4*d.* half-penny. —Pillar Pieces of Eight 5*s.* to 5*s.* 5*d.* 3 farth. ditto Mexico 5*s.* 9*s.* 3 farth.

FROM *Moscow*, That the Cold had been so intense, that an hundred Persons were froze to Death, Birds fell dead in the Streets, and Horses harness'd to the Sledges, were frozen standing stiff as Wood.

From *Persia*, That the Bashaws of *Ormus* and *Bender-Abassi*, with several other principal Men of that Kingdom, have enter'd into a League against the Usurper; so that a Civil War is daily expected, which has been the Drift of the Turkish Councils ever since the Deposition of the *Sophi*.

From *Poland*, That the Grandees are forming private Conventions in their respective Districts; but most of them seem united in this Particular, *viz.* To exclude a Foreigner from the Crown. The Interest of his Imperial Majesty seems so considerable, and necessary to any Candidate, that this Event will probably draw closer the Knot, that seem'd to be loosening in the Life of the late King, (on Account of the Pragmatick Sanction) between him and the Elector of *Saxony*; who prudently seems to lie quiet. *France* on the other Hand seems determin'd to push the Interests of King *Stanislaus*, and has made such a Declaration as may possibly Occasion some future Disturbances.

From *Palestina*, That the Turks, on the *Moors* being defeated before *Oran*, and the seizing two of the Grand Seignior's Ships, had taken all the Churches from the Christians, and committed horrible Impieties on the Holy Sepulcher; Ecclesiasticks and Seculars had been the Gallows, and had the Soles of their Feet flead and rubbed with Salt; others the Nails of their Hands and Feet torn off by Pinchers, and then boiling Pitch, and burning Sulphur pour'd into their Wounds. At *Damascus*, *Rama*, and *Bethlehem* many Monks have been skinned alive.

From *Oran*, That a great Body of *Moors* attacking some *Spaniards* at work upon an Out-Fort, had been defeated with a great Slaughter by the *Spanish* Troops which sallied out of the Town,

with the Governour *Don Ladron de Gueverra* at their Head, who was too brave to be discouraged by the Fate of his Predecessor the Marquis *de Santa Cruz*. Tis now concluded, that the Marquis, not being found among the Prisoners at *Algier*, was the same *Spanish* Commander seen to fall from his Horse in the Battle, being shot through the Body and into the Thigh whom the *Moors* stript of his Cross, Rings and Cloaths, and then beheaded him.

From *Cadiz*, That an *Algerine* Capitana, or Ship of War, had been destroyed by the *Spanish* Squadron; but not before she had landed 300 *Turks*, with Provisions she brought for the *Moors* Camp.

From *Madrid*, That a Deserter having taken Shelter in the *Dutch* Ambassador's Palace, who refused to deliver him up, a Detachment of Guards took him by Force, having killed 3 or 4 of his Excellency's Domesticks. 'Tis added, the King demanded Satisfaction.

From *Brussels*, That on the 21th Instant King *Stanislaus* sent his Act of Abdication, by an Express to *Warsaw*.

From *Germany*, *Prussia*, *Sweden*, *Muscovy*, and *France*, that their respective Sovereigns have order'd their Troops to be in a Readiness, in Case they should have any Occasion to interpose with Force in the Affairs of *Poland*.

From *Corsica*, That the Officers sent thither from *Genoa* to collect the usual Tax, were forc'd to retire, after a great deal of ill Treatment, the Inhabitants refusing to pay it under Pretence that the new-establish'd Form of Government there is not yet made publick.

From *Geneva*, That that City had been blockaded up by the *French*, occasion'd by the Rudeness of some Person, who flung an Apple at the Altar whilst the Almoner to the *French* Minister was celebrating Mass, and threw down the Chalice, just after it had been consecrated; but the Magistrates having deputed four of their Body to his most Christian Majesty, to offer any Satisfaction in their Power, the Blockade is rais'd.

A REGISTER *of* BOOKS *pub-lish'd in* MARCH, 1733.

THE Regard had by Providence to Prosperous Iniquities: A Sermon preach'd before the Rt Hon. the Ld Mayor, &c. at St Paul's, Jan. 30. By Wm Berriman, D. D. Printed for Mess. Ward and Wickstead.

2. D. Thomæ Cragii Jus Feudale & Civile. Editio Tertia, prioribus multa emendation, &c. Printed at Edinburgh, and Sold by George Grafton, in London.

3. The Proceedings at the Old Bailey, on the 21, 22, 23, and 24 of Feb. last, in 2 Parts, by reason of S. Malcolm's Trial at length, pr. 1s.

4. A Short Account of Mortifications, and of the surprifing Effect of the Bark, in putting a Stop to their Progress, &c. Sold by J. Nourse.

5. A Letter to Sir Hans Sloan, Bt, from Wm Stukely, M. D. about the Cure of the Gout by Oils externally apply'd, as prepared by Dr Rogers of Stamford. Printed for J. Roberts, pr. 6d.

6. The Adventures of Prince Jakaya: Or, the Triumphs of Love over Ambition. Being Secret Memoirs of the Ottoman Court. Translated from the Original French. Printed for A. Bettesworth, pr. 4s.

7. The Volunteer Laureate. Inscribed to her Majesty on her Birth Day. By Richard Savage, Esq; No. 2. Pr. for L. Gilliver, pr. 6d.

8. Encomium Argenti Vivi: A Treatise upon the Use and Properties of Quicksilver. By a Gentleman of Cambridge. Printed for Stephen Austen, pr. 1s.

9. A True Copy of the Paper deliver'd by Sarah Malcolm, the Night before her Execution, to the Revd Mr Piddington, of St Bartholomew's the Great, March 6. 1732-3. Printed for J. Wilford, pr. 4d. (See p. 137.)

10. Some Observations address'd to the Author of the Letter to Dr Waterland, &c. In which, from his Words, and Reasoning against the Author of Christianity as Old as the Creation, it is plainly prov'd, that his Letter, Defence, and Remarks, ought all to be burnt, and the Author banish'd.

11. The Close of the Defence of the Religion of Nature and the Christian Revelation, in Answer to Christianity as Old as the Creation: In an Address to Christian Ministers and Christian People. By the late Revd Mr Simon Browne. Printed for R. Ford.

12. A Sermon, preach'd March 15. 1733. at a noted Chappel in Westminster, from their Words of St Luke, Chap. 2d. Ver. 1st. And it came to pass in those Days that a Decree went out that all the World should be TAXED; with some practical Observations and Uses suited to the present Times. By Robert Vyner, D. D. and Rector of the said Chappel. Printed for Humphry Fitz-Drug, at his Office in the Old Jewry, pr. 13d. Half-penny.

13. Remarks on Fog's Journal of February 10. 1732-3, exciting the People to an Assassination. Printed for J. Wilford. (See p. 146.)

14. The Sequel of Mr Pope's Law Case, or farther Advice thereon: In an Epistle to him. By a Templer. With Notes Explanatory, &c. Printed for the Benefit of the Author, pr. 2s. 6d. i. e. for Verse 6d. for Notes 1s. and for the Law Case 1s.

15. The Interest of the Compound Distiller consider'd, with some Observations on the Distilling Trade. In a Letter to a Member of Parliament. By J. Browne, Distiller. Printed for T. Payne.

16. An Answer to Dr Berryman's Remarks on Mr Chandler's Introduction to the History of the Inquisition, by Samuel Chandler. Printed for John Gray, pr. 6d.

17. Proportional Architecture, or the Five Orders regulated by Equal Parts, after so concise a Method, that renders it useful to all Artists. Sold by A. Bettesworth, pr. 2s. 6d.

18. A Proposal for the Relief of Ireland, by a Coinage of Monies, of Gold and Silver, and establishing a National Bank. Printed for J. Worra, pr. 6d.

19. The Ordinary of Newgate's Account of the 8 Malefactors, executed at Tyburn March 5. and of Sarah Malcolm, executed in Fleetstreet, the 7th. Printed for John Applebee.

20. The Political Foundling. Sold at the Pamphlet Shops, pr. 1s.

21. Proposals offer'd for the Sugar-Planters Redress, and for reviving the British Sugar Commerce. In a farther Letter from a Gentleman at Barbados, to his Friend in London. Printed for J. Wilford.

22. A Supplement to the Sermon preach'd at Lincoln's-Inn, on the 30th of Jan. 1732. By a Layman. Address'd to a very important and solemn Churchman, Solicitor-General for Causes Ecclesiastical. Pr. for J. Peele, pr. 6d.
* *The Writer of the Weekly Miscellany having charged the Author of the Sermon with Insolence, and with observing no Measures of Truth or Decency; and having in No. XIII. answer'd his Calumnies concerning the Bp of London's usurping a Jurisdiction over our Colonies; the Layman, in this Supplement, makes no direct Reply to that Answer; but arraigns all Ecclesiastical Authority; and strikes at the whole Office of Priesthood.—Is a Chapter of the Bible, says he, less edifying when read by a Layman, than when read by a Clergyman? &c. Towards the Conclusion he has some Strictures upon the Author of the Miscellany on his having attributed the Wickedness of the Age and the frequent Murders, to the Neglect of observing the Lords Day, and mention'd the Powers of Church-wardens to present all Persons that do not go to some Place of Worship on that Day, with a Hint that the Writings of Atheists and Free-thinkthinkers are one great Occasion of Irreligion — It is not Free-thinking, says the Layman, that fills the Goals, loads the Gallows, and Peoples Exchange Alley: Was Sarah Malcolm a Free-thinker?*

thinker? Did she die one? was Sir J. B—t
or Ravilliac Free-thinkers; or was He one, who
offer'd to murder the late King? Is it Freethinking that absolves Traytors or Criminals of
any sort? I was surprized to hear Compulsory
Laws mention'd as still in force to oblige People
to go to Church. Could any but Persecutors solicit such a Law? No penal Laws whatever
were, or ever could be prompted by a Christian Spirit.

23. Lord *Bacon*'s Philosophical Works me-
thodiz'd, and made English, with occasional
Notes, in 3 Vols. 4to. By Dr *Shaw*. Printed
for Mess. *Knapton*, &c.

24. The Reply of a Member of Parliament
to the Mayor of his Corporation. Printed for
J. Roberts, pr. 6d.

25. Some General Considerations concerning the Alteration and Improvement of Publick Revenues, pr. 6d.

26. Excise Anatomis'd: Declaring that an
equal Imposition of Excise to be the only Cause
of the Ruin of Trade, the universal Impoverishment, and destructive to the Liberties of the
whole Nation. Sold by the Booksellers, pr. 6d.

27. An Appeal to the Landholders, concerning the Reasonableness and General Benefit of
Excising Tobacco and Wine. Pr. for *J. Peele*,
pr. 6d.

28. The Budget open'd; or, an Answer to
a Pamphlet, intitled, a Letter from a Member of Parliament to his Friends in the Country, concerning the Duties on Wine and Tobacco. Printed for H. *Haines*, pr. 6d.
*This Pamphlet uses many Arguments from
the Craftsman; but hints one thing worth Observation, which the Author proposes as a Remedy
for the Frauds committed in the Customs, that
is, to let the Commissioners thereof have the
nominating and advancing their Officers as those
of the Excise have; and then they cou'd better
Answer for their Fidelity and Conduct; and
there wou'd be less Occasion for extending the
Excise.*

29. A Dialogue between Sir *Andrew Free-
port*, and *Timothy Squat*, Esq; on the Subject
of Excise. Being a full Review of the whole
Dispute. Printed for *J. Roberts*, pr. 1s.

30. A Letter from a Merchant of *London*,
to a Member of Parliament; in Answer to a
Letter from a Member of Parliament to his
Friends in the Country, concerning the Duties
on Wine and Tobacco. Pr. for *A. Dodd*, pr. 6d.

31. The Case of the Planters of Tobacco in
Virginia, as represented by themselves; sign'd
by the President of the Council, and Speaker
of the House of Burgesses. To which is added
a Vindication of the said Representation. Printed for *J. Roberts*, pr. 1s.

32. Some Thoughts on the Land Tax, General Excises, and the least burthensome way
of raising Taxes; occasion'd by the *London
Journal* on that Subject.

33. A Collection of Letters from several
Counties, Cities, and Boroughs. Containing
Instructions to their Representatives, to oppose any Extension of the Excise Laws. Printed for *J. Wilford*.

34. A short Letter to the Letter-Writer
concerning the Duties on Wine and Tobacco.
Printed for T. *Warner*, pr. 4d.

35. An Impartial Enquiry into the present
Question concerning Excise: In which the
Advantages arising to the King and Subject,
from raising Duties by Excise, are demonstrat-
ed, and the Objections thereto obviated, &c.
Printed for *J. Roberts*, pr. 6d.

36. An humble Address to the People of
England: Being a Demonstration that a Land
Tax is more prejudicial to Trade and Liberty
than an Inland Duty upon Wine and Tobacco,
Printed for T. *Cooper*, pr. 1s.

37. The Origin and Essence of a General
Excise. A Sermon on a very extraordinary
Occasion, at a noted Chappel in *Westminster*,
on *Wednesday* the 14th of *March*, 1732. By
Robert Wyner Rector of the said Chappel.
Printed for *Humphry Fitz-Drug*, at his Office
in the *Old Jury*.

38. A Letter from the Mayor of the antient Borough of Guzzle-Down, to Sir *Francis
Wronghead*, their R—ve in P—t, in Answer
to his Letter of the 19th of *Feb.* last. Sold by
J. Wilford.

39. A Scheme or Proposal for taking off the
several Taxes on Land, Soap, Starch, Candles,
Leather, Plates, Pots, &c. and replacing the
said Duties by another Tax, which will bring
in more Money, in a more easy equal manner.
Printed for C. *King*, in *Westminster-Hall*, pr. 6d.

40. Some Considerations on Publick Credit,
and the Nature of it's Circulation in the Funds.
Occasioned by a Bill now depending in Parliament concerning Stock-jobbing. Printed for
J. Brotherton, pr. 6d.

41. Historiæ Medicæ. Certe Ægrotantium
enarratæ, &c. Autore *Galielmo Clinch*, M. D.
Printed for *John Clarke*.

42. The Miser. A Comedy. Taken from
Plautus and *Moliere*. By *Henry Fielding*, Esq;
Printed for *J. Watts*. (See p. 138.)

43. The Decoy, an Opera. Printed for *J.
Osborne*.

44. The Mad Captain. A Ballad Opera.
Printed for *Charles Corbet*, pr. 1s.

45. Advice to a Lady. Printed for L. *Gilliver*, pr. 6d. (See the whole p. 149.)

45. *Sappho* to *Adonis*, after the manner of
Ovid. Printed for L. *Gilliver*.

47. The Man of Taste. Printed for L. *Gilliver*, pr. 1s.

48. *Gay*'s Fables Epitomiz'd. Printed for
B. *Creake*, pr. 1s. 6d.

49. The Bacchanalians, A Poem to Mr *Hogarth*. Printed for *A. Dodd*, pr. 6d.

50. Sirs are you mad? Or, a Caution to the
Citti. Printed for W. *Mears*, pr. 3d.

51. An Elegy to a young Lady: In the man-
ner of Ovid. With an Answer, by a Lady,
Author of *the Verses to the Imitator of Horace*.
Printed for *J. Roberts*, pr. 6d.

52. Scanderbeg. A Tragedy. By Mr *Howard*. Printed for *John Watts*.

53. Beauty and Proportion. A Poem. Printed for *Tho. Astley*.

54. The

54. The Royal Hermitage. A Poem. By *G. Lumley,* of *Merton College, Oxon.*

55. Verses address'd to the Imitator of the First Satire of the second Book of *Horace.* By a Lady of Quality. Pr. for *A. Dodd,* pr. 6*d.*

56. To the Imitator of the Satire of the second Book of *Horace.* Pr. for *J. Roberts,* pr. 6*d.*

57. Alma Mater, a Satyrical Poem on the University of Oxford. Pr. for R. *Wellington.*

58. The present State of the Republick of Letters, for *Feb.* 1733. Pr. for *W. Innys.*

59. The Christian's sure Guide to Eternal Glory : or Living Oracles most Comfortable, Holy and Instructive of the Lord Jesus Christ from Heaven, in his Royal Embassy to the seven Churches of *Asia,* as deliver'd to St *John* after his Glorification. Containing, 1. The Names and Titles wherewith he was, is, and must be ever Honoured in Glory. 2. The Comforts and Instructions which all Churches need for their Increase in Faith and Holiness, 3. The wonderful large and gracious Promises of Eternal Life to encourage all Men to Persevere and Conquer. 4. Prayers and suitable Devotions to render the Whole most Useful and Acceptable. *London:* Printed for *Francis Jefferies,* in *Ludgate-street.*

60. A General Dictionary, Historical and Critical; in which a new and accurate Translation of that of the celebrated Mr *Bayle* will be included. The whole containing the History of the most *Illustrious Persons* of all Ages and Nations, particularly those of *Great Britain* and *Ireland,* distinguish'd by their Rank, Actions, Learning, and other Accomplishments. Printed for and Sold by *Nich. Prevost.*

61. The late Lord *Belhaven's* memorable Speeches in the last Parliament of *Scotland,* holden at *Edinburgh* in 1706. on the Subject matter of the then projected *Union:* Wherein the slavish Homage and Respect that the People of *Scotland* should in Time pay to every petty *English* Exciseman, is predicted. Printed for *J. Roberts,* pr. 1*s.*

Weekly *and* Monthly Pamphlets *as before.*

ADVERTISEMENTS.

March 31. *was published,* No. II. *of*

THE Ceremonies and Religious Customs of the various Nations of the known World; faithfully translated from the French Original; and illustrated with above 172 Copper Plates, all beautifully design'd by M. B. PICART, and engrav'd by most of the best Hands in Europe.

The Price of the whole Work, Printed on Dutch Paper Royal, and compriz'd in four large Volumes in Folio, will be but 5*l.* 10*s.* in Sheets which is no more than half the Price of the Original ; to be deliver'd out in Weekly Numbers during the Space of two Years and two Months, at 1*s.* per Number, which will only amount to Three Half-pence per Sheet, and Three-pence per Folio Print.

PROPOSALS *at large, with beautiful* SPECIMENS, *may be seen at the Places where* SUBSCRIPTIONS *are taken in,* viz. CLAUDE DUBOSC, *Engraver, at the Golden Head in Charles-street, Covent Garden ;* THOMAS BOWLES, *Printseller next the Chapter-house in St Paul's Church-yard;* PHILIP OVERTON, *Printseller, near St Dunstan's Church, Fleetstreet;* THOMAS GLASS, *Printseller, next the Royal Exchange Stairs in Cornhill;* J. BOWLES, *Printseller, at the Black Horse in Cornhill ;* J. REGNIER, *Printseller, at the Golden Ball in Newport-street near Long Acre;* J. HULTON, *Printseller, at the Corner of Pall Mall facing the Haymarket;* PAUL FOUDRINIER, *Stationer and Printseller, the Corner of Craigs-Court, Charing-Cross ;* J. KING, *Printseller, in the Poultry near Stocks market ;* MrsMARBECK, *Printseller, in Westminster Hall,* J. CLARK, *Engraver and Printseller in Grey's Inn,* Mr SYMPSON *Engraver and Printseller, near the end of Catherine-street in the Strand,* W. DICEY *at Northampton,* J. ABREE, *at Canterbury,* J. MOUNTFORT, *at Worcester,* F. HOWGRAVE *at Stamford,* W. EVANS *on St James's Back, Bristol,* R. RAIKES *at Gloucester.*

That the Publick may not be impos'd on by invidious Aspersions, Mr DUBOSC faithfully assures them, that this is no spurious Edition, but genuine and compleat in all respects for the Truth of which; and of his various additional Beauties, he refers to his own printed Specimen, and to the *Amsterdam* Proposals, for proof of the vast Difference in the Prices, and not to the original Edition, as some are pleas'd to call Mr LOCKMAN's Translation of three Volumes only, of the present Undertaking.

Just publish'd,

(*In Three Volumes, Folio, beautifully printed on a fine Paper, and adorn'd with upwards of a Hundred Folio* COPPER PLATES, *design'd and engrav'd by the famous* PICART)

THE RELIGIOUS CUSTOMS and CEREMOMIES of ALL NATIONS, compil'd from the most eminent and most authentick Historians and Travellers of different Countries. Translated from the French with Improvements. Printed for N. PREVOST, at the Ship opposite Southampton Street in the Strand ; Mess. Clements and Wilmot at Oxford ; Mess. Crownfield and Thurlbourn, at Cambridge ; Mr Hilyard, at York ; and Mess. Leake and Lobb, a: Bath.

And in the Press VOL. IV. embellish'd with a great Number of Copper Plates, all design'd and engrav'd by the Artist abovementioned translated from the French, (with Illustrations) by Mr John Lockman.

To prevent the Publick from being impos'd upon, it may be proper to take Notice, that a spurious Edition of this Work, is now carrying on engrav'd by Mr Du Bosc, and others, which will be sold as dear as the Original Edition above advertised.

The Gentleman's Magazine:

Lond. Gazette
Lond̄ Jour.
Fog's Journ.
Applebee's ::
Read's :: ::
Craftsman :
D. Spectato?
Grubstreet J
W. ly Register
Free-Briton
opp. Doctor
Daily Court
Daily-Post
Dai. Journal
Da. Post-boy
D. Advertiser
Evening Post
St James's Ev.
Whitehall Ev.
Lōdon Ev. Eg
Flying-Post
Weekly Mis-
cellany.
The Auditor

St John's Gate.

York ::Newc
Dublin 6 ::
Edinburgh :
Bristol :: ::
Norwich 2:
Exeter ::::
Worcester ::
Northampto:
Gloucester::
Stamford ::
Nottingham
Bury Jvarn
Chester ditto
Cerby ditto
Ipswich do.
Reading do.
Leeds Merc
Newcastle
Canterbury
Birmingham
Manchester
Boston::: ¶
Jamaica, &c
Barbados ::

Or, MONTHLY INTELLIGENCER.

For APRIL, 1733.

CONTAINING,

/more in Quantity, and greater Variety, than any Book of the Kind and Price/

I. A View of the WEEKLY ESSAYS, *viz.* Against encouraging Foreign Artifts; Of dapper Men, Specimen of a General Dictionary criticis'd and vindicated; a Voyage to the Island of Love; M. *Voltaire*'s Dedication of *Zaire*; Patental Cruelty, Tenderness; Impertinents, Half Wits, and Coxcombs; a Sacrifice to Dulness; of Happiness, Friendship, Benevolence; Female Drefs; Benefits; Marrimony; Theatres; a humorous Love Letter; *Vulcano* in *Ireland*, &c.

II. POLITICAL POINTS, *viz.* Of Appeals to the People; a Jesuit's Letter; a Scots Prophecy; the Ministry and their Scheme vindicated; condemn'd in a Letter to Sir *Robert Walpole*; Re-

marks on the Proceedings of the Common Council; of Parliaments corrupt and good, K. *Richard* IId's Ministers; the *Craftsman*'s Congratulation; the same proved a Farce, On the E. of *Ch——d*'s Removal; Debates on Sugar Colony Bill.

III. POETRY: Beauty and Virtue beyond Riches; Prologue by Mr *Dnick*; Verses by Bp *Atterbury*; Of Ld *Baltimore* and Mr *Oglethorpe*; On a new Bufto in her Majefty's Grotto, with an Invitation to write on this Subject for a Reward; a Birth-day Hymn; Epigrams, &c.

IV. OCCURRENCES FOREIGN and DOMESTIC; Prices of Goods, &c.

V. REGISTER of Books.

VI. Table of CONTENTS.

By SYLVANUS URBAN, Gent.

LONDON: Printed, for the AUTHOR, and fold at St *John's* Gate: By F. *Jefferie*, in *Ludgate-ftreet*; at the Pamphlet Shops; and by moft Bookfellers.

CONTENTS.

THE
Gentleman's Magazine:
APRIL, 1733.

A View of the Weekly DISPUTES *and* ESSAYS *in this Month.*

Grubftreet Journal, March 29. No. 170.
Sketch of a Criticifm, &c.

MR. BAVIUS,

THE Gentlemen who threaten us with a new Edition of R. STEPHENS'S *Thefaurus,* &c. in their Epiftle to the *Studiofi,* &c. fay, *Jam diutius paucifsimorum hominum vfse cœpit, & non fine ingenti literarum difpendio, nummo immani quantum! vœnivit.* What is *jam diutius cœpit? Jam diutius* for *jam pridem,* I fuppofe, and *cœpit* for *cœperit?* And *nummo immani quantum!* one might take for a Medal of an enormous Size. Why not thus: *Grandi,* or *immani pretio jam pridem cœperit. Cum vœnivit,* wrong Tenfe. What is *ingens literarum difpendium?* What do they mean by *vivifsim?* Who ever faid *demereri literas? Curæ perficiundæ & explicandæ,* I don't underftand. *Citra renatas literas* for *poft renatas. Culturam magis debitam referrent,* is falfe Latin. *Culturam juftius,* or *potiori jure referrent acceptum,* would have been right. *Hiulca fuffecimus,* is, we have put *biulca,* where there were none before. *Accedere operi fubeundo,* is bad.

The Specimen affords ample room for Criticifm. STEPHENS in the Word *Damnofus,* quotes *Jul. Ianus.* Our Editors, not knowing what to make of it, have put it *Jul. Janus.*

Damnare, fays STEPHENS, *genitivo aliquando jungitur, aliquando ablativo;* they ftrike out the *Ablativo,* and put the Citations in another Place. — Inftead of STEPHENS's *Capite ob rem aliquam damnari,*. they have put *Capite aliquem damnare,* and then left it among the Paffives.—In a Quotation from SENECA, they have left out the Word *Creditor,* and made Nonfenfe of it. Under the Words, *Tributis damnare,* they have added, *vulgo contemnuntur;* of which let them tell the Meaning.—*Dubium efse poteft Latinos e Grecia eam traduxifse;* better, *dubium quin traduxerint.*, And then, *afserit* SCALIGER; which SACLIGER, and were does he fay fo?

Not to have read HARDUIN's *Notes* carefully; as well as the GRONOVIUS's, &c. is a Crime in thefe Editors.

CALLIOPIUS.

Weekly Mifcellany, April 21. No. 19.
Extract of an Anfwer to the above.

SIR,

IT was with no fmall Surprize, the Editors of ROB. STEPHENS's *Thefaurus* found themfelves rudely attack'd by a Writer in the (foregoing) *Grubftreet Journal.* — *Jam diutius cœpit,* it feems, is faulty, and muft be alter'd. So that when *Ter. Adelph.* has it, *Haud diu huc conmigrarunt,* we muft read *nuper.—Nummo immani, Grandis Pecunia,* is a common Expreffion with *Tully.— Cum vœnivit* is wrong Tenfe. If there's a Difference between *vœnivit & vœnivit,* our Examiner has took the worft. If any Alteration was neceffary, it fhould be *vœneat,* as that Edition has continued to be fold from its firft Publication to the prefent Year.—*Demereri literas* is juftifiable upon the fame Principles as *De Rep. bene mereri. Civitatem demereri* is ufed by *Tully* and *Livy.* —— *Acceptum,* or *in acceptum*

acceptum referre, was in Allusion to the *Roman* Method of Book-keeping, their *Tabulæ Accepti & Expensi*; instead of which had they used our Method of *Debtor* and *Creditor*, it would have been as true to have said *acceptum referre*, is false *Latin*, as how to affirm *Debitum referre* is. Where is the Difference between *accedere operi subeundo*, or ad *opus subeundum*, and that of *Brut. ad Cic. Accedere ad Remp. libevandam*?

The Objection to *Julianus*, contains two Assertions, 1. That we did not understand it. 2. That we altered it. We are sorry a false print in *Stephens* should escape us, but that we alter'd it, the Copy will confront his Assertion To affirm we did not understand it, depends upon the probability, that a Number of Persons concerned in a Work, where *Julianus* is quoted in almost every Sheet, could not understand it, when they met with it incorrectly printed.—As to *damnare*, it would be injurious to suppose, any one would not be apprised of an ablative Case, when he saw it quoted; if the Citations are differently ranged from the former Edition, it was in regard to Alphabetical Order, which STEPHENS sometimes over-looked.—How *Creditor* comes to be omitted, we are at Loss to Account for; and yet 'tis false to say the Place is Nonsense without it.—All Copies exhibit, *Tributis contemnuntur*, not *condemnamtur*. — We mean *Jo. Scaliger*, in his Notes on *Eusebius's Chronical Canons*.

How does the *Examiner* in his last Paragraph supply this Ellipsis, *as well as to have read them*, or, *as well as not* to have read them? So great a Censor of Inaccuracy ought to have been more accurate. And now let the Unprejudiced Judge between us, and describe to himself what must be the natural Temper of that Man's Mind, who (supposing the Faults he has suggested to be as gross as his own Fancy or Will could frame them) durst not confess, what we with Modesty may insist on, the many valuable Improvements which every where occur, in our Edition, besides that of Paper and Letter, which every body acknowledges to be a great Improvement.

Extract of Mr Oglethorpe's Letter to the Trustees for establishing the Colony of Georgia, dated from the Camp at Savanah, Feb. 10. 1732-3.

GENTLEMEN,

I Gave you an Account in my last Arrival at *Charles-Town*. The Governor and Assembly have given us all possible * Encouragement. Our People arrived at *Beaufort* on the 20th of *Jan.* where I lodg'd with them in some new Barracks built for the Soldiers, while I went myself to view the *Savanah* River: I fix'd upon a healthy Situation about ten Miles from the Sea. The River here forms a Half Moon, along the South side of which the Banks are about forty Foot high; and upon the Top a Flat, which they call a Bluff. The plain high Ground extends into the Country five or six Miles, and along the River Side about a Mile. Ships that draw 12 Foot Water can ride within ten Yards of the Bank Upon the River Side, in the Centre of this Plain, I have laid out the Town; over-gainst it is an Island of very rich Land, fit for Pasturage, which I think should be kept for the Trustees Cattle. The River is pretty wide, the Water fresh, and from the Key of the Town you see its whole Course to the Sea, with the Island of *Tybe*, which forms the Mouth of the River; and the other way you see the River for about six Miles up into the Country. The Landskip is very agreeable, the Stream being wide, and border'd with high Woods on both Sides. The whole People arriv'd here on the 1st of *Feb.* at Night their Tents were got up: Till the 7th we were taken up in unloading and making a Crane, which I then could not get finish'd, so took off the Hands, and set some to the Fortification, and began to fell the Woods. I mark'd out the Town and Common; half of the former is already cleared, and the first House was begun Yesterday in the Afternoon. Mr *Whitaker* has given us one hundred Head of Cattle. Col. *Bull*, Mr *Barlow*, Mr *St. Julian*, and Mr *Woodward*, are come up to assist us, with some of their own Servants.

Your most obedient humble Servt
J. OGLETHORPE.

* *They had order'd*, 1. *That Capt.* Mac-pherson *and* 15 *Rangers (who are Horse-men) do repair to* Georgia, *to abide there for the Protection of Mr* Oglethorpe *and his People, till they be settled.* 2. *That the Scout-Boats do attend them also at the Charge of the Publick.* 3. *That a Present be sent forthwith to* Georgia *of* 100 *breeding Cattle, and* 5 *Bulls,* 20 *breeding Sows, and* 4 *Boars; also* 20 *Barrels of Rice.* 4. *That Col.* Bull *be desired to go to* Georgia *to aid Mr* Oglethorpe *with his best Advice and Assistance.*

From the *Daily Post*, April 2.

A Letter from a Merchant to his Friend in the Country, occasion'd by the Free Briton *of* March 29. (See p. 144.)

SIR,

YOU know I have been a Factor for the People of *Maryland* some Time, of which Character (notwithstanding that Hireling the *Free Briton's* Insinuations) I am not ashamed. What his or his Patron's Aims are, by insolently interfering with the private Accounts and Transactions of Merchants with their Correspondents, may be easily guess'd at. In short, the industrious and generous Trader must be humbled. For People may take it in their Heads to make Comparisons betwixt such a useful and valuable Body, and another Species, whose Characters I won't now draw.

I have had, and still have above 20,000 l. Capital in that Trade, and I declare I would be glad to wind up my Accounts now with 5 per Cent. for my Money, since I have there traded, and I have had no material Losses, but a successful Run of Business. I shall conclude with observing, that (according to the *Free Briton's* modest Scheme) every one who knows the Nature of the Tobacco Trade, will see that our Commissions are to be reduced to scarce a Competency to pay Clerks in the Compting-House of a very middling Merchant, let be for the vast Expence (in that Trade especially) of Necessaries in it.

And as for the exceeding great Burthen the Merchants must feel in the Loss and Expence by their Shipping, sinking so much of their Money, the vast Credit they are obliged to give the numerous Planters, the Risques they run at Home and Abroad, the Trouble they are at, &c. Them truly must all be borne, as an Encouragement to the brave fair Trader, to prevent his vying with the Nobility.

Yours, *A. C.*

Free Briton, April 5.

In Answer to the foregoing Letter.

I am well acquainted, says *Walsingham,* with the Person who sent me the State of the Case between the Planters and their Factors, he is intimately knowing in all mercantile Affairs. I am not surprized that the inimitable *Letter-Writer* should be angry at any Proposals for the Relief of the *industrious Trader,* since he RIOTS *in their Oppression,* and about a Year since, when this Affair was first talk'd of, he gave it as a Reason to divers *honourable Members,* why he *must* and should oppose this Alteration of the Duties, namely, that it would curtail him of a Profit of more than 2000 l. a Year. I leave every reasonable Man to judge, whether this is not a powerful Argument for the Alteration.

As to the Comparisons to be drawn between that *valuable Body* the FACTORS and a SPECIES, meaning the NOBILITY, *Walsingham* fears, that if these *valuable* FACTORS proceed in this extraordinary manner, they will soon convince the HOUSE OF LORDS, and all *reasonable Men,* that they will not be *hurt* by being *humbled.* It is unfair and absurd to say, what is proposed to *relieve* the Oppressed, is done with an Intention meerly to *humble,* &c. No Oppression ever could be redressed without some *Mortification* to the *Oppressor;* but then it is an Act of Justice, and so far it is from being *Insolence* to interfere between the *Planter* and *Factor* in their Accounts, when the *former* complains against the *latter,* that the *Planters* have a Right to demand it from the Justice of Mankind.

I cannot but think the Letter-Writer very unhappy in his applying the Word *Hireling* to *me.* I never was suspected of converting the Favour of Great Men into JOBB-WORK; I always detested the *vile Trade* of solliciting Ministers to espouse a *mercenary Project,* for the sake of any *reserved Profits,* stipulated to myself. When he can lay his Hand upon his Heart and say the same, he will be safe from *Recrimination.*

Walsingham then inserts his Friend's Answer, to this Effect.—Let me tell *A. C.* he himself is a *Hireling,* in being a Factor to the Planters; but why does he not dispute the Facts (See p. 144) instead of calling Names? As to the Assertion in the Letter in the *Daily Post, of Commissions being reduced to scarce a Competency to pay Clerks,* &c. Do this Gentleman's Clerks receive near 2 and half *per Cent* upon the gross Produce of a Hogshead of Tobacco sold for Exportation, the bonded Duties off? What secret Service are they to do for that Sum besides Writing? Doth a *Barbadoes,* a *Jamaica,* a *Carolina,* a *New England,* or *Newfoundland* Factor charge more than 2 and half *per Cent.* Commissions upon the gross Produce of any Goods consigned to them? Why then must the Poor Planters, upon their Tobacco, be obliged, merely from Fiction, in the Cafe of exported Tobacco, to pay more than double Commiffions of what the reft of their Fellow-Subjects do; when by that means principally, they are almoft begger'd, and often brought in Debt by thefe Factors?

As to the Article of Shipping, which the Author of the *Vindication of the Cafe of the Planters* grants the Factors lofe Money by, it is not rightly ftated. Four Hogfheads of Tobacco do not require more Room than 2 Tons of moft other Goods; yet at the Rate of 7l. *per Ton* it's a better Freight than Ships can make from *Barbadoes,* &c. It's well known, that thefe Factors may, and often do hire, or charter good Ships to bring home Tobacco at 7l. *per Ton,* provided they are not to wait for their Lading above 40 or 50 Days. Is it not then monftrous Affurance in thefe Factors to complain of lofing by their Shipping, when they need not fuffer fuch Lofs? Let them imitate the OEconomy of Thofe who let them their Ships, that is, pay their Tradefmen punctually, and not perfuade them to hold parts of Ships with them, and make them wait a long time for their Money, which will oblige Tradefmen to charge in Proportion to fuch Forbearance. In fine, if thefe Factors will not fend more Ships than they are fure of Lading for, in order to get Commiffions from each other, they will have no Reafon to complain on this Head.

The **Auditor**, April 3. No. 25.

The following Letter complains of a publick Oppreffion.

Mr AUDITOR,

I AM a *Perriwig-maker*; and it has coft me a great deal of Pains and Expence to be inform'd of the neweft Fafhions, to oblige my Cuftomers; but of what ufe all this has been to me, you may judge by the Sequel. Laft Week, a young Nobleman, whofe Father I ferved many Years, fent for me, and ask'd me *if I had ever been in* France? I anfwer'd in the Negative, upon which his Honour gave me to underftand, he had no farther Commands for me, being refolved to have no Wig-maker but a *Frenchman,* or one who had worked a great while there. Now, is not this a cruel Cafe, that a Tradefman fhall not be employed merely becaufe he is an *Englifhman,* and has never been out of *England?* Foreigners are fo confcious of this Fondnefs for their Work, that

they often buy Wigs from *Englifh* Wigmakers, and pay more for them than a Nobleman would to the Maker; tho' he makes no Difficulty about the Price to the Foreigner. Yours, &c.

ANDREW FULLBOTTOM.

Far be it from me to difcourage the Ingenious and Induftrious from whatfoever Nation they come; but the above Practice feems quite *unnatural.*

Seignior *Boccalini* tells me, this Infatuation for what is brought from foreign Countries, is only to be met with in *England:* Other Nations invite Strangers among them, and treat them courteoufly, till they get Mafters of thofe Arts and Sciences, thofe Strangers excell in: But an *Englifhman* is never employ'd abroad merely becaufe he is an *Englifhman.* He afferts with fome warmth, that the Name of an *Englifhman* ought not to be conferred on thofe Admirers of Foreign *Gew-gaws,* who boaft all their Cloaths are made at *Paris,* all their Velvets or Silks in *Italy* and *France,* and who will not wear a Lace for a Hat, or a Knee-Garter, if manufactur'd at Home. This fantaftick Tafte for foreign Things is further ridicul'd in the following Letter.

Mr AUDITOR,

I AM a fpruce dapper Spark, and, in Drefs, a very pretty Fellow. Thus accomplifh'd, I made my Addreffes to a young Lady, of a Size fuitable to my own: But met with a Repulfe; which I can impute to nothing but to her having juft before feen, *The great* SAXON. Ever fince fhe makes a jeft of me, and twitts me with a Saying of an impudent *Irifh* Poet, *The Man that is born to be fix foot high, is born to be a great Man.* In Oppofition to which I cite Q. *Elizabeth's* Judgment of a very tall Ambaffador from *France,* that he was like a very high Houfe, in which the upper Apartments are worft furnifhed; I defire her to perufe the GUARDIAN on the Perfections of little Men, and tell her, I am as well qualified to perform all the Duties of a Husband, as the moft affuming Monopolift of Manhood.

Yours, TRIPPANT ERECT.

The AUDITOR agrees; that Height or Lownefs of Size neither obftruct nor promote the Performance of the effential Duties of a married State: Good-nature, and Evennefs of Temper, Virtue and good Senfe, Love and Conftancy are independant of Stature; but fufpects Mr *Trippant* is one of thofe vain Creatures who

who imagine every Woman they converse with muſt be in Love with them; therefore approves his Miſtreſs's Slight; however, tells her, the Woman ought'ro be deſpiſed who values a Man only for his Stature, Bulk or Perſon; ſuch a one is unqualified to afford a Man of intrinſick Worth that Happineſs and Content which ſhould attend the Matrimonial State.   B.

From the **Daily Courant,** April 4.
Of *Appeals to the People.*

POpular *Appeals* are always dangerous, often unjuſt, and never to be uſed, till *Male-Adminiſtration* has been undeniably proved, and Juſtice legally attempted in vain. 'Tis abſolute Cruelty to condemn on Hearſay or Poſſibility; *one Story is good till another is told.*

One Part of our Conſtitution depends ſo much upon another, that no flagrant Enormities can paſs unpuniſhed in either; and if ſo, *Popular Appeals* are an Affront to the Conſtitution; and rather an Arreſt of Publick Juſtice, than a ſpeedier way of obtaining it. Why have the People choſen a Legiſlature, but to obey their Power, and ſubmit to their Decrees? From them there's no Appeal, till 'tis prov'd their Delegates are falſe and unfaithful to their Truſt; an Aſſertion that no Man can yet make with Juſtice.

Nothing is more eaſy than to acquire the Reputation of a *Patriot* by noiſy Declamations in favour of the People. *Self* has ſo large a Share in every Man's Thoughts, that we are ready to embrace every Thing where it ſeems concern'd. This is the true Cauſe why *Libels* on the Government are ſo well receiv'd by the People; and on this Principle ſo many *Patriots* have aggrandiz'd themſelves in our Days. When ſuch a one declares for the *good old Cauſe,* no body enquires into his Integrity; no, we rather chuſe to be ignorant, than be diſpleaſed with the Anſwer; tho' the following Quotation could not be more notoriouſly appoſite to *Satan* than to him,

And thou, ſly Hypocrite! who now
  would'ſt ſeem
Patron of Liberty! who more than thou
Once ſawn'd, and cring'd, and ſervilely
  ador'd?

An indifferent Third-Rate Stateſman will make a tip-top *Patriot,* and thoſe who were but ill-qualified for their Sovereign's Service, make notable Advocates for the People. But have theſe doughty Delegates any *real* Deſign to ſerve their Principals? No; they deſpiſe the People whom they affect to patronize; and, were their own Turn ſerved, would deſert them the next Moment.— 'Tis plain then, that Appeals are generally Impoſitions on their Underſtandings, often Perverſions of their Loyalty, and always an Affront to the Throne.
                                  MEANWELL.

Grubſtreet Journal. April 5. No. 171.
Remarks on the Specimen of a General Dictionary *biſtorical and critical.*

Mr BAVIUS,

SInce the maſterly Criticiſm of *Iſaac de Duobus* appear'd in your Journal (See p. 1100, 1118.) Dr *Alleyn's* New Diſpenſatory has entirely loſt the little Credit it had before. Such Examinations therefore are very ſeaſonable when any Productions are vamp'd up to impoſe on the World.

The Undertakers of the *General Dictionary* have promis'd a Work which they are conſcious they are not able to perform. This will appear from the Article relating to the *Eaſtern Hiſtory,* in which they aſſure us, they " have not had Recourſe barely to *d'Herbelot's Dictionary,* and other Works on that Subject, written in the European Languages, but to the oriental Authors and Manuſcripts." Yet in the Specimen of their Performance, the contrary is evident. They write the Name of *Abaſſa's* Brother *Haron Raſchid;* 'Tis true, ſome foreign Authors write it ſo; but GREAVES, POCOCK, HYDE, and the reſt of the *Engliſh* Authors ſkilled in the oriental Languages, write *Harun Raſid,* or rather *al Raſid,* as the Engliſh Orthography requires. But if they had rather chuſe foreign Authors, why did they not write *Rachid* after the *French,* or *Raſcid* according to the *Italians?* The Truth is, they conſulted none but D'HERBELOT, nor him ſufficiently; for tho' in the Article of *Abbaſſa,* the Name in Queſtion is erroneouſly printed, in the next to it, it is written *Haroun al Raſchid;* and in the Preface is a Reaſon for uſing the *ſch,* inſtead of *ch,* which is the *French* Character for the *Engliſh ſh.*

In like manner they write *Giaffar,* inſtead of *Jaffar.* What Confuſion muſt ſuch Inaccuracy introduce in a Work compil'd chiefly out of foreign Dictionaries, which as they differ in Language, muſt vary in writing proper Names peculiar
                                      to

to Nations which do not use the Roman
Character ? So that if the Authors of the
General Dictionary transcribe Names as
they find them, innumerable Articles
will be placed under wrong Letters, and
the same Names repeated under different
Letters.

Two Faults more are in the Article of
Abassa. The Title of *Harun al Rasid,*
is *Khalifah.* On what Authority have
they written *Khaliff ?* and why not the
old word *Calif,* instead of a new one ?
Why did they forsake D'HERBELOT,
who in the same Article writes *Khalife*
(tho' elsewhere *Khalifah*) and yet follow him, with regard to *Abassides ?* a
word no way conformable to the Arabic
Idiom ? according to which they should
have said the Family, or rather the
Children of *Abbas.* The *Bibliotheque
Orientale* of D'HERBELOT, tho' it contains a vast Treasure of Eastern Knowledge, yet is full of the Faults of the
Press, and Inaccuracies of the Pen, the
Author not living to publish it himself,
and such great Criticks ought, pursuant
to their Engagement, to *correct the Errors* of their *Authors,* and to have begun with him, especially as they had so
fair an Opportunity.

These Faults are committed within the
Compass of three Lines, and that they
might not be obliged to give more, they
have placed the Article of *Abdolonymus*
before it, contrary to alphabetical Order.
In *Abdolonymus* there is nothing which
might not be drawn up from USHER,
MORERY, &c. That they had not
Recourse to the Originals, may be
presumed from the Note D, where both
DIODORUS SICULUS and Q. CURTIUS
are mention'd, but the Places of neither
cited. The Notes are a meer Heap of
Quotations, dry and flat.

Of all the supplemental Articles,
(which are to swell the Work to 6
Volumes) only some of those composed
by the Authors themselves are drawn up
after the manner of BAYLE's.—In a
word the Imposition extends to the very
Impression of the Book. By proposing 6
Volumes the Publick might expect two
entire Volumes of Additions to BAYLE;
but in this they will be deceiv'd for the
Page of the *General Dictionary* is so
much scantier than the *French* Copy,
that supposing the Translation and Original contain an equal Number of Sheets,
Bayle will take up 4 Volumes. The 6
Volumes will cost 10 or 11 *l.* whereas

the compleat Edition of *Bayle* will not
exceed 5 *l.* or 5 *l.* 10 *s.*　　　　　*A. B.*

The **Auditor,** April 6. No. 26.

THIS is a Continuation of the Journal
of a Voyage (begun p. 131.) from
the Kingdom of *Happiness,* to the *Island
of Love.* By the Description which the
Voyager here gives of his Travels, it
appears, that we must make *Mo-
rality* our Friend and *Desire* our Attendant,
if we expect a safe Arrival at this Island.

The first Port we touch at is *Sincerity.*
About the Middle of the Island, delightfully situated on a *Hill,* is *Enjoyment;*
to get at which we must pass thro' the
several Villages of *Hope, Chimera, Fear,
Diligence, Courage,* and *Success;* the last
contiguous to *Enjoyment,* in the Middle
of it is a *Grotto,* called *Rapture;* from
whence a Path insensibly leads to *Contemplation,* and *Retirement.*

Here the Voyager stops, to attend to
the following Reflections of his Friend
Morality. 'How vain, fugacious, and
empty, are all the little momentary Pleasures of Life.' How blind and fond are
we of being deceived! What Pains do
Men take to surmount ten Thousand
Difficulties which lie in their way to
Vice! and then how *soon* is the Appetite
palled, and how *long* does the *Sting* remain upon the *Conscience!* The Balm
which sweetens our passage thro' Life,
flows from a Spring more unsullied than
all the empty Follies of *Human Invention.* *Reason* has Charms to satiate us
if we employ it in surveying the Works
of Creation: The *Melody* of Musick
melts and dies away, but the *Harmony*
of this *Contemplation* will last to all
Eternity.'　　　　　ANTIQUAE.

Mr AUDITOR,

I A'M surprized, Sir, that in your Cri-
ticism on the *Miser* (See p. 138.) you
talk so insensibly of Love ! Why do you
think it strange a *Miser* at threescore
should be *in love ?* If you think the Love
of Gold has so lin'd his Soul, that no o-
ther Love can make an Entrance, you
are mistaken; for if he were made up
of that rich Metal, the Heat and Force
of Love would soon dissolve and melt
him, till he were as free and generous
as if he had never known a covetous
Thought.　　　　　BELVIDERA.

Belvidera should consider, that the
Poet was to draw the Character of a
Miser, and not of a *Miser in love.* Q. C.
The

The Craftsman, *April 7. No.* 353.

FOR Part of this Days Entertainment the *Craftsman* gives us a Letter from a Jesuit in *England* to the Rector of that Order at *Bruffels* in 1627 ; which may be seen in *Rushworth's Collections*, Vol. I. P. 474.

In this Letter the Jesuit gives an Account of the several Steps which had been taken by his Fraternity to propagate their Caufe and difturb the Peace of *England.* We fhall only take Notice of fuch Paffages, for the fake of which the *Craftfman* feems to have inferted the whole Letter.

"The Materials, fays the Jefuit, which build up our Bulwark, are the *Projeĉtors* and *Beggers* of all Ranks and Qualities. Both thefe Factions co-operate to deftroy the *Parliament*, and to introduce *Oligarchy.*

Our Foundation is *Arminianifm.* The *Arminians* and *Projeĉtors* affeĉt Mutation. This we fecond, and enforce by probable Arguments. Firft, we confider the King's Honour and prefent Neceffity ; and fhew how the *King* may free himfelf of his *Ward*, as *Lewis* XI. did. And for his great Splendour and Luftre, he may raife a *vaft Revenue*, and not be beholden to hisSubjeĉts ; which is by way of an Impofition of an *Excise.* Then our *Church Catholicks* fhew the Means how to fettle *this Excife*, i. e. by a *Mercenary Army of Horfe and Foot*, The Horfe fhall be *Foreigners*, and *Germans*, who will eat up the King's Revenues and fpoil the Country.

This Mercenary Army of 2000 *Horfe* and 20,000 *Foot* fhall be taken on Pay, before the Excife be fettled. In forming the *Excife*, the Country is moft likely to rife. If the *mercenary Army* fubjugate the Country then the *Soldiers* and *Projeĉtors* fhall be paid out of the *Confifcations.* If the *Country* be too hard for the Soldiers, they muft confequently mutiny, which is equally advantageous to us. Our fuperlative Defign is to work the *Proteftants*, as well as *Catholicks*, to welcome in a *Conqueror*, and That is by this Means. We hope inftantly to diffolve *Trades*, and hinder the building of *Shipping* ; in devifing probable Defigns, and putting the State upon Expeditions."

§ D'*anvers* next by way of Parallel, gives an Account of the noble Stand lately made by the polite Part of the world againft the Attacks of Mr *H—l* on their Liberties and Properties. This Gentleman has govern'd the *Opera's* and modell'd the *Orcheftre* without Controul. Even *Kings* and *Queens* were to be content with what low Charaĉters he was pleas'd to affign them. This Excefs and Abufe of Power foon difgufted the Town ; his Government grew odious, and his *Opera's* empty. In Order to mend his Affairs, he form'd a *Plan*, without confulting his *Friends*, which he inform'd us would be to the Advantage of the Publick, and of *Opera's* in particular. This he concerted with *his Brother*, in whom *Heat* and *Dulnefs* are miraculoufly united. The *Scheme* is produc'd, and fets forth, that the late Decay of *Opera's* is owing to their *Cheapnefs*, and to the great *Frauds* of the *Doorkeepers*, that the *Annual Subfcribers* were a parcel of Rogues, and made an ill Ufe of their Tickets, by *running* two into the Gallery ; that to obviate thefe Abufes, he had contriv'd a Thing that was better than an *Opera*, call'd an *Oratorio* ; to which none fhould be admitted but by *printed Permits* of one Guinea each, which fhould be diftributed out of *Warehoufes of his own*, and by *Officers of his own naming:* and laftly, that as the very Being of *Opera's* depended on *himfelf fingly*, it was juft that the Profits arifing from hence fhould be for his own Benefit. He added indeed a favourable Condition, that any Perfon aggriev'd might appeal to *three Judges of Mufick*, who might in 7 Years determine it. This *Scheme* difgufted the whole Town, who exclaim'd againft the *infolent and rapacious Projeĉtor of this Plan* ; and he had the Mortification to fee but a thin Audience at his *Oratorio*, and of 260 odd that it confifted of, not above ten paid for their *permits*, but had Money given them to keep them in Countenance.

EPIGRAM.

QUoth *W—e* to *H—l*, fhall We 2 agree, And *excife* the whole Nation ?

          H. *fi, Caro, fi.*

Of what Ufe are *Sheep*, if the *Shepherd* can't fhear 'em ?

At the *Hay-Market* I, you at *Weftminfter—*

          W. Hear Him !

Call'd to Order, their *Seconds* appear in their Place ;   [*Face.*

One fam'd for his *Morals*, and one for his *Tho'* at firft they bad fair, at laft They were croft,   [BORAH loft.

The Excise was thrown up, and De-

Weekly Miscellany, April 7. No. 17.

S I R,

I Am pleas'd with the Approbation universally given of your *Literary* Intelligence. There was something *Generous* as well as *Just* in your late Account of the *French* Tragedy of *Zara.* For, tho' it's reasonable to acknowledge our Neighbour's *Good* Qualities, yet, it's Virtue highly exalted to do it under a Consciousness of exposing *our Ill* ones.

If the *French* are not wrong'd, when consider'd as a *Vain*, while They are in Truth but a *Gay* People, how is it, that, while *we*, who wou'd be thought *Serious* and *Solid*, are disgracing Taste, and Nature, by the Applause we bestow on Trifles ? The *French*, on the contrary, press in Crouds to support the gravest and Sublimest Tragedy produc'd in these Latter Ages.

The following is a short Abstract of the Author's Dedication to Mr *Falkener*, an *English* Merchant. — " You are an *Englishman*, and I was born in *France* ; but the Lovers of Learning are all Fellow-Citizens : *Thinking Men* differ little in Principles, and compose a Republick of their own. I present you then, this Tragedy, as my Countryman in the *Letter'd* World, and my *Intimate Friend* in the other.

I rejoice I can instruct my Countrymen, in what Light a *Merchant* is consider'd among yours ; and with how superiour a Distinction, they support the Dignity of Legislators.

A second Reason which induc'd me to discourse of polite Learning with an *Englishman*, is, That happy *Freedom* of Thought, which, methinks you communicate to my Spirit. ——

THE Man, with whom I hold Discourse,
   New-fashions my Desire,
If brave, methinks, I share his Force,
   If Lively, I'm on Fire.

A Courtier, of a creeping Size,
   Unmans me, with his Dread,
I ape his Cringes and Disguise,
   And learn his pliant Tread.

But, when I meet a fearless Mind,
   His Freedom hardens mine :
I catch his Fire, blaze unconfin'd,
   And dare be bold to shine.

I value myself upon no stronger a Motive, than for having written a Piece, truly *simple.*—I don't propose *Zara* as a Model. The Success it has met with, is owing to the Care I have taken to speak of Love in the tenderest, or most natural Manner.—And I have *hit* the Heart and Taste of my Audiences. A Poet may be sure to please, when he speaks more to the *Passions* than the *Reason* of Men.

Your Countrymen, we fancy, are neither Devout *enough*, to be charm'd with the Zeal of old *Lusignan* (a Character in this Tragedy) nor *Tender* enough to be touch'd by the Sentiments of *Zara* ; you pass here, as more likely to be pleased with the Plots of two *Factions*, than the Intrigues of Two *Lovers.* 'Tis true, you weave as much Love in your Tragedies as we, but your *Heroes* don't express it in so natural a Manner.—The *French* make Love, *like Lovers*, and the *English*, like Poets.

Allow the *French* to be your Masters in Gallantry, and there are other good Things we will permit *you* to teach us. It was from the *English* Stage I learnt the Boldness, to introduce in the Scene, the Names of our Kings ; and of our antient Families ; conceiving this Novelty might give Birth to a new Species of Tragedy, yet unknown among us ; and some Great Genius's will arise to perfect the Idea, of which *Zara* is only a Sketch. As long as *France* protects Learning we shall never want Good Writers : Nature forms in all Ages and Countries, Men of Genius in all Kinds.—To make them *appear*, call them out by Encouragement ; otherwise all the polite Arts may, one Time or other, vanish at once, in the midst of those Stately Establishments, rais'd to invite them."— Thus far, *Voltaire* in his Dedication. *Yours* EUSEBIUS.

NOTE. Mr *Voltaire's* Tragedy, *Zaire*, is written in the *Turco-Christian* Taste ; and is taken from the History of the *Crusades, Orosmanes*, Brother or Son of *Saladin* falls in Love with *Zaire*, Daughter of the last King of *Jerusalem* ; and by a *Frenchman*, who proves to be her Brother, is inspir'd with Jealousy, and at length kills her.

There is in this Tragedy a happy Mixture of *French* and *Turkish* Names and Manners, *Feathers* and *Turbants*, different *Religions* and Maxims ; the Characters are so well kept up, that all is regular and without Confusion.

M. *Voltaire* has prefix'd to this Tragedy a gallant Dedication of it in verse to *Mademoiselle Gossin*, who plaid the Part of *Zaire* ; translated thus.

A Ccept, fair Actress, dear enchanting Maid,
   The Poet's Homage to thy Beauties paid,
Protect my Verse ; 'tis but thy own I give,
Zara is thine ; thy Action bid her live.
                  Those

Those Eyes, that heavenly Voice, so full of Charms,
Compell'd each Critick to let drop his Arms.
Still, as with graceful Ease your Steps you bend,
We find Illusion on those Steps attend,
Inspire the tender Sentiment, the Sigh,
And call the ready Tear from ev'ry Eye.
The Power of Verse almost neglected lay;
Thy heavenly Voice secures his future Sway.
The God of Love, forgot by ev'ry Swain,
Presages from thy Eyes an happier Reign.
Henceforth the Rival Powers, with friendly Strife,   (Life.
Shall claim thee Theirs, and share my future
Both have I serv'd, and one still gives me Law;
From t'other's dangerous Service I withdraw.
—Happy the favour'd Youth! thrice happy He;
Blest with a Smile, enchanting Fair from Thee;
Who in those Eyes his happy Fate explores,
Who dies for Love, who pleases, who adores;
Who spends in am'rous Talk the gayly fleeting Time—!   (but in Rhyme!
—But, ah! the Wretch indeed, who courts thee

London Journal, April. 7. No 719.

THE Ministry, by the proposed Scheme of altering the Duties, have shewn themselves the *best Friends* to the Merchants, notwithstanding what the *Craftsman* says in his last Paper (See p. 145.) " We have been lately told, *That Parliaments don't sit to please Merchants.*" Let him tell us, *who* said this, and on *what Occasion*; for those Words, I am inform'd, says Osborne, were occasion'd by an *injudicious* Speech of a *certain Gentleman,* who, in a Passion said, *The Merchants and Tradesmen would never* FORGET *nor* FORGIVE *this Usage*; to which a Gentleman *justly* replied," That the Parliament of *England* sate to represent the People of *England*; that the Parliament must do their *Duty to the Nation,* whether *Merchants* liked or *disliked* it, *forgave* or not *forgave,* for they did not sit there to *please Merchants* only, but to provide in the best Manner for the Good of *the whole Community.*" This is a *mild* and *gentle* Return to a *weak* and *bold* Threatning of the House.

As to the supposed calling the *Merchants* and *Tradesmen* STURDY BEGGERS, (See p. 140. H.) it seems to be told for the Sake of calling *Sturdy Beggers* ROBERTSMEN. But the Fact is not true : The Gentleman was speaking of the Insolence of *fraudulent Dealers, Breakers of Laws, Runners of Goods,* and *Plunderers* of the King's Revenues; and if he called them *sturdy Beggers,* it's what they deserv'd. Tis therefore Mr *D'anvers,* who confounds the *honest* and *dishonest Tradesmen* who calls them *Sturdy Beggers,* and not the *Gentleman* he refers to, who always carefully distinguishes betwixt them.

Some Writers have justly observed, that the wisest way of raising Money is by *taxing Luxuries.* To this *D'anvers* replies, he will not call what is *above* the *Necessaries* of Life, *Luxuries,* but *Conveniencies,* (See p. 145. H.) for in all *civilized Countries,* the *Conveniencies* of Life are distinct from *Necessaries* and *Luxuries.* Be it so : But these *Conveniencies* should be taxed, and never *Necessaries.* His Quotation from Mr *Addison* is nothing to the Purpose. That Writer could say a thousand useful Things in the most *pleasing* Manner, yet not able to *prove* one; for he had not the *Power* of Reasoning.

As to the *Craftsman* and *Budgeteer's* mad Rant about *Magna Charta* and *Trials per Pares,* it may be answer'd, That tho' *in most Cases,* to be tried by *Juries,* is one Fundamental Part of our Government, yet never *in all Cases.* If *Offenders* against *Excise Laws* were left to *Juries,* the *Frauds* to be prevented by these Laws would not be prevented, because the common People, out of whom *Juries* are generally made, count it *no Crime* to cheat the *King* : Many of them are Smuglers themselves; and when Officers of the Customs have come into Courts with Heads and Arms cut in the Execution of their Office, and Evidence upon Oath hath been given, that such Persons, then present in Court, wounded them, yet the Jury brought them in *not Guilty,* with great Shouts of Joy. Therefore Juries ought not to be allow'd in such Cases.   F. OSBORNE.

Fog's Journal, April 7. No. 231.

LILLT, the Name subscrib'd to this Paper, continues his Ridicule (See p. 146) on a Pamphlet entitled *Remarks on Fog's Journal of Feb.* 10. and in the same ludicrous Strain banters the Writer in, what he calls, five Strokes of Panegyrick, being a true Character of Sir —— and then gives the Reverse of this Picture, in a like Vein, from the same Pamphlet, and calls it a modest, but satyrical Description of *Fog's Journal* of the 10th of *February,* in which he makes the Writer stile that Journal a Panegyrick upon Assassination -- a regular Scheme of Vengeance — a private Murder, a popular Butchery, pointed out by the assas-
sinating

finating Spirit of an infamous Writer, &c.

The great Art of a Statesman is to find a Mystery in Words of the most obvious Meaning; and to explain an inoffensive Expression, or a Jest, into a seditious or treasonable Libel. *Sejanus* was always furnish'd with proper Instruments for this Work. Two of his Creatures impeach'd *Cremutius Cordus*, a noble *Roman*, of High Treason, for having said in his History, that *Cassius* was the last of the *Romans*. The Accusation was made good by the following Argument, *If* Cassius *was the last of the* Romans, *then* Tiberius *is not a* Roman, *consequently not the* Roman *Emperor*.

In the Reign of our *Richard* III. a Citizen of *London*, who liv'd at the Sign of the Crown, was convicted of High Treason for saying in a jocular manner, He would make his Son *Heir to the Crown*. Had I, says *Fog*, liv'd in that Age, at the Sign of another Crown, I should have took warning, pull'd down my Sign, and set up a Begger's Cap in the Room of it. But then, if a *Walsingham* or *Osborne* had liv'd near me, I should have been accus'd of violating the Majesty of a crown'd Head, and of intimating to the People that a sturdy Begger was a better Man, than K. *Richard*.

Another Story *Fog* relates from *La Mottraye's* Anecdotes of *Turkey*, Vol. v. Chap. 17. A *Greek* Merchant, who had lent the late K. of *Sweden*, when in *Turkey*, 10,000 Crowns, for the Recovery of it, went to *Stockholm*. Whilst he was there the King was kill'd, and Baron *Gortz* beheaded. However, the *Swedes* satisfy'd the Merchant, who gave a short Detail of all these Transactions in a Letter to a Friend who was an Officer of the *Janizaries* at *Constantinople*. The Letter by Accident fell into the Hands of the Grand Vizier, who order'd the *Greek*, on his Return, to be brought before him, and then adjudg'd him in this manner, *Thy Letter is a most villainous Writing, and was design'd to excite the* Janizaries *to murder me. I don't believe there was such a Man as* Gortz; *if there was, how durst thou compare me to an Unbeliever, when there was not the least Resemblance betwixt us? Gortz was the Minister of a petty Prince— I am the Lieutenant of the greatest Monarch in the World, the Prop of the Ottoman Empire, and the Guardian of the Sultan. Dost not thou say here, thou Blood-hound, that* Gortz *was beheaded at* Stockholm

in the Face of the Sun at Noon-Day? Does not this intimate to the Janizaries, *that they ought to butcher me at* Stamboul *(Constantinople) in the Face of the Sun at Noon-Day? For* Stockholm *and* Stamboul, *and* Stamboul *and* Stockholm *is the same Thing. And who besides thyself ever presum'd to say, that the Sun shines at Noon in any Place out of the Empire of the* Musselmen?—Having thus said, he seized the Merchant's Effects, and commanded a Slave to strike off his Head. In like manner, the *Remarker's* Scope is to shew the great Importance of Sir R— that he is the only Person able to bear the weight of the Nation; and that if he should happen to slip, or some malicious Fellow shou'd steal behind him and trip up his Heels, down we go, Liberty, Property, the Protestant Religion, with— and—with their B—and Bags—and the whole Train of Excisemen.

Fog concludes with a Prophecy he met with in the *Cotton* Library, sent in a Letter by Sir *Nicholas Throgmorton*, then Q. *Elizabeth's* Embassador in *Scotland*, to Secretary *Cecil*. This Prophecy was deliver'd at the High Cross at *Edinburgh*, by one *Mac Donald*, who was gifted with the second Sight, and is as follows:

Whenne the Heich Priestia of Jesu sal Worschipp Thor and Woden.
And ane Cairnie tinucht sall well with a Millioun of Stalwart and stout Warriourg;
Whenne the Bairng of Iud.Brutug sall refuse to eat Sweeties,
And all the Aprh Earleg of Luddig Coune sall bee Soiners and Clandre Beggarg;
Whenne the Weedg of America and the Beryes of Portingale sall sette al the Searong of Ausd Britapne in a fied Low.
Mokand Fikh a nude burn ag haith nought bren lichtlie seene before.
And Douchtie Scortig Lairdg sall bee sall teed to bere huge Inglig Pachig
Chenne sall cum to pass and sikkerlp bee Stabilist
The Thrid Union, and al Partieg sall bee nae maie.

         W. LILLY.

Berrington's *Evening Post*, April 10.

The sense of the People of England, *in relation to the present Scheme of an* Excise *on Tobacco and Wine, in a Letter to Sir* Robert Walpole.

     S I R,

AS there never was, perhaps, a Time when there was so universal a Dislike to a publick Measure, it is worth while to consider who are in the Opposition,

tion, its Rife, and the Reafons of its Continuance.

Some of the Oppofers, no doubt, are not only Enemies to you, but to the prefent Settlement in his Majefty and his Family. But the giving any juft Handle to thefe Enemies of Liberty and the Proteftant Intereft, ought carefully to be guarded againft.

There are Others whofe chief View is to over-turn the Adminiftration, and introduce a new Sett of Minifters. Thefe perhaps, are not a Few. An Old Minifter muft be the Object of much Hate. Even the Obliged count it painful to be long obliged to the fame Perfon. You, Sir, muft have feen enough of this to confirm the Obfervation. Thefe alfo are to be guarded againft. For, if upon a new Scheme opening, any of Thefe turn upon their Leader, the Generality of Mankind immediately conclude againft it.

But thefe are far from being the Majority in the prefent Cafe, who are declared Enemies to the intended Extenfion of the Excife. No, they are Merchants and Traders; Men in the Intereft of the prefent Royal Family, and under no Refentments and Prejudices to Courts. Among thefe, Oppofition is not confined to the Fraudulent or Unfair Dealers; but the Worthy, Honeft, Publick-fpirited, true *Englifh* Merchant and Shopkeeper, oppofe it as a Project not only vexatious and troublefome, and breaking in upon the Liberties of particular Merchants and Traders; but as it tends to fubvert the Liberties of the Kingdom, and, as to the Benefits propofed by it, a Project thoroughly chimerical.

As to the Rife of this Oppofition, there was Reafon given to fuppofe, that this Scheme was not intended to terminate in an Excife upon Wine and Tobacco; nor did it need much Skill to propagate the Dread of a General Excife. Laft Year, it was dropt, that the Method of Collecting all Duties by way of Excife, was the moft effectual, equal, and juft Way; and feveral Papers and Pamphlets fince, have more openly avow'd this Project. This firft gave the Apprehenfion of fuch a Defign, an Apprehenfion hardly to be eras'd, when the Prefent Winter was ufher'd in, with a profefs'd Intent of turning two Duties into that Channel. And if the prefent Defign is good, with refpect to two Duties, it will be equally good with regard to any other Duties collected to the Cuftom Houfe,

where any fuppofed Frauds may be prevented by this Method of Collecting.

What does the prefent Bill offer in lieu of thefe dreaded Evils? The Frauds complain'd of (in Tobacco) are inconfiderable, compar'd with what are pretended; and thofe too (arifing from the Corruption of Officers) may be better prevented by other Means. The Advance this Alteration will raife, will be a Trifle; and as to the Plantations, and the Bonding here, the One may be reliev'd, and the Other prevented, without the Aid of one Excife Officer. ------- But cou'd the Ends propos'd by it, be fully anfwer'd, as it could not be effected without encroaching on the Liberties of Traders, and as Differences are not to be decided by Juries, I would beg you, Sir, to confider, whether it is worth while to go on with fuch a Scheme, however well intended, tho' it fhould raife three Millions inftead of 300,000 *l.* againft the whole Bent and Genius of a Nation, whofe Paffion is that Love of Liberty, which once made you the Favourite of the People; and that not only at the Hazard of your own Safety and Honour, but at the Hazard of ------- what I dread to mention.

The Zeal and Duty I have for his Majefty, my Love for my Country, and a Regard for the Trading Part of it, have demanded this Addrefs to you. If you, Sir, even † now, fhould decline the Purfuit of fo unpopular a Scheme, your Name will foon be as much honour'd, as it is now defam'd; and you would not want an Advocate in the Breaft of Every One, who would confider You doing This, as purfuing the Good of your Country, in Conformity to the general Senfe of the People. *Tours &c..*

† *The next Day Sir* Robert *in a handfome Manner, and by his own Motion, put off the further Confideration of this Bill to the 12th of* June *next.*

Univerfal Spectator, April 7. No. 235.

When Souls that fhould agree to will the fame,
To have one common Object for their Wifhes,
Look diff'rent Ways, regardlefs of each other,
Think what a Train of Wretchednefs enfues!
Love fhall be banifh'd from the genial Bed;
The Nights fhall all be lonely and unquiet;
And every Day fhall be a Day of Cares.
Fair Penitent.

Parental Cruelty.

AFTER fome Remarks on the Authority of Parents, Mr *Stonecaftle* inferts

inferts a Letter for the Service of a young Lady, to the following Purport.

S I R,

I am the only Child of a Gentleman of ftrict Virtue and Honour. From my Infancy, till of late, he has treated me with the utmoft Fondnefs, which. I have always acknowledged by a dutiful Behaviour. Being of a tender Conftitution, I have refolved upon a fingle Life, and refufed feveral Matches without his being uneafy at it. But a certain Gentleman has lately fo infinuated himfelf into my Father's good Opinion, that he commands me abfolutely to marry him, tho' his Perfon, Temper, and Morals are my utter Averfion.

About a Week ago be din'd with us. After Dinner I retir'd with a Relation to another Part of the Houfe, where I endeavoured to divert her and myfelf on the Harpficord. As foon as the Gentleman was gone, my Father came to us in a violent Fury, broke the Harpficord, tore my Books, and faid a thoufand bitter Things to me, protefting, fince I would not marry at his Defire, he would force me to it; I fainted away; which, I fuppofe, occafion'd my Friend to fay fomething on my Behalf, for which he rafhly told her he never more defir'd to fee her at his Houfe, and would take Care I fhould not be troublefome at hers. An Incivilty he would have been afhamed of at another Time. Alas! How is he alter'd! What cruel Sufferings do I undergo! My Conftitution is too weak to bear them long, and Death is my Choice rather than this hateful Marriage. When my Father reads this Letter, I hope he'll be fenfible of fome Compaffion, and ceafe to perfecute me. I am, &c.

Mr *Stonecaftle* obferves on the Cafe of his *Correfpondent*, that her Non-compliance is not an Act of *Undutifulnefs*, but *Self-prefervation*, and that forcing a Child to marry, is contrary to Reafon, as well as the natural Liberty of every Creature. This he illuftrates by the following Inftance.—A Friend of mine had an advantageous Offer made him for his Daughter; on his acquainting her with it, She in a refpectful Manner, beg'd his Excufe. The Father was greatly difappointed; but foon found his Daughter was pre-engag'd to another of a much inferior Fortune. At this he was under much Concern, but inftead of a rigorous Treatment, ufed the kindeft Arguments to perfwade her to like that which he judg'd moft for her Advantage; whilft with Tears fho in-

treated him not to prefs her to a Match that muft make her very miferable, affuring him fhe would never marry without his Leave. Finding how her Inclinations ftood, the indulgent old Gentleman fent inftantly for the Lover, and joyning their Hands, *Here, Sir,* fays he, *I give you my Daughter, even without your asking: Let that, however, not leffen but inhance the Gift: She might have been Great elfewhere; but, remember, I give her you to make her happy.*

The Auditor, April 10. No. 29.

Quicquide agunt Homines Votum, Timor, Ira, Voluptas
Gaudia, Difcurfus Noftri Farrago Libelli eft.
  Juv.

THE *Auditor* begins this Paper with a fhort Panegyrick to the Memory of *Ifaac Bickerftaff*, Efq; whofe Steps he endeavours to tread in, and to diverfify his Subjects according to the Manner of that agreeable Writer. Next he introduces the following Letter.

Dear Mr. AUDITOR,

I Have once more taken Pen in Hand; and now ye vain Deceivers of our Sex, ye brisk Impertinents, Half Wits, and folemn Coxcombs, expect to have your Follies fhewn, and all yourfelves expofed. And firft, that provoking Blockhead *Petulant*, who, with no more Senfe than is requifite for the Foreman of a Shop, affects the Character of a Wit, and fets up for a Critick. —— He told a Lady, the other Day, fhe fpoke falfe Grammar; and offer'd to prove from *Ariftotle*, that what fhe faid was contrary to the true Nature of *Phrafeology*; yet among his own Sex he never opens his Mouth. He is *dull*, with the Affectation of being *witty*; *foolifh*, when he would appear *wife*; *infipid* where he endeavours to *fhine*, and *difagreeable* where he defigns to *pleafe*.

Then there's little *Jafper Lively*, who has but juft *Latin* enough to read an Elegy in *Ovid*, is perpetually praifing the Majeftick Beauty of *Virgil*, and happy Boldnefs of *Horace*. He has all the Extravagance of a Man of Fire, but not the *Beauty*; the *Hurry*, but not the *Strength* of his Imagination: He is *fpritely*, without Wit; and *ignorant*, not thro' want of, but Pretence to Learning, which makes him go out of his Depth.

Urbanus is the civileft Coxcomb breathing. From a Dutchefs to a Chambermaid, any thing in Petticoats may command him. He is very skilful in varying

ing his Phrafes of Saluration according to the Quality of the Perfon he fpeaks to: He told a great Lady, the other Day, *He fhould be too happy, if fhe would Honour him, with her Commands*; and, meeting her Woman on the Stair-Cafe, defired the *Favour of fome Commiffion*; affuring her *he would be very punctual in the Performance.* He is Welcome, becaufe he is pleafed in all Company: It is not the Merit, or Perfon, but the Woman he pays his Refpects to.

But fee that univerfal Lover, dying *Ned Amorous*, who thinks Love is the moft effential Part of Converfation between the two Sexes. He has been run thro' the Body 2 or 3 Times, yet perfifts to *love without Paffion*, and *figh without Defire*.

Oppofite to thefe are your *Familiarly Rude*, Men of Eftates; who knowing they need but ask to have, treat us in a Manner too grofs to name; they buy Women as you do Horfe-flefh, for the Finenefs of their Limbs.

Under this Clafs may be reckon'd our Modern *Rufticks*; who, as foon as they are of Age, fally out of the Woods, and come up to Town, where they poffefs Beauty they know not how to Value; who know no Mufick beyond the Horn, or Company beyond their Lady Mothers. Gods! are thefe fit Company for Life? This the Reward of Innocence and Beauty? Are thefe the Men we are to *honour* and *obey*? No, rather, as the matchlefs *Diftinna* faid, Let me earn my Daily Bread with a Man of Senfe, than furfeit with a Fortune, and a Fool. Your old Correfpondent. (See p. 74.)

COQUETILLA.

He concludes with an Article of News from the Theatre in *Drury-Lane*, *viz*. That the Managers there had lately contracted with a new Actor, by Birth a D O G, but by Education, Behaviour, and Drefs, a FINE GENTLEMAN. He made his firft Appearance the 5th Inftant, to fo numerous an Audience, that the Manager of the *New Houfe* in CO-VENT GARDEN was oblig'd to difmifs his Company; notwithftanding it was but the *fecond* Night of the Reprefentation of an excellent new TRAGE-DY, called, *The* FATAL SECRET.

Grubftreet Journal, April 12. No. 172.
Dulnefs not to be taxed.

&c. I. IN the feventeen hundred thirty third Year, in the third Month, (COLLEIUS KIBLRUS being Laureat of

Great Britain, France and Ireland; JO-HANNES OLDMIXONUS Hiftoriographer, and EDMUNDUS CURLEIUS Biographer, in chief, of the faid Dominions) there arofe great Sufpicion, Diffatisfaction, and Exclamation among the Merchants and Traders of Great Britain. This Fermentation begun firft among the Dealers in Wine and Tobacco, and was occafion'd by the Leaven of Malice and Wickednefs put into their Mouths by one DEMLTRIUS, and his *Craftfmen*; which they fwallow'd with their Eyes fhut, at the fame Time ftopping their Ears againft the Reprefentations made to them of the Danger and evil Confequences thereof This Leaven was compofed of a large Quantity of acid Liquors, mixed with Alkalis. The former confifted of ftrong Affurances, that fome evil-minded Perfons had refolved to lay an heavy Burden, call'd an Excife, upon Wine and Tobacco, in Time of Peace, in order to extend it hereafter in Time of War, to all Commodities. The Alkalie part confifted of great Commendations of the People's Judgment and Power, Compaffion for their Hardfhips, and good Inftructions as to the Nature of them, in order to procure a Remedy.— This Leaven foon put the Traders in Wine and Tobacco into a great Ferment, and caufed them to make loud Complaints; which were refounded thro'out the Kingdom.

Sect. II. At that Time refided in the Cities of *London* and *Weftminfter*, a great Number of Perfons, who dealt in a Staple Commodity call'd *Dulnefs*; the Trade in which being very extenfive, was liable to Abufes. However, every Man might make ufe of his own or acquired Stock, and utter or vend it to any Part of the Kingdom. Nay, the Clergy, who are under Reftraint as to other Merchandize, had full Liberty as to this, nor were the lefs Canonical, or lefs worthy of Preferment.—Neither was this Kind of Merchandize burthen'd with heavy Impofts, Cuftoms or Excifes. One Branch of this Trade, indeed, which arofe from the daily or weekly Productions of Grubftreet, lay under fome Inconveniencies by the Paper, and Stamp Duty. But notwithftanding this Britifh Manufacture of *Dulnefs* flourifh'd exceedingly.

Sect. III. In the midft of the Noife and Clamour againft an Excife, a certain Projector of Grubftreet propofed a new Scheme (See p. 122, 142) in which he difapproved the Defign of exciting Wine and Tobacco, as hurtful to Courage and Policy,

licy, whereas they are rather assisted by those two Commodities. Wherefore this Grubean Projector ought to be the less regarded, when, instead of an Excise upon Wine and Tobacco he proposes that one be laid on Dulness.

Sect. IV. As soon as the Rumour of this Project had reached the Ears of the Traders in Dulness, it made them all tingle. In this general Consternation they had Recourse to religious Ceremonies, and resolved to offer a large Burnt-Offering to the Goddess of Dulness.

Sect. V. Besides the constant Traders in Dulness, some who were accidentally so, brought their Offerings on this solemn Occasion. These were DEMETRIUS, who brought some Quires of *Craftsmen* reflecting upon K. *Charles* I. FOGGIUS, with near the same Number of Journals taken from printed Books; and BAVIUS, with a good square Bundle of *Grubstreet Journals*, written by a variety of Authors, and perhaps some of them by himself.— The most eminent among the constant Traders were KILPRUS LAUREATUS; and his Offering was nine hundred Weight of translated Tragedy; half that Quantity of stolen Comedy, spoiled in the transmographying; and three hundred Weight of *New-Year* and *Birth-Day Odes*, finely printed in Quarto. CARUS, surnamed (falsely) (BOETROTICUS,) offer'd two Reams of unsold *Courants*. FRANCISCUS OSBORNIUS, offer'd ten Reams of *London Journals*. FRANCISCUS BRITANNICUS offer'd fifteen Reams of *Free Britons*, given away, but returned unread. Lastly, PUFFERUS HYP-ORATORICUS, whose Offering consisted of *Oratory Transactions*, lately anabaptized, *Books of Oratory*, proper *for Gentlemen and Ladies to take into the Country*; a Load of *Accademical Lectures*; *Hyp-Doctors* innumerable as unintelligible; *Orations, Lectures, Sermons, Expositions, Postills, &c.* in Manuscript, all new. There were many others of less Note, among whom, I myself, says this Writer, who have but lately begun Trade, contributed my Mite.

Free Briton, April 12, No. 177.

Remarks on the Proceedings of the COM. MON COUNCIL, *in Reading a Copy of the* TOBACCO-BILL, *April 9th.*

I Was surpriz'd, says *Walsingham*, to read in the *Daily Journal* of the 11th, that the BILL, now depending in the *House of Commons*, was exhibited in the *Common Council*, and a *Copy of that Bill* publickly *read by the Order* and in the Hearing of this Assembly.

If Powers and Privileges are given to any Assembly for Publick Good, as they certainly are, to encroach upon such Rights is making a War against the Publick, and in its Tendency destructive to the People. The *Court of Common Council* are invested with many and great Privileges, given them for the Good of the *City of London*. Whoever attempts to violate these Privileges breaks in upon the Fences of national Liberty; renders Forms and Constitutions precarious; sets Examples to *other Men* to invade *other more essential Forms*, as their Passions or Interests may induce them. Of how much greater Force must this Reasoning be with Relation to the *House of Commons*, the *supreme Representative* of the People?

Of all the Privileges with which the *House of Commons* are entrusted, the Power of *raising Money* is the most important, and most sacred. It is of so tender a Nature that they will not suffer their Money-Bills to be alter'd by the *Lords*, nor the manner of raising Money to be dictated *even from the Throne*. It is that great essential Privilege on which all their other Privileges, and their very Being as a *House of Commons*, and as the *Representative Body of the People*, wholly depend. By having asserted this Power they have preserved their Right of Proceeding, as the *Grand* Inquest of the Nation, and their Share in the *supreme* legislative Power of the Kingdom. They will not allow it to be *debated as any Conference*, nor to be *argued by* Council *at their own Bar*; nor the *Bills to be printed* while depending; nor will suffer their *Clerks to give Copies of such Bills to any but their Members*, and to them *only for their* private Use *in the Debates and Proceedings of the House*.

No Man can deny, that a *Bill for repealing* certain Duties, or *for imposing Duties* in Lieu of those repealed, or a Bill for answering both these Intentions, is a *Money-Bill.* The *Tobacco-Bill* is of such a Nature; for the Commons would not suffer it to be printed; nor would hear Council against it on any Petition. If all this is granted, it may be ask'd, by what means the *Common Council* obtain'd a Copy of this *Money-Bill* whilst depending in the *House of Commons.* Is it possible that a M——r could be so unfaithful to the House, to betray the *Copy of a Money*;

ney-Bill allowed him for his *private* Perufal, as to bring it into a *City Common Council*, to be *tried* Paragraph by Paragraph, at the *Bar* of a foreign jurifdiction, to be arraigned and judged in the Chamber of a Corporation, even after the *Houfe of Commons* had proceeded in it, and had order'd it to be read a fecond Time? That none but a M — r could obtain a Copy— let others judge.

None will difpute that the *printed Votes* were proper to be read in fuch an Affembly, and fufficient Foundation for the *Common Council* to form their *Petition* upon: But to enter into an Examination of fuch Parts of the Proceedings of the *Houfe of Commons*, which the Houfe had *refufed to publiſh*, feems as high an Infringement of the moſt facred Privilege of Parliament as was ever attempted by any *private Man, or particular Community.* I know not why, (adds *W.*) a *Pariſh Veſtry* may not claim as much Liberty of dictating to the higher Powers, as a *City Common Council.* Let me tell the Perfon, who obliged them with a Copy of this Bill, that he committed a PUBLICK ROBBERY. I mention this for the Inftruction of thofe who give any *Copies* of *Office Papers* without Leave of the Government. I have heard there are fuch Perfons, tho' *a worthy Gentleman*, not long fince, made it a Complaint, that the *Clerks of the Cuſtom-houfe* would not oblige him by committing this Crime.

By the *Julian Law* it is termed PECULATUS, and treated as the fame Crime with *Robbing*, or *Embezzling* the publick Treafure. It was punifhed by TRANSPORTATION, *Forfeiture of Goods and Chattels*, and Lofs of all Privileges as a ROMAN CITIZEN, or MEMBER *of the Commonwealth*; as may be feen by the 9th Law, Paragraph the 5th of the DIGEST. Lib. 48. Tit. 13. Tho' the *Civil Law* is not wholly incorporated with the *Law of England*, yet a BRITISH PARLIAMENT may revive the *juſt Decrees* of a ROMAN SENATE.

The *Zuditor.* April 13. No. 28.

Qui fecundum Naturam vivunt, ii fcli beate vivunt. TULL. de Offic.

IT is natural to feek for *Happinefs*; but the Misfortune is, moſt Men make *Pleafure* rather than *Happinefs* the End of their Search. If *Happinefs* follow'd every Man's *Opinion*, it would have as many monftrous *Shapes*, as there are human *Paffions*; and while thefe are liſten'd to it will be a

difficult Task fo to determine human *Happinefs*, as to convince Men of the Truth of it. But this is the Defign of the following Enquiry.

It was faid by a great Emperor and Philoſopher, that *No Man can do any Thing, purely human, well, unlefs he knows the Relation that Thing hath with divine Things: Nor any divine Thing well, unlefs be knows the Relation that Thing hath with human Things.* The E. of *Shaftsbury's* Brother, in his Pteface to his Tranflation of the *Cyropædia*, has an Opinion much of the fame Import.

A Man fhould therefore examine, whether the *Happinefs* he feeks after be confiſtent with his feveral Relations, as Man; if it violate any of thefe Relations, it is not his *proper Happinefs.*

For *Man* is compofed of *Mind* and *Body:* By *Mind* is underſtood a *Principle of Intelligence*, that *conceives* and *reflects*; by *Body*, a certain Quantity of Matter animated by that *Mind.* The Nature of the *Mind* is infinitely fuperior to that of the *Body*; and the *fuperior* Excellence ought always to govern the *inferior.* It follows, that in the *complete Happinefs* of Man, the *fenfual* Pleafures, as being of *inferior* Worth, ought to be fubordinate to the *Mental.* But what Proportion are they to bear? To anfwer this, it will be proper to determine what Man's natural Relations are; —They may be reduced to *Three* principal ones; To *Deity*, to *other Men*, to *himfelf.* Thefe are the *natural Foundations* of Man's Duty, in the Obfervation or Violation of which, he is *happy* or *unhappy.*

Our Duty with refpect to *Deity*, is *Obedience* to Divine Laws: And what are *Divine Laws* with refpect to Man, but Man's *Natural Engagements*, impofed on him by his *human Nature*, which are the Foundations of his two other Duties. And are therefore to be *firſt* follow'd; nor can Man's *Happinefs* be in *that* which obliges him to violate *thefe firſt univerfal Laws*; becaufe in violating thefe he breaks thro' the *Charactariſtick of Man.* Thefe *natural Engagements* are to clear that they cannot be miſtaken by any one that can reafon at all.

Man by the Ufe of his *Underſtanding* becomes fenfible that there is a Deity completely wife and juſt: that the higheſt Wifdom Man is capable of, is to *find out* the *Laws* which *Deity* has eſtabliſhed in the Univerfe, and that his greateſt *Perfection* and *Virtue* is to conform himfelf to the

Laws

Laws impofed by *Deity* on his *particular Nature,* by the feveral *Relations* he hath to the things about him.

Now it is plain that none who own fuch Deity can be *ignorant* of the Rules he is to act by; Here then is a pofitive Relation of *human things* with *divine.*

One Man's Nature being the *fame* as ano-*thers,* infers a *pofitive* Rule of *Juftice* to be obferved from one Man to another, founded in their common Natures: This is the Relation which determines *Man's Duty towards his Fellow Creatures.*

Laftly it is as clearly difcoverable by the human Underftanding, that Deity looks on the whole Species of Mankind alike, and does not give any *one* Power to be defpotically happy in prejudice of his Fellow-Creatures. This *Truth* determines Man's Duty to *himself,* which excludes all *private* or unjuft preference or Partiality caufed by *Self-Love,* and gives Birth to that great Virtue of *Philanthropy.* (See p.183 A)

If it be objected, that tho' Man, by violating thefe natural Obligations, becomes *unjuft,* yet is he *pofitively happy* in the Enjoyment of *that thing* for which he violates thefe *natural Obligations;* it's anfwer'd, that Man's *Happinefs* is his *Good, that* Good conformable to *his whole Na-ture.* Now, by Nature he is tied down to *Laws* common to his kind; and confe-quently his *Happinefs* cannot be out of thofe *natural Laws* which are of *Divine Eftablifhment.* Hence this great Truth, No Man can be *happy* that is not *juft,* that is, if he violates his *natural Duties.*

Should it be afferted, that by the *Laws* eftablifhed for the Government of Society, natural *Ties* are often *violated,* and Op-preffion, and an *unequal Diftribution of human Benefits* fuffer'd: It's anfwer'd, There is *no* fuch Thing as a *perfect Go-vernment;* yet it's neceffary there fhould be Laws, becaufe the Fear of Punifhment will force Men to keep their *Paffions* with-in Bounds. The *lefs Oppreffion* there is, the *better;* and the more even the Orders and Ranks of Men are in a Government, tha lefs room is there to complain of *une-qual Diftributions;* yet there muft be fome *Diftinction* and *Difference;* there muft be *Governors* and *Governed;* the *Firft* muft be exempt from *bodily Labour,* which necef-farily falls to the Share of the *Latter,* and 'tis juft it fhould be fo.

Thus *Human Happinefs* Is nothing but a faithful Obfervation of the *natural Re-lations* of the Human *Creature* to Deity, to Mankind, and to Self.   I

Weekly *Mifcellany,* April 14. No. 11.

Obfervations on the Layman's Sermon pretended to be preached at Lincoln's-Inn, Jan. 30. and on its Supplement.

A IF the *Malice* in this *Sermon* and *Sup-plement* had not been directly pointed at the *Clergy,* the Author needed not have been afraid that the World *could* be fo *partial* to that Order of Men, as to give *any* of them the *Credit* of thefe Perfor-mances, fo much do they exceed any thing

B in their kind that ever came from the Pen of an *Ecclefiaftick.*

His firft Point is, that the Clergy *ought to have no Power,* becaufe Clergymen al-*ways abufe it.*] What is there in *Reafon* or *Fact* to juftify this Affertion? Were thefe Abufes *peculiar* to the Clergy? No;

C they were the *Error* of the Times com-mon to both *Clergy* and *Laity;* when both acted according to the Laws of a *Popifh Conftitution.* If Laws are *bad,* let them be *mended.* If Power is *exorbi-tant,* let it be *reftrained.* This was re-medied by the *Reformation;* and what

D has happen'd *fince* to fhew the Clergy more given to *abufe* Power than other Men? Several Clergymen in the *Commiffion* of the *Peace* make not a worfe Figure than many of their Lay *Brethren.*

This Writer tells us, there's no great Ex-PLOIT *in wearing Gowns and Bands, and broad Hats.* No; neither is there

E fuch *Magick* in them, that as foon as a Man puts them on, he muft needs *com-mence* either *Knave* or *Fool.* Surely there are fome among the *Clergy* as well as *Lai-ty,* who are worthy to be put in Places of Truft: Not that it's *becoming* in *Clergy-men,* to be ambitious of *Civil Offices;*

F but to fhew that in the Eye of the *Law* the Clergy are not fuch MONSTERS as this Writer makes them. If 'tis faid, the Clergy have been ever aiming at an *En-creafe* of Power, 'tis granted. But is this *peculiar* to *Ecclefiaftical Power?* Prero-gative *bears* fometimes upon Liberty;

G Liberty again upon Prerogative. Will you infer from hence, that Power ought not to be put into the Hands of King or Parliament?

Spiritual Power vefted in Clergymen is a much higher Authority, and which cannot be conteﬅed by Chriﬅians. Why

H are thofe unfit to be entruﬅed with Power from *Men,* who are entruﬅed with Power from God? But he denies that Clergymen have *any* Power, but what is derived from the *State;* and avers, that our Con-ﬅitution ftitution is founded on this Principle. But what feems to give him moft Offence, is, the *Power* of *Ecclefiaftical Courts.* There may be particular Reafons, why this Writer, and many *others,* are uncafy at this kind of Power. But this Matter now lies before a *higher Judgment.*

His other favourite Point is, that as the Clergy ought not to have *any Power,* fo neither fhould they have *any Money.* He tells us, That it's computed the Clergy have a 5th Part of our Wealth. Had he confider'd the Matter, he would have diftinguifhed between *Money* and *Land,* and then might he feen the Falfenefs of his Calculation, becaufe the Clergy have no *Property* in the *Perfonal* Eftates of the Laity; therefore he muft mean the *Lands* only. All the Lands of the Nation are ufually valued at 10 Millions; fo that according to him the whole *Revenue* of the *Clergy* amounts to 2 *Millions.*

But for his better Information, about the latter End of K. *William's* Reign, an exact *Eftimate* was taken of the whole Value of the *Clergy's* Revenue, not excepting *Church Lands,* and if it had been *then* equally divided among the *Livings,* it would not have made them 110l. *per Ann.* one with another. Now, fuppofing the Number of Parifhes 10, or 11,000, any *Tradefman* will tell him what every Living would be worth, if 2 *Millions* were to be fhared equally among them. A fmall Increafe has indeed, been made fince, by the *Augmentation* of fome Livings, but which makes no great Alteration in the Accompt. He likewife forgot to deduct the *Tythes* and *Land* now in the Poffeffion of the *Laity.*

But what does this *Incendiary* mean by threatning the *Clergy* with the Refentments of the *Laity ?* Would he infinuate that the *Legiflature* intend, or are *inclin'd* to deprive the Clergy of any Part of their Revenues? Their Conduct on a late Attempt fhews the Contrary.

Would he have it thought the Laity are generally difinclin'd to the Clergy? Let their frequent *Augmentations* of fmall Livings; their annual Liberality to the Widows and Orphans of Clergymen; the Refpect a *worthy* Clergyman always meets with, fatisfy him, there's no Foundation for fuch a Surmize.

London Journal, April 14. N° 710.

Of Friendfhip and Benevolence.

SElf-*good* arifes from *fharing Pleafure* with, and being fenfible we *merit*

ewell of others. The Pleafures of *Friendfhip* and *Benevolence* infinitely furpafs thofe which terminate meerly in *ourfelves.*

Benevolence and Friendfhip differ. The firft is a fettled calm Friendfhip to *Mankind,* as *Friendfhip* is a warm Benevolence to *one* or a *few* Men. So that the benevolent Man is a more noble Character than that of a *Friend;* becaufe he diffufes *more Good* and makes *more People* happy, and fo ftands a more compleat Image and Reprefentative of the fupreme Being, who is *good to all, Father of the World,* and the *Friend* of the Univerfe.

But, *Friendfhip,* as it gives the higheft Pleafure, is fometimes a *dangerous* Virtue, and more to be guarded againft, than *general Benevolence;* which feldom carries a Man beyond *Self-Regards,* nor pufhes him upon unreafonable Acts of Generofity, which often end in his Ruin. This is intimated, when we fay a Man is *too Good,* meaning that he has acted with fo much Zeal for the Good of *others,* as to *diftrefs* his own Affairs. There may be an Excefs in *Virtue* itfelf; for we are to follow her no further than *Reafon* allows. Neither *Benevolence* nor *Friendfhip* oblige a Man to do what *no Reafon can be affigned* for; therefore *none* fhould ruin himfelf to make *another.* The firft great and univerfal Law of Nature is *our own Happinefs;* which we are never obliged to part with, but when *Virtue* and *Happinefs* are inconfiftent. To part with our *own Happinefs* to another, is doing no Good; there is but *one Man* happy ftill. Much lefs can *Friendfhip* oblige a Man to part with his *Life* to redeem another from *Death.* Why fhould he not die as well as, or rather than his Friend; fince the *very Capacity* for all Enjoyment is deftroy'd by *Death?* But we may do a thoufand good Offices, without deftroying our *Health* or *Fortunes.* It would be much better for the World, if no Men extended their Generofity and Benevolence beyond the Bounds of their own *Fortunes* and *Circumftances :* For thoufands of Perfons and *Families* have been reduced to Want, thro' their *thoughtlefs* Benevolence, and *fenfelefs* Friendfhip; and thoufands of *worthlefs,* idle, *extravagant* Fellows, have eaten the Bread of the *Honeft,* Laborious, Induftrious and *Frugal.* Is not this inverting the Order and *Nature* of Things ? Why fhould one Man's *Virtue* be the Support of another Man's *Vice ?*

There's hardly one in a Thoufand *miferable* but thro' *wrong Conduct,* and the *want* ware of *Industry* and *Frugality*; and 'tis encouraging Vice, to be Benevolent to the *Vicious*. Was it not for this *false* Generosity and *vicious* Friendſhip, a great Number of the *Gentlemen*, as they call themſelves, of this Town, that is, idle-Fellows, who eat, drink, and dreſs at the Expence of others, muſt disband, and turn themſelves to the natural Life of Man, *Labour*, or be *ſtarved*.

If all Perſons who had not *Hereditary Fortunes*, were bred to *Buſineſs*, and our good Laws well executed, we ſhould not find half the Neceſſities that are complained of. The trueſt Charity, and juſteſt Benevolence, is employing People in honeſt Labour and Buſineſs; for 'tis reaſonable that thoſe who have ſquander'd away their Fortunes in Luxuries, ſhould be left to labour for their Bread.

Even *Gratitude*, or *Friendſhip* to Benefactors, *the bigheſt of all* Virtues, ſhould never carry a Man beyond the Rules of *Juſtice*; but it will allow him to put his Virtues in the *ſtrongeſt* Light, and his Foibles in the *faireſt* Light; to juſtify ſuch of his Actions as appear *right upon the whole* and *well deſign'd*, tho' the World be againſt it. So far *Gratitude* allows; and if, when a Friend is *diſtreſſed*, one ſhould leap the Bounds of Reaſon, it's an *Error* that has Charms in it; pity that it is an Error! However, it's eaſily forgiven, when we conſider that the *Exceſſes* or *Vices* of Gratitude are leſs pernicious, than ſome *four rigid Virtues* are beneficial.

SOCRATES.

Fog's Journal, April. 14. Nº 232.
Of Parliaments, both corrupt and good.

IN a Compariſon we lately made, ſays *Fog*, between the Senate of *Rome* under the *Caſars*, and the Parliament of *Paris* (See p. 142.) was ſhewn, that by the Corruption of Senates, the People are enſlaved, and that Subjects may taſte Liberty in Governments not free, where the Magiſtracy is uncorrupt. Of both theſe Extremes we have Examples in the *Engliſh* Hiſtory, and in the ſame Reign.

No Prince ever came to the Crown more univerſally belov'd than *Richard* II. Yet by a wicked and blundering Adminiſtration, he loſt the Affection of his People; for the Politicks of theſe Men were wholly employ'd in ſqueezing Money from the People at Home, while the national Intereſt was neglected abroad.

The Parliament could bear no longer with theſe Miniſters; and therefore ſent a Meſſage to the King, declaring, that *De*

la *Poole*, Earl of *Suffolk*, the Chancellor, and *Vere*, the Treaſurer, ought to be removed from all Office and Truſt, and from the Perſon of the King. What gave the greateſt Offence was, that the Chancellor in the King's Name, demanded an extraordinary Supply for the King's Houſhold, or Civil Liſt; to which the Commons returned Anſwer, That they neither could nor would proceed in any Buſineſs, till the King ſhould come in Perſon amongſt them, and remove the Chancellor from his Office; repreſenting further, That it was the antient Cuſtom of this Realm, that the King ſhould call a Parliament every Year; and that if the King eſtranged or withdrew himſelf from his Parliament for the Space of 40 Days, the Members were at Liberty to go back to their Habitations. In Return, the Miniſters to intimidate the Parliament, adviſed the King to tell them,——" That he perceived his Parliament and People intended to make. Inſurrections againſt him, in which Caſe he was reſolved to ſubmit himſelf to his Couſin, the King of *France*, for Advice and Aſſiſtance, rather than truckle to his Subjects". The Parliament returned Anſwer, " That they had an antient Conſtitution, that if the King thro' evil Council, Obſtinacy, or Contempt of his Subjects, ſhould alienate himſelf from his People, and not govern by the Laws of the Realm, it ſhould be lawful for the People to depoſe him, and to ſet up another of the Royal Family".

This brought the King a little to himſelf, he ſuffered *De la Poole* to be impeached, and then asked a Supply. The Commons anſwer'd, That he need not want Supplies, when he could ſo eaſily ſupply himſelf from thoſe who were his and the Nation's Debtors (Meaning the Miniſters.) The Chancellor and Treaſurer were removed, to ſee if it would put the Parliament in a good Humour; it had the deſired Effect, and a Supply was granted; but none were to pay towards this Tax, but Dukes, Earls, Archbiſhops, Abbots, Sheriffs, Knights, Eſquires, Parſons, Vicars, and Chauntry Prieſts.

They conſider'd next, that by the great Corruption of the Place-men, the publick Revenues were ſquander'd, Trade decay'd, the People impoveriſh'd, the Rents of the Gentry impair'd, and the Place-men immenſely Rich, and therefore impowered 11 Lords to hear all Complaints relating to the publick Revenues from the Death of *Edward* III. — and then broke up.

Thus.

Thus having obtained their Point, the Minifters refumed their Places and Practices; and in order to make themfelves Safe, laid a Defign of taking off the Duke of *Glouceſter*, and fome principal Oppofers, at an Entertainment in the City; but this Plot was fpoilt by being communicated to Sir *Rich. Exton*, L. Mayor of *London*, who gave Notice of it to the Duke.

Their next Scheme was to take off all Terrors of Parliament. To which End they tamper'd with the Sheriffs to raife Forces for the King; and to return none to ferve in the next Parliament, but fuch as they (the Minifters) fhould name. The Sheriffs anfwer'd, that thofe who oppofed the Meafures of the Minifters were greatly belov'd by the People; and that as to Perfons to be returned for Parliament, they could not hinder the People from their antient and undoubted Right of free Elections. Upon this Difappointment, they applied to the Judges, who were more Complaifant, and promifed to make the Law fpeak juſt as they would have it.

About this Time, feveral Lords and Commoners, who had confederated to relieve their Country, met at *Havangay* Park, near *High-gate*; of which the King being inform'd, ask'd Sir *Hugo de Lyn*, a crack-brain'd Knight, what he fhould do with thefe Men? The Knight anfwered, " Let us march out and kill every Man of them, and then by God's Eyes you will have deſtroy'd the worthieſt Men, and beſt Subjeۤts in your Kingdom."

The Minifters having mifcarried in their Defign on the Sheriffs, the next Year appointed a Pack of profligate Fellows for Sheriffs fit for their Purpofe, who returned fuch Tools to Parliament as were the very N E G R O E S of Men in Power, and impeach'd all thofe Lords who had oppofed their Mafters, particularly thofe who had been appointed by the laſt Parliament to infpeۤt the Diffipations in the publick Revenues. — When they had done all that was required of them, they were only prorogu'd, which was a ſtrange Innovation in thofe Days, when no Parliament was ever known to fit twice. —— This Harmony betwixt them and the Minifters, robbed the King of the Hearts of his People, whereby he loſt both his Crown and Life.

The *Craftſman*. April 14. Nͦ. 354

Obſervations on the Cafe of the Planters in Virginia, *in a Letter to*—— fee p. 133.

S I R,

I Know not to whom I could better addrefs my Obfervations on *the Cafe*

of *the Planters of Tobacco in* Virginia, than to one who comes *Agent* from that Colony, and who undertakes to *fupport* that Reprefentation.

· The Cafe feems a Petition, defigned to be prefented to Some-body; therefore furely you have gone beyond your Commiffion, in turning it into an Appeal to the People, or rather a Libel upon the Trade.

· The Cafe begins with an Account of the Progrefs of the *Virginia* Trade thro' a long Courfe of Years, the Mifchief attending it through various Changes by feveral Acۤts of Parliament, and the Hardfhips the Planters fuffer from their Factors.] The Acۤts hinted at, that have affeۤted the Tobacco, are thofe made fince the Acۤt of Tonnage and Poundage. It fays, *That the Impoſition by the firſt of King* James II. *was better ſecured to the Crown, than by the Method introduced by the 7th and 8th of King* William. How does That appear? All the Difference between the Bonding under thofe Acۤts, was, that in the firſt, the Importer gave Bond that the Tobacco fhould not be delivered till the Buyer had paid the Duty; in the latter his Bond obliged Him to pay the Duty; and the Reafon for altering this Method was, becaufe the Buyers could not raife fo much ready Money as was neceffary to carry on the Trade in this Manner; therefore they afterwards collected the whole Duty of the Importer, and the Price of Tobacco advanced in Proportion, and the Merchant charged his Commiffion on the grofs Amount of the Tobacco fold. This is one of the Mifchiefs fuggeſted in the Cafe.

· He goes on; The Merchant's Commiffion may be computed to be above an Eighth of the Nett Produce of Tobacco, and in many Sales, to more than the whole Balance coming to the Planter.] This is an idle Suggeſtion; every one muſt know that the Merchant's Commiffion on the *Virginia* Trade is 2 and a half *per Cent.* as ufual; it is not to be underſtood that the Factor is to *enſure* a Market, or to anfwer for a greater or leffer Produce.

The Writer conceives, that the Prohibition to import Bulk Tobacco has produced fome good Effects; but fo long as the Merchant is trufted to keep Tobacco in his own Warehoufes, and the Payment of Duties are under the prefent Method, he apprehends no Expedient will be found adequate to the Mifchief defigned to be remedied.] I am glad to find he allows

ua.

one Act of Parliament, passed in the Time, and sollicited by the present Set of Merchants, hath produced any good Effects: But am surprized at his Objection about Warehouses. Who so fit to have the Custody of Tobacco consigned to 'em, as those who pay Freight and Custom, and sell it? He says, many of the Merchants contract Debts at the Custom-House, far exceeding their Estates, which had occasioned vast Losses to the Revenue.] If that were true, how does it affect the Planter? They don't stand engaged to discharge those Debts; nor are the Instances many. I must remind you, that it's owing to the Credit given under the present Method of collecting the Duty, that the Tobacco Trade is circulated in the Manner it is, whereby the Planters are enabled to maintain and enlarge their Plantations, seat and stock them with Negroes and Cattle to their own Benefit, and the Advantage of Trade and Navigation.

He says, the Planters find an unaccountable Difference in the Weights of their Tobacco there, and when weighed at the Custom-Houses in *Great-Britain*, especially in *London*.] How improbable is it for the Planters to find this Difference? For, till this Year they had very few Weights and Scales in *Virginia*; the Planters seldom weighed the Tobacco they ship'd Home; and those who did, used Stillyards; which is an uncertain Manner of weighing. He should have considered that Tobacco is a *Vegetable*, and wastes till it's full dry.

He farther observes, That upon Enquiry it will appear, that not above one half of the Tobacco, consumed in *Great-Britain*, can have paid Duties.] How comes He so well acquainted with the State of the Revenue of *Great-Britain*? Had he not these Hints from *hence*? Was not this Case cook'd up by their standing Agent here, and sent to *Virginia* to get the Sanction of the Council and Assembly to it?

He allows, that what he offers upon the Subject, may amount only to Conjecture.] He should have kept *Conjectures* to himself, and not have sported with the Reputations of Men in Business.

The Case says, that upon a just Calculation made of the Weights of one Hogshead with another, there will remain a pregnant Suspicion, that a considerable Part of the Frauds must proceed from weighing Tobacco upon landing, either thro' Corruption or Negligence.] Why is not this Suspicion removed? There is

lodged at the Custom-House a Manifest of every Ship's Lading, containing the Mark, Number, and *Virginia* Weight of every Hogshead, signed by the Collectors, &c. in *Virginia*; there are also the Land-waiter's Accounts at the King's Scale; compare them, and discover Frauds if you can. The World will hardly believe, that a Body of People, who have maintained a fair Character thro' the whole Course of their Business, should be so generally Corrupt, as for a Course of Years, to go on in a way of Theft, plundering the Planters of Tobacco, and then defrauding the Government of Customs without Discovery, as is here charged.

As to some other Suggestions, let him instance where the Commissioners of the Customs, ever permitted any Merchant to give Bond for 3 Years successive Importation, that did not in that Time discharge any of the Bonds for the first or second Year's Importation. If he can't, the large Credit the *Case* speaks of, vanishes. As to the 3 Years expiring before Bonds can be put in Suit, I always counted they were payable in 18 Months, and have heard the Commissioners have threatned to put Bonds in Suit when they had run out of the 18 Months, tho' they knew the Tobacco was *bona fide* exported, the Debentures made out, tho' not passed, on Account of a particular Accident.

The *Auditor*, April 17. No. 29.

THE Discourse at our Club the other Night, turn'd upon Female Dress. *Frank Easy* said the Head Dress is equally free from the Over-growth in those of our Great Grand-mothers, and the Dwarfishness that succeeded in the last Age; but the Ladies still retain an Ornament for that Part, which is often unbecoming; namely their *Bridles*, or *Kissing Strings*. This Fashion we owe to the *French* Ladies, who call it *Desespoir Solitaire*, or *Licol*. From the first Appellation, one may attribute the Origin of them to some desponding Lady, willing to have a constant Resource in any extraordinary Fit of Despair. But to judge from the Name, *Licol*, or *Bridle*, one would rather refer it to the Invention of some young Ladies, to keep their Heads in a just Attitude. They took the Denomination of *Kissing Strings*, either from their Proximity to the Lips, or as they serve to hold the Fair-one's Head steddy, or pull her to, if she is refractory. Yes, says *Tom Cyrick*,

Dum

Dum flagrantia detorquet ad oscula
Cervicem, aut facili sævitiâ negat,
Quæ poscente magis gaudeat eripi;

Frank not underſtanding Latin, went on—Nothing illuſtrates a Lady's Judgment more, than her Skill in Propriety of Dreſs; what Colour is moſt agreeable for her Complexion; What Ornament beſt ſuits the Turn of her Face; a thorough Knowledge in this Point often adds Embelliſhment where Nature has been deficient. Thus, *Macvilla*, remarkable for her *Length of Viſage*, *Hollowneſs of Cheeks*, and *Protruſion of Chin*, by a fine laced Mob, drawn from the Cheeks, and tied under the Chin by a *Bridle*, has an *apparent Plumpneſs* in her *meagre* Face. But why *Miranda*, who has the ſweeteſt Dimple in a lovely double Chin, ſhould muffle up that Part which ſhews the moſt eaſyFall to a well-turn'dNeck, is ſurprizing.

Bridles, interrupted *Tom*, may be juſt and proper for the Uſe you mention; But would be more properly uſed for the preſent Set of *unreſtrained Writers*. *Apollo*, in the *Battle of the Books*, preſents a Bridle to *Lucan*, who, had he not given himſelf up to the Impetuoſity of his Genius, would have been a great Poet; theſe Gentlemen have all his Faults without any of his Perfections. How are we incumber'd with their incongruous Pieces, only diſtinguiſhed by their Repugnance to *Nature*, *Decorum*, and *Reaſon*? I would likewiſe propoſe the ſame *coercive Implement* to an Author, who from his ſuperior Talents in Poetry, preſumes to inſult Men of *Honour*, *Merit*, and the moſt *extenſive Beneficence*: Is this paying the Veneration due to the *Manes* of HOMER or VIRGIL, to employ their Beauties in Productions of *Wit*, infamous for *Ill-nature*, and the moſt *ungenerous Malice*?

Some Letters happening to be brought in, put an End to *Tom's* Diſcourſe. *Frank* read the following.

Friend AUDITOR,

THY Animadverſions are approved by the *Brethren*. Thou haſt wiſely rebuked the People of thy Perſwaſion for holding the Habit of the *Friends* in Deriſion; I deſire likewiſe, thou wilt reprove the Women of thy Belief, for as much as they wear their Garments of an *unſeemly Shortneſs*, and *their Feet are running to Evil*, creating Scandal in the Eyes of the *Friends*, and raiſing evil Thoughts in the *Unclean of Heart*.

Thy Friend, EPHRAIM PLAIN.

Frank was highly delighted with *Ephraim's* Letter. The Short Gowns and Coats, ſays he, now in vogue among the Ladies, have often deceived me in the Wearer, when behind her. I have more than once miſtaken a venerable Lady of 60, near 6 Foot high, for a tall Girl juſt taken from the Boarding-School. One would think, from the Tripping-Gate, both young and old affect, they had tuck'd up their Petticoats to run a Race.

What, ſays *Tom*, like *Atalanta*, from Matrimony? No, reply'd *Frank*, they rather imagine by the Agility of their plyant Limbs, which gives an additional Bloom to their Charms, to get them Huſbands. I agree with *Ephraim*, that nothing is more unſeemly, than one of theſe *abridged Gowns*, when the Foot and Leg are without Proportion; but the *ſmall Foot*, *High Inſtep*, and *Taper Ankle*, with which the moſt exact Symmetry in Architecture is not to be compared, ſhould never be hid.

The *Daily Courant*, April 17.

IT is a Doctrine much inculcated by our modern political Writers, that the Senſe of the People is the ſureſt Standard of judging the Conduct of publick Affairs; and that the Adminiſtration ought to be no longer employ'd than their Meaſures, and Perſons are agreeable to them.

But if their Judgment is ſo exact and certain, what Occaſion is there for their Hebdomadal Demagogues, to beſtow ſo much Pains to point to them the Road they ſhould go? Yet theſe Writers firſt tell the People, that they underſtand their own Intereſt better than any can teach them; and then endeavour to impoſe ſuch glaring Abſurdities upon them as none but Ideots could believe.

The People's Intereſt, it is acknowledged, ought chiefly to be regarded. —But notwithſtanding ſo many Compliments have been paid to their Judgment, yet a Multitude of Inſtances might be named, wherein they have been deceived by the moſt contemptible Tools that ever form'd a Faction; the Death of *Socrates*, the Baniſhment of *Cicero*, the Deſtruction of great and flouriſhingEmpires, have been owing to the inconſiderate, ungovernable Rage of the People, fomented by the moſt deſpicable Inſtruments. *Wat Tyler* and *Jack Straw*, *Maſſianello* and *Sacheverel*, *Miſt* and *D'anvers*, have uſed the ſame Arts,with the ſame Succeſs. One would imagine, that by the Uſe lately.

lately made of the Rabble, the very Riffraff and Scum of the Streets of *London* and *Westminster* were one of the conftituent Parts of our Government, and had a Right to direct the Debates, and controul the Refolutions of Parliament. It's hard to fay in what Capacity they acted, unlefs it was as Reprefentative of the C——n C——l of the C—y of L——n; then it muft be acknowledg'd their Addrefs and Behaviour was perfectly conformable to the Will and Inftructions of thofe that fent them. And well was it for *England*, that fuch a noble Spirit was exerted upon this Emergency, when our Liberties and Religion, our Properties, and the Chaftity of our Wives and Daughters were fo eminently concern'd; of which the C——n C——l of *London* were fo firmly convinc'd, that they not only fent their Reprefentatives as above, but they went themfelves to *Weftminfter* to prevent fuch a pernicious Scheme from taking Effect. As they are a very wife Body, they were foon fenfible how much *their* Trade would fuffer by any Enquiry into Frauds. Indeed, had it fucceeded, many *Tobacco Factors*, who boaft they follow'd the *Sheriffs of London* with the City Petition in their own Coaches, muft hereafter have walk'd on Foot, or gone 4 in a Hack, like Lawyers; and inftead of magnificent Houfes in the Country, have been contented with a Lodging at *Iflington*, or an Apartment in *Canbury* Houfe. 'Tis true, whole Provinces in *America*, all the landed Intereft in *England*, and all the poor Manufacturers, and Confumers of thofe Commodities, intended to be the Subject of the propofed Regulation, would have been confiderably eafed and advantaged by it: But ought thofe to be fet in Competition with the important Interefts of thofe valuable Members of the Common-wealth, the Dealers in Tobacco, and Retailers of Wine?

Could any thing add to the Regard which every true *Englifhman* has fo zealoufly exprefs'd for thofe illuftrious Fraternities of *Tobacconifts* and *Vintners*, it fhould be the decent, modeft, and obliging Conduct and Behaviour, which they have fo fcrupuloufly obferv'd thro' the whole Progrefs of this Affair; for, who could behold them moving along in flow, and folemn Proceffion, thro' *Fleet-ftreet* and the *Strand*, humbly to remonftrate againft the *Bill*, without admiring their exact Order, and their modeft and dejected Countenances? Every C——n C——l Man in the Cavalcade having a Chew of

Tobacco in his Mouth, as an Emblem of the Bufinefs he was upon, and fignifying if that Bill fhould pafs, it would probably be his laft.

It was confidently reported, but to befure falfely, that the Diforders and Riots that happen'd afterwards, were promoted by the fame Perfons who came in this fuppliant manner to implore Compaffion of Parliament; and that when they could not obtain their Ends one Way, they were refolved to ufe the Members of the H—— of C——ns as the *Indians* do their Gods; if they don't quickly hear and anfwer their Petitions, to cut and hew them to Pieces: But this is undoubtedly as true as the reft of the Calumnies raifed by the Minifterial Writers againft thofe eminent Merchants, who brew all their own Wine, and thofe honeft Factors, who enrich themfelves, while they fuffer the Proprietors of the Tobacco they fell to want Bread. (See p. 138)

The Daily Advertifer, April 18.

The Author's Vindication of the General Dictionary, *from the Remarks of* A. B. *in the* Grub-ftreet Journal. (See p. 171.)

THO' we are far from entertaining too advantageous an Idea of our *General Dictionary*, yet it does not merit the injurious Cenfure of *A. B.*

A. B's Critique, with regard to the Oriental Articles relates not to Things, but to three Arabic Names, which he affirms are Mif-fpelt. But, are not the fame Names fpelt differently by various Authors? As to the *Abaffides*, we never pretended it was written according to the Arabic Idiom; but as that Word is employ'd by *D'Herbelot*, *Moreri*, and other European Writers, that is Authority enough for us.

A. B. advances a direct Falfehood, when he infinuates, that the Article of *Abdolonymus* was not extracted from the original Authors. Have we not the very Words of *Strabo*, *Hefychius*, *Diod. Siculus*, *Plutarch*, *Quintus Curtius* and *Juftin*, and the Books and Places whence they are borrow'd, cited in the Margin? As to the Critick's afferting, that the Article of *Abdolonymus* is dry and flat, we appeal to our learned Readers, whether 'tis not as entertaining as the Subject would admit.

He would infinuate, our additional Articles are mere Tranfcripts from *Moreri*, and other Dictionaries. The Falfity of this will appear, by comparing our Articles with thofe under the fame Title in *Moreri*, or any other Dictionary.

That

That his Criticifm is the Effect of Partiality and Malice, appears from his fpeaking in Favour of a *complete and accurate Tranflation* (as 'tis call'd) *of Bayle's Dictionary*, in the firft Number of which we have pointed out a great Number of Blunders, which he ought to have mention'd at the fame Time he animadverted upon our Performance.

A. B. is miftaken, when he declares, that our interfperfing *Bayle's* Dictionary with additional Articles, was only an Artifice to draw *over the Subfcribers to our felves, in hopes of a completer Work.* Any Perfon of Tafte and Judgment who compares their Tranflation with ours, will fee we had no Occafion for fuch an Expedient.

The Critick alfo falfely affirms, our Additions will make but one Volume; as will appear from a Comparifon of the Number of additional Articles in our firft 20 Sheets, with thofe of Mr *Bayle.* Now, it may be asked, Whether Gentlemen would not chufe to pay 7 or 8 Guineas for a new, juft, and accurate Tranflation of Mr *Bayle's Dictionary*, with two Supplemental Volumes in his Manner, rather than *6 l.* for a Tranflation of the faid Dictionary only, tranfcrib'd chiefly from the former univerfally exploded one; a Tranflation, the Errors of which are fo numerous, that upon a Computation of 100 to each Number, the Whole, when the Work is finifhed, will amount to upwards of 12,000. The AUTHORS.

Grub-ftreet Journal. April 19. Nᵒ. 173.

Mevius to Francis Walfingham, *Efq; on his Remarks on the Proceedings of the* Common Council of London, *relating to the Tobacco Bill.* (See p. 180)

SIR,

YOUR High Notions of the *peculiar Rights, Powers* and *Privileges* of the *Common Council* of the City of *London*, and the dreadful Confequences of any Attempts to violate them (See p. 181) feem but lately taken up, or you would not have fallen fo feverely about 18 Months fince, (See p. 461, 475, Vol. I.) on that Court's exerting an undoubted *Right* and *Privilege*, in rejecting without reading a Petition for leave to erect an Equeftrian Statue to K. *Wm*: Your Allegations were all anfwer'd by me (See p. 482, Vol. I.) to which you did not reply, perhaps, becaufe I did not addrefs to you. I expect, however you will defend your late Remarks on that Body, as this Letter is addreffed directly to your felf, or retract

the Charge againft them, of their violating or *invading* the Privileges *of the Houfe of Commons*, in reading a Copy of the Tobacco Bill; particularly their Privilege and Power of raifing Money.—Did the Common Council prefume to *debate* or *argue* this Power? Did they prefume to print any *Money* Bill, or clandeftinely procure a copy of it, contrary to the Order of the Houfe?

The grand Objection againft the late *Inftructions* fent from the feveral Boroughs and Counties to their Reprefentatives, was, that the *Inftructors* declared themfelves againft a Bill, of the Nature of which they were altogether ignorant. Here is a large Body of Men, who, by hearing the Bill read, are exactly inform'd of its Nature, and upon that Information ground their Petition againft it; and, for this rational Way of Proceeding, are charged with infringing the Liberties of the Houfe of Commons. So that by this Method of Reafoning, the People are prohibited from Petitioning at all: They muft not do it before they had feen the Bill, or heard the Contents of it; for then they would incur the Charge of Ignorance and Perverfenefs; and they muft not fee the Bill, or here it read, becaufe this *is as high an Infringement of the moft facred Privilege of Parliament as poffible.*

I'm of your Opinion, that the *printed Votes* were a fufficient Foundation to form their Petition upon. But then I think, none can reafonably Difpute, that a Copy of a Bill itfelf is a *more fufficient* Foundation to ground a Petition upon, than any *general Votes* concerning it. And this may ferve to excufe, if not to juftify, the communicating and reading the Bill in that Affembly. — Befides, fince it had been frequently afferted, that this Bill had been vilely mifreprefented by popular Incendiaries, there was no way fo proper to give People full Satisfaction in the real Contents of it, as to read it to them: And 'tis well known, that the reading of it had fuch an Effect upon many, as entirely to change their Opinion.

Having charg'd both the Perfon who communicated the Copy of this Bill, and all thofe that heard it read, with infringing the moft *facred Privileges of Parliament*, you at laft heap an additional Weight of Guilt upon the Perfon who communicated this Bill, and charge him with a *publick Robbery*, adjudged fuch by the *Roman Law*, and ftill held fuch by

the

the *Law of Nations.* In proof of which you quote the Digeſt *ad Legem Jul.* viz. *Senatus juſſit, lege peculatus teneri. eos, qui injuſſu ejus qui ei rei præerit, tabularum publicarum inſpiciendarum deſcribendarumque poteſtatem fecerunt [fecerint]* I wiſh you had favour'd us with a Tranſlation of this Law, as well on the Account of the Perſons againſt whom you was writing, as becauſe it is neceſſary now that all our Pleadings ſhould be in Engliſh, tho' it is of no force with us.

I cannot apprehend, how an Original Bill, read only a ſecond Time, and which probably may never paſs into an Act, can with any Propriety come under the Denomination of *Tabulæ Publicæ, publick Records* or *Writings,* or, as you call them, *Office Papers.* How this Law can extend to any Perſon, who, with the Leave of proper Authority, having taken a Copy of an Original Paper, afterwards ſhews that Copy to others, I cannot imagine.

The Auditor. April 20. No. 32.

THE *Auditor* having been charged with Copying ſome of his Letters from the old *Spectator,* he clears himſelf of that Imputation, and defies ſuch cenſorious Criticks to prove it.

He likewiſe vindicates that Paſſage in his Advice to *Indamora* (See p. 84 R.) where he ſeems to *encourage* young Gentlewomen in her Circumſtances, to accept of an Offer *abſolutely deſtructive of Virtue ;* His Reply is, *A vicious Inclination wants no Encouragement to do a bad Thing, and a Virtuous one can never be impoſed upon, by any Encouragement, in her Opinion of what She ought to do, which will always appear to her what it really is.*

Laſtly, he inſerts a Letter from *Lepida,* who took to reading his Paper from accidentally ſeeing the Title of it upon one of Mr DUTTON's *Flap-Fans,* which ſhe had bought. *N.*

The Craftſman. April 21. No. 355.

PUblick Bleſſings naturally produce publick Rejoicings ; and I cannot but congratulate my Countrymen, ſays *D'anvers,* upon their late memorable Deliverance ; and ſhall leave the Enemies of *Trade* and *Liberty* to humble Themſelves in Sackcloth and Aſhes.

We have the Pleaſure to obſerve, that the *Spirit of Liberty* is not yet extinct in this Kingdom, and that it has been exerted without any ridiculous Adherence to old Party-names, nor relating to our pre-

ſent Diſputes. Therefore every good *Engliſhman* muſt be glad to find the ſilly Denominations of *Whig* and *Tory* loſt in the more ſeaſonable Diſtinction of *Exciſeman,* or *no Exciſeman.*

As this *Coalition of Parties* hath been attended with ſuch glorious Succeſs, 'tis hop'd they will not ſuffer any *Seducer* to divide them again.

'Tis Difficult to ſay, which ſhould be commended moſt, the prudent Vigour of the *mercantile Part of the Nation,* or the publick Spirit of the *landed Gentlemen,* in ſupporting Them. As the Happineſs of both depends on each other, ſo they have juſtly made it a joint Cauſe, and while they continue thus happily united, we may defy all the Powers on Earth to deſtroy our *Liberties* and *Conſtitution.*

It would be ungrateful not to acknowledge the diſintereſted Conduct of ſeveral Gentlemen in high Stations, both *civil* and *military ;* but the general Applauſe of Mankind, and the inward Satisfaction of having done their Duty in ſo critical a Juncture, will amply compenſate for the Loſs of preſent Favour, or the Frowns of Power. (See Occurrence, *April* 14.)

I congratulate my Countrymen, not only on the *Defeat* of the Scheme, but on the *Project* itſelf ; which hath been ſeveral Years in Embryo, but is now cruſh'd ſo as never to riſe again. The gloomy Proſpect is now vaniſh'd, and we may expect to ſee a little Sun-ſhine and fine Weather ; for to whatever Motives the *Projector* and his *Advocates* may aſcribe our late Succeſs, 'tis certainly owing to the general Senſe of the Nation. And from the Diſappointment they have met with on this Occaſion, we may conclude, no *M——r* in his Senſes will revive a *Scheme,* ſo univerſally oppoſed without Doors, and ſo gloriouſly defeated within.

I often pleaſe myſelf, adds *D'anvers,* with reflecting what a Figure this proſperous Struggle will give us abroad, as a *free People ;* and that it will wipe off that invidious Reflection of Mr *Voltaire,* in his Hiſtory of the late K. of *Sweden.* (See Vol. II. p. 702 C)

It always goes againſt me to inſult the *Unfortunate,* or triumph over the *Vanquiſh'd,* I rather compaſſionate the Caſe of Thoſe who have ſuffered themſelves to be dragg'd thro' an Horſe-pond, and be-mir'd, to no Purpoſe, in ſo odious a Cauſe. —— Even the *Projector* himſelf participates of my Pity.

Was I of a contrary Diſpoſition, I am ſuffici'd

furnish'd with the ftrongeft Materials from the Writings of that choleric old Beldame Mrs *Osborne*, who, in one of her fcolding Fits, unluckily exprefs'd herfelf, as you will fee p. 90 C.

As to the *Projector* Himfelf, 'tis hop'd this *Rebuff* will inftruct him to be cautious for the future, how He provokes the Patience of the People. This will be the Way for him to fleep in quiet, without being haunted with continual Dreams of *Murder* and *Affaffination*. At prefent, he may comfort himfelf, that as he has difcovered no Part of the Spirit or Abilities of JULIUS CÆSAR, he need not be afraid of falling in the *fame Manner.* —— If he is refolved to perfift in his *former Meafures*, and verify Madam *Osborne's* Prophecies, it is out of my Power to prevent it with all my Endeavours.

London Journal. April 21. Nº 721.
The publick Advantages of the late Schemes about Tobacco *and* Wine.

EVERY Method of Wickednefs having been tried to render thefe Schemes odious, and to roufe up a Spirit of Difaffection in the Nation, I think it the Duty of every *Englifhman*, fays *Osborne*, to do Juftice to the *honourable Gentleman* who defigned it, and to undeceive the People, who have been notorioufly abufed.

The *Defign* was to take off a Tax unequal, burthenfome, and partial, only *by preventing Frauds* in Duties already laid, to raife feveral hundred thoufand Pounds a Year to the *Publick*, not the *King*; and to apply the Money to the Taking off the *Land Tax*. 'Twas likewife intended to take off the Duties on *Soap* and *Candles*, only by a *new Regulation* of another Tax.

The *Advantages* of this Scheme, as they relate to the *Excife Laws*, the *fair Traders* in *Tobacco* and *Wine*, and the *Nation*, are as follows. Here he repeats what himfelf and others have before faid on the fame Subject. (See p. 66,67,133,141.)

The *Inconveniences* in the Commodities already excifed, would have been remedied, particularly the Enquiry upon Oath in the *Tea Act*; the *prefent Appeal* in all the Excifes abrogated; and a *new Appeal* inftituted of *three Judges*, without any Expence.

Does this fo *truly laudable* a Scheme, fays *Osborne*, deferve the Treatment it has met with? Or rather, doth not the Minifter, who laid thefe *Methods of preventing Frauds* before the Publick, de-

ferve the *Thanks and Approbation* of all difinterefted Men? Hath not his Ear been open to all other Methods? And is it not clear, that *no other Method* can be found to prevent Frauds in Duties on *Home Confumption*. Muft the *publick Revenue* (of which his prudent Care has been one of the greateft Securities) be fuffer'd *Knowingly* to diminifh, to the apparent *Detriment* of the *People*, who muft make good by *other Taxes*, the *Deficiency* of thofe already laid? He took Care to provide a Remedy; and what has been the Confequence? *The Rage* of Men, who have *private Interefts* to carry on againft the *Good of the Publick*, and Paffions to gratify againft Gentlemen in Power, hath alarmed the People, and fright'ned them out of their Senfes. —— The *high Dignity* of the Houfe of Commons hath been bafely trampled on; the Houfe it felf befet, the Members infulted; his Majefty's, and their Country's beft Servants *burnt in Effigy*; and publick Rejoycings made by way of *Infult upon the Court*. Can Government fubfift on this Foot? —— But I forbear at prefent. ——

Univerfal Spectator. April 21. Nº 220.
Benefits Sufpicious.

A Few Days fince, I happen'd, fays Mr *Stonecaftle*, to light upon a Manufcript entitled, *The Art of murdering Benefits*, or an *Effay upon contemplative Favours*. It fhews in general that not one Gift in fo we receive of our Fellow-Creatures, even that of Life itfelf, is worthy of being called a Benefit; and that few or none pafs undifguifed between us, or uncorrupted with bafe Alloy.

I am not of that fufpicious Temper; and if I think more favourably of them than they fometimes deferve, it gains me more in Satisfaction than it lofes me in Safety; 'tis embellifhing the little *Gold* we find in the *Oar* of Converfation, not to defpife the whole *Mafs*, becaufe it has a great deal of *Drofs*. I appeal to any Author, whether the Kifs given by the Carpenter's Wife of *Oxford* thro' her Window at Midnight, to the fpruce Clerk of *Ofney-Abbey* (as related by *Chaucer* in his *Miller's Tale*) would have been fuch a *difagreeable Courtefy* as he inftances, to a Lover fenfible of the Tokens of *good Houfwifry* that were about her Lips, as if fhe had been all Day at her *Spinning-Wheel*.

Another Apology for Benefits is, we often miftake thofe Things for Injuries which

which are real Favours. This is prettily made out in the following *Proposition* and Answer, superscrib'd *The* GARLAND.

BEtwixt two *Suitors* sat a *Lady* Fair,
　Upon her Head a Garland she did wear:
And of th'inamour'd two, the *first* alone,
A Garland wore like her, the *other*, none:
From her *own* Head she took the Wreath she wore,
And crown'd *him* with it *who* had none before:
Thus these two Lovers Brows were *both* about
Bedeck'd with Garland, and *she* set without.
Beholding then these Rivals on each Side,
And equally adorn'd in *Flora*'s Pride;
She from the *first* Man's Head the Wreath he had, 　　　　　[clad t
Took off, and therewith her *own* Temples
And so this *Lady* and the *second* were
In Garlands deck'd, and the *first* Man sat bare:
Now which did she love best, of him to whom
She gave, or him she took the Garland from?

ANSWER.

She grac'd him *much*, on whom her Wreath she plac'd, 　　　[more grac'd t
But him whose Wreath she *wore* she much
For where she *gives*,she there a *Servant* makes,
But makes *herself* a Servant where she *takes*.
Then where she takes, she honours most, and where
She most does Honour, she must Love most dear.

Lastly, The Nature of Benefits themselves is not depreciated by being confer'd on inferior Objects. They rather give Encouragement to expect they would operate more generously were they more nobly center'd. This is illustrated in the following Song.

STREPHON *versus* Tray. Or, *the* AMOROUS CONTEST.

OH what Pain it is to see,
　Can I bear it, can I bear it,
Oh what Pain it is to see,
Can Flesh and Blood e'er bear it?
When *Cælia* does to me deny
A Kiss, which wou'd give Ecstacy;
A Dog my happy Rival be;
Can Flesh and Blood e'er bear it?

Hopes in Complaisance I place,
They deceive me, they deceive me;
Hopes in Complaisance I place,
But all these Hopes deceive me;
I bow, I cringe, but spite alas
Of courtly Airs and artful Face,
Tray fawns with such superior Grace,
That all these Hopes deceive me.

When I Skill in Musick show,
'Twill not please her, 'twill not please her;
When I Skill in Musick show,
Yet still it will not please her;

My Tune, tho' soft, my Voice tho' low,
'Tis vain; my chiefest Notes must bow
To sweet enchanting Ba——wa——waw;
　That Air alone will please her.

Grant, I cry'd, to cure my Woes,
Balmy Kisses, balmy Kisses,
Grant, I cry'd, to cure my Woes,
Some precious balmy Kisses:
In vain my Sighs to move her rose;
From me she flew, and cruel chose
T'apply her Lips to warm *Tray*'s Nose,
　And lavish there her Kisses.

Yet my Heart is fix'd to try
If she'll love me, if she'll love me,
Yet my Heart is fix'd to try
If she at length will love me;
For if thus kind, thus tender she,
Can to so mean a Creature be,
How vastly, vastly more to me,
If once she'd change and love me.

Fog's Journal. April 21. N°. 29c.

MEzeray, in his History of *Harry* III. of *France*, takes Notice, that when weak and corrupt Ministers embarrass the publick Affairs, their Examples debauch the Morals of others, so that the Teint descends to infect Posterity. This he proves in the Example of *Francis* D'o, Superintendant of the Finances, whose whole Merit consisted in finding out Funds to oppress the People. He was remarkable for a certain little low Cunning, of no Use, but to qualify a Man to be a thorough Rogue, and indeed he used to perplex and embarrass the publick Accounts so as it was not easy to fix his Frauds.

The Estates of *Burgundy*, finding the Burthens laid upon them were inconsistent with those Privileges they ought to enjoy by Virtue of their Union with the Monarchy of *France*, sent a Deputation to represent against the prodigious and unnecessary Expence of new *Offices, Employments*, and *Pensions*; the Multitude of Taxes, and the *arbitrary Method* of collecting them, requesting they might be reduced, and put upon the antient Foot.

Francis D'o employ'd all his Address to abate this Resolution, and had Recourse to Reason, Threats, and Promises, telling them among other plausible Arguments, they ought to confine themselves to their own Province, without troubling themselves or the King with that of the rest of the Kingdom.

The Deputies generously answer'd, That the Interest of one Province, or one Man, ought to be inseparable from that of the whole Kingdom.——As to the rest, every
　　　　　　　　　　　　　man

Man was obliged to take Care of his Posterity, and it was his Duty to leave them the same Privileges he receiv'd from his Ancestors; that a vast Fortune raised upon the Publick Ruin was a high Infamy, and expos'd the Possessor to continual Peril; that they did not envy the great Fortunes which Men acquir'd by such Means. They look'd upon it as an indispensible Duty to watch over the Interests of those born under the same Government with themselves, without Regard to any future Recompence; that the Interest of the Publick was a Thing of much greater Consideration than that of any private Man; that it was no more than common Gratitude to assist and defend the lower People, since from their Labour and Industry the Revenues of the Others arose; that the common People are to the Commonwealth what the Foot is to the human Body, which if it be hurt or oppress'd the Nobler Part comes to the Ground; that mov'd by this Sympathy the Nobility of *Burgundy* intreated his Majesty to put an End to the Grievances of the whole Kingdom; for they should think it a Crime in them to conceal the Resolutions, or any Part of the Complaints of their Province; for this Liberty of addressing was a Mark of the Prince's Goodness, and Petitions an evident Proof of the Subjects Obedience; that if guilty Men endeavour'd to shut his Ears against the Remonstrances of his most faithful Subjects, the Crime was not theirs who would undeceive him, but in those who attempted to impose upon him, and had almost banish'd Truth and Justice from the Councils of the most Christian Kings.

It is possible, says *Fog*, when a *Briton* reads what Stands a Parliament of *Paris* made in the glorious Cause of Liberty, he will blush at the Thought of being bought, terrified, or influenced; it will put him upon his Guard, that he do not suffer his good Purposes to be defeated either by too late or too weakly opposing any arbitrary Measure intended against his Country.

The *Auditor*, April 24. No. 31.

Here Love *his golden Shafts employs; here lights His constant Lamp, and waves his purple Wings.*

THE Auditor having (See p. 119. F.) promised his fair Readers a Clue to *Fidelio's pleasing Maze*, inserts a Letter from *Maritus* to that Purpose.

SIR,

WHEN I first resolved upon a married Life, I laid down this Maxim, That I would take only such Steps, as might render that State comfortable and happy. With this View I did not seek an *Overgrown Fortune*, nor could think of giving my *Hand* to a Woman, from whom my *Heart* was likely to be at Liberty. A beautiful *Face* and fine *Shape*, were not *enough* to engage me, if the *Soul* was not fitted to my own too. With such Sentiments as these, I addressed the lovely *Prudentia*, who at last consented to be my Bride.

We have now been married about 7 Years, and I have enjoyed all the Happiness I could desire, or expect from so agreeable a Lady; the Bonds of Affection are strengthened by all the soft Expressions of her Love. *Prudentia* is the same agreeable Creature, and appears still more entertaining: In her I enjoy a *Wife* and a *Friend*, who shares more than half of every *Care*, and more than doubles every *Joy*, and by her mild and gentle Influence, diffuses Regularity, and Goodnature thro' the whole Family. Hence it is, I love Home better than any other Place; and hence, I hope, is laid a solid Foundation for future Happiness, as long as Heaven and Nature will measure out our Existence here.

Learn hence, my Friend, the Way to maintain social Happiness, when all the Effects of wandering Lusts, and lawless Flames expire, or only remain to the Shame and Infamy of the guilty Wretch.

Yours Maritus.

This State seems better calculated for compleat Happiness, than that mention'd by *Fidelio*; however, there is less to fear from the Censures of the World, which *Constantia* must be liable to, tho' her Reason may satisfy her, they are unjust.

Suppose the Consequence of *Fidelio* and *Constantia's* Union has been an only Daughter now grown up, Will *Fidelio* consent she should live with another professing *Fidelio*, as he had done with *Constantia?* Yes, he will say, if another could be found. But as this is difficult, he will hardly trust his Daughter to make the Trial. If so, may we not judge, his Love for *Constantia* was not so great as his Love for his Daughter? And that his not loving *Constantia* at first, in that tender Manner he ought to have done, to have made her his Wife, was the *true Reason of his avoiding a Marriage*, which he ascribes to the Capriciousness of his Temper?

What is here said, the Auditor does

not

not intend as a Reproach to *Conſtantia* and *Fidelio*; but to ſhew, that if in a married State we would follow their Rules, we ſhould know no other Bonds, and avoid that ridiculous Delicacy of being thought obliged to be honeſt, contrary to our Inclinations.

Grubſtreet Journal. April 25. No. 174.

Mr BAVIUS,

THE Maſter of the C—o—t *Garden* Theatre, at the Beginning of this Seaſon, was offer'd a Tragedy, which he allow'd was written in a *good Stile*; and that the *Paſſions were well mov'd*, yet without Alterations he would not play it, nor with, unleſs he dictated them.

A Comedy was likewiſe offer'd, the Dialogue of which, Mr R— own'd, was *eaſy* and *genteel*, the Characters *new* and *drawn from Life*; yet not ſuited to His Taſte, and therefore abſolutely rejected. — M. *Voltaire*'s *Zaira*, tranſlated, met with the ſame Fate.

Let us now examine, what he has brought on the Stage. *Achilles* ſucceeded beyond Expectation; I think, beyond its Deſert. King LOG's *Fatal Secret*, met with the Reception it merited. I now come to his favourite Piece of the *Mock-Lawyer*, for which *Zaira* made room. The Author of the Tragedy firſt mention'd, had a little humorous Piece ſurreptitiouſly taken from him. From this Mr R— got a whole Opera work'd up by a young Gentleman of *Cambridge*, which Opera is now contracted into this Farce.

Let the Town judge if this Man deſerves their Encouragement: Let Authors conſider, if this is the Man to be apply'd to, or even truſted with their Performances. The Managers of the Old Houſe have behav'd ill; the Maſter of the New worſe: If the firſt have brought bad Pieces upon the Stage, it was becauſe they had no better; yet they rejected not a *Zaira*, nor pirated a Copy.

Yours No-BODY.

The following humorous LOVE LETTER, ſays *Bavius*, is copied from the *Norwich Gazette*.

Dear Madam,

IF there be yet no Propoſition towards a Conjunction with you, be pleaſed to accept of this Interjection of my Pretences: For I do Pronouns Ad-verbum, that I deſire to be Adjective to you in all Caſes; for Poſitively I declare, that Comparatively ſpeaking, I ſhould be Superlatively happy, might I Engender with you in all Moods and Tenſes. I hope you will not think me ſo Singular, as not to deſire to have the Plural Number in my Family; or that I am too Maſculine, to be Neuter in Regard to the Fœminine: Wherefore, Dear Madam, let us have our Affections in Common of Two. Far be it from me to decline this Conjugation, tho' I am not the Firſt Perſon, nor the Second, nor the Third, that have ſolicited you to be Subjunctive to his Love. I preſume you will not be in the Imperative, whilſt I paſs from the Optative to the Potential; and that you will permit me to make a Conjunction Copulative of my Propria quæ Maribus, with your As in Præſenti; this will make a Participle of Happineſs, if you pleaſe Actively to give you a Voice to be Paſſive herein: be you but Supine, and I'll be Deponent: Thus you will find it the Optative Part of my Soul, to be a lawful Concord with the Genitive; my whole Income ſhall be a Dative to you for the Preſent; nothing ſhall be Accuſative againſt you for the Future; and your Dear Name ſhall ever be my Vocative, till Death, the great Ablative of all Things, part us.

I am, Dear Madam, &c.

Free Briton. April 26. No. 176.

THE *Craftſman* has (ſee Occurrence April 13.) taken that Liberty with MAJESTY, which I, ſays *Walſingham*, ſhould have thought *ill-becoming of me*, or of any *private Man.* He hath ſet forth an ample Account of the *Riſe and Fortunes, Abilities, and Merits* of a noble Lord, with heavy Lamentations, that the *King* ſhould thus diſmiſs him; concluding that the *World ſeems aſtoniſhed at ſo unexpected an Event,* &c.

What Inſolence is this to the *Throne!* How injurious to the *Noble Lord!* How unfair to *all* Mankind! It is upbraiding the King with his former Favours to this *noble Perſon.* It is reproaching the *King* with the Abilities and Services of this *noble Perſon,* as if thoſe Abilities and Services were ſuch, that no Reaſons could *juſtify* the King in removing him from his Attendance. It's PRESCRIBING to the *Royal Perſon,* in a Manner which relates wholly to the *King.* It is telling him openly, that his Majeſty *removes* Perſons from his Service *in a manner that* aſtoniſhes *his People;* and *at a Time as* requires him to retain thoſe *Perſons in* his Service. As if his *Majeſty* held the *Allegiance*

Allegiance of his Subjects, by the Tenure of keeping this *Noble Lord* in Employment. This *indecent* Usage of the *King*, is an Invasion of his *personal Liberty*, as well as of his *Royal Dignity*.

Suppofing I was as much byaffed in Favour of the C—R of the E—R, as the Author of this Paragraph seems to be in Favour of the late L—D ST—D, would it be allow'd in me, fhould the *King* ever fend for *the Seals* from that *Honourable Person*, to tell the World of his Services and Employments, and how much Men were *aftonished* and *grieved?*

Can it be treating the *noble Lord* with any *real* Friendfhip, to make this *ill-judged* Ufe of his Name and Character, *in Oppofition to the* Perfon *and* Procedure of the *King himfelf*, who chofe him to attend his Perfon on his first Arrival in this Kingdom, retained him when *dif-mifs'd the Court by his Royal Father*, who begun his Reign by *loading him with Favours*, and hath diftinguifhed *almoft every Year* by fome *new Office* or *Honour* conferred on his Lordfhip, who never fuffer'd his Abilities to languifh in Obfcurity, who never fuffe'd any Service to go unrewarded? Can then this *Great Lord* be well treated by any Man, who mal treats the King?

Hath not his Majefty an undoubted Right to difmifs his Servants at *his own* Pleafure: Doth any Man hold an Employment of this Nature by *Right*, or by *Royal Favour?* Will any Man fuggeft, that the King made the *Noble Perfon* L—D ST—D, to make him independant of *his Royal Self?* Is this Removal then to be cenfur'd as ASTONISHING *to the People*, and GRIEVOUS *to the King's moft zealous Friends?* Should not I be *highly cenfur'd*, were I to INSULT the *Noble Lord*,becaufe the King hath difmiffed him? Is it allowable to infult the King, becaufe he hath removed one of his domeftick Servants? Will they allow me to fay what *they themfelves* moft *unworthily* faid of this *noble Lord*, when he was made L—D ST—D? Would it not appear that all *its* Court Favour, exclufive of themfelves is the Subject of their *Cenfure*, fo a *Removal from Court* is the Subject of their *Adulation*.

How unfair is it to bring fuch a Point into Debate? Suppofe we did not allow thofe *Abilities* and *Services*, to the praife of this *noble Lord*, fuppofe there was more than meerly *Royal Will* and *Pleafure* operating in this Affair, fome *Mis-behaviour* or *Miftake* neceffitating his Majefty to remove him, dare any Man explain it?

The *Authority of the House of Lords*, and the *Action* of *Scandalum Magnatum*, would deter the boldeft Man from fpeaking *Truth of a Peer*, if to his *Difadvantage*. Is it fair then to *reflect on the* KING for having *removed a Lord*, who is alledged to deferve more Favour by his *Merit* and *Services?* When the moft *faithful Subject* dare not, in Defence even of his KING difpute thofe Merits!

What I have here faid, concludes *Walfingham*, has been with all Refpect to this *Noble Lord*, who, I truft, will always deferve well of the *King*, notwithftanding the *Craftsman's* invidious Suggeftions. As it can be no *Wrong* to his Lordfhip, that he is removed, I fhall not be aftonifhed to fee him re-inftated in Employment. However the Author of this Paragraph may pretend to be acquainted with the manner of his Lordfhip's *Difmiffion*, as well as his *Lordfhip's* PRIVATE Letter TO THE KING, I take it as proceeding from Perfons who would be diftinguifh'd by making themfelves too free with PRIVATE and SACRED CORRESPONDENCIES.

Defcription of a Vulcano *in* Ireland, *communicated by Letter to the* B*p of* Kilmore.

On the *Kerry* Coaft of the *Shannon*, between the old Caftles of *Dune* and *Lick* (which are half a Mile afunder) and oppofite to tot *Carrick a Holt*, the antient Seat of the Earls of *Clare*, the *Cliffs* rife to a great Height above the Sea, to 1, 2, or 300 Feet perpendicular, from which Height, by the undermining of the *Waves*, they fometimes fall with mighty Violence into the Ocean.

Near two Years ago a Piece of one of thefe high *Cliffs* fell off, whereupon there broke out a Smoak attended with a ftrong *Sulphureous Smell*. I will not take on me to determine whether the *fubterraneous hidden Fire* was the Ocafion of the *Cliffs* falling, or the *Colifion* of the Rocks on that Accident, the Caufe of the Fire; whichfoever of thefe it was, it has continued burning ever fince, and has wafted away fo much of the *Cliff*, that there was falling from time to time a fpace of it about 60 Feet in Breadth, and 100 in Length. Thefe frequent Breaches have made an eafy Defcent to the Sea from the Top of the *Cliff*, which at firft was perpendicular.

By this means I got down, and about *midway* came where I obferved the *Smoak* breaking out: Here I took notice that the *Heap of Earth* which lately fell from the top, was turned into a kind of *Cruft*, which had feveral *Cracks* from whence the *Smoak* iffued out: The mixture of *burnt Clay*; and *Afhes*, and *calcined Stones*, was worth obferving; but the *Heat* was fo ftrong, that (though *Pliny's* Fate had not come
into

into my Mind) I cou'd not wait to be over curious.

From hence I descended *obliquely* to the Bottom of the *Cliff,* where I had a full View of it, and of the *Progress* the *Fire* had made in it. It was entertaining to look up and observe the Different Figures Into which the *Fire* had eat it, and the Variety of beautiful *Colours* according to the different *Minerals* and *Stones* It met with. In some Places, I observed vast *Columns* of the burnt *Cliff* hanging over my Head. In others, *Veins* of melted *Sulphur* and *Allum* congealed as they streamed down the *Rocks,* and hanging like *Icicles.* The whole Face of the *Cliff* seem'd to be a Composition of *red, yellow, black, and white calcined Stones* and Ashes of Clay cemented together by *Streams* of melted *Sulphur* and *Copperas* that run among them like the *Cement* which Masons pour into Walls.

The first thing I met with at the Bottom of the *Cliff,* was a great Number of burnt *red* Stones, from an Ounce to 20 Pounds in weight, which seemed to compose the lowest *Stratum* of the *Cliff.* The Colour of some of these Stones is a bright red, when the *Sulphur* with which they are tinged is washed off, and they taste so strongly of *Copperas* that touching one of them with my Tongue it raised a *Blister.*

Next to these is a *Stratum* of *yellow* Stones, which are of an harder Nature, and seem by the Taste to have more *Sulphur* and less *Copperas* than the former.

The third *Stratum* is a burnt *black* Stone resembling *Irish* Slate, its Taste is sharp like *Allum.*

The Remainder of the *Cliff,* from the *Stratum* of *black* Stone up to the Place where the *Smoak* breaks out, is a compound of the three *Strata,* together with *Lime, Clay, Ashes, Sulphur,* and *Copperas;* and in this Part the *Fire* seems to be more intense than in any other. The Nature of a Fire composed of *Stones* and *Minerals* is such as does not admit of any *great Blaze,* and though it had, the Sun shone so bright that I could not discern it. But I was informed by the Inhabitants, that they see the Flame very plainly by Night, and I could observe the Air over it in a tremulous Motion like the Air over a burning Lime-Kiln.

It is not my Business to search what Mines this Vulcano may contain, nor how far its burning may in Time proceed; I can only say at present, that the red, yellow and black Stones are of Use in Colouring.

The Cliffs are of an amazing Height, and when the Sun shines on them, appear as if they were finely gilded. At the Bottom they are full of large Caves, into which the Sea rolls a great Way, and the Sea-Calves sport innumerably; and while the Waves are foaming and breaking below, there are three very beautiful Cascades of fresh Water, which falling from the Top of the perpendicular Cliffs, are almost quite dissipated before they reach the Sea, insomuch that we took the Mist arising from one of them to be the Smoak of another Vulcano.

Detached from the Cliff into the Ocean,

stands a curious single Rock; it is a regular square Pyramid, in Height and Size some what resembling the Lord Allen's Obelisk, and has on its very Top an Eagle's Nest. And, that Art might not be wanting where Nature has been so bountiful in its Beauties, the two strong old Castles of *Dune* and *Lick* standing on the Brow of high Cliffs that Jut out like Heads into the Ocean, look as they were designed to guard the Entrance of this romantick Bay.

DEBATES on the Sugar Colony Bill in the last Session of Parliament, by which our Readers may guess at the chief Arguments used in the Present Sessions on the said Bill pass'd the 21st of *March* last, and then ordered to be sent up to the House of Lords.

ON the 13th of *Feb.* the Bill *For the better encouraging the Trade of his Majesty's Sugar Colonies in America* was read a second Time in the House of C——ns, when they proceeded to hear Council, which took up several Days. On the 23d the Speaker open'd the Bill to the House; after which

Mr W——n stood up and spoke as follows:

Sir, I find some of the † Council at the Bar have endeavoured to turn the Affair before us into such a Shape, as if the Question to be determined were, whether the *Northern Colonies* or the *Sugar Colonies* ought most to be encouraged by this House. This, *Sir,* is not at all the Question; the Affair in Hand is the Dispute between the *English* and the *French* Commerce: We are now to determine, whether we ought to encourage a *French* Trade, which tends to the Ruin of our own *Sugar Colonies;* for I have not heard it so much as disputed by any Man, but that they must be soon undone, if some Redress be not given to them in Time; and the only Redress they want at present is, that a Parliament of *England* will only do as much as they can to discourage the *French* Sugar Trade. One would really imagine, that such a Proposal would not meet with any Opposition in a *British* House of Commons.

This, *Sir,* being the true State of the Question, I do not wonder to see it twisted and turned into twenty Shapes, rather than to let it appear in its own genuine and natural Colour; but of all the Lights this Affair has been put into, the most invidious is, that of pretending that the Sugar Colonies by this Bill are contriving a Method of putting their Sugars and Rum upon us at any Price they please to demand; that by this Bill they want us to make a Law for enabling them to sell their Sugars and Rum at a much dearer Price than what is necessary. If this, *Sir,* were

† *The Respective Agents for the Northern Colonies viz.* Pensilvania, Massachusets Bay, Virginia, New York, Rhode Island Providence, New Jersey, *and* South Carolina *had obtain'd Leave to be heard by their Council against the Bill.*

truly

truly the Case, I should be against this Bill as much as any Man; but to me it appears evident, that what they want is only to have such a Price for their Sugars and Rum as they can make them at, so as to live thereby: This we ought to grant, if we can. Now, **A** Sir, I think it has been made appear, that the French are our greatest Rivals in the Sugar Trade, and enabled to become so only by the Trade carried on between them and our Northern Colonies; the great Vent they thereby have for their Rum and Molasses, and the easy Access they thereby have to **B** Lumber, Horses, and all other Necessaries for their Sugar Plantations, which are naturally much more fruitful than ours, enabling them to sell their Sugars and Rum at a much lower Price than it is possible for our Sugar Planters to sell at; it is therefore apparent that our Sugar Plantations must be undone, or we must fall upon Means of preventing **C** the French from selling their Sugars so cheap as they do: Those Means are easy; they are every Day in our Power; put a Stop to the Trade that is carried on between our own Colonies on the Continent and the French Sugar Islands, and you must at once a great deal enhance the Price of all French Sugars: The Charges of making their Sugars will then be a great deal more, and their Rum and Mo- **D** lasses will yield them nothing; they must lay all Charges upon the Returns of their Sugars, and therefore it will not be possible to sell them so cheap as they are sold at present. By this Method our own Sugar Colonies will be greatly encourag'd, and the French may be totally undone; whereas, if we leave Mat- ters in the present Situation, the French Su- **E** gar Colonies will be increasing every Day, and in a little Time our own quite destroyed.

But, Sir, it has been pretended, that if we put a Stop to the Trade now carried on be- tween the French Sugar Islands and our Co- lonies on the Continent, it will in a great Measure ruin those Colonies, because it will entirely destroy their Fishery, and also their **F** Trade with the Indians, both which are car- ried on principally by the Means of the Rum and Molasses, which our Colonies purchase at so cheap a Rate from the French Sugar Islands: If there were any Foundation for this, it would indeed be a very great Objec- tion to this Bill; but as our Colonies on the Continent carried on their Trade with the **G** Indians, and also their Fisheries, long be- fore they had either Rum or Molasses from the French Islands, it is plain that nei- ther of those Trades can depend entirely on their Trade with the French Sugar Islands; but, that the Opening of this Trade with those Islands, has not only encouraged the French Sugar Plantations to the great Detri- ment of our own, but has also in a great **H** Measure discourag'd or rather destroy'd the Sale of English Spirits in that Part of the World, which is a considerable Loss to this Country; for it is well known, that before

our Colonies on the Continent of America fell into this destructive Trade with the French Sugar Islands, they made Use of great Quan- tities of English Spirits, both in their Fishing Trade, and also in their Trade with the In- dians. And if we should put a Stop to this Trade with the French Sugar Islands, there is no Doubt but our own Colonies would again fall into their former Method, and would be able to carry on as extensive a Trade with the Indians, and as great a Trade in Fishing, by the Means of English Spirits, as they ever did by the Means of French Rum. Besides, Sir, if some Rum or Molasses were absolute- ly necessary, do not we know that they could have as much from our own Sugar Islands as they had Occasion for, and within a Trifle at as low a Price as they can have the same Sort of Rum or Molasses from the French Sugar Islands; for in Proportion as the French Sugar Plantations decrease, it is certain that our own will be daily increasing; tho' Bar- badoes may perhaps be as much improv'd as the Extent of Ground will admit of, yet Ja- maica, and several other of the Islands belong- ing to us in that Part of the World, will admit of very great Improvement; and if they were all improv'd to the full Extent, they would produce as much or very near as much Sugar, Rum and Molasses, as could be consum'd in Europe and in America. Thus, Sir, to me it is plain, that the Method propos'd by this Bill, is the only proper one for discouraging the French Sugar Plantations, and encourag- ing our own; and this is a Method by which no Part of our own Dominions can be any way injur'd; therefore I must be for the Bill, and for that Reason, Sir, I move that it may be committed.

This Motion was seconded by the Right Hon. H——to W——le; After which

Mr H——to spoke as follows; Sir, I should with all my Heart be for the Bill now before us, if I could find any Thing in it that would encourage our own Trade to the Detriment of that of the French; but really, Sir, I can- not find any such Thing in this Bill: On the contrary, I clearly foresee, that by the Me- thod thereby propos'd, we are going to de- stroy a very profitable Branch of our own Trade, and to do all we can to encourage, or rather set up a new Trade for the French, which they of themselves have never been able to accomplish. We are amusing ourselves with a vain Conceit, that it is impossible for the French to carry on their Sugar Plantations without the Assistance of the Lumber, Horses and other Necessaries, from our Colonies up- on the Continent; and that their Rum and Molasses would be of no Use to them, if they could not dispose of them to the Inhabi- tants of our Northern Colonies. If it were so, the French would permit that Trade to be carried on openly and freely; they would not leave it under the Discouragement of being carried on in a clandestine Manner, by giving great Bribes to the Governours of their Sugar Island.

Islands: We have no Reason to despise the *French* Knowledge as to the Methods of improving any Trade they aim at; and we know they have for several Years been doing every Thing that was in their Power to encourage their Sugar Plantations. Can we then imagine, that they would have left such Discouragement upon the Trade between their Sugar Islands and our Northen Colonies, if they had thought that their Sugar Works or Plantations could not subsist without it? No, they know that that Trade is a great Hindrance to the Improvement of their own Colonies on the Continent, and therefore they have endeavour'd to put a Stop to it by Degrees, but have never as yet been able to effectuate what they proposed; and now we are by a publick Law to contribute as much as we can to the rendering of their Endeavours effectual. I must therefore look upon what is proposed by this Bill, as a Method not at all certain for improving our own Sugar Plantations to the Discouragement of the *French*, but as an infallible Method for improving the *French* Colonies on the Continent to the very great Discouragement of our own; for which Reason I must be against committing the Bill.

Mr A——n P——y. *Sir*, The Affair before us, is of such a Consequence to the Navigation, Trade, and Happiness of this Nation, that it ought to be weigh'd with the utmost Exactness. There may be a great deal said on both Sides. For my own Part, I have not had Opportunities of acquiring so extensive a Knowledge of Trade as the worthy Gentleman upon the Floor, who spoke first in the Debate; but as I have been dealing in Trade ever since my Infancy, I have many Facts to lay before you, and several Things to say on the Subject in hand, which, in my Opinion, ought to make us extremely cautious of laying any Restrictions on the Trade of any Part of our Dominions. But it is now, I think, too late to enter on a Debate of so serious and extensive a Nature; and therefore I am for adjourning the Debate till to-morrow, or any other Day.

Mr A——n B——d. *Sir*, If the House be resolved to proceed, I will speak to the Affair in hand; but if otherwise, I will not now offer to detain them. (*Here he made a Pause, and the Hou's seeming inclined to proceed, he went on as follows.*) In the Question before us, *Sir*, it is certain some Relief ought to be thought of for our Sugar Colonies. But, *Sir*, I am very far from thinking that the Method proposed by the Bill now before us, is the proper one for giving Relief to our Sugar Colonies: It may cramp and injure our Northern Colonies in some Branches of their Trade, but it never can be of any Advantage to our own Sugar Colonies, as long as they make more Sugar than is requisite for answering the Consumption within our own Dominions. I should be glad we could fall upon any way of making the French Su-

gars dearer, but I am afraid all such Attempts will prove chimerical; and I am sure there is no Method proposed by the Bill, now before us, that can in the least answer this Purpose. As to Lumber, Horses, and other Necessaries for Sugar Plantations, which are now brought from our Colonies on the Continent to the *French* Sugar Islands, there is no Provision in the Bill against their being furnished with such Things from thence for the future; and it would be very wrong to make any such Provision; for if they could not have such Things from our Colonies, they would soon fall into the Way of having all such Necessaries from their own Colonies at *Canada* by way of *Cape-Britain*. And thus we should, by a *British* Act of Parliament, do more towards the encouraging, their Settlements at *Canada* and *Cape Briton*, than they themselves with all their Edicts and Arbitrary Power, have been able to do since the first Establishment. In a little Time we might expect to see those Northern Seas swarming with *French* Ships and Sloops, and a great Part of the Trade of our own Northern Colonies being thereby destroyed, our own Seamen must either starve at home, or run into the Service of the *French* to get Bread.

But, *Sir*, granting it were impossible for the *French* Sugar Islands to have what Horses, Lumber and such Things they want from their own Colonies on the Continent, or any other Part of *America* besides our Settlements, they could have Plenty of all those Necessaries from *France* it self. Sugars are such Bulkly Commodities, that they require a great many Ships to bring them to *Europe*, which Ships return to the *West Indies* for the most part in Ballast, so that the Freight Outwards is generally at a very low Rate; by which means they might have all such things from *Europe* for a very little more than prime Cost: And suppose the Price of such Things stood them in a little more than in our Sugar Islands, the Difference would be so small that it would no way enhance the Price of their Sugars in any Market in *Europe*.

As to Rum, I think it is not pretended that the *French* deal much either in the making of vending of it; but it's argu'd that our Northern Colonies purchase all their Molasses from them, and thereby contribute towards the enabling of them to sell their Sugars at the Low Price they do; and that if our People on the Continent of *America*, did not purchase their Molasses of them, they could make nothing of them in any other way: This is really supposing the *French* to be a more stupid People than any of the Native *Indians* on the Continent. They know that Rum is made of Molasses; and is valuable in almost every Part of the World; they understand the Art of Distilling Rum from Molasses, or if they do not, there is no such mighty Secret in the Art, but they may easily learn it. Can it then be doubted, but that if they could not sell their Molasses to our Colonies on the Continent, they would set up Stills and make Rum out of their own Molasses? And could not they sell that Rum in *America*, *Africa*, and *Europe*, as well

well as we do? To this it is anfwered, That their Government would not allow them to make or fell Rum becaufe it would prejudice the Sale of Brandy, which is the natural Product of *France*: But this we have not the leaft Rea- A fon to fuppofe: If the very Being, or even the Well-being of the *French* Sugar Colonies, depended on their making and felling Rum: we cannot fuppofe, that the *French* Government would ruin them, in order to keep up the Price of their Brandies, unlefs we were to fuppofe. that the King of *France*, and all his Advifers, were Mafters of Vineyards, and of nothing elfe: B We may as well fuppofe, that the King of *France* would make an *Edict* for obliging all their Sugar Planters to throw all their Molaffes into the Sea; becaufe if they are made into Rum in any Place, either in *Europe* or *America*, it may prejudice the Sale of *French* Brandies. We muft therefore prefume, that C if the *French* Sugar Planters could not difpofe of their Molaffes in the Way they now do, they would be permitted to fet up Stills and make their Molaffes into Rum, and fend it to *Europe*, to their own Colonies of *Miffiffipi, Canada*, and *Cape-Breton*, in order to fupply all the *Indian* Nations therewith at a cheap Rate; they would likewife be able to fmuggle a great D deal of it into our *Northern Colonies*, and even into *Britain* and *Ireland*, notwithftanding any Precaution we could ufe to the Contrary. We may perhaps, by putting Arbitrary Powers into the Hands of our Commiffioners of the Cuftoms and Excife, make it difficult to bring *French* Rum on fhoar in any of our Dominions; but it would be abfolutely impoffible E to prevent the Sale of it to our Fifhing Veffels, in the *North* Parts of *America*: Ard, thus, in place of buying their Molaffes at the cheap Rate we now do, and having the Advantage of manufacturing them into Rum ourfelves, we fhould give them the Advantage of Manufacture, and buy their Rum at a dear Rate; and in place of giving them F Lumber and other fuch Goods for their Molaffes, be obliged to give them ready Money for their Rum: For as the Sale of our Lumber, Horfes, and fuch Things, even now depends entirely on the Courtefy of the Governors of their Sugar Iflands, if our People could take nothing but ready Money from them in Exchange, no fuch Sale would ever G be allowed of; fuch ftrict Injunctions would be fent over, that their Governors durft never venture to permit, or even to wink at any *Britifh* Ships coming into any of their Ports, and thofe Goods are too Bulky to be fmugled into any Part of the World.

Since then, *Sir*, we cannot make the Coft of the *French* Sugars higher than it is, let us H confider and examine, if we cannot make the Coft of our own Sugars lefs. This, *Sir*, is the proper and only Confideration. We ought never to make Laws for encouraging or enabling our Subjects to fell the Produce or Manufacture of their Country at a high Price, but to conyive all Ways for enabling them to fell cheap; for at all Foreign Markets, thofe who fell cheapeft will carry off the Sale, and turn others out of the Trade. We may indeed confine our own Subjects, to the buying of what Sugars they want from our own *Sugar Colonies*, at any Price; but we have no Power over Foreigners; fo that unlefs our Sugar Planters fell their Sugars as cheap as any other Sugar Planters, we fhould foon lofe our whole foreign Trade as to Sugars: And even as to our home Trade, our Sugar Planters muft all join together, and confider nicely the home Confumption, if they have a Mind to keep their Sugars at a much higher Price, than they are fold for in other Parts of *Europe*: For if they in any one Year make more Sugars than we can confume at home, it will of Courfe run down the Price of all their Sugars for that Year, even at home amongft ourfelves; fuppofing we confume 80,000 Hogfheads of Sugar a Year, if they fhould in any one Year fend home 100,000 Hogfheads, the additional 20,000 which we have no Occafion for, cannot be fent abroad, they muft be fold amongft ourfelves, and the Sale of that 20,000 would run down the Price of the Whole 100,000. So that let us put this Affair in what Shape we will, the Methods propofed by this Bill can never be any real Relief to our *Sugar Colonies*.

There are many Ways, *Sir*, for enabling our Dealers in Sugar, to fell their Sugars at a lefs Price, than they now can: One Method the *French* have long ago chalked out to us. They forefaw the great Advantage of encouraging their *Sugar Colonies*; they knew the Hardfhips that ours labour'd under, from their being obliged to fend all their Sugars to be unloaded in *England*, before they could be exported to any other Part of *Europe*: They knew how greatly this inhanced the Price of our Sugars, at all the Markets in *Europe*; and in order to give their *Sugar Colonies* an Advantage over ours, they gave them a Liberty of fending their Sugars directly to foreign Markets, without unloading, or fo much as touching at any Port in *France*. This is an Advantage over our *Sugar Colonies*, which the *French* Sugar Colonies have enjoyed for feveral Years. Let us then follow the Example of our Neighbours; let us at leaft put our *Sugar Colonies* upon an equal footing with their Rivals. This will be one great Encouragement to them, and it is to be hoped, that in the Courfe of this Bill, a great many others may be thought of, which will be real Advantages to them, without injuring our other Colonies.

C — l B —— *n. Sir*, As the only Difpute now is, Whether this Bill ought to be committed, I think the Gentleman who fpoke laft, has given a very good Reafon for the committing thereof; he faid, that fome Relief ought certainly to be given to our *Sugar Colonies*, if any fuch can poffibly be contrived. I believe every Member is of the fame Opinion, and therefore muft think, that the Bill ought to be committed. We fhall thereby have Time to confider all the Grievances

stances of so weighty an Affair; and to consult with all those of our Acquaintance, who understand any Thing of Trade; and every Member will then have an Opportunity of offering such Clauses and Amendments as he may think proper: In my Opinion, it cannot so much as admit of a Debate, whether the Bill is to be committed or no. The least Delay may be the Occasion of the Loss of the Bill, and therefore I am for committing it immediately.

Mr. O―――pe. Sir, There never was perhaps before this House an Affair of greater Moment, than this. The whole British Trade, all our Colonies and Settlements in America, may be undone, or very much strengthned by the Resolves we are to come to on the present Occasion. Every Man who knows any Thing of the Commerce of this Nation, knows how much the Whole depends on our Colonies in the West Indies. Every Man may see by the Accounts laid before us, what vast Quantities of Goods are every Year brought from thence, by the Re-exportation of which we balance our Trade with almost every Nation; and I believe I may say, that it is owing to this only, that the general Balance of Trade has always continued so much in our Favour.

Let us but consider the vast Quantities of Goods, sent from hence every Year to our several Settlements in the West Indies; and what Numbers of British Ships and British Seamen are employed in the West Indies Trade, and we shall see how much that Trade and those Settlements ought to be the Care of a British Parliament.

Our Sugar Colonies are of great Consequence to us. But our other Colonies in that Part of the World, ought likewise to be considered; from them we have likewise yearly very large Quantities of Goods, such as Tobacco, Rice, Naval Stores, and the like, which contribute not a little towards preserving the general Balance of Trade in our Favour. We ought not to raise one Colony upon the Destruction of another; much less ought we to grant a Favour to any Subject, or to any particular Set of People, which may prove to be against the Publick Good of the Nation in general.

I am convinced, that some Relief ought to be given to our Sugar Colonies, and I shall readily join in any Measure for that End, not inconsistent with the Publick Good: But this, Sir, is no Reason for committing the Bill now before us; for if there is not one Clause or one Article in it proper for the Purpose for which it was designed, we cannot properly go into a Committee upon it; we may in a Committee upon a Bill add Causes, or make Amendments, but we are not to make a new Bill. In such a Case the proper Method would be, to have the present Bill withdrawn, and to have a new Bill brought in; and this will be a much surer and a speedier Method of procuring Relief

for our Sugar Colonies, than by sending up a Bill to the other House, so irregular, or so improper, that they may find themselves under a Necessity of throwing it out, or which is much the same, of letting it drop in their House, whereby our Sugar Colonies will be obliged to continue for one Year more, at least, under the Hardships, which now lie so heavy on them. This Affair being therefore of the utmost Consequence, I must be of Opinion, that it is now too late, and the House too thin for entering upon the present Debate. Besides, Gentlemen, we ought to have a Regard to the Chair, and not subject him to so great and so long a Fatigue; I must therefore join in the Motion, that the Debate may be adjourned till some other Day.

G―les E――le. Sir, As the great Advantage reaped by the Nation, by any Branch of its Trade, or Manufacture, depends on the Exportation; therefore when any Matter of Trade comes to be considered in this House, we ought to regard only those Methods, which may tend towards the encouraging and promoting the Exportation of any Manufacture: Now, as to the Case before us, if our Colonies do not sell their Sugars cheaper, or at least as cheap as the French, Dutch, or any other Nation can do, no Part of that Manufacture can be exported to any foreign Market. I shall therefore be for enabling them to sell cheaper than they do at present, but never for empowering them to exact higher Prices from any of their Fellow-Subjects; being convinced, that no Laws we can make, can oblige Foreigners to pay a higher Price for our Sugars, than that for which they may every Day purchase Foreign Sugars of equal Goodness.

Mr B――d and some others having afterwards declared, that they would rather be for having the Bill committed, than it should be thrown out; because they thought it was necessary to do something that Session of Parliament, towards the Relief of our Sugar Colonies: The Question was thereupon put, for committing the Bill, and it was resolved, that the House would upon Tuesday then next, resolve itself into a Committee of the whole House upon the said Bill.

This Committee was put off till the 6th of March, when the House went through the Bill, and made several Amendments thereunto, and upon the 9th, the Report was made by Mr Winnington, Chairman of the Committee; and the Amendments were agreed to, all except one; a Clause was added, and several other Amendments were made by the House. Then it was ordered, that the Bill with the Amendments should be engrossed. And on the 15th, it was read the third Time, and passed, and Mr Winnington carried it up to the House of Lords, where Witnesses were again examined, and Counsel heard for and against the Bill, but it was there again dropt, as it had been last Year.

Fog's Journal, April. 28. Nº 234.

Court Minions, Oppressors of the People.

THE chief Business of a Court Minion, or *prime Minister*, is to enrich himself and his Family. PALLAS, a manumized Slave of that stupid Emperor *Claudius*, finding the Way to cajole the *Empress*, enrich'd himself with above 8 Millions extorted from the People, after which the base Senate gave him 100,000 *l.* more; but he was ruined by his own Impudence. — Mr *Gordon*, in a Discourse prefixed to the Translation of *Tacitus*, dedicated to Sir *Rob. Walpole*, says, " Was it any wonder the People of *France* gasped under Oppression and Taxes, when the Government was sway'd by *such a Woman*, (the *Queen Regent*) herself govern'd by 'Cardinal *Mazarine*, a publick *Thief*, one convicted of having stolen from the Finances 9 Millions in a few Years; and one, who in the highest Post of *first Minister*, could never help showing the base Spirit of a *Little Sharper*" ?

In Countries where Royal Prerogative is limited by Laws, the Name of *prime Minister* has been always odious. For, if he fills the Great Offices of State, with Men of Honour and Abilities, they will never submit to his Direction; if with his own base Creatures, they will bring his Administration into Contempt— and if he should strive to maintain his Power by an Invasion of the Peoples Liberties, and his Constituent should be weak enough to support him in it, they will probably be involved in one common Ruin. For Men who are born *Free*, will not be aw'd by any *Human Titles*, or frighten'd into Slavery by a £ *Wig*, a *Red Coat*, and a pair of *Jack Boots*.

Universal Spectator, April 28. No. 238.

Of Drunkenness.

MR. *Stonecastle* describes the Vice of Drunkenness, and the fatal Consequences with which it is frequently attended. I remember, says he, I have read somewhere the following beautiful Allegory :-- The Devil having obtained Permission to tempt a young Man, gave him his Choice, whether he would *murder* his *Father*, commit *Incest* with his *Mother* or get *drunk*. Shock'd with the two first Proposals, he chose the latter; the Consequence of which was, he committed the *other two*.--The Moral is plain; a melancholy Instance whereof happen'd about 30 Years ago, Sir *C—y D—g*

and Mr *T—ll*, inseparable Companions and entire Friends, having drank to a very high Pitch, a trifling Dispute arose between Mr *T—ll* and another Person in the Company, and Sir *Ch—y* taking Part against his Friend, the Quarrel was carried to that Height, and Mr *T—ll* thought himself so grosly affronted that he challenged Sir *C—y* to fight him the next Morning with Sword and Pistol. They met accordingly, and the Baronet was shot Dead on the Spot; whose Catastrophe was the more tragical, as his Wedding-day was appointed with a beautiful young Lady. Mr *T—*was try'd, and found guilty only of Manslaughter.

The Auditor, April 17. No. 32.

Credula res amor est.

NOT many Miles from *London* lived a Gentleman and his Lady, blessed with a large Estate, and one only Daughter, over whom he held a strict Hand. *Violetta* (for that was her Name) complain'd of her hard Usage to her Mother, who endeavour'd prudently to pacify her.

It happen'd, a Footman, lately hir'd, overheard some of their Conversations, and thereupon formed a Project in Favour of himself. He artfully told her in a Letter, that he was a Gentleman of Estate, but knowing it not adequate to what her Father requir'd, he had disguised himself the better to inform her of his Love; and concluded by desiring she would give him an Opportunity to speak to her.

Great was her Surprize on reading this Letter; yet, as he was a Gentleman, she thought she might hear his Proposal; and to that purpose directed him to attend her in a Visit to a Neighbour where she was intimate. *Tom* took the Hint, and in the way open'd at large the Subject of his Letter. *Violetta* too readily lent an Ear to *Tom's* well-timed Discourses; frequent were their Meetings when the Family were in Bed, for 3 Months, when *Tom* pretending to settle his Estate, went away, promising shortly to return, and demand his *Violetta.*

Her Mother soon mentioning her Apprehensions, *Violetta* on her Knees owned she was with Child; but hoped her marrying the Gentleman with whom she was contracted, might be some Atonement for her Guilt. The Mother promised to break the Matter to her Father; as she accordingly did the same Evening. He calmly answer'd, he would convey his Daughter the next Day to *London*, where she

she might privately lie in, and when recover'd, might return Home again. The next Day he took her in his Coach; and when they were got about the middle of a Wood, 20 Miles from Home, he proposed to alight, and walk; which they did. He then told her his fixed Resolution, There to leave her, to act as she thought proper. With that, he gave her 100 Guineas, and she saw him drive away.

Being recover'd from her Surprize, she proceeded to *London*, there she took her Lodging in a Garret, and with what she got by her Needle pay'd for it and her Diet weekly. In the same House lived a Gentleman then at Law for the Recovery of an Estate, who often enquir'd, but could never be satisfied who she was.

Violetta's Time drawing nigh, she prepar'd a proper Dress for the Infant she carried, made an Excuse to her Landlady to be absent two Months, set out one Morning, and at Noon arrived at a Farmer's House, told the Woman of it her Condition, and desir'd her to take her in; which the Woman refused 'till *Violetta* shew'd her a Handful of Gold, which prevail'd, and the next Day *Violetta* was brought to Bed of a dead Child.—Here she staid 6 Weeks, and then return'd to her old Landlady, and liv'd the same retir'd Life as before.

About two Years after, the Gentleman before-mention'd, recover'd an Estate of 1500l. a Year; and having obtained leave to speak with *Violetta*, told her, he did not know a Woman so framed to make a Man happy in a Wife as she was; and that he would that Instant marry her, if she pleased. Surprized at so unexpected an Offer, she told him, she could not accept it without letting him into her past Life, which she did very minutely, with Tears in her Eyes.—His Admiration was heighten'd of the Person who had made such ample Atonement for past Folly; married her immediately, and carry'd her to visit her Father and Mother, where every thing was reconciled, and the Father, to make amends for his Barbarity, settled his whole Estate upon her. Ever since she has liv'd in a perfect Scene of Happiness; but the Footman, abandoning himself to all Wickedness, was hang'd for a Murder.

The **Daily Courant.** April 25.

IT's not easy to determine which is the greatest *Farce*,—The late publick *Rejoicings*,—or Mr *D'anvers's Congratulation* of last *Saturday.* (See p. 190 E.) I call it a Farce, because the laying aside

the Scheme for improving the publick Revenues, was the greatest *Blow* to the *Faction*, they have met with thro' the whole Course of their *Opposition.* They thought themselves sure, either that the *Minister* would be *assassinated*, or that there would be *popular Insurrections* in many parts of the Kingdom, before the People could be undeceived. The Design to murder him was so *well* laid, that there wants no Proof—That those who were the *Actors* in that detestable *Tragedy* were not the *Contrivers* of it. And his Enemies have now the *Mortification* to see, that what they vainly flatter'd themselves would be his *Ruin*, has fixed him firmer in the Affections of his *Prince*, and of the *People*, i. e. such of them as are the Friends of the present Establishment, —as for those who are the *Enemies* of their Country,—may He ever be the Object of their *Hatred.*

What are the *Rejoicings* and *Congratulations* we hear so much of, but either a shameful Description of the *Inconstancy* of the *English* Nation, or the only *Refuge* of a *few* designing *Knaves* to conceal their inward Shame and Disappointment?

The *Madness* of the People was to be kept up; therefore a Petition was drawn and signed by the *Druggists* complaining of the *Excise* on *Tea, Coffee*, and *Chocolate.* To promote this, not the *principal Druggists*, but many Traders not concern'd in those Commodities, went from House to House to *solicit* Hands to this *Petition*, which, when offer'd to most of the Principal Dealers in these Commodities, they absolutely refus'd to sign it; nor did it meet with a better Reception by Men in a *higher Station*, in another *Place*; by Men, who had, *many* of them opposed the Scheme for improving the publick Revenue, but changing their Opinion by fifties, resented this insolent Attempt.

Had Mr *D'anvers* deferred his Song of *Triumph*, till this *great Event* had happen'd, he would have been so wise as not to have publish'd it at all. Mr *D'anvers* is to be pity'd in this Step. (See p. 190. H)

The **Craftsman.** April 28. No. 356.

SIR *Walter Raleigh* observes that *there are few great with Kings, who have not used their Power to oppress; who have not only grown insolent and hateful to the* People; *but insolent to* their Prince.

'Tis demonstrable, that *the Happiness of the* Governors *and* Governed *is reciprocal*, especially in *free Countries*; yet the

the former feldom think themfelves eafy in their Adminiftration, unlefs the *latter* yield abfolute and implicit Obedience to all their Meafures. But as the Happinefs of the People depends on keeping the Power of their Governors within Bounds, any *private Man* who becomes an Advocate for the Enlargement of Power, ought to be fufpected, whatever he may pretend.

There are Inftances of *Minifters*, who, having blunder'd themfelves out of a long Series of *Foreign Blunders*, and patch'd up fomething like a *Peace*, could not reft for a Year or two, but were pufh'd on by the fame bufy Genius to run their Heads in the dark againft *Stone Walls at Home*; as if they took a Pride in betraying their Ignorance. We have feen *fuch Men* obftinately purfuing a Scheme, big with Deftruction, and infolently declaring, *it muft and fhall go down*, and fo the Nation ruin'd, becaufe they had gone too far to retreat with Honour. But it muft be the greateft Satisfaction to a People, to fee fuch Men defeated in their Attempts. We have feen an *infolent dominéering Minifter* reduced to the wretched Neceffity of recanting his *abufive Reflections*, and giving up his *infamous Project*, with Tears in his Eyes. We have feen him hurried, by the Confcioufnefs of his own Guilt, into dreadful Apprehenfions of Danger, and skulking thro' *private Paffages* for the fecurity of his Perfon, tho' fupported by Power and inviron'd by Guards. Nay, he hath meanly implor'd the Protection of *that Affembly*, he had long endeavour'd to render ufelefs, and hath been obferv'd to fhudder with Horror at every Propofition for *new Enquiries*.

While *D'anvers* was thus ruminating on the foolifh Conduct of Men in Power, he fell into a Dream, in which he beholds a parcel of *ill-look'd Ruffians*, draging a *grave Matron* (*Britannia*) into a fumptuous Edifice, over the Gates of which were infcrib'd in large Capitals, NO JURIES, no MAGNA CHARTA. Thefe *brutal Fellows* endeavour'd to wreft her *Shield* and *Spear* out of her Hands; but fhe maintain'd her Hold, with a Smile of Indignation and Contempt. While they were offering her thefe Indignities, a Croud enter'd, and one of them prefented her with the *Decree of the Senate*, took her by the Hand, and led her out, where fhe was joyfully receiv'd by a vaft Concourfe of People, who conducted her in Triumph to her old Manfion, the *Temple of Liberty*. And the City was fill'd with Rejoicings.

London Journal, April 28. Nº 722
The People's Liberty, a Prince's Security.

MEN are never obliged to give up their Happinefs to others, nor are they under any Obligations to *Power*, further than that Power is employ'd for their Good. A *French* Hiftorian in his Relation of *Siam*, fays; "The People *muft* bear the *Yoke* under any Prince, and fince 'tis impoffible to bear a *heavier*, they never concern themfelves about the *Fortune* of their Princes. A *Siamefe* will readily die to gratify private Hate, or to be releafed from a wretched Life; but to *die* for their *Prince* or *Country* is a *Virtue* unknown." But *Great Britain* is a Country of *Liberty*, where the People cannot be *injur'd* but by *themfelves*, nor *feel* it, till they have *done* ill, and where the *Prince* is fecur'd by the *wifeft* Counfcllors, and the ftrongeft Guards, the *Laws*.

The higheft Pleafure humane Nature feems capable of, is fharing it with others. The late *Czar* of *Mufcovy*, after viewing the *Academy of Sciences in France*, waited on the young King, and faid, with a Sigh, "I am a King, Sir, as well as you, but with this Difference, you govern *Men*, and I *Brutes*." *Osborne* applies this to the happy Government of his prefent Majefty over a free People.

Weekly Miscellany, April 28. No. 20.

THIS contains the Tranflation of one entire Scene from the *French* Tragedy of *Zara*; (for which fee our next.)

§ The Academy of Chirurgery at *Paris* propofe for this Year's Prize the following Queftion, *What are the Advantages, and Inconveniencies, according to the Difference of Cafes, of Tents and other* Dilatants.

Thofe who contend for the Prize, are defir'd to reafon on choice and well attefted Facts, either in *French* or *Latin*; to diftinguifh their refpective Papers by fome Sentence, Device, *&c.* and this Mark fhall be cover'd with white Paper Seal'd, not to be taken off, unlefs that Piece gains the Prize; they fhall convey their Works to M. *Morand*, Secretary of the faid Academy by the laft Day of this Year 1733. The Prize, which is a Gold Medal worth 200 Livres, to be proclaim'd the firft *Tuefday* after *Trinity Sunday* 1734, and will be deliver'd to the Author himfelf, or the Bearer of his Letter of Attorney, fhewing the Mark of Diftinction with a fair Copy of his Paper.   Ad

Ad Craffum de *Stella*.

NE, puer, dulces reprimas furores,
  Forma quos Stellæ ciet, intuendo
Quæ dolet Nymphis, juvenumque terret
      Pectora flamma.

Virginis tactu licet intumescat
Nec Tagus versa pretiosus unda,
Nec deaurata gremium procella
    Irriget Æther :

Splendide frugi sed optima circum
Dextra Fortuna monumenta fudit,
Quæ beant Illam, neq; sit pudori
    Dat sua sponso.

At Salus vultu sedat & Voluptas,
Gratiæ ludunt teneros per artus,
Et verecundis oculis Amores
    Mille triumphant.

Ast Honor gestus comitatur omnes,
Temperant Candor Ratioq; linguam,
Pectus & castum Pietas perenni
    Consecrat igne.

Æstiment formæ Critici puellam
(Mente si possint oculisq; sani)
Afferent Aurum pretio carere,
    Lumine gemmas.

Stella cui videt, melius Beatus
Audiat, quam si Thamesi remotum
Misceat Gangen, vel uterq; Soli
    Serviat Indus.

Corporis Dotes animiq; summæ
Cum tot occurrant, licet augurari
Vinculo quot Dii bona conjugali in-
    -nectere gaudent.

Ornet Hæc vestrum face Nuptiali
Ducta si lectum, cumulata profer
Dona tu Terra, dabit Hæc vicissim
    Munera Cœli.

HOR. ODE iii. LIB. iv.
Ad MELPOMENEN.

QUem tu Melpomene semel
  Nascentem placido lumine videris,
Illum non labor Isthmius
  Clarabit pugilem, non equus impiger

Curru ducet Achaico
  Victorem, neque res bellica Deliis
Ornatum foliis ducem,
  Quod regum tumidas contuderit minas,

Ostendet Capitolio :
  Sed quæ Tibur aquæ fertile perfluunt,
Et spissæ nemorum comæ,
  Fingent Æolio carmine nobilem.

Romæ principis urbium
  Dignatur soboles inter amabiles
Vatum ponere me choros :
  Et jam dente minus mordeor invido.

O testudinis aureæ
  Dulcemque strepitum Pieri temperas :
O mutis quoque piscibus
  Donatura cygni, si libeat, sonum,

Totum muneris hoc tui est,
  Quod monstror digito prætereuntium
Romanæ fidicen lyræ,
  Quod spiro, & placeo (si placeo) tuum est.

To *Crassus concerning* Stella.

WHY should the generous Youth restrain
  His Love for *Stella's* Charms,
Whose Beauty fills the Nymphs with Pain,
  The Swains with Rapture warms ?

Tho', at her Touch, no Stream supply
  Surprizing Tides of Gain,
And to her Bosom, from the Sky,
  Descend no golden Rain ;

What Fortune yet attends the Fair,
  With Comfort she surveys ;
Nor need it, to the wealthy Heir,
  Uneasy Blushes raise.

Yet is her Shape, by ev'ry Grace,
  Form'd with exactest Art ;
Unnumber'd Cupids, from her Face,
  With certain Conquest dart.

Yet Honour all her Actions guides,
  Reason her Speech inspires,
Religion, at her Heart presides,
  And glows with holy Fires.

Let Criticks, with impartial Eyes,
  Observe the finish'd Maid ;
And Eastern Treasures they'll despise,
  With her Perfections weigh'd.

Happier the Youth, if *Stella* shine
  On him, with kindly Beams,
Than if the *Thames* and *Ganges* join
  Their tributary Streams.

From such a matchless Frame and Mind,
  Our ravish'd Thought descry,
The purest Bliss the Gods design'd
  From *Hymen's* sacred Tie.

Should, to your Arms, this glorious Prize
  By nuptial Vows be given ;
Contribute, you, what Earth supplies ;
  Receive from her what Heaven.

HORACE ODE iii. BOOK iv.
Translated long since by Bp ATTERBURY.

HE, on whose Birth the Lyrick Queen
  Of Numbers smil'd, shall never grace
The Isthmian Gauntlet, nor be seen
  First in the fam'd Olympick Race.

He shall not after Toils of War
  And taming haughty Monarchs Pride,
With lawrel'd Brows conspicuous far,
  To Jove's Tarpeian Temple ride.

But him the Streams that warbling flow
  Rich Tyber's flowry Meads along,
And shady Groves (his Haunts) shall know
  The Master of the Æolian Song :

The Sons of *Rome*, Majestick *Rome*,
  Have fixt me in the Poet's Choir,
And Envy now, or dead or dumb,
  Forbear to blame what they admire.

Goddess of the sweet sounding Lute
  Which thy harmonious Touch obeys,
Who canst the finny Race, tho' mute,
  To Cygnet's dying Accents raise.

Thy Gift it is, that all with Ease
  My new unrival'd Honours own,
That I still live, and living please,
  O Goddess ! is thy Gift alone.

PROLOGUE *spoken at the* Theatre-Royal, Covent Garden, April 21. *by Mr* PAGET, *on Occasion of his attempting King* LEAR; *a young Gentlewoman his Relation then also appearing for the first Time on the Stage in the Character of* CORDELIA.

By Mr DUICK.

HOw many anxious Fears our Minds depress!
Who fain wou'd merit and yet doubt Success!
We sometimes fail by too much Care to please,
And labour in a Scene which calls for Ease:
Or Diffidence untimely intervenes,
Where boldest Fire and Rage shou'd shake the Scenes:
If we too much in artful Rules confide,
Then Nature wou'd be found the surest Guide.
'Various the Ways by which we miss Renown:
But chief the Dread of this discerning Town.
We know your Judgment nice; we know the Stage
Has shewn you too the Wonders of the Age:
With what Excuse, what Plea, shall I appear,
Thus circumstanc'd t'attempt the Part of *Lear?*
What Characters these Scenes have oft exprest,
And all his venerable Glories dress't:
'Tis a bold Task; yet 'tis allow'd by all,
'Tis glorious from the noblest Height to fall.
Advent'rous Emulation is some Praise,
And may at length a mean Performer raise.
As yet but half my Doubts have reach'd your Ears;
Or still my Heart for our CORDELIA fears:
Think what conflicting Thoughts must strive within,
It this her first Appearance in the Scene. [quell
Oh, cheat the drooping Maid: your Smiles can
Her struggling Cares, and all her Griefs repel.
Our mutual Hopes in your Indulgence live,
For dare we claim the kind Applause you give.
'Tis ours, with studious Cares our Skill to raise:
'Tis yours, to sooth those Cares with gen'rous Praise.
O Praise there lives a secret godlike Pow'r,
Creating Merit where was none before:
This kindles first the emulative Fire, [aspire.
Then fans the growing Flame, and learns it to

Verses from the ESSAY *on* MAN. Epist. II.

HEaven formeth each on other to depend,
A Master, or a Servant, or a Friend;
Bids each on other for Assistance call,
Till one Man's weakness grows the strength of all,
Wants, Frailties, Passions, closer still allye
The common Int'rest, or endear the Tye:
To Those we owe true Friendship, Love sincere,
Each home-felt Joy that Life inherits here:
Yet from the same we learn, in its Decline,
Those Joys, those Loves, those Int'rests to resign;
Taught half by Reason, half by mere Decay,
To welcome Death, and calmly pass away.
What e'er the Passions, Knowledge, Fame or Pelf,
Not one will change his Neighbour with himself.

The Learn'd are happy, Nature to explore;
The Fool is happy that he knows no more,
The Rich are happy in the Plenty given;
The Poor contents him with the Care of Heaven.
See the blind Begger dance, the Cripple sing,
The Sot a Hero, Lunatic a King,
The starving Chymist in his golden Views
Supremely blest, the Poet in his Muse.
See! some strange Comfort ev'ry State attend,
And Pride bestow'd on all, a common Friend;
See! some fit Passion ev'ry Age supply:
Hope travels thro', nor quits us when we die.
'Till then, Opinion gilds with varying rays
Those painted Clouds that beautify our Days,
Each want of Happiness by Hope supply'd,
And each vacuity of Sense by Pride.
These build up all that Knowledge cou'd destroy,
In Folly's Cup still laughs the Bubble Joy;
One Prospect lost, another still we gain,
And not a Vanity is giv'n in vain;
Even mean Self-love becomes, by Force divine,
The Scale to measure others Wants by thine.
See and confess, One Comfort still must rise,
Tis this, tho' *Man's a Fool*, yet GOD *is* WISE.

To Dr CHEYNE, *of* Bath.
On Reading his Works.

NOT all the Gemmy Treasures of the East,
Nor yet the Spicy Odours of the West;
Not all the glorious Trophies of the Great,
Would please so much, or form one Joy compleat,
Like that I feel, great wondr'ous Genius, when
I scan th' amazing Beauties of thy Pen;
Like those true Pleasures ev'ry Sense still meets
When lost I wander in excess of Sweets.
'Tis Magick, Powerful Magick, reigns in this,
And proves what *Sydenham* was, 'bright *Cheyne*
With admiration of thy System fir'd,   [is;
Good God, how oft I've read, how oft admir'd!
Over thy [*] Theory I have often run,
Wond'ring I've read, and read to wonder on a
Surpriz'd my ravish'd Senses pause to see
So many Grecian Sages live in Thee.
In Thee I find united all I've heard,
Of *Pitcairne*, *Celsus*, or the [‡] *Coan* Bard.
To distant Nations Fame thy Worth has told;
Thy Name shall live, when Time itself grows Old:
Great as thy Mind, Immortal Praise, 'tis true,
And all, save Adoration, is thy Due.
By thee, how many Thousands live to day,
That else had slumber'd in their Mother Clay!
Long did the Sacred Art in Bondage mourn,
Become the Jest of Fools, or else their Scorn;
'Till Heav'n, to set the fetter'd Science free,
And pit'ing abject Man, created Thee,
Made Thee to act of Gods the Healing Part,
And live a Pillar to the noble Art,
To be the only shining acting Sage,
Not giv'n, but lent from them to heal this Age.
Great Wonder from above, thou Boast of Men,
Accept these Offerings from a Namesakes Pen.
                                          H. C.

[*] Cheyne's *Theory of Fevers;*   [‡] Hippocrates.

In Defence of Lady MARY WORTLEY.

(*See the End of* Juvenal *variorum.*)

THE learn'd *Sulpicia*, of Patrician Race,
  With *Juvenal*, in Satire, fhar'd the Bays.
When Stoicks of their Banifhment complain'd,
Domitian's Edict fharply fhe arraign'd.
But in her Verfes was no Rancour feen,
Strong withrout Rage, reproving without Spleen.
  Such *Wortley* is ; where e'er fhe came, admir'd
By Foreign Courts ; at Home, not lefs defir'd.
Her high Extraction, and her candid Mind
To leffen Merit never once inclin'd.
  But if *Dan Pope*, in a frantick Mood,
Empoifon'd Arrows throws among the Crowd ;
Spares not his Friends, and, as he vents his Gall,
Virtue and Vice both equal Victims fall ;
Then in Defence of Innocence, of Laws,
A noble Champion of a noble Caufe,
Ingenious *Wortley* draws her conqu'ring Pen,
And drives the foul-mouth'd *Cacus* to his Den.
  Thus once a Pedant, by vain Hopes mifled,
Bafely his City's hopeful Youth betray'd.
Camillus fcorn'd the Traytor, and to fhew
His juft Refentment, arm'd the little Crew
With Rods : They, as their Mafter naked ftood,
Him homewards whipp'd, cover'd with Shame
   and Blood.

On the QUEEN's MOUNT at Kenfington.

STill fhall the Lyre for *Richmond*'s Grot be ftring,
  And *Kenfington*'s fair Mount be left unfong?
Leave for a while fublimer Themes, and tell
How much her Tafte in Gard'ning does excell :
Nor thou my Mufe be backward in the Song,
To whom no bafe nor venal Strains be'ong.
  In that Retreat (bleft with the Summer Court)
Where Citizens on *Sunday* Nights refort,
A Royal Mount, erects its verdant Head ;
Rais'd by that Hand, by which are Thoufands fed ;
Here, free from the Fatigues of State, and Care,
Our Guardian Queen ofts breaths the Morning Air :
From hence furveys the Glories of her Ifle,
While Peace and Plenty all around her fmile.
See here (†) rich *Villa*'s raife their lofty Heads,
There *Kent*'s high Hill, and *Surrey*'s flow'ry Meads;
They feem to ftrive, which moft fhall Homage pay,
A like Partakers of fo mild a Sway.
While fhe is there, ye ruder Winds abate,
And *Zephyrs* fan her from the piercing Heat ;
Guard her, ye Angels! from the noxious Air,
As we are hers, be her your chiefeft Care.
  Defcend we from the Mount, lo! all beneath,
Alike delight, alike frefh Odours breath :
Pleas'd, and amaz'd, each fair Defign I view,
And gradually the verdant Courfe purfue;
At ev'ry Step, new Scenes of Beauty rife,
Here, well judg'd Viftos meet th' admiring Eyes :
A (*) River there waves thro' the happy Land,
And ebbs and flows, at *Caroline*'s Command.
No coftly Fountains, with proud Vigour rife,
Nor with their foaming Waters lafh the Skies;
To fuch falfe Pride, be none but *Louis* prone,
All fhe lays out in Pleafure is her own.

(†) *Hampftead* and *Highgate.* (*) *Serpentine River.*

Here nothing is profufe, nor nothing vain ;
But all is noble, and yet all is plain :
So happily do Art and Nature joyn,
Each ftrives which moft fhall add to the Defign.
In fuch a State, were our firft Parents plac'd,
And *Eve* like *Caroline* the Garden grac'd :
Had fhe fuch Conftancy of Mind poffeft,
She had not fell, but we had ftill been bleft.

A Gentleman in Lapland *to his Miftrefs in* England.

WHile for her *Strephon*, faithful *Cælia* fighs,
  Beneath the *Britifh* Suns, and fofter Skies;
And tho' fhe feels the milder genial Ray,
Repines at *Albion*'s more indulgent Day :
Think not dear Nymph, thefe dreary Climes
   remove
My wonted Vows, or quench the Fires of Love;
By thine awak'd my correfpondent Care
Pays Sigh for Sigh, and tells out Tear for Tear.
Tho' the coarfe Heav'ns and melancholy Clime,
Benumb the fhackl'd Feet of ev'y Rhime;
Tho' *Phœbus* God of Wit and Heat retires,
Withdraws his own, and damps the Poet's Fires;
Yet no Degrees my ardent Love controul,
Which burns ev'n here, and glows beneath the
The *Artic Circle* fhall to *Strephon* prove [*Pole.*
Only th' *Æquator* to his boundlefs Love :
The Vows I make, tho' now congeal'd in Air,
When the warm Spring brings back the youthful
   Year,   }
Diffolv'd to Sound, the Salvages fhall hear.
  Sometimes to fmooth the raging Pangs of Love,
From Map to Map, with endlefs Care I rove;
O'er Realms unknown, and various Lands I fly,
O'er Worlds and Seas now travel with my Eye :
From Pole to Pole I range this fpacious All,
Then fingle *Albion*'s Ifland from the Ball,
Albion to ev'ry Region I prefer,
She the World's nobleft Pride, and You of Her.
  Whene'er your Image ftrikes upon my Soul,
It thaws the Clime, and melts the frozen Pole;
The fancy'd Lightnings of your heav'nly Eyes,
Unbind the Rigour of the Northern Skies;
Tho' the pale Sun fheds here a fickly Ray,
And rolls in diftant Skies the feeble Day ;
Tho' Icy Mountains raife confus'dly bright,
And Chains of dazling Hills fatigue the Sight;
Tho' Rocks in hoary Piles around me ftand,
Rife white, and glitter o'er the fhining Land,
Yet full of thee, o'er boundlefs Plains I go,
Bold and impaffive to the driving Snow.
I fee fecure the Clime the Seas reftrain,
And yoke the Ocean in a wintry Chain ;
O'er the green Surge, my boundle's View I caft,
And fafely walk along the dreary Waft ;
Led by thofe Eyes, my Stars, the Main explore,
And Billows n-ver plowed by Ships before.
  While thefe bright Images my Cares beguile,
The Hills grow warm, and the bleak Deferts fmile,
But if to crown my Hopes with full Delight,
My *Cælia*'s Form might blefs my ravifh'd Sight;
I would not envy thofe rich Realms that lie
Beneath the Influence of a fofter Sky;
I'd revel here, tho' circl'd round with Froft,
And find a Paradife on *Lapland*'s dreary Coaft.

By a Gentleman on his BIRTH-DAY.

DO I yet live ? What Heart conceives
The Height and Depth of Love Divine!
Which thus to Life Duration gives,
And Mercies does to Mercies join.
Yet I muſt die; my Sins conſtrain,
And Love, tho' infinite, complies   :
Juſtice and Truth ſevere ordain
That Each, ev'n pardon'd, Rebel dies.
Then quick, nor let that Moment ſtay !
To Chriſt, my Soul, with Tranſport fly:
Bliſsful with Him to live, I'll pay
With Joy the trifling Debt, to Die.
With Him to live I'll gladſom fly,
Nor ſhall my Fleſh this Flight controul;
Since Time the Body can deſtroy,
But not Eternity the Soul.
My Thoughts fromEarth to Heav'n I'll ſtretch,
Where Man in Majeſty ſhall dwell;
Whom, living, Brutes can almoſt reach,
Whom, dead, ev'n Angels ſcarce excell.
While raviſh'd there I range, tho' now
My Joy from fancied Glory ſprings,
Such Raptures ev'n from Fancy flow,
I bleſs the Thoughts and pity Kings.
Can Fancy then ſuch Bliſs diſplay
As mounts o'er Earth's moſt ſplendid Toys?.
Hence, Lord, my panting Soul convey
Where That muſt ſtoop to Real Joys.
Where I my Time (transporting View !)
Shall, Years deſpis'd, by Ages tell,
And then the glorious Task renew
When Mem'ry droops, and Numbers fail.
Thus marching till I find at laſt
(A Courſe of countleſs Ages run)
When One Eternity ſeems paſt,
Another is but juſt begun.

A *Dialogue* between F. Walſingham *Eſq;* and A——n P——*Eſq;*

W. WHat a ſtrange ſtory's this : Of yours
what a job hear I ;
Let me tell you, this act was a publick robbery :
Tranſported you ſhould be to Tobacco plantations.
P. By what law, I beſeech you ? *W.* By the
law of nations.
By the *Roman law* too : read over *Legem Juliam,*
You'll ſee what a learned Civilian I truly am.
P. But this very *law* you ſo patly have hit on,
Can have nothing to do with any *Free Briton,*
W. But I hope ſoon it will : for when ſo injurious
The *common council* is——P. Pray be not ſo furious:
For were this law reviv'd, it would give you the
ſtatus :   [culatus ?
For how can you be pay'd, when there's no *Pe-*

Ingredients to make a Sceptic. *By Mr* S.Duck.

A Little *Learning,* twenty Grains of *Senſe,*
Reſerve a *double* Share of *Ignorance:*
Inſuſe a *little* Wit into the Scull,
Which never fails to makes a *Mighty* Fool ;
TwoDrams of *Faith,* two Tons of *Doubting* next,
let all be with the *Dregs* of *Reaſon* mixt ;
Theſe jarring Seeds when in his Nature ſown,
He'll cenſure all Things, but approve of none.

On the Five Buſtoes erected by her Majeſty in the Hermitage at Richmond.

HIgh on theLiſt of Fame while *Newton* ſtands,
Whoſe ſpreading Beams enlighten Foreign
Lands ;
Whoſe piercing Genius cou'd alone explore
Nature's deep Secrets, unreveal'd before ;
And, on advent'rous Wing tranſported, trace
The ſtarry Wonders of th' Ethereal Space :
While*Locke* with native Force of Reaſon charms,
And *Woollaſton* by Strokes of *Nature* warms ;
While *Piety* and *Learning* both conſpire
In *Clarke,* to fan Religion's ſacred Fire ;
Whoſe milder Rules, to Souls by Paſſion driv'n,
Still kindly point the certain Road to Heav'n ;
[While *Boyle,* whoſe philoſophic Eye cou'd trace
The myſtic Lines of Nature's various Face,
Shall, like the Sun, diffuſive Beams impart,
Inlight'ning all the mazey Wilds of Art ;] •
So long, illuſtrious Queen ! ſhalt thou receive
The choiceſt Honours that the Muſe can give.

On the GROTTO, by Dr S——

LEwis the living Genius fed,
And rais'd the Scientific Head ;
Our Q——, more frugal of her Meat,
Raiſes thoſe Heads which cannot eat.

• ANSWER'D.

OUR Q——n more anxious to be juſt
Than flatter'd, rears the living Buſt
To choſen Spirits, learned Tribe !
Whom, *Lewis* like, ſhe cannot bribe.

ON THE SAME.

ILluſtrious *Caroline,* the Wiſe, the Great,
One Sage is wanting in thy calm Retreat;
Let *Hobbs,* theDoubtful, make the Set compleat.

[*] ANSWER.

CEaſe envious Muſe ! to ſully thus theGreat,
Nor ſtrive the nobleſt Actions to defeat ;
See ! *Boyle,* that Sun of Knowledge, claims
the Umpire Seat.

A *Paper of* VERSES *found behind one of the* BUSTS *in the* GROTTO *at*——

A Place here is—'twas purchas'd cheap,
Thanks, O--D, thy undoing:
And here is built a clumſy Heap,
Thought beautiful in Ruin.
Three Holes there are, thm' which you ſee ;
Three Seats to ſet your A---e on ;
And Idols four—of Wizzards three,
And one unchriſtian Parſon.
In praiſe of *Clark*--obſerve the Joke---
Writes ev'ry Band and Gown ;
And *Lock*'s the Theme of courtly Folk,
Who lov'd nor Court nor Crown.
Fie, Parſons, fie,---fie Courtiers eke,
Leave uninſcrib'd this Wall ;
For could the honeſt Stones but ſpeak,
They'd contradict you all.

Write you for Penfions ?—you'll have none——
For Fame 'tis vain to quarrel ;
Confider---STEPHEN DUCK's but one,
And CIBBER wears the Laurel.

    * ANSWER'D extempore,.

POOR fnarling Bard, who e'er thou art,
    To fcold at Things above thy Reach ;
Thus *Reynard* faid, the Grapes are tart ;
    And Vice will Virtue ftill impeach.
Both on the Living and the Dead,
    In vain thou doft thy Vengeance wreak ;
Should'ft thou go on, thou thoughtlefs Head,
    Thou't make thofe ftony Buftoes Speak.

On the Five Buftoes in her Majefty's *Her-*
mitage.

HOW are thefe venerable fages grac'd,
    To have their Bufto's in this temple plac'd!

And with what nice difcernment has the *Queen*
Chofe out fit worthies to adorn her fcene !
They all, or fciences abftrufe explain, [tain,
Check lawlefs power, and human rights main-
Religion's rules on nature built define,
Or chriftian revelation prove divine :
All fuit her tafte fo much for fenfe profound,
True learning fam'd, and for religion found ;
Here they'll acquire an everlafting name,
By *Caroline* confign'd to deathlefs fame ;
Who'll with thefe fages long herfelf out-live,
And to all future queens a pattern give ;
To her defcendants moft remote will fhow,
That to fuch worthies princes homage owe ;
Should genuine fcience ftudy to acquire,
To the moft ufeful characters afpire,
Trace reafon's rules, abufe of power difdain, ⎫
Chriftian religion as divine, maintain, ⎬
And by fuch models think, and act, and reign. ⎭

On the BUST *of the Hon.* ROBERT BOYLE *Efq; being fet up in her* MAJESTY's *Hermitage at*
Richmond ; concerning which we have fome VERSES *in the foregoing Page, marked thus* [*]

THESE Lines thus mark'd [*] are inferted inftead of better, which the Reader would have
    met with, had not the Undertaker, fince he faw this Inftance of her Majefty's great and
juft Difcernment, been too much indifpofed to apply to his Poetical Friends. We are fatisfy'd this
Hint would be fufficient to bring us a Supply. But as we have been already greatly obliged to
our Correfpondents without any other Return than inferting as many as we well could ; We propofe, agreeably to a Hint given us in a Letter about a Year ago, that THE COPY OF VERSES
on this Subject which fhall be adjudg'd to excell the reft, be rewarded with a Volume of our
Magazine for the prefent Year on Royal Paper, finely bound in Morocco, and properly Letter'd ;
with the Name of the Author if he pleafes. The Gentleman or Lady whofe Piece fhall be judged to merit the fecond Place fhall be entitled to a Volume in Common Paper, handfomely bound,
and letter'd alfo in a proper manner.

    The Refpective Authors, are defired to fend their Performances directed to St *John's Gate*,
and to diftinguifh their Papers, (after the manner of the Academy of *Paris*) by fome Sentence,
Token or Device, to be cover'd with white Paper fealed over it, which fhall not be taken off
untill the Prize is declar'd, which is to be claimed by the Author's bringing or fending a Copy in
the fame Writing fo diftinguifhed. To give Opportunity to the Gentlemen in *Ireland* to try
their Skill, the time of receiving any Performances will be extended to the 1ft of *Auguf.*
Such Verfes as fhall be received before the 25th of *May*, will be early enough to be inferted in our
next MAGAZINE.

    That the Prize may be determin'd impartially the Publifher will engage 5 felect Gentlemen,
in whofe Judgment he can confide, jointly to examine and give their Opinion of the Pieces referred
to their Arbitration ; 3 of this Number to decide the Point in Queftion, and all to declare on their
Honour, they have not writ, or are privy to the writing of, any Piece under Confideration. The
Publifher was the more willing to comply with this Propofal, fince the Buft of this Noble and great Perfonage has been now the
3d Month fet up, and no notice before taken of it.

    If this Method fhould be found to excite a laudable Emulation, it will be continu'd upon fome
new Subject every Year.

    The Prizes to be declared in our MAGAZINE for *December* ; and deliver'd any time after the
10th of *February* next.

    Note. *The 4 Bufts fo often mention'd, ftand in Niches at each quarter in the Walls of the Vault-*
ed Dome, (See a good Defcription given of the Place No. 24, p. 41.) but the Buft of Mr Boyle
ftands higher than thefe, on a Pedeftal, in the inmoft, and, as it were, the moft facred Recefs of the
Place ; behind his Head a large Golden Sun, darting his wide fpreading Beams all about, and
towards the others, to whom his Afpect is directed. To the Dome is an Iron Door by which you
enter, on each fide of it an Apartment to which are Iron Rails ; and each of thefe Apartments is
capable of Receiving more Bufts, if her Majefty fhould think proper in her Wifdom to add any
at the Number already there.

A SONG.

FLy no more, cruel fair, but be kind and relenting,
  Enough has been shewn of contempt and disdain;
  Taste at length the superior delight of consent-
    ing,
For 'tis much nobler joy to give pleasure than pain
  Wou'd you charm men of sense, and engage
    their addresses;
My *Chloe*, of pride, as of painting beware:
For beauty consists more in minds than in faces,
And the maid's almost ugly, that only is fair.

An Address to *James Oglethorpe*, Esq; on his settling the Colony in *Georgia*.

WHILE generous Oglethorpe's *unwearied pain*
  Wakes up a muse from India's *savage plain*;
Warm'd, as she may, with the humane design,
Yet scarcely vain to paint a worth like thine;
Her numbers languid, and unform'd her voice,
Six hopes her credit only from her choice;
When acts so amiably great inspire,
'Tis praise to love, and merit to admire.
Extensive bliss the god-like breast must crown,
That makes each Good of the distress'd his own;
And worthy Heroes ev'ry tear must rise,
Caught from the wretches woe, and mourners sighs;
When if the just impressions fire impart,
And the prompt hand asserts the gen'rous heart;
Sublime beyond applause, the conscious mind
Forstastes the heav'n that form'd him for his kind.
Hence horrors regions, are with joy explor'd,
And squalid wretches feel the day restor'd;
The sons of want the chearful morsel know,
And ease surprizes in the den of Woe.
Nor think the brave enough already done,
The brave shall finish what the good begun.
Oceans in vain their bounds immense oppose,
And speechless horrors to the eye disclose,
The thirst of others good, eternal fame,
Stills the loud storm, and perils lose their name.
Nor less in vain to stay his great efforts,
The arts of cities and the pomp of courts:
Senates, which lately charm'd, with ease he flies;
While from neglect augmented glories rise.
But say, O truly great, if words can shew
The honest joys thy generous bosom knew,
When first the ever-blooming clime you found,
Where George's *name adorns the teeming ground.*
With silent joy the smiling genius stood,
And hail'd thy presence to the living Wood.
When thus thy thoughts; " Here let the wretch
    have peace.
" Too hungry plenty, and the poor increase.
" Nor fear to pine, while wasting nature fails,
" By tedious intervals of scanty meals.
" The gaping young loud-craving new supplies,
" The weeping parent's wretched let denies,
" Nor as when shaking near the frosty pole,
" They trembled more to heap the stinted coal.
" Whilst here luxuriant forests gladly spare
" The sweetest fuel for the choicest fare.
" And when the happily-increasing band
" Farther replenish the inviting land,
" Iberia's manly race a bound shall know,
" And slave contented in the mine below:

" Nor Gallia's sons of new encroachments dream'
" Glad while they taste the Mississippi stream:,
" In peace 'till we preside, in war prevail,
" And the new world allow the British scale."
Thus tho' the failing numbers lag behind
The genuine ardours of thy God-like mind;
They, pregnant with the genius whence they flow,
Suggest a spirit not unlike thy own':
Exalted pleasures in my bosom rise,
And silent tears of joy invade my eyes.
Oft as the bigot's hellish zeal shall flame,
While charity deplores religion's name:
Oft as the lust of tyrants to inslave,
Shall grind the needy, and distract the brave:
Nations shall to the Isle *of heroes run,*
George *calls the wretch of every clime his son,*
He wills them free, and bids them to possess;,
While lightned hearts and grateful Minds confess
To the firm glories of so bright a scene,
Cæsar *and* Ammon's *son, were greatly mean.*
The fame of tyrants, should, if justice sway'd,
Be bowl'd thro' deserts their ambition made;
But sure an endless race shall learn their praise,
Who made the heirs of want, the lords of ease:
The gloomy wood to flowing harvests chang'd,
And founded cities where the tyger rang'd.
Then may the great reward, assign'd by fate,
Prove thy own wish—to see the work compleat;
Till Georgia's *silks on* Albion's *beauties shine,*
Or gain new lustre from the royal line:
Till from the sunny hills the Vines display
Their various berries to the gilded day:
Whence the glad vintage to the vale may flow,
Refreshing labour, and dispelling woe.
While the fat plains with pleasant olives shine,
And Ziura's *date improves the barren pine.*
Fair in the garden shall the lemmon grow,
And every grove Hesperian *apples shew.*
The almond, the delicious fruit behold,
Whose juice the feign'd immortals quaff'd of old.
Nor haply on the well-examin'd plain
Shall China's *fragrant leaf be sought in vain;*
While the consenting climate gladly proves;
The costly balms that weep in Indian *Groves;*
And when in time the wealthy lands increase
Shall bend the curious to the arts of peace;
They with small pains, assisted by the clime,
Shall pull the Anana, *and unload the lime;*
Thro' groves of citron breathe Arabia's *gale,*
And parch the berry, drank in Mecca's *vale.*

A Description of Maryland, extracted from a Poem, entitled, Carmen Seculare, addressed to Ld Baltimore, Proprietor of that Province, now there. By Mr Lewis, Author of the beautiful Poem inserted in our 4th Number, entitled, a Journey from Patapsko to Annapolis.

IF in wish'd progress, thro' these wide do-
    mains,
  Our Lord shall pass, to cheer his tenant
    swains;
With pleasure will he see th' extensive Land,
Adorn'd by nature with a lib'ral hand,

Of *Chesepeake*, fair bay ! she justly boasts,
That swells to wash her *East* and *Western* coasts ;
Whose num'rous, gentle, navigable streams,
In fame would equal *Po*, or nobler *Thames* ;
Smooth-gliding thro' some Poet's deathless song,
Had they in *Europe* roll'd their waves along.

Vast flocks of fowl each river's surface hide,
Amidst them sails the swan with graceful pride ;
From these, the fowler's gun gains plenteous
    prize,
Those that escape the mimic thunder rise,
And clam'rous, in confusion, soar the skies.
Each flood with wat'ry wealth exhaustless stor'd,
With choicest cates supplies the fisher's board.

CERES all bounteous for the Tiller's toil,
Cloaths with her corny stores th' unfallow'd soil.
POMONA yields delicious fruitage here, ;
Unforc'd by art, nor asks the Gard'ners care
Our loaded Orchards bend beneath their weight,
And call for props to bear the dangling freight.

Here, *Flora*, gaily wild, profusely pours
O'er woods, and meadows, hills and dales the
    flow'rs.

Innum'rous herds about our forests graze,
Fearless the deer upon their hunters gaze.
Wolves, panthers, bears, and ev'ry beast of prey,
Fly the inhabitants, and shun the day,
No dreadful hurricanes disturb our skies,
No earthquakes shock the soul with sad surprize,
No sulphurous volcanos vomit fire,
To blast the plains with devastation dire.
No treach'rous crocodiles infest our floods ;
And pois'nous snakes recede to pathless Woods.
The landscap'd Earth shows many a pleasing
    scene.
And fogs but rarely hide the blue serene.

Nor are these blessings of indulgent Heav'n,
To an ingrateful Race of mortals given ;
Here, ev'ry planter opens wide his door,
To entertain the stranger, and the poor :
For them, he cheerful makes the downy bed,
For them, with food unbought his board is
    spread ;
No arts of luxury disguise his meals,
Nor poignant sauce severe disease conceals ;
Such hearty welcom does the treat commend,
As shows the *Donor* to mankind a friend,
Th'at good *Old-English* hospitality,
When ev'ry house to ev'ry guest was free ;
Whose flight from Britain's isle, her bards be-
    moan,
Seems here with pleasure to have fix'd her
    throne.

Here the Poet, by way of Episode, gives an Account of the great Pains and Expence which the Lord Baltimore's Ancestors had been at in seating and cultivating this Province ; with some other Remarks, which we may probably give another time.

Too long, alas ! *Tobacco* has engross'd
Our cares, and now we mourn our markets lost ;

The plenteous crops that over-spread our plains,
Reward with poverty the toiling swains :
Their sinking *Staple* chills the planters hearts,
Nor dare they venture on unpractis'd arts ;
Despondent, they impending ruin view,
Yet starving, must their old employ persue.

If you, benevolent, afford your aid,
Your faithful tenants shall enlarge their trade :
By you encourag'd, *Artists* shall appear,
And quitting crowded towns, inhabit here.
Well pleas'd, would they employ their gainful
    hands,
To purchase and improve your vacant lands.

While some with sounding axes thinn'd the
    woods,
And built the ships to traverse briny floods ;
Others, industrious, would with hasty care
The various Cargoes studiously prepare.
While these, for fish, the wavy world explore,
Those would refine the rich metallic ore,
The husbandman might from his fertile field,
Raise finer flax than *Germany* can yield :
And from our looms,might curious workmen
The linen, emulous of driving snow.   [show,
To feed the worms that form the silky spoil.
Vast mulb'ry groves, spontaneous, crown our soil,
O'er tallest trees our vines wild-spreading rise,
And hide their purple clusters in the skies :
Did art reclaim their too-luxuriant shoots,
And skilful culture tame their sylvan Fruits ;
We might a flood of native wine produce,
And rival *France* in the nectareous juice.

These blessings nature to this land imparts ;
She only asks the aid of useful arts ;
To make her with the happiest regions vye,
That spread beneath the all-surrounding Sky.

An hundred suns thro' summer signs have roll'd
An hundred winters have diffus'd their cold ;
Since *Maryland* has *Calvert's* race obey'd,
And to its noble *Lords* her homage paid :
And now, the laws of mighty time decree
This, for the year of sacred *Jubilee* :
This year, distinguish'd far above the rest ,
That time hath sent, shall be for ever blest !
From your kind *Visit*, shall the people date
And happier *Æra*, mark'd by smiling fate,
To raise the Province from its languid State.

Your presence shall disperse the cloud that
    spreads,
Threatning to rain down ruin on our heads ;
And from the breaking gloom, shall trade display
Her beams, and warm us with a golden ray.

N. B. *We acknowledge the Receipt of several Letters without any subscription ; but must desire our Correspondents for the future to subscribe some Name to their Epistles, if they expect to have any Answer, and always direct to it, John's Gate.*

If A G R I C O L A would signify what Particulars
    would be most acceptable ; we could get them
    earlier than he directs ; we are afraid that the
    whole will take up too much of our Book.

THE
Monthly Intelligencer.
APRIL, 1733.

Sunday, April 1.

Few Days ago, Sir *Simon Stuart*, of *Hartley* in *Hampſhire*, looking over ſome old Writings, found on the Back of one of them a Memorandum noting that 1500 Broad Pieces were buried in a certain Spot in an adjoyning Field. Whereupon he took a Servant, and after digging a little in the Place, found the Treaſure in a Pot, hid there in the Time of the late Civil Wars, by his Grandfather, Sir *Nicholas Stuart*.

Tuesday, 3.

The Hon. *Horatio Townſhend*, Eſq; was elected Gov. of the Bank of *England.* *Bryan Benſon*, Eſq; Deputy Governor. DIRECTORS elected *April,* 4.

Robert Alſop, Eſq; and Alderman.	*John Rudge,* Eſq; *Moſes Raper,* Eſq;
Mr *Robert Atwood*	*Wm Snelling,* Eſq;
John Bance, Eſq;	Mr *Robert Thornton*
Stamp Brooksbank, Eſq;	
Mr *Clement Boehm*	Sir *Edward Bellamy,*
Sir *Gerard Conyers,* Kt. and Ald.	Kt and Ald.
	Thomas Cooke, Eſq;
Delillers Carbonnel, Eſq;	Sir *John Heathcote,* Bar.
Wm. Fawkener, Eſq;	*Henry Herring,* Eſq;
Mr *James Gaultier*	*Matthew Howard,* Eſq;
Samuel Holden, Eſq;	Sir *William Jolliff*
Chriſt. Lethieullier, Eſq	*Charles Savage,* Eſq;
Henry Neale, Eſq;	*James Spilman,* Eſq;

Thursday, 5.

Elected DIRECTORS of the *Eaſt India* Company.

Sir *Francis Child*	Mr *John Ecclestone*
Capt. *Harry Gough*	Mr *William Rous*
Capt. *Robert Hudſon*	*John Drummond,* Eſq;
Dodding Bradyll, Eſq;	Mr *Joſias Wordſworth,* jun.
Abraham Addams, Eſq;	
Benj. Lethieullier, Eſq;	*Matthew Martin,* Eſq;
John Crook, Eſq;	Capt. *Richard Boulton*
Joſias Wordſworth Eſq;	Mr *Miles Barne*
Baltzar Lyell, Eſq;	Dr *Caleb Cotſworth*
John Gould, Eſq;	*Samuel Feake,* Eſq;
Mr *Richard Blount*	*John Savage,* Eſq;
John Gould, jun. Eſq;	Sir *John Lock*
	William Goſſ-lin, Eſq;

Saturday, 7.

His Majeſty order'd 200 Ton of Halfpence to be coin'd for the Uſe of the Publick.

Monday, 9.

Was held a Court of Ld Mayor, Aldermen, and Common Council, the moſt numerous ever known, when a Petition againſt the Bill for Exciſing Tobacco was unanimouſly agreed to. The Ld Mayor open'd the Court with the following Speech,

Gentlemen,

THere is a Bill depending in the Houſe of Commons (a Copy of which I have procured) laying an Inland Dury on Tobacco ; which Dury, it is univerſally agreed, will prove extremely detrimental to the Trade and Commerce of this great City, as well as to that of the whole Nation. And as the High Station which I have the Honour to be in, obliges me to be watchful over every thing that may affect the Intereſt of my Fellow Citizens; I ſhould think myſelf wanting in my Duty, if I neglected to call you together on this extraordinary Occaſion, that you might have an Opportunity to deliberate on an Affair of ſuch Importance, wherein our Liberty and our Property are ſo eſſentially concerned.

Tuesday, 10.

The Sheriffs of *London*, ſeveral Aldermen, and Common Council-men attended by a great many Merchants and Traders of this City, went to the Houſe of Commons to preſent their Petition againſt the Exciſe. There were about 200 Coaches, and moſtly 4 in Coach.

Wednesday, 11.

Mr *Joſeph Kells*, of *Woodbridge* in *Suffolk*, who was ſeiz'd in the Court of Requeſts, for hiſſing at Sir *Robert Walpole*, and raiſing a Riot, &c. was admitted to Bail in a Recognizance of 500 l. Being ask'd if he was not hir'd to come to *Weſtminſter*, ſaid he came to ſolicit againſt the Exciſe.

At

At Night all poſſible Demonſtrations of Joy were ſhewn throughout the City, on Account of the Tobacco Bill being put off to the 12th of *June*. At *Temple-Bar* the Populace burnt a large Figure of a Man-made with Straw, with blue Paper a croſs his Shoulder, and white Paper ſtuck on his Coat to imitate a Star. The Mob were ſo riotous, that they broke the Windows of ſeveral Houſes not illuminated, particularly at the Poſt-Office.

Thurſday, 12.

An Expreſs arrived at *Briſtol* with the agreeable News, that the Tobacco Bill was Poſtpon'd to the 12th of *June*, and tho' 11 o-Clock at Night, the Merchants and principal Traders aſſembled at the Council-houſe, and drank Healths to the worthy 204 and other Gentlemen who oppoſed the Excife Bill. Bonefires were lighted, and Rejoicings were made thro' out the City.

We might inſert many more Accounts of the Rejoycings that have been made in moſt of the Cities and great Towns all over the Kingdom; but it may ſuffice to ſay the Joy has been univerſal; particularly at *Liverpool*, where a *Courant*, containing ſome ſevere Reflections on the Merchants, (ſee p. 138) was publickly burnt.

Friday, 13.

On This Day which gave the finiſhing Stroke to the *Excife Project* in Parliament, his Grace the Duke of *Grafton* was ſent to the Earl of *Cheſterfield*, to ſignify his Majeſty's Pleaſure to him that he ſhould reſign his Staff, as Lord Steward of the Houſehold. The next Morning (as we are informed) his Lordſhip ſent it, accompany'd with a very dutiful and reſpectful Letter to his Majeſty. My Ld *Cheſterfield* had been one of the *Lords of the Bedchamber* to his preſent Majeſty, during moſt of the Time of his being *Prince of Wales*, and, at his Majeſty's Acceſſion to the Throne, he was appointed *Embaſſador Extraordinary to the States General of the United Provinces*, where he ſupported that high Character with the greateſt Dignity, doing Service to his own Country, and gaining the Eſteem of the *States General*. He was ſoon after appointed Lord Steward, and made one of the Companions of the moſt noble Order of the Garter. The World ſeems greatly aſtoniſh'd at ſo unexpected an Event, and Thoſe, who are moſt zealous for the preſent Royal Family, grieve to ſee ſo *able* and *faithful a Servant* diſmiſs'd in ſo critical a Conjuncture.

The ſame Day the Lord *Clinton* was removed from being one of the *Lords of the Bedchamber* to his Majeſty, as alſo from the Poſt of *Lord Lieutenant of the County of Devon*. He had ſerved his Majeſty in theſe Stations, for many Years, with diſtinguiſh'd Zeal and Fidelity.

We give the foregoing Paragraphs at length from the Craftſman, becauſe of the Remarks made upon 'em by the Free-Briton. (See p. 194 E.)

Were Hang'd at *Exeter*, *Samuel Quan*, *Richard Dowling*, and *Thomas Barrington* condemn'd for robbing a Countryman of about 5 or 6 Pounds. They belonged to a Gang who went about playing at Thimbles and Balls, and about ſix Weeks before ſet out in order to travel the Countries. They own'd that in leſs than three Weeks time they had won of Country People upwards of 100 *l.* but abſolutely deny'd the Robbery. *Quan* lately kept an Alehouſe in St *Giles's*, and *Dowling* was a Butcher in *Clare-Market*. *Quan* was tried about twelve Months ſince at the Old-Baily, for an Offence of the like Nature, but acquitted.

Sunday, 15.

His Royal Highneſs the Duke, enter'd the 13th Year of his Age.

Tueſday, 17.

Was held a General Court of the *S. Sea* Company, when the Petition to Parliament for reducing three quarters of their Capital into Annuities, and rendring the Remainder a Trading Stock, ſubject to the Payment of all the Debts due from the Company, and inveſted in all the Claims and Debts due to it, the ſame having been drawn up, purſuant to the Reſolution of a former General Court, was read, and after a ſmall Oppoſition, approv'd; and a Motion being made to add a Clauſe thereto, for preventing any Perſons whatſoever, in the Company's Service, carrying on any illicit Trade to the S. Seas in the Company's Ships, and likewife a ſecond, for preventing the Fallacy of Directors in making out larger Dividends to the Proprietors than their Trade will ſupport; both of them were agreed to, and the Petition, with theſe Additions, were order'd to be preſented to the Hon. Houſe of Commons.

Wedneſday 18.

The Court of Common Council, met at Guildhall, unanimouſly return'd Thanks

to

to the 4 Repreſentatives of this City, for the Regard they had ſhewn to their Repreſenration, and to the Trade and Liberties of their Fellow Subjects, in ſtrenuouſly oppoſing any Extenſion of the Exciſe Laws. They alſo returned Thanks to the Lord Mayor for his Care and Vigilance for the Welfare of the City, and for ſo ſeaſonably calling them together, and laying before them a Copy of the Tobacco Bill, whereby they had an Opportunity of Petitioning againſt it, which was attended with Succeſs. They likewiſe returned Thanks to Sir *Francis Child*, Sir *John Williams*, and Sir *George Caſwal*, Members of the ſaid Court, having Seats in Parliament, for their ſtrenuous Oppoſition to the ſaid Bill.

Saturday, 21.

A Fund having being eſtabliſhed for augmenting ten poor Vicarages by the Arch-Bp of *Canterbury*, in that Dioceſe, the ſeveral Incumbents, received their Allowances for the Year 1732.

The Truſtees for eſtabliſhing a Colony in *Georgia*, received a Letter from *James Oglethorpe*, Eſq; adviſing his ſafe Arrival there, with all the People under his Care on the 1ſt of *February* laſt; that he had mark'd out the Town (ſee p. 168); that they had received great Encouragement from the Aſſembly, Governor, and Council of *Charles Town*; and that a little *Indian* Nation, about 50 Miles off, were deſirous to be Subjects to K. *George*, and to breed their Children in Chriſtian Schools.

Tueſday, 24.

The following Gentlemen were appointed by the Houſe of Commons, to Enquire into the Frauds of the Cuſtoms, *viz.* Sir *John Cope*, Mr *Clutterbuck*, Sir *William Clayton*, Mr *Fox*, Mr *Henry Pelham*, Mr *Edgcombe*, Sir *Philip Torke*, Sir *Ja Heathcote*, Mr *Clayton*, Mr. *Lowther*, Sir *George Oxenden*, Mr *Talbot*, General *Wade*, Mr *Doddington*, Mr *Duncan Forbes*, Sir *Thomas Frankland*, Mr *Winnington*, Mr *Campbell*, Lord *Hervey*, Mr *Horatio Walpole*, and Sir *William Tonge*. There were 491 Members in the Houſe, when the Ballot was taken, *viz.* 211 and 280.

Friday, 27.

Four of the Seven Malefactors, who received Sentence of Death at the *Old Bailey* the 7th Inſtant, were executed at *Tyburn*, *viz. W. Gordon*, *James Ward*, and *W. Keys*, for the Highway, and *W. Norman*, for a Street Robbery. The other

three, *viz. W. Harper*, and *Samuel Elms*, for Street Robberies, and *Eliz. Auſten*, for robbing her Maſter, who pleaded her Belly, and was found pregnant, were ordered to be tranſported for 14 Years.— 'Twas reported that *Gordon* cut his Throat juſt before he was carried out of *Newgate* for Execution, and that a Surgeon ſewed it up: But in the *Daily Advertiſer*, we have the following ſtrange Account. — Mr *Chovet*, a Surgeon, having by frequent Experiments on Dogs, diſcovered, that opening the Windpipe, would prevent the fatal Conſequences of the Halter, undertook Mr *Gordon*, and made an Inciſion in his Windpipe; the Effect of which was, that when *Gordon* ſtopt his Mouth, Noſtrils, and Ears for ſome Time, Air enough came thro' the Cavity to continue Life. When he was hang'd he was perceived to be alive after all the reſt were dead; and when he had hung 3 quarters of an Hour, being carried to a Houſe in *Tyburn* Road, he opened his Mouth ſeveral Times and groaned, and a Vein being open'd he bled freely. 'Twas thought, if he had been cut down 5 Minutes ſooner, he might have recover'd.

This Gordon *was a Butcher, but had been a reputed Highwayman above 20 Years. He made himſelf an Evidence againſt Dawſon, for Robbing the Cheſter-Mail; and was himſelf afterwards tried at Chelmsford for a bold Robbery of the Fiſhmongers Company on Epping-Foreſt: But he brought a Number of Evidences to prove he was in Ireland, and thereby was acquitted.* (See the Trial in the Hiſtory of Executions, for the Year 1730.) *The Robbery he was executed for, was committed between* Knightsbridge *and* Hyde-Park Corner, *about* 7 at Night, on Mr Peters Under Treaſurer of the Temple, of a Hat and Wig, Watch and Ring he took, and being Drunk, and off his uſual Precaution, he was taken with them upon him before* 8; *ſo that on his Trial, he had nothing to ſay in his Defence, but that he was in Liquor.*

Saturday, 28.

White's Chocolate Houſe near the Palace in St *James ſtreet*, kept by Mr *Arthur*, and two adjoyning Houſes were conſum'd by a ſudden Fire. Young Mr *Arthur*'s Wife leap'd out of Window 2 pair of Stairs upon a Feather-Bed without much Hurt. Mr *Arthur* had the Value of 300 l. in Plate and Caſh buried in the Ruins. But

a

a fine Collection of Paintings belonging to Sir *Andrew Fountain*, valu'd at 3000 l. at the least, were entirely destroy'd. His Majesty and the Pr. of *Wales* were present above an Hour, and encourag'd the Firemen and People to work at the Engines, a Guard being order'd from St *James's* to keep off the Populace. His Majesty order'd 20 Guineas among the Firemen and others that work'd at the Engines, and 5 Guineas to the Guard; and the Prince order'd the Firemen 10 Guineas.

Monday, 30.

'Twas talk'd of, with great Certainty, that the Parliament accepts the Executorship of the remarkable Will of the late *Richard Norton*, Esq; (see p. 57.) and that Trustees will be forthwith appointed to try the Validity thereof in the proper Courts, it being contested by the next Heirs to that Gentleman.

BIRTHS.

THE Wife of Col. *Descury*, deliver'd of three Boys.
The Wife of *John Evelyn*, Esq; Representative for *Helston* in *Cornwal*, deliver'd of a son, baptiz'd the 17th instant, the Pr. of *Wales*, and D. of *Newcastle* standing Godfathers, and the Lady-Visc. *Falmouth*, Godmother.

MARRIAGES.

SIR *John Giffard*, Bart. Married to Miss *Arundell*, Niece to the Ld *Arundell*, of *Wardour*.
—— *Wrottesley*, Esq; : : to the Daughter of the Lady *Wrottesley*, of *Staffordshire*.
Geo. *Stourton*, Esq; : : to the Lady *Petre*.
Alexander Hume, Esq; Merchant, : : to the Daughter of the late Sir *Thomas Frederick*, a Fortune of 10,000l.
Thomas Hanmer, Esq; : : to the eldest Daughter of the Ld *Percival*.
Mr *Godfrey Thornton*, of Lond. Mercht. to a Daughter of *Wm Astel*, Esq;
Mr *Gower*, a Relation of the Ld *Gower*, : : to Miss *Pearson*.
Wm Lethieullier, Esq; a Turkey Merchant : : to the 3d Daughter of Sir *John Tash*, with a Fortune of 60000l.
Joseph Hudson, of *Roehampton*, Esq; : : to Miss *Saunders*, of *Little Ormond-street*.
Sir *Theodore Cockburn*, of *Chelsea*, : : to Miss *Dickins* of that Place.
Wm Conolly, Esq; : : to a Daughter of the E. of *Strafford*.
Wm Wotton, Esq; an Ensign belonging to the Train of Artillery, : : to Miss *Seal* of *Threadneedle-street*.

Mr *George Thornhill*, Attorney at Law' : : to the only Daughter of Mr *John Barnes* an Italian Merchant, with 6000l. Fortune.
James Newberry, of *Kingston*, Esq; : : to Miss *Langdell* a rich Heiress of that Place.

DEATHS.

March 30. JOHN *Preston*, Esq; late City Remembrancer, and Clerk of the Vintner's Company.
Thomas Walker, Esq; at *Streatham*.
31. Dr *Fryer*, of the Col. of Physicians.
Ap. 1. *Henry Clark*, Esq; Page of the Back Stairs to the Princesses *Mary* and *Louisa*.
Thomas Western, Esq; of *Dover-street*.
John Leach, Esq; of *Clargis-street*.
2. Mr *Frewen*, an Attorney of *Lincoln's Inn Square*.
The only Daughter and Child of *Wm. Rawlinson Earle*, Esq; Representative for *Malmsbury*, in *Wiltshire*.
The Wife of *Wm Clifton*, Esq; Brother to Sir *Rob. Clifton*, Bart Knt of the *Bath*.
Relict of *Rob. Blois*, Esq; eldest Son of Sir *Rob. Blois*, of *Suffolk*, Bart.
The Wife of *Vigerus Edwards*, Esq; Secretary to the Com. of Bankrupts.
John Ferguharson, at *Dublin*. He married the Lady Viscountess *Mountjoy*.
3. *Rob. Ingram*, Esq; of *Hanover Square*.
4. Revd Mr *Parker*, Rector of St *Michael's Crooked Lane*.
Capt. *Flower*, of *Lime-house*.
Relict of Sir *William Trevor*, Bart at *Kingston*.
5. *Rob. Myddelton*, Esq; of *Chirk Castle*, Representative for *Denbigh*, leaving his Brother *John Myddelton*, Esq; Executor and near 12,000l. *per Ann.*
Revd Mr *Salmon*, Rect. of *Ongar*, *Essex*.
Dr *Kennedy*, one of the Physicians to St *Thomas's* Hospital.
6. The Lady of *Wm Aislabie*, Esq; Representative for *Rippon* in *Yorkshire*; eldest Daughter of the late Earl of *Exeter*.
Mrs *Drew*, Widow, reputed worth 20,000l. which falls to her Son, an Attorney in the *Temple*.
7. The Relict of —— *Rouse*, Esq; reputed worth 50,000l.
The new-born Daughter of *William Aislabie*, Esq;
Mrs *Warren*, a Maiden Lady, in *Soho*, reputed worth 8000l.
Mr *Matthews*, Body-Coachman to her Majesty.
Mr *Maylin*, Brewer in *Southwark*.
8. *Thomas Walton*, Esq; at his House in *Pall-mall*.

Brig.

Brig. *Wallis*, of the 2d Troop of Guards.
9. *John Woolley*, Man-midwife, at *Sheilds*, aged 87. He left one Son and two Daughters, whom by his Will he cut off with a shilling a piece, and left his Estate to two Cousins. About 2 Years ago a Physician of *Exeter* in like manner left his Estate from his only Daughter.

Mr *Thomas Calvering*, a *Hamburgh* Merchant, at *Hummerton*.

Henry Moor, Esq; at *Walthamstow*, in the Commission of the Peace for *Essex*.

The Wife of Mr *William Mills*, the Comedian.

10. Revd Mr *Robert D'Oyly*, Rector of *Frierning*, in *Essex*. About a Year since he gave 300*l*. to the Corporation of the Sons of the Clergy, for the Maintenance of Clergymen's Widows, &c. A few Years since he published a Book, entitled, *Dissertations on God's permitting the Fall of Adam*, &c.

11. Mr *Clutterbuck*, an eminent Merchant of this City.

Revd Mr *Wilcox*, an eminent Dissenting Minister in this City.

12. The only Daughter of *John Sherwood*, Esq; at *Edmonton*.

15. The Relict of Sir *Henry Northcote*, Bart at *Barnstaple*.

18. The Relict of Dr *Gee*, late a Prebendary of *Westminster*.

19. *James Fullerton*, Esq; at *Wandsworth*. The Countess of *Orkney*.

Mr *Conyer*, Dyer, on *Bankside*, *Southwark*, reputed worth 60,000*l*.

Francis Piggott, Esq; at *Midhurst*, *Sussex*.

20. *Edw. Bradford*, Esq; at *Walcworth*.

Mrs *Mary Hancock*, of *Carey street*, a young Lady of 12,000*l*. Fortune.

21. Mr *Trueman*, Brewer in *Shoreditch*, reputed worth 10,000*l*.

Mr *John Thomas*, a noted Chymist, near *Temple-Bar*.

22. Mr *Larner*, Attorney at *Hoxton*.

Lady *Robinson*, at *Putney*, aged 92.

Sir *John Chetwode*, Bart at *Oakley* in *Staffordshire*, and is succeeded by his only Son Sir *Philip Touchet Chetwode*.

23. *John Greenwood*, Esq; at *Bethnal-Green*.

The Infant Daughter of Ld *Limerick*.

24. Col. *Morgan*, Deputy Governor of the *Isle of Wight*, and Representative for *Yarmouth*.

25. *Richard Richardson*, an Officer on Half pay.

John Prolock, Esq; of *Ipswich*, Counsellor at Law. Fearing he should be buried alive, he ordered his Coffin Lid to be made with Hinges, and 4 Persons to attend his Corpse 8 Days after Interment.

Mr *Blundel*, of *Hodsdon*, in *Hertfordshire*, formerly Wine Merchant.

26. Revd *Wm Tanner*, a Nonjuring Clergy man.

Revd Dr *Gatling*.

Mr *Lockman*, Dresser to his Majesty, and Page of the Back-stairs, dy'd lately at *Hanover*.

27. *Thomas Clarke*, Esq; in the Commission of the Peace for *Westminster*, reputed worth 20,000*l*. which devolves upon his Daughter, the Wife of Mr *Curtis*, Wine Merchant at *Lynn*.

28. Dr *Turbett*, a Fellow of the College of Physicians.

PROMOTIONS.

MR *Baker*, Gentleman to the Countess of *Deloraine*, appointed Page of the Back-Stairs to the Princesses *Mary* and *Louisa*.

Ld *Forbes*, appointed Minister Plenipotentiary to the *Czarina*.

Gabriel Johnston, Esq; made Governor of *North Carolina*, in the Room of *George Burrington*, Esq;

Mr *Hickford*, an Attorney, appointed Sollicitor (*pro tempore*) to the Lords of the Admiralty.

Mr *Primer*, formerly City Marshal, made Tipstaff to Mr Justice *Lee*.

The Ld Chief Baron *Reynolds*, declared Ld Chief Justice of the *King's Bench*.

Ensign *Campbel*, of the 3d Reg. of Foot Guards, appointed Capt. of a Company in Gen. *Grove's* Reg. at *Gibraltar*.

Mr *Seymour*, Cadet in the 3d Reg. to succeed Ensign *Campbel*.

Mr *Bernard Hawkins*, made Housekeeper to the Prince of *Wales*, with a Salary of 120*l. per Ann.*

Mr *John Hynd*, appointed Commissary Clerk of the Commissariot of *Dumfries*, in *North Britain*.

John Ld Murray, Brother to the D. of *Athol*, Lieut. in the 3d Reg. of Foot Guards.

Wm Earl *Cowper*, one of the Gentlemen of the Bed Chamber, in the room of the Ld *Clinton*.

John Thompson, Esq; one of the eight Clerks of the Court of *Exchequer*, in the room of *Benjamin Marriot*, Esq; decd.

Robert Reeve, Esq; a Judge in the Court of Common Pleas.

Tho. Abney, of the *Inner Temple*, Esq; Attorney Gen. of the Duchy of *Lancaster*, in the room of Mr Justice *Reeve*.

Counsellor *Comyns*, his Majesty's Counsel at Law for the said Duchy.

Counc. *Wright* made a Serjeant at Law.

M*s*

Mr *David Hopkins*, made Deputy Warden of the *Fleet*.

The Ld *Hinton*, eldeſt Son of E. *Pawlet*, Ld Lieutenant and Cuſtos Rotulorum of *Devonſhire*.

Capt. *Stevenſon* an Exempt ;

Capt. *Miller*, Brigadier ; and

Capt. *Hepden*, Sub-Brigadier in the 4th Troop of Guards.

Mr *Morris*, appointed one of the Surveyors of the Stores at *Plymouth*.

The Marquis of *Lothian*, his Majeſty's High Commiſſioner to the General Aſſembly of the Church of *Scotland*, which is to meet at *Edinburgh* the 3d of *May*.

Sir *Philip Tork*, choſen Governor of the *Charterhouſe*.

William Kinaſton, Eſq; Recorder of *Shrewsbury*

Mr *Mottram*, appointed Meſſenger in Ordinary to his Majeſty, in the room of Mr *Mottram* his Uncle, who reſign'd.

Mr *D'Oyley*, Nephew to *George Trenchard*, Eſq; Member for *Pool*, made Enſign in Gen. *Whetham's* Reg. of Foot.

Mr *Bromley*, Steward to *Hen.Pelham*, Eſq; made Cryer to the Court at *Hicks's-Hall*.

Mr *Lumley*, a younger Brother of the E. of *Scarborough*, appointed Enſign in Col. *Johnson's* Company in the 2d Regiment of Guards.

Wm Lankey, Eſq; appointed Steward to the D. of *Somerſet*.

Mr *Stephen Duck*, the famous Threſher and Poet, made one of the Yeomen of the Guards.

John King, Eſq; elected Coroner for *Middleſex*, in the Room of *George Rivers*, Eſq; who reſigned.

New MEMBERS.

JOHN *Myddelton*, Eſq; choſen Repreſentative for *Denbigh*.

Ld *Wallingford*, for *Banbury, Oxfordſh*

Eccleſiaſtical PREFERMENTS.

MR *Andrew Rockford*, Preſented to the Rect. of *Ottington, Herefordſh*.

Mr *John Feans*, : : to the Donative of *Wooburn, Bedfordſhire*.

Mr *Cartwright*, : : to the Living of *Ferrſey*.

Mr *Edward Hammond*, made Arch-Deacon of *Dorſet*.

Dr *Middleton*, choſen Lect. of St *Bride's*.

Diſpenſations have paſs'd the Seals to enable

Thomas Walk, A. M. of *Brazen Noſe* College, *Oxford*, to hold the Rectory of *Breyer*, in *Bedfordſhire*, with the Rectory

of *Wimmington* in the ſaid County.

John Libanus, A. M. of *Bennet* College, *Cambridge*, to hold the Vicarage of *Wickham*, in the *Iſle of Ely*, with the Vicarage of *Wickford* in the ſaid Iſle.

Thomas Walwyn, M. A. of *Pembroke* College, *Cambridge*, to hold the Vicarage of *Cudham, Kent*, with the Rectory of *Hays* in the ſaid County.

Wm North, M. A. to hold the Rectory of *Langford*, in *Eſſex*, with the Rectory of *Widford* in the ſaid County.

Edward Darby, M.A. to hold the Vicarage of *Woodford* in *Northamptonſh*. with the Rect. of *Edgcotte*, in the ſaid County.

Wm Sealy, M. A. to hold the Rectory of *Allington*, in *Wilts*, with the Rectory of *Bighton*, in *Hampſhire*.

Mr *Humphry Borough*, Chaplain to the E. of *Waldgrave*, to hold the Rectory of *Borley*, in *Eſſex*, [with the Vicarage of *Rede*, in *Suffolk*.

Philip Pipon, M. A. of *Oriel* College, *Oxford*, elected Maſter of the School at *Biſhop-Stortford*, in *Hertfordſhire*, upon the Reſignation of the Revd Mr *Tooke*.

James Hales, A. M. preſented to the Vicarage of *Chart Sutton*, in *Kent*.

John Anderſon, A. M. : : to the Rectory of *Shoreham*, in *Suſſex*.

Mr *Saintclear*, to the Rectory of *Wootten-Baſſet, Wilts*.

Mr *Price*, to the Vicarage of *Langexlah*, in the County of *Glamorgan*.

Mr *Agate*, choſen Reader and Schoolmaſter of the united Pariſhes of St *Mary Magdalen, Milk-ſt.* and St *Lawrence Jury*.

John Williams, D. D. preſented to the Rectory of *Highworth*, in *Hampſhire*.

Mr *Thomas Matthew*, to the Rectory of *Snelton*, in *Lincolnſhire*.

Mr *Smith*, Rector of *Stone* in *Bucks*, to the Rect. of *Hartwel* in that County.

Mr *Berks*, jun. preſented to the Living of *Tuxford* in *Nottinghamſhire*.

BANKRUPTS.

CHarles *Sandys* of *Brecon*, Mercer.

John Lewis of *Spittle, Warwick*, Malſter.

Patrick Crawford of *London*, Merchant.

Henry Popjay, of *Token-houſe Yard, London*, Merchant.

Thomas Paul of *Dartford, Kent*, Vintner.

Geo. *Cicetor* of *Cripplegate, Midds*, Chapman.

John Brown of *Houndſditch, London*, Grocer.

Henry Mackit of *Shadwell, Middx*. Mariner.

Wm Loyd of *Biſhopgateſt. London* Vintner.

Simon Wood of *Tonnmeſh, London*, Factor.

Alvery Baker of *St Giles Cripplegate, Middx*. Brewer.

Tho. Hartlet of *Shipperton, Middx*. Farmer.

FROM *Berlin*, That the Margravine of *Anſpach*, whoſe Conſort is Brother to the Q. of *Gr. Britain*, was ſafely deliver'd of a Prince.

From *Bruſſels*, That the French were preparing to make a handſome convenient Port of *Graveling*, ſituate between *Dunkirk* and *Calais*.

From *Milan*, That the Court of *Spain* demands of the Emperor the Reſtitution of *Rocca-Gulielma* in the Kingdom of *Naples*, which is reckon'd a Fund of 260,000 Crowns.

From *Naples*, That the little Territory of *Caſa Nova* in *Calabria*, was, by an Earthquake, ſunk 29 Feet into the Earth, without throwing down a Houſe. The Inhabitants being warn'd by a prodigious Noiſe in the Air, eſcaped into the Fields, and only 5 Perſons were kill'd.

From *Verſailles*, That Monſ. the Duke of *Anjou*, died there the 7th Inſt. aged two Years, 7 Months, and 8 Days being Born *Auguſt* 30, 1730.

From *Conſtantinople*, That a great Body of Turks, which were marching to ſuccour *Babylon*, had been defeated by the *Perſians*, who afterwards made themſelves Maſters of that great and populous City. 'Tis added, that the late depoſed Sultan *Achmet* had, within a few Months, loſt four of his Children, *viz.* 2 Princes, and 2 Princeſſes, the Occaſion of their Deaths being unknown.

From *Paris*, That the Card. *de Fleury* lately accoſted the Queen after this manner; Madame, " The King your Conſort is as deſirous as your Majeſty to ſee the King your Father upon the Throne of *Poland*: He will ſpare for nothing to bring it about: The *Polanders* can tell you, how many Millions *France* has already ſcatter'd among them; and we have had Recourſe to all the Negotiations Policy ſuggeſted: We have even gone too far; for a Declaration of the King's has made all *Europe* tremble: People every where imagin'd they ſaw the four Quarters of it in Flames: But, *Madame*, the Affairs o *France* will not permit her to proceed farther: If Money and Perſuaſion will not do, we cannot pretend to make uſe of Force".

From *Seville*, That Don *Joſeph Patinbo*, Prime Miniſter to the K. of *Spain*, was in Diſgrace.

From *Vienna*, That the Affairs in Diſpute about *Don Carlos* are accommodated by Mediation of *Great Britain*.

From *Breſ.ia*, That the Maſter of a Band of Muſick belonging to the Cathedral of that City, died there, after a Life ſo abſtemious, that he had eaten nothing for 32 Years paſt but Herbs boil'd with a little Salt over a Lamp, having never once in that Time had any Fire. His dead Body being expoſed to the View of the Populace, a Woman, who had been a long Time Lame in both her Hands, no ſooner touch'd the Corpſe but ſhe was immediately cur'd, and ſeveral others, many Years Blind. A Surgeon no ſooner made an Inciſion in the Body, but the Blood iſſued in a Stream; which ſo far confirm'd the Reputation of the New Saint, that if a Detachment of Soldiers had not been ſent for to guard the Body, it had been pull'd to Pieces by the Populace out of pure Devotion for the Sake of the Reliéts.

From *Warſaw*, That all the Lodgings in that City were taken up by *French* Gentlemen of Diſtinétion. At an Entertainment the *French* Embaſſador gave, he not only dealt out great Quantities of Viétuals to the Populace, but made a conſiderable Preſent to each of the *Poliſh* Lords invited.

From *Parma*, That *Don Carlos* meeting the Hoſt as it was carried thro' the Cities to a poor Woman, he got out of his Coach, and accompany'd it on Foot to the Chamber where the ſick Perſon lay, when having ador'd it, he retired, leaving a Purſe of Money upon the poor Woman's Table.

From *Paris*, That the Parliament has publiſhed an Arret, ſuppreſſing ſeveral Books, wherein the *Conſtitution Unigtnitus* is propoſed as the *Rule of Faith*, and has ordered a Proſecution to be commenced againſt two Pariſh Prieſts, for refuſing the Sacrament to certain of their Pariſhioners on Account of their being *Appellants* from the ſaid *Conſtitution*.

Cadiz, That 4 Sallee Rovers had put to Sea, with Deſign to make Prize of all fhriſtian Veſſels they can maſter, without reſpeét to any Nation.

From *Frankfort*, That the Princeſs, only Daughter of the late *Margrave* of *Bareith*, who had for ſome Time profeſſed the Roman Catholick Religion, embraced the Proteſtant Faith on Thurſday in Faſter Week, and received the Communion the ſame Day at *Bareith*, from the Hands of a Proteſtant Miniſter.

Towards the End of the Month.

Course of Exchange.	STOCKS	*Monthly* BILL *of Mortality, from* March 27. *to* Apr. 24.
Amsterdam — 35 *a* 34	S. Sea 102 $\frac{1}{4}$	Christned { Males 682 / Females 708 } 1380
Ditto at Sight 34 10	—Annu. 111	Buried { Males 1158 / Femal. 1140 } 2298
Hamburgh — 34	Bank 150 $\frac{1}{4}$	Died under 2 Years old — 1003
Rotterdam — 35 1 $\frac{1}{4}$	India 158 $\frac{1}{8}$	Between 2 and 5 — 215
Antwerp — 35 5	3 *per C. Ann.* 102 $\frac{1}{4}$	Between 5 and 10 — 80
Madrid — 42 $\frac{1}{2}$	M. Bank 116	Between 10 and 20 — 60
Bilboa — 41 $\frac{3}{4}$	African 28 *to* 30	Between 20 and 30 — 129
Cadiz — 41 $\frac{7}{8}$	York Buil. no Transf.	Between 30 and 40 — 199
Venice — 49	Royal Aff. 107 $\frac{1}{2}$	Between 40 and 50 — 186
Leghorn — 50 $\frac{1}{8}$	Lon. ditto 13	Between 50 and 60 — 161
Genoa — 53 $\frac{1}{8}$	Eng. Copp. 1*l.* 18*s.*	Between 60 and 70 — 117
Paris — 32 $\frac{1}{8}$	Welsh ditto 1*l.* 10*s.*	Between 70 and 80 — 77
Bourdeaux — 31	Bank Cir. 6*l.* 10*s.*	Between 80 and 90 — 54
Oporto — 5 4 $\frac{1}{2}$	India Bonds 5*l.* 7*s.*	Between 90 and 106 — 17
Lisbon — 5 5 $\frac{1}{4}$ *a* 4 $\frac{1}{4}$	3 *p. Cent* ditto 2*l.* 10	2298
Dublin — 11 $\frac{3}{8}$	S. Sea ditto 2*l.* 14*s.*	

Price of Grain at *Bear-Key, per* Qr.		Buried.	Weekly Burials
Wheat 23*s.* to 25*s.*	P. Malt 20*s.* to 22*s.*	Within the walls, 184	*April* 3 — 576
Rye 12*s.* to 16*s.*	B Malt 16*s.* to 19*s.*	Without the walls, 715	10 — 541
Barley 13*s.* to 17*s.* 0*d.*	Tares 20*s.* to 22*s.*	In Mid and Surry, 903	17 — 603
Oats 11*s.* to 16*s.*	H. Pease 16*s.* to 18*s.*	City and Sub of Westm. 496	24 — 578
Pease 18*s.* to 20*s.*	H. Beans 18*s.* to 22*s.*		

Prices of Goods, &c. in *London.* Hay 1*l.* 16*s.* to 2*l.* 0*s.* a Load.

Coals per Chaldron 25s. to 26s.
Old Hops per Hun. 3l. to 6l.
New Hops 9l. to 10l.
Rape Seed 10l. to 11l. per Last
Lead the Fodder 14 Hun. 1 half on board, 14l. to 16l. 00s.
Tin in Blocks 4l. 00s.
Ditto in Bars 4l. 02s. exclusive of 3s. per Hun. Duty.
Copper Eng. best 5l. 05s. per C.
Ditto ord. 4l. 16s. to 5l. per C.
Ditto Barbary 70l. to 80l.
Iron of Bilboa 14l. 10s. per Tun
Dit. of Sweden 15l. 10s. per Tun
Town Tallow 31s. 35s. per C.
Country Tallow 30s. to 34s.

Grocery Wares.

Raisins of the Sun 30s. 0d. per C.
Ditto Malaga Frailes 19s.
Ditto Smirna new 21s.
Ditto Alicant, none
Ditto Lipra new 19s.
Ditto Belvedera 20s.
Currants old none
Ditto new 45s.
Prunes French 18s.
Figs 20s.
Sugar Powd. best 54s. a 59s. per C.
Ditto second sort 46s. to 50s. per C.
Loaf Sugar double refine 8d. Half-penny a 9d. per lb.
Ditto single refin. 56s. to 64s. per C.
Cinamon 7s. 8d. per lb.
Cloves 9s. 1d.
Mace 15s. 0d. per lb.
Nutmegs 8s. 7d. per lb.
Sugar Candy white 14d. to 18d.
Ditto brown 6d. per lb.
Pepper for Home cons. 16d. Farth.
Ditto for exportation 12d. half-p.
Tea Bohea fine 10s. to 12s. per lb.
Ditto ordinary 9s. to 10s. per lb.
Ditto Congo 10s. to 14s. per lb.
ditto Pekoe 14s. a 16s. per lb.
ditto Green fine 9s. to 12s. per lb.
ditto Imperial 9s. to 12s. per lb.
ditto Hyson 30s. to 35s.

Drugs *by the lb.*

Balsom Peru 14s. to 15s.
Cardamoms 3s. 3d.
Camphire refin'd 18s.
Crabs Eyes 1s. 8d.
Jallop 3s.
Manna 26s. a 4s.
Mastick white 3s. 6d. to 4s.
Opium 9s. 00d.
Quicksilver 4s.
Rhubarb fine 25s. a 28s.
Sarsaparilla 3s. 0d.
Saffron Eng. 27s. 00d.
Wormseeds none
Balsom Capaiva 2s. 6d.
Balsam of Gillead 20s. 00d.
Hipocacuana 5s.
Ambergreece per oz. 8s.
Cochineal 18s. 3d. per lb.

Wine, Brandy, *and* Rum.

Oporto red, per Pipe 36l.
ditto white 24l.
Lisbon red 35l. a 40l.
ditto white, 26l.
Sherry 26l.
Canary new 30l.
ditto old 36l.
Florence 3l. 3s per Chest
French red 30l. a 40l.
ditto white 20l.
Mountain malaga old 24l.
ditto new 20 to 21l.
Brandy Fr. per Gal. 6s. to 6s. 8d.
Rum of Jamaica *7s. to 9s.*
ditto Low. Islands 6s. 4d.
Spirits Eng. 30l. per Ton.

GOLD in Bars, 3*l.* 18*s.* 4*d.*—Ditto in Coin 3*l.* 18*s.* 3*d.* to 4*l.* 1*s.*—SILVER in Bars, Standard, 5*s.* 4*d.* half-penny.—Pillar Pieces of Eight 5*s.* to 5*s.* 5*d.* 3 farth. ditto Mexico 5*s.* 5*d.* 3 farth.

A REGISTER of BOOKS publish'd in APRIL, 1733.

THE State of the Ecclesiastical Courts delineated. With some Remarks on the Resolutions of the Committee appointed by Parliament for their Inspection and Reformation. And the Method of Proceeding in the Ecclesiastical Courts compar'd with Trials by Juries at the Common Law. Printed for J. Brotherton.

2. A Just Imitation of the First Satire of the Second Book of Horace. In a Dialogue between Mr Pope and the Ordinary of Newgate. Printed for W. Mears, pr. 6d.

3. The Life and genuine Character of Dr Swift written by himself. Printed for J. Roberts, pr. 1s.

4. A Sermon in Vindication of our Saviour's frequent Use of Parables. occasion'd by an Objection in Christianity as old as the Creation. By Edward Sandercock, Printed for Theodore Sanders.

5. A proper Reply to a Lady, occasion'd by Verses address'd to the Imitator of the First Satire of the Second Book of Horace. by a Gentleman. Printed for T. Osborne, pr. 6d.

6. An Epistle to Mr Pope; Occasion'd by Bentley's Milton, and Theobald's Shakelpear. Printed for L. Gilliver.

7. Ulysses, an Opera. Printed for J. Watts, price 1s.

8. An impartial Catechism; or a Faithful Enquiry into some principal Things of the Christian Religion : Wherein all that is Humane is duly consider'd and fully exposed without Prejudice, Priestcraft, or Party Views. By Newman Darash. Sold by J. Roberts.

9. The Proceedings at the Old Baily for the City of London, and County of Middlesex, on the 4th, 5th, 6th, and 7th, of April.

10. Observations on the Life of Cicero. Printed for L. Gilliver.

11. A new Essay on Muscular Motion. Founded on Experiments, and Observations on the Newtonian Philosophy. By Browne Langrish Surgeon. Printed for A. Bettesworth. pr. 2s.

12. The Clerk's English Tutor, shewing the Practice of the Courts of King's Bench and Common Pleas, as they are now settled. With great Variety of English Precedents, conformable to the Statute 4 Geo. II. C. 26.

13. The sly Subscription; or the N—b Monarch, &c. With Sir Briton's Speech to Sir Politick. Printed for T. Tibbit, pr. 1s.

14. The fair Suicide; being an Epistle from a young Lady to the Person who was the Cause of her Death. To which is add'd some Verses occasion'd by the foregoing Epistle, by a Gentleman. Printed for R. Wellington, pr. 6d.

15. A Letter from a Layman to the Author of a Sermon preach'd by a Layman at Lincoln's-Inn, Jan. 30. 1733. pr. for T. Payne, pr. 6d.

16. Memoirs of Affairs of State ; Containing Letters written by Ministers employ'd in Foreign Negotiations, from the Year 1697, to the latter end of 1708. With Treaties, &c. publish'd by Christian Cole, Esq; some time Resident at Venice. Sold by Mess. Bettesworth and Hitch.

17. Some Reasons, in a Letter to a Member of Parliament, setting forth the Defect of our Laws in the Punishment of execrable Murders, and for changing that of Hanging into something more severe. Pr. for J. Roberts, pr. 4d.

18. Idea Juris Scotici ; or, a summary View of the Laws of Scotland. In three Parts. Correspondent to Persons, Rights, and Actions.

19. The True History of Dr Robin Sublimate, and his Associates; or, Bob turn'd Physician. Wherein the whole Art and Mystery of a certain kind of Quackery is fully laid open, &c. Printed for T. Jones in the Strand, pr. 6d.

20. The Projector's Looking Glass ; being the last dying Words and Confession of, &c. Printed by T. Tibbett, pr. 6d.

21. The young Christian's Prayer Book. Dedicated to the young People in Birmingham, and at Coseley. By Samuel Bourn. London: Printed for R. Hett, in the Poultry, 1733. (Pr. Stitch'd in Blue Paper, 1s. 6d. Bound 2s.)

22. The Standard of Equality in Subsidiary Taxes and Payments, or a just and strong Preserver of publick Liberty. Printed for J. Dickenson, pr. 6d.

23. A Reply to the Vindication of the Representation of the Case of the Planters of Tobacco in Virginia. In a Letter to Sir I. R. from the Merchants of Lond. Pr for R. Charlton, pr. 1s.

24. French Excise; or, a Compendious Account of the several Excises in France, and of the Oppressive methods of collecting them. Printed for M. Smith, pr. 1s.

25. Seasonable Reflections, occasion'd by the Bills expected in Parliament, relating to the Duties on Wine and Tobacco. Printed for J. Critchley, pr. 6d.

26. Remarks on a Bill now depending in Parliament, intitled, For the better regulating the Proceedings of Ecclesiastical Courts. By a Right Revd Prelate. Printed for G. Sumtor, pr. 6d.

27. The Returning our Spirits to him that gave them. A Funeral Sermon occasion'd by the Death of the late Revd Mr Daniel Wilcox. By James Wood. Pr. for John Oswald, pr. 6d.

28. The Ordinary of Newgate's Account of the Malefactors executed at Tyburn the 25 instant. 6d.

29. The Duty of Gratitude to God and Man. A Sermon preach'd on Sunday, Feb. 11. 1732-3. in the Parish Church of Gravesend, destroy'd by Fire in 1727, and since rebuilt by Act of Parliament. By Thomas Harris, M. A. Printed for J. Roberts, pr. 4d.

30. Sermons on several Subjects. By James Foster. Printed for J. Noon.

31. The Commodity Excised ; or, the Women in an Uproar. A new Ballad Opera, as it will be privately acted in the Secret Apartments of l'Intineer

ners and Tobacconisti. By Timothy Smoke. Printed for the Author, pr. 6d.

32. *Rome Excis'd. A new Tragi-Comi-Bal-lad Opera. Printed for the Bookfellers, pr. 1. 6d.*

33. *An Excise Elegy: or, the Dragon over-thrown. A new Ballad, pr. 6d.*

34. *The City Triumphant: or, the Burning of the Excise-Monster. A new Ballad, pr. 6d.*

35. *Sedition, a Poem. Pr. for J. Rob. pr. 6d.*

36. *An Essay on Man. Epistle II. Printed for J. Wilford, pr. 1s.*

37. *A Song by the then Poet Laureat in Praise of Milk, as it was sung before K. Charles the second and the whole Court on May Day, occasion'd by Edmund the Gardener getting Rose the Dairy Maid with Child. Printed for J. Roberts, pr. 3d.*

38. *Robin's Progress in eight Scenes; from his coming to Town, to his present Situation. With Mr Frank Lyn's Remarks thereon, pr. 1s.*

39. *Augusta Triumphans: or, London and Liberty. Verses schosen'd by the Citizens Petition on Tuesday the 3d of April 1733, against the Bill for the further Extension of the Excise, pr. 6d.*

ADVERTISEMENTS.

Now in the Press, the fourth Edition of

NO. X. and No. XI. of the *Gentleman's Magazine*, in the former of which was the remarkable Will of *Samuel Travers*, Esq; not printed elsewhere; and the latter containing, among other Things, the Dispute about the Common Council of *London* refusing Leave to erect a Statue to K. *William*. Tho' we cannot at present furnish Gentlemen with one of these Numbers singly, we have a few Sets bound both in Large Paper and Small.——Not only the abovemention'd Will of Mr *Travers* was originally Printed in our *Magazine*, but likewise the following Pieces, several of which have been well receiv'd. On Mrs *Oldfield*. Ld *Carteret* and Speaker *Onslow* compared. Epigram on a Lady stung by a Bee. Gossip's Tale. Lady's Delight. A Winter's Thought. The House-keeper, a Tale. A Dialogue on the Times. A short Table, shewing what Stamps are requir'd by Act of Parliament for any Instrument or Writing whatever. See No. 3. The Amorous Duellists. Bath Beauties. On Dice. Farewel to *Bath*. On Love. E. of *Leicester's* remarkable Letter in Q. *Elizabeth's* Reign, to the Borough of *Andover*. See No. 8. Cure for the Gout. On the Nativity of Christ. Complaint to *Dorinda*. Elegiac Song on the Death of *Edward Bell*, Esq; Spring Gardens. Irish Bishop. Sweeper's Courtship. To a Lady on her Grotto. Epilogue. Translation of Mr *Parry's* Account of *Carolina*, and his Proposals for making a Settlement there. See p. 1020. Verses by a Gentleman. The Trial of *Eleanor Beare* of *Derby*. To a Painter, drawing the Poet's Mistress. A Taylor's Will, in *Ilchester* Goal. On being expell'd a Lady's Company. *Anna* & *Carolina*. To *Nathaniel Payler Monckton*, Esqr The Mock Lover. The Shepherd's Complaint. Trustees for the Colony of *Georgia*, with their Places of A-bode. A Dialogue between a Beau's Head and his Heels. The Miser. Mr *Thompson's* Conditions for surrendering himself; tran-scribed from us into a Daily Paper. Love in V——. Love and Friendship, and three Answers. *Integer Vita*, &c. translated. Tobacco, a Tale. The first of *March*, Latin and English. Old Man and Ass, a Fable abridg'd. *Hor. ad Lydiam*, translated by Bp *Atterbury*. On Mr *Pope*. Acrostick on the Nakedamians. On Presenting an Irish Boy to the present Ld Mayor. Verses by the E. of O——y, to Mrs B——r. On the Return of the Sun. Two Kentish Freeholders. On Excises, &c.

Just publish'd,

For the Use of Families, beautifully printed in Two Volumes in Octavo, adorned with 34 Copper Plates, engraven by Mr Sturt,

DUPIN's EVANGELICAL HISTORY, Or, the Records of the Son of God, and their Veracity, demonstrated in the Life and Acts of our blessed Lord and Saviour Jesus Christ, and his Holy Apostles. Wherein the Life of the blessed Jesus is related in all its Circumstances according to the Order of time. His Parables, Miracles, and Sufferings set in a just Light, and defended from all Oppositions, of wicked and designing Men.

Printed for R. *Ware*, at the Bible and Sun in Amen Corner, near Paternoster-Row, pr. 8s.

Also may be had at the same Place.

I. The large House Bibles, Folio, with six Maps of Geography, and a brief Concordance for the more easy finding out of the Places therein contained. By *Joseph Dowbame*, M.A. Bound in Calf Leather——1l. 8s. per Book, And with Mr *Sturt's* Cuts 2l. 5s. ditto On fine Paper with Cuts——3l 3s. ditto.

II. The History of the Old and New Testament. Extracted from the sacred Scriptures. To which are added, the Lives, Travels and Sufferings of the Apostles; with an exact Historical Chronology of such Matters as are related in the Holy Bible. Illustrated with Two Hundred Sixty Cuts, in Folio. By R. *Blomer*. price 2l. 10s.

III. A Treatise of Architecture, with Remarks and Observations. By that excellent Master thereof, *Sebastian le Clerk*, Knight of the Empire, Designer and Engraver to the Cabinet of the French King, and Member of the Academy of Arts and Sciences, necessary for young People who would apply to that noble Art. Engraven in two Hundred Copper Plates. By *John Sturt*. Translated by *Chambers*. pr. 10s. 6d.

The Gentleman's *Magazine:*

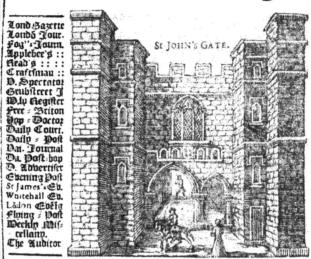

ST JOHN'S GATE.

Lond Gazette
Lond's Jour.
Fog's Journ.
Appleber's ::
Read's :: ::
Craftsman ::
D. Spectator
Grubstreet J
Wkly Register
Free = Briton
Hyp = Doctor
Daily Court.
Daily = Post
Dai. Journal
Dai Post-boy
D. Advertiser
Evening Post
St James's Eb.
Whitehall Eb.
Lndon Ebsg
Flying = Post
Weekly Mis-
cellany.
The Auditor

York = News
Dublin 6 :::
Edinburgh 2
Bristol :: ::
Norwich 2 ::
Exeter 2 : ::
Worcester ::
Northampton
Gloucester ::
Stamford ::
Nottingham
Bury Town
Chester ditto
Derby ditto
Ipswich dit.
Reading dit.
Leeds Merc.
Newcastle C.
Canterbury :
Birmingham
Manchester
Boston ::: ¶
Jamaica &c.
Barbados ::

Or, MONTHLY INTELLIGENCER,

For MAY, 1733.

CONTAINING,

/more in Quantity, and greater Variety, than any Book of the Kind and Price/

I. A view of the WEEKLY ESSAYS, *viz.* The ungrateful Lover; old Age not contemptible; Moral Reflections upon Arts and Sciences; of Superstition; Contemplation, and the Works of Nature; of Clandestine Marriages; Infidelity; Penitence of Mr *John Hampden*; a Lady in a Strait betwixt two; the Fiddlefaddle Club; of Freethinking, a young Master of 68; Mr *Rich* vindicated; the Church of *England* defended; Maternal Cruelty; of Charity Schools.

II. POLITICAL POINTS, *viz.* Of Parliaments, People, and Parties; of Impostors and Projectors; Monosyllables; On the Marriage concluded between the Prince of *Orange* and the Princess Royal, their Characters and Fortunes;

of giving up Ministers; the late Tumults at *Westminster* censur'd and defended; the Lord Mayor and Baron *Thompson*; Legality of the late publick Rejoycings canvass'd; Debates in Parliament, relating to the Charitable Corporation; Vindication of a Paragraph relating to the E. of *Ch---d*; refuted; the Case of our Sugar Colonies stated; Druggists Petition, &c. &c.

III. POETICAL PIECES. A Scene in *Zaire*; of Infidelity; Fate of Womankind; to a Lady; on *Maryland*; W. and P. Epigrams; Songs, &c. &c.

IV. OCCURRENCES FOREIGN and DOMESTIC; Prices of Goods, &c.

V. REGISTER of Books.

VI. Table of CONTENTS.

By *SYLVANUS URBAN*, Gent.

LONDON: Printed for the AUTHOR, and sold at St *John's Gate*: By F. *Jefferies*, in *Lugate-street*, at the Pamphlet Shops; and by most Booksellers.

CONTENTS.

THE
Gentleman's Magazine:
MAY, 1733.

A View of the Weekly DISPUTES and ESSAYS in this Month.

The Auditor. May 1. No. 33.
Amor omnibus idem.   Ovid.

Mr AUDITOR,

Have lived 5 Years with a Man I entirely loved; he always used me with Complaisance; but above half the Time has been in the Country; and then I could never hear from him; it is now six Months since I saw him, when he assur'd me he should return in 3 Days. I cannot help having the greatest Regard for this Ingrate, tho' had I never known him, I should not have been what I shall ever remain, the most wretched of all living Things. I beg your Advice, which when he reads in your Paper, he may have a little more Regard for the Person he has ruined.

DIANA NONESUCH.

I find *Diana* is one of *Fidelio's* Band of Lovers. I have always observ'd that *Love* has made more Wretches than *Hymen*. She is fallen into the general Mistake of her Sex, and flatters herself it is possible to revive a dying Passion. When once we cease to love, we cease for ever. Let *Diana* convince herself of this Truth, and alter her Conduct and Opinion, and not flatter herself she can ever recall the *kit Vagus*.

Mr AUDITOR,

I Was born in the last Century, and have gone thro' a good Number of Years with the Esteem of many, the true Friendship of a worthy Few, and ever declined above two thirds of the *Parties of Plea-*

sure propos'd to me; holding it as a constant Maxim, to spend at least one half of my Time in keeping Company with myself. Thus did I hope to go on; but find an unspeakable Alteration in the Ways and Manners of People towards me. If I walk in publick the Women cast a disdainful Stare at me; and the Men cry with Contempt, *What an old Hag?* The worthy Friends I mentioned being dead, I thought to replace them among those I believed my *Contemporaries*; but the Repetition of trivial Events, favourite Stories of themselves, and a *chronical Distemper paraphrased on*, were the constant Conversation I met with; which, however, confirm'd me in an Opinion, that a Life misspent is the greatest Evil; for in old Age, how greatly entertaining and improving would Those be, who had made a good Use of it? I left them, to see if I could be better entertained among the young Folks; but soon had enough of these. As soon as I came into a Room, my Dress made them burst into a Laughter. My Shape (being a Yard shorter than the Fashion) added to their Entertainment.—Pray, Sir, is old Age *contemptible*, or *shameful*, if unattended with *Youthful Affectation*, extravagant *Passions*, or *Vice?* I am reduced to shelter myself in Solitude, tho' I am fond of Society. Pray tell young People they may chance to grow old; and old People they have lived to very little Purpose. CONSTANTIA ISSOLEA.

Mr AUDITOR,

AN odd sort of a Fellow walks by our Door every Day very fast, in a plain Frock, a Hat two Inches higher in the Brim than any Body's in the World, with

the

the Addition of a rusty silver Lace, a dark Bob Wig without Powder, and I believe a dirty Shirt; he puts one out of Countenance by staring in one's Face, then snuffs his Nose, and walks off——Some believe he is a Spy; others, a Money-Lender, and is constantly watching to see if none of his Debtors are running away. My Mama's Maid told me, she believ'd he was cross'd in Love; but there does not seem Softness enough in his Composition to be sensible of that tender Passion: I rather fancy, he is the *wandering Jew*, so much talk'd of in the Country. - Pray, Sir, don't he ought to be taken up, and made to give an Account of himself? I assure you, not a Maid-Servant about *Temple-Bar*, will go out after 'tis dark, for fear of the black Man.   BIDDY CURIOUS.

This individual Person is my Friend *Tom Oynick*, who happening to stumble into the Company of some Ladies, by the help of his *Eccho's* heard himself convey'd to the whole Company under the Denomination of the *wandering Jew*. Tom was pleas'd at the Conjectures about him, but a little picqued at being thought incapable of Love in it's nicest Delicacy. *Frank Easy* took this Opportunity to be very merry with the Austerity of my Friend's Appearance. *Tom* made him no Answer; but desir'd me to acquaint my Female Correspondent, that if Beauty could make such a rough Clown as *Cymon* attempt such heroick Actions as he did for the sake of his *Iphigenia*, she would not be so severe a Critick, as to think the Addition of a little Sense would be any Obstacle to the feeling a Passion that affects the Mind equally with the Body.

Free Briton, May 3, No. 180.
Remarks on Fog's *Journal*, of Feb. 10.

SInce the *Craftsman* makes such a Design as an *Assassination*, the Subject of Ridicule, (see p. 191 B 203 E) I shall, says *Walsingham*, make some Extracts from the REMARKS on *Fog's Journal*, of Feb. 10, exciting the People to an *Assassination*. (see p. 72.)

Upon reading the said *Journal*, it appears to be a *Panegyrick upon* ASSASSINATIONS, a regular Scheme of Vengeance and Destruction against the present Ministers. It came in Consequence of a long Series of Papers published in that *Journal* to asperse those Ministers as Enemies of Liberty, who are its Bulwarks and Guardians. And that the *Writers of Fog* might

shew that they could equal their *Falsehood* with *Cruelty*, they proceeded in this barbarous Paper of *Feb.* 12. to shew how the Ministers (or in *Fog's* defamatory Meaning the *Enemies of Liberty*) are to be taken off, that is, by butchering the *Principal Minister*.

Vasconcellos, it seems, was *Prime Minister of Portugal*; a lawless Tyrant in an arbitrary Kingdom. Him *Fog* would make, without the least Resemblance of Character, the Parallel of a lawful Minister in a free Country, and would defame Sir *R—t W—e*, as a *Vasconcellos*, that his End may be as tragical as his. The Steps to the Massacre of *Vasconcellos* are minutely described as an instructive Story, how a few *Gentlemen* of Courage and Spirit may rescue their Country from Slavery.   What a Scene of Butchery and low Barbarity hath this *bloody Miscreant* proposed as fit for a brave and humane People to practise! And what End is this execrable Cruelty to procure? The End, *Fog* says, is the transferring of the Crown. The Death of the Minister is desired as an Expedient to dethrone the King. So that, in the Opinion of the *Jacobites* themselves, Sir *R—t W—le's Assassination* is now the only *Chance* the *Pretender* hath.

Monstrous and horrible Design! How unlike that of the *Portugueze!* They shook off a foreign Yoke. This Design is to impose a *Popish Prince* upon a *Protestant People*; and to *Sacrifice a King* who holds his *Crown* by the same Tenure, as his People hold their Liberties.

The *Auditor*, May 4. No. 34.

THis Paper is a Journal of a Voyage to the Island of ARTS. The first Port the Voyager landed at was that of *Encouragement*, in the Island is a beautiful Village called *Perfection*, and the only Residence of the Deputy Governors, who are called *Masters*. The Traveller was so delighted with the Beauty, Order, Harmony, and Proportion, that appear'd in the various Objects of the Place, that he had no Desire to return to the Island of *Happiness*. (see p. 131) upon which his Friend *Morality* thus dissuaded him;

If you weigh the agreeable Charms which here so much engage your Admiration, in the Balance with *Eternity*, of what Use are they to it? Something more Divine should lead us thro' this short Stage of Life, to that Place where we shall discern the Circuit of the whole Creation. Yet I would not advise you totally to deprive yourself of these innocent Amusements, only so to value them, that they do not prove a Snare to you in your Passage to Futurity.   Grubs

Grubstreet Journal, May 3. No. 175.
Of Superstition, Reliques, &c.

Mr BAVIUS,

THERE has been lately published a Posthumous Piece, intitled *Observations upon the Prophecies of* Daniel *and the Apocalypse of* St John, by Sir ISAAC NEWTON. On *Chap.* XI. 38, 39, of *Daniel* he observes, The Heathens were delighted with the Festivals of their Gods; and unwilling to part with those Ceremonies; therefore *Gregory,* Bp of *Neocæsarea* in *Pontus,* to facilitate their Conversion, instituted annual Festivals to the Saints and Martyrs; hence the keeping of *Christmas* with Ivy, Feasting, Plays and Sports, came in the room of the *Bacchanalia* and *Saturnalia*; the celebrating *May-Day* with Flowers, in the room of the *Floralia*; and the Festivals to the Virgin *Mary, John* the Baptist, and divers of the Apostles, in the room of the Solemnities at the Entrance of the Sun into the Signs of the Zodiac in the old Julian Calendar. In the Persecution of *Decius, Cyprian* order'd the Passions of the Martyrs in *Africa* to be register'd, in order to celebrate their Memories annually with Oblations and Sacrifices. This disposed Christians towards such a further Veneration of the Dead, as shortly ended in the Invocation of Saints, by attributing to their dead Bodies, Bones, and Reliques, a Power of working Miracles. In propagating these Superstitions, the Ring-Leaders were the Monks, and ANTONY was at the Head of them: For in the End of *Anthony's* Life, *Athanasius* relates these were his dying Words to his Disciples, *Do you take care to adhere to* Christ *in the first place, and then to the Saints, that after Death they may receive you as Friends and Acquaintance into the everlasting Tabernacles. Think upon these things, perceive these things, and if you have any regard to me, remember me as a Father.* This could not but inflame the Monks with Devotion towards the Saints. Hence came that Noise about the Miracles done by the Reliques of the Saints in the Time of *Constantius*; and hence *Athanasius,* by a prophetick Spirit, hid the Bones of *John* the Baptist from the Heathens, in the hollow Wall of a Church, that they might be profitable to future Generations."

In order to refute this heavy Charge unfairly quoted by Sir *Isaac,* against *Antony,* it will be necessary to give the latter part of his Life, writ by *Athanasius.*

" The Egyptians loved to bury the Bodies of good Men, especially of Martyrs, and wrap them in Linnen; yet not to hide them in the Earth, but to place them on Beds, and to keep them in their Houses; thinking they thereby honour the Departed. But *Antony* frequently desir'd the Bishops to inform the People better concerning this Practice. And fearing lest they should do to his Body in the same manner, he retir'd to the inner Part of the Mountain where he formerly resided; and there falling sick, he exhorted his two Disciples, who had attended him in that ascetick Life 15 Years, to persevere in the Doctrines and Faith they had received from him, to avoid Conversation with Schismaticks: and *rather* to adhere to *Christ in the first place* &c. (repeating the Words above recited) after which adding, " Do not suffer any to take my Body into *Egypt,* left they should deposite it in their Houses. For upon this very Account I came hither. Do you bury my Body, and let no one, except yourselves, know the Place."

Now let the impartial Reader judge of Sir *Isaac's* Assertion, " that *Antony* was at the Head of the Monks, who were Ringleaders in propagating several Superstitions; particularly in attributing to dead Bodies, Bones, and other Reliques of Saints and Martyrs, the Power of working Miracles." So far from it, that he declared it unlawful to keep such dead Bodies above Ground, and took particular precaution in relation to his own.

It is supposed, in excuse of Sir *Isaac,* that this Work of his was an unfinish'd Piece.   Yours, *Ecclesiasticus.*

London Journal. May 5. N° 723.
Of the Parliament, People, and Parties.

THO' the *highest Regard* is due to the Rights and Liberties of the People, yet a *just Regard* is owing to the Constitution; two Parts of which, *viz. King* and *Lords,* are *hereditary.* So that the People have no Power properly their own, but the *House of Commons,* which ought to be rever'd as the best and greatest Security of our Properties.

The late *indecent* Treatment of this August Assembly, makes it necessary to say something concerning their *Rights* with respect to the *People:* For tho' the *Craftsman* says, " the *late Scheme* was crushed by *so high an Authority* as that of the *People,* and by the *original Power* of the People in their *collective* Body," a notion abfolutely *democratical*, yet there is but *One Authority* in this Kingdom, That of *King, Lords*, and *Commons* making Laws; not have the People any *Authority* againft or over the Legiflature; for while the *Conftitution* is preferved, the *original Power* of the People in their *collective* Body can't exert itfelf, or have a *Being*, becaufe it's *loft* and *fwallow'd up* in their *Reprefentatives*, whom they chufe to *judge* and *act* for them. For tho' the People may *petition* or *modeftly reprefent*, yet the Members are to act according to their *own Judgments*. They are not (as a *certain Perfon* ignorantly faid) the *Attornies* or *Creatures* of the People, but are chofen for their fuperior Underftandings, Abilities, and Integrity, to judge and act in their ftead; to fay otherwife is an Infult upon common fenfe, and the higheft Affront to that honourable Houfe, and changes the very Nature of Government into a *Democracy* or *Popular* State. So that to *halloo* the People on to the Ufe of their *original Power*, while the Conftitution is facredly preferv'd, is little fhort of halloing them on to Rebellion; which, without Breach of Charity may be faid of the prefent boafted *Coalition of Parties*, was defigned by two of thofe Parties. This *Coalition* did not fpring from the *Senfe* of the Nation, or the *Hearts* of the People, but was chiefly owing to the *particular unlawful Interefts* of fome, and to the *implacable Malice* of others againft the Government and Miniftry. The *Jacobites* and *Tories* are the fame Men, only with this Difference, that the *Jacobites* are *real Enemies profefs'd*, and the *Tories real Enemies not profefs'd:* Yet the *Craftfman* infinuates, that the Denominations of *Whig* and *Tory* are very *filly*, and ought to be abolifhed; (See p. 193 A) and that a few *circumftantial Differences about Government* fhould not be regarded; this Doctrine has been taken up by fome *deluded Whigs* during the *Heat* of the late Difturbances. But, is the Difference between the Doctrine of *Indefeafible Hereditary Right*, to ferve the *Pretender*, and the Doctrine of a *Legal Parliamentary Right* to the Crown, nothing but *Circumftantial?* Is it only *Circumftantial*, whether we have a Popifh Bigot, or one of the Illuftrious Houfe of *Hanover*, firm to the *Proteftant Caufe*, and in the *Intereft of Liberty?* Whether we have *Tories* at the Helm of Affairs, ever plaguing us with Acts of Power turn'd into, without or againft *Acts of Parliament*; or whether

we fhall have *Whigs* at the Helm, faft Friends to our *Natural Rights?*

The *Jacobites* and *Tories* do indeed at prefent pretend they are for *Liberty*; but 'tis only a *Pretence*; 'tis neceffary for them to affume this Principle; for it's impoffible they fhould oppofe any Government or Adminiftration upon their *own Principles*. To *delude* the *Whigs*, and break the *Whig* Intereft, is the Game they are now playing all over the Kingdom. For which Reafon the *Whigs*, whether in or out of Power, ought to *unite ftrongly* againft all the Plots and Contrivances of their *real* Enemies and *pretended* Friends.

We fee to what Pitch of Wickednefs the *Malice* of fome who call themfelves *Whigs*, joined to the *Artifices* of the *Jacobites*, with an *infamous Traytor* at their Head, have carried Things. What then is the Duty of the Friends of the Government but to join againft the united Force of thofe Men, who had rather fee the *Nation perifh*, than themfelves *not in Power*.

Univerfal Spectator, May 5. N° 239.
Of Contemplation, and the Works of Nature.

SPeculative People are really your Men of Pleafure. Senfual Enjoyments are confin'd within a narrow Compafs, and the Repetition of them palls upon the Appetite : But the Subjects of Contemptation are next to infinite, and every Thought we beftow upon them makes us wifer, happier, and better, enlarges our Faculties, and enables us to proceed farther. To behold, examine and underftand the Operations and Defigns of the *Almighty*, and from thence to admire, adore, and imitate his Wifdom and Goodnefs, is, probably, the Employment of *Angels* and *bleffed Spirits*, and the Mind of Man bufied in the fame manner enjoys the utmoft Felicity it is here capable of.

This delightful Seafon of the Year, when every Thing, animate and inanimate, feems contending which fhall beft declare the Goodnefs of its Creator, muft furely awaken the reafonable *Soul of Man* to Contemplation.

[Here Mr *Stonecaftle* inferts a Letter from Meff. *Furbur, Cafsteels*, and *Collins*, informing the World of the Progrefs they have made in Printing on 12 *Copper Plates* an exact *Delineation* of 400 different Sorts of the moft curious and uncommon Fruits, agreeable to their Propofals; (See Vol. I. p. 420.) and that the *Prints* will be ready for their *Subfcribers* at at the End of *July* next. The Price one. Guinea plain, two Guineas Colour'd.

After a further Recommendation of this Work, and some Commendations of the *Flower-Pieces* done by the same Gentlemen, Mr *Stonecastle* falls into the following Soliloquy.]—What an ample Field for Contemplation is here laid open to us! What a Scene of Wonder and Admiration! What a Check to the Pride and Vanity of Man, whose utmost Knowledge is unable to account for the meanest of these Productions! Can he find out wherefore the *Violet* is array'd in Purple; why the *Sun-Flower* glows with Yellow, the *Lilly* appears in White; by what Chimistry, Nature, from the same Soil, extracts the different *Juices* of innumerable Sorts of *Fruits?* Can he tell how the *Apple* and *Cherry* become round; the *Pear* and *Fig* oblong? How the *Walnut* acquires a hard Shell, whilst the *Mulberry*, growing near it, is so tender skinn'd? Why hang the *Grapes* in Clusters? Why grow some *Fruits* on lofty Trees, some on Bushes, and others on theGround?—If these Things, which seem so trifling,are beyond the Reach of human Understanding, how great must Man's Folly and Presumption be, when he takes upon him to comprehend the Dispensations of the Almighty, impeach his Justice, and direct his Wisdom, in the Government of the Universe!.

But laying aside these serious Reflections, there are a great many Cases, wherein this Work must prove useful and instructive. Those who have Gardens may be instructed wherewith to store them; and those who have none may supply that Want by an exact *Representation* of all that the most stately Gardens yield: Here are shewn the Advantages of *Art* and *Industry*, which even in this Northern Situation can bring to Perfection such an Abundance of those *Fruits* and *Flowers* which are the Natives of the more pleasurable and sunny Climes.

These Collections must be of service to the *Pattern-Drawer*, *Embroiderer*, *Painter*, *Carver*, *Enchacer*, and numberless other *Designers*.

A certain ingenious young *Lady* painted a dozen beautiful *Fans* from the 12 *Flower-Pieces*, soon after they were published. While she was thus employ'd, a *Gentleman* made his Addresses to her and marry'd her to the Surprize of every Body. During the Courtship, being told that his *Mistress* had neither *Beauty*, nor

Fortune, he reply'd, That is true, but *She knows how to spend her Time*.

Fog's Journal, May 5. N° 235.
Of Impostors and Projectors.

IN great and populous Cities, we frequently see some enterprizing Spirit start up, who lives meerly by imposing on the Publick. I have heard, says *Fog*, of a Couple of extravagant Fellows, who having spent their Patrimony, consulted how to subsist for the future. One propos'd the Highway; but that was objected to as dangerous. They therefore concluded to pitch upon some Trade where Ignorance would not be easily discover'd; for it would be easier to set up for a Statesman than a Taylor. But as being made a Minister depended on the Favour of others, they ought to find out something that might depend on themselves; and as Law and Physick were Professions which requir'd but little Stock, they fixed upon these. This being agreed upon, they drew Lots, and one was dubb'd a Counsellor, and the other a Doctor. In the Course of their Practice, one ruin'd his Clients, the other kill'd his Patients; and so both grew eminent, roll'd in their Coaches, and left great Estates.

There are other Impostors inferior to these, who draw small Sums out of Peoples Pockets, by certain little Deceits. But of all the Raree-Shew-Men commend me to a certain impudent Fellow, who at first profess'd nothing but Legerdemain, or Slight of Hand; but afterwards fell into a Trade of exhibiting Monsters to the People. He produced some new Monster every Year for a considerable Number of Years; and to all his Monsters gave surprizing Qualities, which they had not; and when the People complained of a Bite, he carried it off with an impudent Sneer, swearing, the next Monster should makeAmends for all that was past, and then he certainly produced a worse. Thus he went on, till the People threaten'd to have him punished as an Impostor.

At length he resolv'd to strike one bold Stroke for all, and found out a Monster, by which he proposed to make himself easy for ever. Nothing ever made so much Noise as this Monster, for the Projector kept several *Zanies* in Pay (who by the By had never seen it) to praise and extol it; and he was grown so prodigal that he promised every Man a Pension for Life, who would cry it up to thePeople. I heard one of 'em one day haranguing the

Crowd

Crowd, with a wonderful Account of this *curious Curiosity*, being the most *monstrous* Kind of a *Monster* not to be parallell'd in the whole World. The Doctor does not hang out a Picture of his Monster, like other vulgar Projectors, but gives you an Opportunity of paying your Money before Hand, and if you should not like it, you may all go to the D——l.

Here the Doctor himself advanced, and gave a long Detail of the Beauty, Strength, and other Excellencies of his curious Monster. " It has travelled, says he, thro' most parts of *Europe*; and no less a Person than the most Christian King stood Godfather, and the States General Godmother to it at the Font. Yet, considering its wonderful Qualities, I ask no more than 500,000 *l*. for a Sight of it; a Trifle! I know you will give me double that Sum after you have seen it; but I won't take it, for I don't value Money. In the mean Time if any Man pretend to disparage my Monster he is a Rascal, a Son of a W——e, and I'll stick in his Skirts for it as long as I live."

The whole Crowd immediately smoak'd the Doctor; for they knew he was a notorious Liar; besides, many of them had seen this Monster both in *France* and *Holland*, where she had devour'd whole Families, and so terrify'd the People, that they fled from it every where. She would eat in a Morning 500 Bushels of Salt without Bread. I have seen an Account of what she drank in one Day, *viz.* 1000 Gallons of strong Beer; 500 Gallons of Cyder; 450 Gallons of Mead; 400 Gallons of Metheglin; 375 Gallons of Perry; 250 Gallons of Gin double distill'd; 220 Gallons of Usquebaugh; 200 Gallons of Brandy; besides a proportionable Quantity of common Spirits.

The Projector had a felonious Trick of letting her loose at Night, when She used to devour every thing that fell in her way, would eat Starch, Soap, Candles, and devour Washballs like Pills; she once broke into a Shoemaker's Shop, and eat 152 Pair of Jackboots, besides Shoes and Slippers; then into a Sadler's, where she devour'd 22 Saddles, Pummels and all. While People were consulting how to get rid of this Monster, she chanc'd one Night to light into a vast Magazine of *Tobacco*, of which she devour'd as much as would have fill'd 22 Hogsheads, which purg'd its villainous Carcass incessantly for about 16 Days, and then she like the famous Dragon of *Wantley*, kick'd,——did something else ——and dy'd.

The News was no sooner known abroad, but all publick Demonstrations of Joy were shewn, and a thousand Songs were made in praise of Tobacco, like that on *Moor* of *Moor-hall* for killing the great Dragon of *Wantley*.

The Projector fled his Country; however the Magistrates publish'd an Edict, by which he was condemn'd to be hang'd in Effigie, which was executed accordingly; and his Riches, the Fruits of so much Impudence and Lying, were seiz'd upon, and apply'd towards the Maintenance of the Poor. Such was the capricious Fate of the most renowned Doctor *Ferdinando Ferdinandi* of most blundering Memory; of whom it was pleasantly said, that what he gained by his Face, he lost by his Head.

The *Daily Courant*, May 5.
Of Clandestine Marriages; in a Letter to a Member of Parliament.

SIR,

YOU say 'tis unanimously agreed that an effectual Stop ought to be put to Clandestine Marriages; but the Question it seems, is, what will be an effectual Stop? That a Dissolution of such Marriages would be so, is also agreed: But Difficulties arise about the Lawfulness and ill Consequences of such Dissolutions.

If any ill Consequences are apprehended from the Dissolution of Marriages between *Adult* People, let the Laws stand as they do, and such People suffer for their own Rashness: But I cannot apprehend any from the Dissolution of Marriages of Infants, comparable to those dismal Consequences of ruining Families.

As to the Lawfulness of dissolving such Marriages, I might refer you to the Arguments debated in the Council of *Trent*, where, tho' that wonderful Maxim, then wrong applied, carried the Point, *viz.* *Factum valet, quod fieri non debet*, it might have been answer'd by another, *Quod fieri non debuit, infectum esto.* Consequently the Arguments for Dissolution must appear strongest to any that do not hold Matrimony to be a Sacrament.

But leaving the Popish Laws, let us consider the Laws of God in this Case. *Numb.* XXX. 3, 4, 5. may be referred to Vows of Oblation, of Virginity, or other Matters; but the Reason of it holds as strong in the Case of Matrimony; which Vow ought no more to stand, if disallow'd by a Father, than a Vow *in any* of the other Cases : For (*Exod*. xxii. 16,17.)
the

the Power of Matrimony was entirely lodg'd with theFather. Thefe *Jewifh* Laws are not to be accounted as merely Ritual, but Part of their political Law, and founded on the eternal Laws of Nature and Reafon, which look upon a Man's Children as the neareft and deareft Part of his Property. For the fame Reafon our own Laws will not fuffer a Minor to contract a Debt. And it feems very hard, that Boys and Girls fhould have a Power of ruining themfelves by Marriage, when they have not the Power of borrowing 20 *s.*

Further, if the Marriages of Children without their Parents Confent be declared Whoredom, and the Iffue of fuch Copulation illegitimate, it would prevent Jilts and Chambermaids from inveigling young Gentlemen, and deter young Ladies from incurring the Cenfure of Whoredom; and I cannot think fuch Proceeding inconfiftent with the Laws of God; however to prevent this Sort of Whoring, there may be Clogs and Hindrances laid in the Way; as that no Licenfe fhall be granted without the Oath of both Parties; that known, and fufficient Sureties be required to the Bond; that the Parent or Guardian be prefent at the Marriage; That not to be celebrated in any Church, but where the Parent or Guardian of the Minor lives, and by a Clergyman well known. If any Perfon above Age, marry the Son or Daughter under Age of his Mafter or Miftrefs, in whofe Family they are, or have been Servants within the Space of a Year, without the Confent of the faid Mafter or Miftrefs, that all fuch be guilty of Petit-Treafon. This likewife to be extended to young Gentry boarding or l°dging in fuch Family. And all Aiders, Abettors, *&c.* to be Principals.

If annulling thofe Marriages *ipfo facto,* without Sentence, may be liable to Inconveniencies, fuppofe a Power be lodg'd with the Bifhop, out of whofe Court the Licenfe proceeded, to hear the Cafe in a Summary Way, at the Motion of the Parent of the Minor, and if any Fraud appear'd, to declare the Marriage null by Sentence, and the Offenders to be affigned over to the Law.

But if thefe Sort of Marriages cannot be diffolved, fcarce any Penalties will deter fuch People from them who defign to make their Fortunes. Needy Clergymen may be found to perform the Office, who may not be found to undergo the Penalty. What Satisfaction is it to the Parent, that the Official or Surrogate be turned out of his Place? That the Perfon taking the Oath be excommunicated? That the Bond be fued and recovered? That the *Son-in-Law* be imprifoned 5 Years, by the Statute of *William* and *Mary?* Or that a Child hath forfeited all his Eftate to the next Heirs? Thefe are Penalties upon the innocent Father, and the betray'd Child is undone for Life; and all the Remedy yet allowed by the Laws doth but double the Affliction; for which Reafon moft Parents decline any Profecutions, and thereby Villains are encouraged, hope for Forgivenefs, and at length a Reconciliation. *Tours, T. S.*

The **Craftfman,** May 5. No. 357.
On *Monofyllables.*

Mr *D'anvers,*

IT has been objected to the *Englifh* Language, that we have too many Monofyllables. For my Part, I can't help confidering thefe *little Bodies* as the nobleft and moft fenfible Part of our Language, as breathing the very Genius of the *Britifh* Nation, and like that, are ftrong, bold, good, and great.

Of all the antient Writers, *Saluft* and *Thucydides* are the fhorteft. The *latter* of Thefe (fays the moft copious Orator in the World) feems to have *more Sentences than Words.* But according to a Plan, which I have defign'd, future Writers may have *as many Sentences as Syllables.*

The clofer we follow all Languages to their fountain Heads, the more we fhall find them fimple, clear, and unmixt. The Languages of the *Eaft,* from whence all others flow, have the fhorteft Words. The *Chinefe* is the moft copious, yet confifts almoft entirely of fingle Syllables.

But to my Scheme; If *Minifters* would introduce my *fhort Language* into all Congreffes, Preliminaries, *&c.* what Time, Words, and Expence would be faved? A great *Man,* 'tis faid, ought to be Mafter of *many Words;* but if he has but two *little fnugg Monofyllables* at hisCommand, He may do his Bufinefs effectually. By the Help of *thefe,* and a *magick Wand,* He may fee his Charm laft, till a noble Fortune is raifed; unlefs he over-exerts himfelf; and then he'll never be able to lay the *Spirit of the People,* raifed thereby.

I have already the Satisfaction to behold one of the moft important Affemblies in the World, giving a Sanction to my *Scheme,* and I glory in the Honour of it. We have feen the Wifdom of the Nation

tion employ'd with the utmost Vehemence, whether AYE or No should carry the Point. Old hath been the Enmity, and frequent the Skirmishes between these *two Particles*; tho' the AYE's have commonly got the better, being supported by a large Body of powerful and wealthy Auxiliaries; yet the No's not long ago got a signal and complete Victory. To *Them* is owing that a Scheme for importing *wooden Shoes* into this Kingdom hath been lately defeated; and the Publick may expect farther Benefits from the Vigilance of these *little Patriots.*

All the Nations in the World are divided into two great Bodies of *Monofyllables*, of near affinity to the AYE's and No's, and distinguished by the Names of the IN's and OUT's. The IN's are always the richest Party, tho' the OUT's are commonly the honestest Men; but as I am one of the OUT's myself, I shall say no more about that.

I am glad Exception has been taken against the Word PENSION, as of too great Extent, and tho' its Annihilation hath been deferr'd from Year to Year by a *pious, untemporaliz'd Set of Men,* the Day may come, when an honest Impeachment of such an over-grown Word will succeed. However, I rejoice with my Countrymen that, *in all future Elections for Members of Parliament,* there can be no BRIBE.

But tho' I profess myself a Patron of *Monofyllables,* I would not be thought to defend them all. The Word FRAUDS shall have no Quarter; and I heartily wish the *Committee* lately appointed to enquire into them, may not prove a *Committee* of SAFETY.

The Time has been, when the Body of the Nation rose in Arms against two of my greatest Favourites, and entirely abolished them; I mean CHURCH and KING; but they are since happily restor'd. I with Pleasure observe, the People have no Inclination to be made SLAVES; but seem desirous to preserve a due Balance between the Power of the CROWN and the Protection of the LAWS.

I should be glad to see the infamous Word SCREEN scratch'd out of the *English* Vocabulary. Indeed the *great Engrosser of it* hath lately endeavoured to patch it up for his *own Use*; but I cannot think it will prove any lasting Security to Him, being so far worn in the Service of others.

There is one pretty *Monofyllable,* which

will ever keep its Ground. We shall always know what is meant by a TAX. This Word, tho' necessary, yet if made common, grows nauseous, especially if it swells itself into an EXCISE.

For the same Reason I shall never attempt to suppress these fashionable Monofyllables, WAYS and MEANS, which are become almost constitutional.

Panegyricks, I suppose, will be sent me on the Virtues, Beauties, and Rhetorick of GOLD; and the most *eminent, ministerial Writers* will give undeniable Assurances, with what Pleasure they shall always *handle* so weighty an Argument. Some of them may modestly insist on a PLACE only.

Those ill-sounding Words STOCKS, JOBBS, and DEBTS, should be discarded, but I am afraid they will prove too hard for me. But TRADE will meet with many Advocates. The *French* may perhaps insist on giving up our Right to the FLAG; and the *Spaniards* may tell us, We shall lose our EARS. But I shall oppose the Pretensions of *these Gentlemen,* whatever Encouragement they may receive from *some other Persons.*

Numberless Instances of *material sturdy Monofyllables* crowd to come under my Pen; but I must put them off till the 12th of *June.* My chief Difficulty will lye in reducing *proper Names* to my fixt Standard. To do This I must haveRecourse to Abbreviations, not by way of Reproach; for I dare say, if the great *Elizabeth* were to revive, she would rejoice to hear her honest People of *England* for ever endearing to Themselves, the Memory of good Queen BESS. I shall take the same Liberty with *one Gentleman,* who seems to know no Bounds, and shall now and then give him a BOB, since the Nation hath already born so many from him.

But I grow prolix; and shall therefore conclude in one Word, YOURS.

Weekly Miscellany, May 5. No. 21.

Of Infidelity.

WHoever recollects either the excellent Writings publish'd in Defence of *Christianity,* or the weak and baffled Objections of its *Enemies,* may be surprized at the Progress of *Infidelity* among us, but cannot ascribe it to the Force of its Arguments, nor the Decay of Religion to the want of Evidence; we must look out for some *external* Reasons.

The first Thing to be assigned as the Cause of this prevailing Malady is, the *Reigning*

Reigning Luxury of the present Age, greatly exceeding what was ever known to our Forefathers. This renders Vice more frequent and extensive, and engages us in the Practice of Crimes the most inconsistent with *Religion.* The Vices of Luxury are seldom corrected but by *Poverty* or *Disability.* Besides it is giving Strength to Lust, and paving the Way for *Avarice* and *Oppression,* it spreads a fatal Indolence over the Mind, and Religion itself must be parted with rather than the darling Passion, and such Notions as best agree with the Company Men keep.

This dreadful Evil has operated the same Way in all Times and Places; 'twas Luxury raised the Sect of *Sadduces* among the *Jews*; and propagated the Distinction between the civil and political Religions of *Greece* and *Rome,* till at last, instead of lopping off the Errors, it had almost rooted out the Belief of *Providence* and a *Future State*; nor did their *Liberties* long out-live their *Religion.*

In this State of Things, if ever, we surely want a *Reformation*; but (which is another Cause) never was there a greater want of *Discipline.* In the Guilty, an Uneasiness under all Restraints, a Disaffection to our Constitution, *Civil* and *Ecclesiastical,* and a Contempt of all Things sacred and serious; while perhaps too tender a Regard to *mistaken Liberty,* makes those, who might otherwise interpose, exert themselves more gently, than was ever done in this or any other Nation. In Consequence of this, and as a new source of this Calamity, is the *bad Taste, wrong Delicacy,* and *false Politeness,* that direct the Sentiments, and influence the Conduct of our People, both in *Manners* and *Learning.* As to the *former,* instead of examining whether this, or that Action *should* be done, we only enquire whether it *be* done, especially by People weakly thought *Polite.* As to the latter, 'tis true, never were more Scholars, nor *fewer* good Ones. Instead of applying ourselves to good *old Authors,* who taught *manly Sense* and *solid Virtue,* we read trifling *News Papers* and silly *Pamphlets,* stuffed with little Objections, which neither the *Authors* nor their Readers know the Force of. Let these Gentlemen consider, that *Objecting* and *Answering* require very different Talents. A little *Vivacity* is sufficient for the first; but *Judgment, Patience,* and *Attention* are necessary for the latter. I have known many Christians, who could have appeared laudable *Deists,* but

have met with few *Deists,* that could shine on the opposite Side of the Question.

But the *Original,* and the most *standing Cause* of Infidelity, is *Popery.* The *Truth* of *Miracles* has been weaken'd by *counterfeit Ones*; the *Truth* of *Testimony* by the Doctrine of Lying for the Service of the Church; and the *Certainty* of our *sacred Records,* by *uncertain Traditions.* Nay, the Papists actually encourage the Growth of *Irreligion,* to favour the Point of *Infallibility.* With this view *Jesuits* go masqu'd under the Character of *Deists.* Look over the List of our *Infidel Authors,* and we shall soon remember *what* they have been, and *where they were bred.* Horrible as this their Policy is, they have more to plead for themselves than we have. They think we shall be *damn'd* for being Hereticks, and shall *but be damn'd* for being Atheists; so that they imagine they do *us* no Injury, while they promote their own *Advantage.* — These Thoughts were occasion'd by reading the following *Remonstrance* of Mr *Jn Hampden,* against the Errors of Father *Simon.*

HAving been in a most eminent Manner under God's afflicting Hand, I think myself obliged to examine my Conscience concerning the Causes for which it has pleased his Divine Wisdom to inflict so many signal Judgments upon me for Years last past. And I do freely confess, that, among many other heinous Sins whereof I am guilty, there is one especially which causes me great Trouble, and to which I was principally drawn by that Vanity and Desire of Vain-glory, which is so natural to the corrupted Hearts of Men. The Particular is this, That notwithstanding my Education was very pious and religious, and the Knowledge I had of the Certainty of the Truth of the Christian Religion, yet, to obtain the Reputation of Wit and Learning, which is so much esteemed in the World, I was so unhappy as to engage myself in the Sentiments and Principles of the Author of the Critical History of the Old Testament; which yet I plainly perceived did tend to overthrow all the Belief which Christians have of the Truth and Authority of the Holy Scriptures, under Pretence of giving great Authority to Tradition, which afterwards is easily twined and accommodated, as best suits the Interest of those who take upon them to cry it up.

I likewise acknowledge, that tho' I had but very weak Arguments to support my Libertine Opinion, such as I believe I could have easily answered, and as could not make any Impression, but upon those who are willing to cast off the Yoke of their Duty, and O-

bligation

bligation we are all under to live in the Fear of God; yet I was fo rafh and foolifh, as to pretend I thought there was great Strength in them, when I infinuated them, rather than opened them, to fome of my familiar Acquaintance; and, I am afraid, I have contributed thereby to caft fome of them into Opinions, and perhaps Practices, contrary both to the Truth, and the Commandments of the Chriftian Religion.

I do likewife acknowledge, that having difcourfed freely with the Author of the Critical Hiftory, and having heard from his own Mouth that he allowed yet lefs, the Authority of the Books of the New Teftament, than thofe of the Old, which fhould naturally have obliged me to avoid all Communication with him; yet I furnifhed him with Money to execute a Defign which he framed of a Critical Polyglot Bible; which after the Declaration he made to me, I think I ought to have confidered as a Defign which tended to deftroy the Certainty of the Books of the New Teftament as well as of the Old.

This Confeffion I make with all poffible Sincerity, and with much Grief, for having offended God by fo great a Sin, for which I heartily beg Pardon of Him; and I do earneftly befeech all thofe that may to any Degree have been feduced, either by Difcourfes or Examples, that they would ferioufly reflect upon the Danger they are in, that they may be delivered from it in Time, and from fuch Judgments of God as he hath been pleafed to lay upon me.

This Confeffion I have written and figned with my Hand, to the End that if I fhall die before I can fpeak with thofe I have perverted by my Example, they may return to themfelves and to God as I do, by folemn Proteftation which I make to them, that the Opinions I have taught them were nothing but the Effects of my Pride and Vanity, which I unfeignedly condemn, defigning to live and die in thofe contained in this Paper.

J. HAMPDEN.

The Auditor, May 8. Nº. 35.
Jamque Opus exegi.

GENTLEMEN *and* LADIES,

I Have endeavour'd during the Space of 3 or 4 Months to awaken you out of different kinds of Lethargy, and tried by all means I could think of to raife in your Minds a Defire for Entertainments of this Kind; well knowing, that where there is no *Defire to improve*, there can be no *Improvement*, I will not attribute my ill Succefs to your *Want of Tafte*, but rather to your being taken up with Entertainments that afford you a more *Senfible* Delight : Cards and Affemblies,

publick Spectacles, and the *Mall*; News and Politicks, have long prevailed over thofe Minds which *Intereft* had left *difengaged*. In a word I am convinced your Minds are not yet ripe for fuch a Defign; and therefore refolve to give it over for the prefent.

Perhaps this little Attempt may raife your Curiofities before next *Winter*. If I find the leaft Inclination in you to fee me again, I fhall endeavour to make myfelf as agreeable as I can. But I don't think myfelf quite rich enough to lofe 100*l*. a Year for your Entertainment.

I muft not conceal the handfome Behaviour of Mr *Peele*, Publifher of this Paper, who finding I had been at a confiderable Expence, abfolutely refufed to accept of his Due by Agreement.

I return Thanks to thofe who have favour'd me with their Correfpondence; and fhall take it very kindly, if they would continue, during the *Summer* Interval, to favour me with fuch Reflections as occur to them on all Subjects, inclofed to Mr *J. Peele*, Publifher of the AUDITOR. *Tour Real Friend,*

The AUDITOR.

Mr AUDITOR,

WHEN a Child, I was fo frighten'd with Stories of Spirits, &c. that I find it even now impoffible for me to lie alone; I have therefore determin'd to marry. I have two Lovers, whofe Characters I will give you, and defire you to tell me which will make the beft Husband.

PRUDENTIUS and LEVIS are their Names: The *firft* ftarts a grave Subject, and fays, he loves to hear me reafon upon it; defcribes the Charms of Retirement in the Country with a Friend; tells me my Faults; advifes me to read; preffes me to a Conclufion and to make him happy; proffers to fettle a Jointure on me equal to his Eftate; was never known to do a ftingything, nor ever to fpend *two* Guineas where *one* wou'd do, is a perfonable handfome Man; is very polite but a little precife; not fond of Dancing, but in private Company likes it; never very merry, but always chearful; tells me he fhall never be completely happy without me, nor will ever marry another. *Levis* diverts me with Stories, Scraps of Poetry, and new Songs, which he fings delightfully; fwears, every Moment fpent out of *London*, except at *Bath* or *Tunbridge*, is Death; vows I have no Faults; fnatches every Book out of my Hand, and tells me my Eys were never made

made to be caſt down, but, like the Sun, to revive all they ſhine on; proteſts, while he is my Slave he would not change to be a King, and could go on thus for ever; declares all he has ſhall be mine; nobly ſpends as faſt as it comes; has the *Je ne ſçai quoy*, and is polite to exceſs, yet ſeems *ſan ceremonie*; loves Dancing extravagantly, and dances like an Angel; is the merrieſt Creature alive, and never ſits ſtill two Moments; and is loudeſt in a Laugh; vows he ſhall die if he has me not; and really he looks ſo——But, Sir, I beg your Opinion, and am &c.

JENNY WRONGHEAD,

P. S. I had almoſt forgot to tell you, I hate the Country, am very merry, and laugh a great deal, love Dancing beyond any thing, and Singing to Diſtraction: *Bath* and *Tunbridge* are ſo good for one's Health, that you will not blame me, if I love them too in their proper Seaſons.

The *Auditor* ſays, ſhe need only read her own Letter to determine for herſelf. *M.*

Free Briton, May 10. No. 184.

On the Propoſed Marriage of the Princeſs Royal with the Prince of Orange.

I AM far from regretting, ſays Mr *Walſingham*, that I had the leaſt Share in our diſagreeable Debates; and I rejoice when I ſee that happy Occaſion wherein we muſt all agree. When we conſider how much we owe to the *Proteſtant Succeſſion*, in his Majeſty's Royal Family; that the unmoleſted Exerciſe of Religious Worſhip, and the peaceable Poſſeſſion of Liberty and Property; the Toleration of *Proteſtant Diſſenters*, and the Protection of the *Church of England*, have wholly derived their Security from this illuſtrious Family, no *Engliſh* Heart can be too warm for the Support of that Royal Dignity, and for the Propagation of that Royal Blood, whoſe Power, whoſe Virtues have ſo many Years been the Source of ſuch infinite Good to theſe Nations. Whilſt the Royal Line was broken, and the Succeſſion doubtful, to what Fears, to what Attempts from abroad were we expoſed? When the *Proteſtant Succeſſion*, in the preſent Royal Family, took Place, we were at once deliver'd from the Fear of a *falling* Proteſtant Line, and from the Apprehenſions of a *Popiſh Invader.*

His Majeſty has been diſtinguiſhed beyond all the Princes of *Europe*, by a numerous Royal Iſſue. He aſcended the

Throne with this uncommon Felicity, that *Seven of his own Children* were living to ſecure the Succeſſion in his Line; two Princes, his Sons, the Favourites of his People; and *Five Illuſtrious Ladies,* his Daughters, from whoſe Marriages we might promiſe our ſelves a large Acceſſion of Strength to the *Proteſtant Cauſe.*

The Marriage of *Her Royal Highneſs* the PRINCESS ROYAL is of infinite Importance to the People of *England*; ſhe is at preſent *Third in Succeſſion* to the Crown; and her Iſſue muſt inherit, in Caſe the Iſſue of her Royal Brothers ſhould fail. The Choice of an Husband for her Royal Highneſs is therefore of the utmoſt Import to the *Britiſh* Nation, as well as to neighbouring Kingdoms.

His Majeſty's Affection, as well to his his Subjects, as to his Daughter hath at at once provided for the Security of their mutual Happineſs; and hath wiſely deſtin'd Her to a Family, where his Subjects have always placed their *greateſt* Foreign *Security,* namely, to a Prince of the Houſe of ORANGE. Our glorious Deliverer, K. WILLIAM III. was related to us, as Prince of *Orange,* by a double Alliance of this Kind. He was reſpectively the *Son and the Husband of a Daughter* of the Britiſh *Crown.* On whom then, but on a Prince of HIS *Blood,* can his Majeſty with greateſt Gratitude and Wiſdom beſtow his *Eldeſt Daughter?* To whom can the *Princeſs Royal* of *Great Britain* of Right belong, but to a Prince of the *Houſe of Naſſau?* Indeed it is moſt juſt that That *illuſtrious Houſe,* which, during ſo many Ages, hath been the Guardians of Mankind, and the Aſſerters of Liberty, ſhould thro' every Generation *mix in Blood;* and be *allied in Intereſt* with the *Royal Line of Britain.*

Her *Royal Highneſs,* when beſtowed on ſuch a Prince, will leave us, to ſupport the Intereſts of *Britain,* and the Liberties of Mankind, in a Country where ſhe will be moſt capable of aſſiſting both. The excellent Examples of her Royal Parents will now be repreſented by her Royal Highneſs to another People. We ſhall thus be indebted for Part of our national Glory to the *Wiſdom* and *Care* of the QUEEN, which hath ſo happily form'd the Minds of her Royal Offspring; and by means whereof the *Princeſs Royal* hath diſtinguiſh'd herſelf by the fineſt Accompliſhments which a Court can produce, or a Kingdom admire. To great and uncommon Livelineſs of Genius ſhe h ath joined the moſt elegent Attainments of the moſt liberal Education. A maſculine Underſtanding ſoftened with the tendereſt Affections of her Sex : A Knowledge of Languages, and a Love of letter'd Science, added to the moſt refined Taſte of Muſick, and of all the moſt polite Arts. Qualities like theſe will make deeper Impreſſions on the Heart of her Royal Husband, than even thoſe Charms which he receives to his *envied* Embraces. Happy the Nation by whom ſhe is given in Marriage as the *Daughter of the Crown!* and moſt happy the Prince whom they juſtly eſteem moſt worthy of ſuch a Conſort! (ſee p. 248)

Her R. Highneſs hath ſeen all the Bleſſings of Liberty, and been taught to love it. She leaves us, to improve the generous Leſſons which this Country hath taught her, for the Benefit of a People by whom Liberty is as dearly prized, ſo that if ever the Fate of *Britain* ſhould require it to be tranſplanted back again into this Kingdom, we may not have the Misfortune to find it grown *foreign* to a FREE *Conſtitution.*

In this View we cannot but congratulate ourſelves; and we have the higheſt Reaſon to wiſh this *excellent Princeſs* all Felicity, from an Alliance ſo nearly connected with publick Good.

Grubſtreet Journal, May 10. Nº 176.

Mr BAVIUS,

'TIS a juſt Obſervation, that thoſe Men who deal in ill-nature want Wit; and that thoſe Women, who pretend to be above being diverted with the trifling Gallantries and Chit-chat, ſo agreeable to the reſt of their Sex, do not abound in ſuperior Senſe.

We are call'd The *Fiddle-faddle Club,* from the Innocence of our Converſation; becauſe we neither ſcandalize our Neighbours, nor talk of Things above our Capacities. The Club conſiſts of Seven; never admitting any of the He-creatures, for fear of a Set of hideous decay'd Toaſts in the Neighbourhood, who are ever on the Watch to murder our Reputations.— The firſt of our Club is Lady TIPTOE, who being paſſionately fond of the upper Part of her Face, wears Heels like Stilts, to overlook the Croud, where ſhe appears to the greateſt Advantage; for *Tip's* Eyes are fine, and ſhe has the beſt Fancy in a Ribbon of any of us. The next is Lady *Fanciful,* whoſe greateſt Pride is in her Foot, who-buckles her Shoes, and ties

up her Stockings with the greateſt Nicety imaginable. She was the firſt in ſhort Petticoats, furniſhes the Company with polite Whimſies, and has the tip-top Gait in the World. The Third is Lady *Lazy,* who is ſo agreeably weak, that ſhe often borrows a Hand to ſtir her Tea, and feed her Noſe with Snuff. Nothing moves her but the Sound of a Fiddle; for ſhe dances to Admiration. The 4th, *Cecilia Thoughtleſs,* is the Delight of the whole Company; ſhe has a Voice like *Cuzzoni*; and plays upon the Hapſicord to a wonder, all by the Ear; for the dear Creature could never attend to Notes.—But nothing can compare to Miſs *Love-Mode*; ſhe walks ten Miles a Day, when it's the Faſhion; and when it's Polite to ſit ſtill, ſhe can't go croſs the Room. She dotes on China, and had bought a beautiful ſet of Plates for 50 Guineas, when an ignorant Wretch ask'd if they were Delft. This threw her into a moſt violent Paſſion. The 6th of our Aſſembly is Miſs *At-all:* She is certainly the beſt Mimick in the World; ſhe diſplays Ld *Tinſel* and Sir *Ruſtick Racer,* and every ugly Puſs, and old Maid in Town in ſuch lively Colours, that ſhe'd make you half die with Laughing. This, with the Character of dear *Coquetilla,* you will allow, muſt make our Set compleatly agreeable to all People of true Taſte. She has a large ſhare of Beauty, and . is a Maſter-piece in the Art of pleaſing. Her Quickneſs is ſo ſurprizing, that Wit is never loſt upon her. Laughing becomes her to *Diſtraction*; for her Teeth are prodigiouſly fine. Nor can any thing diſturb the Tranquillity of her Temper, unleſs ſhe's obliged to hobble out of a publick Place without a pretty Fellow.

We meet twice a Week to ſettle Faſhions, and talk over the Beaus, and all the pretty Things that have been ſaid to any of us. Our Employment, when not at the Club, is to dreſs in the Whims invented there, to get our Faſhions follow-ed; and to make new Conqueſts. And nothing pleaſes us better than to have our Faſhions approved by the *Beau Monde,* nor concerns us more than to have them neglected and over-look'd; which is a Mortification we now daily meet with. Ever ſince the deteſtable Topic of *Exciſe* has been in vogue, every Head has been fill'd with it. The Day the Bill was put aſide (oh barbarous Diſappointment!) we went to a Ball, dreſs'd in new invented Puffs; and when we expected they ſhould employ the Thoughts and Tongues

of

of the whole Company, they were not in the least obferved, and the whole Difcourfe run on the Dragon *Excife*; which has thrown us all into the Spleen. If you don't advife the *polite* World not to turn Politicians, we fhall never recover. We' fhall wait with Impatience to fee our Wrongs publifhed; which if you perform fpeedily, you will oblige.

THE FIDDLE-FADDLE CLUB.

§ This Paper continues a former Difcourfe (fee p. 179.) where the Writer introduces feveral Authors as terrify'd with a Rumour of a Tax to be laid upon Dulnefs; to avert which they brought their refpective Labours to make a Burnt Offering to that Goddefs. In this, and the 174th Journal, the fame Authors are reprefented as making a large Pile of their feveral Labours, upon a Table where old refufe Books are expos'd to Sale in *Lincolns-Inn-Fields*; to this Pile PUFFE-RUS with a *Hyp-Doctor Extraordinary* fet fire. But PUFFERUS, not relying wholly on the Virtue of religious Duties, injoin'd all Perfons, who had any Veneration for the Goddefs of DULNESS, to repair to her Chapel near the Shambles in *Clare-market*, on *Wednefday, April* 28, and to bring each of them a Shilling.

The Time being come, the great PUF-FERUS enter'd the Roftrum; from whence he deliver'd a long Oration, *entirely new*, in Juftification of the intended Excife upon Tobacco and Wine; at the End of which he faid, he had *unanfwerably anfwer'd* all Objections againft inland Duties; and concluded, that as it was morally certain that the Bill would pafs, he could not apprehend that the Project of an Excife upon Dulnefs would take Effect. However he propofed, that a Committee fhould be chofen out of the Congregation, to confider of all dutiful ways to oppofe the Execution of any fuch Scheme. A Commitee was chofen accordingly, of which PUFFERUS made himfelf Chairman. After fome Debates, they came to a Refolution, that a Letter of Advice and Inftruction be fent to their Reprefentative in Parliament; and that Mr *Carus*, Mr *Osbornius*, and Mr *Britonius* do immediately prepare and draw up the fame. This was done prefently, and had fo good an Effect, that the Project was entirely laid afide.

Fog's Journal. May 12. N° 236.

Of giving up Minifters.

IN the Reign of K. *William* III. the Nation was out of Humour with thofe Minifters, who made the Partition Treaty, and in a manner call'd out for the Impeachment of thofe who advifed it; and it was urg'd, that they fhould be oblig'd to give an Account in what Manner they came by their Fortunes.

When a Controverfy lies betwixt the Plunderers and Plundered, the whole Body of Plunderers muft unite to defend their Leader, or Leaders, perhaps without any Reafon urg'd in their Juftification; but the Cant will be, that the King ought not to give up his Minifters. This is well remark'd upon in a Difcourfe publifh'd in that Reign about the Time of the above Treaty.—Part of which is as follows:

It has ever been the Cuftom of bad Men to cover their Ambition, Corruption and *Rapine*, with the Pretence of their Mafter's Service. They make him believe that their Greatnefs advances his Intereft; whereas he is often weak for want of that Wealth and Power, which they fhare among themfelves; yet we fcarce meet with one Inftance of a Prince, who, in his Diftrefs, has been affifted from the Purfes of his Minifters. But of all the falfe Suggeftions made by Men in Power, none are fo dangerous as thofe infinuated in the Cabinet; by which, the Ears of Princes have been poyfon'd, and induced to purge, till the Body Politick was quite exhaufted of all its good Spirits.

Some Princes have thought it Politick to nourifh Factions in their very Courts; but preferv'd themfelves neuter, to try to make both Sides fubfervient to their Defigns; but no Prince that could help it, ever let Faction grow national; however, if they could not prevent it, they never lifted themfelves on either Side; and *Henry* III. of *France* is a memorable Inftance, how fatal it is for the Sovereign to become the Head of a Party.

Partiality is the little Weaknefs of private Men, and unbecoming the Greatnefs of a Prince, whofe Favour fhould fhine on all alike; otherwife, he has the Service only of the worft Part of the People, and is often forced to protect the Bad againft the Good, and even to defend that Male-Adminiftration, by which himfelf has fuffer'd.

They who were for engroffing the Prince to themfelves, infinuated, that becaufe many Great Men retired, it muft be that they bore ill Will towards the Government. But why did thefe Men, confpicuous for Underftanding, Reach, and Expe-

Experience, suffer others to ruin that Country which it was in their Power to save? No doubt it was because they did not like the Administration of Affairs, nor the Persons with whom they were to be join'd, nor willing to mix in desperate Councils, nor participate in the Blame of what they should not be able to hinder; therefore some refused Employments, others laid down white Staves, the Secretary's Seals, the Great Seal, and other Offices of high Trust, rather than Act against the Interest and Constitution of their Country.

But when these Errors may be corrected, which a few commit, at the Expence of the whole Kingdom; when Things will bear a right Examination, all Parties will chearfully come in, and the best Men be most eager to assist the State with their Purses, Councils, Endeavours, and Affections.

A King never wants Assistance, who is for looking into Abuses; and their Faction, whose Interest it is to protect Male-Administration will be found very weak, when he is in earnest to have what is amiss amended; because but a few are Gainers by Government, and a Multitude are injur'd by it.

Weekly Miscellany, May 12. No. 22.
Of Freethinking and Freethinkers.

S I R,

THE following Extracts are taken from the excellent Works of some of our celebrated Writers, a little modified, and incorporated with some thing of my own.

The Subject is *Freethinking* and *Freethinkers,* who openly propagate their vile Tenets, with no other View, than to destroy all Rule and Order, to rob a good Man of his *Hope,* and for Mischief's sake only, to subvert the established Rule of Things, and on pretence of promoting *Morality,* propagate such Tenets, as must ruin all *Morals,* as well as *Religion,* and leave the Commonalty an abandon'd Race of Profligates.

The *Clergy* are the principal Butt of their Fury and Outrage; and some late Pieces shew us the *Usefulness* of that *Sacred Order,* by the *Pains* those Enemies of *Religion* take to decry it. A celebrated Author says, these Men give up all Title to *Freethinkers* in the genuine Sense of the Word, with the most apparent Prejudice against a *Body of Men,* whom a good Man would be most careful not to violate.

I allow, and you have owned (see p. 182) some will intrude, who are of Tempers unbecoming their Function; but it seems very hard, that therefore the *whole Order* must be vilified. But, is not the *Christian Faith* attacked by the same rude Hands? And I fear the Order itself suffers as much, with some People, for the sake of the Christian Precepts it is its Duty to propagate, as for the *Faults* of any of its *Individuals.*

If *Religion* is the *strongest* Tye of *Human Society,* are not those its common Enemies, who endeavour to establish their impious Notions upon the Destruction of *Religion?* Our Modern *Freethinkers* are a set of *dry, joyless, dull* Fellows, who want *Talents* to make a Figure upon *benevolent and generous* Principles; that think to surmount their own *natural Meanness* by laying *Offences* in the way of such as endeavour to excel upon the *received* Maxims and *honest* Arts of Life. What *Satisfaction,* what *delicious Libertinism* do they enjoy, after getting *loose* of the Laws which confine the *Passions* of other Men? Are not the *Leaders* of this growing Sect *sober Wretches,* who have not *Fire* enough to be further *Debauchees,* than meerly in *Principle?* Thus do *heavy Mortals,* only to gratify a *dry Pride of Heart,* give up the Interest of *another* World, without *enlarging* their Gratifications in *this.*

The *Freethinker* is unacquainted with the Emotions of *great Minds* turned for Religion; and is untouch'd with any such Sensation as the *Rapture of Devotion.* They have neither Taste nor Capacity for what they decry, and are more *Blockheads* than *Atheists;* they are as capable of writing an *Heroick Poem,* as making a *fervent Prayer.* Thus *low* and *narrow* in their Apprehensions, yet *vain,* they are naturally led to think every thing they *do not* understand, *not* to be understood.

The Atheistical Fellows of the last Age, *revell'd* in Excesses *suitable* to their *Principles;* but our Freethinkers lead recluse Lives only to disturb the Sentiments of *other Men.* When such Writers pretend to inform the Age, *Mohocks* and *Cutthroats* may set up for *Wits* and *Men of Pleasure.*

The *Thoughts* of a *Freethinker* are employ'd on certain *minute Particularities* of *Religion;* the *Difficulty* of a *single Text,* or the *Unaccountableness* of some *Step* of *Providence* or *Point of Doctrine* to his *narrow Faculties,* without comprehending

hending the *Design* and *Scope* of *Christianity*; the *Perfection* of human Nature, the *Light* it hath shed abroad in the World, and the *close Connection* it hath as well with the Good of *publick Societies*, as with that of *particular Persons*.

The *Christian Religion ennobleth* and *enlargeth* the Mind beyond any other Profession or Science. The Perfections of the *Deity*, the Nature and Excellence of *Virtue*, the Dignity of the *human Soul*, are display'd in the *largest* Characters. The Greatness of Things is *comparative*. *Astronomy* opens the *Mind*, and enlarges the *Judgment* with regard to the *Magnitude of extended Beings* : But *Christianity* produceth an universal Greatness of Soul, Philosophy encreaseth our Views in every Respect; but *Christianity extends* them to a Degree *beyond* the Light of Nature.

How *mean* must the most exalted Potentate on Earth appear to that Eye which takes in innumerable Orders of blessed Spirits, differing in Glory and Perfection? How little must the *Amusements of Sense* seem to one engaged in so noble a Pursuit, as the *Assimilation of* himself to the *Deity*, which is the proper Employment of every Christian? Let any Impartial Man judge, which hath the *nobler* Sentiments, which the *greater* Views; He, whose Notions are stinted to a *few* miserable *Inlets of Sense*, or He, whose Sentiments are raised above the *common Taste*, by the *Anticipation* of those Delights, which will *satiate* the Soul when the *whole Capacity* of her *Nature* is *branched out* into *new Faculties*? He, who looks for nothing *beyond* this short Span of Duration; or He, whose Aims are *co-extended* with the *endless Lengt* of *Eternity*? He, who derives his Spirit from the Elements, or He, who thinks it inspir'd by the ALMIGHTY? *A. B.*

Universal Spectator, May 12. No. 240.

SIR,

MR *Sprightly* is a young Gentleman about 68, who will be call'd only Master *Bob* ; as the Ladies, who will be called *Misses* till they are married, so says he, if any Body calls me other than *Master*, till I have a Wife, I shall take it as an Affront; you see the *French* have no other Word than *Garçon, Boy,* for those our unmannerly Tongue calls *Batchelors*. *Sprightly* is a great Antiquarian; and being ask'd, why the *French*, were a more sprightly active People than the *English* ? For the same Reason, says *Bob*, that a

Frog is a more nimble Creature than an Ox. Every Animal receives a Tincture from its Food; and no doubt Men partake of the Nature of the Animals they feed upon. This may be observ'd from the Difference between our own Quality and our Rusticks: The former, who have a light Diet, are tender and delicate, and little distinguishable for their Nicety and Indolence from our Ladies; whereas our Country People, who are accustom'd to Swine's Flesh, Beef and Mutton, are selfish, greedy, strong, and sheepish. Q. *Elizabeth*'s Maids of Honour were robust *bona Roba's*, who would shake a Man by the Collar on the least Affront, as the late *ingenious* Mr *Durfey* has observ'd,

> And many a Roman Nose I've rap't,
> When I was a Dame of Honour.

This must be attributed to their Diet. They breakfasted on cold roast Beef, or a Beef Steak. To strengthen my Opinion all Physicians agree Hare is a melancholy Meat; because Men participate of the Nature of that Animal by feeding upon it. For the same Reason the Blood of a Stag prolongs Life.

This leads me to consider the Variety of Tempers among Men, even the Difference in the same Man, and recalls to Memory the Fables of the antient Poets, who were the first Philosophers. The Fable of *Prometheus* forming a Man from the Members of different Beasts, hinted at the various Passions we are subject to. In Conformity to this Fiction, we give Men Epithets from the Beasts they most resemble. A Man who gives a loose to his Passions, we call a *Brute* ; one who loves Money, a *Swine* ; the lascivious Man, a *Goat* ; the brave, a *Lion* ; the meek a *Dove* ; the Coward, or rather *Cowheart*, as having the Heart of a Cow ; the Fable of the *Centaurs*, a Creature compos'd of Man and Horse, shews how difficult it is to make our Reason and our sensual Inclinations, agree because this Union depends upon a thorough Knowledge of ourselves, which is the most important Point of Wisdom, so important that the greatest Men of Antiquity thought that excellent Precept, *Know thy self*, could come from no other than a God.—

Hence Mr Sprightly *takes an occasion to make a Digression, to recommend a Scrutiny into our Actions*. The Pythagoreans, says he, did this thrice every Day. S. crates made a doubt whether he could ever be able to comprehend himself. And concludes with that Saying of *Cicero*,

That

That our Lives ought to be compared to an eloquent Harangue; they ought to be all of a Piece; and the way to have them so, is, in Mr *Sprightly's* Opinion, to bring every Day's Action before the Tribunal of our Conscience. *A. B.*

London Journal, May 12. Nº 724.

Of Kings, Ministers, and People.

SIR *Wm Temple* justly observes, "That there is a certain *Restlesness of Mind and Thought*, which seems inseparably annexed to our Natures and Constitutions, unsatisfied with what we are, or at present possess, and ever troubling or corrupting the Content and Happiness of our Lives. From this *Original Fountain* issue those *Streams of Faction*, that, with some Course of Time and Accidents, over-flow the wisest *Constitutions*, treat the *best* Princes and *truest* Patriots like the worst *Tyrants*, and most seditious Disturbers of their Country, and bring such Men to *Scaffolds* as deserve *Statues*. The most extraordinary Persons have fallen Victims to the wicked Arts of Men, who cover their own *Ends* under those of the *Publick*; who, not only discover Miscarriages where they are, but *forge* them where they are not; who quarrel first with the *Officers*, and then with the *Prince* or *State*; who make *Fears* pass for *Dangers*, and *Appearances* for *Truth*; who misrepresent *Misfortunes* for *Faults*; and under the Pretence of *Patriots*, *undermine* the Credit and Authority of the *Government*, on purpose to set up *their own*."

This is a perfect Description of the *pretended Patriots* of our Days. Not a *Paragraph* in History, nor a *Reflexion* made by an honest *Historian* upon *arbitrary* and *tyrannical* Government, but is made *parallels* with the *present* Government.

The *Craftsman* began a late Paper with Sir *Walter Raleigh* and Dr *Prideaux.* (see p. 202. H) And what is the *infamous* Use he makes of this? Why, to insinuate to the People, that such is the State of Things *in our own Country.* Instead of shewing the *real Difference* between those Governments and Ministers and the *present*, not only Ministers are threatned with Assassinations and Murders, but the Government itself with a *Dissolution.* To this Purpose is a Passage in one of these weekly Libellers (see p. 201 E) The last *Craftsman* has likewise a remarkable Passage (see p. 230 G) The

Sense of which can be no other than this, *That* CHURCH *and* KING *are going to make* SLAVES *of us*; and that the People say, they will not be made *Slaves*, tho' it be at the Price of the Destruction both of CHURCH and KING; and therefore *To Arms*; *Britons! Strike home.*

To this End are the *High Authority* and *Original Power* of the People trump'd up; but it is our great Felicity that the Constitution has been preserv'd without them ever since the *Revolution*, excepting *some Attempts* in the four last years of Q. *Anne*; when the same *execrable Traytor* was at the Head of *Power*, who is now at the Head of *Faction*, and at the Head of *some of those Whigs*, who then counted him the most execrable Traytor that *England* ever bred.

The Writers who make these *Infamous Parallels*, at the same Time roar out against *Bribery and Corruption*: But can there be a Corruption *equal* to that of infusing into Peoples Minds, that *legal* and *limited* Monarchies are the same as *arbitrary* and *illegal* Tyrannies? Thus are the People taught to *Speak Evil of Dignities*, and to lose all Reverence for *Government*, and the *Persons* of our Governors; and are insensibly led into such fatal *National Prejudices* by *two Incendiary Journals*, that I tremble to think of what may be the Consequence of so *unexampled* a Licentiousness, almost *inconsistent* with the very *Being* of Government.

Not that they bring any *Reasoning* which is *conclusive*, or *Parallel* that is *just*; and they know they have no Occasion for *Truth*; for in *free Countries* the People are prone to *believe* ill of Men in Power; and from this *Disposition* greedily swallow *any Materials* for Truth, which the Enemies of the Government throw before them. Thus these Journalists have often produced Scraps of *History* not *Argument*, to prove, "That a *wise King* would put away his Minister when he became *odious* to the People." But all the Instances from the *Gavestons, Spencers, Empsons,* and *Dudleys,* and from K. *Charles* and the D. of *Buckingham,* are only Instances of *weak Kings* and *wicked Ministers.* What have we to do with these? Is it a Consequence, that because some Kings of old ought to have dismiss'd *wicked* and *arbitrary* Ministers, when the People assembled in *Parliament* desir'd it, that therefore a King of *England* should give up a Minister, who never advised his Majesty to one *arbitrary Action,*

Action, only becaufe there is a *Clamour* raifed againft him amongft the *vulgar* and interefted Men, led on by the *Crafty* and *Ambitious*? This would be to eftablifh Iniquity by a *high Authority* indeed. If *Minifters* are to be thus treated, 'tis the greateft *Misfortune* to be the *greateft Men*; who feem rais'd up to Power, only to be *thrown down*; and adorned for *Sacrifice* rather than for *Glory*. But his Majefty knows, that the only way to fit *eafy* and *firm* upon his Throne; is to govern by *the Laws of the Land*; to be *fteady* in the Support of his Friends, and not to *fear* his Enemies: This is the way to be King.

The *Craftfman*, May 12. No. 358.

I Was in hopes, fays D'*anvers*, that the *Projector of Excifes* would have pocketted up his late Difgrace, and inftructed his Advocates to fhew fome Marks of Contrition and Humiliation. But it feems he infolently perfifts in the Uprightnefs of his *Scheme*, and gives us to underftand, it is only laid afide for the prefent, in Compliance with the unreafonable Prejudices of a felf-interefted, or mifguided Multitude. Nay, he hath manifefted his Defign, by taking a mean Advantage againft thofe who oppos'd his Meafures. He may think this a politick Step to convince the World he has not loft Ground, and to deter others from prefuming to controul his Will in any future Project. But it feems as if he took Delight in Storms of State; tho' he hath given Proof he wants Courage to weather them.

I was led into thefe Thoughts by fome Papers, publifhed in Behalf of Excife, even fince the Demolition of that *execrable Project*; particularly one, intitled, *An Englifhman's Thoughts on the late Danger of the Conftitution*, printed in the *Daily Journal* of the 27th paft.

I fhall confine my Remarks to that Part of it, which relates to the *Methods employ'd to oppofe the late Bill, for extending Excifes*. " If it fhall ever happen, fays he, That publick Meafures are influenced and directed by any Confideration, but the *Reafon of Things*, and the *Good of the Community*, the Happinefs, the Safety of a *free People*, and the very Being of a *well-ballanced Conftitution* are at an End."] This I grant, and am glad to find a *minifterial Writer* pleading for the Freedom and Independency of Parliament. I hope *thefe Gentlemen* will not for the future, indecently reflect on a *Bill*, for

preventing any unwarrantable Practices in that *auguft Affembly*; for, the fecret Influence of a *Bribe*, or a *Penfion*, is more dangerous to the *Freedom of Parliaments and Conftitution*, than the *open Petitions*, or *Inftructions* of the People to their Reprefentatives, againft any deftructive Scheme. However *uncommon* thefe Methods have been, they are fully warranted by the fundamental Laws of our Government, as well as the frequent practice of our Forefathers.

But we are told, *The People are too ignorant of the general State of Affairs, to be intrufted with the important Power of governing the Government*: *That fuch Ignorance is unavoidable, unlefs* Minifters *are to communicate their Difpatches to the World, and our Enemies be acquainted with every Step we defign againft them*.] Whatever Force there might be in this Argument, as to *foreign Affairs*, in Time of *War*, it is nothing in a Point of *Domeftick Government*, which the Body *of the People* muft underftand better than any *Minifter of State* whatfoever.

As to their attending the *Houfe of Commons* with a Petition in a *tumultuous Manner*, I appeal to every impartial By ftander, whether fo large a Concoufe of People ever behav'd with more Decency, or Regard to the Dignity of the Place. The *Merchants* and *Traders* difmiffed their Servants as foon as they got out of their Coaches, that they might commit no Diforders. Nay, they did not attend the *Sheriffs* with their *Petition*; but went fome Time afterwards, and appeared only in the *Court of Requefts*, and adjoyning Coffee-houfes, peaceably, to folicit againft the Bill.

If there happened any little Infult, or Diforder, in the Evening of that Day, when the Bill was put off, it ought to be imputed to that Exuberance of Joy, which is apt to break out on fuch Occafions. The Merchants never encourag'd any fuch Outrage. If the fame Spirit difcover'd itfelf thro' out the Kingdom, and the *Projector* was contemptuoufly treated *in Effigie*, it is what he might expect, and ought to be look'd upon as a very moderate Satisfaction for his Endeavours to opprefs them in *Reality*.

He tells us, " The *wifer* and *better Part of the Kingdom* fee no Reafon for Exultation meerly becaufe an honeft Attempt to prevent notorious Frauds hath not been attended with Succefs; *nor any other propofed in its Room*."] I fhould
be

be glad to know where these *wise* and *good* Men live. If they should discover themselves as a *Party* I believe they would appear to consist of *Projectors, Pensioners* and *Excisemen.* I cannot add *Placemen* to the Number, several of them having been obliged to resign some of the best Employments in the Kingdom, meerly because they were so short-sighted as not to discover the *Honesty* of that Attempt. Unless I am mistaken, a Motion was made in the *House of Commons* for a Committee, to enquire into the *Frauds of the Customs,* several Days before this Paper was published. As this Motion arose from *those Gentlemen,* who opposed the *Excise Scheme,* they have purg'd themselves from the Imputation of being the *Patrons of Fraud;* and tho' this Enquiry is not fallen to their Lot, we may assure ourselves the Business will be effectually done by Those who are chosen for that Purpose. I shall only recommend to their Thoughts an Observation of the late Ld *Shaftsbury.* " I know very well, *says He,* many Services are done to the Publick for the sake of a *Gratuity;* and that *Informers,* in particular, are to be taken Care of, and sometimes made *Pensioners of State;* but I shall never allow my Esteem on any other Man than the *voluntary Discoverers of Villany and hearty Prosecutors of their Country's Interest.* And I know nothing greater, or nobler, than the undertaking and managing some *important Accusation;* by which some *high Criminal of State,* or some form'd *Body of Conspirators against the Publick,* may be arraign'd, and brought to Punishment, thro' the honest Zeal, and publick Affection of a *private Man.*"

We are told, *the Commissioners in all Counties, ease themselves, and lay disproportion'd Burthens upon their poorer Neighbours.*] This seems an odd Compliment to almost all the landed Gentlemen in *England* worth 100 l. *per Ann.* and comes very improperly from the Advocate of a *Minister,* who hath publickly declared, that whatever Inequality there may be, he looks upon all Methods to alter it as impracticable; and that He will never attempt it.

I shall conclude with desiring the *mercantile and trading part of the Kingdom* to keep themselves on their Guard; since the *great Projector of their Ruin,* still persists in his *Scheme,* and threatens to revive it; nor think themselves safe, while *such a Man* hath any Power or Credit in

the Kingdom; for if they suffer Him to recover Strength, they will fall unpitied, and perhaps undefended.

The *Daily Courant,* May 15.
An Answer to the foregoing Craftsman.

AFter Gentlemen have been actually assaulted and wounded, by a rude and lawless Rabble, spirited up by *D'anvers,* and convened by the inferior Tools of his Faction; when he has found that those who were doomed Victims to the Malice and Ambition of implacable Malecontents, were providentially preserved from the wicked Designs formed against them, then the whole Affair has been turned into a Jest: Those that escap'd the Ponyard, were baited with the basest and most abusive Language from an insolent and desperate Rabble, met together in such open Defiance of the Laws, to awe and comptroll the Debates of Parliament; and this Rabble, which did actually attack several of the Members, has in Terms of great Tenderness been represented by Mr *D'anvers,* as the *mercantile Part of the Nation, substantial Tradesmen, and sober Citizens,* who came down to *Westminster,* as humble Supplicants, to implore the House of Commons to reject the Bill for altering the Duties on Tobacco; a great Compliment truly to the *Mercantile Part of the Nation!*

But to fix all these Riotous Proceedings on the *Merchants and Traders,* he says, *They dismissed their Servants as soon as they got out of their Coaches.* If then the Persons present, when these Outrages were committed, were chiefly *Merchants and Traders,* either Mr *D'anvers* is guilty of a very injurious Reflection upon that useful and worthy Body of Men; or they must be the Authors of all the Violence and Outrage offer'd to the Members of the House of Commons on this Occasion; for how light soever he may make of the Matter, the Parliament was of Opinion, it was an Offence of so flagrant a Nature, and such an Indignity and Insult upon them as to deserve their Censure and Resentment, and they adjudg'd such Transactions a notorious Breach not only of the Laws of the Land, but also of the Privilege and Freedom of Parliament.

He allows there were *some little Insults and Disorders committed.* This Confession is so extraordinary from him, that we may, without any forced Inference, conclude it to have been a dangerous Riot. But he says, *such little Insults can't be pre-*
vented

vented in a great Multitude. No; therefore the Law has made such mobbish Meetings a Capital Offence; a Law which one of the reputed Writers of the *Craftsman* was most zealous in promoting, tho' he is since dissatisfy'd with it. But no great Stress ought to be laid on the Actions, Principles, or Writings of this Gentleman, whose Character is a perfect Contradiction to itself, fixt and constant to nothing but Malice, Envy, and Revenge; mourning for the Prosperity of his Country, exulting upon any Misfortune he imagines has happened to it, and, like *Nero*, setting it on Fire, and then singing Songs of Joy and Triumph, while it is consuming in Flames.

Grubstreet Journal, May 10. No. 177.
The Master of the New House vindicated.
Mr BAVIUS.

IN your 174th *Journal*, (see p. 194) one of your Correspondents affirms, that Mr RICH refused a Tragedy, which he allowed was writ in a *good Stile, and that the Passions were well moved*] Mr R—PH offer'd a Tragedy, to some Passages of which Mr RICH objected, but did not insist on his dictating the Alterations

Mr R— is likewise accus'd of rejecting a Comedy, the Dialogue of which he own'd, was *easy* and *genteel*, the Characters *new, and drawn from the Life*.] Mr RICH knows of no such *Comedy*, so offer'd him.

Again, That M. VOLTAIRE's *Zaira* translated, met with the same Fate.] Mr A. HILL shew'd Mr RICH a Translation of two or three Scenes in the 3d Act of *Zaira*; which he said was done by his Brother. Mr RICH found no Fault; but told Mr H—LL he could not oblige him without breaking previous Engagements.

The last Article of Accusation is, that Mr R— got a whole Opera work'd up by a young Gentleman of *Cambridge*, out of a Piece surreptitiously taken from the Author of the first mentioned Tragedy.] One Mr C-MBE, a Clergyman, submitted a comic Piece to Mr RICH, who thought it had Merit but too thin of Characters. About the same Time Mr P—*the* young Gentleman of Cambridge, shew'd Mr RICH another comic Piece. Out of these two Mr RICH judged it possible to make an agreeable Entertainment. Accordingly Mr P— and Mr C—MBE, jointly made a compleat Opera, and for 40l. Mr C—MBE agreed to give up his Right in it to Mr P—. A Day or two before the Money was to be paid, Mr RICH was informed that the Piece belonged to Mr R—PH; and suspecting some Imposition, he acquainted Mr P— with what he had been told. Mr P— went to Mr C—MBE, and expostulated with him. Mr C—MBE appeared very much confused, but insisted on the 40l. and pleaded his Right of Possession to the Work. Mr P— here broke off with Mr C—MBE, and returned the Copy he had from him to Mr RICH, which was intitled *The Gallant Schemers*, thereby to convey it to the right Owner. After this the *Mock-Lawyer* was cast into the Shape it now is, without keeping in any Part of Mr C—MBE's Copy, Fable, or Manners: Yet Mr RICH is accused of ungenerous and fraudulent Practices, whose Friend was near being defrauded of 40l. by a scandalous Imposition. Either Mr C—MBE came with R—PH's Consent; or he imposed both on Mr RICH, and Mr R—PH, who ought therefore to declare, in his own Name, Mr C—MBE to be the Thief and Impostor; if he would not lie under a Suspicion of a Combination with him.

I have formerly shewn the Unworthiness of the Managers of *Drury-Lane* Playhouse. (see p.120.) This I shall further make appear in the Difference betwixt them, and the Master of *Covent Garden* House; in their Dispositions. The former refused two Persons a Benefit this Season, to whom they have been obliged; and that after three of the Managers had absolutely promis'd it. Mr RICH, on the first Application, consented to let one of those Persons have a Benefit at his House, from no other Motive than the Difficulties under which the Person labour'd in his Circumstances; to whom Mr RICH lay under no Obligation.

Yours, SOMEBODY.

Free Briton, May 17, No. 182.
On a Report of the Lord Mayor of London's distinguishing between publick Rejoycings and Riots. (see Occurr. 11.)

WHEN I behold, says Mr *Walsingham*, the present LORD MAYOR of LONDON, whose *virtuous Extraction*, ready Wit, and great Abilities, have render'd him as fit for Magistracy, as his *notorious Attachment* to the Liberties of his Country, and his *incomparable Zeal* for the Protestant Succession in his Majesty's Royal Family, and his *Aversion to a Popish Pretender* (whom he hath so frequently and so *piously* abjur'd) have so wor-

H h

worthily recommended to be the higheſt Magiſtrate in this great City, ſitting in the Chair, I muſt acknowledge it an effectual Confutation of all the idle Clamours, that the Faction againſt the Conſtitution have lately gained *too much Footing* in the City of *London.*

I cannot therefore avoid taking Notice of every Thing that relates to him in *his Adminiſtration of* that *Authority* with which he is inveſted (*Thanks be to God*) FOR ONE YEAR: And therefore I attentively read an Article in the common News-Papers, *That his Lordſhip had given it in Charge to the Grand Jury for the Ci-ty of* London, *at the laſt Seſſions at the* Old Bailey, *that, in the* Inqueſt *tken to be taken of ſuch Offences, Crimes, and Miſdemeanours, as had been committed within the Body of the County, they ſhould carefully diſtinguiſh between* Riots *and* publick Rejoycings *for any Good which had been done:* And *that the* Foreman *of the Grand Jury thanked his Lordſhip in a ſolemn Manner for this* weighty *and* uſeful Inſtruction.

Now, with humble Submiſſion, this Intelligence cannot be true. Pray conſider the Fact. Here is an Inqueſt to be taken; and the *Lord Mayor,* who hardly ever yet gave the Charge to the Grand Jury ſince the *Old Bailey* hath been a Court of *Oyer and Terminer,* is made to give them a *ſtrict Charge*—To what purpoſe? To inſtruct them that they *carefully diſtinguiſh* between *Riots* and *publick Rejoycings for ſome Great Good* lately done. Can this be true? Certainly not; 1. For that *no Great Good* hath been done. 2. That there have been *no Rejoycings for Great Good,* but rather for *great Miſchief.* 3. Becauſe it muſt ſhew his Lordſhip *apprehended* that *ſuch* rejoycings *might,* and *would be preſented* by the Grand Jury as *riotous* Proceedings againſt the Peace of the Crown, the Good of the City, and the Laws of the Land.

Neither can I believe the Grand Jury could return his Lordſhip *ſuch Kind of Thanks.* For, is it poſſible to ſuppoſe that the Grand Jury could not have known, without this Inſtruction, *how to diſtinguiſh* ſuch *Rejoycings* from riotous *Proceedings?*

Nor could this Procedure be true of this *honourable Magiſtrate;* as the Diſtinction, he is ſuppoſed to make, is *illegal* and *abſurd,* an Attempt to ſet up a *Diſpenſing Power* in a *Grand Jury of London,* under the *Direction of a Lord Mayor,* and directly tending to *miſlead* them in that *impartial* Enquiry, which *by their Oaths*

they are ſworn to make. For, by the *Common Law,* no *poſſible Diſtinction* can exiſt between *Riots* and *publick Rejoycings* made on any Account but this, *that ſome Rejoycings have at certain Times been made in a* peaceable, lawful *manner, without ſuch Circumſtances as deſcribe and conſtitute a* RIOT. A publick Rejoycing, *even for ſome Good* which hath been done, may be a moſt *miſchievous, tumultuous, riotous* Proceeding; and the Grand Inqueſt, in ſuch Caſes, are to preſent the *whole Fact,* namely, That *under* Pretence of rejoycing for an Inſtance of Good, *the Peace was broken,* and the Perſons of divers of *his Majeſty's Subjects were inſulted.*

If Magiſtrates can inſtruct *Grand Juries* to *diſpenſe* with their *Oaths and Conſciences;* if the *Lord Mayor of London* can charge the *Grand Inqueſt of London* to ſet aſide the Law of the Land for the Convenience of a Party, and to interrupt the free Execution of Juſtice, the *Magiſtracy of the City of London* would be a Power ſet up in Oppoſition to the Laws. Such a Perverſion of the *Grand Inqueſt of this City* would call aloud for ſome Animadverſion from the *Grand Inqueſt of the Nation.*

Who then can poſſibly believe a Paragraph which makes his Lordſhip act in *avowed Contempt and Defiance* of the unanimous Reſolutions, and the moſt ſolemn Declarations of the HOUSE OF COMMONS, notified to him by the four *Repreſentatives of the City of London?* Is it poſſible to believe, after a *lewd, riotous, diſorderly Rabble,* had, in the Court of Requeſts, and the Avenues to the Houſe of Commons, *inſulted* and *aſſaulted* ſeveral Members, under Pretence *of Rejoycing,* that the *Lord Mayor* himſelf ſitting in the Seat of *Juſtice,* could *inſtruct the Grand Jury* to *diſtinguiſh ſuch Proceedings from Riots,* becauſe *pretended to be* publick Rejoycings for a great Good lately done? This would be giving out a *Leſſon of Advice* to all the Grand Juries in all the great Towns, whoſe Charters give them the Privilege of Counties, to *diſpenſe* with their Oaths for the Convenience of a *Party.* Whoever then ſhall countenance Attempts ſo directly tending to deſtroy the Liberty of the ſupreme Legiſlature, is an ENEMY *to the Conſtitution of the Kingdom,* an *Invader of the Peace and Liberties of his Country,* is UNFIT *for all Kinds of publick Truſt,* and ought to be treated as a BETRAYER OF MANKIND.

PRO-

PROCEEDINGS *in last Session of* PAR-
LIAMENT.

UPON the 25th of *Feb.* Mr *Sandys* (according to Order) reported from the
Committee, to whom the Petition of the
Charitable Corporation was referred, the Result of their Enquiry as to the Time, Manner, and Circumstances of *George Robinson*,
Esq; and *John Thompson*, withdrawing themselves into Places beyond the Seas; whereupon it was ordered, that Leave should be given
to bring in a Bill, for the Appearance of
George Robinson, Esq; at a certain Time to
be fixed in the Bill; and it was also ordered,
that Leave should be given to bring in a Bill,
to encourage and compel *John Thompson*,
Warehouse-keeper to the Charitable Corporation, and his Accomplices, to surrender
themselves with the Books and Effects of the
said Company, at a certain Time, to be fixed in the Bill.

W——m W——s W——nn presented to the
House, a Petition of *Mary Leafe*, Wife of
Thomas Leafe, (who some Days before had
been by Order of the House, confined a close
Prisoner to *Newgate*, without the Use of
Pen, Ink, or Paper, or any Person's being
admitted to speak to him, for prevaricating
in his Evidence before the said Committee)
alledging, that her Husband was deprived by
such Restraint, of Subsistance, and wanted
the common Necessaries of Life for his Support, and therefore praying that the
House would give Leave, that the Petitioner
might have Access to her Husband. Upon
his presenting of this Petition, he informed
the House, that when the Petitioner put
this Petition into his Hands, he told her,
that he would not so much as desire that she
might have free Leave to go and come, but
that if she had a Mind to be confined with
her Husband, he would move for it; to which
she consented; and therefore he moved, that
she might have Leave to confine herself with
her Husband, if she thought fit. Whereupon,
G——les E——ke stood up and said, Sir, I
wish the Gentlemen of that Committee would
inform us, whether this *Leafe* has been guilty of any new Crime since his Confinement
to *Newgate*; for by what is proposed it would
seem to me, that he has since been guilty of
some very heinous Crime; you confin'd him to
Newgate for his Prevarication, but now you
are going to inflict a much more severe, an
unheard-of Punishment, upon the Man; you
are going to confine his Wife in the same
Room with him, and that without any thing
of his asking; for I do not find that he joins
in the Petition. (See Vol. II. p 769.)

Mr C——r. *Sir,* I should be glad the
worthy Member, who spoke last, would shew
us, how it was in the Power of Mr *Leafe* to

join in the Petition with his Wife; for he
having been confined without the Use of Pen,
Ink, or Paper, or any Person to speak to him,
I cannot easily comprehend, how it was possible for him to join in any Petition.

Some Members were for admitting her;
but at last Sir R——t W——le and Mr W——n
having taken Notice, That since his Confinement to *Newgate*, there might have been
several Things concerted among his Accomplices abroad, which his Wife, by being admitted at any Rate, could convey to him, and
might also convey to him Instructions how he
was to behave, and what to answer to any
Questions that might be put to him, whereby he would be rendered more obstinate, and
more able to conceal the Truth from the
Committee. The House thereupon ordered
the Petition to lie upon the Table.

Then was debated the Question about expelling of *George Robinson*, Esq; Many of
the Members were for expelling him immediately; for that though they were to endeavour by Rewards and Punishments to bring
him over in order to make a Discovery; yet
they were to have a particular Regard to their
own Honour: That it was proposed to grant
him a general Indemnity by Act of Parliament; and putting the Case that he thereupon came over, and made as full and as ample
a Discovery as could be desired; yet he would
still continue a Rogue, notwithstanding of
such Compliance, and therefore it would be
very improper that he should continue a
Member of that House; and for that Reason it would be necessary to expel him, before
the bringing in of this Bill for a general Indemnity; for if the Bill were once passed, he
might next Minute take the Benefit of it,
and they could not in Honour afterwards expel him; because it would be inflicting a
Punishment upon him, for a Crime for which
he had an Indemnity by Act of Parliament.

To this it was answered, by the Gentlemen of the other Side of the Question, That
they wished the expelling or not expelling of
him had not been mentioned upon that Occasion: The only Thing they had then before
them, was to contrive Means for prevailing
upon him to come over and make a Discovery
of that whole Affair: That if they should
then expel him, it would be terrifying him
from coming over at the same Time that they
were inviting him to come, which would be
a very inconsistent Manner of Proceeding:
That besides, it was not regular for them to
proceed directly to the expelling of him, without giving him Time to be heard; by the
Report then made to them, there was no
Crime as yet proved against him; by that
Report they could take no Notice of any
Thing but his Bankrupcy, and as to that he
ought at least to have time to be heard before

he

he were expelled; That the Honour of the House was as much concerned in Proceeding regularly even against a Rogue, as in not fitting with a Rogue; and therefore they were against so abrupt a Method of expelling him.

The Reply to this was, That by the Report then made to them, it appeared, that a Statute of Bankrupcy had been issued against him; that thereby his whole Estate, Real and Personal was vested in the Commissioners, and consequently he could not have the Qualification as to Estate that was necessary for every Man in order to entitle him to his Seat in that House: That moreover, by the Laws relating to Bankrupts, a Bankrupt was declared to be out of the King's Protection; he was in a manner an Outlaw, and therefore could not continue a Member of that House; and for that Reason they thought that the Bankrupcy alone was sufficient Ground for that House to proceed immediately to the expelling of him.

To this it was answered by the Gentlemen of the Law, That the Question as to a Man's being a Bankrupt or no, could not properly come before them, more especially before he had submitted and acknowledged himself a Bankrupt; that a Statute of Bankrupcy's being taken out against a Man, was no incontrovertible Proof of his being a Bankrupt; because, if upon his Petition it should appear that he was not a Bankrupt, the Statute would be superseded: It was true, they said, that by one of the Laws against Bankrupts in Q. *Elizabeth's* Time, a Man who was declared a Bankrupt according to that Statute, was declared to be out of his Majesty's Protection; but that there had been very few declared Bankrupts according to that Act; they did not know if there ever was any one but Mr *W——d* of *H——*; and that therefore no Argument could be drawn from that Statute as to the Case in Hand.

In this Debate Mr *P——n* proposed, that the Bill of Indemnity to be brought in as to *Robinson*, should contain an Exception as to the Privilege of his sitting in that House, by which they would leave themselves at Liberty to act as they thought proper, supposing he should appear and take the Benefit of the Indemnity to be granted him: To this it was objected, that the sending up of such a Bill to the other House, would be giving them a Power to intermeddle in an Affair relating to the Privilege of that House, which was not at all proper to be done; and therefore it was proposed to have the Indemnity Special; but this likewise was objected to, as being what would not be effectual for the purpose intended; because upon such an Indemnity it was not to be presumed that *Robinson* would come over; he could not be thereby secured against Parliamentary Censure; and therefore he

would never trust to any Special Indemnity.

This Debate was carried on for a long time on both Sides, with a great deal of Accuracy and fine Reasoning, but the Spirit of the House being strongly bent upon using all Means for procuring Justice to the injured Proprietors of that Corporation, the Debate went off without any Motion, and the abovementioned Bills were ordered, and brought in upon the 7th of *March*; upon which Day they were both read a first and second Time, and committed; and an Instruction was given to the Committee, to alter and make both the Bills into one, which was done accordingly next Day in the Committee. The Day after, viz. the 9th, the Report was made, and the Bill was ordered to be engrossed; and on the 13th, the Bill was read the third Time, passed, and sent up to the House of Lords; where it was soon passed.

On the 3d Day of *April*, this Affair occasioned some new Dispute; for the Day being then passed, on which *Robinson* and *Thompson* were to appear by the Act abovementioned, and neither of them, but particularly the said *Robinson*, not having appeared or surrendered himself in the Terms of the said Act; it was moved, That he might be expelled: But some of the Members took Notice, that by the said Act, he might within the Time limitted surrender himself to either House of Parliament; and though he had not surrendered to that House, yet they did not know but that he had surrendered himself to the other; and therefore they moved, That a Committee should be appointed to inspect the Journals of the Lords, and to report to that House, whether any, and what Proceedings had been before the Lords, in Consequence of an Act passed that Session, entitled, An Act to encourage and compel George Robinson, Esq; and John Thompson to appear, &c. But to this it was answered, That according to the Terms of the said Act, the said *Robinson* might have surrendered himself to the other House, and might thereby have freed himself from the Pains, to which he was by the said Act subjected, in case of his not appearing and surrendering; but that they had nothing to do with, when they came to consider, whether or no he ought to be expelled; because in that Question, they had nothing to consider of, but whether or no he had attended the Service of the House according to Orders; if he had, it would appear by his answering for himself in his Place, or by some Member's rising up and making an Excuse for him; if he had not, he was guilty of a high Contempt of the Orders and Authority of that House, for which he ought to be expelled; and that therefore they had not in the present Question any Business with the Journals of the other House.

At

At last the Question was put upon this Motion, and it was carried in the Negative. Then the House came to a Resolution, *nemine contradicente*, That *George Robinson*, Esq; having been charged in Parliament with being privy to and concerned in many indirect and fraudulent Practices, in the Management of the Affairs of the Charitable Corporation for Relief of industrious Poor, by assisting them with small Sums upon Pledges, at legal Interest; and with having got into his Hands very large Sums of Money belonging to the said Corporation; and being returned a Burgess to serve in this present Parliament for the Borough of *Great Marlow*, in the County of *Bucks*, and having never attended the Service of that House, although required so to do, was guilty of a high Contempt of the Orders and Authority of that House. And then next they resolved, *nemine contradicente*, That the said *George Robinson*, Esq; should be for his said Offence expelled that House.

On the 20th of *April*, the Order of the Day being read, for receiving the further Report from the Committee, to whom the Petition of the Proprietors of the Charitable Corporation was referred, the Serjeant at Arms attending the House, was ordered, to go with the Mace into *Westminster-Hall*, and into the Court of *Requests*, and Places adjacent, and summon the Members there to attend the Service of the House; and he being returned, Mr *Sandys* read the Report in his Place, together with the Appendix thereunto, and the same was ordered to be taken into Consideration upon that Day se'nnight, and such a Number of Copies of the Report with the Appendix was ordered to be printed, as should be sufficient for the Members of the House.

On that Day se'nnight, viz. the 27th, the Report was again read at the Table, and was ordered to be taken into further Consideration, on *Tuesday* then next; and accordingly on *Tuesday*, viz. the second of *April*, the House proceeded to take the same into their further Consideration as follows, viz.

Part of the said Report, relating to the Examination of Mr *John Harrison*, Accomptant to the Petitioners, and the Account by him produced, was read.

Resolved, That it appears to this House, that the Money paid in upon the Capital Stocks of the Charitable Corporation, for Relief of industrious Poor, by assisting them with small Sums upon Pledges at legal Interest, was upon the 15th Day of *Feb.* 1731, 353,817 *l.* 10 *s.* (See Vol. II. p. 578, 579.) and the Notes and Bonds, issued by the Committee and Assistants of the said Corporation, and then standing out, were 145,515 *l.* amounting in the Whole to 499,332 *l.* 10 11. And that the Pledges and Securities to make good the same, amount to no more than

77,507 *l.* 3 *s.* 24. 3 Farthings; so that there remains a Loss of 421,825 *l.* 6 *s.* 9*d.* Further

Resolved, That it appears to this House, that by the Charter granted to the said Corporation, the Choice of Officers, making of By-Laws, and the Management of the Affairs and Business of the said Corporation, are directed to be by a general Court.

And they also came to the several Resolutions following, viz.

Resolved, That it appears to this House, that under Colour of a Resolution of the General Court of the said Corporation, on *Nov.* 2. 1725, impowering the Committee of the said Corporation to begin and proceed in lending Money upon Pledges, and in order thereto, to chuse proper Officers, and agree upon Houses, and to prepare By-Laws to be laid before the General Court, and to do and perform all such other Matters and Things, as relate to the carrying on the Business of the said Corporation, the Committee of the said Corporation have from that Time taken upon them to appoint Officers; and to make Orders for the Management of the Affairs of the said Corporation, without the Approbation of a General Court.

Resolved, That it appears to this House, that 396,069 *l.* 11 *s.* 8 *d.* farthing is charged to be lent out upon Pledges at the Offices belonging to the said Corporation in *Fenchurch-Street*, and *Laurence-Pountney-Hill*, tho' no more Goods are to be found, to answer the same, than what upon a Valuation, amount to 40,000 *l.*

Resolved, That it is the Opinion of this House, that the taking the Key of the Warehouse in *Fenchurch-Street*, out of the Hands of Mr *Wainwright*, Accomptant of the said Corporation; who had given large Security, and ordering the same into the Hands of *Nathaniel Lovell* their Messenger, who had given no Security, was one principal Cause of great Losses to the said Corporation.

Resolved, That it is the Opinion of this House, that the discharging Mr *Clark*, Surveyor of the Warehouses belonging to the said Corporation, after he had made Observations upon the Insufficiency of the Value of Pledges, without examining into the Truth of the said Observations, and the not appointing another Surveyor in his room, gave a great Opportunity to *John Thompson*, their Warehouse-keeper, to defraud the Corporation, and was one other principal Cause of great Loss.

Resolved, That it is the Opinion of this House, that the permitting Borrowers to negotiate their Business, in the Names of *Rich. Woolley*, and *Tho. Warren*, and other Agents and Officers of the said Corporation, as Brokers, and not in their own Names, has been the Occasion of many Frauds, and very great Loss to the said Corporation.

Next

Next Day the House came to the following Resolutions, viz.

Resolved, That it is the Opinion of this House, That the impowering the Officers at the Warehouse in Fenchurch-street belonging to the said Corporation, to lend any Sum whatever upon one Pledge, with the Consent of any one of the Committee or Assistants, by any Writing under his Hand, has been the Occasion of great Loss, and is contrary to the Intent and Purpose of the Charter of the said Corporation.

Resolved, That it is the Opinion of this House, That the impowering John Thompson, the Warehouse-keeper of the said Corporation, to lend as far as 2000 l. upon any one Pledge at his Discretion, has been another principal Cause of the great Loss sustained by the said Corporation.

Resolved, That it is the Opinion of this House, That the neglecting to take an Account from Time to Time of the several Pledges said to be made to the said Corporation, and to enquire into the Reality and Value of them, and to inspect into the Warehouses of the said Corporation, were great Breaches of Trust, and were other principal Causes of great Loss to the said Corporation.

Resolved, That it is the Opinion of this House, That the erecting or issuing Cash-Notes and Bonds, without the Authority or Consent of a General Court of the said Corporation, was a great Breach of Trust, and another principal Cause of the Loss sustained by the said Corporation.

Resolved, That it is the Opinion of this House, That the Committee and Assistants of the said Corporation acquainting the several General Courts, called for declaring Dividends, That they had cast up the Books, examined the Accompts, and considered their Profits, without having ever inspected the Warehouses, to see whether they had any Pledges for the several large Sums of Money lent, and sometimes without having seen any Account whatsoever, in order to induce the General Courts to make large Dividends, was an infamous Contrivance to give his Majesty's Subjects a false Notion of the Value of the Shares of the said Corporation, that some of the Committee and Assistants might the more easily dispose of their own Shares at exorbitant Prices.

Resolved, That it appears to this House, That the several Licences granted for augmenting the Capital of the said Corporation to 300,000 l. and 600,000 l. were obtained upon false Suggestions and Representations, and were applied for to the Crown without any Order of a General Court, or Court of Committee of the said Corporation, and in a private and clandestine Manner, and kept Secret for some Months, for the private Advantage of some of the Committee and Assistants, and their Agents, during which Time great Numbers of Shares were bought by them.

Resolved, That it appears to this House, That Copartnerships have been entered into between some of the Committee and Assistants and some Agents and Servants of the said Corporation, in which the Cash of the said Corporation has been employed, and great Sums stand embezzeled.

Resolved, That it appears to this House, That many notorious, fraudulent, and indirect Practices have for some Years last past been carried on by Persons concerned in the Direction and Management of the said Corporation, their Servants, Agents, and Accomplices, to the utter Ruin of many of his Majesty's faithful Subjects, in manifest Violation of the Trust reposed in them, and contrary to the Intention of their Charter.

On the 8th, the House resumed again the Consideration of the said Report, and Resolved, that the R.H. Sir † Robert Sutton, Kt of the Bath, Sir Archibald Grant, Bart, Dennis Bond, Wm Burroughs, Esqs; Mr George Jackson, Mr Benj. Robinson, Mr Wm Squire, George Robinson, John Thompson, Rich. Woolley, and Tho. Warren, having been guilty of many † notorious Breaches of Trust, and many indirect and fraudulent Practices in the Direction and Management of the Affairs of the Charitable Corporation, and having thereby occasion'd great Losses to many of his Majesty's Subjects, ought to make a just Satisfaction for the same.

And it was order'd, that Leave be given to bring in a Bill, to restrain the said Gentlemen, all except Wm Squire, (who was before absconded, or gone out of the Kingdom) from going out of the Kingdom, for the Space of one Year, and until the End of the then next Session of Parliament; and for discovering their Estates and Effects; and for preventing the transporting or alienating the same; and for obliging the said Wm Squire to surrender himself; also a Bill was order'd to be brought in for the Relief of the Sufferers in the Charitable Corporation.

Both these Bills speedily passed, but the House of Lords expunged out of the first, the Names of Mr George Jackson and Mr Benj. Robinson.

On the 16th came on the Affair of Ballou's Letter, (see the Original French and the Translation of it Vol. II. p. 768.) which was order'd by both Houses to be burnt by the Hands of the Common Hangman (see Vol. II. p. 773, 785 A B)

† On further Examination of this Affair next Session Sir Robert Sutton and Dennis Bond, Esq; were judged guilty only of a Neglect of Duty. (See Occurrences May 3.)

The *Craftsman*, May 19. No. 359.
Vindication of a Paragraph relating to the E. of Ch―'s Removal.

MR D'ANVERS,

THE *Free Briton* of *April* 26. (see p. 194) hath arraigned you of high Crimes and Misdemeanours, in That *you have given a Detail of the K―g's Proceedings, in dismissing a noble Lord, &c.* particularly for the following Sentence; *viz.* " The World seems greatly *astonish'd* at so unexpected an Event; and Those, who are most zealous for the present Royal Family, *grieve* to see so able and faithful a Servant dismiss'd, in so critical a Conjuncture. " (see p. 212.) But,

In the first Place, the Fact is not truly stated; for you gave no Account of the *noble Lord's Rise and Fortune.*—His *Rise* was no more than This, that a Person of great *Quality, Fortune,* and *Talents,* bred up in *Courts,* happen'd to arrive at great Employments. This does not seem very *astonishing.*—His *Fortune,* I believe, has not been much increas'd by his *Posts:* But such a Mistake may be easily accounted for in Mr *Walsingham,* who by his Intimacy with *one great Man,* imagines *Rise* and *Fortune* are inseparable.

But he lays the greatest Stress upon the Words *astonished* and *grieve.* As to the *first,* I affirm the good People of *England* have a natural Right to be *astonished. Astonished* is so far from being arrogant or disrespectful, that it is enjoyn'd us as a Duty by the great Governour of the Universe, *Mark me, and be astonished! Tremble, and be astonished!* and some small Degree of it is certainly due to his *Vicegerents.* That this manner of Expression in the present Case was particularly respectful, will appear by the *Negative* of the Proposition; for suppose the *Craftsman,* after an Enumeration of his Lordship's Services, had said, *that the World is* NOT *astonish'd at such an Event;* would it not have been construed into a scandalous Insinuation, that the noble Lord was dismiss'd, because a *faithful* and *able Minister* does not suit with the present Times? The Word *astonish'd* therefore implies an humble Resignation to the Royal *Pleasure,* without any curious Enquiries into the Reasons, by which it acts. It is the *Ignorance* only of the Cause, not *any* Suspicion that a *Cause* is wanting, which produces the *Astonishment;* and therefore Mr *Walsingham,* who is in the *secret of Affairs,* is in the Case of an A-

stronomer, who laugh'd at the *Astonishment* of the Vulgar, during the *late Eclypse.* Dear Mr *W.* be so good as to cure us, inferior Mortals, of this *offensive Astonishment,* and unravel the Mystery in plain Terms. In one Place, you seem to impute this Event to *Errors* and *Infirmities,* but afterwards insinuate so terrible a Cause, that to speak it out would be *Scandalum Magnatum.* But you, *Sir,* always preserve such a Decency of Expression that you are pretty safe from Prosecutions of that Nature; tho' I am glad to hear you have received farther Assurances, and are now *at full Liberty to enjoy the Disgrace of this noble Lord, whenever your* Genius prompts you, *or your* Patron *directs you, without any Apprehensions of* Breach of Privilege, *Actions of* Scandalum Magnatum, *or even* a Cudgel. I could not conceal my Joy, upon hearing of the candid Message you lately receiv'd; and wish you could prevail on your *Patron* to give poor *Francklin* some gracious Promise of Indemnification from the *Cudgels and Flails of the Law.*

If there was any thing really blameable in the Form of Expression, the *Craftsman* had a pretty good Apology, that he was let into it by the general Example of his Countrymen, who have been *astonish'd* at almost every Thing that has happen'd in the World for several Months past, both as to the *political Maxims* advanced and defended, and the *Events* which have occurred. Is it not *astonishing* that a *great Minister* should be baulk'd in his Design of passing a most beneficial Law, even during *this Parliament;* or that He should acquire *new Credit* and *Authority,* by being burnt and treated with other Marks of Indignity, in all the great Market-places of the Kingdom?

As to the other Term, I will undertake to prove, that it is likewise the Duty of every good Subject to be *grieved,* when the *Crown* loses the Service of an *able Minister,* be the Cause what it will, whether it be for his *Misbehaviour,* or by a *Misrepresentation* of his Actions.

The *Craftsman* used the Word *grieve,* no otherwise than being *sorry,* or concern'd; whereas Mr *W.* changes it into *grievous,* which implies, that the *noble Lord's* Dismission was *burthensome* and *oppressive* to the People.

I must here beg Leave to be somewhat *astonish'd* at Mr *W's* Intimation, that if his *Patron* were turn'd out, He would drop Him at once, and not afford Him a com-

commemorative Paragraph, setting forth his *Foibles*, &c. This is a little ungenerous in Mr *W.* who hath received so many Favours at his Hands, but when that fatal Hour arrives, as one Day it must, I hope somebody will do *the Honourable Gentleman* that last Office.

Mr *W.* is often deficient in point of Proof, his only Argument is a *tautological Syllogism*, or *Premises*, which prove the contrary of his *Conclusion*, and consists in several Times repeating the *Proposition*, or *Conclusion*, which ought to be proved. When he descends from *Assertions* to *Reasoning*, he often mistakes in his Conclusion, of a *Negative* for an *Affirmative*. For Example, your mentioning the *Abilities* and *Services* of a *Minister* is set forth as upbraiding the King with his Favours; whereas it is *commending* his Majesty; for no Man can be *upbraided* for favouring *Merit*; had you said *Disservices* and *Inabilities*, his Conclusion would naturally follow.

As for *identical propositions* (as That of *deserving Favour by Merit*) They ought to be excused in Mr *W.* as the *only Truths* he deals in. Therefore, if the *Craftsman* had given us the censur'd Proposition in different Terms; *that the World seems greatly astonished, and Those, who are most Zealous for the present Royal Family,* grieve *to see so unable and so unfaithful a Servant continu'd in Power, in so critical a Conjuncture*; in such a Case He would have been justly chargeable with abusing a *certain Person in a high Station*; and perhaps with reflecting on the K—g, for continuing his Favour to so *worthless a Wretch.*

I cannot conclude without congratulating Mr *W.* on the glorious Harvest of Scandal, which this Season is like to produce; for as *Court Favour* is the only Criterion of *Merit* in his Eyes, so every Man who happens to lose an *Employment*, or the Countenance of his *Patron*, becomes at once the Object of his Resentment, and is sure to smart under the Lash of his Pen.   *Yours, &c.*

§ S I R,

THE Account of the Druggists Petition, in the *Daily Courant* of *April* 25, (see p. 111,) being wrong stated, it's thought necessary to inform the Publick that the Considerations which induced them to take that Step, were, to be relieved from the Trouble and Oppression of the *Excise Laws*; and if possible, put a Stop to the

Smuggling Trade. To this Purpose, a great Number of them met at the *Swan in Cornhill*, in Feb. last. Then a Committee of 12 was chosen to conduct the Affair. They apply'd to *the first Commissioner of the Treasury*, but without Effect. Thereupon *that Committee* was dissolved, and another chosen, to prepare and solicit a *Petition*; and to get Hands to it, two ways were offer'd, *viz.* Either *to call the People together, or to send it to their Houses.* The *Committee* thought there was not Time for the *first*, and therefore took the *last Method*, and deliver'd their Petition to one of their *Agents*, to call upon the *Dealers* the next Day; not to *solicit Hands*, but to give such as pleased an Opportunity to sign it; and this he did *alone*. In this manner it was promoted and obtained. It was signed by all *Dealers*, and by *Them* only; and if the greatest Part of them were *Men of no Substance*, it can be owing to nothing but the *oppressive Laws*, from which they sought Relief. In the Votes it was called a *Petition from the Druggists, Grocers, China Men*, and *others dealing in Coffee, Tea*, &c. which may justify its being signed by many who are not *Druggists*. The Reason why all the *Principal Druggists* did not sign it is, some were of the late *Committee*; others had left off this Branch of Trade, to avoid the Slavery of *Excise Laws*. Those who refused to sign were *Ten*; and the only Reason they gave was, They feared the Time was too short, and wished they had gone to *Parliament*, when they went to the *Treasury*.

London Journal, May 19. No. 725.

On the intended Marriage of the Princess Royal with the Prince of Orange.

THIS Marriage naturally puts us in Mind of that illustrious Prince of *Orange*, who deliver'd us from the Two greatest Evils, *Popery*, and *arbitrary Power*, for which a *grateful People* placed the Crown on his Head, whereby such a *happy Ballance of Power* was settled between King and People, as *firmly secured* our Liberties, which before were *precarious*. 'Tis hard to determine which to admire most, his Majesty's *Gratitude*, in giving back, as it were, the Crown to a Family, by Means of whose Virtues he received it; or his *high Regard* to his People, by giving them a *stronger Security* of their Liberties.

This *Gratitude* in his Majesty is a Piece of *Natural Justice*; for no sooner was the

the Crown placed on the Head of King *William*, but he immediately got a Bill into the House, *For declaring the Rights and Liberties of the Subject, and settling the Succession of the Crown*, and labour'd hard, by means of the House of Lords, to have a Provisoe in Favour of the Princess *Sophia*. But the *Jacobites* and *Tories* so prevail'd in the House of Commons, that their Lordships Provisoe was disagreed to. The King used his utmost Endeavours to bring the Commons to a Compliance, and declared in Council, That his Queen, the Prince and Princess of *Denmark* desired it as well as himself; but the Birth of the D. of *Gloucester* soon put an End to the virtuous Design, which, upon that Prince's Death, the King resumed; and a little before his Dissolution, fixed the *Crown* and our *Happiness*. Hear his Words;

My Lords and Gentlemen.

" Our great Misfortune in the Death of the D. of *Gloucester* hath made it absolutely necessary, that there should be a further *Succession to the Crown* in the *Protestant* Line, after Me and the Princess: The *Happiness* of the Nation and the *Security* of our Religion (which is our chiefest Concern) seems to depend so much upon This, that I cannot doubt but 'twill meet with a *general* Concurrence; and I earnestly recommend it to your *early* and *effectual* Consideration. "

This Marriage must give the highest Joy to *every Heart truly English*; for tho' we have no *immediate* Concern in it; yet we are happy that *Ages* and *Generations* to come may be happy by this very Match. May we ever be as grateful to the House of *Hanover*, as that *Illustrious House* is *just* to us, and our *Natural* and *Civil* Rights.

But tho', by the *Goodness* of Providence, and the *Wisdom* of Laws, we are placed in the best Situation for Happiness that ever People experienced, we make a hard Shift to be *miserable*. 'Tis the *Nature* of *Englishmen*, and observed by all Foreigners, to be *peculiar* to us. There may be indeed another Spring of our *political* Uneasinesses; we are *free to find Fault*; and because we *can* we *will*. Thus *Humour and Pride* often produce *Factions* in a State, but not so often as *Ambition* and *Self-Interest.* " A great Cause of *Discontents*, under the best Government, (as Sir *Wm Temple* observes) is the *unequal Condition* that must neces-

sarily fall to the share of so many and so different Men that compose them: All are easily satisfied with themselves and their own *Merit*, tho' they are not so with their *Fortune*; and when they see others in better Condition, whom they think less deserving, they lay it upon the ill Constitution of the Government, the Partiality or Humour of Princes, or the Negligence or Corruption of Ministers. "

The *Use* we are to make of this Humour is, to adhere to our *Senses* and our *Reason*; both which assure us, we are as happy as 'tis in the Power of any thing *without* us, to make us; all the rest depends upon *ourselves*, and the *right Use* of our *inward* Faculties.

Fog's Journal, May 19. No 237.

Of governing by a Party.

WHEN an Administration endeavours to govern by a Party, 'tis presum'd their Designs are bad. This will appear if we examine the Conduct of *Catherine of Medicis.* She was the Wife of *Harry* II. and had Influence over Affairs, not only in his Life, but during the successive Reigns of her 3 Sons, *Francis* II, *Charles* IX. and *Henry* III. She was of a most restless Ambition, and brought with her into *France* some *Italians*, her Countrymen, who wanting to make their Fortunes, put her upon many Things, which gave Offence to the People; who being offended, were ill treated for being so.

In the Life of her Husband, she caress'd the Dutchess of *Valantinois*, the King's Mistress, and thereby found Means to gratify her darling Passion, the free Exercise of Power; for the King could refuse her Nothing. when he found her so complaisant. When the King was dead, and her Son *Francis* II. a Minor, succeeded, the Regency of Right belonged to the K. of *Navarre*, a Protestant. From that Minute she began to favour the Protestants; but at length prevailed on that Prince to resign the Regency. Then she banished the Dutchess of *Valantinois*.

Francis being dead, and *Charles* IX. succeeding, her Power continued, and she still cajol'd the Hugonots, having for that Purpose, employ'd a couple of Bishops without Religion or Morals, to associate with the Chiefs of the Hugonot Party, and to insinuate to them, that she was well affected to their Opinions in Matters of Religion. Nay, she published an Edict, to release those who had been imprison'd on Account of Religion: But at the same

I i   Time

Time employ'd the Conftable and others to inftill Fears and Jealoufies into the Minds of the Roman Catholicks; fo that both Parties might hate one another; which at laft ended in the cruel and inhuman Maffacre of the Hugonots on St. Bartholomy, which was projected at Court, and executed by the direct Orders of the Queen Regent, and Part of it in her Prefence. It being over, and fancying fhe might ftill keep the reft of the Hugonots in her Intereft, fhe caufed it to be given out that this Maffacre was committed by the *Guifes*, known Roman Catholicks; but they were fo offended at it, that they infifted that the King fhould write to the Provinces and Parliament of *Paris*, that what was done, was all by his own Order, which was accordingly done, with this Excufe, that the Admiral, and fome Chiefs of the Hugonots had form'd a Confpiracy to deftroy the King and all the Royal Family, even the K. of *Navarre* and Prince of *Conde*.

Many were the Cabals of the Court, fometimes with one Party, fometimes with another. Now the Catholicks were to be managed; and the *Guifes*, viz. the Duke and his Brother the Cardinal, were both affaffinated in the King's Palace at *Blois*; and all thefe Things fell out while *Catherine of Medicis* govern'd the Councils of *France*.

The Reafon of fuch contradictory Meafures, *Mezeray* tells us, was, that the Court was eternally griping after Money, Taxes, Impofts, and Excifes were continually multiply'd upon the People, and the Hugonots were carefs'd to ftrengthen the Court againft the Difcontents thefe Proceedings muft occafion; but when the Difaffection became dangerous, then the Catholicks were to be gratify'd by the Perfecution of the Hugonots; thus the Paffions of different Parties were play'd againft each other, to fleece and opprefs both.

We may find in our own Hiftory, the fecond Part of the fame Game. After the Murder of K. *Charles* I. when the World faw *Oliver's* Defign of ufurping the Government to himfelf, he fell into this Trick of cajoling of Parties. The Prebyterians, who firft refifted the King, were outed of all Employments, and *Oliver* joined the Independents, a Party, he thought better able to fupport him; the *Levellers* were alfo countenanced in their Turn; but thefe, finding themfelves cheated in the Promifes made them by *Cromwel*, join'd with the *Agitators*, another Party; from

whence it was apprehended, they would diftrefs the wicked Meafures of thofe at the Helm; therefore it was thought fit to court the Presbyterians again; and feveral of their Preachers were employ'd to make Propofals to their Leaders; but to their Honour, they would not come in.

All this Shuffling with Parties was to ftrengthen the Government againft the Difcontents, which Standing Armies, Excifes, and other Taxes, raifed in the People; and will always be practifed with the fame Views.

Let thofe who are fo courted confider, that they are making Chains for themfelves, and that when a Party has given up its whole Intereft to fome rapacious Minifter, upon the bare Promife of fome Favours to themfelves, when they have gone to demand the Performance, have been fob'd off with, *This is not the Time.* If they are not facrificed as the Hugonots, the beft that can happen to'em, is to fhare Oppreffion with their Fellow-Subjects.

How happy is it for a Nation, when fuch Defigns have been fet on Foot, that the Undertaker has not had Parts equal to the Michief he intended; when all Sects and Parties have taken the Alarm, fhook Hands, and wonder'd they could ever have been Enemies upon the Account of fuch trifling Diftinctions as cunning Knaves made ufe of to divide them.

Weekly Miscellany. May 19. No. 23.

IN this Paper Mr *Hooker* gives us an Account of the Rife and Progrefs of Charity Schools. He fays this Defign was firft fet on Foot in 1698, and has fince diffufed itfelf thro' the whole Nation, and that at this Time there are within the Cities of *London* and *Westminster*, and Bills of Mortality, 132 Charity Schools. This Defign meeting with fuch Encouragement, *Truftees* were chofen in each Diftrict to overfee the Managment of the *Mafters* and *Miftreffes*, and to prefcribe Rules and Orders in each School; and *Treafurers* were appointed. In 1706 thefe Truftees form'd themfelves into a voluntary Society, and chofe a Chairman, to prefide and fummon Meetings, which have been regularly continued to this Time, where Orders from Time to Time have been agreed upon; and in the Year 1729, Rules and Orders for the better Regulation of the faid Schools were recommended to the feveral Truftees of Schools in the Country; which being laid before the *Archbiftops* and *Bifhops*, they were by them, under
their

their Hands, approved and eſtabliſhed; and are here inſerted: But as theſe Rules and Orders are calculated ſolely for the Uſe of thoſe Schools, and as each undoubtedly have them, we think it needleſs to repeat them here.

Univerſal Spectator, May 19. Nº 241.

IS fill'd with Quotations from *Pope's* *Homer*, with Remarks to ſhew the *Hoſpitality*, *Humanity*, and *Benevolence* of the *Antients*, after the Manner we have given the Reader Specimens of, p. 116, 130.

The Flying Poſt, May 22.
A Character of the Prince of Orange.

JOhn *William Henry Charles Friſo*, Pr. of *Orange* and *Naſſau*, Hereditary Stadtholder, of *Frieſland* and *Groningen*, and Stadtholder by Election, of *Guelderland* and the County of *Zutphen*, is the Poſthumous Son of *John William Friſo*, Pr. of *Orange*, &c. by *Mary Louiſa* Princeſs of *Heſſe Caſſel*, Siſter to the King of *Sweden*, by whom he had alſo a Daughter, the Princeſs *Anne*, born *Sept.* 21, 1710.

The late Pr. of *Orange*, Heir (by a Will in his Father's Life-time) to the Eſtate of K. *William* III. ſignaliz'd his Valour during the laſt War in the *Netherlands*, but was unfortunately drowned in his Coach the 5th of *July* 1711. O. S. in ferrying over the *Amer* at *Moërdyke*, in his Paſſage from the Army to the *Hague*, to meet and conſult with the K. of *Pruſſia*. His Princeſs however was ſafely delivered of the preſent Prince, *Auguſt* 21 following, to the univerſal Joy of the 7 Provinces. He was baptized the 10th of *September* following, the States General being Godfathers.

The firſt publick Act recorded of him was, laying the Foundation Stone of the New *Town-houſe*, a fine Building at *Leuwarden*, *April* 2, 1715, when he was little more than 3 Years and a half old: On the 2d of *November* 1723, the States of *Guelderland* and *Zutphen* unanimouſly choſe him their Stadtholder, Captain General and High Admiral; and on the 4th wrote a Letter to the States of *Holland* and *Weſt-Frieſland*, wherein " they declare his Election to be of vaſt Concern to the true Intereſt of the Province, and of its Inhabitants; the Pr. of *Orange* and *Naſſau* being the only Inhabitant born in this State, who can juſtly have this Noble Dignity conferr'd upon him, ſince he is already Stadtholder of 2 of

the 7 Provinces without reckoning our own; and ſince the illuſtrious Anceſtors and Relations of this Prince have done our State, in Times both of War and Peace, the moſt important Services that could be done for the Advantage and Safety of their Country".

By the Inſtructions which the States of *Guelderland* and *Zutphen* drew up for the Regulation of his Conduct, he was to have a Regiment of Foot, and the Diſpoſal of every Poſt that fell in it, beſides 5000 Florins Annuity out of the Revenues of their Province, and the Stadtholder's Quota of all the Fines, of Fiefs, and their Diſpatches:

Tho' the States of *Holland* and *Weſt-Frieſland* remonſtrated againſt this Act of *Guelderland* and *Zutphen*, yet the firſt Time his Highneſs arrived at the *Hague*, he was received with all imaginable Marks of Reſpect and Affection by the People, and the ſeveral Colleges of the Republick.

The firſt Viſit this Prince paid to his preſent Majeſty of *Great-Britain*, after his Acceſſion, was in *June* 1729, when his Majeſty paſſed thro' *Holland* to *Germany*.

The 16th of *September* following, his Highneſs was inſtalled Stadtholder of *Groningen*, and, the next Month, of *Guelderland*. In *November* 1730, he was at the *Hague* with all his Retinue, to join in the Celebration of the Birth-Day of his *Britannick* Majeſty, and was received with univerſal Joy.

In *Auguſt* 1731, he took upon him the actual Functions of his Dignity of Stadtholder of *Frieſland* and *Groningen*, &c. Being 21 Years of Age the 21ſt of *Sept.* he celebrated his Birth-Day with great Magnificence at *Leuwarden*; and two Days after was introduced into the Aſſembly of the States of *Frieſland*, where he was inſtalled Stadtholder, and Capt. General of that Province.

The Prince being now his own Maſter, made ſeveral Removes in his Family, and recalled ſome truſty Servants who were not permitted to wait on him during his Minority. (See Foreign Affairs, Vol. I. *Nov.* 1731, p. 503.)

In *Septem* 1732, He was in the Camp at *Oſterbout*, where he conſtantly attended theGenerals in their daily Exerciſe and Motions of their Troops; and General *Hompeſch* had the Honour to give him the firſt Military Inſtructions. This Application of his gain'd him the Love of all the Troops and gives all Proteſtants
Reaſon

Reaſon to hope he will maintain the Honour and Glory ſo juſtly gain'd by his illuſtrious Anceſtors.

The Revenues of this Prince are computed at about 60,000 *l.* a Year. It is ſomewhat remarkable, That as King *William*, then Prince of *Orange*, was marry'd on his Birth-Day, to the Eldeſt Princeſs of *England*, ſo the preſent Pr. of *Orange* is to be married (as it is credibly reported) on his Birth-Day, to the Princeſs Royal. *Tua eſt Lavinia Virgo.* His Motto is, *Tandem fit Surculus Arbor,* which belonged to his Anceſtor Prince *Maurice.*

Grubſtreet Journal. May 24. No. 178.

IN this Paper, *A. B.* replies to the Authors Defence of the *General Dictionary, hiſtorical and critical,* againſt this Writer's Criticiſm upon their *Propoſals* and *Specimen* of the Work. (See p. 171,188.) Their Defence, ſays *A. B.* of their Manner of Spelling the *Arabic* Names, is ſo weak, that I ſhall obſerve, that ſuppoſing the particular Criticiſm related merely to the Mis-ſpelling of three Arabic Names, they cannot pretend ſuch an Objection, if well grounded, is trifling, ſince they have declared in their *Specimen of Errors,* that *ſuch Mis-ſpelling of Names creates Confuſion in Hiſtory*; and had engaged in their *Propoſals, to correct the Errors with which the Authors they uſe abound.*

Affirms, in Contradiction to their Aſſertion, that moſt of their additional Articles, are mere Tranſcripts from *Moreri,* and other Dictionaries, and gives ſome Inſtances.

It was no Falſhood to affirm, that their Additions on the Foot of the *Specimen,* would amount but to one Volume: But if the Quantity of Additions are to be determined, by comparing thoſe in the firſt Number with the Articles of *Bayle,* they will ſwell not only to two Volumes, but to ten. So that the whole Work will conſiſt of 15 Volumes, inſtead of 6. May it not therefore be concluded, Their Inſinuation, that their Work will not coſt above 7 or 8 Guineas, is an Artifice to draw in the Publick to pay at leaſt 20 ?

As to the other Tranſlation of *Bayle,* which, ſays *A. B.* they inſinuate I am partial to, I will undertake to find more, and greater Errors in two Pages of their firſt Number, than are contained in their *Specimen* of Errors. Let the Reader only look into the 11th and 35th Pages.

§ Mr BAVIUS,

MR SOMEBODY, contrary to his Promiſe to give us his *Remarks* upon every *Petit piece* exhibited upon *Drury-Lane* Stage this Seaſon, has been ſilent on two Occaſions, which might have provoked his Spleen, and employed his Satire.

The young, ſmart, primier Miniſter, who has a kind of hereditary Right to — Ignorance, and theatrical Power, to manifeſt his poetical Capacity, brought on a *Thing* of his own Writing about a Month ago, called *The Mock Officer,* or *The Captain's a Lady.* Tho' he introduced it at his own Benefit, when his Friends were preſent, yet the Contempt ſhewn to it was ſo unanimous, that the Audience would not ſtay to hear out all the poor, low Nonſence, prepared for their Entertainment. I might here Remark on the Modeſty of this little Spark, in emulating Mr *Wilks,* in his moſt celebrated Part, *Sir Harry Wildair.* — And this Contempt of his *Mock Officer,* I preſume, provoked him to ſet about an incomparable pretty Paſtoral of 2 Acts, called *Damon and Daphne,* with which he entertained the Town on *Monday* Night. This Piece is a rural Tragedy; and indeed it ſucceeded in the *moving* Way, for it obliged beſt Part of the Audience to *move off,* before it was half over. In this Performance, the ingenious Son has not only *out done his own uſual Out-doings*; but has even exceeded his great laureated Sire in paſtoral Writing.

§ The laſt Letter is from Mr *Ralph,* who vindicates himſelf from the Aſperſions of Mr *Somebody* (See p. 241.) and ſolemnly proteſts, that he neither ſaw nor heard of the Letter which ſeems to be the Ground of the Liberties taken with him, tho' the Farce (ſays he) which Mr *C—be* offered to Mr *R* — was really my own, yet Mr *C—be* did not come by it by any fraudulent, or indirect Practice. No, adds Mr *Ralph,* I gave it him to do what he pleaſed with it, becauſe I my ſelf was weary of fruitleſs Applications. He was to appear as the Author too; neither did I know what Bargain he had made, nor was I to ſhare in the Profits. Whom therefore could I injure ? — On the other Hand, if Mr *C—be* had been illegally poſſeſſed of the Copy, and this Gentleman had thought himſelf in any Danger from me, 'twas eaſy to find me, and clear the Affair at once. — RALPH.

Of

Of unjustifiable Marriages.

AS there is now under consideration a Bill to prevent Clandestine Marriages, it would be very proper for Somebody to endeavour to get some salutary Clauses added to prevent unhappy Marriages; with suitable Penalties to be Inflicted on those that should be found Delinquents: As for Example; when two young thoughtless Fools, having no visible way to maintain themselves, nor any thing to begin the World with, yet resolve to marry, and be miserable, let it be deemed *Petty Larceny*.—If a younger Brother marries an Old Woman, purely for the sake of a Maintenance, let it be called *se defendendo*.—When a rich old Fellow marries a young Wench, in her full Bloom, I would have it made *Felony without Benefit of Clergy*.—When two old Creatures, that can hardly hear one another s—t, but hauk and cough Night and Day, and can propose not the least Comfort to themselves in the Thing, yet will marry together to be more miserable, let them be deemed *non compos*, and sent to a Mad-house.—When a Lady marries her Coach-man, or a Gentleman his Cook-maid (especially if there are Children by a former Marriage) let them both be *transported* for fourteen Years.—When a man has had one Devil of a Wife, and buried her, and yet will marry a Second, let him be brought in *Felo de se*, and buried in the High-way accordingly.—When a Woman in good Circumstances marries a Town-rake not worth a groat; if she's betrayed into it, let it be called *Accidental Death*: But if she knew it, make it single *Felony*, and *singe* her in the Fist.—When a Man with no Children marries a Woman with five or six, and *vice versâ*, let the Delinquent stand thrice on the *Pillory*, lose both his Ears, and suffer one Year's Imprisonment —If a Man marries a Woman of ill Fame, knowing her to be so, let him be condemned to have a pair of Horns painted on his Door, *in perpetuam rei memoriam*; or if she be a known Scold, then a couple of Neats Tongues painted there.—And when a Man or Woman marries to the disinheriting of their Children, let them suffer as in cases of *High-Treason*.—When a Woman marries a Man deeply in debt, knowing him to be so, let her be sent to the *House of Correction*, and kept to hard Labour for three Months; and if he deceived her, and did not let her know his Circumstances, let her be

acquitted, and he be doom'd to beat Hemp all Days of his Life.

Free Briton, May 24. No. 183.
The Craftsman *answer'd* (see p. 247.)

SIR,

IT is so long since you and I corresponded, that I begun to fear my evil Genius had betray'd me into your good Opinion; but to my great Comfort, I perceived in your last Paper you set me forth as *sunk very low in the Esteem of Mankind,* meaning *yourself.*

You tell us, that a *noble Lord,* having lately *lost* his Employment, Mr *Walsingham* immediately seiz'd his *Character* as *lawful Prize,* and fell to *tearing it to pieces* with his usual *Alacrity* and *Decency.*] What a silly Falsehood is this! The Charge lies against yourself; you treated *his* Character as *a Pretence* to *censure* the KING who dismiss'd him. The *Author of this Paper* then thought, and still thinks such Treatment, an *Act of great Insolence* to the ROYAL PERSON, and not a little injurious to the *Noble Peer* himself. But it's very consistent with your Character, when you cannot defend your *insolent Usage of the* KING, to raise an Alarm, that the *Noble Lord's Character* is seized as *Prize,* and is *tearing* in Pieces. How came you to betray *such an Abhorrence of your own Office,* that the worst Thing you thought you could say of your Adversary was, what all the World have said of yourself? — *He tears Characters in Pieces!*

Mr *Walsingham,* as petulant and as malicious as you represent him, is far from being at Enmity with the *Noble Lord,* notwithstanding all your Endeavours to set his Lordship and him at *variance.* I always did, and shall continue to *treat his Lordship* with the greatest Decency, and Respect, his Message to *me* having been a very *civil one,* containing no such *abusive Expressions* as the *pert* little *Author* of the Paper before me hath suggested.

But it seems he has incurr'd your Displeasure, by *charging* you with certain *Crimes committed against the King.* I have heard of a *Criminal,* who was in the same Warmth of Passion *against an Indictment,* and threatned to *swear the Peace* against the *Judge* who tried him, for *putting him in Fear* of his Life.

I apprehend the natural Import of your Paragraph of *April* 19. to be, that the KING *had* astonished *the World,* and grieved *the most zealous Friends of his Royal*

Royal Family; by dismissing, &c. and in this View I looked on *you* as making this *Noble Lord's* Ability and Service *reproachful to the King*, who had rewarded them so, as there could be no Pretence of thus *insulting his Majesty with them*.

In Answer to this Charge, you have given us a *Thing* which you call a *humourous* Letter containing a *learned Dissertation* upon those *two* important *Words*, Astonished *and* Grieve. Wherein you would prove you have a Right to be astonish'd, whenever you please, at his Majesty's Royal Proceedings; and *grieve* at his *Conduct*, without supposing it *grievous*.

What *little ridiculous Punster* has thou taken to thy Assistance? Prithee, *Caleb*, make the best Use of your *new Converts*. If they *can tag* Rhimes, *make* and *sing Ballads*, employ them in their *proper* Vocations; but don't expose yourself and your Friends, by *taking them in* to write *Craftsmen*.

You seem to be still more incensed against Mr *W.* for speaking of your Offences in the Manner and Language of the *Attorney General*.] But why this *Nibbling* at Mr *Attorney*? Did it ever, my Dear, do you any Service, to affront that *Learned and Honourable Person*? Why don't you sing your *old favourite Ballad*, by way of Triumph over him?

Sir *Pb——p* well knows,
That *Innuendoes*
Will serve him no longer in *Verse* or in *Prose*.

You make several *wonderful* Discoveries. In one place you inform us, that the *Noble Lord* hath made no Additions to his Fortune by his Employments; as if his Lordship's O *Economy* was a *fit* Subject to be *joked upon*; or you less *insolent* in presuming to declare, that *the* KING *had astonished the World*, &c. Fine Reasoning truly!

You say, *Astonishment is the Attribute of* GOD *himself*, and that it must in some Degree be the Attribute of his *Vicegerent to astonish the Earth*.] Well then, *his Majesty* is, it seems, the *Vicegerent* of GOD ALMIGHTY for this Time. A while ago you talked about SIGNOR MONTAGNA, and of a *King* who made the *lowest Character in the whole Drama*. Indeed, it is a refined way of proving, that you did *not affront the King*, when you told him, *He had astonished his People*; because the *Holy Scriptures* enjoyn us to be *astonished* at the *Great God*. This passage to be sure was meant as the finest *stroke* of Humour in this Pious and Loyal Performance.

Well, but you insist, the *People of England* have a *Right to be astonished*. Well said, Mr *D'anvers*; stand up for our Rights and Privileges; and I will add, for your Comfort, with Regard to the Exclusion of *your* able *and* faithful *Friends* from his Majesty's Service, you will probably have the Blessing, to hold and exercise this *divine Right of being astonished* as long as you live.

To shew your *Skill in Logick*, you put the *Negative* of your Proposition.] *Dear Mr D'anvers*, is it candid in you, who are deeply read in *Ramus* and *Duns Scotus*, to set your *logical* Strength against a plain Man, whom, you *say*, hath not the *Power of Reasoning in him*? Were I to answer you in the same way, I should tell you, that *both* your *Positive* and *Negative* are full of *Insolence* to the King. Supposing you did shiver with some little *Fit of Surprize*; that the Hopes of your Party were *ruined* when the *Noble Lord* was dismissed, must you run abroad *babbling* and *bellowing*, We are *astonished! ruined! undone for ever!*

I believe you was *greatly astonished*; and well you might, my Dear; this unexpected Event has dissipated the Dream of a NEW MINISTRY which thy *Patrons* held themselves most sure of. How many anxious Nights and waking Hours have been employed, to *plan* the illustrious *Junto*? wherein you, Sir, was to have been *not an unworthy Member*. Tell us, was not you *getting into your Coach and Six*? and pleasing yourself in the Triumph you should have over all the Authors that ever trolled about Town in their Chariots?

You tell me *I have received Assurances, and am at* full Liberty *to enjoy the Disgrace of this* Noble Lord, *without any Apprehensions* of Breach of Privilege, Actions of Scandalum Magnatum, *or even a Cudgel*.] To be serious here; his Lordship did send a very candid Message: But were it possible for him to have mention'd a *Cudgel*, I might have told him, that a *Cudgel* was no *Part* of the *Privilege* of a *Peer*; but that *every Commoner of England* has an *equal Right to use it* for the Preservation of his Person, and will *return* it, tho' offer'd by the *Hand of a Peer*; and if a *Peer* should appoint a *Deputy* for that purpose, I should assign him over to the *venerable Society of Chimney Sweepers*, nor should scruple to lay the aforesaid *Cudgel over the Shoulders of the Peer himself* where ever I met him. If *you*, Mr *D'anvers*

D'anvers, or any of your *Family,* are willing to try this Point with me; I have as *trusty* a Truncheon as one would wish to handle: But don't come in *the Dark,* three in a Concert, with *Bludgeons* and *Blunderbusses* to demolish a *single Man.* I dare say, his Lordship gave you no Authority to *mis-recite* his *Message* in this Manner: and it is a little indiscreet in you to abuse *an Intimacy* you have but just been honour'd with. If you ask his Lordship for a sight of the Answer to his Message, you will find the Author of the FREE-BRITON reply'd, *That if there were any just and honourable Motives, requiring him to speak with Freedom of so great a Person, it would not be the Fear even of Penalties, and much less of Insults that should deter him.* But I shall discuss this Matter more at large in a *Paper Extraordinary.*

Yours, FRA. WALSINGHAM.

The Craftsman. May 26. No. 360.

AN *insolent Minister,* defeated in his Projects, is like an *old Fox,* caught in a Trap, who beats Himself to Death, in struggling to get loose. Just such a Spectacle we have in the Person of a *great Projector,* who hath unluckily *fallen into the Pit which he had digged for others;* and endeavours to extenuate his Disgrace by a thousand little Arts, which serve only to plunge him deeper in the Mire. However baffled, he obstinately perseveres in the Uprightness of his *Scheme,* and an avow'd Resolution to *revive* it at a convenient Opportunity, which can only serve to keep up the Spirits of the People, and unite Them in his Downfal.

I shall here, says *D'anvers,* make some cursory Remarks on a delicate Performance, entitled *An Examination of the late Conduct of the Ministry, with Respect to the Duties on Tobacco and Wine.*

The first four Pages are fill'd up with the usual Adulation to the *Patron of these Writings,* who is represented as not quite frighten'd out of his Wits at an *Execution in Effigie;* but however he may swagger, like Captain *Bluff,* whilst the Enemy is at a Distance; yet Fear and a guilty Conscience carry him off, like *Teague's Legs,* whether he will or no. His *Advocate* seems so sensible of This, that he harangues very pathetically on the late *Mock-Executions,* and asserts, *that the same Person, who play'd that Farce of Assassination, would make it a real Tragedy, if they could do it with Impunity.*——What

a sad Thing it is to be troubled with a *wounded Spirit*? I have done all in my Power to cure the *honourable Gentleman* of these Apprehensions (see p. 191 B) for I look upon *Assassination,* tho' perpetrated against the *worst Man,* ever in Power, as robbing the *Gallows,* or the *Scaffold.*

The Gentleman proceeds to examine the *late Project, for excising Wine and Tobacco,* and tells us, *This was not originally a Court Scheme; but took its Rise from the Grievances and Discouragements of the Tobacco Planters; as may be seen at large in their Case.]* An Assertion absolutely false. Was not the *Case* first cook'd up at home, and then sent to a *Minor Minister* abroad, with Orders to draw *the Assembly of Virginia* into it, with specious Pretences that the Decay of their Trade was owing only to the want of such a Regulation in the manner of collecting the Revenue, as their *Representation* tended to promote? If this was not the Case, how came it that the *Projector* himself should be able to give us Notice of *such a Scheme* long before *this Representation* arrived; or why was the *Gentleman,* who brought it, thought worthy to be rewarded with a *particular Honour,* besides a large *Gratuity* from Those who sent him? Why was not this *Representation* laid before the *House of Commons,* as the Groundwork of a *Bill,* calculated for the Service of the *Planters?* I wish, however They and our other Colonies may find that Relief, Protection, and Encouragement which myself and some *Gentlemen* have long endeavour'd to procure for them.

Next he takes the chief Cities and Corporations of *England* to Task, for presuming to *petition* and *instruct* their Representatives against the *Bill.* This he calls a *dangerous Innovation,* tho' as old as our *Constitution* itself; and tells us *that if it is suffer'd to grow into a Custom, it will be a Thorn in the side of* Power, *that no Strength will be able to remove;* and therefore proposes to pluck it out, and plant it in the *side of Liberty,* but I, says *D'anvers,* think it much better where it is. There are already too many Thorns in the *side of Liberty;* such as *Septennial Acts, Riot Acts, Standing Armies,* &c. which I am afraid *no Strength will be able to remove.*

He puts an Objection against his *Patron,* which is not easily answer'd. " It may be ask'd, *says he,* Why these Bills were not prosecuted, with *Resolution,* as They were

were projected with *Wifdom*?"] The Reafons he affigns, are admirable. He tells us it was *poftpon'd on the fame Principles it was firft form'd, the Good of the whole.*] I believe the People would have taken it more kindly, if he had defifted a little fooner; for his yielding to their Importunities at laft, after he had brought the Point to a *Crifis*, look'd as if he had more Regard to his own *Intereft* than their *Sentiments*; and that he gave it up, becaufe he found upon Enquiry, he could not carry it. We are inform'd, indeed, by his *ingenious Advocate*, that *it is plain by all the Divifions that it was in his Power within Doors*; and, *if we may believe the* Craftfman's *Declamation on* Standing Armies, *he could have fecur'd it without.* —— *An undeniable Proof, that the Perfons in Power made this* Sufpenfion of the Bill, *a Compliment to the prefent Difpofition of the People.* Yet in the next Paragraph owns, that his *Patron* could not have carried the *Bill*; for amongft other Reafons, in Defence of this *lively Expedient*, (the Sufpenfion of the Bill) he mentions it as one, that it *prevented the Triumphs of the Oppofition in* fetting it entirely afide.

The Remainder of *this Pamphlet* is fill'd with grofs Flattery to his *Patron*, and the fafhionable Abufes upon all *Oppofers*. I have the Honour, fays D'*anvers*, to partake of his Scandal, as a *pert Demagogue*, the *Bully of the People*, and a *Writer of Libels on Record.* But I forgive the Author, and fhall never envy Him the more honourable Character of being the BULLY *of an odious* Minifter, a TOOL *of* State, and a PENSIONER *upon Record.*

Fog'ſ Journal, May 25. N° 238.

The Cafe ftated betwixt the Sugar Colonies · in the Iflands, and thofe on the Continent of America.

St. Chriftophers, Jan. 19, 1732-3.

THIS Day, on my Arrival here, I met with a Monthly Pamphlet for *Sept.* 1732, where, in the Account of the Debates in Parliament, Mr O—*pe* is introduced as faying, I *remember there was once a Petition prefented to this Houfe by one County, complaining, that they were injured in their Trade, as to the Sale of* Beans *by another, modeftly praying that the other County fhould be prohibited to fell* Beans. [See p. 938 C Vol. II. our Magazine, No. XXI. for *Sept. being the very Book this Writer refers to.*]

But, fuppofe one County was able to produce *Beans* enough for all the Occafions the Nation has for *Beans*, and could hardly produce any thing elfe, and was therefore encouraged by the Nation; if another County, better adapted for other Produce, i. e. *Hops*, fhould drop that, and take to the raifing of *Beans*, and occafion a want of *Hops*, where would the Abfurdity be, if the *Bean*-County, thus injur'd in its Sale, fhould petition that the other County fhould be prohibited felling *Beans*? This Cafe is not unlike that of the *Southern* and *Northern* Colonies of *England*, in the former whereof there is Land enough, and which is fit for nothing elfe, to produce Sugar fufficient for all the Occafions *England* has for it, and likewife to fupply foreign Markets. Hence it follows, that if any of her other Colonies, fhould neglect or diminifh its own proper Productions, and pretend to produce *Sugar*, it would be the Intereft of *England* to reftrain them. Tho' the *Continent* Colonies of *England* cannot produce *Sugar*, yet, which is worfe, they fupply our Rivals in the *Sugar*-Manufacture, with Materials to raife *Sugar*, viz. Lumber, Horfes, Provifions, without which they could not rival us in that Trade.

Mr O—*pe* lays no fmall Strefs on the Extent of our Dominions on the Continent, and he might have added their People, which I take to be more than 500,000. Whereas all the Inhabitants of our *Sugar* Colonies, White and Black, Men, Women and Children, are not near that Number: But 'tis not the Quantity of Land, or Multitude of People in Colonies, that inrich the Nation they belong to, unlefs they are both properly employ'd. What Advantage the *Northern* Colonies can bring to their Mother Nation in the Productions of *Cattle* and *Provifions*, let themfelves fhew, only let it be remembred, that Lumber, Tobacco, Rice, Hemp, Flax, Pitch, Tar, Pot-afh, Wine, Oyl, Silk, Copper, Iron, &c. are all out of the Queftion, becaufe moft of thefe the National Intereft requires the *Continent* Colonies to be employ'd in. If any Gentleman would know the Nation's Profit from the fmall Quantity of Land, that is poffible at prefent to be cultivated in her *Sugar* Colonies, he will find in a fmall Tract, entitled, *The prefent State of the Britifh Sugar Colonies confider'd*, That *Barbadoes*, which does not contain much more than 80,000 Acres of Manurable Land, and but a few Number of Hands, has for many Years

Years, down to 1731, yielded annually to the Publick in the Nett Proceed of Sugar at a *Medium* Price   320, 000*l*.

Rum and Molasses———	80, 000
Ginger, Cotton, and Aloes—	20, 000
Duty to the Crown———	50, 000
Home Freight———	66, 000
Commissions, Port Charges, &c. ———	22, 600

   558, 600

And the Custom-House Books will prove further that the Sugar of *Barbadoes*, is scarce above one fourth of what is produced yearly in all the *British* Sugar Colonies.

I am not a little pleased to learn from so sure an Authority as Mr O—pe's, that *the Gentlemen concern'd in the* Board of Trade, *are as exact and diligent in all Matters, which fall under their Consideration as any* Board *in* England. Had their Predecessors been as strict and careful in their Enquiries, the directing the Motions of the several Colonies to the general Interest of the Nation, could not have proved so troublesome as it now does; their Ignorance was the more inexcusable, because Mr *Davenant* inform'd the Publick in 1698, of several particulars very proper to be known in regulating our Colonies, which had they been regarded by that *Board*, might have done a deal of Good, · and saved abundance of Expence to the Nation.

Tho' I am no great Friend to the settling of *National* Colonies *any where* on the Foundation of *private* Charities; and tho' a certain *Dean*, who founded a College at *Bermudas*, met with a general Approbation, he has lately given the World a Demonstration what the most plausible Scheme formed (at the distance of *Great-Britain* from *America*) upon naked Theory, and such *borrow'd*, or *hackney* Intelligence as can be picked up, are like to come to: yet such are my Resentments of the Miseries, of the Unfortunate, and the Necessity there is of a better Barrier, that I heartily wish Mr. O—pe, and those concerned with him in the Undertaking, all the Success they desire; provided the Colony they mean to settle be not suffer'd to go upon such Produce, Trade or Manufactures, as interfere with those of *Great-Britain*, or her other Colonies, as it would tend to. *destroy the mutual Dependance that the People of all the* British *Dominions ought to have upon each other*; for, as Mr *Gee*

observed, *the interfering of Colonies with their Mother Nation would do much hurt to the Nation, and end in no good to the Colonies.*

[The foregoing Discourse upon our Sugar Colonies is somewhat of the latest, however, to oblige our Readers in the Plantations, we have inserted it, and likewise the following Sketch of the Bill that is now past for their Advantage and Relief, *viz.* " After 25 *Dec.* 1733, 9 *d.* *per* Gallon is to be paid for Rum and Spirits made in the *American* Plantations not belonging to his Majesty, on Importation to the *British* Plantations; 6 *d. per* Gallon for Molasses and Syrups; and 5 *s. per* C. Weight for Sugar and Paneles, to be paid in *British* Money. No Sugars, Paneles, Syrups, or Molasses of the *British* Plantations, to be imported into *Ireland*, unless shipped in *Great-Britain*. Duties paid for Sugar or Paneles imported from the *British* Plantations after 24 *June*, 1733, to be repaid on Exportation within the Year. An Allowance of 2 *s. per* C. Weight more than formerly to the Exporter for Sugars refined in *Great-Britain*. Sugars may be imported from the *Spanish* or *Portuguese* Dominions, as formerly.]

Weekly Miscellany, May 26. No. 24.

A *Vindication of the Church of* England, *against* Mr Neal's *Reflections.*

THE Design of Mr *Neal's History of the Puritans*, is to introduce the *Geneva* Plan of Church Government and Discipline, or some thing nearly like it. To accomplish which he represents the *Church of England* as founded in Violence and Bloodshed, its Constitution contrary to the Word of God, and invading Christian Liberty; expressing much Displeasure at almost every Thing done at the *Reformation*, and severely treating the great and worthy Instruments of it. On the contrary, he recommends the Patrons of the *Geneva* Model in the strongest Terms: What must the Inference of this be, but that the corrupt Church should be abolish'd, and a *purer* placed in its Room? The first Volume of this History was published about the Time that the *Dissenters* wrote so many Pamphlets upon the *Test Acts*; and by comparing the Principles, and Language of these Pamphlets with Mr *Neal's* History, there appears a *concerted* Scheme to subvert the *Establishment*, and that the Repeal of the *Corporation* and *Test Acts*, was only the first Step.

K k   'An

An anonymous Writer, in his Anſwer to Mr *Neal*, ſhews, 1. That Q *Elizabeth* was not, as Mr *Neal* repreſented her, a *Papiſt* in her Heart, but ſincerely deſigned to aboliſh Popery, and took the propereſt Meaſures to that great End. 2. That the *Reformation* eſtabliſhed under her Reign, in reſpect to *Doctrine, Government,* and *Worſhip,* was agreeable to *Scripture,* and *Primitive* Uſage, and not liable to the Objections of Mr *Neal.* 3. He clears the then Government, Miniſtry and Biſhops, from Mr *Neal's* Charge of *Cruelty* and *Perſecution,* in the enforcement of Conformity to the *Religion Eſtabliſhed.*

In regard to the Doctrines of the Church of *England,* he anſwers two Objections; *viz.* First, That our *Articles* are drawn up with ſuch Latitude of *Expreſſion, that Men who do not agree in* Every Point *of Doctrine, may yet* Subscribe. This our Author obſerves, to be a great Inſtance of the *Moderation* and *Wiſdom* of the Compoſers, ſo to expreſs controverted Points, wherein learned and good Men differ'd in Opinion, as to unite them in excluding general Notions which they all agreed to condemn. In this he agrees with Bp *Burnet,* who ſays, in his Hiſtory of the Reformation, that by the means of ſuch Moderation, *the Church of* England *has been, ſince that Time, the Sanctuary and Shelter of all Foreigners, the chief Object of the Envy, and Hatred of the Church of* Rome, *and the great Glory of the Reformation.*

Secondly, *That our Church requires Subſcription to Articles, directly and expreſly countenancing the moſt* Rigid *Notions of the* Calvinists. For the Confutation of this Objection, he refers to a Piece entitled, *an Apology for the Church of* Eng. which proves the Articles drawn with a Latitude to admit a Subſcription from *Arminians* as well as *Calviniſts.*

As to the Hiſtorian's Complaint of *Perſecution* and *Cruelty,* in the Enforcement of *Conformity* to the Religion *eſtabliſhed,* this Writer anſwers, that the *Puritans* did not deſire a *Toleration,* but an *Eſtabliſhment* of their own Scheme, ſuch as would have kept all others, in particular the *Lutherans,* and the Friends of K. *Edward's Reformation,* out of the Church; as they did not deſire a Toleration themſelves, ſo they *would not grant it to others.*

At the end of this Work, is a Collection of *notorious* and *ſhameful* Inſtances of *Diſhoneſty* in Mr *Neal's Repreſentation* of

Facts and *Quotations;* as *leaving out* part of a Sentence or Paragraph, which alters the Senſe; and even *adding* Words or Sentences to ſerve his purpoſe; with other the like infamous *Artifices* to *conceal,* or *diſguiſe* Truth. No doubt the Anſwerer has been exact in his Facts, becauſe he is ſo particular in his Quotations and References. But beſides this the *general Practice* of theſe Writers confirms ſuch a Suppoſition. A *fair* and *ingenuous* Writer is ſcarce ever to be met with among them.

BRITANNICUS.

London Journal, May 26. No. 726.

Of Petitions to Parliament.

THE *three Powers,* of which our Conſtitution conſiſts, are naturally ſuch a Check one upon the other, that their ſeveral *diſtinct Intereſts* will preſerve them from growing into *one ſingle Power:* and if in Time to come (as in Times paſt) *one* of theſe Powers ſhould get the better of, and ſwallow up the others, the *Conſtitution* is gone, and our *Liberties* loſt, tho' the *People* was that Power, and become the *Conqueror.*

The *high Authority* of the People, and their *original Power,* therefore, put about, at this Time, to juſtify a late *ſcandalous Treatment* of the Houſe of Commons, is an Authority unknown to our Conſtitution and abſolutely *democratical.* Our Repreſentatives, on whom the Power of the People is devolved, may if they pleaſe, aſk our Advice, and we may *give* it them without asking, and *petition* them to act according to it; this is all we can do, we can't *command* them. If we don't like what they have done, we are at Liberty, when the Time is expired, to chuſe others: But to ſend *threatning* Letters, and *inſolent* Inſtructions, *authoritative* Orders and Commands to the *ſupreme* Legiſlature, and after that come up by Thouſands; to beſet their Houſe, to affront them as they paſs, to ſpit in their Faces, to joſtle ſome, ſtrike others, and burn them in Effigy all over the Kingdom, is very little ſhort of Rebellion. But if a Parliament ſhould from wrong Principles, private Intereſts, Attachments to, or *Malice againſt* a Court, (as in K. *William's* Time) give into *Meaſures,* or make *Laws,* which break in upon or weaken the Conſtitution; then *the Original Power* of the People is return'd into their own Hands, and 'tis their Duty to oppoſe oppofe by all proper Methods, the Defigns even of the Parliament it felf.

In the laft Year of K. *William*, fome Gentlemen of *Kent*, to their immortal Honour, *petitioned* the Parliament, that our *Religion* and *Safety* might be effectually provided for; "*That their* LOYAL ADDRESSES *might be turn'd in to* Bills of Supply, *that his Majefty might be* ENABLED POWERFULLY *to affift his Allies.*"

The *French King* had then acknowledg'd the *Pretender* to be King of *England*, he had feized on *Spain*, ftood ready to fwallow up all *Europe*, and overturn the *Proteftant Religion* and *Liberty*; while *the Parliament* of *England*, the Majority of which was *Jacobites*, did nothing but fend LOYAL ADDRESSES to the King, whom they *hated*.

The *Petition*, therefore, was founded on the higheft Reafon; our *Religion*, *Liberties*, and every Thing valuable, depended upon the Behaviour of the *Parliament*; who, not doing their Duty, was *hated* by the People, *diffolved* by the King, and another chofe in its ftead, which did *Juftice* to the Kingdom.

But tho' there was the *ftrongeft Reafon* for *Oppofition* to this Parliament, yet the Gentlemen of *Kent* only *humbly implor'd*; and were, for THAT, committed to the *Gatehoufe*, " as guilty of a *fcandalous, infolent, and feditious Petition*, tending to deftroy the *Conftitution of Parliaments*, and to *fubvert* the eftablifhed Government of thefe Realms." But we have lately feen Petitioners *threaten, inftruct, order and command*, nay, charge the Houfe with overturning *Magna Charta*, only becaufe they were going to hinder fraudulent Dealers from cheating the Nation. Thefe Petitions, and the Actions committed afterwards about the Houfe and Kingdom, are indeed *Scandalous*, &*c.* and tend to fubvert the Government.

In compliance with feveral Importunate Sollicitations, we infert here a fhort Extract of the Method obferved by the Truftees, in peopling of the Colony of Georgia. (See Vol. II. p. 1017.)

THAT the Mother Country fhould not be robbed of any Hands ufeful to it, the Truftees ftrictly examine thofe who defire to go over, and make other Enquiries, to find out whether they can get a Subfiftance here; therefore they will admit no Sailors, no Husbandmen or Labourers from the Country, none who would leave their Wives and Fami-

lies without a Support, none who have the Character of lazy, immoral Men, or any in Debt, without confent of their Creditors.

Thofe the Truftees fend over have all Expences of Paffage defray'd, and are furnifh'd with Arms, Working-Tools, Seeds of all kinds for their Land, and Provifions for a Year. And proper Perfons are appointed to inftruct thofe that are ignorant.

As Experience has fhown the Inconvenience of private Perfons poffeffing too large Quantities of Land in our Colonies, by which means, the greateft Part of it muft lye uncultivated, and the Occupiers are thrown at fuch a Diftance, that they can neither affift, or defend one another; the Truftees fettle the People in Towns, a hundred Families in each: And allot no more Land than what can with Eafe be cultivated, and yet will afford a fufficient and handfome Maintenance. They divide each Man's Share into three Lots; *viz.* One Lot for a Houfe and Yard in the Town, another for a Garden near the Town, and a third for a Farm at a little Diftance from the Town. Thefe Lots are all to be laid out, and the Houfes built by joint Labour and Affiftance; and when finifh'd, Chance is to determine, who fhall be the Proprietors of each of them; by this Conduct no Man will have reafon to complain, fince Fortune alone can give the Preference.

As they will not be fuffer'd to alienate their Lands without Leave of the Truftees, none certainly will go over, but with a Defign to be induftrious; and as they will be fettled in fuch a Frugality, none who can live here, will think of going thither, where, tho' they will have a fufficient and plentiful Maintenance, they will have no room for Luxury, or any of its attendant Vices.

Univerfal Spectator, May 26. No. 241.

Maternal Cruelty.

MR SPECTATOR,

I Was not a little pleafed with your Sentiments, of paternal and filial Duties in refpect of Marriage (See p. 177 H.) There is no fuch thing as determining Felicity for another; People muft be happy their own Way, or not at all; Opinion here is every Thing, and againft that all Arguments are fruitlefs.

Cordelia, an agreeable young Lady, and Daughter to a Gentleman of a large Fortune

tune at *White-hall*, by a maternal Authority was strictly confin'd. At length she got abroad, when at the approach of the genteel *Costillo* she found her Heart surpriz'd with the soft Engagement of the little Deity. And after a long Combat between Duty, Misery, Modesty, and Love, the mad:, an Offer of herself to him —— He had too much Honour to take an Advantage of her Innocence, and married her in three Days. *Costillo* is endow'd with many excellent Qualities, tho' unhappy in a want of Fortune equal to his Merit, yet has a Spirit above doing a mean Action. However, neither his Person nor Accomplishments have made any Impression on the Minds of *Cordelia's* Parents, who continue an uncommon Hatred to him, and imprison, use ill, oppress and destroy her whom they ought to assist and save, from the Effects of a mercenary Temper, and a tyrannical Revenge on the innocent Husband, who is driven to *Paris* to avoid their Resentment and the Chagrin of seeing his Wife *Mal-traited*, who is already reduced to a walking Anatomy by her Mother's ill Usage. *Yours* T I M O L E O N.

THURSDAY, MAY 31. The *Free-Briton* and *Grub-Street Journal* of this *Date*, we refer to our next.

ADDRESS of the House of LORDS to His Majesty, on his acquainting them with the intended Marriage of the Princess Royal, &c. (see p. 266. 233.)

Most Gracious Sovereign,

WE *Your Majesty's most dutiful and loyal Subjects, the Lords Spiritual and Temporal in Parliament assembled, beg Leave to return Your Majesty our most humble Thanks for Your most gracious Message, and for Your Goodness in acquainting us, that Your Majesty has received, from the Prince of Orange, Proposals for a Treaty of Marriage between the Princess Royal, Your Majesty's Eldest Daughter, and that Prince; and to express at the same Time the just Sense we have of Your Majesty's tender Care and Concern for the Interests of Your People, and for the further Security of the Protestant Succession to the Crown of these Realms, in having been pleased favourably to receive the Instances made by the Prince.*

When we consider the many great and signal Advantages that these Kingdoms have received from a strict Union with the House of Orange, it is with Pleasure

we observe Your Majesty's present Disposition to give a Princess, so deservedly dear to Your Majesty, and esteemed and admired by all Your People, to a Branch of that House.

The Distinction with which Your Majesty is, upon this Occasion, graciously disposed to honour his Highness the Prince of Orange, is a fresh Proof of Your Majesty's unalterable Resolution to preserve to Your People those Liberties, which Your late Royal Predecessor, King William the Third, of ever glorious Memory, came to restore.

These, Sir, being our Sentiments, and, as we persuade our selves, those of the whole Nation, we beg. Leave humbly to assure Your Majesty, That we will readily and chearfully concur in every Thing that may contribute to the concluding and perfecting an Alliance that will tend so much to the farther Security of the Protestant Succession to the Crown of these Realms, and to the Encouragement and Support of the Protestant Interest in Europe.

ADDRESS of the H. of COMMONS, on Do.

Most Gracious Sovereign,

WE *Your Majesty's most Dutiful and Loyal Subjects, the Commons of Great-Britain in Parliament assembled, return Your Majesty Our most Dutiful Thanks for being graciously pleased to communicate to Us Your Royal Intentions of concluding a Marriage between the Princess Royal and the Prince of Orange.*

The happy Prospect of seeing this Alliance entered into and concluded with a Prince, whose Family has always distinguished it self in Support of the Protestant Religion and in Defence of the Liberties of Europe, gives us the greatest Satisfaction: We remember with Gratitude the great and infinite Benefits procured to this Nation by that illustrious House; and We cannot but promise Our selves a further Security to the Protestant Succession to the Crown of these Realms from the Renewal of that Union, which gave Birth to and laid the Foundation of this inestimable Blessing.

And We beg Leave to assure Your Majesty, that, to demonstrate Our Duty, Zeal, and Affection to Your Majesty, and to testify the just Sense We have of the singular Merits and eminent Virtues of the Princess Royal, We will enable Your Majesty to give her such a Portion, as may conduce to her future Happiness, and to the supporting her Royal Highness with Honour and Dignity.

A

A Translation of one SCENE *of* Mr VOL-
TAIRE's *fine* Tragedy *of* ZAIRE, *which
had a Run of* 36 *Nights at* Paris.

Enter Lusignan : *(led in, by two Guards)* to Chatillon, Nerestan, *and* Zara.

Luf. WHere am I? what forgiving angel's voice
      Has call'd me, to re-visit long lost day?
Am I with christians?--I am weak--forgive me--
And guide my trembling steps,--I'm full of
    years.----
Yet, *Misery* has worn me, more than age ;
--Am I, in truth, at liberty ? *(seating himself.*
Cha. You are :
And ev'ry christian's grief will end, with yours.
Luf. O light ! ---O ! dearest, far, than light !
    that voice !----
Chatillon ! is it you ?------my fellow martyr ?---
And, shall our wretchedness, indeed, have end ?---
In what place are we, now ?--my feeble eyes,
Difus'd to daylight, long, in vain, to find you.
Cha. This *was* the palace, which your Fa-
    thers built----
'Tis, *now*, the son of *Noradin*'s seraglio.
Zara. The master of this place---the mighty
    Osman,
Distinguishes, and loves to cherish, Virtue ;---
This generous *Frenchman*, yet, a stranger, to you,
Drawn from his native soil, from peace, and rest,
Brought the vow'd ransoms, of ten christian slaves
Himself, contented, to remain, a Captive.----
But, *Osman*, charm'd, by greatness, like his own,
To equal, what he lov'd, has given him, *Tou.*
Luf. So, gen'rous *France* inspires her social sons !
They have been, ever dear, and useful, to me !---
Wou'd, I were nearer to him--Noble fir,
            (Nerestan approaches.
How have I merited, that you, for me,
Shou'd pass such distant seas , to bring me blef-
    fings,
And hazard your own safety, for my sake ?
Ner. My name, fir, is *Nerestan*--born in *Syria*,
I wore the chains of flav'ry, from my birth ;
Till quitting the proud crescent, for the court,
Where Warlike *Lewis* reigns, beneath his eye,
I learnt the trade of arms ;--the rank, I hold,
Was but the kind distinction, which he gave me,
To tempt my courage, to deserve Regard.
Your fight, unhappy prince, wou'd charm his eye;
That best, and greatest, monarch, will behold,
With grief, and joy, those venerable wounds,
And print embraces, where your fetters bound you;
All *Paris* will revere the cross's martyr ;
Paris, the refuge, still, of ruin'd kings !
Luf. Alas ! in times, long past, I've *seen* its
    glory ;
When *Philip*, the victorious liv'd--I fought,
Abreast, with *Montmorency*, and *Melun* ;
D'*Espaing--De Negle*---and the far-fam'd *Coureys*
Names, which were then the praise, and dread,
    of war !
But, what have I to do, at *Paris* now ?
I stand upon the brink, of the cold grave ;----

That way, my journey lies,--to find, I hope,
The KING of kings ; and move remembrance,
    there,
Of all my woes, long suffer'd, for his sake.---
You gen'rous witnesses, of my last hour,
While I yet live, assist my humble prayers ;
And join, the resignation of my soul.------
Nerestan ! *Chatillon* ! and you, fair mourner !
Whose tears do honour to an old man's sorrows,
Pity a father,---the unhappiest, sure !
That ever felt the hand of angry heav'n !
My eyes, tho' dying, still can furnish tears :
Half my long life, they flow'd, and still *will* flow ;
A daughter, and 3 sons, my heart's proud hopes,
Were all torn from me, in their tend'rest Years ;
My friend, *Chatillon*, knows, and can remember---
Cha. Wou'd I were able to *forget* your woes :
Luf. Thou a pris'ner, with me, in *Cæsarea*,
And, there, beheld'st my wife, and two dear sons,
Perish, in flames---they did not need the grave
Their foes wou'd have *denied* them !--I beheld it;
Husband ! and father ! helpless, I beheld it !
Denied the mournful privilege, to *die* !----
If ye are saints, in heav'n, as, sure I ye are,
Look, with an eye of pity, on that brother,
That sister, whom you left--if I have, yet,
Or son, or daughter---for, in early chains,
Far from their lost, and unassisting, father,
I heard, that they were sent, with numbers more,
To this *Seraglio*, hence to be dispers'd,
In nameless remnants, o'er the east, and spread
Our christian miseries, round a faithless world.
Cha. 'Twas true--for, in the horror of that day,
I snatch'd your infant daughter, from her cradle ;--
But, finding ev'ry hope of flight was vain,
Scarce had I sprinkled, from a public fountain,
Those sacred drops, which wash the soul from sin,
When, from my bleeding arms, fierce *Saracens*
Forc'd the lost innocent ; who, smiling, lay,
And pointed, playful, at the swarthy spoilers !----
With her your youngest, then, your *only* son,
Whose little life had reach'd the fourth, sad, year,
And, just, given sense, to *feel* his own misfortunes,
Was order'd, to this city.------
Ner. I, too, hither,
Just, at that fatal age, from lost *Cæsarea*,
Came, in that crowd of undistinguish'd chris-
    tians.
Luf. You ?--came you thence ? Alas ! who
    knows, but you
Might, heretofore, have seen my two poor
    children ?
Ha !--madam !--that small ornament, you wear,
                        (Looking up.
Its form, a stranger, to this country's fashions,
How long has it been yours ?
Zara. From my first breath, sir------
Ah !---what !---you seem surpriz'd ! why should
    this move you ?
Luf. Wou'd you confide it, to my trembling
    hands ?
Zara. To what new wonder, am I now referv'd !
Oh, sir ! what mean you ?

Luf. Providence! and heaven!
O, failing eyes! deceive ye not my Hope?
Can this be possible?---yes---yes---'tis she!
This little cross, I know it by sure marks,
Oh! take me, heav'n! while I can die with joy---
  (*Sinking to the Ground.*
Zara. O I do not, fir, diftract me---rifing thoughts,
And hopes, and fears, o'erwhelm me!
Luf. Tell me, yet,
Has it remain'd, for ever, in your hands?
What! both, brought, Captives, from *Cæfarea,*
  hither?
Zara. Both, Both------
Ner. Oh, heav'n I have I then found a father?
Luf. Their voice! their looks!
The living images, of their dear mother!
O! thou; who thus, canft blefs my life's laft fand,
Strengthen my heart, too feeble, for this joy;---
  (*rifing.*
Madam! *Neroftan!*---help me, *Cbatillon*---
Neroftan! if thou ought'ft to own that name,
Shines there, upon thy breaft, a noble fcar,
Which e'er *Cæfarea* fell, from a fierce hand,
Surprizing us, by night, my child receiv'd?
Ner. Blefs'd hand!---I *bear* it, fir,---the mark
  is there;
Luf. Merciful heaven!---
Ner. kneeling. O, fir!---O *Zara,* kneel.
Zara kneeling. My father? Oh!
Botb. Oh!
Luf. O, my loft children!   [ing you,
Laf. My fon! my daughter!--- loft, in embrac-
I wou'd now *die,* left this fhou'd prove a dream.
Cba. How touch'd is my glad heart, to fee
  their joy!
Luf. Again, I find you---*dear,* in *Wretchednefs;*
D, my brave fon-and, thou, my namelefs daughter
Now diffipate all doubt, remove all dread;---
Has heav'n, that gives me back, my children,--
  given 'em,
Such, as I loft 'em?---come they chriftians to me?
One weeps---and one declines a confcious eye!
Your filence fpeaks---too well I underftand it.
Zara. I cannot, fir, deceive you---*Ofman's* laws
Were mine--- and *Ofman* is *not* chriftian.
Luf.! Ah! my mifguided child!---at that fad
  word,
The little life, yet, mine, had left me, quite,
But, that my death might leave thee, loft, for ever.
Sixty long years, I fought the chriftian's caufe,
Saw their doom'd temple fall, their power de-
  ftroy'd:
Twenty, a captive, in a dungeon's depth,
Yet, never, f or myfelf, my tears fought heav'n,
All, for my children, ofe my fruitlefs pray'rs;
Yet, what avails a father's wretched joy?
I have a daughter---and my God an enemy------
But, 'tis my guilt, not hres---thy father's *prifon,*
Depriv'd thee of thy faith---yet---do not lofe it;
Reclaim thy birth-right-hink, upon th: bloo d,
Of twenty chriftiankings---tthat fills thy Veins;
'Tis heroes blood---the blood of faints and martyrs!
What wou'd thy mother feel, to fee thee thus?

She, and thy murder'd *brothers* --- think, they
  call thee,
Think, that thou fee'ft 'em ftretch their bloody
  arms,
And weep, to win thee, from their mard'ter's
  bofom.------
Even, in the place, where thou betray'ft thy god,
He *died,* my child, to fave thee --- turn thy eyes,
And fee, for thou art *near,* his facred fepulchre;
Thou can'ft not move a ftep, but, where, *be* trod!
Thou trembleft---oh! admit me, to thy foul;
Kill not thy aged, thy afflicted, father:
Take not, thus foon, again, the life, thou gav'ft
  him,
Shame not thy mother,--nor betray thy GOD.
--'Tis paft---repentance dawns, in thy fweet eyes,
I fee bright truth, defcending, to thy heart,
And, now, my long, loft child is found, for ever.

On INFIDELITY.

From the WEEKLY MISCELLANY.

WHEN Infidelity *unmaſk'd appears,*
  Nor knows herſelf the ugly form ſhe wears;
When ſacred writ is made the ſcoffer's theme,
And ſmartlings think it witty to blaſpheme;
* *When prophecies are ſaid to fail their day,*
And their intent allegoris'd away;
When truth is bullied from her antient ſeat,
† *And miracles reſolv'd into a cheat:*
What modeſt muſe, ev'n in Apollo's ſpite,
Wou'd not now pluck a quill, and dare to write?
Oh! cou'd I pierce, like Juvenal's ſharp ſtyle,
Or wound, like courtly Horace, with a ſmile!
Theſe modern arts I wou'd expoſe to view,
And ſhew what ſome degen'rate minds purſue;
To pluck up all religion by the root,
And level man with the unthinking brute,
To baniſh ſacred virtue from our Coaſt,
And (their laſt effort!) kill Aſtrea's ghoſt;
That lawleſs pow'r might authorize the will,
And glutton appetite enjoy her fill.
Have not theſe principles debauch'd the land?
Have they not put a ſword in murder's hand?
And ſent deſpair, dire harbinger, before,
To fool the rich, and tyrannize the Poor?
Hence villanies of each degree have ſlow'd,
And ev'ry day been kalender'd with blood!
Thus J—nk—s fell; thus fell the wretched pair,
That knew not their own ſinleſs babe to ſpare;
And do the authors of theſe miſchiefs live?
Can mercy, be it infinite, forgive?
Forgive it cannot, tho' a while it may
Forbear, and to repentance grant a Day;
Tho' patient Juſtice be a while implor'd,
To ſtay the fall of her uplifted ſword;
Vengeance will come, as ſure as Death will come;
And fix their ſad unalterable doom.
To this we leave them, and with chriſtian care
Give the juſt alms of pity, and of pray'r:
But let POPE's *numbers check theſe haughty jets,*
Or honeſt HOOKER *in his nervous proſe.*

---

* Collins.   † Woolfton.

A DIALOGUE *between the* Rt Hon. Sir
R—T W—LE, *and* W—M P—Y, *Esq; in*
Imitation of Horace. Ode IX. Lib. 3. (See
the Ode and another Imitation, p. 111.)

W. WHile I and you were cordial friends,
  Alike our interest and our ends,
I thought my character and place
Secure, and dreaded no disgrace.
No statesman, sure, was more carest,
Or more in his good fortune blest.

P. While I, your other self, was deem'd,
And worthy such renown esteem'd ;
E'er great NEWCASTLE won your heart,
And in your council took such part,
I was the happiest man in life,
And but with tories had no strife.

W. NEWCASTLE, noble and polite,
Whom GEORGE approves, is my delight,
His loyal merit is his claim,
For him I'd hazard life and fame.

P. Me St *John* now, whom every muse
And every grace adorns, subdues ;
Attach'd to him, I've learnt to hate
Your person, politicks, and state.

W. What if our former friendship shou'd
Return, and you have what you wou'd ?
If, for your sake, the noble duke
Sh'u'd be discarded, and forsook ?

P. Tho' St *John* now my fury warms,
And all his measures, have such charms ;
Tho' he is fond, indiff'rent you,
Our ancient league I'd yet renew,
For you I'd speech it in the house,
For you write Craftsmen and caresses ;
For you with all my soul I'd vote,
For you make friend, impeach, and plot,
For you, I'd die ; —what wou'd I not ?

Written by the lord L—NE, *in a window*
of the Tower, when under confinement there, over
the name of R. WALPOLE, *who had been con-*
fined in the same room in 1712. (See p. 239 l. 9.)

GOOD unexpected, evil unforeseen,
  Appears by turns, as fortune shifts the
  scene :
Some rais'd aloft come tumbling down amain ;
And fall so hard, they bound, and rise again.

To a gentleman, who had bound up some
of SWIFT's *and* POPE's *Poems, with*
one of F———'s *Plays.*

SAY wretch, what enmity, what rage
  Cou'd thus provoke thee to profane
The pure inimitable page
Of POPE, and our unrival'd DEAN?

Not PHALARIS, with tyrant heart,
 Cou'd half thy savage glory claim :
He, only rack'd the mortal part,
 But thou attempt'st to murder fame.

Thy F———'s labours thus to save,
 Extreamly elegant, and nice is ;
Like wise Egyptians, from the grave
 Preserving carcasses with spices.

In this position, be assur'd,
 He's more conspicuously undone ;
For MERCURY's but more obscur'd,
 By being plac'd too near the SUN.

The FAREWELL.

ADieu, foolish wanton, to all thy loose charms,
  Adieu to the pleasures, I found in thy arms ;
I scorn such mean conquests as others can win,
And despise fairest Lodgings where all may crowd
On these musical strings no more will I play (in
To which each pretender has a counterfeit key.

 Whilst absolute monarch I reign'd o'er your
NoCajus in Caja was ever more bless'd : (breast,
But since you've debauch'd your allegiance by
  stealth,
And chang'd love's dominion for lust's common-
  wealth,
I'll quit that frail empire, which once I held dear,
And let puny states your gross *Netherlands* share.

The Condition of Womankind.

HOw hard is the fate of poor womankind,
  Forever subjected, and always confin'd ;
Our parents controll us untill we are wives,
Our Husband's enslave us the rest of our lives.

Tho' fondly we love, yet we dare not reveal,
But secretly languish, compell'd to conceal ;
Deny'd every freedom of life to enjoy, (coy.
We are sham'd if we're kind, and blam'd if we're

To a Lady on reading Sherlock upon Death.

MIstaken fair, lay SHERLOCK by,
  His doctrine is deceiving ;
For whilst he teaches us to die,
 He cheats us of our living.

To die's a lesson we shall know
 Too soon, without a master,
Then let us only study now
 How we may live the faster.

To live's to love : To bless, be bless'd
 With mutual inclination :
Share then my ardour in your breast,
 And kindly meet my passion.

But if thus bless'd I may not live,
 And pity you deny,
To me at least your SHERLOCK give,
 'Tis I must learn to die.

To the Author of the Essays on Man, on his being Anonymous.

YE churchmen, laymen, scholars, wits, draw
  near ;
All who have sense, or want it, study here.
Say, has no generous eye the writer found ?
No pension rais'd him, and no laurels crown'd ?
So, where * the sev'nfold inundation brings
Mysterial plenty, and autumnal springs,
To some bold ox the stupid *Memphian* bends,
Nor traces *Nile*, tho' *Nile* from Heav'n descends.

   * *Egypt.*

Further Extract of the POEM *address'd to* Ld
BALTIMORE. (*See our last, p. 210.*

SUch, gracious fir, your province now appears,
How chang'd by industry, and rolling years,
From what it was!——
When, for the faith your ancestors had shown,
To serve two monarchs on the *English* throne ;
Cecilius, from the *royal Martyr*'s hand, * 1632.
Receiv'd the * charter of this spacious land.
Incult, and wild, its mazy forests lay,
Where deadly serpents rang'd, and beasts of prey:
The *Natives* jealous, cruel, crafty, rud :,
In daily wars declar'd their thirst for blood.
Oh, if the *Muses* would my breast inflame,
With spirit equal to the glorious theme !
My verse should shew to the succeeding age,
(Would time permit my verse to 'scape its rage;)
What toils your great *Progenitors* sustain'd,
To plant and cultivate the dreary strand.
What virtue in *Cecilius'* bosom glow'd !
Who with ‖ unsparing hand his wealth bestow'd,
Exhausting treasures from his large estate,
His infant-colony to cultivate ;
To humaniae a barb'rous, savage race,
And for industrious men provide a dwelling-place,
Maturest wisdom did his *Act* inspire,
Which ages must with gratitude admire ;
By which, the planters of his land were freed
From feuds, that made their parent-country bleed;
Religious feuds, which, in an evil hour,
Were sent from hell, poor mortals to devour!
Oh, be that rage eternally abhorr'd !
Which prompts the worshippers of one mild*Lord*,
For whose *salvation* one *Redeemer* dy'd,
By war their *Orthodoxy* to decide !
Falsely religious, human blood to spill,
And for *God*'s sake, their fellow-creatures kill!
Horrid pretence ——
Long had this impious zeal with boundless ⎫
Sway, ⎟
Most dreadful, urg'd o'er half the earth its way, ⎬
Tyrannic, on the souls of men to prey : ⎟
'Till great *Cecilius*, glorious hero! broke ⎭
Her bonds, and cast away her cursed yoke.
What praise, oh *patriot*; shall be paid to thee ⎫
Within thy province ‡ *conscience first was free!* ⎬
And gain'd in Maryland *its native liberty.* ⎭
To live beneath the blessings of her smile,
Numbers of *Albion*'s sons forsook their Isle ;

‖ *Ld* Cecilius *was at the Charge of sending
Ships, with People, and Provisions, to seat
and cultivate* Maryland ; *which Charge a-
mounted to* 40,000 l. *the Interest of which
Money He never receiv'd, by any Profits he
had from thence. See Ld Baltimore's Case,
deliver'd to the Parliament of* England, *in
1715.* ‡ *By an Act in* 1649, *allowing Liberty of Conscience to All, who profess their
Belief in* JESUS CHRIST. * *By the
said Act, a Fine was impos'd on such as
should call their Fellow-Planters any of those
Party-Names by which the Factions of Religion then in* England *were unhappily distinguish'd.*

In ships prepar'd by *Baltimore*'s command,
They came to cultivate his subject land :
And all, who could not for themselves provide,
Were by his kind paternal care supply'd. (dwell,
    That men of diff'rent *Faiths* in peace might
And all unite t'improve their public weal ;
* *Opprobrious names*, by which blind guides engage
Their blinded *Proselytes*, in deadliest rage ;
Sunk in *Oblivion*, by the wise *Decree*
Of *Calvert*, left his land from faction free.
    But whither flies the muse ? —, his curring ⎫
blame,   [*Theme*, ⎬
While thus she wanders, devious from her ⎭
Above her Flight ascends *Cecilius'* Fame !
    Him *Charles* succeeded ; the couragious son
Advanc'd the work his parent had begun ;
To cheer the planters by his gracious smile,
And by his presence animate their toil ;
Fir'd with the bold adventure, scorning ease,
He left the pompous court, and pass'd the Seas:
His frequent visits eas'd his tenants care,
When they were wounded deep with grief severe:
To drive away the planters from their lands,
Th' outrageous *Natives* came in hostile bands ;
Revengeful, cruel, restless, they pursu'd
Their enemies, and, ruthless, shed their blood:
Returning from his daily toil, at night,
The husband often saw with wild affright,
His darling wife, and infants, robb'd of breath,
Deform'd, and mangled by dishonest death.
The wise *Proprietor* his cares addrest,
To stop these ills, and heav'n his labours blest ;
Disarming of their rage the savage race ;
Extending o'er the land the shield of peace.
The planters, of their Foes no more afraid, ⎫
In plenty liv'd, pursuing gainful trade ; ⎬
And to their parent-land large tribute paid. ⎭
But to their *Lord*, for those incessant cares,
In which, the fire, and son employ'd their years;
For so much treasure spent---what gains accrue ?
Small their amount! ---perhaps in distant view,
He saw th' advancing province would afford
An ample income, to some future *Lord*:
But e'er his progeny receiv'd that gain,
A round of years had roll'd their course in vain.
    At length, to you, great fir, has fortune paid
The int'rest of the debt, so long delay'd ;
And ev'ry future year that runs his race,
Shall to your revenue add large increase :
If you, my *Lord*, afford your gen'rous aid,
If you inspirit our decaying trade.

We are informed that the Hibernian *Poetess has
been long indisposed, which probably may have
retarded the Publication of her Poems, and
therefore we defer inserting* M. D.'s *satirical
Lines on that Subscription, till we hear farther.
The Verses on the Subject proposed for a Prize in
our last Magazine came too late to be inserted,
except some, the Writers whereof will on due
Consideration, find not proper for us to publish.*
Mr H. C. *Pray excuse us for the same Reason. Sir, It is
with us as you hope, and we hope will be always.*

THE
Monthly Intelligencer.
MAY, 1733.

Wednesday *May* 2.

IN the Afternoon was an Eclipse of the Sun; it was observed from the Top of St. *John's Gate* to begin 46 Minutes after 5, and to end 31 after 7. by St. *Paul's* Clock. Total Duration 1 Hour 45 Minutes. The greatest Obscurity was about 5 Parts in 6.

Thursday, 3.

The Commons address'd his Majesty to order the Attorney General to prosecute Sir *Archibald Grant*, Bart. *W. Burroughs*, Esq; *WmSquire*, *George Robinson*, Esq; *Rich. Woolley*, and *Thomas Warren* for indirect and fraudulent Practices in their Management of the Affair of the Charitable Corporation. (See p. 246. D)

The Ld Bishop of *Bristol* was installed at that City, by his Proxy the Rev. Mr *Sutton*, one of the Prebendaries, and Rector of St. *Leonard's Bristol.*

Friday, 4.

The E. of *Burlington*, Knight of the Garter, &c. resigned his Gold Staff, as Captain of the Band of Gentlemen Pensioners. His Countess likewise resigned her Place of Lady of the Bed-Chamber to her Majesty.

Saturday, 6:

A Fire broke out at *Aylesbury*, which in less than 2 Hours, consumed above 30 Houses, together with Barns, Stables, and a vast Quantity of Corn and Hay.

Monday, 7.

Alexander Hume, Earl of *Marchmont*, one of the 16 Peers of *North Britain*, resigned his Place of Ld Register of *Scotland.*

Some Fishermen on the Flats of *Sandwich*, seeing a young *Grampus* with his Tail above Water, they lugg'd it into the Boat; on which it made a hideous Roaring, which the old one hearing, came to his Assistance, following the Boat, blowing up the Water higher than a House, wetting the Men very much, and pursuing so eagerly, that, for want of Water, she fell on her Side; and then the Boatmen took her also; being open'd, they found in her about a Bushel of small Fish, *viz.* Eels, Mullets, Mackarel, &c. Some of two Pounds weight. The old one near as big as a Whale, weighed about 700 *lb.* Weight, was almost 11 Feet long; had a Teat near her Tail, and about a Quart of Milk in her; the young one had no Fish in her Belly, weigh'd about 200 *lb.* and was 7 Feet long.

Tuesday, 8.

His Majesty signify'd by a Message to the Parliament, that a Contract of Marriage was far advanced, between the Princess Royal, his eldest Daughter, and the Prince of *Nassau-Orange*, Hereditary Stadtholder of the Provinces of *Friesland* and *Groningen.*

Wednesday, 9.

Both Houses waited on his Majesty with Addresses of Thanks, (see p. 263.) for communicating to them the said intended Nuptials: To which his Majesty return'd the following Answer;

To the HOUSE of LORDS.

My Lords,

I Thank *you for this Mark of your Affection to me and my Family: It is a great Satisfaction to me to find that the intended Marriage between my Daughter and the Prince of* Orange *is so agreeable to you.*

You may be assured, that I shall make the Preservation of the Liberties of my People, my chief Care and Concern.

To the HOUSE of COMMONS.

Gentlemen,

I Give you my Thanks *for this new Instance of your Duty, and Affection. Nothing can be more acceptable to Me, than your great Readiness in complying with*
this

this Demand, and the Perſonal Regard you have ſhewn to Me and my Family.

The Committee of the S. Sea Company, appointed to examine the 30 Articles referr'd to them, made their Report, which the Court ordered to be printed, and voted 600 *l.* to the Secretary, Clerks, &c. employ'd by the ſaid Committee, including contingent Expences.

Friday. 11.

A Cauſe was try'd in the Common Pleas at *Weſtminſter*, between Mr *Freeman*, a Plaiſterer, Plaintiff, and *J— C----*, Eſq; a Juſtice of the Peace, Defendant, for extorting a Shilling from him for a Diſcharge, tho' there was no Warrant granted, nor was there a Clerk to pretend a Demand for the ſame. It was likewiſe prov'd to be his daily Practice to take Money for binding over, granting and diſcharging of Warrants, which the Judge obſerv'd was a great Abuſe and contrary to Law. The Jury gave a Verdict for the Plaintiff and one Shilling Damage and Coſt of Suit.

Saturday, 12.

Ended the Seſſions at the *Old Baily*, when the 3 following Perſons received Sentence of Death, *viz.* *John Jones*, for robbing 2 Gentlemen on the Highway near *Tottenham High Croſs*; *John Davies*, for robbing three Waggons on *Hounſlow* Heath; and *Henry Hart*, for robbing a Woman in Moorfields of a Blanket. *Solomon Powers*, found guilty of Manſlaughter in ſhooting *Grace Neal* with a Muſquet, was burnt in the Hand. Twenty Two caſt for Tranſportation, *Wm Sambatch*, convicted of a Miſdemeanor, in procuring 2 Sheets of Lead, value 9 *l.* from Mr *Creed*, in the Name of Mr *Criſp*, to be pillory'd, impriſoned 6 Months, and pay a Fine of one Mark.

From the *London Evening-Poſt.* 12.

The Beginning of this Week, (*Tueſday* S.) when the Grand Jury met at *Guildhall*, they received, firſt, their uſual Charge, and then *were directed* to enquire into the late Burnings, Rejoycings, &c. in Anſwer to which the Ld Mayor (to his immortal Honour, adds *D'anvers*) told them, they were to diſtinguiſh between *publick Rejoycings* for any Good done, and *Mobbing* &c. And *yeſterday* at the *Old Bally* the Foreman of the Grand Jury addreſſed himſelf to the Rt. Hon. *John Barber*, Eſq; Lord Mayor, on the Bench, in theſe Words, *We the Grand Jury of the City of* London, *return*

your Lordſhip Thanks for your ſeaſonable Advice and Inſtructions, as well as for your juſt Diſtinction between Publick Rejoycings and Riotous Mobbings. —— This ſeeming a Miſrepreſentation of the Caſe, Mr Baron *Thomſon*, thought himſelf ſo nearly concern'd in it, that he judged it proper to publiſh that Part of his Charge, which this Paragraph ſeem'd to reflect upon, as follows,

Gentlemen,

*Y*OU have heard the Act read againſt *Tumults and Riotous Aſſemblies. I am ſorry that I can obſerve to you, that there has been lately outrageous Proceedings of that Kind in this City. Let the Pretences for ſuch Aſſemblies be what they will, all Licentious Rabbles and their Mobbiſh Proceedings ought to be diſcountenanced, not only by the Magiſtrates, but by all who wiſh to preſerve the Government, the Laws, and our Excellent Conſtitution. Every Man who thinks ſeriouſly, muſt be ſenſible of the ill Conſequences that are likely to proceed from ſuch Diſorders: They are, as the Act expreſſes it, a Diſturbance of the publick Peace, are uſually fomented by thoſe who are diſaffected, and tend to the endangering his Majeſty's Perſon and Government. I do not know whether any of theſe Offences may be laid before you: If they ſhould, I preſume, Gentlemen, that you would do your Duty in your Station. But I ſpeak this chiefly as a Caution and a Warning, that it may be known there are Laws in Being very ſevere againſt ſuch Offences. And as I am always rather for Mercy than Severity, and for preventing Miſchiefs, than be under the Neceſſity of puniſhing the Authors of them; I hope it will have the Effect, that we ſhall hear of no more ſuch for the future. I thought it my Duty to ſay thus much, and I could not ſay leſs upon ſuch an Occaſion.* WM THOMSON.

Sunday, 13.

Between 2 and 3 in the Morning, the Watchmen of St. *Paul's Covent Garden* and St. *Martin's in the Fields* ſeized 1100 Weight of uncuſtom'd Tea, 3 Men and a Boy on 4 Horſes, were taken, 2 of the Men were ſubſtantial Farmers at *Rye.* There were 9 of them in all, but 5 made their Eſcapes with drawn Cutlaſſes in their Hands.

Thursday 17.

His Majeſty went to the Houſe of Peers, and ſign'd the following Bills, *viz.* For granting an Aid to his Majeſty by a

Land-

Land-Tax. —— For repealing the Duty on Geneva and other compound Liquors. —— For preventing vexatious Suits at Law, and for the better Recovering of small Debts in the Principality of *Wales*. —— Relating to the Holding of County Courts. —— For filling up of *Fleet* Ditch. —— For repairing *Arundel* Port in the County of *Sussex*. —— The *Berkshire* Road. —— The *Hertford* Road. —— The *Ipswich* Road, and the Two-pennies Scots Bill. —— A Bill for the Encouragement of the Importing of Sugar from his Majesty's Plantations in *America*. *Tiverton*, *Horsly-down* and *Old-street* Church Bills. And 20 private ones.

About two in the Morning, the Watch stopt two Women in *White-cross Street*, with Baskets on their Heads, containing 117 Pounds of Tea, which being secured in the Watch-house, two of the Watchmen went with the Women who offer'd to shew them the House where they believ'd there was more. Being come into *Bumbill-Row*, one of the Women crying out, *Robbers*, *Robbers*, the Smugglers came up, and so beat one of the Watchmen about his Head with the Handles of their Whips, that he died in a few Hours.

Friday, 18.

Mr *Duncan*, Minister from the Pr. of Orange, for the Negotiation of the Marriage of his Highness with the Princess Royal, had a private Audience of their Majesties.

BRISTOL *May* 21. 1733.

To the Rt Worshipful Jn King, *Esq; Mayor, and the Worshipful the Aldermen of the City of* Bristol, *met at the Guildhall, at an Adjournment of the Quarter Sessions.*

WE the Grand Jury for the said City and County, take the Liberty of acquainting your Worships, that we have seen the Extract of a Letter, printed in the *Daily Courant* the 19th of *April* last, that highly reflects on the Conduct of the Rt Worshipful the Mayor, for the Rejoycings he encouraged on the Suspension of the Excise Bill, —— and as in Duty bound, we have made Enquiry into the several Facts there asserted, and find many of them to be false and scandalous; and we are well informed that Mr Mayor took necessary Caution to prevent any Excess of Joy, that such extraordinary News might naturally happen to produce. We do therefore present the said Extract of a Letter, dated the 14th of *April* last as a scandalous Libel, and desire your Worships will treat it as It deserves.

Tuesday, 22.

The Ld *Anne Hamilton*, resign'd his Post of Ensign in the First Reg. of Foot

Guards, as did Capt. *Whitworth*, his Command of a Troop in Brig. Gen. *Churchill*'s First Reg. of Foot Guards.

Thursday, 24.

The Court of Delegates, appointed to enquire into and decide the Cause (See Vol. II. p. 627) between Mrs *Katherine Weld*, Daughter to the Ld *Aston*, and her Husband, *Edward Weld*, Esq; for Insufficiency, confirm'd the Marriage, and decreed the Sufficiency of the Husband. There were present the Ld *Delawar*, Dr *Wilcox* Bp of *Rochester*, Dr *Tanner* Bp of St *Asaph*, Ld Ch. Baron *Reynolds*, Mr Baron *Comyns*, Sir *Henry Penrice*, Dr *Tindal*, and Dr *Kynaston*, who admonish'd them to live together with Unity, Love and Content, as Man and Wife.

Arthur Onslow, Esq; Speaker of the H. of Commons, and Chancellor to the Queen, transmitted to the Provost of Queens College, *Oxon*, a Benefaction of 1000 *l.* given by her Majesty, towards finishing the new Building of that College, of which the Queens Consorts of *England*, are, by the Charter of *Edward* III. declared Patronesses in Succession.

Monday, 28.

John Jones and *Jn Davis*, condemn'd for Robberies on the Highway, were executed at *Tyburn*. *Davis* feign'd himself sick, and desir'd he might not be ty'd in the Cart: But when he came to the Tree, while the Hangman was fastening the other's Halter, he jumpt out of the Cart, and ran over 2 Fields; but being knock'd down by a Countryman, was convey'd back and hang'd without any more Ceremony. *Jones* confessed he had been Confederate in several Robberies with *Gordon*, lately executed.

Wednesday 30.

Their Royal Highnesses Princess *Amelia* and *Caroline*, having been to drink the Waters at the Wells by the New River Head in the Parish of St. *James Clerkenwell*, almost every Day for the latter Part of this Month, there was so great a Concourse of the Nobility and Gentry, that the Proprietor took above 3 *l.* in a Morning. And this being the Birth-Day of their said Royal Highnesses, as they passed thro' the Spaw-field, Mr *Cook*, who keeps a Publick House therein, saluted them with 21 Guns, and in the Evening there was a great Bonfire near the Place, in Honour of the Day, when Mr *Cook* fired his Guns again several Times; a Custom he observes on Birth Days of the Royal Family. The Day was also kept as usual at Court

The Scheme *of a* Lottery *for Relief of the Sufferers by the Chav.Corporation.*
The Price of the Tickets 4 *l.* each.
That the Tickets shall be expressed in the Words following, viz. *This Ticket, in case it be drawn a Prize, intitles the Bearer to the Payment of the Prize, so drawn, within 40 Days after the Drawing is finish'd:* And that the Money be receiv'd and paid at the Bank.

	l.		l.
Benefit 1 of	10000	----	10000
1 ---	5000	----	5000
3 ---	3000	---	9000
4 ---	2000	---	8000
20 ---	1000	---	20000
40 ---	500	---	20000
200 ---	100	---	20000
400 ---	50	---	20000
1200 ---	20	---	24000
26300 ---	10	---	263000
28169		amounting to	399000

First drawn   500
Blanks 96831 Last drawn   500
125000   400000

Thursday 31. Sir *Joseph Jekyl,* Master of the Rolls, gave 500 *l.* his Lady 100 *l.* towards the Setling of *Georgia;* besides which the Trustees received 100 *l.* from the E. of *Abercorn,* 150 *l.* collected in the Parish of St *Margaret, Westminster,* and other Benefactions, this Month.

BIRTHS

THE Princess of *Hornes,* Daughter to the E. of *Aylesbury,* deliver'd of a Daughter at *Brussels.*
The Lady of the E. of *Pomfret,* deliver'd of a Daughter, who was baptiz'd the 25th instant, the D. of *Manchester,* standing Godfather, the Princess R.yal, and the Dutchess of *Bolton,* Godmother.
The Lady of the Resident *Hoppmann,* deliver'd of a Daughter.
The Wife of *John Larocbe,* Esq; Representative for *Bodmyn* in *Cornwal,* deliverd of a Son.
The Wife of *Wm Rawlinson Erle,* Esq; Representative for *Malmsbury, Wilts,* deliver'd of a Son and Heir.

MARRIAGES.

LD *Wm Hamilton,* married to Miss *Haws,* Daughter of *Francis Haws,* Esq; a South Sea Director in 1720. able to give her 40,000 *l.*
George *Wrighte,* Esq; Member of Parliament for *Leicester* :: to the only Daughter of Sir *Thomas Clarges,* Bart.
Mr Justice Lee, :: to Mrs *Melmoth* worth 20,000 *l.* Relict of an eminent

Merchant of that Name.
Mr *Williams,* of the Custom-house, to the Daughter of the Rev. Mr *Richardson* late Rector of *Allhallows, London Wall.*
Mr *James Barclay,* a Dutch Merchant, Grandson to *Robert Barclay,* the famous Apologist, :: to Miss *Sally,* Daughter of of Mr *John Freame,* Banker, and Deputy Governor of the Lead Corporation.
Mynheer Bentinck, one of the States of *Holland,* 2d Son to the Countess of *Portland,* and Brother in Law to the D. of *Kent,* :: to a Dutch Lady of vast Fortune.
Sidney Stafford Smith, Esq; of *Sevenoaks* in *Kent,* :: to a Daughter of Sir *Cha. Farnaby,* Bart.
George Pitt, of *Stratfieldsea, Hampsh.* Esq; :: to Miss *Wyndham,* a rich Heiress.
M. *Van Notten,* a Dutch Merchant :: to the 2d Daughter of the late *David Bosanquet,* Esq; a Fortune of 8000 *l.*
Sir *John Leigh,* of *Addington, Surry* Bar. of 3000 *l.* a Year, aged near 70 :: to Miss *Wade,* about 18, Daughter of Mr *Wade,* Apothecary at *Bromley* in *Kent,* who lately cur'd Sir *John* of a Mortification in his Toe.
Mr *Wagg,* Hop Merchant in *Southwark* :: to the eldest Daughter of *George Baker,* of *Haukhurst* in *Kent,* Esq; with a Fortune of 6000 *l.*
Morgan Keene, of *New Sarum, Wilts.* :: to Miss *Roberts,* of *Craven-street* in the *Strand,* a Fortune of 6000 *l.*
Henry Norris, Esq; Son of Justice *Norris* of *Hackney* :: to Miss *Handley.*
Farely, Esq; of *Oxfordshire* :: to Miss *Harriot Pitt,* Sister to Miss *Fitt* one of her Majesty's Maids of Honour.
Wm Medcalfe, Esq; :: to Miss *Afflock,* both of *Cambridgeshire.*

DEATHS.

Apr. 8. THO. *Coleman,* Esq; Resident at the Court of the Great Duke of *Tuscany,* at *Pisa;* He Married Mr *Pulteney* Wife's Sister.
27. Monf. *Picart,* at *Amsterdam,* the most celebrated Engraver of this or any other Age. He imbib'd the first Rudiments of his Art under his Father, called *Picart the Roman,* which he finish'd under the famous *Le Brun.*
28. The Rev. Mr *Parker,* at *Richmond,* Chaplain to the Ld *Digby.*
29. Mrs *Philadelphia Mohun,* Daughter of *John* Ld *Mohun,* who did signal Services for K. *Charles* I. during the Civil Wars. She was 80 Years old and a Maid, and Great Aunt to *Charles* Ld *Mohun.*

kwn, kill'd in a Duel with the late Duke *Hamilton* in *Hyde Park*, *Nov*, 15. 1712.

30. *James Fleet* Efq; Son and Heir to Sir *Jn Fleet*, formerly L'd Mayor of *London*.

May 1. Sir *Tho. Wifeman*, Bar. at *Eaft-Grinftead*, *Suffex*. Dying unmarried, and without Brothers, the Title is extinct.

2. *John Winter*, Efq; at *Kenfington*. Mr *Beverly*, Clerk of the Cheque of the King's Yard at *Deptford*.

3. *Fiennes Harrifon*, Efq; Son of the late Sir *Edw. Harrifon* ; *Clarkenwell*.

Mr *Bowles*, Searcher in the Port of *Briftol*. The Wife of Mr *Woodyer*, who kept the *King's Arm's* Tavern on *Ludgate-Hill*, of a wound fhe receiv'd a few Days before from her Husband with a Cleaver on the Side of her Head.

Mr *Abraham Chambers*, Banker.

Mr *Henworth*, a Merchant of this City. *Jofeph Saxfon*, Efq; a Hamburgh Mercht reputed worth 12,000 *l.* and 200 *l.* a year.

Mr *Zachariah Zouch*, Clerk to the Bench of Juftices for *Surry*.

† Mr *John Underwood*, of *Whittlefea* in *Cambridgefhire*. At his Burial, when the Service was over, an Arch was turn'd over the Coffin, in which was placed a fmall piece of white Marble, with this Infcription, *Non omnis moriar*, 1733. Then the 6 Gentlemen who follow'd him to the Grave fung the laft Stanza of the 29th Ode of the 2d Book of *Horace*. No Bell was toll'd, no one invited but the 6 Gentlemen, and no Relation follow'd his Corpfe ; the Coffin was painted Green, and he laid in it with all his Cloaths on ; under his Head was placed *Sanadon's Horace*, at his Feet *Bentley's* Milton ; in his Right Hand a fmall Greek Teftament, with this Infcription in Gold Letters εἰ μὶ ἐς τῷ ςαυτο, J. U. in his Left Hand a little Edition of *Horace*, with this Infcription, *Mufis Amicus*, J. U. and *Bentley's Horace* under his Arfe. After the Ceremony was over they went back to his Houfe, where his Sifter had provided a cold Supper ; the Cloth being taken away the Gentlemen fung the 31ft Ode of the 1ft Book of *Horace*, drank a chearful Glafs, and went Home about Eight. He left near 6000 *l.* to his Sifter, on Condition of her obferving this his Will, order'd her to give each of the Gentlemen ten Guineas, and defir'd they would not come in black Cloaths ; The Will ends thus —— *Which done I would have them take a chearful Glafs, and think no more of* John Underwood.

Ch. Frewin, of *Leicefter Square*, Efq;

Lowther, 3d Son of Sir *Jofeph Pennington*, at *Cambridge*.

7. *George* E. of *Cholmondeley*, General of the Horfe, Governor of *Guernfey* and *Kingfton upon Hull*, Col. of the 3d Troop of Horfe-Guards, Ld Lieut. and Cuftos Rotulorum of *Chefter* and *North Wales*, and F. R. S. He was fucceeded by his only Son *George* Vifc. *Malpas*.

John Hall, Efq; at *Rippon*, *Torkfhire*.

8. Mrs *Mead* at *Aylesbury*, laft Surviving Sifter of *Wm Mead*, Efq; of that Place.

10. *Barton Booth*, Efq; the celebrated Tragedian, one of the Patentees of *Drury Lane* Playhoufe. He was efteem'd the greateft Scholar and Actor the *Britifh* Theatre could ever boaft. What he wrote himfelf concerning another Perfon was very applicable to him, *viz. Haud ignobili Stirpe oriundus, nec Literarum rudis humaniorum ; Rem Scenicam permultos feliciter Annos adminiftravit ; juftoq; Moderamine & Morum Suavitate, omnium, infra Theatrum, Obferuantiam, extra, Laudem, ubique Benevolentiam & Amorem, fibi conciliavit.*

11. *Cornelius Arnold*, Efq; aged 87, Counfellor at Law, at *Roehampton*.

13. Mr *Moneliy*, Sword-Cutler to moft of the Nobility.

The Rev. Mr *Carey*, Vicar of *Iflington*.

14. *James Avery*, Efq; at *Rochefter*.

15. *Tho. Grahame*, Efq; Apothecary to his Majefty.

Wm Shaw, Efq; Train-Bearer to the Lord Chancellor.

Capt. *Dundafs*, Commander of his Majefty's Sloop *Drake*, lately at *Lisbon*.

James Wroughton, Efq; of *Efcot* in *Wiltfhire*, who married the Countefs Dowager of *Abington*, who furvives him.

Mrs *Mafon*, of *Careyftr* worth 10,000 *l.*

16. Relict of the late Sir *Hale Hooke*, and Wife of Dr *Lilly* for 20 Years paft.

17. *Francis Moult*, Efq; formerly an eminent Chymift.

Roger Stewart, Efq; at *Taunton*, *Somerfetfhire*.

18. The Rev. Mr *Chifeull*, Vicar of *Walthamftow*, *Effex*.

19. Mr *Elicot*, an eminent Watchmaker in *Swithin's Alley*.

Mr *James Jenner*, an eminent Mafter Builder in *Grofvenor-ftreet*.

The Wife of ———— *Croven*, Efq; nearly related to the Ld *Craven*.

21. *John Mainwaring*, Efq; of *Mile-end*.

Sir *Richard Cox*, Bar. who in 1706 was Ld Chancellor of *Ireland*, and one of the Lords Juftices of that Kingdom.

Robert

Robert second Son of the Ld *Hobart*.
Mrs *Rouse*, Sister to *Wm Conolly*, Esq; of *Ireland*.
The Lady *Gore*, Mother to the late Sir *Ralph Gore*, at *Dublin*.
The Lady *Dungannon*, in *Ireland*.
23. *Thomas Carpenter*, Esq; of the *Homme*, near *Weobly* in *Herefordshire*, and left his Estate (about 300 *l.* a Year) to his Cousin the Ld *Carpenter*.
Sir *Brook Bridges*, Bar. High Sheriff for *Kent*, at *Godnestone* in that County.
24. The Rev. Mr *Thomas Fydell*, in *Clarges-street*.
25. Miss *Judith*, only Daughter of Justice *Gough*.
John Combs, Esq; at *Hertford*, formerly Turkey Merchant worth 20,000 *l.*
Sheppard, Esq; in *Red Lyon-Square*.
Thomas Price, Esq; of *Buckinghamshire*, at *Bath*.
28. The only Daughter of *Shallet* Esq; in *York Buildings*.
Mr *Deputy Tombes*, wholesale China Man in *Leadenhall-street* worth 20,000 *l.*
Mr *Charles Harris*, a Wholesale Haberdasher in *Bread street*.
30. Capt. *Lovibond*, Son to a Master in Chancery of that Name.

PROMOTIONS.

LD *Carmichael*, appointed Col. of a Company in the 3d Reg. of Guards.
John Lightfoot, Esq; made Chirographer of the Common Pleas, in Reversion.
Ld Visc. *Lonsdale* appointed Ld Keeper of the Privy Seal, in the Room of
The D. of *Devonshire*, made Ld Steward of his Majesty's Houshold, in the Room of the E. of *Chesterfield*.
Mr *Wiseman*, Clerk of the Cheque at *Woolwich*, made Clerk of the Cheque at *Deptford* Yard; in the Room of Mr *Beverly* deceas'd. And
Mr *Russel*, late Consul at *Algiers*, succeeds Mr *Wiseman* at *Woolwich*.
Mr *Barnet* of *Burlington-street*, married to a Relation of the Countess of *Suffolk*, made Supervisor General of the Salt Duties in *Scotland*, in the room of Sir *Henry Rollo*, Bar. deceas'd, with a Salary of 150 *l.* per Ann.
George F. of *Moreton*, appointed Vice Admiral of *Scotland*, in the Room of the E. of *Stair*. 2000 *l* per Ann.
Robert Ld *Walpole*,—Custos Rotulorum for the County of *Devon*, in the Room of the Ld *Clinton*.
Gilbert Fleming, Esq; —— Lieutenant General of the Charibbee Islands, and

likewise of the Island of St *Christopher*, in *America*, in room of *Wm Mathew*, Esq.
James Wedderburn, Esq; —— Clerk of the Common Pleas in South *Carolina*.
Robert Burnet, Esq; —— Secretary to; *Nova Cæsarea*, or *New Jersey*, in *America*
Philip Gery, Esq; made Lieut Col. to Brigadier Gen. *Churchill's* Reg. of Dragoons in the Room of
Charles Armand Powlett, Esq; Lieut. Col. of the 2d Troop of Horse Grenadiers, and Deputy Governor of the *Isle of Wight*.
Capt. *Compton*,—Commander of his Majesty's Sloop *Drake* in the room of Capt. *Dundas*, deceas'd.
The Ld *Lovell*—Capt. of the Band of his Majesty's Gentlemen Pensioners, in the room of the E. of *Burlington*, who resign'd. And
Robert Coke, Esq; the said Ld's Brother, ——Vice-Chamberlain, in the room of Ld *Wm Beauclerc*, deceas'd.
James Cockburne, Esq; Paymaster to the Royal Reg. of Artillery, made Secretary to the D. of *Argyle*, as Master-General of the Ordnance.
Thomas Fane, Esq; made Customer Inwards for the Port of *Bristol*.
Sir *Charles Wager*, elected Master of the Corporation of Trinity House at *Deptford*, for the ensuing Year.
Dr *Wadsworth*, and Dr *Jurin* chosen Governors of St *Thomas's* Hospital.
Capt. *Tollard*, made Commander of the *Pearl* Man of War.
Capt. *Eaton*, succeeds Col. *Bragge* in a Company of the 3d Reg. of Guards; and Capt. *Legge* succeeds Capt. *Eaton* as Capt. Lieut. of the Coldstream Reg.
Sir *Wm Billers*, made Col. of the Blue Reg. of Train'd Bands, in the Room of the late Sir *Gilbert Heathcote*.
Dr *Hall*, chosen Physician to St *Thomas's* Hospital.
Thomas Webster, Esq; made Ensign in a Company in the 2d Reg. of foot Guards
George, E. of *Cholmondeley*, appointed Lieut. of the Counties of *Montgomery, Flint, Merioneth, Carnarvon*, and *Anglesea*; and likewise of the County of *Chester*, City of *Chester*, and County of the same; and also Custos Rotulorum of the County of *Chester*; also Steward of the Royal Manor of *Sheen* in *Surry*, in the Room of the late Earl his Father.
Sir *Robert Salusbury Cotton*,—Lieut. of the Country of *Denbigh*.
Capt. *Jekyl*,——Major to Brig. Gen. *Churchill's* Reg. of Dragoons, in the Room of *Philip Gery* Esq;

Mr

Mr *Mailand*---Enfign in Col. *Legg's* Company in the 3d Reg. of Foot Guards, in the Room of Enfign *Campbell*.

Mr *Leblange* made Enfign in the Cold Stream Regm. in the Room of Ld *Anne Hamilton*, who refign'd.

Major *Wardour*, appointed Lieut Col. of the 2d Troop of Horfe Guards, in the Room of *Lewis Dives*, Efq; who refign'd.

Capt. *Edwards*, an Exempt in the faid Troop, made Major in the Room of Major *Wardour*.

Major *Soron*, made an Exempt in the Room of Capt. *Edwards*.

Capt. *Marchant*, Sub-Brig.—Brigadier in the Room of Capt. *Soron*; and *Mathew Hall*, Efq;—Sub-Brigadier in the Room of Capt. *Marchant*.

Mr *Berry*, Quarter Mafter in Brig. Gen. *Dubourgay's* Reg. appointed Enfign of a Company in the fame.

New MEMBERS.

THE Ld *Sidney Beauclerc*, a Brother of the D. of *St Albans*, chofen Reprefentative for the Borough of *Windfor*.

Maurice Bocland, Efq; for *Yarmouth* in the *Ifle* of *Wight*, in the room of the Ld *Malpas* now E. of *Cholmondeley*.

Leonard Smelt, Efq; rechofen for the Borough of *North Allerton* in *Yorkfhire*, having been made Clerk of the Ordnance.

Wm Rawlinfon Erle, Efq; for *Malmsbury* in *Wiltfhire*, having been made Clerk of the Deliveries of the faid Ordnance. See p. 1084.

Ecclefiaftical Preferments *conferr'd on the following Reverend Gentlemen.*

JOHN *Wilcox*, M. A. prefented to the Vicarage of *Collumpton*, *Devonfhire*.

Mr *Jennour*, chofen Lecturer of the United Parifhes of St *Olave Old Jury*, and St *Martin's Ironmonger Lane*, inftead of Dr *Trapp*, who refign'd.

John Anderfon, M. A. prefented to the Rectory of *Shoreham*, *Kent*.

Mr *Fiddes*, of *All-Souls* College in *Oxford*, made a Prebendary of St *Pauls*, in the room of Dr *Godolphin*, deceafed.

Mr *Tho. Swallow*, Vicar of *Writtle* near *Chelmsford*, prefented to the Living of *Stondon*, *Effex*.

Mr *Henfhaw*, to the Rectory of *High Ongar* in *Effex*, worth upwards of 300 l. per Ann.

Mr *Wm Goodwin*, made a Prebendary in the Collegiate Church of *Brecknock*.

Mr *Tho. Leland*, prefented to the Vicarage of *Corthnew*, *Cornwal*.

Mr *Simon Hardy*, to the Rectory of *Cottingham*, *Norfolk*.

Mr *Charles Dixon*, to the Vic. of *Kingfton* and *Iford*, *Suffex*.

Hugh Lewis, D. D. appointed Prebendary of the Free Chapel of St *George* in the Caftle of *Windfor*, void by the Refignation of Dr *Bland*.   And

Edward Martin, L. D.——Prebendary in the faid Chapel, void by the Death of *Wm Wade*, M. A.

Mr *John Nicoll*, Head Mafter of *Weftminfter* School, made a Doctor in Divinity in a Convocation at *Oxford*.

Dr *Secker*, inducted into the Rectory of St *James's* at *Weftminfter*.

Mr *Northey*, prefented the Vicarage of *Clumford* in *Kent*.

Mr *Wm Jones*, to the Vicarage of *Llanllibet* in *Flintfhire*.

Dr *Thomas Rymer*, appointed to preach before the Houfe of Commons on the 29th Inftant, being the Reftauration of K. *Charles* II.

Mr *Clarke*, one of the Senior Fellows of St *John's* College, chofen Senior Burfer to that Society; and

Dr *Williams*, and Mr *Regifter*, admitted Senior Fellows.

Mr *John Wilkinfon*, prefented to the Rectory of *Milborn Port*, *Somerfetfhire*.

Difpenfations have pafs'd the Seals to enable

Mr *Smith*, Chaplain to the Bp of St *Davids*, to hold the Vic. of *Stone*, together with the Rectory of *Hartwell Bucks*.

John Wilcox, M, A. to hold the Rectory of *Zelemonachorum*, *Exon*, together with the Vicarage of *Collumpton*, in the faid County; and

Whadham Chandler, M. A. Chaplain to the Bp of *Durham*, to hold the Rectory of *Bifhop's-Wereham*, with the Rectory of *Wafhington* in the faid County.

Mr *Lacon Lamb*, prefented to the Rectory of *New Town* in *Monmouthfhire*.

BANKRUPTS.

THomas *Woodyer*, of *Ludgate hill*, Vintner. *George Heyliger*, of *London* Merchant. *Wm Whitehead*, of *Old Bethlehem*. Turner. *Tho. Grayhurft*, of *Shoreditch*, Mid Brewer. *Tho. Ball*, of *Tamworth*, *Warwick*, Chapman. *Jn. Wynell*, of *Wyldftreet*, Mid. Victualler. *Tho. Ryley*, of St *Martins* in the *Fields*, Mid. Chapman. *John Triquett*, of *Stepney*, *Middlefex*, Dyer. *John Whitehead*, of *Southwark*, *Surry*, Dyer. *John Corbery*, of *Shoreditch*, Mid. Weaver. *John Butcher*, of *London*, Carpenter.

IT is advised from the *Hague*, That Mr *Finch*, the *British* Minister, had notified to the States General, the Conclusion of a Marriage between the Prince of *Orange* and the Princess Royal of *England*, with whom he is to have 80,000 *l.* given her by the Parliament, and 10,000 *l.* a Year settled on her by the King during her Life. That this News had terribly disconcerted four or five Gentlemen there, who before had thwarted every Thing proposed to the Prince's Advantage. On the other Hand, the Friends of the Prince congratulate one another upon the Success of this Affair, hoping his *Britannick* Majesty and the whole Nation will have his Interests at Heart, and give a better aspect to his Affairs than they have lately had.

From *Oran*, That a Body of *Moors*, to the Number of 9000 Foot, and 2000 Horse had attacked Fort St *Ferdinand*, but were repulsed by the *Spaniards* with the Loss of above 1500 Men, after an obstinate Skirmish.

From *Amsterdam*, That Letters from *Batavia* advise, that about a Year and a half ago, Orders were sent to that Settlement, to turn out part of the Regency, and to prosecute the Governor of *Ceylon*, for his abominable Tyranny in putting scores of innocent Persons to Death. The Officer being arrived at *Batavia*, did execute his orders there; but coming to *Ceylon*, tho' back'd with some hundreds of Soldiers, and 20 pieces of Cannon, the Governor saluted him with all the Guns of the Fort, charged with Ball, and made him retire; Whereupon it was resolved by the States General, to send 6 Men of War and 4000 Land-Forces to *Ceylon*, for fear this rebellious Governor should deliver up the Place to the *Moors*, or the People of the Country.

From *Versailles*, That her most Christian Majesty was delivered of a Princess.

From *Paris*, That the Disputes about the Bull *Unigenitus*, are again grown to such a Height, as must seemingly end in the downfal of the Authority of Parliament, or of the Jesuits, unless accommodated; the Parliament being resolved to hazard another Exile, rather than part with a Tittle of their Jurisdiction; and the Majority of the Bishops, the Pope's Nuncio, and the Jesuits, being resolv'd, if possible, to overturn it.

From *Warsaw*, That several Confederacies were form'd, in Relation to the ensuing Election of a King, all unanimous in the Exclusion of a Foreigner. That the *Czarina* had resolv'd to oppose the Election of K. *Stanislaus* with all her Forces, and frankly declared as much to the *French* Minister. The Emperor also has sent to *Warsaw* an Act of Exclusion against the said King; notwithstanding which, that Prince stood fairest to be elected K. of *Poland*: However, the Friends of the Elector of *Saxony* did not despair. There was a Dispute between the *Russian* Minister and Mr *Woodward*, who refus'd to give Place to the former.

From *Warsaw*, *May* 25. That the Dyet of Convocation had held its last Session on the 22d, and then agreed to and sign'd a general Confederacy in good Order, having first Sworn not to Elect a Foreigner as above. The Day of Election was fixt for the 25th of *Aug.* But a Protest was enter'd by the *Dissidents*, who had been excluded.

From *Berlin*, *May* 30. That the Nuptials of the Prince of *Anhalt* with the Princess *Albertina*, were celebrated with great Splendour and Magnificence.

From *Rome*, That Card. *Coscia* was sentenced to be imprison'd ten Years in the Castle of St *Angelo*; suspended from all Active or Passive Voice in the Election of a new Pope; declared to be excommunicated, and only to be absolved by the Pope at the point of Death; and what is worse, to restore all the Money he had received contrary to the Tenour of the Apostolick Bulls.—— But is allow'd 1000 Crowns a Year for his Subsistence, a Priest and a Servant to attend him, and the Privilege of two Rooms and a Gallery.

From *Gibraltar*, That the three *English* Men of War, which had been at *Tetuan*, to demand Satisfaction of the King of *Morocco*, were return'd without obtaining it; and were preparing to Sail towards *Sallee*, to cruize upon the Rovers of that Place.

From *Seville*, That the King of *Spain* was making Armaments both by Sea and Land, not only greater, but of a different Nature from those of last Year; viz. 23 Men of War, 17,000 Land Forces, and a vast Number of small Vessels, Transports, &c.

From *Marseilles*, That the *Capitana* of *Algiers*, of 80 Guns, and two other large Ships of the *Turkish* Squadron going to the relief of *Oran*, were cast away in a Storm, many thousand Soldiers drown'd, and the rest who 'scaped to *Scio*, refused to embark again.　　**STOCKS**

Towards the End of the Month.

Course of Exchange.	STOCKS
Amsterdam — 35 *a* 34	S. Sea 103 $\frac{3}{8}$
Ditto at Sight 34 10	— Annu. 110 $\frac{1}{2}$
Hamburgh — 34	Bank 150 $\frac{1}{8}$
Rotterdam — 35 1 $\frac{3}{4}$	India 162 $\frac{1}{4}$
Antwerp — 35 5	3 *per* C. *Ann.* 102 $\frac{3}{8}$
Madrid — 42 $\frac{1}{4}$	M. Bank 116
Bilboa — 41 $\frac{3}{4}$	African 30
Cadiz — 41 $\frac{7}{8}$	York Buil. no Transf.
Venice — 49	Royal Aff. 107 $\frac{1}{2}$
Leghorn — 50 $\frac{1}{8}$	Lon. ditto 13 $\frac{1}{8}$
Genoa — 53 $\frac{1}{4}$	Eng. Copp. 1*l.* 18*s.*
Paris — 32 $\frac{5}{8}$	Welsh ditto 1*l.* 6*s.*
Bourdeaux — 31	Bank Cir. 6*l.* 00*s.*
Oporto — 5 4 $\frac{1}{2}$	India Bonds 5*l.* 13*s.*
Lisbon — 5 5 $\frac{3}{8}$ *a* 4 $\frac{3}{4}$	3 *p. Cent* ditto 2*l.* 4*s.*
Dublin — 11 $\frac{7}{8}$	S. Sea ditto 2*l.* 15*s.*

Monthly BILL *of Mortality,*
from Apr. 24. *to* May 29.

Christned	Males 835	Females 809	1644
Buried	Males 1393	Femal. 1464	2857

Died under 2 Years old	1251
Between 2 and 5	335
Between 5 and 10	135
Between 10 and 20	82
Between 20 and 30	170
Between 30 and 40	219
Between 40 and 50	236
Between 50 and 60	183
Between 60 and 70	132
Between 70 and 80	73
Between 80 and 90	30
Between 90 and 100	11
	2857

Price of Grain at *Bear-Key, per* Qr.

Wheat 22*s.* to 26*s.*	P. Malt 21*s.* to 23*s.*
Rye 12*s.* to 16*s.*	B. Malt 19*s.* to 21*s.*
Barley 13*s.* to 17*s.* 6*d.*	Tares 20*s.* to 22*s.*
Oats 10*s.* to 15*s.*	H. Pease 16*s.* to 18*s.*
Pease 20*s.* to 21*s.* 6*d.*	H. Beans 18*s.* to 22*s.*

Buried.	
Within the walls,	227
Without the walls,	850
In Mid and Surry,	1138
City and Sub of West	642

Weekly	Burials
May 3	586
8	574
15	560
22	586
29	551

Prices of Goods, &c. in *London.* Hay 1*l.* 16*s.* to 2*l.* 0*s.* a Load.

Coals per Chaldron 25*s.* to 26*s.*
Old Hops per Hun. 3*l.* to 4*l.*
New Hops 7*l.* to 9*l.*
Rape Seed 10*l.* to 11*l.* per *Last*
Lead the Fodder 19 *Hun.* 1 *half on board,* 15*l.* to 16*l.* 00*s.*
Tin in Blocks 4*l.* 00*s.*
Ditto in Bars 4*l.* 02*s. exclusive of* 3*s. per Hun. Duty.*
Copper Eng. best 5*l.* 05*s. per C.*
Ditto ord. 4*l.* 16*s.* to 5*l. per C.*
Ditto Barbary 90*l.* to 100*l.*
Iron of Bilboa 15*l.* 05*s. per Tun.*
Dit. of Sweden 16*l.* 10*s. per Tun*
Town Tallow 36*s.* 00*s. per C.*
Country Tallow 1*l.* to 15*s.*

Grocery Wares.

Raisins of the Sun 31*s.* 0*d. per C.*
Ditto Malaga Frailes 19*s.*
Ditto Smirna new 21*s.*
Ditto Alicant, none
Ditto Lipra new 19*s.*
Ditto Belvedera 20*s.*
Currants old none
Ditto new 45*s.*
Prunes French 17*s.*
Figs 20*s.*
Sugar Powd. best 54*s. a* 59*s. per C.*
Ditto second sort 46*s.* to 50*s. per C.*
Loaf Sugar double refine 8*d. Half-penny a* 9*d. per lb.*
Ditto single refin. 56*s.* to 64*s. per C.*
Cinamon 7*s.* 8*d. per lb.*
Cloves 9*s.* 1*d.*
Mace 15*s.* 0*d. per lb.*
Nutmegs 8*s.* 7*d. per lb.*
Sugar Candy white 14*d.* to 18*d.*
Ditto brown 6*d. per lb.*
Pepper for Home consf. 16*d.*
Ditto for exportation 12*d. Farth.*
Tea Bohea fine 10*s.* to 12*s. per lb.*
Ditto ordinary 9*s.* to 10*s. per lb.*
Ditto Congo 10*s.* to 14*s. per lb.*
ditto Pekoe 14*s. a* 16*s. per lb.*
ditto Green fine 9*s.* to 12*s. per lb.*
ditto Imperial 9*s.* to 12*s. per lb.*
ditto Hyson 30*s.* to 35*s.*

Drugs *by the lb.*

Balsom Peru 14*s.* to 15*s.*
Cardamoms 3*s.* 3*d.*
Camphire refin'd 17*s.*
Crabs Eyes 1*s.* 8*d.*
Jallop 3*s.*
Manna 2*s.* 6*d. a* 4*s.*
Mastick white 4*s.* 6*d.*
Opium 9*s.* 00*d.*
Quicksilver 4*s.*
Rhubarb fine 25*s. a* 28*s.*
Sarsaparilla 3*s.* 0*d.*
Saffron Eng. 27*s.* 00*d.*
Wormseeds none
Balsam Capaiva 2*s.* 9*d.*
Balsam of Gillead 20*s.* 00*d.*
Hipocacuana 5*s.*
Ambergreece per oz. 8*s.*
Cochineal 18*s.* 3*d. per lb.*

Wine, Brandy, *and* Rum.

Oporto red, per Pipe 36*l.*
ditto white 24*l.*
Lisbon red 35*l. a* 40*l.*
ditto white, 26*l.*
Sherry 26*l.*
Canary new 30*l.*
ditto old 36*l.*
Florence 3*l.* 3*s per Chest*
French red 30*l. a* 40*l.*
ditto white 20*l.*
Mountain malaga old 24*l.*
ditto new 20 *to* 21*l.*
Brandy Fr. per Gal. 6*s.* to 6*s.* 8*d.*
Rum of Jamaica 7*s.* to 0*s.*
ditto Lew. Islands 6*s.* 4*d.* to 10*d.*
Spirits Eng. 30*l. per Ton.*

GOLD in Bars, 3*l.* 18*s.* 4*d.* — Ditto in Coin 3*l.* 18*s.* 3*d.* to 4*l.* 1*s.* — SILVER in Bars, Standard, 5*s.* 4*d.* half-penny. — Pillar Pieces of Eight 5*s.* to 5*s.* 5*d.* 3 farth. ditto Mexico 5*s.* 5*d.* 3 farth.

A REGISTER of BOOKS publish'd in MAY, 1733.

THE Patriot, an Epistle to the most Noble *Philip*, E. of *Chesterfield*, one of His Majesty's most Hon. Privy Council, and Knight of the most Noble Order of the Garter. By Mr. *Stanhope*. Printed for *John Cooper*, price 6 d.

2. A Letter to the Rt. Hon. Sir *Rob. Walpole*, concerning the Election of a K. of *Poland*, the Claim of K. *Stanislaus*, the Views of the House of *Austria*, and the Interest of *Great Britain*. By *Charles Foreman*, Esq; Printed for *J. Wilford*, pr. 1 s.

3. A Letter to *Caleb D'anvers*, Esq; Printed for *J. Chrichley*, pr. 6 d.

4. Of Publick Good. An Epistle to the Rt. Hon. *John* E. of *Stair*. Printed for *J. Wilford*, pr. 6 d.

5. The Loyal; or, Revolutional Tory. Being some Reflections on the Principles and Conduct of Tories; shewing 'em true Friends to the present Establishment, some of the Capital Pillars of the Constitution, and worthy of Royal Trust and Confidence. By a Friend to the Church and Constitution. Pr. for *Wilford*, price 1 s.

6. Revolution Politicks: Or, a compleat and regular Collection of above a 1000 Reports, Lies, and Stories, which were the Fore-runners of the great Revolution in 1688. Sold by the Booksellers.

7. An Impartial Enquiry into the late Conduct of the City of *London*, relating to the Excise Bill. By a Common Council Man. Pr. for *J. Roberts*, price 6 d.

8. Lord Blunder's Confession; Or, Guilt makes a Coward. A new Ballad Opera. Sold by the Booksellers, price 1 s. 6 d.

9. The Whole Proceedings upon the Tryal of *Rob. Marral*, alias *Bold Bob*, &c. &c. Sold at the Pamphlet Shops, price 6 d.

10. How do you after your Oysters? Better than you after your Tobacco. Sold by the Booksellers, price 6d.

11. Putt, or Refusal; An Answer to a Pamphlet sign'd *Magna Charta*, or Change Alley excised by the prating Sir *John*, who lately got a Simple Running only by casting up certain Numbers on a Blank Paper. Printed for *J. Roberts*.

12. Remarks on the History of the Test; in which some Mistakes are corrected, and some Prejudices obviated. Pr. for *J. Roberts* price 6 d.

13. A Discourse made to a Person in a Country Parish Church, *Oct.* 1. 1732, doing Penance for the Sin of Fornication. Most humbly recommended to the Consideration of the Committee of the Hon. House of Commons, of the Enquiry into the Abuses of the Ecclesiastical Courts. Pr. for *J. Clark*.

14. The Sugar Colony Act, the Brandy and Geneva Act, Amendment of Vexatious Arrests, and Law English. At the King's Printing House.

15. Change Alley excised: Or, The Bears and the Bulls in an Uproar. Printed for *W. Webb*, price 6 d.

16 Reasons for Explaining and Amending the Act for the better Regulation of Juries, in a Letter to the Rt. Hon. *Arthur Onslow*, Esq; Speaker of the House of Commons, concerning a Clause in that Act, which gives a Power to the Master of the Crown Office, to strike Juries for the Trial of the Subjects of *England*, at the Motions of the King's Attorney, in Actions, Informations, or Indictments, for Misdemeanours brought at the King's Suit. Printed for *T. Cooper*, pr. 4 d.

17. St. *James's* Park, a Comedy, as it is acted every fine Day, between the Hours of 12 and 2, during the Season, with a Prologue and Epilogue, and a Song on Mopsa's bare Bottom. Printed for *John Cooper*, pr. 1 s. 6 d.

18. The Classic Quarrel. A Tale. By the Author of a proper Reply to a Lady. Printed for *Thomas Osborne*.

19. Poems on several Occasions. By *J. Banch*. Printed for *J. Roberts*, pr. 2s.

20. An Essay on Man. Epistle III. Printed for *J. Wilford*, pr. 1s.

21. The Minor; or, Letters Satyrical, Panegyrical, Serious and Humorous on the Present Times. Shewing the great Improvement, of Wit, Poetry, Learning, &c. Printed for *J. Roberts*, pr. 1s.

22. The Lure of Venus: or, a Harlot's Progress. An Heroi-comical Poem. In 6x Canto's. By Mr *Joseph Gay*. Sold by *J. Wilford*, pr. 1 s. 6 d.

23. The Man of Honour. A Poem. Printed for *J. Wilford*, pr. 6 d.

24. The British Hero: A Poem sacred to the immortal Memory of *John* late Duke of *Marlborough*, Prince of the Roman Empire, &c. Printed for *F. Clay*, pr. 1s. 6 d.

25. The Female Politician: or, the Statesman unmask'd. A Novel. Printed for *J. Huddlestone*.

26. All Vows kept. A Comedy. Printed for *A. Bettesworth*.

27. The Mock Marriage: of, a Lady and no Lady. A new Ballad. Inscribed to a certain Peer, and an Hibernian young Lady, who were lately wedded in Jest, but bedded in Earnest. Sold by the Booksellers.

28. The Neuter; or, a Modest Satire on the Poets of the Age. By a Lady. Dedicated to the Rt Hon. *Mary Wortley Montagu*. Printed for *T. Osborne*, pr. 6d.

29. Human Ordure, Botannically consider'd, the first Essay of the Kind ever published in the World. Printed for *F. Cogan*, pr. 6d.

30. Chelterne and Vale Farming, explain'd, according to the latest Improvements. Containing the Nature and Improvement of the four Clays, four Loams, four Gravels, four Chalks, and three Sands. By *W. Ellis*. Sold by *J. Parker*.

31. A

31. A Treatise on Carpentry. In which are contained the most concise and authentick Rules of that Art, in a more exact Method than has yet been made publick. By *Francis Price*: Sold by *W. Meadows*, pr. 5s.

32. A Dissertation on the Power of the Church in a middle way, betwixt those who screw it up to the highest with the Papists and Scotish Presbyterians on the one Hand, and the Eastians and Followers of *Hugo Grotius*, who on the other Hand do wholly reject the intrinsick Spiritual Authority wherewith Jesus Christ hath vested the Rulers of his Church. Auct. P. M. Eccl. Scot. Direptæ & Gementis Presb. Printed for *G. Strahan*.

33. A second Letter to the Rt Revd *Richard* Ld Bp of *Litchfield* and *Coventry*, in Defence of a former Letter to his Lordship; wherein that injur'd Society call'd Quakers, are impartially defended against his Lordship's Vindicator. Sold by *J. Roberts*, pr. 1s. 6d.

34. A Dialogue on Devotion, after the manner of *Xenophon*: In which the Reasonableness, Pleasure, and Advantages of it are consider'd. To which is prefix'd, a Conversation of *Socrates*, on the Being and Providence of God. Translated from the *Greek*. Printed for *Richard Hett*, pr. 1s.

35. The whole of the Proceedings in the Arches Court of *Canterbury*, in a Cause between the Hon. Mrs *Katherine Weld*, Daughter to the Ld *Aston*, and *Edward We'd*, Esq; her Husband. Sold by the Booksellers.

36. The Art of Nursing: or, the Method of bringing up young Children according to the Rules of Physick; for the Preservation of Health and prolonging Life. Printed for *J. Brotherton*, pr. 2s.

37. Philosophical Conversations on the Existence of Bodies, a Vacuum, the Properties of Motion, &c. Translated into English by *Thomas Dale*. Printed for *W. Innys*.

38. Philosophical Translations No. 425 for the Months of *September* and *October*, 1732. Printed for *W. Innys*.

39. Glory and Gravity Essential and Mechanical. Wherein the Objects and Articles of the Christian Faith are exhibited; as they were originally and successively reveal'd, Hieroglyphically, by Representations in Figures. And as words were adapted to, and Letters reveal'd to record the Ideas of those Figures; the Words are so explain'd, and each by the other illustrated. With some account of the Origin and present State of the Doctrine of the Adversary. By *J. H.* Sold by *Tho. Green*.

40. Remarks on some Observations address'd to the Author of the Letter to Dr *Waterland*, by the Author of the Letter. Printed for *J. Peele*, pr. 6d.

41. A Letter to *Wm Pulteney*, Esq; concerning the Administration of Affairs in *Great Britain* for several Years past, and the present State thereof. With Observations on our Polemical Writers. Pr. for *J. Roberts*, pr. 6d.

42. The Proceedings of the Old Baily for the City of *London* and County of *Middlesex*, on the 10th, 11th, and 12th, of this instant *May*. Printed for *J. Wilford*, pr. 6d.

43. A Journal of his Polish Majesty's Camp at *Redewitz* in *Saxony*. Pr. for *L. Gilliver*.

44. The Report of the Committee appointed to inspect and examine the several Accounts of the S. Sea Company, laid before the General Court of the said Company the 16th of *June* last; and added to the Committee for Law Suits, for the Prosecution of Capt. *Wm Cleland*, and Mr *James Dolliffe*. Printed for *W. Wilkins*, pr. 1s. 6d.

45. Ingratitude: To Mr *Pope*. Occasion'd by a Manuscript handed about, under the Title of Mr *Taste*'s Tour from the Land of Politeness to that of Dulness and Scandal, &c. Printed for *J. Dormer*, pr. 1s.

46. The Secret History of *M—d—lla*. Containing a faithful Account of her Birth and Parentage; her Amour with a Gentleman in *Ireland*, &c. Together with the whole Series of her Amours with Count *Ons—lavio*, and their Extraordinary Nuptials, &c.

47. The Life of that Excellent Tragedian *Barton Booth*, Esq; late one of the Managers of the Theatre Royal in *Drury Lane*. Printed for *J. Cooper*.

48. An Apology for Sir *Rob. Sutton*. Printed for *T. Warner*, pr. 1s.

49. A Letter from a Member of Parliament for a Borough in the *West*, to a Noble Lord in his Neighbourhood there, concerning the Excise Bill, and the Manner and Causes of losing it. Printed for *J. Roberts*, pr. 6d.

50. Appendix ad Marmora Oxon: Sive Græcæ trium Marmorum recens repertorum Inscriptiones, &c. By the Editor of the Oxford Marbles. Sold by *W. Bowyer*, pr. 1s. 6d.

51. A Treatise address'd to his Grace the Metropolitan of all *England*, to make the Corporation of Clergymen's Sons more useful to its Members, and as the Numbers of those Objects of Compassion, from the Certificates given into the Corporation, have been computed to amount to at least 3000. By *Robert Tate*, a Clergyman's Son. Sold by Mr *Strahan*.

52. A Demonstration of the Will of God by the Light of Nature, in eight Discourses. Printed for *F. Cogan*.

53. A Scheme of the true Appearances of the Satellites of Jupiter at *London* 1733; the first commencing at 10 o'Clock in the Evening of *May* 22, and ending the 8th of *October*. By *Ch. Leadbetter*. Sold by *J. Wilcox*.

Books publish'd in Numbers, viz.

Sir *Walter Raleigh*'s History of the World. *Rapin*'s Hist. of *Eng*. Sir *Roger Lestrange*'s *Josephus*. Acta Regia. *Bayle*'s Hist. and Crit. Dict. No. 10. pr. 1s. Universal Hist. No. 7. pr. 3s. 6d. Modern History. *Oxell*'s Roman History. History of the Popes. Sir *Richard Baker*'s Chronicle. *Moll*'s Description of *England*. *Campbell*'s History of the Bible. *Stackhouse*'s History of the Bible. Ordinary of *Newgate*'s Account. Historical Register. Political State. Monthly Mercury. *Keating*'s History of *Ireland*. No. 30, being the last.

A D-

The Gentleman's Magazine:

Lond. Gazette
Lond. Jour.
Fog's Journ.
Applebee's ::
Read's : : : :
Craftſman ::
D. Spectator
Grubſtreet J
Wkly Regiſter
Free - Briton
Hyp - Doctor
Daily Court.
Daily - Poſt
Dai. Journal
Da. Poſt-boy
D. Advertiſer
Evening Poſt
St James's Eb.
Whitehall Eb.
London Eb'ſa
Flying - Poſt
Weekly Miſ-
cellany.

St JOHN's GATE.

York 2 News
Dublin 6 :::
Edinburgh 2
Briſtol : : : :
Norwich 2 ::
Exeter 2 ::
Worceſter ::
Northampton
Glouceſter : :
Stamford : :
Nottingham
Bury Journ.
Cheſter ditto
Derby ditto
Ipſwich dit.
Reading dit.
Leeds Merc.
Newcaſtle C.
Canterbury
Mancheſter ::
Boſton ::: ¶
Jamaica. &c.
Barbados : .

Or, MONTHLY INTELLIGENCER,

For JUNE, 1733.

CONTAINING,

(more in Quantity, and greater Variety, than any Book of the kind and Price.)

I. A View of the WEEKLY ESSAYS, *viz.* Ld *Shaftſbury* on Raillery; The Lay-Preacher confuted; of Madneſs and Folly; Management of the Stage and Mutiny of the Players; on Impudence; Freethinking and Toleration; Reflections on Life and old Age; on Converſation and Reading; News-Papers banter'd; a Miſer making his Will; Meditations on Life and Death, Solitude, &c.
II. POLITICAL POINTS, *viz.* Mr *Walſingham's* Defiance; of national Virtue; Vogue; Irony, and publick Rejoicings, Rights, Natural and Civil; Coalition of Jacobites, Tories and Whigs; Power productive of Enemies; Exciſe Scheme palliated; the Miniſtry unjuſtly defamed; Proceedings and Debates in Parliament; National Debt; Lords Proteſts; *Walſingham* and *D'anvers* ſcolding; chief Clauſes of the Exciſe Bill; curious Preamble for a Peerage Patent; Garbling the Army, dangerous to the Conſtitution; Miniſterial Writers ſelf-confuted; wicked Policy of dividing the *Nation*, &c.
III. POETRY: A Song by Dr *Swift*; Prize Verſes on her Majeſty's Grotto; Characters from the State Dunces; Epigrams, &c. ſeveral New. *See the Contents.*
IV. OCCURRENCES FOREIGN and DOMESTIC; King's Speech; Acts paſs'd; Cauſes tried; Deaths; Births; Promotions; Removals; Prizes of Goods, &c.
V. REGISTER of Books.
VI. Table of CONTENTS.

By SYLVANUS URBAN, Gent.

LONDON: Printed for the AUTHOR, and ſold at St *John's Gate*: By F. *Jefferies*, in *Ludgate-ſtreet*; at the Pamphlet Shops; and by moſt Bookſellers.

CONTENTS.

THE

Gentleman's Magazine:

JUNE, 1733.

A View of the Weekly DISPUTES *and* ESSAYS *in this Month.*

Grubſtreet Journal, May 31. Nº 179.

Mr BAVIUS,

IS the Province of a *true Critic to* point out the Beauties, as well as the Defeĉts, of a Work of Learning. Whoever, is not thus impartial in his Deciſions, deſerves the utmoſt Contempt and Indignation. How far Mr A. B. the Writer of two Letters in your *Journals*, (ſee p. 171, 252.) againſt the *General Dictionary*, will ſtand this Teſt, we ſhall now examine.

He writes with Paſſion ; cenſures generally, tho' his Exceptions are particular, whilſt he palliates the flagrant and numerous Errors of a pretended *Tranſlation of* Mr BAYLE'*s Dictionary.*

In his firſt Letter he charges us with not having Recourſe to Originals ; this we refuted, of which he took no Notice in his Reply. He affirms that the Article of ROBERT ABBOT, an *Engliſh Biſhop*, is tranſlated from *Moreri*, and the *Supplement*, yet that Article is Mr BAYLE's. He aſſerts, *there is ſcarce an Article of our Additions, but what contains ſome groſs Errors, and that our Work is more faulty than the pretended Tranſlation in all Reſpects.* This we defy him to prove. He charges us with a *hardy Falſehood for denying that ſeveral of our Articles are meer Tranſcripts from Moreri, and other Dictionaries.* What we inſiſted upon, and ſtill do, is, that even theſe Articles are not tranſcribed from thoſe Dictionaries, ſince we have illuſtrated them with Notes,

which are generally the moſt conſiderable Part of thoſe Articles. Neither is it true, that we have ſuppreſs'd the Names of the Authors from whom we have borrow'd part of the Text of a few of our additional Articles in our 1ſt Number. Nothing can be be more untrue than his Aſſertion that our Additions will ſwell to ten Vols.

However, Mr A. B. makes no Objection to our Tranſlation of Mr *Bayle's* Articles ; whereas we can point out above 2000 Errors and Omiſſions in the 10 Numbers in their pretended Tranſlation. In ſhort, his Objections relate almoſt wholly to ſome of the Oriental Articles in our 1ſt Number, chiefly with Regard to the Orthography of the Names. We grant there are ſome Inaccuracies of that Kind in it, which we have ſince remedied by conforming to the *Engliſh* manner of writing them in our 2d Number. Mr *Bayle* has committed ſome Errors of as great Importance, in his oriental Articles ; and *D'Herbelot* himſelf is by this Critic acknowledg'd to be very inaccurate : Yet who would explode thoſe two valuable Writers on that Account only ?

In our 2d Number we have corrected and ſupplied Mr *Bayle's* Articles of *Abulfaragus* and *Abulfeda*, ſhewn ſeveral Errors of *D'Herbelot*, given a conſiderable Extract from an Arabic MS. and drawn all our Articles in Mr *Bayle's* Manner.

Our third Number will exhibit many Corrections of *Moreri*, *Collier*, &c. And the Article of Mr *Addiſon* will ſhew our Accuracy in doing Juſtice to the eminent Writers of our Nation. And we can aſſure the Publick, we are poſſeſs'd of an Arabic Manuſcript, containing above 600 Lives of illuſtrious Perſons, never yet

yet printed, nor tranflated into any European Language.

Whatever Mr A. B. may think of our
Defign, yet Foreigners have thought our
Additions worthy of being tranflated; as
appears by an Advertifement in the *Amfterdam Gazette.* The Authors.

Free Briton, May 31. No. 184.
The *Craftfman* having, fays *Walfingham,*
mifreprefented the Meffage fent me by
the E. of Ch—— it is verbatim as follows; to the Author of the *Free Briton.*

London May the 2d, 1733.
Sir,

THE E. of C——, *whofe Secretary I
have the Honour to be, has order'd
me to wait upon you with his Service,
and acquaint you, that he has read your*
Free Briton *of Thurfday laft, in which
you exprefs your felf to lye under fome
Difficulties, and feem to have a Check
upon you on Account of* Scandalum Magnatum, *which prevents your writing fo
freely as you are able. His Lordfhip defires you would be under no Apprehenfions in the World; and affures you, upon
his Honour, that he will not profecute you,
nor caufe any Infult to be given you, on
that Account; and defires that for the
future you would fpeak out upon his Subject, and fay to the World whatever your
own Imagination may furnifh you with.*
Yours * * *

Upon the Receipt of this Letter, fays
Walfingham, I addreffed one to his Lordfhip to the Effect following.

London May the 10th, 1733.
My Lord,
I was greatly furprized at a Letter left
me, by your Lordfhip's Command. I am
as truly *forry* for the Occafion, as I am
aftonifh'd at the Contents, it is my Mif-
fortune to be mifunderftood by your Lordfhip. For, Could I have imagin'd, there
were any *juft* and *honourable* Motives requiring me to fpeak with Freedom of fo
great a Perfon, it would not have been
the *Fear of Penalties, much lefs of Infults,*
which could have deterred me. (See p.
255) I muft ever acknowledge this Meffage to be the ftrongeft Evidence I have
met with, of a brave and great Mind,
that fcorns to fhelter its Actions from
Enquiry, by the inglorious Advantage of
Powers or Privileges. I fay not this
from Fear or Flattery: But as I never
entertained an unworthy Thought of your
Lordfhip, this Inftance of your generous

Nature compels me ever to think and
fpeak of you with the higheft Veneration.

If I mention'd the Power of the Peerage, as a Bar to any free Reflections on
the Character of Peers, I mention'd it only to fhew, that it was *unfair,* and *highly difingenuous,* to bring *great Names* into publick Debate, fince fuch apparent
Difadvantages attended fuch Difquifitions.

This I faid to reprove the Writer
whom I animadverted on, whom I believed no Friend of your Lordfhips, but
a Perfon doing you *Wrong* in an avowed
Attempt to render a Sacred Name *unpopular on your Account,* which I could
never imagine pleafing or grateful to your
Lordfhip. And however you are pleafed
to indulge me this Liberty with refpect
to *yourfelf,* I am not fure you can excufe
it in me as it relates to his *Majefty,* fhould
I explain any affair which wholly relates
to the *King* and *your Lordfhip.*

This Liberty I then difclaimed, as
having nothing to explain to your Lordfhips Difadvantage, and if I had, ftill I
difclaimed it, as not prefuming even *in
Defence of the Throne, to explain for the
Throne;* which fhews the little Candour
and Decency of that Perfon who caft *invidious Colours* on the *King's Procedure*
which the moft faithful Subject was not
at Liberty to explain. Subfequent to and
much inferior to thefe Confiderations, was
the Point I mention'd relating to the
Rights and *Power of the Peerage.* But
tho' I am fafe on that Account, yet your
Lordfhip ought not to be difrepectfully
treated, nor his *Majefty's* Wifdom or Juftice *commented on for removing even the
higheft Officer* of his own *Houfhold.*
I am &c.

Whilft I was waiting the Event of my
Anfwer the Writer of the *Craftfman* ac-
quaints the World, *that I have received
Affurances* &c. (fee p. 247 B)

What a Reprefentation is this of the
Noble Earl's Meffage! And yet *unfair*
and *difhoneft* as it appears, let all Men
judge, whether the *Craftfman* could
have *played with the Words* of that Meffage, or *mifreprefented their Meaning* in
this manner, unlefs he had been *allowed
a Sight of that Meffage.* If then he was
allowed a Sight of it, he muft have
grofsly abufed the *Noble Lord's Indulgence;*
and if his Lordfhip did *knowingly fuffer*
that Writer to fuggeft, that his Lordfhip,
in his great Mercy, had fpared me from
a *Cudgel,* I infift upon it, his Lordfhip
muft, by that very Proceeding have *departed*

parted from his Honour, *and violated his own* Promise, *that he would not cause any* Insult *to be given me on his Account ;* since this *of itself* is the *greatest Insult* any of his Friends were *capable of giving me.*

It is therefore apparent, that the *Crafts-man* hath by this *Misrepresentation of* the *Message,* treated the *Noble Earl* in a very unbecoming and unpardonable manner ; for it is not consistent with his Lordship's Honour or Justice, that he should cause or approve of such an Insult to be given ; and His good Sense must convince him that it's ridiculous, to tell any Man he will not cause any Man to be cudgelled when that Person never *craved his Mercy,* or *dreaded his Power.*

However, if my vindicating his Majesty from the insolent Charge of the *Craftsman,* of *having dealt* unjustly *by his Lordship,* be resented by *the Earl ;* and *he thinks it Mercy* to me, that he neither *complains of me to the Lords,* not *sues me in Westminster-Hall,* nor causes me to be *cudgelled,* I humbly implore him *to take back his* gracious Assurances, I *release* him from all his *Promises,* and willingly leave him in full Possession of *his Complaints, his Actions,* and *even his* Cudgels.

As I know the Regard which I owe to *Honour and Titles,* yet I shall think it my indispensible Duty to vindicate the Name and Honour of the *King,* whoever thinks fit to insult him on any Pretence: And if any *Noble Lord* of *smaller Personages,* shall think such a Vindication an Affront to *themselves,* I hope they will not scruple to avenge it on Me, by *such Weapons* as they shall think *most suitable* to their own *Quality,* and never offer me *any Exemption* of this Kind.

The *Craftsman,* June 2. Nu. 361.

Of National Virtue.

THE vigorous Opposition to a late *execrable Scheme* gives a just Idea of a brave People struggling for their Liberties ; and notwithstanding the Noise, which the *Projector* and his *Advocates* have made about some little Insults from the Populace, they ought rather to admire their Forbearance and Moderation.

That our *Passions* have the principal Share in all our Pursuits, and are the Mediums, by which (under the Guidance of *Reason*) the Author of Nature intended human Affairs should be conducted, are undoubted Truths ; and the highest Virtue we seem capable of, is That of direct-

ting our *Passions,* to those Objects that tend chiefly to communicate Happiness to others, in Conjunction with ourselves.

From the Prevalence, or Depression of *this Principle,* a Standard may be erected by which the real Intentions of Governors, and consequently the Expediency of farther Submission, or just Resentment, may be discover'd. The flourishing Condition of the *Roman* Commonwealth was always in exact Proportion, as these *noble Sentiments* were countenanced by Those who held the Reins of Government.

Now let us enquire what Footing *this Principle of Virtue* has got in this Island ; what Patronage it receives from Men in Power ; and by what Means it hath been several Years in Decline. This we shall best discover by mixing with various Company, and attending to the Manner, in which most popular Points are treated.

The *Tools of Men in Power* are generally shunn'd by Men of Integrity, and are compell'd to converse with one another ; yet it frequently happens that a virtuous modest Man falls into their Company. If such a Person presumes to differ in Sentiments from any of these worthy Gentlemen, and expresses his Dislike of the publick Measures, the first Thing they salute him with, in Imitation of their *Master,* is a broad Grin, succeeded by an indecent Laugh. This occasions Warmth and Resentment ; upon which his Pulse is felt, and Remedies prescribed, to cure *Insanity* and *common Honesty;* which *these Gentlemen* look upon as inseparable.

If he proceeds to delineate the visible Steps of *Men in Power* to enslave the People ; and proposes gentle Means to stop the Progress of these Enormities, he is treated as an *Incendiary,* an *Encourager* of *Riots* and unfit for *civil Society.*

Among People, whose *good Breeding* and *Politeness* are their chief Aim, Matters of Importance are differently treated. To These, all Subjects are of equal Consequence, with this Exception, that the most trifling have their greatest Attention.

If *Politicks* are introduced, it is by way of Diversion. How deeply so ever the *Liberties of the Subject* are concerned in the Question, the only Point regarded is, the Dexterity, by which the *opposite Party* was outwitted in carrying it for or against the People. This Disregard in matters of the greatest Concern, hath as real, tho' not so wicked a Cause as the Vigilance of those, who subsist upon the Reward they receive from their *infamous*

Em-

Employment of putting all Virtue out of Countenance. It is not difficult to point out the Spring of this fashionable Indifference, when we see all Opposition to *Men in Power*, how just or reasonable so ever, attributed either to implacable Hatred and Revenge, or a sordid Expectation of playing the same Part, and the Possibility of disinterested Views in publick Affairs absolutely deny'd, tho' accompanied with a Conduct strictly conformable to such Views; when we see so little Regard paid to Merit, or common Decency, that the Price of every Man's Conscience, who opposes, is as confidently talk'd of as the *infamous Schemes* he opposes; when *Corruption* is contended for as the only Principle of Action; that Mankind was born for *Servility*; and that the *Liberties of the People* are absolutely incompatible with our Constitution.

I would not be thought, says *D'anvers*, to cast an Odium upon *good Breeding* and *Politeness*. I know many, whose *good Breeding* has not yet brought them into the Vogue of Indifference. My Design is to shew what an unhappy Influence these fashionable Doctrines seem to have had among some Men; and how easy it is to be lull'd asleep with *State Opiates*.

I have, indeed, the pleasure to observe many brave Men, in whom a Zeal for their Country is too deeply ingrafted, to be affected by any such impertinent Attempts, and the People in general demonstrate they have not yet taken Leave of their *Liberties*, in an Instance, that will for ever endear their Memories to Posterity; and if this great Event is in any Measure owing to the Zeal of some *particular Persons*, it evinces the Necessity of keeping a watchful and jealous Eye over our *Liberties*, as the only infallible Security of them.

But tho' I have the highest Opinion of my Countrymen in general, I cannot suppose them Proof against all Temptation, especially that of *Vogue*; and when I see with what infamous Views the Custom of laughing at all Pretences to *national Virtue* is introduced among us, supported with a regular Body of Men, set a part to decry *this Principle*, I tremble at the Consequence; and if in expressing my Abhorrence of *these Practices*, I betray too much Warmth, I have the Satisfaction to know that it proceeds from my Zeal for the Preservation of *those Liberties*, which from a fashionable Disregard of them may be lost for ever.

Fog's Journal, June 2. No: 239.
Of Irony, and Publick Rejoicings.

A Man no sooner does something which recommends him to the good Will of his Countrymen, but the Ministerial Hacks behave as if they thought it their Duty to abuse him for it. The Grand Jury of the City of *London* having thought fit to thank the Lord Mayor for the Distinction he made between Riots and Rejoycings, Mr *Walsingham* look'd on it as a sufficient Ground for abusing both one and the other. (See p. 241, 266.) But he has laid aside his usual manner of declaiming, and attempts to be arch; a Charge never laid upon him by his most severe Criticks, yet there is nothing in this way of Writing unworthy of Mr *W*. Men as great as himself have placed their chief Glory in being counted arch Wags. He therefore only imitates his Betters, and when he attempts that Figure call'd *Irony* he seems to know himself, and the Strength of his own Genius; for a most excellent Critick has given us the following Definition of it;

Irony is not a Work for groveling Pens; but extremely difficult even to the best. It is one of the most beautiful Strokes of Rhetorick; and when a Bungler attempts it, his misshapen Work with this awkward Polishing becomes entirely deformed, as the false Beauty of Paint upon a Lady's Face is less desirable than no Beauty at all, and the Pertness of a shallow Fop more disagreable than his Silence.

But Mr *W*.'s Irony has a Delicacy in it peculiar to the Man. He begins his Paper with a mock Encomium on my Lord Mayor; next takes notice of what he read in certain Papers of Intelligence of my Lord Mayor instructing the Grand Jury at the *Old Baily*. Now, if a Man was inclined to cavil, he might object to this in point of Veracity; for, what is here hinted at did not pass at the *Old Baily*. But this would be mere cavilling; for Truth is not Mr *W*.'s Vocation, and as old *Falstaff* said, *Every Man ought to live by his Vocation.*

Where he speaks of the unfeigned Rejoyings made for the Suppression of the Excise Bill, (see p. 242 E, F) how logically he draws his Consequences! *No great Good hath been done; therefore there have been no Rejoycings for great Good, but rather,* as wise Men tell us, for *great Mischief*. Indeed the *Irony* seems to be dropt here, but is taken up again the next Sentence,

tence, for there it is a *great Good* again: But he might have learnt this dodging way of reasoning from some Legerdemain Patron, who might be a great Virtuoso at Cups and Balls — *Here you have it, and there you have it not.*——— We may guess at the *wife* Men that tell us the dropping of the Excise is not a great Good, but a great Mischief. We may confine them to Two, near a-kin to each other, whose Wisdom is just fit to tally with his Wit and Veracity.

The Ld *Shaftsbury* observes, that, "*To describe true Raillery perhaps would be as great a Task, and as little to the Purpose, as to define good Breeding—None can understand the Speculation except those that have the Practice, yet every one thinks himself well-bred, and the most formal Pedant fancies he can rally with a good Grace and Humour. There can't be a more preposterous Sight than an Executioner and a Merry Andrew acting their Part upon the same Stage; yet this is the real Picture of certain Writers—they are no more Masters of Gravity than they are of good Humour—the first runs into harsh Severity, and the last into an aukward Buffoonery; like Children, who at the same Instant are both peevish and wanton. I don't wonder, therefore, to hear those publick Lamentations, that whilst the Writings of their Adversaries are so current, their Answers to them can hardly make their way into the World. Dulness is a Millstone able to sink any Book—the Temper of a Pedagogue suits not with the Age, and the World, however it may be taught, will not be tutor'd. If one who is neither a Philosopher nor a Gentleman, encroaches upon the Character of both, and appears alike capable of the Reason of the first, as the Raillery of the other, what wonder if the Product of such a jumbled Brain be ridiculous to the World.*

Next *Fog* gives us the Sentiments of *Cives Liberatus,* a Correspondent, upon publick Rejoycings.

He says, That Joy ought to be in Proportion to the Danger escaped; that the Citizens of *London* lately apprehended their Liberties and Trade in some Danger, and likewise their Birthright of being Master of their own Houses and Goods; they look'd on the late Scheme as design'd to alter the antient Constitution of this Kingdom; that as it was lawful to oppose it, it could not be unlawful to rejoyce at its Miscarriage; that in all Ages it has been usual for the People to shew

their Dislike to Projectors of Things like this; that the People in general did, upon the first News of the Danger they had escaped, make themselves a little merry with the Projector, and what they did, shew'd rather a Contempt than Cruelty and ill-Nature. But the strongest Reason for Rejoycing he quotes from a Book, once in great Esteem among Christians, but which Mr *W.* may look upon as a Satire upon the Conduct of some very good Friends of his. This Book is the Holy Bible, and the Passage quoted is from *Deut.* XXVIII. 47, 48, 49, 50, 51.

London Journal. June 2. No. 727.
Of *Rights,* Natural *and* Civil.

THE Enemies of the Government being deeply engaged to *unite all the Parties* in the Kingdom against the *Ministry,* and to that End play off the *Rights* of the *People* against the *Rights* of the Government, by asserting, That the *Represented* ought to have an *Influence, Power,* and *Authority* over their *Representatives,* it is become necessary to explain the Origin, Nature and Extent of *Rights,* Natural and Civil.

All *Right* ariseth from the *Nature* of Man, and his *natural Relation* to other Men; which is *Equality;* for all Men are, by Nature, *equal.* Which is true, not withstanding the *natural* Difference of *Understanding, Strength,* or even *Goodness;* for these give no Right over another's Person or Property. Hence it follows, that no Man, or Set of Men, have any *Right* over others without their own *Consent.*

As this is true of *Natural,* so is it of *Civil* or *Political Rights,* which arise only from *Consent. Birth* gives no *Right;* nor can there be any *hereditary Right,* but what is settled by *Law* and *Compact. Conquest* gives no more *Right* to govern, than the *superior Power* of a *Highwayman* gives a *Right* to an honest Man's Money or Life. The *Consent* of the People constitutes a Government for their common Protection against the Invasions of wicked Men upon their *Natural Rights;* for *Natural and Political Rights* are the same, and differ only, as one is the *Security* of the other.

Thus 'tis evident, That *all Right* comes from the *People;* that there is no *just Power* but what is derived from *them,* and ought in *every Instance* to be exercised for their *Good;* yet it does not follow, that when a Government is settled even by *Consent,* that the *People* have a *Right,*

Right (while the Conſtitution is preſerved)
to exerciſe * *Authority* and *Power* over
the *Government* by Threatning, Ordering,
&c. according to the *Craftſman,* who ſays,
The late Treatment *of the Houſe of Commons was ſuch an* Influence, *as the* Nature of our Conſtitution *requires.* (See p.
239.) But I ſay, ſays *Oſborne,* the *Nature*
of our Conſtitution is entirely *ſubverted*
by it; that the Houſe of Commons ſhould
be under no *Influence,* but that of their
own *Reaſon;* and that they are *better
Judges* (having no private Intereſt in the
Caſe) concerning Points of *domeſtick Government, Trade,* and *Taxes,* than (what
D'anvers calls) the *whole Body of the People,* that is, the Dealers in *Tobacco* and
Wine, and their Dependants, of *London,
Briſtol,* and *Liverpool;* to whom are joined *Jacobites, Tories* and Male-content
Whigs; therefore their *Petitions* ſhould
have run in this Strain;
  "We are the *whole Body of the People of
England, trading in* Tobacco *and* Wine,
by Virtue of the high Authority *and* ori-
ginal Power *preſiding in our collective Body, do peremptorily command you our* Repreſentatives, Attornies, Servants, *and*
Slaves, *to do as we bid you; and We ſtrictly
charge you, (as you value our* high Diſpleaſure) *not to make any Laws to reſtrain us from defrauding the Government
and prejudicing the fair Trader".* This is
the Senſe of the late Petitions as *juſtify'd*
by *D'anvers's* Doctrine of the *Original
Power of the People* over their *Repreſentatives,* which with his Scheme of making a *Coalition of Parties,* are of the *high*

* *This Authority, when not forcibly wreſted
from them by an unjuſt Invaſion, reſides in the
collective Body of the People: And tho' for the
more convenient Exertion thereof, it be intruſted
with, and delegated to a certain Number, choſen
from Time to Time by the People out of their own
Body; yet it is always to'be ſuppoſed exerted according to the general Senſe of the whole collective Body, who accordingly acquieſce in the Determinations of this Select Number, as ſpeaking
and declaring the Senſe of Things. But,*
  *Whenever the whole collective Body is appre-
henſive, that their Repreſentatives, from a miſapprehenſion of any Caſe, are going to exert their
Authority, contrary to the general Senſe of that
Body, whoſe Authority they are entruſted with
and in whoſe ſtead they act; it is neceſſary ſuch
general Senſe of the collective Body ſhould be
ſignified to them: which is ſo far from being any
Abridgment of their Authority, that a Determination according to ſuch general Senſe is a further Sanction as it is an Approbation of their
Proceeding.* —— Letter ſign'd *Anglus* in the
Grubſtreet Journal, *June* 7.

eſt Conſequence to all *true* Lovers of Liberty and the *Conſtitution,* that is, to the
Whigs. This new *Democracy,* or *Government of the People,* may, if encouraged,
come to Tumults, Inſurrections, and open
Rebellion.
  The *Coalition* endeavour'd at, is a *Coalition* of *Jacobites, Tories,* and *Whigs.*
To do what? Why, to turn out the Miniſtry. What are the *Whigs* to get by
that? Do they expect that Sir *Wm* ——
(a *Jacobite,* at the Head of *Jacobites* and
Tories, and who hath many Years labour'd
to get Start of the *other Gentleman,* who
is, or *hath* been at the Head of the Male-
content *Whigs,*) is taking all this *Pains* to
obtain *another,* or a better *Whig Miniſtry?*
Will the *Whigs unite* with Men who are
declared Enemies to the *Government,* the
Revolution, the *Royal Family,* the *Conſtitution,* and to the Intereſts of *Liberty?*
Will not the Conſequence be, *Breaking
the Whig Intereſt.* Yes, ſay ſome *angry,
deluded, diſappointed Whigs,* — "Better
broke than kept; for are not the *Whigs*
turn'd *Tories?* And the *Jacobites* and *Tories* turn'd *Whigs,* and almoſt the only
Whigs we have left? Is there not a Book
lately publiſhed, call'd, *The Loyal and Revolutional Tory,* which aſſerts ſuch to be,
The Capital Pillars of the Conſtitution, and
ought to be received into Places of *Truſt,
Confidence,* and *Profit,* by the preſent
Royal Family?" ——
  'Tis true, theſe Things are ſaid; but
but what have they done to prove their
Converſion? Have they *really* renounced
thoſe Doctrines that are *inconſiſtent* with
the *Revolution* and *Act of Settlement?* Did
they not *join* in with, and *wiſh* well to
the Rebellion in the late King's Time?
Have they not ever ſince the *Revolution*
conſtantly voted for *ſuch Men only,* who
have done all they could to *oppoſe* the Government? And ſhall we now receive
them into our Boſoms? No, let the *Whigs*
heartily unite againſt the next Election:
For if a Parliament be obtained by the
Union of *ſome of the Whigs,* with the
Jacobite and *Tory* Intereſt, it cannot be a
Whig Parliament: And the terrible Conſequences of a *Tory* Parliament, let every
Man conſider, who is concerned for the
true Intereſts of England.

Weekly Miſcellany. *June* 2. No. 25.
Obſervations on the Layman's Sermon,
continu'd *from* p. 182.

THE Inſolence with which this Writer has treated the whole Order of
the

the Clergy is beyond Example, and his Artifice *too thin* to conceal his Design against *Christianity it self.* He tells us he is a *Christian.* So did *VVoolston*; so does *T—d—l:* But if we measure this Writer's Regard to the *Gospel*, by that he shews to the *Institutions* of *Christ*, and to those *Appointments, Human* or *Divine*, which have been made for their *Defence* and *Security*, it is impossible to mistake his *Views.* For, is there *one* of them that has escaped his *Censure* or *Ridicule?* I shall confine the Subject of this Paper to the *Appointment* of the *Lord's-Day*, which I will at present suppose *merely* Human, What Provisions *our Laws* have made to secure the Reverence due to this Day is well known. But how does this Writer treat these Laws? Why, he *starts* at the very *naming* them, and cries out *Popery* and *Persecution.* The Alarm, I suppose he took from our *Miscellany* of *Feb.* 24. (See p. 88.)

He is *surpriz'd to hear of compulsory Laws still in Force to oblige People to go to Church, and asks whether such a Law (if there be one) can be reconcil'd to the Principles and Laws of Toleration?* Who ever said there are any *such* Laws now in Force? What *was* said, is, that *there are Laws yet in Force which oblige all Persons, not otherwise reasonably hinder'd, to resort every Lord's-Day to* some *Place of religious VVorship*; which I hope is not inconsistent with *our* Laws of *Toleration*, which extend to *Protestant Dissenters of all Denominations*, who are permitted to go where they please, provided it be *some where.* Therefore the Execution of *Penal Laws* upon *Absenters*, is so far from *interfering* with, that it pursues the very *Sense* and *Spirit* of the *Act* of *Toleration.*

But by the *Principles of Toleration* this Writer means, I suppose, his *own* Principles; he thinks it an *Infringement* on the *Liberty* of the *Subject*, that any one should be obliged to resort to *any* Place of publick Worship. For he says, No *Penal Laws* were, or ever could be prompted by a *Christian Spirit.* Is it *just* and *Christian to force any Man to hear what or whom he does not like?* Would a High-Churchman care to be forced to hear a *Presbyterian Preacher, suppose in a Country where there were no other, as in Geneva?* What has he to do at *Geneva?* The Question concerns *our own Country*, where he may find *some* Christian Communion, with which he may join con-

sistently with his *Conscience.* Where then is the *Persecution?*

The only Supposition pertinent to the Argument, is, of a Man who has no *Choice* left, either to go to *no* Place of Worship, or some where to hear *what he does not like.*] This can be only the Case of *Roman Catholicks* and *Unbelievers*, for whom our Law allows no *Toleration. Papist* then, or *Infidel* we must suppose him. If a *Papist*, he must naturally say, that *Popery* has as *good a Right* to *Toleration* as any other Religion. If *Unbeliever*, let him declare himself, and *every* Congregation where the Name of *Christ* is named, will naturally cast him out. But so long as such Gentlemen keep on the *Mask* of *Christianity*, how is it *possible* that Laws *should* distinguish them? Or how can they complain, if, when they come to *Church* to *qualify* themselves for *Places*, the Government *presumes* 'em to be what they *pretend*; and as *Christians*, obliges them to go to *Church*, or *elsewhere*, on other Occasions?

I believe this is the first Attempt ever known to *justify* an *absolute Contempt of all* religious Worship. With what Views? Why, That *Faith*, and *Orthodoxy*, and *Creeds*, and the *Church* (the Source of *infinite Mischiefs*) may be demolish'd, and *full Scope* left to *Free-thinking*, which *never* did any Harm! If he means that all the bad Things done in the World are not the Effect of *Free-thinking*, or that Men may be very wicked under the *Mask* of Religion, he tells a *stale Truth*, which serves no Purpose. But if any one should say, that in Proportion, as Men get the Habit of *thinking* themselves out of *Christianity*, they do not commonly grow worse than *Heathens*, it would be a Proof of nothing but great *Partiality* and little *Observation* or *Knowledge* of the World. If one is to judge of *this Lay Divine's* Opinion by the Sentiments of some of his *Brother Free-thinkers, Self-Murder, Lying, Lewdness, &c.* may pass as *no Vices*, or perhaps as some of the *Refinements* of the Age.

I don't suggest that all who shew Irreverence to the *Lord's-Day*, have Designs against *Christianity*; yet, if ever the *Sunday* should come to be treated, *generally*, without Distinction, we should be in a fair Way of losing that little Religion which is left among us. It is hardly possible that Laws should provide against all Abuses; but *Religion* and *good Sense* would easily supply the Defects of Law;

Laws; and I should be glad to see so much of *both*, that Persons of *Distinction* would make a Scruple of taking those Liberties on the *Lord's-Day*, which if an *Alehouse-keeper*, or a common *Carrier* should be guilty of, the Law would subject him to a *Penalty*.

RICHARD HOOKER.

Universal Spectator, *June* 2. Nº 243.
Madness and Folly, ally'd.

THIS Paper seems to be a Comment on a *Courant* upon the same Subject, published in *Nov.* 1731. (See p. 490. Vol. I.)

After giving some different Accounts or Causes of the Inequality of human Understanding, the Author proceeds to shew in some Instances the Effects produced by those Causes; all which being specifically treated of in the said *Courant*, we need not repeat.

Grubstreet Journal, June 7. No. 180.
Of the Management of the Stage.
Mr BAVIUS,

'TIS notorious, that many and grievous Complaints have been made of the Insolence of Stage Tyrants, towards Writers, who were so unhappy as to stand in need of their Favour; and 'twas the best Behaviour that could be expected from those who consider'd every Poet as one that asked an Alms, and themselves as the Lords Commissioners for dispensing the Charity of the Muses. But however great and notorious the Imposition was, there seem'd no Prospect of Redress so long as the Management was in such Hands, as there appeared little Probability of a Change.

At length one of the Managers, for a large Consideration, sold half his Share to a Gentleman. The Death of another made way for a 2d Alteration. But tho' both the new admitted Sharers (who had half the Patent) diligently apply'd themselve to regulate the Conduct of the Theatre, and resolv'd to treat Authors like Gentlemen, to act all Plays that had any Prospect of Success, and even to refuse the rest with Humanity and good Manners; yet one little Creature, only the Deputy and Representative of his Father, was turbulent enough to balk their Measures, and counterbalance all the Civility and Decency in the other Scale. In short, he has behav'd, during the whole Season, the first of his Reign, and the last, as if there was neither Author or Actor in the World, of any Consequence,

but his Father and himself. To remedy this, the Gentleman who bought into the Patent first, purchased his Father's Share, and set him down in the same obscure Place from whence he rose.

Now 'twas presum'd, every Obstacle to Peace and good Order was remov'd; not considering, that he who was so imperious in Power, would be seditious out of it; or that a Man who receiv'd so much Money for his Share of the Patent would immediately try to render it of no Value by putting himself at the Head of this Faction. But they were deceiv'd. While the Patent was in the Hands of the Players, none of them thought it unreasonable, if they were duly paid, that the Managers should divide the rest at the End of the Season. But as soon as it came into the Hands of Gentlemen, who had bought it at a prodigious Expence, PISTOL himself was the first to perswade them they were free before, but now Slaves; that they ought to mutiny, set the Patent at Defiance, and ruin those who had made the Purchase. The Consequence was a Combination among the Players to set up for themselves. Accordingly the *Antient* display'd his Standard, beat up for Volunteers, and offer'd to inlist all who came, almost on their own Terms. They are to have as much Salary as they have now; to share the Profits at the End of the Season; and to be all Managers as well as himself; to sit equal Judges on Authors, and divide the Tyranny of using them as they please; like the drunken Sailors in the Play, they are all to be *Viceroys*; PISTOL desir'd only to be *Viceroy over them.*

Yours MUSÆUS.

Mr BAVIUS,

THE late Dispute between the Patentees and Players of *Drury Lane* Playhouse induc'd me to consider the Conduct of both Parties.

The *English* Theatre hath risen for a Series of many Years under the Patronage of Princes, and appeared in greater Lustre than any other: And, what is more extraordinary, the most eminent Writers in the Dramatick way, have been Players; of which *Shakespeare* and *Otway* are immortal Instances.

I believe no Nation can boast so many excellent Writers for the Stage, nor so many inimitable Performers. But as Wit, good Sense, and Politeness were absolutely necessary to support the Character and Dignity of the Scene, the Management of the Theatre was always entrusted to

Per-

Perſons qualify'd to judge of all Performances to be introduced in that Place.

Sir *Richard Steel* for ſome Years had
it under his Direction, and as eminent as
he was, ye he thought it not unworthy
of him, to join with thoſe profeſſed
Players, Mr *Booth,* Mr *Wilks,* and Mr
Cibber; becauſe it might be ſuppoſed
that their own Intereſt as well as the
Honour of the Stage, would make them
induſtrious to ſupport it in full Credit.

Hence we may perceive, that the
Management of the Theatre has been
always committed to Perſons who had
given ſome publick Proof of their Capacity to judge, what would be moſt
inſtructive or agreeable to the Taſte
of an *Engliſh* Audience. Whether the
preſent Patentees are qualify'd for ſuch a
Task let the Publick judge. As they have
bought the Management of that Houſe,
they will naturally promote their own
Advantage, and not the Reputation, Intereſt,. or Encouragement of their own
Company, or the Authors. Whereas, if
the Profits ariſing from the Stage, were
to become Rewards to thoſe who were
the Ornament, and Support of it; if by
any extraordinary Merit, Perſons might
riſe, thro' ſeveral Gradations, to ſhare in
the higheſt Advantage; this only would
make the Theatre appear in its true
Glory, and our Age might produce a new
Oldfield, and a new *Booth,* to delight
and entertain the wiſe and generous.

Tours PHILO DRAMATICUS.

Free Briton, June 7. No. 185.

FOR the Subject of this Day's Entertainment Mr *Walſingham* gives the
Publick, Part of a Pamphlet lately printed
entitled *A Letter from a Member of Parliament for a Borough in the Weſt, to a
Noble Lord in the Neighbourhood there,
concerning the* Exciſe-Bill *and the Manner and Cauſes of loſing it.*

The Obſervations which ſeem moſt to
claim our Regard in this Extract are,
That ſome Gentlemen, who laid the Exciſe on *Soap, Candles,* and *Leather,* were
the moſt Zealous Oppoſers of the *Exciſe*
upon *Wine* and *Tobacco*; yet do not call
that (as they do this) *a Badge of Slavery.*
Again, there has not been *one new Tax*
laid in his preſent Majeſty's Reign. As
to the preſent intended *Alteration in the
Revenue,* it was evidently calculated for
the Benefit of the Publick in general, to
eaſe one great Part of the People, without laying any new Impoſition on the

reſt; and his Majeſty's Part of the Duty
was ſtill to continue under the *Cuſtoms.*

What therefore could the Court or the
Miniſtry gain by this Project, beſides the
Reputation of curing execrable Frauds,
and of relieving the Land? What Influence or Service could accrue to the Miniſtry from two or three additional Exciſemen in a County, eſpecially when
almoſt half the number of conſiderable
Officers of the Crown were to have been
dropped, namely, the Receivers General
of the *Land Tax.* NOTE, that by the
preſent Laws of Cuſtoms and Exciſe,
the *Commiſſioners of both,* or the *Commiſſioners of the Treaſury* for the Time
being, have Power to create *as many
Officers as they pleaſe.*

Univerſal Spectator. June 7. No. 144.
On Impudence.

THE Contraſte, or Oppoſite to every
Virtue, generally bears ſo much
falſe Similitude of the Virtue, that it's
not eaſy to give our Commendation where
it is alone due. *Avarice* deceives under
the Appearance of *Frugality,* and *Profuſion* under the Form of *Generoſity.* Particularly, Impudence is ſo nearly ally'd
to a noble Generouſneſs of Spirit, and a
laudable Aſſurance, that it's no Wonder
the Commonalty generally miſtake it for
thoſe Qualifications. The ſurpriſing Impudence of a Criminal, who contemns approaching Death, is not by the Vulgar
diſtinguiſh'd from the heroic Conſtancy
of a ſuffering Great Man. Hence Impudence is ſo ſucceſsful, as it has a glaring
appearance of Virtue. At the Bar it recommends itſelf under the Diſguiſe of
Eloquence, can never be convinc'd, but
with an obſtreperous Torrent of Tautology and unmeaning Phraſes, will bear
down Learning, Law, and Senſe. In the
Profeſſion of Phyſick, the Judgment and
Experience of an *Eſculapius* will be
equall'd by the arrogant Impudence of a
Quack. Even in the Pulpit, a ſtrong
Pair of Lungs have been eſteem'd Rhetorick; and incoherent common-Place Oratory, for ſound Senſe and cloſe Reaſoning.

Impudence will make a Man engage
in an Undertaking unequal to his Abilities, furniſh him with Spirits, inſpire him
with Confidence, and give an Aſſurance
of ſucceeding. How many, with this
Quality alone, have thought themſelves
the propereſt Perſons for the higheſt Offices in Church and State; with this a
Man may be a Scholar without Learning,

a Courtier without common Civility, a Statesman without Prudence, a Prelate without Religion, and a Judge without Honesty.

Impudence is the most successful Procurer of Power, Honour, and Riches. An impudent Man will never think he has less Abilities for being reproach'd with Ignorance; stedfast in his own good Opinion he persists in doing Wrong; nor is concern'd that his Fame is prostituted if he obtains his Point; he is loud against those Vices he is himself guilty of, that credulous People may think him innocent.

Impudence is of general Use as it covers all Imperfections, and takes away even Suspicion itself; but the Attainment of it is not easy. To form such a Man there must be a good natural Genius as well as acquir'd Perfections, a proper Turn of Mind, and Cast of Features. The largest Share of Mankind are forced to use their utmost Industry before they can entirely shake off the remaining Symptoms of Modesty.

Impudence would hardly bear such a Sway was it not owing to a Kind of Wrong Modesty; nor would so many lay a false Claim to Merit, if it was not neglected by those who had a real Title to it. *Eugenio* is a Man of polite Learning, has a delicate way of Thinking, and a particular Happiness in expressing his Thoughts; yet, thro' a false Modesty, thinks he can never speak well enough, so passes for a hum-drum Fellow; while *Loquax,* who is ever prattling is thought a Man of Spirit and Vivacity. Nor is this false Modesty confin'd to the Men only. *Dulcinea* has an exquisite Voice, yet can never be persuaded to sing to any but her Mamma or her Aunt. *Cleora* is the tenderest, fondest Wife imaginable; yet, when among those who have a gayer Notion than to love a Husband, is asham'd of being thought so. *Lactilla* is an excellent Manager in her Family; yet on her Visiting Day nothing can flutter her more than to praise her *Oconomy. Chloe* attends publick Prayers, and has private Devotions; yet if *Coquetilla* accuses her of Formality, she'll deny her Piety, and be asham'd of her *Religion.*

Concludes with a Letter from *Penelope Proper,* giving an Account of an old Fashion lately reviv'd among the Ladies of wearing Sticks; and hints that the Ladies at *New Tunbridge Wells* and the *Park* would not toss their Sticks about with that threatning military Air they usually do, if they would but learn to *limp.*

London Journal. *June* 9. No. 728.

A Minister of State must naturally make Enemies, in Proportion to the **A** *Extent* and *Continuance* of his Power. He never *obliges* but he *disobliges.* It's no Wonder then, to see Ministers *abused,* and Men in Power *defamed*; the *best Servants* supplanted, or undone, by the *Worst,* when we consider the *Number* and *Malice* of their Enemies, and the *vile* **B** *Methods* by which the *Bad* undermine the *Good.*

Here Mr *Osborne* gives a high Encomium on the great Services and excellent Qualities of a Minister whom he had full in View, and whom he has seen treated with much Malignity and Virulence, **C** as tho' he had been guilty of all the Crimes which Human Nature, in its most Degenerate State, was ever capable of; and for which 'tis impossible to assign one Reason, but the *Extent* and *Continuance* of his Power. We have seen this Spirit exerted to the full in the *Craftsman,* more especially in the last (see p. 281) which seems **D** wrote by *new* and more capable Hand, than any that hath yet appeared in that Paper

He sets out with two Principles that are very true, " That one Passions have the *principal Share* in all our Pursuits; and that our *highest Virtue,* is, the *directing our Passions* to those Objects which **E** have the greatest *Tendency* to communicate Happiness". By this *infallible Standard,* I am willing the Minister's Actions should be tried. But what Use does he make of it; or how, from *this Principle, prove* his Point against the Minister? Why, **F** thus; by boldly asserting, without *Argument,* or *Facts* to support it, That all the *Attempts* and *visible Steps* of the Gentlemen in Power are to *enslave the People,* &c. (See p. 111.) Fine *Reasoning,* truely! 'Tis hard to determine which is the greatest *Folly* or *Wickedness* of this **G** way of *Talking,* under a Pretence of *Reasoning*; laying down a Principle to try a Man, which is the *Tendency of his Actions*; and them *asserting,* that all his Actions are *bad,* without attempting the *least Proof* of an *Assertion,* on which *alone depends the whole Farce of all his Argument.* He hath mentioned, indeed, an **H** *infamous Project,* and an *execrable Scheme*; but the *Infamy* and *Execrableness* lay only in *those Actions* which rendered it *unpopular.*

This Gentleman, it seems, is angry, that

that he and his *Club of Patriots* are treated so freely, and their Opposition said to spring from Hatred, *disappointed Ambition*, &c. But why should they not be so treated, if by their Actions, they shew those were their *Motives* ? That they do so, is plain : Don't they give every Vote with the Court, when *in Power* ; and against it, when *out of Power* ? Have we not seen the same Man approving Actions as *right* ; yet, the next Day, upon taking a *Staff* out of his Hand, damning all those Actions as *wrong* ; and upon putting that *magick Wand* into his Hand again, all Things have been *right* again ? Do these Men expect to be call'd *Patriots* ?

The asserting, as they do in all their Weekly Libels, That the *Principle* of publick Virtue, or Love of Country, is lost, may be a Truth which they *feel* ; but I believe, *national Virtue*, and a true Sense of *Liberty*, is higher now than ever it was in *England*, and will, no Doubt, be exerted when proper Occasions are given. But what would they have Men do ? Knock out their Brains against Stone Walls ? — Or fight for Fighting-Sake ? 'Tis a *national Vice* to oppose Power, when 'tis not employ'd against the Good of the Publick. Opposition is then only Patriotism, when it exerts itself against *publick Wickedness* in High Places. But these Patriots *see Evils* which *No-body* else sees ; ——— and won't see *the Good*, that *every Body* else sees. But thro' Hatred to *one Man*, from Motives all *Personal*, and not one *National*, will not acknowledge they either *see* or *feel*. They make the People *disaffected*, and then gravely say, *the Ministry* do it. They have been *the Causes* of every Evil, which this Nation hath felt ever since the present Royal Family came to the Crown ; yet lay all the Evils they have *created* at the Door of the Ministry.

PROCEEDINGS *of the House of Commons in the Sessions* 1732.

ON Feb. 10, Mr *Turbill* presented to the House, Copies of all Proceedings, Papers, &c. in his Custody, relating to the Sale of the Estate of the late E. of *Derwentwater*. But being asked, if he had the original Minute Book, in which were the Proceedings relating to the said Sale ; he acquainted the House that he had brought it along with him, and that it was in the Lobby ; whereupon he was ordered to bring it in, which he accordingly did ; and then it was ordered, that he should lay before the House all the original Minute Books, which were in his Cus-

tody, relating to the Sale of the forfeited Estates, which he accordingly did the next Day.

On the 17th, Mr *Turbill* was ordered to attend the House next Morning, with the Books of Contracts of the forfeited Estates ; the Books, in which the Conveyances of the forfeited Estates were entered ; the two original printed Particulars of the Estate of the said late Earl of *Derwentwater*, set up to Sale the 11th of *July*, 1723 ; and the original printed Particular of Mr *Charles Ratcliff*'s Annuity of 200*l*.

On the 22d, all the said Books, Instruments and Papers, were referred to the Consideration of a Committee ; and the Lord *Gage* was directed by them to move the House, that such Persons as the Committee should think proper to be examined upon the Subject Matter of their Enquiry, should be examined in the most solemn Manner ; which was ordered accordingly.

On the 30th of *March* the Report of the Committee was read and taken into Consideration ; whereupon it was resolv'd, *nem. con.*

1. That on the 30th of *July* 1723, *Matthew White*, Esq; was declared the Purchaser of an Annuity of 200*l*. during the Life of *Charles Ratcliffe*, issuing out of the Estate of *James* late Earl of *Derwentwater*, with all the Arrears thereof, from his Attainder, for 1201*l.* 1*s.* without due Notice of Time or Place for exposing such Annuity to Sale ; and without the Presence of a sufficient Number of Commissioners and Trustees, as requir'd by the Act appointing such Commissioners.

2. That *William Smith*, Esq; did on the 11th of *July* 1723, for the Consideration of 1060*l.* contract for an Estate of *James* late Earl of *Derwentwater*, mention'd in a Particular, publish'd by the said Commissioners and Trustees, to be of the annual Value of 5013*l.* subject to the Annuities and Incumbrances in the said Particular mention'd ; and to be sold during the Continuance of an Estate in Tail-Male, vested in *Charles Ratcliffe* in Remainder, Expectant on the Death of *John Ratcliffe* under Age, and without Issue-Male, which Contract was on the 30th of the same *July*, vacated and torn out of the Book of Contracts, and a new one then procur'd and dated as on the 11th, by which the said *William Smith* not only obtain'd the said Remainder in Tail, but also the Reversion in Fee of the said Estate for the same Sum of 1060*l.* altho' a sufficient Number of Commissioners and Trustees, as requir'd by the Act, was not present either on the 11th or 30th of the said *July*, nor had any Notice been given of exposing to Sale the Reversion in Fee of the said Estate.

3. That *Matthew White* and *William Smith*, Esq; were present on the 30th of the said *July*, when *Samuel Allen*, Secretary to the said Commissioners and Trustees, sign'd the Names of Sir *Thomas Hales*, and Sir *John Eyles*, to the respective pretended Contracts made with the said *White* and *Smith* on the said 30th of

July

July, when no Commissioner and Truftee, but *Dennis Bond*, Efq; and *John Birch*, Serjeant at Law, were prefent.

4. That the contracting for the Sale of the aforefaid Eftates, by a lefs Number of the Commiffioners and Truftees than four; and the not giving 15 Days Notice at leaft, of fuch Sales, was a manifeft Violation of the Act of Parliament for the Sale of the faid Eftates, highly injurious to the Publick, and a notorious Breach of the Truft repofed in fuch Commiffioners and Truftees.

Upon thefe Refolutions it was order'd that Leave fhould be given to bring in a Bill to declare and make void the feveral Contracts, and the Conveyances made in Purfuance thereof, of the Eftate of the late E. of *Derwentwater*, to *William Smith*, Efq; and alfo of the Annuity of 200 l. during the Life of *Charles Ratcliffe*, with the Arrears thereof to *Matthew White*, Efq;

After which the Houfe refolved, *nem. con.* That any Commiffioner and Truftee, appointed by the faid Act, directing or permitting the Secretary of the Commiffion, or any other Perfon, to fign the Name of any abfent Commiffioner and Truftee, in order to make up the Number of Commiffioners and Truftees, requir'd by the faid Act, to any Sale, Contract, &c. was guilty of a Violation of the faid Act, and of a high Breach of Truft.

After which a Motion was made, that it fhould be refolved, That any abfent Commiffioner and Truftee appointed by the faid Act of Parliament, impowering any Perfon to fign his Name for him, in order to make up the Number of Commiffioners and Truftees requir'd, to Matters of Form in Proceedings under the faid Act, was guilty of a great Irregularity in the Execution of the faid Act. But a great many Members of the Houfe being of Opinion, That it was as great a Violation of the Act, and as high a Breach of Truft for any abfent Commiffioner to impower any Perfon to fign his Name for him, in order to make up the Number of Commiffioners requir'd, as it was for any Commiffioner prefent to direct or permit any other Perfon to fign the Name of any abfent Commiffioner, in order to make up the Number of Commiffioners prefent; therefore they were for amending this Motion. However, after a long Debate, the Queftion was put and carried for the Motion, 175 againft 140; whereupon a 2d Refolution was made in the Terms moved for.

Then they read that Part of the Report which related to *Dennis Bond*, Efq; a Member of the Houfe, who, after being heard in his Place, withdrew, and it was *Refolved*, That he was guilty of a notorious Breach of Truft repofed in him, as a Commiffioner and Truftee for Sale of the forfeited Eftates for the Ufe of the Publick; then it was *Refolved, nem. con.* That he fhould for his faid Offence be expell'd the Houfe.

That Part of the Report which related to *John Birch*, Serjeant at Law, a Member of the Houfe, was next read, who being heard in his Place, withdrew, and it was *Refolved*, That he was guilty of a notorious Breach of Truft repofed in him, as a Commiffioner, &c. after which it was *Refolved*, That he fhould for his faid Offence be expell'd the Houfe.

And laftly, That Part of the Report which related to Sir *John Eyles*, Bart, a Member of the Houfe, was read, and he being heard in his Place, withdrew; and the Recital of a Conveyance entred in a Book belonging to the faid Commiffioners and Truftees was read; then it was *Refolved*, That he was guilty of a great Irregularity as a Commiffioner and Truftee for Sale of the forfeited Eftates, by empowering Mr *Samuel Allen*, Secretary of the Commiffioners and Truftees, to fign his the faid Sir *John Eyles*'s Name, when abfent, in order to make up the Number of Commiffioners and Truftees required by Act of Parliament, to Matters of Form in Proceedings under the faid Act. And it was ordered, that he fhould for his faid Offence, be reprimanded in his Place by Mr Speaker. (See p. 716. Vol. II.)

And the Lord Vifc. *Gage*, having been Chairman of the Committee for enquiring into this Affair, and having been at a great deal of Pains in detecting this fraudulent Sale, thro' the whole Courfe of which, his Lordfhip had behaved with that Honour, Integrity and Impartiality, which becometh a true Patriot; it was refolved, *nem. con.* That the Thanks of the Houfe fhould be given to his Lordfhip, for the great Service he had done the Publick, in detecting the faid fraudulent Sale; (fee the Speaker's Thanks, and his Lordfhip's Anfwer p. 817. Vol. II.

On the 6th of *April*, the Lord *Gage* prefented to the Houfe a Bill for making void the feveral Contracts for Sale of the faid Eftate to *William Smith*, Efq; and alfo the Annuity of 200 l. and the Arrears thereof during the Life of *Charles Ratcliff*, to *Matthew White*, Efq; and the feveral Conveyances made in Purfuance of the fame; which was then read the firft Time, and ordered to be read a fecond Time on *April* 19.

On the 17th of *April*, were prefented to the Houfe and read, a Petition of *William Smith*, Efq; and alfo of *Matthew White*, Efq; praying to be heard by their Council againft the faid Bill; which Petitions were ordered to lie upon the Table 'till the fecond Reading of the Bill, and that the Petitioners, if they thought fit, might be then feverally heard by their Council againft the faid Bill. And it was ordered that Mr Attorney General fhould appoint Council to produce and manage the Evidence at the Bar of the Houfe, at the fame Time for the Bill. And the former Order for the fecond Reading of the faid Bill being difcharged, the Bill was ordered to be read a fecond Time on the 21ft of *April*

Here-

Hereupon a Motion was made, and the Question proposed, that the Witnesses, to be examined for and against the said Bill at the second Reading thereof, should be examined in the most solemn Manner. This occasioned a long Debate in the House. Those that were against the Question represented, That the House of Lords had always insisted, That the House of Commons being no Court of Judicature, had not therefore a Power to examine Witnesses in the most solemn Manner, at the Bar of their House; That tho' this Power had always been claimed and insisted on by the Commons, yet it was a Point still in Dispute between the two Houses; and that if the House of Commons should on that Occasion make use of this disputed Power, it would occasion a Breach between the two Houses, which might not only prove to be the Loss of the Bill then under Consideration, but might be of much worse Consequence, by putting a full Stop to all the publick Business of the Nation; for, whenever any Breach happened between the two Houses, it proved always a very difficult and tedious Matter to re-establish Harmony between them; so that their coming to any such Resolution might entirely unhinge the Government, and bring the whole Kingdom into Confusion.

On the other hand, those that were for the Question, declared the great Concern they had for the Bill then under Consideration, and for the publick Quiet; but said, that the true Method of preserving the publick Quiet, was, for each House to take Care to preserve those Powers and Privileges which properly belong to them; for if that House should begin to yield up, or not exert a Power they had always enjoyed, only because the other House pretended to dispute their having any such Power, they might come at last to be stript of all the Powers and Privileges they ever had or could pretend to: That it was well known, that the House of Commons had always been used to empower their Committees to examine Witnesses before them in the most solemn Manner; and it was very odd to pretend, that the House itself could not make use of that Power which they every Day delegated to their Committees. It might perhaps be pretended, that as the House of Commons was no Court of Judicature, they could not therefore administer an Oath; but that was not now to be brought into Dispute, because they might get such of the Members as were Justices of the Peace to administer the Oath to the Witnesses, upon which Oath the Witnesses might afterwards be examined at the Bar of the House; or they might get one of the Judges to come to the Speaker's Chambers to administer the Oath to the Witnesses, which was no new or unheard of Method; for that there was upon their Journals a Precedent for the same, and that Method was then allowed of by the other House without any Dispute: That even as to their

having a Power of administring an Oath in the most solemn Manner, they hoped that there was no Member of that House who doubted thereof; and if it were to be brought into Dispute, it could be proved to the Conviction of all impartial Men: The House of Commons was certainly a Court of Record; their being such, had been admitted of by the other House in the most solemn Manner, as appeared by the 6th of *Henry* VIII. *Chap.* 16. By which it was enacted, 'That no Knight, &c. should depart from the Parliament without Licence of the Speaker and Commons, to be entered on *Record*, in the Clerk of the Parliament's Book, in pain to lose their Wages. This was an indisputable Testimony of their being a Court of Record, and as such they certainly had a Power to administer an Oath in any Affair, which came properly before them; but as there was a Precedent for examining Witnesses in the most solemn Manner at the Bar of their House, without bringing their Power of administring Oaths into Dispute, if the present Question was agreed to, they might follow that Precedent, and thereby prevent all Occasion of Dispute between the two Houses.

These were the chief Arguments made use of in this important Question; but most of the Members were so desirous to have the Bill passed into a Law, that they were not for any thing that might occasion the least Demurr in the passing thereof, if it could be possibly avoided; and were of Opinion that it was not at all absolutely necessary to examine the Witnesses at the Bar of the House, in the most solemn Manner, upon Occasion of the Bill. After all, the previous Question being put, *viz.* That that Question be now put, it passed in the Negative.

On the 21st, the Council for and against the Bill were called in; the Bill was read a second Time, and the Council were heard in Part: On the 24th the Council were heard to an End, and the Bill was without any Opposition committed to a Committee of the whole House. After which it passed both Houses.

ON *April* 18. Mr *Wyndham* reported from the Committee, to whom the several Lists of the Officers, and their Deputies belonging to the several Courts in *Westminster-Hall*, and elsewhere, with the Lists, Accounts and Tables of Fees claimed by them, which were presented to the House in the then last and present Session of Parliament; and also the Lists, Accounts, and Tables of Fees of the Officers and Servants belonging to the Judges of the several Courts in *Westminster-Hall*, and the Circuits, the Associates, and Clerks of Assize, presented to the House in the Session of Parliament preceding the last, were referred; the Matter as it appeared to them, with the Resolutions of the Committee thereupon, which were agreed to by the House *nem. con.* and were as follows, *viz.*

1. That

1. That the long Difuse of publick Enquiries into the Behaviour of the Officers, Clerks and Ministers of the Courts of Justice, has been an Occasion of the Increase of unneceffary Officers, and given Encouragement to the taking of illegal Fees.

2. That the Interest, which a great Number of Officers have in the Proceedings of the Court of Chancery, has been a principal Cause of extending Bills, Answers, Pleadings, Examinations and other Forms, and Copies of them, to an unneceffary Length; to the great Delay of Justice, and the Oppreffion of the Subject.

3. That a Table of all the Officers, Ministers, and Clerks, and of their Fees, in the Court of Chancery, should be fixed and eftablished by Authority, which Table should be registered in a Book in the said Court, to be at all Times infpected gratis; and a Copy of it figned and attefted by the Judges of the Court should be returned to each House of Parliament, to remain among the Records,

Whereupon it was refolved, nem. con. That an humble Addrefs be prefented to his Majefty, that he would be pleafed to give Directions, that a Survey should be taken of the Officers, Clerks and Ministers of the Courts of Juftice in this Kingdom; and that an Enquiry should be made into their Fees, in order to reform the fame, and to eftablish what are reafonable and legal, in fuch Manner, as his Majefty in his great Wifdom shall think fit.

ON April 26. A Petition of the Court of Directors of the S. S. Company, pursuant to a Refolution of the Proprietors of the faid Company, then lately agreed upon in a General Court, (fee p. 721, Vol. II.) was offered to be prefented to the House, for Leave and Authority to convert 3 4th Parts of their prefent Capital Stock into Annuities, attended with an Interest of 4 per Cent. per Ann. payable out of the Company's Funds; and that the remaining 4th Part, after the Annihilation of a Million thereof, by Application of that Sum intended that Year to be paid the faid Company, to that Part of the Capital, and paying off a Million of their Bonds therewith, may not be fubject to a further Redemption, without the Company's Confent, till the S. S. Annuities are reduced by Redemption to be equal to fuch Capital; and therefore praying that the faid Company might be enabled to put the Premifses in Execution, in fuch Manner as to the House should feem meet, And the Order of the House of the 4th Jan. laft, against receiving Petitions for private Bills after the 2d of March laft being read, it was thought proper to delay the Affair till next Seffion of Parliament; when a Bill pafs'd to this Purpofe, and received the Royal Affent June 13, 1733.

ON the 9th of May, Mr Wluningion made a Report from the Committee appointed to view the Cottonian Library, &c. Whereupon the following Addrefs was prefented to his Majefty,

Moft Gracious Sovereign,

WE your Majefty's moft dutiful and loyal Subjects, the Commons of Great Britain in Parliament affembled, having taken into our Confideration the great Collection of valuable Records belonging to this Nation, and the Neceffity of tranfmitting them down fafe and entire for the Ufe of our Pofterity, humbly beg Leave to reprefent to your Majefty the State, in which we found them, together with the Inconveniencies, that may arife from their remaining in their prefent Situation.

A great Part of the Cottonian Library, with the Variety of curious and ufeful Matters therein contained, has (notwithstanding the late Fire at Afhburnham Houfe) by the great Diligence and Attention of the Truftees been preferved: And that the Publick may not for Want of due Care be gradually deprived of fo noble and generous a Benefaction, we beg Leave to recommend it in the moft particular Manner to your Majefty's Confideration, Favour and Protection.

The feveral Places affigned for the Prefervation of all thefe ineftimable Monuments of Antiquity, are too narrow, and confined for their Reception, and fome of them in a very ruinous and dangerous Condition.

We find alfo fome Records not depofited in their proper Office, but either remaining in private Hands, or in Places not affigned for publick Records, nor under the Care of any ftated Officer.

Nor has the antient Method of removing Records from the Offices, wherein they are originally formed, to fuch Places, as are appointed to preferve them, been duly obferved, chiefly for Want of Room in the prefent Qffices allotted for their Reception.

Great Inconveniencies have arifen to the Inquirers after this ufeful Knowledge, not only from thefe Difficulties, but alfo from the undiftinguished and confufed Manner, in which fome of the Records of this Kingdom have been kept, there being no general Kalenders or Indexes to the Whole, which with proper Encouragement may be compleated by Perfons of Skill and Ability, and would probably bring to Light many material Remains of Antiquity, which from the Difficulty of Accefs have long lain unknown and neglected.

The prefent fhort Enquiry, imperfect as it is, has produced an Inftance of this, by difcovering amongft the antient Records, That Directions for Works of this Kind have been formerly given by your Majefty's Royal Predeceffors,

Your faithful Commons beg Leave further humbly to reprefent to your Majefty, That as the Publick Intereft is concerned in providing more fecure and decent Repofitories for the Records of this Kingdom, fo the Publick Faith is engaged for the better Reception and Prefervation of the Cottonian Library, fo generoufly given for the Publick Service,

And

And as there is at present little or no Allowance to the Keeper of the said Library, we humbly submit it to your Majesty's Consideration, whether, if a proper and reasonable Stipend were granted to him, it would not engage him to perform his Duty with great Care and Diligence.

Having thus with the greatest Humility laid the State of the Records of this Kingdom, and of the *Cottonian* Library before your Majesty, we assure ourselves, that it will be intirely agreeable to your Majesty's gracious Disposition, to transmit to future Ages these Monuments and Remains of Antiquity, so necessary and useful to the Knowledge and Preservation of our excellent Constitution, which we hope will go down to Posterity, together with the Family under which it now flourishes, as inseparable Blessings to this Nation.

Your faithful Commons do therefore most humbly beseech your Majesty, that you will be graciously pleased to give such Directions (as your Majesty in your great Wisdom shall think fit) for the better Reception, and more convenient Use of the Publick Records of this Kingdom, and of the *Cottonian* Library.

And we beg Leave further to assure your Majesty, that whatever extraordinary Expences are incurred by the Directions your Majesty, in your great Wisdom, shall think fit to give on this Occasion, shall with great Chearfulness and Unanimity be provided for, and made good by your faithful Commons.

The Lords Protests, 1733.

Die Mercurii 30 Maii 1733.

Moved to resolve, *That it is the Opinion of this House, that the Produce of the Sinking Fund should be applied, for the future, towards redeeming such Taxes as are most grievous to the Subject, oppressive to the Manufacturer, and detrimental to Trade.*
Which being objected to, After Debate, The Question was put upon the said Motion, And it was resolved in the Negative.

Dissentient.

1. Because we conceive, That it would have been extremely for the Honour of the House, and for the Service of the Publick, to have this Resolution entered in our Books, at a time when we have so far consented, in Compliance with the House of Commons, to a Bill, by which near Half a Million collected from the Sinking Fund, in several Years, is appropriated to the Service of the present Year.

2. Because the Sinking Fund being composed of the Surplusages of Funds originally granted as Security to the Creditors of the Publick; and these Surplusages arising chiefly from a Reduction to 4 *per Cent.* of the Interest granted them, for the most Part at the Rate of 6 *per Cent.* we cannot but think, that

this Saving ought to be applied, according to the most inviolable Rules of Equity, and according to the known Design, and the repeated and solemn Engagements of Parliament, to a gradual Discharge of the Principal to these Creditors of the Publick, who have parted with a Third of their Revenue in this View, and upon this Confidence.

3. Because we apprehend, That the Method of applying large Portions of the Sinking Fund to the Service of the current Year, must, in Effect, perpetuate the Debts and Taxes which lye on the Nation, and is therefore injurious to the Publick. Had this whole Fund been strictly applied from the Beginning to its proper Use, we think it may be demonstrated, not only that much more of the National Debt might have been discharged, but that those Taxes, which are most oppressive to the Poor, and most prejudicial to Trade, might have been already taken off, since upwards of 480,000 *l. per Ann.* belonging, as we conceive, to this Fund, has been applied to other Uses.

4. Because we apprehend, That it cannot be for the Good of the Nation, nor consequently for the Honour of Parliament, to separate those Interests in the particular Appropriations of the Sinking Fund, which were so wisely and so justly united in the original and general Design of it (the Interest of the Nation, and the Interest of the Proprietors of the National Debts) the former was intended to be eased, and for that Purpose the latter were to be cleared as soon as possible. If it be said therefore, that the Creditors of the Publick do not desire to be cleared any faster than they are in the present Method, nor object to the Application of Part of the Sinking Fund to other Uses, we apprehend that no Argument, which ought to avail in a House of Parliament, can result from such an Assertion, because we conceive, that, in every Instance of this Kind, in every Application of the Sinking Fund, or of any Part of it, we are to look on our selves as obliged, not only, to be just to the Creditors of the Publick, but to be careful of the Ease of the People, to keep the particular and general Interests united, as they originally were, and not to sever them. If, in Fact, the Creditors of the Publick do not object to the Application of such large Proportions of the Sinking Fund to other Uses, than to the Payment of the Debts, it may be said, that no Injustice is done them by any such Application, according to the known Maxim, *Volenti non fit Injuria.* Nay, it may be deemed for their private Interest, to have such beneficial Mortgages continued to them as long as possible, and they may desire therefore not to be cleared any faster than they are likely to be in the present Method. But we apprehend, that it cannot

cannot be for the Interest of the Nation to have these Mortgages continued any longer, than is absolutely necessary to discharge the Debt secured by them, and that we, by Consequence, who are Trustees for the People, ought to desire and endeavour, that the Debts may be discharged, and the Load of Mortgages be removed as soon as possible. In this manner, Publick Faith would be strictly kept, Justice would be done, and no Injustice could be done to the Creditors of the Publick. In the other Method, and by diverting such large Portions of the Sinking Fund, if it should be granted, that no present Injustice was done to the Proprietors of these Publick Debts, yet must it be allowed, as we apprehend, that great Injury is done to the Nation, unless it can be proved, that the unnecessary Continuation of Debts and Taxes, is a National Benefit.

5. Because we conceive, That if the whole Produce of the Sinking Fund were not to be applied to the Discharge of the Publick Debts, it would be much more for the Ease of Trade, and Advantage for the Nation, that some of those grievous Taxes, out of which it arises, should cease, than that they should be continued to supply the current Service at 4 *l. per Cent.* which might certainly be supplied by other ways at a cheaper Rate. These Taxes are not only grievous in themselves, but almost intolerable, by the Manner of collecting them under the Laws of *Excise*: Laws so oppressive to the Subject, and so dangerous to Liberty, that every Man who wishes well to his Country must, in our Opinion, desire to see them put to a speedy End. Most of these Taxes were laid during the Necessity of two long and expensive Wars, and were granted only for Terms of Years, that so the Principal and Interest of the Loans made on them might be paid off in a certain limited Time. Thus the Nation consented to pay, in some manner, a double Tax, in order to avoid the long and uncertain Continuance of such grievous and dangerous Impositions; and, according to the first Design, many of them would have been very near the Expiration of their Term at this Hour. The Wisdom of Parliament indeed thought fit afterwards to throw these Taxes, and the Method of discharging these Publick Debts, into another Form, which now subsists. But we cannot conceive, that this was done with a View for continuing our Taxes and our Debts the longer; on the contrary, we are sure it was done in the View of discharging both the sooner; and it is this very View which, we apprehend, must be fatally disappointed, if the present Method of diverting any Part of the Sinking Fund from the Payment of the Publick Debts be suffered to continue.

6. Because we apprehend, That this Method may create the utmost Uneasiness in the Minds of his Majesty's Subjects, and may tend, if not timely prevented by the Wisdom and Authority of this House, to diminish their Affection for his Person and Government. Hitherto, whilst they have labour'd under the Weight of Taxes, and groan'd under the Oppression of *Excise Laws*, the Hope of seeing speedily an End to both, has been their sole Consolation; but nothing can maintain this Hope, except a due Application of the entire Sinking Fund to the Discharge of those Debts, for the Discharge of which these Taxes were intended and given. If some Part of this Fund therefore continue to be mortgaged off, and other Parts to be applied to the current Service, even in the midst of profound Peace, this Hope must sink, and Despair arise in its stead. We insist with greater Concern and Earnestness on this Point, from our Observation of what has lately pass'd on the Occasion of Attempts to extend the cruel and arbitrary Methods practised under the *Laws of Excise*, and naturally and necessarily, as we apprehend, flowing from them. If any new Law of this kind had passed elsewhere, it could not have prevailed in this House; but we think it the more incumbent upon us, after such an Attempt, and such National Resentment expressed against it (both which are of publick Notoriety) to promote, as effectually as we are able, the Quiet and Happiness of his Majesty's Reign, by cutting off any Hopes or Fears which may be still entertain'd, that such a Project will, at some Time or other, succeed. And to this good and laudable End, we conceive, that nothing would have contributed more than such a solemn Declaration of the Sense of this House as is contained in the Question.

Bedford,	Bridgwater,	Litchfield,
Craven,	Ker,	Sunderland,
Gainsborough,	Bruce,	Coventry,
Winchelsea and	Carteret,	Strafford,
Nottingham,	Masham,	Thanet.
Gower,	Bathurst,	
Tweedale,	Shaftsbury,	

Die Sabbati, 2d. Junii 1733.

THE House being moo'd to appoint a Committee to examine into the Proceedings of the South-Sea Company.

After Debate,

The Question was put, *Whether a select Committee shall be appointed of Twelve Lords, to be chosen by Ballot, to examine into the Transactions and Proceedings of the* South-Sea Company, *from Feb.* 2, 172c. *and to lay their Report before this House.*

Resolved in the Negative.

Content 79   Not Content. 7c.

Dissentient

Diffentient.

1. Because the present Debt of the Kingdom being almost wholly incorporated into the Three great Companies, it behoves the Legislature who are the proper Guardians of the Publick Creditors, to take all possible Care that they suffer no Injury in their Estates, by any Frauds committed in the Management of them: For tho' the Directors are chosen by a General Court, they are invested with such extensive Powers, (that they are capable, by abusing their Trust, of doing infinite Mischief to the Proprietors unless their Proceedings are vigilantly watch'd and controul'd by that supreme Authority under whose Sanction they act, and by which only such Practices can be effectually prevented or punished.

2. Because this House having been induced, by the Reasons before-mention'd, to begin an Enquiry into the Management of the *South-Sea* Company, we apprehend, that our Honour is engag'd to answer those Expectations which the Publick had so justly conceiv'd from it; and since the advanced Season of the Year will not permit us to finish this Examination during the present Session of Parliament, we apprehend a Committee was the only proper Way left to unravel such dark and intricate Affairs, which require a very nice Inspection into many voluminous Books; it appearing to us, by what we have seen and heard at our Bar, that the Accounts of this Company have been kept in a very confus'd, irregular, and unwarrantable Manner, in order, as we apprehend, to conceal Frauds, and defeat all Enquiries.

3. Because the great Distresses and Calamities of the Year 1720 having been occasioned by the Directors, at that Time, declaring such extravagant Dividends as the Company was not able to support: The Legislature have, in all their Acts relating to this Corporation, which passed since that Time, taken the utmost Care to prohibit and restrain the Directors from being guilty of the like Practices; yet notwithstanding this, they have been so far from taking Warning from the Examples made of their Predecessors, that it appears by the Accounts laid before this House, that although by the Cash which came into their Hands, and by the Sale of Four Millions of Stock to the Bank, and by the Loans of Stock and otherwise, they were sufficiently enabled to pay off the Debt of five Millions, four hundred thousand Pounds then owing to the Company, as in Justice and Prudence they ought to have done; yet influenc'd, as we have Reason to believe, by the corrupt Views of some few, who may have assumed to themselves the whole Management of the Affairs of this Corporation, they left great Part of their Debt on Bonds at Interest unpaid, and by unwarrantable Dividends out of the Money, in Order to give a fallacious Value to their Stock, Multitudes of His Majesty's Subjects have been defrauded; and they have, without the Knowledge of the Proprietors, not only dissipated above 2,300,000 *l.* received from the Directors Estates, but they have likewise brought a new Debt of 2,000,000 *l.* upon the Company, and thereby diminished the Capital of every Proprietor's Stock, by which means great Injury and Injustice have in numerous Instances been done to Orphans and the Reversionary Heirs of these Estates, to the great Dishonour of the Publick Faith, and Discredit of the Nation.

4. Because, although the Directors applied to Parliament in the Year 1727, for their Authority to dispose of the Produce of the Estates of the forfeiting Directors, pretended to be then remaining in their Hands; yet it appears by the Accounts now before us, that the greatest Part of this Money had been before actually divided out in extraordinary Dividends; and when, in Order to give some Colour to these Proceedings, they obtained an Act of Parliament to dispose of these Estates, they never called a General Court to acquaint them with the State of this Account, or to take their Directions for the Application of any remaining Part of these Estates, notwithstanding they were expressly requir'd so to do by the said Act.

5. Because there is Reason to believe, from a general View of the same Accounts, that there are many Articles hitherto unexamined, under which a Multitude of Frauds may be concealed, such as Buying, Selling, creating or issuing Bonds, imploying irregularly the Cash of the Company which lay in their Hands, whilst the Proprietors were paying Interest for Money borrowed out of the Bank, in transacting Stock Abroad, and selling fictitious Stock at Home, with many other Practices of the like Nature, too long and various to be particularly explained: For these Reasons, we conceive it to be absolutely necessary to have appointed a Committee, as the only Method to distinguish the Few who probably are Criminals, from many Gentlemen, who may at present lie unjustly under the same Imputation; especially at a Time, when a Bill was actually depending for dividing the Capital of this Company, Three Fourths into Annuities, and leaving the remaining Quarter to be a Trading Stock, with a large Debt and Demands upon it unliquidated, and the Value of it consequently unknown; which should it pass into a Law, will, in all probability, promote and encourage the Infamous Practice of Stock-Jobbing, to the Ruin of great Numbers of His Majesty's Subjects.

6. Because the other House have frequently appointed

appointed Commissioners to Inspect the Publick Accounts during the Interval of Parliament, as the only practicable Method of arriving at any Knowledge in such Affairs; a Method indeed too much disus'd of late Years: We therefore apprehend, that no just Objection, either was or could be made to a Committee, which is perfectly agreeable to the Nature of our Constitution, cannot be of any Prejudice to the Company; and being confin'd to a particular Enquiry, can give no Grounds of Apprehension to any, but those who are afraid it may lead to farther Discoveries of iniquitous Contracts and corrupt Bargains, in the Settlement and Transactions of this Company since the Year 1720, which *some Persons* have endeavoured with so much Industry to conceal.

7. Because we think it highly expedient, at this Time, to vindicate the Publick Faith of the Nation, lest Foreigners should be Induced, by the many Instances of *Fraud* and *Corruption* which have been of late discovered in other Corporations, suddenly to draw their Effects out of own Funds; and thereby totally destroy *publick Credit*, and plunge us in inextricable Difficulties.

8. Because the Arts made use of to divert us from our Duty, and defeat this Enquiry, give us Reasons to prosecute it with fresh Vigour; for Impunity of Guilt (if any such there is) is the strongest Encouragement to the Repetition of the same Practices in future Times, by Chalking out a safe Method of committing the most flagitious Frauds, under the Protection of some *corrupt* and ALL-SKREENING MINISTER.

9. For these Reasons we think ourselves under an undispensible Obligation to vindicate our own Honour, by leaving our Testimonies in the Journals of this House, that we are not under the *Influence of any Man whatsoever*, whose Safety may depend on the Protection of *Fraud* and *Corruption*; and that we entered upon this Enquiry, with a sincere and just Design of going to the Bottom of the Evil, and applying to it the most proper and effectual Remedies.

Bedford	Tweedale	Bridgewater
Strafford	Cobham	Chesterfield
Bathurst	Coventry	Carteret
Litchfield	Stair	Berkshire
Suffolk	Montrose	Bruce
Masham	Winchelsea	Marchmont
Shaftsbury	and	Thanet
Craven	Nottingham	Gower

NOTE. *The Protests on passing the Mutiny Bill, and rejecting the Pension Bill, are to the same Effect as the Protests thereon, last Session to which they refer; See Vol. I. p. 215. Vol. II. p. 815, 816, Vol. III. p. 134, 135.*

The **Craftsman**, June 9. N°. 194.

MR *Walsingham* having spun out Papers (see p. 194,253, and 28.) from one little Paragraph of Home News in the *Craftsman*, (see p. 212,) Mr *D'anvers* bestowes a good Deal of Banter upon him on Account of the various Steps he has taken to make himself eminent as a Writer, and wonders that any Man in Power, however distress'd for *Advocates*, should trust his Cause with such a giddy, *truant Youth*, without Wit, Learning, or Knowledge of the World. His first Attack, says he, was upon a Gentleman who had often disturb'd his *Patron* in his golden Dreams; and having demolished him, he fell upon several other conspicuous Characters in the *House of Commons*, both living and dead. After this, the *Lord Mayor, Aldermen, Common-Council,* and *Representatives* of this City (*except one upright Man*) fell under the same severe Discipline. To these were added all the considerable *Merchants* and *Traders* in the Kingdom, who had the Insolence to controul the last glorious Efforts of his *Patron*, a GENERAL EXCISE.

This noble-spirited Freedom gave him new Credit with his *Master*, who immediately enlarged his *Pension*, and ordered him to bespeak an *Equipage*, suitable to his Character.

From this Time the *great* Mr *Walsingham* assumed a higher Stile, and in every Paper discovers his *new Dignity*. He takes Leave of the *lower House* to exercise his censorial Power against the Peers of the Realm, who have discover'd any Opposition to the Will of his *Patron*; and a *noble Lord* is severely handled for having had the Misfortune to lose a *good Place*, and retain a *good Character*. When I unwarily inserted that Article of News, I little apprehended it would raise such a Storm in Mr *W*'s Breast. But it produced a long *Free Briton* containing a learned and critical Comment on those obnoxious Words, *astonish,* and *grieve,* with some polite Strokes on his Lordship's Character, and a broad Intimation that he could lay some terrible Things to his Charge, if he was not restrained by the *Privilege of Peerage.*

His Lordship being unwilling to check so aspiring a Genius, remov'd his Scruples, by a Message,. to which Mr *W*. returned a *respectful Answer,* (See p. 28.) However, the Beginning of this fine Answer is a little out of Character; for he he tells the *Noble Peer that he is* truly for-ry (*i. e.* grieved) *for the Occasion, and* aftonifhed *at the Contents of his Lordfhip's Letter.* The very Words which occafion'd the Difpute between us. As a *Free Bri: ton,* no Doubt, *this Gentleman* hath a Right to any Words in the *Englifh Language*; but according to his own Doctrine (fee p. 280. E.) it is a very high Infult to tell a *Peer of the Realm* that He grieves and is *aftonifh'd* at any Thing that comes from Him.

There likewife feems a fmall Incon-fiftency between his *firft Paper,* upon this Subject, and another Paffage in his *An-fwer to the Noble Peer.* In *one,* he tells us, that the *Authority of the* Houfe of Lords, *and the Action of* Scandalum Magnatum might deter the boldeft Man *from fpeak-ing Truth of a Peer*; and, for his ownPart, *He darrs not do it.* In the *other,* he fays, *Nothing can deter* him, *and that he is incapable of* Fear; or, in other Words, He is of a fudden grown *bolder than the boldeft Man alive*; nay even *bolder than himfelf*;

But I am really *grieved* and *aftonifhed,* that Mr *W.* fhould decline to make any Ufe of his late *Indemnity,* in explaining the Reafons of his Lordfhip's *Difmiffion.* Inftead of That, he affures the *Noble Peer, be hath nothing in his Power to ex-plain to his Difadvantage.* It may be ask'd, Why Mr *W.* fhould infift fo much on the *Privileges of the Peerage,* as a Re-ftraint, when it was no Reftraint? To this he readily anfwers, that what he faid, was defigned only *as a Reproof to the Writer of the* Craftfman; and that it was *unfair and highly difingenuous to bring great* Names *into publick Debates*; yet fhews in every Page of his Writings, that the *higheft Characters* are at his Com-mand; even that *facred* and *awful* Name, which fills up the greateft Part of his Differtations on this *Subject.* NAY, in one, *he fubmits it to the* Royal Judg-ment, *whether I have not been guilty of great Infolence to the* Royal Perfon. Thus the King is nominated Arbitrator between a Couple of *Weekly Writers*; an Honour I could never prefume to expect or ask. But it feems the whole Power of the Kingdom is at Mr *W's* Service.

My Correfpondent in his Letter un-luckily mentioned an Exemption from the Danger of a *Cudgel,* amongft other Immunities contain'd in the *Meffage.* But Mr *W,* infifts that the Word *Infult* was only mention'd in it; he calls this a *Mifreprefen-*

tion *of his Lordfhip's Meaning*; yet argues from it, that *my Correfpondent muft have been allowed a* Sight *of that Meffage*; where-as the contrary Conclufion is more natural. However, Mr *W.* infers, that the *Noble Lord* ought to have kept *this Meffage* an abfolute Secret; and that his fuffering any Writer to *play upon it,* was a *Viola-tion of his Honour and Promife*; *fince,* fays he, *this was the* greateft Infult *any of his Friends could give* Me.—See how the *Gen-tleman's* Prowefs grows upon him! He not only refolves to return *Blows for Blows* from whatever Hand they come, but threatens to drub *all the Nobility round,* if they prefume to infult him in this Man-ner.—What a terrible Creature is this Mr *Walfingham!* —I fhudder at the Thoughts of him, but hope my Age will protect me. As he call'd upon his *M—j—y* to ftand *Umpire* between *us Two,* he has return'd his *M——y* the Favour. (See p. 281. E.) and declares himfelf *his Champion in ordinary,* without any Regard to the Claim of Mr *Dimmock.*

I fhall conclude, fays *D'anvers,* with requefting Mr *W.* to intercede with his *Patron,* to grant me the Liberty of *fpeak-ing out to the World,* without any Appre-henfions of *Meffengers,* or *Special Juries*; and I affure him, if he can prevail with his *Patron* to fhew this Regard for *Li-berty,* I will not give it up with a poor, fneaking Declaration, that *I have nothing in my Power to explain to his Difad-vantage, and that I never entertained an unworthy Thought of him*, but I will make a free Ufe of *his Indulgence,* for my own Juftification, and the Emolu-ment of the Publick.

Fog's Journal. June 9. Nº 240.

IN this Paper Fog drolls upon the little Arts and Subterfuges his Adverfaries make ufe of, in want of Argument, to keep themfelves from finking. It almoft pities me, fays he, to fee what miferable Shifts their Patron has been reduced, to make himfelf appear of fome Con-fequence. Since his Project has been drop'd fo little Tricks have been ufed to deceive the People in the Country in all Circumftances relating to it. The Papers that are Weekly fent into the Country, and given *gratis,* are the Vehicles of in-numerable Falfehoods. In one of thefe you read what was never dreamt of, that the Tax upon Soap and Candles, in Cafe the Excife had fucceeded, were to be taken off.

There

There have likewife been manufcript Letters fent to feveral little Boroughs, by particular Perfons, who have a peculiar Intereft in deceiving them. One, fays *Fog*, I have feen, fent to a certain Borough in *Devonfhire*, and addreffed to one Mr *Sk — er*, and fign'd *W. T.* which he begins in thefe Words.

Tou will perhaps, be furpriz'd at this, when I acquaint you, that the Excife on Tobacco was Yefterday drop'd by Sir — by putting off the Bill to the 12th of June next. He did it in an exceeding fine Speech, with a full Juftification of the Propofal, and an Excufe to the Freeholders of England *for dropping what was intended, and wou'd have proved, for their Eafe, had the Publick been enabled to collect, and receive what is now by Law due to the Publick.* As to the Juftification Mr *W. T.* fpeaks of, I will venture to affirm, fays *Fog*, No-body heard any fuch Thing but himfelf, unlefs a bold Affertion, without Proof, could be called fo. As to his Excufe to the *Free-holders*, had he made one, they would hardly have thank'd him for it, becaufe it was they who forc'd him to quit his Hold. They exerted their whole Strength in the Prefervation of the Trading Intereft, whereby they prov'd at once their publick Spirit, and good Senfe; knowing the Interefts of their two Bodies are infeparable. Perhaps, Mr *W. T*, your Mafter might think to fet the Landed, and Trading Intereft at Variance with each other, in Hopes of drawing fome Support to his finking Caufe, but it won't do. —— He is a little too well known.

As what follows is a notorious Falfehood, I fhall give it in your own Words, *viz. After the Houfe was up Yefterday, an infamous Mob in the Court of Requefts, made a direct Attack on Sir —'s Perfon, which muft, and would have ended very fatally, if his Friends about him, and the Juftices, and Conftables attending, had not, with great Difficulty, carried him fafe, and unhurt to his Coach.*

It is certain, fuch a Number of People affembled together, upon a Point, wherein their very Liberties were concern'd, never behav'd with greater Decency. The infulting Language they receiv'd from feveral of the Mercenaries, could not provoke them to make fuch a Return as it deferv'd, knowing the leaft Difturbance would have furnifh'd thefe People with a Pretence to reprefent thefe Meetings as riotous Affemblies, and be made an

Argument in Favour of the pernicious Scheme then depending; therefore their Refentment was only fuch as is fhewn againft an Actor who has play'd his Part Ill, and this is reprefented as an Attempt to Murder. I can't forbear repeating here, what was faid by a Man of Quality on the fame fide of the Queftion with Mr *W. T's.* Mafter, who having feveral ridiculous Affaffination Pamphlets fent him, (See p. 224) upon Reading part of one of them, committed the whole Cargo to the Flames, with this remarkable faying, *He is not worth Powder and Shot, by G——*

In the Conclufion, Mr *Sk——r* is order'd to affirm all the Contents of this fine Letter to be true, a very hopeful Employment! I thought all Things of this Nature had, properly fallen within the Province of thofe two renowned Politicians, *Osborne* and *Walfingham.* As to the Part Mr *W. T.* acts in this Affair, there is fome Excufe, if it be true, that he is an humble Hanger-on upon Sir.— In this Condition he fhould be confider'd as pleading his own Caufe.

The Weekly Mifcellany, June 9. N°. 26.

Remarks on the Layman's Sermon, *&c.*

IN the *Supplement* to the *Layman's Sermon*, the Author cites a Paffage out of *Rufhworth* to the following Effect, *viz. About this time (in the Year 1636) the New Statutes for the Univerfity of* Oxford *were finifhed and publifhed in Convocation. The Preface difparaged K.* Edward VIth's *Times and Government; declaring that the Difcipline of the Univerfity was difcompofed by that King's Injunctions, and that it did revive and flourifh again in Q.* Mary's *Days under* Card. Pool, *when by the much to be defired Felicity of thofe Times, an in-bred Candour fupply'd the Defect of Statutes.*

The Lay-Preacher then proceeds, —— *Was there ever in any Declaration, even from the* Vatican, *more of the Popifh Stile and Spirit? The Times and Government of that pious Proteftant and Reformer* Edward VIth, *are traduced by an* Englifh Convocation; *the Days of that Popifh Bigot* Q. Mary *are wifh'd for, and a* Romifh Cardinal *is mentioned and extolled for his Church Government; Popifh Superftition, Brigotry, and blind Obedience are reprefented as* Inbred Candour.

Unfortunately for this Author, that very Body of Statutes, with the Preface mentioned by *Rufhworth*, and thus com-
mented

mented on (publish'd for Probation in 1634, and finally confirmed in 1636) is still in Being in every College Library in *Oxford*, and the original Manuscript, reposited in the Archives of the University.

To shew that *Rushworth* has misrepresented, and the *Lay-preacher* greatly injured the Compilers of these Statutes, the following are the Words refer'd to.

Edoardo sexto ad Clavum sedente novo sudatum est Molimine; Dati Vindices, sed e Senatu Regio, non Academico; qui Statutorum Specimen (ut paribus Musculis uterque Oculus moveretur) Utrique Academiæ commune exhibuerunt. Præscribente Rege, & Lenocinante Novitate, primo visum Opus admitti: Sed quia constrictum nimis & angustum erat, Illo extincto statim & ipsum conclamatum est; & illud solummodo præstitit, quantum satis est ut memoretur fuisse.

Paulo post potiente Rerum Maria *sub Cardinalis* Poli *Auspiciis idem recruduit Labor; designati qui in publici Regiminis Excessus, & Defectus animadverterent. Nova exinde data Leges, sed pari cum prioribus Angustia; Idemq; fere Jugum, tantum aliis Manibus impositum. Interim tamen inter incerta vacillans Statuta viguit Academia, colebantur Studia, enituit Disciplina, & optanda Temporum Felicitate Tabularum Defectus resarcivit innatus Candor, & quicquid Legibus deerat, Moribus suppletum est.*

Let the *Lay-preacher* point out in what Words the Government of *Edward* VI. is traduced for his having unsettled the *Popish Discipline*; let him produce his Authority for saying this Cardinal *was extoll'd for his Church Government*; or shew, in the Clauses recited, one single Word concerning either the *Church*, or *Church-Government.*

Upon the whole it appears, that the Authors of this Preface have (without any Aid from the *Vatican*) related two bare Matters of Fact; First, that Commissioners appointed by *Edward* VI. endeavour'd to compile a proper Body of Statutes for the University; but they not being a *Senatu Academico*, their Design proved abortive, and was dropt at the Death of that Prince.

Secondly, That in Q. *Mary's* Time this Design was resumed by Card. *Pool*, and Persons appointed by him to carry it on; but still without Success, the *Popish* Card. is so far from being extol'd, that both he and his Commissioners are used with great Freedom. *In the Days of*

that *Popish Bigot* Q. Mary *are guilty for.* How does this appear? Why, truly, the Author of this Preface tells us, that by the desirable Felicity of those Times the *Candour* and *Morals* of the *University* supply'd the Defect of *written Laws.* But where is the *Popery* in all this? Why, *optanda Temporum Felicitas*, can signify nothing but the Days and Government of a Popish Queen; then it follows, that *Studia, Disciplina, & Mores*, must be Fire, Faggot, and Gun-powder.

By this Time the *Lay-preacher* must be reduc'd to acknowledge either, 1. That he never saw this same Preface; or, 2. That he is ignorant of the Language in which it is written; or, *Lastly*, That he has knowingly, and willfully published to the World a gross and notorious Falsehood.   OXONIENSIS.

Grubstreet Journal, June 14. No. 181.

The Case of the Patentees and Players of *Drury-Lane.*

MR BAVIUS,

Instead of examining the Causes of the Dissention between the Patentees of *Drury-Lane* Theatre, and the Actors, a Method which seldom has any Effect, (it being the Privilege of a *Free-born Englishman* not to be convinced by any Reason that does not fall in with his own.) I shall endeavour at something that may at once please both Parties, and at the same Time promote the publick Good.

The Case is this. — The whole Company of Comedians think proper to withdraw themselves from his Majesty's Service, and prefer a Commonwealth to that Form of Government, under which they have hitherto acted. For this they plead a natural Right, which every collective Body of People has in the Disposal of their Lives and Labour.

Every Age has its particular Humour, Whim, or Caprice. The Progress towards the Erection of 50 new Churches in the two late Reigns; some produce as an Instance: 'Tis not impossible but we may distinguish ourselves by building 50 new Theatres, at least as well frequented. The last Winter open'd with three constant Play-Houses, and as many for Opera's. Every Parish will shortly have one.

Things being in this happy Train, what remains but that the Male-contents of *Drury-Lane*, pitch upon a proper Place in which to fix their Residence. Necessitous People indeed; might settle where there is the best Prospect of Gain; but theirs is a different Cafe. Whatever Ends 'Mr C—b—+ may have, yet every other Creature concerned, has acted in a brave Contempt of Self-Intereft: Neither Bribes nor Penfions could foften them: For indeed, by what other Names can we call the immenfe Salaries of Mr A. H—l-m, and Mr Wm M—ls? What elfe could make the fober Mr M—ls quit a comfortable Certainty; or engage old J—n-n in Contentions, of which he will not probably live to fee an End? As for the Women, it's no Wonder the Managers, being but two Men, were not able to fecure them againft fo many Rivals. Whatever be the Motive upon which thefe Ladies act, 'tis plain they have a like Contempt of Self-Intereft with the Men, and are equally qualify'd for the College in *Moorfields*, than which, for the Convenience of Surgeons, it's Largenefs and Vicinity to the Pegafus, no Place is more proper.

As to the Managers, they have now an Opportunity of raifing the Dignity, and fupporting the Decency of the Stage. The Manner in which it has been hitherto fupply'd, by taking Perfons of the loweft, and moft profligate Characters, is, no doubt, the Reafon why Gentlemen of Senfe and Learning prefer Starving, to a comfortable Subfiftence in fo ill Company. But this Evil, thus happily removed, 'tis probable the Univerfity will foon fupply us with a regular and judicious Company of Players at a much lefs Expence. Nor are our Hopes confined to the Univerfity alone, fince we fee fo many Gentlemen of the Inns-of-Court fo much better verfed in the Laws of the Stage, than in thofe of the Land. I had once thought it a piece of Juftice, that the unfortunate Members of our Society, who have long ftarved by Writing for the Stage, may be provided for in the Character of Actors. But befides the Inconvenience of the Lownefs, and Profligacy of the Perfons, I fear, it would be impoffible to confine them to any Rule or Agreement, or bring them to any Apprehenfion of the Sentiments of thofe Authors, whofe Works we would fee reprefented. As for the Female Part of the Company, every Charity-School will fupply a dozen Wenches of more decent Education and Character, more Health, Youth, Beauty, and Genius, than the common Run of Actreffes. One Seafon's good Inftruction would qualify them for all the Bufinefs of the Stage.   *Yours*, &c.

§ Mr *Bavius*, next inferts a Scene from *Vanbrugh's Æfop*, where the Players are reprefented as having revolted from their Patentees, fhewing for Caufe feveral frivolous Complaints; all which Æfop liften'd to with great Attention; and when they had done, he told 'em the following Fable.

E. I'll tell you what, Sirs———
I once a pack of beagles knew ---
That much refembled I know who:
With a good Huntfman at their Tail,
In full Command,
With Whip in Hand,
They'd run apace
The chearful chace,
And of their Game were feldom known to fail.
But being at length their chance to find
A Huntfman of a gentler kind,
They foon perceiv'd the Rein was flack,
The Word went quickly thro' the pack ——
They one and all cry'd *Liberty* ;
This happy Moment we are free,
We'll range the Woods,
Like Nymphs and Gods,
And fpend our Mouths in praife of Mutiny.

With that old *Jowler* trots away,
And *Bowman* fingles out his Prey :
Thunder bellow'd thro' the Wood,
And fwore he'd burft his Guts with Blood:
Venus tript it o'er the Plain,
With boundlefs hopes of boundlefs gain :
———*Juno*, fhe flipt down the Hedge,
But left her facred Word for Pledge ;
That all fhe pick'd up by the by———
Shou'd to the publick Treafury ;
And well they might rely upon her ;
For *Juno* was a Bitch of Honour.
In fhort, they all had hopes to fee
A heavenly crop of Mutiny,
And fo to reaping fell :
But in a little time they found,
It was the Devil had till'd the Ground,
And brought the Seed from Hell.
The pack divided, nothing throve ;
Difcord feiz'd the Throne of Love :
Want and Mifery all endure,
All take Pains, and all grow Poor.
When they had toil'd the live long Day,
And came at Night to view their Prey,
Oft alas, fo ill they fped,
That half went Supperlefs to Bed.

At length they all in Council fate ;
Where at a very fair Debate,
It was agreed at laft,
That flavery with eafe and plenty,
When Hounds were fomething turn'd of twenty,
Was much a better fate,
Than 'twas to work and faft.

The

The Patentees in their Case publish the Salaries of each Actor per Week, to shew how little Reason they had to mutiny, viz.

To Mr *Colly Cibber*, from the Time of letting his Share, till he left the Stage 12*l.* 12*s. per Week.* Mr *The. Cibber* 5*l.* and his Wife's whole Salary till her Death, without doing the Company any Service the greatest Part of the Winter; and his own also, during the Time of his being ill, who perform'd but seldom till after *Christmas.* Mr. *Mills,* jun. 3 *l.* under the same Circumstances with Regard to his Wife. Mr *Mills* sen. 1 *l. per Day,* for 200 Days certain, and a Benefit, clear of all Charges. Mr *Johnson* 5*l.* Mr *Miller* 5*l.* paid him eight Weeks before he acted, besides a Present of 10 Guineas. Mr *Harper,* 4 *l.* and a Present of 10 Guineas. Mr *Griffin* 4 *l.* and a Present. Mr *Shepard* 3 *l.* Mr *Hallam,* for himself and Father (though the latter is of little or no Service) 3 *l.* Mrs *Heron* 5 *l.* rais'd from 40 *s.* last Winter, yet refus'd to play several Parts assign'd her, and acted but seldom this Season. Mrs *Butler* 3 *l. per Week.*

By these and other Salaries, with the incident Charges, (besides Cloaths and Scenes) the Patentees are at the daily Charge of 49 *l.* odd Money, each Acting Day.

The Free-Briton. June 14. No. 186.

MR *Walsingham* here makes Reprisals on the *little Insignificant* Under Writer of the *Craftsman,* as the sole Author of that Paper of *June* 9. which W. calls a *flat, foolish, and childish Invective* against him, filled with *peevish, stupid Stuff.* The Writer of it having, adds he, been expell'd his College, became a Libeller of the Ministry, for whom he had been an unsuccessful Scribler; upon this being hired as a *Hack* by the Patrons of the *Craftsman* to convey their Resentments to the Publick, the *little Creature* grew conceited, and had the Impudence to think himself a Wit; and, not content with being despised as a *very low Implement,* resolved to be treated by all the World, as of a very odious Species of Vermin. For being now become, *in his own Opinion, a Wit,* he fancied he had *no Occasion for Morals;* falls to Libelling a *Right Rev. Prelate,* and 'abus'd a *Clergyman,* his *intimate Friend,* for Writing in that Prelate's Defence. *Walsingham* bestows other Epithets on him, as *Malicious, Mercenary,* &c. and

justifies his own Censures of the Common-Council of *London;* as drawn from him by the necessary Defence of K. *William's* Memory; and insists that the Character of a noble Peer, is no way indecently or otherwise mention'd by him than to rescue his present Majesty's Royal Person from the Indignity and Insult offer'd by the Patrons of the *Craftsman;* which Insult *W.* observes they have evaded defending or speaking to, and put their little *Hack* into the Controversy to render Censure *Contemptible,*

So Proteus, hunted in a nobler Shape Became, when seiz'd a Puppy or an Ape.

Fog's Journal. June 16. N° 241.

Extracts from the EXCISE BILL.

AS fine a Thing as the Excise Project was, the Projector and his Faction kept all the Beauties of it to themselves till the Minute it was produced in order to be pass'd into a Law. This was sufficient Cause to suspect something in it that wou'd not bear Examination.

The Lord Mayor, Aldermen, and Commons of the City of *London,* for procuring a Copy of this Bill, have been censur'd as guilty of a high Breach of the Privilege of Parliament. (see p. 180.) But with no less Ignorance than ill Manners; for there's an Officer, call'd the City Remembrancer, whose Business it is to attend the House of Commons, to take Copies of all such Bills as may affect the Trade of the City; neither is there any Vote, Resolution, or Order of the House now subsisting, by which this Privilege is taken away.

But as this Bill is yet extoll'd by some, we shall quote such Clauses from it, as made one Side very fond of it, and set the rest of the World as much against it.

Be it enacted, That all the Powers, Authorities, &c. which in an Act made in the 12th Year of the Reign of King *Charles* II. (Entitled an Act for taking away the Court of Wards and Liveries &c.) or by any other Law now in Force relating to his Majesty's Revenue of Excise upon Beer, &c. be provided for levying and paying the Inland Duty, by this Act impos'd, as fully and effectually, as if all the Powers, Authorities, &c. were particularly repeated. *And* for the better securing the said Inland Duty upon Tobacco, it is further enacted that all Tobacco imported into this Kingdom from any of the British Plantations, upon the

Entry

Entry thereof at the Cuſtom-houſe, and charging the ſame with the further Subſidy of one Penny in the Pound, granted by the ſaid Act of the 9th of K. *Wm.* III. ſhall be forthwith put into a Warehouſe provided for that Purpoſe at the Charge of the Importer or Owner thereof, and approved by the Commiſſioners for the Inland Duty, if in the Port of *London,* or by Officers appointed by ſuch Commiſſioners, if in Out-Ports, and ſhall not be taken out from thence upon any Account, otherwiſe than is herein after mentioned, *viz.* Such Tobacco as ſhall be ſold to be conſumed in *Great-Britain,* or intended ſo to be, ſhall be deliver'd out upon Payment of the ſaid Inland Duty, by this Act impoſed, in the manner following, *viz.* The Proprietor or firſt Buyer, or whom he or ſhe ſhall appoint, ſhall make an Entry with the Collector or Receiver of the ſaid Inland Duty, of ſo much Tobacco remaining in ſuch Warehouſe, as he or ſhe intend to take out, and pay down in Ready Money the ſaid Inland Duty; the ſame Method to be uſed in Out-ports; and upon producing a Warrant or Certificate, ſign'd by ſuch Collector or Receiver, certifying the Payment of the ſaid Inland Duty, to the Keeper of ſuch Warehouſe where the Tobacco has been put upon Importation and Entry thereof as aforeſaid, and upon producing a Certificate, from the Collector or principal Officer of the Cuſtoms of the Payment of the ſaid further Subſidy for ſuch Tobacco, according to the Proviſion herein after mentioned, the ſaid Keeper of ſuch Warehouſe ſhall deliver thereout ſo much of the ſaid Tobacco for Home Conſumption, as ſhall be mention'd in ſuch Warrant or Certificate to have paid ſuch Duty and further Subſidy. And the Keepers of ſuch Warehouſes ſhall thereupon give to the Proprietor or firſt Buyer, or the Perſon by him or her appointed, a Permit or Certificate to accompany the ſaid Tobacco, to be ſign'd by the Officer attending ſuch Warehouſes, to be appointed by the Commiſſioners for the ſaid Inland Duty to prevent the Seizing thereof, and to be produced to the Officers of, and for the ſaid Inland Duty for the Diviſion or Place where ſuch Tobacco ſhall be carried within the Time in ſuch Permit limited, during which Time, and no longer, ſuch Permit ſhall continue in Force; and as to ſuch Part of the ſaid Tobacco as ſhall be intended for Exportation, the ſame ſhall be deliver'd out of ſuch Ware-

houſes unto the Proprietor, &c. upon ſuch ſufficient Security to be firſt given by Bond to his Majeſty, with Sureties, that the ſame and every Part thereof ſhall be exported, and not relanded in *Great Britain,* which ſaid Security ſhall be diſcharged without Fee or Reward, upon producing ſuch Certificate to ſ Officers as aforeſaid, that is to ſay, to ſuch of the Tobacco as ſhall be enter'd for, or, landed in *Ireland,* the Iſland of *Guernſey, Jerſey, Alderney, Sark,* or *Man,* the Condition of the Bond ſhall be to bring a Certificate in Diſcharge thereof within

from the Date of the Bond, to be ſign'd by the proper Officer of the Cuſtoms reſiding there, and for Tobacco enter'd for any other Place, to bring a Certificate under the common Seal of the Magiſtrate in any place beyond the Seas, or under the Hands and Seals of two known *Britiſh* Merchants, being at ſuch Place, importing ſuch Tobacco was there landed, or upon Proof by credible Perſons, that ſuch Tobacco was taken by Enemies or periſh'd in the Seas, the *Examination and Proof thereof being left to the Judgment of the ſaid Commiſſioners* of the Cuſtoms. *Provided,* that if any ſuch Proprietor, &c. ſhall be minded to manufacture any Part of ſuch Tobacco ſo taken out for Exportation, it ſhall be lawful for ſuch Proprietor, on giving Notice to the Officer for the ſaid Inland Duty, appointed to attend the Warehouſe, of the Place where he or ſhe intends to manufacture the ſame. *And* farther, that ſuch Tobacco ſo manufactur'd for Exportation, ſhall be kept apart from all Tobacco for Home Conſumption, and that   Days before the ſame ſhall be exported, Notice ſhall be given to the Officer, that he may ſee the packing up of the ſame, and attend the putting it on Board the Ship, which is to receive it under the Care and Inſpection of the Searchers, and the Exporter of ſuch manufactur'd Tobacco to give Security by Bond, as before requir'd, every Perſon offending in the Premiſes ſhall   the ſaid Tobacco and together with   and alſo the ſum of   And farther, that the Value of ſuch Tobacco ſo exported, ſhall always be rated at the Price of the beſt Tobacco of the like Sort, as it ſhall at ſuch Time bear and ſell for in *London. And* further, that before any ſuch Proprietor, &c. ſhall be permitted to export ſuch Tobacco he ſhall declare upon Oath, before the taking out his Coquet, or giving Bond, that

that the said Tobacco is really and truly intended by him to be exported in the Ship therein mention'd, and is not intended to be relanded in any Part of *Great Britian*. And that whoever shall not make due Entries upon Importation, or not bring it to the Warehouse appointed for that Purpose, or shall re-land any of it after Exportation, all such Tobacco shall be   And the same shall and may be   by any Officer of the Customs, for the said Inland Duty, and the Person, &c. offending shall together with   *Provided,* that if any Dispute arise, the Proof shall lie on the Owner or Claimer, and not on the Officer. And for preventing Clandestine carrying any such Tobacco out of the Warehouse, the Keeper or Keepers thereof shall keep one or more Books, wherein to enter an exact Account of such Tobacco brought in or carried out, and of the Days and Times when, and how much thereof was deliver'd out for Home Consumption, and how much for Exportation, and the Name of the Person or Persons and for whose Use, and transmit the same every   Months, or oftener, upon Oath, to the Commissioners, with an exact Account of what is remaining in the said Warehouse, which the said Commissioners are hereby injoined within   to appoint some Person or Persons to inspect and examine, and if upon such Examination any Fraud appears in the said Books or Accounts, the Officer or Officers offending herein, shall not only be   but also shall   for every such Offence the Sum of   And farther, that it shall be lawful for the Proprietor or Proprietors of such Tobacco so to be lodged to affix *one Lock to every Warehouse,* and to keep the Key, and for the Officer or Officers attending such Warehouse to fix one other Lock and to keep the Key, and the Proprietor or Proprietors, may, in the Presence of the said Keeper or Keepers, Officer or Officers attending, view, sort, separate, and receive out of such Warehouses such of his Tobacco therein lodged, intended either to be consumed in *Great Britain,* or exported to Foreign Parts.

NOTE, *Blanks were left for the Time, Sums, Penalty and Forfeitures,* &c.

The **Craftsman**, June 16. N° 363.
Preamble to a Patent.

AN Antiquary of *Oxford* having obliged Mr *D'anvers* with a Manuscript he found in the *Bodleian* Library, he gives it us in Latin first, and then a Translation of it, to the Effect following.

WHEREAS our trusty and well-beloved Counsellor *** hath distinguished Himself in the most notorious manner by his uncommon Loyalty and incredible Attachment to our Interest, which is equally obliging to us, and hath manifested the same Respect to our *dearest Consort,* lest an ungratefulNeglect of so *egregious a Person* should render us unworthy of so many important Services; and since He hath at length vouchsafed to *wear the highest Titles,* as well as *deserve them;* our Will and Pleasure is, He should be advanced to that exalted Station, which his own singular Modesty hath too long declin'd. A Man who, even in the Bloom of his Years, apply'd himself to *beneficial Studies,* and return'd enrich'd with a plentiful Harvest from the barren Wilds of *Scotland.* His Years, as they advanc'd, more than answer'd the Expectations of his Youth; especially in that ever-memorable Year, when the Distresses of Thousands, drawn in by the fraudulentExecution of a plausible Scheme, had almost driven the Nation to the last Extremities. In this critical Juncture, He allay'd the Heats and Animosities of the People, by a CERTAIN CONTRACT *with a great money'd Company;* which He had the consummate Address to draw up with his own Hand; and when the Turn was serv'd, to dissolve and annul with the same *political Craft* and *glorious Falshood.* Having therefore signaliz'd Himself above all his Countrymen in the arts of *raising Money,* We thought fit to place Him at the Head of our *Treasury;* where, however profusely he dissipated the *publick Money,* we saw it immediately refunded into our Exchequer with *ample Interest.* His unparallel'd Capacity for squeezing Money out of every Thing sufficiently display'd his Abilities for the *Office* which We had conferr'd upon Him; of which He lately erected to Himself a Monument in *Ireland* more durable than his *own Brass;* but He reserv'd the noblest Effort of his Genius for his own Country, when He made that glorious bold, and desperate, tho' alas! fruitless Attempt to EXCISE the Commodities of all Countries, and cut off something from every Man's Property, for the Benefit of us and our Government. He is also endowed with a most amazing Fluency of Speech by which, under a Cloud of mysterious Words

Words, he can conceal the Secrets of State, from the prying Eyes of *seditious Malecontents*. By thefe Means, He hath long thunder'd in the Senate, as *fole Dictator*, the *Reprefentatives* of the People being oblig'd to concur with his Meafures, either by his *Power*, or *more agreeable Applications*. He hath likewife ftudied *foreign*, as well as *domeftick Affairs*; and having wifely obferv'd our Trade at the greateft Height in Times of Peace, he firft thought of reclaiming his Countrymen from their *Brutality to Strangers*; nay, he form'd a Scheme of Alliance with our moft *implacable Enemies*; for having been always averfe to *Wars*, and an Admirer of *Peace, Trucrs, Congreffes, Negotiations* and *Treaties*, He put us to no lefs Expence in purchafing a *Reprieve from Wars*, than it coft our *mad Heroes of old* in carrying on and concluding them; hence it is, that there's fcarce a Nation upon Earth, with whom we are not link'd in clofe Confederacy; and whilft we are oblig'd to affift fo many States, we may rely on their reciprocal Affiftance upon any Emergency.——Yet have not the Welfare and Intereft of the *Soldiery* been difregarded, fince in the midft of an *undifturbed Peace*, we can review a *Standing* Army within our own Walls.——What a Protection are *Thefe* to their Fellow Subjects! What a Terror to foreign Nations! What an Ornament to our Cities! Moreover, We have frequently advis'd with this *pacifick Hero* concerning the Management of *Ecclefiaftical Affairs*; fince he is not inferior to any Prelate of our *Church*, either in Piety, Learning, or moral Virtue. His Intimacy with our *Bifhops* hath proved advantagious to us on feveral Occafions; for thofe *folemn Fathers*, always intent upon the *one Thing needful*, are convinced of the Advantages of a good Underftanding between the *Mitre* and the *Crown*, have always promoted whatever tended to augment our *Revenue*, enlarge our *Prerogative*, or a Compliance with our Will. ——Whereas therefore our *Soldiers* revel at their Eafe; our Merchants are reliev'd from the Fatigues of Commerce; and fuch Perfons invefted with the *Epifcopal Dignity*, as even the moft inveterate Adverfaries of our Church would rejoice to fee exalted; for all thefe Bleffings We acknowledge ourfelves indebted to the Vigilance, Fidelity, and unwearied Application of a *fingle Minifter*. What then remains, but that We confer upon this *incomparable Patriot*, who, whilft a Com-

moner, obtain'd the Honour of *two Ribbons*, the only Title wanting to his Merit? ——*Know ye therefore* &c.

I wifh, fays D'*anvers*, my Friend had let us known the Occafion of this *curious Piece*, for I cannot find any Minifter in the *Englifh* Hiftory, whom it fits in every Particular. The Character of *Villars*, D. of *Buckingham*, feems to fuit it beft, as the *whole Power of the Kingdom was monopoliz'd in his Hands*; as he had the Honour of the *Blue Ribbon* whilft a Commoner; and was the firft Minifter who endeavour'd to naturalize *Excife* in this Kingdom. After all, I muft leave it to the Reader to determine, whether it was a *real Preamble*, or only the Sport of a political Satirift upon fome over-grown *Monfter of Power*, in former Times.

Univerfal Spectator, June 16. No. 245.

AFter fome moral Reflections upon Life, it's Uncertainty, and the various Purfuits of Men thro' the different Stages of it, Mr *Stone-caftle* gives fome Account of his own; that he is now arriv'd to his grand Climacteric, and can with Pleafure furvey the *Track of Life* he has ran thro', having fpent the former part of it in acquiring Knowledge, in imbibing the Sentiments of *Virtue*, and in doing fuch Acts as Virtue prompted him to, which he thinks can be equall'd by Nothing but the Pleafure his *old Age* affords, in having dedicated that to the Infpiring his Countrymen with the Love of Good, and expofing the Follies of a trifling Age. Tells us, he is fenfible of the *Decay of Life* by the *Increafe of Infirmities*; yet hopes he fhall without *Reluctance*, filently drop into the *Grave*, like *Fruit full Ripe to be gathered*. Thefe Reflections he fets in a ftronger Light, in a Contrafte contain'd in a Letter from his old Friend *Harry Eafy*, labouring under a Complication of Difeafes and Infirmities.

Dear *Harry Stonecaftle*,

WHat a detefted Thing is *old Age!* I am now fcarce the *Shadow* of what I was: The Springs of my Body are worn out in *Luft* or *Riot*. Pains are my Tormentors by *Night*, and a thoufand Infirmities difturb the Quiet of my Day. My *Spindle Legs*, once the Admiration of a *Ball-Room*, lie ufelefs in a Chair before me; my once *round plump Cheeks* are now ftitch-fallen, and full of Wrinkles. The *Lips* which have kifs'd the fineft Beauties, are now fodden with a *continual* al *Drivel*; and my *Taſte*, once exquiſite, is now ſo loſt, that I could not be ſenſible of Pleaſure from the *Height of* Luxury. I'm forſaken by Men of *Wit* as being *nauſeous*; nor can I blame *them*, when I would, if poſſible, forſake myſelf.

Theſe Miſeries I could endure; but how can I allay the *unextinguiſhable Fear* I have of *Death*. My *Deſpair of ſomething* (which I would not willingly believe) ſometimes tempts me to put an End to a Life ſo full of *Torment*; —— but when I have reſolv'd to perform the *Dictates* of my *Madneſs* —I *ſtart* —Fear ſeizes me — I'm afraid of I know not what —Of that which I once ſo *wittily ridicul'd* — A *future Being*; What that *Being is*, or whether it may afford a State of *Puniſhment*, lays open ſuch a Wilderneſs of Thought till I have loſt myſelf in *Confuſion.* ------ Such is my Terror, while you ſeem willing to meet Death. But why need I fear? — My *Honour*, and *Honeſty* have been undoubted; I have neither injur'd nor oppreſs'd any. *Tou* indeed have been *Su-perſtitious*, and follow'd the Dictates of *Religion*, implicitly paid a Deference to *that*, which from the Principles of *Nature* I denied; you put a Confidence in the Tales of *Prieſts*, while I was alone govern'd by the Dictates of my own *Fancy*. But ah! too late I find, *Reaſon*: is not ſufficient to guide our *Lives*, when it cannot ſupport us in the *Anguiſh* of *Death.* —Vain is all the *Morality* I boaſted of: I am ſenſible I have *err'd*; —For, what is *Honour* without Piety, or being *Faithful* to my *Priend*, when I have been a *Rebel* to my *God*? ——Every Man who will conſider *Death*, will find Reaſon inſufficient to make him *eaſy*, to calm his *Soul*, and to give him that *Serenity* of *Mind* you expreſs. Why then will a *reaſonable* Man *live* according to a Syſtem in which no *reaſonable* Man *dare die*? — You may perceive the *Anguiſh* of my *Soul*; — I can no more—H. *Eaſy*.

London Journal, June 16. No. 729.

On *Conversation and Reading*.

THE following Verſes, ſent me by a young Gentleman, ſays *Osborne*, were occaſion'd by a Diſpute about the Difference of Speaking from the *Underſtanding*, and Speaking from *outward Senſe*; it being aſſerted, that ſome Minds are like Blanks, and have no Ideas but what proceed from ſuch Objects as ſtrike the *Eyes* and *Ears*.

To SOCRATES.

Thought, you *affirm*, and Speech in grave
    Diſpute,
The *Reas'ning Human, and Unreas'ning Brute*,
Diſtinguiſh ſole; (*as ſubtle Sages teach*;)
And prove the Miniſter of *Thought*, is *Speech.*
Hence Speech once *granted to proceed from Thought*,
The Soul (you urge) *with richeſt Fancy fraught,*
Strives to get free, unable to ſuſtain
The Preſs of Images that croud the Brain;
And, faſt as Matter new Supply affords,
Her Labour eaſes in proportion'd Words.
This, as a certain Axiom you profeſs;
But learn, there is no Virtue in Exceſs:
For, if this dark Philoſophy implies.
That to be very loud, is to be wiſe;
It argues, by the ſame inverted Rule,
That Silence is the Burthen of a Fool.
Speech ſprings from Thought; *yet none admire the Vine*
That yields the largeſt Growth, but pureſt Wine.
Firm as my Faith, this Maxim I maintain,
H—a's C**ÆLIA**, *and my* FLAVIA, *ſhew it plain.*
That C**ÆLIA** *ſpeaks with Eaſe, may be made out*;
But that ſhe Thinks *the while, admits a Doubt*:
And FLAVIA, *'tis confeſs'd, oft ſilent ſits*;
But that ſhe Thinks *the while, no Doubt admits.*
C**ÆLIA**'*s Diſcourſe is what ſhe ſees or hears,*
Robb'd of all Senſe, ſtop but her Eyes and Ears;
FLAVIA'*s, from Senſe, aſſumes a purer Riſe*;
She hears and ſees with mental Ears and Eyes.
C**ÆLIA**'*s a ready Sheet, in order lay*
The Preſs, ſtamp what you pleaſe, 'twill ſerve the Day;
FLAVIA'*s a Book, with treaſur'd Learning ſtor'd,*
Conciſe of Stile! a Sentence in a Word;
At Home deſerted, C**ÆLIA** *roams Abroad,*
In hopes of Chance-Acquaintance on the Road:
But FLAVIA *rarely deigns Abroad to roam,*
Becauſe ſhe's better entertain'd at Home.
In Seats ſo diſtant from each other dwell
The Pow'rs of Talking *much, and* Thinking *well*:
For Words, *the faithful Agents of the Mind,*
Are prix'd, not by the Number, but the Kind.

Socrates, after a little Comment on the foregoing Verſes, ſays, a facetious Gentleman of his Acquaintance, wiſhes, *That all the Books in the World were burnt, becauſe then we ſhould know who had any Senſe* of their own. I am not quite ſo *Gothick*, ſays *Socrates*, yet could wiſh, that inſtead of poring over Books 6 Hours in a Day, Men would think at leaſt as many Hours as they read; and that after they have read an Hour or two, they would lay the Book aſide, walk about the Room, recollect the *Senſe* of the Author;

and

and then examine whether that Sense be *true* or *false* ; for a Man may remember the *Words*, and not understand the *Sense* of the Author : But if he can relate in his own Words what he hath read, he may A be assur'd he understands the *Sense*, which he is then to *examine* by general Principles of Reasoning whether it be *true* or *false*. This is the Way to form Great Men, while the other Method of reading, remembring, and never *examining*, hath made *Blockheads and Slaves* of all the g World. We are never to *suppose* any Book *true*; nor any Person *right* ; but *try* both Book and Person by these *eternal Truths*, of which *no Man* need be ignorant. To *Reason* all Things must *submit*, but that must *submit* to nothing. The Exercise of our Reason is the only way to make us *wise* and *good* Men : By that we C shall see what *can*, and what *cannot* be known ; and *make use* of the one, and *neglect* the other : It will render us *serviceable* and *agreeable* ; and make us capable of *receiving* and *giving* Knowledge : We shall, by this *Examination*, see so little Evidence for most of those things which are talk'd of with such an assuming D Air of Importance, that we shall lose that *dogmatical* Spirit, which is the *Bane* of all *Societies*.   SOCRATES.

The *Free-Briton*, June 21. No. 187.

Of False Patriotism.

THE greatest Frauds are carried on under the most venerable Names ; Ambition and Avarice dare not confess their selfish Views. The *Love of Country* in Men aspiring to Rule is often a Pretence only ; this ought to awaken every F Man's suspicion.   is one of the wisest Sayings recorded of *Satan, Does Job serve God for nought?* And it is a wiser Question for the People to ask concerning such Patriots, *Why all this Zeal for the Country, is it to serve us or yourselves?* If it should happen that any of these virtuous G Patriots should discover their Venality, and demand as their Price special Advantages to themselves, in Default of which they threaten to overturn the Government of a Country ; to shew such Inconsistencies between the Professions and Practices of such Persons, is treated as H a capital Crime against Virtue itself, and one sort of Evidence that the *Magistrates* are employing their Influence to depress the *Love of Country*.

It cannot but be matter of Ridicule,

when we see Patriotism become a common Name for all sorts of Men embark'd in Opposition to the Government. Hath a Man been impeached for Crimes and Treasons, and convicted thereof by his Flight ; saved, yet labouring the Destruction of that Government to which he owes his Pardon? — He is a PATRIOT. If another abetted that Person in his wicked Design, to betray our *Commerce* to the *French* by a *Bill* in Parliament, and in his Attempt to make Liberty of Conscience penal under the Name of *Schism*, engaging with him in the *Jacobite* Cause ; opposing, distressing the Government for almost 20 Years, in every Instance which came before the Publick. And as he had been the *Instrument of his Male Administration*, becoming the *Pupil of his Sedition and Calumny* ; *He too is* a PATRIOT. If a third was disgusted by seeing a *greater Person* than himself made a Secretary of State, or a *wooden-Spoon* of a *Lawyer* angry that, as he sunk in Fees, he did not rise in Preferment ; — *These are* PATRIOTS *also*. Or if a *solemn Pedant* should think to avenge his Exclusion from Employments of Importance, by laying out his *inimitable Dulness* in *voluminous unintelligible* REPORTS, for stripping innocent Men of their Fortunes, and screening the Guilty in their Crimes, merely to E gratify a *Great Male-content's Mistress*: Or if *Hurlo Thrumbo* employ his Eloquence in *weeping* one Day over his Crimes against the Ministry, and *abusing their Persons* on the next : Or if *Judas Iscariot*, who would sell the Blood of any Man for 30 *pence*, nay, *three Half-pence*, whose Reputation is so bad, that no Ministry ever thought it prudent or safe to employ him ; *all these are* PATRIOTS. And so is *J-n-th-n F—rw—d*, who opposed a late Scheme for *altering the Revenue*, because he thought it might lessen the *Transportation of Felons*, by lessening the Number of *Runners of Goods*. And so is CYDER who foisted an Article into an *A— of P—t*, by which a Person, who was never out of the Kingdom, is said at the Peril of his Life to have brought a Manufacture into it. And in Consideration of the Merit of the said Person, in having once had a Brother, who had the Merit of having brought the said Manufacture hither, Mr *Cyder* obtained a due Reward for that Person (see p. 719, 985) of which a *competent Share* was by *private Bargain* reserved to his own Use ; and this

this is PATRIOTISM; and these are the Men who, notoriously wanting that generous Passion, *Love of Country*, yet have the Assurance to pretend they abound with it more than all other Men.

Grubstreet Journal, June 21. No. 182.

A Banter on News-Papers.

*D*Emocritus observing the many trifling, false, and contradictory Articles published in the News-Papers, sends Mr. *Bavius* the following,

Domestick News. From *Leaden-hall-street* we hear, that the *East-India* Company design to purchase the *Monument*, to make a Present of it to the Great *Mogul* for a *Tobacco* Stopper. — From *Kensington*, that *Phillis*, the favourite Bitch of the Countess of *Stiff-rump*, was safely delivered of two very pretty male Puppies, to the unspeakable Joy of that noble Family. — From *Battersea*, that Mrs *Mambrino*, the good old Woman that cuts for the Simples, has had great Practice of late, particularly from many Proprietors of Yorkbuildings, and Adventurers in the Charitable Corporation; and some young Citizens who kept Country Houses. From *Yarmouth*, That no *Red-Herrings* have appeared in the Seas this *Mackarel* Season, which is thought to be very ominous. But this being Ship-News, we impatiently wait for more certain Information.

Diseases. Hot-cockles 2. Span-ku 5. Long-fives 13. Ganthaddock 15. Palsy in the Elbow 7. Crinkums 3. Hidebound 4. Pip 2. Don't-know-howishness 5. Stoppage in the Breath 415. In all 479.

Casualties. A fat Carman stepping over a Kennel, broke his Shoe-buckle; a Lady fell down and crack'd her Maidenhead; an old Lady caught a violent Cold by leaving off a Diamond Ring.

Imports. Some *French* Fashions of the newest Cut; several Bales of *Jesuitical* Equivocations, and mental Reservations; of Infidelity Ten Tons; but our Markets being over-stock'd, it bears a low Price. From several Countries, Singers, Dancers, Harlots and Harlequins.

Exports. Twelve dozen of Custards; 18 dozen of Gooseberry-Tarts; several queer Dukes, rum Dukes, sad Dogs, bitter Bitches, silly Curs, Coxcombs, and Convicts. From *Scotland*, That a scorbutick Distemper abounds there exceedingly; and that Scrubbing Posts are to be erected by Subscription at 4 Miles distance throughout the Kingdom.

Drogheda in *Ireland*, A poor Woman was lately delivered of a Male Child without a Shirt.

From our Sugar Colonies in *America*, that the last Year's Sugars are very sweet; that Rum is apt to make People drunk and quarelsome.

Foreign News. From *Amsterdam*, That the Dutch are great Lovers of Butter and F—ing. A Treaty of Marriage is on Foot between *Mynheer van Slabber-chops*, and a Daughter of the *Heer van Stink-a-pace*, a young Lady of great Accomplishments, and a vast Fortune. — From *Poland*, That he is likeliest to be elected King, who distributes his Money into the most proper Hands. — From *Constantinople*, That the Grand Signior has many Concubines, but mortally hates the Whore of *Babylon*. — From *Rome*, that the Pope has got the Gout in both his Feet; and is very willing to dispense with the Ceremony of Kissing his Toe. — From *France*, that the Bull *Unigenitus* is likely to be baited by the *Jansenists*, till he will not be able to roar any longer. — From *Spain*, That the common People are lazy, proud, and poor; the Women Priest-ridden, and the Inquisitors as great Rogues as ever.

The Craftsman, *June 23. N° 364.*

Of Garbling the Army.

I Think it my duty, says Mr *D'anvers*, to acknowledge the Honour Mr *Walsingham* has done me in his last inimitable Production; (see p. 301.) for tho' it's impossible not to feel the Poignancy of his Satire, yet he hath such a peculiar Delicacy in conveying it, that I cannot find in my Heart to be angry with him.

In a late Paper (see p. 248, F) I congratulated this *great Personage* on the ample Materials which this Season was likely to afford him, for exercising his Genius in courtly Invective. He hath seen my Prediction partly accomplish'd, by the Dismission of some other *noble Lords* from their Employments. Being sensible that Mr *W*'s Valour equals his Wit, I shall not presume to express either my *Grief* or *Astonishment* at the Dismission of a *noble Lord from his Post of Colonel of Horse*; but I hope Mr *W.* will allow me to be *concern'd* that his Lordship should have done, or not done, thought or not thought something or other, that hath brought his *Patron*'s Displeasure upon him. (See p. 195. F. 254. H.)

I cannot indeed be *astonish'd* at this

Event

Event, since on the very Day after which her late Majesty, in a Speech from the Throne, denounced DESTRUCTION against such as delighted in War, this noble Lord was remov'd from his *Regiment of Dragoons*. I presume therefore neither the World, nor his *Lordship* can be astonish'd, since, no Doubt, the same way of thinking and acting hath again put him in the same Situation.

Neither will I suffer myself to be griev'd, since *Grief* implies some Degree of Esteem for the *Person*, who is the Object of it. Far be it from me, as it is from Mr *W.* to have any Regard for a *Person*, who hath received the least Mark of *ministerial Displeasure!* It is but common Candour to suppose that some *secret Demerit*, hath not only justify'd, but call'd for his Disgrace.

My only Concern is for the *Persons in the Administration*, whom *this Event* may affect, and which their Enemies may use as a Handle of adding Numbers to those whom they have already deluded.

I am the more confirm'd in this apprehension by the Discourse of a *Male-content Politician*, which I heard t'other Day at a Coffee-house. *It is strange, said he, That a Man, who was turned out of one Regiment in the last Year of Q. Anne, should be now turned out of another by Persons protesting to act upon opposite Principles. If the Commissions of Officers are so precarious, how precarious must those Liberties be, which depend singly upon the Virtue of such Officers?* I have heard that the noble Lord *lately dismiss'd hath, for these 30 Years past, distinguished himself as* a good Soldier, *and* a good Citizen. *When such Men are removed, there must be some Designs laid, which render it unfit for Them to be trusted. However, it will cause a Reduction of the Army next Year; for the chief Argument for keeping it up was, That as it had never been garbled, it could not be intended for any ill purposes;* and a noble Duke, *whose just Influence in the House of Peers is well known, declared,* That if one *single Officer* was removed, on account of his *Civil Conduct*, he would from thence forwards be against the Army. — I should not lay much stress on these Arguments, if I did not find them confirm'd by Mr *Walsingam* himself in his Paper of *March* 9. 1731-2. *An Army, says he, must be first garbled and modelled, before it can be dangerous. Let the Orators against Armies shew an In-*

stance *in the present Reign, or Administration, where any Officer was discharged the Service, for being* disagreeable to the Ministry. *If such Schemes should ever be projected, do we imagine the* two Houses of Parliament can, or will overlook such Schemes *when discover'd? Will not such* Schemes be the strongest Arguments against these *Troops?* (See p. 645. Vol. II.) We must therefore conclude, that this *noble Lord* was not dismissed either for being *disagreeable to the Ministers*, or because He would not serve *Ministerial Projects. This Event* then must be attributed to different Motives, perhaps to his want of Courage, or Conduct in *Military Affairs*; and I wish Mr. *W.* would set us right in this Affair by those *Authentick Informations*, which he receives upon all such Occasions.

But if any *Minister* should hereafter attempt to *garble* and *model* the Army, by turning out Officers without any pretence of Misconduct in their *military Capacity*, I agree with Mr *W.* that *the two Houses of Parliament cannot overlook* such *Schemes; they will be the strongest Arguments against* a Standing Army.

Commissions in the Army are different from *Employments in the Royal Household*, upon which he descanted so amply in the Case of *another noble Peer* lately dismiss'd; (See p. 195 E.) for we have Mr *W's* Word that ours is a *National Army*, and kept up only by *Parliamentary Authority*, for the Protection of our *common Liberties*. If therefore the Legislature cannot defeat the unwarrantable Influence of *such a Minister* over the *Officers of the Army*, it will follow from his own Reasoning that *these Commands* are incompatible with Seats in Parliament, upon the Freedom of which the Preservation of our *Liberties* absolutely depends; nor can any *Gentleman of Honour* be fond of sitting in either House upon *such Terms*; especially if the *Minister* should extend his Power to the Protection of every *dirty Stock-jobber*, who may have served his purposes to the Ruin of Thousands. This would be degrading the *Gentlemen of the Army* into the lowest of all Instruments, the Tools of a *Corrupt and an All-screening Minister*.

When K. *William* was press'd by some of his *Ministers* to dismiss Sir *George Rooke* for opposing some of their Measures in Parliament, he gave them the following Answer —— *No*, said he, *If you have any Thing to allege against his Conduct in in the* Navy, *I may comply with your Request, but I will never discharge a brave experienced Officer, who hath always behaved himself well in my Service, for no other Reason than his Conduct in* Parliament.

Fog's Journal, June 23. N° 242.

AND be it farther Enacted, That after the said Day of no Tobacco shall be sold or exposed to Sale, unless when intended for immediate Consumption, in any Quantity, not exceeding Ounces; but in some Warehouse, enter'd as aforesaid to be approved of by the Commissioners for the Inland Duty hereby granted, for the keeping Tobacco after Importation, and Entry thereof at the Custom House, upon Pain of and the Value thereof, together with *And be it enacted,* That after the said Day of where any Tobacco shall be sold or deliver'd out to be manufactured from any enter'd Place in any Quantity above the Weight of the Officer, for the said Inland Duty, for the respective Divisions or Places, where the same shall be sold and deliver'd, shall be obliged upon Request of the Seller, thereof without Fee or Reward to give to the Buyer, or Manufacturer thereof, Certificates in Writing, expressing the Quantities delivered and the Names of the respective Buyers, Sellers, and Manufacturers, sign'd by the said Officer, and certifying that the Duty thereon charg'd by this Act hath been paid, or that the said Tobacco had been condemn'd and forfeited, or was Part of such Stock in Hand as aforesaid. Which Certificates shall be produced to be left with the Officer of the Division, into which the said Tobacco shall be carried, to satisfy that no Duties are to be answered for the same, and that the Seizing thereof may be prevented. *And be it farther Enacted,* That from, and after the said Day of no Tobacco exceeding the Quantity of be remov'd, from any Part of the Kingdom, without a Permit or Certificate sign'd by one or more Officers expressing the Name and Place of Abode of the Buyer, Seller, Proprietor, Manufacturer, or other Person, upon whose Account such Tobacco shall be removed, and the Quantity and Kind of the said Tobacco, and that his Majesty's Inland Duty charg'd thereon by this Act, was paid, or that the same had been condemned as forfeited, or was Part of such Stock in Hand as aforesaid, on Pain of which shall be found carrying from one Place to another without such Permit or Certificate, together with

And be it farther Enacted, That after the said Day of the Commissioners for managing the said Inland Duty are hereby impowered to provide and deliver to the respective Sellers of, and Dealers in such Tobacco as aforesaid, printed Books of Permits, with Counter parts, and proper Blanks for inserting the Quantity Name and Place of Abode of such Dealer in Tobacco, and of the Person to whom such Quantity is to be sent, and also the Day of the Month and Year; which Book, with Counter-parts, every such Dealer in Tobacco is hereby required to keep to be inspected by the Officer, for the said Inland Duty; and every such Dealer in Tobacco shall before sending out any Quantity of Tobacco not exceeding nor under * [first enter in the Permit and Counter-part the Day of the Month and Year, Names of the Place, and Person the said Tobacco is sent to, with the Quantity such Permit shall serve for; and if any Dealer &c. shall send out any Quantity of Tobacco not exceeding and under] without such Permit, or first having made all such Entries in the said Permit and Counter-part shall not produce to the Officer for the said Duty the Counter-part of such Permits, and likewise the Permits that shall not have been made use of, when he shall demand the same, he, she, or they shall for any the said Offences the Sum of *And be it farther Enacted,* That after the said Day of no Seller of, or Dealer in Tobacco shall send out with any one Permit more than one Quantity of Tobacco, on Pain of

And be it farther Enacted, That if upon Inspection, the Counter-part of any Permit that shall have been taken out of such Permit-Book for sending out any such Tobacco as aforesaid, and examining the Stock of any such Dealer in Tobacco, there shall not appear a suitable Decrease to answer the Quantity mentioned, the Surplus Quantity of Tobacco, over and above what ought to have been remaining in such Stock, be deemed, and taken to be brought in without any Permit, and shall be All Permits shall express a Time therein limited, during which, the same shall continue in Force, and within that Time shall be produced, and left with the Officer of the said Inland Duty of the Division where such Tobacco shall be carried to, to prevent the Seizing thereof. *And it is hereby farther Enacted,* That all Persons, who shall Deal in Tobacco after the said Day of shall keep an Account of all such small Quantities of Tobacco not exceeding the Weight of in one Parcel as he or they shall sell in each Day, and shall every Night enter into a Book an Account of the gross Quantity of the said Commodity sold and deliver'd in that Day in such small Quantities as aforesaid; and such Dealers in Tobacco shall also keep one other Book, wherein they shall severally enter every Parcel of Tobacco above the Weight of which he, she, or they shall sell or deliver in each Day, which said Book shall be deliver'd upon Demand to the respective Dealers in Tobacco, by the Commissioners &c. PROVIDED

---

* *What comes between these* [ ] *was left out in* Fog *thro' incorrectness.*

always, that no Dealer in Tobacco shall have more than one such Book of each Sort at the same Time, and when filled up, the same being return'd to the Officer from whom they were receiv'd, upon the Oath of such **A** Dealer as aforesaid, or Servant who kept the same, and made the Entries therein, of the Truth of such Entries, one more Book or Books shall thereupon be deliver'd to such Dealers, in the Room of such Books, so return'd, and the said Books so kept by such Dealers in Tobacco, shall be produced and laid before the Officers for the said Inland Duty **B** as often as they shall call for, or request the same, the better to enable them to keep Account of the Increase and Decrease of the Stock of such respective Dealers. *And it is hereby Provided and Enacted*, that if any such Dealer in Tobacco shall neglect or refuse to keep such Books, or to make such Entries therein, or to Permit the Officers of the said **C** Inland Duty to inspect them, or shall not return the said Books according to the Directions of the Act, or shall make any false Entry in such Book or Books, the Person or Persons offending therein, shall for every such Offence the Sum of *And be it Enacted*, That after the Day of

It shall be lawful to and for the Officers of the said Inland Duty by Day to enter into all and every Warehouse &c. made use of for keeping or manufacturing Tobacco by any Person or Persons, Bodies Politick or Corporate, and by weighing or otherwise to take an Account of the Quantity and Sorts of all Tobacco brought or remaining in such Place as aforesaid, in the weighing whereof **E** the Persons dealing in, or manufactureing Tobacco, or some Persons on their Behalf, shall be assisting to the said Officers, and shall keep sufficient Weights and Scales to be made use of for that Purpose. And if any such Person shall hinder or refuse the said Officer, to enter into such Warehouse, &c. or to take such Account as aforesaid, or neglect to **F** keep sufficient just Weights and Scales shall keep any false Weights or Scales, or shall neglect or refuse to assist the said Officers in weighing as aforesaid, or shall hinder or obstruct any of the said Officers in the Execution of the Powers and Authorities hereby given, the Persons offending therein, shall for every such Offence the Sum of **G**

PROVIDED that in Case any Officer for the said Inland Duty by this Act granted shall have Cause to suspect that any Tobacco is fraudulently conceal'd in any Place whatsoever either enter'd for keeping or manufacturing the same, or not enter'd, with Intent to defraud his Majesty of his Duty thereon. then, if such Place shall be within the Cities of *London* or *Westminster*, or the Weekly Bills **H** of Mortality, upon Affidavit made by such Officer before the Commissioners for the said Inland Duty hereby granted, or any of them; or in Case the same shall be in any other Part of *Great Britian*, upon Affidavit

made by such Officer, or before more Justices of the Peace of the County, or Division where such Officer shall suspect the same to be conceal'd, setting forth the Ground of Suspicion, it shall and may be lawful for the said Commissioners or Justices of the Peace respectively before whom such Affidavit shall be made, if they shall judge it reasonable, by special Warrant under their respective Hands and Seals, to authorize such Officer by Day; but if by Night, then, in Presence of a Constable, to enter such Place where he shall so suspect any Tobacco to be fraudulently conceal'd, and to all Tobacco there found so fraudulently conceal'd together with ; and if any Person whatsoever should obstruct any Officer from entering such suspected Place or in the Tobacco which shall be therein found fraudulently conceal'd, the Persons offending therein for every such Offence the Sum of *And be it Enacted* that if after the said Day of any Person shall assault, resist, molest, or hinder any Officer of the Customs, or of the Inland Duty by this Act granted, in the due seizing or securing of any Tobacco which may be seized by Virtue of this or any other Act now in Force, or hereafter to be made, or shall by Force rescue any such Tobacco after the same have been seized or shall attempt or endeavour so to do, or after such Seizure shall stave, destroy or damage any Vessel or Package wherein the same shall be contained, all Parties offending shall for every such Offence the Sum of *And it is hereby farther Enacted* that all as well specifick as pecuniary relating to the Inland Duty by this Act imposed, or to any Seizures made in Pursuance of this Act, shall be sued for, levied and recovered, or mitigated by such Ways, Means and Methods as any Fine Penaly and Forfeiture is or may be recovered or mitigated by any Law or Laws relating to his Majesty's Revenue of Excise, or any of them, *subject to the Alterations herein after mentioned*, or by Action of Debt, Bill, Plaint or Information in any of his Majesty's Courts of Record at *Westminster*, or the Court of Exchequer for *Scotland*; and that of every such shall be to his Majesty, his Heirs and Successors, to be applied to such Uses as are herein after mention'd, and the other to him or them who shall seize, inform or sue for the same. PROVIDED always, that such Persons as for the Time being shall in Pursuance of this Act be appointed Commissioners for the said Inland Duty on Tobacco, or of them, and also

Justices of the Peace within their respective Districts shall have and exercise the same or like Jurisdiction, Power and Authority, and may judge, determine, mitigate or order in all Cases and Matters relating to the said Inland Duty upon Tobacco, as the Commissioners of Excise upon Beer &c. or two Justices of the Peace, may exercise, adjudge, deter-termine, mitigate or order, in like Cases, in relation to the said Duties of Excise, and that the Judgment which shall be given in Pursuance of this Act by the said Commissioners and Justices of Peace respectively, shall be and are hereby declared to be subject only to such Appeal as is herein after-mentioned.

As I want Room, says Fog, I shall omit that Clause relating to three Farthings in the Pound, which was to be secured to the King during his Life, and upon which, no Drawback is allowed upon Exportation; but I wou'd recommend it to be read by Mr *Osborne* who asserts so often, that the King was to be no Gainer by this Scheme; I shall also omit that Clause, in which there was a Penalty upon all Dealers, who do not enter at the Excise Office all Warehouses, &c. made use of for keeping or manufacturing Tobacco.

Fog omits the Clause whereby the imposing an Oath to make the Dealers in Coffee Tea and Chocolate accuse themselves or forfeit 20 l. *was to be repealed; also the Clause which appointed three Judges in Westminster-Hall, or the Judges of Assize, to hear and determine, in a summary Way, all Appeals from the Commissioners of Excise. (See p.* 133 B)

Universal Spectator, June 23. No. 246.
Old Age Whimsical.

Mr STONECASTLE,

I Am a dying, or rather a dead Man, for I have been deluded to make my last Will and Testament, tho' I am not quite fourscore. As soon as, on the Persuasion of the young Rascal my Son, I began the Prologue, *In the Name of*, &c. I immediately felt a strange Palpitation at my Heart. This dissipated, as I was disposing of my Body and Soul; but when I came to dispose of my Goods and Chattels, my Distemper return'd, a Palsy in my Tongue hinder'd my Speech, yet with infinite Labour I pronounc'd, *I do — constitute — my — Son to be my Sole —* Here I made a full Pause, nor could I for a Quarter of an Hour, utter — Heir and Executor. That damn'd Article over, I went on tolerably to bequeath Lady Gay love, my dear loving Consort, those necessary Tracts I have by me, call'd Crumbs of Comfort, the Government of the Tongue, and a Bible, well knowing from her Court Breeding her Desire of Novelty, and being assur'd nothing can be more new to a modern polite Lady.

But how inexpressible are the Agonies I went thro', before I could resolve to follow the Example of those frugal Men who squander some Thousands away in building Hospitals: Charity covers a Multitude of Faults, therefore I subscrib'd to Hospitals 1000 l. With some Reluctance

I bequeath'd 1 s. to my Nephew Harry Truewit of the Middle-Temple, to purchase The Clerk's Companion, or Secretary's Guide; recommending to him the serious Perusal of it instead of Plays, Poems, &c. for the Study of that Book alone gain'd me two Plumbs. Then with as much Reluctance as Imprudence, I left my Doctor a Diamond Ring. All my strong convulsive Fits return'd in appointing the Sum of 500 l. to Betty my Cook-maid; but I recover'd a little when I consider'd, that was the only Legacy for which I receiv'd any Favours in my Life time. After some Pangs at other Legacies, I sign'd, seal'd, and saw it witnessed. —— Scarce was the Ink dry, and wax cold, but my Son, Wife, Doctor and Legatees were reckoning how long I could last. —— Thus you see the Inconveniencies that they, who love their worldly Goods, run into by making Last Wills and Testaments. I recommend it therefore to every wealthy Brother, not to kill himself before his allotted Time, but unconcern'd for Sons, Wives, Brothers and Friends, to die intestate, and generously leave that Wealth they have, by Right or Wrong obtain'd, to common Lawyers, and Civilians, to be divided among them all, as the disputing Heirs at Law may judge most proper.
Thrifty Gripe.

Weekly Miscellany, June 23. No. 28.
A Meditation in Solitude.

Mr HOOKER,   Cl—d, Yorkshire.

THE Season of the Year tempting most People of Condition into the Country, I conceived the following Paper, the Production of a young Author, would be no disagreeable Entertainment.
Yours, &c.

MAN, during his whole Pilgrimage thro' Life, should never lose Sight of that fix'd Point, which is the ultimate End of his Being; he should ever remember he is dust, and that his Kindred with the Earth is enobled by that Breath of Life within him, which allies him to Deity, and bids him think on Mortality. A due Reflection upon his human Part should qualify his Vanity; and the Contemplation of his Spiritual Nature should rectify his Ideas with Regard to the Objects of Sense, and lift up his Soul to Heaven, and thus prepare him for the Society of Beings of a superior Order.

I am now amusing myself in these Walks of Solitude, where methinks I am thus whisper'd by one of my invisible

ble Attendants. " Mortal, confider thou muft e'er long be one of us, and then in what Light wilt thou regard the Actions of thy prefent Life? The Confcioufnefs alone of a well-acted part will fecure that uninterrupted Happinefs which we enjoy, when thou *entereft into the Houfe* A *of thy Eternity.*" This throws me upon Meditating what a fmall Part of my real felf this Body is, and how much extravagance and idle Solicitude is employ'd in providing for it. For, what is this Carcafe but a living Sepulchre? The continual Fluxion of its conftituent parts evinces how little of it I can call myfelf, and B how little even of that Little will be remaining when mingled with its kindred Duft. What then becomes of all its Faculties and Senfations? Shall my Duft, paft into a Thoufand different Shapes and Pofitions, eaten of Worms, fhot up into Vegetables, tranfmigrated by an endlefs Diverfity of Changes, blown about by the C Winds, diffipated by the Waters —— fhall thefe fcatter'd Fragments be ftill confcious of any thing; or re-unite to a thinking Subftance? This is the Province of Omnipotence.

But I have a Soul, a Reflective part, the Spring of Life and Action. Here is D my real felf, and the only part that will furvive all Changes. This Body is no more effential to the Well-being or Perceptions of the Soul, than a material Body occafionally affumed, is to an Angel. But as the Organs of this Body are the prefent E Inlet of Senfe, and the Inftruments of Knowledge and Conception, it imports me to have a conftant Regard to the State of Separation, when the Soul fhall draw its Ideas from the Fountain of Light, without the Interpofition of any grofs Medium. I fhould therefore betimes difengage my Thoughts and Affections from F the Earth and Senfe, and now and then ftrike into the Paths of more abftracted Thinking. In order to this, the Mind muft be furnifhed with fpeculative Truths, and Meditations of a more exalted Turn than fuch as ordinarily refult from the Matter of human Commerce, or the Objects about us; elfe, how unprovided fhall I G come into that World of Spirits, where my Entertainment and Commerce muft be altogether Spiritual, and for which I fhall have no Tafte without a preparatory Exercife! What a difmal Emptinefs muft the Soul find in itfelf, which in this H Life has been entertain'd with nothing but bodily Pleafure! What a horrible State of Diftraction and Defpair muft we

conceive it, to be perpetually catching at what will for ever fly from us! Deprived of the very Support of Being, the chearing Beams of divine Influence, and finking in an eternal Void and Defolation of all Things! Here is Hell, *the never-dying Worm, the unquenchable Fire* of a tortur'd Confcience! Upon this I confider the Words of Mr *Cowley*, but in an improved Senfe,

What fhall I do to be forever known,
And make the World to come my own?

An inactive Contemplation will not anfwer this End; but I am to exert fuch Talents as God has blefs'd me with, to his Service, and to the Benefit of Mankind. Whether this may fet me in any more honourable Point of View, either in thefe lower Regions, or after my Removal, concerns me not; but this I may promife myfelf, that it will procure me a more favourable Reception among the Company of exalted Spirits, where the Exercife and Degrees of our Virtues here will determine our Rank and Eminence. The very Reflection gives me a Foretafte of—Something the Soul opens and grafps at, fomething the Imagination is even feized of, but faints in the Retention, and which I can even at this Diftance perceive and partly enjoy.

Mr *Hooker* here fubjoins the following beautiful Lines from Mr *Norris*'s Poem call'd the *Profpect*, as very appofite.

What a ftrange Moment will *that* be,
My Soul, how full of Curiofity,
When wing'd and ready forth'eternal Flight,
On th'utmoft Edges of thy tottering Clay.
Hovering and wifhing longer Stay, [Sight!
Thou fhalt advance, and have Eternity in
When juft about to try that unknown Sea,
What a ftrange *Moment* will *that* be!
But yet how much more ftrange *that* State
When, loofen'd from th' Embrace of this clofe
Mate,
Thou fhalt at once be *plung'd* in Liberty,
And move as fwift and active as a Ray
Shot from the lucid *Spring* of Day!
Thou who juft now waft clogg'd with dull
Mortality,
How wilt thou bear the mighty Change, how
Whether thou'rt then the *fame* or no! [know
Then to ftrange Manfions of the Air,
And ftranger Company, muft thou repair!
What a new Scene of Things will then appear!
This World thou by *Degrees* waft taught to
Which leffen'd thy Surprize below, [know,
But Knowledge *all at once* will *overflow* thee
there;
That World as the firft Man did *this*, thou'lt
Ripe-grown in full Maturity. [fee,

STATE *of the* NATIONAL DEBT *Provided, or Unprovided for, by* PARLIAMENT, *as it stood,* Dec. 31. 1731. *and* Dec. 31. 1732. *Together with the Produce of the* SINKING FUND, *and to what* DEBTS *contracted before* Dec. 25. 1732. *it has been apply'd.*

	Amount on Dec. 31. 1731.				Between Dec. 31. 1731, and Dec. 31. 1732.					Amount on Dec. 31. 1732.			
EXCHEQUER.					Increase		Paid off						
	l.	*s.*	*d.*	*q*	*l.*	*l.*	*s.*	*d.*		*l.*	*s.*	*d.*	*q*
Annuities for long terms, being the Remainder of the Original Sum contributed and unsubscribed to the S. S. Com.	1837033	9								1,837,033	9		
itto for Lives, with Benefit of Survivourship, being the original Sum contributed.	108100									108,100			
Ditto on two or three Lives being the Sum remaining after deducting what is fallen in by Deaths.	134282	14	8	3		2,783	6	8		131,499	8		3
Ditto at 9l. per Cent. per Ann.	161108	6	1							161,108	6	8	
Ditto on Lottery, Anno 1710.	109290									109,290			
Ditto on the Plate-Act 6 Georgij I.	312000									312,000			
Ditto on the Nevis and St Christopher's Debentures, at 3l. per Cent.	37821	5	1	1						37,821	5	1	1
Exchequer Bills on the Victuallers Act, Anno 1726.	481400									481,400			
Ditto made out for Interest on old Bills exchanged.	2200									2,200			
Annuities at 3l. 10s. per Cent. per Ann. for the Year 1731.	400000									400,000			
Duties on Salt revived, Anno 1732.					500,000	40,000				460,000			
EAST-INDIA Company.													
By two Acts of Parliament 9 W. Regis, and by two others 6 & 10 Annæ.	3200000									3,200,000			
Bank of ENGLAND.													
On their original Fund, at 6 per C.	1600000									1,600,000			
For cancelling Exchequer Bills 3 Georgij primi Regis.	1500000									1,500,000			
Purchased of the S. Sea Company.	4000000									4,000,000			
Annuities at 4l. per Cent. charged on the Duty on Coals since Lady-Day, 1719.	1750000									1,750,000			
Ditto charged on the Surplus of the Funds for Lottery 1714.	1250000									1,250,000			
Ditto for Lottery 1731.	800000									800,000			
SOUTH-SEA Company.													
On their Cap. Stock and Annu. per Act 9 Georgij primi Regis.	31302203	5	6	2		1,000,000				30,302,203	5	6	2
	48985438	12	9	2	500,000	1,042,783	6	8		48,442,655	6	1	2

EXCHEQUER Dr.	*l.*	*s.*	*d.*	*q*	Per Contra. Cr.	*l.*	*s.*	*d.*
To Cash of the Sinking Fund, on Dec. 31, 1731.	364799	16		1	BY Money issued towards discharging the National Debt, between Decem. 31. 1731. and Dec. 31. 1732.			
To the produce of the Sinking Fund, between Dec. 31. 1731,								
On the	632876	16		2				
On the	315731		1		By paid the S. Sea Company.	1000000		
On the S. Sea Company Fund	148725	4	10	3				
Tax on Papists	196	19	2	2	Ballance, Dec. 31. 1731.	462329	16	3
	1462329	16		3		1462329	16	3

Q q

The Daily Courant. No. 22.

To——Efq; in *Somerfetfhire*.

SIR,

YOU tell me that the great Motive to your *Converfion* from the Sentiments of the *Male-contents*, was their A Violence againft the *Minifter*, and their repeated *Declarations*, that they would never fuffer either *King* or *Kingdom* to have any Quiet till they had remov'd him. Horrid Refolution! Men can no longer be in Doubt of what thefe People aim at, when they behold them threaming thofe B in the *Adminiftration*, exciting *Difcontents* thro' the *Nation*, at the fame Time that they thwart his Majefty's Meafures, and openly (as in laft *Saturday's Craftfman*) traduce both HIM and his ROYAL CONSORT. See p. 307.

In the Clofe of laft *Seffions of Parliament* an *Enquiry* was fet on Foot, not to any purpofe, but a *Report* was made that the *Mini-* C *fter* by his *Intereft* would prevent the coming at proper *Perfons* to be examined; far from impeding the *Enquiry*, he did all he could to forward it. After much Noife the *Thing* dropt; tho' fome, with fhamelefs Confidence, have fince *protefted*, they were hinder'd from diving to the *Bottom*, (See p. 295.) in flat Contradiction to the Knowledge of *All* who attended to the *Affair*. It is wonderful to hear Men on this Occafion revive their old Phrafe of *Skreening*; which if applicable any where, it muft be to a *Committee* of their own, notorious for having fo confounded the *Evidence*, in relation to the *Enquiry* before them, E as to render it impoffible to diftinguifh thofe who were in the *Secret* of the *Fraud*; whereby they have defeated the *Publick Juftice*, as they oppofed *Publick Charity*. Had the *Miniftry* thus behaved, how had their *Speakers* bellow'd, and their *Authors* triumph'd? But as it is, Mr——is *afhamed*, and Mr *D'anvers* F is *filent*.

Another Inftance of their want of *fhame* and *Loyalty* is, their careffing any body who will but *rail at*, and libel the *Adminiftration*. A few Weeks ago they pick'd up a patchwork Pamplet of a pragmatical *P----f-----n*, after it had been refufed by the Bookfellers, and its Author had attempted by Letters to G extract Money for delivering it up, and, after new vamping it, thruft it into the World, with the Sanction of Friend *Franklin's* Name, the fure Report of *Scandal*. Little Credit, however, has their Acquifition gained them. The Revd *Scribbler* is fit only to officiate (as he commonly does) as the *Marker* of a *Billiard-Table* in *Town*, and a Sot in a *North Country* H Ale-houfe with a *Tapfter* in the *Country*. The Publick will fcarce want Diverfion, fince they have thus recruited their Band of *Sedi-*

tion Spreaders, and have got *two* or *three* witty Lords, who have nothing now to do ——— but write.

You will, I dare fay, do all in your Power to ftop the Current of Difaffection in your part of the Country; and therefore I fhall tranfmit you fuch Helps as I can. At prefent, I can only inform you, that a grand *Piece* is on the *Tapes* at D---wl---y, in which the Difcontented, and the *Difcarded*, the old *Snarlers* at the *Minifter*, and new *Band* of detected *Caballers*, are all to have their fhares; and if it produce nothing, why then ——— are all miftaken, and muft try what Spirit they can infufe at Country Meetings, brew Sedition at *Horfe-Races*, and perhaps practife again upon the *Diffenters*. Yours R. E.

London Journal. June 23.

IN this Paper *Osborne* defends the Miniftry, and gives them the Title of *Patriots* for *keeping Peace abroad*, and *preferving the Conftitution at Home*. As to the Cry raifed by their Oppofers, of *Standing Armies, Places and Penfions, Bribery and Corruption*, he appeals to *any* Man of Senfe, whether, if the oppofing Gentlemen were in Power, we fhould not have as large an Army, and as many Places and Penfions? From whence he argues againft their pretended *Patriotifm*, after the fame manner we have before fhewn in feveral Places, and therefore need not repeat it.

Grubftreet Journal. June 28. No. 183.

Mr BAVIUS,

THE late Accounts of the Progrefs and Succefs of Mr *Taylour* the Oculift, brought to my Mind a Story of *Sefoftris*, a King of *Egypt*, who being many Years Blind, was reftor'd to Sight, by looking (as the Author has it) at a Woman who never knew any Man befides her Husband. This induced me to believe the Doctor Married, and that many of his famous Cures were due to the conjugal Fidelity of his Wife. With thefe Thoughts I clofed my Eyes to Sleep, and fell into a Dream.

I had (methought) been the *Sefoftris* of *Great-Britain*, and was inconfolable for the Lofs of a Senfe which the Beauty of my fair Countrywomen gave me fo many Opportunities of gratifying; but was comforted by reflecting on their Virtue which gave me fo eafy a Remedy.

Big with this Hope I fent for the pious *Sophrona*; but fhe looked on my Blindnefs as a Judgment from above. Next I fent for *Saphira*, noted for exact Regularity in domeftick Life; but fhe was fo fatigu'd

by

by being at a Mafquerade, that fhe could not poffibly get abroad. Many fuch little Excufes I had from others. *Delia*, who fince her Husband's Death, had wholly devoted herfelf to Mourning and Solitude, might, doubtlefs ihave done the Bufinefs, if fhe could have been feen; but the Meffenger had no fooner told his Errand but her Footman, a young handfome Fellow, pertly anfwer'd, his Lady was not to be fpoken to.

Thus difappointed, I fummon'd my Council, and defir'd their Advice, they offer'd to fend for their feveral Ladies; I thank'd them, but remembring that they all ufed Spectacles, I chofe rather to truft to the Daughter of one of them, who being but 7 Years old was betrothed to her Father's Ward. To this it was objected, that not being of Age to confummate, this inchoate Marriage did not entitle her to the Privilege of a Matron.

All this while I had forgotten my own Wife, who then enter'd the Room, and, to my unfpeakable Joy, immediately open'd my Eyes; which fhe did by the loud thundering Rap of her Chairman at the Street Door, when I heard the Watch cry paft 3 o'Clock and a Moon light Morning. OCULATUS HENROOST.

The Free-Briton, June 28. Nº. 188.

Corruption fometimes neceffary.

MR Walfingham *inferts a Difcourfe to demonftrate the Neceffity of Corruption, fometimes, in Adminiftring the Publick; acknowledging however, that it entails very bad Effects on Society.*

When *Cefar* was contriving the Deftruction of the Commonwealth, the beft Men in *Rome* thought no Means but Corruption could fave it; even *Cato* approved the Defign, and contributed to the Sum raifed by the Nobility to carry the Election of *Bibulus*. And *this* good Patriots muft do; for, that which promotes the common Happinefs cannot be ill in itfelf, and is only bad when ill applied, and then it's neceffary to defeat it, by over-bidding, and out-buying it. (See Vol. I. p. 346, &c.)

It is to be lamented, fays he, that Mankind are corrupt in themfelves, wherefore it is no Crime but a meritorious Action to get them off from their Favourite Follies, and gain them by Perfuafion, humouring, or even buying them.

The Craftfman, June. 30 Nº 634.

THE *Projector* we hear ftill continues, fays D'anvers, to difperfe Pamphlets

about the Country; particularly one, intitled *a Letter from a Member of Parliament for a Borough in the Weft to a noble Lord* &c. (See p. 287 F.) but it is fo wretched a Performance that we may fafely truft it among our Countrymen; inftead of any particular Animadverfions upon it, I fhall prefent the Reader with fome Extracts from another little Treatife lately publifhed on the other Side of the Queftion, intitled *a Letter from a Member of Parliament to his Friend in the Country* &c.

The Author firft confiders the mutual Dependency between *Kings* and *Parliaments*, the Neceffity they lie under of each other, and the Convenience each is, *to the other*; then fhews how careful our Anceftors were in all their Acts to bind up the Prerogative from raifing Money without Confent of Parliament; and that the granting a Sum annually for ever would render Parliaments ufelefs. *Pafquerus*, Advocate General in the K. of *France*'s Chamber of Accounts, tells us, that *Charles* V. *procur'd, by Confent of the three Eftates thefe Aids for Defence of the Realm, to be granted for three or four Years together; that this Confent of the People at firft was That, which gave Occafion to the King to take it without Confent*; from whence he concludes *that* France *muft not eafily admit, tho' once, what they would not agree to for ever?* This would have been our Cafe had we been infatuated enough to have changed an *annual Tax* into *perpetual-Excife*. But we muft not imagine they would have been contented only with laying their Hands on *Tobacco* and *Wine*; no, the fame plaufible Pretence of *Frauds* might with equal Juftice, have been extended to other cuftomable Commodities.

He concludes, That if it fhall appear that this *Scheme* would have deftroy'd the very *Being* of *Parliaments*, it muft be granted that the Day it met with its Doom fhould be enter'd as a *Red-letter Day* in future Calendars, and celebrated as long as a *former Deliverance*, which tho' more bloody in its Execution, yet, in its Confequences, would not have been fo fatal to the Conftitution; and that as long as the 5th of *Nov.* is commemorated, the 11th of *April* will not be forgotten.

Fog's Journal, June 30 Nº. 243.

IN this Paper *Fog* difcourfes on that old Trick of Minifters of State to fomeṇt Divifions

Divisions among the People when Opreſſions were intended, and gives an Inſtance from the Hiſtory of *Venice*. But why ſuch Methods ſhould be taken in this Country, and at this Time, cannot be eaſily accounted for, yet ſays he, we ſeePamphlets diſperſed all over the Country, to ſtir up Hatred and Animoſity betwixt the landed and trading Intereſts of this Kingdom.

It happens fortunately for the Nation, that this Deſign ſhould come from one whoſe bad Intentions to the Publick are already ſo well known, that there can be no great Danger of his Succeſs; and indeed, both he and his Mercenaries begin to be conſcious of it themſelves; for the Writer of *the Letter to the Free-holder* is forced, in order to gain a little Credit, to diſclaim all Acquaintance with him, however his many falſe Aſſertions ſhow whoſe Troop he rides in. This Pamphlet certainly contains a Remedy for the Poyſon it carries, and will be ſo far from ſetting the People together by the Ears, that it muſt have a contrary effect; and ſhews the Neceſſity of the People's continuing their Unanimity, ſince the Exciſe Scheme is ſtill juſtify'd, ſo that the Projector wants but an Opportunity to bridle us with it.

Thus he has declared himſelf an Enemy to Trade, wherefore it is hop'd it will thrive the better, ſince it had declin'd ſo much while he pretended to be a Friend to it. And now, forſooth, the Merchants are all Cheats——no, no; had they been ſo, they would have come to a better Underſtanding with him; who has ſtood the Friend and Champion of ALL Gentlemen of that Character, without excepting even *Ch—rs, S-tt-n* and *B----nd.* That he bears no good Will to the Freeholders is certain becauſe they bear none to him, having with the greateſt Unanimity and Spirit, ſuccour'd the Trading Intereſt in the Day of its Danger. On Examination we ſhall find that the Glorious 205 poſſeſs at leaſt four times as much of the Lands of *England* as thoſe who voted for the Bill; however, as Regiments, Salaries and P——s may paſs forFreeholds, they muſt make a conſiderable Figure in the Freeholders Liſt.

It happens that a certain Gentleman has blunder'd himſelf into ſo dangerous a Situation, that down he tumbles 10,000 Fathom, unleſs the good People of *England* will be ſo kind to quarrel amongſt themſelves about ſome Trifle or other. —— There is no raiſing Diviſions now about Religious Ceremonies; and thoſe bewitching Words of *Whig* and *Tory,* have loſt their Magick; what remains to be done

for an unfortunate poor Devil, whoſe Safety depends upon our Confuſion, but to make a Quarrel betwixt the Freeholders and Traders of *Great-Britain,* to keep his Head on his Shoulders? It is for that, and to keep themſelves in for Life, that Mr *W. T.* or Sir *W. T.* writes lying Letters into *Devonſhire,* and the ingenious *J—n D—nd* into *Scotland,* worthy of being made the Hero of theSecondpart of the*State-Dunces.*

Extract of a Letter from the Courant, *April 19, preſented by the Grand Jury of Briſtol, as a ſcandalous Libel.* See p. 207.

Briſtol, April 14.

THE News of the Fall of the Exciſe-Bill, being brought us by Sir *A— E-*'s Meſſenger, our M——r ſent to all our Church-wardens to have their Bells tuned; all the Schoolmaſters in Town were order'd to keep Holiday; the Boys were employ'd in making Squibs, and the M——r erecting a Battery behind his Houſe, on which he planted ſeven great Guns, to the great Annoyance of the ſmall Beer in the Square. Faggots and Tar-barrels were erected into monſtrous Bonfire-Piles, and ſome Ships ſhewed their dirty Colours; few of the Fires were without ſome Inſtruments of Execution. In the Council, I am told, a new ſet of Healths was drank. This I think was the moſt ſcandalous Affair I ever ſaw; and it is ſomething extraordinary that the Supreme Civil Magiſtrate of a C—n, whoſe Duty and Office it is to preſerve the Peace, and preventTumults, ſhould be the firſt principal Promoter of them.

The Reſpective LISTS, *containing the Names of 21 Members each, which were balloted for April 24. to be a Committee to enquire into the Frauds of the* CUSTOMS, *with the Number of Votes to each Name.*

Sir John Cope	294	Mr Walter Plumer	207
Mr Clutterbuck	293	Sir John Barnard	206
Sir William Clayton	292	Mr Gybbon	208
Mr Fox	292	Mr Palmer	206
Mr Henry Pelham	291	Mr Sandys	206
Mr Edgcombe	291	Lord Limerick	205
Sir Philip York	290	Lord Morpeth	204
Sir John Heathcoate	290	Mr Alderman Perry	204
Mr Clayton	289	Mr Wm Pulteney	204
Mr Anth. Lowther	289	Mr H. Furneſe	203
Sir George Oxenden	289	Sir Edward Stanley	202
Mr Charles Talbot	289	Mr Tho. Wyndham	202
General Wade	288	Sir Francis Child	201
Hon. Geo. Doddington	288	Mr Robert Dundaſs	220
Mr Duncan Forbes	288	Sir Wm Wyndham	200
Sir Tho. Frankland	288	Mr Geo. Compton	199
Mr Winnington	288	Mr Edmond Waller	197
Mr Campbell of Pembroke Shire	288	Mr Edward Harley	196
Lord Hervey	287	Mr William Noel	196
Mr Horace Walpole	285	Sir John Cotten	194
Sir William Yonge	284	Sir Thomas Sanderſwright	191

N. B. We defer the *London Journal,* and *Weekly Miſcellany* to our next.

Prize VERSES, No. I. *(See p. 208.)*
On the FIVE BUSTOS in the QUEEN's GROTTO.

OFT has the muse her heav'nly skill pro-
    phan'd,
And wealth, or power, her venal voice obtain'd:
Tyrants, and ravagers of human race,
Her partial aid has rais'd to honour's place.
Strange ! that the softer notes of sacred verse, 5
Shou'd the dire wastes of horrid wars rehearse,
Or take from glitt'ring grandeur trifling themes,
Or wild ambition, and its frantick dreams,
Yet pay to heav'n-born science mean regard,
And leave fair *virtue to her own reward.* 10
O ! let such Obloquy no longer stain
BRITANNIA's sons, or blast the Muse's strain:
A theme presents will honour all their lays,
BRITANNIA's queen deserves their utmost praise:
To Æras yet unknown her fame shall last, 15
And triumph, when the bounds of time are past.
Behold her venerable cell!——she builds,
No pillar hung with spoils of martial fields,
The clam'rous drum, the swords destructive
    gleam,
Or tubes, whose wombs with dreadful thunders
    teem : 20
More noble trophies CAROLINE delight,
Which the wrapt mind to studious thoughts invite.
Amid surrounding glooms her Grot she founds,
Deep silence reigns thro' all the solemn bounds:
Not more sequester'd was the sacred shade, 25
Where NUMA nightly to ÆGERIA pray'd;
Nor more divine that nymph of heav'nly race,
Than the great guests that fill this hallow'd place.
With conscious awe the trembling muse essays,
Too weak her voice to sound their matchless
    praise. 30
    BOYLE *the benighted paths of science clears,*
Like Phœbus who to chase the mists appears.
The human mind LOCKE *intimately knew,*
And in eternal lines her pourtrait drew.
Thy pages, WOLLASTON, *distinctly show* 35
The truths and duties which from nature flow:
Thine, CLARK, *display religion's milder charms,*
Which the pleas'd soul to heav'nly rapture warms.
NEWTON *the volume of the skie unseals,*
And all th' amazing miracle reveals; 40
That skie, illustrious sages, must decay,
And all the works of nature shrink away,
But your establish'd fame shall still endure,
Amid the wrecks of failing worlds secure.
    Thou, too, protectress of the good and wise,
At whose command these awfull Bustos rise,
Thro' all succeeding ages shalt receive,
The noblest praise the voice of fame can give:
For thee *Philosophy* extends her views,
For thee each *Poet* cultivates his muse, 50
For thee *Religion* plumes her heav'nly wings,
And *Truth* from her celestial fountain springs.
If in all future annals *Britain* stands
Th' amaze and envy of surrounding lands,
If there is fixt the seat of every muse, 55
If every science there her dwelling choose,
If every virtue, every social grace,
Distinguish blest BRITANNIA's happy race:
Thy bright example shall be own'd the cause,
And the whole world unite in thy applause. 60

PRIZE VERSES, No. II.
ODE *on the* BUST *of the Hon.* ROBERT
BOYLE, *Esq; in her* MAJESTY's *Grotto.*

NATURE, O BOYLE ! tho' hid in night,
    Her laws, to THEE, were clear as light,
Such worth again where shall we meet?
Or where a queen so good, so great?
    In vain we wish, in vain we burn;
Seasons in these will ne'er return,
On earth another BOYLE can't shine,
Nor such a queen as CAROLINE.
    While then this GROTTO thus is grac'd,
So long shall BRITISH wonders last.
Merit supported by the throne
Shall give to fame, a lasting STONE.

CHARACTERS from the STATE-DUNCES;
    A POEM, inscrib'd to Mr POPE.

LET dull Parnassian *sons of rhime, no more*
    Provoke thy satire, and employ thy power ;
New objects rise to share an equal fate,
The big, rich, mighty, Dunces of the State,
Shall Ralph, Cooke, Welstead, *then engross thy rage,*
While courts offend a H——, Y——, *or* G——:
Dulness no more roosts only near the sky,
But Senates, Drawing-rooms, with garrets vye ;
Plump p—rs, and beardless bards, alike are dull,
St James's and Rag-Fair, club fool for fool.——
    Hence the long train of never-ending jars
Of warful peaces, and of peaceful wars,
Each mystic treaty of the mighty store,
Which to explain, demands ten treaties move:
Hence scarecrow navies, floating raree-shows,
And hence Iberia's *Pride and* Britain's *woes.*——
——*Here, proxy.pamphlets, spun from Prelates brains;*
There, the smooth jingle of Cook's *lighter strains ;*
Here Walsingham's *soft lulling Opiates spread ;*
There glowny Osborn's *quintessence of lead:*
With these the statesman strove to ease his care,——
While Dulness rules, say, shall her sons despair?
O'er all she spreads her universal sway,
K—gs, Pr—tes, P—rs, *and rulers all obey;*——
Full open mouth'd N——e *there behold,*
Aping a Tully, *swell into a scold,*
Grievous to mortal ears;——*as at the place*
Where loud-tongu'd virgins vend the scaly race.
——*See* H——n *secure in silence sit,*
No empty words betray his want of wit
If sense in hiding folly is express'd,
O H——n! *thy wisdom stands confess'd.*
To Dulness sacred curse for ever true,
Thy darling Caledonian, *goddess, view.*
Th' pride and glory of thy Scotia's *plains,*
And faithful leader of her venal swains,
Loaded is not 'tis, beneath a servile weight,
The dull laborious packhorse of the state.——
Here E——ex, A——m—le *(for senates sit)*
And W——by *the wise in council sit,*
Here lordly G——n, G——m, *ever dull,*
By Birth a senator, by fate a f——l.
    Lo! to yon bench now, goddess, turn thine eyes,
And view thy sons in solemn dulness rise,
All dozing, wrinkled, grave, and gloomy, see
Each form confess thy dull Divinity;
True to thy cause, behold each trenchar'd sage
Increas'd in folly as advanc'd in age :

    R r   Her

Here Ch—r learn'd in mystic prophecy,
Confuting Collins, makes each prophet lie:
Poor Woolston, by thy Smallbrook there assail'd,
Goals sure convinc'd him, tho' the Prelate fail'd.
 But chief Pastorius, ever grave and dull,
Devoid of sense, of zeal divinely full,
Retails his squibs of Science o'er the town,
While Charges, Pastorals, thro' each street resound,
These teach a heav'nly Jesus to obey,
While those maintain an earthly Appius sway.—
 Who would not trim, speak, vote, or conscience pawn,
To lord it o'er a see, and swell in lawn?
If arts like these, O S——k, Honours claim,
Than thee none merits more the prelate's name:
Wond'ring behold him faithful to his see,
Prove parliaments dependent to be free.—
 Lo! o'er yon flood H—e casts his low'ring eyes,
And wishful sees the reverend turrets rise.
While Lambeth opens to thy longing View,
Hapless! the Mitre ne'er can bind thy brow:
Tho' courts should deign the gift, how wondrous hard
By thy own Doctrines still to be debarr'd;
For if from change such mighty evil springs,
Translations sure, O H—e! are sinful things.
 Full plac'd and pension'd see H—r—o stands,
Begrim'd his face, unpurify'd his hands;
To decency he scorns all nice pretence,
And reigns firm foe to cleanliness and sense.
How did H—r—o BRITAIN's cause advance!
How shine the sloven and buffoon of France!
In senates now, how scold, how rave, how roar,
Of treaties run the tedious train-trow o'er!
How blunder out whate'er should be conceal'd!
And how keep secret what should be reveal'd!—
 Silence! ye senates, while environ'd Y—e
Pours forth melodious nothings from his tongue.—
 —There W—— and P—'s, goddess, view,
Firm in thy cause, and to thy Appius true;
Lo! from their labours what reward betides!
One pays my army, one my navy guides.—
 Form'd for the softer arts, shall H——y strain,
With stubborn politicks his tender brain;
For ministers laborious pamphlets write;
In senates prattle, and with patriots fight!
Thy fond ambition, pretty youth, give o'er,
Preside at balls, old fashions lost restore—
 Behold a star emblazon C—n's coat,
Not that the knight has merit, but a vote.
And here, O goddess, numerous wrongheads trace,
Lur'd by a pension, ribbon, or a place.—

Answer to the State DUNCES

TO love and hate all human pow'rs submit;
 The strength of reason, and the life of wit:
To them the mind a willing homage pays;
And prejudice, unseen, each heart betrays.
O prejudice! unbounded is thy reign;   5
Great dullness toils but to augment thy train:
Nor are her sons thy votaries alone;
Thou mak'st a PULTNEY's eloquence thy own.
With patriot zeal still cover private hate;
And when his vows are finish'd, make him great: 10
No Chief's more fit thy empire to maintain,
Could friendship bind him in her sacred chain,
Truth we applaud, yet sacrifice to thee;
Not Phoebus, nor the nine, can set us free.
See POPE to thy almighty influence bend;   15
To Virtue and to Bolingbroke a friend!

Unequall'd bard! yet still with mortal mind,
Or false to freedom, or like bigots blind.
Can fires of flav'ry cheer a Briton's bowl?
Can St JOHN's treasons feast a patriot-soul?   20
Has ALBION then a son, who can forget
BRITANNIA weeping, and the monster's threat?
The tyrant-boast of penalties and pains;
While conscience trembled at the hell-forg'd chains?
See St John brooding intellectual night;   25
And ev'ry pow'r of wit made slave to spite:
When will thy crimes be full, thou false to all!
Still envy, malice on thy aid will call.
Still will a PULTENEY join, a POPE commend;
* To Virtue only and her Friends, a Friend.   30
To Freedom ever sacred be my pen,
Freedom! that makes us great, that makes us men.
Could I, Dan POPE, once reach thy lovely strain,
No more should party rage that word prophane;
Then should my verse the wounds of treac'ry heal, 35
And faction's brood to ev'ry eye reveal;
Fair LIBERTY should every charm display,
PEACE beauteous smile, warm'd with her genial ray;
In her blest Eden ev'ry virtue grows,
Folly and baseness are alone her foes;   40
Full are her cities, nations crowd her gates,
Obedient plenty on her scepter waits;
Just to her cause, and to Britannia true,
Oh! could my muse the glorious theme pursue
With equal strength, BRUNSWICK should crown
 my lays,   45
While faction's tribe is doom'd to † Whitehead's
 praise.
Hear the vain bounce, with scandal quite grown mad
N—c—e is a dunce, his voice is bad;
G—n is grave and dull; a dunce is Y—ge,
For melody is natural to his tongue: 50
'Tis dulness governs all, ev'n J—'s brains;
There's not a day in which he takes no pains:
H—r—y's a dunce, 'tis prov'd; for he can write;
He's little too; nay more, the lord can fight:
There's W—n and P—m dunces plain,   55
One pays the army, and one guards the main:
That W—m is one, thy proof can't fail,
For heretofore he drank a mug of ale.
Rash sightless thing, of poetry beware;
Go read thy dunces G—n, S—k, H—re: 60
Ask injured POPE thy fawning to excuse,
Nor like thy ‡ APPIUS thy own Friend abuse;
Henceforth be dumb, and merit honest fame,
Lest W—m should hapless hear thy name:
Alas! what fatal star betray'd thy Youth,   65
As innocent of state affairs, as truth,
On thy first voyage to be repairless split,
Poor bard! to think that calling fool was wit!
In thy low scandal ever buried lie,
Beneath the notice of an human eye;   70
No, pity rises, PULTENEY's smiles be thine,
With WALPLE's foes may'st thou at Dawley dine;
Alien to good, unworthy e'er to hear
How WALPOLE's musick wins th' impartial ear;
I've seen his truth each guileful knot untwist, 75
Till faction wonder'd how he could exist,
Felt the sweet charm, and spite of selfish hate,
Retir'd abash'd, and in just silence sate.

* See No. 26. p. 150.
† Whitehead, the Author of the State-Dunce.
‡ He makes Appius abuse his Friends.

Mr POPE's EPITAPH on Mr GAY.

A Manly wit, a child's simplicity,
The morals blameless, and the temper free,
Words ever pleasing, yet sincerely true,
Satyr still just, with humour ever new;
Above temptation in a low estate,
And uncorrupted, even, among the great:
A safe companion, and an easie friend,
Belov'd through life, lamented in thy end.
Those are thy honours; not that here thy bust
Is mixt with heroes, or with kings thy dust:
But that the worthy and the good shall say,
Striking their achLng bosoms, Here lies GAY.

To Mr POPE, on the SAME.

ENtomb'd with kings tho' GAY's cold ashes lye,
A nobler monument thy strains supply.
Thy matchless muse, still faithful to thy friend,
By courts unaw'd, his virtue darts commend.
Lamented GAY, forget thy treatment past,
Look down, and see thy merit crown'd at last.
A destiny more glorious, who can hope?
In life belov'd, in death bemoan'd by POPE.

—On his being Author of the ESSAY on MAN.

THE muse, O P— some cynick reas'ners blam'd
And beauties which they could not taste, defam'd:
But when to verse, philosophy you join,
Thy force of reason proves the muse divine.
So gold, the worth unknown, to some appears,
'Till a new lustre from the mint it bears;
Then with devotion they the coin behold,
George gives the stamp, and adds new worth to gold

On the number of the members who voted against the late bill of excise being the same with the amount of the first eight square numbers in Arithmetick; viz.

$$1\!-\!1$$
$$2\!-\!4$$
$$3\!-\!9$$
$$4\!-\!16$$
$$5\!-\!25$$
$$6\!-\!36$$
$$7\!-\!49$$
$$8\!-\!64$$
$$\overline{204}$$

HEre's a health to the glorious two hundred and
four,
Who hinder'd excise-men from ent'ring our door:
Which had they once enter'd, their cursed intrusion
Would soon have been follow'd by a train of confusion.
When th' old world by a flood was o'erwhelm'd, Eight
found grace,
Scap'd that general excise, and renewed the race:
Eight prevented it here, making each an oration;
Near two hundred begat, by vocal propagation.
Whom acting so soundly, so roundly, on the square,
To the sum by eight figures produc'd we compare.
For the first eight square numbers amount to no more,
Than the mystical sum of Two hundred and four.

EPIGRAM.

THE scheme oppos'd! and letters writ
By friends to—neither trade nor wit.
But hold—the wou'd-be-patriots say
Explain the riddle, sir, we pray.
The friends to trade then can't be those,
Who cheat their country, friends, and foes.
And he that knows scarce how to write,
Sure must be deem'd a learned wight.
Since these then gave the senate rules,
Sirs, whether are you knaves, or fools?

The Statues ADDRESS to Ld COBHAM, on his Return to his Garden at Stowe.

FROM every muse, and every art, thy own,
Thy bow'rs our theatres, thy mind our throne,
Hail, to thy virtues manumiz'd from state!
Hail, to thy leisure, to be wisely great!
Fetter'd, by duties, and to forms enslav'd,
How timely have thy years a remnant sav'd!
To taste that freedom, which thy sword maintain'd,
And lead in letter'd ease, a life unpain'd.
So Scipio (Carthage fall'n) resign'd his Plume,
And smil'd at the forgetfulness of Rome.
O, greatly bless'd! whose ev'ning sweetest shines,
And in unclouded slowness, calm declines!
—While free reflection, with reverted eye,
Wane'd from hot noon-tide, and a troubled sky,
Divides life, well: the largest part, long known
Thy country's claim— the last, and best, thy own.
Now like the masters of the world, go shine:
Be Charles's *life, and* Dioclesian's *thine.*
Form thy own pow'r; dependant peace create
And shade distinction, from the storms of state.
With pray'rs, and praise, thy toil, like heav'n's,
be paid,
And guard the growing world, thy hands have made.
There, while, detach'd, thy self supported Soul
Resumes dominion, and escapes controul;
Moves, with a grandeur, monarchs wish in vain,
Above all fears, forms, dangers, hopes, and pain;
A glance, sometimes, from thy safe summit, throw,
And see the dusky world look dim, below.
Through the dark throng, discern huge slaves of pride,
Should'ring unheeded happiness aside;
Thwarted, and push'd—and lab'ring into name;
And dignify'd, with all the dirt, of fame.
Then with a smile superior, turn away;
And lop th' exub'rance of some straggling spray.
Wind, through thy mazes, to serene delight,
And, from the bursting bubbles, shade thy sight.
Yet—where thou shin'st, like heav'n, behind a cloud,
Moving, like light, all-piercing, tho' not loud,
The muse shall find thee, in thy bless'd retreat;
And breathe this honest wish, at COBHAM's *feet:*
Fresh, as thy lakes, may all thy pleasures flow!
And, breezy, like thy groves, thy passions blow!
Wide, as thy fancy, be thy spreading praise!
And long, and lovely, as thy walks, thy days!

The Retirement. By Dr BROOKES.

WElcome peaceful, calm retreat!
Far from common ills of fate,
Welcome joys before unknown!
E'ry pleasure, e'ry blessing,
E'ry bliss that's worth possessing,
Here delights, and here alone.

Let aspiring minds pursue
Dang'rous greatness, guilded woe,
Tortur'd with ambitious care;
Here such empty dream's despising,
Far from falling as from rising,
I avoid the tempting snare.

Heaps of wealth amass'd in vain
Give the sordid Miser pain,
Waking dread his bosom rends;
But content my wishes bounding,
An soft peace my bed surrounding,
Downy sleep my call attends. Frand

Fraud and envy, guilt and fear,
Breed no dire confusion here,
  Perfidy no refuge finds ;
Here no superstition reigning
Crowds of fancy'd ills containing,
  Preys on weak unthinking minds.

Innocence and spotless love
Truth and honour round me rove,
  Exil'd from the guilty town :
Chearfull studies time beguiling,
Wing the moments, ever smiling
  Till my latest sands fall down.

A SONG, by Dr SWIFT.

FLutt'ring spread thy purple Pinions,
  Gentle Cupid, o'er my Heart ;
I a Slave in thy Dominions,
  Nature must give way to Art.

Mild Arcadian, ever blooming,
  Nightly nodding o'er their Flocks,
See my weary days consuming,
  All beneath yon flow'ry Rocks.

Thus the Cyprian Goddess, weeping,
  Mourn'd Adonis, darling Youth ;
Him the Boar, in silence creeping,
  Gor'd with unrelenting Tooth.

Cynthia, tune harmonious Numbers,
  Fair Discretion string the Lyre,
Sooth my ever waking Slumbers,
  Bright Apollo lend thy Choir.

Gloomy Pluto, King of Terrors,
  Arm'd in adamantine Chains,
Lead me to the Chrystal mirrors,
  Wat'ring soft Elysian Plains.

Mournful Cypress, verdant Willow,
  Guilding my Aurelia's Brow,
Morpheus hovering o'er my Pillow,
  Hear me make my dying Vow.

Melancholy smooth Meander,
  Swiftly purling in a round,
On thy margin Lovers wander,
  With thy Flow'ry Chaplets crown'd.

Thus when Philomela drooping,
  Softly seeks some silent Mate,
See the Bird of Juno stooping,
  Melody resigns to Fate.

VERSES made at Sea.

NO more ye muses, tell of verdant plains,
  Where beauteous nymphs are sung by coward
    swains ;
Where DAMON, big with love, to forrests goes,
And am'rous towns to trees declare their woes ;
Where squeaking pipes the fair one's worth proclaim,
And docile woods learn to repeat her name :
Where askilst sighs the winds to PHILLIS bear,
And DAMON only dyes in metaphor.

I like love-scenes drawn from the wat'ry plains ;
Fraught with stout heroes and intrepid swains ;
Where PORTS are pretty PHILLIS's ; and towns,
When destitute of nymphs, in love with towns ;
Where sails are th' only leaves which DAMON sees,
And lovers talk to masts instead of trees ;
Who never sigh but when the zephyrs fail,
Then send a breeze of sighs t' improve the gale.

In regal state see here the sovereign swain
(The winds his guards) rides o'er the subject main :
Hark! with majestic voice, untaught to squeak ;
Steady ! he cries, and struts along the deck :
The words far distant cabins quickly learn,
And steady ! steady ! echoes from the stern.
His heart impatient, he, tho' billows rise,
And leagues divide, salutes her with his eyes :
On top-mast perch'd, when guns and trumpets fail,
They march before to tell the am'rous tale.
Does night approach ? e'en then he skims the deep,
And flyes to kiss his mistress when asleep.
Quick-sands and rocks he scorns, fir'd with her charms,
Nor quits his course till harbour'd in her arms ;
O, if that bliss severer fate denyes,
He acts the lover honestly, and—dyes.

PLOT for PLOTS or, The BITER BIT.

DO not, perspiring peer, disdain
  To make your own for ever,
New risen from Hibernia's main,
  A VENUS form'd so clever.

She'll not disgrace with blood too mean
  The stock whence you descended :
With vergers was her sire the dean
  In dignity attended.

'Tis much beneath a noble station,
  With sanguine hopes to warm her,
Only to please a brutish passion ;
  Then leave the blooming charmer.

CUPID, as full of wiles, resenting
  Such snare design'd the fair one ;
From ambuscade sly HYMEN sent in,
  To fix the luscious baron.

HYMEN, a bitter-sweet old grig,
  Snatch'd up his flaming taper ;
Vow'd, if his honour took a jigg,
  That he should pay the scraper.

Thus MULCIBER did MARS ensnare
  The Cyprian dame enjoying ;
He coop'd 'em in a cage of iron,
  As they were sweetly toying.

The queen of love, in toils enclos'd,
  Flash'd from her radiant eyes :
The hero storm'd to be expos'd
  The banter of the skies.

PHOEBUS compos'd a jocund ditty ;
  And BACCHUS sung a catch, sir :
COMUS, intolerably witty,
  Affirm'd he'd found his match, sir.

This only difference lies the case in :
  MARS VULCAN's bed polluted ;
His bride for concubine embracing,
  The peer himself cornuted.

Then cherish, fragrant sir, a dame
  That will exactly suit you ;
Who doubly arm'd to conquest came,
  With cunning, and with beauty.

Let CL—ND—N glory in her charms ;
  Boys lisping call you daddy :
Believe there's pleasure in her arms,
  Tho' she's your lawful lady.

A2

An ODE.

I Envy not the proud their wealth,
 Their equipage, and state:
Give me but innocence and health,
 I ask not to be great.

I, in this sweet retirement, find
 A joy unknown to kings:
For sceptres, to a virtuous mind,
 Seem vain and empty things.

Great CINCINNATUS, at his plow,
 With brighter lustre shone,
Than guilty CÆSAR e'er could do,
 Tho' seated on a throne.

Tumultuous days, and restless nights,
 Ambition ever knows;
A stranger to the calm delights
 Of study and repose.

Then free from envy, care, and strife,
 Permit me, heav'nly pow'rs,
To pass a pure unblemish'd life,
 And crown with peace my hours.

A RECEIPT to cure a *love* fit.

TYE one end of a rope fast over a beam,
 And make a slip noose at the other extream;
Then just underneath let a cricket be set,
On which let the lover most manfully get;
Then over his head let the sucket be got,
And under one ear be well settled the knot.
The cricket kick'd down, let him take a fair swing;
And leave all the rest of the work to the string.

GULLIVER and MÆVIUS, an EPIGRAM.

YOU seldom see a clown without his cur,
 Thus Mævius goes dogs-trot with Gulliver:
As sharper is attended with his setter,
That snaps the copy, this procures the letter.

On the POET LAUREAT's being put out of the *House* of Lords.

C——R (the wonder of a brazen age)
 Always a hero, off or on the stage,
The other day, in courtesy, affords
His lovely phyz, to grace the house of lords:
Quite free from pride, he humbly condescends
To treat the very smallest peers, as friends:
With sneer, or grin, approves each grave debate,
And smiles when brother dukes support the state:
On the learn'd bishops bench looks kind---enough,
And offers good lord KING a pinch of snuff.
Whilst thus he rains his favours on the crowd,
An old rough Earl his swift destruction vow'd;
Regardless of th' imperial crown he wore,
Regardless of the bays and brains he bore;
A voice as hoarse as SUTHERLAND's gave law,
And made the king, the fop, the bard, withdraw.
O C——R, in revenge, your wrath forbear,
This once, your stupid, stingless, satire spare,
And with dull panegyrick dumb each peer:}
Like rhyming bell-man's ghost haunt their abodes,
And frighten them with birth or new-years odes.
If banish'd thence, you still may shine at——;
There p——rs and scoundrels equally resort;
Unmatch'd in all, superiors never fear;
But since you're peerless, scorn the name of Peer.

To Mrs MARTIN, on her leaving *Leigh,* By the REV. Mr W——

WHile from our ravish'd eyes yon distant stray,
 And leave unblest the silent walks of Leigh,
Think how your Swains your tedious absence mourn
In fruitless sighs, and wish for your return.
TEME's limpid stream, which once might justly boast
Upon its verdant banks the fairest Toast,
Pleas'd to reflect the beauties of your face,
As on its surface you serenely gaze,
In gentle murmurs now complaining flows,
And joyns with us in sympathetick woes:
The scaly race forget their sportive leap,
To mourn your absence in the owzy deep.
The lofty pines, beneath whose ample shade,
You oft have gayly smil'd, or talk'd, or read;
Neglected feel a sensible decay;
Put off their verdure, languish, fade and die.
Haste then, O lovely fair! recerse your flight,
And with your presence bless our longing sight:
Revive these languid bow'rs, and fading groves,
Once happy scenes of joys, and tender loves.
The spring shall then appear in all its bloom,
And Philomela's song conduct you home;
The fields and meads their choicest flow'rs prepare,
To deck your bosom or adorn your hair;
The tuneful muse shall then attempt your praise,
In nobler strains and more exalted lays;
Happy, if on her song you chance to smile,
And with your Approbation crown her toil.

The POET's IMPORTANCE.

THE glow-worm scriblers, of a feeble age,
 Pale twinklers, of an hour, provoke my rage:
In each dark hedge, we start and insect fire,
Which lives, by night, and must, at dawn, expire:
Yet, such their number, that their specks combine:
And the unthinking vulgar swear, they shine.
Poets are prodigies, so greatly rare,
They seem the tasks of heaven---and built with care;
Like suns,---unquench'd, unrival'd, and sublime,
They roll, Immortal, o'er the wastes of time:
Ages, in vain, close round, and snatch in flame;
High, over all, still shines the Poet's name:
Lords, of a life, that scorns the bounds of breath,
They stretch existence----and awaken death.
Pride of their envied climes! They plant renown,
That shades the monarch's, by the muse's, crown:
To say, that Virgil, with Augustus, shin'd,
Does honour, to the lord of half mankind,
So, when three thousand years have wane'd away,
And Pope is said t'ave liv'd, when George bore sway,
Millions shall lend the King the Poet's fame,
And bless, implicit, the supported name.

On SICKNESS. (See p. 312.)

FROM this vain world, where ills abound,
 And joys, but few mix'd, are found,
Where restless foes those few insist,
And friends are impotent at best,
My wearied soul, good Lord, remove
To bowers of bliss and friends above.
I said: when lo! this pray'r preferr'd,
Stern sickness (frightful guest!) appear'd;
I started, frown'd, and cry'd, be gone,
From one already half undone.
Can pain a cure for sorrow be?
I'm enough wretched without thee.

Weak man! who errs a thousand ways,
And censures what deserves his praise!
The hideous form so seiz'd my thoughts,
I then th' intrinsick worth forgot.
But welcome, guest ; for now I find,
Tho' seeming cruel, thou art kind:
Kind, as I wish'd; and lead'st the road
From this vain world, to heav'n and God.
To heav'n and God I'll press the way,
Tho' grim the pilot, rough the sea:
Who can his course reluctan bend,
When that's the port, and he the friend!

The RECONCILEMET, from *Hor.* Ode, 9 *L.* 3.
See the Original with another Translation, p. 148.
and an Imitation, p. 268.

Damon. WHile I with love your breast con'd warm,
          While me alone to please you'd strive ;
Con'd loll upon no other arm,
  I was the happiest youth alive.

L. *While you could love none more than me,*
  Nor 'stead of Lyddy, Chloe *boast ;*
Lyddy *was then the* happiest *she,*
  The fairest maid, the brightest toast.

D. *That* Chloe *charms I'll not deny,*
  To th' lute who sweetest notes can give:
For whom I won'd not fear to die,
  Would dying make my Chloe *live.*

L. *Me* Strephon *charms; who with each breath*
  Vows mutual constancy *and truth :*
For whom I twice would suffer death;
  Would death but spare my lovely youth.

D. *But --- if of love our broken knot*
  Venus *should kindly tie again;*
Should charming Chloe *be forget*
  And slighted Lyddy *once more reign?*

L. *Then won'd I chuse, tho' fairer he,*
  Than fairest planet in the sky,
Thou light as cork; as rough as sea,
  With thee to live, with thee to die.

On the *Craftsman's* AYE *and* NO. (See p. 230.)

WHEN *from the axe good* D'anvers *flew,*
  And to his king for mercy cry'd ;
His gen'rous king the axe withdrew,
  And yes to all he ask'd reply'd.

His monarch's goodness to repay,
  When mov'd to act against the foes
Of him who gave him life,——'twas nay——
  And all his voice could breath were no's.

Oh George, *hadst thou this* Craftsman *known,*
  The sentence had not seem'd amiss,
For life when cringing to thy throne,
  Hadst thou said no, *instead of* yes,

Yet tho' his pen so long has rev'd,
  Let him in time chastise his quill;
That law, whose aye *has often sav'd,*
  May one time have a no *to kill.*

On the *Lay-man's Sermon,* (see p. 298.)

THy countrymen, good Charles, are still the same ;
  They murder'd once thy body, now thy fame.
By venal Scots thou to the block wast led,
Betray'd when living, and bely'd when dead.
All peace be to thy soul, much injur'd prince:
The sires sold thee, their sons their country since.

Mrs B—R to the E. of O—Y on his promise to sup with her.

THO' *the muse had deny'd me so often before,*
  I ventur'd this day to invoke her once more.
She ask'd what I wanted? I said, with delight,
Your lordship had promis'd to sup here to-night ;
And, on an occasion so much to my honour,
I hop'd she'd excuse me thus calling upon her.
  To this she reply'd, with disdain in her looks,
If that be the case—go summon your cooks.
  In answer I told her how little you eat ;
That in vain I should hope to regale you with meat;
That she knew wit and humour to you were a feast,
Who had, tho' no stomach, an excellent taste.
  This calm'd her resentment, she paus'd for a while;
Then the goddess propitious reply'd with a smile,
If with humour and wit you'd have him delighted,
What need I be call'd?—let the dean be invited;
The business is done, if with him you prevail;
For a Boyle *and a* Swift *will each other regale.*

To Mrs A—a K—y with a present of Fruit.

THO' *the peach, and the plumb, with* Apollo *conspire,*
  To present you their softness, and sweetness, and fire,
Their aid is in vain, for what can they do,
But blush, and confess themselves vanquish'd by you;
Where virtue, and wit, with such qualities blend
What mortal, what goddess would dare to contend?

As the Poetical Pieces from *Gratus* and *Love-much*, came too late to be inserted this Month, they will have leisure to review them. We shall be glad of *Gratus's* Correspondence, without putting him to any Charge.

We are obliged to *Cleophilus,* &c. for their good Wishes; they may be assured we shall continue our best Endeavours for the Entertainment of all our Readers ; We could insert here many Encomiums bestow'd upon our Magazine, not only from private Letters, but from publick Attestations: But it being, as Mr *Addison* has somewhere observ'd, the most difficult Thing in the World for a *Man* to talk with any tolerable Decency, when he is speaking of himself, we shall therefore decline mentioning any Particulars of that Kind, as we have often, what some might think necessary in our own Justification. For the same Reason Mr *Bennet* must excuse our not accepting his Defence from the scandalous Abuse he mentions. As he owns it ill-grounded, he might conclude we despised it and the illiterate Author. Our Readers who complain of the smallness of the Print, are desired to consider, a larger would be a great deal cheaper to the Publisher, and that all the Letter we now use, being entirely new, is very near as legible as the Size we formerly printed on, tho' it contains a 6th Part more in almost every Page than any other Monthly Pamphlet ; wherefore our Advertisement of *more in Quantity* and *greater Variety* than any Book of the *Kind* and *Price,* is most strictly true; notwithstanding it has been objected to by those, who, to the Surprize of all that have observed the difference, use the like Expression in a very hyperbolical Way.

THE
Monthly Intelligencer.
JUNE, 1733.

Friday, 1.

THE Court of *King's-Bench* gave Judgment against *Wm Rayner*, formerly convicted for publishing a Hieroglyphical Paper, call'd, *Robin's Game*, or *Seven's the Main, viz.* To pay a Fine of 50*l.* 2 Years Imprisonment, and give Security for his good Behaviour for 7 Years.

Monday, 4.

A Proclamation was published to oblige Ships arriving from *Tripoli*, which is now visited with the.Plague, to perform 40 Days Quarentine.

Wednesday, 6.

At a General Court of the *S. Sea* Company it was agreed that the Moneys arising from the Sale of the late Directors Estates had been employ'd for the Service of the Company, and to their Satisfaction.

Saturday, 9.

Came on at *Drs Commons*, before Dr *Bettesworth*, Dean of the Arches Court of *Canterbury*, a Cause between the Rev. Mr *Goole*, Rector of *Aynbam* in *Oxfordshire*, Plaintiff, and Mrs *Hudson*, alias *Boyce*, Wife of *John Boyce*, Esq; of *Oxford*, Defendant, concerning a Marriage Contract, prior to her Marriage with Mr *Boyce*. Sentence was given in Favour of Mr *Boyce's* Marriage.

Monday, 11.

His Majesty enter'd on the 7th Year of his Reign; theDay was observ'd as usual in this Metropolis, but with more Loyalty and Rejoicing than ever at *Greenwich*, where a Boat compleat with a fineOrange-colour'd *Arning*, given by Colonel *Bell* Comptroller of the Post Office, was row'd for by 6 Watermen from *Woolwich* to that Place. The 2d Man had 10 s. and the 3d 5 s. to drink his Majesty's Health.

Tuesday, 12.

A Chapter of the most noble Order of the Garter was held at St *James's*, when the Prince of *Orange*, the D. of *Devonshire*, and the E. of *Wilmington*, were elected Knights Companions.

Wednesday, 13.

His Majesty went to the House of Peers, where the House of Commons being come, the Rt Hon. *Arthur Onslow*, Esq; their Speaker, recommended to his Majesty, in a fine Speech, the several Bills that lay ready for the Royal Assent: He took Notice likewise of the particular Business of this Session of Parliament; and concluding with high Encomiums on the intended Match of the Princess Royal with the Prince of *Orange*, and on her Royal Highness's personal Virtues, he presented to his Majesty the Bill for her Royal Highness's Portion. After which his Majesty was pleased to give the Royal Assent to,

1. An Act for enabling his Majesty to apply 500,000*l.* out of the Sinking Fund, for the Service of the Year 1733, and for the further Disposition of the said Fund, by paying off one Million of *S. Sea Annuities*; and for enabling his Majesty, out of the Monies arisen by Sale of Lands in the Island of St *Christopher*, to pay the Sum of 80,000*l.* for the Marriage Portion of the Princess Royal, and 10,000*l.* to the Trustees for establishing the Colony of *Georgia* in *America*; and for making good all Deficiencies and Charges by taking Broad-Pieces into the Mint, out of the Coinage Duty; and for appropriating the Supplies granted in this Session of Parliament; and for issuing to the Sub-Dean, Treasurer, and Steward of the Collegiate Church of St *Peter*, *Westminster*, out of the Monies reserved for building fifty new Churches, 4000*l.* for the Repair of the said Church, and 1200*l.* for finishing the Dormitory belonging thereunto.

2. An Act for the converting a further Part of the Capital Stock of the *S. Sea* Company into *Annuities* redeemable by Parliament, and for settling the remaining Part of the said Stock in the said Company. (See p. 292 H)

3. An Act to explain and amend an Act entitled, An Act for the better Regulation of Attornies and Sollicitors.

4. An Act for enlarging the Time for Exportation of Tea.   5. An

5. An Act for the further Encouragement of the Whale-Fiſhery.

6. An Act for making perpetual the ſeveral Acts therein mentioned for the better Regulation of Juries; and continuing the Act for regulating the Manufacture of Cloth in the *Weſt-Riding* of *Yorkſhire*, except one Clauſe; and for continuing an Act for the more effectual puniſhing wicked and evil diſpoſed Perſons going armed in Diſguiſe, and to prevent the cutting or breaking down the Bank of any River, or any Sea Bank; and to prevent the malicious cutting of Hop-Binds; and for continuing the Act 14 *Car.* II. for preventing Theft and Rapine upon the Northern Borders of *England*.

7. An Act to enable Perſons to ſue for Adminiſtration of the Will of *R. Norton*, Eſq;

8. An Act for the better Regulation of Laſtage and Ballaſtage in the River Thames.

9. An Act for the Relief of Pariſhes, and other Places, from ſuch Charges as may ariſe from Baſtard Children born within the ſame.

10. An Act to oblige Ships coming from Places infected more effectually to perform their Quarentine.

11. An Act to recover and preſerve the Navigation of the River *Dee*, in the County Palatine of *Cheſter*.

12. An Act for making effectual ſuch Agreement as ſhall be made between the Charitable Corporation and their Creditors.

13. An Act for appointing Commiſſioners to Examine, State and Report, who of the Sufferers in the Charitable Corporation are Objects of Compaſſion; and for giving Relief to ſuch Sufferers, and for enforcing the Laws made againſt Foreign Lotteries; and for empowering the ſaid Commiſſioners to hear and determine the Claims of ſuch Creditors and Proprietors of the ſaid Corporation, as have not made their Claims within the Time limited by an Act made in the laſt Seſſion of Parliament.

14. An Act to prevent the coining or counterfeiting any of the Gold Coins, commonly called Broad-Pieces.——And to 11 private Bills. After which his Majeſty made the following moſt gracious Speech, and then prorogued the Parliament to the 26th of *July*.

My Lords and Gentlemen,

THE Seaſon of the Year, and the Diſpatch you have given to the Publick Buſineſs, make it proper for Me to put an End to this Seſſion of Parliament.

Gentlemen of the Houſe of Commons,

I return you My Thanks for the Proviſions you have made for the Service of the current Year; I have never demanded any Supplies of My People, but what were abſolutely neceſſary for the Honour, Safety, and Defence of Me and My Kingdom, and I am always

beſt pleaſed, when the Publick Expence are ſupplied in a Manner leaſt burthenſome to My Subjects.

My Lords and Gentlemen,

I cannot paſs by unobſerved the wicked Endeavours that have lately been made uſe of to inflame the Minds of the People, and by the moſt unjuſt Miſrepreſentations to raiſe Tumults and Diſorders, that almoſt threatned the Peace of the Kingdom; but I depend upon the Force of Truth, to remove the groundleſs Jealouſies that have been raiſed of Deſigns carrying on againſt the Liberties of My People, and upon your known Fidelity, to defeat and fruſtrate the Expectations of ſuch as delight in Confuſion. It is My Inclination, and has always been My Study, to preſerve the Religious and Civil Rights of all My Subjects; let it be your Care to undeceive the deluded, and to make them ſenſible of their preſent Happineſs, and the Hazard they run of being unwarily drawn, by ſpecious Pretences, into their own Deſtruction.

Mr *Joſeph Kells*, bound over to the *King's Bench* (See p. 212) was diſcharged from his Recognizances.

Princeſs *Amelia* left off drinking the Waters, at New *Tunbridge Wells*, (See p. 267) and order'd 25 Guineas for Mr *Reaſon* Maſter of the Wells, 3 Guineas apiece to the Servers of the Water, and one Guinea to each of the other Attendants.

Thurſday, 14.

About 100 Perſons, 50 of whom were able to bear Arms, embarked for *Georgia*, furniſh'd in every Reſpect by the Truſtees.

At a Seſſions of Admiralty held at the *Old Bailey*, Capt. *Rice Harris* was try'd for the Murder of *Richard Beard*, one of his Men, on the Coaſt of *Guiney*, on the 2d of *June* 1731, by barbarouſly beating him with a Cat of Nine-Tales, on his refuſing to go aloft to furl the Sails, on which Account he allow'd him no Proviſions, ſo that he died in a few Days, declaring the Captain was the Cauſe of his Death. The Jury found him Guilty; Death.

Monday, 18.

Sir *Charles Kells*, Sir *Tho. Frankland*, and *Tho. Winnington*, Eſq; Lords of the *Admiralty*, held a Board at *Portſmouth*, and appointed the Maſter's, &c. of a new Academy in his Majeſty's Yard there, for the receiving and inſtructing 30 young Gentlemen in Maritime Affairs.

Tueſday, 19.

A Cauſe was try'd at *Guildhall* before Mr Juſtice *Page*, between a Weaver of *Spittlefields*, Plaintiff, and a young Gentlewoman, Defendant, on a Note ſuppoſed

Poſed to be herHand-writing,for 4000*l*.pretended to be given to the Plaintiff as a Security or Confirmation that ſhe would be married to him, and afterwards would-not; but the Court committed him to *Newgate* for publiſhing the ſaid Note, it appearing to be falſe, forged, and counterfeit, he knowing it to be ſuch.

Wedneſday 20.

The *S. Sea* Company in a General Court reſolv'd to allow a further Time for bringing in their Bonds to be mark'd 3 and half *per Cent.* to the 20th of *July*, about 300,000*l.* having not been brought in: And as the Attorney General's Opinion was, that the Company had nor a Right to diſpoſe of their Trade, the Conſideration of Sir *Thomas Fitzgerald,* the *Spaniſh* Agent's Propoſals, for giving the Company an Equivalent for their Trade, was adjourned till the Diviſion of their Capital into Annuities and a Trading Stock ſhall take Place.

Thurſday, 21.

In the Court of Exchequer at *Weſtminſter,* was try'd a Cauſe, wherein the King and the Eaſt India Company were Plaintiffs, and *James Naiſh,* Eſq; one of their late Super-Cargoes, Defendant, for importing Gold unlicens'd, and without paying a Duty of 5 *per Cent.* to the Company, as by Law requir'd. The Jury found that he had imported Gold to the Value of 26,864*l.* and as to the Penalty on it, they brought in their Verdict Special, which is to be argu'd before the Barons of the Exchequer.

At a Tryal in the Court of Common Pleas at *Weſtminſter,* Mr *Bellinger, Worceſter* Carrier, had a Verdict for 25*l.* with Coſts, given him againſt Mr *Simms* at the Swan at *Knightsbridge,* for detaining the Horſe that *Gordon* the Highwayman was taken upon, and had ſtolen from the ſaid *Bellinger,* who tender'd the Money for the Charge of keeping. The Horſe was adjudg'd to Mr *Simms.*

Friday, 22.

A Cauſe was try'd in the Court of Common Pleas *Weſtminſter,* letween a Tallow-Chandler, Plaintiff, and a Doctor that undertakes to cure mad Perſons, Defendant, for an Aſſault and Battery, and falſe Impriſonment of the Plaintiff for ſeveral Days in the Doctors Houſe. It appeared that the Doctor, in Confederacy with the Plaintiff's Wife, under pretence of viſiting his Brother in *White-Chappel,* whom they affirm'd to be dying, convey'd him in a Coach to the Mad-Houſe, where they confined him 4 or 5 Days, till his Wife and her Confederates had made a

way with his Effects. The Jury gave a Verdict for the Plaintiff, and 100 *l.* Damage with Coſts.

A Cauſe was try'd at the *Marſhalſea* Court, *Southwark,* wherein a Quaker was Plaintiff, and a Child of 4 years old, and her Guardians, Defendants. The Child had a ſore Finger, which the Plaintiff pretending to Cure, it turn'd to a Mortification, and he cut it off, brought in a Bill of 15 *l.* arreſted the Child and confined her ſeveral Weeks in the *Marſhalſea* Priſon. But the Plaintiff not being bred a regular Surgeon he was Non-ſuited; and the Court order'd the Bayliff into Cuſtody.

Saturday, 23.

At a General Court of the *Eaſt India* Company, *Joſiah Wadſworth,* Eſq; (Chairman) acquainted the Court, that the 200,000*l.* paid to the Government for prolonging their Charter for 30 Years, had occaſion'd the reducing their Dividends to 6 *per Cent. per Annum,* but now upon conſidering the State of their Trade both at Home and Abroad, they might divide 3 and half *per Cent.* for the Half year at Midſummer; which was agreed to.

Saturday, 30.

At the Seſſions at the *Old Baily,* receiv'd Sentence of Death *Wm Robinſon,* alias *Cecil,* for Robbing a Gentlewoman at her own Door of a Cloak and 14 *l.* *Roſe Moreton,* for privately ſtealing 24 Guineas and ſome Silver from her Maſter.

Several Members who voted againſt the exciſing Tobacco were met on Returning to their Corporations by great numbers of People of all ſorts, received Thanks, and were treated with great Honour.

BIRTHS

THE Lady of Sir *Rowland Hill,* of *Hawkſton, Salop* Bar. only Daughter of Sir *Bryan Broughton* of *Staffordſhire,* Bar. deliver'd of a Son and Heir.

The Lady of Earl *Cowper,* of a Daughter. 24, The Lady of the Ld *Charles Cavendiſh,* Brother to the D. of *Devonſhire,* deliver'd of a Son.

The Lady *Baltimore,* delivered of a Daughter at *Annapolis,* the 7th of *May* laſt. The Lady of the Lord *Naſſau Powlett,* deliver'd of a Son. Sr *Cha. Blackwell's* Lady, of a Daughter.

MARRIAGES

DR. *Thomas Tanner,* Bp. of St. *Aſaph,* married laſt Month to Miſs *Scot'ow,* of *Thorp* by *Norwich,* a Fortune of 15,000*l.* Mr *Nelthrope,* at *Lincoln* —— to Miſs *Strong* with 4000 *l.* Fortune.

Robert Coke, Efq; Vice-Chamberlain to her Majefty, younger Brother of the Lord *Lovel*, — to the Lady *Jane Holt*, Relict of *John Holt*, Efq; and Sifter to the late D. of *Wharton*, and to Sir *Wm Morice's* Lady.

William Trumbal, Efq; of *Finchamftead Park, Berks*, only Son of Sir *Wm Trumbal*, Secretary of State to K. *William*, — to the fecond Daughter of the Ld Vifc. *Blundell*.

Geo. Venables Vernon, of *Sudbury, Staffordſhire*, Efq; — to the youngeft Daughter of *Thomas* late Ld *Howard of Effingham*.

Sir *John Giffard*, of *Burfbal, Leicefterſbire*, Bar. to the eldeft Daughter and Coheir of the late *Richard Arundell Bealing* Efq; with 40,000 *l*. Fortune.

Wm Villiers, E. of *Jerfey*, — to the Dutchefs Dowager of *Bedford*, Daughter to the D. of *Bridgwater*.

Jofeph Warkman, Efq; of *Gloucefterſbire*, to Mifs *Bridges*, with a Fortune of 15,000*l*.

Thomas Hankey, Efq; 2d Son to Sir *Hen. Hankey*, Knight Alderman, and one of the Sheriffs of *London*, — to a Daughter of Sir *John Barnard*, Kt. and Ald. of the fame

George Wrighte, Efq; one of the Reprefentatives for *Leicefter* ——— to the only Daughter of Sir *Thomas Clarges*, Bart.

Robert Scot, Efq; Reprefentative for *Forfar* in *Scotland*, — to a Daughter of Col. *Middleton*, with a Fortune of 5000 *l*.

Mr *Jn Souton*, Silk-Dyer — to a Daughter of the late Rev. Dr *Lake*.

Dr *Clark*, one of the Phyficians to *Guy's Hofpital* — to the Relict of — *Jacobs*, Efq; with 12,000 *l*. Fortune.

Mr *Thom. Giles*, a Flanders Merchant — to Mifs *Cranidge*.

Thomas Horfeman, Efq; a *Weft-India* Merchant — to the only Daughter of Mr *Jorden* Hop Merchant in *Thames-ftreet*, a Fortune of 8000 *l*.

DEATHS.

May. 22. DR. *Woodhoufe*, at *Nottingham*.
28. Robert *Bene*, Efq; fenior Alderman of *Norwich*, aged 80.

30 *John Moth*, Efq; at *Kenf. Gravel-Pits*. *Cha. Bailiff*, Efq; at *Chippenham, Wilts*. Mr *Pickering* Rector of *Lamberburft, Kent* Dr *Saxbridge*, Dean of *Ferns, Ireland*.

June 1. *John Markham*, Efq; lately arriv'd from the *Eaft-Indies*.

John Hammond, of *Covent-Garden*, Efq;
2. The Lady of Sir *Hugh Clopton*, of *Stratford upon Avon, Warwickſb*. lately Ktd.

3. *Geo. Sayer*, Efq; near *Lenham* in *Kent*.
4 *Hicks Burroughs*, Efq; Engroffing Clerk of the Houfe of Commons.

Mr *Mayo*, a *Weft-India* Merchant,

5. *James Lloyd*, Efq; in *Redlion-Square*.
Mr *Arthur Heron*, Rector of *Morton, Effex* Mr *Somers*, a Clerk in the Stamp-Office.
The Relict of — *Sneyde*, Efq; *Strand*.
6. Geo. *Brailsford*, a *Portugal* Merch. *Wm Hickford*, Efq; at *Dixon, Gloucefterſb*.
Humphry Hardwick, Efq; Vice-Confull, lately at *Lisbon*.

Capt. *Blount*, Brother to the late Sir *John Blount*, South-Sea Director.

Capt. *Saunders*, belonging to the Guards.
7. *Twifdale Erſkine*, Efq; Nephew to the Solicitor General for *Scotland*.

8. Mr *Jabez Moloch*, a Jew Merchant. *Jofeph Stewart*, Efq; at *Lalam, Midſx*. Mrs *Editha Pope*, Mother of *Alexander Pope*, Efq; the celebrated Poet. aged 93.

She was laſt furviving of the Children of *William Turner*, Efq; of *York*, who by *Thomaſine Newton*, his Wife, had 14 Daughters, and 3 Sons, two of which died in the King's Service in the Civil Wars, and the eldeſt retired into *Spain*, where he died a General Officer. She lived with her Son (her only Child) from the time of his Birth to her Death ; and was carried to the Grave by 6 poor Men, to whom were given Suits of a dark, grey Cloth, and followed by 6 poor Women in the fame fort of Mourning. She was Interred near the Monument of her Husband, on which is the following Infcription. *D. O. M. Alexandri Pope, Viro, Innocuo, Probo, Pio, Qui vixit annos 75 Obiit 1717. Et Edithæ Conjugi, Inculpabili, Pientiſſimæ, Quæ vix. annos 93. Ob. 1733. Parentibus Bene-merentibus, Filius fecit.*

Mrs *Erſkine*, Sifter to the E. of *Buchan*.
10. Mrs *Howland*, Widow at *Beddington, Surry*, a great Fortune.

Capt. *Daniel Burges*, formerly an Officer in the *Eaft-India* Company's Service.
11. Sir *Anthony Abdy*, Bar. fucceeded by his Brother, now Sir *Wm*.

James Arne, Efq; in *Cavendiſb-Square*.
Mrs *Belledine*, Widow, in *Panton-ftreet*.

Sir *Nevil Hickman*, Bar. eldeft furviving Son to Sir *Willoughby Hickman*, formerly Reprefentative for *Lincolnſbire*. His Son Sir *Willoughby* a Minor, enjoys the Eftate.

Mr *Bailiff*, one of the Sixty Clerks in Chancery, reputed worth 10,000 *l*.
12. *James Chapman*, Efq; at *Stockwel, Surry*, a Hamburgh Merchant.

Capt. *Glover*, at *Ifleworth*.

Elizabeth, Countefs Dowager of *Caftlehaven*, in *Ireland*, and Baronefs *Audley* of *Heleigh* in *England*, much lamented.

— *Gouldborough*, Efq; at *Bromley* in *Kent*.
13 Mr *Mayo*, a Diffenting Minifter, at *Kingfton* upon *Thames*.

Mr *Walling*, Baptift Minifter, *Southwark*.
Robert

Robert Banks, Esq; one of the Commissioners of the Sewers in the City of *York*.

Miss *Elizabeth*, Daughter of Mr *Tombs*, late China Man in *Leadenhall-street*, who about a Fortnight ago left her 12,000 *l*.

14. Sir *William Chapman*'s Lady.

The Rev. Arch Deacon *Neal*, in *Ireland*.

15. The Ld *Darcy*, only Son of Judge *Jessop* of *Lincoln's-Inn-Fields*. About 2 Years ago he chang'd his Name by Act of Parliament, to possess the Title and Estate descended to him by his Mother. The Title goes to — *Darcy*, Esq; a Relation, now Page of Hon. to his Majesty.

Dr *Herbert* Chaplain to the 1st Reg. of Guards at Sea, on his Return from *Georgia*, whither he accompanied Mr *Oglethorpe*.

17. Capt. *Lovemore*, at *Cirencester* in *Gloucestersh*.an old Commander in the Navy.

Capt. *Thomas Biggs*, aged 90, an Officer in the Army, in the Reign of K. *Char*.II.

Wm Burton, Esq; at *Stoke-Newington*.

Cap. *Jn Farlow*, an old Officer in the Navy

— *Milner*, Esq; of *Hatton-Garden*, in the Commission of the Peace for *Middlesex*.

18. *Robert Monger*,Esq; Wine Merchant

Mr *Wm Bullock*, a Comedian of *Goodman's-Fields* Theatre.

19. Mr *Dixon*, Deputy Closet-keeper to his Majesty.

Joseph Mellish, Esq; at *Blyth* in *Yorkshire*.

The Lady *Lee*, so called from her Marrying *Jn Lockhart*,Laird of *Lee* in *Scotland*.

20. Mr *Andrew Lumisdean*,an Episcopal Minister, and Bishop at *Edinburgh*.

21. Mrs *Eliz. Watson*,aged 95, a Maiden Lady. She left 300 *l*. to the Poor of the Parish of St *George's Southwark*.

22. Mr *La Roche*, a Wine Merchant.

Nathaniel Roffey, Esq; Distiller, and in Commission of the Peace for *Surry*.

Capt. *Berkley*, Commander of the *Tyger*, in his Passage from *Dixey'sCove* to *Barbadoes*.

Benjamin Peake, Esq; chief Agent to the Royal *African* Company, at *Cape-Coast Castle* the 7th of *March* last.

Relict of *George Darby*, Esq;

The Wife of *Samuel Turner*, Esq; in Child-bed, in *Great Ormond-street*.

Sir *Thomas Hatton*, Bar. at *Long-stanton Cambridgshire*. He is succeded by his Brother (Sir) *John*.

Smith Hollinsworth, Esq; in the Commission of the Peace,at *Appleby* in *Leicestersh*.

23. Dr. *Wadsworth*, late Physician to St. *Thomas's Hospital*.

Capt. *James Plunket*, formerly Commander in the *East-India* Service.

Capt.*Armstrong*, an old Sea Commander.

Mr. *Wilson*, Brewer in *Black-Fryers*.

25. *John Shannon*, Esq; at *Abingdon*,

formerly a Merchant of this City.

27. Mr *Smith*, the City Bricklayer.

Sir *John Stonehouse*, Bart. Kt of the Shire for *Berks*, the 9 last Parliaments. And succeeded by his Son (Sir) *John*.

28. The Rt. Hon. Earl of *Sutherland*, one of the 16 Peers for *Scotland*, Kt.of the Thistle. P. C. Lord Lieut. Sheriff and Hereditary Admiral of several Shires and Isles in *Scotland*. His Grandson, call'd Lord *Strathnaver*, succeeds in Honour and Estate.

Mr *Chappellow*, Needle-maker in *Albemarle's-street*, reputed worth 15,000 *l*.

29. Mrs *Bellasyse*, a Relation of the Lord *Fauconberg*, in *Bloomsbury*.

PROMOTIONS,

HEnry *Bland*, Esq; appointed by the *Turkey* Company, Secretary of the Embassy at *Constantinople*.

The Right Hon. the Lord *Lovell*, made joint Commissioner with the Hon. *Edw. Carteret*, Esq; for executing the Office of Post-Master General, in the Room of Gov. *Harrison*, who dy'd in *November* last, from which time Mr *Carteret* had a Commission to act alone.

Thomas Farrington, Esq; has the Grant of the Office of Auditor of his Majesty's Revenues in *Wales*, in the Room of *Sidney Godolphin*, Esq; deceas'd.

Gabriel Johnson, Esq; appointed Captain General, and Governor in Chief of *North Carolina* in *America*.

Isaac Gardner, Esq; made Apothecary General to the Army, in the Room of *Thomas Graham*, Esq; deceas'd.

John Lord *Hervey*, Son and Heir apparent to the E. of *Bristol*, call'd up to the House of Peers, by the Title of Baron *Hervey* of *Ickworth* in the Coun.of *Suffolk*.

James Brudenell,Esq; appointed Groom of the King's Bed-Chamber.

Mr *Nailor*,made one of the Clerks Assistants to the House of Commons, in the Room of Mr *Burroughs*, deceas'd.

E. of *Tankerville* made Master of his Majesty's *Buck Hounds*.

Col. *Read*,promoted to Ld *Albermarle*'s Regiment of Foot at *Gibraltar*.

Col. *Fuller*, succeeds Col. *Read*, as Major in the 1st Reg. of Guards.

Archibald, E. of *Ila*, appointed Keeper of the Great Seal of *Scotland*, in the Room of the Duke of *Montrose*.

The E. of *Jersey* made one of the Gentleman of the Bed-Chamber to the Pr.of *Wales*

Sir *Wyndam Knatchbull*, Bar. appointed High Sheriff of *Kent*, in the Room of Sir *Brooke Bridges*, Bar. deceas'd.

Earl of *Kintore*, appointed Kt. Marshal of *Scotland*, in the Room of Ld *Binning*.

John, Duke of *Athol*——Keeper of the Privy Seal of *Scotland*, in the Room of the Earl of *Ila*.

John E. of *Crawford*, one of the sixteen Peers of *Scotland*——Gentleman of the Bedchamber to the Pr. of *Wales*, in the Room of the E. of *Tankerville*.

Rich. Aldworth, Esq;——Deputy Ranger of *Windsor-Forest*, in room of Col. *Negus*, dec.

Rowland Robinson, Esq; presented to the Command of a Company of Foot on the *Irish* Establishment.

Mr *Jn Collyer*, appointed Deputy Closet Keeper to his Majesty, in the Room of Mr *Dixon*, deceas'd.

Thomas Bold, Esq; Barrister at Law Brother-in-Law to Ald. *Champion*, elected Bailiff for the Borough of *Southwark*.

Robert Westley, Esq; and *Michael Hilderdson*, Esq; elected Sheriffs of *London*.

Solomon Ashley, Esq; chose Governor and Capt. *Abill*, Deputy Governor of the York-Buildings Company, in the room of Col. *Horsey* and his Son.

Mr *Craggs*——a Surveyor in the Brewery

James Rutherford, Esq; Representative for the Shire of *Selkirk* in *Scotland*, made Commissary for *Peebles* in *Scotland*.

Robert Holsford, *James Lightbourn*, *John Bennet*, *Wm. Kynaston*, and *Francis Elde*, Esqs; 5 of the Masters in Chancery, constituted Commissioners to Examine which of the Sufferers in the Charitable Corporation are entitled to the Advantages arising from the Scheme of the new Lottery. *The Persons entitled to Relief are to take the following Oath viz. That the Value of their Real and Personal Estate and Effects, exclusive of their Share, Notes and Bonds in the Charitable Corporation, after a Deduction of so much as will be sufficient to satisfy and discharge all their just Debts, did not on the 25th Day of Dec. 1732, exceed the Sum of 5000l.*

Lord *Harry Powlett*, next Brother to the D. of *Bolton*, and Kt. of the Shire for *Hants*, appointed one of the Lords Commissioners of the Admiralty in the Room of Sir *Charles Wager*, made first Commissioner in the Room of Ld *Torrington* deceas'd.

Ld Viscount *Shannon*, made General of the Horse, in the Room of the late E. of *Cholmondeley*.

Col. *Richard Kane*, appointed Governor of *Port-Mahon* and Island of *Minorca*, in the Room of Ld *Carpenter* deceas'd.

Philip Anstruther, Esq; Representative for the Burghs of *Crail*, &c. and Colonel of a Regiment of Foot, made Lieut. Gov of the said Island in the Room of Col. *Kane*.

George Wade, Esq; Lieut. General of his Majesty's Forces, appointed Governor of *Port William*, Fort *George*, and Fort *Augustus*, in *North-Britain*, in the Room of Major General *Syburgh*, deceas'd.

Major General *Russel*——Governor. And Maj. *James* St. *Clair*, —— Lieut. Gov. of *Berwick upon Tweed*, and *Holy-Island*, in the Room of Major-General *Russel*.

Major General *Sutton*, Representative for *Newark upon Trent*, appointed Governor of the Island of *Guernsey*, in the Room of the late E. of *Cholmondeley*.

Major *Bennet*, of the 2d Troop of Life-Guards, made Gov. of the Island *Scilly*.

Mr *Mountague*, 2d Son to Col. *Mountague*, made Captain Lieut. in his Father's Regiment of Foot.

The Earl of *Selkirk*, one of the 16 Peers for *Scotland*, made Lord Clerk Register of *Scotland*, in the Room of the Earl of *Marchmont*, remov'd.

Peter Campbel, Esq; Member for *Elgin* in *Scotland*, made Lieu. Gov. of *Portsmouth*.

Robert Mac Carty, Esq; Commander of his Majesty's Ship the *Rumney*, made Governour of *Newfoundland*, and the Fort and Garrison of *Placentia*.

The E. of *Albemarle*, appointed to the Command of the Third Troop of Life Guards, in the Room of the E. of *Cholmondley*, deceas'd.

George Howard, Esq; —— Gov. of *Cowes* Castle in the Isle of *Wight*.

Henry E. of *Pembroke*, appointed to the Command of his Majesty's own Royal Regiment of Horse in the Room of Ld *Cobham* who was removed.

Lord *Monson*, made Captain of the Band of Gentlemen Pensioners, *and not Lord Lovel as mentioned in our last*, p. 270.

Artillery Company of London. Sir *Charles Peers*, chosen President, Sir *Gerrard Conyers*, Vice-President, Sir *John Eyles*, Treasurer, *Robert Alsop*, Esq; *and* Sir *Henry Hanky*, Lieutenant Generals, Col *Ferris*, and Major *Osgood*, Major Generals.

Ecclesiastical Preferments conferr'd on the following Reverend Gentlemen.

MR *Tho. Keith*, presented to the Vicarage of *Sawbridgeworth*, *Leicestershire*.

Mr *William Amprons*, —— to the Vicarage of *Foxdale Suffolk*.

Mr *Le Plain*. —— to the Vicarage of *Buckingham*, *Salop*.

William Marble, A. M. chosen Fellow of *Christ's* College *Cambridge*.

Mr *Blomberg*, to the Vicarage of *Fulham*, Mr *Edward Beacon*, —— to the Living of *Watterfield*, *Suffolk*.

Mr *Thomas Stackhouse*, to the Vicaridge of *Beenham*, *Berks*.

Mr *Wm Buttonshaw* —— to the Living of *Hackington* near *Canterbury*.

Mr *Tobias Swinden*, to the Rector of *Kingsdown*, *Kent*.

The Bankrupts in our next.

IT is advised from *Berlin*, that on the 12th Instant the Nuptials of the Prince Royal of *Pruſſia*, and the Princeſs of *Beveren* were celebrated at *Saltzdabl* with great Magnificence.

From *Oran*, That a Detachment of *Spaniards* had intercepted a Convoy of 600 Camels, loaded with all ſorts of Proviſion, and Ammunition, going to the *Algerine* Army, which being alarmed thereat, marched directly out of their Camp to retake it, but the *Spaniards* being ſuccour'd from the Garriſon, a bloody Action enſued, which ended in the Defeat of the *Moors*.

From *Petersburg*, That the Princeſs *Ann* of *Mecklemburg*, had made publick Profeſſion of the Greek Religion, to qualify herſelf for the Honour intended her by her Aunt the *Czarina*, the chief of which is no leſs than ſucceeding her in the Empire. The Undertaking, interrupted by the Death of *Peter* the Great, of digging a Canal along the Borders of *Tartary* as far as *China*, will be carry'd on again. The Great *Mogul* having promis'd to encourage and protect the *Ruſſian* Commerce throughout his Territories.

From *Stockholm*, That the K. of *Sweden*, as Landgrave of *Hiſſe-Caſſel*, had acceded to the Guaranty of the Pragmatick Sanction.

From *Warſaw*, That by the Excluſion which the Dyet of Convocation have paſſed upon Oath, to any Foreign Candidate, K. *Staniſlaus* ſeems to ſtand faireſt to be elected K. of *Poland*; on this Apprehenſion the Emperor, and the Czarina, exert themſelves to prevent a Choice ſo diſagreeable to them, and have Troops in readineſs to enforce their Perſuaſions and Remonſtrances. Many of the Members of the Dyet have, ſince it broke up, complain'd that the Oath was extorted from them, and have apply'd for a Diſpenſation from it to the Court of *Rome*, which is known to favour the Elector of *Saxony*. —*Bavius* in the *Grubſtreet* Journal makes a ſly Remark, *viz. We Proteſtants are much wiſer, who can give ourſelves a Diſpenſation in ſuch Caſes.* And *Mævius* the following Poetical Reflection,

Bleſt realms! where no hereditary right (wight
Intail'd, unchang'd, exalts ſome changeling
But one, in whom all Princely arts have ſhone,
By fair Election mounts the canvas'd Throne:
Unbrib'd, unaw'd, where Patriots ſmiling ſee
Two Foreign Armies march to keep them free.

From *Grand Cairo* in *Egypt*, that the *Turks* having heard that the *Spaniards*

had taken *Oran*, and defeated the *Moors* and *Turks* ſeveral Times, without giving them any Quarter, were ſo enraged, that they reſolved to deſtroy all the Chriſtians in that Country; that they had deprived the *Roman* Catholicks, as well as the *Greeks* of their Churches, and exerciſed the moſt outrageous Cruelties upon the *Franciſcans*, whoſe fine Church and Houſe they had demoliſh'd, and in order to exterminate the *Chriſtians* and *Europeans*, mixed Lime with their Meal, whereby ſeveral loſt their Lives.

From *New England*, That on the 13th of *March* laſt two *Spaniſh* Men of War, of 60 and 70 Guns, and full of Hands, took 4 *New England* Ships near *Tortuga*, where they had been to lade Salt, and chaſed others which were under Convoy of the *Scarborough* Man of War, Capt. *Durell* of 20 Guns, who fought ſeveral Hours, till the reſt of the Fleet, in Number 32, got ſafely off.

Plantation Affairs.

LEtters from *South Carolina* inform us, That the Affairs of that Province are in the utmoſt Confuſion; Mr St *John*, Surveyor-General, and Deputy Auditor of the Province, has been in Cuſtody ever ſince the 10th of *Feb.* laſt. Mr *Cooper*, one of the Aſſiſtant Judges, with moſt of the Gentlemen of the Law have been committed for endeavouring to obtain Writs of *Habeas Corpus* to enquire into the Legality of ſuch Commitments. The People in Trade are much alarm'd at the late Attempts to encreaſe the extraordinary Quantity of Paper Money, and to ſuſpend the *Habeas Corpus* Act, which Proceedings have put a ſtop to all Buſineſs.

From *Georgia*, That the People there are all in good Health, and go on briſkly with the Town of *Savannah*, and are in perfect Amity with all the Indians; and that they have erected a Battery of ſeveral Pieces of Cannon in a Fort that commands the River.

From *Annapolis Royal*, That about the 14th Inſtant at 8 o'Clock in the Morning it ſeemed very ſerene, tho' the Sun did not ſhine out, neither was it overſpread with black Clouds, or the Air foggy. About 9 enſued a Darkneſs, which viſibly increaſed as the Sun approached the Meridian. Between 11 and 12 it became ſo dark, that the People were obliged to light Candles. This ſtrange *Pheuzmenon* was the more extraordinary as there was no poſſibility of an Eclipſe at that Time.

From *Jamaica*, That the run-away Negroes are become very troubleſome, having taken a Town in the Mountains which had been forced from them.

Towards the End of the Month.

Course of Exchange.	STOCKS	*Monthly* BILL *of Mortality, from* May 29, *to* June 26.
Amsterdam 35 *a* 34 11	S. Sea 106 $\frac{1}{4}$	Christned { Males 620, Females 665 } 1285
Ditto at Sight 34 10	—Annu. 110 $\frac{7}{8}$	
Hamburgh— 34	Bank 150 $\frac{3}{4}$	Buried { Males 993, Femal. 1005 } 1998
Rotterdam— 35 1	India 163 $\frac{1}{4}$	
Antwerp — 35 4	3 *per C. Ann.* 103 $\frac{3}{4}$	Died under 2 Years old — 877
Madrid —— 42 $\frac{1}{4}$	M. Bank 116	Between 2 and 5 — 188
Bilboa —— 41 $\frac{1}{8}$	African 29	Between 5 and 10 — 63
Cadiz —— 41 $\frac{3}{8}$	York Buil. no Transf.	Between 10 and 20 — 52
Venice —— 49	Royal Aff. 107 $\frac{1}{2}$	Between 20 and 30 — 129
Leghorn — 50 $\frac{7}{8}$	Lon. ditto 13 $\frac{3}{8}$	Between 30 and 40 — 143
Genoa —— 53 $\frac{5}{8}$	Eng. Copp. 1 *l.* 18 *s.*	Between 40 and 50 — 183
Paris —— 32 $\frac{5}{8}$	Welsh ditto 1 *l.* 6 *s.*	Between 50 and 60 — 157
Bourdeaux — 31 $\frac{3}{4}$	Bank Cir. 7 *l.* 07 *s.*	Between 60 and 70 — 101
Oporto—— 54 $\frac{1}{2}$	India Bonds 5 *l.* 11 *s.*	Between 70 and 80 — 72
Lisbon—— 55 $\frac{1}{2}$ *a* $\frac{3}{4}$	3 *p. Cent* ditto 4 *l.* 4 *s.*	Between 80 and 90 — 27
Dublin—— 11 $\frac{7}{8}$	S. Sea ditto 2 *l.* 15 *s.*	Between 90 and 100 — 6
		1998

Price of Grain at *Bear-Key, per* Qr.		Buried.	Weekly Burials
Wheat 20 *s.* to 25 *s.*	P. Malt 15 *s.* to 19 *s.*	Within the walls, 193	*June* 5 — 578
Rye 12 *s.* to 14 *s.*	B. Malt 15 *s.* to 18 *s.*	Without the walls, 601	12 — 513
Barley 11 *s.* to 13 *s.* 6 *d.*	Tares 14 *s.* to 15 *s.*	In Mid and Surry, 780	19 — 454
Oats 7 *s.* to 11 *s.*	H. Pease 13 *s.* to 15 *s.*	City and Sub of West 424	26 — 453
Pease 15 *s.* to 17 *s.*	H. Beans 14 *s.* to 17 *s.*		

Prices of Goods, *&c.* in *London.* Hay 1 *l.* 16 *s.* to 2 *l.* 0 *s.* a Load.

Coals per Chaldron 25 *s.* to 26 *s.*
Old Hops per Hun. 3 *l.* to 6 *l.*
New Hops 7 *l.* to 9 *l.*
Rape Seed 9 *l.* to 10 *l. per Last*
Lead the Fodder 19 *Hun.* 1 *half on board,* 14 *l.* to 16 *l.* 00 *s.*
Tin in Blocks 4 *l.* 00 *s*
Ditto in Bars 4 *l.* 02 *s. exclusive of* 3 *s. per Hun. Duty.*
Copper Eng. best 5 *l.* 05 *s. per C.*
Ditto ord. 4 *l.* 16 *s.* to 5 *l. per C.*
Ditto Barbary 70 *l.* to 100 *l.*
Iron of Bilboa 14 *l.* 10 *s. per Tun*
Dit. of Sweden 15 *l.* 10 *s. per Tun*
Town Tallow 36 *s.* 00 *s. per C.*
Country Tallow 1 *l.* to 10 *s.*

Grocery Wares.

Raisins of the Sun 31 *s.* 0 *d. per C.*
Ditto Malaga Frailes 19 *s.*
Ditto Smirna new 20 *s.*
Ditto Alicant, 18 *s.*
Ditto Lipra new 19 *s.*
Ditto Belvedera 20 *s.*
Currants old none
Ditto new 45 *s.*
Prunes French 18 *s.*
Figs 20 *s.*
Sugar Powd. best 54 *s. a* 59 *s. per C.*
Ditto second sort 46 *s.* to 50 *s. per C.*
Loaf Sugar double refine 8 *d. Half-penny a* 9 *d. per lb.*
Ditto single refin. 56 *s.* to 64 *s. per C.*
Cinamon 7 *s.* 8 *d. per lb.*
Cloves 9 *s.* 1 *d.*
Mace 15 *s.* 0 *d. per lb.*
Nutmegs 8 *s.* 7 *d. per lb.*
Sugar Candy white 14 *d.* to 18 *d.*
Ditto brown 7 *d. per lb.*
Pepper for Home conf. 16 *d.*
Ditto for exportation 12 *d. Farth.*
Tea Bohea fine 10 *s.* to 11 *s. per lb.*
Ditto ordinary 9 *s.* to 10 *s. per lb.*
Ditto Congo 10 *s.* to 14 *s. per lb.*
ditto Pekoe 8 *s. a* 14 *s. per lb.*
ditto Green fine 8 *s.* to 12 *s. per lb.*
ditto Imperial 10 *s.* to 16 *s. per lb.*
ditto Hyson 24 *s.* to 28 *s.*

Drugs *by the lb.*

Balsam Peru 14 *s.* to 15 *s.*
Cardamoms 3 *s.* 3 *d.*
Camphire refin'd 17 *s.*
Crabs Eyes 2 *s.* 5 *d.*
Jallop 3 *s.*
Manna 2 *s.* 6 *d. a* 4 *s.*
Mastick white 3 *s.* 8 *d.*
Opium 11 *s.* 00 *d.*
Quicksilver 4 *s.*
Rhubarb fine 25 *s. a* 30 *s.*
Sarsaparilla 3 *s.* 0 *d.*
Saffron Eng. 28 *s.* 00 *d.*
Wormseeds none
Balsam Capaiva 2 *s.* 9 *d.*
Balsam of Gillead 18 *s.* 00 *d.*
Hipocacuana 6 *s.*
Ambergreece per oz. 11 *s.*
Cochineal 18 *s.* 3 *d. per lb.*

Wine, Brandy, *and* Rum.

Oporto red, per Pipe 36 *l.*
ditto white 24 *l.*
Lisbon red 30 *l. a* 00.
ditto white, 26 *l.*
Sherry 26 *l.*
Canary new 30 *l.*
ditto old 36 *l.*
Florence 3 *l. per Chest*
French red 30 *l. a* 40 *l.*
ditto white 20 *l.*
Mountain malaga old 24 *l.*
ditto new 20 to 21 *l.*
Brandy Fr. per Gal. 6 *s.* to 5 8 *l.*
Rum of Jamaica 7 *s.* to 0 *s.*
ditto Lew. Islands 6 *s.* 4 *d.* to 10 *d.*
Spirits Eng. 26 *l. per Ton.*

GOLD in Bars, 3 *l.* 18 *s.* 4 *d.*—Ditto in Coin 3 *l.* 18 *s.* 3 *d.* to 4 *l.* 1 *s.*—SILVER in Bars, Standard, 5 *s.* 4 *d.* half-penny.—Pillar Pieces of Eight 5 *s.* to 5 *s.* 5 *d.* 3 farth. ditto Mexico 5 *s.* 5 *d.* 3 farth.

A REGISTER of BOOKS publish'd in JUNE, 1733.

AN Examination of Archdeacon Eachard's Account of the Marriage Treaty between K. Charles II. and Q. Catherine, Infanta of Portugal. By Dr Colbatch. Printed for W. Thurlburn, price 2 s.

2. A Second Letter to Wm Berriman, D.D. In which his Review of his Remarks on the Introduction to the History of the Inquisition, and the Characters of St Athanasius and Martyr Laud, are farther stated and supported. By Samuel Chandler. Printed for John Gray, pr 6 d.

3. A Reply to the Defence of the Dissertation or Inquiry concerning the Gospel according to St Mathew: Wherein is shewn that the Author has left the said Dissertation or Inquiry in many Instances without Defence, and that he has effectually defended it in none. By Leonard Twells. Printed for R. Gosling.

4. The Life and Humorous Adventures of William Grigg of Snarlton in Suffolk. Being a true History of many curious, memorable, and extraordinary Exploits. Published from the Original Manuscript, preserved in the Grubstreet Vatican. By a Native of Grubstreet. Printed for T. Cooper, pr. 1 s.

5. A General History of Printing from the first Invention of it in the City of Mentz, to its Propagation and Progress thro' most of the Kingdoms of Europe, &c. in one Volume 4to. By S. Palmer, Printer. Printed for A. Bettesworth, price 10 s. 6 d.

6. The Philosophical Transactions (from the Year 1720, to the Year 1732.) abridged, and disposed under general Heads; By Mr Reid and John Gray, A. M. F. R. S. in 2 Vols 4to. Printed for W. Innys and R. Manby, with the Approbation of Dr Halley and other Principal Persons of the Royal Society.

7. A Serious Address to Men in Business concerning the right ordering their Affairs; with Advice in Case of those who have unhappily managed. In two Discourses on Prov. xxvii. 23. By John Ford. Printed for R. Ford.

8. A View of the Real Power of the Pope, and of the Power of the Popish Clergy over the Laity; with an Account how they use it. To which is added, the seven Discourses of Abbe Fleury upon his Ecclesiastical History of the first 1400 Years after Christ. Published by T. H. Esq; Sold by J Nourse, pr. 3 s. 6 d.

9. A Sermon preached at St Sepulchre's Church, April 5, 1733. at the Yearly Meeting of the Children educated in the Charity Schools in and about the Cities of London and Westminster. By Robert Ld Bp of Peterborogh. Sold by J. Downing.

10. Obedience to Government: A Sermon preached before the Hon. House of Commons, at St Margaret's Church Westminster, on May 29. 1733. By Tho. Rymer. Printed for S. Billingley, price 6 d.

11. The Resurrection of the same Body, as asserted by St Paul: A Sermon in the Parish Church of Great Torrington on Easter-Sunday, March 25, 1733. By Samuel Johnson, M. A. Printed for L. Gilliver.

12. Advice to an aspiring young Gentleman of Fortune, in Imitation of the Fourth Satyr of Persius.

13. The State Dunces. Inscrib'd to Mr Pope. Printed for J. Dickinson. pr. 1 s. See p317

14. The Satyrist; in Imitation of the Fourth Satire of the first Book of Horace. Sold by Mrs Dodd, pr. 1 s.

15. The London Merchant Triumphant; or Sturdy Beggars are brave Fellows. A new Ballad. Printed for T. Reinshaw. pr. 6 d.

16. The Lover's Pacquet: Or, The Marriage Miscellany, with the newest mode of Courtship, &c. Printed for T. Reynolds, pr. 1 s

17. Mr Taste's Tour from the Island of Politeness, to that of Dulness and Scandal. Printed for S. Slow, pr. 1 s.

18. The Opera of Operas: Or, Tom Thumb the Great. Sold by the Booksellers, pr. 1 s.

19. The Humorous Miscellany: Or, Riddles for the Beaus. Inscrib'd to the Earl of Cardigan. By E— B— Printed for S. Slow price 6 d.

20. The Lady's Slip at Bath. Sold at the Pamphlet Shops, pr. 1 s.

21. The Manners of the Age in Thirteen moral Satyrs, written with a Design to expose the vicious and irregular Conduct of both Sexes. Printed for Jer. Batley.

22. Poems on Affairs of State, collected from the Daily, Evening, and Weekly Papers. To which is added, the History of the Traytors, Edric the Father, and Edric the Son; and of the Settlement of the Danes on the English Throne. Printed for J. Roberts, price 9 d.

23. A Short History of Prime Ministers in Great Britain. Printed by H. Hains, pr. 6 d.

24. A Letter to the Freeholders of Great Britain. Printed for J. Peele, pr. 6 d.

25. A Warning Piece for London; or a Completion of several Prophecies of the Old Testament in these our Days. By Barnaby Beckworth, Lithotomist and Student in Astrology. Printed for J. Roberts, pr. 6 d.

26. The Statesman's Progress: Or, Memoirs of the Life, Administration, and Fall of Honly Chan, Primier Minister to Abenfadir, Emperor of China. In a Letter from a Spanish Father Missionary, to his Friend at Madrid. Printed by P. James, pr. 6 d.

27. The Protests of the Lords in Parliament in 1733. To which is added the State of the National Debt. See p. 293 E.

28. A Bill for Repealing several Subsidies,

dies, and an Impoſt now payable on Tobacco of the Britiſh Plantatiohs, and for granting an Inland Duty in lieu thereof; being the propoſed Law for an Excife on Tobacco. Printed for *W. Webb*, pr. 6 *d.*

29. A Letter from a Member of Parliament to his Friend in the Country; giving his Reaſons for his oppoſing the further Extenſion of the Excife Laws; and ſhewing, That had the late Attempt ſucceeded, it had been deſtructive of Parliament, and fatal to the Conſtitution. Printed by *H. Haines*, pr. 6 *d.*

30. Free Thoughts concerning Souls. In Four Eſſays. By the Author of the Impartial Enquiry, *&c.* Printed for *R. Robinſon*, price 2 *s.*

31. The Drone detected. Or, A Letter to *Euſtace Budgell*, Eſq; Author of the Bee. Being a ſufficient Anſwer to his Letter to every Perſon in *Great Britain.* Printed for *J. Jolliffe*, price 2 *d.*

32. The Expence of Univerſity Education Reduc'd. In a Letter to *A. B.* Fellow of E. C. Printed for *G. Strahan.*

33. The Mirrour: A Collection of Miſcellany Letters on ſeveral Subjects. To which is added, the Trial and legal Convic-

tion of *Alexander Pope* of Dulneſs and Scandal in the High Court of Parnaſſus. Price. 1 *s.*

34 Inſtructions for Planting and Managing Hops, and for raiſing Hop Poles. Printed for *D. Brown*, price 1 *s.*

35. A Friendly Epiſtle to the Author of the State Dunces. Sold by *E. Cooke*, pr. 6 *d.*

36. The Loſs of Liberty. A Poem. Printed for *J. Roberts*, pr. 1 *s.*

37. A Serious Diſſuaſive againſt Subſcriptions for Horſe Racing.

38. Remarks on the ſaid Pamphlet.

39. An Anſwer to the Remarks, being a further Diſſuaſive againſt the Horſe Races. Printed for *Whitworth* at *Mancheſter*, and may be had at St *John's Gate*, if beſpoke.

40. A Satyr on the new *Tunbridge Wells*. Being a Poetical Deſcription of the Company's Behaviour to each other; a ſevere Satyr on the Beaus, Court Ladies, *&c.* Sold at the Pamphlet Shops. pr. 6 *d.*

41. The Court Dunciad. Sold at the Pamphlet Shops, pr. 1 *s.*

42. An Eſſay concerning Rational Notions. To which is added, The Proof of a God. Printed for *W. James.*

Books Publiſh'd in Numbers as uſual.

Note, There are three or four different LISTS *of the Members who voted for and againſt the Exciſing Tobacco, each of which is advertiſed againſt as very imperfect, by the fictitious Publiſhers of the other; and that which pretends to moſt Accuracy, is condemn'd as an Impoſition by the* Craftſman, *who promiſes one (to be given away) that ſhall be Genuine.*

ADVERTISEMENTS.

TICKETS in the LOTTERY for the Year 1733. Bought and ſold by *John Ward,* at the LOTTERY-OFFICE, over-againſt the Swan-Tavern, in *Exchange Alley*; where Numerical Books will be kept during the Drawing; and alſo a Regiſter Book, where any Perſon, entering their Numbers at Six-pence *per* Ticket, may have an immediate Account ſent them of their Succeſs, if in Town, and by the firſt Poſt to any Part of *Great-Britain.* (*See the Number and Value of the Benefits in our laſt Magazine p. 268.*)

N. B. Benefit Tickets are to be paid at the *Bank*, within forty days after the Drawing of the Lottery, without any Deduction.

Any Perſon may come to the Office thro' Mr *Walthe's* Shop, at the *Golden-Ball*, over-againſt the *Royal-Exchange.* There are not three and a half Blanks to one Prize.

Juſt Publiſh'd, the Eighteenth Edition,
Of *DYCHE's* Guide to the Engliſh Tongue,

IN Two Parts. The Firſt proper for Beginners; ſhewing a natural and eaſy Method to pronounce and expreſs both common Words and proper Names, in which particular Care is had to ſhew the Accent, for preventing vicious Pronunciations. The Second for ſuch as are advanced to ſome Ripeneſs of judgment; containing Obſervations on the Sounds of Letters and Dipthongs, Rules for the true Diviſion of Syllables, and the Uſe of Capitals, Stops and Marks, with large Tables of Abbreviations and Diſtinctions of Words, and ſeveral Alphabets of Copies for young Writers. Price 1 *s.* Sold by R. Ware at the Bible and Sun in Warwick Lane.

Alſo may be had juſt Publiſh'd,

II. The Spelling Dictionary: Or, a Collection of all the common Words in the Engliſh Tongue by T. Dyche, Price 1 *s.* 6 *d.* or both bound together 2 *s.* 6 *d.*

(For the Uſe of Schools) the third Edition, of

III. The Fables of PHÆDRUS, who (was made a Denizen of Rome by Auguſtus Cæſar) under the following Heads, *viz.* The Weakeſt goes to the Wall; Chuſe the leaſt Evils; be content in your Station; All covet all loſe; Keep not too great Company, &c. Rendered into familiar Engliſh by THO. DYCHE. Price 1 *s.*

IV. A Deſcription of Three Hundred Animals, viz. Beaſts, Birds, Fiſhes, Serpents and Inſects. With a particular Account of the Whale Fiſhery, Extracted out of the beſt Authors, and adapted to the Uſe of all Capacities, eſpecially to allure Children to read, Illuſtrated with Copper Plates, whereon is curiouſly Engraven, every Beaſt, Bird, Fiſh, Serpent or Inſect, deſcribed in the whole Book. Price 2 *s.* 6 *d.*

V. Tradeſman's Guide. Containing a Liſt of all the Stage Coaches and Carriers; with an Account of all the Fairs and Market Towns in England. Price 1 *s.*

The Gentleman's Magazine:

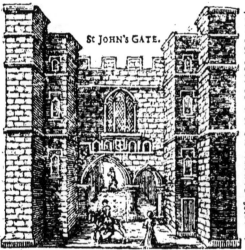

St John's Gate.

Lond Gazette
Lond̄ Jour.
Fog's Journ.
Applebee's ::
Read'g :: : :
Craftsman ::
D. Spectator
Grubstreet J
Wkly Register
Free-Briton
Hyp-Doctor
Daily Court.
Daily-Post
Dai. Journal
Su. Post-boy
P. Advertiser
Evening Post
St James's Ev.
Whitehall Ev.
Lōdon Ev'g
Flying-Post
Weekly Mis-
cellany.

York 2 News
Dublin 6 :::
Edinburgh 2
Bristol :: : :
Norwich 2 ::
Exeter 2 : : :
Worcester : :
Northampton
Gloucester ::
Stamford : :
Nottingham
Bury Journ.
Chester ditto
Derby ditto
Ipswich dit.
Reading dit.
Leeds Merc.
Newcastle C.
Canterbury
Manchester :
Boston ::: ¶
Jamaica, &c.
Barbados :

Or, Monthly Intelligencer,

For JULY, 1733.

CONTAINING,

(more in Quantity, and greater Variety, than any Book of the Kind and Price.)

By SYLVANUS URBAN, Gent.

LONDON: Printed for the AUTHOR, and sold at St *John's* Gate: By F. *Jefferies*, in *Ludgate-street*, at the Pamphlet Shops; and by most Booksellers, 1733. *Where may be had* Compleat Sets, *or any* Single Number.

Juſt Publiſhed,

THE PHILOSOPHICAL TRANSACTIONS (from the Year 1720 to the Year 1732,) abridg'd and diſpos'd under their ſeveral Heads, by Mr *Reid* and *John Gray.* A. M. F. R. S. in two Vols. 4to, being a Continuation of the Abridgment done by Mr *Lowthorp,* and Mr *Jones.*

Printed for *W. Innys* and *R. Manby,* Printers to the Royal Society, at the Weſt End of St *Pauls.*
N. B. This Abridgment by Mr *Reid* and Mr *Gray,* being begun by our Approbation, and encouraged by many Members of the Royal Society, who have revis'd and improv'd their own Papers,
we believe the ſame from our Knowledge of the Abilities of the Compilers to be well executed.

John Arbuthnot, M. D. F. R. S.
Robert Barker, M. D. F. R. S.
James Bradley, Prof. Aſtron. Savil. Oxon, F. R. S.
George Campbell, F. R. S.

J. T. Deſaguliers, L. L. D. F. R. S.
Martin Folkes, V. P. R. S.
John Hadley, V. P. R. S.
Edmund Halley, L. L. D. Reg. Aſtron.
  Prof. Geom. Savil. Oxon, V. P. R. S.
William Jones, F. R. S.

John Machin, Prof. Aſtron. Greſh: Sen R. S.
Colin Mac-Learin, F. R. S.
Abraham de Moivre, F. R. S.
James Stirling, F. R. S.

This is to give Notice, that

THE
Gentleman's Magazine:
JULY, 1733.

A View of the Weekly DISPUTES *and* ESSAYS *in this Month.*

Weekly Miscellany. June 30. No. 29.

R. *Hooker* informs us, that Mr. *Oldmixon* has lately, very lately, printed a Piece, which he gives a- **A** way at his House in *Southampton-Buildings*, under the Title of *a Reply to the groundless and unjust Reflections upon him in three* Weekly Miscellanies (See p. 117, 129, 140) but so little to his Justification **B** that Mr *Hooker* thinks it deserves rather Banter than a serious Answer.

Oxoniensis had charged him with being in Concert with Mr *Ducket* to impose a Cheat on the World, by making Mr *Smith* Author of a Lye, in saying, that the scandalous Expression concerning Mr *Hampden*, in the *History of the Rebellion*, **C** was foisted in by the Editors.

The Reply sets forth, that some Years before the Discovery was talked of, Mr *Oldmixon*, in the Preface to *Clarendon* and *Whitlock compared*, had charged that very Expression on the *Author* of the History, not on the *Editors*; therefore if **D** it was inserted by the *Author*, it could not be *foisted* in afterwards by the *Editors.* Cavillers may still object, that Mr *Oldmixon*, tho' he had formerly charged the Expression on the *Author*, did, notwithstanding, think fit *since* to charge it on the *Editors*, and consequently that he might be concerned with Mr *Ducket* in *inventing* the pretended Evidence of Mr *Smith*, as thinking such a positive Testimony would be more satisfactory to the World than his own bare Assertion.

That there is a Cheat somewhere is certain, because the Passage is to be seen under the Historian's own Hand. (See p. 146 G.) but where shall we fix it? Why, it is likely to fall at last upon one that

is dead, and *cannot deny it*, Mr *Smith*, who imposed upon Mr *Ducket*.

It was expected that Mr O. would have reply'd to the *Reasons* offer'd in Support of the Genuineness of the History. (For which Mr *Hooker* fairly offers him a Page in his Paper, since he pretends he is refus'd it in others.) But hold there; he is not to be catch'd by such a Youngster as *Oxoniensis*. He was engaged in a useful Work that will make waste Paper of *Clarendon* and *Echard*, and which is now ready for the Press. And I cannot, says Mr *Hooker*, but congratulate the World, upon the intended Publication of a 2d Volume of his History, not inferior to be sure to the first. As to Materials, Method, Style, Diction, Language, and Fidelity, the Historical Talents of this Writer were never yet question'd by any of his Admirers, tho' the rest of the *malicious World* have denied him, at least, *one* necessary Qualification. *Ne quid falsi dicere audeat, ne quid veri non audeat.* R. HOOKER.

Extract from Mr Oldmixon's *Answer to the foregoing* Miscellany, *viz.*

'T IS false that I was concern'd with Mr *Ducket* in inventing the Story, I was not known to Mr *Ducket* at the Time it was written to me in the Country, by a Person whose Veracity Dr *Oxoniensis* knows and dares not object to.'

What could hinder my believing that Mr *Ducket* spoke Truth, when the foisting in such shocking and false Expressions to *serve the Cause*, was so agreeable to the Character of all that were said to be concerned in it? Mr *Ducket's* Letter, in which he offers to attest it, remains with Mr *Cox* under the *Royal Exchange*.

He aims awkwardly at Raillery, in misrepresenting my bringing a good Character of Mr *Hampden*, from *Whitlock* and *Ludlow*, that the Passage was not genuine; Stupid to a Prodigy! I brought it to prove, That the Expreſſion about *Hampden* being, for that Reaſon, ſlanderous and untrue, it was more for the Hiſtorian's Credit to think any one ſaid it rather than himſelf. If he will make me ſay, That the *Clarendon Hiſtory* is not to be named the ſame Day with Gen. *Ludlow*'s. I defy him, and any of his *Profeſſors* in Hiſtory to prove that it is; or that there is one Fact in the former, on the Parliament Side, fairly repreſented. There are Hundreds of Charges of Miſrepreſentations againſt that *Hiſtory*, in the *Critical Hiſtories*, and *Clarendon* and *Whitlocke* compar'd; let them diſcharge it of them if they can.

In the Book at *Bartlet's Buildings*, (See p. 146, H) which he poſitively ſays was depoſited there for ſight; and the Gentleman poſitively denies he was authoriſed to ſay it, the Expreſſion about *Hampden* is not in the *Body* of it, but in the *Margin*, referr'd to by an *Aſteriſk*.

I am, oblig'd to him for his ingenuous Recommendation of my *ſecond Volume* of the *Hiſtory of England*, That *it will not be inferior to the firſt*, as to Materials, Method, Style, Diction, Language and Fidelity; tho' he might have left out the Words *Diction* and *Language*, which I ſuppoſe he added for the ſake of that uſeful, declamatory Figure *Tautology*. He ought to know that *Diction* is the technical Word for the *great Poetry*; *Language* is the ſame for *Comedy, Fſſays,* &c. and *Style* particularly apply'd to *Hiſtory*.

As to the making waſte Paper of *Clarendon* and *Echard*, I do not recollect that I ſaid it of *both*; but, whether I ſaid it or not, aſk Mr *T*—— in the *Strand*, and Mr *M*——on *Tower-Hill*, Whether it is true, or not?

London Journal, June 30. No. 731.

MR *Osborne* continues to argue againſt the Power and Authority of the People over their Repreſentatives, from it's Tendency to a *total Diſſolution* of the Government and Conſtitution, by making the *People* the *Legiſlature*

Next he proceeds to make ſome Obſervations on the *Craftſman*, (See p. 307.) who traduces the K——as *garbling* the Army to ſubdue the People to tyrannic Sway, only becauſe he hath diſmiſſed a *noble Lord from his Poſt of Colonel of Horſe,* who was turned out once before, that is immediately after the *Peace*, in the *Four laſt Years of Q. Anne*. But, ſays *Osborne*, no Inſinuation can be more villainous than

that the N—Perſon was diſmiſſed for *the ſame way of Thinking and Acting*. He was then diſmiſs'd for making a *glorious Stand* againſt *Meaſures* calculated to *overturn* our Liberties, and bring in the *Pretender*. Can the *ſame way* of Thinking and Acting be the *Cauſe of Diſmiſſing* the ſame *Perſon* at this Time? Are the Actions of the Court the ſame now, as in the Four laſt Years of Q. *Anne*? It muſt be a *different Way* of Thinking and Acting; and what Wonder? Are Men always the ſame? Don't they grow peeviſh with Age and Infirmities? Don't they carry about them *ſtrong Paſſions*, which bear them ſometimes, like a Torrent, againſt all Principles of Reaſon? — Have we not of late heard of *Perſons* ſigning a moſt *notorious Libel* that ever was drawn (ſee p. 293. 295. againſt the Adminiſtration, who, not long ago, would have abhorr'd the *Drawers* and *Signers*? Have we not heard of *undutiful*, and almoſt ſeditious Behaviour, not *in the Houſe*, but *out of the Houſe*? Have we not heard of *Factious Aſſemblies* kept at ——? Why ſhould we ſuppoſe ſome *Deſign laid by* the Court which an *honeſt Man* can't come into? Why not rather ſuppoſe, that the ſame Perſon who was once for *Liberty*, is now for *Faction*?

The ſame Charge of a Deſign to enſlave the Nation is made in a Pamphlet call'd, *The Hiſtory of Prime Miniſters*, wherein a *Man in a high Station* is accus'd of promoting a deſtructive Change of Manners, and of throwing into his Maſters Hands ſuch an *abſolute Power* as may be ſufficient to protect him againſt the whole Kingdom. But for Proof, not one Action is brought, except of *Miniſters dead* ſeveral Hundred Years ago. Here lies the Argument; one *John Gray*, a *Norfolk* Man, in K.*John's* Reign, ſo oppreſſed the People by cruel and arbitrary Actions, as to cauſe his Maſter to be hated, and at laſt poyſon'd, therefore Sir R—W— a *Norfolk* Man, does the ſame now. This is the *Reaſoning,* and this the *Honeſty* of our *Patriots*, who, in their *parallel* Hiſtories are always fond of bringing in a Queen. The Queen and *Tho. Becket*! The Queen and *Suffolk*! &c. To which nothing ought to be ſaid, but that there is no Poſſibility of adding to the *Villainy* of the *Suggeſtion*. —

Thus are *theſe Patriots* perverting the Minds, corrupting the Judgments, and alienating the Affections of the People from his Majeſty and his Government; yet charge this *Alienation of Affections* to the *Actions* of the Miniſtry. This, perhaps, may be

Matter

Matter of Sport to Men who wish for a *Change of Hands*; but ought to awaken the Vigilance and Attention of the *Whigs*, and particularly of the *Protestant Dissenters*, who should consider, that if thro' *false Prejudices*, and *little Resentments*, they either join with the Enemy, or grow *cool* and *indifferent*, Liberty is gone.

Daily Courant, July 3.

A 2d Letter to —— Esq; (See p. 314)

THE Design of the Writer of this Letter is to request the Assistance of the Gentleman he writes to, in rendring abortive the Scheme of the *Male-contents* in the Western part of the Kingdom. To that End he communicates to him the following particulars of it to him.

A *noble Person*, says he, of your Acquaintance, having differed sometimes in his Sentiments from the *Ministry*, has had it intimated to him, that, provided a strong Interest could be made in the *North*, the *Western* Counties might be prevailed on to shew bolder Signs of Dissatisfaction, than hitherto the *Heads* of the *Male-contents* have dared to express. The *Purport* of these Insinuations is, doubtless, that by proper Methods, they may be excited to speak the *Language* of the *Discontented* and *Disaffected*, in *Petitions* or *Addresses*, from which the *Faction* would quickly bellow on the Topicks of *Publick Danger* and *instant Ruin*, if the *Prince* should refuse to hearken to the *Voice of the People*; for such would the *Clamours* be called of but *two* or *three hot headed Corporations*. But I am in no pain for these Threats; nor can I dread from the *People*, what is so apparently against their *Interest*, and what, if they should *attempt*, must prejudice them by its *Effects*.

However, as the *Recess of Parliament* is the Harvest of the *Male contents*, in which they have Leisure to corrupt the *Country*; I send you some Minutes to enable you to answer their most florid *Orators*. We are sensible that *Men* of the *greatest Rank* among them will stoop to the most contemptible Methods of stirring up Sedition, and bringing over *Converts* to the Party. 'Tis therefore I send you this short *Brief* of the Merits of our *Cause*.

First, I observe, that the Safety or Danger of the *Common-wealth* depends strongly on the Disposition of the *Prince*. Monarchs of fierce and haughty Spirits, who set a greater Value on Glory, than on the Welfare of their Realms, often begin their Conquests by subduing those who dispute their Will at Home. *Kings* of soft and indolent Tempers, are liable to be corrupted by Favourites. But while we have a brave, generous, honest and religious Prince on the Throne, careful of his Subjects, and satisfied with the ample Territories that of Right belong to him, what have we to fear?

Next to the *Disposition* of the *Prince*, the *Publick* Safety depends much on the Disposition of his *Ministers*. Where they are Foreigners, Men of low Births, bad Characters, and desperate Fortunes, the Subjects have every Thing to fear. But when we behold none but our Countrymen; *Nobles* of the best Families and Fortunes, in greatest *Credit* at Court, and in the highest *Offices*; when we distinguish among the Ministry those glorious Patriots, who, in a late Reign, by a vigorous Opposition, defeated the formidable Conspiracy enter'd into by a *wicked Administration* to overturn our Constitution, and introduce *Slavery*, that they might continue *Engines* of *Oppression*, why should we distrust them; or imagine that they should at once sacrifice their own Interest, and that of the Publick? Experience hath demonstrated in their Favour. When the *most Noble Person*, against whom the *Malice* of the *Faction* is chiefly bent, came last into Office, the *Publick Affairs* were in the most *deplorable Condition*, occasion'd by the Event of the *South Sea Scheme*; a Project strenuously opposed by the *present Minister*; our *Transactions* with *Foreign Powers* in great Confusion, the *Jacobites* elate. Let us remember, how those Heats and Discords have been gradually cooled, and *Publick Credit* revived; how by a Series of wise and well-timed *Treaties*, our Perplexities with *Foreign* Courts have been untwisted, and a solid *universal Peace* established; how the open and secret Attempts of the *Pretender* and his Adherents, have been overthrown, with the Assistance of ONE, who, out of Spleen, is now *Building* up what he then out of *Zeal* towards his *Country* destroy'd. In fine, comparing the present Posture of *Affairs* at *Home* and *Abroad*, with what they were in 1721, no honest Man will deny, that the Epithets *Wise*, *Able*, and *Industrious* for the *publick Good*, are due to the *present Ministry*, and particularly to that *Honourable Person* so often libelled by the CRAFTSMAN.   R. F.

The *Free-Briton,* Ju'y 5. No. 189.

MR *Walsingham*, from another Writer, tells us, That as no good Minister can be safe, where mischievous Minions

nions prevail, fo neither can a Prince or his State. *James* the 5th of *Scotland,* had not only, fays he, a fair Opportunity of eftablifhing a lafting Peace with *England,* but alfo of fucceeding his Uncle *Harry* the 8th, *Mary* the only Daughter of that Prince being declared illegitimate, when he courted *James* to a clofe Alliance. Nothing could promife better to *Scotland,* nothing more Honourable to the *Scotch* King. He accepted the Propofal, and the *English* Ambaffadors return'd highly fatisfy'd. But K. *James* had Minions of more prevalence than his Council, his Honour, or Intereft. To thefe Minions, fome of 'em Clergymen, the Bifhops apply, and engage them to diffuade the King. They frightened him with the Word *Herefy,* faid it was grown up in *England,* and was growing faft in *Scotland,* and fhew'd him how by fuppreffing it he might enrich himfelf with the Eftates of the Hereticks.

The K. liften'd to the Propofal, till the Laird of *Grainge* his Treafurer, an honeft, bold Man, convinced him of his Error. The next Step therefore was to ruin the Treafurer, by defaming him to the King. " He was proud, a Heretick, carried an *English* New Teftament in his Pouch; nay, fo arrogant, that he would not proftitute his Son's Wife to his Majefty's Pleafure." For not obeying in this laft, when the venerable Prelates had put the King on fending for the Lady, whom they reprefented to be very fair, the Treafurer was very near being Imprifon'd; but tho' he efcaped that Danger, he could not prevail with the King to keep his Promife with *England*; fo was he ruled by his Minions. *Harry* the 8th rages, vows Revenge, and fends an Army to lay *Scotland* defolate. The *Scotch* King too raifes Forces, but Forces without Heart, as commanded by his Minion *Sinclair.* The Lords and Principal Officers, thro' Indignation refufed to fight, nay fuffer'd themfelves to be taken Prifoners. The Army thus overthrown, the Kingdom expofed, and the K. reduced to Anguifh and Difgrace, all Mouths were open'd againft the Bifhops; amongft the reft his Majefty, having now his Eyes epen, let fall fome Expreffions againft them, for which they took fevere Vengeance. Such Men never retract, never forgive. The troubled State of the Kingdom did not move them. They had learnt the Art of making an *Italian Poffet,* and with this they fhut up the Days and Reign of *James* the fifth. Were not thefe notable Directors of a Monarch's Power and Confcience? But they were Popifh Pre-

lates; whereas the Proteftant Clergy are meek, confcienrious, difintereffed, fincere and no ways ambitious of Rule.

Such was the Fate of this Prince, poffefs'd of many good Qualities, but undone by being feduced to forfake honeft and worthy Advifers, to follow deceitful, felfifh and corrupt.

Grubftreet Journal, July 5. N°. 184.

Proposal for a Theatrical College.

Mr BAVIUS,

NOthing, I think, can more promote the Glory of a Prince, which is the Good of his People, than the eftablifhing and endowing a Theatrical College.

Exeter Change, now to be fold, might be turned into a fpacious Theatre; and there is Ground enough in the other part of the Eftate to erect the adjoining College with two Wings, one for the Apartment of the Men; the other for the Women. Thefe to be under the Direction of one Head Governor; competent Salaries to be eftablifh'd, with other Profits, and neceffary Provifions for Officers, Servants, &c. This would be a handfome Subfiftance for our decay'd Gentry; or for thofe who have deferved larger Eftates, and better Fortune in the World. None fhould be admitted who have not had a genteel and liberal Education. If any of either Sex fhould lofe their fair and honeft Character, to be expell'd, and the Delinquents Place immediately fill'd up. This would encourage Virtue, difcountenance Vice, advance Education, and be the means of perfecting Theatrical Entertainments, as well as the Performance of them.

The Governor ought to be a Gentleman of the beft Underftanding in Theatrical Affairs, to examine all Plays, and dramatical Entertainments; to order all Decorations of the Stage; and to inftruct young Players in their feveral Parts; in all which he might have the Affiftance of proper Perfons, who fhould have a handfome Allowance. This would be the greateft Glory, as well as Advantage to the Nation, the beft of Diverfions, and a new Sort of Charity. Foreigners would not then find our Theatres, which fhould be Fountains of Wit, Fountains of Folly. What muft they think of our Mafters, &c. or indeed of the whole Nation, who encourage fuch defpicable Wretches in all Degrees? But our new Theatrical College would make us admir'd by our Neighbours, and probably induce them to follow our Example.

PHILO-BRITANNUS.

The

The **Craftsman**, July 7. Nº 366.

A Modern Whig's Political Creed.

ABout 5 Years ago, says *D'anvers*, I gave the political Creed of a *Modern Whig*, in Opposition to the original Principles of *that Party*; but the *ministerial Writers* have since added several new Articles, especially the following *viz.*

That *the People in Office and Favour at* Court *ought to engross* all the Lands in the Kingdom.

That *to assert the* King's Parliamentary Title, *in Opposition to* Hereditary Right, *is bordering upon High-Treason.*

That *the* Majesty of the whole People *is invested by our Laws in the Person of the* King.

That *the* Crown *ought to have a pecuniary Influence over the* House of Commons.

That *the* People *have no Right, in their* collective, *or corporate Capacities, to instruct their own* Deputies; *even in Cases, which affect their Trade and Liberties.*

That Excises, *which deprive the Subject of* Trials by Juries, *and expose his Business to the* Inquisition *of Crown Officers, are the most effectual means of promoting* Trade.

That *standing Armies are the best Preservative of* publick Liberty; *especially when duly garbled and modelled to ministerial Purposes.*

Let History determine whether *these Tenets* are not diametrically opposite to the very first Principles of *that Party*; or, whether *Whiggism* was not originally founded on *popular Liberty*, in Opposition to the Encroachments of *Prerogative*, and the *Power of the Crown*; and whether our pretended Whigs have not borrow'd their Arguments from the *Tory Writers* of former Reigns, in behalf of a *perpetual Revenue, Excises, pensionary Parliaments,* and *standing Armies*?

Indeed of late, the Names of *Whig* and *Tory* have been happily laid aside, the Consequences of which the *Ministerial Writers* apprehending, spare no Pains to divide us again. This is the Burthen of Mother *Osborne's* Reveries, for several Weeks past, who exerts all the little Pathos in her Power, to set the People of *England* together by the Ears about *Shadows*, that her *good* Patron may have an Opportunity of running away with the *Substance*: But every Attempt of this kind serves only to unite them more closely in that *honest Confederacy*, on which the Preservation of their *Liberties* absolutely depends.

One great Topick of Complaint is, that *Opposition* gives Strength to the *Tory Party* and may endanger the *present Establishment*; whereas it hath been manifestly carried on entirely on *Whig-Principles*; th. Principles of the *Revolution*, on which this *Government* was founded, and on which only it can be supported. The *Ministerial Writers* are so sensible of this, that they have been obliged to dress up a strange Monster, called *Republican-Jacobitism*, or something between a *Commonwealth* and an *absolute Monarchy*; which they hop'd would frighten the People into their Arms for Protection; but have seen their *Bugbear* treated with Contempt.

One thing is to be admir'd in the Writings and Conduct of *these Gentlemen*; tho' they are always angry at any Coalition of Parties, where the *Country Interest* is concerned, yet are they fond of Proselytes on the *other side of the Question*, and spare nothing to gain them, however formerly tainted with *Tory, Jacobite,* or even *Popish Principles*. A little dutiful Compliance gives a Place amongst the best Friends of the Government.

These Writers tells us, our present Misfortunes and Disturbances are owing to the *Gentlemen in the Opposition*; in this perhaps they are not altogether in the Wrong; for, if they reckon the Loss of the *Excise Bill* a Misfortune; I grant, says *D'anvers*, it was entirely owing to the pertinacious Opposition of these *Gentlemen*; who have likewise been very officious in their Endeavours to reduce our *Army, Debts,* and *Taxes*; to discover *Frauds* in great Companies, and to punish the *Authors* of them, to prevent *Corruption, Stock-jobbing,* and all *Misapplications of the publick Money*; besides other *Attempts*, that may have disturbed a *certain Gentleman*; but of which the People have manifested their Sense in a Manner, that will for ever do Honour to the *British* Nation abroad, and may be a Warning to *some Persons* at home.

It is true, all *Opposition* naturally creates Ferment and Contention; but should *Ministers*, be left to do as they please?

Liberty and *Property* are neither *Whig,* nor *Tory*, but common to all Men, and therefore all Men will naturally rise in their Defence, when They see these invaded. The *late Project* was universally look'd upon as such an Attempt, and consequently united the Body of the Nation against it. The Progress of this Opposition was indeed attended with some Warmth and Resentment; but to whom must it be
im-

imputed? To Thofe who were neceffita-
ted to ftand up in their own Defence; or
to Him, who reduced Them to that Neceffity? Who may be moft properly faid
to delight in *Confufion*, and *inflame the
Minds of the People*? Thofe who oppofed
an *unnatural Scheme*, or He, who projected and perfifted in it till it created *Tumults and Diforders*, that almoft threat-
en'd the Peace of the Kingdom!

As to the *Pretender*, if he has any
Hopes, as I wifh he may have none,
they can be grounded on nothing but the
Profpect of fome *corrupt, all-bribing,
all fcreening, all-excifing Minifter*; who,
being confcious of his own Guilt and the
publick Hatred, may endeavour to draw
his Mafter into ruinous Projects, under
fpecious Pretences in Hopes of efcaping
unobferved Himfelf, amidft the general
DESTRUCTION.

But if ever fuch a *Monfter of Power*
fhould arife in this Country, We rely on
the Vigour of an *uncorrupt* Parliament to
defeat his Schemes; and as the Time is
drawing near, when the People will have
an opportunity of fhewing their Sentiments, We doubt not They will fet a
Mark upon every Man, who appears in
a *certain Lift* as an Enemy to their *Trade*
and *Liberties*, and make Choice of thofe
only, in whom they have Reafon to confide, either from their former Services,
or their known Characters in the World,
without any Regard to little *Party-Dif-
ferences*, or *Diftinctions*.

London Journal July 7. Nᵒ. 732.
*Anfwer to the Argument in the laft
Craftfman, That the late Bill about
Tobacco and Wine would hurt Trade,
injure the Conftitution, and deftroy Par-
liaments.* (See p. 315.)

ALL Hands are employ'd, fays *Ofborne*, to render the M—r odious,
yet his Enemies conftantly complain of
Papers and Pamphlets fent all over the
Kingdom in his Juftification. Very arrogant truely! But they feem to imagine
the Game their own. The *Nation*, fay
they, is againft the M—r, and he muft fall.
If by *the Nation*, they mean all wifh him
out, and themfelves in; *unfair Traders,
Smugglers*, &c. or thofe who have been
deceived by *falfe Reprefentations* of Men
and Things; they are certainly right: But
Men of Senfe, unprejudiced, and not immediately interefted, and Thoufands a-
mong the *Tradefmen*, don't think the
worfe of him for this Bill. They know it

was a *juft* and *equitable Defign* to do National Juftice, to prevent Frauds, and increafe the publick Revenues without any
new Tax. But a *Letter from a Member
of Parliament to his Friend in the Country*,
quoted by the laft *Craftfman*, endeavours
to prove it dangerous Conftitution: His
whole Argument ftands thus: *The Harmony which has fubfifted between King
and Parliament, hath been from the neceffity they lie under of each other: But
this Bill would have* taken away that neceffity, *by furnifhing the King with Money enough* in Perpetuity, *inftead of Duties,
annually granted and appropriated.* -- But
this Bill would not have deftroy'd *that
Neceffity*; therefore the Conclufion is falfe.
Indeed, if the Bill would have raifed Money enough in Perpetuity to fupply *all Taxes* now *annually* raifed, and to be raifed in
future, and fo the Army paid, and Charges
of Government defray'd; and all this
Money left *unappropriated*, then the Conclufion would have been juft: But this is
not the Cafe; the Bill laid no *new* Duty,
and only alter'd the *old* into a more effectual Method of Collection; therefore the
Conftitution muft be *the very fame* as before. As to the *Additional Money* to be
brought into the *Exchequer* by this Bill,
Care might have been taken, that it fhould
not be employed by the Crown *at Pleafure*. What that Money would have been
no Body can tell; but fuppofe it would
have ferved to have taken off the *Land
Tax*, could not this *Additional Money* have
been *Annually appropriated* by Parliament
to *neceffary* Services? But 'tis faid, the King
may *feize* this Money: It may be fo; and
fo he may break thro' all the Laws of
England; but if he fhould feize Money
appropriated for the *Nation's Ufe*, he would
be a *publick Robber*; and if a King fhould
ever come to *robbing Exchequers*, as K.
Charles II. did; we know our *Remedy*.

What trifling Arguments are thefe!
For, befides the Confideration of the *annual Appropriation* to be made, is 3, or 4,
or 500,000 *l.* a Year, enough to deftroy
the *mutual Neceffity* and *Dependance* of
King and Parliament on each other.

Ay, but fays the Author of the Letter,
*We are not fo weak as to imagine, they
would have ftopp'd at Tobacco and Wine*.
Prove what you fay. The People at the
Revolution might with equal Juftice have
objected to 1 *s.* on the Land, becaufe it
might have ferved as a Precedent to the
laying 3, 4, and 5 more, and fo on.
But any thing will ferve for Argument,
which

when Men have ſtrong *Intereſts* and *Prejudices* ; for nothing elſe could have made a Scheme, which had hut one Inconvenience attending it, *viz.* a little Trouble to a few Tradeſmen, ſo generally diſliked. *Oſborne* ſays, he is ſatisfy'd, and unprejudiced Men will conſider, that the Miniſter's Deſign was the publick Good.

Weekly Miſcellany, July 7. No. 30.

Remarks on Mr Chandler's *Introduction to his Tranſlation of* Limborch's *Hiſtory of the Inquiſition.*

Mr HOOKER,

IN the abovemention'd Piece I have obſerv'd many Facts, plainly miſrepreſented, which diſcover the Prejudice and Bias of the Author. This Charge I ſaw made good by Dr *Berriman's Remarks* in ſeveral Particulars of the *4th* and *5th* Century. Where the Dr touches upon Part of Archbiſhop *Laud's* Character, he ſeems to expect ſome other Hand would enter more fully upon that Province, and *chaſtiſe* his Adverſary *in that and other Parts of* Engliſh *Hiſtory.* I have therefore determin'd to take Notice of one extraordinary Paragraph :

Having mention'd the Over-throw of Biſhops and Common-Prayer in *England,* and the Eſtabliſhment of the *Presbyterian Diſcipline,* he proceeds thus.-- *The Writers of the Church-Party think this an everlaſting Brand of Infamy upon the Presbyterians. But how does this throw greater Infamy upon them, than the Subverſion of* Presbytery in Scotland, *and the impoſing Canons and Common-Prayer upon that Nation, doth on* Laud *and his Creatures?* The ſame Arguments that will *vindicate the Alterations made in* Scotland *by the* King *and the* Biſhops, *will vindicate thoſe made in* England *by the* Parliament *and the* Presbyterians.

As to the firſt of theſe, if the Archbiſhop had been the Perſon who procured it in a peaceable and legal Manner, I believe it would not have been reckon'd among his Crimes. But this is falſe in Fact. *Spotſwood* maintains, that the Government of Biſhops was receiv'd in *Scotland* from the firſt Eſtabliſhment of Chriſtianity : And it continu'd at the Reformation, till *Andrew Melvil,* who had learnt another Platform at *Geneva,* raiſed an Oppoſition to it in *1575* ; and in *1580* got their Juriſdiction diſallow'd by an Act of Aſſembly, and, their Temporalities taken away by Act of Parliament, in 7 Years

more, which K. *James,* in 1606 got reſtor'd by the ſame Authority, and in 1610 their Eccleſiaſtical Juriſdiction, when he obtain'd ſome of their nominal Biſhops to receive Conſecration in *England,* and then go back to their own Country to confer the Order on more ; *Laud* then being but a private Clergyman.

The other Thing charged upon the Archbiſhop, is his introducing the Liturgy or Service-Book in *Scotland* ; and mention'd as a Balance for our Sectaries putting it down at Home. But I except both to the Fact and the Parallel. When K. *James* had reſtor'd the Biſhops, this Thing was reſolved on in 1616, and ſome *Scots* Biſhops were appointed to compile a Liturgy accordingly. The Service-Book was made, tho' not brought into Uſe, before the Death of K. *James.* After K. *Charles's* Progreſs into that Kingdom, this Buſineſs was reſumed ; the Liturgy reviſed by the *Scots* Biſhops ; and tho' framed upon the Model of the *Engliſh* Liturgy, yet vary'd ſo as not to ſeem preſcribed to them from the Church of *England.* The Uſe of it after this, was requir'd by the King's Authority, with the Advice of the Privy Council of *Scotland,* as agreeable to Law, as the tumultuous Rejection of it was illegal and unwarrantable. *Laud* might have a Hand in conducting the King's Councils, and in conferring with the *Scots* Biſhops : But as the Legality of the whole Proceeding is not liable to any juſt Exception, Mr *Chandler* ſhould have made a wide Difference between that Tranſaction and the Overthrow of our Eſtabliſhment at Home. K. *Charles* in his *Declaration concerning the Tumults in Scotland,* printed 1639, (from whence follows a large Quotation,) clears *Laud* from projecting or preparing the Thing, and ſhews that it was done by *Scotſmen* according to Law, and eſtabliſh'd by himſelf in diſcharge of his Duty and Conſcience.

The **Daily Journal,** July 7.

To ―――― *Eſq; in* Somerſetſhire.

SIR,

YOU tell me that the *Sticklers* againſt the *Miniſtry* would perſwade every 'Borough, that, to have their *Liberties* ſafe ; they are to reject, at the next Elections, whoever voted for the *Bill of Exciſe.* That this is an unjuſt Way of Proceeding, I will endeavour to demonſtrate. The chief Heads of a *Member's* Duty

in

in Parliament are, 1. The Care of *their* particular Concerns who *Elect* him; and 2. The maintaining the *Constitution*, and doing every Thing neceffary for the Safety, Eafe, or Reputation of the Government, *i. e* the *Publick*. If a Gentleman difcharges his Confcience. in all thefe Refpects, his *Electors*, in *Juftice*, ought to chufe him again. The *Teft* of what is for the Safety, Eafe, or Reputation of the *Publick*, muft be every *Member's private Judgment*, which his *Electors* prefume fufficient by conftituting him their *Reprefentative*; and if *he* keep that *unbiaffed*, nothing more can be expected from *him*. Let us now fee how far the *Bill* for altering the Method of collecting the *Duties* on *Tobacco*, clafhes with what is here laid down.

The Reafons affign'd for making this *Alteration* were, That prodigious *Frauds* are committed in the prefent Method of Collection, and not to be prevented while under the *Commiffioners* of the *Cuftoms*; that thefe *Frauds* induced a *Neceffity* of raifing a *large Sum of Money* on the *Subjects*; that the prefent Methods of levying the *Duties* were found fo grievous to the Planters of this *Commodity*, as to occafion their loudeft Complaints; that by the propofed *Alteration*, all thefe Evils would be effectually cured; the whole Duty collected into the *Exchequer* at a *fmall Expence*, with fcarce any Danger of Fraud or Embezzlements; a large Addition made to the *publick Revenue*, which might be apply'd in Eafe of thofe grievous, unequal Taxes heretofore impofed; the Planters deliver'd from their *Oppreffions*; and thefe Advantages purchafed at the Expence only of Smugglers, and other unfair Dealers. (See p. 121.)

As to *Frauds* in the *Cuftoms*, undeniable Teftimonies have been already *laid* before the World, and many. more will fhortly appear: From whence it will be evident, that the *Government* has been deprived of fome 100,000 *l.* a Year by the Cheats in this Commodity. The Planters, with inconteftable Reafon, afcribe their Sufferings to the collecting, thefe *Duties* by way of Cuftom. How much the *Publick* would gain from the *Variation* of the prefent Method. is not eafily laid down; but the Experience of 2 or 3 Years would have nearly determin'd it. (See p. 122 E.)

That the pofitive *Inftructions* of a *Corporation*, without any Reafons affigned, or againft Reafon, are not fufficient to bind up the *Hands* of a *Member*, muft be admitted, otherwife our *Boroughs*, like the *Towns* in *Holland*, would in fome meafure be *independent States*. The utmoft therefore that can be infifted on, is, that *Members* pay a Regard to the Directions of their *Conftituents*, if thofe Directions are confiftent with the *Intereft* of their Country. The Reafons affign'd in the late *Inftructions* were, That the Bill was calculated to *overturn* the *Conftitution*, by giving too much *Power* to the *Crown*, and to ruin Trade, by incumbering it with *Permits*, &c. Now, if on debating the Matter, it plainly appeared that it would not be attended with fuch Confequences, then might the *Members* vote for its becoming a Law, in Difcharge of their *Duty* towards the *Common Wealth* in general, notwithftanding their *Conftituents* being *mif-inform'd*; and this fhould confequently incline the *Electors* in their Favour.

Grub-ftreet Journal. July 12. No. 185.

An *Account* of a journey to PARIS, in a letter from a COUNTRY SQUIRE to his PAPA.

Paris in France, this 16th of June, annoq; Domini 1733. in the 7th year of K. GEORGE the fecond

Ever honoured Sir, mon pere,

*A*Fter *my humble duty remember'd to you hoping you are in good health, as I am at this prefent writing; this is for to let you know, that we left Dover laft tuefday was three weeks, to faile upon the maine ocean fea; and having a bloudy ftrong gale of wind, we gott to Callis in foure houres: but I did not half like it, for I was moft confumed fea fick; and our DICK was fo abominablie bad, that I thought he would have been vivat rex, and dy'd upon the fpott: he muted, and caft to that degree, as if he would have brought up his very pluck and harflet. We had no fooner landed, but we were hurryed to the governor, and then to the cuftomhoufe, where we had a mortall deal of trouble with my portmantle; and DICK had fire to have left the bag where was all my cleane linnen, and old fhoets. And as neither DICK nor I underftood then one word of French, we had like to have been bamboozled; but by the help of a well-fpoken Englifh gentleman. a very handfom bodyed perfon in the face, (whom I found was a drawer at the filver lyon tavern there,) we gott out of that fcrape, and he very civilly carryed us to the houfe where he had the honour to ferve. There we lived in clover, and there I found two Englifh travellers going to Paris: the one a huffing young fpendthrift, with a blue-purple-fcarlet coat on, all bedizened with lace; a filly puppy, that could neither play at putt, nor all-fowers, but wanted me, forfooth, to play at quadrill; which I knew*

to

no more of than the pope of ROME: so I smelt the Lay, and shun'd him. The other was an Oxford scholler, just come from Cambridge, a meer ninny: his first question was, if I was acquainted with the Classicks? and I in return, asked him, if he was acquainted in Essex; and let him know you was of the Quorum, and that I was your son, and heir: but as for the family of the Classicks, I was sure there was no such in our country, or none of any note: upon this he grinn'd, and turn'd away upon his heele, and so I found the fellow was a foole. And I was glad I got sheere of him; and resolved to keep no English gentlemen company: because, first and foremost, they spend their money at no rate, and I do not desire such conversation, because I know it argufies nothing, and their pretenses of friendship are nothing but blandation: and I resolving to live within compass, (do you, Sir,) design'd to go to Paris in the waggon; and DICK was of the same opinion. But when I call'd for a reckoning,——(blood and thunder!) I may say, that there was the Devil to pay——but, as the saying is, necessitas non habet leggs; so I paid it, with as good a will, as if I had swallow'd a hedge-hog.

We set out early one morning, in company only with three Frenchmen (very clever gentlemen indeed:) one of them spoke pretty good, bad English, and had been footman to a half pay officer; the second was a rope-dancer; and the third taught dogs to set; and the like; but surely, they were the most complaisant gentlemen, that ever were borne or christened. Whatever I said, they said so too: if I sweez'd, they bow'd; if I laugh'd, they did the same; if I yawn'd, they stretch'd their jaws; and so forth. We were ten days in getting to Paris; some times I rode, and sometimes I walk'd, and pass'd thro' many townes and cities: but I knew better than to puzzle my braines to remember their names: which would argufie nothing at all, if so be I came for improvement, and the like of that. My fellow travellers were so mortal civil to me, that I cou'd do no less than bear their expences, tho' I was forced to use some violence (as it were) to ingage them to accept of it; however, I lost nothing by it; for in return, they taught me French as fast as hops, so that by the time we got to Paris, I could say we Mounseer and non Mounseer as well as the best of them, and so con'd our DICK too. But they all said they never knew any body that ever learn'd so much in so short a time; and I am of the same mind too, tho' I say it, that shou'd not say it, and that's a proud word; but mum for that——tace is Latine for a candle.

At Paris, by advice of my friend the foot-man I took lodgings at a friends of his, at a sixsouse ordinary, up two pair of stairs, in a back-lane, because of cheap living. For, thinke I to my selfe, as I came here only to see fashions, I may as well do that, out of a window up two paire of staires, as out of a parlour: and to save charges DICK lies with me, but is dismally afraid of spirits, and of things walking, because he can't speak a bitt of Latine.——And for my owne part, I resolve (as the saying is) to keep only the best of company: so I found a sufficient number of very polite gentlemen, that lodged in the same house that is to say, two journey-men taylors, (natives of Ireland,) two Itallian fidlers, and the chief toad-eater to a very noted mountebank: but, sure, and sure! had you but seen how they all bowow'd, bow'd to, and complimented me, you would have taken your corporall oath, that they were men of quallity, and knew that E was somebody. I seldom go abroad, because I can see the world fast enough out of my chamber window: but when I do go out, one, or more, and sometimes all these civil gentlemen wait on me: and poor DICK is so afraid of being lost, that he either takes holde of my sword, or the Lappet of my coate, whenever I go into the citty. And as I never weare my best cloathes for fear of danking them, so he never wears his new livery, lest people should take me for some lord, and murder me for my money, or cutt his throat for the sake of his cloathes. I don't go to a play, because they say sad naughty women are there: and I have been at court but once, and I will insure you, that I will never go twice; for I think in my heart, that it is as fine a sight, to see our quarter sessions. But it seems my merit could not be hid there: for I am told, by one, that heard it from the king's corn-cutter, that he was inform'd by one of the pages in waiting, that he thinks he heard the cardinal say, as how as he almost thought, that I was some body of distinction if the truth was known, and the like of that.

I must not forget to tell you, that they are all here either Papishes or Roman catholicks, and I like them at no price: so that when I have seen fashions one week more, I designe to returne from beyond sea, in order, Sir, to make you a grandfather, if I live and do well, as the saying is. The whole citty have their eye upon me, especially the ladies, who, I am told, are all in love with me: and every one saies, I am vastly improved by travelling; and that I am so witty, and so wise, that they never saw the peer of me in all their borne dayes: and as I have now seen the world I hope the gentlemen of the county will be so wise, as to put me up, for one, at the next election.

Pray my love and service to Mrs PEGGY, and bid her prepare to be happy,——she knowes well enough what I meane. DICK remembers his love to all the fox-hounds, particularly to Dutches, and desires of all love, that if she lyes in, he may be put downe for a puppy. So no more at present, but my love to TOM JACKSON, and goodman HICKUMBOTTOM, and to the parson, and his aunt, which is all from

Dear PAPA,

Your ever loving son till death,

W. BOOBYKIN.

P. S. Here is a vast cunning man lives at the very next door: he proffers for a luidore, (as they call it,) to learne me to make spells, and charms, and love powders, and will teach me to raise the devil, into the bargaine: which I think may be of great use to me at elections, and is fur-

foxhunting, and so forth. And as I have a com-
pacity for any witty thing, I have a huge mind
to learne: and he tells, if I will turn papish, he
will give me the true receipt to make the philosophers
stone, that will turne every thing I touch, into
gold, and silver, and money, and the like: but I
shall beg his diversion for that, for I han't a
mind to be damn'd, at present; and hope I never
shall, if I live and do well, and so forth, as the
saying is.　　　W. B.

Universal Spectator, June 30, July 7, 14,
No. 247, 248, 249.

IN the first of these Papers is an Account of the Death of *Henry Stone-*
castle, of *Northumberland,* Esq; in the
the 2d of his being succeeded by his Nephew *Henry Stonecastle* of *Lincoln's-Inn,*
Esq; in the 3d, of the Characters of the
Club which is settled to carry on the *Spec-*
tator with him.

The *Senior* of this Society is Sir *Jas-*
per Truby, turn'd of *Sixty,* of uncommon
Good Nature and *Jocularity,* free from
the *Petulance* of *old Age,* of a *sound*
Judgment, and a large *Experience* of
Things: He was a *Turkey Merchant,*
and having gain'd a *handsome* Fortune,
he gave up his Business to enjoy the Product of his *Industry.* As he knows the
getting of *Money,* he knows the *Value* of
it; he is *Generous* without *Profusion,* and
Frugal without *Avarice*; he is never
better pleas'd than when he is shewing
his *Love* to Mankind: In a Word, he is
a *loyal Subject,* a *true Englishman,* a *good*
Citizen, and an *agreeable Friend.* Sir
Jasper was married about his 30th Year
to a Lady with whom he now lives in
the most affectionate Love, but has lost
all his Children.

The next is Mr *Worthy,* a Gentleman
of *University Education,* once a *Fellow*
of a *College,* but having a plentiful Fortune, quitted his *Books* to converse with
Men. Being of a Studious Disposition, he
chuses to live a *Batchelor,* of a *Philoso-*
phic Turn, excellent *Morals,* general
Learning, and is a *good Christian.* From
a long Acquaintance with *Classical Au-*
thors, he has an excellent Taste for *polite*
Literature.

The next Gentleman is distinguish'd by
the Name of the *old Flanderean,* his real
Name is *Platoon,* he served under the D.
of *Marlborough* in all his *Campaigns,*
and ever since the Peace he has been on
Half-pay. The Captain has good Sense,
but a *rough* Carriage and manner of Expression; he is so *unfashionably* blunt, as
to speak as he *thinks,* but *speaks* as scarce
any but himself *dare*: He pays no De-

ference to *Titles,* but will tell a Peer he
wants *Sense,* and a Lady she wants *Mo-*
desty; yet his *Satire,* tho' *severe,* is not
malicious, and his *Wit* is excus'd as not
proceeding from *Spleen.* His *Dress* is
entirely *a la mode de Campaigne.* He is
very *Humane,* strict in his *Honour,* constant in his *Friendship,* an Enemy to *none,*
but a Friend to *all.*

Opposite to the Captain sits the Courtly
Harry Careless, who thinks it the greatest Character in Life to be a Man of *Wit*
and *Pleasure.* He has a peculiar Negligence, dresses well, keeps the best Company, and is in Favour with the *Ladies*;
yet is a good *Scholar,* reads *Virgil,* and
is not unacquainted with *Homer.* He furnishes the Club with the Gallantry of the
Town, and tells a Story with a Happiness peculiar to himself; is always *easy,*
and generally *smiling.* Among the Fair
he is esteem'd for his Judgment in Fashions: He sometimes comes late to the
Club, but as he staid to hand some *cele-*
brated Toast to her *Chair,* was engag'd in
the *Mall,* or something of *like Impor-*
tance, he is excus'd. *Harry* always en-
livens the *Club* by *easy Conversation* and
good *Humour,* and is therefore their Favourite.

The next is Mr *Truewit,* a Gentleman
of distinguishing Taste, which is just and
delicate, of a lively Imagination, corrected by a Strength of Judgment; he
has a pretty Vein of *Poetry,* and is an
excellent Critick.

The Character of *Harry Stonecastle*
himself is given by Capt. *Platoon,* who
tells us *Harry* is in his 40th Year, about
20 of which he has been a Member of
Lincoln's Inn, but made no further Progress in the Law than a few Pages in the
Doctor and *Student,* and had just dip'd
into *Coke* upon *Littleton.* From a whimsical Notion that he was too modest for
the Bar, he never apply'd himself to the
Study of it; and therefore he is scarce
known to any in his *Inn* but his *Laun-*
dress and a *Bencher* or *two*: With these
Oddities he discovers *good Sense,* and some
Learning: Sometimes you will find him
among a Knot of *Jews* in the *Alley,* and
sometimes listning attentively to a *Spa-*
niard on the *Change*; he has been taken
by the Gravity of his Face for a *Project-*
or, and by his *Taciturnity* for a *Jesuit!*
From the *minutest Occurrences* he is
drawing *Apothegms,* and *Maxims of Life.*
In short; he is a *queer, moralizing, comi-*
cal Fellow.

The

The **Daily Courant**, July 13.

TO a generous Mind, it's a most affecting *Speculation*, that the *Passions* have often the Afcendency over *Reafon*, even in Perfons remarkable for *fine Senfe* and *Underftandings*, *Envy* and *Ambition* feem the moft violent. Antient andModern Authors abound withInftances of this Kind. The D. of *Guife*, in the Reign of *Henry* III. of *France*, was fo fenfible of his own *allowed* Merit, that neither the Refpect of the *Miniftry*, or the *Favour* of the *Prince* appeared to him capable of doing him fufficient Juftice. Soaring ftill above the Duty of a Subject, he began to encourage Factions, fet up Grievances to charm the *Populace*, and at length became the Head of a *League* formed for the Security of the *Catholick Religion*, even under a biggotted Catholic Prince. His Schemes fucceeding for a confiderable Space, he was the Darling of the Mob, fo much adored by the *Citizens* of *Paris*, that they rofe in his Favour, and infulted the *King* in his Palace, from whence he fled to a fafer *Place*, ill-mounted, and with but few Attendants. Not long after the *Duke* was, by his Majefty's Command, affaffinated at *Blois*.

The famous E. of *Effex* was a *Nobleman* of the fame Stamp; fo boifterous, fo full of his own Merit and Services, that he attempted to impofe *Laws* on the Queen in her own Court, and excited a Rebellion in the Streets of her *Capital*; for which, notwithftanding the *Favour* he once ftood in, he fuffered on the *Scaffold*; tho' the Rafhnefs of his laft *Treafon* made it fo ridiculous, that the *Relation* thereof is fcarce credible.

But, as the common Adage obferves, *No Man becomes exceffively wicked all at once*, fo no *Party* in their Beginning carry Things to *Extremities*. Oppofition heats them; this Warmth and repeated Difappointments blow them at laft into a Flame. Men in thefe Circumftances fay any thing, and believe all things; fancy *Obftinacy* a *Virtue*, and miftake the *Shouts* of their own *vociferous Dependents* for the *Voice* of the *Nation*.

Thefe Obfervations are beft illuftrated by comparing them with the Behaviour of our prefent *Malecontents*.

In the *Dawning* of their *Difcontents*, when the *Ambition* of *rifing* had thrown them from what they *poffeffed*, when they began to publifh thofe *Sentiments* which had grown upon them in *Difgrace*, and to detect thofe *Errors* which they could not fee while in *Office*, there was fome Decency in their Language: They had but juft deferted their *Attachment* to their *King*, and broke off their Friendship with the *M—*; in hope therefore that their *appealing* to the *People* would engage the *Court* to comply with their Demands, they preferv'd good Manners, and left a Door open to Reconciliation.

But when the Steadinefs of his prefent *Majefty* convinced them, that all fuch Hopes were vain, they not only indulged the groffeft Scurrility, Calumny and Falfehood againft the *Adminiftration*; but, beginning with ridiculing *Reviews*, and HIM who appointed them, they proceeded, and have fpared their *S——n* as little as they have done his *Servants*. The *Hiftory* of *England* has been ranfack'd for both Purpofes, and the *Execution* of MINISTERS, and the *dethroning* and *murdering* their MASTERS have been pointed out by the fame *Hands*.

Papers and *Pamphlets* were not the only Weapons they ufed againft the *King* and his *Adminiftration*; the H— of C— echoed with their *Declamations*, and *Antiminifterial Harangues* were heard in *another Houfe*; but met with the Reception they deferved. On which the *Junto* at *B—ul—y* profcribe the *Majority* of both H—s, and order their *Heralds*, Fog and *D'anvers*, to proclaim them *Hirelings* of *a Minifter*, *corrupt Penfioners*, and *Traytors* to the *People*.

To call upon thefe Men for Proofs would be loft *Labour*: But there is one Inftance on behalf of the *M——*, which will do more Honour to the *Adminiftration*, than all the Journals, Harangues and Libels of the *Craftfman* have done, or can do them Difcredit; namely, the BALLOT for the CUSTOM-HOUSE COMMITTEE; it was declared to be the *Criterion* of the *Friends* to the prefent *M—*, and the *Friends* to a *thorough Change*, perhaps of —as well as— . On this important Occafion, if Bribery, Corruption and Penfions had been the only *Ties*, why might they not have *deferted* who were againft the *M—* in their *Hearts*, and only bound to him by *venal Engagements*? Or how came there to be fo large a *Majority*, if fome of thofe who were *terrified* by *Clamour* in another *Inftance*, had not voted according to their *Confcience* here, when they knew they might do it fafely.

The *Freeholders* too, having fhewn, on various Occafions, little Refpect to the Inftructions of the *Malecontents*, the

U u D——wl——y

D—ckl—y *Committee*, have directed their *Limners* to depict them as so many debauched, idle, ill-principled, mercenary Boobies, who are ready to give up their Consciences, Country, and Liberties to whoever will *purchase them*, and are now distributing Lists and Orders, with which whatever *Counties, Cities*, or *Boroughs*, refuse to comply, they are to be stigmatiz'd with the *blackest Reflections* the *Faction* can invent.

On the whole, it is evident, that the present Opposition is form'd on a Set of *Positions*, which for Modesty, Truth and Justice, have not their Match since the Fall of LUCIFER, the first PSEUDO-PA-TRIOT, and his *Evil Angels*.

R. FREEMAN.

London Journal. July 14. N° 733.
Old and Modern Whigs; Court Whigs, and the Political Creed *of the Male-content Whigs.*

A Witty Author says, The Difference between *Fools* and *Madmen* is, *Fools* reason *wrong* from *right* Principles, and *Madmen* reason *right* from *wrong* Principles; as, when they fancy themselves *Kings*, they speak in the *Sublime*, and put on the *Port* and *Majesty* of Kings. Such *Madmen* are the present *Antiministerial* Writers; they assert, *That we are going to be enslaved;* They believe, like their Brethren in *Bedlam*, what hath no Foundation in Nature or Fact, and from thence reason right; for *Opposition* and *Resistence* is certainly a *Duty*, when there are *Designs* and *Attempts* to overturn the Constitution and introduce arbitrary Power. Yet there is not *one Step* taken towards it.

All who write in Defence of the Government and Ministry, are called Writers for *Arbitrary Power*, and *Modern Whigs*, who are departed from the Original Principles *of that Party*. From a few mangled Sentences of some Writers, the *Craftsman* gives (see p. 339.) a *political Creed* as the *Credenda* of the *Court Whigs;* tho' 'tis impossible to produce any *Whig Writer against Courts*, who hath built on truer *Principles* of Liberty, than have been laid down in the Course of these Papers, tho' wrote in *favour of a Court*.

But it seems the *Whigs* are chang'd from what they were in the Reigns of *Charles* II. and *James* II. and so they ought to be, in their *Practices*, tho' not in *Principles;* and the Reason is, *Courts are changed*. Their Opposition was Pa-

triotism, because those *Courts* carried on *Designs* against the *Liberties* of the People. But, would not the *Whigs* be as mad as the *Malecontents*, to *oppose* and *resist*, when the Reason for *Opposition* and *Resistance* is ceased? So that the *Modern* and *Old Whigs* differ indeed in their *Actions*, tho' not in their *Principles*, and so do the *Craftsman's* good Friends and Confederates, the *Tories*. The *Old Whigs* practised *Resistance* to *Arbitrary Power*, and the *Modern Whigs*, Obedience to *legal Power*, and are *right* in both; but the *Old Tories* taught and practised *Passive Obedience* to *Arbitrary Power* and *Lawless Government*, and the *Modern Tories* teach and practice *Active Resistance* to *legal Power*, and *just Government*, and are *wrong* in both.

The *Difference* also between the Writings of *L'Estrange* and Bp *Parker*, in those Reigns, and the Writings of the *Court Whigs* in this, is as great as between Light and Darkness, yet the *Craftsman* says, they are the *very same*. The first wrote for the Court, but for *Arbitrary Power, Prerogative above Law*, for *Persecution* and *Tyranny* over *Conscience;* and the latter now write in Defence of *Legal Power, Prerogative according to Law*, and for all the *Civil* and *Religious Rights* of Mankind; yet, it seems, they are *the same!*

Now, says *Osborne*, I will give him a Creed for his Creed; or the *Credenda* of the *Male-content Whigs*, or *Whigs run mad*.

They believe, That the *People of England*, in their *collective* Body, have a Right to *command Obedience* from the Parliament, and over-rule their Proceedings; and that these *Sovereign Lords* and *Supreme Judges*, THE PEOPLE, are the *Legislature of England*.——That our *Monarchy* ought to be turned into a *Democracy;* that we have no Occasion for *Kings* nor *Lords;* and that the *Bishops* should be turned out of the House of Lords, because they are for the *present Government*——That 'tis the Duty of the People to *resist* a *good Government, equally* as a *bad*——That *true Whiggism* consists in *perpetual Resistance*.——That *Jacobites* and *Tories*, nay, even *Papists*, are as heartily for the *Revolution*, and the present *Royal Family*, as the *Whigs*.——That because *Jacobites* and *Tories* cannot oppose but on *Whig Principles*, therefore those of them in the Opposition, are *thorough Whigs*.——That because the *Whigs* in K. *Charles's* and K. *James's* Reign, opposed

poled

poſed *illegal Acts*, and *arbitrary Power*; therefore the *Whigs* ſhould *now oppoſe legal Acts*, and *juſt Government.* — That whenever the King *diſmiſſes* a Servant, whom THE PEOPLE like; or *keeps in* a Servant whom they diſlike: then his Majeſty is ſetting up *arbitrary Power*; and if he preſumes to *diſmiſs an Officer* in the Army, then he is *garbling* and *modelling* the Army, to enſlave the People.—That Sir R— W—, that *Monſter of Power*, is for bringing in the *Pretender*; becauſe in a general Confuſion, he may have a Chance to eſcape, in the *Dark*, that dreadful Puniſhment, which otherwiſe will come upon him in the *Light*.

Theſe are ſome of the *Credenda* of our *Malecontent Whigs*, by which they have turned our Government, as their own Heads are turn'd, Topſy-turvy.

The *Craftſman* ſays, "all *Party Differences* and *Diſtinctions* are Shadows." But I, ſays *Osborne*, affirm they are *Subſtance*, and of the *utmoſt Importance*. Let Hiſtory and Facts determine whether there is not a *real Difference* between Parties, ſuch a *Difference* as greatly affects the *Happineſs* or *Miſery* of the Kingdom.

The **Craftſman** July 14. No. 367.

SIR,

A *Portugueze Carpenter*, with ſome Friends, paſſing by a *Crucifix* erected on the Road near *Lisbon*, his Companions pulled off their Hats as uſual; but he took no Notice of it. Being asked the Reaſon, he reply'd, He could not bring himſelf to worſhip a *Croſs*, which he made but Yeſterday out of his own *Crabtree*. This carries a good Moral, and is an Inſtance that the ſudden Elevation of an unworthy Object, inſtead of acquiring Dignity, will only be attended with Contempt and Ridicule.

The Matter muſt, in ſome Meaſure, anſwer the *Dignity* intended to be given it. Let the moſt ingenious Artiſt repreſent *Jove* with his Eagle and Thunderbolt in Straw, or *Alexander the Great* in Mud, the God, the Hero, and the *Artiſt* will all three become contemptible.

The ludicrous Image of St. *Taffy*, hung up every firſt of *March*, juſtly excites the Reſentment of the brave *Cambro-Britons*, who cannot patiently ſee their *Patron-Saint* repreſented in Straw and Ticking.

The Anniverſary, national Juſtice, executed every 5th of *Novemb.* on the *Devil*, the *Pope*, and their Adherents, would make deeper Impreſſions on the Minds of my Fellow Subjects, if thoſe Perſonages were exhibited in nobler Materials. For this Reaſon, when a *famous Projector* was treated in the ſame manner, on the 11th of *April* laſt, he was equip'd in a Manner ſuitable to his Character; which had ſuch an uncommon Effect on the Populace, that a *certain learned Gentleman* thought it his Duty to interpoſe. (See p. 191. C.)

I look upon a *firſt Miniſter* as a *political Carpenter, Carver* or *Statuary*, and to have a ſort of delegated Power of Creation, which in former Ages was carry'd to great Exceſſes, both by *political* and *real Sculptors*. *Caligula* made a *Conſul* of his *Horſe*. *Nebuchadnezzar* made a *golden Image*, which he order'd all his Subjects to worſhip, tho' *le Clerc* thinks the *golden Image* was only typical, and denoted the King's *firſt Miniſter*, to whom he had given all his Power. As to our *modern Sculptors* one may ſee at *Hyde Park-Corner*, what abſurd and incongruous Figures they expoſe to View.

I knew a Statuary in the Country, who had a Quarry of Stone of a bad Sort, porous, and ſuſceptible of *Dirt* and *Corruption*. Being a very impudent Fellow and of a flippant Tongue, he made the Country believe, there was no good *Stone* but his, and no good *Sculptor* but himſelf. They all employ'd him, but at laſt found his Materials bad, and his Workmanſhip worſe; and were obliged, for their own Security, to get rid of it as ſoon as they could, and to prop in all Haſte to prevent Ruin.

This would be the Caſe of ſuch a *political Sculptor*, who ſhould deal in Nepotiſm, and cut only out of his own Quarry; the ſame Materials not being fit for all ſorts of Figures. For Inſtance, ſhould a *firſt Miniſter* be nearly related to a Perſon, who had neither Head nor Heart to recommend him; who began the World with being laugh'd at as a Buffoon, and became ſtill more ridiculous by attempting to be grave; ſaucy and inſolent when Merry, and abſurd when Serious; long a Joke for being dirty, and ten times more ſo by endeavouring to be clean; equally ignorant and ſelf-ſufficient; equally greedy of Money and Power, and equally incapable of uſing either; whoſe Experience in Buſineſs ſerved only to give him Pride without Dignity, and Preſumption without Knowledge; if ſuch a Creature, by his Relation to a *firſt Miniſter*, be erected into a Miniſter, the Workman would be exclaim'd againſt, and the Work deſpis'd.

Horace (I mean *Quintus Flaccus*) gives a humorous Account of a *Priapus*, that, the

the Workman had cut into a God from a useless, dirty Log of Wood. He makes this *Priapus* express his Astonishment at the Change of his Condition, and at his finding himself in the Gardens of the Court, after his former, nasty Habitation; and he talks in a Strain of Dirt and Obscenity, becoming his Extraction. But the Employment the Poet assigns him at last of scaring Crows and f—t—g at old Women, is so proper that no body envies his Godship. JOHN ENGLISH.

§ The *Craftsman, from his own Chambers,* informs us, that the News-Papers continue to give us pompous Accounts of the Manner, in which several Cities and Corporations have received *those Gentlemen* who opposed the *Excise-Bill;* and says, if we may credit private Advices, *another Set of Gentlemen* are distress'd how to behave, or justify their late Conduct. Many of them, 'tis said, congratulated their Neighbours on Defeat of the *Scheme,* and gave themselves an Air of being against it; but the *Lists,* now published, have undeceived the People, and reduc'd *those Gentlemen* to several Shifts.

Some of 'em are so modest as to confine themselves at home; while their Creatures are employ'd to put the best Gloss they can upon a bad Cause; and *corrupt,* where they cannot *persuade.*

Others put a bold Face on the Matter, and persist in it sturdily that they opposed the *Project* in some Shape or other. For this purpose, they have procur'd false Lists to be dispers'd, to impose on those, whose Confidence they have already abused.

Some ingenuously acknowledge they were for the *Scheme,* but allege, they did it to prevent *Frauds,* and relieve the *Land-Tax.*

But of all their Arguments, none pleases me so much as this. *It is true,* say they, *we voted* for the Excise; *but did it only to gain Credit with the* Projector, *and by those Means prevail'd upon him to drop it.* I am told *this Plea* hath been already used in several Boroughs, and I shall not be surprized to hear that the *Projector* hath issued out Certificates of this kind to every one of his Creatures, assuring their Corporations, that it was solely at *their Request,* he laid aside such a glorious Project.

But I think the best way for *these Gentlemen* would be, to take the Advice of one of their Advocates in the *Courant, June* 19, who proposed that every Gentleman, who voted for the *Excise,* should be catechis'd upon a little Stool by the Minister, and be obliged to explain the Grounds and Motives of his Conduct, in the Face of a full Congregation.

Daily Courant, July 17.

SIR,

THE *Craftsman* of last *Saturday,* (see p. 347) is divided into a Letter of *Raillery* on the *M—y,* and certain gross *Reflections* on the *House of C—mm—ns.*

The *Letter* is made up of low Wit, and Scraps of Learning, scandalous Insinuations, and studied Buffoonery; a new Stile surely in political Debates! but I had forgot it drops from the Quill of a *Terræ Filius,* inured to Punning, Railing, and Libelling, ever since he was expelled the *University* for blowing up Sedition, and for his dissolute Life. But, will *Raillery* contribute to the Good of the *Publick?* Will humorous Stories convince Men of Understanding, that the *M—y* are such as Mr *English,* alias Mr *Amb—ß,* would represent them? Or should a worn-out *Oxford* Jest prejudice the *Reputation* of a *Person* in considerable *Employments,* without any *Pretence* to Proof? Are *Sneer* and *Banter* all the *Weapons* in the Power of the *Faction?*

What does all that is suggested in this extraordinary Letter amount to, more than this, That the *M—r* hath procured an Office for his *Relation,* who on that Score is exposed to all the *Jests* and *Sarcasms* of the *opposite Party?* Is there any thing in it which should make the *People* angry, or the *M—r* ashamed? Did not *Burleigh, Clarendon,* and *Godolphin* raise their *Relations* to great Employments? And were not many of those *Relations Ornaments* to the Nation? Nay, the *Gentleman* against whom this *Invective* is pointed, is as much distinguish'd for *personal Virtues,* as any Man who has possess'd the *Place* he holds within the Reach of Man's Remembrance. But all this is nothing; he is still a *W—;* and therefore entitled to all the hard Names *Pog* and *Caleb* can give him.

We now proceed to Mr *D'anvers's* Remarks on the Conduct of certain Members of the *House of Commons,* as improbable as the *Adventures* of *Gavagantua* and *Pantagruel;* only, as *Caleb's* Genius falls short of *Rablais,* so the Story is not so well put together. The Falshood is too glaring to give any Pleasure. However, I entreat him to give us a little Light into the following Queries.

1. If there be any *Instance* of a *Member's* denying that he voted for the *Excise-Bill,* or pretending to *congratulate* his *Neighbours* on its being *lost* or *postponed?*

2. If

2. If any *Gentleman* who voted with that *Bill* ever pretended to draw up a *false List*, or if such *false Lists* have been procured or published by any Persons suspected of having to do with the *Administration*?

3. What *Member* of the *House* corrected, at the Desire of a *Person* infamous for Publishing *Libels*, the *List* of the *Members*, and some other *Particulars*, in a late *Pamphlet* said to contain the *Proceedings* in the last *Sessions*, &c?

4. What *Members* of either *House* have advanced their *Quota* towards Printing 12,000 Lists of the *Members for* and *against* the *Excise Bill*, and of Lords *for* and *against* the *S. Sea Enquiry*, which have been given *gratis* thro' all the Kingdom; thro' which also *Orators* have been dispersed, to persuade the People their Liberties are in Danger?

5. If any *Person* can be *named*, who has claimed the *Merit* of advising or prevailing on the *M——* to consent to the *Postponing* of the *Bill* in Relation to the *Tobacco* Duties, or the *Resolutions* in regard to the *Wines*?

Let the *Craftsman* give a direct answer to these *Demands*, because if the 3d and 4th Queries be true, then his Patrons are guilty of notorious Breach of *Duty* as *Members* of *Parliament*, and of scattering *Sedition*, and endeavouring to disturb the *Peace* of their Country; and if the 1st, 2d, and 5th, *Queries* be *false*, the *Craftsman* of last *Saturday* is a *Bundle* of *Seditious Lies*, tending to wound the Characters of Gentlemen of *Worth* and *Fortune*, and abusing them for their Conduct in *Parliament*; which is contrary to the *Laws*, to *Reason* and *Humanity*, dangerous to the *Constitution*, and shocking in the Eyes of every *honest Man*.

R. FREEMAN

Grubstreet Journal, July 19. No. 186.

Mr BAVIUS,

ENglishmen boast, that there is no Body of Laws better calculated for the preservation of Property and Liberty, and for deriving to us all the Blessings of Society, than those of our Country. Under the Dispensation of wise and upright Magistrates, with a happy Propensity to Obedience in the People, they flow evenly thro' the whole Community, and administer Refreshment to every Member. But, where there is no general Disposition in the Subjects chearfully and spontaneously to pursue the Paths of Equity, the best Magistrates find it extremely difficult to administer Justice.

As Laws cannot be duly administred without various Degrees, and subordinate Ranks of Men; so when the Souls of such Men are deeply stained with Dishonour and Immorality, how pernicious to Society may they be? In such a Case, so far is the most excellent System of Laws from being a Blessing to a State, that they become the greater Instruments of Oppression and Engines of Mischief.

Tho' the late Statutes have excellently provided against the Extortions of those Miscreants, Counter and Sheriffs Officers, Bailiffs and their under Strappers, yet the best Laws are bare-facedly violated, or artfully eluded. Since the Fees of these Gentlemen have been ascertained, and 24 Hours allowed to the Party in Custody, before he can be legally turned into Prison, they have found out another way to make themselves ample Amends for the Loss of their former Opportunity of Oppression. Are they apprehensive the unfortunate will give the Plaintiff immediate Satisfaction? They run him immediately to a Spunging-House, and Mr *Officer* will be sure to be out of the Way till the 24 Hours are expired, unless *the Prisoner bleeds freely.*

The Artifice of Capt. SPUNGE is of the same Stamp; no Evidence or Testimony from the Suitor will satisfy his tender Conscience. How does he *know the Plaintiff, or his hand-writing*, tho' he has all the Evidence that would satisfy a Court of Justice? Thus this Infidel must confine the Prisoner, till his Confederate Oppressor Mr OFFICER shall think fit to show his Countenance of Humanity.

Besides, these Officers have a Number of *Satellites* called Runners, who live in the Atmosphere of these Harpies, and are employed to feel the Pulses of the Prisoners, lest Mr OFFICER should let slip the critical Minute when the Purse Strings are drawn. After this Crew have put the Prisoner to all the Difficulties and Expences in their Power, their Honours are highly affronted, if they are not complimented with a Present extraordinary for their great Civility.

So contemptible indeed are the Offices of these Men-eaters grown, that *few* but ignorant and narrow-minded Wretches will throw themselves into such Employments. Amongst Men of such a Complexion, Benevolence and Humanity are treated as Folly and Weakness; and good Sense, and an honest Heart, persecuted as Invaders of their Properties.

Hence

Hence we may form an Idea of what important Consequences to the Publick are a good Capacity of Difcernment, and a beneficent Difpofition in the other intermediate Practicers; and how much it is the Duty of every Magiftrate to inculcate thefe Principles, and extirpate their Oppofites. The good Effects of all Laws are more or lefs enjoyed, as thefe noble Qualities prevail, or fink, amongft Practicers.

I fhall conclude with obferving, That as the Clergy are, from their Profeffion, injoined to fet Examples of Virtue and Religion beyond all others; fo, in right Reafon, ought thofe who are concern'd in adminiftring of the Laws to excell others in brave and worthy Examples of Juftice, and every focial Virtue. Every Offence committed againft the Laws, by its Adminiftrators and Practicers, in the Execution of their Offices is aggravated according to their Height and Dignity in that Profeffion.   PUBLICOLA.

PROCEEDINGS *in the laft Seffion of* PARLIAMENT.

AN Attempt to change fome Cuftoms, by Reafon of the Frauds committed in them, to an Inland Duty, or Excife, having made the greateft Noife, and having ended only in an Enquiry into the faid Frauds; we think proper to begin with the Proceedings thereon.

April 19. Refolved, Nem. Con. That a Committee be appointed to enquire into the Frauds and Abufes in the Cuftoms, to the Prejudice of Trade and Diminution of the Revenue.

Refolved, That the Number of the faid Committee be one and Twenty, and be chofen by way of Balloting, on *Tuefday* the 24th.

April 24. The Members having been Summon'd by the Serjeant at Arms to attend, the Clerks went on each fide the Houfe with Glaffes to receive from the Members the Lifts of Perfons Names to be the faid Committee.

Order'd, That a Committee examine the faid Lifts, and Report on which 21 Perfons the Majority falls.

April 25. Lord *Vere Beauclerk* reported from the Committee, that they had examin'd the Lifts, and that the Majority had fallen on the firft of the Lifts mentioned p. 515. in which we defire our Readers to correct three Miftakes made in fome Copies at the beginning of the Impreffion, viz. for *Foe* read *Fox,* for *Lewthier,* read *Lowther,* and for *Novel,* read *Noel.*

The Accounts relating to *Tobacco* and *Wines* laid before the Houfe were transferred to this Committee.

June 7. Sir *John Cope* made the Report to the Houfe. From whence follows a fhort Extract.

THE Committee, to avoid Confufion in their Enquiry, have examin'd the Frauds committed in each Branch of the Revenue fingly; and obferving that their Papers of Information related chiefly to Frauds in the Tobacco Trade, they proceeded in that Branch firft. They take Notice of the great Care and Caution that is ufed by the Commiffioners in appointing Numbers of Officers over a Ship from her Arrival in the River till fhe is brought to the Keys to unlade her Freight, to prevent any Tobacco being landed without paying or fecuring the Duties. Notwithftanding which they have full Proof of many notorious Frauds.

The principal Fraud committed at Importation is, the fetting down in the Landwaiter's Books, by which the Duty is computed and paid, lefs Weight than the Hogfheads imported do really weigh: which is one of the principal Complaints made by the Merchants at *Briftol* in 1721, and was this year made by the Planters in *Virginia*, by their Agent Sir *John Randolph*, who informed the Committee, that the ufual Weights in *Virginia* were and are from 800 to 550 Pounds, that the utmoft allowance for Wafte in the Voyage was 8 *lb*. on every hundred Weight, but believes it cannot be fo much, having an Account of his own from *Briftol,* where he finds a Wafte of no more than 15 Pounds in a Hogfhead of 800 Weight.

The Hogfheads imported from *Maryland*, weigh at a Medium, 700*l*. weight.

In *June* 1727, *John Midford* imported, in the *Wm* and *Jane*, from *Virginia*, 301 Hogfheads, the Weight of which, as taken by the Landwaiters, was 199,257 *lb*. wt.

The true Weights	230,150 *lb*. wt.
Difference, (the Duty of which loft)	30,893 *lb*. wt.
In 1729, the Weights of 17 Hogfheads as taken in the Landwaiters Book, amount only to	8961 *lb*. wt.
The real Weights of the fame, as by the Account of Sales, were	12334 *lb*. wt.
Difference, (the Duty of which was loft)	3373 *lb*. wt.

. The

The Medium of 355 Hogsheads imported in the same Ship, of which these 17
were part, being no more than 521 *lb.* wt.
there is Reason to believe the like Fraud
was committed in the whole Parcel.

An Account of Sales deliver'd to a
Planter in *Virginia*, shews, that 4 Hogs-
heads were charged in the Landwaiters
Books 483 *lb.* wt. less than the real
Weights.

Mr *Randolph* acquainted the Committee with a Fraud, since 1726, by short
Weights at Entry of 485 Hogsheads of
Maryland Tobacco, whereby the Merchant got 30 Hogsheads clear of Duty.

In *September* 1731 Mr *Philpot* having
discover'd a Fraud, went to the Merchant,
who gave him 100 Guineas to conceal it,
which he then did; but has since paid
the said 100 Guineas to the Commissioners,
and made a Discovery; and by examining the Landwaiters Books and comparing them, there appears very great Reason to suspect a multitude of Frauds of
this Nature.

Some of the Frauds at Exportation,
in order to obtain Debentures which the
Exporters are not legally entitled to are
by shipping corrupt or damaged Tobacco,
mixed with Dirt, Rubbish and Sand; and
by shipping Stalks alone stripped from
the Leaf, which by Law are to receive
no Drawback.

In the Year 1704, or 1705, *Tho. Parr*,
Esq; of *Datchet*, had consigned to his
Care in *Holland*, 8 or 900 Hogsheads of
Roll Tobacco, in each of which · Rolls
was contained a Piece of Lead of 2 or 3
Inches thick, and 6 or 7 Inches long, for
which the Merchants had obtained a
Drawback for the Duty as Tobacco.

But one of the greatest Frauds on Exportation is, by the unfair Traders endorsing on the Back of their Coquets
greater Weights than the Hogsheads contained, and so discharging Bonds for more
than the real Exportation; whereby large
Quantities of Tobacco will remain in
their Hands without Payment of Duty.

May 12, 1733, an Entry was made by
one *Cox* of 8084 *lb.* wt. of Roll Tobacco
for Exportation; but, on Examination
there was no more than 6825 *lb.* wt. upon which the whole Quantity was seized.

In *September* 1732, Mr. *Peele* entered
in the *James* and *Mary*, from *Maryland*,
310 Hogsheads of Tobacco, for which he
paid the Duty in ready Money; near 200
Hogsheads of which he sold in *October*
following, to Mr *Hyam* for Exportation,

and they were immediately exported.
It appears on these 200 Hogsheads, that
the Duties paid at Importation, according to the Weights in the Landwaiters
Books, were short of the real Weights
by 13292 *lb* It appears on Exportation,
that the Certificates sworn to by *William
Cameron* for Mr *Peele*, to obtain Debentures, was to discharge Bonds given on a
former Entry for *Virginia* Tobacco, imported in *November* 1731. That the En-
dorsement on the Coquet, made by Mr
Peele, in Order to receive the Debentures,
exceeded the real Weights actually shipped, by 8288 *lb.* so that the Total of the
Pounds Weight intended to be gained by
this Fraud, amounts to 21580.

Another Fraud the Committee take Notice of, is, that of Relanding, after having Debentures for the Drawbacks;
which Tobacco so relanded is sold for
home Consumption under the Market
Price, in prejudice to the fair Trader. Of
this they give several Instances, particularly in the Isle of *Guernsey*, *Jersey*, and
Man. Mr *Howel*, who lived many years
in *Flanders*, has frequently observed several Quantities of Tobacco imported into *Ostend* and *Dunkirk*, and there re-
packed in Bales of 100 *lb.* wt. each, and
then again put on Board *English* and *Irish*
Vessels, that waited there for that Purpose, and were employed in relanding
it in *England* and *Ireland*. About 12
Month ago nine *British* Vessels were ta ;
king in Cargoes of Tobacco for this Purpose at *Dunkirk*.

The Vessels employ'd thus in the Smug-
ling Trade, take out Clearances for the
Ports of *Spain*, *Portugal*, or some other
foreign Country, in order to produce, in
Case they are met with on the Coast of
Britain or *Ireland*.

There have likewise been considerable
Quantities of Tobacco run without payment of Duty; of this kind have been
seized and condemned, 958,745 *lb.* wt.
since *Christmas* 1723, including the Tobacco relanded after Exportation.

Another considerable Fraud, discover'd
in 1728, was the ·stealing and pilfering
Tobacco from Ships in the River; this
Fraud was called Socking; and was carried on for several Years by Tidesmen on
Board, Porters on the Keys, Mates, Boat-
swains and Crews, Lightermen, Coopers,
and others in the Merchants Service : On
this Discovery 2 Tidesmen, 1 Cooper,
and 2 Lightermen were convicted, and
order'd for Transportation; 1 Boatswain,
1 Tides-

1 Tidesman, and 1 Porter were whipp'd on the Keys; and about 150 Tidesmen and inferior Officers, were dismissed. 20 Tons of Tobacco were seized in Houses by the River side; of which 22,741 *lb.* wt. was condemned and forfeited. This Tobacco was sold by the Receivers to several considerable Dealers in Town.

The great Temptations to commit these Frauds, both at Importation and Exportation, arises from securing the Duties by bonding, and discharging these Bonds at Exportation. The Abuse is, the discharging Old Bonds by new Importations, contrary to Law and Oath; by which the Merchant gets into his Hands a considerable Sum of Money to the Hazard of the Revenue.

Another Loss to the Nation in general, from this Method of Bonding, arises from the Temptation Factors are under to export or sell for Exportation, the Tobacco in their Care, without Regard to Price, and merely to discharge their Bonds; whereby Foreign Markets are over loaded, the Fair Trader undersold, and the Planter injur'd in his Sale, and some times brought into Debt, while the Factor receives his full Commission even for the Duty bonded and drawn back, by such hasty Exportations. This appears by the Memorial of the Council in *Virginia* sent to the Board of Trade in 1713, and confirmed by Mr *Hyam*, and Sir *J. Randolph.*

The Method of discharging old Bonds by new Importations, is likewise very injurious to the Sureties bound with the Merchants; since by this Means they continue subject to the Debt long after the Tobacco, for the Duties of which they were bound, has been either exported, or sold for Home-Consumption; which has been the Case of almost all who were Security for such Merchants as died, or broke indebted to the Crown, many of whom have been undone thereby.

The Frauds and Abuses in TEA and BRANDY are grown to so great a Height, and carried on in such an outrageous Manner, not only on the Coast, but even in *London*, by Gangs of Armed men as seems to call for the Assistance of the Legislature to put a Stop to their Progress. The Number of Custom-house Officers who have been beaten, abused, and wounded since *Christmas* 1723, are no less than 250, and 6 murder'd; no less than 251,.320 *l.* Wt. of Tea and 652,924 Gallons of Brandy seized and condemned, and upwards of 2000 Persons

Prosecuted. Besides which 229 Boats and and other Vessels have been condemned, 185 of which have been burnt, and the Remainder employed in the Service of the Crown.

Gabriel Tomkins, a noted Smugler now in the County Goal of *Surrey* for returning from Transportation, deliver'd in a List of several Grocers and Shopkeepers in *London, Westminster,* and *Southwark* with whom he dealt about 3 Years ago for 15 or 20,000 *l.* wt. of Tea and Coffee in a Year.

In the next place the Committee enter'd upon the Frauds and Abuses in the Customs on Wine, and find that no more had been condemned since *Christmas* 1723 than 2208 Hogsheads, altho' the Commissioners of the Customs in 1725 had received Informations upon Oath that there had been run in *Hampshire, Dorsetshire* and *Devonshire* from 1723 to 1725, 4738 Hogsheads; and on Enquiry 30 Officers were dismiss'd, and Informations enter'd against 400 Persons, 38 were committed to Goal, 118 admitted Evidence, and 45 compounded for their Offences.

In the Appendix to the Report, the Committee set forth at large their Examinations of several Persons, who were either concerned in, or were well informed of many notorious Frauds and Abuses in the Customs. Among the rest is that of *Joseph Shakell*, formerly Warehouse-keeper and Porter to Sir *Randolph Knipe*; and he informs, that the Ship *Churchill Galley* arrived in the River from *Dantzick*, loaded with Linnen and Pot-ashes; that by Sir *Randolph's* Direction he got two Landwaiters for his Purpose, who enter'd in their Books about half the Quantity landed, for which Service he gave them a Bank Bill of 70 *l.* Of another Ship which brought a Parcel of Buckrams, Sir *Randolph* having made a short Entry of about half the Quantity, he gave the Landwaiter 3 Guineas to let it pass besides his Bill Money for passing the Bales without opening them. At another Time Sir *Randolph* gave two Landwaiters for making a short Entry of Linnen and Pot-ashes 60 *l.* At another Time Sir *Randolph* gave two Landwaiters 20 *l.* a-piece for the like Service. At another Time he paid the Officers 10 *l.* a-piece on the like Occasion. That during the Informant's 12 Years Employment under Sir *Randolph*, above an Hundred Ships had arrived from *Russia, Riga,* and *Petersburgh* with Hemp, and Flax on Sir *Randolph's* Account;

count; in some of which the Landwaiters, had allowed him 20 Tons more than was enter'd, who were always paid accordingly.

Mr *Gilbert Higginson*, who has been in the Tobacco Trade about 20 Years, on his Examination, inform'd the Committee that he knows very great Frauds and Abuses have been committed, both in the Importations and Exportations of Tobacco, but chiefly occasion'd between certain Merchants and certain Officers; and he really believ'd from particular Informations, some Persons have discharged their Bonds with about 2 thirds of the Number of Hogsheads they imported; and that the Revenue hath suffered by such Practices the best Part of 100,000 Pounds *per Annum* in this Port of *London*, for some Years last past; besides a great deal of Prejudice done to the fair Traders.

This Report and Appendix take up 103 Pages in Folio, yet the Committee observe, that the Shortness of the Session, would not allow them to make it so compleat as they might otherwise have done, and that the Number and Intricacy of the various Frauds render a thorough Disquisition almost impracticable.

GRANTS for the YEAR 1733.

	l.	s.	d.
For 8000 Seamen for 13 Months at 4 l. per Man per Month	416000	0	0
The Ordinary of the Navy and half Pay	311405	19	8
For the Support of Greenwich Hospital	10000	0	0
For Ordnance for Land Services	77806	11	3
Ditto Extraordinary Expences	1374	6	1
Provision for 17709 Land Forces at home	651484	17	1
Ditto Plantation, &c. Forces and Garrisons	104835	8	1
For Out Pensioners of Chelsea College	33128	15	5
Expences not provided for by Parliament	7256	8	8

See last Year's Grants, No. XX. p. 919.

For the ARMY.

Townshend Andrews, *Esq*; Deputy Pay-master.
Francis Whitworth, *Esq*; Surveyor of his Majesty's Woods
John Cornwallis *Esq*; Equerry to the Prince
Sir Thomas Robinson, Bart.
Thomas Lewis of Hampshire *Esq*;
Sir Archer Croft, Bart. Commissioner of Trade
Sir Richard Lane,
Henry Pelham, *Esq*; Pay-master of the Army
Horatio Walpole *Esq*; Cofferer
Sir William Yonge, Commissioner of the Treasury
Sir Robert Walpole, Chancellour of the Exchequer, and first Commissioner of the Treasury
Lord Hervey, Vice Chamberlain
Joseph Danvers, *Esq*;
Lord Malpas, Master of the Horse to the Prince
Charles Talbot, *Esq*; Solicitor General
Thomas Clutterbuck, *Esq*; Commissioner of the Admiralty
Colonel Bladen, Commissioner of Trade
Sir Philip York, Attorney General

Proceedings on the Army.

Feb. 5. SIR *Charles Turner* reported from the Committee appointed to consider of the Supply granted to his Majesty. That it is their Opinion, That the Number of Men for Guards and Garrisons in *Great-Britain, Guernsey,* and *Jersey,* for the Year 1733, be 17709 Men, Officers included.

On the second Reading of this Resolution, it was moved to be recommitted, but the Question being put, it passed in the Negative.

Resolved, and *agreed,* That a Sum not exceeding 651,484 17 1¼ be granted to defray the Charge of the said Forces.

A Motion was made, and the Question put, That an humble Address be presented to his Majesty, to desire that he would be graciously pleased from his earnest Desire to ease his People of every Charge, not absolutely necessary, and his Regard to the Constitution of this Kingdom to take the first favourable Opportunity of making a Reduction of those Forces, which this House hath Voted in pursuance of the Estimate laid before them by his Majesty's Direction; it passed in the *Negative* Yeas 239. Noes 171.

On this Occasion there were great Debates for two Days; in which the following Gentlemen Spoke, exactly in the order they are placed; but as the Arguments were not very different from those in the Preceding Sessions, (see p. 935, 6, Vol. II. P. 3, 4, 135, 136, Vol. III.) we shall not trouble our Readers with any Account thereof at present.

Against the ARMY.

Lord Morpeth
Edward Harley, Esq;
Henry Rolle, Esq;
Edward Digby, Esq;
Thomas Bramston, Esq;
Sir John St Aubin
Sir Thomas Saunderson
Sir Joseph Jekyl, Master of the Rolls
Sir William Wyndham
William Shippen, Esq;
Thomas Wyndham, Esq;
Sir John Barnard
Thomas Palmer, Esq;
William Pulteney, Esq;
Sir John Hind Cotton
Watkin Williams Wynn, Esq;
William Bromley, Esq;
Sir Walter Baggot
William Gwyn Vaughan, Esq;
Thomas Geers Winford, Esq;
Charles Cholmondeley, Esq;
Sir Wilfrid Lawson
Samuel Sandys, Esq;
George Heathcote, Esq;
Philip Gybbon, Esq;

Free Briton. July 19. No. 191.
Revolution Principles of the Tories.

AS wife Governors pay a Deference to the Inclinations of the People, so this Deference ought to engage their Love and Gratitude to that Government that yields it. But to insult a Prince, or a Government for having taken *Counsel from the People*; to treat the *Dignity of Parliament* disgracefully, and *supreme* Power with Reproach, for that Candour and Deference which hath been shewn to the popular Inclination, is a *Crime against the People*; as it is an Act of Ill-usage to those who have shewn them all Indulgence.

Good Sense and good Intentions make Men moderate and well-natured, when successful. A bad Heart and mean Understanding are the Prompters of Insolence in the Minions of Fortune. Such Insolence ill recommends any Man to be trusted with Power; it shews him to be a Tyrant without it: What then would he be with it? It is of the Essence of Arrogance, to think itself right in all its Doings, and at the same Time to act outrageously in every one of them. The same overbearing Spirit, which shall in one *Craftsman* call it SEDITION, to complain of a *City Common Council*, even to the Citizens who chose them and were betrayed by them, shall in another *Craftsman* (see p. 348. B.) defame 265 MEMBERS of *the House of Commons*, as Enemies to their Country, for having laid aside a *Bill*, chiefly in Compliance with the popular Opinion. The same tyrannical Spirit, which can claim Impunity, even whilst it is *insulting the Head that wears the* Crown, can assume the *ridiculous Air of protecting a* Coroner *even by a* CUDGEL; can first advise a *solemn Invitation to publick Enquiry*, with a full Promise of Indemnity, and then *proceed to search J——rn——ls for Precedents*, how a Complaint may be made.

I have known, says *W.* the same Equity and Candour that thus resented this Liberty of Animadverting on the Case of *one Peer* of this Kingdom, be warmed into Raptures on a stupid and infamous Libel (see p. 317.) on 30 or 40 Lords of the *greatest Rank* and Consideration, an impudent Invective, that called the D. of *G——n* a LOOBY, the E. of *G——m* a FOOL, the E. of *I——l——y* a PACKHORSE, the D. of *N——e* a SCOLD. the Ch——r of the *Ex——r* a BLOCKHEAD, with other Phrases, equally curious, and elegant, bestowed upon the E. of *W——l——ngt——n*, Duke of St. *A——*, D. of

D——f——rt, E. of *E——ff——x*, E. of *Alb——le*, the L. *O——w*, the L. *H——vey*, the Bp of *S——y*, the L. *T——ngt——n*, the L. *H——ngt——n*, the Rt. Hon. *H——y P——b——m*, Esq; the *Att——ney* and *Soll——r Gen——l*; nay, upon Col. *P——y*, the ONLY BROTHER of the *Honourable Person* who is the *Hero of the Libel*; and all this without any sort of Provocation.

By such Insolence and Outrage, which would justly deprive them of the Character of *Gentlemen*, do these Persons pretend to the *first Titles of Virtue*. They are like a *most noble Colonel*; they would give a huge Sum of Money for a *good Name*, as the best Commodity they can carry to Market, and the most effectual Means to *bubble* Mankind. They would delude us by calling themselves *Whigs*, whilst they are labouring to subvert a *Whig-Establishment*, and tells us, that *the Tories*, with whom they join, to a Man, are acting upon *Revolution-Principles*. (See p. 339.)

I never doubted that the Tories were acting upon *Revolution Principles*; nor suspected them of *Non Resistance* and *Passive Obedience* under the *Protestant Succession*; and I dare answer for the *Pretender*, however he has been hurt by the *Revolution*, he is no Enemy to *Revolutions*. I remember a Ship fitted out some Years ago in his Service, and which his late Majesty caused to be seized at *Genoa*. This *had the glorious Name of the* REVOLUTION; and was, without Doubt, *designed to procure one*. Prodigious Recommendation of the *Tories* to the *Whigs*, that the *Tories* are acting upon *Revolution Principles!* Prodigious Merit of such *Whigs*, who are engaged in the Cause of a *Revolution!* This inverts the Order and Basis of our Constitution. We know that *the Revolution* of 1688 was only to be supported by *the Protestant Succession*; but how a *Protestant Succession* can be supported by a Revolution, is beyond my Abilities to find out.

When the *Tories* of the *City of London* treated K. *Wm* with so much Insolence, and denied him a Statue, (see Vol. I. p. 448) and when *Fog* defamed that *excellent Prince* without Rebuke from the *Craftsman*, I understood it all as proceeding on *Revolution Principles*: But in View to a *Revolution of their own.*

When *these Tories* and their new *Allies*, insulted and assaulted the *Members* of the House of Commons, for the Liberty they took of *Speaking and Voting* in Parliament, I never disputed this to be done on *Revolution-Principles*. And when a *Scarlet Gown* made

made a Speech at the O—— B——y, to perfuade a *Grand Jury*, that *Rejoycings could not be Riots* (fee p. 266.) however outrageous in their manner, I did as clearly conceive it to be made on *Revolution Principles*, as it was contrary to all the *Principles of Law* and *Justice*; nor fhould I think the faid *Scarlet Gown* more fincerely attached to *Revolution-Principles*, even fhould I fee the folid Proof of a *Journey to R——me* with Remittances for the Advancement of *Revolution-Principles.* There is indeed a filly Scandal goes about the World, that this fame *Scarlet Gown* hath a great Averfion to Germans; but this muft be impoffible, confidering *whom he* hath the Honour to be ally'd to.

When we behold Patriots, who have voted againft the *Proteftant Succeffion*, from the firft Procefs of the Act of Settlement in its Favour, to the prefent Hour of *its Eftablifhment*; when we fee thofe who engaged in Rebellion againft the King, and thofe who refufed to fign the Affociation againft the Pretender; when we fee thefe Patriots thus oppofing the Government, in fpeaking and writing *per Tela, per Ignes*, with a *Tool fent over from a Convent of Jefuits abroad*, and another *expelled from a Univerfity at Home*, who begun his Hoftilities againft the Government by declaring, that *Nature would rebel againft Principle*; affifted by a *beneficed profligate Hiftoriographer of prime Minifters*;—— Who can remain unconvinced, that they are proceeding, in the moft cordial and uniform Manner, on *Revolution Principles*? But in Cafe they fucceed in their *Scheme of a Revolution*, whether they will make their *Succeffion* altogether *Proteftant*, may continue a Doubt, till we fee how they have blanched their *Ethiopian at Dawley*, and whether that *fable* Patriot's *Confcience is* ever likely to be fair complexioned.

If we take this Word *Revolution* in every Senfe, I think they are entitled to the free and full Ufe of it. If I fhould review B——ke's Life, and fee him in one Month abjuring the *Pretender*, in the next taking the Oaths as *Secretary of State* to this very *Pretender*, and in two or three Months afterwards betraying all that *Pretender's* Affairs to the *Prince on the Throne*, I fhould think this a mighty *Revolution*, if not in his Principles, yet in his Conduct. Or, if I fhould fee another great Patriot, who, notwithftanding he had been loaded with infinite Favours, could not be obliged by any, oppofing a Court from his

Diflike, not of their Meafures but of his Preferments, making overtures to be reinftated, and then, returning to his Oppofition with all Fury; worfhipping the rifing Sun on the opening of a new Reign, and, on his Difappointment of Power, invading that very Prince in his *private Life*, and *perfonal Character*, with injurious and unmanly Invectives, I fhould not fcruple to declare my Opinion, that fuch a Man was much addicted to *Revolutions*: And, if I fhould ever fee him transfer his *Allegiance* from *one Title* to *another*, I fhould not think it more wonderful, or unnatural in him, than the transferring of his Affections from a *W——le* to a *B——ke*.

When we confider that a *Revolution of Government* is defired, we cannot wonder that the moft *beneficent*, the moft *indulgent* Acts of the *ftanding Government* fhould be *unfairly* and *invidioufly treated.*

That the *Craftfman*, who hath no Juftification of the whole Courfe of his Writing, if the *Liberty* of appealing, from the Reprefentatives to the Reprefented, be denied him, fhould, of all Men, term it Seditious, to bring a Complaint before the *Citizens of London* againft the *Common-Council* of that *City*; that the Authority of the *Houfe of Commons*, which was always facred to us *Whigs*, fhould be outragioufly dealt with; that *one* particular *Peer* fhould be protected from Animadverfion, *even by a Cudgel*; and that, at the fame Time, *Dukes, Earls, Secretaries of State*, and *Lord Chamberlains*, fhould be deftin'd to Abufe *by Dozens*: I fay, thefe ftrange Inconfiftencies need not furprize us, when we confider that they may be all fully accounted for on *Revolution-Principles*. And when we confider, how the *Jacobitifm of certain Tories*, and the *trimming Spirit* of our *Patriot Whigs* ftand in need of fuch Principles, we may be fure they will *always beftow their Panegyricks on the Doctrines of* Resistance, *whilft it is their Bufinefs to* Resist; and that they will be fond of *every Meafure* which introduced this Government, provided fuch Meafure may be adapted to *overthrow it*.

The Englifhman, No. I.

IN *Berington's* Evening Poft was formerly publifhed an occafional Entertainment, entitled the *Templer*, of which we gave feveral Extracts, (fee p. 52, &c. Vol. I.) As we are willing to do Juftice to every new Author that appears with any

any probability of pleasing, we shall take the same Liberty with one who now makes his Appearance in this Paper under the Title of *The Englishman.*

The Author in his first Number explains the glorious Title of *Englishman,* and lays down his Plan; which in short is, that in treating on any Subject, he will neither flatter Governors, nor court Opposition, but will write impartially; nor can pay so ill a Compliment to his Countrymen, as to think he shall be therefore the less acceptable.

The Englishman. No. II.

PErhaps no Book published of late Years has done more Service to General Liberty, than RAPIN's *History of England.* As Persons of all Denominations have read and recommended it with great Zeal; so almost all Men, since the Publication of it, seem to entertain the same Sentiments about *Government* and *Subjection;* and no One can read the Publick Writers of our different Parties, without observing, how little appears at present of the Distinguishing Nonsense of former Times upon those two important Subjects. As I conceive, great Part of this Good has arisen from the right Understanding of our History, and the many just Reflections made upon it, I could not be altogether silent in Commendation of what has contributed to this happy Event.——But that which should give *Englishmen* still greater Pleasure, is the Use which the Translator makes of this Work, in his DEDICATION to his Royal Highness the *Prince of Wales.* Instead of the fulsome Flattery and Panegyrick, common to Pieces of that Kind; the Design of this Writer appears so worthy, and the Sentiments so truly honest, that I cannot do him a higher Honour, than to give the Publick the Dedication itself. At the same time, the Reader will observe, there cannot be a more amiable Idea, nor an Idea of truer Dignity, given of the Prince to whom it is address'd, than, that the Way of paying Court to Him, is not by offering the false Incense of Adulation, but by approaching Him with that Plainness and Truth, which is becoming a *Freeman* and an *Englishman.*

To His Royal Highness FREDERIC, PRINCE of WALES.

SIR,

MY presuming to offer to Your Royal Highness this Translation, is in some measure justified by the Nature of the Subject, and Reason of the Thing. For History, however useful to others, is infinitely more so to a Prince, and particularly the History of that Crown He is born to wear. How instructive, as well as agreeable, must a fair and impartial Narration of the Lives and Actions of a long Series of Predecessors be to Him! And that such is the following History, originally penned by a Foreigner, who had no Party to serve, or Interest to promote, may be undoubtedly concluded from the universal Approbation it every where meets with.

Here then, as from a faithful Monitor, un-influenced by Hopes or Fears, Your Royal Highness will learn, in general, That to a Prince nothing is so pernicious as Flattery; nothing so valuable as Truth: That proportionable to his People's Liberty and Happiness will be his Glory and Strength: That true Valour consists not in destroying, but protecting Mankind; not in conquering Kingdoms, but defending them from Violence: That a Prince's most secret Counsels, Motives and Pursuits, will probably one day be published and vigorously judged; and, however flattered whilst living, yet when dead, he will be treated as his Actions have deserved, with Honour or Reproach, with Veneration or Contempt.

More particularly, Your Royal Highness will Here perceive, that foreign Acquisitions and Conquests were generally fatal to England; all Increase of Empire burdensome to her, except That of the Ocean, which can never be too extensive, as it enlarges and protects her Trade, the principal Fountain of her Riches and Grandeur.

But above all, you will Here see the Origin and Nature of our Excellent Constitution; where the Prerogatives of the Crown, and Privileges of the Subject, are so happily proportioned, that the King and the People are inseparably united in the same Interests and Views. You will observe, that this Union, though talked of by even the most Arbitrary Princes with respect to their Subjects, is peculiar to the English Monarchy, and the most solid Foundation of the Sovereign's Glory and the People's Happiness.

Accordingly, you will Here constantly find, that in the Reigns where this Union was cultivated, the Kingdom flourished, and the Prince was glorious, powerful, trusted, beloved. On the contrary, when, by an Arbitrary Disposition, or evil Counsels, fels, it was interrupted, the Constitution languished, mutual Confidence vanished, Distrust, Jealousy, Discord arose; and when entirely broken, as was unfortunately sometimes the Case, Confusion and Civil Wars ensued.

As this Union, so essential to our Government, was by Your Royal Grandfather and is by His Present Majesty, Your Royal Father, steddily adhered to; so it is with extreme Satisfaction presumed, that the same Adherence will distinguish Your Royal Highness's future Reign: a Presumption grounded upon Your many noble Endowments, but chiefly on that Foundation of all other, as well as Royal, Virtues, a generous Mind, which naturally abhors Oppression and Tyranny.

Presuming on this known Generosity, I most humbly intreat Your Royal Highness's gracious Acceptance of this Address and Translation; and beg leave to have the Honour of subscribing myself, with profound Respect and Submission,

S I R

Your ROYAL HIGHNESS'S

Most humble, most dutiful,

And most obedient Servant,

N. TINDAL.

. I think the *Englishman* should have observ'd to his Readers, that the Prince was so pleased with this plain Dedication, that he gave the Author a Gold Medal worth 40 Guineas.

The **Craftsman**, July 21 N° 368.
Mr Danvers's *Political Faith.*

HAving given my Readers, says D'anvers, the political Creed of a *Modern Whig,* (see p. 339) it may be expected that I, who profess myself an *old Whig,* should present them with a *Counterpart* to it. Indeed I find myself anticipated by the learned Madam *Osborne*; (see p. 346 E.) but as she hath not hit exactly on my *Principles of Government,* I shall proceed to state the principal Articles of my *civil Faith,* which are as follows, *viz.*

1. That Government was originally ordained for the Good of the *Governed*; and that the *supreme Magistrate,* whatever he is called, is properly the *Servant of the People,* when consider'd in their collective Capacity, tho' superior to every Individual.

2. That all *absolute Governments* are tyrannical Usurpations on the *natural Rights of Mankind,* and originally founded in Force, or Fraud.

3. That altho' our Government is commonly call'd a *Monarchy,* yet it partakes very much of democratical Principles, and is therefore properly styled a *limited, mixed Monarchy,* or a sort of *regal Commonwealth.*

4. That as the Essence of our Constitution consists in keeping a *proper Ballance* between the several Branches of the *Legislature,* the utmost Care ought to be taken to secure the *Freedom of Elections without Doors,* and the *Virtue of our Representatives within.*

5. That *Liberty* is the Birthright of *Englishmen* and *Britons,* solemnly confirm'd to them on many Occasions; and if any future Prince should attempt to deprive them of it, they have an undoubted Right to resist him by Arms, notwithstanding their *Oaths of Allegiance,* which are only conditional, whilst the Prince observes his own *Oath.*

6. That the late *glorious Revolution,* and the *present Establishment in the Protestant Line* were founded on these Principles, and cannot be justify'd on any other.

7. That the *present Royal Family* being seated on the Throne by the Consent of the People in Parliament it is our Interest and Duty to support them in it, as long as they comply with the Design of their Establishment, and observe those *Limitations,* with which the Succession is circumscribed by Law.

8. That *Prerogative* is a Word of no determinate Meaning, and was first invented in arbitrary Reigns to supersede the *Law,* and impose upon the People. No Prince, since the *Revolution,* hath a Right to any *Prerogative,* which is contrary to *Law,* or can *dispense with the Laws of the Land.*

9. That all *standing Armies,* in Times of Peace, more than are absolutely necessary for the immediate visible Ends of Government, are inconsistent with the Nature of a *free Country,* and will always furnish Matter of Umbrage to Men of Sense and Reflection.

10. That all Divisions of the People into *Parties* and *Factions,* about unessential Points of Government or Religion, tend to weaken the Foundation of *Liberty,* and may be used to subvert our *Constitution.*

11. That *Taxes* ought to be made as easy, as the Circumstances of Affairs will admit, both with Respect to the *Sums raised,* and the *Manner of collecting them,* especially on all Commodities, which affect the *common Necessaries of Life,* our Trade and Manufacture.

12.

12. That as all Opposition to a *good Administration* is undoubtedly *factious* and *wicked*; it is equally certain that Opposition to a *bad Administration* is the strongest visible Mark, which any Man can give his Country of *Patriotism* and *publick Virtue*.

These are my Principles, to which my Writings have been agreeable. I have not, like the *Court Writers*, laid down *good Propositions* and retracted them in the *Application*. I shall say no more at present, of my Principles as a *Whig*; but it may not be improper to give the particular Reasons, which induced me at this Time to make a publick Confession of them.

It hath been constantly objected against the *Craftsman*, that the *Gentlemen*, supposed to be concerned in it, have had no other End than to supplant the *present M—rs*, and work themselves into their Places; that therefore they have obstructed wise and prudent *Measures*; or, at least, would do the very *same Thing*, if they were in Power.

Now, I think it is generally believed that *a certain Gentleman* is at length winding up his Bottoms, and endeavouring to make a decent Retreat; this therefore I judge a proper Juncture to assure my Readers, that the *Alteration of Persons* hath not been the only Point pursued in these Papers; for which Reason I am determined not to lay it down, till they are convinced themselves that *something farther* was intended; and I hope will be happily effected. Let Power be in what Hands it will, it ought to be watch'd; and if any *future Minister* should pursue the same Measures lately opposed, he must expect the same Treatment from the Assertors of Liberty. I must declare before Hand against all *Patching* and *Screening*, which will be so far from satisfying, that it will exasperate the Nation, and perhaps blow them into a Flame. On the contrary, when I see a stedfast Resolution taken to promote the Honour, Interest, and Ease of the Nation, I shall be glad to lay down my Pen, and wear out the Remainder of my Life in Peace and Serenity of Mind.

As I have long had the Honour to be called the *Mouth of a Party*, and represented as the *Vehicle*, made use of by the *Gentlemen in the Opposition* to convey their Sentiments to the World, I thought it incumbent upon me to declare myself publickly as a Writer. Whether I speak the Sentiments of *these Gentlemen* at present, I know not; but I have discharged my own Conscience, and shall leave the World to judge whether I or Mrs *Osborne* write most like a WHIG RUN MAD.

Fog's Journal, July 21 No. 246.

FOG shews by what kind of Politicks the *French* Ministers have been enabled to deprive the People of their Liberties.

We have, says he, taken Notice in former Discourses, why it was thought necessary that all the Powers of the Estates of the Kingdom should be transferr'd to the Parliament of *Paris* (See Vol. II. p. 834, 858, 944, 1052.) which is now as much the Representative of the Kingdom, as those Estates were formerly of the whole People, and have on many Occasions exerted their Power, even in Opposition to the Court; wherefore the Ministers did all they could to abridge their Power; for publick Liberty is a terrible Bar in the Way of Men in great Affairs, for every Knave would be safe, if he could.

That the Ministers might therefore live without Controul, it was necessary that the Parliament of *Paris*, the Clergy, Nobility, Magistracy of the Town, and the trading Interest should be all brought into a Kind of Dependence upon the Court.

The Nobility were drawn in to loiter their Time at Court in Luxury and expensive Follies, that having so wasted their Estates, they might be obliged to hang upon a Minister for a Pension, or a Government, to support their Rank.

As to the Church, its primitive Hierarchy did not seem calculated to support Tyranny in the State, the Bishops were elected by the inferior Clergy, and afterwards indeed confirm'd by the Pope; but even this last did not bring them under the Influence of the Court; the first Attempt made towards it was at a Time, that the Court of *France* was embroil'd with that of *Rome*, the former gain'd over a few of the Bishops, and being resolv'd to clip the Pope's Authority in Spirituals, caused them to assemble and take on them the Name of a National Council, or National Assembly, in which they declar'd that the Pope had no Authority to excommunicate Kings; that none of his Bulls had any Force, unless they had the Sanction of a general Council; with some other Thing, which shew'd plainly, that they aim'd to place in the King and his Ministers that Infallibility which they denied to be in the Pope.

The

The King took to himself the Right of naming all the Bishops exclusive both of the Clergy and of the See of *Rome*; the Ceremony of sending a *Conge D'Elire* to the inferior Clergy is a meer Farce, tho' it's an Acknowledgment that the Right of electing is in the Clergy. Hence the Clergy of *France*, are now one of the chief Supports of Arbitrary Power.

The *French* Ministers have never been able to gain over the whole Body of *French* Bishops upon any Occasion; for which various Reasons have been assign'd; first, that they are generally chosen out of the Prime of the Nobility; that some of them are bred up in Sentiments of Generosity, and Notions of Honour; and that they are not burthen'd with Wives and Children, which was sometimes made an Excuse for yielding to Corruption. However, the Ministers have a Party sufficient among them as it is.

The next Thing done towards establishing arbitrary Power in *France*, was, to humble the People by Clogs and Incumbrances upon Commerce. To this Purpose most of the Branches of Foreign Trade were monopoliz'd, and certain Persons, for Considerations, best known to the Ministers, obtained Grants and Charters for trading to this or that Part of the World, exclusive of all other Subjects. *In good Governments, says a French Author, it is usual to prohibit importing Merchandizes that shall hinder the Sale of Home Manufactures, but to forbid the Subjects to export Home Manufactures, is a Hardship peculiar to* France; *the Effect is, it has sunk our Commerce, and engaged all those Monopolizers to become Champions for Arbitrary Power.*

Next the Taxes laid upon Wine, Salt, and some other Things essential to the Living of the Poor increas'd the Price of Labour; so that when Monf. *Colbert* erected Manufactures, he found the *English*, and some other Nations, were able to under-sell the *French* in Foreign Commodities, because free from those Taxes, which must be continued in *France*.

The next to be gained over were the Magistrates of the chief Cities and Towns, and these were managed various Ways; many were drawn in by being promis'd Coats of Arms to them and their Families; others were tempted for a Post in the Army given to a Son, Brother, Nephew, or a Cousin, &c. For such trifling Considerations did many of them sell that Part of the Liberties of their Countrymen which were intrusted with them.

Could the Parliament of *Paris* have been gain'd over, Arbitrary Power would have been fix'd in *France* as firm as an immoveable Rock; but here the Ministers met with such Oppositions and Difficulties as must turn to the everlasting Glory of the *French* Nation. *Mezeray* takes Notice that in the Reign of *Henry* III. 24 Edicts for raising Money upon the People, were presented to the Parliament by the Court to be verify'd, and that only three of them pass'd. Not only Edicts for raising Money but for extending the Regal Power and Prerogative, have been refused; even the Ministers have not been able to gain one Voice, when the Thing in Question has had the least Tendency towards Oppression. This being the Case, there have been eternal Contentions betwixt the Court and Parliament; so that when the Court has met with Repulses, they have banish'd the Parliament, and sometimes executed the Edict without its being register'd at all. ——But what may not Ministers do in Countries where there are standing Armies? But as this Point has never been given up by the Parliament, the *French* comfort themselves with this Reflection, that while their Parliaments preserve their Integrity, they have a Chance of recovering their Liberties one Time or other.

Some have wonder'd that the *French* Ministers never found Means of introducing a certain Number of Tools of their own into that August Assembly; for so they might have ruin'd the Nation, and have boasted that they made the Laws of the Land the Rule of their Administration. ——It is much safer said a *French* Gentleman, for the Ministers, that Things should remain as they are; at present the People are in hopes of better Times; but if their Parliament should be turn'd into an Assembly of Court Slaves, they would see that they were bought and sold, and would send such a Parliament to the Devil.

Weekly Miscellany. July 21. No. 32.

The Benefit of Religion.

MR HOOKER,

THE only Motive of Action to an intelligent Being is *Happiness*; either *present* or *future*; i. e. the Satisfaction that accompanies, or the Good that we believe will follow any Action. To propagate Religion and Virtue is more worthy a rational Agent, than to disturb the Order of Society and destroy the Happiness of Mankind, by corrupting their Principles and Manners, and is it not natural to suppose, that

that a Confcioufnefs of Acting properly and beneficently fhould carry with it more Satisfaction, and the Expectation of greater Good in Confequence, than *Infidels* can *receive* or *expect* from their unwearied Endeavours to propagate Infidelity! How is it then that the greater Good, as a natural Caufe, does not produce the greater Effect? Shall we fay, that thofe who declare for Religion and Virtue do it not upon *real Conviction?* That cannot be generally the Cafe. And yet how fhall we, otherwife, account for their Conduct? If they have the Intereft of Religion and Virtue *fincerely* at Heart, how can they fit unconcerned when the Enemy is fo openly and vigorously attempting its Deftruction?

But if thefe act an inconfiftent Part, by fhewing an Indifferency to Things worthy their moft active Zeal, thofe who are labouring to introduce a General Corruption in *Principle* and *Practice*, muft be confidered as mere *Lunaticks*, and *Fools*. For they are bringing upon Mankind a general Calamity, of which themfelves muft unavoidably be common Sharers. If Injuftice, Inhumanity, Oppreffion, Murder, &c. be (as has been publickly afferted) no Crimes, it is fhocking to imagine the Scene of Diftraction that muft inevitably enfue. Such is the wretched Condition, to which the *Modern Free-thinkers*, thofe *Friends* of *Mankind*, would reduce us and themfelves!

Others engaged in the fame Caufe, act with more Caution and Referve. They would be thought to allow the *Diftinction between Good* and *Evil*, and a *Moral Obligation* grounded upon it, but deftroy its Force, by taking away its Sanction. *Virtue* they pretend, requires no Sanction befides the Reward it confers upon its Followers. And having thus provided for the Security of *Virtue*, they deny a *Providence* and *future State*, by which they *weaken* her *Influence*. Let the Happinefs, or Mifery, which *accompanies* the practice of Virtue be ever fo great, if Men are perfuaded that over and above thefe *Natural* Rewards and Punifhments, they fhall certainly receive others, fuperadded by the *pofitive Will* of their Creator, here is an *auxiliary Force*, an *additional* Motive. And therefore whoever attempts to *weaken* Men's Belief of a *future State*, or to leffen their Apprehenfion of the *Degree* of future Happinefs or Mifery, is a declared *Enemy* to *Virtue* and to *Society*, let him carry his abftracted Notions of Things ever fo far, in Refpect to their *Eternal Relation* and *Fitnefs*. The *Obligation* and *Force* of Oaths, univerfally

efteemed the grand Security of *Social Good*, is wholly deftroy'd, if you take away the Belief of a *Providence* and a *future State*. And from this Way of Reafoning it follows, that all Deiftical Notions, are lefs *ufeful*, than the Belief of *Chriftianity*.

As to thofe who disbelieve, not only the Truths of Revelation, but Natural Religion too, they are utterly inexcufable to common Senfe, to their own Intereft, and to the Community, if they offer to make a *Convert*. A *Wife* Infidel (if *Wifdom* and *Infidelity* could meet in the fame Perfon) would be more fearful of communicating the *Infection*, or of being known to have it, than if he had the moft invenom'd Plague upon him. If the Legiflature does not think fit to *banifh* fuch *Traytors* the *Kingdom*, every private Perfon ought to banifh them his *Houfe* and *Company*.

PHILANTHROPUS.

London Journal July 21. No. 734.

THE Defigns of the Writers againft the Court being to *divide* and *break* the *Whig Intereft*, Mr *Osborne* refolves to do all in his Power to *unite* and *ftrengthen* it.

The Authors of the *Craftfman* affuming the Character and Principles of *Whigs*, is only to *deceive*; becaufe they are conftantly traducing the *Whigs*, levelling them with *Jacobites*, and the moft rancour'd Enemies of the Government, and exhorting them to *divide* and *join* with them. What honeft *Whigs* are thefe! Suppofe a *zealous old Tory*, to prove his Sincerity, fhould tell his Brethren, that the only Way to fupport their Caufe, was to *divide*, and *join* with the *Whigs, Republicans*, Presbyterians, &c. Would not this be full as *reafonable* as the *Craftfman's* bidding the *Whigs* break themfelves to pieces, and join *the Enemies* of *Liberty*, the better to fupport the *Caufe* of *Liberty*.

The *Enemies* of the Government are, indeed, playing a natural Game, for they may get by the Change: But, what are the *Whigs* doing? Tearing out their own Bowels; and gravely telling us, all *Diftinctions* fhould be drop'd, but that of *Court* and *Country Party*. But how ridiculous is it to talk of fuch a Diftinction, when there is *no Foundation* for it; fince at this Time there is no *Court Party* againft the *true Interefts* of their *Country?* But as *Facts* will better convince than *Reafoning*, Ofborne produces an *Inftance* when there was a *Reafon* for a *Country Party*; by which we fhall difcern there is *no Reafon* for one now. The

The *Opposition* and *Resistance* to the *Court* in K. *Charles* I. time, and the forming a *Country Party*, was absolutely necessary, because the *Court* was trying all Ways to *set up a Government above and against Law*. Doctrines were taught at Court, published by Authority, and sent over the Kingdom, in these Words: *That the King is not bound to observe the Laws of the Land, concerning the Subjects Rights and Liberties; and that his Royal Will in imposing Taxes* without Consent of Parliament, *binds the Subjects Conscience under pain of* Eternal Damnation. And in Consequence of these Doctrines, no Parliaments were called for 12 Years together, during which Time a few Courtiers met in one place, as *Privy Counsellors*, and sent forth *Proclamations* as Law, and then the *same Men* met in the Star-Chamber and executed those *mock Laws* with the utmost Rigour, and it may be justly said, That *that* Reign *was one continued Violation of the Laws of* England; King *Charles* IId's Reign, consisted chiefly of *Tricks of State*, against Law, Equity, and Liberty; and K. *James* II. openly avowed a Power of *Dispensing* with all Laws.

In these Reigns, therefore, there was *Reason* for a *Country Party*; and so there was in the 4 last Years of Q. *Anne*, when *Bedford's* Book of *Hereditary Right* was published, by the Court, with a full Design to prejudice the Title of the El. of *Hanover*; when *Schism Acts* and *Occasional Acts* were made, and Resolutions form'd to take away the *Dissenters Votes*, because *Friends* to the House of *Hanover*; and all those Things done by the *very Men*, whom we are now taught to receive into our Bosoms, as Persons more true to the Interest of the present *Royal Family*, and *the Cause* of Liberty, than the *Whigs* themselves. Good God! Can this be said against the *Experience and Feeling* of almost every Man in the Kingdom, and yet *believed*? What *Dryden* said of *Priests* holds as true of these *deluded Whigs*,

> *That Courtiers Vows, and Harlots Tears,*
> *Are* Truths, *to what they tell*.

Why must we have a *Country Party*? Against what? Against a *legal* Government; against King, Lords, and Commons, making *reasonable* Laws; against an *Administration* governing absolutely by those Laws, and consulting the Good of the Community? Would we have a *Country Party* against our Country, for such would be a Party *against the Court*? Let the *Whigs* say, whether they don't really think the *Constitution* of *England* is more secure in the Hands of *Whigs*, than in the Hands of *Tories* and *Jacobites*? Whether they think that Men, who, tho' some of them *invited* the Prince of *Orange* over, Yet were against settling the Crown upon him, and who distressed him thro' his whole Reign, That Men, who came absolutely into Schemes, in the Close of Q. *Anne's* Reign, to bring in the *Pretender*; who enter'd into a Rebellion against the *late King*, and who have ever since, constantly voted for Gentlemen distinguish'd by their *Disaffection* to the Government, Whether these Men, are Persons with whom the *Whigs* should *unite*, to preserve a *Revolution Government*, and support the *Glorious Cause* of *Liberty*? And then say, whether there is any possible way to preserve the Blessings we enjoy, but *firmly uniting the Party* known to be always *for Liberty*, against *all other Parties* known to be always *against Liberty*; till they lately put on a Shew of it, on purpose to *deceive*?

The **Daily Courant.** July 20.

MR *D'anvers* having (see p. 347) paid Sir *R. W.* his usual Compliment proceeds (F) to acquaint us, that his Brother Mr *H. W.* at his first setting out into the World, was laughed at for *neglecting Dress*, and *loving a merry Joke*.

I have known the Gentleman traduced, for many Years; have seen him in all his Humours, in his grave and merry Vein, and can solemnly protest, that I never heard him joke at his Inferiors with *Insolence* and *Ill-nature*, but his Jests were ever season'd with a certain good Nature that took away the Sting; and has more than once recalled to my Mind the famous Character of his Name-sake HORACE, *Omne vafer vitium ridentis Flaccus Amici Tangit & admissus circum præcordia ludit*.

In his merry Vein with his Equals or Superiors, I have observed a decent Freedom, becoming a Gentleman.

As to his serious Vein, I have been surpriz'd he could have found Leisure to make himself Master of so many different Branches of Knowledge, which it would be excusable in a Man of Business to be in some Measure ignorant of.

That worn-out Joke of his being a Sloven, is too ridiculous to be taken Notice of. I have seen People justly laugh'd at, and despised, for being over-nice in their Dress, but never before for being unaffected and careless.

Mr *Danvers's* Charge of Ignorance and Self-

Self-sufficience, is not applicable to this Gentleman. As to his being *equally greedy of*, and *incapable of using either Money or Power*, I am sorry Œconomy and a necessary Care in providing for younger Children, should subject any Gentleman to the Imputation of being covetous. If *he is incapable of using Power*, his being greedy of it signifies nothing, because he could do neither Good nor Harm with it. I never heard that Experience in Business could give Dignity; it may, indeed, in little Minds, create a sort of *Pride*; but an Experience of this Nature, must be founded on natural good Sense, and can hardly be the Occasion of Pride. But it seems yet more impossible for *Experience to exist without Knowledge*, which Mr *D'anvers* seems to assert, when he says, That this Gentleman's Experience serves only to give him Presumption without Knowledge.

If one was to expose the Characters of some of the Principals in the Opposition, the Avarice of some, and the Profuseness of others; I am afraid the Scenes of Wickedness and Lewdness would be too shocking; therefore I shall forbear. Yours, &c.

The *Free-Briton*. July 26.

THE last preceding Free Briton *was an Extract from Cato's Letters, on the Method great Men take to become Popular. This is likewise copy'd from that Author, to shew the Effects of Party Prejudices, as applicable to the present Times.*

It is surprising what minute and contemptible Causes create Discontents, Disorders, Violence and Revolutions amongst Men; what a small Spring can actuate a mighty and many-headed Multitude; and what mighty Numbers one Man is capable of drawing into his Disgusts and Designs. It is the Weakness of the many, when they have taken a Fancy to a Man, or the Name of a Man, they take a Fancy even to his Failings, adopt his Interest right or wrong, and resent every Mark of Disfavour shewn him, however just and necessary it be. Nor are their Resentment and Fondness the less violent for being ill-grounded: If a Man makes them drunk once or twice a Year, this Injury is a Kindness which they never forget; and he is sure of their Hearts and their Hands for having so generously robbed them of their Time, their Innocence, and their Senses. Cato proceeds to give several Instances of Party Prejudices, and then concludes, I would only desire it to be considered, what Infamy and Contempt it reflects

upon the human Species to be thus apt to run into Discord and Animosities upon such wretched and unmanly Motives; and what Monsters and Impostors they must be, who begin, or manage, or heighten those absurd Contentions amongst any Part of the Race of Men, already too unhappy by the Lot of Nature.

Weekly Miscellany. July 28. No. 32.
Christianity and Infidelity examin'd.

IF one was to credit the bold Assertions, every Day given out in Print and Conversation, Christianity has neither Worth nor Proof on its Side, and the modern Infidels are the only Men of strong Reason and sound Sense. But the loudest Pretensions are not always the best warranted. Look into their most masterly Performances, and if you draw a Line over the declamatory Parts, the Defamation, Calumnies, Forgeries, Falsehood, and some Truths artfully inserted, there will not be an Argument left, that can influence a Man of Reason to quarrel with the Religion of his Country. If then these Writers quarrel with it on such Grounds, they must either be Men of no Reason, or their Reason must be perverted, and their Understandings darken'd, by vicious Habits.

A good presumptive Argument, that this is the real Source of Infidelity, i., all eminent Learning and Virtue in the known World have been, and still are on the religious Side of the Question, opposed by the Ignorant, Loose, Profligate, Debauch'd, and Turbulent, impatient of Religion, on account of the Restraints it lays on their Lusts and Passions.

The Time of spreading these Doctrines helps us to form the same Judgment of their Original; an Age when Avarice, Luxury, and Wantonness have broke in upon the Nation in Consequence of the *South Sea Year*, fatal to *Property*, but much more to *Virtue*.

But there is no need of presumptive Arguments, when we have the Doctrines themselves to prove the Point. Is it possible any Men could bring themselves to assert, that every Man's Reason is of itself able to carry human Nature to its highest Perfection; That God can discover his Pleasure but once, and but one way; That all new Revelation is not only superfluous but impossible? That the Relations of Things are the Law of Man, and that he is able to see all things with their several Relations; That nothing
can

can be true which we cannot fully comprehend and measure; and God can command nothing without giving his reason for it? That Men have no Occasion for Instructions to awaken them to Duty? That all which Heaven requires of Man is to search his Head and Heart for what is agreeable to himself, and that to pursue this, will be Virtue and Happiness? That therefore all Laws divine and human, except what a Man thus makes for himself, are Impositions on the natural Liberties of Mankind?

In pursuance of this Scheme it has been publickly avow'd, that Vice is beneficial to the State, and more so than Virtue; that it would be for the Interest of the Nation to have publick Stews; that one Man is not made for one Woman; but that Polygamy, Concubinage, and even Sodomy is lawful; that all Ordinances are useless. Thus the Bands of Society have been loos'd, and the Foundations of Government sapp'd; hence Disregard of Authority, Loosness, a Ferity of Manners; Theft, Fraud, Rapine, Murders, Debauchery; Presumption, Despair, Phrenzy, Madness; Self-Executions, and making away Infants out of a Principle of Benevolence. (See Vol. II. p. 723.) These are the natural Consequences, and visible Effects of the new Scheme, and the Issues of a corrupt Heart,

It will be said, some Patrons of the Modern Scheme are as sober and chaste as other People. If so, we must seek some other Principle of Action in such; but then it cannot be a better than those above-mention'd; because Doctrines, big with such monstrous Consequences, cannot proceed from a good one. Some Vices, less notorious than others, are yet more mischievous. Pride and Vanity can swell the Heart of Man. The Love of Novelty, Ambition, Envy, Pique, Revenge, have carried People incredible Lengths. Some chuse to be famous on any Terms.

Its no wonder if the indolent, luxurious, wanton, conceited, seditious, weak and corrupt part of Mankind, are fond of an Idol that has something in it to court every one's vicious Taste. It is indeed observ'd to the Honour of Christianity, that it carries the Marks of Truth and divine Force, because without Artifice, or Violence it spread over the Earth in a little Time, tho' its Precepts were irreconcileably uncomplaisant to the Practices of a debauch'd World. What then, but its incontestable Evidence and direct Influence

on the Good of Society, cou'd make Prejudice and Depravity bow down before it?

It is easy to fix Absurdities, which no body maintains, on Religion, and then running at her with Rage and Fury; A Treatment like to that, which Christians suffered, when they were sewed up in the Skins of Animals, and then worried to Death.

To laugh is very easy; and the greater and better a Thing is, the more liable it is to undiscerning Banter. *Virgil* has been travestied, and the Heroes of the *Iliad* ludicrously personated by Frogs and Mice; but are either of those two Poems, therefore read with the less Admiration? Ridicule is no Test of Truth. The Christian Religion is, and will be, as lovely, certain, and beneficial, as if Infidels had never wagg'd their Heads, loll'd their Tongues, or shook their Sides at her. **X.**

London Journal July 28. No. 735.
Remarks on Mr D'anvers's *political Creed*

THO' Mr *D'anvers*'s *Civil Faith*, (See p. 357.) is, *in general*, the Faith of all the *Whigs*; yet 'tis not exactly *Orthodox*, according to our *Constitution*; and even *this Creed* he has always retracted in the *Application*.

His first Article, that the King is *the Servant of the People*, i. e. *inferior*, is false; for the K. of *England* is as *truly superior to all the People*, as He is to every *Individual*: The whole People is only a Collection of *Individuals*; and, if the King is *Superior* to *each Individual*, He is *Superior to All*; that is, to the *Whole People*. But this *Distinction* was trump'd up to justify the late *tumultuous*, and almost rebellious Proceedings; about which Time this Doctrine of the *original Power* and *high Authority* of the People, in their collective Body was set up against the Government. But the *whole People*, in their collective Body, have no *other Right* than *each Individual*; that is, to defend themselves when they are injur'd. The King hath a *real* and *essential Part* of the *Legislature*, and the *whole executive Power* of the *Laws* is in his Person; by Virtue of which he is SUPREME in all Causes, and over ALL PERSONS. The *People* have no *Power* nor *Authority* while the *legal Government subsists*; but Kings, Lords, and Commons have *all Power and Authority*, as the *Legislative Power* of the Kingdom; and the King hath all *Power and Authority*, as to the *executive Power* of the Kingdom. This is his *Right* or *Prerogative* according

cording to Law. He hath likewise a *further Prerogative*; that is, as Mr LOCKE observes, a Power lodged in him to be exercised for the Good of the People, *in all those Cases*, in which 'tis impossible *Laws* should provide.

Calling our Government (as the *Crafts-man* does) a *Regal Common-wealth*, is either using Words in a very uncommon Sense, or else a *dangerous Innovation*. *Venice* is indeed a *Ducal Aristocracy*, and only a *Nominal Power* in the Duke; and if in *England, all real Power* was in the *People*, and only a *Nominal Power* in the *King*, then the Phrase *Regal Common-wealth* would be just; but it is not so.

His Ninth Article I agree to; and leave him to make the most of the Concession.

His 10th Article is also true; but whether People are for or against the *Revolution*, and the *Present Establishment*, is not an *unessential Point* of Government; so that, if the People are thus divided, 'tis then, for *the Good* of the Kingdom, and *the Preservation* of Liberty, that they should be *so distinguished*.

His 11th Article I absolutely agree to, *That all Opposition to a good Administration is factious and wicked*. This *factious* and *wicked* Part have the Antiministerial Writers been acting these several Years; Mr *D'anvers* hath wrote in *direct Opposition* to the grand Principle he hath laid down, *That 'tis our Duty to support and stand by an Administration as long as they comply with the Design of their Institution*. Agreed, and no longer. And I am content to put the whole Issue of the Controversy upon this single Point.

But why do we talk about Administrations, and *Ministers*, when (according to the *Craftsman*) the Ministry is going to be *changed*? The plain *English* of all that he says upon this Head is this, " If there is a Change of Ministry, or, if the Ministry is to be *new medell'd*, then we will *oppose them* with as much *Malice* and *Injustice*, as we have done the *present Ministry*. We have not contended merely for an *Alteration of Persons* (God knows our Hearts) but for *such an Alteration* as shall terminate in the *Authors* and *Confederates* of the *Craftsman*, that *glorious Triumvirate, P—W— and B—Therefore* whatever Changes are made, we will never lay down our Pens till SOMETING FURTHER, which we *solely* intended, that is, *ourselves in Power*, be happily effected " If this is not their Meaning of *something further*, they must either in-

tend a *Change of Government*. or, which God of his his infinite Mercy forbid, *chopping off the Head of the M——r*. That would be *something further*, indeed.

But let them not be deceived; neither his Head, nor Person, nor Estate, nor POWER are in Danger. Let not his *Friends*, therefore, be imposed upon by the *Artifices* of his *Enemies*; for these are only *Lies of the Day*, to *discourage* them from acting vigorously *in his Service*, which from the Part he has already acted, may be justly call'd, *The Service of the Nation*. OSBORNE.

The **Craftsman**. July 28. No. 369.

Remarks on the Report from the Committee of Enquiry *into the Frauds in the Customs*.

I Shall first, says D'*anvers*, explain the Occasion of *this Enquiry*. Whilst the *Excise Bill* was depending, the *Advocates* for it, insisted on the Multiplicity of *Frauds*, and that the Nature of them were such, as nothing but the Power of *Excise-Laws* should be able to prevent them. The Gentlemen, on the *other Side*, acknowledg'd there might be very great *Frauds*, and declared they were ready to come into any Method to remedy them, not tending to the Destruction of *Trade* and *Liberty*, as they apprehended an *Excise* did. Hereupon one of the Representatives of this City, a great Trader in *Tobacco*, moved for an Account of *Frauds in that Commodity* for ten Years past, to be laid before the House, which appeared to amount to so trifling a Sum, that the Persons, who started the Objection, insisted no more upon it; but the Gentlemen on the *other side*, having defeated the *Excise Scheme*, resolv'd to purge themselves from any Imputation of designing to countenance *Frauds* of any kind. For this purpose an *honourable Gentleman* proposed, that a *Committee* be appointed to enquire into the *Frauds and Abuses of the Customs in general*.

A *certain Gentleman* was very much perplexed with the Motion, but having mumbled the Thistles a while, continued to the Enquiry, and it was resolved, That the Committee should be chosen by *Ballot*, a Method of voting originally design'd to prevent all unwarrantable Influence; but what was his Conduct upon this Occasion? Why, he summoned all his Creatures together, in a most unprecedented manner, and having told them, in a slabbering Speech,

Speech, what a terrible Combination of all Parties was form'd against him, conjured them, in a moſt pathetick Manner, to ſtand by and ſupport him againſt the Deſigns of his Enemies, for if they ſucceed againſt me, ſays he, the next ſtep will be to turn you all out of your Places, to fill them with Creatures of their own.

Then he went round the whole Aſſembly, Man by Man, ſqueezing them very feelingly by the Hand, and preſenting 'em at the ſame Time with a Liſt of 21 *Gentlemen* (17 of whom were in Employments of great Profit) beſeeching them to Vote for it, if they had any Regard for *Him* or their *own Intereſt*. By theſe Methods he ſucceeded; and *one of his Advocates* hath ſince very judiciouſly triumph'd upon it. (See p. 345. F.) Let the World judge how far *ſuch Methods* are conſiſtent with the Nature of our *Conſtitution*, or the original Intention of *Balloting*.

As to the *Report* itſelf, I cannot, ſays *D'anvers*, forbear admiring the peculiar Eloquence of the Style, in which it is drawn up; but when we reflect on that *glib Genius*, who is named the Compiler of it, we cannot wonder that it far exceeds all former Productions of the ſame Kind.

The *Committee* begin with acquainting the Houſe, that they proceeded with the *utmoſt Diligence* in examining the Matters referr'd to them. Indeed no *Diligence* ſeems to have been wanting to procure Information; for it appears that *Smuglers*, *corrupted Officers*, and Perſons taken out of Goal were produced as Witneſſes. Nay, they had Recourſe ſo far back as 1704 for one Inſtance of *Fraud*, and in ſeveral Places take Notice of *Suſpicions* and *Conjectures* of Perſons under Examination, inſtead of *Facts* atteſted by proper Vouchers. I don't mention this as a Reflection on *theſe Gentlemen*; no, I ſpeak it to their Honour, to ſhew that they executed their Truſt, as became their Duty to the Houſe; yet they ſeem to be conſcious, that their Diſcoveries will not entirely come up to the Expectation of the Publick; which they impute to the *Want of Time*, and the *Extenſiveneſs of Frauds and Abuſes in the Cuſtoms*, which I am afraid would, on Examination, appear to be the Caſe in *other Branches of the Revenue*.

The *Gentlemen* obſerve, they begun their Examination with the Frauds in the *Tobacco Trade*, becauſe of *the great Importance of that* Trade *to the Nation*; *the Greatneſs of the Loſs to the Revenue*; and

the *Complaints of the* Planters in VIRGINIA. I was a little ſurprized to find the *laſt Article* amongſt their Inducements, ſince it's well known how *that Repreſentation* was obtained, and after we have received Accounts from *Virginia* of their being as much alarmed at the Conſequences of an *Exciſe*, as the People of *England*. But I confeſs the *Gentlemen* had ſufficient Inducements of another kind, to begin with *this Branch of the Cuſtoms*; I mean to juſtifie the Charge brought againſt the *Tobacco Merchants*, that they were concerned in *fraudulent Dealings*, and to ſhew the Neceſſity of putting the *Laws of Exciſe* in Force againſt them. But the *Tobacco Merchants*, in general, are not juſtly anſwerable for all the *Frauds*, mentioned in theſe Papers; ſome of which were firſt diſcover'd by *their Aſſiſtance*; and others tranſacted by *little Dealers in that Commodity*.

It likewiſe appears to me that the whole Amount of Frauds hitherto diſcover'd in the *Tobacco Trade* is ſo far from being enormous, that it is really too trifling to be mentioned, when reduced from *Pounds of Tobacco* to *Pounds Sterling*; eſpecially when compared with the large Extent of *that Trade*, and the Great Weight of Duties upon it, which will always be the Occaſion of *Frauds* in every Commodity burthened with them.

If the Planters ſuffer any Hardſhips under the preſent Regulations, they muſt be aſcribed to the ſame Cauſe; for when it is conſider'd that the *Duties upon Tobacco* amount to above 5 *Sevenths of the original Value*, which the *Planter* is not able to pay himſelf, the Perſons who advance the Money, will make an Advantage of it, as they juſtly may, and very probably ſome of them have been guilty of Extortion; but that this would be redreſſed by an *Exciſe*, is not yet ſatisfactorily explain'd.

The *Committee* next examine the Frauds and Abuſes in TEA and BRANDY; but as theſe *Commodities* are already *exciſed*, I am at a Loſs to gueſs for what purpoſe theſe *Frauds* are exhibited to the Publick; unleſs to convince them of a Truth which ſome Perſons have endeavour'd to conceal, viz. *that thoſe Branches of the Revenue which are already under an* Exciſe *are as liable to Abuſes as Thoſe under the* Cuſtoms.

The Frauds diſcover'd in the *Wine Trade* are ſo inconſiderable, that they hardly deſerve any Animadverſion, for they affect only

only a few *little Smuglers* on the Coasts, whom all the Laws in the World will never totally restrain, whilst the *Height of Duties* lays so strong a Temptation in their way. *Gallies*, *Dragoons*, and even *Death* itself are not able to suppress them in *France*.

It is acknowledged, thro' the whole *Report*, that most of the *Frauds* and *Abuses* mentioned, have been committed by the Connivance of *little Officers*. It these Gentlemen could have found *Time* to go thro' their Enquiries, They might have traced *this Iniquity* to its Fountain head, as the *other List*, I am told, resolved to do, without Regard to *Persons*. They might have found, that some of the chief Posts in the *Custom-house* were *Patent-Places*, held in Trust for Persons, who never go near their *Offices*, but leave them to *Deputies*, with little or no Salaries besides *Perquisites*, which is only a more genteel Word for *Bribery* and *Corruption*. It would have appeared, that ONE GENTLEMAN, in particular, who enjoys *two of the greatest Posts in the Administration*, hath another held in Trust for him in the *Custom-house*, for two Lives, which annually costs the Nation more Money than all the Frauds in the *Tobacco Trade* amount to for several Years past.

Whilst this continues to be the Case, who can wonder to hear of *Frauds* and *Abuses* in publick Offices? But the Remedy is easy and obvious. Let us either resume these great *Sine-cures*, and settle handsome Salaries upon *Those*, who actually do the publick Business; or make the *Principals* answerable for the *Frauds* committed by the Collusion of their *Deputies*. This would prove infinitely more effectual than that ridiculous Project, for preventing the *Effects of Corruption* by an *Excise*, whilst the *Cause* is suffer'd to remain.

There is another bad Effect, attending the Practice of *holding great Employments in Trust*; i. e. if it should ever find its way into the *House of Commons*; for as all Employments in the Receipt of the Revenue are incompatible with a *Seat in Parliament*, such a clandestine Method as this, would not only be an Evasion of the *Law*, and a burthensome Imposition on the *Publick*, but might be made the Instrument, under a bad Administration, of subverting our *Constitution*.

To conclude. The only way to prevent an iniquitous Commerce between the *Corrupter* and *Corrupted*, is by removing

the Temptation, that is, by making some sort of Regulation amongst the *Officers of the Revenue* as just mentioned, and lowering the *Duties*, which appear most grievous, as far as the Exigencies of State will possibly admit.

Fog's Journal, July 28 Nº. 247.

I Have lately received repeated Intelligence from a certain Country famous for Dumplins and dull Heads, that an Itinerant Quack has lately strolled about the Country, amusing the People with a Thousand idle Stories of what great Things he has perform'd in his Travels.

Your Quacks generally have but one Medicine, which Medicine is to cure all the Diseases in the Weekly Bills; it is just so with the Quack, of whom we are speaking; he has been heard to say in his Speech to the People, and with a grave Face too,—*If there be any amongst you, who is apprehensive of being Poor, let him take these Pills*. But nothing has been more diverting to me, than the odd and fantastick Catalogue of his Cures.

I remember among the rest, that he pretends to have cured the K—g of F—t of a Looseness in his Pocket, and that this Prince has made so perfect a Recovery, that he now saves his Money, and is observ'd to grow exceeding rich. His next Cure was upon his Im—l M——y, whom he pretends to have cured of all Attachments to his Neighbours, or Dependance upon his Al——s, so that he now pursues his own Interest as if they were not to be relied upon.——The next in the List is, that he once cured a whole Nation of their Trade, with all the Symptoms of Repletion, which are generally the Consequences of it; so that you cou'd see Thousands sit with their Arms across without being embarrass'd with any Business;——but the most ridiculous of all was, that he shew'd some scurvy Drawings, which he said were the Pictures of several Prelates and Pastors of the Church, (of what Church I can't say; but I suppose of the Church of *Rome*) these he pretended had been all his Patients, and he wished himself at the Devil, if he had not cured them all of the Christian Religion.

This Quack has lately taken upon himself the Name of Sir *Sidrophel* the *Rosicrucian*, and he was attended by a Zani, whom he called his Man *U baccum*, tho' it was suspected by some, that they were both of a Family, and as two Harlots, when

when they set up in Partnership, are Maid and Mistress by Turns; so Sir *Sidrophel* and *Whaccum* were Master and Man by Turns, and it is not doubted but they were equal Sharers in the Profits of every Cheat. As to Sir *Sidrophel*, many who had seen and observ'd him upon this Peregrination were of Opinion, that he was the same Person, who under the Name of *Ferdinando Ferdinandi* for many Years followed the Trade of exhibiting Monsters for Money, (See p. 227.) and now thought it adviseable to change his Name.

Whaccum was one of those that breed up themselves; but when he arrived at the Age of Manhood, it is said that his whole Estate, Real and Personal, might amount to about two Shirts and a Rag, and as all Creatures are endued with a Kind of Instinct towards Self-Preservation, *Whaccum* cast about how he should live in the World; to this purpose he got himself introduced to a great Lady, who was very rich, and famous for her Benevolence and good Nature, to beg some Employment from her. This great Lady ask'd poor *Whaccum* a most unlucky Question, for she desired to know of him what he was fit for? *Whaccum* has own'd a thousand Times since, that he never was so puzzled in all his Life, he scratched his empty Head, and attempted to look wise; but cou'd return no Answer—*Vox faucibus hæsit*—The good Lady observing the Perplexity into which she had thrown him, sent him away, telling him she wou'd give him a Month to answer that *Enigma*; at the Month's End *Whaccum* returns with all the Marks of Success in his Countenance, and having presented himself before the Lady, said to her, Madam, you desired to know what I was fit for, then your *Ladyship must understand that I am fit for* — *every Thing*. This is noAnswer, says the Lady, I desire to know what you understand. Oh! answers *Whaccum*, there is nothing easier than to answer that, then your Ladyship must know, that I understand—I had found it out once; but now I think on't, I have forgot it.—Thus *Whaccum* thought to get off by attempting a Joke.

The Steward, who was present, says, One of your Ladyship's Gardens is infested with Crows and Jackdaws, he wou'd make an excellentScarecrow—A Scarecrow! replies *Whaccum*, no I thank you for that, I had much rather be an Embassador; so refused the only Employment for which he was duly qualified.

To return to Sir *Sidrophel*; he was one of those who have not Invention toStrike out any thing even in Roguery—all his Artifices were such as had been practised over and over by other Quacks; but then he wanted their Conduct to carry him thro'; for the chief Address of a Quack consists in being able to conceal his Ignorance, but here Sir *Sidrophel* fail'd; for by a wrong Turn in his Head he was ever exposing himself this way,—the more he was known, the more he was despis'd, and his Practice universally cried down.—When he found the Spirit thus rising against him, he told the People they were all dim sighted, and *Whaccum* made a long Harangue to prove it, telling them, that the Doctor, to shew hisGood-nature, was willing to cure them of this new Distemper for nothing, by a Method altogether new; but some of them being inquisitive, found it was to be done by putting out their Eyes.

All these things put together obliged Sir *Sidrophel* to go a Journey, and visit a Province where he thought he had some Friends——his Pockets were full of Money, and he was resolv'd to have Fame; tho' he paid for it.—In this Progress *Whaccum* was of great Use not only in diverting the Mob with Grimace, but he promiss'd a thousand of them to make them Great Men, if they wou'd only say Sir *Sidrophel* was a good Doctor; to others Money was scatter'd for the same Purpose.—As amongst the Multitude there must be some Knaves, some Fools, the Fools were won by Promises, and the Knaves prevail'd upon for the *Ready*, to hollow for the Doctor; but Sir *Sidrophel* went a Step further to support a rotten Reputation; for as *Alexander* the Great of old intending to visit the Oracle of *Delphos*, sent a large Bribe privately to the Priests to salute him the Son of *Jupiter Ammon*; so Sir *Sidrophel* having a Desire to shew himself in all his Glory in a Country Town, did upon certain Considerations engage some Priests there to acknowledge him a Doctor.

It was agreed between them that he was to enter the Town in a triumphant Manner, attended by all his Hirelings—*Whaccum* led the Van with a Yard of dirty Shirt hanging out before, and as much behind, scratching his Head with one Hand, and pulling up his Breeches with the other; next came Sir *Sidrophel* himself, a goodly Countenance bronz'd over; they proceeded either to a Tavern, a College, or a Hall, where their Friends who had been retain'd for this Purpose waited to receive them. Sir *Sidrophel* was no sooner enter'd, but one of the Company, who was promis'd at least to be made a Parish Beadle for this Service, advances towards him, and in the Name of his Brethren presents him with the Diploma of Doctor, either in a Gold, a Silver, or a Brass Box, I don't care which; Sr *Sidrophel* answer'd thisHarangue with another altogether in Praise of himself, except a little Digression in Favour of *Whaccum*. *Whaccum* next makes a Speech in Praise of himself and Sir *Sidrophel*; Sir *Sidrophel* he extoll'd as the greatest Doctor, and himself as the most finish'd *Zani* in the World; but he concluded his Speech by telling the Company, that they look'd a little sheepish and out of Countenance, as if they were asham'd of what they were doing; but, my Friends, adds he, take Courage, be like Sir *Sidrophel* and me, for you see we are asham'd of Nothing.

The Evening concluded with a magnificent Feast, for Sir *Sidrophel* spared no Cost, and indeed he need not, for he was only treating the Fools with their own Money: The Glass went about freely, and the old Saying was made good, that when the Wine is in, the Wit is out; for Sir *Sidrophel* being call'd upon for a Toast, drank Success to Frauds in all Trades and Professions whatsoever; *Whaccum*'s Toast was, that the World might be govern'd by *Quacks* and *Zani*'s; the more they drank, the more foolish they grew, and discover'd not only their former Tricks, but those they intended to commit.

Next Day they departed in the same State, Sir *Sidrophel* appearing as full of Glory as *Sancho* when he was made a Governor, and *Whaccum* as proud as *Sancho*'s Ass drest up in new Trappings to accompany his Master to his Government; every Body laughing at the Farce; for there was not a Woman or a Child in the Town but knew that Sir *Sidrophel* paid for his Diploma.

Now I have finish'd my Story, it is likely all the World will look upon it as a mere Fable.——I own it is a Fable, and it is likely I shall be ask'd where is the Moral.

All I can say, is this, *That every Man who affects popular Applause by a Conduct that is neither wise nor honest, is a kind of a Sir* Sidrophel, *and like him must have Recourse to Tricks to purchase even*

the Appearance of it, and every Man who abets and supports such a one, is a kind of a Whaccum.

If we should carry our Reflections a little farther, I will suppose that a Man in a great Station, who has an infinite Number of Things at his Disposal, and who has rais'd a great Estate from little or nothing, may create a Number of Dependants in the Country where he was born, by drawing many from all Ways of Industry to hang intirely upon him, and it would be no Surprize that he should be cried up by these; but if I should see this very Person opposed, even in his own Country, by those who were reputed the Men of the greatest Worth and Honour in it, I should think him a Wretch indeed. As for my own Part, were I the greatest Man in the Kingdom, I should be ashamed to boast of a little Popularity in a Country Town, at the same Time that I was hang'd in Effigie in every other Part of the Kingdom; and it has often been found by Experience, that Popularity is like some Plants, that never spread, if they are forced.

If there be a Person in the World in such a Situation as is here described, I will tell him a Story.——Cromwell *riding into the City amidst a Number of Spectators, and a Mob hollowing about him,* Lambert, *who accompanied him at the Head of the Troops, seem'd mightily pleas'd with the Shew and Applause; but* Cromwell *observing what the Hollowers consisted of, said to* Lambert, *Cousin, Cousin, there would be a much greater Croud, and ten times the Shouting, if you and I were both in a Sledge going to be hang'd.*

Foo's *Journal of the 7th and 14th are taken up with the Lists of the Voters for and against the Tobacco or Excise Bill; but as they are in almost every body's Hand, we did not think it needful to insert them, and the less so, since somebody has been so sagacious as to publish a correct List of that kind, in Octavo, on purpose to bind up with the Monthly and Quarterly Books, and at so small a price as* Two Pence.

The Account of the Proceedings in Parliament to be continued in our next.

The diverting Advertisement of a Sale at Temple Oge, which Mr A···· hints at, was written by an Ingenious Gentleman, a Correspondent of ours at Scarborough, Decem. 1732, with Regard to that Place, and sent to the Universal Spectator, who foisted in a Word with a double Entendre; from thence the Dublin Papers lately took it, only changing the Place; and with that Alteration it was injudiciously copied by some London Newswriters, as a Piece of Irish Wit. This, we imagine Mr A····· will think a sufficient Reason for our not inserting it last Month, and especially since he may see it Vol. II. p. 109;

PRIZE VERSES, No. III. (*See p. 208, 317.*)
On the QUEEN's GROTTO. *An* ODE.

THink not, *my friend,* devouring age
    Shall e'er on sacred science prey,
Or Volumes of the learned sage
    Can, like to common things, decay.

BRITANNIA's *Queen* asserts their cause;
    For them the sculptor's art employs;
For them from regal state withdraws,
    To taste of much serener joys.

The awful *Busts* of men renown'd
    For various skill her GROTTO grace,
Where simple elegance is found,
    And solemn silence guards the place.

There sweetest contemplation dwells,
    Dispensing bliss a thousand ways;
The clouds that clog the mind dispells,
    And nature's choicest store displays.

Ye venerable shades! look down,
    Or leave a while your blest abodes;
And pleas'd the grateful tribute own
    That lifts you to the rank of gods.

PRIZE VERSES, No. IV.
On the QUEEN's GROTTO.

WHAT land BRITANNIA, e'er was blest
    as thine,
For usefull learning and the sacred sons
Of science fam'd? Now far more happy still
Since CAROLINE delights to grace desert,
And with the smiles of *approbation* raise
To more *distinguish'd* heights those aweful names
To all MINERVA's *faithfull vot'ries* dear.

Behold the *humble* GROTT, by royal guest
Ennobled, and for contemplation form'd,
Admits the *venerable busts* of those
Whose various skill, while living, found no peer.

BOYLE first arose, and, like the *morning star,*
Gave joyful promise of the *day's* approach:
With *patient search* he from the *plain effect*
Trac'd the *remoter cause;* and, with success,
Into the secret springs of nature div'd.

LOCK, bravely bold, threw off the *galling yoke,*
With which the *Stagirite* for ages past
Enslav'd the free-born minds of dastard men:
He pointed out the paths of *sacred truth,*
And lent to feeble reason friendly aid.

Then NEWTON, *wond'rous man!* still higher soar'd,
Describ'd the laws by which the *shining Orbs,*
That through the *boundless void* incessant roll,
Perform their *course* encircling; how they keep
One *certain track,* by bonds invisible
Confin'd, nor through the liquid *aether* stray.

But, if to elevate our minds above
This earthly frame, to guide our devious steps
To the blest realms of light, where angels dwell,
Deserve superior praise, O WOOLASTON, to thee,
And thee, O CLARK, it justly does belong.

PRIZE VERSES, No. V.
On the ROYAL GROTTO.

THY groves, O *Richmond,* now may vie,
    With old *Parnassus'* sacred hill,
The *Muses* here their voices try,
    And *Bards* the heav'nly rapture feel.

Here *Carolina,* sapient queen,
    Revolves the labours of the wise,
And leaves the courts tumultuous scene
    To trace the wonders of the skies.

Semiramis, thy mighty walls,
    Thy tomb too, *Artemisia,* yields,
Disgrac'd each female structure falls,
    Compar'd to that our sovereign builds.

Her GROTTO venerably wild,
    Seems like *Calypso's* fabled cell,
Or that where from the world exil'd,
    The peaceful *Hermit* loves to dwell.

The *Bustos* rear'd by her command,
    Thro' ev'ry age shall speak her praise,
While *Science* lives in *Britain's* land,
    Or *Bards* to merit tune their lays.

RICHMOND. A BALLAD.
Tune of, To you fair ladies now at land.

FROM o'er the park, and meadows fine,
    Just as the sun does rise;
To you, who, till the clock strikes nine,
    Do ne'er unclose your eyes;
Then over snuff, and tea, and news,
Your summer hours contented lose.

'Tis sweet to taste the morning air,
    Where fawns around one play;
And drops of dew, as diamonds fair,
    Strew all the glitt'ring way:
To view the hill, the stream, the trees,
To hear the birds, and feel the breeze.

The crowded street is your delight,
    And rat'ling coach to hear;
The watchman's solemn voice by night,
    Is musick to your ear:
Tom ask not when the violet blows,
Nor care you for the opening rose.

Here I, secure from strife and care,
    Seek, when the ev'ning's nigh,
My little room that's clean and square,
    And but one story high;
Where envy cannot find a place,
Nor malice shew her sallow face.

Let sordid minds, of wealth possess'd,
    To mammon altars raise;
Ambition be with power bless'd,
    And vanity with praise:
But fortune is a fickle dame,
And double-tongu'd, alas! is fame.

Give me, hard penury to chase
    From haunting of my door;
And let a chearful temper grace
    My small, but honest, store:
To this do all my wishes tend,
The useful book, the faithful friend.

WARBLETTA : A Suburbian Eclogue.
By a GENTLEMAN of PARNASSUS.

NOT ev'ry temper rural scenes delight:
    Begin, my Muse, a low suburbian flight.
Love, who invades the rural nymphs and swains,
No less a tyrant in the *suburbs* reigns;

'All, more or less, his pains or pleasures know, 5
" For what's too high for love? or what's too low?
Begin, my Muse, WARBLETTA's woe rehearse,
Who oft in cadence clear has sung thy verse.

WARBLETTA--sweetest of the throng that squalls
Melodious ballads--at the end of Paul's; 10
She, whose love-sonnets with persuasive strain,
Cou'd maids, 'tis said, and prentice-boys detain;
Who on EXCISE, the ever-famous song,
Cou'd sing so loudly----and yet sing so long;
Alluring a wide-gaping motley band, 15
Whilst in their pockets div'd some nimble hand:
No more her vocal pow'r in publick tries,
But weeping to a neighb'ring gin-shop flies;
There pensive on a runlet sits alone,
And, blending gin with tears, thus makes her moan. 20

GALLOWAY TOM, inveigling renegade,
The bane of ev'ry fond believing maid!
Curs'd be the day, when first I heard his name,
And kindred warblers chaunt aloud his name.
Curs'd be the hour, when first I saw his face, 25
So smartly impudent, and void of grace.
Well I remember it amidst the throng,
How, at first sight, I faulter'd in my song;
Gaz'd--sigh'd, and gaz'd, and ev'ry sweeter tone
Practis'd, and levell'd at his ear alone. 30
Quick he perceiv'd, and gain'd my blunder side;
Kiss'd me, swore roundly, and as roundly ly'd.
How my heart leap'd at his flatt'ring words to meet,
When the knave vow'd he'd wed me at the Fleet!
Persuaded--and I bought a copper-ring, 35
When he, false wretch! intended no such thing.
Like a brass shilling neatly silver'd o'er,
His vows have pass'd--but they shall pass no more;
The silver's worn away, and now, alas!
His perfidy appears more plain than brass. 40
Wicked o'erseers defraud the wretched poor;
The justice squeezes the starv'd padding whore:
Yet overseers and justices I see,
O TOM! are much--much honester than thee.
Think, varlet, think, to raise thee half-a-crown, 45
How readily I pawn'd my sunday-gown!
To thee in Bridewell, for no goodness, pent,
What victuals brought I! and what money lent!
Yet all that money--which I earn'd so hard,
I've known thee lose upon a single card. 50
Releas'd I saw thee fly to Brick-dust MOLL;
Yet now return--and I'll forgive thee all:
I could, I fear, be once again deceiv'd,
Again believe thee---as I once believ'd.
O TOM, return, forget to throw a main; 55
And burn thy cards which a lord's purse might drain.
Lords may be wicked at their virtue's cost,
Since titles guard 'em, when their virtue's lost.
Great rogues may plunder a whole common-weal;
But thou'dst be hang'd in hemp, if thou show'dst steal.
To great ones then thy lewdness quite resign,
And be thou honest, TOM, and only mine.
Come, quickly come, upon my once-lov'd breast,
Repose thee---sink within my arms to rest.
If cares oppress thee, I'll divert my love 65
With Patient GRIZEL--and a GRIZEL prove.
For thee all day with open throat I'll toil;
With thee at night, well-pleas'd, divide the spoil;
For thee a spicy hot-pot I'll prepare;
For thee a nice sheep's-head I'll dress with care. 70

Will not these win thee?----Add to these the joy,
Which nightly shall our waking hours employ.
Hard-hearted wretch! in vain, in vain I sue,
Rougher than winds to a well-powder'd cue.
The habit of thy temper now appears; 75
Oh!--thou wast nourish'd sure by Huckley-bears.
Like burning brandy my warm bosom glows,
Whilst thine is like a wint'ry puddle froze.
What, tho' in ballad so much skill I boast!
So long have reign'd St Giles's fav'rite toast! 80
By pur-blind fiddlers have been often ply'd,
As often all their hated suits deny'd!
Nor voice, nor person for my TOM has charms;
And whilst ungrateful he thus shuns my arms,
Frantic I make some airy bulk my bed, 85
Where chilling winds fly whistling round my head;
Whilst lazy muddy channels bubling creep,
Inviting (tho' in vain) my eyes to sleep
My chearless eyes are ever waking found,
When dismal watch-men walk their mid-night round; 90
Or at their peaceful stands securely snore,
While robbers, at their elbows, force a door.

Yet. TOM, return; or quickly tell me where
I may, with open arms, approach my dear.
Tell me, ye brighter nymphs of Drury--say; 95
Saw you my perjur'd varlet go this way;
Imbrowned hunters of fam'd Wapping--tell,
Does he amidst your winding alleys dwell;
Ye maids, where'er he strays, his courtship shun:
Near--you'll believe--believing--be undone. 100
Cruelly thus of ev'ry joy bereft,
Lost in my quiet, and my bosom cleft;
Such are the Eng'ring sorrows of my mind,
E'en in Geneva no repose I find.
No more shall love-sick ditties swell my throat; 105
SMUT shall no more obtain a warbling note;
Against EXCISE I'll raise my voice no more,
She said--and dozing sunk upon the floor.
The maudlin matrons cry'd--Pray mark her fall!
The pow'r of gin from love defend us all. 110

VERSES addrest by a Gentleman of the Church
of ENGLAND to a ROMAN Catholick Lady.

From *Faulkner's Dublin* Journal, *July* the 7th.

I Yield! I yield, all conqu'ring maid!
   Your charms triumphantly prevail!
Such wond'rous beauty must persuade;
   Tho' fathers, popes, and councils fail.

Blest change! an heretic no more,
   I gaze convinc'd; and, with surprise,
I listen to your silent lore;
   A sudden convert of your eyes.

Like inspiration's heav'nly ray,
   Lo! truths divine your face can teach;
You look what Bellarmine show'd say;
   You smile beyond what doctors preach!

Against that innocence, and bloom,
   What fool of reason can dispute?
Ye serious triflers, foes of Rome!
   Can you that air, and shape refute?

From such ambassadors of heav'n
   All schismaticks wou'd learn their duty;
And soon, by mother-church forgiv'n,
   Become the proselytes of beauty!

To

To such fair agents in the cause,
 The proudest prince wou'd rev'rence pay;
Senates repeal oppressive laws,
 And all implicitely obey!

Cou'd Rome *such missionaries send,*
 Her glory to the skies won'd tow'r,
Her empire to the poles extend,
 And both the India's own her pow'r!

No wretch, who rashly meets your eyes,
 By words can their effulgence paint;
No cold protestor then denies,
 The worship of a female saint!

I hear a seraph, while you sing!
 Each fibre feels the thrilling lay:
My raptur'd soul is on the wing:
 With ecstacy I die away!

My fancy bright ideas warm;
 Hail, fairest of thy lovely kind!
With all the graces in thy form,
 And all the Virtues in thy mind!

I see perfection on her throne!
 My errors I'll no more pursue!
Infallibility I own!
——Infallibility——in you!——

WOMAN'S hard FATE. *By a Lady.*

HOW *wretched is a woman's fate,*
 No happy change her Fortune knows,
Subject to man in every state,
 How can she then be free from woes?

In youth a father's stern command,
 And jealous eyes controul her will;
A lordly brother watchful stands,
 To keep her closer captive still.

The tyrant husband next appears,
 With awful and contracted brow;
No more a lover's form he wears,
 Her slave's become her sov'reign now.

If from this fatal bondage free,
 And not by marriage chains confin'd;
But blest with single life can see,
 A parent fond, a brother kind.

Yet love usurps her tender breast,
 And paints a phoenix to her eyes,
Some darling youth disturbs her rest,
 And painful sighs in secret rise.

Oh, cruel pow'rs, since you've design'd,
 That man, vain man! should bear the sway,
To a slave's fetters add a slavish mind,
 That I may cheerfully your will obey.

The ANSWER. *By a Gentleman,*

HOW *happy is a woman's fate,*
 Free from care, and free from woe,
Secure of man in ev'ry state,
 Her guardian-god below!

In youth a father's tender love,
 And well-experienc'd eye,
Restrains her mind, too apt to rove,
 Enamour'd with a toy.

Suppose her with a brother, blest,
 A brother sure is kind;

But in the HUSBAND *stands confest,*
 The father, brother, friend.

'Tis man's, to labour, toil, and sweat,
 And all his care employ,
Honour, or wealth, or pow'r to get;
 'Tis woman's to enjoy.

But look we on those halcyon *days,*
 When woman reigns supreme;
While supple man his homage pays,
 Full proud of their esteem.

How duteous is poor Strephon's *love!*
 How anxious is his care!
Lest gentle Zephyrs *play too rough,*
 And discompose the fair.

Then say not, any pow'rs ordain,
 That man should bear the sway;
When reason bids, let woman reign,
 When reason bids, obey.

We should have been more thankful for the following Birth-Day Verses had they been sent in MAY, the Month they belong to.

To the Rt Hon. the Lady ELIZABETH BOYLE, *Daughter to the Rt Hon.* JOHN *Earl of* OR-RERY, *on her Birth-Day,* May 7. 1733.

MAY *each new year some new perfection give,*
And all the mother in the daughter live;
May'st thou her VIRTUES *to the world restore!*
And be what Henrietta *was before.*
And when revolving years mature thy charms,
When pride of conquest thy fair bosom warms,
May some great youth, for ev'ry grace renown'd
With taste and science blest, by VIRTUE *crown'd,*
By Virtue guarded from ambition's wiles,
Superior both to fortune's frowns and smiles,
Who wears the honours of a glorious name,
Yet to distinction bears a nobler claim;
Like a new star, in native lustre bright,
That boasts no radiance from reflected light.
Allow'd the rising genius of his age,
By every excellence thy heart engage;
Like him who bless'd thy mothers nuptial state;
But O! may heav'n give thine a longer date.

Imitation of a Greek Epigram; occasion'd by the Rt Hon. the E. of ORRERY's *Verses (see p. 319) to Mr* POPE *upon his Epitaph on Mr* GAY.

WHilst Phœbus *to the* NINE *repeats the lay*
 Design'd *to grace the monument of* GAY,
Much they admire the numbers of the god,
And much that equal praise which BOYLE *bestow'd.*
Just your applause he answers; from these lays,
By grief inspir'd, now springs superior praise.
Thus when slain Hyacinth *requir'd my woes,*
Flow'rs ever-blooming from my tears arose,
Yet thus admir'd, thus prais'd, I grieve whilst BOYLE
Transfers to POPE *the glory of my toil;*
Transfers in numbers with such sense and fire,
As He might own with pride, and I inspire.
Nor triumph (daring youth!) in this success,
Soon thy robb'd honours shall my wrongs redress;
Men shall assign to me a nobler gift,
*Thy * Verses to my other favourite* SWIFT.
* See p. 40.

Verses

VERSES written by Dr SWIFT.
See the Occasion p. 110.

A Paper book is sent by Boyle,
  Too neatly gilt for me to soil.
Delany sends a silver standish.
When I no more a pen can brandish.
Let both around my tomb be plac'd,
As trophies of a muse deceas'd;
And let the friendly lines they writ
In praise of long departed wit,
Be grav'd on either side in columns,
More to my praise than all my volumes.
To burst with envy, spite, and rage,
The Vandals of the present age.

The TRIUMVIRATE.

THree WILLS with great, but diff'rent ta-
    lents born,
The present British parliament adorn.
W—m with liveliest thoughts his audience charms,
Sh—n's strong reason the guilty GREAT alarms;
P—y with sharpest wit his satyr arms.
No M—r with all his pension'd band,
Can long this brave triumvirate withstand,
W— be wise, and seek some safe retreat;
Don't think that F—d and G—t, which made thee
    great,
Can stem the torrent of a nation's hate.

E CONTRA.

ONE Robin still three doughty WILLS defies,
    And mocks the venom of their weekly l—s.
His vigilance protects our rights and laws,
While fortitude defends the patriot's cause.
Spite of all calumny, in him we find,
An open gen'rous heart, and steady mind;
Solid his reas'nings are, and strong his sense,
Noted for calmness, as for eloquence.
Unmov'd, he pitying, looks down to see,
The vain efforts of the united three.
While Britain's safety is the statesman's care,
He runs no danger, and can know no fear:
Had the three power, equal to their hate,
W—le wou'd then be crush'd, but still be great.

From the WOMAN of TASTE. A Poem.

WOuld you a daughter should in taste excell,
    First teach her how to dance, and then to spell,
Let her be learn'd and virtuous by degrees,
And always use her feet before her knees;
Pay less her head to tutor than her heel,
The posture's more polite to step than kneel.
'Twill shew the girl a nymph of taste indeed,
To learn her gamut, if she quits her creed,
Preferring play to pray'r, and wit to grace,
For fear at court she else may lose a place;
The maids all mad to turn their sister out,
Who shames their order—and appears devout.

From the COUNTER-PART to the STATE-DUNCES.

COU'D I, oh D'anvers! with thy spirit write,
    Or virtue charm thee, and the truth delight;
Walpole might then accept the offer'd praise,
And live immortal in the deathless lays,

Caleb, by all thy wit and art's confess'd;
E'en vice looks beautiful, by thee when dress'd,
And we grow fond of what we should detest.
Thy matchless talents, and thy nervous sense,
But stronger prove the patriot's innocence;
For shou'd thy skill the conscious great assail,
No subterfuge, no art could such avail;
But here, almighty truth will still prevail.
D'anvers, thy name includes a pow'rful band,
Wit, learning, envy, there go hand in hand:
There lively B——ke genteel, severe,
Whose sense is sterling, and whose diction's clear,
Hopes, by his satire, to redeem his post;
And gain, by wit, what treachery has lost.
There B——l poyson spreads, but cloaks his rage,
And apes the Stoick thro' the labour'd page:
Tho' calm and smooth th' envenom'd periods glide,
His warmth discovers what his art won't hide:
This little champion for Britannia's cause,
Whose quill protects our liberties and laws,
Who once rul'd modes with spectatorial air,
And wrote instructions to improve the fair;
Now undertakes to criticise the great,
And dubs himself the censor of the state.
Won'dst thou be still caress'd, still entertain'd?
Mistaken bard, resume thy pleasing vein;
Thro' ev'ry maze, the fond Coquet pursue,
Lay all her foibles open to her view;
Make her desist from each affected grace,
And rest contented with her nat'ral face.
Let dress of beaux employ thy utmost care,
Check monstrous fashions, lash the solitaire;
Let growing follies rouse thee to the war.
Nature has trac'd thee out this path to fame,
And B——l's thus may match his kinsman's name.
But hold; shou'd I each character pursue,
And name each hero in this hostile crew,
Whose single force the guilty might alarm,
Whose views are dang'rous, while their reas'nings
    charm;
Tho' smooth my lines as Wh——d's verse shou'd flow,
With all his art I shou'd too tedious grow.
Let me, howe'er, advise this to useful youth,
Whom party-rage engages against truth.
Leave thou state-wrangles to experienc'd age,
Let Sh——n, P——y, W——m, mount the stage,
These have invention equal to their rage:
These have perplexing arts, grown old and sour
In a long tedious vain pursuit of pow'r.
But if thou art determin'd to write on,
And pleas'd to be harmoniously undone;
Art fonder of a poet's empty fame,
Than with Lycurgus, to enrol thy name;
Doff rather choose to be a pope than ‡ king,
Join truth to art; to both good-nature bring;
Hadst thou done this, thou hadst retriev'd the lawn;
And Walpole, as a faithful patriot, drawn.
Hadst trac'd his actions, and from them hadst shewn,
His zeal for Britain's sons, and for her throne;
Spoke him humane, disinterested, just,
True to his country, faithful to his trust:
Ready to hear, as ready to relieve,
Firm to our rights, and the prerogative:
Hadst sung a statesman, who has never swerv'd,
Refusing honours, offer'd, and deserv'd. —
Open, unbiass'd, eloquent, sincere,
His hands unsullied, and his conscience clear.

‡ Lord Chancellor.

Such Walpole is, and such thy song had been,
Had not thy wit been over-rul'd by spleen.
What pity, Wh——d, envy shou'd abuse,
So young, so moving, and so sweet a muse;
That she who warbles with enchanting grace,
Shou'd fright th'enraptur'd with a satyr's face!
P——y, in history well vers'd acts o'er,
The parts of rebel lords in days of Tate:
* Fitzwalter, P——y, lives again in thee,
But in a Walpole, we a † Pembroke see.
The Junto, who with rebel bravous ado,
To servile arts and base detraction fly;
If these all fail, to sooth invet'rate hate,
Like those of old, they'll over-turn the state:
But vain those hopes, while such the tim'ne surround
As W——d's numbers have been taught to wound.

*Chief of the Conspirators in the reign of K. John.
† See the History of K. John, and Henry III.

The PROJECTOR'S SOLILOQUY.

LOOK back, survey the Lists of Time,
     See with what Ease I've rul'd the Roast,
My Power sweeping all away,
     My Name one constant shining Toast.
O'er mighty Men without Controul
     I've bore a long and glorious Sway:
And must I now to Beggers yield
     With shame and vile Disgrace the Day?
Can after such a Strength of Force
     My great Ambition brook Disgrace?
No, No! I'll look a second Time
     The Sturdy Beggers in the Face.
And if they are not really such,
     I'll drain their full to empty Purses,
And then sit pleas'd amidst my Bags,
     Defying all their fruitless Curses.

To the AUTHORS of the BEE.
By the Rev. Mr *Lloyd* of *Glidem Sutton, Cheshire*.

WHen spring luxuriant thro' all nature reigns,
     Blooms in the blood, and revels in the veins;
The BEE excursive seeks the flow'ry field,
Or sucks the sweets which garden glories yield:
Returning home, into his hive he pours
The juice of aromatick herbs and flowers:
So you, the bloom and quintessence extract
From ev'ry weekly-wit, and well wrote tract:
With all the flowers of speech adorn each page,
And dart your sting at a degenerate age.

N. B. We make not the least Pretence to the Merit of
the last line, but have some grounds to hope our Readers
will find this Epigram in other Respects applicable to our
Magazine; as the Writer of it has acknowledg'd.

From the FRIENDLY-EPISTLE to the Author of the STATE-DUNCES. (See p. 317.)

SUppose I should an equal freedom take,
     And call thee fool or dunce for scolding's
     sake,—
Thy conscience sure wou'd justify my muse;
For thine hath been of naughty names profuse:
Or if resentful of thy Satire's Rage,
Suppose I should the grumbling crew engage,
Anti-State-Dunces! hardly rul'd by law,
And, in thy manner, men of Figure draw,—
'Twere easy work,—reprisals might be made,—
I have a hundred blockheads in my head,

Commons and Peers, deserving to be scourg'd,—
And so they shall, if more my muse be urg'd,
     But now, my Lad, I'll only from the clan,
Select and sketch thy idol of a Man,
Not as my fancy views him, but by truth,
A thing unknown to thy ill-tutor'd Youth!
I know thou'lt stare, and cry, It is not he!
No more like P——y, by the Lord, than me!
Yet such he is, tho' far beyond thy Ken,
God's justest likeness among Sons of Men!
Meek! generous! friendly! merciful! and just!
Patient! forgiving! faithful to his Trust!
Unsordid and unselfish! modest! kind!
Of purest manners! and of gentlest mind!
Ever observant of establish'd laws!
No devotee to popular Applause!
Unchangeable! undeviating! brave!
So good, he needs not cry to Christ to save!
     Such is the *Patriot* in such hands as mine:
But, oh! how alter'd, when he falls in thine!
Thy Epithets, however meant, are wrong,
And quite confound the purpose of thy Song;
Make nonsense sense, and truth on falshood raise,
Thy praise all satire, and thy satire praise!
Or vainly imitating *Master* POPE,
Dost thou like fame, and like protection, hope?
Ah! touch not nettles, lest they have a sting—
Remember ICARUS's feeble wing;
ULYSSES' bow which none but he could draw,
And, tho' thou laugh'st at manners, dread the law:
I fear, young man, not persons of the great,
Their dulness, nor their vices mov'd thy hate,
Thy prejudice and bigotry's the cause:
Thy soul's a slave, a rebel to the Laws.
Yes,—or to faction and her friends a friend;
Thy muse, audacious, wou'd not thus offend.
     But can such ill-plac'd stingless satire vex?
Whom does it hurt, whom injure, or perplex?
Thy mind's intention only can provoke,—
There's murder in't: thy muse is but a Joke.
If she can wound, 'tis only them, whose ways
Thou mak'st the wretched subject of thy praise:
Ill-fated P——y! damn'd alive in rhime!
Hast thou not acted some prodigious crime,
Some meritoriously flagitious fact,
To bring curst Panegyrick on thy back?
To wip the poet's mercy, who makes bold,
At liberty, and virtue's sons, to scold?
Save us, kind heaven, preserve thy chosen seed
From blessings, that wou'd blast us all indeed!
     Take my advice,—read WILLIAM LILY o'er,
And night and day on CATO's disticks pore,
Learn morals, wisdom, decency and sense;
Nor Poet, till thou'rt better taught, commence.
But if thou'rt destin'd to be damn'd indeed,
If providence thy misery hath decreed,
If 'tis thy fate to rhime, for god's sake try,
Whether thy muse can work an eulogy.
     Were it in praise of any thing that's evil,
St—n, the POPE, PRETENDER, or the DEVIL,
For praise of merit and illustrious men
Is far beyond thy naughty nature's ken.
'Tis virtue's work; and he who wou'd excel,
Shou'd know his genius and his subject well:
Else, blund'ring, he'd egregious faults commit,
Call STANHOPE stupid, W——Y a Wit,
ARGYLE a coward, DELAWARE too dumb,
NUMPS a fine speaker, and the SPEAKER dumb!

The Citizen's Proceffion, or, the Smugglers
Succefs, and the Patriot's Difappointment.

Tune, The Abbot of *Canterbury.*

YOU Puts that have Land, and you Cits that
　　have none,
You fair traders who pay, and you fmuglers who
　　fhun
All duties on wine and tobacco, draw near,
And you a fair ftate of the matter fhall hear;
　　　　　　　　　　　　(*Derry,* &c.

How of late a fam'd Bill, brought in parliament,
The *Frauds* on *Tobacco* and *Wine* to prevent,
Was dropp'd by the clamour of fmuglers and
　　knaves,
Who to Confcience and Honefty fcorn'd to be
　　Slaves.　　　　　　　*Derry,* &c.

An *Alderman-Factor* roar'd loud 'gainft the bill,
Which to his private pocket did bode fo much ill,
To be ftripp'd of 4,000 a Year who'd bear it?
Vile flav'ry to be tax'd thus to publick Spirit!

Then, what's to be done? the factors all cried:
« Join the poffe of vintners, *Bar—d* replied;
« Let's frighten the rabble with fome wholfome
　　lies.
« I have it — the word fhall be, *General Excife.*

A *General Excife!* fays one with a fneer,
On *Commodities twain?* the word will not bear.
« No matter for that, quoth *Bar—d* again,
« Full well I remember the reign of the queen;
« Then words without meaning had heavenly
　　　　　　　　　　　　(charms,
« When paffive obedience loud founded to arms,
« When the city for *Withers, Cafs, Newland* & *Hoar,*
« Cry'd, *no trade,* and elected thofe *untrading* four.
« To lead mobs by reafon's an idle pretence,
« Mobs ceafe to be mobs, when govern'd by fenfe;
« Then give out the word, try what it will do;
« And if that don't fucceed, cry out, *Liberty* too.

The project fucceeded, the rabble took fire,
And of rabbles for reafon in vain you enquire:
Their reafon is curfing; they rail at excife;
And each *Slave* to *Delufion* for *Liberty* cries.

Thus a found, before facred, was blafphemed by all
The mob of the city, the great mob and fmall;
As in the word *Liberty,* no good they faw
But *cheating* the *Publick,* and *baffling* the *Law.*

Their leaders, the factors, wrote circular letters;
And the wife common council-men, following
　　their betters,　　　　　　(calf,
By hand-bills warn'd all honeft knaves within
To fupport the dear cheat now ready to fall,

To make a brave ftand, all cloath'd in their beft,
For *Freedom of Fraud,* in the court of requeft;
But begg'd they would borrow fome gentlemen's
　　Coaches,　　　　　　　　　(es.
To grace their fine fhow in their *modeft* approach-

You'd have laugh'd to have feen the fpruce cits
　　run about,　　　　　　　　Rout;
Borrowing chariots and coaches t' attend at the
Of widows and maids they got many a Score,
And cramm'd themfelves in by two and by four.

The proceffion was aukward, but made a great
　　fhow;
For the Coaches like cuckolds were all on a row;
Their arms the moft uniform ever were borne,
For each for his creft wore a gallant *Stag's Horn*
　　　　　　　　　　　　(van?!
Would you know in this cavalcade who led the
It was my L—d M—y—r, a true *Perkin's* man:
Phenomenon Wilkins (pert coxcomb) was there,
And furly old *Harris* fnarl'd loud in the rear.

This rabble, as rabbles are brave 'gainft a few,
When they faw themfelves 40 to 1 good and true,
Infulted the members as by them they pafs,
If thofe offer'd to reafon, thefe bray'd like an afs.

With them our *Mock-Patriots* join'd the loud cry;
And others from *Pannick* were known to comply:
Some doubted their *Principals* at the next choice;
And fome thought the *Mob's* was the publick voice.
　　　　　　　　　　　　(trade,
Thus a bill to cure Frauds, and protect the fair
By the bellowing of fmuglers, its exit hath made:
The publick's ftill cheated, and each wanton cit
Sneers at the Landholder, to fee how he's bit.

Thefe fmuglers now fwear, let the laws but alone,
And in a fhort time all the lands are their own,
For they foon fhall get money to purchafe, and
　　then　　　　　　　　　　(Men.
They will take of the land-tax, and live like great

The landholders poor will foon wail the loft bill,
When they find themfelves damn'd to pay 1s. ftill,
And fee fmuglers enjoy more indulgence than
　　they,
Who in *Liberty's caufe bore the heat of the Day.*

Shall they be reftrain'd too from planting their field
With tobacco *, or whatever elfe it would yield,
For the fake of our trade, while fmuglers are free
From paying juft taxes, *is this liberty?*

Thefe *patriots* anfwer, *no matter for that.*
To bring all to confufion is what they'd be at:
They defpair of a fhare in the adminiftration,
Unlefs they fucceed in diftracting the nation.

Next they brought in petitions, and try'd all their
　　ftrengths,
The divifion difcover'd they'd gone too great
　　lengths:
Then they try at a *ballot;* a *ballot* but fhows
Whoever we have, we will have none of *Thofe.*

By thefe we may learn our *fham patriots* defigns,
They will encourage *frauds on tobacco and wines;*
Yet rail at *corruption,* and *penfions,* and *places,*
Which let them enjoy, and you'll gain their
　　good graces.

But thefe *patriots* find they're moft damnably bit,
Who made themfelves fure, if they gain but this
　　hit,
To win the whole game, and fo bring all about;
But *no noes are got in, tho' great noes are turn'd out.*
　　　　　　　　　　　　Derry, &c.

* Planting of Tobacco is prohibited in this Kingdom, by
an Act made 12. Car. II. for the Encouragement of our
Trade.

The Pig. *A* TALE.

SOME husbands, on a winter day,
  Were met to laugh their spleen away,
As wine flows in, and spirits rise,
They praise their consorts to the skies.
Obedient wives are seldom known,
Yet all could answer for their own,
Acknowledg'd each as sovereign lord,
Abroad, at home, in deed, and word;
In short as absolute their reign, as
Grand Seignior's over his sultanas.   10
For pride, or shame to be out done,
All join'd in the discourse, but one.
Who, vex'd so many lies to hear,
Thus stops their arrogant career.

'Tis mighty strange, sirs, what you say,
What! all so absolutely sway?
In *England*! where *Italians* wish
Have plac'd the women's paradise?
In *London*! where the sexes flower
Have of that *Eden* fix'd the bower?   20
Fie! men of sense to be so vain,
You're not in *Turkey*, nor in *Spain*,
True *Britons* all; I'll lay my life,
None here is master of his wife.

These words the general fury rouze,
And all the common cause espouse.
Till one with voice superior said,
(Whose lungs were sounder than his head)
I'll send my footman instant home,
To bid his mistress hither come;   30
And, if she flies not at my call,
To own my power before you all,
I'll grant I'm henpeck'd, if you please.
As *Sh——k*, or as *Socrates*.

Hold there——replies th'objector sly,
Prove first that women never lie;
Else, words are wind—to tell you true,
I credit neither them, nor you;
No, we'll be judg'd a surer way,
By what they do, not what they say.   40
I'll hold you severally that boast,
A supper at the loser's cost,
That if you'll but vouchsafe to try
A trick I'll tell you by and by,
Send strait for every wife quite round,
One mother's daughter is not found,
But what before her husband's face
Point blank his orders disobeys.

To this, they one and all consent,
The wager's laid, the summons went.   50
Mean while he this instruction gives,
Pray only gravely tell your wives,
Your will and pleasure is to invite
These friends to a boil'd pig to night.
The commoner the trick has been,
The greater chance have you to win,
The treat is mine, if they refuse;
But if they boil it, then I lose.

The first, to whom the message came,
Was a well born and haughty dame;   60

A saucy independent she,
With jointure, and with pin-mony,
Secur'd by marriage-deeds from wants,
Without a separate maintainance.
Her loftiness disdain'd to hear,
Half thro' her husband's messenger,
But cut him short with—how dare he
'Mong pot-companions mention me?
He knows his way (if sober,) home,
And if he wants me, let him come.—   70
  This answer, hastily return'd,
Pleas'd all, but him whom it concern'd.
For each one thought his wife on tryal,
Would brighter shine by this denyal.
  The second, was a lady gay,
Who lov'd to visit dress and play,
To spark it in the box or ring,
And dance on birth-nights for the king.
Whose head was busy wont to be
With something else, than cookery.   80
She hearing of her husband's name,
Tho' much a gentlewoman, came;
When half inform'd of his request,
A dish, as he desir'd it, drest,——
Quoth madam, with a serious face,
(Without enquiring what it was)
You can't sure for an answer look,
Sir, do you take me for your cook?
But I must haste a friend to see,
Who stays my coming for her tea.   90
So said, that minute out she flew.
What could the slighted husband do?
His wager lost, must needs appear,
For none obey that will not hear.
  The next, for housewifry renown'd,
A woman notable was own'd,
Who hated idleness and airs,
And minded family affairs;
Expert in every thing was she,
At needle-work, or surgery: 100
Fam'd for her liquors far and near,
From richest cordials to small beer:
To serve a feast she understood,
In *English*, or in foreign mode;
What e'er the wanton taste could choose,
In kickshaws, sauces, or ragoos:
She spar'd for neither cost nor pain,
Her welcome guest to entertain.
Her husband fair accosts her thus:
To night these friends will sup with us. 110
She answer'd with a smile, my dear,
Your friends are always welcome here.
—But we desire a pig, and pray,
You'll boil it;—boil it! did you say?
I hope you'll give me leave to know
My business better, sir, than so:
Why ne'er in any book was yet
Found such a whimsical receit:
My dressing none need be afraid of,
But such a dish was never heard of.   120

I'll roast it nice, but shall not boil it,
Let those who know no better, spoil it.
—Her husband cry'd, for all my boast,
I own, the wager's fairly lost.
And other wives, besides my love,
Or I'm mistaken much, may prove
As chargeable as this to me,
To show their pride in housewifry.

Now the poor wretch that next him sat,   130
Felt his own heart go pit a pat:
For well he knew his spouses way,
Her spirit brook'd not to obey,
And never yet was in the wrong—.
He told her with a trembling tongue,
Where, and on what, his friends would feast,
And how the dainty should be drest.
—To night, quoth (in a passion) she?
No sir, to night it cannot be;
And was it a boil'd pig you said?
You and your friends sure are not mad.   140
The kitchen is the proper sphere,
Where none but females should appear,
And cooks their orders, by your leave,
Always from mistresses receive.
Boil it! — was ever such an ass?
I pray, what would you have for sauce?
If any servant in my pay
Dare dress a pig that silly way,
In spite of any whim of yours,
I'll turn her quickly out of doors.   150
For such a thing, (nay never frown)
Where I am mistress, shall be done.
Each woman wise her husband rules;
Passive obedience is for fools.

This case was quickly judg'd; behold!
A fair one of a softer mold;
Good humour sparkled in her eye,
And unaffected pleasantry;
So mild and sweet she enter'd in,
Her spouse thought certainly to win: 160
(Pity, such golden hopes should fail,)
Soon as she heard th' appointed tale.
My dear, I know not, I protest,
Whether in earnest, or in jest,
So strange a supper you demand,
Howe'er, I'll not disputing stand,
But do it freely as you bid it,
Prove but that ever woman did it.
—This cause, by general consent,
Was lost for want of precedent.   170
Thus each deny'd a several way;
But all agreed to disobey.

One only dame did yet remain,
Who downright honest was, and plain,
If now and then her voice she tries,
'Tis not for rule, but exercise.
Unus'd her Lord's commands to slight,
Yet sometimes pleading for the right.
She made her little wisdom go,
Farther than wiser women do.   180

Her husband tells her, looking grave,
A roasting pig I boil'd would have;
And to prevent all pro and con,
I must insist to have it done.
Says she, my dearest, should your wife,
Get a nick name to last for life?
If you resolve to spoil it, do;
But then I hope you'll eat it too.
For, tho' 'tis boil'd to hinder squabble,
I shall not, will not sit at table.   190
She spoke, and her good man alone,
Found he had neither lost nor won.
So fairly parted stakes: the rest
Fell on the wag that caus'd the jest,
" Would your wife boil it? let us see."
Hold there, you did not lay with me.
You'll find, in spite of all you've boasted,
Your pigs are fatted to be roasted.
The wager's lost, no more contend;
But take this councel from a friend.   200
Boast not your empire, if you prize it;
For happiest he, who never tries it.
Wives unprovoked best obey,
And that you'll find the safest way.
But if your dear ones take the field,
Resolve at first to win or yield;
For heaven no medium ever gave,
Between a sovereign and a slave.

INSCRIPTION *on a* MONUMENT *erected in
the East Cloyster,* WESTMINSTER ABBEY.

Reader,
If thou art a Briton,
Behold this tomb with reverence and regret,
Here lye the remains of
DANIEL PULTENEY:
The kindest relation, the truest friend,
The warmest patriot, the worthiest man.
He exercised virtues in this age,
Sufficient to have distinguished him in the best.
Sagacious by nature,
Industrious by habit,
Inquisitive with art,
He gained a complete knowledge of the interest of Britain,
Foreign and domestick;
In most, the backward fruit of tedious experience;
In him, the early acquisition of undisputed youth.
He served the crown several years:
Abroad, in the auspicious reign of queen ANNE;
At home, in the reign of that excellent prince K. George I.
He served his Country always:
At court Independent;
In the senate unbiassed.
At every age, and in every station,
This was the bent of his generous soul;
This the business of his laborious life.
Publick men and publick things
He judged by one constant standard,
The true interest of Britain.
He made no other distinction of party;
He abhorred all other.
Gentle, humane, disinterested, beneficent.
He created no enemies on his own account:
Firm, determined, inflexible,
He feared none he could create in the cause of Britain.
Reader,
In this misfortune of thy country, lament thy own:
For know,
The loss of so much private virtue
Is a publick calamity.

N. B. Several other Poetical Pieces are come to hand,
and shall be inserted the first Opportunity.

THE
Monthly Intelligencer.
JULY, 1733.

Tuesday, 3.

AT a Court of Aldermen and Common Council, Michael Hillersden, Esq; elected on *Midsummer* Day one of the Sheriffs of this City, paid a Fine of 620 l. to be excused from serving the said Office.

'Tis confidently reported, that a Squadron of 20 Men of War will shortly be sent to the *Baltick* under the Command of Admiral *Stewart*.

Wednesday, 4.

A Waggon laden with Silver, which had been taken from a *Spanish* Privateer by the *Garland* Man of War some Months since, arrived at *London* under a Guard of Sailors.

Count *Kinski*, the Imperial Envoy, demanded of our Court the Succours stipulated by the Treaty of *Seville*, to act in Conjunction with the Emperor's Forces in Case of a Rupture, in relation to the Affairs of *Poland.*

Thursday, 5.

A Proclamation was issued for summoning the Peers of *Scotland* to meet at *Holyrood House* at *Edinburgh*, to elect a Peer to sit in the House of Lords in the Room of the E. of *Sutherland*, decd.

Friday, 6.

At the Assizes for *Berks, John Whitaker* was condemn'd for a Robbery on the Highway, *Joseph Farmer* for Felony.

Began the Publick Act at *Oxford*. About one o'Clock the Revd Dr *Holmes*, President of St *John's College*, Vice-Chancellor, with other Members of the University in their proper Habits, and a vast Concourse of Persons of Distinction, repair'd to the Theatre, to hear the Speeches and Disputations. On *Sunday*, Mr *Handel's Te Deum* and Anthems were perform'd in St *Mary's Church*. On *Monday*, the Vice-Chancellor, accompany'd by the Heads of the Houses, the Doctors in their Boots and Robes, and the other Members of the University properly habited, repair'd again to the Theatre, where was a vast Concourse of Nobility, and other Persons of Distinction of both Sexes. The Ceremony was then perform'd of creating 84 Masters of Arts, one of whom was the Ld *James Beauclerck*. After which the Gentlemen who were Inceptors in the Degree of Doctor in several Faculties, held Disputations for some Time, and at length were created in their Turn, *viz.* Doctors of Divinity, Dr *Isham*, of *Lincoln College*; Dr *Ballard*, of *C. C. College*; Dr *Robinson*, and Dr *White*, of *Merton Coll.* Dr *Bliss*, of *Worcester Coll.* Dr *Attwell*, of *Exeter Coll.* Dr *Cockman*, Head of University Coll.— Not in Holy Orders; Dr *Fanshaw*, of *C. C.* and Dr *Green*, of *Queen's Coll.*— Doctors of Physick, Dr *Aldersey*, *Manaton, Pitt* and *Peters*, of *C. Ch.* Dr *Adee*, and Dr *Healy*, of *C. C. Coll.*—Doctors of Law, Dr *Secker*, of *Exeter Coll.* and Dr *Pocock*, of *C. C. Coll.* The Vice-Chancellor concluded the Act with an elegant Oration in Praise of Learning, the Honours of it, and the Methods used in that University for obtaining them, On *Tuesday* Mr *Handel's* new Oratorio, call'd *Athalia*, was perform'd with vast Applause, before an Audience of 3700 Persons. The same Morning the Gentlemen who receiv'd their Degrees made their Offerings at St *Mary's Church* as usual, and afterwards heard a Latin Sermon. *Wednesday* was held a Convocation, in which Father *Courayer*, who fled from *France* about 7 Years ago, on Account of a Book he wrote in Defence of the Validity of the *English* Ordination, returned Thanks to the University for the Honour they did him two Years since, in presenting him with his Degrees: He was present in his Robes during all the Ceremonies in the Theatre. A *Terræ Filius* had been appointed, and appear'd in his Character, but was not suffer'd to make his Speech. [*See a List of the* Performances *p.* 384.]

Saturday 7.

At *Wincheſter*, five Men receiv'd Sentence of Death, *viz.* Two for robbing the *Exeter* Coach; one for Forgery; one for Horſe ſtealing; and one for robbing his Fellow Servant.

Thurſday 12.

Arrived in the River the *Reſolution*, with 3 large Whales, the Fins are computed to be about 3 Tons. She was one of the *S. Sea Greenland* Ships. Her Succeſs is aſcribed to an Inſtrument for ſhooting the Harpoons at the Whales, by which 2 of the 3 were caught. By an Act paſſed the laſt Seſſions of Parliament for encouraging the Whale Fiſhery, the owners are entitled to 300*l*, being 20*s*. *per Ton* on the Ships Burden; upon the whole 'tis apprehended they will clear 1000*l*. by the Voyage. But the Succeſs of a *Dutch* Ship arrived this Month in the *Texel*, call'd the *Beemſter*, Cap. *John Shot*, is very extraordinary; ſhe catch'd no leſs than 15 Whales; part of whoſe Fins and Blubber ſhe was oblig'd to put on board other Ships.

Saturday, 14.

The Aſſizes ended at *Chelmsford* for the County of *Eſſex*, when *Richard Caſs* was capitally convicted of two Robberies on the Highway, and likewiſe for Horſeſtealing. He was the Perſon principally concern'd with *Davis* in his Robberies, who attempted to make his Eſcape out of the Cart at *Tyburn*. (See p. 267.)

Monday, 23.

The Parliament, which ſtood prorogued to *July* 26, was again prorogued to *Oct.* 9. A Proclamation was at the ſame Time iſſued, offering a Reward of 50*l*. for every Deer-ſtealer that ſhall be convicted of deſtroying the Deer in any of his Majeſty's Chaſes and Foreſts.

At *Shrewsbury* Aſſizes was try'd the Validity of the Marriage of *Nicholas Williams*, late of *Carmarthen*, Eſq; deceaſed, with Mrs *Mary Jones*; Spinſter; after a Trial of 12 Hours a Verdict was given in Favour of Mrs *Jones*, and for the Marriage.

Friday, 27.

At the Aſſizes at *Croyden*, *William Garbe*, a Weaver, receiv'd Sentence of Death, for Robbing a Woman in *Bird-cage Alley, Southwark*; alſo *Robert Wilſon*, a Boy, for ſetting Fire to his Maſter's Dwelling houſe and PaperMills at *Cobham*, but was repriev'd for Tranſportation.

A Computation was made, that within 12 Months paſt 800,000 Quarters of Corn had been exported from *Great Britain* to *Portugal, Spain, Eaſt France;* and *Italy*, at above a Million Sterling the Purchaſe, to the great Advantage of this Kingdom, in general, and the landed Intereſt in particular.

Tueſday 31.

The Grand Juries *&c.* aſſembled this Month in ſeveral Counties, took into Conſideration the Nomination of Gentlemen to repreſent them in the Parliament to be Choſen next Year; in which they generally had regard to thoſe that Voted againſt the Tobacco Scheme; And where any were nominated of different Sentiments, the ſtrongeſt Oppoſition imaginable was ſet on foot; and Meaſures taken to ſhew their Strength and Numbers on on each Side.

On Sir *Robert Walpole's* Arrival at Great *Yarmouth* in *Norfolk*, he was received by the Corporation in their Formalities, under the diſcharge of the Cannon, and Conducted to the Guild-Hall, where the Mayor deliver'd him a Parent conſtituting him High Steward of the Corporation for Life, in a Silver Box; on which Sir *Robert* made a very handſome Speech: Afterwards a moſt ſumptuous Entertainment was provided for him by the Corporation, and all poſſible Marks of Reſpect ſhewn him.—On his proceeding to *Norwich*, he was met about three Miles off that City, by the Biſhop, Dean, Clergy, near 1000 Citizens on Horſeback, and a great Train of Coaches, amidſt the Joyful Acclamations of a very numerous Body of People, and was preſented with his Freedom in a GoldBox, on which Occaſion he made a very elegant Speech, and promiſed to promote their Trade in General, and particularly the Woollen Manufacture. *Horace Walpole* and *Walter Bacon* Eſqs. were nominated Candidates for that City againſt next Election; *Robert Coke* and *William Morden* Eſqrs for the County, by a vaſt Appearance of Gentlemen and Free-holders; however Sir *Ed. Ward* and Mr. *Brantbwayt* were put up in Oppoſition, for the City, Sir *Edmund Bacon* of *Garboldiſham* and Mr *Woodhouſe* for the County, who had all the Signs of a ſtrong Intereſt.

A great Stir was made in *Cheſhire* upon the Arrival of the E. of *Cholmondeley* Governour of *Cheſter* Caſtle, and Sir *R. Groſvenor*, one of the Repreſentatives of that City; the former was met by about 1000 Gentlemen and Citizens on Horſeback and in Coaches, and conducted thro' the the City with great Acclamations, to the Caſtle. The Cry was, *Confuſion to the Male Contents, and Proſperity to the Na-*

vigation of the River Dee: But Sir *Robert* was attended by near 4000 Gentlemen and Freemen on Horseback, about 40 Coaches, 19 with 6 Horses, who were two hours passing thro' the City; Many of the Freemen had gilded Tobaccco Leaves in their Hats. The Cry was, *No Excise*, and the Music play'd to the Tune of *A begging we will go*. The Gentlemen and Free-holders present unanimously agreed to Vote at next Election for *Charles Cholmondeley* and *John Crewe* Jun. Esqrs, a-gainst Sir *Robert Salisbury Cotton*, Bart. who was for the Tobacco Bill. On the same Account the E. of *Tilney*, was opposed at the Assizes for *Essex* by Lord *Walden*, join'd by Sir *Robert Abdy*, for whom the Gentlemen and Freeholders almost una-nimously declar'd. And the like Interest is making in other Places against the next Election.

Samuel Sandys, Esq; was met the 25th on his Return to *Worcester* by several hun-dred Inhabitants wearing Woollen and Tobacco Caps, who testified their Grati-tude for his Zealous opposition to the To-bacco Bill, *&c.* wishing Prosperity to all who stood in Defence of Trade and Liberty.

Dennis Bond Esq; who had been con-cerned in the Charitable Corporation Af fairs (See p. 246 D) on his Return to *Corf Castle*, was received with such Marks of In-dignation that he was obliged to leave the Town with all his Attendants, for fear of worse Treatment.

Sir *Henry Gough* Bart. Member for *Tot-ness* in *Devonshire*, on his return to his Country Seat near *Birmingham*, was met in that Neighbourhood, by above 500 Gentlemen &c. on Horse-back, who ex-press'd their grateful Acknowledgments for his Services in Parliament, by his firm Attachment to the Liberties of his Coun-try, and the Interest and Prosperity of the *fair Trader*.

At the Assizes for the County of *Derby* the following Address of Thanks of the High Sheriff and Grand Jury was present-ed to Sir *Nathanael Curzon*, Bart. God-frey *Clarke*, Esq; the Ld *James Cavendish* and *Charles Stanhope*, Esq; Representatives for the County and Town of *Derby*.

Gentlemen,
We the High Sheriff and Grand Jury for the County of Derby, *beg Leave to take this Opportunity of returning you our most sincere and hearty Thanks for your unwearied and steady Application, in be-half of ourselves and the rest of our Fellow*

Subjects, when our Liberties and Proper-ties were of late so remarkably attack'd.

Gentlemen,
It shall be our Study upon all Occasions to acknowledge the Obligations, we lie under to you, and to assure you with what Zeal and Esteem, we desire to be account-ed, Honoured Gentlemen, your most oblig-ed Humble Servants.

Sir *John Gonson*, Sir *Robert Baylis*, Sir *Francis Child*, Sir *William Billers*, Knts. *William Peer Williams*, *William Mel-mouth*, *Edward Baber*, *Micajah Perry*, *John Milner*, *Marmaduke Allington*, *Tho-mas Lane* and *John Howe*, *Esqrs.* appoin-ted Commissioners for making a Survey of all the Officers, Clerks and Ministers of the High Court of Chancery, and to enquire what Fees, Rewards and Wages they, their Substitutes and Under-Clerks, may and ought to take, and what have been unjustly encroach'd on the Subject; and what Oppressions, Extortions, and Exacti-ons any of them have committed,

The Weather was so excessive hot most part of this Month, that it was scarcely tolerable to Man or Beast. Several Hor-ses dy'd on the Roads, and Numbers of People being tempted to go into Rivers and Ponds to cool themselves, above 20 were drown'd within the Bills of Morta-lity. Much Mischief was also done by Lightning. Some Gentlemen thought the Season too hot to take a Journey to visit their Corporations.

BIRTHS.

THE Lady of the Count *de Montejo*, the *Spanish* Ambassador, deliver'd of a Daughter at *Powis* House, *Ormond-street.*

Ld Visc. *Middleton*'s Lady, of a Son & Heir.

Mr *Horace Walpole*'s Lady, of a Daughter.

Ld *James Cavendish*'s Lady, of a Son.

The Wife of *Thomas Pelham*, Esq; Repre-sentative for *Lewes*, deliver'd of a Son.

The Wife of *Charles Montagu*, Esq; Nephew to the Earl of *Halifax*, of a Son.

DEATHS.

July 1. MR *Charles Weftgarth*, Clerk of the *Weftern Road*, in the Gen. *Poft-Office*; a Gentleman endow'd with many valuable Accomplifhments.

3. The Revd Dr *Burton*, Canon of Chrift Church College, *Oxford*.

Councellor *Horfeman*, an eminent Conveyancer.

4. Capt. *James Williamfon*, an Officer on Half-pay.

Benjamin Beaumont, Efq;

Sir *John Stonhoufe*, not dead, as mentioned from the Papers at the End of laft Month, when we had not time to enquire out the Truth.

FOREIGNERS. The Marquis de *Grimaldo*, at *Madrid*, formerly Prime Minifter of *Spain*, aged 73.

The D. of *Veraguas*, Brother-in-Law to the D. of *Liria*, eldeft Son to the D. of *Berwick*, aged 56.

The Baron *de Fief*, High Chamberlain to the K. of *Sweden*.

Count *Maximilian*, of *Martiniz*, at *Vienna*, Privy Counfellor to the Emperor, Chamberlain of the Golden Key, and Knight of the Golden Fleece, aged 70.

Count *Ottocar*, of *Staremburgh*, ibid.

6. *John Rayner*, Efq; at *Mortlake*.

Tho. Miffing, Efq; at *Stubbington* near *Gofport*, an eminent Merchant, and Contractor for the Victualling of *Gibraltar*.

Mr *John Letton*, Wine Merchant, in *Leicefter Fields*.

The Revd Mr *Weekfy*, who had been 53 Years Minifter of *Sherfton, Wilts*.

The Relict of Counfellor *Vernon*, who died about 18 Years ago.

8. Capt. *Francis Wife*, formerly Captain in a Regiment of Dragoons.

10. Mr *Thompfon*, a Brewer at *Millbank, Weftminfter*.

11. *John Farlow*, an *Italian* Merchant.

Samuel Burton, Efq; Alderman, and Reprefentative for *Dublin*.

John Page, Efq; Alderman of *Dublin*.

13. Mr *Holford*, of *Botolph Lane*, Orange Merchant.

——*Partridge*, Efq; at *Thetford, Norfolk*.

Mrs *Mary Sacheverel*, a Maiden Lady of a large Fortune, in *Red-lyon Street, Holb*.

14. Mr *Moate*, one of the Stampers of the Stamp Office.

Mr *Delander*, a noted Watchmaker, near *Temple-Bar*.

Mr *Benj. Birch*, an eminent Surveyor.

Wm Gardiner, Efq; formerly a *Virginia* Merchant.

Mrs *Boynton*, a Maiden Lady of good Fortune.

Mr *Jofeph Hare*, a noted Mufick-feller, in *Cornhill*.

William Chainey, Efq; In the Reign of Q. *Anne*, he was Gauger General of the Excife, and difcover'd great Frauds committed by the Brewers and Purfers of the Navy, for which the Houfe of Commons in that Reign voted him a Reward of 500 l. In the Reign of K. *George* I. he was made Gauger General of the Cuftoms. At his Death and fome Years before, he ferved Mr Ald. *Parfons*, for which he had upwards of 300 l. *per Annum*.

17. Capt. *Campion*, formerly Commander of the *Dreadnought* Man of War.

The Revd Mr *Goftling*, near 60 Years Minor Canon of *Canterbury*, Vicar of *Littlebourn*, Chaplain to his Majefty, Sub-Dean of St *Paul*'s, and a Prebendary of *Lincoln*.

Mr *Graves*, the City Huntfman.

Richard Kingborough, Efq; one of his Majefty's Juftices of the Peace for *Middlefex*.

18. Mr *Adanfon*, Table Decker to the Ladies of the Bedchamber.

20. Lady *Frankland*, aged near 80.

Capt. *J. Barton*, at *Bromley, Middlefex*.

21. *Alexander Montgomery*, Efq; who behav'd gallantly as an Officer in the Service of K. *Charles*, and K. *James*, II. But having entertained fome Scruples, refign'd his Poft, and liv'd retir'd.

22. *Kempthorne*, Efq;

Mr *Thompfon*, an eminent Packer in *Coleman Street*.

Williams, Efq; in *Pickadilly*.

Thomas Jones, Efq; Major to Lord *Tyrawley*'s Reg. of Foot.

23. Cap. *Bower*, a Sea Officer; in St *Mary Axe*.

Mr *Gregory*, formerly a Linnen Draper in *London*.

Rob. Onflow, Efq; related to the Speaker; at *Malden, Effex*.

24. The Revd Mr *Jenkins*, formerly Mafter of *Gray's Hofpital, Kent*.

Mr *Woodftock*, Engine-keeper, and Bricklayer of the Palace of St *James's*.

Mr *Baker*, one of the Surgeons of St *Thomas's* Hofpital.

The Revd Mr *Williams*, of *Magdalen* College, *Oxford*.

John Fownes, Efq; of *Kittery Court, Devonfhire*.

The Revd Dr *Edward Morfe*, Rector of *Gatton, Surry*, and of *Chalfont St Peter, Bucks*.

The Wife of *Legh Mafter* Efq; Member of Parliament for *Newton, Lancafhire*.

The

The Revd Mr *Sadler*, Rector of *Frath*, *Northumberland.*

Capt. *Glanville*, an old Land-Officer, at *Sevenoak, Kent.*

26. Mr *Dawson*, a wealthy Sugar-Baker in *Basinghall Street.*

The Wife of *John Robinson*, Esq; in the Commission of the Peace for *Westminster.*

Mr *Bell*, Master Attendant of his Majesty's Yard at *Deptford.*

28. *John Cheeke*, Esq; above 40 Years Marshal of the High Court of Admiralty.

31. *Thomas Woodford*, Esq; who arrived last Year from the *East Indies.*

PROMOTIONS.

Wm Heathcote, of *Hursley*, near *Southampton*, Esq; created a Baronet.

Sir *Edward Crofton*, Sir *Henry King*, and Sir *Thomas Prendergaft*, made Privy Counsellors of *Ireland.*

George Proctor, Esq; made Steward of the Castle of *Windsor*, and of the Courts of Record there; also Clerk to the Constable and Keeper of the Seals of the said Courts.

Robert How, Esq; and *James Colebrooke*, jun. Esq; made Chirographer of the Court of Common Pleas.

Walter Campbell, Esq; made Receiver General and Cashire of the Customs in *Scotland*, in the Room of *Munro Graham*, Esq;

James St Clair, Esq; — Col. of the late Ld *Cathcart's* Reg. of Foot.

Mr *Samuel Heathcote*, — Yeoman of his Majesty's Bread Pantry.

E. of *Godolphin*, — Gov. of *Scilly*, and *George Bennett*, Esq; Lieut. Gov.

Hon. *John Fane*, Esq; created Baron of *Catherlogh* in *Ireland*, and made Captain and Colonel of the first Troop of Life Guards; in whose Room

Sir *Robert Rich*, appointed to the Command of the first Troop of Horse Grenadier Guards.

George Liddel, of *Hammer*, Esq; — Register of Seisines for *Orkney* and *Zetland.*

Edward Turner, of *Ambroseden*, *Oxfordshire*, Esq; created a Baronet.

E. of *Pembroke*, appointed Ld Lieut. &c. of *Flintshire.*

Mr *Richard Owen*, — Ensign in Sir *Charles Hotham's* Reg. And

Mr *Thomas Rodd*, Lieut. in the Royal Reg. of Welch Fuzileers.

Daniel Lambert, Esq; elected Sheriff of *London* and *Middlesex*, in the Room of *Michael Hillersden*, Esq; (See p. 377.)

Mr *Jabez Harris*, who was Clerk of the *North Road*, in the General Post Office, appointed by the *Post-master General* Clerk of the *West Road*, in the Room of Mr *Westgarth* deceased, to take Place at *Michaelmas* next.

Mr *Richard Dickerson*, Bye Night Clerk appointed to succeed Mr *Harris.*

Mr *John Sawtell*, Eldest Assistant appointed Bye Night Clerk.

David Munro, Esq; made Captain of Gen. *Tatton*'s own Company; and *Christopher Mitchel*, Esq; — Lieutenant in the same Regiment.

Mr *Edward King*—City Huntsman.

Mr *John Woodstock*—Bricklayer, &c. to the Palace of St *James's*, &c. in the room of his Brother deceas'd.

Capt. *Barclay*, an Officer on Half-pay, made Major to Ld *Tyrawley's* Regiment

Michael Hillersden, and *Radcliff Smith*, Esqs. chosen Governors of St *Bartholomew's* Hospital.

Mr *Eager*, appointed Master Attendant of the King's Yard at *Chatham.*

Ecclesiastical Preferments *conferr'd on the following Reverend Gentlemen.*

MR *King*, of *Christ Ch. Coll. Oxon*, collated to the Rectory of St *Michael's, Crooked Lane.*

Mr *Price*, presented to the Rectory of *Langevelach, Glamorganshire.*

Mr *John Marsh*, — to the Rectory of *West Cliff*, near *Dover.*

Mr *Strickland Gough*, — to the Rectory of *Nesse Prango, Salop.*

Mr *Smith Muchall*, — to the Rectory of *Routon, Staffordshire.*

Mr *Wm Borlace*, — to the Rectory of *Sexby, Lincolnshire.*

Mr *Gilbert Jackson*, of *C. C. College, Oxon*, — to the Rectory of *Botley, Southamp.*

Mr *Ford*, — to the Rectory of *Wookey, Somersetshire.*

Mr *John Howell*, — to the Rectory of *Mervall, Cornwall.*

Francis Clerke, L. L. D. — to the Rectory of *North Bewsleete, Essex.*

Mr *Sneyd*, of *Staffordsh.* — to the Rectory of *Heningham, Essex.*

Mr *Arthur Bransby*, — to the Rectory of *Great Coates, Lincolnshire.*

Henry Rand, A. M. — to the Rectory of *Berstod, Kent.*

Wm Speed, M. A. — to the Rectory of *Thornbury.*

Mr *John Bury*, — to the Vicarage of *Stebbing, Herefordshire.*

Mr *Wm Haward*, — to the Rectory of *Roding Aythorpe, Essex.*

Mr *Street* — to the Living of *Islington.*
Rich.

Rich. Rock, M.A. presented to the Vicarage of *Stroud* in *Gloucestershire*.

Mr *Lloyd*, Usher of *Westminster* School, — to the Rect. of *Burtborpe Gloucestersh.*

Mr *Christopher Brockell*, — to the Rectory of *Briggsby*, *Lincolnshire.*

Mr *Gray*, — to the Rectory of *Althorne*, *Essex.*

Mr *Thomas Williams*, — to the Rectory of *Lawwoman*, &c. *Cardiganshire.*

Mr. *Naylor*, presented to the Vicaridge of *Othorn*, *Torkshire.*

Mr. *William Eberson*, to the Vicarage of *Cole Kerby*, *Torkshire.*

Mr *B. Smith*, presented to the Vicarage of *Lenton*, *Torkshire.*

Mr *Plummer*, Rector of *Bilton*, *Warwickshire*, to the Rectory of *Culworth*, *Northamptonshire.*

Dr *Barton*, succeeds Dr *Burton*, as Canon Residentiary of C. C. C. *Oxford.*

Dispensations have pass'd the Seals to enable

Mr *Gregory*, to hold the Rectory of *Carlton*, *Nottinghamshire*, with that of *Widmorepole* in the same County.

Mr *Peter Bevis*, Batchelor of Civil Law, to hold the Rectory of *Silferton*, with that of *Warkleigh*, both in *Devonshire.*

Mr *Rich. Chapman*, M.A. to hold the Rectory of *Friendsbury*, *Kent*, with the Rectory of *Cobham*, in the same County.

Mr *Thomas Hurdis* to hold the Vicarage of *Laughton*, *Suffex*, with the Rectory of *Sutton cum Seaford.*

Mr *Penifton Booth*, made Chancellor of St *Paul's* Cathedral, vacant by the Resignation of Mr *Jones.*

Mr *Whiddon*, chosen Pastor of the Dissenting Congregation at *Kingfton*, in the Room of the Revd Mr *Mayo*, decd.

MARRIAGES.

THE Ld Visc. *Weymouth*, married to the second Daughter of the Lord *Carteret.*

The Revd Mr *Sturges*, one of the Prebendaries of *Winchefter*, — to the Daughter of the late Revd Mr *Louth*, one of the Prebendaries of that Cathedral.

Capt. *Maurice*, formerly Commander of a *Weft India* Ship, — to a Daughter of Mr *John Worth*, of *Worth*, *Devonshire*, with 5000 *l*. Fortune.

Mr *John Gifford*, of *Devonshire Square*, Merchant, — to Miss *Brooks*, with a Fortune of 15,000 *l*.

Simon Ld *Frafer*, of *Lovat*, a *Scots* Nobleman, — to Miss *Primrose Campbell*, Coufin German to the D. of *Argyle.*

Mr *Adam Bummieu*, a noted Diamond Cutter near *Stocks-Market*, — to Mifs *Duvor*, a *French* Lady.

Mr *Turner*, an eminent Linnen Draper in *Fleet Street*, — to Mrs *Pinckney*, of *Southampton Street.*

John Lawton, Efq; Clerk of the Securities of the *Excife* Office, — to Mrs *Cooper*, Widow, with 30,000 *l*. Fortune.

Wm Smith, of *Clement's Inn*, Efq; — to Mifs *Gibfon*, of *Westminster.*

The Ld *Trynham*, — to Mifs *Powell*, Sifter to the Lady of Sir Fr. *Curzon*, Bart.

John Bullock, jun. Efq; of *Norfolk Street*, in the *Strand*, a Student at *Cambridge*, — to Mifs *Bullock*, a young Lady of 20,000*l.*

Mr *Bernard*, a noted Hop-Merchant in *Thames Street*, — to the eldeft Daughter of Mr *Allen*, a Wholefale Hofier in *Thames Street*, with a Fortune of 10,000*l.*

Mr *Stephen Duck*, the famous Threfher Poet — to Mrs *Sarah Big*, Houfe-keeper to her Majefty at *Kew-green*, who gave her a Purfe of Guineas and a fine Gown.

The Hon. Mr *Bofcawen*, Son to Lord Vifc. *Falmouth*, — to a Daughter of Sir *Philip Meadows.*

Steph. Winthorp, Efq; of *Walbrook*, Merchant, — to a Daughter of Alderman *Davy* of *Exeter*, a Fortune of 10,000 *l.*

Mr *Bruce*, a Diffenting Minifter — to Mifs *Molly Street* of *Pinner.*

Mr *George Stedman*, a Quaker, Woolftapler in *Southwark*, — to Mifs *Houfe*, of the fame Perfuafion.

BANKRUPTS.

E D. *Oldfield*, of Newcaflle under Line, Stafford, Vid. William *Lawrence*, of Hertford, Taylor.
William *Gofling*, of Hilborough, Norfolk, Draper.
Williams *Adams*, of Princes R. Weftminfter, Upholder.
John *Payne*, of New-Brentford, Middlefex, Baker.
James *Tildefly*, of Liverpool, Merchant.
Thomas *Shute*, of Melkfham, Wilts, Mercer.
Richard *Scott*, of Appleton, Yorkfhire, Woollstapler.
John *Lekrux*, of London, Merchant.
Edward *Mawde*, of Rochdale, Lancafhire, Chapman.
Henry *Geale*, of Gravefend, Innholder.
Zachæus *Breedon*, of Iflington, Middlefex, Mer.hant.
Abner *Grantham*, of Norwich, Factor.
James *Brooks*, of Chilmark, Wilts, Mercer.
David *Ketcherel*, of Canterbury, Chapman.
William *Rathborn*, of Chefter, Merchant.
John *Webb*, of Taunton, Somerfetfhire, Sergemaker.
Robert *Geale*, of Gravefend, Victualler.
John *Main*, of the Strand, Taylor.
Robert *Paulling*, of Pudding Lane, London, Victualler.
John *Graham*, of Rouel, Cumberland, Salefman.
Charles *Wood*, of Southwark, Chapman.
Daniel *Newman*, of Fetter-lane, London, Victualler.
Sir Thomas *Bury*, of Eton, Merchant.
William *Mafon*, of Coleman-ftreet, London, Currier.
William *Stirling*, of London, Merchant.
William *Caw*, of London, Merchant.
Chriftian *Redfern*, of Park-Place, Middlefex, Taylor.
John *Gent*, of Stone, Staffordfhire, Chapman.
John *Prieft*, of Oxford Road, Middlefex, Victualler.
Theophilus *Clayton*, of Norwich, Upholfter.
Jofeph *Woodward*, of Towerhill, London Corn'factr.
James *Trinder* Jun. of Hounflow, Middlefex, Innholder.
William *Onyon*, of Gofwel-ftreet, Maid, Coachmaker.
Gregory *Cording*, of Dulverton, Somerfet, Mercer.

The Order of the Philological Performances at the *OXFORD* Act, *see p.* 377.

William Nicholas, Commencer in Arts of Corpus-Christi College, *open'd the* ACT. In Prose.

CONCENT. I.

LOrd *Barry,* eldest Son of the E. of *Barrymore,* of Brazen-Nose College. *On the Oxford Act.* In Responsive Verse. — 2. Viscount *Castlecomer,* of Christ-Church. *To the KING.* In Lyric Verse. — 3. Sir *Henry Furnese,* of Christ-Church, Bart. *On the* ROYAL FAMILY. In Heroic Verse. — 4. Ld *Romney,* of Christ-Church. *On the Princes of* ORANGE. In Heroic Verse. — 5. Mr *Senhouse,* Fellow of New-College. *On the Printing Press.* In Prose. — 6. Mr *Tracey,* eldest Son of Ld Viscount *Rathcule,* and Sir *Ed. Newdigate,* Bart. both of University College. *On the Oxford Almanack for the Year* 1733. In Responsive Verse. — 7. *Godfrey Clarke,* of New College, Gentleman-Commoner. *On the Orrery.* In Heroic Verse. — 8. *Robert Hoblyn,* of C. C. C. Gentleman Commoner. *On Medals.* In Lyric Verse. — 9. *Wm Hasseldine, Wm Bracebridge,* and *Tho. Hily,* of Magdalen-Colledge. *On the Doctrine of Flowers.* In Responsive Verse. — 1c. Mr *Crew,* of Hart-Hall. *On Learning and Virtue.* In Prose. — 11. *Rich. Sutton Yates,* Gentleman-Commoner of Queen's. *On her Majesty's Bounty to that College.* In Heroic Verse. — 12. *George Brodrepp,* of Univ. Coll. Gentleman Commoner. *On the Bounty of Dr Radcliff.* In Lyric Verse. — 13. *Henry Baynbrigg Buckeridge,* of St John Baptist Coll. Gentleman-Commoner. *On the sacred Dramatic Music, or Oratorio.* In Lyric Verse.

CONCENT. II.

1. Ld *Guernsey,* Son of the E. of *Aylesford,* of Univ. Coll. *The Praise of true Magnificence.* In Lyric Verse. — 2. *Edmund Gibson,* Son of the Bp of *London,* of Christ-Church. *On the Colony of Georgia,* In Heroic Verse. — 3. *Lewis Langton,* and *Thomas Baber,* of Magd. Coll. Gentlemen-Commoners. *The Beau and Academic.* In responsive Verse. — 4. *Edwyn Sandys,* Fellow of New Coll. *On Hales's Vegetation.* In Heroic Verse. — 5. Mr *Potter,* Son of the Bp of Oxford, of Christ Church. *Opinion Queen of the World.* In Prose. — *Richard Sutton,* of Wadham Coll. Gentleman-Commoner. *On the Burning of the Cotton Library.* In Lyric Verse. — 7. *Thomas Medley,* of St John Bapt. Coll. Gentleman Commoner. *On the Botanic Garden.* In Lyric Verse. — 8. *Welbore Ellis,* and *John Roberts,* Students of Ch. Church. *Pyrrho Reviv'd.* In Responsive Verse. — 9. Mr *Drake* of Baliol Coll. Mr *Murray,* third Son of Lord *Elibank,* of the same Coll. *The ancient Statues. The modern Statues.* In Prose. — 10. *Giles Eyre,* of Madg. Coll. *The Praise of Optics.* In Heroic Verse. — 11. *George Coke,* and *Lewis Jones,* of Ch. Church, Gentlemen Commoners. *Defence of* CLARENDON. In Responsive Verse. — 12. *Thomas Smallbrook,* of Trinity Coll. Son of the Bp of *Coventry* and *Litchfield.* ASHMOLE'S MUSÆUM. In Heroic Verse. — 13. Mr *Mills,* of C. C. C. Gentleman Commoner. *The Parish Priest.* In Heroic Verse. — 14. *Powel Snell,* of Baliol Coll. Gentleman-Commoner. *The English Malady.* In Heroic Verse.

CONCENT. III.

George Randolph, Commencer in Arts of All Souls College, *concluded the* ACT. In Prose.

SOUTH CAROLINA.

April 7. The Commons House of Assembly, in order to justify their late Proceedings in committing several Gentlemen to Custody, (see p. 329.) came to the following vigorous Resolutions; *viz.* That it is the undeniable Privilege of that Assembly to commit such Persons as they judge deserve it; That Freedom of Speech and Debates, ought not to be impeached or questioned in any Court or Place out of that House; That it is a Contempt and Violation of the Privileges of that House to call in Question any Commitments of the *Commons House of Assembly;* That no Writ of *Habeas Corpus* lies in Favour of any Persons committed by that *House* during its Sitting; That any such Proceeding, except in *Assembly,* was an express Contradiction of the *Declaration of Right,* 1 *Will. & Mav. cap.* 2. That the Messenger attending the House do make no Return, or yield any Obedience to such Writs of *Habeas Corpus;* And that the *Chief Justice* be acquainted with these Resolutions that the said Writs may be superseded, as contrary to the Law, and the Privilege of the House,

April. 13. The Chief Justice made a Speech in Council complaining of the foregoing Resolutions as tending to the Dissolution of all Government, in which Speech he charges the Lower House of Assembly with disallowing his Majesty's undoubted Prerogative, renouncing Obedience to his Writs of *Habeas Corpus,* and assuming to themselves a Power to abrogate and make void the Laws; and therefore advise the Governor and Council to dissolve them.

April, 19. *Francis Tonge,* Esq; made a Speech to the Council, wherein he defends

fends the Proceedings of the Lower House; and gives this State of the Case, *viz.* I find, *says he, Dr Cooper's Commitment is for superintending the Deputy Surveyors in laying out Lands contrary to Law, and the Governor's Warrants, which tends to the creating litigious Disputes, and involving the Country in the utmost Confusion. Mr Greeme's Commitment is for that he, as Attorney at Law, filled up and sign'd a Capias ad Respondendum against John Brown, Messenger of the House. That of Mr Rowland Vaughan is for an open and notorious Affront and Contempt offered the House, by serving a Writ of Habeas Corpus on John Brown, Messenger, when he was actually in the Execution of his Office.* He maintain'd these several Charges by shewing that the Privileges of that House were the same as those of the House of Commons in *Great Britain.*

April 20. The Upper House came to several Resolutions wherein they approve what had been done by the Lower House with Regard to Commitments; are of Opinion, that the Commons House have the same Privileges as the House of Commons in *England*; that the *Resolutions* of the Commons House of Assembly do not strike at his Majesty's Prerogative, as suggested in Mr *Chief Justice's* Speech, and that his Expressions therein, as relating to the Commons House, are unprecedented; and declared that the Speech of *Francis Tonge,* Esq; is agreeable to their own Opinion.

May 10. Mr *Loy'd* made a Speech in the Lower House in which he took to pieces that which the Chief Justice had made; and in Conclusion proposed, and the House came to, the following Resolutions, *viz.*

Resolved, *That the Resolutions of this House, which the Chief Justice (falsly and maliciously) says, tend to the Subversion of all Government, disallowing his Majesty's undoubted Prerogative, are, on the quite contrary, calculated to support Government, as well as to preserve his Majesty's Prerogative.*

Resolved, *That it is very ignorant, or malicious, in the Chief Justice to say, that this House assume to themselves a Power to abrogate and make void the Laws of the Land; because they ordered into Custody some of their Fellow-Subjects, for committing notorious Grievances contrary to Law; and others for Breach of Privilege and Contempt of this House, a-*

greeable to the known Practice of the *House of Commons* in *Great Britain, and that of this Province.*

Resolved, *That is is the Opinion of this House, that Robert Wright Esq; the present Chief Justice, by his Speech, and other Actings, appears to be unjustly prejudiced against the People of Carolina, unworthy the Honourable Employment he now bears; and that it would tend to his Majesty's Service, and the Tranquillity of this Province, that he were immediately suspended.*

By Order of the House,
I. *Amyand,* C. D. C.

From GEORGIA.

Savannah, May 20, Mr *Oglethorpe* return'd from *Charles* Town the 18th and found here the Chief Men of all the Lower Creek Nation, to the Number of 50 Persons with their Attendants who were come some of them a Journey of 5 Days to treat of an Alliance with the Colony. Mr *Oglethorpe* received them in one of the New-houses the same Day. Their Address was to the following Purpose; they first claimed all the Ground to the South of the River *Savannah*; but as He who had given the *English* more Wisdom, had also sent them here for their Instruction, so they freely gave up their Right to all the Land they did not use themselves, and offer'd to go and attack the *Cheroqueese* who they heard had slain some *English,* if Mr *Oglethorpe* would Command them, declaring a love for him and his People. The Articles of Traffick being agreed on, a Laced Coat, Hat and Shirts were given to each of the Chiefs, some Cloth for their Attendants, a Present of Gun-powder, Irish Linnen, Tobacco, Pipes, Tape of all Colours, Bullets, and 8 Cags of Rum to carry Home to their respective Towns. Thus the Peace being concluded, Mr *Oglethorpe* having recommended the care of the People and of carrying on the works to Mr *James St Julian* and Mr *Scott,* return'd to Charles Town.——The *James,* Capt *Toakley,* 110 Tons, and 6 Guns, arrived here on the 14th with Passengers and Stores. This Ship rode in 2 Fathom and a half Water close to the Town at Low Water-mark. The Captain received the Prize appointed by the Trustees for the first Ship that should unload at this Town, where is safe Riding for much larger Vessels.

FROM

FROM the *Hague*, July 15. The Solemnity of installing the Pr. of *Orange* Kt of the Garter, was perform'd in the *Orange Hall* of his Highness's House in the Wood near this Place. This Hall is one of the finest Rooms in the World for Painting, the Trophies of the Great Founder of the Republick being there painted by *Rubens*. In this Hall were erected a Throne for the King, and a Stall for the new Knight, each having a Canopy over it, with the Arms of his Majesty and those of his Highness. Round the Hall were Galleries rising gradually, which were crouded with Gentlemen and Ladies of Distinction. Mr *Finch* and Mr *Anstis*, Herald at Arms, invested his Highness with the Ornaments of the Order with the usual Ceremonies; and every Body admired the good Grace with which the Prince performed his Part. He then return'd to his Apartment, but first shewed himself to the People, who made the Wood, as well as the Hall, ring with Huzzas and *vivat Orange*. Being return'd to the Hall his Highness was surrounded by the Ladies who admir'd the Richness of his Hat, which was half-covered with Diamonds and Pearls. At 3 o'Clock was a magnificent Repast, to which were invited the three Stadtholder Provinces to the Assembly of the States General, the Council of State, the Chamber of Finances, and other Lords of the First Rank; a long List of Healths were drank, and 8 Casks of Wine were given to the Populace.

From *Constantinople*, That the *Ottoman* Forces, sent to the Succour of *Babylon*, had been defeated in three successive Engagements by *Kouli Kan*, the Persian General, in Consequence of which he was become Master of the Place.

From *Dresden*, That the Electress of *Saxony* was deliver'd of a Prince.

From *Paris*, That they had prepar'd a Number of Bridges to throw over the *Rhine*, and all necessary Provisions are made to form a powerful Army on the Side of *Alsace*, and that they had also fitted out 18 Men of War of the Line.

From *Auvergne* in *France*, 'That the Inhabitants of a Village situate on the Side of a Mountain a League in Length, perceiving on the 23d past the Earth in Motion, ran precipitately with their Cattle to some Distance, and in a Moment after saw their Houses fall into an Abyss, which the opening of the Earth had made and the next Day, nothing was discover'd

more than Rocks and a yellowish Earth. But the People were yet more surpriz'd to find a new (and as high as the former) Ridge of Mountains and Rocks, which extended to the middle of the Plain, and bars up the Highway between *Clermont* and *Isoire*. The Earth kept working for some Time, Swelling in some Places, and Sinking in others, and the new Mountain shook surprisingly. All which happen'd without Smell, or Smoak, or any other Noise, than that of the Fall of the Houses. It had been observ'd a long Time before this happen'd, that the Earth often crack'd, and form'd Chinks of half a foot long, but no Bottom could be found.

From *Turin*, That the King of *Sardinia* had declared, he will observe an exact Neutrality, in case the Affairs in *Poland* should occasion a War in Europe.

From *Berlin*, *July* 2. The Nuptials of the Prince of *Beveren*, with the Princess *Charlotte* of *Prussia*, were celebrated with great Magnificence.

From *Warsaw*, That the *Poles*, rather than bear the least Shadow of Controul over their Election, will call in the *Turks* and *Tortars*. They were actually making Levies and every 30th Man was obliged to serve, by Order of the Senate and Primate, who hath put off the Election for two Months, in order to favour *Stanislaus*, it being impracticable for the *Imperialists* and *Russians*, who seem resolv'd at all Hazards to oppose him, to keep the Field in the Winter.

That the Palatin of *Podlachria* who distinguish'd himself in the late Dyet of Convocation, by a strenuous Opposition to the Oath of Confederacy, on his Return into the Country, engaged 3000 Gentlemen to oppose the said Oath with Life and Fortune; had declar'd himself the Head of their Party, and did not doubt of being shortly join'd by a great Part of the Kingdom, notwithstanding what has been given out of the Unanimity in Favour of *Stanislaus*. That, in order to avoid the Troubles which the ensuing Election was likely to create, almost all the Foreigners, with several of the moderate *Poles*, were retiring into *Prussia*, with their Families and Effects.

From *Copenhagen*, That the King of *Denmark* had granted the *French* Squadron a free Passage thro' the *Sound*, provided they did not fall upon any of the Allies of that Crown.

STOCKS

Towards the End of the Month.

Courſe of Exchange.	STOCKS	Monthly BILL of Mortality, from June 26, to July 24.		
Amſterdam 35	S. Sea 105	Chriſtned { Males 660 } 1316		
Ditto at Sight 34 10 ¾	—Trading Stock 92	{ Females 656 }		
Hamburgh— 34	—Bonds 2 l. 12	Buried { Males 960 } 1889		
Rotterdam— 35 1	—Annuties 109	{ Femal. 929 }		
Antwerp — 35 4	—Ditto new 107 ⅛	Died under 2 Years old — 887		
Madrid —— 42 ½	—dit. 3 per C. 100 ⅛	Between 2 and 5 —— 130		
Bilboa —— 41 ⅛	Bank 150	Between 5 and 10 —— 63		
Cadiz —— 41 ¼	---Cir. 7 l. 12 s. 6 d.	Between 10 and 20 —— 48		
Venice — 49	India 160	Between 20 and 30 —— 129		
Leghorn — 50 ⅞	—Bonds 5 l. 7 s.	Between 30 and 40 —— 159		
Genoa —— 53 ½	Ditto at 3 per C. 4 l.	Between 40 and 50 —— 135		
Paris —— 32 ½	Million Bank 116	Between 50 and 60 —— 141		
Bourdeaux — 31 ½	African 28	Between 60 and 70 —— 87		
Oporto—— 5 4 ½	Royal Aſſ. 105	Between 70 and 80 —— 67		
Lisbon— 5 5 ½ 4 ¼	London Aſſ. 13 ¼	Between 80 and 90 —— 34		
Dublin— 10 ⅞	Eng. Cop. 1 l. 16	Between 90 and 100 —— 4		
	Welch ditto 1 l.	1889		

Price of Grain at Bear-Key, per Qr.

			Buried.		Weekly Burials
Wheat 20 s. to 24 s.	P. Malt 15 s. to 20 s.	Within the walls, 174		July 3 —— 509
Rye ' 22 s. to 24 s.	B. Malt 15 s. to 19 s.	Without the walls, 525		10 —— 514
Barley 11 s. to 13 s. 6 d	Tares 14 s. to 15 s.	In Mid and Surry, 781		17 —— 401
Oats 7 s. to 11 s.	H. Peaſe 13 s. to 15 s.	City and Sub of Weſt 409		24 —— 465
Peaſe 17 s. to 25 s.	H. Beans 14 s. to 17 s.	1889		1889

Prices of Goods, &c. in London.　Hay 2 l. a Load.

Coals in the Pool 22 s. to 24 s.
Old Hops per Hun. 3 l. to 8 l.
New Hops 9 l. to 10 l.
Rape Seed 10 l. to 11 l. per Laſt
Lead the Fodder 19 Hun. 1 half on board, 14 l. to 16 l. 00 s.
Tin in Blocks 4 l. 00 s
Ditto in Bers 4 l. 02 s. excluſive of 3 s. per Hun. Duty.
Copper Eng. beſt 5 l. 15 s. per C.
Ditto ord. 4 l. 16 s. to 5 l. per C.
Ditto Barbary 70 l. to 80 l.
Iron of Bilboa 14 l. 10 s. per Tun
Dit. of Sweden 15 l. 10 s. per Tun
Town Tallow 30 s. to 32 s. per C.
Country Tallow 28 s. to 32 s.
Salt 4 s. to 4 s. 6 d.

Grocery Wares.
Raiſins of the Sun 28 s. 0 d. per C.
Ditto Malaga Frailes 19 s.
Ditto Smirna new 20 s.
Ditto Alicant, 18 s.
Ditto Lipra new 19 s.
Ditto Belvedera 20
Currants new 45 s.
Prunes French 18 s.
Figs 20 s.
Sugar Powd. beſt 59 s. per C.

Ditto second sort 46 s. to 50 s. per C.
Loaf Sugar double refine 8 d. Half-penny a 9 d. per lb.
Ditto single reſin. 56 s. to 64 s. per C.
Cinamon 7 s. 8 d. per lb.
Cloves 9 s. 1 d.
Mace 15 s. 0 d. per lb.
Nutmegs 8 s. 7 d. per lb.
Sugar Candy white 14 d. to 18 d.
Ditto brown 7 d. per lb.
Pepper for Home conf. 17 d.
Ditto for exportation 13 d. Farth.
Tea Bohea fine 10 s. to 11 s. per lb.
Ditto ordinary 7 s. to 9 s. per lb.
Ditto Congo 10 s. to 14 s. per lb.
ditto Pekoe 9 s. a 14 s. per lb.
ditto Green fine 8 s. to 12 s. per lb.
ditto Imperial 10 s. to 16 s. per lb.
ditto Hyſon 24 s. to 28 s.

Drugs by the lb.
Balſom Peru 14 s. to 15 s.
Cardamoms 3 s. 3 d.
Camphire refin'd 19 s.
Crabs Eyes 2 s. 5 d.
Jallop 3 s.
Manna 20 d. a 33 d.
Maſtick white 4 s. 0 d.

Opium 11 s. 00 d.
Quickſilver 4 s. 3 d.
Rhubarb fine 25 s. a 30 s.
Sarſaparilla 3 s. 0 d.
Saffron Eng. 28 s. 00 d.
Wormſeeds 3 s. 5 d.
Balſam Capaiva 2 n 9 d.
Balſam of Gillead 18 s. 00 d.
Hipecacuana 7 s.
Ambergreece per oz. 12 s.
Cochineal 18 s. 3 d. per lb.

Wine, Brandy, and Rum.
Oporto red, per Pipe 36 l.
ditto white 24 L
Lisbon red 30 l.
ditto white, 26 L
Sherry 26 L
Canary new 30 l.
ditto old 36 L
Florence 3 L per Cheſt
French red 30 L a 40 L
ditto white 20 L
Mountain malaga old 24 L
ditto new 20 to 24 L
Brandy French per Gal. 7 s.
Rum of Jamaica 7 s.
ditto Leu. Iſlands 6 s. 4 L
Spirits Eng. 26 L per Tun.

A REGISTER of BOOKS publish'd in JULY, 1733.

THE Theatric Squabble, or the P—ct, a Satire, In which the Characters of them and the Actors are properly distinguish'd. Printed for *A. Dodd*, pr. 6 *d.*

2. A Friendly Epistle to the Author of the State Dunces. pr. 6 *d.* (See p. 373.)

3. Primitiæ Poetices: Sive illustrium veterumque Poetarum Sententiæ, Printed for *John Pemberton*, pr. 1 *s.* 6 *d.*

4. The vocal Miscellany. A Collection of above 400 celebrated Songs; many of which never before published, for *J. Hazard*, pr. 3 *s.*

5. The second Part of the State Dunces. Inscrib'd to Mr. *Pope.* Printed for *J. Dickenson*, pr. 1 *s.*

6. The Citizens Procession: Or, The Smuggler's Success, and the Patriot's Disappointment. A Ballad, pr. 4 *d.* (See p. 374.)

7. Diligence in the Christian Ministry necessary to be found in Peace. A Sermon occasion'd by the Death of the late Rev. Mr *Daniel Mayo*, M. A. By *Wm Harris*, D. D. Printed for *Rich. Ford.*

8 The Woman of Taste, in a 2d Epistle from *Clelia* in Town, to *Sappho* in the Country. Printed for *Jer. Batley*, pr. 1 *s.*

9. The Oxford Oyster-Women, a Poem. To which is prefix'd a Hymn to the Moon. Sold by the Booksellers.

10. The Life of the Stage: A Collection of the best Plays of the best Poets, bound in eight neat pocket Volumes, pr. 1 *l.* 7 *s.* 6 *d.*

11. The Counterpart to the State Dunces. Printed for *W. Mears*, pr. 6 *d.* (See p. 372.)

12. The Terræ Filius Speech, as it was to have been spoken publickly at the Theatre in *Oxford*. Sold by the Booksellers, pr. 6 *d.*

13. The Oxford Toast's Answer to the Terræ Filius's Speech, for *J. Wilford*, pr. 6 *d.*

14. The Wrongheads, A Poem. Address'd to Mr *Pope.* By a Person of Quality. Sold by *T. Astley*, pr. 6 *d.*

15. A Translation of the second Satire of *Perseus.* By *T. Brewster*, A. M. Printed for *W. Bowyer.* pr. 6 *d.*

16. Athalia, and Deborah, two Oratorio's, or sacred Drama's; also *Acis* and *Galatea*, Printed for *J. Watts.*

17. Marci Hieronymi Vidæ Hymni de Rebus Divinis. Printed at *Oxford.*

18. The Magick Glass; or Visions of the Times. Printed for *T. Cooper*, pr. 1 *s.*

19. A Discourse on the Blessing of a good Government, and on the Wickedness of Disaffection and Sedition. In which the Nature of our Constitution is consider'd, &c. Printed for *J. Roberts*, pr. 6 *d.*

20. A most exact Alphabetical List of the Members who voted *for* and *against* bringing in the Bill of Excise; also of the Lords who voted *for* and *against* the Enquiry into the Frauds of the South Sea Company on a Sheet of Royal Paper, pr. 6 *d.* The same, with Improvements, in a half Sheet 8vo. fitted to bind with the Monthly and Quarterly Books, pr. 2 *d.*

21. Two Addresses to the King against an Excise on Wine and Tobacco. Printed for *J. Roberts*, pr. 4 *d.*

22. Acts of the last Session of Parliament and the Ten last Sessions preceding. Sold by *S. Keble.*

23. 1. The Report with the Appendix, from the Committee of the House of Commons, appointed to enquire into Frauds and Abuses in the Customs. pr. 2 *s. d.*

24. The Report with the Appendix, from the Committee to whom the Petition of the Proprietors of the Charitable Corporation was referr'd, pr. 3 *s.* Printed for *R. Williamson.*

25. A second Essay upon the Nature, Manner, and End of Christian Revelation. In which is contained a full Distinct Answer to all that is material in *Christianity as old as the Creation.* By *Christopher Robinson*, M. A. Printed for *J. Pemberton*, pr. 2 *s.*

26. The Expences of University Education Reduc'd. In a Letter to A. B. Fellow of E. C. Oxon. The 2d Edition, with a Postscript. Printed for *G. Strahan.*

27. A short Review of the Quick-Silver Controversy, in a Letter to *Dover*, By a Mercurialist.

28. An Essay concerning the Effects of Air on human Bodies. By *John Arbuthnot*, M. D. Printed for *J. Tonson.*

29. An Examination of the Sketch, or Plan, of an Answer to the Book, entitled, *Christianity as old as the Creation*, laid down in a Letter to Dr. *Waterland*; wherein the Tendency to the Subversion of Christianity, and all Religion is expos'd. By *John Clarke* of *Hull.* Printed for *Battesworth and Hitch*, pr. 6 *d.*

30. Exercitatio Geometrica de Descriptione Linearum Curvarum. Auctore *Gulielmo Braikenridge.* Printed for *R. Hett.*

31. Spectacle *de la* Nature; or Nature display'd. Being Discourses on such particulars of Natural History as were thought proper to excite the Curiosity, and form the Minds of Youth. Printed for *J. Pemberton.*

32. 1. Oratio de Vanitate Luminis Naturæ Habita 2 *April anno* 1733, in Communi Universitati *Andreapolitana* auditorio: Quum Rectoris dignitatem annuam deponeret Auctor *Archibaldus Campbell*, S. T. P.

33. Remarks on Mr *Innes's* Critical Essay on the antient Inhabitants of the Northern Parts of *Britain* and *Scotland.* Sold by *J. Gray*, pr. 1 *s.*

34. *Job's* Creed, or Confession of Faith. A Sermon occasion'd by the Death of the Rev. Mr *Edward Wallin.* By *John Gill.* Printed for *A. Ward*, pr. 6 *d.*

35. Relative Holiness. A Sermon preached at the Consecration of the Parish Church of St *John* in *Southwark*, June 15, 1733. By *William Richardson*, M. A. Printed for *W. Hinchliffe*, pr. 6 *d.*

36. The Friendly Apparition: Being an Account of the moſt ſurprizing Appearance of *Sarah Malcolm's* Ghoſt to a great Aſſembly ofh er Acquaintance at a noted Gin Shop; on occaſion of a late Affront offer'd to her Memory by burning her Effigy, and of the *Alexanders* being taken up again. Sold at the Pamphlet Shops, pr. 6 *d.*

37. Diſaffection to the Government dangerous to the Liberties and deſtructive to the Happineſs of *Britain*, Or, ſome Conſiderations on being deceiv'd. Printed for *J. Roberts.* pr. 6 *d.*

38. A View of the Articles of the Proteſtant and Popiſh Faith. On a Sheet of Royal Paper. Sold by *J. Downing.*

39. A Liſt of the Priſoners that were try'ed at *Croydon*, at the laſt Aſſizes held there. Printed for *J Appleb**ee*.*

40. A Brief View of Eccleſiaſtical Juriſdiction as it is at this Day practis'd in *England*. Addreſs'd to Sir *Nathaniel Curzon* Bart and the reſt of the Gentlemen of the Committee appointed by Parliament for enquiring into the Abuſes and Corruptions of Eccleſiaſtical Court Juriſdiction. Printed for *J. Peele.*

41. An Account of the ſeveral Loans, Benefactions and Charities belonging to the City of *Coventry.* Printed for *W. Ratten* there.

42. An Enquiry into the Methods, ſaid to be now propoſed in *England*, to retrieve the Sugar Trade. By the Author of the Detection of the State and Situation of the preſent Sugar Planters at *Barbadoes.*

43. A Diſſertation on Unity in Trinity, and Trinity in Unity. Printed for *R. Ford.*

44. *Virgil's* Paſtorals, by *J. Stirling*, A. M. In a new Method, and better adapted to the Capacity of Youth than any yet Printed. It has the Proſaic Order of Words; an Alphabetical Vocabulary; the Themes of the Verbs; a Table which ſcans every Line, *&c.* Sold at the Author's School in *High Holbourn.*

45. Acts of Aſſembly paſs'd in the Aſſembly of *Barbadoes.* Printed by *John Baskett.*

46. The Proceedings of the *Old Bailey*, for the City of *London*, and County of *Middleſex.* on the 28*th*, 29*th*, and 30*th* of June laſt, Printed for *J Wilford.*

47. Campanologia improved; or, the Art of Ringing made eaſy, by Plain and Methodical Rules and Directions, whereby the Ingenious Practitioner may, with a little Practice and Care, attain to the Knowledge of Ringing all manner of Double, Tripple, and Quadruple Changes; with Variety of New Peals, upon five, ſix, ſeven, eight and nine Bells. As alſo the Method of calling Bobs for any Peal of Tripples from 168 to 2520 (being the Half Peal:) Alſo for any Peal of Quadruples, or Cator's from 324 to 1140. The Third Edition, corrected. Printed for A. Betteſworth, and C. Hitch, at the Red-Lion in Pater-noſter Row, pr. 1*s.* 6*d.*

88. *Spiramina, or Reſpiration Review'd;* being Chiefly the Arguments of that great Philoſopher by Fire *Johannes Baptiſta Van Helmont*, diſcovering certain uſes of the Lungs not Commonly obſerved, and aſſerting that they have not that alternative Motion that is generally aſcribed to them, but that in a ſound-Man they are porous, pervious to the Air, and Conſtantly at reſt: Humbly offer'd with ſome Additions to the Conſideration of the Curious and Inquiſitive by *M. J.* Sold by the Bookſellers in *London*, pr. 6 *d.*

ADVERTISEMENT.

THE Ceremonies and Religious Cuſtoms of the various Nation of the known World; faithfully tranſlated from the French Original, and illuſtrated with above 172 Copper Plates, all beautifully deſign'd by M. B. Picart, and engrav'd by moſt of the beſt Hands in Europe.

The Price of the whole work, Printed on Dutch Paper Royal, and compriz'd in four large Volumes in Folio, will be but 5 *l.* 10 *s.* in Sheets which is no more than half the Price of the Original; to be deliver'd, out in Weekly Numbers during the Space of two Years and two Months, at 1 *s.* per Number, which will only amount to three Half-pence per Sheet, and Three pence per Folio Print.

PROPOSALS *at large, with beautiful* SPECIMENS, *may be ſeen at the Places where* SUBSCRIPTIONS *are taken in, viz.* CLAUDE DUBOSC, *Engraver, at the Golden Head in Charles-ſtreet, Covent Garden;* THOMAS BOWLES, *Printſeller next the Chapter-houſe in St Paul's Church-yard;* PHILP OVERTON, *Printſeller near St Dunſton's Church Fleet-ſtreet;* THOMAS GLASS, *Printſeller near the Royal Exchange Stairs in Cornhill;* J. BOWLE, *Printſeller at the Black Horſe in Cornhill;* J. REGNIER, *Printſeller, at the Golden Ball in Newport-ſtreet near Long Acre;* J. HULTON, *Printſeller, at the Corner of Pall Mall facing the Haymarket;* PAUL FOURDRINIER, *Stationer and Printſeller, the Corner of Craigs-Court, Charing Croſs;* J. KING, *Printſeller, in the Poultery near Stoks market;* Mrs MARBECK, *Printſeller, on Weſtminſter Hall,* J. CLARK, *Engraver and Printſeller in Gray's Inn,* Mr SYMPSON *Engraver and Printſeller, near the end of Catherine-ſtreet in the Strand.*

That the Publick may not be impos'd on by invidious Aſperſions, Mr DUBOSC faithfully aſſures them, that this is no ſpurious Edition, but genuine and compleat in all reſpects for the Truth of which, and of his various additional Beauties, he refers to his own printed Specimen, and to the Amſterdam Propoſals, for proof of the vaſt Difference in the Prices, and not to the original Edition, as ſome are pleas'd to call Mr LOCKMAN's Tranſlation of three Volumes only, of the preſent Undertaking.

The Gentleman's Magazine:

St John's Gate.

Lond.Gazette
Lond. Jour.
Fog' Journ.
Applebee's :
Read's :: ::
Craftsman :
D. Pyctato:
Grubstreet J
Wh.Register
Free-Briton
Imp. Doctor
Daily Court
Daily Post
Dai.Courna
Dai.Post-boy
Advertiser
Evening Post
St James's Ev
Whitehall Ev
Lndon Ev bfg
Flying - Post
Weekly Misc.
cellany.

Hogh - News
Dublin 6 :::
Edinburgh 2
Bristol ::::
Norwich 2:
Exeter 2 :::
Worcester ::
Northampton
Gloucester::
Stamford::
Nottingham
Bury Journ.
Chester ditto
Derby ditto
Ipswich do.
Reading do.
Leeds Merc.
Newcastle C.
Canterbury:
Birmingham
Manchester
Boston ::: ¶
Jamaica, &c.
Barbados ::

Or, MONTHLY INTELLIGENCER.

For AUGUST, 1733.

CONTAINING,

more in Quantity, and greater Variety, than any Book of the kind and Price,

I. Proceedings and Debates in last Session of Parliament, *viz.* On the Motion to Address; the Pension Bill; Army; Supply; *Spanish* Depredations; Sugar Colonies; Lords and Commons Addresses, &c.

II. Weekly Essays, *viz.* Of Pride in Men of Worth; Religion and Infidelity; Of Oppressions in the Courts of Equity; hard Words in Preaching ridicul'd; of the *Indians* bordering on *Georgia*; Quickfilver dangerous; a Lesson for bad Husbands.

III. Political Points, *viz.* On the present Rejoicings; Excises in *B----ke's* Administration; Excise-Scheme calculated; the present Crisis; an Artifice of the *Craftsman*; *Fog's* and a certain Gentleman's Friendship for the Dissenters; *Craftsman's* Remarks on the Committee of Enquiry examin'd; *Bob* and *Will*; Encomium on *Rysbrack's* Statue of King *William*; the City of *Bristol's* Judgment and Generosity; the Power of the People defended; the Act of Settlement; broke thro'; Candidates for the Crown of *Poland*.

IV. Poetry. To the Ld *Weymouth* on his Marriage with Miss *Carteret*; the Flying Fair; on seeing a Lady Blush; *Martial's Phillis* match'd; *Sappho* imitated; The Wandering Heart, from *Catullus*; the DIVINE of Taste; Golden Legend or honest Lawyer; Prize Pieces Riddles; Female Wish; Epigrams, &c.

V. Domestic Occurrences, &c.

VI. Prices of Goods, Grain and Stocks.

VII. Foreign Affairs;

VIII. Books and Pamphlets.

IX. A Table of Contents.

By SYLVANUS URBAN, Gent.

LONDON: Printed for the AUTHOR, and fold at St *John's Gate*, By *F. Jefferies*, in *Ludgate-street*; all other Booksellers; and by the Persons who serve Gentlemen with the News-papers. Of whom may be had Compleat Sets, or any single Number. A few on Royal Paper.

CONTENTS

Just Published,

THE PHILOSOPHICAL TRANSACTIONS (from the Year 1720 to the Year 1732,) abridg'd and dispos'd under their several Heads, by Mr *Reid* and *John Gray*, A. M. F. R. S. in two Vols. 4to, being a Continuation of the Abridgment done by Mr *Lowthorp*, and Mr *Jones*.

Printed for *W. Innys* and *R. Manby*, Printers to the Royal Society, at the West End of St *Paul's*.

N. B. This Abidgment by Mr *Reid* and Mr *Gray*, being begun by our Approbation, and encouraged by many Members of the Royal Society, who have revis'd and improv'd their own Papers, we believe the same from our Knowledge of the Abilities of the Compilers to be well executed.

John Arbuthnot, M. D. F. R. S.
Robert Barker, M. D. F. R. S.
James Bradley, Prof. Astron. Savil. Oxon, F. R. S.
George Campbell, F. R. S.

J. T. Desaguliers, L. L. D. F. R. S.
Martin Folkes, V. P. R. S.
John Hadley, V. P. R. S.
Edmund Halley, L. L. D. Reg. Astron. Prof. Geom. Savil. Oxon, V. P. R. S.
William Jones, F. R. S.

John Machin, Prof. Astron. Gresh. R. S.
Colin Mac Laurin, F R. S.
Abraham de Moivre, F. R. S.
James Stirling, F. R. S.

THE
Gentleman's Magazine:
AUGUST, 1733.

PROCEEDINGS *and* DEBATES *in last* Session of Parliament.

JANUARY 16, 1732-3.

IS Majesty being come to the House of Peers and seated on his Throne, and the Commons sent for, Open'd the Sessions with a most Gracious Speech. See p. 38.

In the House of Lords, the Marquis of Lothian, (seconded by Lord Lovelace) moved an Address of Thanks, which was agreed to without any Objection, and presented the 17th, being as follows.

Most Gracious Sovereign,

WE Your Majesty's most Dutiful and Loyal Subjects, the Lords Spiritual and Temporal, in Parliament assembled, do in all Humility return the Thanks of this House, for Your Majesty's most Gracious Speech from the Throne. It is owing to the happy Success of Your Majesty's Counsels and Negotiations, that Your Majesty now assembles Your Parliament for no other Reasons, but the ordinary Dispatch of the Publick Business; and Your Majesty being graciously pleased to express such great Satisfaction in giving us an Opportunity of humbly offering our Advice to the Throne upon such Affairs, as shall require the Care and Consideration of Parliament, we think it incumbent on us, in return, to consider that Part of our Duty to be the highest Honour and Privilege of this House, which, as we have always enjoyed, so we beg leave to assure Your Majesty, we will never abuse.

We will use our utmost Endeavours to proceed in such manner in the speedy Execution of the great Trust reposed in us, that the People may be fully sensible, that no unreasonable Heats or Animosities shall delay or interrupt our Deliberations, and that the true Interest of our Country, the present and future Ease of our Fellow Subjects, and the Publick Good of Great Britain shall outweigh all other Considerations, though covered by any specious Pretences whatsoever. Upon these Foundations, we may be confident, that our Resolutions will be agreeable to Your Majesty, by being beneficial to the whole Nation.

See His Majesty's most Gracious Answer p. 38.

In the House of COMMONS an Address of Thanks was, after some Debates, resolv'd

on the 16th, reported the 17th, and presented the 18th, being as follows,

Most Gracious Sovereign,

WE Your Majesty's most Dutiful and Loyal Subjects, the Commons of Great Britain in Parliament assembled, humbly beg leave to return Your Majesty Our most Sincere and Hearty Thanks for Your most Gracious Speech from the Throne.

The Situation of Affairs, both at Home and Abroad, gives Your Faithful Commons the Highest Satisfaction, and fills their Hearts with the deepest Sense of Gratitude to Your Majesty, being fully sensible that the Present Happiness We enjoy, is the entire Effect of Your Majesty's Wisdom and Resolution.

Such Supplies as shall be necessary for the Honour, Safety, and Defence of your Majesty and your Kingdom, shall Chearfully and Effectually be raised by Your Faithful Commons, with all possible Duty to Your Majesty, and a just Regard and Concern for those We represent.

We also beg Leave to assure Your Majesty, that in all Our Deliberations, as well in raising the Supplies, as in the Distribution of the Publick Revenues, We will pursue such Measures, as will most conduce to the Present and Future Ease of Our Fellow Subjects, and such as are agreeable to Your Majesty's known Goodness and Gracious Intentions towards Your People, and the constant Endeavours of Your Faithful Commons, shall be [consistent with the Honour and Justice of Parliament,] and [with the Trade, Interest, and Liberty of the Nation.]

That Our Proceedings may carry with them the Weight and Credit, which ought always to attend the Resolutions of the Commons of Great Britain, and that the necessary Dispatch may be given to the Publick Business; We will use Our utmost Endeavours to avoid all unreasonable Heats and Animosities, nor suffer Our Selves to be diverted, by any specious Pretences whatsoever, from steadfastly pursuing the true Interest of Our Country, which, in Pursuance of Your Majesty's most Gracious Recommendation, from Your great Example, and Our own indispensible Duty, shall upon all Occasions be Our first and principal Care.

See His Majesty's most Gracious Answer p. 38.

De-

Debate, *Jan.* 16, *on the* King's Speech.

The Hon. Commons being return'd to their House, and the Session constituted by reading a Bill (*viz.* that for preventing clandestine Out-Lawries) His Majesty's most Gracious Speech was read; upon which

H——*y* B——*ley*, Esq; after taking Notice of the present happy Situation of Affairs at Home and Abroad, and that the present. Tranquility was entirely owing to his Majesty's great Wisdom and prudent Conduct, (by which he had surmounted all those difficulties thrown in his Way by the Enemies of the Nation, for which a great many Acknowledgments of Thanks were due,) moved that an humble Address be presented to his Majesty to return thanks &c. as in the Terms above, except the Clauses mark'd thus [ ]

J——n Kn——*t*, Esq; seconded the Motion for Thanks, as most due to his Majesty's good Conduct, and hoped the House would unanimously agree thereto.

Sir *J——n* B——*rd* then said, I shall always be ready to make all proper Acknowledgments of Thanks to his Majesty; but I do not really know what the Hon. Gentleman means by the Words, *We will endeavour to avoid all unreasonable Heats and Animosities, and not suffer ourselves to be diverted by any specious Pretences whatsoever.* I hope, Sir, there never were, nor ever will be any *unreasonable Heats* or *Animosities* in this House. And if any Man shall ever be vain enough to endeavour or impose upon this House, by making use of *specious Pretences* for concealing Designs he dare not openly avow, I hope there will always be in this House Men of Understanding and Integrity to expose such Attempts; but if any Gentleman happens not to like what is said by another, cannot he oppose it, without being guilty of any *unreasonable Heat* or *Animosity*, or making use of *specious Pretences*? I must say, Sir, the desiring such Words to be put into our Address looks as if the Gentleman was conscious that something is to be brought before us this Session which he foresees will meet with a warm Opposition; and I hope no Gentleman will be precluded by these Words, from giving his Sentiments freely upon any Question that may occur. If any thing should happen to be proposed in this House, which evidently appears to be inconsistent with the Liberties or the Trade of this Nation, I hope the Indignation of every Man that thinks so, will rise against such a Proposition, and that he will oppose it with that honest Warmth as becomes every Man who has the Happiness of his Country really at Heart. But in a preceding Part of the Motion made by the Hon. Gentleman: He proposes for us to say, *That we will raise the Supplies in such manner as will most conduce to the present and future Ease of the Subject.* Now, Sir, I must take notice that there seems to be a great Jealousy without

Doors, as if something were intended to be done in this Session that may be Destructive to our Liberties and detrimental to our Trade. There is such a Jealousy among all Sorts of People, and in all Corners of the Nation; therefore we ought to take the first Opportunity to quiet the Minds of the People, and to assure them, they may depend on our Honour and Integrity, that we never will consent to any thing that may have the least Appearance of being destructive to their Liberties, or detrimental to their Trade; for which Reason, Sir, I move for an Amendment, and that these Words, *And such as shall be consistent with the Trade, Interest and Liberty of the Nation,* may be added to the Motion.

S——l S——ys, Esq;] Sir, I can see no Occasion for saying that we will endeavour to avoid all *unreasonable Heats and Animosities, and not suffer ourselves to be diverted by any specious Pretences*; 'tis never to be presumed that we shall ever fall into any unreasonable Heats or *Animosities*, or suffer ourselves to be diverted by *specious Pretences* from steadfastly pursuing the true Interest of our Country. I must say, Sir, I think it a little strange, that after this House has sat so quietly so many Sessions; after it has granted so many and so considerable Supplies; I say, Sir, it seems to me a little strange, that we should now in such a particular manner be put in mind of our Duty, and desired to avoid all *unreasonable Heats and Animosities.* As for the other Part of the Motion for an Address, I think the Amendment proposed is not only very proper, but absolutely necessary, and therefore I second it.

W——m S——n Esq;] Sir, I have always been against long Addresses; I am ready enough to agree to an Address of Thanks; but such Address ought to be in the most concise Terms, and the most general Words: This was the ancient Usage, and I find but few of our old Customs altered for the better: However, if we must make long-winded Addresses, I think we ought to take some Notice of the Jealousies and Suspicions without Doors. There is at present a most remarkable Spirit among the People for defending their Liberties and their Trade, in Opposition to Attempts they expect are to be made against both: From all Quarters we hear of Meetings and Resolutions for that purpose; and this Spirit is so general, that it cannot be ascribed to any one Set of Men: They cannot be branded with the Name of Jacobites or of Republicans. No; the whole People of *England* seem to be united in this Spirit of Jealousy and Opposition; and it ought not to be entirely neglected. 'Tis well known I am no Friend to popular Remonstrances; a Man that is a Favourer of Monarchy, can't well approve of such Measures. But a thorough Contempt of them may produce the most terrible Effects.——I look on it, Sir, as a most certain Maxim, that the People never would so generally complain, unless some way hurt when they find themselves hurt, they will, they have a Right to complain, and it is our Duty to take Notice of their Complaints; but at the same time we ought to have a Regard to the Honour and Dignity of Parliament; for which Reason I shall beg leave to add to the Amendment proposed, these Words, *and such as shall be consistent with the Honour and Justice of Parliament.*—This was approved of by Sir J——n B——rd and Mr S—ys; then

Mr C——r of the E——r said,—I now rise up. Sir, to do what is not usual for me to do; I rise up to second a Motion made by my worthy Friend who spoke last. I was really of Opinion, that his Majesty's Speech was in such Terms, that no Exception could have been taken to any one Word of it; and the Motion for an Address of Thanks was so short, and so agreeable to it, that I could not imagine any Objection could have been made. His Majesty recommends the avoiding of *unreasonable Heats and Animosities,* and, in Answer, the Hon. Gentleman who moved for the Address, proposed, that we should say that we would avoid all *unreasonable Heats* and *Animosities.* In my Opinion, there cannot be a more proper Return to that Part of the Speech: his Majesty surely did not thereby intend to preclude any Man from offering his Sentiments freely on whatever may be proposed. If any thing be proposed inconsistent with the Publick Good, no Opposition thereto can be called an *unreasonable Heat* or *Animosity;* nor is such an Opposition any way comprehended in the Words made use of by his Majesty.—As for the Amendment proposed to the other Part of the Motion, it really seems liable to the same Objection; 'tis not to be presumed that we will do any thing that is inconsistent with the Honour and Justice of Parliament; if any such thing should be proposed, it would without doubt be rejected with Scorn. And as for the Trade of the Nation, I do not know what the Gentlemen mean thereby; but as to what I mean by the Trade of the Nation, I hope nothing will ever be brought into this House that is or can be Detrimental thereto; if there should it would most certainly be rejected. I know of nothing to be brought in, that can any way injure the Trade of the Nation; but if any thing can be proposed for the Improvement thereof, I shall very readily agree to it, and so I hope will every Gentleman in this House.—I agree with the Hon. Gentleman who spoke last, that the Complaints of the People are not to be neglected, when they are sincere and true; if the People are hampered in their Trade, or in any other way hurt, they must feel it, before they begin to complain; in such Case, 'tis our Duty not only to hear their Complaints, but to find out a Remedy, if possible: But they may be taught to complain before they feel any Uneasiness. However, let their Complaints be real or imaginary, well or ill founded, it does not signify to the present Question. If the Gentle-

men think it necessary to add the Words proposed, the adding or not adding of them is to me a Matter of absolute Indifference.

W——r Pl——r, Esq;] I do not know, Sir, whether or no the People may be taught to complain when they feel no Hurt; but I am sure, if they are taught not to complain, they will at last feel the Hurt most severely; and then perhaps their Complaints may signify nothing, they will be contemned even by those who have done them the greatest Injuries.

Sir J——n B——d.] Sir, If the Hon. Gentleman on the Floor thinks our Trade can be hurt by what the People seem to be afraid of, he must think that he understands Trade better than all the Traders in England; or must mean by the Trade of the Nation something different from what is thereby meant by all those that are concerned therein. I thought, Sir, I had given a sufficient Reason for adding the Words I proposed; but since it has been insinuated that they are liable to the same Objection the Words first taken Notice of by me, are liable to, I must explain myself a little further. It is certainly to be presumed, that this House will never agree to any thing that is destructive to the Liberties, or derrimental to the Trade of the Nation; I am sure, if ever we do, we shall do what's inconsistent with the Honour and Justice of Parliament. This, Sir, is certainly not to be presumed; yet we find there are very general Apprehensions, that some such thing is intended; and for this Reason I moved for the Amendment; but there are no Fears, of our falling into *unreasonable Heats and Animosities;* his Majesty, I hope, never had any such Jealousy, I am sure the Body of the People apprehend no such Misfortune; therefore, there is no Reason for such Words in our Address.

The Question was then put, and the Amendments proposed were agreed to without any Division. After which,

Sir T——s A——n.] Sir, I can't in any Address to be presented to his Majesty, approve of saying what I don't believe to be true. It is proposed that we should congratulate his Majesty upon the *Situation of our Affairs both abroad and at home.* This I can't agree to, because I do not really think them in the best Situation. Are not the *French* still going on in fortifying the Harbour of *Dunkirk,* contrary to the Faith of the most Solemn Treaties? We can't now say, that the *French* are our *good Allies;* and by their Behaviour in this Particular we may see that we can't much depend on any of the Treaties subsisting between us and them; this very Affair we may perhaps in a little time hear made use of as an Argument for our keeping up a numerous Standing Army in time of Peace; and can we express a Satisfaction at the *present Situation of our Affairs,* as long as there is any such Argument left?—Besides, have our Merchants yet had any Redress for those Depredations committed upon them by the *Spaniards?* Is not that Affair still put off, notwithstand-

ing

ing the moſt explicite Engagement entered into by the famous Treaty of *Seville*; that Treaty! which we have heard ſo much applauded, and by which we entered into Engagements of the greateſt Conſequence. On our part it has been moſt punctually performed, and yet our Merchants are ſtill waiting for that Reparation which in Juſtice is due to them, which by the moſt ſolemn Engagements has been ſtipulated for them, and which was, the only Stipulation in our Favour contained in that Treaty. Shall we then ſay, that we are *ſatisfied* with the *preſent Situation* of our Affairs, while the Cries and Complaints of our injured and unredreſſed Countrymen are daily meeting us in every Corner of the Streets?—Again, as to our Home Affairs, is not our Trade daily decaying? even our ſtaple Manufacture is almoſt quite undone. There is ſcarcely any ſort of Trade in a thriving Condition, but that in *Change-Alley*, and there, ſuch abominable Frauds are daily practiſed, that many honeſt well-meaning Men have thereby been totally ruined and undone. Does not almoſt every Seſſion open to us ſome new Scene of Villany? Theſe Calamities are almoſt univerſal; they do not fall upon ſingle Perſons, or upon a few, but upon Multitudes at a time; and may be owing in a great Meaſure to ſome of thoſe Perſons who have in their Hands the Management of publick Affairs: While ſuch fraudulent Practices are ſuffered, and our Trade thereby ſo much injured, can we approach the Throne, and ſay in ſuch a ſolemn manner, that we are *ſatisfied with the Situation of our Affairs*? For my part, I am not; and therefore move that theſe Words, ſhould be left out, or ſome way altered.

Upon this the Rt Hon. Mr S——r acquainted him, that by the Orders of the Houſe, and the conſtant Forms of Proceedings, the making of an Amendment to any Part of a Motion, was an Approbation of every preceding Part of that Motion; and as that Part of the Motion which he propoſed to amend, preceded that which the Houſe had agreed to amend, therefore they could not now receive his Motion.

This laſt Motion being thus dropt, the Queſtion was put upon the Motion made by Mr B——ly as amended by Sir J——n B——rd and Mr Sh——n, and was carried without any Diviſion; whereupon the Preceding Addreſs was drawn up and preſented as above.

DEBATE, Jan. 31. *On bringing in the Penſion Bill.*

S——l S——y, Eſq;] Sir, I take the Opportunity of the preſent leiſure from other Buſineſs to Mention a Bill that for two or three ſucceſſive Seſſions has paſſed this Houſe and been as often thrown out in the other. What their Reaſons (ſee p. 134.) were, I ſhall not pretend to gueſs; but I think it never met with any real Oppoſition in this Houſe. And as I am convinced it is a good Bill, and ab-

ſolutely neceſſary for preſerving our Conſtitution, I hope it will force its Way at length thro' all Oppoſition. The Bill I mean is for making more effectual the Laws in being, for diſabling Perſons from being choſen Members of, or ſitting or voting in this Houſe, who have any Penſion during Pleaſure, or for any Number of Years, or any Office held in Truſt for them. This is the Bill which I have here ready to offer to the Houſe, and which is the very ſame, Word for Word, with that which in the very laſt Seſſion had the Approbation of this Houſe; I therefore think it quite unneceſſary to move the Houſe for Leave to bring in ſuch a Bill; but my Motion ſhall be, for Leave to bring up the the Bill which I have now in my Hand.

T——t W——n——n, Eſq;] Sir, As to the Bill mentioned by the Hon. Gentleman I have nothing to ſay againſt it; and I don't know but that the Bill the Hon. Gentleman has prepared, may be the very ſame with that which had the Approbation of this Houſe laſt Seſſion; I believe 'tis the ſame; but the conſtant Practice of this Houſe has been, at leaſt for 100 Years paſt, that no Bill ſhall be brought in till Leave be firſt asked and granted, and I can ſee no Reaſon why it ſhould be altered in the preſent Caſe. It is indeed my Opinion, that in no Caſe it ought to be altered; for if we ſhould again fall into the ancient Method, and allow every Member to preſent whatever he pleaſed, the Houſe might be ſurprized into things which might be very improper, and perhaps altogether inconſiſtent with the Honour and Dignity of this Houſe. For this Reaſon, Sir, I think the Motion ought not to be complied with; and therefore I move for the Order of the Day.

Sir E——d S——h.] Sir, Since the Hon. Gentleman has aſſured us the Bill now in his Hand, is the very ſame with that which in laſt Seſſion had the Approbation of this Houſe, I muſt be of Opinion, that there is nothing extraordinary in the Motion he has made. We are told, that it has been the conſtant Practice of this Houſe for many Years, that no Bill ſhall be brought in without having firſt obtained the Leave of the Houſe for ſo doing; Why, this is the very thing the Gentleman has moved for: He has moved for Leave to bring up a Bill which he tells you is the very ſame with that you have already ſo often approved of; There can be nothing Irregular in ſuch a Motion; and therefore, Sir, I ſecond it.

Sir W——m Y——ge.] I do not wonder, Sir, to ſee the Gentleman who made the firſt Motion, perſevere in the ſame thing; but I muſt confeſs I am a little ſurprized to hear ſeveral State Topicks every Year renewed and inſiſted on, notwithſtanding their having been ſo often diſapproved of by a Majority of the Houſe. I am really quite tired with hearing the ſame Arguments repeated over and over again every Seſſion. The Hon. Gent. ſhould not have ſaid the Bill he mentions

:ioned had always paſſed even in this Houſe without Oppoſition ; ſome Gentlemen appeared againſt it, and teſtified their Diſlike to it. But let the Bill be a good thing, or a bad thing, the Manner in which the Gentleman deſires to have it introduced, is very extraordinary. 'Tis indeed a Privilege of the Members of the other Houſe, that any Lord may offer a Petition or Bill to the Houſe without asking Leave ; but this Privilege the Members of this Houſe have, for the ſake of Decency and Order, given up long ago ; and I can ſee no manner of Reaſon for our reaſſuming it, or for our beginning now to extend our Privileges beyond what they have been for ſo many Years paſt. As to the bringing of Bills into this Houſe, the uſual Motion is for Leave to bring in ſuch a Bill as is propoſed ; but this is a new ſort of Motion ; 'tis a Motion for Leave to bring up ſuch a Bill ; which I am ſure there is in the preſent Caſe no manner of Occaſion for, and therefore I really think the Motion ought to be rejected, it ought to have a *Negative* put upon it ; but ſince the worthy Gentleman near me has waved that Point, and has moved for the Order of the Day, therefore I ſhall now only ſecond his Motion.

W——y P——y Eſq;] *Sir,* As for the firſt Motion, there is nothing in it but what is warranted by Precedents of late Years, therefore I ſhall be for it. But I can't but take Notice of what the worthy Gentleman who ſpoke laſt was pleaſed to ſay, as to the ſame Arguments being repeated every Seſſion, though the Majority had often determined againſt them. I could never yet think that the Determination of the Majority could alter the Nature of Right and Wrong ; or that ſuch a Determination could make a good Argument a bad one, or a bad Argument a good one. If a Gentleman happens to be of the Minority, he muſt at that time ſubmit to the Determination of the Majority ; but he may ſtill be convinced that he was in the Right : Let the Majority determine as often as they will, I ſhall always be ready to offer thoſe which I take to be good Arguments againſt any thing that I think is wrong, or in Support of what I think is right. The worthy Gentleman ſeems to be much afraid leſt the Members of this Houſe ſhould reaſſume any ancient Privilege, or extend thoſe they at preſent enjoy ; I can ſee no Reaſon for his being ſo mighty cautious in this reſpect ; but what is now propoſed, is really no Re-aſſumption of any old Privilege, nor is it an Extenſion of any Privilege we now enjoy ; it is only neglecting a Piece of Form upon an Extraordinary Occaſion, when there appears to be no manner of Uſe in obſerving it.

Sir J——n R——t] *Sir,* I wonder to hear it Inſiſted on, that the Motion firſt made is ſo unprecedented ; I remember a Bill preſented in the ſame, or rather more extraordinary manner, and that was, the laſt Suſpenſion of the *Habeas Corpus* Act ; many now in the

Houſe may remember that the Gentleman who brought in that Bill, ſtood cloſe at the Bar of the Houſe, when, after informing the Houſe of the Danger that the Crown and the Kingdom were in from the rebellious Plots then carrying on, and that it was at that Juncture abſolutely neceſſary to empower his Majeſty to ſecure the Perſons of thoſe whom he ſuſpected to be plotting againſt our Eſtabliſhment, he then informed the Houſe, that he had prepared a Bill for that Purpoſe, and therefore moved for Leave to bring it up ; which was immediately granted, and the Bill was I believe that very Day twice read, and ordered to be committed : This, *Sir,* was ſomething more extraordinary than what is now moved for, becauſe the Bill then ordered to be brought up, was a Bill that had never been before this Houſe, and conſequently no Member of the Houſe could be any way appriz'd of the Contents thereof ; whereas the Bill now in Queſtion, has frequently had the Approbation of this Houſe.

Mr C——r of the Ex——r.] *Sir,* What the Hon. Gentleman has been pleaſed to move for, is certainly an extraordinary Method of Proceeding, and never followed but on ſome very extraordinary an! preſſing Occaſion. As to the Precedent mentioned, it was one of the moſt extraordinary Occaſions that ever can happen, and in a Caſe that required the utmoſt Diſpatch. I can't think there is any Compariſon between that Caſe and the preſent ; there is in the preſent no Neceſſity for going into any Extraordinary Method. We have Time enough for obſerving the ordinary Methods of Proceeding. The Fate of the Bill does no ways depend on its being brought in this very Day. If the Gentleman ſhould move in the uſual manner for Leave to bring in a Bill, and Orders ſhould be thereupon given by the Houſe to ſome Gentlemen to prepare and bring in the ſame ; can it be ſaid that this Method will occaſion the putting it off for this Seſſion ? Therefore, *Sir,* I hope the Gentlemen will not inſiſt upon this extraordinary Method of having Leave to bring it up immediately.

S——l S——y, Eſq;] *Sir,* I ſhall be very far from making any Compariſons between the Caſe in Hand, or between any Caſe, and that which immediately concerns the Safety and Preſervation of the Crown. But, as I had aſſured you that the Bill in my Hand, was the very ſame with that which had before been approved of by this Houſe, I thought it quite unneceſſary for the Houſe to obſerve that Ceremony of ordering ſome Gentlemen to prepare and bring in a Bill which was already prepar'd. I don't deſire to bring any thing into this Houſe without firſt having the Leave of the Houſe ; yet I can't think, that though the ancient Method of Proceeding were revived, the Houſe would be in any Danger of being ſurprized into any thing : For no Bill can paſs till it has been three times read, and has paſſed through a Committee. It is not the

the Restraint we have laid ourselves under, that prevents the House's being surprized; It is the Necessity of having the Bill so often read before it can pass; for when a Gentleman has moved for Leave to bring in any Bill for the Purposes he mentions, the House can't know whether the Bill prepared and brought in be according to their Orders, till it be once read: Some Gentlemen might move for Leave to bring in a Bill, and upon obtaining such Leave, might bring in a Bill of a quite different Nature; but this would probably be discovered on the first Reading, the Bill would without doubt be thrown out, and whoever endeavoured thus to impose on the House, would probably meet with a most severe Censure. ——But the present Dispute really seems to be between the Words *to bring up,* and the Words *to bring in*; for my part I am quite indifferent in this Affair; whether I have Leave to bring it up now, or to bring it in a little while hence, does not in my Opinion signify much; if I have Leave to bring it up, I must immediately take a Walk to the Bar; if I have Leave to bring in a Bill, and am ordered to prepare one for that purpose, I shall take a Walk the same Way in a very little time; But for the Bill itself, I do think it of such Consequence, that if there were any Method by which we could shew a more than ordinary Regard to the Bill, that ought certainly to be observed.

The Rt Hon. Mr S——r then read from the Journal of the House of the 9th Year of his late Majesty's Reign, the Precedent mentioned by Sir J---n R----t, and said, Gentlemen, the usual Method of proceeding in this House, as to the bringing in of Bills, Is, first to move for Leave to bring in a Bill for such or such Purposes, and that being agreed to, the House then orders some of their own Number to prepare and bring in the Bill; this is the usual Method, but in the Precedent I have now read to you it appears the then Solicitor General moved for Leave to bring up such a Bill, which was granted, and he immediately brought up the Bill, and the same was read a first time; from which it is plain that Mr Solicitor, when he made his Motion, informed the House, that he had prepared such a Bill, and had it then ready to be laid before them, and therefore he moved for Leave to bring it up, which it seems the House at that time complied with.

Upon this some Members suspecting that he was, in Pursuance of this Precedent, going to put the Question on the Motion made by Mr S——s, they called out No, no. *Whereupon, he said,* Gentlemen, as to the Affair in hand, or any Affair that comes before this House, I am not to appear of one side of the Question nor of the other. It is my Business to take Care that the Orders and Methods of Proceeding be regularly observed. In all Questions about Order I am to inform you, of what has been formerly done in the

like Cases, and to take Care that all Decency and Order be observed both in our Debates and Proceedings: In all Cases I am to observe those Directions the House shall be pleased to give, and in the present Case I only desire to know from you, what Method you will observe, whether you are inclined to follow the Precedent now read to you, or if you are inclined to proceed according to the Method usually observed: But I must put you in mind, that if you proceed according to the usual Method, Decency requires that the Bill should not be brought in immediately after the Order for preparing and bringing in the same; it is necessary that some Time should intervene between the Order for preparing it, and the presenting of it to the House; and therefore I must desire that those Gentlemen who shall be ordered to prepare and bring it in, may not go immediately to the Bar, and tell us, that they have according to Order, prepared such a Bill, and are ready to bring it in.

Sir W——m pr.---m.] Sir, I am surprized to hear any Fault found with Gentlemen insisting upon their Opinions, notwithstanding their having been disapproved of by a Majority in former Sessions. I do not think Sir, that the Majority's being of a contrary Opinion can ever be made use of as an Argument for convincing Men that they are in the wrong: Minorities, notwithstanding their being out-voted, may still have as good an Opinion of their Opinions, as the Majority of theirs. It has often happened, that what has been disapproved of by the Majority in one Session, has been approved of by a Majority perhaps in the very next Session; and as to the Bill now in hand, it has been two or three times approved of by the Majority of this House, and as often rejected or disapproved of by the Majority of the other House; what their Reasons were I do not know, but I am of Opinion, that the same Reasons against the Bill were not offered to the Members of this House, that were offered to the Members of the other; for if they had, it would probably have been disapproved of, and rejected by the Majority even of this House. From hence it appears that the Majority's being of any one Opinion is no infallible Sign of that Opinion's being right. This I thought myself obliged to take notice of, that those Gentlemen who happen to be generally of the same Opinion with the Majority, may not from thence conclude that they are certainly right. As to the Matter now in Dispute, I really think it is of no Moment: Whether the Gentleman shall have Leave to bring up the Bill, or to bring in a Bill, is to me a Matter of so much Indifference, that I can't find out a Reason why the Gentleman's Motion should have been opposed; for to order a Gentleman to prepare a Bill, after he has told us that he has prepared one, and that 'tis the very same with what the Majority of this House has in former

mer Sessions approved of, really seems to me to be a little incongruous: I can find out no Reason for Gentlemen's insisting on this Piece of Incongruity, unless it be that they have a Dislike to the Bill itself. We certainly **A** ought in general to observe the usual Method of Proceedings; but surely, we ought not to observe any customary Method, when the observing it appears to be in itself absurd.——

Mr S——s at last not insisting on his Motion, but agreeing to have the Bill brought in according to the usual Method, the Question was put for Leave to bring in the Bill, **B** which was agreed to without any Opposition; and Mr *Sandys* and Sir *Edm. St.Auley* were ordered to prepare and bring in the same. Then the House resolved itself into a Committee of the Supply; and as soon as that was over, Mr *Sandys* presented the said Bill to the House, which was received and read the first time, and ordered to be read a **C** second time.

Debate Feb. 2. *On the* Army.

In a Committee to consider further of the Supply granted to his Majesty (the Secretary of War being ill,)

T——d A——s, Esq; Dep. P——M——r, moved **D** *that the Number of Forces for the Year* 1733 *be* 17709 *effective Men, Officers included*; (See Vol. II. p. 882) and was seconded by

Fr——t Wh——th, Esq; Surveyor of his Majesty's Works.

Ld M——th, in Opposition thereto, moved, *that the Number be only* 12,000 *Men.*

E——d H——ly Esq; seconded his Motion, and a warm Debate ensued, which turning **E** chiefly on the same Topics, as in the preceding Session, we shall not enlarge on the Particulars, but refer to Vol. II. No. XX. for Aug. 1732. p. 882, 3, 4, 5, 6.

The Speakers for the first Motion were the first 11 in the List for the Army (See p. 353) and the Speakers for the second, were the first 15 in the opposite List. **F**

The chief Arguments for the first Motion, were, That though the publick Tranquillity was now established, yet the Preservation thereof depended on so many Accidents, that it could not be certainly relied on, therefore we ought always to be in such Circumstances as to be able not only to defend ourselves, but likewise to fulfill all our Engagements to **G** our Allies: That there was still a very powerful Party in the Kingdom, firmly attached to the Pretender, and daily watching an Opportunity to disturb the Quiet of the Nation, by endeavouring to overturn the present happy Establishment; and therefore it was necessary to keep up an Armed Force sufficient to dissipate any sudden Insurrection that might be raised by such Men: That this **H** Party was still more audacious and more to be dreaded, because they were spirited up by a great many seditious Libels, daily spread

abroad even by those who pretended to be Friends to the Protestant Succession, and to the Illustrious Family now on the Throne.

Sir A——r C——ft said, ' That the continuing of the same Number of Forces was the ' more necessary, because to his Knowledge ' Popery was increasing very fast in the Country, for that in one Parish which he knew, 'there were no less than seven Popish ' Priests; and that the Danger from the Pretender was the more to be feared, because ' they did not know but that he was then ' breeding his Son a Protestant.'.

Mr C——r of the E——r took Notice ' That ' a Reduction of the Army was the chief ' thing wished for and desired by all *Jacobites* ' in the Kingdom; that no Reduction had ' ever been made, but what gave fresh Hopes ' to that Party, and encouraged them to raise ' Tumults against the Government; and he ' did not doubt, but that if they should resolve ' to reduce any Part of the Army, there ' would be Post-Horses employ'd that very ' Night to carry the good News thereof to the ' Pretender and his Adherents beyond Seas.'

H——e W——le said, ' That the Number of ' Troops then proposed was absolutely necessary to support his Majesty's Government, ' and would be necessary as long as the Nation enjoyed the Happiness of having the ' present Illustrious Family on the Throne.

The chief Arguments made use of against the first Motion, and for the second, were, That if they gave any Credit to his Majesty's Speech at the Opening the Session, which they were in Duty bound to do, the Tranquillity of *Europe* never was, nor ever could be on a more firm Basis than at present, therefore a Reduction was now to be made in the Army, or never to be expected. As to the Pretender, they did not believe that there was any considerable Party for him in this Nation: That Pretence had always been a Ministerial Device made use of only for accomplishing their own Ends; but in reality a meer Bugbear, for that his Majesty reigned in the Affections of his People; upon that his Majesty's Security depended, and if it did not depend on that, the Illustrious Family now on the Throne could have but little Security in the present Number, or in any Number of Standing Forces, that could be kept up for its Defence: That if there was any Discontent in the Nation, it was owing to the keeping up such a numerous Standing Army in Time of Peace, whereby the People were subjected to many Hardships which they were never before acquainted with: That the People of *England* had never gone into any violent Measures, against the Prince or the Throne, but when the Prince or those employ'd by him were first in the Fault: That this Maxim was so generally true, that in our whole History there was no Instance to the contrary, but only that which happened in the Reign of King *Charles* I. therefore, if there was any Uneasiness among the People, the

proper

proper Remedy was, to remove those things which were the Causes thereof: If the Ministers should change their Measures, the People would certainly alter their Minds. That the *Dutch* were by the Situation of their Country in a much more dangerous State than we are or can be in, yet had then resolved on a Reduction of their Army; therefore they thought we could have no Pretence for continuing ours.

Sir W----m W----m said, ' That though the general Arguments in the Affair before them, had often been canvassed in that House, yet, *says he,* the Debate of this Day seems to me something new: In former Years the Gentlemen who argued for a Standing Army in Time of Peace, always argued for its Continuance only for one Year longer; but Gentlemen have now thrown off the Mask, and are daring enough to declare, that the same Number of Forces must always be kept up; And made as it were a Part of our Constitution. We have already continued the Army so long, that some Gentlemen have told us to day what no Man would have ventured to have told us a few Years ago, and if we continue it but a little longer, it may be in the Power of some Gentlemen to talk to this House in Terms no way agreeable to the Constitution or the Liberties of our Country. To tell us, *Sir,* that the same Number of Forces must be always kept up, is a Proposition full fraught with innumerable Evils, more particularly this, that it may make wicked Ministers more audacious in propagating Schemes inconsistent with the Liberties, destructive to the Trade, and burthensome on the People of this Nation. In Countries governed by Standing Armies, the Inclinations of the People are but little minded, the Ministers place their Security in the Army, the Humours of the Army they only consult, with them they divide the Spoils, and the People are plundered by both. ' In this Country, his Majesty has the Hearts, Hands and Purses of all his Subjects at his Service, and may he have them always, but I hope they will never be in his Power. His Majesty desires no such thing; he never can desire it; he depends only on the Affections of his People; and therefore, Sir, I am convinced that the Demand of so numerous a Standing Army, never could come from him: It is no way necessary for his Support, whatever it may be for theirs who now desire to have it continued.'

Mr R----*le,* among other things, said, ' To him it appeared that in order to preserve ourselves against one who might perhaps prove a Tyrant, we were going to establish 18,000 Tyrants, and to make their Establishment in some measure a Part of our Constitution: That in order to be free of a Religion which we think a bad one, we are resolved to have none at all: As to the Party for the Pretender, he could not believe, there was any such thing: It was nothing but a mere Pretence, and the making use of it on all Occasions,

could not but make him call to Mind, that wicked and blasphemous Saying of Pope *Leo X.* who on a Procession's passing by while he was at an elegant Entertainment, said to his Cardinals, *Quantum profuit nobis hæc fabula Christi!* ' He concluded with these Words: ' Let us do as our Forefathers used to do; *Let us remove the Wicked from before the King, that so his Throne may be established in Righteousness.*

Mr P----y, among a great many other smart things, said, He could not but be diverted with some Arguments then, and on former Occasions made use of for keeping up a Standing Army. Last Year, *says he,* we were told that a Popish Solicitor was a dangerous Man to the Government, (See Vol. II. p. 885 B) and now a Popish Solicitor has spawned out Seven Popish Priests, and even the Post-Horses I find have joined in this traiterous Confederacy.

As to the Argument drawn from the Reduction of the Dutch Forces, it was replied, That the Reduction mentioned was not then agreed to by the States-General: It was a great Question, whether it would or no, and if it should, it was only a Reduction of the last Augmentation; whereas the last Augmentation had been reduced by us long ago: So that the Dutch were now only a going to make that Reduction, which we had made upon the first Prospect we had of seeing the Tranquillity of Europe established; and though the Reduction proposed in Holland should be made by them, yet they would still have a much greater Number of Standing Forces, in Proportion, than what was proposed to be kept up in this Kingdom.

Mr C----r of the E----r,] I cannot but take Notice of an Observation made, as to the People's never carrying their Resentment to any Pitch against the Prince upon the Throne, unless the Prince or those employed by him were first Guilty of some Fault. The Gentleman was pleased to admit of one Exception to this Rule, and that was in the Case of K. *Charles* I. But he ought to have admitted of another Exception, in the time of the King the very last upon the Throne; I do not know what Pitch of Resentment the Gentleman may mean, but I am sure there were some People who carried their Resentment against that King to a very high Pitch, and it cannot be said that he was ever guilty of any Fault, or that those employed by him had then at least been guilty of any; yet some People carried their Resentment so high, that they appeared in Arms to dethrone him; thank God they did not succeed; they happened luckily to be defeated by the small Number of Regular Forces we had then in the Kingdom, which were much inferior to them in Number. Such, Sir, was our great good Luck at that time; but I must say, those Gentlemen who desire to have the Country left as void of Defence as it was then, can have but little Regard for our present happy Constitution, or the Security of the Illustrious Family now on the Throne.

At last the Question was put on the Motion made by T----d A----a Esq; and it was agreed to, 239 to 171.

Di-

DEBATE, Feb. 5. On the ARMY,

In which the other Gentlemen in the Liſts refer'd
to p. 353. ſpoke in their Turns.

W—n W—ms W—e Eſq; On the Report
of the Reſolution of the Committee, to the A
Houſe, moved for *recommitting that Reſolution.*

W—m B—y Eſq; ſeconded the ſaid Motion, and, a Debate enſued, in which the Arguments were near the ſame as before given.

Mr C—ch indeed added That he wonder'd
to ſee Gentlemen ſo jealous of Incroachments
upon our Conſtitution at a time when it was
in its greateſt Vigour, and ſhone forth in its B
pureſt Luſtre.

Mr W—m, in anſwer, gave a ſuccinct, hiſtorical Account of our Conſtitution, the ſeveral Dangers it had been in, and Changes it
had gone through; and from thence ſhewed
that it was very far from being now in its
greateſt Vigour, but that on the contrary,
many bad Cuſtoms had crept in of late, of
dangerous Conſequence to our Conſtitution, C
and might prove to be the Cauſe of its Overthrow, if ſome effectual Remedy was not
ſpeedily applied.

At laſt the Queſtion was put for recommitting the Reſolution, but was carried in
the Negative, 207 to 143; after which the D
ſaid Reſolution, and the other Reſolution the
Committee had come to, (See p. 353.) were
agreed to by the Houſe, without any Amendment or Diviſion.

Then L..d M....th repreſented the bad
Circumſtances of the Nation by reaſon of
the great Debts, and the many Taxes the People groaned under, and therefore concluded E
with a Motion, *That an humble Addreſs be*
preſented humbly to deſire his Majeſty, to take
the firſt favourable Opportunity of making a Re-
duction of the Forces agreed to, &c. (See p. 353.)

This Motion was ſeconded by S....l S....s
Eſq; and the other chief Speakers in favour
of it were, Sir W...m W...m, W....m
P....y Eſq; W....m S....m, Eſq; and F
G....ge H?...te, Eſq;. The Arguments made
uſe of in general were, *The great Neceſſity for*
taking all Opportunities to reduce the publick Ex-
pence; that thereby ſome of thoſe Taxes might
be taken off, which at preſent lay ſo heavy on our
Trade and our Manufactures, that moſt of our
Neighbours were enabled to underſell us in foreign
Markets: That the keeping up of a ſtanding
Army in time of Peace, without abſolute Neceſ- G
ſity was altogether inconſiſtent with the Liber-
ties of this Nation: That though there might
be at preſent a Neceſſity for the Forces agreed to
yet that Neceſſity might ceaſe in a few Months;
and it would then become neceſſary both for the
Eaſe of the Nation, and for the Preſervation of
the Conſtitution, to disband ſome of them: That
though the King was always to be preſumed
thoroughly acquainted with the Circumſtances of H
the Nation, and inclined to contribute to the pub-
lick Welfare, yet it had ever been the Cuſtom of
that Houſe, and was their Duty to addreſs the
King upon Matters of great Conſequence; in or-

der to recommend to his Majeſty thoſe Meaſures
which they thought would conduce moſt to the
Happineſs and Safety of the Nation.

The Speakers againſt this Motion, were
Mr. S—r G—l, Ld H—y, H—y P—m,
Eſq; and Mr C—r of the E—r. Their Arguments in general were, *That the preſenting ſuch*
an Addreſs was in ſome Meaſure inconſiſtent with
the Reſolution they had juſt agreed to: It was
reſolving that the Forces for the Year 1733 ſhould
be ſo many; and addreſſing that they ſhould not
be ſo many; that theſe two Reſolutions following
one another upon their Journals would appear to
be very extraordinary: That beſides, the preſent-
ing of ſuch Addreſs would be diſreſpectful to his
Majeſty, as it would be a ſort of Inſinuation
that his Majeſty might neglect the firſt Op-
portunity of reducing the Army; and thereby leſ-
ſening the publick Charge; and as they never yet
had the leaſt Occaſion, it would be now unjuſt to
harbour any ſuch Suſpicion: That in many Caſes
it might be the Cuſtom, and the Duty of that
Houſe, to addreſs the Throne on particular E-
mergencies, but in a Caſe that regarded his Ma-
jeſty and his Adminiſtration in ſuch a general
Manner, as the Caſe in hand did, it would in
moſt diſreſpectful; they might as well addreſs his
Majeſty to govern according to Law, or not to
incroach upon the Conſtitution; and an Addreſs
in ſuch Terms would, they believed, be allowed
to be ſhewing a very high Diſreſpect to the King
upon the Throne.

Mr S—n having inſiſted a good deal on his
Majeſty's knowing how much the Nation was load-
ed with Debts and Taxes and how inconſiſtent
it was with our Conſtitution, to keep up a Stand-
ing Army in Time of Peace, and therefore his
Majeſty, he was ſure, would not look on their pre-
ſenting of ſuch an Addreſs as any way diſreſpect-
ful to him; and ſome of his Expreſſions on this
Subject having been taken notice of, and pretty
much animadverted on by the Gentlemen of the
other ſide, he Reply'd, That he could not but
look on himſelf as a very unfortunate Member in the late Reign he had incurred the
Diſpleaſure of many Gentlemen, and undergone a ſevere Cenſure of that Houſe, for ſaying it was one of the greateſt Misfortunes of his late
Majeſty's Reign, that he did not know our Lan-
gnage, and was unacquainted with our Conſti-
tion; and now, ſays he, I find I have diſobliged ſeveral Gentlemen by ſaying that his
preſent Majeſty well knows the Circumſtances of
the Nation, and is acquainted with our Conſtitution. But let them take it as they will, I
muſt think that his Majeſty is thoroughly acquainted with both, and therefore will look
upon ſuch an Addreſs as proceeding from that
honeſt Concern we ought to have for thoſe
who ſend us hither, and not as proceeding from
any Diſreſpect towards him; and thoſe we
repreſent muſt be highly pleaſed to ſee us ſo
watchful of all Opportunities to leſſen their
Charge.

At laſt the *Queſtion was put, and the Houſe*
come to a Diviſion, but it was carried in the
Negative 203 *to* 136.

DEBATE

DEBATE, *February* 7.

This was on a Motion to raiſe the Supply *without creating any New Debt, on any Fund whatſoever,* which paſs'd in the Negative. The Deſign of the Motion with the Arguments thereon will be taken Notice of in another Place, where we muſt mention the Affair again.

DEBATE, *Feb.* 13. On the *Spaniſh* Depredations.

Sir W——d L.——a begun to this Effect. *Sir,* The many and great Loſſes our Merchants have ſuſtained by the Depredations committed on them by the *Spaniards,* are well known to every Gentleman in this Houſe ; and likewiſe that by the 2d Separate Article of the Treaty of *Seville* all thoſe Affairs were to be adjuſted in the Space of 3 Years. As the Time is now expired, I hope, our Merchants have already got, or are ſoon to receive a ſufficient Reparation for all their Sufferings : This is an Affair on which the Happineſs of many private Men depends, and is of ſo much Conſequence both to the Honour and Trade of this Nation, that it is incumbent upon us, as Members of this Houſe, to enquire into it ; and therefore, I *move, That an humble Addreſs be preſented to his Majeſty, that he will be graciouſly pleaſed to give Directions, that there may be laid before this Houſe, Copies of the Reports made by his Majeſty's Commiſſaries in Spain, together with all Letters and Papers relating thereto ; and what Satisfaction has been made to the Subjects of Great Britain for the Loſſes they ſuſtained by the Depredations of the* Spaniards *in Europe, or in the Indies, purſuant to the 2d Separate Article of the Treaty of Peace, Union, Friendſhip, and mutual Defence between the Crowns of* Great Britain, France, *and* Spain, *concluded at Seville on the 9th of November,* 1729.

This Motion for an Addreſs being ſeconded, Mr C——r of the E——r ſaid, Sir, ſuch an Addreſs may, if Gentlemen inſiſt on it, be preſented to his Majeſty, but I can now aſſure you, there is as yet nothing that his Majeſty can lay before you ; for tho' by the Treaty of *Seville* the Commiſſaries of the two Nations were to ſettle all the Affairs referred to them by that Treaty, within the Space of 3 Years from the date thereof ; yet by reaſon of ſeveral unforeſeen Accidents, they never could meet ſo as ſo enter upon Buſineſs, till *Feb.* laſt. Since that time they have been proceeding upon the Affairs referred to them, but as yet nothing is brought to that Maturity, as to be proper to be laid before this Houſe. The Delays they met with, made it neceſſary to prolong the Time for ſettling thoſe Matters, and therefore it has been agreed between the two Nations, that

the 3 Years ſhall be computed from *Feb.* laſt, and by that time it is to be hoped all thoſe Affairs will be ſettled in ſuch manner, as will give full Satisfaction to every Member of this Houſe, and full Reparation to every one of the Subjects of *Gr. Britain,* who has met with a real Injury from the *Spaniards.*

W——m P——y Eſq;] There is a Term made uſe of in the Exchequer called *Nichil,* which has been ſome times uſed by the Gentleman who ſpoke laſt, and has often been given as an Anſwer to this Houſe, when Accounts of the Produce of ſome certain Branches of the Revenue have been called for. Now as to the preſent Affair, it may be there has not yet been any thing done, or at leaſt not brought to Maturity, to be proper to be laid before this Houſe : This may be the Caſe, tho' it is a little ſurprizing that in ſo long a time there ſhould have been nothing done ; however, ſuppoſing that it is the Caſe, then his Majeſty may give us this Exchequer Term for Anſwer ; he may tell us there has not been any thing done : It is from his Majeſty only, that this Houſe can properly have an Anſwer : Even ſuch an Anſwer we are not to take from any Subject whatſoever. And as the preſenting of ſuch an Addreſs to his Majeſty will ſhew our Conſtituents that we are careful of the Affairs of the Nation, and have a Concern for the Merchants who have been ſo great Sufferers by the Depredations committed by the *Spaniards ;* therefore, I am for agreeing with the Motion.

Sir T——s A——n,] If in all this time there has been nothing done by thoſe Commiſſaries, I am much afraid this Affair may be ſpun out to a very great Length. I do not know but it may laſt as long as the Gentlemen employed as our Commiſſaries may live ; for as they have thereby a good Salary and all their Charges borne, they may not perhaps be too haſty in concluding the Affairs referred to them ; on the other hand it is to be preſumed, the *Spaniards* will make all the Excuſes they can invent, for delaying their making that Reparation which in Juſtice they ought to do, and which we are engaged in Honour to inſiſt on. It is therefore our Duty, as Members of this Houſe, to deſire from time to time to know what is doing in an Affair in which both the Intereſt and Honour of the Nation is ſo much concerned, in order to prevent all unneceſſary Delays, and to ſatisfy the World that this Nation does not tamely put up ſuch Injuries.

J——n C——t, I ſq;] Sir, I muſt do the Gentlemen employ'd the Juſtice to declare, that to my Knowledge, they very much deſpiſe the Salaries they have from the Publick, and are puſhing as much as poſſible the Accommodation of all the Affairs referred to them, in order that they may return home

to

to look after their private Affairs. I am very ſure there is not one of them who, for the Sake of the Salary, would have gone out of the Kingdom, or ſtay one Month in *Spain*. It was the Hopes only of being ſerviceable to their Country, that prevailed on them to go thither, and they are doing as much as lies in their Power to render their Service as be- **A** neficial as poſſible to their Country ; the ſooner that Affair is brought to a Concluſion, the more beneficial will their Service certainly be. This I know to be the Caſe, but if it were otherwiſe, his Majeſty would certainly take Care that no unneceſſary Delays ſhould **B** be allowed in an Affair of ſuch Conſequence, and will lay before this Houſe an Account of all the Proceedings in that Affair as ſoon as it can be conveniently done ; and therefore I muſt be of Opinion, that there is no Occaſion for our preſenting any ſuch Addreſs.

W---m P---y, Eſq;] *Sir*, We may depend on it, that his Majeſty will take all poſſible Care of this, as well as of every other Affair that regards the Honour or Happineſs of the Nation, but his Majeſty muſt employ others under him, and as they may be dilatory or negligent, therefore it is the Duty, and has always been the Practice of this Houſe, to enquire into the Management of Affairs **D** of great Conſequence. In the preſent Caſe, I am for the Addreſs propoſed, becauſe it will be a Spur to the Miniſters, to procure as ſpeedy and as ample a Satisfaction to our injured Merchants, as they can poſſibly get. Our having taken notice in the laſt Seſſion of the *Spaniſh* Depredations, procured, I believe, thoſe Inſtructions ſent laſt Summer to **E** his Majeſty's Ships of War in the *Weſt Indies*, and was the chief Cauſe of ſending ſome of our Ships to the *Spaniſh* Coaſt to demand Satisfaction. One of the Captains did in purſuance of theſe Inſtructions ſend his Boat with his Lieutenant on ſhore to demand Satisfaction ; but the *Spaniards* were ſo far **F** from complying with ſo juſt a Demand, that they made the Lieutenant and the Men Priſoners ; whereupon he, like a brave *Engliſh* Captain, ſeized the firſt *Spaniſh* Ship he could meet with : But I have been ſince informed that this *Spaniſh* Ship has been reſtored, tho' the *Engliſh* Ship has not, nor the **G** Owners of it received any Satisfaction. How we came to reſtore this Ship, before they had agreed to releaſe our Ship, is more than I can comprehend ; for as they had done the firſt Injury, they ought to have been obliged to have made the firſt Reparation. As to the Gentlemen employed as our Commiſſaries, I don't know whether they deſpiſe their Salaries or no, but I am ſure if they continue as long in *Spain* as one Gentleman ſeems apprehenſive they may, it will verify what I ſaid in this Houſe in relation to thoſe Af-

Vol. III. No. XXXII.

fairs, that it were better for the Nation, and the Sufferers, to have yielded up the Affair at firſt, and to have given the Money ſuch Commiſſion might coſt the Publick, to be divided among them ; for as it is, I am afraid, if the Charges that Commiſſion has and will ſtand the Publick in, were to be deducted from the Sum we may recover from the *Spaniards* by way of Reparation, very little will remain to be divided among the plunder'd Merchants.

Mr *C---r* of the E---r,] *Sir*, I do not know where the Hon. Gentleman got his Information, in relation to the Reſtitution of the *Spaniſh* Ship, but I can aſſure him it is wrong ; for at the ſame time that Orders were diſpatched for releaſing the *Spaniſh* Ship, Orders were diſpatched from *Spain* for reſtoring the *Engliſh* Ship and Cargo, and her not being reſtored is not owing to any Neglect here, or at the Court of *Spain*, but to the Shifts and Delays made uſe of by his Catholick Majeſty's Governors in the *Weſt-Indies*, who notwithſtanding their having received expreſs Orders for delivering up that Ship and Cargo, had found out ſome new Pretences for delaying the ſame.

W---P---, Eſq;] *Sir*, I cannot but with Pleaſure obſerve, that if a War ſhould happen between *Spain* and us, we muſt certainly get the better of them ; for our Governors and Officers in the *Weſt-Indies* are, it ſeems, moſt punctual and exact in obſerving Orders from hence, even tho' they may be not much to their own private liking ; whereas it appears that his Catholick Majeſty's Governors and Officers in thoſe Parts have but little Regard to the expreſs Orders they receive from him ; he, it ſeems, has no Authority over his own Officers, and conſequently in caſe of a War, we ſhould have a very conſiderable Advantage.

H---o W---k, Eſq; and *C---l B---s* ſpoke alſo againſt addreſſing, but all ſeemed to be pretty indifferent, and the Gentlemen of the other Side inſiſting upon their Motion, therefore it was at laſt agreed to without any Diviſion ; and the Addreſs having been preſented, Mr Comptroller reported, on the 16th, his Majeſty's Anſwer, which was to the very ſame Effect as Mr *C---r* of the E---c had ſaid before. (See *p.* 400. G H)

Proceedings and Debate, Feb. 21. In the Committee on the Sugar Colony Bill, *T---s W---n*, moved for a Reſolution, *That no Sugar, Paneels, Syrops, or Melaſſes, nor any Rum or Spirits, except of the Growth or Manufacture of his Majeſty's Sugar Colonies* **H** *in America, ſhould be imported into* Ireland, *but from Great Britain only.*

W---r C---y, Eſq; oppoſed this Motion, and ſaid in Subſtance, That he would join in any proper Meaſures for encouraging our Sugar Colonies, but he could not agree to the alter-

Ccc

ing the Laws as they then stood with respect to the Importation into *Ireland* : That the allowing of Rum to be imported directly into *Ireland* from any of our Colonies in the *West-Indies*, was with Design to discourage the Consumption of *French* Brandies in that Kingdom ; which Design would be entirely overthrown by that Resolution ; for if it should be made necessary to bring Rum to, and enter it in *England*, before it could be carried to *Ireland*, it would very much enhance the Price of it, by which the Consumption thereof would be diminished, and the Consumption of *French* Brandies consequently increased : That it was unreasonable to lay such a Restriction on the Trade to *Ireland*, because that Kingdom was a Part of our own Dominions, and contributed very considerably to the Riches and Power of *England* : That besides, if a Law should be made in the Terms of the Resolution proposed, it would probably embroil us with some of our Neighbours : the *French* might look on it as a Breach of the Treaty of *Utrecht*, which stipulates, that the Trade between *France* and us should remain on the same footing it was on at that Time ; and the *Portuguese* would certainly look on it as a Breach of the Treaties subsisting between us and them, because by such a Law the Importation of *Portugal* Sugars directly into *Ireland*, would be expresly prohibited.

J—n S—pe, Esq;] As to enhancing the Price of Rum in *Ireland*, and thereby discouraging its Consumption in that Kingdom, no such Consequence could ensue from the Resolution proposed, because there might still be as much Rum as was requisite for the Consumption in that Kingdom imported directly thither from our own Sugar Colonies in *America*; what was proposed by the Resolution moved for, was only to prohibit the direct Importation of any of the Commodities mentioned therein, from any of our other Colonies in *America*, and with good Reason, because it appeared, that what was imported directly into *Ireland* from the other Colonies, was generally the Produce of the Foreign Sugar Colonies in that Part of the World, whereby the Trade of those Colonies was very much encouraged and improved, to the Ruin of our own Sugar Colonies in *America*. Tho' we are to look upon *Ireland* as a Part of our own Dominions, yet we ought not to allow them to encroach upon any Branch of the Trade of *England*, which they are always endeavouring ; and if we did not take care to keep that Country under the Yoke, they might in time grow so rich as to be able to throw it off, which they would perhaps willingly do, if ever it should happen to be in their Power : As to *Portugal*, some Words might be put in, for obviating any Exception that might be taken by them.

Hon. *G—ge D—n*, Esq; said, He was sorry to differ from his Hon. Friend, but he had always looked on Prohibitions in Trade as of dangerous Consequence, and never to be laid on it, unless absolutely necessary : we had no Reason to be jealous of *Ireland* ; that Country had always appeared loyal and zealous for his Majesty, and for the present Royal Family ; they had generally behaved as good Subjects, at least for many Years last past ; and he believed the best way to keep them so, was to give them all proper Encouragement, and to shun as much as possible laying them under any particular Restraints or Disadvantages : That he looked on that Kingdom in a very different Light from what some other Gentlemen seemed to view it in ; the People thereof he always considered as a Part of ourselves, and he hoped they, or at least the most of them, never did, nor ever would look upon themselves as being under any Yoke, but that of the Government and Laws of their Native Country.

H—o W—le, Esq;] As to what was proposed by the Regulation moved for, he did not think there was any thing in it contrary to the Treaties of Peace or Commerce subsisting between us and any of our Neighbours ; it was only a Regulation of Trade within our own Dominions, and had no Relation to the Trade of any of our Foreign Neighbours. If we were to prohibit the Importation of any one of their Commodities into any Part of the *British* Dominions, they might perhaps have Reason to take it amiss ; but what was now proposed, was not a general Prohibition, it was only the appointing of such particular Places within our own Dominions for the Importation of such Commodities, and prohibiting the importing of them at some other Places : As this regarded only our Trade among ourselves, no Foreign Power could take any just Exceptions thereto ; but however, since there was no Design of prohibiting the Importation of *French* Spirits, or *Portugal* Sugars, directly into *Ireland*, therefore he would propose an Amendment, to the Resolution, viz. *That no Sugar, Paneels, Syrups, or Melasses, of the Growth, Product or Manufacture of any of the Colonies or Plantations in* America ; *nor any Rum or Spirits of* America, *except of the Growth or Manufacture of his Majesty's Sugar Colonies there, be imported into* Ireland, *but from* Great Britain *only.*

Which was agreed to without any Division.

T—s W—n, Esq; then moved, *That a Duty of* 4s. *per Hundred Weight, Sterling Money, be laid on all Foreign Sugars and Paneels imported into any of his Majesty's Colonies or Plantations in* America. Which was agreed to without any Opposition.

C—t

C---l M---n B---n, *moved the two following Resolutions, viz.* 1. *That a Duty of* 6 d. *per Gallon, Sterling Money, be laid on all Foreign Melasses and Syrups imported into any of his Majesty's Colonies or Plantations in A-merica.* 2. *That a Duty of* 9 d. *per Gallon, Sterling Money, be laid on all Foreign Rum imported into any of his Majesty's Colonies in America.*

Sir J---n B---d observ'd, That as the Trade stood between our Northern Colonies and the *French* Sugar Islands, it appeared that our Colonies bought Melasses of them at a very low Price, and distilled them into Rum, by which they provided themselves at a small Charge with the Rum that was necessary for them in their Trade with the *Indians*, and in their Fishing Trade. They had, it was true, most of the Materials for making this Rum from the *French*, but the Manufacture was all their own, and thereby a great many of our Subjects in that Part of the World were employed and maintained: That such a high Duty on *French* Melasses, and the Difficulty of running such a bulky Commodity, would lay them under a Necessity of manufacturing it themselves, so that our Subjects would lose all their Employment, and instead of buying Melasses in their natural Dress from the *French*, they would be obliged to purchase the same manufactured into Rum, whereby the *French* Sugar Islands would take of them at least three times the Money they took formerly. It would be easy to carry that Rum, and sell it in a Smuggling way to our Fishing Vessels at Sea, and even to run it into every one of our Colonies on the Continent of *America*. The Sea-Coast belonging to us in that Part of the World is of such a vast Extent, and hath so many little Harbours and Creeks, the Roads are so little frequented, and the Towns so open, that it would be impossible to prevent the Running of *French* Rum on shoar, or the Conveying it from one Town to another after it is landed. No, not even if we should send thither the whole Army of Excise Officers we have here. The sending of them thither might indeed add a great deal to our Happiness in this Country, but all of them together could be of no Service for such a Purpose in that Country. That as to the Laying a Duty both upon Foreign Rum and Melasses, he would not be altogether against it, but then it ought to be only a small Duty, for the Sake of giving an Advantage to our own Sugar Colonies, not such a high Duty as was in a manner equal to a Prohibition; for that was granting a Monopoly to our Sugar Islands, with respect to a Commodity absolutely necessary for our Northern Colonies both in their Fishing Trade, and in their Trade with the native *Indians*; and as the

French were our Rivals in both those Trades, we were about giving them a certain Advantage as to these Trades, without doing them any Harm as to their Sugar-Trade; for if they sold Sugar and Rum cheaper than our Colonies did, they would have Vent enough for all they could make, they would have a stolen Market for it in the *British* Dominions, and an open Market in all other Parts of the World.

C---l M---n B---n said, That he had often heard our Army of Excise Officers set in a very terrible Light, and represented as of the most dangerous Consequence to the Liberties of the Nation; but now he heard it urged that this whole Army would not be able to reduce our Northern Colonies, and he was sure if they were not, there was no Fear of their being able to reduce this Nation. But without sending any of that Army to *America*, he hoped there would be no such things as Smugling in that Part of the World; it was to prevent such a pernicious Practice, that be proposed only laying a Duty on Foreign Rum, not a Prohibition, and the Duty he proposed was no higher than was absolutely necessary for putting our Sugar Islands on an equal Foot with the *French*.

Sir J---n B---d] That he had said that our whole Army of Excisemen would not be able to prevent the Running of *French* Rum in that Country; he did not mention *reducing* the Country; but he believed it would be much easier to reduce the Country, than to prevent the Running of *French* Rum in it, in case what was then proposed should take effect: That if the Gentleman really meant to prevent Running, he was very unfortunate in what he had proposed, for he had proposed the only Method that could be thought on for encouraging the Smuggling Trade, which was that of laying on a high Duty, equal, if not above, the first Price of the Commodity on which it was laid.

There were several other Gentlemen spoke upon this Subject, viz. S---l S---s Esq; A---n P---y, Ld V---t P---l, J---n D---d, G---ge H---te Esq; Captain E---d V---n, J---n C---t Esq; and Sir W---m S---d---n; *some of whom were against the two Resolutions proposed, some for amending them, and some for agreeing. At last the Question was put, and they were severally agreed to without any Division.*

The two following Resolutions were agreed to without any Opposition, viz. 1. *That all the Duties charged on the Importation of all Sugars and Pannels of the Growth, Product and Manufacture of his Majesty's Colonies and Plantations in* America, *into* Great Britain, *be drawn back on Exportation of the same.*

2. *That a Drawback or Allowance of* 2 s. *per Hundred Weight on all Sugars refined in and exported from* Great Britain, *be paid on the Exportation thereof ever and above all Drawbacks or Bounties now payable thereon.*

Sir J---n B---d seconded the last and
said.

said, That these two were the only Resolutions they had come to, which in his Opinion would be of any real Use to our Sugar Colonies and particularly the last he was glad to see moved, because he hoped it would make them think of some other things relating to our Trade, which stood in need of some such Redress. There were several Foreign Materials imported into this Kingdom liable to Duties on Importation, which Duties were drawn back if the Materials were again exported in the same Shape, but if manufactured and made more valuable by the Labour of our own People, neither the Merchant nor the Manufacturer could draw back the Duties, even though they should afterwards export the same; and could shew that this new Manufacture was made of Materials that had paid a Duty on Importation, and would have had a Drawback on Exportation, if they had been carried out rough as they were brought

in: This he said was a scandalous Oversight when these Duties were first imposed, but more scandalous that in so long a time it had never been amended. Several Examples of this could be given, but he would then only mention the Duties on Foreign Hemp, Flax, Cordage, &c. which was drawn back, if the Goods should be exported in the same Condition they were imported, but if these very Goods should by the Labour of our own People, be manufactured into Cables and other Tackle for Shipping, and then exported, the Exporter could not have any Drawback: This, was a great Loss to that Branch of our Trade which was very considerable, but would be much more if it were not for this Hardship.

These Resolutions being reported on the 22d were agreed to by the House, and a Bill was order'd to be brought in pursuant thereto, which passed into a Law. (See p. 256-7.)

[*To be continued.*]

Weekly ESSAYS and DISPUTES in AUGUST, 1733.

Free Briton, Aug. 2. No. 198.

Of Pride in Men of Worth.

THE Investigation of human Nature is not more difficult than greatly useful; however hard it may be to trace the Springs of Action, to mark the characteristical Passions of Men, and to see thro' their various Disguises; whoever undertake it with Deliberation, will in many Respects be wiser from their Enquiry, and receive a real Benefit, especially, if, while they watch the sinister Views, and ridiculous Foibles of others, they are humble enough to search their own Hearts for the same Infirmities.

There is a Weakness, indeed, which sometimes is the Misfortune of Men whose Worth and Understanding we hold at no mean Rate, namely, a Self-Satisfaction, which, when it grows immoderate, renders all Science vain and unprofitable. This Fondness for a Man's self makes his Worth less amiable, his Virtues lose their sociable Appearance, and his Knowledge, or Ability, is treated without Respect, because he shews them to the World, as proud Grandees do the Honour of Birth and Quality, to insult their Inferiors.

Where this overgrown Self-Satisfaction is blended with every bad Quality, we have no Reason to be sorry that the

Man is marked with so forbidding a Characteristick. It would be the Blessing of Society, if all bad Men were unsociable; since the Innocent and well-meaning would never be tempted to put themselves into the Hands of notorious Inhumanity.

But where Men, whose Intentions are good, and whose Hearts are naturally kind, debauch their Understandings thro' insatiable Lust of Applause, it gives ample Occasion for Wonder, Regret, and Ridicule. How many do we daily behold of this Sort, familiar to those who are infinitely raised above them, and stately to those in their own Rank of Life? Others make use of the Privilege of the most indulgent Friendship, only to exercise the most unfriendly and distasteful Authority; where there ought to be the easiest Conversation, they assume the most imperious Dictatorship, where cordial and endearing Kindness claims all possible Tenderness, & mutual Condescension, they assert a proud, unsociable Superiority of Character; others, not satisfied with usurping the Name of Superiority, officiously thrust themselves into a Kind of Management over their Friend and his Affairs; these consider the frankest Temper, the easiest Humour, or the most friendly Disposition only as so many Advantages in Favour of their own assuming and arbitrary Spirit. At the same Time that such Men treat all the World in this magisterial Manner, how do they swell with Resentment, whenever their undoubted Equals treat them with decent Familiarity, or in any Man-

Manner lefs expreffive of Homage and Reverence, than they are pleafed to arrogate to themfelves ? Such a Spirit makes Perfons infupportable to their Friends, and theirFriends grow indifferent to them; it cuts off Men of Senfe from the Enjoyment of their intrinfick good Qualities, and deprives them of the Affection of many,who fly from them as from aPlague.

The Truth is, there cannot be a harder Task than to bear that Behaviour from a Friend, which fubjects a Man to worfe Treatment, than if he were in the Power of an Enemy.

As what has been here faid, is only of that Kind of Pride which corrupts Men of Worth, we have neverthelefs Reafon to wifh them well inSpite of their Foibles, and we cannot wifh them better than that they may fee thefe Failings. Extreme Pride and Infolence are ill Signs of an elevated Mind, often fure Proofs of one that is mean and groveling, always of a Judgment mightily corrupted and milled. Even their Boafts of Affection for their Friends, will be treated as favouring more of Ambition, and Delight to govern, than really to oblige. Such Men might juftly be alarmed, did they confider how much they provoke the Spleen and Refentment of others. Mankind have no Reafon to bear Infolence, efpecially where they ftand on equal Terms, both of Power and Obligation. Such Infolence occafions many fharp Reflections, many invidious Remembrances. The proud Man's Profperity, like the Tyrant's Power, is obnoxious to all Men, becaufe he himfelf is the only Man who enjoys Satisfaction in it; whilft Affability; like, juft Government, collects and cherifhes all Men under its Wings ; So that the meaneft are in good Humour with the greateft,and can bear to behold the moft elevated Grandeur, without repining at that Man's Felicity from whofe Influence all feel fome Degree of Comfort, and none find Caufe of Complaint. DIOGENES.

The **Daily Courant.** Aug. 2.
Expoftulation on the prefent Rejoicings.

WHAT a ridiculous Figure fhall we make in the Eye of Pofterity when they fhall read of the Clamours raifed thro' the Nation on Account of the Bill for altering the Manner of collecting the Duty uponTobacco; and of theHuzza's and Acclamations with which the moft furious Oppofers of that Bill were conducted into their refpective Countries?

They will conclude their Anceftors were certainly mad, becaufe they will find nothing in the Bill which ought to occafion the leaft Joy for the Mifcarriage of it.

No great Credit, indeed, ought to be given to thofe pompous Accounts, which by their Style and Manner look as if they were the Handy-work of Mr *D'Anvers*, and fent down by the Gentlemen themfelves, who were to be the Heroes of the Hiftory, and by them tranfmitted back again to be inferted in the News-Papers.

This will appear the more probable, if one confiders by whom, and on what Occafion thefeSongs of Triumph were made. Indeed had thefe Champions been met only by the Dealers in Tobacco and Wine, the Report might have deferv'd fome Credit; but when, like *Saul* and *David*, they are ufher'd in by their Thoufands and ten Thoufands, it lofes all Probability, and they defeat their own Defigns, by carrying them beyond all Bounds of Prudence, Temper, and Moderation; therefore thefe Accounts muft be utterly falfe; or the People abfolutely infatuated. The former feems rather to be the Cafe. Every Gentleman who has a Seat inParliament, when he retires into the Country, may be congratulated on hisArrival by his Friends and Neighbours, who, if he keeps a good Houfe, and isfree of his Beer, will croud about him, and be taught to fay or do any thing that he fhall direct them, and will hollow out either for, or againft an *Excife*, as is moft fuitable to their Patron's Humour. But this is not the Way to know the Senfe and Difpofition of the People. No Doubt but if the Friends of the Adminiftration had ufed the fame Methods, and took the fame Pains, as their Enemies have done, they might have procured as many Addreffes and Remonftrances in favour of the *Excife Scheme*, as the others have done in Oppofition to it, and met with as gracious a Reception from their Conftituents.

The *Craftfman* would make us believe, there is not a Gentleman in the Intereft of the Adminiftration, that durft fhew his Head in the Country; while thofe who oppofed the Meafures of the Miniftry are looked upon as Saviours and Deliverers of the Nation: But if the Kingdom were to be fairly polled, and every Man's Opinion is to be taken *feriatim*, 'tis highly probable two Parts in three would declare, that they did neither know not care what the Scheme was,or ever thought about it; and that the Majority of the reft reſt would freely own, that they were ſold and underſtood it to be a Project for a *General Exciſe.*

But no Induſtry has been wanting to exaſperate the People againſt ſome Gentlemen, who have deſerved better of them than any of thoſe that pretended to exclaim againſt their Conduct. Was the Ld B——e a better Miniſter, or an honeſter Man than the Honourable Perſon he has been libelling and reviling for ſo many Years? Would an Exciſe upon *Wine* and *Tobacco* (the Rigour of Exciſe Laws too being abated) have been of more dangerous Conſequence to Liberty, or a heavier Burden upon the Poor, than the Exciſe upon *Soap* and *Candles*? Yet not only That, but alſo the Exciſe upon *Starch, Paper, Paſte-Board, Silk, Callicoes Linnens, Stuffs, Hides, Silver-Wire,* &c. were the Works of Ld B——'s Adminiſtration; not to mention the Bill he brought into the Houſe of Commons, for reſtraining, or rather taking away the Liberty of the Preſs, which he has ſince made uſe of with ſo much Indecency and Virulence againſt other Miniſters. Theſe, and many others of the like kind, were the glorious Feats of this illuſtrious Perſon whoſe Conſcience, ſince he has been a Patriot, is become ſo ſqueamiſh that he ſtrains at a *Gnat*, tho' when he was a Miniſter he could ſwallow a *Camel.*

The **Craftſman,** Auguſt 4, No. 370.
The Exciſe *Scheme would not have anſwer'd the End propoſed of taking off the* Land-Tax.

EVery body knows, that a *Land-Tax* of 1 *s.* is laid for 500,000 *l.* which muſt have been raiſed on *Tobacco* and *Wine,* in order to take it off the Land: But we muſt firſt ſuppoſe, that the *Frauds,* committed in the Duties on *thoſe two Commodities,* do amount to that Sum; and that an *Exciſe* would have effectually put a ſtop to them. The *miniſterial Writers* pretended at firſt that the *former* was the Caſe, and the *latter* would be the Conſequence; and even the *Projector* was not aſhamed to inſiſt on both theſe Points in the *Letter to his Electors,* with that unlucky Motto, *Magna eſt veritas, et prevalebit.* He propoſed to raiſe 200,000 *l.* of this annual Sum on *Tobacco,* and 300,000 *l.* on *Wine.* But it appear'd, on Examination of this Affair in Parliament, that the whole nett Duties upon *Tobacco* did not amount, *communibus annis,* to much above 200,000 *l.* a Year, and the Seizures not to

above 1400 *l.* a Year at a Medium, from *Chriſtmas* 1724 to 1731. And theſe Seizures have continued to decreaſe conſiderably ſince 1728, at which Time the Government was put into a Method of detecting and preventing ſeveral Frauds in this Trade by that very Body of *Merchants,* who have been ſince ſo ill treated. Can then the *Frauds undiſcover'd* amount to as much as the *whole* nett *Duty;* or would an *Exciſe* have brought them all to Light? Even the *Projector, within Doors,* did not pretend to advance the Duties on *Tobacco,* by the Alteration, above 30,000 *l.* a Year; and *other Gentlemen* demonſtrated, it would not really be advanced much above *a 3d part of that Sum,* ſuppoſing the *ſame Importation* and an entire Stop put to all *Frauds.*

But ſuppoſe the Duties would have been increaſed 30,000 *l.* a Year, ſtill 470000 *l.* would have been wanting to make up the propoſed 500,000 *l.* in Lieu of the *Land-Tax of* 1 *s.* which muſt therefore have been raiſed by an Improvement of the Duties on *Wine.* It appear'd by Accounts laid before the Houſe, that the *whole Duties upon this Commodity* came to little more than 500,000 *l. per Ann.* at a Medium from *Chriſtmas* 1724, to 1731; and the Seizures for the ſame Term, not to above 7300 *l.* ſo that 469300 *l. per Ann.* the remaining part of the ſaid 500,000 *l.* muſt have been raiſed by an *extraordinary Importation of Wine,* or by the wonderful Operation of *this Scheme,* in detecting all the myſterious Practices of the *Wine-Brewers,* and putting a Stop to thoſe daring Delinquents, the *Smuglers.*

As ridiculous as this way of reaſoning may ſeem and is, it contains the whole Force of the Arguments advanced in Favour of the *late Scheme.* But as *ſinking Men* will catch at a Twig, it's no wonder the *Projector* ſhould endeavour to work up the *landed Men* into a Belief that his only Deſign was to eaſe them, and that all this Load of Infamy is fallen upon Him purely on *their Account.* They have not indeed, thought ſo; nay, have join'd with the *trading Intereſt* againſt Him. This, no Doubt, is enough to put any *Miniſter* upon Earth out of Humour.

But if we ſhould ſuppoſe, againſt all moral Certainty, that the late Project would have raiſed the *whole Sum propoſed,* yet the old Queſtion will recur, whether a People who have expended above 200 *Millions,* for the Support of their *Liberties,* within theſe 50 Years paſt, and ſtill

Till pay above 5 *Millions* every Year, ought to give them up at last for the Sake of saving 500,000*l*. a Year in their national Expences; especially when that Saving might be easily made, consistent with our Constitution, by a proper Reduction of the *Army*, the Suppression of *useless Offices*, and *exorbitant Pensions*?

It likewise deserves a Remark, that none of the Money suppofed to be raifed by an Improvement on *Wine* and *Tobacco*, could have been apply'd to the Ease of *Landholders*, as the Laws now stand; for those Duties being appropriated to particular Uses, the Application of them to any other would be a Violation of publick Faith. But if the Publick thinks there is no Weight in such an Argument, I must insist on it, that a *Million* might have been taken out of the *Sinking Fund* for the current Expences this Year, as well as 500,000*l*. by which means the *Land-Tax* might have been abolish'd without an *Excise*, as well as with it; but this was only a shoeing-Horn to draw the *landed Gentlemen* into the *Scheme*; and had They been so weak, the Confequence would have been a Diminution of the Revenue, which would have necessitated the continuing, if not encreasing the *Land-Tax*; perhaps, I might add, that the Pretence of Frauds and Abufes in Collection of the *Land-Tax* might be made an Argument, some Time or other, for converting that Duty into an *Excise*.

I am far from recommending the Mifapplication of the *Sinking Fund*, folemnly appropriated by feveral Acts of Parliament to the Payment of our *Debts*, and formerly called *facred* and *inviolable*. This was the Language of a Book published about 7 Years ago, entitled an *Essay on the publick Debts*, approv'd by a *certain Gentleman*, who then call'd Himself the Father of the *Sinking Fund*; but has drawn many a pretty Sum out of it since, however, under a Pretence, that the Money did not properly belong to it: But this Year he has publickly took *half a Million* from it, without any Distinction or Pretence whatfoever; and I shall not be furprized, if he should demand the *whole Produce* next Year, for the current Expences of the Government.

But if it should be judged proper to difappropriate this *boasted Fund*, I think it will be much better apply'd to the Reduction of Duties most burthenfome on the *Necessaries of Life, Trade and Manufactury*, then to the *current Service of*

the *Year*. This will give the moft effectual Relief to the *British Landholders*, by rendering *Provisions* and *Labour* cheap: For as Mr *Locke* obferves, Taxes, however contriv'd, do, *in a Country, where their great Fund is in Land, for the moft Part terminate on* Land.

Mr *de Witte* has a pretty Allegory concerning the wrong Policy of burthening *Trade* and *Manufactures*. The Antients, says he, have compared these inconfiderate People to *Mice*; who being to live on the Fruit of an Orchard, and finding the *Roots of the Trees* relish'd well, they eat of them, by which Means the Trees, for want of *fufficient Root*, bore lefs Fruit, and the *wifeft* of them told the others the Reafon of it, but were not believed by the *foolish* and *greedy Mice*, who continued gnawing the *Root*. The following Year many of the *Trees* having loft their *Roots* and *Fibres*, were either blown down by the *Storms*, or killed by the *Froft*, which the *foolish Mice* judg'd was the Caufe of it, and not their eating the *Roots*, and so continued feeding on, till the Trees were so diminished, that both the *wife* and *foolish Mice* muft either die of Hunger, or feek a better Habitation.

Tho' this Fable is adapted to the Point in Debate, yet it is not entirely applicable to our Cafe, at prefent; for the *foolish* and *greedy Mice* have not yet carry'd their Point; and I hope the *honeft Country Mice* will always be on their Guard againft any Attempts of their *Brethren at Court* to draw them into the fame Snare.

London Journal, Auguft 4. No. 736.
On the prefent dangerous Crifis.

THE Accession of the Houfe of *Hanover* to the Crown of these Realms, it was expected, would have put an End to all *great civil Diffensions*; but no fooner was the Difpute ended, Sword in Hand, between the *Jacobites* and *Whigs* in the Beginning of the late Reign, but the *Whigs* began to quartel among themfelves; then they agreed for fome Time; till *Ambition* form'd a Party among the Friends of the Government, which, joining with its *real Enemies*, is grown formidable. How thefe Difcontents were revived, for what Ends, and with what Confequences upon the Safety, Honour, and Power of the Kingdom, let thofe anfwer to God and Man who have been the Authors and Promoters of them.

Sir *Wm* Temple hath juftly obferv'd, *That a weak or unequal Faction may*

ferve

serve perhaps to animate the Vigour of a Government; but when it grows equal, or near proportioned in Strength and Number, and irreconcilable by the Animosity of Parties, it can scarce end without some violent Crisis *and Convulsion of State.*

This we should do well to think of before Thinking be too late, and our Distempers incurable. Most of the great *National* Contentions and *State* Distempers *heretofore*, arose from *real National Grievances*, Attempts of the Court upon the Rights and Liberties of the People; but our *present Distempers* flow solely *from ourselves*; for the Court hath done us no Ill; we have no *real publick Grievances*. The Question is, *Who shall be greatest*; a Question in which the People are no way concern'd, but as 'tis more reasonable that they should adhere to Persons in the Administration who have govern'd by Law, than to appear for Persons out of Power, acting from *meer personal Views*, to the Disturbance of the Peace and Prosperity of the Kingdom, and from no other Principle than the *Destruction* of the *Ministry*, whom they have not been able to prove guilty of one *National* Crime.

They have talk'd, indeed, of *Bribery* and *Corruption, Places and Pensions, standing Armies,* &c. But *these Sounds* are only to frighten Children; for there ever were the *same Complaints* under all *Ministeries.* But the *Faction* being sensible of their *Inability* to produce either *Fact* or *Reason* to prove any Thing done by the Min stry against *publick Good*, lay their whole Stress upon the Word *Excise*; the People were made to believe that *Ill* was designed them in the late Scheme for *preventing Frauds* in the Customs; whereas there was no Evil in it, but the *additional Trouble* to a *few* Tradesmen, which could not be helped. But to assert, that the Scheme was prejudicial to TRADE and LIBERTY, is as *senseless* as 'tis *wicked*; which may be demonstrated in a few Words.

No *Taxes* on *Home Consumption* can be prejudicial to *Trade*, but what raise the Price of Goods so high that the People can't *reach* them: But *here* there was no *New Tax* laid: It was only a *Continuation* of the *Old Tax*, with such a *new Manner* of collecting it, as would greatly *Benefit the Fair-Trader*, by hindering *Smuggling: Trade*, therefore, it could not *prejudice* but *promote*. Neither could it affect *Liberty*; for Liberty is *Govern-*

ment by just and equal Laws, which *secure* our Persons and Properties, and leaves us in the *free Exercise* of our rational Faculties. Now, which way does *the Scheme* about *Tobacco* and *Wine*, affect our *Liberties?* The *Faction* seems to talk of *Liberty* without *Ideas*; for *all Liberty* but that of doing what is *right*, is *Licentiousness*; and not a *Blessing*, but a *Curse*. The *Liberty of Smuggling, Defrauding* the Government, and *prejudicing* the fair Trader, is a Liberty inconsistent with the *Rights of others*, and ought, therefore, to be prevented, tho' the Consequence be a little more Trouble to Tradesmen; nor have They a *Right* to be *exempt* from that Trouble, which is *absolutely necessary* to prevent *great Frauds*, and so encourage the fair Trader.

To talk then of the Scheme's being prejudicial to *Liberty*, is most *ridiculous* Cant and *popular* Phrenzy; nor could such a Notion ever have prevailed, had it not been artfully put about by the *Heads* of the Faction, to sink the M———r; and then *ecchoed* back by the Friends to Smuggling and Clandestine Trade; till at last it came to be generally believed, that *all Things* were to be *excised*, and *all Men* made *Slaves.*

From this State of the Case it appears, that the *People* have no Concern in the Dispute, but to *do Justice* to the *Injured.* Can there be greater *Injustice* and *Insolence*, than that a set of Men, because *not in Place*, should *combine* and write *Weekly Libels* against the Government, and tell his Majesty, that, chuse what Ministry he pleases, *they* will follow them; *they* will have no patching nor screening; *they* will never lay down their Pens, till SOMETHING FARTHER be done; and that if Power be lodg'd in any Hands but *their own, they* will oppose it. (see *p.* 356.)

Who knows the Consequences of this State-*Bullying?* this *Hectoring* of the *King* and *Government?* Things seem *ripening* for Action; and we know there are Men at the Head of the Malecontents, a MAN, at least, *desperate* enough for any Measures. The *Friends* of the Government should therefore *firmly unite* against them, and no longer give the Enemy an Occasion to expect a *Change*, not of *Ministers* only, but of *something further*, of *Government* too.

Concludes with a Story told him about an Honest Tory of the Defection of a great many Whigs, who exceed the Tories in their Freedom of Speech; but *Osborn* borne advifes the Tory not to depend on their Affiftance; they will, fays he, have Senfe and Honefty enough to unite againft you and all your Meafures.

Weekly Mifcellany, Aug. 4. N° 34.

Religion and Infidelity, a Dream.

METhought, fays this Writer, I found myfelf engaged with a mixed Multitude of both Sexes and all Ages, in climbing a large Hill, not only craggy, but fteep, which made it irkfome to thofe who had impair'd their natural Strength, or carry'd any great Matter of Burthen. To direct our Journey there was a dubious Light that grew clearer as we came nearer the Summit: Which, however, few would have been able to gain, had it not been for the kind Offices of feveral Perfons who reach'd out their Hands to all, that would accept of their Affiftance. The Brow of the Hill was terminated by a Partition impenetrable, except at one Opening, which was thro' a Gate of the plaineft Order, exceeding low and narrow.

Having, without much Difficulty, gain'd Admiffion, I faw, feated on a Table rais'd Altar-wife by two Steps, a female Perfonage, whofe Countenance was a happy Mixture of Majefty and Sweetnefs; her Eye was difcerning, her Tongue perfuafive, and her Head incircled with a Glory: In her Right-hand fhe held the Sun, near which ftood *Truth*: In her Left-hand was a Book, with the Portraiture of a Lamb bearing a Crofs upon it, a rich Veftment flow'd down to her Feet. On the firft Step to the Altar ftood two Figures, one with a piercing undazzled Eye, looking ftedfaftly upward; the other with a modeft but chearful Afpect: On the Step above ftood a third Figure, whofe Heart feemed on Fire, and her Look moft affectionate, and charming. Pointing my Eye upward the fame Way, the Figure on the firft Step was looking, I faw Glory rifing above Glory, till I was loft in the immeafurable Height. Cafting my Eye downwards I had on each fide the moft beautiful View of Lands, Rivers, Seas, Ships, Cities, &c. Turning myfelf to the auguft Perfon fitting before me, I could not help applying to her that fine Paffage in the Book of Pfalms—*The King's Daughter is all glorious*, &c.

In a Fit of Tranfport I returned to the Wicket of Admiffion to communicate my Joy to thofe on the Outfide of it,

(Gent. Mag. Vol. III. N° XXXII.)

fome of whom being too tall, difdain'd to ftoop and enter; others were too big. The fame Fate befell fome Ladies with their Hoops, which rather than bend, they skudded back-again as faft as they could. Others had their Pockets fo ftuff'd as made their Paffage impracticable. Some I faw ftanding full before the Gate, in View of the Glories within, yet without the laft Effort to enter; the Reafon was, their Eyes were fo diftorted and awry, that they did not fee what they feemed to look upon. The next Company confifted of Men and Women, who came up in Couples: A Torch was borne before them, at Sight of which a fide Door opened and admitted them. Several other Couples claimed the fame Benefit, but were refufed, becaufe they had not the Torch with them. Thefe were follow'd by a Company preceded by a Torch, but in another Order; for here each Man, leading feveral Females, defired the Entrance might be enlarged: They were told there had been Inftances of fuch Admiffions, but that thefe Doors had been long clofed up, they muft therefore either feparate or retire; they chofe the latter.

Thefe, with many others, returned the Way they came, and found no Difficulty in the Defcent. An irrefiftible Curiofity pufh'd me after them to a Plain at the Foot of the Hill: In the Middle of it on a large Bladder, fate an ugly Phantom which, upon a nearer Infpection, I found to be the fame Figure I had, when awake, sketch'd out for an Emblem of *modern Infidelity*, (fee p. 262 G.) at which every Company, as they arriv'd, ftopp'd and bow'd. Her Retinue was numerous: Thofe of them which I could diftinguifh by their Drefs or Actions wore, *Banter, Laughter, Prejudice, Ignorance, Difcord, Clamour*, and *Curiofity*: Before her ftood *Pride* a-tiptoe; at her Feet loll'd *Flattery*. In one Hand fhe wav'd a *fmall Taper*, and in the other held a *Quarto Book*. Proclamation was made for Silence to hear the Oracles of *Reafon*. After fome plain Things, it was pronounced to the liftening Crowds, That the *Part* was bigger than the *Whole*, and the *Taper*, flaring above their Heads, larger and brighter than the *Sun*; that the Stature of the *fhorteft Man* might extend as high as the Lengths of all the Individuals there prefent put together; and that the *fineft Buildings* were not to compare for Beauty with the *Ruins* of thofe Buildings. At the Conclufion, the Company was difmifs'd

D d d   with

with Tapers in their Hands to try their Goodness, by finding their Way thro' an immense Labyrinth, full of Bogs and Precipices, cross Paths, perplex'd Windings and illusive Turns, without a Spark of Light to direct them, but what they carried. They enter'd the Place with Frolick and Inadvertence; but had not sported long before *Return* became impossible; and Mirth and Wantonness changed into Confusion and Lamentation. Cries were heard from every Quarter, of Persons whose Tapers were gone out, tearing themselves with Bushes, running against Trees, plunging into Waters, or tumbling into Pits. Many, sick of endless Wanderings, run their Heads into Halters, or finish'd their Misery with Poison and Daggers. In the midst of this Distress, several Persons offer'd to extricate them, onCondition they put outboth their own Eyes, which had so misled them, and implicitly following their Conductors: Some accepted the Terms without examining the Credit of their Guides.

Grown weary of viewing these Scenes of Horror, I recover'd the Plain, where the Author of all this Mischief sate, just at the Instant, when a Sword of Fire issued from the Mouth of the Matron seated on the Summit of the adjoining Hill, and proceeded to the Place where I was. As it came near the Idol, the Taper in her Hand grew dim, because many of its strongest Rays flew off, and incorporated with the approaching Flame, to which they seem'd congenial. The radiant Weapon prick'd the Monster's Seat, which gave a loud Crack, and sunk to the Earth with its Burden; whose Womb, bursting with the Fall, the Bowels gush'd out, and with them a vast Quantity of loathsome dissonant Animals, whose Bustle and Hurry, with the Explosion of the Bladder, waked me.   X

Fog's Journal. Aug. 4. N° 148.
Of Oppressions in the Courts of Equity.

PHilopatros, sends Mr *Fog* a Discourse on the Number, and Intricacy of our Laws; which, he observes, give a Suitor, who has a wealthy or powerful Adversary, a very discouraging Prospect of Success from the Justice of his Pretensions. 'Tis not, says he, the Laws only that want to be rectify'd, but the Practice of them much more. The Courts of Equity, (especially the Chancery) intended to mitigate the Rigour of the Common Law, are become the greatest Grievances of the

Subject; being the most dilatory and expensive of any other.

The Forms of Bills and Answers might be much shorten'd, by leaving out unnecessary Repetitions; the same Faults are found with the unnecessary Forms in taking Depositions of Witnesses; the Impertinence of Registers in drawing Orders, which recite former Orders that might as well be produced; and in decretal Orders they repeat the whole Substance of the Bills and Answers, and every Council's Argument, which are of no Use, but a vast Addition to the grievous Load of that Office; the Price paid upon every Sheet is intolerable, considering how little they contain; the exorbitant Fees to Council, and even to their Clerks are insupportable.

Expedition-Money is anotherGrievance, of which the Courts of Law are as guilty as that of Equity. In the Courts of Equity, if a Person has a Decree given against him, and he absents himself, his Estate is enter'd upon and sequester'd to pay the Debt; but the Oppression lies in the Manner of levying it, which is done by Sequestrators who seize and sell all personal Estates, and receive the Rents and Profits of Real Estates, till payment be made of Debt and Costs. The Sequestrators put in Bayliffs, who live at Discretion; scarce ever appear themselves, yet charge 6s. 8d. a Day each, during the Sequestration; the Plaintiff indulges them in it, as believing he is to hold the Estate till Payment of Debt and Charges; the Master allows these Demands, and reports so much due, alledging 'tis the Practice of the Court so to do. If you apply to the Court, you are either sent back to the same Master, or told, you are not to stand in Contempt of the Court, and have no Right to be heard, till you have obey'd its Decrees; whereas, really, the Defendant do's not refuse Payment thro' Obstinacy but Disability; yet the Sequestration continues, the Charges eat up the Estate, and the real Debt is not paid at last; and the Reason is, the Court of Equity can't give Damage, and therefore the Defendant must be punish'd with Costs for an unavoidable Contempt. This is so far from doing Justice or Equity, either to Plaintiff or Defendant, that 'tis really plundering them both. 'Tis vain to say in Excuse, that this is the Course of the Court; for if it be so, it ought to be changed; and it requires no Act of Parliament to enable such a Change,

Judges

Judges of thefe Courts having it in their Power to redrefs all thefe Grievances, as they are not Laws, but Points of Practice only.

I have, on the contrary, known a Judgment obtained in the King's Bench for a Debt againft a Clergyman, and for Nonpayment a Writ iffued to the Bifhop to fequefter his Spirituals, which was committed to one Sequeftrator only under Security to account, who agreed with the Churchwardens of the Parifh, to collect the Tythes fequefter'd, for 20 L. a Year. When the Debt was near paid, the Debtor apply'd to the Court that the Sequeftrator might account; a juft Account, and Vouchers for every Article were given and allow'd, except that for collecting; the Account was referr'd to the Mafter of the Office, who reported 10 *l. per Ann.* fufficient. The Sequeftrator charged nothing for himfelf and made it appear, that he had actually paid 20 *l. per Ann.* and that nobody would collect it under that every thing that could be raifed out of the Premifes was collected and fold to the beft Advantage, and more made of it by 20 *l. per Ann.* than ever the Defendant himfelf made of it; the Sequeftrator demanded no Fees for himfelf, yet the Court confirm'd the Mafter's Report.

There's no Doubt which of thefe Courts has a Right to the name of Equity. The King's Bench did not err in oppreffing the Defendant for his Contempt, or countenanced the Sequeftrator or his Subftitutes to plunder him, as the other Method of Practice certainly does.

'Tis hop'd therefore our Chancellors have comply'd with this Practice only as they have found it fo ufed, rather than as they thought it juft, and that a Remedy will fpeedily be applied, efpecially fince Enquiry is now to be made into the Fees of all the Courts. PHILOPATROS.

The *Daily Courant,* Aug. 7.
SIR,

AMong the *Craftfman's* many Artifices none has fubfifted fo long as treating their Antagonifts with an Air of Contempt, and affuming to themfelves all the Learning, Wit, and Honefty in the Nation. This Humour diffufes itfelf from the Patrons to the Patronized, from the Railers at Power in the Senate, to the Difperfers of Treafon among the Mob; each of them calls his Oppofers, Blockhead, Fool, Blunderer, Robber and Pickpocket. It may be the *Craftfman* will tell me I call Names as faft as he or his Affociates. Be it fo. But then I produce Facts in Support of what I fay; and if they difpute the Veracity of the Charge, the Recordof B——ke's Conviction will ftrike them dumb. (See p. 406. D)

Can Mr *D'Anvers* produce any Inftance of a Miniftry fupporting themfelves for a dozen Years together in Favour, not only of the Prince, but of that Body who are the fupreme Judges of Perfons offending againft the State; while thofe who fought and had fworn their Deftruction were continually watching their Tranfactions, and omitting Nothing which might excite either legal or popular Vengeance? Or, fhould there be fuch an Inftance, can their Safety be imputed to any Thing but their Innocence? And is not this the prefent Cafe?

To draw Parallels, to frame Satyrs, to burlefque Patents, are Engines which might be played againft any body in a high Station, and are Proofs only of the Envy of their Authors.

R. *Freeman,*

Grubftreet Journal, Aug. 9. N° 189.

Mr BAVIUS,

THE following Epiftle was actually fent to a Country Clergyman (who ufed hard Words in his Sermon) by a Gentleman who accidentally came into his Church and heard him. Country Curates fhould confider that their Academic Terms and pedantic Expreffions are mere Greek and Hebrew to poor Husbandmen, probably to the Squire himfelf. The Performance of Divine Service in an unknown Language was one great Occafion of the Reformation, and has ever fince been efteemed a monftrous Abfurdity. Too many of our *London* Divines are not entirely free of this Error, whereby they deprive the illiterate Part of their Audience of that found Doctrine they might expect from Men of their known Abilities. Yours, AB. CD. &c.

N. B. Thefe Writers fhould have told us that the following Letter was printed feveral Years ago, and not have given it in a Manner as if lately printed.

To the moft Deuteronomical Polydoxologift, Pantophilological Linguift, Mr——— *Archi Rabbi Sophi Diotrephes,* &c.
SIR,

THE unanimous and humillimous defiderations, as well of your parochian, as hic-et-ubiquetarian, illiterate, femipaganian auditors, beg leave fubmiffively to 'emonstrate, That altho' by your specious proems, and spacious introductions, promising great perspicuity in predication, you endeavour to inveigle our affections in order to indoctrinate our agricolated intellects; yet through the caliginous sublimity of internexed conundrums, tonifruating with obstreperous cadencies, you rather obfuscate than illuminate our A-b-c-darian conceptions, so that we generally return not at all edified, but puzzled, confounded, and astonished. We therefore for our souls good, (in bonne esperance, that your urbanity will not be exasperated at the presentation of these our cordial desires) do from the nadir of our rusticity almacanterise to the very zenith of your unparalleled sphere of activity, in beseeching your exuberant genius to nutriate our rational appetites with intelligible theology, suitable to our plebeian apprehensions, and to recondite your acroamatical locutions for more scholastic auscultators. For, while our first, second, and third selves, together with our domesties, all of Ignoramus's offspring hear you gigantize in lycophronian and pharigenous raptures, in words we never met with in holy writ, as Corollaries, Ephemeris, and such other heterogeneal language, without dilucidation of their genuine signification, we lose the whole system of your doctrine, in admiration of your eximious erudition. Being therefore under a panic timidity, lest we should see a restauration of the dialect of Babel, and that some sesquipedalian circumforaneous saltimbanco should mount the rostrum, and after your example, should in spagirical bombast repuzzle the quintessentials of our ingeniosities, with more amalgamations, cohobations, and fixations: we beg you to call to mind S Austin's saying, _Mallem ut reprehendant grammatici, quàm non intelligant populi: I had rather that the grammarians should blame, than that the people should not understand me._

And now, egregious Sir, we supplicate your clemency, not to look upon these lines as derogatory to your most exquisite parts and profound science: for we rather admire such superlative acquisitions; which however we humbly opine, are more proper to be displayed among learned academicians, than mechanical and agrestical auditors. And we exstimate ourselves abundantly justified in this our humble application by the authority of S PAUL, much greater than that of S

AUSTIN, who says, interpreted in plain English, _If I know not the meaning of the voice, I shall be unto him that speaketh a barbarian; and he that speaketh shall be a barbarian unto me,_ 1 Cor. xv. 11. And thus having copulated our plebeian endeavours, we exosculate the subumbratión of your subligacles: and sooner shall the surges of the sandiferous sea ignify and evaporate, than the cone of our duty towards you be in the least unconcatenate or dissolved, always wishing you health and happiness,

A, B, C, D, E, F, &c.

Free Briton. Aug. 9. N° 194.

MR _Walsingham_ first draws a Comparison between _Fog_ and the _Craftsman,_ wherein he allows the _former_ the superior Genius and most _Sneer,_ but the _latter_ the most Malice. _Caleb hates the Government from Spleen against the Administration; Fog hates the Administration from Spleen against the Government;_ but both agree in praising all who have _left their Places,_ if not from an _Affinity of Principles,_ yet from a _Similitude of Fortunes. Fog_ has lately so for conform d to the _Craftsman_ as to mourn over the Removal of a P—r of N—th Br—n, even on Account of his _Service_ and _Attachment_ to the _Protestant Succession._

Fog has a considerable Merit; he is coming to Terms with our _Protestant_ Dissenting _Brethren,_ and tells us, _That the_ Churchman _hath now taken the_ Quaker and Presbyterian _into his Bosom, because they have lately united with him in a particular Cause._ Formerly, indeed, Churchman _were for_ Cutting their Throats, _because at Church_ Prayers _were said by a_ Common prayer Book, _and at Meeting_ without one. (See p. 316, H.)——But will you, Mr _Fog,_ be always in this rare Humour? Suppose they should not continue in your System of Politicks, will you let them _live_ saying Prayers _without_ a _Common-Prayer Book?_ or else, if you should relapse, who knows but their Heads, being _in your Bosom, their Throats_ may be in more than ordinary _Danger!_ I ask, because I have observ'd certain unfriendly Emotions in you to the _Dissenters._ Don't you remember, my Dear, a nice Distinction you formerly made, between the _Oaths of Churchmen_ and the _Affirmations of Quakers?_ Did you not call it the _Oath of a Christian_ opposed to the _Word of a Quaker?_ And may you not as nicely distinguish between the

Throat

Throat of a Quaker and the *Throat of a Chriftian*, till at laft fome of our Friends at *St Omers* may fatisfy your Confcience that the *Sixth Command* of the *Decalogue*, was only meant to guard the Lives of *Chriftians*, and that it is no *Murder* to *cut the Throat of a Quaker*?

I beg further fome Explanation of the Word *Bofom*. I never heard of any *Repeal* or *Explanation of the Sacramental Teft*, in Favour of *Diffenters*, either made or intended by *Churchmen*. So that you may as well fay, the *Diffenters* are in *Abraham's Bofom*, as in *Churchmen's*, unlefs their Kindnefs be like that of a certain *ingenious Animal*, fomething a-kin to you, who hugs a *Kitten* to Death with violent Fondnefs. I hope you don't mean *to banter* my *Proteftant Brethren*, for any Service you fuppofe they have done your Caufe. God knows, *this Bofom* of yours will be but a bad Lodging, if your Heart is as *ftony* as it ufed to be.

There is another Point which wants to be explained. You fay, in your laft *Journal*, *That English Horfes are known to be* very fleet, *and* fome Gentlemen *may foon have Ufe for fuch to carry them from a Danger they never met with at a Review.*] That Word *Danger* is as myfterious as the Word *Blow* in *Guido Vaux's* Letter; and, to be fure, is fome Hint to a Friend to provide himfelf with a *fwift Horfe*, for a feafonable Efcape out of this Country. It cannot certainly be *Civil Officers*, who are never concern'd in the *Reviews* of *Military Appearances*. It cannot be the *Gentlemen of the Army*, whofe *Bravery* and *Fidelity* were never fufpected: Who then is it we are to look on as *threatned with Danger?* It can neither be the *Clergy*, nor *Lawyers*, nor the *Army* nor *Minifters of State*, nor even S— S— *Directors*; Is it then the K——, and the Princes of his *illuftrious Family*? I have heard it affirm'd, that all the Rage a-gainft the *prefent Adminiftration*, was really directed againft the *Foundations of our Eftablifhment*. Is *Fog* too of this Opinion? Is the Man, who forrows in the Difgrace of thofe who fupported the *Proteftant Succeffion*, of Opinion, that the K— and his Children muft provide themfelves with fleet Horfes, to efcape a Danger worfe than thofe they have met with at Reviews?

Is the *Quaker* and *Presbyterian* taken into the *Churchman's Bofom* becaufe they have helped to promote this Caufe, of *driving the K— out of this Country!* No;

They will abhor fuch a Caufe, and the Help which hath been given it, affured as they are in the Words of this Writer, that *they are to have their Throats* cut, *becaufe they fay their* Prayers *without a* Common-Prayer Book.

If this is the End of *attacking the Adminiftration*; I think too much cannot be done to fupport it, whofe Being thus ftands declared to be effential to the *Proteftant Succeffion*, and to the *Liberties of Britain*.

It is however our Comfort, that neither *his M—* hath any occafion to fly, nor will ever fubmit to Flight, even when he cannot fave us. This is our Security and the juft Support of our Adminiftration, whofe Fidelity he hath tried, and whofe Service he hath approved, will be *his Security*.

Weekly Mifcellany, Aug. 11. N° 35.

THE Writer of a Letter in this Paper highly applauds the Undertaking of eftablifhing a Colony in *Georgia*; beftows large Encomiums on the Founders of it; and adds, that a Subfcription is now open'd by the Truftees for the religious Ufes of the Colony, a Church is to be built and endow'd at *Savannah*, and a Clergyman, well recommended, is fent over on the Foot of an annual Salary, to refide as the firft Minifter of it there. Thefe early Expreffions of Zeal in the Truftees, gives us juft Ground to hope, that a better Face of Religion will be preferv'd in *Georgia*, than appears in many of our *American* Settlements; and that many Obftacles which have hitherto defeated all Attempts to gain the *Indians*, may be gradually remov'd. And as a Confirmation of his Hopes, the Writer gives the following Part of a Letter from *James Oglethorpe*, Efq; at *Georgia*, to the Hon. —— in *London*. Dated the 9th of *June* laft.

THERE feems a Door opened to our Colony towards the Converfion of the *Indians*. I have had many Converfations with their chief Men, the whole Tenour of which fhews there is nothing wanting to their Converfion, but one, who underftands their Language well, to explain to them the *Myfteries* of Religion; for as to the *moral* Part of Chriftianity they underftand it and affent to it. They abhor *Adultery*, and do not approve of *Plurality* of *Wives*. *Theft* is a thing not known among the *Creek* Nation, tho' fre-

frequent, and even honourable, amongst the *Uchees*. *Murder* they look upon as a most abominable Crime, but do not esteem the killing of an *Enemy*, or one that has injur'd them, Murder. The Passion of *Revenge*, which they call *Honour*, and *Drunkeness*, which they learnt from our Traders, seem to be the two greatest Obstacles to their being truly Christians: But upon both these Points they hear Reason; and with respect to drinking of *Rum*, I have weaned those near me a good deal from it. As for *Revenge*, they say, as they have no executive Power of Justice amongst them, they are forced to kill the Man who has injured them, in order to prevent others from doing the like; but they do not think that any Injury, except *Adultery*, or *Murder*, deserves Revenge. They hold, that if a Man commits *Adultery*, the injur'd *Husband* is oblig'd to have Revenge, by cutting off the Ears of the *Adulterer*, which if he is too sturdy and strong to submit to, then the injured Husband kills him the first Time that he has an Opportunity so to do with Safety. In Cases of *Murder*, the *next in Blood* is obliged to kill the Murderer, or else he is looked upon as infamous in the Nation where he lives; and the Weakness of the executive Power is such, that there is no other way of Punishment but by the Revenger of Blood, as the Scripture calls it. For there is no coercive Power in any of their Nations. Their Kings can do no more than *perswade*. All the Power that they have is no more than to call their old Men and their Captains together, and to propound to them, without Interruption, the Measures they think proper. After *they* have done speaking, all the others have Liberty to give their Opinions also, and they reason together till they have brought each other into some unanimous Resolution. These Conferences in Matters of great Difficulty have sometimes lasted two Days, and are always carried on wih great Temper and Modesty. If they do not come into some unanimous Resolution upon the Matter, the Meeting breaks up; but if they are Unanimous (which they generally are) then they call in the young Men, and recommend to them the putting in Execution the Resolution, with their strongest and most lively Eloquence. And, indeed, they seem to me, both in Action and Expression, to be thorough Masters of true Eloquence; and, ma-

king Allowances for badness of Interpreters, many of their Speeches are equal to those which we admire most in the *Greek* and *Roman* Writings. They generally in their Speeches use *Similies* and *Metaphors*. Their *Similies* were quite new to me, and generally wonderful proper and well carried on. But in the *Conferences* among their chief Men they are more *Laconick* and concise. In fine, in speaking to their young Men they generally address to the Passions; in speaking to their old Men they apply to Reason only. For Example, *Tomo-chi-chi*, in his first set Speech to me, among other Things said, *Here is a little Present*, and then gave me a *Buffalo's Skin*, painted on the Inside with the Head and Feathers of an *Eagle*. He desired me to accept it because the *Eagle* signified *Speed*, and the *Buffalo Strength*. That the *English* were as swift as the Bird, and as strong as the Beast; since, like the first, they flew from the utmost Parts of the Earth over the vast Seas; and, like the second, nothing could withstand them. That the Feathers of the Eagle were *soft*, and signified *Love*; the Buffalo's Skin *warm*, and signified *Protection*; therefore he hoped that we would Love and Protect their little Families. One of the *Indians* of the *Cherichee* Nation being come down to the Governor upon the Rumour of the War, the Governor told him that he *need fear nothing, but might speak freely*. He answer'd smartly, 'I always speak freely; what should I fear? I am now among my Friends, and I never feared even amongst my Enemies.' Another Instance of their short manner of speaking was, when I ordered one of the *Carolina* Boatmen, who was drunk, and had beaten an an *Indian*, to be tied to a Gun till he he was sober in order to be whipped; *Tomo-chi-chi* came to me to beg me to pardon the Boatman, which I refused to do, unless the *Indian*, who had been beaten, should also desire the Pardon for him. *Tomo-chi-chi* desired him so to do; but he insisted on Satisfaction by the Punishment of the Man; upon which *Tomo-chi-chi* said, 'O *Fonseka* (for that was his Name) this *Englishman* being drunk, has beat you; if he is whipt for so doing, the *Englishman* will expect, that, if an *Indian* should insult them when drunk, the *Indian* should be whipt for it. When you are drunk you are quarrelsome, and you know you love to be drunk, but you don't love to be whipt.' *Fonseka* was convinced, and

beg-

begged me to pardon the Man. As foon as I granted it, *Tomo-chi chi* and *Fonfeka* ran and untied him; which I perceived was done to fhew that he owed his Safety to their Interceffion.

The Craftfman. Auguft 11. No. 371.
Of the Hanover Succeffion, and its Foundation.

IT is our great Happinefs that his prefent Majefty's Dominion is founded upon a better Title than either the *Jus Divinum* or *Hereditary Right.* He owes it purely to the Voice of the People in Parliament. He got it by their Favour, and will keep it by their Affection. The Limitations and Conditions, by the due Obfervance of which he is entitled to it will ferve as a Rule to fecure to his Pofterity the Hearts and Purfes of their Subjects to all Eternity. His Predeceffors had not the fame Advantages. They were bred up in a Notion that their *Prerogative* intitled Them to do what they pleas'd; nor were the Privileges *of the People* fo firmly afcertain'd.

Machiavel lays down this Pofition; *That no Government can long enjoy Liberty, unlefs it be frequently brought back to its firft Principles.* It is the Nature of all Governments to degenerate, therefore he recommends a frequent Renewal of the Conftitution. The frequent Revolutions in this Kingdom have preferved us a *free People,* when *Liberty* is loft in almoft every other Part of *Europe.*

The *laft Revolution* has done more for us than any of the reft, I mean not that brought about in favour of the Prince of *Orange,* but that by which the *prefent R. Family* were feated upon the Throne. This happy Change in our Government, tho' not called a *Revolution,* is the moft Important we have had, and has amounted within a few Degrees of that Reduction to the *firft Principles of Government* which *Machiavel* recommends; and had we ufed the fame Caution to prevent *new Dangers,* as to redrefs *old Grievances,* our Liberties had been deliver'd to Pofterity, after a Thoufand Years, more fecure and durable, than at the beginning of the Commonwealth.

The Power of unlimited Monarchs owes its Rife to the Abufe of the firft Truft repofed in them, fays Cardinal *Bentivoglio.* *Of Old, Kings were no more than Chiefs, or principal Magiftrates in States Republican and free.* It ought to give every *Englifhman* the higheft Satisfaction to find our Conftitution fo nearly refembling primitive *Liberty.* Our Princes have Authority given them to defend the *Laws of the Land,* but not to break them. The People will no longer fuffer themfelves to be duped into an Opinion, that *regal Authority* muft inevitably import an *abfolute Dominion;* and juftly look on the Word *King* as fignifying no other than a *third Eftate,* fuperior to every Individual, yet inferior to the collective Body of the People whofe Advantage and Profperity were the only Caufes of its Exiftence.

The *Act of Settlement* has obtained all thefe great Advantages for us. *That Compact between Prince and People,* formerly treated as a mere Chimæra, is no longer to be difputed. In *that Act* are contained certain Stipulations and Conditions, under which the Prince has confented to accept, and by which Tenure he only holds his Crown. By thefe Means every Subject may know the Extent of his Prince's Power and the Meafures of his own Allegiance. '

Two *fundamental Points* of this our fecond *Magna Charta,* are, *Firft, That the King fhould never leave his* Britifh *Dominions without Confent of Parliament;* and fecondly, *That He fhould never engage* England *in any Broils relating to his Foreign Territories:* but we have fince abandon'd *thefe two Points;* the *firft* foon after his late Majefty's Acceffion; the other in that ever-memorable Refolution of the Houfe of Commons, by which we engaged *to fupport and maintain his Majefty's* German *Dominions with the utmoft Efforts of* Great Britain.

The remaining Articles of the Act of Settlement are of fuch a Nature, that we have no Reafon to fear they will be difpens'd with. The Advantages arifing from a Settlement eftablifhed on the Foot of *Liberty* are fuch, that whoever endeavours to raife the *Prerogative* one Step higher than it ftands at prefent, or even argues in Favour of fuch Conduct, is the worft of Traytors, and deferves the Curfe and Hatred of the whole Community.

Sir *Wm Temple,* obferves of the *Dutch Republick,* That this ftomachful People, who could not endure Impofitions under a *Spanifh* Government, have fince been inured to them in the higheft Degree under their own *popular Magiftrates.* The Reafon of their general Content was this, that They found every one fubject to the *fame Law;* So with us, the *Act of Settlement* binds the *Prince* equally with the meaneft *Peafant.*

The

The Benefits of this excellent Establishment are not so easily discover'd, till some Abuses happen. But if ever a *weak* and *corrupt Administration* should arise; if an *evil Minister* should embezzle the publick Treasure; if he should load the Nation in Times of Peace, with Taxes sufficient to maintain a War, and under the pretence of secret Services, should expend the Money to line his own Pockets, to stop the Mouths of his hungry Dependants, to bribe some future Parliament, to patch up a Peace with foreign Powers, offended by a Series of Provocations and Blunders: if he should perswade his Sovereign that his Security consisted in the Continuance or Increase of the *publick Debts*, and that his Grandeur was founded on the *Poverty of his Subjects*; if the Nation should ever fall under these unhappy Circumstances, they will find the Excellence of a *free Constitution*. The publick Discontent will discover itself only in faint Murmurs; the Nation will wait long, before they engage in desperate Measures, that may endanger a Constitution, from which they expect a sure, tho' perhaps a dilatory Justice upon such an *enormous Offender*.

These are the Advantages of our present happy Settlement; let us resolve to preserve it inviolate, and ourselves in the Condition for which all Men were originally design'd, that is of a *free People*.

London Journal, August 11, No. 737.
Observations on the Craftsman's *Remarks on the Report of the Committee to enquire into Frauds in the Customs.* (See p. 364.)

MOST of the *Frauds* discover'd are *undeniably proved*, by Persons of undoubted Veracity: But that there are among the Witnesses some *Smuglers, corrupted Officers,* &c. is no wonder; *honest Men* will not be in wicked Confederacies. This Objection therefore is trifling, and so is the other, *That the Frauds here laid open are not worth troubling the Nation about;* for the *late Bill* was not only intended to *prevent* such *Frauds as are discover'd* but those that are *not discover'd*, which may infinitely exceed the other.

This *Scheme* therefore was the most *reasonable* and *honest*, the best calculated to *prevent* Frauds and benefit the *fair Trader*, that could enter the Heart of Man; and for which the People of *England* ought highly to esteem the Minister, for taking Care that the *full Duty* be paid

on every *Commodity* taxed; because *That* will enable the Government to remove some *burthensome Taxes*, or prevent *new ones*.

As for *the Occasion* of this Enquiry, which the *Craftsman* arrogates to *himself* and his *Associates*, 'tis granted, that their Motion for *appointing a Committee*, might be the Occasion of this *Report*, but not of the *Enquiry*; or *This* was made by the Ministry, long before the late Sessions of Parliament, and they had the *Materials* and *Evidences* by them, which were the *Foundation* and *Reason* of the late Scheme.

Now let us see what *the Opposition* would have done, if by Ballotting they had got *their List*; why truly, they would have *enquired* who had *Patent Places, demolish'd them, resumed great Sine-Cures,* or made the *Principals* answerable for their *Deputies*, (See p. 365 B) What wild romantick Stuff is this! they would not *reduce* one Place. But if these *Patent-Places*, &c. were demolish'd, it would signify nothing towards removing the Evils complained of; unless they imagine, that when *Principals* come *to act* as *Deputies*, they will *immediately grow honest*. The way to cure the *Evil* is, to put it *out of the Power of* Men to defraud, as *Warehousing* and *Excise* would have done.

One Word about the *Craftsman's* Speech (See p. 364 G) What an *unprecedented* way of talking is this! to call near 300 Members of the House, *Creatures* and *Prostitutes*; and asserting, That every Member was *brib'd* before he *voted!* May it not be more reasonably supposed, that a *certain Gentleman*, not yet a *Minister*, summon'd his Creatures, presented them with another List, and made the following Speech:

Gentlemen,
You know we have long labour'd, in vain, to destroy this *Monster of Power*, this *domineering Minister*; but now he has destroy'd himself; *Excise* will sink him, you see we have set all the Nation against him; let us follow our Blow, unite firmly, and Vote for *these Men*; (here's a List:) If we get a *a Majority* to enquire into Frauds, we may get a Majority to *impeach* him; then is our Business done; when you, Sir, shall be S— of S—; you in the T—y; you in the E—r; you in the A—y, &c. But if we miscarry in this Point, we must have Recourse to our old dull tedious Method of working

working him out by *Journals, promising* Places and Penfions, and actually diftributing large Sums againft the next E—n; for tho' *Bribery* and *Corruption* be a *Sin,* yet we may *bribe* againft Bribery, and *corrupt* againft *Corruption.* The *End* is good, and *Matt. Prior* has told us,

The End muft juftify the means;
He only fins, who Ill intends:
If then it is to combate Evil,
'Tis lawful to employ the Devil.

Thus fpoke the Hero; the Affembly fhouted for Joy, and fo departed.

Fog's Journal. Auguft 11. Nº 249.

FOG entertains us with an Account fent him by *Weftmonaftirienfis,* of a Squabble among a Crowd of Boys who had been *collecting,* not by way of *Excife,* but *begging* Money for a Bonfire on a memorable Occafion, when the whole City was illuminated. The Conteft was, who fhould be *Cafh-keeper;* fome were for *Bob,* others for *Will.* Several Objections were raifed againft *Bob's* Character, as that he was a *fly Rogue,* not faithful to his Truft, had finer and greater Variety of *Play-Things* than any *Mafter* in *England;* that he laid out a great deal of Money in *Squibs, Serpents, and Crackers,* at improper Times; that he was lavifh to *foreign Bonfires;* and money had been expended in Faggots, tho' they never had but fneaking Fires. Upon this the oppofite Party urg'd a great many Things in *Bob's* Defence; at laft, the Queftion being put, it was carried againft pilfering *Bob* by a confiderable Majority. Then they hurried poor *Bob* to a Juftice of Peace, who fent him to *Bridewel* to beat Hemp, till he had refunded all his illgotten Bawbles, and the Money he had clandeftinely funk.

Will being now invefted in *Bob's* Poft, they read over a Lift of all the Loyal and Difloyal in the Parifh, according to *Bob's* Report of them; but proceeding to raife their Contribuions, were always difappointed at the Houfes of the *Former,* and as unexpectedly fuccefsful at Thofe of the *Latter.* Among the Number of Refufals, that from the *Laureat* was not the leaft wonder'd at; for inftead of Money, he fent them his Ode, which would make but a *poor Blaze,* in Honour of his Majefty. Indeed they would fain have fpar'd it, and try'd to fing it to fome Tune; but in vain; fo gave it to a Man that was going by *to light his Pipe.*

‡ Then follows a Remark of Mr *Camden* (*Gent Mag.* Vol. 3. No. xxiii.)

on the Eftablifhment of the *Roman* Legions in *Britain,* fent to Mr *Fog* by *Cornavius* to the Effect following;

"Thus by a *Standing Army* a Yoke of Slavery is impofed upon the *Britifh* Nation, which before was never without Terror hung upon the the Necks of its Inhabitants; from thence they proceeded to load them with Taxes, Excifes and other intolerable Impofitions, and obliged them to fubmit to Publicans or Excifemen, who took an Account of their Goods or Properties, and who, like Harpies or Bloodfuckers, liv'd upon the Life and Spirit of the People: They regifter'd all People Eftates, in order to exact certain Sums of Money! They will not fuffer the Inhabitants to ufe or plead their antient Laws, but the whole Magiftracy is eftablifhed by an arbitrary Power, under the dreadful Apprehenfions of Axes and Halters! Every County or Province hath its governing Officer, and every City its ruling Magiftrate. The Judges affemble every Term, and end Law-Suits; they being exalted in a lofty Chair or Seat, declare their proud and arrogant Opinions, being furrounded by Numbers of Bailiffs, Attornies, and other ignorant Pettifoggers, where Rods (worfe than Scorpions) are prepared for the Backs of the People, who being difarm'd of all Strength, are forc'd to fubmit to their fevere Difcipline! And every Year fome Lord or other eminent Perfon is oblig'd to change or furrender his Office, or fly his Country, or hold up his Hand at their black Tribunal! Yet, all this is not fufficient to fatisfy cruel Minifters! They make it a principal Part of their Bufinefs to promote Factions, and encourage Strifes among the Populace; and on fome Perfons beftow Penfions and Places, that they may have Tools enough to enflave the whole Nation.

Grubftreet Journal. Aug. 16. Nº 192.

BELLUM MEDICORUM.

Who can decide, when doctors difagree,
And foundeft cafuifts doubt, like you and me?

Mr BAVIUS,

THE late introduction of quickfilver into phyfical practice, has been the caufe of great expence of Chriftian ink, and unchriftian fcolding between the æfculapian combatants. And, which is the merrieft jeft of all, they pretend to give no one reafon why it is good for

E e e   fome-something, or nothing; nor account in the least for its *modus operandi :* which however, is not a greater wonder, than to see so many hundreds run into the whim of swallowing it as they do, to the quantity of several pounds weight; some for one distemper, and some for another; but great part of them, because they ail nothing, or are they don't-know-howish. Some pretend to have received wondrous benefit from it; some to have got marvellous mischief: others that it had done them neither good nor harm. Now to all such I would give this wholesome advice, to leave off whilst they are well. Let any man of common sense but consider these two things, (viz.) if it does not pass into the lacteals, it cannot associate with the blood, and so it will pass through the intestines without any effect, except such a one as it had on Mr *Booth* the tragedian; that is, mortified them from one end to the other. And if it does pass the lacteals, it must cause bloody work in some of the smaller vessels, and at best a salivation, that may prove fatal.—Let any one read Dr *Turner's Answer* to Dr *Dover's last Legacy to his Country*, and he will find much satisfaction in this controversy, if wit and learning, blended with experience and impartiality, can give him any. There is a fair account both of its tragical and comical Effects. Amongst the last, there is this remarkable one: A certain quick-silver lady dancing at a public assembly, the quicksilver she had taken that morning, flew out at her but-end, and all bespangled the floor! Which, by the glaring light of the many candles, the gentlemen took to be brilliants, and stooped down to take them up accordingly; but finding it was only quicksilver, and judging from whence it came, they cry'd out that some lady had scatter'd her diamonds; which moved much laughter amongst the gentlemen, and blushing amongst the ladies.

We are a people strangely given to quackery and novelty, and I make no doubt but the cry would run as much in praise of hasty-pudding, or even of the use and excellency of cow-heels, if half a dozen leading people, with a medicaster at the head of them, did but bellow out the wonderful cures they had perform'd. A few years ago, the whole nation, run a madding after the reverend Doctor *Hancock's* practice of drinking cold water, in almost every distemper, just as quick-

silver is cry'd up now. Till at last up-starts some merry fellow, by the name of *Gabriel John*, and exposed the Doctor and his practice, in such a ludicrous, but witty manner, that from that time, the custom dwindled, and grew out of use.

But as people are commonly most fond of what is prohibited, (especially the ladies) I am for every one's having liberty to die their own way; to that end, I am for recommending this mineral to be sold at all coffee-houses and brandy-shops. It would sound harmoniously to hear the guests call out, " Here boy! a dish of coffee, with two-penny worth of quick-silver: or, " Here landlord! a quartern of gin, and a quarter of an ounce of mercury." As to the ladies, let them introduce it to all their tea-tables, instead of cold nants. Let a small phial be emptied in each lady's dish that wants mercury in her tail, or is troubled with too much health, or that has the vapours to any fashionable degree. Only let it be a standing rule in each family, that all the quicksilver that every lady scatters from her lower end at such assemblies, shall be for the sole use of the servants that attend the tea-table. Let there be likewise free liberty to all to take it their own way, whether boiled, raw, stewed, fryed, and even broiled, if proper gridirons be procured for that purpose, that will not let all the fat run into the fire. And it is to be hoped, that with proper observation, every lady that takes it, will become a barometer, and foretell the weather by the rise and fall of the quick-silver in her guts, as well as any weather-glass whatever : which may be of vast advantage to tradesmen that take country houses, and for the increase of their substance, ride out of town from minding their shops and business two or three times a week, for the sake of country air, and because they are afflicted with too much health in the city. It will also be very convenient for the ladies themselves, thus to fore-know the weather, when it will be most proper to pay visits, or to lie a-bed and contrive, &c. These things I submit to your consideration.

But who would run, that's moderately wise,
A certain danger for a doubtful prize?

Weekly Miscellany, Aug. 18. N° 36.

Of Scepticism.

Mr HOOKER,

I Have often heard learned and religious Men wonder at the great increase of of *Scepticks* and *Freethinkers*: Now, I have often wonder'd that they do not increase much faster than we fee them at prefent, confidering the many Prerogatives and Privileges annex'd to their Quality. As 1ft, A Man may fet up in this Way with ever fo little Stock of Learning and Natural Parts, and yet flourifh in his Bufinefs. Let the moft arrgant Dunce but rail againft Priefts, burlefque the Scriptures, and banter every Thing facred and ferious, with a proper Degree of Affurance and Petulancy, and immediately he rifes up a Wit, and a Man of Senfe, and receives the Compliments of many a profound and *freethinking* Brother. The *Illiterati*, who, 'tis reckon'd, conftitute two Parts in three of the whole Nation, from a natural Ambition of Honour and Refpeft, incline to that Party, in which they may fhine and make a Noife with fo little Abilities and Attainments. What an excellent Afylum is this fceptical Society for a Man, that has juft Learning enough for the Appearance of a Scholar, but not enough to fecure him from blundering! You remember an Hero of the freethinking Club, that crowded a certain *Difcourfe* of his with Abundance of Extracts from *Greeks* and *Latins*,to the pleafant Entertainment of his *Orthodox* Adverfaries. What a Jeft were his *Rabbies at Sichem*, and his *fuch-like Prodigies*? yet was this Man extoll'd by his little Affociates, like a fecond *Grotius* or *B——y*. What a Number of enormous Errors in Hiftory and Criticifm have the Learned difcover'd in the famous Mr *T——l——d*? Yet was he a *Coryphæus* of the Sect. Now, who would not turn *Sceptick*, to eclipfe the *Grævius's*, *Gronovius's*, *Bocharts*, *Voffius's*, *Peatfons*, and *Stillingfleets*, without a thoufandth Part of their Knowledge? Whereas, not an hundred fuch Writers as *T——l*, on the Side of Chriftianity, would have ever acquir'd a Name, but funk immediately into Oblivion. 'Tis a bold and glaring Paradox, a wild and aftonifhing *Noftrum* ftarted with Confidence and Conceit, and defended with incorrigible Obftinacy that gives uncommon Talents of Reafon and Wifdom to a *C——b* or an *A——l*.

Again; what a convenient Privilege is it, to mifreprefent Authors, *antient* or *modern*, to mifquote or mif-tranflate, to curtail or interpolate, and force 'em into Service, without hurting your Honefty, or difquieting your Confcience! This is fo much a *Peculiar* of *freethinking* Writers, that, *a Letter to &c.* feems penn'd by fome ingenious *Academic* of that Turn.

One Privilege more claim'd by a *Freethinker*, and which no other Perfon has the Liberty of ufing, is, He may rail and ftorm, and call you Rogue, Cheat, Hypocrite, traduce whole Orders and Faculties of Men, yet his Invective is innocent and polite, and the Author a *Gentleman*. The groffer the Abufe, the fmarter the Sentence; and the deeper the Wound, the finer the Edge that makes it. Thus are the poor *Ecclefiafticks* rattled off by the *G——ns* and *T——ls*, and *R——ds*, by *Rights of the Church*, *Independent Whigs*, and long *Laymens Sermons*. Yet do but give a little Severity to your Pen againft them, and what an Outcry is made againft the *Orthodox*! *This is the Spirit of Orthodoxy*! *Spiritual Thermometer*! *Holy Fire*! *Cant of Bigots*! *Dogmatical Divines*! *Oppreffors of Reafon*! *Perfecution*! *Uncharitablenefs*. Alas, who would write for Religion, if thefe be the Terms? or who would read him that does? Who would be fetter'd with fo lifelefs and miferable a *Moderation*, that he muft not do Juftice to the Caufe he defends, nor rebuke and ridicule the moft foolifh and wicked Abfurdities? You too, Mr *Hooker*, muft be filent, for fear of offending a tender and touchy *Freethinker*. *Frange mifer calamos, vigilataque prælia dele.* **CANTAB.**

London Journal. Aug. 18. N° 738.

The late Tobacco *Scheme would have anfwer'd the End propofed.*

THE *Craftfman* endeavours to prove, That the Scheme about *Tobacco* and *Wine* would not have raifed 500,000 *l*. His Proof lies thus: The *Projector* himfelf, he fays, allow'd, *within Doors*, that the *Tobacco Scheme* would bring in no more than 30,000 *l*. But this, fay *Osborne*, *I know* to be *falfe*. Well, but in the famous *Letter* to the Electors *without Doors*, it was propofed to raife 200,000 *l*. on *Tobacco*, and 300,000 *l*. on *Wine*. But how can that be, fays this *Sagacious Reafoner*, when the *whole nett* Duties on *Tobacco* don't amount to much above 200,000 *l*. a Year; the Seizure not to 1400 *l*. a Year at a Medium of 7 Years? Can, therefore, the *Frauds undifcover'd* amount to as much as the whole *nett* Duty? (See p. 406.)

Osborne anfwers: The Number of Hogfheads of *Tobacco*, *annually imported* into *Great Britain*,are between 60 and 70,000; about

about 2 *thirds* of which are exported; so that there would remain for *Home-Consumption* about 23,000, if no part of that which was *exported* was *re-landed* or *run upon the Coasts.* The Duties on 23,000 Hogsheads at 15 *l.* per Hogshead, come to 345,000 *l.* yet at present, by the *Frauds Inwards* and *Outwards,* it produces Nett into the *Exchequer* little more than 150,000 *l.* Whence it follows, that the Duties, *were there no Frauds,* would be more than *doubled,* tho' no part of those 40,000 Hhds *exported,* were *re-landed* or *run,* the contrary of which is highly probable from the *Facts* in the *Report*; (See p. 351 H) which if true, there may be near 40,000 Hogsheads *consumed at Home,* the Duties on which would amount to 600,000 *l.* a Year, and so we should get 350,000 *l.* a Year by Tobacco, more than the *present Duty* brings in. But if *no part* of what is *exported,* was *relanded,* yet if there were no *Frauds* Inwards nor Outwards in the *one Third Part consumed at Home,* the Duties would come to 195, or 200,000 *l.* more than they do at present; whereby we should get as much as was proposed *without Doors* in the *Letter to the Electors*; and whence it follows, that the *Frauds undiscover'd* would amount to more than *the whole nett Duty* hath done for several Years past.

This is a full Proof from *probable Premises,* that the Tobacco would have done more than its part towards easing the Freeholders of 1 *s.* in the Pound.

But, says *D'Anvers, ought we to give up our Liberties* for the sake of such a *Saving?*] This is no Question, but among *designing Knaves*; for there is *no part of Liberty* given up by the *Scheme.*

Another *terrible Objection* against the Scheme is, *Not a Farthing of this Money could have been applied to the Ease of the Landholders, as the Laws stand at present.*] No! Why then we should have *alter'd the Laws.* These Duties being appointed to *particular Uses,* don't make *the Application* of the supposed *advanced Sum* to *other Purposes,* a *Violation of publick Faith*; for, if the *publick Faith* is *preserved* by the *Application* of the *present Duties,* then all that the Scheme brought in more, might be *applied* to ease the *Landholders,* or any thing else the Parliament thought fit.

Nothing is more ridiculous than to talk of a Law as *sacred* and *inviolable*; every Law ought to be *changed,* when more Good can be done to the Publick by chang-

ing it: The *Sinking Fund* itself is no more *sacred* than any *other Law*; and 'tis the Duty of the Parliament to apply that Money in such a Manner as the *whole People* may be most *eased* and *benefitted.* To talk, therefore, of *sacred Depositums* not to be diverted from their original Purpose, is to talk like an *Enthusiast,* or a Madman; for, if 'tis better that the Debts be paid off *very gradually*; and, that Interest Money be no *lower,* then this *sacred Depositum* should be so applied, as to *take off Taxes* burthensome to the *poor,* &c.

As to what the *Craftsman* asserts, That the *Scheme* would have necessitated the *encreasing the Land Tax,* by the *Diminution* of the Revenue; which would have been the unavoidable Consequence of making those *Commodities* of Tobacco and Wine *dearer,* and the *Consumption* less, he might as well have said, *Those Commodities* would have been *dearer* without the least *new Tax,* or *additional Duty*; and the Revenue would have been *diminished,* by being *increased.*

The *Free-Briton* August 16. No. 195.
On Mr Rysbrack's *Statue of K.* William III. *Heroes, Sculptors,* &c.

IT ought to be had in everlasting Remembrance, says Mr *Walsingham,* That when the COMMON COUNCIL of *London* refused *even to* READ a *Petition,* to erect a *Statue,* at the *Expence* of the Petitioners, in Honour of K. *William* III. (See p. 448) the *City* of BRISTOL, of their own *free Will,* raised a Statue at their *common Charge,* with a Magnificence worthy of his Fame, and of their *Affection* to his Memory.

The Statue Mr RYSBRACK hath formed with infinite Application and Success, is worthy of publick Attention; not only as it regards the *Memory* of K. WILLIAM, but as it is a *Work of Genius,* and will do Honour to this Nation. Methinks I see the Spirit of Antiquity sublimely expressed in every Stroke. It was thus that Senates dedicated Statues to their Gods and Patriots. Thus *private Genius* bore its Part in *publick Love.* The *Sculptor and the Statuary* vied in their Works with *living Nature,* whilst the *General* and the *Judge,* ambitious to be the *Subjects of those Arts,* vied in their Actions with the *immortal Gods.* But now the *Artist* and the *Hero* are alike rare, because that *divine Flame* which animated both, hath wanted due Encouragement.
Sir

Sir *Wm Temple* obferves, that *Cervantes* contributed more than all Men to fink the *Glory of the* Spanish *Nation.* The Ridicule of their *Enthufiafm* made the *Love of Glory* abate among them. Warmed by this Fire both *Art* and *Heroifm* are animated. The fame Spirit which fired *Alexander* formed his *Apelles* and *Praxiteles.* The HERO breathes in his *Statues,* and lives on his *Medals*; nor was *Alexander* more a Hero, than *Apelles* and *Praxiteles* were *Painters,* and *Statuaries.*

On the contrary, our *Heroes* and *Statuaries* have too often borne an even Proportion with the *Genius* and *Parts* of each other. Sublime *Genius* hath fo rarely appear'd in *Government,* or in Arms, during thefe laft Centuries, that it feemed not the *Growth of the Times.* It might give an *Englifhman* juft Concern, that the *Delight* and *Prodigy* of his Country, the invincible D. of *Marlborough,* fhould, in that ftupendous Pile, erected to the Memory of his Merits and Archievements, be fo ill requited by the *Statuaries* of his Times, that they could do him no more Honour, than by a vile Conceit over his Gate, of a *dreadful Lion,* the Supporter of the *Britifh Arms,* tearing to pieces a *miferable Cock,* being *Gallus* in Latin, fignifies alfo a *Frenchman.* From this *deteftable Abufe of Statuary* that *great* Man refcu'd his Fame. His *fuperior Genius* in *Arms* raifed him a Trophy worthy of himfelf, by taking the *Bufto of the late* French *King* from the *Gates* of LISLE, and placing it on a *Front* of *Blenheim.*

It is a Felicity, we have Reafon to be proud of, that the *two* greateft *Men,* whom the modern Times have known, or the *Englifh Armies* were ever led by, K. *William* III. and the D. of *Marlborough,* have lately had RYSBRACK to give them Life and Likenefs in *Brafs* and *Marble.* Q. *Elizabeth,* thought the execrable Reprefentations of her Perfon, by *wretched Imitators,* fo injurious to her Dignity, that fhe caufed them to be deftroyed in an *ignominious* Manner. No Hand can give the *Expreffion of a Hero* to any Figure, unlefs he is bleft with Genius to *conceive* the Reality of *Heroifm.* There muft be the *true Sublime* in the Artift's Imagination, otherwife he will never reach or defcribe the *Sublime* of fuch an *elevated Character.*

The Misfortune of the Moderns in general hath been, that they have made no Diftinction between *Artifts* and *Mechaniks,* but have rewarded *Science,* as if they were paying the Price of *meer* dull *Drudgery.* There is hardly any Price too large for the Works of a perfect Mafter; his Reward ought to be in Proportion to his Genius. I is a melancholy Circumftance, when Men of *fublime* Capacities have not *Scope for* ingenious *Induftry,* have not Leifure, Liberty, or Recompence for fuch Labour, as might carry Art to its higheft Excellency. Too many, inftead of being infpired with Emulation, and incited by Encouragement, to feek after fuch Attainments, have been doomed to the unwerthy Fortune of *work-ing for a meer* Livelihood; whilft the Generality of Men have neither had *Judgment* to difcern, or *Generofity* to reward thofe Arts, which in Ages paft would have fecured the Artift *boundlefs Wealth and Immortality.*

It hath indeed been fometimes feen, that Princes have had *Tafte* and *Difcernment* equal to their high Fortune. An *Emperor* was the Patron of TITIAN, and a *fovereign Pontiff* cherifhed the divine RAPHAEL. Thus *Charles the Fifth* raifed the *Venetian School,* and *Leo the Tenth* was the Founder of the *School of Lombardy,* where fo many excellent Painters were bred, and fuch marvellous Pictures were wrought. But fince thofe Times, that Country hath not feen *any fuch Encourager* of Science, and for that Reafon only hath not feen any fuch *great Mafters.*

Carlo Maratti, the beft *Roman Painter* of this laft Age, faid excellently well, when one of the *Roman Princes* cenfured him for the *exceffive Sums* which he demanded for his Paintings; "The World, *faid he,* owes a *vaft Debt* to the Great Men, who wrought in thefe Schools before me, and as their *lawful Succeffor* I demand the *Payment of* their *Arrears.*"

BERNINI had *Louis the Fourteenth* to reward him, and deferved fo munificent a Prince for his Patron. Is is to the Honour of the *Britifh Court,* that the Queen, who now adorns it, and as an *ingenious Foreigner* hath obferved, was *born to encourage the whole Circle of Arts,* hath taken *Statuary* into her Protection, and made her Retirement illuftrious by thofe *Monuments of Genius,* which fhe hath chofen to grace it. Nor is her Love to *learned Men,* and to the *Statuary-Art,* more diftinguifhing in this Inftance, than her *peculiar Affection* to this Country, and to the *Natives* of *Great Britain.* Whilft BACON and BOYLE, Sir ISAAC NEWTON and Dr CLARKE, LOCKE and WOLLAS-

TON,

TON, employ the Hand of RYSBRACK, and are placed in *her* GROTTO, her own *Leibnitz* is not allowed a Place there.

Whilst *Statuary* hath this Protection in the *Court* of *Great Britain*, I do not wonder to see RYSBRACK encouraged by so many of the *British Nobility:* It hath been allowed in his Praise, that he never undertook any great Work but with an *Industry* which far *exceeded his Reward,* and always shewed he wrought more for *Reputation,* than *any other Recompence.*

I am sorry, that the *modern Taste* hath been the lowest of all the *modern Attainments.* What a Passion hath prevailed for *Old China,* whilst the finest *Arts of Sculpture* have languished for want of Encouragement! What a Profusion of Expence does every noted *Toyshop* cost the *Beau Monde,* yet how small a Part of this Expence contributes to the Encouragement of *Genius* or *Science !* I verily believe, if *Praxiteles* himself had been an *English Sculptor,* and not been known in the late *Duke of Devonshire's* Life-Time, he would have found his Art of less Profit to himself, than to be a *Seller of Old Cloaths in Monmouth-street ;* and I have known those, who have carried his Art to a very great Height, less known and rewarded, than perhaps they might have been, had they laid out their *Time and Parts* in the antient and elegant Science of *a Taylor.*

The Schools of Antiquity, which have left us the noblest Memorials of *antient Genius* in Statuary and Sculpture, arose in the *free Commonwealth,* where the STATE itself was the *Patron and Rewarder of* SCIENCE. It seems a Promise of the same *Encouragement to* Science, when *Cities, in their corporate Capacity,* countenance such Works: And I will speak it for the *Honour* of BRISTOL, that *their City* hath as much distinguished *its Judgment in their Election of an Artist,* as *its Generosity* in the *Reward assign'd him.*

Having said so much of *Statuary,* as worthy the Protection and Care of a great, a *free,* and *wise* People, I will add, that, in the Countenance which we give to *Men of Genius,* we ought *wholly* to consider *Genius.* We should never take PARTY into the Affair, nor prefer a *bad* or *indifferent* Hand to a *good one,* on the *Score of Politicks.* I know not whether RYSBRACK be *Whigg* or *Tory.* I know him to be a *good Statuary,* and believe him to be an *honest Man* and *impartial Sculptor.* If he hath made a Busto of Sir

R——t W——le, he hath made a Monument for the late D——l P——y, Esq; Formerly indeed *Parties* were not so charitable ; SYMONDS, the most excellent Sculptor of all the Moderns, was, on a Tryal in *K. Charles the Second's* Time, wherein he shewed his infinite *Superiority* over all his Competitors, rejected by his Judges, and removed from his Office, only for having been unfortunately employed as an *Engraver* under O. CROMWELL.

It is owing to such *Wretchedness of Spirit,* that, not only the *Coins,* but even the MEDALS, which are to transmit the *Busto's,* and remarkable Incidents in the Lives of *our* PRINCES to all Posterity, have been the *meanest* of all *Performances,* and very scandalous *Caracatura's* of the *Royal Persons,* whom they were designed to represent, and whom *they* ought to represent, with all the Graces of a *masterly* Conception and Expression.

The **Craftsman,** August, 18. N° 372.

IT is pleasant to consider, what ridiculous Things are done by Men, who plead a sort of Title to the highest Offices of Government by Pretences of extraordinary Skill in *political Affairs.* They fancy that a *Minister* hath nothing to do but to form a *Party,* strong enough to support him at *Court,* and to carry on his Business in *national Assemblies.* When this is done, by a proper Distribution of Places, Pensions and Honours, He thinks he is a finish'd *Politician,* and drives on the Chariot of Government thro' thick and thin, and thus Flatterers extol him as a person of infinite Address. But this is only the Quackery of Government ; and requires no more Skill than packing a Jury, or carrying a Cause in *Westminster-Hall* by Subornation and false Evidence. The true Art of Government consists in a general Knowledge of Mankind, and the particular Disposition of the People to be governed. This is the most glorious and solid Foundation of Power, in a *free Country ;* for there is but little Difference between a People's being govern'd *according to the Will of their Rulers,* and in a Manner *contrary to their own Will.* One is the Consequence of the other, and both may be call'd *arbitrary Government.*

Tho' this be a self-evident Truth, yet nothing is more common amongst the *Minions of* Courts than to despise the Sense and Voice of the *People.* They are call'd the *Mob,* the *Vulgar,* the *Rabble,* &c.

&c. and treated, as if they had no more to do in Matters of Government than the Beasts of the Field. I do not mean, says *D'anvers*, the *Mob* or *Dregs* of a Nation, loose, idle, vagabond Wretches, but the Body of the *common People* in general, whose *natural Capacities* we shall find as docible and intelligent, in their Way, as Men of a much higher Rank. View them in a *moral Light*, they will appear, generally, as honest in their Dealings, as cordial in their Friendships, and as true to all their Engagements, as any *Courtier*, or *Minister of State* in the Kingdom. Even in *political Affairs*, we shall not find the *poor Tradesman* or *Country Farmer* so stupid as commonly represented by *Court Writers*. They judge of publick Measures, both in Peace and War, by the Effects, which they produce on their *Trade* and *Dealings*; a much surer Criterion than That, by which Gentlemen of Fortune are apt to form their Opinion of these Affairs. What, then, have these Men done to deserve such Treatment as they have lately receiv'd? But let us trace this Matter a little farther, with Regard to the *Constitution*.

It is acknowledged by the *Gentlemen on the other side*, that all Power was originally deriv'd from the *People*, and will revert to *Them*, whenever the *Constitution* is dissolved; that is, when our Governors break their Covenant with us.

If the *Majesty of the whole People is invested by our Laws in the Person of the King*, as Mr *Walsingham* asserts; it will follow, that the *Majesty of the King consists in the collective Majesty of the People*; I am sure his lasting Security is in *their Affection*.

Nor can I agree with *these Writers*, that the *People* have divested Themselves of all their *natural Authority*, by forming Themselves into *Society* and submitting to the Rules of *Government*; for by our Constitution, in some Cases, They have a greater Jurisdiction than the *King* himself. The Determination of *Property*, and the Power of *Life* and *Death* depend on the Verdict of an *English Jury*, composed of the *common People*. The King hath no Power to punish any Man, even for *High Treason against his own Person*, without the Judgment of the People, legally impanell'd upon a *Jury*. He is intrusted, indeed, with a Power to put the *Decisions of the People* in Execution; and in Cases *Criminal*, may remit the Punishment He cannot inflict; but

in all Disputes about *Property*, the *King* hath no Power to reverse, or dispense with the Judgment of the *People*; a Privilege they still continue to enjoy, by their *own glorious Spirit* and the honest Vigour of their Representatives, in Opposition to *Those*, who lately endeavour'd to deprive Them of it, in one of the most valuable Branches of *Property*.

This leads to another great Instance of the *Power of the English People*; whose distinguishing Characteristick it is, above all other Nations, *to obey Laws of their own making*. The *House of Commons* are only the *Deputies*, the *Trustees*, or (as Sir *R. Steele* called Them) the *Attornies of the People*, chosen to represent their Sense in Parliament; for which They formerly received *Wages* and *Instructions* from their Principals. The *latter Practice* hath been newly revived with great Success; and as the *former* is intirely laid aside, Care ought to be taken that They may not receive *Wages* from any else. A vast Power is still vested in the *People of England*, by this Right of *electing the House of Commons*. When Parliaments were only *annual*, or even *triennial*, this Power was much greater than at present, by returning so often. But even as the Law now stands, the whole Power of the *House of Commons* must revert to the *People* once at least in *seven Years*; and as that Time is now drawing near, it cannot be doubted that They will make a proper Use of it. I shall only put Them in Mind, that, if the *septennial Act* should not be repealed before the next Election, the *Length of the Term* ought to inspire Them with double Vigour.

How ridiculous therefore is it to argue that the *common People of England* have no Right to intermeddle in *publick Affairs*, nor Capacity to judge of Them? Will any Man pretend to deny, that the Happiness of *England*, and the very Being of our Constitution depends on a *free and uncorrupt Parliament*? Is not the Right of electing *that Branch of the Legislature*, which has the chief Power over the *Purse of the Nation*, reposed by our Constitution in the Body of the *People*? Does not *this Right* imply a Capacity of judging who are proper Persons to be intrusted with such a Power? and, where They are left to Themselves, do They not commonly discover a sufficient Capacity? I am not singular in my Opinion; *Cato* says, in his Letter to the *Freeholders March* 1722, (near a Year, after Sir

R.

R. W. was sworn into his present Places.)
—*If you did but know,* Gentlemen, *how you are used above by* Those, *who think it worth their Time to flatter you below and to your Faces, you would not want Admonition. You are called the Mob, the stupid Herd, the Dregs and Beasts of the People; and your Interest is never thought of by* those Men, *who thus miscall you; Men, who have no more* WIT, *much less* HONESTY *than your selves; whose Sauciness is owing to* Wealth, *plundered from you. It depends now on your selves, whether you will deserve these base and reproachful Names, or not. Shew that you are* MEN, *and you will be used like Men; but if you sell your selves, like* Beasts, *the* Purchasers *will have a Right to sell you again, and make honest Gains out of a villainous Bargain.*

The same *base and reproachful Names* have not only been repeated, but wonderfully improved, and extended to *Persons,* who never before pass'd under the Denomination of a *Mob.* The *principal Merchants* and *Traders of England* have now the Honour to be rank'd amongst the *Dregs of the People,* treated as a Gang of *Smuglers, Pedlars* and *perjured Rascals,* who cheat the *King,* and impose upon their *Fellow Subjects.* For this Reason *Fetters* were actually prepared for Them; and when They came down to *Westminster,* in a legal Manner, to supplicate the Parliament against so cruel an Expedient, They were scouted by the *Projector,* and branded with the infamous Name of STURDY BEGGARS.

This Appellation hath however discovered the Spirit of the *Man,* and united Them all against Him, for their common Security. It hath likewise brought a *good old Time* into Fashion, and made it the favourite Entertainment in all publick Assemblies, *without the Verge of the Court.*

It is really astonishing that He should persist in these Insults, or encourage his *Advocates* to renew Them, after so memorable a Defeat, and the Rebukes he hath met with in most of the chief Towns and Corporations in *England.* But *Quos Jupiter vult perdere, prius dementat.*

Let us suppose that a *great Man,* upon travelling the Road, should be thrown into a Ditch, and seeing some Country Fellows not far off, should call out to Them in the manner following; Hark'ee, you RASCALS, *come hither and help me out of the* MIRE.—Would it not be natural for

an honest Rustick to reply; *Waunds, Sir, if you can't keep good Words in your Mouth, you may lye and rot there for us?*

I have heard a Story of a *French Bishop;* who (being a Man of Quality, as the Bishops general are in *France*) thought it beneath his Dignity to address his Flock in the usual Style, *Mes cheres Freres,* or *dearly beloved Brethren;* but began his Sermon thus; *Canaille Chretien, ecoutés la Parole de Dieu;* Ye CHRISTIAN SCOUNDRELS, *listen to the Word of God!—* But what was the Consequence? Why the whole Congregation went immediately out of Church, and left the *proud Bishop* to preach by Himself.

The *Merchants* and *Traders of England* have lately been used in just the same complaisant Style by our *Lay-Primate.* But as they live in a *free Country,* they have already discovered some Marks of their Resentment, and perhaps, may soon express it in a more effectual Manner. The *Spirit of Liberty* is so generally diffus'd amongst Them, that it cannot be easily suppress'd. Let the *Projector* call Them *Scoundrels* and *Beggars,* as much as He pleases: but, I thank God, it is in their own Power not to be made *Slaves.*

I shall conclude with an Observation of the Ld *Clarendon* on the great Earl of *Strafford,* whose pernicious Measures brought not only his *own* Head to the Block, but likewise That of his *unhappy Master,* by endeavouring too long and obstinately, though at last in vain, to screen Him from the Justice of the Nation. *Of all his Passions,* says the noble Historian, *his Pride was most predominant; which a moderate Exercise of Ill-fortune might have corrected and reformed; and which was by the Hand of Heaven strangely punished, by bringing his Destruction upon Him by two Things, that He most despised, the People and Sir* Harry Vane.

Grubstreet Journal, August 23 No. 191.

FRiend *Ezra,* in a Letter from *Norwich,* makes several Remarks on M. VOLTAIRE's *Letters* concerning the *English* Nation lately publish'd; instances in many Particulars wherein *Voltaire* charges the *Quakers* with Ceremonies, Customs, and Sayings which they never use; proves him guilty of Contradictions and Nonsense; and concludes, " Such a Collection of Lies, as he has pack'd together in p. 17, 18, 19, 20, 21, I never read; and at which, indeed, I wonder'd not, when I heard, that *active Man,* when in *England,* had

had an excellent Knack of *Multiplying* a Small Sum to a greater, in a — by way of *Erafement, &c.* Nor is it to be thought ftrange, that he has fcribbled thefe *ridiculous* Paffages about us, when it feems to be his whole Bufinefs, to make a *Droll of Religion.*

A new Candidate for the Crown of Poland.

My dear Coufbin BAVIUSH,

I Mufht informe you, my deare Joy, that all my pofhterity were BAVIUSHES,— both fhirnames and chrifhen names, boyefh and girlefh, were every mothers fhon of them named BAVIUSH. And as I find that your *Shournall* comes out every day onefh a week, and that you are a fhecretary, and can read and write, you may do your relafhiofi very great mufh kindnefs. For arra joy ! in the firfht and fecond plaafh,. I mufht be after on telling you, that I have long had a petifhion in my pocket, to be made a great man; and have waited for that purpofh upon two lords footmans, my old acquaintance by mother's fhide ; who all-both promifhed to get me into bifhnefs very fhpeedily, one time or other, in the black guard, or eufhtom houfh. But indeed now, I have got no-ting at all, nor that nither. Therefore my requefht is, that as there is now hereafter, a very great opportunityefh to do a fhmall mattersh for your he-coufhin, my owne fhelfe, that you will be graceoufly pleafhed, to maake me king of Poland, till fhomething better may be done for me. I mufht tell you, my dear coufhin, this may faave mufh chrifhan bloodfhed, and many good catholick livefh. For I will have no fightingfh, nor quarrelingfh, but only prayingfh to the Pope and St PATRICK, and burning of hereticklh, and drinking of ufhqubaugh, and eating bonny clabber and potatoefh, and fing lilliburleero.

If you pleafh, deare coufhin, to put me on board the Frenfh fquadron, with coufhin STANISLAUS, we may be both king of Polands ; or he may be king, and arra ! I may be king over him, which will be as well, for the better : and then, coufhin, you fhall be knighted, and be a great lords, or an excifhman ; and I will marry your godmother, and maake a man of her.—But I mufht defire of you, to lend me five pundfh, to buy me an equipage ; or if you have not fo mufh ready monyfh abroad, in the houfhe, let me have forty fhillingfh, and give me bond for the refht. I defire your fpeedy anfwer, by the next pofht, fhome day before Chrifhmas, by the firft return of the carryer, and write carrifh paid ; becaufe I have no monyfh to pay the porterifh, and owe my landladyefh two ninepenfhes for lofhing in her garret, a fortfhight and two weekfh. Thufh, my dear

joy, in doing your fhelfe no good, and me no hurtfh, you will allways fometimefh oblige bote my owne fhelfe, and all my predeceffhors, to the end of the worldfh. And now, deare joy, if it be needlefh, and I fhould come fhort, of failing to be king of Polands, I petifhion your neglifhence, that I may be made a man-midwife, or a confetfhioner, or a boot-catcher in fome ale-houfe, that is a great inn, indeed now ; and fho I refht your owne deare coufhin,

DEARMOT MAC BAVIUSH.

The **Daily Courant**, Auguft 22.

Reply to the Craftfman.

IN the Adminiftration of the Gentleman who fpeaks fo feelingly in the *Craftfman* (See p. 415.) the act of Succeffion, tho' as much a Law then as now, was a *Ballad* and *wafte Paper*, the *Minifter* of the Prince and his Memorial were treated in fuch a manner as tho' the Succeffion was *fecured to the Pretender*, elfe his Seat in the Houfe of Peers had not been deny'd his prefent M—y.

This Sneerer on the *Parliament's* Refolution to fupport his Majefty's *German Dominions*, ought to remember, it was at a Time when thofe *Dominions* were threatned with an *Invafion*, on account of the Meafures his Majefty had taken to fecure *our* Trade, endanger'd by the Eftablifhment of the *Oftend Comp.* Where then was the Injury done to thefe Nations, by an Act that our own National Honour and Security were concerned in, unlefs his Majefty is to be worfe treated than an *Ally?* and how are we hurt by his late or prefent Majefty's Vifiting their *German Dominions?*

Every *Briton* wifhes the Act of *Settlement,* and every other Law which reafonably circumfcribes the Prerogative, and fecures Liberty, may be for ever preferved inviolate. If there be a Man who would extend the Prerogative beyond its legal Bounds, or a Villain who wou'd mifreprefent the Conduct of a juft Prince, to make the People uneafy, let him have the *Curfe* of, and fall a Victim to, his injur'd Country. (See p. 415 G)

The great Security we now enjoy is *Primarily* owing to the *Courage, Wifdom,* and Succefs of the *Immortal* K. *William,* and thofe *Patriots* who brought about the *Revolution*; but I confefs, was not *complete* till the Act of Succeffion took Place. This we had almoft fatally proved, when the late *Queen's Miniftry* (amongft whom were the L— B——d and Sir W——

W——)

E f f

W——) complimented her Majesty more on her *indefeasable hereditary Right,* than upon her *Parliamentary Title;* and brought the deluded People to offer her the *Incense* of *Passive Obedience, and Non-Resistance.* Then indeed our *Rights* were *precarious;* but now the *Crown* claims only by that *Compact,* which is as binding to the *People* as to the *Prince,* and enter'd into for their *Benefit,* as well as his *Honour.* J. ENGLISH.

The **Craftsman,** August 25. No. 373.

MR *D'anvers* begins with a Defence of some of his late Papers, which, with his *Political Creed,* had offended the *Ministerial Advocates;* Particularly, where, in defining the Nature of our Government, he called *it a sort of* REGAL COMMON-WEALTH, (See p. 357. A) The Word *Commonwealth,* says he, does not always signify a *Democracy,* or *popular State;* but is often applied to all sorts of Government, as *Poland, Venice,* &c. and I added the Word *regal,* to distinguish it from a *simple Commonwealth;* and as our Government is lodged in *three different Estates,* it can't be properly called a *Monarchy,* any more than an *Aristocracy,* or *Democracy,* because it partakes of all.

I had likewise asserted, says *D'anvers,* That *the late Opposition had been carried on entirely on* WHIG PRINCIPLES, *the Principles of the* REVOLUTION. (See p. 339. A) Upon which *these Gentlemen* reply'd, Nobody deny'd them to be *Revolution-Principles,* since us'd to effect *another Revolution,* (See P. 354) But I declare, I mean only *those Principles,* which brought about the *late Revolution,* in Favour of K. *William.* I am likewise charged with saying, *I am not determin'd to lay down this Paper, till my Readers were convinced, that* something farther *was intended, than an* Alteration of Persons; by which 'tis insinuated that the *Constitution* and *present happy Establishment* are marked out for Destruction: (See p. 364 G) But my only Meaning was, an *Alteration of Measures.* Thus well-meaning People are alarmed with Apprehensions of Designs against the Government, where Reformation of Abuses, and Preservation of our Constitution are only intended.

Great Pains have been taken to possess the *Protestant Dissenters* with such an Opinion, to frighten them into the Measures of *Those,* who have no great Reason to expect their Assistance. For this End, They have been told that the *Pro-*

testant Succession is in Danger from the present Opposition; and that if a *certain Gentleman* be removed, They have nothing to expect but immediate Persecution. But they are too wise to be so imposed on; and too well acquainted with the *present State* and *Temper of the Nation,* to be terrify'd with such Bugbears.

But how came *this Gentleman* to be such a Friend and Patron of the *Dissenters!* 'Tis true, he voted and spoke against the *Schism Bill;* But he as warmly opposed the Repeal *of that Act,* in the late Reign.

The Author of the *Independent Whig* has a Passage to this Purpose: Mr W*—— was once their* (the Dissenters) *great Favourite. They see how* HE *served them. Have they found others much kinder?*

This Mr *W——* was a *Country Gentleman* when he opposed the Repeal of the *Schism Act,* as well as when he voted against passing it; whatever were his private Reasons, 'tis certain in both Cases, he acted in Opposition to the *Gentlemen then in Power;* and therefore the *Dissenters* are under no Obligation to Him, on that Account.

What has been done since to deserve their Favour? 'Tis well known what Part he, and his Creatures, acted last Year, with Regard to the *Sacramental Test;* tho' what the *Dissenters* ask'd and expected was only in Pursuance of *repeated Promises.* But, it seems Matters of greater Consequence, then in Embryo, made it *improper* to perform them; and the Event has shewn how heartily concern'd he was for their *civil Interest,* tho' *Reasons* of State would not permit him to make Them easy in their *religious Affairs.*

Probably the same Game may be play'd over again at this Juncture, when *their* Assistance is become so necessary to a *certain Gentleman;* they will, likely, be caress'd and cajol'd with Promises of great Matters to be done for them, if they will only concur with him in the Choice of a *new Parliament,* as well as of *Corporation-Magistrates* at the approaching Election: But let them remember what this Gentleman told them last Year, as well as what hath pass'd since, and then judge whether he can have any Inclination, or Power, to do any Thing for Them. Let Them consider, that their Interest is the same with ours; and as they joined cordially with the rest of their Countrymen, in opposing the late Attempt upon our *common Liberties,* I hope They will not be be induced to enable the *Projector* to revive and execute his Scheme.

I shall conclude with a short Address to my Readers of all Denominations.

Gentlemen,

IT is now *manifest, by the unusual Applications made throughout the Kingdom, that the Choice of a new Parliament is a Point of the utmost Consequence. If you continue to exert that truly publick Spirit, which has already discover'd itself amongst you, we may still live to see the Accomplishment of our Wishes, in the flourishing Condition of our Country, which nothing can so effectually destroy as a Division amongst yourselves; and depend on't, no Artifices will be left untry'd to create such a Division. Be therefore on your Guard, and shew you are in earnest, by rejecting such Persons as have already deceiv'd you, and espousing Those, who have proved faithful to their Trust.*

Fog's Journal. August 25. No. 251.
Substance of a Letter from Bobadillo, *to the Primate of* Poland.

May it please your Highness,

SInce the Administration of Affairs has been wholly committed to my Management, I have so notably bestir'd myself, that, without Vanity, I may conclude my Name and Character have reached your Ears. But as my Renown and Exploits at home may have been only transmitted to you by my most notorious Adversaries, such as haughty Landlords, ignorant Merchants, useless Traders, paltry Shop-keepers, and audacious Handy-Craftsmen, it will not be superfluous to give some Account of my Residence and Conduct.

Know, then, I am at least Third in Power, in an Island call'd *Utopia*, which, with another adjacent one, the new *Atlantis*, forms a powerful Kingdom. A bold, hospitable sort of People, but so stiff-neck'd, and obstinate that it's almost impossible to persuade them out of their Senses, or to convince them, that I and one or two more under my Direction, understand their Interest better than they do themselves.

Tho' our *Archon*, or chief Magistrate's Power is limited, yet we (that is to say I) who administer Affairs, have found Means to be as absolute as we please, that is, we can promote our Creatures, wreak our Malice against insolent Opposers, appear prodigal, yet amass immense Treasure. — From this last Consideration I presume I am no unworthy Candidate for your vacant Throne; for notwithstanding the Fertility of *Poland*, I have heard, Money does not abound there, which is owing to the Excellence of your Laws and Customs. This is agreeable to my

Maxim, that the surest Method to prevent Insurrections, is to enslave the People.

I am also assured, that your King's Power is very extensive, your Nobles absolute, and the People Slaves. Most excellent Constitution! I envy'd Condition! this Scheme I shall pursue, with this Difference, that to preserve Peace and Quiet I will make all the *Palatines* my Pensioners.

It may be fancied, that when the Merchants, Farmers, Mechanicks, &c. are exhausted, it will be difficult to find Supply for our craving Appetites, but there is Wealth enough to last my time, and I never trouble my self about what may hereafter be.

I persuade my self I shall meet with your Eminence's Concurrence in our material Point, the Improvement of the Revenue of the Crown. I am inform'd, that the yearly Income of your late King, never amounted to 100,000 Crowns, which was entirely swallow'd up by his Courtiers and Pensioners. My Ambition for a Diadem, is very vehement, I must acknowledge; but unless you consent to my Measures for encreasing the Revenue, I shall remain in *Utopia*, since the obtaining a greater Sum, than the whole Income of your Crown, is to me only the Exercise and Amusement of one Morning.

I have only to add, that it is not wholly Ambition or Avarice, which prompts me to run a Crown-hunting; (for both those are pretty well gratify'd where I am;) but, to let your Highness into a Secret, I see a Storm gathering against me, and it is high Time to look out for a Retreat somewhere. I am, &c.
BOBADILLO.

Universal Spectator. August 25. No. 255.
A Lesson for bad Husbands.

SIR *Jasper Truby*, appearing under a deep Concern at the *Club*, being importuned, declared the Reason of it in the following Terms. I have just received the News, said he, of the Death of *Eudoxia*, a Lady to whom I was formerly *Guardian*; I married her to a polite young Gentleman, of good Sense, Family, and Fortune, as the most effectual means to make her Life happy. The first Six Years of their Marriage was a continued Scene of *Felicity* and *reciprocal Endearments*: But how unaccountable are the *Madnesses of Men!* Notwithstanding all his *good Sense, Love* for his *Wife,* and *Care* for his *Children,* this *fond, careful* Husband turn'd a *Debauchee!* Corrupted by a Set of *Men of Pleasure,* he lost his *Innocence* and his *Virtue.* This unexpected Course of Life ran him in *Debt,* and threatned his Family with *Poverty* and *Misery.* His Wife in all the *Agonies of Grief,* pour'd out her Complaints for the Conduct of a *Husband* she *still lov'd*; he receiv'd her Remonstrances with good *Humour,* and some Concern,
and

and mov'd by the moſt irreſiſtible Power of her *Tears*, ſwore the moſt *ſacred Oaths* in Promiſe of *Amendment*. But infatuated to his looſe Companions, he loſt the Remembrance of his *Oaths*, *Wife* and *Children*. *Eudocia*, tired out with *vain* Interceſſions, wrote the following Letter, which ſhe made her *little Boy* and *Girl* carry him one Morning, when he was Sick with his Evening *Debauch*.

My Dear Husband,

How can I believe you love me, when you perſevere in what will terminate with my Death, and the Ruin of your Children? You profeſs a Fondneſs for your Children ; *let then theſe* little Orators *plead in their own Behalf. Look on them my Dear, with the Tenderneſs of a Father, and think of their being abandon'd to* Shame *and* Want: *Shall the Darlings of your Soul, the Offsprings of your Love, accuſe their Father for their Miſery?* —— *Look once more on your* Supplicant Babes; *obſerve their Concern impreſs'd on them by their Mother's* Tears, *and* Nature *muſt prevail. Do not you feel all the* Pangs *of Remorſe? All the Agonies of Love and Nature? Does not your Heart ake? your Soul melt?—Save, oh! ſave then your* Children, *otherwiſe deſtin'd to Poverty and* Sorrow.——*As for your* Eudocia, *ſhe has felt too deep an Impreſſion to ſurvive it long.*—

Here ſays, Sir *Jaſper, Guilt, Love* and and *Nature* moving all his Paſſions, he burſt into Tears ; the innocent Cries of his Children added new Tortures to his *Agony.*—He ſnatched both up in his Arms, and haſtened to *Eudocia's* Chamber: He found her on the Bed, drown'd in Tears, deſpairing of Succeſs, and forming to herſelf the moſt terrible Proſpect of future Calamities: He ran into her Embraces, and kiſs'd her and her Children a thouſand times over, and when his *Paſſion* would permit him, thus began, " You have conquer'd, my *Eudocia*, a *diſſolute unthinking Husband*: I ſee my *Follies*, and it's yet in my Power to retrieve my *Fortune*, and make you and theſe dear *Infants* happy."—*Eudocia*, with an Extaſy, flinging her Arms about his Neck, *Perſiſt*, ſays ſhe, *my dear, dear Husband, in your Reſolution, nor let theſe* BABES *ſuffer by your* Perfidy.—*As for me, I have but a ſmall ſpace to live ; my* Sorrows *have been too great: But to demonſtrate your* Love *to me, be careful of our* Children.—Unable to utter more, with a tender *Look*, bowed her Head and expir'd. Who can conceive the Agonies of the fond *convicted* Man when he heard his *Children* lamenting their *Mother*, dead with Grief for the *Miſconduct* of their *Father* ; when he ſaw the *tendereſt Wife* fall a *Victim* to an *unthinking Husband?*

The Free Briton, Auguſt 23. No. 196. *is only a Letter of* Cato's, *which he quotes againſt the* Craftſman, *to ſhew that in all Governments there are Politicians who are Enemies*

to the *preſent Eſtabliſhment, not becauſe it is an ill one, but becauſe they themſelves are not in it.*

London Journal, Auguſt 25. N°. 739.
The Craftſman, *a traiterous Libel.*

THE *Craftſman of Aug.* 11 (See p. 415.) declares our new *Magna Charta* (the *Act of Settlement*) broke, the *Conſtitution* diſſolved ; and is nothing leſs than an Introduction to a *Declaration of War* againſt his Majeſty.

The *Act of Settlement* is call'd the *Compact between King and People* ; as tho' there was none really exiſting to that Period of Time. All our *Rights* antecedent to this *ſecond Magna Charta*, are treated as chimerical Things ; but now we have, it ſeems, *poſitive Laws* againſt our Kings ; and the *Conditions* and *Limitations* in the *Act of Settlement*, are the ONLY TENURE by which the King holds his *Crown*; and *Two of the fundamental Points* of this Act, the *Craftſman* plainly inſinuates, are broke thro' ; the *Inference* from which is, that the People are abſolved from their Allegiance ; or, in his own Words, *are no longer bound to obey.*

But the *Act of Settlement* is not a *Change of Government*, as the *Craftſman* aſſerts ; nor are its *Articles fundamental, ſacred, or unalterable*. The Government, the Rights of the *Crown*, and thoſe of the *People*, were the ſame before. There are, indeed, no human Laws *unchangeable* ; if the *Legiſlative Power* hath taken away *Two* of theſe reſtraining Articles, the *Conſtitution* is the ſame. But, if the King, by his ſole *Power*, had diſpenſed with, or broke thro' theſe Articles, he would have *invaded* the Laws, and violated his Coronation Oath ; but this is not *pretended* to be the Caſe ; and he never left his *Britiſh* Dominions, or deſires to ſupport or increaſe his *German*, without *Conſent* of Parliament.

What, therefore, the *Craftſman* hath ſaid about theſe two *fundamental Points* in the Act of Settlement is Nonſence : 'Tis not only *ridiculous*, but *Treaſonable* to inſinuate, That the King hath broke thro' the *Conſtitution*, and that the People are abſolved from their *Allegiance*, when his Majeſty hath broke no Law.

Another *Point* propagated among the People is, *That tho' the King is ſuperior to every Individual, yet he is inferior to the Collective Body of the People.* An Aſſertion abſolutely falſe and *tending to Treaſon* : For what is the *whole People* but *all the Individuals?* to every one of them, the King is, even by this Author, acknowledg'd *Superior.* This ſhews the *Aſſertion* to be compleat Nonſenſe. But beſides, 'tis *againſt Law*; for the King is, by the Laws of *England*, in all *Cauſes, and over all Perſons*, Supreme, i. e. in his *Executive* Power.

Some Eſſays being unfiniſh'd, are defer'd to our next that they may appear to better Advantage.

PRIZE

PRIZE VERSES, No. VI.

On the QUEEN *and the* BUSTOES *plac'd in her* GROTTO.

DEscend from heav'n, *Urania,* sacred guest,
And now with all thy fervours warm my breast,
To the high theme of CAROLINA's praise,
And each distinguish'd sage, my numbers raise.
Say, what ennobles most a royal name,
And wins a glorious, an immortal fame?
Not the bright crown. the proud triumphal car,
With all the trophies of successful war,
How many thousand kings have sunk to dust,
Their mem'ries and their names for ever lost?
A thousand victors in oblivion lye,
Whose loud applause once shook the vaulted sky?
Why are they shrouded in eternal night?
'Cause unillumin'd with fair virtue's light:
'Tis virtue only wins th' immortal prize,
Virtue, more durable than earth or skies!
'Twas this, *Britannia,* taught the blooming maid
To slight the crown which at her feet was laid;
In vain the charms of empire tempt her youth
To deviate from the paths of sacred truth;
How justly heav'n in her pious zeal approves,
And gives a crown to guard the faith she loves!
By her example, ye distinguish'd fair,
Who the same awful heights of empire share,
By her example, form each royal grace,
And show'r down blessings on your subject race.

Virtue and science! lo they both unite,
And blaze in CAROLINE with matchless light!
From splendid scenes which females most admire,
Behold the solitary *Queen* retire!
She seeks her humble *Cell,* and turns her eyes
Where the five venerable *Bustoes* rise;
Then feeds on thoughts, sublime which raise the mind
Above the trifling cares of humankind;
With *Boyle,* the secret springs of nature views,
And the coy pow'r thro' all her wilds pursues.
With *Wollaston,* revolves the moral tyes
Which mutually from conscious beings rise;
Beings, in one great common int'rest joyn'd,
And all dependent on th' eternal mind.
Now, *Locke,* the human soul's extensive pow'rs
(Thy own great theme) employ her studious hours;
Then wafting soft from empyreal skies,
Religion like a blooming cherub flies
Lur'd by persuasive *Clarke;* the royal breast
Receives with rapture the celestial guest:
And now she leaves the earth, and wings her flight
With *Newton* thro' unbounded fields of light;
Enraptur'd, tracks the planets wandring way,
And orbits where excentrick comets stray:
Millions of worlds possess the vast profound!
Millions of suns with planets circling round!
Planets, which secondary planets grace,
Endless the wonders of th' ethereal space!
These are the studies which a *Queen* admires;
String to her praise, ye bards, your sounding lyres,
In ev'ry clime repeat her honour'd name,
And spread thro' her your own immortal fame.

O *Richmond,* happy in so great a guest!
Whose praise shall all thy pleasing scenes out-last;
Thy *palaces* to wasting time may yield,
Thy *hill* be level'd with the humble field;
Old *Thames* may fail, or choose a diff'rent way,
And thro' remoter plains his waves convey;
But *Carolina's* fame no damage fears
From the wild ravage of a thousand years;
Her *Grotto* fate shall from oblivion save,
Till fainting nature seeks a final grave.

PRIZE VERSES, No. VII.

On the QUEEN's *Grotto.*

Dignos laude viros musa vetat mori.

HAil, royal dome, adorn'd with solemn state,
In mem'ry of the wise, the good, the great!
No more let strangers boast of *Greece* or *Rome,*
Wisdom's fair temple now is found at home.
Behold the monumental marbles rise,
What forms, what features strike the gazing eyes!
How awful, how to life each count'nance wrought
In stone, profoundly grave, as, when alive, in thought.
First rank doth learning's generous patron claim,
Himself a noble mirror of the fame;
Strict piety in whose sagacious mind,
And lib'ral arts in happy conceit joyn'd,
Seraphic BOYLE, thy search in nature's store
Was but to learn t' admire thy maker more!
See rev'rend CLARK, whose pleasant lips were hung
With sweeter strains than flow'd from *Nestor's* tongue.
How venerable his stile! how strong his sense!
How soft, how moving, is his eloquence!
How dread his warnings from the sacred word!
Learn justice, mortals, hence, and fear theLord.
Alas! in vain are all persuasive Arts
(Tho' from a CLARK) to melt obdurate hearts;
Reason and rhetorick in vain combine,
'Till heav'nly pow'r assays, and grace divine.
Ingenious LOCKE, 'twas nobly of thee design'd
T'assert the native freedom of the mind,
To disembarrass us of prejudice,
And mark th' extremes of reason and caprice,
To break th' ignoble fetters of the soul,
And range in quest of truth without unjust controul:
Thou teachest how by conscious mental act
We form, associate notions, and abstract;
Declar'st th' original and vast extent
Of thought, belief, opinion, and assent,
Laborious knowledge teems in every line,
And *Plato's* fam'd ideas yield to thine.
Thine essay, wond'rous man! shall ever live,
And to thy learned name perpetual honours give.
See next that sun of art well skill'd to draw
A just description of the primal law.
In equal balance WOLLASTON perpends
The moral weight of actions and their ends;
And states their moments; tut'ring heedless youth
To speak, to act, to live eternal truth
Sets in an easy, but surprising light,
The mathematic principles of right.
Mankind admires in this new form to see
A demonstration of morality,   B*u*

But where's the great incomparable sage,
The ornament and wonder of his age?
Huygenius, Tycho, Kepler, high in fame,
Bow to the honours of an *English* name.
The system never was from errors free,
Till NEWTON rose and said, Let darkness flee.
Thus have I seen the sun compel to flight
At once the gloomy horrors of the night,
And pour thro' th' universe his own impetu-
    ous light.
Thy principles, illustrious sir, proclaim
Nature and NEWTON meant the very same.
Who has explor'd like him the planets course,
Their gravitating and projectile force?
NEWTON without a rival reigns alone,
Prince of the new philosophy, his own.
Such was his genius, such his vast command,
T' improve what science e'er he took in hand;
What e'er he touch'd, howe'er abstruse his theme,
He clear'd the rubbish, and refin'd the scheme.
Thro' the wide world his various learning flies,
His fame is only bounded by the skies;
Prodigious man! accept my feeble lays,
A mortal tribute to immortal praise.
Nor thou remain unsung, fair CAROLINE,
In whom the graces with the muses joyn;
By hon'ring these great names in lasting stone,
To ev'ry *British* heart thou hast endear'd thine
    own.
This, of thy glory, is no mortal part,
Great patroness of piety and art.
How bright thy virtues, O illustrious Queen,
And numr'ous as a constellation seen!
In vain my muse attempts the long detail,
Unequal is her strength, her numbers fail;
These monuments of virtue thou didst raise
In deepest silence better speak thy praise.

PRIZE VERSES, No. VIII.

To her MAJESTY, *on her* GROTTO.

WHile, *matchless queen,* amid your *lov'd* retreat
   You deign to build the *muses* sacred seat,
Thy *chosen sages* from the tomb *remand,*
And bid 'em *rise* beneath the *sculptor's* hand;
Britannia's hopes indulge the *bright presage,*
And from thy *Æra,* date her *classic age.*
On the *state volume* now, the *labour'd piece*
Applauded work of *Rome* or antient *Greece.*
No more shall *fame* with *partial honours* smile
To shame the *muses* of thy *happier isle;*
Thy *grotto* shall with their *triumphs* vie,
And *greater names* a *loftier verse* supply.
Not with more *awe* the *pious chief* essay'd
To view the *wonders* of that *hallow'd shade,*
Than we thy *venerable* CELL survey,
And to it's *honour'd guests* our *solemn visit* pay.
O could my *muse* obtain the *secret power*
To trace *thee* in thy calm *sequester'd hour,*
When from the *splendid courts* admiring train
Thy *lonely feet* the *wonted covert* gain,
There (*only conscious to heav'n's purer eyes,*)
Pleas'd, shou'd I mark thy *warm devotion* rise,
See *humble majesty* at *large* express,
In all its native noblest glories dress'd;
Then view the*/ seated queen* in deep amuse
Each *reverend bust* with *earnest gaze* peruse,

Till *dewy tears* her *tender conflict* tell,
And own the *merit* she rewards so well;
Or while, perhaps, to *studious arts* inclin'd,
She reads th' *immortal labours* of their mind,
An *intervening glance* her thought relieves,
And the *lov'd form* her *silent praise* receives.
If LOCK present his *deep judicious page,*
Apparent *truths* her *pleas'd assent* engage;
Great man! who with *laborious search* defin'd
The *powers, and compass,* of the *humane mind.*
Or if experienc'd BOYLE's *sagacious schemes*
Invite her thoughts to *philosophic themes;*
They yield before his *all discovering ray,*
And *science* triumphs in *unclouded day.*
When WOLLASTON delineates *natures laws,*
(*How lovely, the resembling draught he draws!*)
Or CLARK, religion's heavenly truths proclaims,
And with his powerful lore the soul enflames,
Her looks the *pleasing energy* disclose
And her *rais'd breast* with *sacred rapture* glows,
If NEWTON writes of *gravitation's* force,
Or traces *colours* from their *lucid source,*
Abstrusest themes beneath *her knowledge* fall,
She reads with *ease,* and comprehends 'em *all.*
Amazing artist! whose *discerning eyes*
Search'd the *vast systems* of th' *illumin'd skies,*
Taught what *fixt laws* the *circling orbs* obey,
And first describ'd the *comet's* devious way.
  Hail ye *great sages!*—her *delightful cares,*
O may no *fate* the *lasting work* impair!
May your *own fame* a *sure duration* give,
And make the *sculptor's labour* ever live.
Yet if, *illustrious queen,* her fond request
The *muse* might offer, to thy *gen'rous breast,*
When with *like favours* thy *unwearied hand*
Prepares a-new to *bless* a *grateful land,*
Thy *Milton,* oh! thy *Britain's Orpheus* grace,
And *introduce him* to the *sacred race;*
Thy late indulgence * amply has display'd
How well thy love esteem'd the darling *shade;*
Approve him still, the merit will be known
When age disfigures the *resembling stone.*—
  Yet—thy own *virtues* shall a trophy raise,
And swell thy annals with *distinguish'd praise.*
—Let the rear'd bust the deep inscription fail,
And time at length o'er nature's self prevail,
Thy worth, *imperial fair!* shall *firm* endure,
And in *eternal skies* a *nobler fame* secure.

  * *Her Majesty's royal Bounty to Mrs* Clark, *the surviving Daughter of Mr* Milton.

PRIZE VERSES No. IX.

On the BUSTOES *in her* MAJESTY'S *Hermitage.*

HOW vain are pleasures which arise
   From all the giddy world calls great;
Pleasures which godlike souls despise,
  For those beyond the pow'r of fate.

Scepters and crowns, those envy'd things,
  Ne'er yeilded yet substantial joy;
But the delights that wisdom brings
  No adverse fortune can destroy.

These solemn truths great EDWARD * knew,
  When he to mourn his darling son,
To SHENE's † sequester'd groves withdrew,
  The empty pomp of courts to shun.

But

  * *Edw.* III.   † *Part of* Richmond.

But wiser far our spotless queen,
  Who ne'er by grandeur's charms misled,
Now loves *that* solitary scene
  To converse with the learned dead.

At her command a lonely GROTT
  Arises, beautifully wild,
With BUSTS, of those whose envy'd lot
  Attracts her nice election, fill'd.

There BACON stands, an awfull name!
  Who nature's ample bounds survey'd,
And wonders of the world's vast frame,
  And learning's secret wealth display'd.

There noble BOYLE, to virtue dear,
  Whose happy genius, peircing mind,
And painfull search did science clear
  Philosophy from rust refin'd.

There LOCK we view, whose matchless skill
  Taught feeble reason how to climb;
And curbing fancy's headstrong will
  Makes wit with judgment sweetly chime.

And there sagacious NEWTON's plac'd
  Who well the starry regions knew,
The laws which bound the planets trac'd,
  And could their devious tracks pursue.

There WOLLASTON, whose volume shows
  He knew th' extent of nature's law,
Could combat virtue's deadly foes,
  With precepts he from thence did draw.

CLARKE too is there, whose sacred theme
  Supported firm with reason's force,
Wins for religion our esteem,
  Of every solid bliss the source.

Not antient *Rome's* admired fane,
  Where all their fabled gods did dwell,
Equals this small selected train,
  Or rivals CAROLINA's cell.

Nor shall, if bards can aught presage,
  Her fame e'er die, to time a prey,
But to the world's most distant age
  Their works her glory shall convey.

To the Rt Hon. Ld Visc. WEYMOUTH on his
late Marriage with Miss CARTERET.

By Dr BOWDEN, *Author of the* POETICAL
Essays lately publish'd.

WHile crowds, my lord! applaud your happy choice,
  The muse attempts the theme with grateful voice,
Tho' low her notes, and unobserv'd her song,
Doth in the louder murmurs of the throng;
Yet are her raptures true, her duty paid,
Tho' sung to rocks, and utter'd in the shade;
Yet shall the vocal rocks resound the lays,
And vocal groves the nuptial consort raise,
While birds are witness to the artless strains,
And hymen, hymen echo's o'er the plains,
How oft they bear me in the russet vale,
And low brow'd downs repeat the ev'ning tale?
And when Aurora's curtains gild the sky,
Swift as her beams the gentle tidings fly.

  How blest th' alliance where no int'rest rules?
The bane of bliss, and perquisite of fools?
Where love its full unmingled joy displays,
And reason dictates while the heart obeys?

Where wisdom, innocence, and beauty joyn
To make the destin'd object all divine?
Well might such charms e'en rigid Romans win,
And in soft bondage captivate a Thynne.
Virtue, like hers, con'd envy's sting disarm,
And with one smile unwilling spoils charm;
Sprung from a peer whom matchless virtues grace,
And stamp a lasting lustre on his race;
Alike Mecænas to the muse, and state,
Whom foes must love, and malice cannot hate.

  How gay the country, and the fields how dress'd
When first the fair these rural regions bless;
While sylvan choirs conduct her o'er the plains,
And as she smiles the meadows smile again;
The jocund swains dance rustic carols round,
And Pan loud piping propagates the sound;
The distant dales the harmony prolong,
And babbling fountains murmur out a song;
Blithe Fauns, and Naiads on the banks are seen,
And hail her guardian goddess of the green.

  Welcome bright Nymph to these poetic villa,
These savage forests, and romantic hills:
Like Sybil saints you consecrate the grove,
And each soft scene breathes innocence and love;
The rugged wilds a gentler air assume,
And sudden verdures brighten thro' the gloom
To these lone walks you unknown day diffuse,
And warm these accents of the rustic muse.
'Twas thus Minerva civiliz'd the swains,
And spread politeness o'er Arcadia's plains.

  Still may your joys increase, illustrious pair
Not flush'd by fortune, nor depress'd by care,
Till beauteous offsprings in your likeness smile,
And add new graces to Britannia's Isle.

To SYLVANUS URBAN, Gent.
SIR,

THE Lines I herewith send you are the Complaint of two Gentlemen of your acquaintance whom I chuse to mention by the Names of Damon and Strephon. They have been rusticating in a Village not many miles from the Metropolis, which tho' not frequented by the Beaumonde, has several pleasant Heaths and green Lanes about it, where they generally take their Evening Walks; which Way soever they chance to steer, it is their Fortune to meet two unknown fair Ladies whose Coyness will not permit them to make that Acquaintance which they flatter themselves with the Hopes of obtaining by your Publication of the following Address in your Magazine for August; for they expect thus to be haunted and tormented as long as the fine Weather favours their Evening Excursions.
  Yours &c.

To CAMILLA and FLAVIA.
The Invitation: Or, the FLYING FAIR.

OR on the heath, or in the lane
  The wand'rers we pursue;
But our pursuit is still in vain,
  The chace we must renew.

When e'er we meet, it is by chance,
  They tempt us but to shun;
They lead us thro' a fairy dance,
  And loyter but to run.

The harvest ripe in yonder field
  Does to the reaper bend:
The fair ones, if they're ripe, shou'd yield,
  And bless the faithful friend.

If shepherds times were those, you'd know
The nymphs who grace the plains,
Still home at night with pleasure go,
To meet their happy swains.
The shade we take attends the fair,
For you we sought the grove;
We want no walk, nor ev'ning air,
Our want is you and love.

On seeing a LADY blush.

ON CELIA's eyes with pleasure as I gaz'd,
    And thence a thousand doubts and raptures
Whilst lost in ecstacy I fondly trace   (rais'd,
The num'rous charms of her bewitching Face,
A sudden change her blushing cheeks disclose,
The LILLY was contending with the ROSE.
The rival flow'rs disputed empire there,
Ambitious each to serve and grace the fair:
Long was the contest, doubtful the success;
Each resolute, and each for conquest press'd,
At length the bloody rose, unus'd to yield,
Appears triumphant on the beauteous field.
Flush'd with a victor's fury, on he prest,
And of the centre of her cheek possess'd,
Thence hurl'd the panting foe upon her breast,
There doom'd to live the vanquish'd still remains,
Whilst in her cheeks th' insulting conqu'ror reigns.

LIB. 12. Epig. 66. MARTIALIS.

FOrmosa Phyllis nocte cum mihi tota
    Se praestitisset omnibus modis largam,
Et cogitarem mane quod darem munus,
Utrumne cosmi, nicerotis, an libram,
An baeticarum pondus aere lanarum,
An de moneta Caesaris decem flavos:
Amplexa collum, basioque tam longo
Blandita, quam sunt nuptia columbarum,
Rogare caepit Phyllis amphoram vini.

In ENGLISH,

WIth me fair *Phillis* pass'd the night,
    And strove to please with new delights
At at the dawn I musing lay
How all her favours to repay,
In china ware, or tea, or snuff,
Or in some gaudy piece of stuff,
She clasp'd my neck, and chuck'd my chin,
And softly beg'd a quart of gin.

The two following Odes were sent from the North
to the Weekly Miscellany, *to illustrate some obser-*
vations on the Greek and Latin Languages to
this Purport. " The *Greek Language*, is the
Fountain of Poesy and Elegance; the Original of the finest Pieces that have entertain'd
the World ever since it had a Taste of polite
Literature; and hence Criticks may learn to
approve with Judgment, when they are pleased to like any thing in an Author.
As to the *Latin*, tho' it is a noble Language,
the Dialect of all the Learned, is concise
and readily written, yet it is barren and
harsh in Comparison of the *Greek*; its Ver-
sification is far from being so flowing and
harmonious as that, where a happy Distribution of Vowels makes the poetical Lan-

guage perfectly Musical. In a word, the *Latin*
is an imperfect Tongue, raised out of the
several Dialects of the *Greeks*, but vastly inferior to it. Its Authors are likewise mere
Copyers or Imitators, tho', it must be allow'd,
they are generally Improvers.

From the Greek of SAPPHO.

MORE than mortals blest is he,
    That sighs, and looks, and sits by thee,
And hears thy voice so softly sweet,
Breathing rapture, breathing wit;
And sees the dimpled smiles that break
Round thy soft withdrawing cheek,
Whilst on him thou roll'st thy eyes,
And enjoy'st his tender sighs:
Do the gods, in all their bliss,
Taste an happiness like this?
For me, no sooner I descry
The least sparkle of thy eye,
But thro' my veins a tingling flame
Thrills and runs thro' all my frame,
While my floating senses rove
In dream of bliss and trance of love.
In vain my falt'ring tongue I try,
The accents half come forth and die.
I hear no more, no more I see,
Impassion'd all, and all is thee!
I shiver now, and now I sweat,
My pulse is high, my heart on fret;
Then panting, pale, and breathless lying,
Trembling, fainting, swooning, dying,
My pulse is stopt, my spirits fail;
And life does in a sigh exhale.

From the Latin of CATULLUS.

MY heart has play'd me slip to-day,
    An't strangely fills my head,
That, as 'tis us'd to run away,
'Tis to Belinda fled,

Yes, he is fled, my wanderer
Of beauty's fort possest,
Perhaps now chides my idle care
From her relenting breast.

But what if I in charge should give
Her not to entertain,
But rate my wanton fugitive,
And send him home again?

Would she her captive thus forego,
And lose my little sinner;
And not expect a kiss or two
To so much grace should win her?

But then, if she myself should noose,
And there is room to fear:
To stay or go, is hard to choose!
Venus, your counsel here.

The DIVINE of Taste.

SIccus before the university preaching,
    Cites not a text in all his courtly teaching,
Yet from all preachers SICCUS bears the bays;
All praise the priest, who preach'd his hearers praise.
Amongst the learned skulls not one was seen to nod;
So much the word of man excell'd the word of God.

The golden LEGEND.

On a Lawyer who gain'd a cause of 500 l. return'd 400 to his client, and had it recorded
in his parish church.

DID RAMUS *gain a cause? This should be told*
In the bright letters of immortal gold,
But did he once restore what he'd lay'd hand on?
This must deserve a golden memorandum,
And pity 'tis, since those so fair appear,
But all his deeds were thus recorded here.

The PRIEST and LAWYER.

SAid a priest to a lawyer, you've a knavish old mule
And you, said old RAMUS, *are an ass—and*
a fool:
From pulpit the clerk rebukes this disgrace,
And ACHITOPHEL *curses and damns to his face:*
Soon, at Westminster, RAMUS *replies to the wit,*
And the priest coram nob. *summons up by a writ:*
The judge was incensed at learn'd NOSTRADAMUS
The jury displeased with honest old RAMUS.
The dispute now may end, since no mortal denies,
That they're equally honest and equally wise.

VERSES occasioned by the foregoing

THis sharp Epigram's point, thus divided in two,
Cannot pierce near so deep, as some single ones do,
The conduct at church, and in Westminster-hall,
Prove both equally fools, but knaves not at all.
Tho' in learning and sense each was par to the other,
Yet one fool might be much more a knave than his
brother.

To a young GENTLEMAN on his re-
turn from INDIA.

By Mr M. BROWNE.

REfresh'd to our desiring eyes,
Amid the pleasure you infuse,
Let my glad thoughts in numbers rise,
And bring a welcome from the muse.

As yet a mother's fondest love
Prints on thy cheek its tender seal;
Her eager eyes unweary'd rove,
Till tears her inward transport tell.

E'er the dread ocean safe resign'd,
The dear reviver of her ease;
She trembled at the gentle wind,
And chid the whisper of the breeze.

Thy sire with close-enfolding arms
Receives thee in his warm embrace,
Pleas'd to behold her softer charms,
Resembled in thy manly face.

Upheld by his obliging hand,
Fain wou'd my verse his favours own;
O may his lovely Virtues stand
A Pattern for th' engaging son.

Lo, where his younger hope appears,
(Bless heav'n the dear deserving Youth)
Companion of thy growing Years,
And partner of thy native truth.

A useful life, a virtuous name,
Shall kindly bless the ripen'd pair,
Prolong their date, advance their fame,
And crown the happy parent's care.

(Gent Mag. Vol. III. N° xxxii.)

While, generous family,—your joys,
Your merit—warm my grateful lays,
The genius that her art employs
Sinks with the weight of love and praise.

By a Gentleman desiring to be admitted
into the assembly of LADIES at the last
WARWICK RACES.

HAIL, *beauty's ever-smiling train!*
Propitious, hail! each lovely guest!
Whose charms adorn Varvicia's *plain,*
Whose presence glads her genial feast.

While victors panting for renown,
O'er num'rous realms extend their sway;
Let this my fond ambition crown,
This radiant circle to obey.

Might I (my duty to approve)
The nectar bear to each gay Toast;
No fav'rite in the court of JOVE
Shou'd such distinguish'd honours boast.

But if too rashly I presume
On goddesses reveal'd to sight,
And meet TIRESIAS' *hapless doom,*
May HOMER's *wit the lost requite.*

Fir'd by your influence divine,
I'd all his happy flights out-do;
His song as far excell'd by mine,
As his fam'd HELEN *is by you.*

A DIALOGUE occasion'd by a late Interview be-
tween a COURTIER, and a PATRIOT.

C. SIR JOHN much joy t'ye. P. Joy! of what, I pray sir?
C. We hear your country styles you PATRIOT. P.
Ay sir?
C. A style none but sir JOHN deserves to wear,
A style and title none at court can bear.
P. Well and our thanks to them for this their grace;
But I expect from you sir some good place.
C. E'en take your choice sir. P. What means this? C.
No joke sir,
LORD of your HOUSE, go stink of LEES and SMOAK sir,
Presumptuous knight, t' expect a place at palace,
Who dar'd not do a thing worth e'en the gallows!

The FEMALE WISH.

GRant me, ye gods, a calm retreat,
Where I may pass my days:
Far from the low mean follies of the great;
Free from the vulgar's envious hate,
And careless of their praise.

Bless'd with a faithful female friend,
Thus let my time slide on;
But when my ev'ning sun shall downward tend,
And fleeting life is at an end,
I'll quietly be gone.

Just so some tender blossom that has stood
In the recesses of some secret wood,
Unruffled by the winds, feels slow decay,
Hangs down its head, and gently dies away.

To a YOUNG LADY.

POLLY, *from me, tho' now a love-sick youth;*
Nay, tho' a poet, hear the voice of truth.
POLLY, *you're not a beauty, yet you're pretty:*
So grave, yet gay; so silly, yet so witty:
A heart of softness, yet a tongue of satire:
You've cruelty; yet, ev'n in that, good-nature.

Now

Now you are free, and now reserv'd a while;
Now a forc'd frown betrays a willing smile.
Reproach'd for absence, yet your sight deny'd;
My tongue you silence, yet my silence chide.
How won'd you praise me, shou'd your sex defame;
Yet, shou'd they praise, grow jealous and exclaim!
If I despair, with some kind look you bless;
But, if I hope, at once all hope suppress.
You scorn; yet, shou'd my passion change or fail,
Too late you'd whimper out a softer tale.
You love; and yet your lover's plea reject;
Shun, yet desire; discern, and yet suspect.
Such, POLLY, are your sex---part truth, part fiction,
Some thought, much whim, and all a contradiction.
                                    R. SAVAGE.

A Gentleman at LEYDEN to one at CAMBRIDGE.
SIR,   JULY 17. O. S.

WITH braying asses, howling dogs,
     With squeaking mice, or croaking frogs,
Poets and painters may amuse,
For such devices can't abuse;
Carve roguish boys, or waggish foxes
On stoppers, or tobacco boxes:
Or by just emblem paint out truth,
For age, a grave; a cradle, youth:
But not describe an ape for man;
Or for a woman draw a fan;
Nor for a weazle hunt a hare,
A dog for cat, or bull tor bear;
Nor move a forest on the flood,
Or hang a herring in a wood:
Tho' in burlesque, and *Dutch* design,
The picture course, and verse not fine,
Each *Dutchman* laughs at sight so odd,
A head of brawn, and tail of cod.
Surrounded by canal or flood,
With post of fir, or wall of mud;
With men of trade each street abounds,
Who cast up pence, or sum up pounds,
Who thrive in peace, and gain in war,
By casks of pitch, or tubs of tar;
Something or nothing, always doing,
From *Van Trump*, down to *Vander Bruin*.
With drowsy gate and clumsy size,
Most wond'rous grave, and wond'rous wise;
With canvas frock, and speckled shirt,
With air of lead, or mien of dirt,
Slide on the ice, and safely ride on,
From *Amster-Rotter-dam* to *Leyden*;
With cheese and butter who regale,
O'er caus of mum, or mugs of ale;
Who can't afford, or wont allow
A cheek of ox, or heel of cow.
Here we buy hadocks, or eat oysters,
As slovenly as in your cloysters;
No sauce, yet fish; no fire, yet smoak;
With a bad butler, and worse cook;
With nasty flaggons spoil our cloaths,
And on our napkins wipe our nose;
Excessive loud, or very low,
As humours stagnate, fancies flow;
By knock-down argument maintain,
By dint of fist, or dint of brain;
Pray to a *Saint*, or sing a *Psalm*:
And do no good, tho' do no harm:

In reason weak, by passion strong;
Bold in opinion, never wrong.
Trenchar'd professor's lecture hear,
How flows the tide, or rolls the sphere;
But their solutions are not good,
Or cannot well be understood:
For worse and worse our *Hum-drums* grow,
And study much, but little know:
Dream on as in a *College* way;
That is, all night, and all the day.

On CELINDA making a Collection of Poetry

TO high *Parnassus'* shady seat,
   The muses ever green retreat;
To *Helicon's* smooth gliding stream,
A beauteous guest Celinda came;
She came; and as she pass'd along
Amazement seiz'd the tuneful throng:
E'en Phœbus, he whose piercing eye
Can all the wide creation spy,
Confess'd the wide creation o'er,
He ne'er saw one so bright before:
E'en when in *Thetis'* mirrour clear
His own reflected beams appear.
And now the nymph with graceful air,
Thus to each muse addressi'd her pray'r,
She spoke---and silence reign'd around:
The winds forgot their murm'ring sound,
The list'ning birds forgot their song;
The streams the painted meads among,
In mute attention ceas'd to glide;
And Aganippe stopt it's tide.
Hear me; ye sacred nine, she said,
(So may your lawrels never fade)
Hear me the pleasing cause relate,
Why thus I sought your blissful seat;
Look here (and then a book she shew'd,
That rich with *Purple* binding glow'd)
This book, O Muses, 'tis my will
That you with poetry shou'd fill.
With joy the present I'll receive;
The present you alone can give.
She said, the willing nine obey,
And each their proper tribute pay:
Melpomene gave elegy,
The loftier ode Calliope;
Thalia offer'd pastoral:
The nymph with smiles accepts them all.
But Cupid, who where-e'er she came,
Incognito pursu'd the dame,
Sudden reveal'd himself to light:
Celinda started at the sight.
Muses to me restore the book,
(Inrag'd he cry'd with threatning look:)
No poetry shall here be seen,
But what is wrote by Cupid's pen:
The fair no incense shou'd receive,
But that which suppliant lovers give;
To fill this book is Venus' care;
What business have the muses here?
To fill this book! not thousands more
Con'd e'er contain the endless store
Of praises, which her merits claim,
And love wou'd write on such a theme.

A RIDDLE.

ONE *thing at once the fam'd de Witte confefs'd,*
Was all his wifdome'er prefum'd to do :
And that they're wondrous artifts all atteft,
Whoe'er among the ladies can do two :

Then tell ye, Britifh *fages, if ye know,*
Nor in your breaft my name a fecret keep,
At once who all thefe different things can do,
Can ftand, and run about, and fing, and fleep.

On the Lady E. H. Painting.

COSMELIA'*s charms infpire my lays,*
Who fair, in nature's fcorn,
Blooms in the winter of her days,
Like GLASSENBURY *thorn.*

COSMELIA, *cruel at fourfcore,*
Like bards in modern plays,
Four acts of life pafs guiltlefs o'er,
And in the fifth fhe flays.

If e'er impatient of the blifs
Into her arms you fall,
The plaifter'd nymph returns the kifs,
Like Thisbe, *through a Wall.—*

A RIDDLE.

THink not, fair ladies, I'm a cheat,
Tho' I have never feen as yet
A hand I could not counterfeit.

And if to brutes my birth I owe,
And fo my pedigree's but low,   5
By education a friendly aid,
What great improvements may be made!
'Twould be unkind that birth t' upbraid ;
Art took me from my mother's fide,
And did a kinder nurfe provide :   10
Whofe care fo far prevail'd, that foon
I found my native roughnefs gone.
And from the rule which nature takes,
In the more lovely works fhe makes,
(As when her wifdom ftrives to grace 15
With eyes and lips the human face,
In double births her work is feen,
And each to other proves a twin :)
'Tis thus I in the world appear,
No fooner live, but am a pair.   20

But fuch my pride, Oh ! fhame to tell !
I ftill endeavour to conceal
Thofe beings who gave me mine ; I mean
My fecond being—but in vain :
We're fo alike, that who they are   25
My every feature muft declare.
By them I was train'd up to arms,
And made the guard of female charms :
And tho' I feem of gentle mein,
At combates I have often been.   00

But tho' I feem to threaten war,
To fhew, how much I peace prefer,
The deareft friends have found in me,
When they wou'd friendfhip's laws decree,
A well-known proverb to declare,   35
How very intimate they are.

By th' youth I'm claim'd for ravifh'd blifles
And made the fee of ftolen kifles ;
When with a tender tread, for fear
His ftep fhou'd wake the fleeping fair,
He prints upon her melting lip
The happy forfeiture of fleep.

I've fuch obliging ways about me,
There's fcarce a vifit made without me :
And I am drefs'd where'er I go,   45
To fympathize with joy, or woe.
When I at funerals appear,
My fable robes I always wear ;
And have a fuit of white befide,
When ever I attend the bride.   50

I'm feldom known, I muft confefs,
To boaft of riches, or of drefs :
It is my chiefeft care to hide
The radiant diamond's fparkling pride ;
To keep the emerald's lovely green,   55
And the gay ruby's blufh unfeen ;
And all that I affect of ftate,
Is only to be plain and neat.

But ne'erthelefs I can't deny,
I'd fo far pleafe the public eye ;   60
That, ftay, till I'm retir'd, and you
All my rich furniture may view.
So when my lord is gone to town,
The houfe and gardens may be fhown.
—Then may the youth a treafure fee :   65
To touch it would a blefling be ;
The richeft, fofteft ivory !
May fee of gems a radiant fcene,
By the wearer polifh'd o'er again :
May fee a faphire proud to bear   70
A ringlet of the fair one's hair ;
Which is itfelf as proud, to fhow
On whofe fair neck the treafure grew.
Then too the happy bride may fee
Her pledge of bridal conftancy ;   75
Which, in a plain-wrought circle bending,
Denotes a love that knows no ending ;
And fhews, the ornament fhou'd be
Of trueft love, fimplicity.

Ladies, who have a hand at guefling,   80
Know, it is you I am addrefling :
And by this time, the mufe depends
You have me at your finger's ends.

PRINCEPS AURIACI, and the other Poem,
fent us from *Oxford,* being in *Latin* are too
long for our Magazine; but if we could be
favour'd with correct Copies of all the Performances at the *Act,* they fhould be printed in a more advantageous manner.
Mr. *P.P.*'s Verfes *To the Queen,* having before
been publifhed, can't be admitted in competition for the *Prize,* but Originals of a moderate Length will be received till *November.*
Having fo many other new Pieces, we muft
defer the Confideration of *H. S.*'s, Mr *M.*'s,
R. S.'s, *H. C.*'s, *G. E.*'s to next Month.

THE
Monthly Intelligencer.
AUGUST 1733.

Wednesday, 1.

THE Books were opened at the Bank to receive from those who had given in their Names the first payment of One Pound *per* Ticket in the Lottery, granted for the Relief of the Charitable Corporation.

A great Meeting of Dissenters was held in *London*, and several other Parts of the Kingdom, to celebrate the Day, it being That wherein the Schism Bill was to have taken Place, but was prevented by the Death of the Queen; by which Bill the Dissenters would have been debarred the Liberty of educating their own Children.

Thursday, 2.

At a General Court of the S. Sea Company a Dividend of 2 *per* Cent. was agreed upon for the Half Year ending at Midsummer, and the Dividend Warrants to be made payable the 17th Instant. 'Twas also resolv'd that the Committee of Trust should immediatly proceed to the Sale of the remaining part of the late Directors Estates, and apply the Money to pay off those Bonds that have not been brought in and mark'd for 3 and half *per* Cent. The Bonds which are to be thus paid off, amount to 65,300 l. besides 13,000 l, which have not been brought in pursuant to a former Resolution to receive one half of the Principal, and the Interest on them to cease from Michaelmas next.

At the Assizes held at *Wells* for *Somersetshire* Mr *Charles Jones* was tried for the Murder of Mr *Price* at *Bath* in a Duel, some time ago, for which he fled to *Holland*, but surrender'd against the Lent Assizes, several Gentlemen gave him the Character of a peaceable Person, and other Circumstances appearing in his Favour, he was acquitted.

Six Thimble-players were tried for a Robbery on the Highway; when one *Cox* swore, that one of them struck the Money out of his Hand, and the others took it up and made off; upon which they were found guilty: But the Judge would not pass Sentence before he consulted his Brethren, it being a doubt *whether they put the Person in Fear of his Life?* If not, 'twill be single Felony only, and Transportation.

Tuesday, 7.

Was publish'd a Proclamation offering a Reward of 50 l. for every Deer Stealer convicted, for any Fact committed between the 20th of May last, and the 29th of September 1734.

Saturday, 11.

About this time His Majesty ordered 3000 l. for repairing and beautifying the Palace of *Holyrood-House* at *Edinburgh*.

Her Majesty order'd a Mount to be rais'd in *Richmond* Gardens, for a Prospect of the *Thames* and adjacent Country. Also the Bust of Lord *Bacon* to be placed in her Grotto.

Monday, 13.

At the Assizes at *Newcastle* four Persons receiv'd Sentence of Death, but only two order'd for Execution. It's observ'd that no Person has been hang'd at that Town for 30 Years past.

Wednesday, 15.

In *Little St. Helen's Bishopsgate-street* was discover'd by some Workmen a *Roman* Pavement, which by the Inscription had been laid about 1700 Years. The Work was Mosaick, and the Tiles not above an Inch Square. Several humane Bones of large Size being found also, it seems to have been a burying Place of note.

Some of the Apothecaries Company being in the Neighbourhood of Rochester, gathering Simples, according to annual Custom, a merry Gentleman told the People they were come to measure the Land, in order to lay it under an Excise; upon which they came upon the Simplers with Scythes, Pitchforks, &c. and oblig'd them to take to their Heels.

The

The Truſtees for the Co-
lony of *Georgia* received out
of the Exchequer the Money
given by Parliament for encouraging that Undertaking
viz. } 10,000 00 0

Given before by ſundry Perſons 3,723 13 9 A
Diſburſed to June laſt 2,254 17 9

Came Advice, that near 20 Sail of Merchant Ships were loſt in a Hurricane the
30th of June at St Chriſtophers.

Friday, 31.

The Duties upon *French* Brandies imported in this and the two Preceding
Months, amounted to upwards of B
200,000 *l.*

To give our Readers an Idea of the
preſent Struggles in moſt Parts of the
Kingdom, with a View to the next E-
lection of Members of Parliament, we
ſhall only inſtance in the Application C
made to the Freeholders for the County
of *Kent*, whoſe Votes are deſir'd (on the
Country Intereſt) for Lord VANE, and Sir
EDW. DERING, *Being Gentlemen both
Well-affected to the preſent Conſtitution of
the Government in Church and State, zealous Oppoſers of the late* Exciſe Scheme, D
*and ſteady Aſſerters of the Religious and
Civil Rights and Liberties of their Fellow-
Subjects.* —— And their Votes are deſir'd (on the Court Intereſt) for Ld MID-
DLESEX, and Sir GEO. OXENDEN, Bart.
*Being Gentlemen diſtinguiſhed for their
Revolution Principles, and Affection for
the Proteſtant Succeſſion in the illuſtrious* E
houſe of Hanover; *Oppoſers of all Schemes
for unneceſſarily encreaſing and perpetu-
ating the unequal and heavy Tax upon
Land, to the manifeſt Wrong and Ruin of
the Country Intereſt, and ſtrenuous Advocates for the common Rights, Privileges,
and Liberties of* ALL *their Fellow Subjects.* F

Fifty Tons of Half-pence and Farthings
were order'd to be coin'd at the Tower
for the Service of *Ireland.*

The *French* Fleet conſiſting of 12 Men
of War and a Frigate, with K. *Staniſlaus*
on board, having been ſeen paſſing by
Dover, Admiral *Stuart* was order'd to G
Portſmouth, to haſten the Equipment of
a Squadron of Men of War, ſuppoſed for
the *Baltick.*

Thurſday the 6th of *September* was appointed for the Prince of *Orange's* Em-
barking for *England.* An *Engliſh* Gentleman, who comes in his Retinue, brings H
with him ſome fine Prints of King *William* and Queen *Mary*, curiouſly grav'd in
Holland, and as large as Life.

Remarkable Advices *of various Kinds.*

MR *Paul*, a Surgeon at *Stroud* in *Glou-
ceſterſhire*, lately extracted from the
Kidneys of a Woman, by an Inciſion
through her Back, a rough Stone as large
as a Pidgeons Egg, and made an entire
Cure; it is the firſt of the Kind ever perform'd in this Kingdom; the Caſe will
ſoon be Publiſhed.

At *Uſingen*, in Count *Naſſau's* Gardens,
an *Indian* Plant, named *Cereus Indicus
Serpens*, one Evening in *July* laſt, about
Sun-ſet, began to open its Bud, which it
had puſh'd out about a Month before, and
was at full Bloom at one in the Morning,
in the ſhape of a Rummer, affording an
agreeable Smell, ſo ſtrong that the Houſe
was filled with it. The Stemmata within were of a ſulphurous Colour, with
white, oval, pointed Leaves. The Bloſ-
ſom which was about 12 Inches diameter,
clos'd at Sun-riſing, and ſo faded away,
the whole Bloom being but of a Night's
Duration.

At *Guarda* in *Portugal*, one Father
Antonio Sequeira d'Albuquerque, who had
been 86 Years Canon of the Cathedral
Church, in *May* laſt, when he was 114
Years old, cut an entire new Set of Teeth,
ſmall, regular, and white as Ivory: His
long, white Beard turn'd black, as did his
Eye-brows, and the Hair on his Head.
He had retain'd the perfect uſe of his
Senſes; his Nerves, relax'd by Age, began to contract, and his Muſcles ſeem'd
filling out with a Juvenile Robuſtneſs;
when a Fever ſeizing him, he died.

Mr *Bond*, of *Bondvill* in the County of
Armagh, in *Ireland*, preſented the Lord
Primate with a Stalk of Flax which carried above 200 Boles, each Bole containing 8 Grains of Seed; which is a Proof
that the Lands in the North of *Ireland*
may be improv'd to great Advantage.

Near *Chabli*, in *France*, 3 Women being a-breaſt, two of their Heads were
ſtruck off by Lightning, and carried 50
Paces, but ſhe in the middle received no
Hurt.

B I R T H S.

THE Lady of Sir *John Heathcote*, Bt.
deliver'd of two Daughters.

The Lady of the E. of *Thanet*, deliver'd of a Son.

The Lady of *John Bryan*, Eſq; deliver'd of a Son.

The Lady of Sir *John Harcourt*, deliver'd of a Daughter.

The Lady of *Geo. Clinton*, Eſq; of a Son.

MARRIAGES.

MR *Morgan*, Doctor of Musick, at *Westchester*, Married to Miss *Wilton*, a Fortune of 30,000 *l.*

—— *Skinner*, Esq; —to Miss *Barbara Ople*, of *Newington*, with a Fortune of 30,000 *l.*

Miss *Vanfleet* of *Budge Row*, a Fortune of 8000 *l.* to an eminent Dutch Merchant.

Dr *Richard Osbaldiston*, Dean of *York Cathedral* — to Mrs *Elizabeth Fairside* with 20,000 *l.* Fortune.

Philip Sercoate, Esq; —to the Dutchess Dowager of *Cleveland.*

William Gape, whose Brother was late Representative for *St Albans*, — to the Daughter of Tho. *Putland*, Esq; of *Chelsea.*

The Son of Tho. *Turner*, Esq; Recorder of *Bury St Edmunds* —to the Youngest Daughter of Sir *Thomas Gery*, late Master in Chancery, with a Fortune of 20,000 *l.*

Mr *Clermont*, a *Portugal* Merchant— to Miss *Leglese*, Daughter of a noted Wine Merchant.

Mr *Cotton*, a young Gentleman of about 27 Years of age, —to Mrs *Morgan* of *Bethnal-Green*, Widow, aged 72, with a Fortune of 10,000 *l.*

Tho. *Martin*, Esq; —to Mrs *Jane Little.*

John Willis, Esq; eldest Son to the Bp of *Winchester*—to the only Daughter of Col. *Feilding.*

Ld *Sinclair*, a Peer of *Scotland*—to the Countess Dowager of *Southesk.*

Mr *Caleb Lloyd*, a Grocer at *Bristol*, — to a Daughter of Mr *Colsworthy*, a Merchant at *Exeter*, with a Fortune of 4000 *l.*

James Wells, of *Wardington*, *Oxfordsh.* Esq; —to a Daughter of the late Sir Thomas *Harvey* of *London.*

The E. of *Pembroke*—to Miss *Fitzwilliams*, late Maid of Honour to her Majesty.

Sir *James Nicholson*, of *Edinburgh*, Bar.—to the Relict of *Robert Arbuthnot*, Esq; late Auditor of the Exchequer.

Tho. *Ackworth*, of *Northamptonshire*, Esq; —to the Daughter of —— *Garbet*, Esq; of *New Bond-street.*

George Mangay, Esq; — to Miss *Dunstar*, of *Green-street*, *Soho.*

Richard Thompson, Esq; 2d Prothonotary of the Court of Common-Pleas — to Miss *Pen Cave*, Sister to Sir *Verney Cave*; Bt

DEATHS.

July 29. JOHN *Hall*, Esq; of *Channells*, in *Norfolk.*

30. *John Woodhouse*, Esq; at *Charlton.*

Thomas Frith, Esq; at *New-Windsor.*

Dr *Richardson*, Master of *Peter-house*, and Fellow of *Eaton College*, *Cambridge.*

31. The Lady *Isabella*, Relict of Sir *Wm Wentworth*, and Mother of the E. of *Strafford.*

Aug. 2. *Sam. Colebatch*, Esq; one of the Sealers in Chancery, and Groom of the Larder to his Majesty.

3. *Seth Adams*, Major of the White Reg. of Trained Bands of this City.

Joseph Frewen, Esq; at *Gravesend.*

Mrs *Harrison*, aged 104, at *Hampstead.*

4. Mrs *Jane Killegrew*, at *St Albans*, Daughter of the late Adm. of that Name.

Tho. *Whitfield*, Esq; at *Brentwood*, *Essex.*

5. Tho. *Mason*, sen. of *St Mary Axe*, Esq;

7. Sir *Clobery Noel*, Bart. Knight of the Shire for the County of *Leicester.*

Sam. Joel, Esq; at *Richmond*, *Surry.*

Mr *Nath. Smith*, Tanner in *Southwark*, reputed worth 20,000 *l.*

8. Tho. *Powell*, Esq; at *Reading*, *Berks.*

9. *Sam. Newton*, Esq; in *Aldermanbury.*

Henry Henley, Esq; of *Leigh*, *Somersetsh.*

Major *How*, at *Edinburgh.*

The Revd Mr *John Teard*, Dean of *Achonry*, at *Dublin.*

10. Mrs *Love*, a Maiden Milliner in *Westminster.* She left 300 *l.* to the Charity Children of the Free School in *Totbill Fields*, and 200 *l.* to her Maid, with her Stock in Trade.

The Revd Mr *Rowland Woodward Hill*, Rector of *Hodness* in *Shropshire.* He left 100 *l.* per Ann. to the New Theatre at *Cambridge*; and 100 *l.* to poor Clergymen's Widows in the County of *Salop.*

11. *Thomas Davison*, Esq; formerly in the Commission of the Peace for *Middlesex*, reputed worth 20,000 *l.* and 500 *l.* per Ann.

12. *Edward Coke*, Esq; Brother to the Rt Hon. the Ld *Lovell.* He is succeeded in his Estates by his younger Brother the Hon. *Rob. Coke*, Vice-Chamberlain to her Majesty.

The Revd Mr *John Swain*, M. A. of *St John's College*, *Oxford.*

13. *John Boyer*, Esq; formerly Hamburgh Merchant.

John Boggas, of *Hawley*, *Suffolk*, Esq;

George Sparks, Esq; at *Chelsea.*

The Revd Mr *James Hales*, at *Wanstead*, in *Essex.*

14. *Jn Booth*, Esq; Steward to the D. of *Montagu*, reputed worth 40,000 *l.*

15. *Sam. Webb*, Esq; in the Commission of the Peace for *Middlesex*, and many Years Treasurer of the *London* Workhouse, *Bishopsgate-street.*

The Revd Mr *George Cooke*, Vicar of *Warfield*, in *Windsor Forest.*

16. *John Rowbray*, Esq; formerly Cupbearer to K. *James* II. aged 94.

John Warwick, Esq; at *Richmond.*

Dr *Matthew Tindal*, Author of the *Rights of the Christian Church*, and of *Christianity as old as the Creation*, of which he left a 2d Volume finished, and bequeathed it to *Eustace Budgell*, Esq; his Executor, together with 2,000 Guineas. The Residue of his Estate he left to his Nephew, the Rev. Mr *Tindal*, Translator of *Rapin*'s History. He was aged near 80; had been reconciled to the Church of *Rome* in the Reign of K. *James* II. but after the Revolution gave his Opinion against those who acted at Sea under his Commission, and so came into Favour with the reigning Prince. In *Parker*'s Ephemeris, 1711, is erected a Scheme of his Nativity.

17. ——— *Selwyn*, Esq; formerly a *Spanish* Merchant.

John Wise, Esq; of *Essex*.

The Relict of Sir ——— *Bard*, Knt. near *Watford*, in *Hertfordshire*.

John Soames, Esq; at *Uxbridge*.

18. The Relict of the late Sir *Tho. Cole*, in *Grosvenor-street*.

Mr *Raymond*, Brewer at *Ratcliff-Cross*:

19. Mr *Tate*, Serjeant at Mace at the *Poultry* Compter.

21. *Jn Blowing*, Esq; an old Commander in the *West-India* Trade.

——— *Cole*, Esq; at *Warden-Hall, Essex*.

22. *Tho. Towers*, Esq; at *Bansted, Surry*.

23. *Tho. Bridges*, Esq; at *Clapham*, reputed worth 20,000l. and 500l. per Ann.

Mr *Lane*, an eminent Surveyor and Architect. He built *Guy's Hospital* in *Southwark*, and was worth 20,000l.

David Edwards, Esq; at *Rhid Grose*, near *Carmarthen*, in *South Wales*. He left the Bulk of his Estate to his Brother, the Master of *Daniel*'s Coffee-house near *Temple Bar*.

The Revd Mr *Webb*, Brother-in-Law to *Anthony Henley*, Esq; Representative for *Southampton*. He had a Living in *Oxfordshire* worth 400l. per Ann. in the Gift of the said Mr *Henley*, but contested by Sir *Richard Mill*, Bart.

The Relict of Sir ——— *Young*, Bart. at *Staines*, in *Middlesex*.

John Waters, of *Deptford*, Esq; possess'd of an Estate of 4000l. per Ann.

The Relict of the late Rev. Mr *Fleming*, a Dissenting Minister, worth 15,000l.

James, Countess Dowager of *Macclesfield*, Relict of the late Earl; and Daughter and Coheir of ——— *Carrier*, of *Wirksworth, Derbyshire*, Esq;

26. *John Abbot*, Esq; formerly a *Hamburgh* Merchant.

Miss *Honeywood*, related to General *Honeywood*.

27. Monf. *Moinor*, a famous Musician,

Sir *James Fleetwood*, at *Hammersmith*.

29. The Wife of *Daniel Hopkins*, Esq; Deputy Warden of the *Fleet* Prison.

Capt. *Brooks*, Commander of the *Mary* in the *West-India* Trade.

30. Mr *Simpson*, Warehouse-keeper to the Company of Stationers.

The Relict of ——— *Lawson*, Esq; of *Westerham*, in *Kent*.

Ecclesiastical Preferments *conferr'd on the following Reverend Gentlemen*:

MR *Peter Bevis*, ——— to the Rectory of *Silverton*, *Devon*.

Thomas Walk, A. M. presented to the Rectory of *Bletso*, in *Bedfordshire*.

Mr *Hurdis*, to the Vic. of *Laughon, Suff.*

Mr *Gilbert Jackson*, ——— to the Rectory of *Botley, Southampton*.

Philip Barton, L. L. D. made Canon of *Christ Church, Oxford*.

Mr *Thomas Remington*, ——— to the Vic. of *Warter, Yorkshire*.

Mr *Cook*, ——— to the Living of *Inford, Wilts.*

Mr *John Hale*, ——— to the Rectory of *Standen Massey, Essex*.

Mr *Samuel Cove*, ——— to the Rectory of *Stringworth, Leicestershire*.

Mr *Hammond*, ——— to the Archdeaconry of *Dorset*.

Mr *Gregory*, ——— to the Living of *Carlton, Nottinghamshire*.

Mr *Samuel Robinson*, ——— to the Rectory of *Lamberhurst, Kent*.

Dr *Holdsworth*, ——— to the Rectory of *Chalfont St Peters, Bucks*.

Dr *Owen*, ——— to the Rectory of *Stoughton, Huntingdonshire*.

Dr *Bignall*, ——— to the Rectory of *East Farndon, Northamptonshire*.

Mr *W. Boudrey*, ——— to the Vic. of *St Lawrence, Reading*.

Mr *Proctor*, to the Living of *Frowden, Somersetshire*.

Mr *Broom*, ——— to the Rectory of *Pulham, Norfolk*.

Mr *John Collings*, ——— to the Rectory of *St Mary de Crypt, Gloucester*.

Mr *Oliver Lampstone*, ——— to the Rectory of *Thirske, Yorkshire*.

Mr *Thomas*, ——— to the Rectory of *Wandsworth, Surry*.

Mr *John Francis*, ——— to the Rectory of *Harbledown* and Vic. of *Brabourn, Kent*, and is succeeded by

Mr *Charles Norris*, in the perpetual Curacy of *Nackington, Kent*.

Mr *George Wightwick*, A. M. elected Minister of the Dissenting Congregation at *Kingston upon Thames*.

Mr *John Worſley*, to the Vicarage of *Numington, Yorkſhire*.

A Diſpenſation is paſs'd to enable *Edw. Villiers*, M. A. Brother to the E of *Jerſey*, to hold the Rectory of *Merſton Bygott, Somerſetſhire*, with the Rectory of *Froom Zelwood*, in the ſame County.

John Tregenna, M. A. Chaplain to the Counteſs Dowager of *Caſſills*. of *North Britain*, to hold the Rectory of *Roch*, in *Cornwal*, with the Rectory of *Manegan* in the ſaid County.

PROMOTIONS.

MR *Maſon*, appointed Table-keeper to the Ladies of the Privy Chamber, in the Room of Mr *Adamſon* dec.

Capt. *Cockran* —— Gentleman Uſher Quarter Waiter in ordinary to her Majeſty, in place of *Richard Hill*, Eſq; who reſign'd to him,

Capt. *Bowley*—Major of the Ld *Tyrawley's* Reg. of Foot.

Mr *Powel*—one of the Gentlemen of the Chapel Royal at St *James's*, in Place of the late Mr *Goſtling*.

Mr *Symmonds*, Dep. Sealer, made Sealer in Chancery, in the room of the late Mr *Colebatch*.

Mr *Criſpigney*—Marſhal of the Court of Admiralty, in the room of *John Cheeke*, Eſq; decas'd.

E. of *Dunmore*—Knight of the Thiſtle in the room of the E. of *Sutherland*, dec.

D. of *Argyle*—Colonel of his Majeſty's own Royal Reg. of Horſe-Guards, in the room of the D. of *Bolton*, remov'd.

Ld *Cathcart*—Col. of a Reg. of Horſe in Ireland, late Sir *Rob. Rich's*; and is ſucceeded by

Sir *Adolphus Oughton*, Bar. in the Command of a Reg. of Dragoons; who is ſucceeded by

John Robinſon, Eſq; as Lieut. Col. to the 2d Reg. of Foot-Guards.

John Folliott, Eſq; —firſt Major; and *Henry Pulteney*, Eſq; —ſecond Major of the ſame Regiment.

Mr *Samuel Sharpe*—Surgeon of *Guy's Hoſpital*, in the room of the late Mr *Baker*.

Ld Viſc. *Percival*, of *Ireland*, created Earl of *Egmont* in that Kingdom.

Ld Viſc. *Lymington*, made Ld Lieut. and *Cuſtos Rotulorum* of the County of *Southampton*, and Warden and Keeper of the New Foreſt *Hampſhire*, in the room of the D. of *Bolton*.

Mr *John Colebatch*—Groom of the Larder to the King, in Place of his late Brother.

Ld *Malton*—Ld Lieut, of the *Weſt Rid-*ing, and *Cuſtos Rotulorum* of the *North* and *Weſt Riding* in the County of *York*.

Mr *Nicholas Bulling*,—Dep. Sealer in Chancery, in the room of Mr *Symmonds*.

Thomas de Grey,—Comptroller of the Firſt Fruits and Tenths, in the room of *John Harbord*, Eſq;

D. of *Montagu*,—Governor and Capt. of the *Iſle of White*, and Governor of *Carlsbrook Caſtle*, and Conſtable and Doorkeeper of the ſame, and Steward Receiver and Bailiff of all Manors, Lands &c. within the ſaid Iſland in the room of the D. of *Bolton*.

Lieut. Gen. *Evans* ſucceeds the D. of *Argyle* in the Command of the Queen's own Reg. of Horſe.

Brig. *Tyrrel*—Gen *Evans* in his late Reg. of Dragoons; and

James Sinclair, Eſq;—Brig. *Tyrrel* in his Regiment.

Major Gen. *Sutton*, made Governor of the Iſland of *Guernſey*, &c.

Mr *Young*,—Steward of St *Katherine's* near the *Tower*, in place of the late Mr *Newton*.

Mr *Edward Ruſworth*, appointed Deputy to his Father who is Regiſter of the Arches Court of *Canterbury*.

Mr *Knowler*, choſen Recorder of *Canterbury* in the room of Mr *Crayford*, &c.

Mr *Pye*, Attorney appointed a Commiſſioner of Bankrupts in the room of *Wm Shaw*, Eſq; dec.

Receivers General of the LAND TAX *for the preſent Year, viz.*

Nicholas and Edward Dewy, Eſqrs for Suſſex.
Nathan'el Thorn, Eſq; for part of Devon.
Timothy Boldaſton, Eſq; for part of Norfolk.
Richard Reddal, Eſq; for Bedford.
James Hays, Eſq; for Berks.
Edward Parſons, Eſq; for Whitehall and St James's.
Benjamin Darby and Peter Baker, Eſqrs for Somerſet.
James Phillips, Eſq; for South Wales.
Thomas Lane, Eſq; for Brecon, Radnor, and Glamorgan.
Thomas Giſbourn, Eſq; for Derby.
John Owen, Eſq; for Lancaſter.
William Satees, Eſq; for Durham and Northumberland.
Robert Clayton, Eſq; for Hereford.
John Fletcher, Eſq; for Cumberland.
James Baily, Eſq; for Stafford.
William Dowſe, Eſq; for Huntington.
Thomas Clifford, Eſq; for Monmouth.
John Berry, Eſq; for Nottingham.
Richard Corbet, Eſq; for Surrey.
Allen Whitiford, Eſq; for Scotland.
Samuel Robinſon, Eſq; for London, Middleſex and Weſtminſter.
William Elliot. Eſq; for Cornwal.
George Gee, Eſq; for Eaſt and North Riding of York.
John Bird, Eſq; for Warwick and Coventry.

BANKRUPTS.

STanclift Parkins, of Southwark, Surry Carpenter.
John Falconer of George Lane, London, Merchant.
William Stanier, of Shrewsbury, Salop, Draper.
Henry Burtenſhaw, of Huſterpoint, Suſſex, Tanner.
Tho. Meade, of the Strand, Middleſex, Linen Draper.
John Bound, of Ringwood, Southhampton, Tanner.

FRom *Petersburgh*, that a Body of 15,000 *Tartars* of *Crim*, attempting to force a Paſſage thro' the *Czarina's* Territories to join the *Turkiſh* Army in *Perſia*, were repulſed by the *Ruſſians* under the Command of the Prince of *Heſſe-Hombourg* with a great ſlaughter.

As nothing certain can be gather'd of the preſent Election in *Poland*, it may not be improper to give a ſhort sketch of that of King *Auguſtus*, from the Abbot de *Parthenay's* Hiſtory. So fine a Subject, ſays he, merits ſo much the more a juſt and ſincere Writer, as it has been disfigured by M. de *Voltaire*, who ſtudying to embelliſh his Work, was not much concern'd, whether his Descriptions were true. Witneſs that of *Altena* and the Siege of *Riga*.———— After the Death of *Sobieski*, the Affairs of *Poland*, were greatly embarraſs'd. The *Turks* and *Tartars* ravag'd it; the *Czar* demanded that the King to be choſen ſhould renounce ſome of his Titles, and a Civil War under the Name of a Confederacy, broke out in *Lithuania*. Several Princes intrigued for the Crown, who, by the Addreſs of the Miniſter of *France*, were ſet aſide in favour of the Prince of *Conti*; then a Party was form'd, ſupported by the Emperor, for raiſing to the Throne *Frederic Auguſtus*, Elector of *Saxony*. The General Dyet open'd the 15th of May, 1697; and after ſome ſharp Conteſts, Card. *Radziewski*, the Primate, declared the Prince of *Conti* King, with the Acclamations of more than 80,000 Gentlemen. But *Auguſtus* being choſe by another Party, enter'd *Poland* with an Army, and ſoon brought over many to his Intereſt. The *French* Party decreaſed ſenſibly by the abſence of the Prince of *Conti*, and the Delay of the Remittances and Troops he promis'd the Republic. The Abbot de *Polignac* and the Primate proteſted againſt the Election of *Auguſtus* as illegal, the Proclamation having been made by a Biſhop, in prejudice of the Rights of the Primate, and without the Conſent of the Republick; the Dyet of Confirmation unanimouſly confirmed the Prince of *Conti*; and ſigned a Confederacy in Defence of their Religion and Liberty. *Auguſtus* ſurmounted all theſe and other Difficulties. Firſt the Place where the Royal Ornaments were kept, being poſſeſs'd by his Adverſaries he broke it open. The Second Difficulty, that by the Laws of *Poland*, the King muſt be crown'd by the Arch Biſhop of *Gueſna*, Primate of the Kingdom, was provided againſt, by declaring that Arch-biſhoprick vacant. Another Difficulty was, the Law order'd, that the deceas'd King ſhould be buried before the Coronation of his Succeſſor. This they eluded by performing his Obſequies in Repreſentation; after which the Biſhop of *Cujavia* proceeded to the Ceremony of Coronation. This occaſioned a Satire, entitul'd, *The Arguments of the Acts of the Comedy of Warſaw*; Act I. *A King without a Diploma*. II. *A Funeral without a Corpſe*. III. *A Coronation without a Primate*. IV. *A Dyet, without Nuncios*. V. *Proteſts without Effect*. During theſe Tranſactions the Prince of *Conti* caſt Anchor before *Dantzick*. Soon after he came to *Oliva*, and was again proclaimed King, was deſired to enter *Poland*, and promiſed Aſſiſtance; but was oblig'd to retire to *France*, after ſeeing *Mariembourg*, the only Place he relied on, open its Gates to the *Saxons*.

From *Warſaw*, That the Troops of the *Czarina*, to the Number of 50,000 Men, had enter'd *Poland*, under the Command of General *Leſlie*, who had declared by a Manifeſto in her Majeſty's Name, it was only to preſerve the Freedom and Rights of Election.

From *Dreſden*. That the *Saxon* Forces with a Train of Artillery, were in Motion towards *Poland*. The *Lithuanians* having determined to make that Elector their King, if not King of *Poland*, and this too conſiſtent with their Oaths, not to Elect a Foreigner; they having trac'd his Descent from the famous *Jagellan* Duke of *Lithuania* and K. of *Poland*.

From *Calais*, That a French Squadron of 18 Men of War well provided, was ſail'd for *Dantzick* with K. *Staniſlaus* on board and a fair Wind.

From *Paris*, That the King of *Spain* was diſpos'd to make a Diverſion in the *Milaneſe* with an Army of 18,000 Foot and 7000 Horſe in favour of the *French* in caſe of War with the Emperor. But that they expected to be oppoſed on the *Rhine*, where they had a large Army ready to enter the Empire, by the King of *Pruſſia*.

From *Danzick*, That the Primate had called a Council, wherein it was reſolved to oppoſe the *Ruſſians* with all the Forces of the Republic. P. S. There is now a Report that the Primate is dead. 'Tis affirm'd, that M. *Leuenwold*, the Ruſſian Miniſter, was ſhot at, upon which he had retired from *Warſaw*.

Towards the End of the Month.

Courſe of Exchange.	STOCKS	Monthly *BILL of Mortality,* from *July* 24, *to Aug.* 28.
Amſterdam 35 2	S. Sea 104	
Ditto at Sight 34 11 ½	—Trading Stock 83	Chriſtned { Males 834 } 1603 { Females 769 }
Hamburgh— 34 4	—Bonds 1 *l.* 19	
Rotterdam— 35 3	—Annuties 105	Buried { Males 1313 } 2614 { Femal. 1301 }
Antwerp — 35 5	—Ditto new 107 ⅛	
Madrid — 42 ¼	—dit. 3 *per* C. 97 ½	Died under 2 Years old --- 1317
Bilboa —— 41 ⅛	Bank 145	Between 2 and 5 ---- 213
Cadiz —— 42 ⅛	---Cir. 7 *l.* 12 *s.* 6 *d.*	Between 5 and 10 ---- 73
Venice —— 49	India 152	Between 10 and 20 ---- 49
Leghorn — 50 ⅞	—Bonds 4 *l.* 5 *s.*	Between 20 and 30 ---- 151
Genoa —— 53 ½	Ditto at 3 per C. 2 *l.*	Between 30 and 40 ---- 197
Paris —— 31 ⅞	Million Bank 116	Between 40 and 50 ---- 215
Bourdeaux – 31 ½	African 27	Between 50 and 60 ---- 173
Oporto—— 54 ½	Royal Aſſ. 102	Between 60 and 70 ---- 117
Lisbon—— 5 5 ½ a ¾	London Aſſ. 12 ¼	Between 70 and 80 ---- 66
Dublin—— 11 ⅞	Eng. Cop. 1 *l.* 16	Between 80 and 90 ---- 35
	Welch ditto 1 *l.*	Between 90 and 100 ---- 8

Lottery Tickets for the Receipts 4 *s.* 6 *s.* Diſcount.　　2614

Price of Grain at Bear-Key, *per* Qr.		Buried.	Weekly Burials
Wheat 23 *s.* to 26 *s.*	P. Malt 20 *s.* to 22 *s.*	Within the walls, 205	*July* 31 --- 491
Rye 13 *s.* to 16 *s.*	B. Malt 16 *s.* to 19 *s.*	Without the walls, 778	*Aug.* 7 --- 475
Barley 13 *s.* to 16 *s.* 6 *d*	Tares 18 *s.* to 20 *s.*	In Mid and Surry, 1052	14 --- 556
Oats 10 *s.* to 15 *s.*	H. Peaſe 16 *s.* to 19 *s.*	City and Sub of Weſt 579	21 --- 545
Peaſe 20 *s.* to 22 *s.*	H. Beans 19 *s.* to 23 *s.*	2614	28 --- 546
			2614

Prices of Goods, &c. in *London.* Hay about 1 *l.* 16 *s.* to 2 *l.* a Load.

Coals in the Pool 24 *s.* to 26 *s.*
Old Hops per Hun. 2 *l.* 10 *s.* to 4 *L.*
New Hops 5 *l.* to 6 *l.* 10 *s.*
Rape Seed 10 *l.* to 11 *L.* per Laſt
Lead the Fodder 19 Hun. 1 half on board, 14 *l.* to 16 *l.* 00 *s.*
Tin in Blocks 4 *l.* 00 *s.*
Ditto in Bars 4 *l.* 02 *s.* excluſive of 3 *s.* per Hun. Duty.
Copper Eng. beſt 5 *l.* 15 *s.* per C.
Ditto ord. 4 *l.* 16 *s.* to 5 *l.* per C.
Ditto Barbary 70 *l.* to 80 *l.*
Iron of Bilboa 14 *l.* 10 *s.* per Tun
Dit. of Sweden 15 *l.* 10 *s.* per Tun
Town Tallow 30 *s.* to 32 *s.* per C.
Country Tallow 28 *s.* 32 *s.*
Salt 4 *s.* to 4 *s.* 6 *d.*

Grocery Wares.
Raiſins of the Sun 28 *s.* 0 *d.* per C.
Ditto Malaga Froilas 19 *s.*
Ditto Smirna new 20 *s.*
Ditto Alicant, 18 *s.*
Ditto Lipra new 19 *s.*
Ditto Belveatra 20
Currants new 45 *s.*
Prunes French 18 *s.*
Figs 20 *s.*
Sugar Powd. beſt 59 *s.* per C.

Ditto ſecond ſort 46 *s.* to 50 *s.* per C.
Loaf Sugar double refine 8 *d.* Half-penny a 9 *d.* per lb.
Ditto ſingle refin. 56 *s.* to 64 *s.* per C.
Cinnamon 7 *s.* 8 *d.* per lb.
Cloves 9 *s.* 1 *d.*
Mace 15 *s.* 0 *d.* per lb.
Nutmegs 8 *s.* 7 *d.* per lb.
Sugar Candy white 14 *d.* to 18 *d.*
Ditto brown 7 *d.* per lb.
Pepper for Home conſ. 17 *d.*
Ditto for exportation 13 *d.* Farth.
Tea Bohea fine 10 *s.* to 11 *s.* per lb.
Ditto ordinary 7 *s.* to 9 *s.* per lb.
Ditto Congo 10 *s.* to 14 *s.* per lb.
ditto Pekoe 9 *s.* a 14 *s.* per lb.
ditto Green fine 8 *s.* to 12 *s.* per lb.
ditto Imperial 10 *s.* to 16 *s.* per lb.
ditto Hyſon 24 *s.* to 28 *s.*

Drugs by the lb.
Balſom Peru 14 *s.* to 15 *s.*
Cardamoms 3 *s.* 3 *d.*
Camphire refin'd 19 *s.*
Crabs Eyes 2 *s.* 5 *d.*
Jallop 3 *s.*
Manna 20 *d.* a 33 *d.*
Maſtick white 4 *s.* 0 *d.*

Opium 11 *s.* 00 *d.*
Quickſilver 4 *s.* 3 *d.*
Rhubarb fine 25 *s.* a 30 *s.*
Sarſaparilla 3 *s.* 0 *d.*
Saffron Eng. 28 *s.* 00 *d.*
Wormſeeds 3 *s.* 5 *d.*
Balſam Capaiva 2 *s.* 9 *d.*
Balſam of Gillead 18 *s.* 00 *d.*
Hipecacuana 7 *s.*
Ambergreaſe per oz. 12 *s.*
Cochineal 18 *s.* 3 *d.* per lb.

Wine, Brandy, and Rum.
Oporto red, per Pipe 36 *L.*
ditto white 24 *L.*
Lisbon red 30 *l.*
ditto white, 26 *L.*
Sherry 26 *l.*
Canary new 30 *l.*
ditto old 36 *L.*
Florence 3 *L.* per Cheſt
French red 30 *L.* a 40 *L.*
ditto white 20 *l.*
Mountain malaga old 24 *l.*
ditto new 10 *l.* to 24 *l.*
Brandy French per Gal. 7 *l.*
Rum of Jamaica 7 *s.*
ditto Leew. Iſlands 6 *s.* 4 *d.*
Spirits Eng. 26 *s.* per Tun

A REGISTER of BOOKS publish'd in AUGUST, 1733.

MTulli Ciceronis de Naturâ Deorum Libri tres. Cum Notis integris Pauli Manucii, &c, Recensuit, suisque Animadversionibus illustravit ac emaculavit *Johannes Davisius*, Coll. Regin. Cantab. Præses. Editio Tertia, emendatior et auctior. Proftant apud *J. and J. Knapton*.

2. *Synopfis Medicinæ* : Or, a Summary View of the whole Practice of Physick. Being the Sentiments of the moft celebrated Authors in all Ages, relating to Diseases, their Causes and Cures; with moft Cases in Surgery and Midwifry; with Observations, &c. By *John Allen*, M. D. and F. R. S. Tranflated by himfelf with large Improvements. In II. Vols 8vo. Printed for *J. Pemberton*.

3. Reflections on Man, and his Relation to other Creatures. Shewing, that we derive our Natural Knowledge of Religion and the Deity from that of our felves, and not from abftract and curious Speculations. Printed for *J. Wilford*; price 2 s.

4. The gradual Revelation of the Gofpel from the Time of Man's Apoftacy: Set forth and explained in 24 Sermons preached at *Bow* Church at the Lecture by the Hon. *Robert Boyle*, Efq; in the Year, 1730. 1731, 1732. To which is added a Sermon concerning the Duty of Shunning the Converfation of Infidels and Hereticks; &c. By *Wm Berryman*, D. D. Printed for Mr *Ward*.

5. The Duty of not conforming to this World. A Sermon preach'd before the Univerfity of *Oxford*, at St *Mary's*, on Act Sunday 1733. By *Thomas Cockman*, D. D. Printed for *Richard Clements* at *Oxford*, and *Thomas Osborne* in *London*.

6. Letters concerning the *English* Nation, viz. On the Quakers, Church of *England*, Presbyterians, Dr *Clarke*, Parliament, Government, Trade, &c. By Mr *De Voltaire*. Printed for *C. Davis*.

7. Les Avantures de *Telemaque* Fils D'*Ulyffe*. A new Edition, with Cuts and Maps. Sold by *J. Brotherton*,

8. The State Mutineers: Or a Play-house to be Let. A Tragi-Comi-Farcical Ballad Opera. By a Gentleman late of *Trinity College, Cambridge*. Printed for *Richard Wellington*. price 1 s.

9. The Fancy'd Queen. An Opera. Printed for *Charles Corbett*, pr. 1 s.

10. The Oxford Act: A new Ballad Opera, as it was performed by a Company of Students at *Oxford*. Sold at the Pamphlet Shops.

11. The Hiftory of Harvides and Lupella. Sold at the Pamphlet Shops.

12. The Quack Triumphant; Or, The N——r——ch Cavalcade. Sold at the Pamphlet Shops.

13. A Poem on her Majefty's Rebuilding the Lodgings of the Black Prince, and *Henry*.

V. at Queen's College Oxford. By Mr *Tickell*. Printed for *J. Tonfon*. ●

14. The Merry Mufician: Or a Cure for the Spleen: Being a Collection of Songs and Ballads, fet to the Violin, &c. Printed for *J. Tilmafh*. price 3 s.

15. The Blanket: A Poem in Imitation of *Milton*. By *John Lloyd*, M. A. Printed for *Jer. Batley*. price 6 d.

16. The Ancient and Modern Hiftory of the Loyal Town of *Rippon*. Adorned with Cuts, a South Weft Profpect and a new Plan of the Place; together with fome Account of the Antiquities and prefent State of *Beverley*, *Pontefract*, *Wakefield, Leeds, Kirkham, Keighly, Skipton, Knaresborough, Tadcafter*, and many other remarkable Places in the County of *York*; with their Monuments and Infcriptions, containing alfo a Letter to the Hon, *John Aiflable* Efq; a Poem defcribing the Beauties of his Seat at *Studley Park*, &c. and the Happy Reign an Eclogue. Collected and Printed by *T.* Gent. of *York*, Sold by the Bookfellers in *Yorkfhire*, and Meff, *Betteſworth* and *Hitch, London*. 8vo. price in Calf 4 s 6 d.

17. The Hiftory of *York*, by the fame Author price bd. 4 s.

16 Killing no Murder. Briefly difcourfed in three Queftions. By Col. *Titus*, alias *William Allen*. Sold by *T. Boteman*. price 6 d.

17 The Heretical Tree of Popery, reprefenting the Origin, Gradual Progrefs, and prefent State of Popery, and proving their peculiar Doctrines to be the Branches of Ancient Herefies, and condemned by the truely Chriftian, Primitive Church. Neatly engraved on a Copper Plate, Sold by *Hen.* Overton. pr. 2 s. 6 d.

18 The Wooden Age; a Satyrical Poem, infcrib'd to *William Pulteney*, Efq; Sold by the Bookfellers. price 6 d.

19 The Tufcan Treaty: Or, *Tarquin's* Overthrow. A Tragedy Printed for *J. Watfon*.

20 An Effay on the Improvement of Midwifery, chiefly with Regard to the Operation, By *Edmund Chapman*. Printed by *A. Blackwell*, price 2 s.

21 The Court Medley ; Or, Marriage by Proxy. A new Court Opera. Sold by the Bookfellers. price 1 s 6 d.

22 The Secret Hiftory of *Mama Oello*, Princefs Royal of *Peru*. Sold by the Bookfellers. price 1 s.

23 The Sturdy Beggars: A new Ballad Opera. Sold by *J. Dormer*, price 1 s. 6 d.

24 Minifters and private Chriftians compared to Salt: In three Sermons from *Luke* 14, 34. 35. printed for *John Ofwald*. pr. 1 s.

25 A Differtation on the Gravel and Stone, fhewing their Nature, Difference, and Symptoms; The Method of curing them; How to remove their Fits; And to prevent them for the future. Sold by *J. Ifted*. pr. 1 s 6 d.

26 Com

26 Commentarium Nofologicum, Morbos Epidemicos et Aeris Variationes in Urbe *Eboracenfi* Locifque vicinis per fedecem Annos graffantes complectens. Authore *Clifiono Wintringham*. Impenfis *J. Walthoe*.

27 The laft Will and Teftament of the famous Free Thinker *Matthew Tindall* L.L.D. Containing 1ft. His Bequeft of 2000 Guineas to *Euftace Budgel*, Efq; with Directions for publishing the Works he left behind him, and his Motives for conftituting that Gentleman his Executor. 2dly. Mr. *Parker's* moft remarkable Calculation of Dr. *Tindal's* Nativity in the Year 1711. 3dly. A Particular Account of his Sickneſs Death and Writings. Printed for *E. Curl.*

28 A Collection of Letters extracted from the moft celebrated French Authors. In *French* and *Englifh.* The *Englifh* by *Tornworth Reresby,* Efq; Printed for *J. Walthoe.*

29. An Account of the burning of the City of *London,* as it was publifhed by the Special Authority of King and Council in the *London Gazette* Sept. 3. 1666, Sold by *W. Mears.*

30. Dr *Warren's* Epiftle to his Friend, of the Method and Manner of curing the late raging Fevers, and of the Danger, Uncertainty and Unwholefomeneſs of taking the *Jefuit's* Bark. Tranflated from the Latin by *Maurice Shelton,* Efq; fold by *D. Brown.* price 2 s.

31. The Chriftian's Sure Guide to Eternal Glory: Or, Living Oracles moft Comfortable, Holy and Inftructive of the Lord Jefus Chrift from Heaven; Containing, 1. The Comforts and Inftructions which all Churches need for their Increafe in Faith and Holineſs. 2. The wonderful large and gracious Promifes of Eternal Life to encourage all Men to Perfevere and Conquer. 3. Prayers and fuitable Devotions. Printed for *F. Jefferies* at the *Bible* and *Crown,* in *Ludgate-ftreet.*

Where may be had.

French and *Englifh* Common prayers. The *Welch* Bibles with Notes or without, and all Sorts of Bibles and Common Prayers whole Sale and Retale.   Alfo

The Ladies Mifcellany price 2 s.

A complete Lift of the Voters for and againft the Excife 8vo pr. 2d.

Juſt Publiſh'd.

No. XII. Vol. I. No. XII. Vol. IV.

THE Ceremonies and Religious Cuftoms of the various Nations of the known World; faithfully tranflated from the French Original, and illuftrated with above 272 Copper Plates, all beautifully defign'd by M. B. PICART, and engrav'd by moft of the beft Hands in Europe.

The Price of the whole work. Printed on Dutch Paper Royal, and compriz'd in four large Volumes in Folio, will be but 5 l. 10 s. 50 Sheets which is no more than half the Price of the Original; to be deliver'd, out in Weekly Numbers during the Space of two Years and two Months, at 1 s. per Number,

which will only amount to three Half-pence per Sheet, and Three pence per Folio Print.

PROPOSALS *at large, with beautiful* SPECIMENS, *may be feen at the Places where* SUBSCRIPTIONS *are taken in,* VIZ. CLAUDE DUBOSC, *Engraver, at the Golden Head in Charles-ftreet, Covent Garden;* THOMAS BOWLES, *Printfeller next the Chapter-houfe in St Paul's Church-yard;* PHILP OVERTON, *Printfeller near St Dunftan's Church Fleet-ftreet;* THOMAS GLASS, *Printfeller next the Royal Exchange Stairs in Cornhill;* J. BOWLES, *Printfeller at the Black Horfe in Cornhill;* J. REGNIER, *Printfeller, at the Golden Ball in Newport-ftreet near Long Acre;* J. HULTON, *Printfeller, at the Corner of Pall Mall facing the Haymarket;* PAUL FOUDRINIER, *Stationer and Printfeller, the Corner of Craig-Court, Charing Croſs;* J. KING, *Printfeller, in the Poultery near Stoks market;* Mrs MARBECK, *Printfeller, on Weftminfter Hall,* J. CLARK, *Engraver and Printfeller in Gray's Inn,* Mr SYMPSON *Engraver and Printfeller, near the end of Cathirine-ftreet in the Strand.*

That the Publick may not be impos'd on by invidious Afpertions, Mr DUBOSC faithfully affures them, that this is no fpurious Edition, but genuine and compleat in all refpects for the Truth of which, and of his various additional Beauties, he refers to his own printed Specimen, and to the Amfterdam Propofals, for proof of the vaft Difference in the Prices, and not to the original Edition, as fome are pleas'd to call Mr LOCKMAN's Tranflation of three Volumes only, of the prefent Undertaking.

Juſt Publiſh'd,

For the Ufe of Families. (beautifully printed in two Volumes 8vo.) adorned with 34 Copper Plates, engraven by Mr. STURT.

DUPIN's EVANGELICAL HISTORY: Or the Records of the SON of GOD, and their veracity, demonftrated in the Life and Acts of our Bleffed Lord and Saviour Jefus Chrift, and his holy Apoftles. Wherein the Life of our Bleffed Jefus is related in all Its Circumftances according to the Order of Time. His Parables, Miracles, and Sufferings fet in a juft Light and defended from all Oppofitions of wicked and defigning Men.

Printed for R. Ware, at the Bible and Sun in Amen-Corner, near Pater-Nofter-Row. Price 8 s.

Where may be had juft publifhed

1 An Hiftorical Narration of the whole Bible. In two Parts, The firft treating of the old Taftiment, with the various Hiftories of the Lives and Travels of our Bleffed Saviour and his Appoftles. With a Summary of the of the Matter, Doctrine, Scope and Divine Anthority of all the Canonical Epiftles; and an Explanation of feveral chief Heads in the myfterious Book of St John's Revelation. By J. Hammond, D. D. and curioufly adorned with Cuts, engrav'd by John Sturt. Price 4s. 6d.

2. The large HOUSE BIBLES. Folio, with fix Maps of Geography and a brief Concordance for the more eaſy finding out of the Places therein contained, by J. DOWNHAME, B. D.

Bound in Calf Leather— — 2 l. 8 s. per Book.
And with Mr. Sturt's Cuts, at — 2 l. 5 s. ditto.
On a fine Paper with Cuts — — 3 l. 3 s.

3. A curious FIELD'S BIBLE, Folio with fine Cuts, In two Vols. Bound in Turkey Leather. Price 20 l. And

4. One on Imperial Paper, Three Volumes, with fine Cuts— Price 30 l.

Likewife the greateft Varie y of all Sorts of Bibles and Common Prayers, in feveral various Bindings, with or without Cuts, by Wholefale or Retale

St John's Gate.

Lond Gazette
Lond Jour.
Fog's Journ.
Applebee's : :
Read'g :: ::
Craftsman :
D. Spetator
Grubstreet J
W. Ip Regifter
Free=Briton
Hyp=Doctor
Daily Court
Daily=Post
Dai. Cournal
Da. Post=boy
D. Advertiser
Evening Post
St James's Eb.
Whitehall Eb
London Eb Eîg
Flying=Post
Weekly Mis-
cellany,
General Eve-
ning Post

Post 2 News
Dublin 6 :::
Edinburgh 2
Briftol : ::: :
Norwich 2:
Exeter 2 ::
Worcester ::
Northampton
Gloucester ::
Stamford ::
Nottingham
Bury Journ.
Chester ditto
Derby ditto
Ipswich do.
Reading do.
Leeds Merc.
Newcastle C.
Canterbury :
Birmingham
Manchester
Boston ::: ¶
Jamaica, &c.
Barbados : :

Or, MONTHLY INTELLIGENCER.

For SEPTEMBER, 1733.

CONTAINING,

more in Quantity, and greater Variety, than any Book of the Kind and Price.

I. Proceedings and Debates in Parliament continu'd, *viz.* Speeches on the Excise Scheme; Sinking Fund; Foreign Auxiliaries; Army; Navy; Land Tax, &c. by several Members of both Houses; (fee the Contents.)

II. Weekly Essays, *viz.* A Warning to young Ladies; of the Court of Chancery; Infidelity; Some-body and No-body; Remarks on Mr *Gordon's* Translation of *Tacitus*; Of Censure; Painting, Sculpture, and Statuary; Encomium on the Fair Sex by a Physician.

III. Political Points, *viz.* Capt. *Gulliver's* Flying Island; Defence of the English Government; Dissenters vindicated; address'd, and courted on both sides; Political Game of Chess; Rise and Repeal of the Schism Bill; Freeholders Catechism; Mr *Walsingham's* Patron

no Friend to the Dissenters; the contrary maintain'd.

IV. Poetry. A London Eclogue; The pert and fantastical Lady; happy Lover; *Sly* and *Lovett*; the Modern Freethinkers *Goliah*; the despairing Lover; Cupid at *Bath*; the Nymphs of the *Thames*; Praise of Virtue; the happy Pair; on the Marriage of the Pr. of *Orange* with the Princess Royal; to Mrs *Pritchard*, appearing on the Stage; an Ejaculation; Riddles answer'd, *&c. &c.*

V. Domestic Occurrences, Deaths, Marriages, Promotions. The Speech of *John Barber*, Esq; Lord Mayor, and of Sir *William Billers*, Lord Mayor Elect.

VI. Prices of Goods, Grain and Stocks.

VII. Foreign Affairs;

VIII. Books and Pamphlets.

IX. A Table of Contents.

By SYLVANUS URBAN, Gent.

LONDON: Printed for the AUTHOR, and sold at St *John's Gate*: By F. *Jefferies*, in *Ludgate-street*; all other Booksellers; and by the Persons who serve Gentlemen with the News-papers. Of whom may be had Compleat Sets, or any single Number. A few on Royal Paper.

CONTENTS.

It is desired that all Letters to the Author of this MAGAZINE may be directed to St JOHN's GATE, in which Case they will always come to hand sooner than otherwise.

Tuesday October 2. 1733. This Day is publish'd.

[PRICE THREE HALF PENCE.]

The GENERAL EVENING POST.

TO be continued every Tuesday, Thursday, and Saturday; in which will be contain'd the best and freshest Account of all Foreign and Domestick News, with whatever else can render a News-Paper useful and Intelligent to the Publick.

Printed for, and sold by J. Roberts in Warwick-Lane where Advertisements are taken in, also by Cæsar Ward at the Ship between the Temple-Gates in Fleetstreet, London.

THE
Gentleman's Magazine:
SEPTEMBER, 1733.

Proceedings and Debates in laft Seffion of Parliament.

EB. 21. the *Penfion Bill* (*V.* p. 394. A) was read a 3d time, paffed, and was fent up to the Houfe of Lords.

Feb. 22. his Majefty gave the Royal Affent to feveral Acts (See p. 99, E)

Debate on the Motion to take 500,000 L from the Sinking Fund.

Feb. 23. The Houfe refolved itfelf into a Committee to confider of raifing the Supply granted to his Majefty.

Sir R—— W——, C—r of the Ex——, ftood up, and fpoke in Subftance as follows:

Sir, Laft Seffion this Houfe came to a moft reafonable Refolution, to eafe the Landed Intereft of 1 s. in the Pound upon the Land Tax, by granting in Lieu thereof a Duty on Salt for three Years. By this the Landed Intereft, which has many Years borne fo great a Share of the publick Expence, has in this laft found a moft fenfible Eafe; if any Method can be fallen on for continuing this Eafe, fuch Method ought certainly to be followed. As I had the Honour of moving for that Refolution, the Approbation I then met with encourages me now to move for another, which I hope will be equally agreeable, viz. *That it is the Opinion of this Committee, that towards raifing the Supply granted to his Majefty, there be iffued and applied the Sum of 500,000 L. out of fuch Monies as have arifen for the Surplus, Exceffes or Overplus Monies, commonly called the Sinking Fund, over and and above what hath been applied to the Payment of one Million, towards difcharging the National Debt, purfuant to an Act of the laft Seffion.*" This Motion, I hope will meet with the Approbation of this Houfe; for it has always been my Opinion, and I believe every Man's, that the Publick Expence ought always to be raifed according to that Method which is the leaft burthenfome to the People: By this Method we fhall provide for a great Part of the current Service of the Year without laying any Burthen whatever on the People, and without doing Injuftice to any Man. The Cafe of the *Creditors* of the Publick is now very much altered from what it was; the Competition among them is not now which of them fhall be firft, but which of them fhall be the laft paid; therefore Gentlemen need not now apprehend, that any of the publick *Creditors* will look upon the Houfe's agreeing to this Motion as an Injuftice done them, on the contrary they will look on it as a Favour, and would be glad that a much larger Part of that Fund were to be applied in the fame manner. And this Motion ought the rather to be agreed to, more efpecially by thofe who have a Regard for the Landed Intereft, becaufe we can thereby continue to the Landed Gentlemen that Eafe which we granted them laft Year; whereas if this Motion fhall appear not to be agreeable to the Committee, then I, or fome other Gentleman of this Houfe, muft move for a Land Tax of 2 s. in the Pound, there not being, fo far as I know, any other Way or Means left of providing for the current Service of the Year.

W——m P—lt—y, Efq;] Sir, Tho' I was aware of the Motion now made by the Hon. Gentleman, yet I was in hopes that what he has now moved for was not all that he was to open this Day to the Committee we are now in; and therefore I fhall conclude with a Motion of a different Kind. But, there is another Thing, a very terrible Affair impending, A monftrous Project! Yea more monftrous, than has ever yet been reprefented! It is fuch a Project, as has ftruck Terror into the Minds of moft Gentlemen within this Houfe, and into the Minds of all Men without Doors, who have any Regard to the Happinefs or to the Conftitution of their Country. I mean, that Monfter, the Excife! That Plan of Arbitrary Power, which is expected to be laid before this Houfe; therefore I am for having the Whole of that Gentleman's Defigns laid before this Committee at once, and a fufficient Time given to confider the Whole, before we come to a Refolution on any Part.——Of late Years, Gentlemen have been led, I do not know how, into a Method very different from what our Anceftors did always obferve. In former Times the general or particular Grievances were firft examined, confidered, and redreffed in Parliament, before they entered upon the granting

of

of Supplies; but lately we have been led in-to a Method of granting all the Money neceſ-ſary for the publick Service among the firſt Things we do. The Malt, Land-Tax Bill, and ſuch Bills, are now in every Seſſion the Firſt things that appear upon the Journals of this Houſe; and when theſe things are finiſhed, the Gentlemen in the Admini-ſtration generally look on the whole Buſineſs of the Seſſion to be over. If this Houſe ſhould then enter upon any diſagreeable En-quiries into Grievances, we might then per-haps be told, that the Seaſon was too far ſpent, that it was neceſſary for Gentlemen to return home to mind their private Affairs; we might probably be obliged to defer to another Seſ-ſion what the Welfare of this Nation required to be determined in the preſent. I hope, Gentlemen will again begin to follow the wiſe Method obſerved by our Anceſtors, and keep ſome Security in our own Hands for our ſitting till we have heard and redreſ-ſed all the Grievances of our Fellow-Subjects, There are ſeveral things which we ought to examine into before this Seſſion ſhall be con-cluded. Does not every Gentleman expect an Application to be made to us from the *South Sea* Company? That Company has now made choice of a Set of honeſt Proprietors to be the Directors of their Affairs; they are enquiring into the State of them and as they muſt examine into the Management for ſome time paſt: they will ſtand in need of a Parliamentary Relief, and it ought to be granted them.——The Hon. Gentleman ad-dreſſes himſelf in a very particular manner to the Landed Intereſt; I hope every Gen-tleman in this Houſe has a Regard for the Landed Intereſt; but I hope the Landed Gentlemen of this Houſe are not to be bullied into any *Miniſterial Jobs*, by telling them, that if they do not agree to ſuch a Motion, a Land Tax of a *s.* in the Pound muſt be moved for. I hope, *Sir*, the Landed Gen-tlemen will never be induced to conſent to any thing that may undo the Nation, and overturn the Conſtitution for ſo ſmall a Bribe, as that of being free from the Payment of a *s.* in the Pound Land Tax, and for one Year only. The landed Gentlemen of this Nation have often ventured their All in their Country's Cauſe, and it is an Indignity of-fered to them to imagine, that their paying or not paying ſuch a Trifle as 1 *s.* in the Pound Land Tax will be of any Weight with them, when it comes in competition with the Welfare and the Happineſs of their Coun-try.——The Sinking Fund, that ſacred Depoſit for extinguiſhing the Debts, and aboliſhing the Taxes which lie ſo heavy on the Trade and the People of this Nation, ought never to be touched; It has of late been too often robbed; I beg pardon, *Robbing* is a harſh Word; I will not ſay robbed; but upon ſe-veral Occaſions there have been conſiderable Sums nipped away from it: Upon the Demiſe of his late Majeſty a large Sum was taken

from the Sinking Fund, and applied to the Civil Liſt; by the taking off the Salt Duty another large yearly Sum was taken from it; the People are now again charged with that Duty, but no Reſtitution has been made to the Sinking Fund. And now it is propoſed to ſnip off of it 500,000*l.* at once.————At this Rate the People of the Nation muſt for ever groan under the Taxes they are now ſubject to, and our Trade la-bour under Difficulties and Diſcouragements. Is this, *Sir*, conſiſtent with the Welfare or Happineſs of the Nation? Is this the Method by which the Landed Gentlemen are to be eaſed of a *s.* in the Pound Land Tax?——The Hon. Gentleman has been called, and once had the Vanity to call himſelf *the Fa-ther of the Sinking Fund*; but, if *Solomon's* Judgment was right, he, who is thus for dividing the Child, can never be deemed the true Father. But I ſhall allow him the Ho-nour of being the Father of two other Chil-dren lately brought forth in this Nation, a Standing Army and an Exciſe; but as for the Sinking Fund, he ſeems now to, renounce all Pretences of being the Father thereof, I ſhall not now, *Sir*, enter further into the Merits of the Motion that the Hon. Gentle-man has been pleaſed to make, becauſe I hope a proper Time will be allowed for Gen-tlemen to conſider of a Queſtion of ſo great Conſequence; therefore I conclude with a Motion for the Chairman to leave the Chair.

Mr C——r of the E——r.] As for the Gen-tleman's ſaying I had the Vanity to call my-ſelf the *Father* of the Sinking Fund, I muſt ſay, that whether I was vain of being thought ſo or no, I remember a Time when the E-ſtabliſhing of that Fund was treated as a monſtrous Project, and then I was obliged to father it; but no ſooner was it found out to be a good and a right thing, and a Project that was both feaſible and agreeable to the Intereſt of this Nation, but other Gentlemen endeavoured to rob the real Father, whoever he was, of the Glory of being the Father of that Child. As for the other monſtrous Pro-ject ſo much talked of, which ſome Gentle-men now endeavour to ſhew in ſo terrible a Light, I doubt not but that in a little time it will appear in a quite different Shape to the impartial and unprejudiced Part of the Nation. Let it be what it will, I am re-ſolved to propoſe it; and if I have but a very little Time, I ſhall lay it before you for your Conſideration: I have no Doubt but that upon a thorough Examination, it will be found to be for the general Intereſt of the Nation, and for the Advantage of every fair Trader in particular; and this I am ſo much convinced of, that I believe I may live to have it told me I was not the Father of it, but that other People had thought of it before me. I never as yet inclined to do that which I thought was ill; I am afraid of doing ſo; but I never ſhall be afraid of doing Good either to my Country, or to

private

private Men, so far as is consistent with the Interest of my Country. As for the Sums which have been taken from the Civil List they were not taken from it by me, they were taken from it by the Authority of this House; I was only one of those who consented to it; and particularly as to the Sum which was taken from the Sinking Fund upon the Demise of the late King, and given to the Civil List, the Hon. Gentleman who sits near me agreed to it as well as I, but our Motives for agreeing were perhaps very different.——The Sinking Fund was established for Payment of the Debts of the Nation, but still it was left subject to Disposal of Parliament; if upon any Occasion it shall appear that a Part of it may be more properly applied to some other Use, the Legislature has certainly a Power to apply it in that manner which they shall judge to be most for the publick Good, and for the Interest of the Nation in general. This is the proper Question now under our Consideration; we are now to determine, Whether the Sum of 500,000 *l.* shall be applied this Year towards the Ease of the Landed Interest, where it is absolutely necessary to give some Relief, or, if the Whole shall be this Year applied towards the Payment of the Publick *Creditors* who do not so much as wish or desire it. This is the plain State of the Question; and I could hardly have expected that it would have stood a Debate.

Sir *J—n B—d.*] Sir, As to the Project which the Hon. Gentleman seems to be afraid of being robbed of the Glory of, I believe he may be very easy in that respect; for my part I am so far from believing, that when it appears in Publick, it will procure either Honour or Glory to the first Projector, whoever he be, that I am firmly convinced it will turn out to be his eternal Shame and Dishonour, and that the more the Project is examined, and the Consequences considered, the more the Projector will be hated and despised.——As to the Question now before us, it affords me a most melancholy Consideration; I own, that the Landed Interest, as well as every other Interest, stands very much in need of Relief; I allow that by what the Gentleman now proposes, the Landed Interest may meet with some immediate Ease, and I will likewise easily grant, that it may in our present Circumstances be agreeable to the Creditors of the Publick; but, while I have the Honour to be a Member of this House, I am not to consider the immediate Ease of the Landed Interest in particular, nor the present Pleasure of the publick Creditors;—— I am to consider the Welfare of the Nation in general, both as to the present, and as to future Times; and as I am convinced that what is now proposed will in the long run be contrary to the Interest of the Nation in general, I therefore declare my Dissent. ——In all Affairs which come before this House, we are to have a due Regard to Posterity, and the Question now before us is, *Whether we shall give a present Ease to the Landed Interest of 1 s. in the Pound Land Tax, by unjustly loading our Posterity with the Payment of 500,000 l. and the Interest thereof from this present Year? or, Whether we shall continue to pay the 1 s. in the Pound Land Tax, and thereby free the Nation of a Debt of 500,000 l. and our selves and Posterity of a new Debt of 20,000 l. which must be yearly incurred for the Payment of the Interest upon that Debt, till the principal Sum be satisfied and paid?* This is the Question before us, and whoever considers it in this Light, must conclude, that what is proposed, is robbing of our Posterity of 500,000 *l.* and the growing Interest thereof, for the Sake of a trifling present Ease to ourselves. If the Landed, or any Interest, could be relieved by reducing the publick Expence, it would redound to the Glory of him who had the Honour of being the Author thereof; but to ease ourselves by loading our Posterity, is a poor temporary Expedient of short-sighted or self-interested Politicians, and the Author of such an Expedient must expect the Curses of Posterity, and can never expect present Thanks from any but such as are as short-sighted, or as self-interested as himself.——I hope, I shall not now be taxed with affecting Popularity, or with speaking Provincially, or as a Member for the City of *London,* as I have often been on other Occasions; for as to the present Question, I consider it entirely in a National View. As a Member of this House I shall always look upon myself as one of the Representatives of the People of *Great Britain,* and I hope every Gentleman who has the Honour of being a Member of this House, will always do the same. I hope it will never be in the Power of any Man to make the Landed Interest range themselves in Opposition to the trading Interest of this Nation; but if ever such a wicked Design should take Effect, if the Members of this House should ever be brought to talk and to vote provincially, or as Members for Cities or Boroughs, or as Members for Counties; if the former were to join together against the latter, it is easy to determine on which side the Majority would be. The Hon. Gentleman who made the Motion, now seems to aim at the Affectation of Popularity among the Landed Gentlemen; this I am really surprized at, considering how often he has taxed me, and other Gentlemen in this House, with Affectation of Popularity as a most heinous Crime.——The *Creditors* of the Publick are, perhaps, at present unwilling to be paid off, because they have a greater Interest for their Money from the Publick, than they can have any where else; this is one, but not the principal Reason for it; for the chief Reason is, the Method and Manner of paying them: If a considerable Part of their Debts were to be paid at once, and a reasonable Notice given of such Payments being to be made, they could then diſpoſe of their Money to as good an Advantage for themſelves, and much more to the Advantage of the Trade of this Nation; but in the preſent Method the Payments are ſo ſmall, and the Warning ſo ſhort, that many of them do not well know how to diſpoſe of the ſmall Sums they receive, and therefore are unwilling to receive any in that manner: However their Inclinations be, it is certainly the Intereſt of the Nation to have them ſoon all paid off, and therefore no Part of what is appropriated to their Payment, ought to be converted to any other Uſe: Their Unwillingneſs to receive Payment is ſo far from being an Argument againſt paying them, that on the contrary it ſhews, that they have a better Bargain from the Publick than they can in the ſame way have from any other Perſon; and therefore, if it were poſſible to borrow Money at a lower Intereſt; if it were poſſible to add to the Sinking Fund, the Publick ought certainly to do it, in order to pay off thoſe who are now *Creditors* of the Publick at ſo high a yearly Intereſt.——I hope it will be thought that I am ſincere in what I ſay, ſince I am in every reſpect talking againſt my own private Intereſt; I have a Part of my Eſtate in Land, and therefore ought to be for reducing that Tax; I have another Part of my Eſtate in the Publick Funds; and conſequently I ought to be as fond as other Men of not being paid off, and having as high an Intereſt as I can poſſibly get from the Publick; and the remaining Part of my Eſtate I have in Trade, as to which alſo I ſpeak againſt my own Intereſt; for as a Trader I ought to be againſt paying off the Publick Funds, becauſe the Intereſt of Money will be thereby reduced; and though it may ſeem a Paradox, yet it is certain, that the higher the Intereſt of Money is in any Country, the greater Profit the private Trader will always make: In a Country where the Intereſt of Money is high, the Traders will be but few, the general Stock in Trade will be but ſmall; but every Man who is a Trader muſt make a great Profit of what Money he has in Trade.

J—phi, D—a—rs, Eſq;] I am ſo far from ſeeing any Inconvenience in what the Hon. Gentleman has propoſed, that, conſidering how little Occaſion there is at preſent for paying off any of the Publick Debts, I am ſurprized at his Modeſty in asking ſo little from the Sinking Fund; for, if he had asked the Whole, it would have been reaſonable for us to have given it him, ſince it is for the Support of a Government under which we enjoy ſo many Bleſſings, more particularly that of the free Exerciſe of our holy Religion. The Landed Gentlemen bore the greateſt Share of the late War; by that they have been loaded with many heavy Taxes; by that were all thoſe Funds created out of which the Plumb Men of the City of *London* have made moſt of their Eſtates, by which they are enabled to deck their Wives in Velvets and rich Brocades, while poor Country Gentlemen are hardly able to afford their Wives a Gown of Lindſey Woolſey. The Landed Intereſt has long laboured under the greateſt Diſtreſs, and therefore we ought to embrace every Opportunity of giving them Relief.

Sir *W—m W—m,*] I have the Honour to ſit in this Houſe as a Knight of a Shire, yet I look on myſelf as one of the Repreſentatives of the whole Body of the People of *England*, and therefore I ſhall never endeavour to find out a Diſtinction between the Intereſt of the Landed Gentlemen, and that of the Nation in general; whoever does endeavour it, will ſoon find himſelf diſappointed. I know that ſince laſt Seſſion of Parliament it has been moſt induſtriouſly given about in the County which I have the Honour to repreſent; *O Gentlemen! The Knight of your Shire was againſt eaſing you of 1s. in the Pound Tax Land.* If it was done with this Deſign to do me a Diſſervice, I ſhall leave thoſe who did it, to brag of their Succeſs. For I am ſo conſcious that my Behaviour in that Affair then was right, that were I to plead Merit with my Conſtituents upon any one Vote I ever gave in this Houſe, it would be upon my Way of voting in that very Affair; for I ſhall always be againſt ſacrificing the publick Happineſs of the Nation, or the Security of our Conſtitution, to any ſuch mean and ſordid View, as that of a little preſent Eaſe in the Land Tax.——The Sinking Fund, is a Fund I have always had the greateſt Veneration for; I look on it, as appropriated to the relieving the Nation from that Load of Debts and Taxes it now groans under; I take it, to be ſo abſolutely appropriated to that Uſe, that if upon any preſſing and unlooked-for Emergency, we ſhould be neceſſarily obliged to borrow a little from it, the ſame with Intereſt ought to be repaid by ſome Tax to be raiſed within the Year. I have indeed been always afraid that ſome enterprizing Miniſter might be tempted to ſeize upon it, or ſome Part of it, in time of War; but I little dreamt of ſeeing any Attempts made upon it in a time of the moſt profound Tranquillity. It is to me a melancholy Conſideration to think of the preſent vaſt Load of the National Debt; 45 Millions Sterling and upwards! all contracted ſince the Revolution! This muſt be a melancholy Conſideration to every Gentleman that has any Concern for his Country's Happineſs; but if the Motion now made to us ſhall be agreed to, how diſmal will this Conſideration be rendered, when we reflect upon the little Appearance that there will then be of this Debt's being ever paid? Is the Publick Expence never to be leſſened? Are the People of *England* always to pay the ſame heavy and grievous Taxes? Surely, if there is ever a Time to be looked for of eaſing the People of this Nation, the Preſent is

the

the time for doing it. But, when I reflect upon what was done last Session, I am really afraid of proposing any Relief for the poor Manufacturers and Labourers of this Nation; I do not think we can trust ourselves: The Salt Duty was taken off by this House as the Tax the most grievous to the Labourer and the Poor of this Nation, and the Sinking Fund was thereby diminished; for the Relief of the Poor we did consent to this Incroachment on that sacred Fund, but that very Tax was again laid on, because some Gentlemen pretend to have found out, that the Landed Gentlemen of *England* were poorer than the Poor. At this rate the Whole of the Sinking Fund may by degrees be exhausted, and the Poor of the Nation not relieved from any one Tax they now groan under.——Last Year, Sir, the Salt Duty was laid on for three Years in Lieu of 1 s. in the Pound Land Tax for one Year, and this was pretended to be a Relief to the landed Interest; but it was then evidently made appear, that it was no Relief even to any Landed Gentleman in *England*, unless he was a Man of a plentiful Land Estate. And it was then also made appear that the People of the Nation was to pay above a Million for the 500,000 l. thus saved in the Pockets of the Landed Gentlemen. And now this Year the Sum of 500,000 l. is to be taken from the Sinking Fund in Lieu of 1 s. in the Pound Land Tax; this likewise will be found to be much such another Relief as that of last Year. We are to save this Year in the Pockets of the Landed Gentlemen 500,000 l. but this Sum must hereafter be paid by the Nation some time or other: If it be paid next Year, we then pay 520,000 l. for it, if not till two Years hence, we pay upwards of 540,000, and if it is not paid till 15 or 16 Years hence, by computing Interest upon Interest, which in such Cases must always be done, the Nation must then pay above a Million for the 500,000 l. Ease, now pretended to be given to the Landed Gentlemen: This is the least Sum that it will cost the Nation; but if to this we add what might be saved by the abolishing of some of those Taxes which now lie heavy upon Trade, and which cost the Nation more in levying than the neat Produce ever amounts to, then it will appear, that the Nation must be infinitely a greater Loser by this Ease now pretended to be given to the Landed Interest. Let any Landed Gentleman consider this, and at the same time let him consider that the Lands of *Great Britain* stand ultimately obliged to pay all the Debts we owe, in case our present Funds should fail, which they may probably do by the Decay of our Trade, if it continues long under the Difficulties it at present labours under; let any Landed Gentleman consider this, and then let him determine whether he and his Posterity owe. Thanks to the Gentlemen who now pretend to be so great

Friends to the Landed Interest.——What can these Gentlemen say, who are thus for loading Posterity? Can they imagine that there will ever be a Time of more profound Tranquility? or less Occasion for publick Expence? Or, that our Posterity will be in much better Circumstances than we are? I am sure if we propose the last, we must shew some more Regard to the Trade of the Nation than has been shewn for some time passed; we must think of relieving the poor Tradesmen and Manufacturers from the many and various kinds of Taxes they now groan under; and we must avoid all Occasions of loading the Publick with the Payment of Interest, by providing within the Year for the current Service of the Year: To this the Motion how made is directly contrary; for the not paying off of an old Debt is the same with contracting a new, and subjects the Nation to the same Expence with respect to the payment of Interest. But I hope we shall have another Day to consider of this Question; therefore I shall now only conclude with the seconding of the Motion for the Chairman's leaving the Chair.

H——y P——m Esq;] As other Gentlemen have their melancholy Considerations, the most melancholy Consideration I have is, that notwithstanding our having a Government under which we enjoy our Laws, our Liberties, and our Religion, to the utmost Extent, yet it is absolutely necessary to put the Nation to a very great annual Charge, in order to support that Government against the Foreign Enemies both of our Constitution and Religion, supported and encouraged by our Factions and Divisions at home: This is the Reason that we cannot, by a Saving in the Publick Charge, give that Ease to the Landed Interest which is become absolutely necessary to be given, and since we cannot with any Safety to the Constitution, or to the present happy Establishment, give that Ease by a Saving in the Publick annual Expence, we must therefore resolve to give it in that manner which will be least Burthensome to the People, and that I take to be the Method which is now proposed to us. ——Gentlemen may talk as they please of what was done last Session, but I can say that in all Places where I have since been, I have had the Pleasure of having the Universal Thanks of the People for the Ease then given to the Landed Interest: Whatever Gloss may now be put upon that Affair, yet I know that some Gentlemen who appeared against it, were heard to say at the time, that that Affair was first mentioned, *This is a most damnable Project! It will please the Country too much, therefore we must endeavour to render it abortive.* I will indeed do the Gentlemen the Justice to believe, that they then spoke as they thought; and they then did what they could to prevent the Success of a Design by which his Majesty's Administration has gained the Favour of the Generality of the Landholders in *England*.——I have as great a Regard for Posterity, as any Gentleman in this House, therefore I shall never be against any thing absolutely necessary for conveying to Posterity the many Blessings we now enjoy under the present happy Establishment. What is now proposed, is not a throwing of any new Load upon Posterity; it is only a disposing of that Money. which always has, and still is at the Disposal of Parliament: We have a Right to dispose of it in that manner which we think most conducive to the general Interest of the Nation, and what is now proposed, is only an exercising of that Right, and thereby granting an Ease to the most oppressed Part of his Majesty's Subjects, at a Time, when there is no pressing Demand for applying the Money either to that Use for which it was at first intended, or to any other Use whatever. This is a Question that in my Opinion requires no time to consider of; it is granted by every Gentleman who has spoke in this Debate, that the Creditors of the Publick do not desire to have their Money; and it is likewise granted that the Landed Interest stand in great Need of Relief; it cannot therefore be doubted but that the Parliament may and ought to apply at least a Part of that which is not so much as wished for by the Publick Creditors, to the Relief of those who are now in so great Distress; especially since no Relief can be given to them by any other Means: For which Reason, I shall be for agreeing with the Motion made by the Hon. Gentleman near me.

Mr *W*——*r*,] It is known I believe by every Gentleman in the House, that *Scotland* pays little or no Part of what is raised for the Use of the Sinking Fund, and for the small Part they do, or ought to contribute towards that Fund, they have already received an Equivalent; so that by what is now proposed that Part of the Nation is not to contribute a Shilling towards this 500,000 *l*. which is to be applied for the current Service of the Year: Now, I should be glad to know by what Article of the Union they are to be free from paying any Part of so large a Sum for the current Service of the Year. I find by some Accounts called for, and now lying on our Table, that there has been but a very little paid by the People of that Part of the Island, towards the Support of the Government, and I believe that the little, has generally been distributed among them in Pensions, Rewards and Gratuities.

J——*ph T*——*r Esq;*] There are some People in this Nation whose Case is such; that the more they owe, the greater Advantage they make, and the richer they grow; those are the Bankers of *London*, and of the other great Cities in this Nation: It would seem by the Motion now made to us, that some Gentlemen imagine the Case of the Nation to be the same; but I cannot be of their Opinion, and therefore I shall be against agreeing with the Motion.

Besides the Gentlemen above-mentioned, there were several other Gentlemen spoke in this Debate, viz. Mr S——r and the L——d T——l, for the Motion; the Hon. E——d D——y, G——ge H——te, P——p G——n, S——l S——t, and T——s P——r Esqrs spoke against it, and for the Speaker's leaving the Chair; at last the Question Whether the Speaker should leave the Chair was put, but carried on a Division in the Negative 245 against 135; after which the Question was put upon the first Motion, and carried without any Division.

Then was moved and resolved without Opposition, *That it is the Opinion of this Committee, that towards raising the Supply granted to his Majesty, the Sum of 1 s. in the Pound, and no more, be raised in the Year 1733, upon Lands, Tenements, Hereditaments, Pensions, Offices, and Personal Estates, in that Part of Great Britain called* England, Wales, *and the Town of* Berwick *upon* Tweed; *and that a proportionable Cess (according to the 9th Article of the Treaty of Union) be laid upon* Scotland,

2d Debate on the foregoing Subject.

Feb. 26. *These Resolutions being reported, and the Question moved, for agreeing with the Committee as to the first Resolution, there ensued a Debate to the following Purport.*

S——*lS*——*s, Esq;*] Notwithstanding the long Debate in the Committee upon this Resolution, I cannot now let it pass without taking Notice of the bad Consequences it may be attended with. The Constant Method heretofore, of providing for the current Service of the Year, has been to grant annual Supplies to be raised by Taxes which were granted for that Purpose, consequently only for one Year. It would have been High Treason in any Officer to levy such Tax after the Expiration of the Year for which it was granted. By this Method our Kings have always been under a Necessity of calling Parliaments frequently; if the King wanted a Supply, there was no Tax subsisting by Law, out of which he could get it, and therefore he was obliged to call a Parliament to grant him a new Supply, and to impose a new annual Tax for that purpose. Of this nature, is the Land Tax; it has never been granted for more than one Year at a Time. But, we now are going to give up that Tax which we have always in our own Hands, and which we may grant or not, as we see occasion; and in the room thereof to substitute a Tax, or at least a Method of providing for the current Service of the Year, which we have not in our Power, the Taxes by which the Sinking Fund is raised being all granted for ever, and may be levied without any new Authority from Parliament. By this, we clearly point out a Method by which some future ambitious Prince may provide for the current Service of the Year without the Assistance of Parliament, from whence he may judge the Parliaments are

unneces-

unneceſſary, and will certainly lay them aſide as ſoon as he finds them thwarting of his Meaſures. I know, it will be told me, that it would be as illegal and criminal to apply the Revenue of the Sinking Fund to the current Service of the Year without the Authority of Parliament, as it would be to levy Taxes without any ſuch Authority ; but, is a very great Difference between the that Caſes ; in levying a Tax contrary to Law, every Officer employed knows that he acts with a Rope about his Neck, and therefore it would be difficult for the moſt powerful Prince to get Officers that would be ſo employed ; whereas in levying thoſe Taxes appropriated to the Sinking Fund, there are none guilty, but a few of the chief Officers who connive at the Miſapplication. Another material Difference there is, between thoſe two Caſes ; The levying of any Tax *contrary to Law* gives immediately the Alarm ; every Man thinks he is robbed of his Property ; and as the whole People in the Nation would on ſuch an Occaſion take the Alarm, ſo it would be eaſy to ſtop ſuch a Prince in the beginning of his Tyrannical Career. But tho' an ambitious Prince and his Miniſters ſhould miſapply the Produce of the Sinking Fund, by converting it to the current Service of the Year, the Body of the People would be no ways alarmed, becauſe they would find that they were not obliged to pay any Taxes but thoſe which they knew to be due by Law ; on the contrary, they would probably be well pleaſed with the new ſort of Government, becauſe they would find themſelves, for ſome time at leaſt, free from the Payment of thoſe Taxes which had formerly been annually raiſed by Parliament ; and thus before the Body of the People could be made ſenſible of the Tyranny they were under, the Arbitrary Power of the Prince would be eſtabliſhed, and the Fetters of Slavery riveted upon the People. I cannot but dread the Conſequences of the Reſolution now before us, and therefore I could not let ſlip this Opportunity of again declaring my Diſſent to it.

W——m Sb——n, Eſq;] *Sir,* There was no Occaſion for ſo ſolemn a Preparation (*a*) for what I have to ſay ; but as I did not give you any Trouble in the Committee, I will now beg leave to ſay a few Words to the Queſtion. I have, in many Debates heard Parliamentary Faith much inſiſted on ; particularly laſt Seſſion, when it was propoſed that *Scotland* ſhould pay equally with *England* towards a Duty which was then raiſed, or rather revived, and applied to the current Service of the Year, a certain Hon. Gentleman inſiſted, that it was a Breach of Parliamentary Faith. I wonder to ſee that Gentleman now ſo forward for committing a Breach of Parliamentary Faith. I remember, when the Law we are now going to break thro', was brought in, the Gentlemen who brought it in, told us, that it was to be looked on as a fundamental Law of the Realm, and therefore to be always had in the greateſt Reverence and Eſteem ; that no Attempt was ever to be made for encroaching upon or altering it ; and that the Surpluſes or Exceſſes of the Funds thereby eſtabliſhed were always to be religiouſly and ſacredly preſerved, and appropriated to the paying off the Debts of the Nation : He then ſaid, that upon the ſtrict Obſervance of this Law, the Credit and future Happineſs and Glory of this Nation entirely depended ; and in purſuance of what he ſaid, the Words of the Law were made very plain and expreſs, that all the Exceſſes and Surpluſes there mentioned ſhould be appropriated to the diſchaſging the Principal and Intereſt of ſuch National Debts as were incurred before the 25th of *Dec.* 1716, and were declared to be National Debts, and not provided for by Parliament, in ſuch manner as ſhould be directed by any future Act, *and to or for no other Uſe whatever.* By theſe Words it is plain that the Sinking Fund is not abſolutely at the Diſpoſal of Parliament ; the Parliament may direct what Debts are to be paid off, but cannot direct thoſe Surpluſes and Exceſſes to another Uſe beſides that of paying the National Debts before the Year 1716, without repealing that Law ; and as all the Publick Creditors have as much a Right to have their Principal paid as their Intereſt, we certainly cannot divert the Fund appropriated for the Payment of their Principal without their Conſent, no more than we can divert the Funds appropriated to the Payment of their Intereſt ; it is a Breach of Parliamentary Faith in the one Caſe as well as in the other. Upon the Faith of this Law, ſo many became ſoon afterwards Purchaſers of our publick Funds, that we have ſince been enabled to reduce the Intereſt payable upon them, and thereby conſiderably increaſed this ſame Sinking Fund ; can it be then ſaid, that Parliamentary Faith is obſerved towards thoſe Purchaſers, if, without their Conſent, that Law be broke thro', which was the greateſt, perhaps the only Temptation for them to purchaſe ? I am really ſurprized to hear Gentlemen argue as they do upon the preſent Subject ; but, I remember that the Author of, at leaſt he who brought in that Law, was a Country Gentleman, therefore I don't at all wonder to ſee a Miniſter of State endeavour to tear down any Monument erected by a Country Gentleman ; but I would have Gentlemen reflect, that he that pulls down a Monument of Glory, erects to himſelf a Monument of Infamy. For my part, I have always been a Country Gentleman in this Houſe ; I am afraid — afraid I ought not to ſay,

---

(*a*) As ſoon as he roſe up to ſpeak, Mr D——n——n moved for clearing the Galleries of all ſuch who were not Members, which was done accordingly.

ſay, for I deſire to continue always to be a Country Gentleman; therefore am for preſerving inviolated this Monument of Glory erected by an honeſt Country Gentleman; and for this Reaſon, Sir, I cannot agree with the Committee in the Reſolution now before us.

Sir W——m Y——ge.] Sir, As we had the Sentiments of moſt Gentlemen on the Subjects now before us in the Committee, I was in hopes the Reſolution would now have been agreed to without further Debate; but I find it is otherwiſe. An Hon. Gentleman preſents to be in great Fear, and to dread dangerous Conſequences from this Reſolution; but how any Gentleman can be at preſent under ſuch Apprehenſion I cannot comprehend; there cannot be any Colour of Reaſon for it, as long as the preſent Royal Family poſſeſſes the Throne; it can never be ſuſpected that his preſent Majeſty, or any of his Illuſtrious Family, will ever think Parliaments uſeleſs, or make any Attempt for laying them aſide; ſuch a thing might indeed very probably happen, if by a *Revolution*, I ſhall never give it the Name of a *Reſtoration*, the Pretender to his Majeſty's Crown, or any of his Deſcendents, ſhould get Poſſeſſion of the Throne; the Creditors of the Publick might then indeed deſpair of ever having either Principal or Intereſt, they would be told that none of the Publick Debts ought to be paid, becauſe contracted without any Legal Authority, and for keeping the Rightful Heir from the Crown: Parliamentary Faith would then be laughed at, and thoſe Taxes, which are now appropriated and faithfully applied to the Payment of the publick Creditors, would then be all at once converted to the Support of Tyranny and Arbitrary Power. This would certainly be the fatal Conſequences of ſuch an unhappy Revolution; but how invidious is it, ſo much as to ſuſpect any ſuch Deſign in his Majeſty, or any of his Family who ſhall ſucceed to the Crown! Their Title to the Crown flows from the Authority of Parliament, and entirely depends on the Preſervation of our preſent happy Conſtitution; how then can it be ſuppoſed that they will deſtroy Parliaments, ſince by the Deſtruction of them they would certainly deſtroy themſelves? But I find, thoſe groundleſs Jealouſies and Fears are pretended not only in this Houſe, but they are induſtriouſly ſpread through all Parts of the Nation; I had myſelf a Letter lately from the Corporation I have the Honour to repreſent, *deſiring me not to conſent to any Extenſion of the Exciſe Laws, becauſe our Parliaments would be thereby render'd uſeleſs*: This Letter came by the Poſt, by whom it was wrote, I do not know; however from thence I conclude, that it has been repreſented to the People in that Country, *that if a certain Scheme now upon the Anvil ſhould ſucceed, Parliaments would be render'd quite uſeleſs,*

and *would be laid aſide*. The Vulgar and the Ignorant Country People may be poſſeſſed with ſuch Fears; but I little expected to have heard any ſuch Arguments made uſe of in this Houſe. I am indeed ſurpriſed to hear it ſo much as inſinuated, that the preſent Reſolution is any Breach of Parliamentary Faith, or that the publick Creditors have a Right to demand that no Part of the Sinking Fund can be applied to any thing but to their Payment. The Caſe of the Sinking Fund is very different from thoſe Taxes which are appropriated towards the Payment of their Intereſt: It was upon the Faith of this laſt Appropriation, that they lent their Money, and therefore they cannot be diverted to any other Uſe without their Conſent; but the Sinking Fund was eſtabliſhed long after, there was no Money lent to the Publick by any Man upon the Faith of that Fund; and therefore it is entirely at the Diſpoſal of Parliament; the Legiſlature may convert it to any Uſe they pleaſe without the Conſent of any Man, or of any Body of Men; as to the Diſpoſal thereof we are under no Reſtraint but that of the Publick Good; and as I am convinced that what is propoſed by this Reſolution is the beſt thing we can do for the Publick Good, therefore I ſhall be for agreeing with our Committee.

W——m P——y, Eſq;] The Fears which my Hon. Friend has expreſſed are moſt juſt and reaſonable, however groundleſs they may appear to the Gentleman who ſpoke laſt. His preſent Majeſty is known to us, we know that all his Deſigns are juſt and honourable, and we know that he will not allow himſelf to be miſled by any guilty Miniſter; he is too good to think of trampling upon the Rights and Liberties of the Subject, for the ſake of protecting any high Criminal whatever. But, we cannot certainly know what is to happen hereafter; we cannot depend on the Diſpoſitions, the Humours or the Deſigns of all the Princes, even of the preſent Royal Family: Who knows but a Prince not yet born may ariſe, who finding himſelf poſſeſſed of a Revenue wh'ch he may raiſe by virtue of the Laws in being, and which he knows to be ſufficient for the Support of his Government without any Aſſiſtance from Parliament, may from thence conclude that Parliaments are uſeleſs to him, and therefore reſolve to lay them aſide. The preſent Royal Family has as good a Right to the Crown, as ever any Family had that ſwayed the Scepter of this Kingdom: their Right to the Crown no more depends upon Parliaments than the Right of any former Royal Family ever did; and yet we know that ſome of our former Kings have had Views of overturning the the Rights and Liberties of the People. The only Barrier againſt ſuch Deſigns, is to take all proper Care that it ſhall never be in any

future

future Prince's Power: This is what has hitherto preserved our Liberties, and this is our only Security in time to come. The Hon. Gentleman has, I do not know how, lugged in the Pretender to this Debate; I am sure the mentioning of that Bugbear was very foreign to the Subject, but is the Pretender the only Person we have to fear? no, these is no Prince in *Europe* from whom we have less to fear than from him; he has so little Interest in this Nation, that our Liberties can never be in any Danger from him; and I hope the present Royal Family will always be so fully possessed of the Hearts and Affections of the People, that it never will be in the Pretender's Power to do us any Harm. The only Hopes he can ever have, must arise from the Arbitrary Designs of the Prince upon the Throne, and therefore we ought carefully to avoid all those Measures, which may give a Foundation for the forming of any such Designs in any time to come.

Sir W——m W——m, I did not design to give the House any Trouble this Day; but such Insinuations are thrown out, by some Gentlemen, as I cannot with Patience sit still and hear. I generally observe, that when proper Answers cannot be made to what Gentlemen advance, then *Jacobitism* is brought in; and because some Gentlemen differ from others, therefore they must be taxed with the terrible Name of *Jacobite*: I wish, that Gentlemen would resolve for the future always to give us Arguments and not Names for the Support of their Opinions. For my own part, I will leave it to the whole World to judge, who most pursue the Principles of the Revolution, They who are for supporting the Government in that way which is most easy, and least burthensome to the People, or they who are for doing it in a way which is so odious and so burthensome to the whole Nation.——Whenever there are any just Fears of the Pretender; if there ever shall happen to be any real Designs in his Favour, which I hope never will, then I shall do as I always have done, I shall shew by my Actions what my Principles are. I believe, I stand in the Opinion of Mankind acquit of any Imputation of *Jacobitism*, as much as the Hon. Gentleman over the Way, or any Gentleman in this House; therefore, I as much despise the Imputation, as I despise being always a servile Assentator to every thing proposed by the Administration. But as such Insinuations have been often thrown out against me in this House, I must let Gentlemen know that it is a Treatment which I think inconsistent with the Dignity of this House, and which I will no longer bear with.

W——m S——s Esq;] I believe, I have no Occasion to make any Professions of what I am; but I must take Notice that in private Life, any voluntary Securities granted to Creditors, after the borrowing their Money, are as binding upon the Granter, and ought to be as religiously observed, as those granted at the time the Money was lent: And I cannot think but that the Case is the same with respect to publick Transactions. I do not know but that some Gentlemen in this House may be offended at my so much as mentioning the Reign of K. *James* II. yet on this Occasion I must mention it; that unfortunate Prince took many wrong Steps, ran himself into great Difficulties, and at last lost his Crown, by following too implicitly the wicked Counsels of a bad Minister, and that very Minister most basely betrayed and at last deserted his Master. One of the greatest Misfortunes of that Prince, and that which contributed most to his Overthrow, was his keeping up a Standing Army in time of Peace; he did it indeed without the Consent of Parliament, but he did it at his own Expence; he did it without Consent of Parliament, because he could not find a Parliament so mercenary and corrupt enough to give their Consent.

Besides the Gentlemen above-mentioned, Mr. C——r of the E——r, and the L——d T——d spoke in favour of the Resolution; and T——s W——m Esq; spoke against it. At last the Question being put, it was carried to agree with the Committee, without any Division: After which the Question was put upon the 2d Resolution, and agreed to without Opposition, and a Bill order'd to be brought in accordingly.

DEBATE On the Call of the House, and the EXCISE SCHEME.

Feb. 27. The Order of the Day for the Call of the House being read, and a Motion made for adjourning it till that Day Fortnight,

Sir J——n R——t spoke in Substance as follows: I do not rise up to oppose putting off the Call till this Day Fortnight; that I shall easily agree with; but there being a certain Scheme to be brought into this House which seems to be of very great Consequence to the whole Nation, I wish, that the Call of the House may be appointed to be about the Time that Scheme is to be laid before us.——We have been long in Expectation of seeing this glorious Scheme, which is to render us all compleatly happy, we imagined, as had been insinuated to us in the preceding Session, that it was to come in lieu of the 1 s. in the Pound Land Tax, as a Supply for the current Service of the Year; but in this we are disappointed; that Measure has it seems been altered, and we have seen this Ease as to the Land Tax otherways supplied. I do not know, whether the Scheme itself has lately met with any Alterations or Amendments, but I hope if it be to be laid before us in this Session, that it will not be put off till towards the End when Gentlemen are tired. If a Scheme of that Consequence be at all brought in, it certainly ought to be brought in when the House is full, that it may be considered and approved

proved or rejected by as many Members as can possibly be brought together. As soon as the time for its being brought in shall be fixed, and the Call of the House accordingly appointed, then, I shall take the Liberty to move for Letters to the Sheriffs, as has been often practised on the like Occasions.

Mr C——r of the E——r.] As to the Scheme mentioned by the Hon. Gentleman who spoke last, I am resolved, very soon to make a Motion to some such Purpose, as enquiring into the Frauds of the Publick Revenue. If a Call of the House be appointed for this Day Fortnight, I believe I shall be fully determined between this and that time, and so be able to move for a Committee; the House may then appoint a Day for going into the Committee, so that every Member may have Notice to attend if he pleases.—I do not, I never did desire to surprize this House into any thing, nor had I, thank God, ever any Occasion to use the low Art of taking Advantage of the End of a Session: But when the House does resolve itself into some such Committee as I now mention, I will then lay before that Committee a Scheme which I have long thought of, which is, I am convinced, for the Good of the Nation, and which, if agreed to, will improve both the Trade of the Nation and the publick Revenue. I never had any Intention to propose it as a Supply for the current Service of the Year; I was always sensible that no such thing could be done; but if it be agreed to, and if, upon a Trial, it be found to bring in any Addition to the Publick Revenue, this House may then dispose of the Increase in the following Session of Parliament as they shall judge proper; till then it cannot be appropriated, because till then it cannot be known what the Amount may be. When that is once ascertained, it may then be brought in Aid of 1 s. in the Pound Land Tax, and thereby that Ease may be continued to the poor Landholders for Years to come, if so the future Parliaments shall think fit.—As for the Scheme's having received Alterations and Amendments, I don't know, but it may: I never thought my self so wise as to stand in no Need of Assistance; on the contrary I am always ready to receive Advice and Instruction from others, and I shall always be ready to add, alter, or amend any thing I have thought of, by the Advice of those who are conversant in such Affairs. The Scheme I have talked of, I have not only examin'd by myself as thoroughly as I could, but I have taken from others all the Assistance I could get; and in all my Enquiries in relation thereto, I have chose to consult with those who, I knew, had a perfect Knowledge of such Affairs, and had no particular Interest in view; nor any private End to serve; from those who may have By-ends of their own, I never can expect impartial Counsel, and therefore I have in this, as well as every other Affair, thought it ridiculous to ask their Advice. Such as it is, I shall be soon ready to lay before you; then I shall give you all the

Information I have had in the Affair, and will be most ready to hear and receive all the Information or Instruction that can be given by any Gentleman in this House.—It's certain, there are daily very great Frauds committed in the collecting of the Publick Revenue, and if any method can be fallen on, *to prevent these Frauds, and to enable the publick to receive what is so now justly and legally entitled to*, it ought to be embraced, and the Author thereof, whoever he may be, would deserve the Thanks of his Country; for it would not only be a great Advantage to the Publick Revenue, but to every honest and fair Trader in the Nation; because that where-ever a Tax is laid on, and not collected regularly and duly from every Man subject thereto, it is really making the fair Trader pay to the Publick, what the fraudulent Trader turns into his own private Pocket, and thereby the Smuggler is enabled to undersell the fair Trader in every Commodity he deals in, by which all the fair Traders in the Nation must be at last ruin'd and undone.

Sir W——m W——m.] *Sir I have not had the Honour of being let into the Secret of this extraordinary Scheme, but by all that I could ever hear of it, I believe, when it is laid before us, the Question will appear to be, whether we shall sacrifice the Constitution to the preventing of Frauds in the Revenue. This, I take to be a very material Question; and therefore I think it is necessary to have a full House; for which Reason I shall be not only for Letters to the Sheriffs, but also I hope that every Gentleman in this House will write to such of his Friends in the Country as are Members, and intreat them to give Attendance on that important Day*

Sir J——n B——rd.] *Sir, When the Hon. Gentleman is prepared to lay his Scheme before us, I hope he will move for some general Committee; if he does, I shall not give the House any Trouble; but if he moves for a Committee to consider the Frauds in any particular Branch of the Revenue, I shall take the Liberty to oppose it, because there are Frauds in every Branch of the Revenue, and perhaps I shall be able to shew, that there are as many Frauds in other Branches of the Revenue, as there are in those which the Hon. Gentleman has a Mind now to take a particular Notice of. I must think, that the attacking or Enquiries at present to the Frauds committed in any particular Branch, is like singling out a Deer from the Flock in order to be hunted down; she is to be the first Sacrifice, but the whole Flock are to be hunted down at last: This, I believe, is the Case, and if I have been rightly informed, this very Scheme in its first Conception was for a general Alteration of the Method of collecting the publick Revenue: It was for a General Excise; but that it seems was afterwards thought too much at once and therefore we are now, it seems, to single out only one or two Branches, in order that they may be first hunted down; but the very same Reason that may prevail with us to subject any one Branch of the Revenue to the Laws of Excise, may afterwards prevail with us to subject every Branch to those Arbitrary Laws; and as such Laws are in my Opinion absolutely inconsistent with*

Lib rty

Liberty, therefore I must think that the Question upon his Scheme, even alter'd as it seems it is, will be, whether we shall endeavour to prevent Frauds in the collecting of the Publick Revenues, at the Expence of the Liberties of the People?— For my own part, I never was guilty of any Fraud; I put it to any Man, be he who he will, to accuse me of so much as the Appearance of a Fraud in any Trade I was ever concerned in; I am resolved never to be guilty of any Fraud. It is very true, that these Frauds are a very great Prejudice to all fair Traders, and therefore I speak against my own Interest, when I speak against any Method that may tend towards preventing of Frauds; but I shall never put my private Interest in Ballance with the Interest or the Happiness of the Nation: I had rather beg my Bread from Door to Door, and see my Country flourish, than to be the greatest Subject in the Nation, and see the Trade of my Country decaying, and the People enslaved and oppressed.

H—y P—m Esq;] I wish this Scheme, be it what it will--- were laid before us; for till it is, I believe we shall every day be falling into some Debate or another about it, without knowing any thing of it. I do not know where the Hon. Gentleman who spoke last got his Information, but as I have had the Honour to converse sometimes with those who always knew most about this Scheme, I can assure him that there never was any such thing intended as a General Excise, nor was there ever any Design of making a general Alteration in the Method of collecting the publick Revenue. But I shall not at present say any thing further upon the Subject, because I think it a little odd to enter into Debates about what we know nothing of.

A—n P—ry, likewise spoke upon this Occasion in Vindication of the Merchants dealing in the Wine and Tobacco Trade. After which the Question was put, and the Call of the House was put off till that Day Fortnight; and it was ordered, That no Member of the House should presume to go out of Town without Leave of the House; that no Leave should be asked for any Member to go out of Town, but between the Hours of One and Two; and that Mr Speaker should write circular Letters to the Sheriffs and Stewards of the several Counties of Great Britain, requiring the Attendance of the Members on that Day Fortnight; and that the House would proceed with the utmost Severity against such Members, as should not then attend the Service of the House. Then

S—l S—ys Esq; moved for the House to resolve, that such Members of that House, who should absent themselves without Leave of the House, should be reputed Deserters of their Trust and Neglecters of that Duty they owed to that House and their Country. Whereupon several Members got up, some as may be presumed to have seconded this Motion, but. *H—o W—le,* Esq; was pointed to, who said, That he was against the Motion the Honourable Gentleman had been pleased to make as being a very extraordinary one, and such as there was then no Occasion for, and therefore he moved for

the Order of the Day, which Motion was immediately seconded.

Sir J....n R....t said, *That the Motion his Friend had made, was perhaps a little extraordinary, but it was upon a very extraordinary Occasion, and not without Precedent, and therefore he would be for it.*

Sir W...m Y...ge said, That an Hon. Gentleman over the way had said, that *every one of them ought to write to their Friends in the Country and desire them to give Attendance,* but if the Motion then made should be agreed to, they might in his Opinion, save themselves the Trouble; for that no Member then in the Country would think he had one Friend in the House, if any such Resolution should be made against him.

Mr. S....ys said, *That what he had moved for, was so far from being without Precedent, that there was a Precedent for it but very lately, and that was in the famous Case of Dr. Sacheverel; when that Affair was before the House, there was such a Resolution made, and from thence it was that he took the very Words of the Motion.* Then the Question was put upon the Motion for the Order of the Day, because of its having been seconded before the other Motion was seconded, and that being carried in the Affirmative, the other was dropt.

Feb. 23. The Pension Bill was read the first time in the House of Lords; and after some Debate, a Motion was made for rejecting it, upon which it was moved to order, that the same should be read a second time on the Tuesday following, and after further Debate the Question was put, whether the said Bill should be read a second time? which was resolved in the Negative by 68 to 25; whereupon a Protest was entered for the Reasons entered in the Journals of that House the 21st of March 1729, and the 2d of March, 1730. (See Vol. I. p. 215) and was signed by the Noble Lords following, viz.

Scarsdale,	Coventry,	Litchfield,
Northampton,	Berkshire,	Bruce,
Foley,	Gower,	Bridgwater
Strafford,	Oxford and	Bathurst,
Aylesford,	Mortimer.	Montjoy.

On the 4th of April was laid before the House of Lords, according to their Desire, a State of the National Debt, which see P. 313.

DEBATE March 6. in the House of LORDS on the Bill for punishing Mutiny and Desertion.

Assoon as the Order of the Day was read for the House to resolve it self into a Committee on the said Bill, it being the only Opportunity that House can have to take into Consideration the Number of Forces to be kept up in the Kingdom. The E. of O....rc made a strong and pathetic Speech against keeping up so numerous a standing Army in time of Peace, and concluded with moving for reducing the Number to 12,000 effective Men, including Invalids.

I i i

The

The E. of *W.. ea* ſeconded the Motion, and ſhew'd, the dangerous Conſequences of keeping up ſo great a Number of Regular For-ces within the Kingdom in time of Peace; among which, this he ſaid was one, *That it made Miniſters of State more daring than other-wiſe they durſt venture to be, both in contriving and executing Schemes that were burthenſome to the Peopl; Schemes that never could enter into the Heads of any but thoſe who were drunk with an Exceſs of Power.*

The E--l of C----d.] My Lords, *Whatever be the bad Conſequences of keeping up a great Number of Regular Forces in any Country, no Argument drawn from thence can be any way applicable to the Number of Regular Forces pro-poſed by the Bill now before us; only* 17 *or* 18,000 *Men; ſuch a ſmall Number is ſo far from being dangerous to the Liberties of this Nation, that it is abſolutely neceſſary for their Preſervation and the Support of our preſent happy Conſtituti-on. Before we can ſuppoſe that the ſaid Forces may be of any dangerous Conſequences to our Li-berties: We muſt ſuppoſe them to be able to hold the whole Body of the People under Subjection; and the Gentlemen of the Army to be all of them ſuch abandoned Creatures, as that they will join together unanimouſly in the wicked Deſign of en-ſlaving their Native Country: In the preſent Caſe, neither of theſe Suppoſitions can be made;* 17 *or* 18,000 *Men can't be able to hold the whole Body of the People of Great Britain under Subjection; we have I hope many hundred thouſands of brave Men in Great Britain, who would riſe in Arms, and ſoon ſwallow up ſuch a handful of Men, if they ſhould be but once ſuſpected of joining in any Deſign againſt the Liberties of the People. And, I have ſo good an Opinion of the Gentlemen em-ployed in the Army, that I believe no Lord in this Houſe can ſuppoſe, any great Part of them would join in any ſuch wicked Deſign; if any Attempts were to be made upon our Liberties, I am perſuad-ed that the Gentlemen of the Army would be the firſt to appear againſt ſuch Attempts, and would join heartily; and, I hope, unanimouſly in the Defence of their Country.*

The M---s of Tw---le.] My Lords, *I am ſo far from being of Opinion that the Number of Re-gular Forces propoſed by this Bill to be kept up, is abſolutely neceſſary in a Time of the moſt pro-found Tranquillity, that I am thoroughly con-vinced no ſuch Number would be neceſſary even in the Time of the moſt raging War; and, for the Support of my Opinion, I have the Experience of all paſt Ages. In the Time of the late War there was never any ſuch Number kept up within the Kingdom, and yet how were all the At-tempts then made againſt our happy Eſtabliſh-ment? The unnatural Rebellion raiſed againſt his Late Majeſty, is a convincing Proof how little neceſſary it is to keep up ſuch a Number as now propoſed: There was then a very formidable In-ſurrection againſt the Government, and yet that Inſurrection was defeated by a very ſmall Hand-ful of Regular Forces, a much leſs Number than what is now propoſed to be kept up; for we all very well know that that Rebellion was defeated before the Arrival of any of the Foreign Troops* which were then brought into the Kingdom. The Rebels were ſubdued, and all were ſoon af-ſer obliged to ſubmit, or to fly from their Native Country. I wiſh indeed that ſame other Mea-ſures had been afterwards purſued, with regard to thoſe who were engaged in that unjuſt and un-natural Affair; the Government might perhaps have made a better Uſe of their Succeſs; for if I am rightly informed, not 11. of the forfeited Eſtates ever came to the Publick, they were all applied to the Payment of the Commiſſioners and Officers employed to enquire after them. It is not eaſy to determine exactly what particular Number of Regular Forces may be abſolutely ne-ceſſary for preſerving a juſt Government; but I am ſure, the beſt way of determining is, from the Experience of paſt Times; and whatever Num-ber may be neceſſary for ſupporting a juſt Go-vernment, I am as ſure, that any Addition made to that Number, is a Step towards the Sup-port of an unjuſt and an Arbitrary Government. The Number now propoſed, is not the only thing to be regarded in the preſent Queſtion: It is true, there is but 18,000 propoſed to be kept up, but we all know that in the manner that this 18,000 is modelled, they may upon any Emergency be ſpeedily augmented to 40,000 effective Men: And that Number, if they ſtood unanimouſly together, would, I am afraid, be able to ſupport and render ſucceſsful any Attempts againſt the Liberties of the Nation, notwithſtanding the great Numbers of brave Men we may have in Great Britain. I have as good an Opinion of the Officers now employed in the Army, as any Man can have; but they are not immortal, nor are we ſure that they will always be continued in Command, or be ſucceeded by Men of the ſame Virtue and Honour: If any Prince, or Chief Miniſter, ſhould ever form Deſigns againſt the Liberties of the People, he will firſt model the Army, diſmiſs all the Men of Honour, and put Creatures of his own into their room, and thus the Nation may be undone before any Man can fly to its Relief. I muſt therefore think that the keeping up of ſo great a Number of Regular For-ces is a turning that Civil Government under which we have for ſo many Ages preſerved our Liberties, into a Military ſort of Government, under which no Country ever did, or can preſerve either their Liberties or their Properties; under ſuch a Government, the Poſſeſſions of every Man muſt entirely depend upon the Good-will of the Chief Officers of the Army; the poor Farmers and Tradeſmen muſt ſubmit to be plundered and mal-treated by every common Soldier, and the Men of the beſt Families in the Nation may of-ten be obliged to ſue in the moſt humble manner to thoſe who were formerly their Footmen or Me-nial Servants. This is a moſt terrible State, and therefore I muſt be for agreeing to the Re-duction propoſed.*

The D---ke of N---c--le.] My Lords, *I ſhould be very glad to agree to the Reduction propoſed, or to any Reduction; if I thought it any way ſafe for us to do ſo; but, we never as yet made any Reduction in our Army, but it encouraged our Enemies both at home and abroad to make Attempts towards diſturbing the*

the Quiet of the Nation ; we might perhaps with a lefs Number be able to defeat any Infurrection that could be made againft the Government, but then we never could be at Quiet for any confiderable Time, the Enemies of the Government would be always forming Plots and Defigns againft It ; and the only Method for preventing any fuch, and for preferving Peace among ourfelves, is to keep up fuch a Number of Regular Forces, as may take away from fuch Men all Hopes of Succefs : The Number propofed is the leaft that can be thought fufficient, and if it were much greater than it is, there would be nothing to be feared from it under his prefent Majefty, or any of his illuftrious Family ; which is eftablifhed upon the Principles of Liberty, upon the Principles of the Revolution, and it is by fuch Principles only that they or the Liberties of the Nation can be fupported ; neither can be deftroyed without involving the other in the fame Deftruction ; therefore I never can have any Fears of any Number of Forces kept up under his Majefty or any of his Family. Laft Year, I obferved that none of your Lordfhips declared openly againft keeping up any Number of Forces, or any Army at all ; you feemed all to agree that it was neceffary to keep up fome Regular Forces, yet all thofe who then appeared for a Reduction, joined together in voting againft the whole Bill ; they were againft having any Bill at all for the Punifhment of Mutiny and Defertion ; from whence I muft conclude, that all thofe who were then for a Reduction, chofe rather to have no Mutiny Bill, nor any Regular Army, than not to have that Number reduced which they had propofed. I do not know, what the noble Lord meant, when he talked of Men's being drunk with Excefs of Power ; I do not know any Man that is fo, or that has any Opportunity of being fo ; nor do I know of any Schemes that have been, or are to be attempted, that are burthenfome to the People. I have indeed fome Guefs at what Scheme the Noble Lord points, but I believe when that Scheme comes before us, it will appear to be agreeable, at leaft to all the honeft Part of the People, and beneficial to the Nation in general. If the Gentlemen who are to propofe it, did not think it fo, they never would attempt it ; but if they are convinced it will tend to the Improvement of Trade and the Revenue, I fhould think them very weak, if they were intimidated by Clamours raifed againft it, by Men whofe Private Intereft or Malice has prompted them to oppofe what they muft know to be for the Publick Good. It is true, the Publick Tranquillity is to all outward Appearance at prefent pretty fecure, but our Tranquillity both at home and abroad depends upon fo many Accidents, that it would be very imprudent in

us to make any Reduction this Year. At prefent there are perhaps fome very ftrong Reafons for us to be upon our Guard ; we may perhaps very foon have Occafion for Regular Forces, but I cannot explain myfelf, I beg Leave not to do it ; however, I may fay, that I never will be for a Reduction, unlefs the Publick Tranquillity fhall happen to be in fuch a State as may be much more certainly depended on, than at prefent. It is certain there are two great contending Powers in Europe, between whom there is and will be a perpetual Rivalfhip, fo that it is impoffible for us to be in an abfolute Cordial Friendfhip with both at one Time ; while we keep ourfelves in a good State of Defence at home, we fhall always be independent of either ; but if we fhould ftrip ourfelves of our own proper Defence, we muft then truft entirely to one of thofe Powers to defend us againft the other, by which means we fhould foon be brought into an abfolute Dependence upon one of thofe Powers, and fhould be obliged to join in every Meafure that fuch Power could propofe to us. And as I am convinced that the Number of Regular Forces now propofed to be kept up, is abfolutely neceffary for our own proper Defence, at leaft for this Year, I muft be againft making any Reduction.

The E--l of S----d.] My Lords, I readily grant there is, and I hope, always will be a continual Rivalfhip between the two great contending Powers of Europe ; for if ever that Rivalfhip fhould ceafe, which it never can but by one of them being fwallowed up by the other, it would be an unlucky thing for this Nation, as well as all the reft of Europe ; but, are we to keep up a numerous ftanding Army as long as that Rivalfhip fhall continue ? If fo, we muft never think of any Reduction : No, that Rivalfhip has already continued many Ages, yet we have fupported ourfelves againft both, without having ever kept up any Standing Army ; this new fort of Defence has been but lately thought on, and never can be a proper Defence for this Nation : The only way we have to fecure ourfelves at home, to make ourfelves confiderable abroad, and to force a Refpect from both thefe contending Powers, is to do as we have always formerly done, to put our whole Truft in our natural Strength, our Fleet, and the natural Bravery of our Men in general ; as long as we truft to this, and obferve a Neutrality as to both thefe contending Powers, we fhall be courted by both ; we may fall in fometimes with the one, and fometimes with the other, according as may beft fuit our own Intereft and the Circumftances of Affairs : By fuch a Management we fhall always be able to hold the Balance of Europe in our own Hands, and never have Occafion to court the Friendfhip, or fear the Refentment of any Power on Earth. But if we be-

gin

ẟin to purſue contrary Meaſures; if we be always the firſt to enter into Alliances with the Powers of Europe, and the original contracting Parties in moſt Treaties, we thereby give the Power of holding the Balance of Europe out of our Hands; and the neglecting our Fleet and our Militia, for the ſake of keeping up a Standing Army, will ſoon render us contemptible to every one of our Neighbours, unleſs we reſolve to keep up a much more numerous Army than what is propoſed by this Bill, and ſuch a Propoſition will, I hope never be approved of by a Majority of either Houſe of Parliament. A Standing Army and a Military Law has, my Lords, been always inconſiſtent with the Liberties of the People: The Officers and Soldiers under ſuch a Regulation are always obliged to give the moſt implicit Obedience to their Superior Officers; they muſt not enquire whether their Orders be according to Law; if they do, they are guilty of Mutiny, and may be immediately ſhot for any ſuch Diſobedience. The chief Commander of an Army muſt always be veſted with an Arbitrary and Abſolute Power over the Army, and if his Army be numerous, he may eaſily by their Means extend his Power over the whole People of the Country where ſuch an Army is kept up; and therefore, my Lords, in all Countries where the People have any Regard to their Liberties, they ought never to keep up a greater Number of Regular Forces than are abſolutely neceſſary for the Security of the Government, and for the Preſervation of the Country againſt any ſudden Invaſion by a Foreign Enemy. We have the Happineſs to be ſurrounded by the Sea, we know how difficult and expenſive it is to make any Invaſion upon us with any great Body of Men; any ſuch Invaſion we muſt have a timely Warning of, and by having our Militia in good Order, and our Men, as they were formerly trained up to Arms and Military Diſcipline, we ſhould always be able to draw, upon any Occaſion, and in any Place within the Iſland, a great Army together, to oppoſe our Enemies, if they ſhould happen to have the good Fortune to eſcape our Fleet at Sea. In our preſent Circumſtances, and conſidering the happy Situation of our Country, I muſt be of Opinion, that 12000 Men are abundantly ſufficient for all the good Uſes we can have for them, and therefore I ſhall give my Aſſent to the Reduction propoſed.

The D—ke of A—le.] I agree with thoſe Lords who ſay, we ought to truſt to our Fleet; we have good Reaſon to do ſo, and we accordingly do put a great Confidence in our Fleet. It is happy for us that we are ſurrounded with the Sea; for if there were any Communication by Land between our Neighbours and us, inſtead of the ſmall Number of Regular Forces now propoſed, it would be neceſſary for us to keep up at leaſt three times the Number: Let us but conſider the great Armies that are kept on

Foot by our Neighbours, and then we muſt conclude, that if they could invade us by Land, a Regular Army of 60,000 Men would hardly be ſufficient for our Defence; and beſides this, we ſhould be obliged to be at a great Expence in fortifying all our Cities and Towns, to prevent our Country's being over-run by any ſudden Invaſion, or after any unfortunate Battle. Theſe Misfortunes and theſe Charges we are kept free from, by our being ſurrounded by the Sea, and as long as we have a Fleet ſuperior to that of any one of our Neighbours, it is hardly poſſible for them to invade us with any conſiderable Armament; but, My Lords, we are not to truſt entirely to our Fleet for protecting us againſt a ſmall Force; a ſmall Fleet may be ſo ſpeedily prepared, an Invaſion with a ſmall Force may be ſo ſuddenly made, that the Troops may be landed before we have any Account of their Imbarkation; at leaſt ſuch a ſmall Fleet may be got out to Sea, before we have any Account of their Deſign; and if they be once got into the wide Ocean, it is well known how eaſily they may eſcape being met with by our Fleet. If ſuch a thing ſhould happen, if ever a ſmall Number of Regular Forces ſhould be landed, and we had no Regular Forces to oppoſe them at their landing, what would be the Conſequence? Why, we might be ſubdued before we could have it in our Power to make any Reſiſtance; for it is not to be ſuppoſed, that the Militia of this or any Country could make any Reſiſtance againſt a Body of Regular and Well-diſciplined Veterans; Numbers of Men are very little to be depended on; the Men may be perſonally brave, but if they want Diſcipline, a very numerous Body of Men may be eaſily defeated by a Handful of Regular and Well-diſciplined Soldiers: This we may be convinced of from Hiſtory; this we may ſee, if we but attend to what happens every day in other Parts of the World.—I have heard Gentlemen contemn the *Spaniſh* Armada, which was fitted out in Q. *Elizabeth's* time againſt this Nation; but in my Opinion, it was lucky for this Country that they never got to the Shore; they had 16,000 Veteran and Well-diſciplined Troops on board, which were to have been reinforced with as many more as ſoon as the Fleet could return to fetch them: I am afraid, if that Armada had not been diſſipated by Storms and Winds, that wiſe Queen would not have found a great deal of Safety in the Militia which ſhe had raiſed, ſhe would have found even the greateſt Number of them but a very unequal Match for ſuch a Body of Well-diſciplined Veterans: And but lately we were again in great Danger from the ſame Country; then indeed they did not pretend to be a Match for us at Sea, and for that Reaſon they prepared for an Invaſion upon us with a ſmall Number of Troops, and did it ſo privately and ſo ſpeedily, that they might have been landed before we knew any thing of their Deſign, if their Fleet had not again been diſſipated by the Storms : They had then, 'tis true, but a ſmall Number of Regular Forces, but few as they were, if we had had no Regular Forces to have oppoſed them, they would have been ſufficient for the Deſign, conſidering the great Aſſiſtance they would have got from the Diſaffected of our own Men that would have joined them at their Landing: Even notwithſtanding the Regular Forces we then had on Foot, we do not know what would have been the Conſequence of their Landing ; it would at leaſt have involved our Country in a Civil War, our Liberties and all that is dear to us would have again been at Stake. Such Deſigns, will always be forming againſt us, if we reduce our Army too low, and would probably be the Conſequence of our agreeing to the Reduction propoſed.——It is certain that every Country muſt have ſomething to truſt to for its Defence, ſome Power to protect it againſt Invaders ; if it has not a Regular Army of its own Subjects there muſt be ſome other ſubſtituted in the room thereof. I have conſidered this Queſtion as much, I believe, as any Man ever did ; I have converſed with a great many Gentlemen upon the Subject, and I have read, I believe, all that ever, was wrote upon the Head ; and the Whole, in my Opinion, may be reduced to theſe *Three Expedients,* which are propoſed in the room of a Standing Army of our own Subjects ; to wit, *our Fleet, our Militia, or an Army of Foreign Auxiliaries.*

As to truſting altogether to our Fleet, Experience ſhews us the Precariouſneſs of ſuch a Dependance ; beſides theſe Inſtances, what Danger were we in, in the Year 1708? The Invaſion might very probably have taken Effect, notwithſtanding our Fleet, if the French Commanders had had diſcretionary Orders, but happily for us they had peremptory Orders to land only at a particular Place, and it not being in their Power to land there, their Orders did not permit them to land at all. In that Country the Cuſtom then was, for the King's Council to direct both their Generals and Admirals in every particular Part of their Conduct ; a Lady perhaps gave Directions to the General when to fight, and a Secretary of State, who perhaps never ſaw a Ship gave Orders to their Admiral how to ſail : To this it was we owed our Safety ; for by the Orders their Admiral had, he could not well avoid being met with by our Fleet ; but this was not the only thing that then ſaved us ; that Invaſion might have taken Effect, if it had not been for a Private Pique between two great Ladies at the Court of France, by which their Preparations at Dunkirk were retarded, and their Fleet kept from ſailing ſeveral Weeks, whereby we had Time to fit out that Fleet which prevented their landing at the Place they were ordered to.——Even the happy Revolution, is an Inſtance how little a Fleet is to be depended on ; K. Wm in his Way to England came in Sight of the Engliſh Fleet, which was able enough to have fought him, but the Winds were ſo contrary, that it was impoſſible for it to come up with the Dutch ; if it had, that glorious Attempt, by which we recovered our Liberties, might have been defeated: By this Accident we then recovered our Liberties, but if we ſhould ever reſolve to truſt entirely to our Fleet, the ſame Accident may hereafter be the Cauſe of our loſing them.

The Second Expedient propoſed in room of a Standing Army, is the Militia: Now, conſidering the preſent State of our Militia, I believe, it will not be pretended we can truſt to them ; I confeſs, the Militia of a Country may be brought under ſuch exact Diſcipline, as to make them almoſt equal to any Regular Troops : but, ſuch a Thing is not to be done in this Country : We now ſee how much Grumbling is occaſioned by the Militia's being called out to exerciſe but once a Year, and from thence we may judge what would be the conſequence if they were to be called out once or twice a Week, which would be abſolutely neceſſary, to keep them ſo well-diſciplined as to be depended on for immediate Service. I have often heard it inſiſted on, that the keeping up a Standing Army raiſes Diſaffection to the Government ; this I cannot agree with, but from what I daily ſee, I muſt conclude, that the laying the whole Militia of the Kingdom under a Neceſſity of marching out to exerciſe once or twice every Week, would raiſe a moſt terrible Diſaffection againſt the Government, and the more terrible, becauſe the Diſaffected would not only have Arms in their Hands, but would have ſome ſort of Skill in uſing them.

I have ſeen a great many Projects for keeping our Militia under a good Diſcipline, but all in my Opinion, Impracticable, Ineffectual, or much more Expenſive to the Publick than the Regular Army now kept up. But, My Lords, ſuppoſing the Militia could be kept under exact Diſcipline, is a Soldier in a Red Coat more dangerous to our Liberties than a Soldier in a Black, a Blue or a White Coat? I can ſee nothing more terrible in Red than in any other Colour, nor can I think an Army in Red more dangerous to our Liberties than an Army in Black ; nay, the Latter may be the moſt dangerous of the two ; they have certainly done much more Miſchief to Mankind, and to this Country in particular. As to the Power of the King, it is the ſame over the Militia, as over a Standing Army ; he has an abſolute Command, names all the Officers, and, if he were to make any Attempts upon our Liberties, might as eaſily model the Militia, as the Army.

As for the Officers and Soldiers of the Army's being obliged to obey their Superior Officers without any Limitations, it is certain, they are not ; they are obliged to obey only legal Orders ; illegal they may diſobey with Impunity. If I were at the Head of my Regiment, and ſhould order them to ſhoot a Gentleman innocently paſſing by, might not my Regiment refuſe to obey any ſuch Orders? Can it be ſaid that they would be found guilty of Mutiny, or condemned to be ſhot by a Court-Martial for ſuch Refuſal? No, their Conduct would be approved of by any Court-Martial, and the Perſon condemned, who gave the illegal Orders. The Officers and Soldiers of the Army are therefore in this as well as in moſt other reſpects ſtreſs upon the ſame Footing with thoſe of the Militia, or at leaſt upon the ſame Footing that the Militia muſt be put on, before they can be made uſeful for the Defence of the Nation.

Thus it appears, that with reſpect to our Li-berties, a Standing Army of our own Sub-jeſts can be no more dangerous than a Well-ordered and a Well-diſciplined Militia; and by late Ex-perience we find, that they behaved after the ſame manner, when they found Attempts were making againſt the Liberties of the Nation: In the Reign of the late K. James, the Army be-haved in the ſame manner as the Militia had done under his Father. It is a ſort of Article of Faith among ſome People, that no Attempts were made againſt our Liberties in the Reign of K. Charles I. But the Caſe is far otherwiſe; his whole Reign, at leaſt from the Beginning to the Year 1641, was a continued Scene of the moſt Arbitrary and Oppreſſive Meaſures; what by his Court of Star-Chamber, and his Spiritual Courts (of theſe Laſt, I think, we have ſome ſtill remaining) did not he oppreſs the Subjeſt in the moſt unprecedented manner? Even the firſt Set of Miniſters he had, began to encroach upon the Liberties of their Country; but after them he got a Spiritual Prime Miniſter, an Archbiſhop, who ſoon drove the Nail to the Head, and laid the People under a Neceſſity of taking Arms in Defence of their Liberties: That King and his Miniſters had taken all poſſible care to model the Militia, he had the ſupreme Command over them, he had named ſuch Officers over them as he thought would do whatever he pleaſed, but when Affairs were come to this Criſis, that they ſaw they muſt fight either for the Liberties of the People, or againſt them, many of theſe Officers the King had named took Party againſt him, and the Orders of thoſe for him were in many Places deſpiſed by the Private Men. The Army under his Son behaved in the very ſame manner, and it will always be ſo; in Caſe of a Civil War the Army being Part of the People, will certainly behave as the People do, every Man will join that Party which he thinks moſt in the Right.

As to Auxiliary Troops, I believe no Man will pretend that we ought to keep a Standing Army of Foreign Auxiliaries; if we ſhould call ſuch to our Aſſiſtance, we are not very ſure they will go out again at our Deſire: It has been juſt-ly obſerved by a great Author, that whatever Country truſts her Defence to Foreign Auxili-aries called in to our Aſſiſtance, would not always leave us whenever we had a Mind; yet Expe-rience has ſhewn us, that we cannot always de-pend upon their coming to our Aſſiſtance as ſoon as called. The late unnatural Rebellion afforded us an Inſtance of this; his late Majeſty I am ſure had done nothing to deſerve that Treatment, yet ſuch a dangerous Inſurrection broke out againſt him, and we had at the ſame time ſo few Troops of our own, that we were obliged to ſend to our Allies for that Aſſiſtance which they were enga-ged by Treaties to give us: Unluckily it happen-ed, the Dutch for ſome time before had been ſo much addicted to that Political Maxim of re-ducing their Army, that they were not in a

Condition to make good their Engagements to us: ſo that we were obliged to hire Troops in Germany and to wait till they marched down to the Dutch Garriſons, before we could have a Man of the Dutch Troops to march to our Aſſiſtance: And we had at that time ſo few Troops of our own, that for ſome time after my Arrival in Scotland, I had but 1600 Men to make Head againſt al-moſt as many thouſands them up in Arms in that Country againſt the Government. It is very wrong to imagine that in Time of Danger the whole Regular Army we have can be brought together; it muſt in ſuch Caſes be divided, and a Detachment left at every Place where any Danger may be dreaded; ſo that even from the Number now propoſed, it would not be poſſible to form a a Body of five or ſix thouſand Men in any Part of the Kingdom, except juſt about London.

The Dutch Auxiliaries did at laſt arrive, though not till after the Rebellion was in a great meaſure defeated: But, I ſhall never de-ſire to ſee any more Foreign Auxiliaries in this Country. I have been long in the Service of the States General; I was once a General in their Army, from whence one would expect that I might have had as much Authority over their Troops as any Britiſh General could have, and yet I had a very great deal of Difficulty to keep them in Order: They were mighty apt to miſtake a Friend for a Foe, eſpecially if they ſaw any thing that was worth taking. I was an Eye-Witneſs of the many Hardſhips our beſt Subjeſts ſuffered from theſe Foreign Auxiliaries, I then did what I could to remedy them, and in order to prevent any ſuch for the future, I ſhall always be againſt any Meaſure which may tend towards laying the Government under a Neceſſity of tai-king in Foreign Auxiliaries.

I cannot imagine how ſome People have got into a way of thinking, that the Liberties of all the Countries in Europe have been over-turned by Standing Armies; I do not know one Country in Europe, whoſe Liberties have been ſo overturned. The Liberties of Rome were in a great meaſure overturned by the Luxury and Corruption crept in among the People long before the Time of Julius Cæſar; and in his Time, their Standing Army was ſo far from being the only Means of overturning the Liberties of Rome, that the greateſt Part of the Standing Army joined againſt Julius Cæſar; but he had a Deviliſh Head of his own, ſo that by his own good Conduct, and the Bravery of his Troops, he got the better of his Enemies, tho' they had the greateſt Numbers even of Regular Troops of their Side. If the Romans at that time had had no Standing Army, would not the People, would not the very Mob have done the ſame? every Man who had Courage, or who could be perſuaded to go to fight, would have joined that Party he liked beſt: the Commander, who could make the beſt Uſe of thoſe that joined him, would have got the Advantage; and the victorious Army would have had it in their Power to have ſettled the future Form of Government upon what foot-ing they had a mind.

It is the ſame with reſpect to all the other Countries

Countries of Europe *where Arbitrary Power is established. In* France *their Liberties were overturned long before they had a Standing Army;* A *the oldest Corps of Regular Troops in* France, *is the Regiment of* Picardie; *which was raised only in the first or second Year of our* Q. Elizabeth, *and, it is well known, long before that time the Liberties of the* French *were entirely destroyed. In* Spain, *their Priests destroyed the Liberties of the People; and it is by means of their Inquisition, that their Arbitrary Government is to this day supported;* B *by means of that terrible Spiritual Court, their Priests support their own Despotick Rule not only over the People, but over the Court, and Army too. In* Sweden, *it was likewise their Priests that established an arbitrary Rule, and it was by their Army that their Liberties were restored; in* Denmark *a House of Commons surrendered up their Liberties to the Crown; and thereby enabled their King to get himself declared the Absolute and* C *the Arbitrary Sovereign over the whole Cuntry.*

Thus, My Lords, we may find, that a Standing Army never had the chief Hand in destroying the Liberties of their Country; nor indeed can it be supposed they ever will: Can it be supposed that any Man of Common Sense, who has a good Post in the Army, and the Laws of his Country for his Protection while he behaves well, will ever join in Measures for subjecting himself to D the uncontrollable Will and giddy Pleasure of any one Man? He must know, that true Honour and Virtue, or a faithful Performance of his Duty could then be no Protection to him; his Life, Estate, and every thing dear to him, must then depend on the

mere Pleasure of a Court; and every Man knows, about Courts, true Honour and Virtus often falls a Sacrifice to Whispers, deceitful Insinuations, and false and private Accusations: Is it then reasonable to presume, that the Gentlemen of the Army, bred Strangers to the low Arts and vile Practices usual about Courts, will ever give up that honourable Dependance they have upon their own Behaviour and the Laws of their Country, for the sake of a slavish Dependance upon any Court whatever: For my part, it is not possible for me to suspect any such thing, therefore I cannot from thence draw any Argument against keeping up a Standing Army in this Country. But the small Army now proposed is only for protecting the Peace and Quiet of the Country against sudden Invasions, or against little Insurrections, or rather Mobs that may be raised by a few discontented Subjects. The main Strength of this Nation, and that upon which we principally depend, is the Superiority of our Fleet, and the Bravery of our Men in general: Let us continue to preserve the present Superiority we have as to our Fleet; and cultivate Bravery and Military Discipline as much as possible among our Men in general; but do not let us, for the sake of groundless Jealousies and pretended Fears, expose the Peace of our Country to be disturbed by every Neighbouring State who shall take it in their Heads so to do, or by every Subject who shall be prompted by his Resentment or Ambition to rebel against the Government of his Country.

[*To be continued.*]

The Names at length, both of Lords and Commons, may be seen in the List of Parliament, printed at St John's Gate.

A View of the *Weekly* DISPUTES *and* ESSAYS *in this Month.*

The **Craftsman**, Sept. 1. No 374.

Letter to the *Craftsman* contains several Quotations from Capt. *Gulliver's* Voyages; E which, says the Writer, had a certain *Projector* well weigh'd, he F would have found an easier Method of *Taxing the People,* and supporting a *crazy Administration.* In his Voyage to *Laputa,* the Captain fell into the School of *Political Projectors,* some of whose Maxims are here cited.

One *Doctor* proposed that, upon the Meeting of a *Senate,* certain Physicians should attend at the three first Days of their Sitting; and, at the Close of each Day's Debate, feel the Pulse of ever Senator; after which, having maturely considered and consulted on the Nature of the several Maladies, and the Method of Cure, they should, on the 4th Day, return to the

Senate-House, attended by their Apothecaries, stored with proper Medicines; and, before the Members sate, administer to each of Them Lenitives, Aperitives, Abstersives, Corrosives, Restringents, Palliatives, Laxatives, as their several Cases required; and according as these Medicines should operate, repeat, alter, or omit them at the next Meeting. This *Project,* would be of much Use for the Dispatch of Business, where *Senates* have any Share in the Legislative Power; beget Unanimity; shorten Debates; open a few Mouths, close many more; curb G the Petulancy of the Young; correct the Positiveness of the Old; rouze the Stupid, and daunt the Pert.

As to Ways and Means, one *Professor* was for laying a Tax upon *Vices,* but a second proposed to tax all the Qualities of H Body and Mind, for which Men chiefly value Themselves, the Rate to be more or less, according to the Degrees of excelling, the Decision whereof should be left

in

intirely to their own Breaſt. The higheſt Tax to be upon *Men,* who are the greateſt Favourites of the *other Sex,* and the Aſſeſſments according to the Number and Nature of the Favours They have received; for which they are allowed to be their own Vouchers. *Wit, Valour* and *Politeneſs* were likewiſe propoſed to be largely taxed, and collected in the ſame Manner. But as to *Honour, Juſtice, Wiſdom* and *Learning,* they ſhould not be taxed at all, becauſe They are Qualifications ſo ſingular that no Man will allow them in his Neighbour, or value Them in Himſelf. Either of theſe Ways of raiſing Money would be much more equitable and conſiſtent with Liberty than ſome lately attempted.

He gives us one Citation more concerning the Political Government of the Kingdom of *Laputa,* or the *flying Iſland,* the King of which hath ſeveral Dominions on the Continent below; and what follows relates to his Method of ſuppreſſing *Inſurrections* amongſt them.

If any Town ſhould *Mutiny,* fall into *violent Factions,* or refuſe to pay the *uſual Tribute,* the King hath *two Methods* of reducing Them to Obedience. The *firſt* is by keeping the *Iſland* hovering over ſuch a Town, and the Lands about it; whereby He can deprive Them of the Benefit of the *Sun,* and afflict the Inhabitants with Death and Diſeaſes. If the Crime deſerve it, They are at the ſame Time pelted from above with great Stones; againſt which They have no Defence, but by creeping into Cellars and Caves, whilſt the Roofs of their Houſes are beaten to Pieces. But if they ſtill continue obſtinate, or offer to raiſe *Inſurrections,* He proceeds to the *laſt Remedy,* by letting the *Iſland* drop directly upon their Heads, which makes an univerſal Deſtruction both of Houſes and Men. However, This is an Extremity, to which the Prince is ſeldom driven; neither, indeed, is He willing to put it in Execution; nor dare his *Miniſters* adviſe Him to an Action, which, as it would render Them odious to the *People,* ſo it would be a great Damage to their *own Eſtates,* which lye all below; for the *Iſland* is the King's Demeſn.

But there is ſtill, indeed, a more weighty Reaſon, why the Kings of this Country have been always averſe from executing ſo terrible an Action, unleſs upon the utmoſt Neceſſity; for if the Town, intended to be deſtroy'd ſhould have in it any tall Rocks, as it generally falls out in the

larger Cities, a Situation probably choſen at firſt with a View to prevent ſuch a Cataſtrophe; or if it abound in high Spires, or Pillars of Stone, a ſudden Fall might endanger the *Bottom,* or *Under-Surface of the Iſland;* which, although it conſiſts, of *one intire Adamant,* two hundred Yards thick, might happen to crack by too great a Shock. Of all this the *People* are well apprized, and underſtand how far to carry their Obſtinacy, where their *Liberty,* or *Property* is concern'd; and the *King,* when He is higheſt provoked, and moſt determined to preſs a City to Rubbiſh, orders the *Iſland* to deſcend with great Gentleneſs, out of a Pretence of Tenderneſs to his *People,* but indeed for Fear of breaking the *adaman-tine Bottom;* in which Caſe, it is the Opinion of all their Philoſophers, that the *Loadſtone* could no longer hold it up, the whole Maſs would fall to the Ground.

The Obſervation which the Writer makes upon the whole is, Tho' the Politicks of *Laputa* are no way applicable to our Government, yet every one may be ſaid, in a metaphorical Senſe, to have an *Adamantine Bottom,* or to be ſupported by the *Affections of the People,* which ought to be kept firm and compacted by the magnetick Virtue of a *wiſe and upright Adminiſtration.*

London Journal. Sept. 1. No. 740.

AMong the ſeveral Arts which the Gentlemen in the Oppoſition make uſe of to traduce, one is, by affirming againſt the cleareſt Evidence of Facts, " *That our Government* is not, at *preſent,* ſo good as it was in its *Original;* and that it muſt be reduced to its *Primitive Purity.* For which purpoſe *Machiavel* is quoted (See p. 415.) But this *political Maxim* can only be applied to Governments worn out with Age, broken and never amended, nor renewed; excellent in their *Original,* but deſtroy'd by the Vices of great Men, contending for Power; whereas the *Reverſe* is true of our Government, which was *bad* in the *Beginning,* made better by Degrees, and is brought to *Perfection* at laſt. The *primitive Purity* of our Government was that the People had no Share in the Government, but were *Villains,* Vaſſals, or Bondſmen of the Lords; a ſort of Cattle bought and ſold with the Land. The very *Parliaments of* old were compoſed only of Eccleſiaſtical and Civil *Tyrants* called *Abbots, Priors, Barons,* &c. The Kings, indeed, were *not abſolute* over the

Barons; but both *King* and *Barons* were *abfolute* over the People. *Property* they had none; but both their *Labour* and their *Blood* were the *Property* of their *Lords*, till the Power of the *Barons* was deftroy'd by *Henry* VII. and the Power of the Church by *Henry* VIII. Af-ter *that*, they got Wealth and Power, and by Degrees, Liberty. The *Revolution* fixed and fettled that Liberty, fo well, that to fecure our Happinefs, is not to go back to the *firft Principles* of our Go-vernment, but to *keep fteadily* to the *laft*. To go further, would be to weaken that *juft Ballance* now fettled between *Pre-rogative* and *Liberty*, the *Rights* of the *King* and the *Rights* of the *People*, which are abfolutely *diftinct*; as thus;

The *Rights of the People* confift in *fra-ming* their own Conftitution, and *chufing* their own Governors. But as long as the *Conftitution* is *preferved*, and the Chief Magiftrate acts by the *Laws* of the State, the *People* have no *Power* nor *Au-thority*. K. *James* II. diffolved the Con-ftitution, by invading the Laws; the People fent him away, and chofe another King. This was *right*. But till another King acts as He did, the People have no fuch Right, nor any Power but to chufe their own *Reprefentatives*, and try their Fellow Subjects. This is not a *natural Authority*, as the *Craftfman* calls it, but *Legal*; for, there is no Authority in *Eng-land*, but *Legal*. But the Perfons they chufe, are not (as that *profound Politician*, Sir *Rich. Steele*, calls them) *the Attornies* of the People, but *Legiflators*, fent up by the People to *judge* and *act* for their Good. They cannot be chofen to *repre-fent the Senfe of the People*, becaufe 'tis impoffible *the Senfe of the People* about *fu-ture Tranfactions*, fhould be known. If the Members were to do this, they muft fend to the People whatever is brought into the Houfe, who muft then meet in their *Collective* Body; that is, all the *Freeholders* and *Freemen* muft affemble, debate upon, and *agree their Senfe*, before their Reprefentatives can have Authority to act. This fhews the Abfurdity of *re-reprefenting the People's Senfe*, which is all Cant, to ferve a *late* Turn: For Men muft act according to their *own Reafon*, tho' againft the Senfe of all the World.

The *Rights of the King* are as plain. The *Craftfman*, indeed, fays, " That the King is only trufted with the *Execu-tive Power*." But, this is not true: The King is *an Effential Part* of the Legifla-

(*Gent. Mag.* Vol. 3. No. xxxiii.)

ture; and the *People* can no more make Decifions without him, than he can with-out them. The *Decifions* which bind the Nation, are not the *Decifions of the Peo-ple*, but of *King, Lords*, and *Commons*; by which Decifions or Laws, the King, as the *Executive Power* of the Kingdom, is obliged to act: And while he thus acts, he is *Superior* to *all Perfons*, whether in their *Collective* or Noncollective Capacity.

In thus ftating the Rights of the *King* and *People* I hope, fays *Osborne*, the *Craftfman* will not call this abufing the People. I know of no Writer on the Side of the Miniftry, who hath, as he fays, call'd the *Body* of the People *Mob*, the *Vulgar*, &c. (fee p. 422 H) And 'tis a manifeft Slander upon a *certainGen-tleman*, to fay he call'd *the Body of the People, Sturdy Beggers*; he only pleafant-ly faid, that when a numerous Body of Tradefmen, well fed and well cloath'd, came as *Petitioners*, and *look'd*, at the fame Time, as tho' they came to *give*, not *receive Law*, that, if they were *Beg-gers*, they were *Sturdy Beggers*. But what is this to the Body of the People ? How *four* and *fevere* are thefe Antimini-fterial Writers, that they won't fuffer a Man to *laugh* ! 'Tis a Sign they are as much out of *Humour*, as out of *Power*.

But this is one of their Arts to fet the People *againft the Miniftry*, in which they will find themfelves greatly miftaken, as they feem to apprehend, or they would never have been driven to the low Shifts of cajoling the 'Diffenters. (See p. 426 H) But the Diffenters underftand their own and Country's Intereft better, as *Englifh-men* and *Proteftants*, than to be deluded by a Writer, who, while he is courting them, and blaming the Conduct of the M——r towards them, about the *Teft*, dares not own the *Juftice* of the *Repeal*.

The *Daily Courant*, Sept. 1.

IT's evident from the laft *Craftfman* (fee p. 426.) that the *Club* publifhed their *Political Creed* (fee p. 357.) with Defign to delude fome honeft Whigs, par-ticularly the Proteftant Diffenters, who have been generally reputed (perhaps un-juftly) to incline to the*Republican* Scheme. The Prefident of the *Club* well remem-bers what Effect this had in the Time of his Adminiftration, when the Diffenters, in Addreffes from all Parts of the King-dom, were reviled as *Republicans*. They can hardly forget what follow'd that direful Prelude, that Watch-word given

out

out by that glorious Minister B——ke. Now indeed they are absolutely safe from all such Treatment, and are as well affected to his Majesty's *Title* and *Government* as any in the Nation. But it is pleasant to see the *Man* who formerly marked them out as Enemies to their Country under this *Appellation*, now courting their Favour by assuming the same Character himself. He does, indeed, out of his pious Regard to the *King*, allow our Government to be a *Regal Commonwealth*, a Doctrine which the *Dissenters* can't but look upon as absurd and ridiculous, and with respect to the Author, as the most arrant Grimace. This appears from his manner of supporting this ingenious Conceit. " The Word *Commonwealth* is not used, says he, in the strictest Sense to signify a *Democracy* or *popular State*, but is often applied to all sorts of Government without Distinction."— Allowing this, would any one, who wou'd give an Idea of this, or any Government, use a Word which suits all Sorts of Government without Distinction? and equally applicable to *England*, *France*, or *Poland*? Neither does he mend the Matter by saying *he means a Republick with a King at the Head of it*; for *Republick* being the same as *Commonwealth*, this Notion is still applicable to all the Kingdoms upon Earth; tho' it is obvious, that *Monarchical Government* is of various Sorts, and of different Degrees.

A *mixt Monarchy* most exactly suits the Constitution, and includes both the *Rights* and *Prerogatives* of the *Crown*, and the Share which the *Lords* and *Commons* have in the *Legislature*. And this great Politician was once as Zealous to strain the *Prerogative* of the *Crown*, not only to the Prejudice, but to the utter Dissolution of the other *Estates*. And the *Act of Settlement*, which he pretends to be the *Rule* of his *Political Faith*, was once the most disgustful Thing in the World to him. Yet this Man has the Face to appear as an *extraordinary* Friend to Liberty, an Advocate for *Dissenters*; and if he can meet with any of a Republican Taste, endeavours to consolidate them with his Party. This *is* he who addresses the People in the most important Affair that can come before them, the Choice of a new Parliament. BRUNO.

Weekly Miscellany, Sept. 1. N° 38.

GIVES a Treatise on the Parliament of *Paris*, which we have had before, (See p. 563, 564.)

Universal Spectator, Sept. 1. No. 256.
A Warning to young Virgins.

Mr Spectator,

IF *Misery* is a Claim to your *Patronage*, none can have a greater than myself. I am the Daughter of a Country Gentleman, who gave me a virtuous and polite Education; my Life was retir'd, innocent, and happy, 'till about last Spring, my rural Innocence and my Person, attracted the Desires of a young Gentleman lately come from *London*. As he had every Charm to *captivate*, he soon gain'd my Heart. There was now nothing wanting but the *Marriage Ceremony*; the Day was *fixed*, but he by some *unsuspected* Excuse had it *deferr'd*. At this *Juncture* his *Passion* seem'd to *encrease*, his *Vows* of *Love* and *Constancy* were doubled; he *sigh'd* — *wept* — *kneel'd* — *swore*; he urg'd, that as the Day was fix'd, The Ceremony was but an *empty Form*; and that in the Eyes of *God* we were by our mutual *Vows*, Man and *Wife*—*Conquer'd* by his *Tears* and his *Charms*, trusting in his *Oaths* and his *Arguments*, He prevail'd, and *I* was ruin'd.—In a few Days his fond Endearments were converted into the *coldest Indifference*; he made a little Quarrel with my Father, took Horses for *London*, and abandon'd me to *Misery* and *Shame*.—Inexpressible was my Grief; but alas! I have lately found too evident Signs of my bearing about with me a *Babe*, an *innocent* Partner of its Mother's *Wretchedness* and *Disgrace*—How shall I stand the *Reproach* of my *Parents*, and be able to see their *Agonies*, too *great*, perhaps, for them to *bear*.——Must my Child, for its *Father's Villainy*, inherit its *Mother's Shame*—These Thoughts are insupportable! Heaven keep me from destroying myself; let this *barbarous* Action be publish'd; perhaps, stung with *Remorse* the Ingrate may *relent*, and make me *Reparation*, at least it may secure other fond Maidens from the *Misery* of the wretched SYLVIA.

Fog's Journal, Sept. 1. No. 251.
Of the Court of Chancery, &c.

ALL Oppression which has the Law for its Sanction is more cruel in itself and more fatal in its Consequences, than any Acts of Injustice committed by private Men. The common Law having no Power to distinguish Objects of Pity; to remedy this, was instituted the High Court of Chancery, which is the Repository

tory of the King's Conscience; and therefore it is called the *Court of Equity*. But the Chicane and Tricks of this Court, are such, as gave Occasion to Mr *Dryden* to say, *Who gains the Cause is but the* last *undone*.

The expensive Methods of obtaining Justice in Chancery, and the vexatious Delays in the M——s of that Court, cast an Odium, not only on it, but the Law in General, and make this highest Tribunal in *Great Britain*, worse than the Inquisition in *Portugal*.

The Office of a M——r in Chancery is only to state Facts, that are too tedious for the Court to look into, and to adjust Bills of Costs. From the Nature of the Office, Expedition to Suitors, was the End proposed by its Institution. These Offices are in the Gift of the Chancellor, the more valuable they are the more is got by their Sale, or the better Provision for a Relation.

Notwithstanding some wholesome Measures taken some Years ago to obviate Oppressions, yet the M——s take arbitrary Steps to bring the Fortunes of Suitors into their Hands.——*Dormer* having embezzled the Effects of Suitors by Stockjobbing, and other infamous Practices, to the value of 25,000*l.* an Order was made in 1725, for the M——s to bring in their respective Accounts of Cash and Securities in their Hands; and that no more Money should be lodg'd with them. This Order they evade by the following Method: When a Receiver is appointed of the Rents of an Estate in Litigation, each of the Parties nominate two, whose Names, with their Securities, are laid before the M——rs, who appoint their own Creatures, their Clerks, or Country Attornies, Persons wholly unknown to either of the Parties, by which they get the growing Rents and Profits into their own Hands; the Master is to pass their Accounts, which they make intricate and vexatious, to give their Imployer (the M——r) the Opportunity of an infinite Number of Warrants and Summons's; and in Case of an exorbitant Allowance to the Receiver, his Partner the M——r, spends a Year or two in going thro' the Account, and there is no other Remedy than by taking Exceptions to the M——r's Report, which is full as dilatory and vexatious as the original Suit; and as at the Close of a Chancery Suit, *the Suitors rarely have Money to spare*, in that Case these Abuses are not to be remedied, and they must stand or fall by the M——r's Determination.

Where a Receiver has had only a Year's Rent to account for, the M——r has frequently taken two Years, to peruse and finish his Accounts, by which the M——r or Receiver, or both, have had the Benefit of the Suitors Money so long. Where some have apply'd to set aside the M——r's Receiver, the Delay and Cost of it is excessive; an Instance of which lately happen'd upon M——r E——d, who took so long Time in appointing another Receiver, on the former's being removed, as to let the long Vacation come on, by which the Estate suffer'd prodigiously.

The M——s, to vex Suitors who oppose them, join the Solicitors in contriving to spend 2 or 3 Years in taxing a Bill of Costs, which makes the taking 100 *l.* off a 300 *l.* Bill, by Warrants and Attendances, rather a Loss than a Benefit. Then they glut their Revenge by making a bad Report, by which the Parties are put to the Charge and Delay of arguing Objections and Exceptions. The Cause of Lord *Falconbridge* against Mr *Fitzgerald* affords numberless Instances of this Kind.

Another View the M——s have in appointing Receivers, is to make Parties in petty Corporations, in order to influence Elections. The Attornies agree with the M——s to oppose the Election of Those who have appeared for the Amendment of the Law, whom they term common Enemies. In all Cases the M——s serve one another, by taking and giving Recommendations in their respective Countries.

The Warrant or Summons is but 2 *s.* but the M——s have introduced a Practice that Solicitors do not attend till the third Summons, and then perhaps, the M——r is to attend in the House of Lords or elsewhere: But is not this picking the Suitor's Pocket of 6 *s.* and of thrice 6 *s.* 8 *d.* for the Solicitor's Attendances? And when the M——r attends, one or other of the Solicitors will be sure to be absent; the M——r directs another Warrant; and when all attend, which is rarely under the tenth Warrant, they do as little Business as possible; which is the Reason that a short plain Account takes up about 7 Years, and a long and intricate Account 20, 30, or 40 Years; which by two Men of understanding might be settled in so many Days; an Instance of which is upon Lord —— being made Chancellor; he was shock'd to hear Exceptions taken to a Report upon an Account that had been 40 Years in a M——r's Office, and that there was reason to set aside the Report, and to send the Parties to begin the Ac-

Account anew: He granted a Commission to four Gentlemen, who in 14 Days settled that long Account to the Satisfaction of the Court and the Parties. The Ch—r has since found how detrimental to his Interest the lessening the Value of the M—r's Office would be.

Again, it's usual to pay the M—r for 10,000 Sheets of Copy, where 100 would be more than sufficient.

Another intolerable Grievance is, Consequences of Country Attornies acting as Council at Quarter Sessions, who have raised their Fees from 3s. 4d. to two and three Guineas, while the Barristers who are often Brow-beat, get no greater a Fee than 10s. The Barristers at *Whitechapel,* and other Courts about Town, where Attornies are excluded from pleading, have but a Crown Fee, which is settled, and what they would be satisfied with at the Sessions, were Attornies excluded. The Ignorance of Attornies causes many irregular Orders, the reversing of which is the chief Business of the *King's Bench.* The present Backwardness of most Tenants in paying Rent is owing to the Calamities brought on them by Country Attornies, who introduce the Practice of acting as Barristers at Quarter Sessions, by prevailing on a M—r in Chancery to attend at the Spring Sessions; they are complimented with the Chair; then admit their Creatures the Attornies, who return the Favour at their Client's Expence. This Practice was abolished in the largest County by Men of Fortune, who attend the Quarter Sessions. In other Counties the Justices being mean Men are under the Influence of Attornies, who generally have the finest new built House in every Market Town: But it is not so only in this Nation. Monsieur *Belzac* tells the following Story. *The Inhabitants of a certain Valley in* France *had lived in the most perfect Friendship, till an Attorney came amongst them; immediately nothing but Processes and Appeals to the Parliament of* Thoulouse. *After they had spent all their Money, they began to consider what could occasion this wonderful Change; all agree, there was no such thing before the Arrival of that Attorney. Upon which they drove the Harpy out of their Country, and their pristine Tranquillity was entirely restored.*

The Free Briton. Sept. 6. No. 298.

Of Censure.

CEnsure, says Mr *Addison,* is *the Tax a Man pays to the Publick for being* eminent. All the illustrious Persons of Antiquity, and indeed of every Age, have passed thro' this fiery Persecution. There is no Defence against it but Obscurity; it is a Kind of Concomitant to Greatness, as Satires and Invectives were an essential Part of a *Roman* Triumph. But True Honour is infinitely above the low and lying Arts of Scandal. A brave Man is always the last to report an ill Thought of his Enemy; whose Fame he will forbear, as he scorns the Imputation of Revenge. Generous Natures, with Pleasure, discover a Truth to any Man's Advantage, nor ever suppress it for the sake of little sordid Resentments. *Shakespeare* seems to imagine Calumny more criminal than even the *Crimen peculatus.*

——*Good Name in Man or Woman*
Is the immediate Jewel of their Souls.
Who steals my Purse steals Trash; 'tis something, nothing;
'Twas mine, 'tis his, and has been Slave to Thousands:
But he who filches from me my good Name,
Robs me of that, which not enriches him,
And makes me poor indeed.

Walsingham applies this Observation on Calumny to the Usage a certain Minister has met with, who has been branded undeservedly even with the Name and Qualities of the Devil, by the *Craftsman* and other Antiministerial Declaimers. When a Minister, says *W.* falls under their Displeasure, they conceive him accountable for all the Corruptions in the Nation. The Pestilence and Famine, if they happen in his Time, are laid at his Door; just as in the late Queen's Reign, the great Storm of Wind, was said in a Sermon to be a Judgment on the Administration.

Grubstreet Journal, Sept 6. N° 193.
Remarks on the Free Briton; see p. 420.

De pictore, sculptore, fictore, nisi artifex judicare — non potest.

TO be a complete Judge of *Painting, Sculpture,* and *Statuary,* it is necessary to have had a *proper Education* in some famous Academy; to have studied for several Years the Graces of the most celebrated Works, antient and modern, in the Originals, or at least in their best Copies; and to have conversed with the most celebrated Artists of the Age, to enable him to discern the nice Strokes and Touches of Art, which distinguish the Hands of Artists, and are imperceptible to all but such.—But has Mr *W.* this Discernment; and how did he attain it? That

That he has it we are assured, because he exerts it upon proper Occasions; and he might attain it by *Inspiration* or *Enthusiasm*, attended with a *suitable Encouragement*; to which two Causes he ascribes the Appearance of the greatest Men among the Antients, both in Arts and Arms; yet he owns, there now and then rises, even in *later Ages*, a *sublime Genius*, as well in *Art*, as in *Heroism*; both which are *animated* by the same *Fire* and *Spirit*, (that of *Enthusiasm*,) and gives for Instances, K. *William*, the D. of *Marlborough*, and Mr *Rysbrack*. 'Tis pity he could not produce one Example more to accompany Mr *Rysbrack*, that so the modern Instances of *Art*, might have equall'd those of *Heroism*. Had he view'd the Monuments in *Westminster Abbey*, he might have seen the Works of one, who has *expressed the Spirit of Antiquity*, tho' in a different Manner, and who may succeed Mr *Rysbrack*, with as little Disadvantage to his own Reputation, as the D. of *Marlborough* succeeded K. *William*.

But after all, I must represent to the World the malicious Remarks of some envious Persons, upon this very Panegyric. They say, that this Paper, like the rest of his Compositions, consists of an indigested Heap of high-flown Tautologies, which convey no Meaning to the Reader; that where he has attempted to use rhetorical Figures, he has inverted and set them upon the wrong End; that there is not only false Reasoning in it, but even false Grammar; that one Part of it contradicts another; that there are several historical Mistakes, and one egregious Blunder which overturns his whole Panegyric, and entirely destroys the Reputation of his Judgment in the Art of Statuary. For, in order to do honour to Mr *Rysbrack*, he has attributed to him the Bustoes, *those Monuments of Genius, which her Majesty hath chosen to grace her* GROTTO; which unfortunately happen to be the Work of another, and as some think, a much inferior Hand. Upon which account, they say, that if Mr *Rysback*, out of Gratitude for this affectionate Zeal without Knowledge, should think fit to exert *the greatest Profusion of his Art* upon Mr *Walsingham's* own Bust, as the properest Present for him; in order to render it more *antique*, it ought to be adorned with the Ears of MIDAS.

To the foregoing Remarks, *Bavius* subjoins his own, *viz.* That *Praxiteles* was no *Painter*, and flourished some Years before *Alexander* was born; and that *Apelles* was no *Sculptor*, nor *Statuary*; and hopes Mr *W.* will give a *Dissertation* upon these *Statues* and *Medals* of *Apelles* and *Praxiteles*, which he seems to have lately seen. (See p. 421.)

Weekly Miscellany. Sept. 8. No. 39.

A Writer, who signs *Christianus*, expresses his Zeal for Religion by recommending the Imitation of Clergymen the Example of their learned Brethren of the last Century; who, in a united manner, printed a Set of admirable Discourses to oppose Popery, and to reconcile Protestant Dissenters to our holy Mother the Church. Our Danger now from Infidelity, says he, is not less, and wishes some learned Clergymen, and others, would combine, and publish a plain and judicious Defence of the Christian Religion in all its Parts, each Man concern'd submitting his Performance to the Perusal and Correction of all. For the main Reason why young Fellows turn Infidels, is because they have not studied the Grounds and Reasons of the Christian Religion, and, for want of proper Directions, being left to themselves, they neglect this Business as a dull and heavy one, and having nothing to say in its Defence, and not caring to be laugh'd at, pick up from loose Books and loose Company, some trifling Cavils, commence Unbelievers, and scoff at Religion.

The **Craftsman.** Sept. 8. No. 373.

Of the English *Constitution.*

A Ccording to a certain Set of Writers, our *excellent Constitution* is no better then a Jumble of incompatible Powers, which would fall to Pieces of Themselves, unless upheld by the honourable Methods of *Bribery* and *Corruption*; for how else can any Man plead for the Necessity or the Fitness of *Places* and *Pensions*, or any *pecuniary Influence* among the Members of the *House of Commons?* If any such *Dependance* or *Bias* were really necessary, it would prove that the *Form* of our Government itself was defective to a degree of Ridiculousness; that it was a *Constitution*, having a *Representative of the People* which must be engaged *not to represent them*, and not to vote and act, as They would, if uninfluenced by *private Interest*, and *corrupt Motives*. Now, if such an *Influence*, or *Dependance*, was universal and unlimited throughout the *whole House*, the Monarchy

chy would be *absolute*; and every Degree of *this Influence* tends to *arbitrary Power*. *Such Influences* therefore the Friends of Liberty must guard against; which is not setting up a *new Form of Government*, but preserving the *old*.

Our Constitution is a fleeting Thing, which at different Times hath differ'd from itself, as Men differ from themselves in Youth and Age; but still is the same. At the *Revolution* it received a considerable Strength by *that Act*, called the *Declaration of Rights*. About 5 Years after this, we obtained the *Triennial Act*, which was an additional Security to our Liberties. K. *William* passed also several other Acts, viz. for securing to us *free Parliaments*, and consequently our *Constitution* and *Liberties*, to prevent *double* and *false Returns*; to prevent *Bribery*; to prohibit *Commissioners of Excise sitting in the House*; and a Clause in the *Act of Settlement* provided, that after his *Decease*, and the Decease of the then Princess *Anne*, no Person who had *any Office, or Place of Profit, under the King, or received any Pension from the Crown, should be capable of serving as Member of the House of Commons.*

Another Instance of the Advantage, accruing to the Cause of *Liberty*, under the Reign of that *glorious Deliverer of our Country*, was his complying with the Desire of his *People* and *Parliament* in reducing the *Standing Forces of England* to about 7000 Men, which good Acts in favour of Liberty ought to be inscribed on the Pedestal of his Statue, as well as his delivering us from Popery and Slavery.

I mention these Things, says *D'anvers*, because *some Persons* are often defying People to instance in any *one Article of Liberty*, or *Security for Liberty*, which we once had, and do not still enjoy. Are *long Parliaments* the same as frequent Elections? Is the Circumstance of having almost 200 *Members of the House of Commons*, in Offices, the same Thing as having a *Law*, which would have excluded all *such Persons* from sitting there? Is an Army of about 17,000 Men for *Great Britain*, at the Expence of 850,000l. *per Ann.* the same Thing as an Army of 7000 Men, at the Expence of 350,000l. *per Ann.* for *England*, besides about 3000 Men for *Scotland*? Is the *Riot Act*, which establishes *Passive Obedience* and *Non-resistance* by Law, even in the utmost Extremity, the same Thing as leaving the People at Liberty to redress themselves?

In the Reign of Q. *Anne* an expensive War involved the Nation in a heavy Debt, which occasioned several *Duties* and *Taxes*. This is of no Advantage to the Cause of *Liberty*, as it makes the *Crown* the annual Receiver of near 50 *Millions of the People's Property*; besides increasing its Weight and Influence by a vast Number of *Officers*. In this Reign an Act passed to repeal the *Clause* abovementioned of the 12th of K. *William* relating to the holding of Places in the *House of Commons*, but a *Clause* was *inserted*, by which certain Persons holding *Offices*, were incapacitated from sitting in the *House of Commons*, as well as all Persons, holding any *new Places*, created since 1705; likewise, that all Persons, who, after their Election in Parliament, shall accept any *Office of Profit* under the *Crown*, were made incapable of sitting, unless *Re-elected*. In the 5th of her Reign She passed the *Qualification Act*, which requires every Member for a Borough to have 300l. *per Ann.* and for a County 600l. *per Ann.* and other good Laws. But if any of these have not their due Force, by Reason of some concealed *Evasions*, since found out, what can be more reasonable than to apply an effectual Remedy? Is it not of greater Consequence to *prevent* such *Evasions* than any *little Frauds in the Customs*? If the Laws formerly contrived for securing to us *free Parliaments* and frequent *Elections* have been repealed, it is natural to desire a Recovery of them. If the *publick Debts* so incumber us, that we could not engage vigorously in a War, *for our own immediate Interests*; or, if they are so circumstanced, that they may render our *Liberties* less secure, what can be more reasonable than to lessen them, by managing the national Expence with all possible Frugality, and shunning all Occasions of encreasing it?

If the *ministerial Advocates* would be thought to have any Sense of Liberty, or *Revolution Principles*, let them come fairly to *these Points*; but if they are resolved to drudge on in their old Road of calling *Jacobite* and *Republican*; they must expect to continue in the Contempt they are at present.

London Journal. Sept. 8. No. 741.
A Letter to the Protestant Dissenters.

GENTLEMEN,

FEW Men *know* you better, or *since* you more than myself. I am also a *true general Protestant*, attach'd to no religious

ligious Party, nor *averse* to any ; for the *Church of England*, but not against the *Dissenters* ; for the *Dissenters*, but not against the *Church* : † I am for you *all*, as long as you all act like *Christians* and *Protestants*. § This qualifies me to see the *Truth* ; and I will *speak* it too ; for 'tis *now* absolutely necessary, in this *general Clamour* and *Discontent*.

Clamours and *Discontents* ever were, and will be, as long as *Liberty* lasts : Not the Days of Q. *Elizabeth*, nor the more happy Days of our *glorious Deliverer* K. *William* were without them. There are, at *Hatfield*, a Closet full of Pamphlets and Papers, wrote against that great Statesman *Burleigh* ; which, under his own Hand, he calls *Libels 'against me while I was a Minister of State* ; and in the *State Tracts* are more *cruel Satyres* and *Invectives* against K. *William* and his Ministry, than against his present Majesty and Ministry. But it doth not follow that the *Measures* of the Court were then against the *Interest* of the Country. We know how Libels are produc'd in *England* ; and the true *Cause* of all the *Virulence* retailed in the *Craftsman* and *Fog* ; The *Causes* are not in the *Court* or *Ministry*, but in their Enemies, who are defied to prove *one Action* they have done against our *Constitution* or *Liberties*. These *Clamours* and *Discontents* must therefore arise from another *Quarter*, and first from some Differences among the *Whigs in Power*. All could not be pleas'd : Those who were not, fell a *Railing*, and set up a Weekly Journal, which, with the Help of another *Jacobite* Journal, hath poyson'd the Nation ; and 'tis impossible the *best Ministry* could preserve *popular Affection* and *Esteem* against Papers constantly *misrepresenting* all their Actions.

The *Jacobites* and *Tories* lay very quiet from the Rebellion in the late Reign, till a long Time after the *Craftsman* appear'd, and so *wisely* let *him* do the Work ; which, while the *Whigs* were united, they had neither *Power* nor *Credit* to do. But now the Work is done, these *Jacobites* appear under all Shapes, of *Whigs*, *Freethinkers*, and *Republicans*.

† A Writer in the *Grubstreet*, who signs WITCH OF ENDOR, *Sept.* 20, in a bantering Strain, says, it was the Intent of the facetious old Lady (*Osborne*) to make us laugh by giving us an Imitation of an Anabaptists Sermon.

§ *Indifference* about Religion, qualifies a Person to *see* the Truth. O! *Lepidum caput! Grub. ibid.*

You, Gentlemen! are some of the *fastest* of the *real* and *original* Friends to the *Revolution* and *Hanover Succession*. Consider, therefore, what Part it becomes you to act, to preserve those invaluable Privileges you enjoy, as *Englishmen* and *Protestant Dissenters*. As *Protestant Dissenters*, indeed, you have not *all you* wish, nor all I wish ; there's *one Thing* wanting, and *but one* ; for you have seen the *Occasional* and *Schism Acts* repeal'd ; but the *Test Act* remains unrepeal'd, which obliges you that have Places in the Government to go *once* to Church, and take the *Sacrament*. * This Act, I think ought to be *repeal'd* : But the *Ministry* thought it not *proper*, when you ask'd for it ; N for they don't consider Things in a *Philosophical* or *religious*, but in a *Political* View only ; and say in their Justification, " *That they must*, as Servants *of their King and Country*, *do what appears best for the Peace and Happiness of the Kingdom, at* every Juncture ; *that tho' Things may be* reasonable *in themselves*, *yet all Seasons are not equally proper to do them in* ; *that* all Parties *and Bodies of Men are to be* consider'd, *just as they relate to the Good of the* Whole *; that tho' the* Dissenters merit *every Thing from the Royal Family*, *and from the Kingdom*, *which Reason can demand*, *yet* some Regard *is to* be had to the Principles, *or, if you please, the* Prejudices *of the Church of England* *; that there are at least* Six Millions *of* Church People, *to* One Million *of* Dissenters, *that* great Numbers *of the Laity*, *and a Majority of the* Clergy, *are yet against the Repeal*, *and say, that the* Test *is a very small Evil to you, because you are grown into generous Sentiments of Religion*, *and scarce one in a thousand counts* Communion *with the Church of England* sinful ; *and therefore 'tis not worth while to remove so small an Evil*, *and*

* In the *Miscellany*, *Sept.* 15. Mr *Hooker* tells Mr *Osborne*, he has in this Letter advanced some Things which affect the Honour of his Majesty, the Safety of our *Establish'd Religion* and *Government*, and even the Reputation of the *Dissenters*, and calls upon him to answer *Crito*'s State of the *Test* Affair, as laid down in some of the first *Miscellanies* (see p. 7.) or publickly retract his Charge, That the Establishment of the *Test* is *unjust*, and ought to be repealed.

‖ That is, Ministers have no Religion, *natural* or *reveal'd*. O! fy, good Woman, what could provoke you to be so severe upon your Friends ? *Grub*.

and which shortly *may be none at all, at the Hazard of a much greater, to be* fear'd *from a vastly more numerous Body of* Men *; that both* Clergy *and* Laity *are* growing into *the same Sentiments of Liberty with yourselves, so that you will soon meet in the same general* Opinions *of Religion and Government; and then, they will be willing to grant your Desire; or, you will be too wise, to have occasion for it; that you may obtain that in a little Time without Difficulty, which, when you desired it, was attended with great Difficulties; that they are entirely in your Interests, and will do what you request, in this Point, as soon as it's consistent, with the general Interest; that Prudence, and your high Regard to the publick Peace bid you wait the proper Season and then* ‖STRIKE; *what that Season is you* can't be ignorant." 'Tis certain, next *Winter* cannot be that proper Season. You see what Use the *Enemies* of the Government and Ministry have made of a *late Scheme;* and do you think they are able to bear another Body of Men at the same Time thundering in their Ears, the dreadful Cry of *the Danger of the Church,* joined to that of *Excise,* and the *Danger* of the Loss of *Liberty?* Who is *sufficient for these Things?* The last Reason, why they can't do it *next Winter* is unanswerable, unless the *Whigs* are united. But *you* and *I* may differ in our *Maxims of policy;* and the *Ministry* may be *mistaken:* What then? Must this *Mistake* be wrought up into *such a Crime,* as to make a *sober, virtuous,* and *rational* People, be guilty of the greatest *National Crime, breaking the Whig Interest,* and *hazarding their Happiness,* which now they are *sure* of? for that must be the Consequence of the *Dissenters generally opposing* the present Ministry.

February 15.

WHoever has made impartial Observations on *publick Affairs,* since the *Restoration,* must be convinced, that the Preservation of the *Religious* and *Civil* Rights of the People, is founded on the *Whig Interest;* and that the vigorous *Assistance of the Protestant Dissenters* is absolutely necessary to the Preservation of it. For, notwithstanding all *Distinctions* are laugh'd at, yet *Whigs* and *Tories, Jacobites* and *Papists,* are the *same* Men, and have the *same general Principles, Views* and *Designs* they used to have. This plainly appears from a Pamphlet, published at the Close of the last Session of Parliament, entitled, *The Loyal or Revolution Tory;* the Design of which is to shew, That tho' the *Whigs* were the *favour'd People,* yet, from their late *ungrateful* Conduct, they ought to be cast off, and themselves taken into their Places. *We never find, says that Writer, any* National Calamities or Enormities *committed in the State, but at such Junctures as the* Jacobites *and Dissenters had the Power of turning the Scale in Counsels of State.* Again: *We can never suppose the Dissenters, who have so long desir'd the Destruction of the Establishment of the* Church, *to be destitute of Schemes for that purpose, or want Inclinations to put them in Execution.*

If the *Revolution Tory* is thus severe upon you, what will the *Anti-revolution Tories* be? of which you are, probably, convinced there are *Two* to *One.* Is it not Time to look about you, when these your mortal Enemies are lifting up their Heads, and *asserting* their *exclusive Right* to Royal Trust and Confidence? Don't you *tremble* at the Consequences of letting *Tories* and *Jacobites* into the Administration? Were *these Men* ever in *Power,* without doing Things *destructive* to our *Civil* and *Religious* Rights, with a View to subvert the *Constitution,* as settled since the *Revolution?*

Yet *bad* as they are, they must come into Power, upon the *Breaking of the Whig Interest,* and which must be broke, if you *oppose* the *Court Whigs* at the next Election: For you know, that the *Church Whigs* and *Dissenters* together, when the most firmly united, are not *equal* in Number to the *Jacobites* and *Tories,* and have been always forced to supply the *Defect* of *natural Strength,* with great Art. But upon your Revolt, there must be *a Majority of Tories.* The Consequence of a *Tory Parliament,* must be a *Tory Ministry,* who will do you all *possible Mischief.* Some *Malecontent Whigs* are so sensible of this, *viz.* Mr *S. R.* &c. that *they* begin bravely to oppose them. Besides, can you be sure, whether a Court may not think it as reasonable to be *forced by Tories,* as you think it reasonable to *vote with Tories?* Can you tell how far they will *resent* your opposing them? Whether they will not represent you as a *turbulent, antimonarchical, seditious, gloomy, murmuring* Race of Men, never satisfied with

‖ The Writers both in the Grubstreet *and* Miscellany *are at a loss what* Osborne *means by this terrible Word.*

with your *present Condition* ; ever for infringing upon *the Prerogative*, and Undermining the *Church* ? Whether the *Ministry* are right or wrong, in refusing the Repeal of the Teft Act, *at this Time*, is hardly worth confidering ; nor Whether ANY SINGLE MINISTER hath *erred* in his Conduct towards you, which, I think, he has : But it's certainly worth confidering, above all Things, Whether we fhould preferve our *Civil and Religious Liberties*, or wantonly throw them *all* away, becaufe we want *one* ? which *one* the *Tories* would not give you ; and the *Craftfman* who is the Mouth of all the *Independent Whigs*, hath declared, they are for keeping a NEUTRALITY between the *Church* and *Diffenters*. F. OSBORNE.

Weekly Mifcellany, Sept. 15. No. 40.
Of Infidelity.

Mr HOOKER,

ONE of the favourite Topicks of the Infidels, in private Converfation, is *the Number of their Profelytes*. Moft Men of Senfe, they fay, are of their Party ; this they cannot account for, but from the general Knowledge and Learning now fpread among the People, which other Ages *formerly* wanted. But this is falfe in Fact ; for from the Revival of Learning at the Reformation, down to the Death of Sir *Ifaac Newton*, the moft eminent Men in all Arts and Sciences, have almoft univerfally been ftrict Adherers to the Chriftian Faith. Tho' they differ in fome Points, yet they were united in their Belief that our Religion came from God. This has unexceptionably been made appear by the prefent *Bp of London*, who collected the Sentiments of Mr *Addifon*, Mr *Locke*, &c. into one Volume. To put the Matter beyond all Doubt, it may be proper more minutely to trace out the Origin of that Spirit of Unbelief, which fo vifibly reigns among us. You have already attempted fomething of this Kind ; (fee p. 230.) to which the following Branches may be added.

Firft, *the impious Violation of the moft folemn Oaths,* whether form'd as a Teft for the Security of the Prince's Perfon, or defign'd for the better executing of civil Trufts, or for the more faithful collecting the publick Revenue. From hence they proceed to other Impieties, and having worn off the Senfe of God's avenging Providence, they ftruggle hard to get rid of the Belief of that Religion, whofe Precepts they are refolv'd not to practife.

(Gent. Mag. Vol. 3. No. xxxiii.)

Near a kin to this, is the wicked Behaviour of fuch modern *Arians*, as have fubfcribed thofe *Articles* which they believe the Reverfe of ; fuch Articles as the Church expected to be fecured by the moft ferious Teft. The Church and State may be fairly defended for impofing proper Tefts, becaufe no Society *can* fubfift without fuch Securities, provided they do not multiply *needlefs* Temptations.

Not only the Conduct of the *Arian Subfcribers*, but *Arianifm* itfelf, or the Revival of it, has been another Means of drawing Men off from the Belief of Chriftianity. I do not charge it upon the *Nature* of Arianifm *as fuch*, nor can I fee why the Difputes about the Divinity of Chrift's *Perfon* fhould alter the Evidence for the Divinity of his *Commiffion*. However, feveral even of the *Arian* Writers have begun in *Herefy*, and ended in *Infidelity*. Dr *Clarke*, it muft be acknowledg'd, always made a Diftinction between Things *above* Reafon, and Things contrary to Reafon. But the generality of this Party have notoriofly run greater Lengths.

Laftly, Their ftrong Prejudices againft the Clergy, on Account of their many Defeats and Difappointments, may have difinclin'd many from the Belief of that Religion from which the Clergy muft derive all their Efteem and Support. Had the Clergy, *in all Times and Places*, been the general Pefts of Society, as their Enemies reprefent them, I fhould think their Inftitution could not proceed from a wife and good Law-giver ; but no Hiftory informs us that they have been fuch. They are Men, and have their Faults, but their Faults fhould not be magnified or multiplied, or their Virtues be concealed. Yet fo it is ; and the Clergy being render'd fufpected, the common Enemy is permitted to infufe his Poyfon, while no Remedy muft be receiv'd from the Hand of the Phyfician.

The **Craftfman.** Sept. 15. N° 376.
Of the Game of Chefs.

Mr D'anvers,

CHefs is, perhaps, the only Game that is play'd at for nothing, and yet warms the Blood and the Brain as much as if the deepeft Stakes were laid. No Perfon ever flatters at this Game by underplaying himfelf. I remember but one Inftance of fuch an Adulation. An excellent Player at the Game at Chefs, got a good Employment by fuffering himfelf to be beat by a Firft *Minifter*, in the late Reign.

L l l   at

There's a Story of two Persons of Distinction, the one lived at *Madrid*, the other at *Rome*, who plaid a *Game at Chess* at that Distance. They began when young, and tho' they both lived to a very old Age, yet the Game was not finished. One of them dying, appointed his Executor to go on with the Game. Their Method was, *Each Don* kept a *Chess Board*, with the Pieces ranged in exact Order, in their respective Closets at *Madrid* and *Rome*; having agreed who should move first, the *Don* informs his Playfellow at *Rome*, by Letter, *that he had moved his* King's Pawn *two Moves*, the Courier speedily returns, and advises his Antagonist, that the Minute after he had the Honour to receive his, *he likewise moved his* King's Pawn *two Paces*, and so they went on.

This Play is a Contention who can lay the deepest Designs; and the several Motions and Powers of the Pieces are as follow. The Names of the Pieces are King, Queen, Bishop, Knight, Rook, *and* Pawn. The chief Personage, except the *King*, is the *Queen*. But she has infinitely more Power than her *royal Consort*; and has all the Motions of every Piece, except the *Knight*; his Motion being continually indirect or oblique. He, indeed, is the only Character, that always professes to act by Stratagem, or Fraud; but his Motion being particular, he must be a bad Player that does not guard against him.

The next in Quality to the *Queen* is the *Bishop*, who always takes Post on the Side of *her Majesty* or the King, is of very little Use in the Beginning of a Game, and is by Profession never obliged to move upon the Square, as even the *Rooks* and *Pawns* do, and therefore marches cross the Board from Angle to Angle. At the Close of a Game, he is of some little Use, tho' he seldom *gives Check to the* King, and rarely acts without the Assistance of the *Queen* or *Knight*. He often supports indeed, by his Presence, any Design they undertake. The *Bishops* are of so indifferent Account, that in old *Chess-Boards* they are describ'd as *Fools*, and distinguish'd with *long Bars* and *Bells*.

Next to the *Bishop* is the *Knight*, who does great Execution by Surprize. You often see him jump over the Heads of the *Nobles*, and thin the Ranks of the *Plebeians*, whose professed Enemy he is. When he is guarded by the *Queen*, he makes dreadful Havock, and often *Check-mates* the *King*. This is done, by forcing *his Majesty* into such a Situation, that he is as it were lock'd up, and disabled from moving, without being taken Prisoner by some *other Piece*. But such is the Regard to *Majesty*, that, when this happens, the Game is quite over; and the Conqueror only says this Word, *Mate*; the Inventors of this Diversion imagining, that a *King* incapable of acting, was as *no King*.

The Person next the *Knight*, is the *Rook*; but in old Boards he is called a *Castle*, or *Tower of Defence*; and acts always upon the Square. When the King is in Danger of being *Check-mated*, he rescues him; and such is their Power, that *two Rooks* are equal to a *Queen*.

In the Front of *King, Queen, and Nobles*, is placed the whole Body of the *Pawns*, or *Commonalty*, as their best and natural Guard. Their Motions are upon the Square; and if well conducted, are sure of Success. If properly supported they will break into the Ranks of the Enemies *Infantry*; push thro' the *Nobles*, and take a vacant Seat in the Upper House. Then they are called *Noblemen*. Some of these *Pawns*, or *Commoners*, even in that Capacity, shew uncommon Foresight, and defeat the Designs of a *Knight*, or a *Bishop*, with great Address. I have known some of them march with great Discipline and Order, even till they had almost inclosed the Enemy, and then they have obliged them to break their own Ranks, and submit with great Loss and Disgrace to the Force of a *Scheme* formed long before, to reduce them; but then they must be led by experienc'd Generals; for a false Step in such an Enterprize may prove of bad Consequence.

The *Free-Briton*. Sept. 20. No. 100.
On the Rise and Repeal of the Schism Bill.

MR *Walsingham* answers that Assertion of the *Craftsman*, That a certain Hon. Gentleman opposed the Repeal of the *Schism Bill* (see p. 426. B) and clears up that Affair by giving a short Account of the Proceedings thereon from the Journals of *both Houses*.

May 12, 1714. Sir *Wm Wyndham* moved that the Statute of the 13th and 14th of K. *Charles* II. entitled *an Act for the Uniformity of publick Prayers*, &c. might be read, and a Bill was order'd to be prepar'd by Sir *Wm Wyndham*, Mr *Cholmondeley* of *Cheshire*, Ld *Down*, Mr *Campion*, Mr *Dixie Windsor*, &c.

May 21. Sir *Wm Wyndham* presented the Bill *to prevent the Growth of Schism*.

May 26. Sir *Wm Wyndham* was made Chairman

Chairman of the Committee on the Bill, when a Clause being offer'd to be added, to exempt from Penalties, such as should teach to read the Old and New Testament, and the Common Prayer Book, it was rejected; and the Bill, at his Motion, order'd to be engrossed.

June 1. The *Schism Bill* passed; and Sir *Wm* was order'd to carry it to the Lords; which being return'd with Amendments, Sir *Wm* was order'd to carry it back, and acquaint the Lords that the House had agreed to their Amendments.

Mr *Walsingham* having thus shewn, that Sir *Wm Wyndham* was the *Father of this Bill*, he then names the *Peers* who enter'd their DISSENT *on the Journals* when the Lords passed the Bill. Those who stand in ROMAN *Letters* being *now living*, those in *Italicks* dead, viz.

(*Herbert* E. *of*) *Torrington*, *Dorchester*, (*late* D. *of Kingston*,) SOMERSET, *Bolton*, DORSET and *Middlesex*, GRAFTON, *Devonshire*, TOWNSHEND, CARLISLE, *Scarborough*, *Sunderland*, DERBY, *Cornwallis*, *Lincoln*, *Orford*, *Nottingham*, *Somers*, *Radnor*, *Rockingham*, *Haversham*, *Foley*, W. *Lincoln*, (WAKE) *J.* Ely, (Moore) *Jo. Bangor*, (Evans) W. St *Asaph*, (Fleetwood) *Jo.* Landaff, (Tyler) *Schomberg*, LEICESTER, MONTAGU, *De Longueville*, (*late* E. *of Sussex*) *Hallifax*, *Cowper*, GREENWICH, D. of ARGYLL.

Next he gives some Account of it from a Tract, entitled, the *Secret History of the White Staff*, to justify the E. of *Oxford* from the wicked Proceedings of the late Ld B——ke, written under the View, and from the Informations of that *Noble Earl*, and affirming, *that the* Schism Bill *was* castrated *by his Lordship; that he took out the most* malicious *and* persecuting *Part, which the* Wild-fire Men *had formed to ruin Families, and* oppress *the People;* and that these *Wild-fire Men* were Bp A——TT——RB——RY, who *sollicited* this Bill, Ld B——L——NGBR——KE, who *closed* with it; and Sir W——M W——ND-H——M, who *negotiated* it.

In 1718, a Bill had its Rise with the Lords, which was entitled, *An Act for Strengthening the Protestant Interest*. This *repealed the Schism Act*, and likewise *another Act of the* 10th *of Q.* Anne *for preserving the Protestant Religion, by better securing the Church of England:* And in this *complicated Condition* it was opposed in *both Houses*, as being clogged with more than it ought to contain, namely, with *another Repeal*, besides THAT *of the Schism Act*. It was therefore held *unparliamentary*, and being a Matter of *religious Dispute*, near kin to that which occasion'd the Rebellion, it was judg'd unseasonable. Many *eminent Whigs* in both Houses voted against the Bill as thus circumstanced: *But none of them voted against it as repealing the Act*, FOR PREVENTING THE GROWTH OF SCHISM.

As the late D. of D——v——nsh——re and E. C——wp——r, both of unexceptionable Characters, acted and reasoned in *this Manner*, no *Whig* can imagine, that they opposed the *Complication of two Repeals* in one Bill, from any *View of voting against the Repeal of the* SCHISM-BILL.

Now will any *Whig* or *Dissenter* imagine, that the *Honourable Person*, now accused, who govern'd himself in Concert with *two such excellent Men*, either meant or voted on that Occasion *from Opposition to the Repeal of the Schism-Bill*, consider'd *singly* of itself. When it is further consider'd that Mr P——Y himself, spoke and voted in the same Manner, is it possible, that Mr P——Y, who knows *he never had any such Meaning*, as to vote *against repealing the Schism-Bill*, can *honestly* do otherwise, than acquit such *Whigs*, as were then his *Confederates*, of this defaming Charge?

Whoever reviews the Conduct of the *Great Name* so unjustly aspersed, will find, that in all Parts of his Life, he hath been the *warmest Friend*, and *kindest Benefactor* of the *Protestant Dissenters*. Who more *heartily* and *formidably* opposed those persecuting Laws against the *Dissenters* proposed in the Beginning of Q. *Anne's* Reign, than He? If then he differ'd from others, concerning the Conjunction of *two Repeals* in one *Act*, and the *Season* of attempting it, is this to be weighed *against the whole Course of his Life*?

However the *Whig Lords* might object to such a complicated Bill, yet none of them left his Name on Record, as a *thorough Enemy to the passing of the Bill*; nor did the *opposing Whigs* in the *House of Commons*, vote against it on the *third Reading* there. The TORY Lords, who PROTESTED against *passing this Bill* for strengthening *the Protestant* Interest, and who opposed it, as well for that it *Repealed the Schism Act*, as the *Act of the* 10th of *Q. Anne*, there are now living, St——rsd——le, Angl——f——y, W——st——n F. of Arr——n, M——sb——m, N——th——mpt——n, Ux-br——dge, Str——ff——rd, B——th——rst, Br——ce, L——t.b——ld, M——ntj——y Visc. W——ds——r.

From the GRUBSTREET JOURNAL.
SOMEBODY *to* NO-BODY.

Invisible Sir,

I ONCE thought myself a Person of the
greatest Importance; but I find you are
as famous as my great Self; but with little
Reason; for, tho' there may be some sorry
Scrubs of the Family of the *Any-Body's*, that
may out of Vanity claim Kindred with the
Some-Body's, yet, upon Search in the Herald's
Office, it is found, they come originally from
the *No-Body's*. And since the Honour of
my Atchievements is too often attributed to
you, and your Roguery as commonly laid
at my Door, I think it high Time to tell
you, I renounce you, and if I meet you, I'll
piss upon you, help yourself how you can.

I was but yesterday in a Coffee-house,
where a Politician gravely said, I wonder
who will be King of *Poland?* The Answer
was, *No-body* can tell.—Do you think the
Czarina's Fleet will engage the *French* Squadron? *No-body* knows.—Will *France* fall out
about quarrelling? The Answer is the same,
Now, Sir, you—fib—; for 'tis I, and not
you, that are privy to these Things—Is it
not strange that *No-body* should want to be
thought *Some-body?* It is plain, therefore, that
Some-body is better than *No-body*, and is better
acquainted in the Cabinets of Princes,
than e'er a *Nobody* under the Sun.

In a certain Parish, where the Parson, for
the Good of Souls, is often non-resident
a Friend of mine asked, who preach'd in
his Absence? he was answer'd, *No-body.*—
This I think must be a Lie, because I know
your Education and Want of Talents. However, my Friend says 'tis true; and that often, when the Parson himself preaches, you
only are awake; yes truly! *No-body* is awake; *No-body* minds what's said.

I was mightily pleas'd when I read of several Maiden Assizes, and that *No-body* was
to be hang'd at divers Places: But as all
the News-papers are sad Liars, except the
Grubstreet Journal, I shall mind none but
that for the future. Who broke all the Windows last Winter at Foot-ball? *No-body*. Nay,
some say you are an Incendiary, and wrote
most of the threatening Letters, and set
fire to all the Houses that have been burnt
by unknown Villains. What can you say to
that? Nothing at all! For *No-body* did it.

You have likewise caus'd a Report, that
in many Shops in this City, *No-body* minds
how things go; takes any Care; knows how
long the Man will hold it; *&c.* which
none but a vain Coxcomb, like yourself,
would pretend to know. And *No-body* pretends to know how many Weddings, Births,
and Burials we shall have next Winter; to
find out the Longitude, and the perpetual
Motion, the Philosophers Stone, and can tell
how many F—ts go to an Ounce—But this is
all *Gasconade*; and I challenge thee to meet
me at the *Oratory*, where you are generally
an Auditor, and dispute the Matter fairly with me there. But if you are afraid,
challenge you to meet me behind Montague-House, where you have been often wounded
—If you refuse, I will post you for a Coward. I expect your Answer by *Any-body*, and
am your sworn Enemy   SOME-BODY.

From the GRUBSTREET JOURNAL.
NO-BODY's *answer to* SOME-BODY's *Letter.*

MR PRATE-A-PACE,

SIR,

I Read your huffing Letter, and I'll tell you
a Secret, which all the World knows, but
yourself;—and that is, (come a little nigher
to me.—)you are a very silly Coxcomb—Nay,
don't start, for it's true:—and take it from
me, that *Nobody* cares a pin for ye;—*No-body*
dares dispute with ye;—*No-body* dares fight
with ye; and, in a word, *No-body* dares do
any thing with ye.—

What signifies scolding about Family or
Honesty? I can prove, that *No-body* is older
than *Some-body*, or than *Any-body*; that there
has been an hundred to one more of the
Some-body's hang'd, than of the *No-body's*; and
that the *Some-bodys*, are therefore the greatest
R—s—Pray, who first thought of the Excise Bill?—Who petition'd against it;—who
mobb'd, and broke Windows for its being
lost?—Who rais'd a hundred and fifty Lies
about it; Why, *Some-body*, to be sure.—
And, in a Word, all the Villainy, that is
committed, when the naked Truth comes
to light, is always found to be by *Some-body*,
altho' *No-body* generally bears the Blame at first,
the more is the Shame:—So that I would
not have you boast too much of your Family.
—If I say I have found the Longitude, I can
prove it; which none of the *Some-body* can.

I wonder how you can have the Confidence to mention the *Oratory*. How often
has Mr *Orator* kindly invited you and Mr
Any-body; promising, with the greatest Assurance, that you should hear *new and uncommon Observations upon Subjects never treated
of in any other Pulpit:* And yet neither of you
would come, except when you could get in
for Nothing? Nay, you not only absented
yourself, but was so base as to traduce that
great Man, as very ignorant. Upon which,
tho' he has many times challenged you to
a fair *Disputation*, yet you never dared to
appear. And tho' I have been so kind as
frequently to appear for you myself on those
Occasions, and have even obligedMr *Orator*
to be silent, particularly on Wednesday Evenings: yet, instead of returning me your
Thanks, you now endeavour to expose me
for taking your Part, and even challenge me
to dispute with you in the very same Place;
which makes your Ingratitude as flagrant
as your Impudence.——Nor is your Folly
less remarkable in requiring me to appoint
a *Time* for this *Disputation*, when you acknow-

knowledge, that I am *generally an Auditor* there. Why therefore did not you come and meet me?——Come the very next Sunday, when I will make it evident to the World, that as it is generally agreed, that *No-body* is able to dispute with Mr *Orator*, so *Some-body* is not able to dispute with *No-body*.

But do not imagine, that I chuse to dispute, in order to decline fighting: for, let me tell you, that *No-body* loves fighting, for fighting sake: and as my Honour is concerned, *Nobody* (whom you now so much despise) will turn you inside outwards, and make an Hermaphrodite of ye.——I'll teach you how to bully a Man of Honour! I will.——And now, to compleat your Vexation, I do assure ye, that *No-body* does know who will be King of *Poland*, if you are never so angry at it; and likewise whether the *Muscovite* and *French* Fleet will fight if they meet, and who will beat; and, in one Word, *No-body* knows whatever will happen next Year, both by Sea and Land; but you shall not know a Word of it if you fret your Guts out.——Be sure you meet me without a Second, and make your Will, that you may not walk when you are dead, for not settling your Affairs: for *No-body* will as surely kill you, as that you are now alive.——Say your Prayers, put on your long Sword, come open-breasted, and die bravely, by the invincible Hand of your mortal Enemy

NO-BODY.

The Craftsman, Sept. 22, N° 377.

Extract from the FREEHOLDER's POLITICAL CATECHISM.

Question. WHO *are you?*
Answer. I am *T. M.* a Freeholde of *Great Britain.*

Q. *What Privilege enjoy'st thou by being so?*
A. I am a greater Man in my civil Capacity, than the greatest Subject of an arbitrary Prince; because I am governed by Laws, to which I give my Consent; and my Life, Liberty, and Goods cannot be taken from me, but according to those Laws. I am a Freeman.

Q. *Who gave Thee this Liberty?*
A. No Man. It is a natural Right; Man is born to the Exercise of it, as soon as he has attain'd to That of his Reason; but that my *Liberty* is preserved to Me, when lost to a great Part of Mankind, is owing, under God, to the Wisdom and Valour of my Ancestors.

Q. *Wherein does this Liberty consist?*
A. In *Laws* made by the Consent of the People, and the due Execution of *those Laws.* I am free, not *from the Law,* but *by the Law.*

Q. *Wilt thou stand fast in this Liberty?*
A. Yes verily, by God's Grace, I will; and I thank this good Providence that I am born a Member of a Community governed by *Laws,* and not by *arbitrary Power.*

Q. *What do'st thou think incumbent upon Thee, to secure this Blessing to thyself and Posterity?*
A. To believe aright concerning the fund-

amental Articles of the Government, to which I am subject; to act on all Occasions conformable to this orthodox Faith; to oppose, with all the Powers of my Body and Mind, the Enemies of our good Constitution, their secret and open Abettors, and to be obedient to the King, the supreme Magistrate.

Q. *Rehearse the Articles of thy political Creed?*
A. I believe that the supreme, or legislative Power of this Realm resides in the *King, Lords,* and *Commons*; that his Majesty K. *George* II. is sovereign, or supreme Executor of the Law; to whom, on that Account, all Loyalty is due; that *each of the three Members of the Legislature* are endowed with their particular Rights, and Offices; the *King,* by his royal Prerogative has the Power of determining and appointing the Time and Place of the Meeting of Parliaments; that the Consent of *King, Lords,* and *Commons is necessary* to the Being of a Law, and all the *three* make but *one Lawgiver*; that as to the Freedom of Consent in making of Laws, those *three Powers are independent,* and each bound to observe the Laws that are made.

Q. *Why is the Legislative Power supreme?*
A. Because it gives Law to all.

Q. *What mean'st thou by Loyalty to the King?*
A. I have heard that *Loy* signifies Law; and Loyalty *Obedience according to Law;* therefore He who pays this Obedience, is a loyal Subject; and He, who executes the King's Commands, when contrary to *Law,* is disloyal and a Traytor.

Q. *Is it not a Maxim in the Law, that the King can do no Wrong?*
A. It is; for since *Kings* do not act by themselves, but by their *Officers,* and *inferior Magistrates*; the Law provides against any undue Exercise of their Power, by charging all Kinds of Male-Administration upon their *Ministers*; the great Regard, paid to the *King* by this Maxim, laying him under an indisputable Obligation, not to skreen his *Ministers* from publick Justice, or publick Enquiry.

Q. *What do'st mean by the* royal Prerogative?
A. A discretionary Power in the *King* to act for the *Good of the People,* where the *Laws* are silent, never *contrary,* but always subject to the *Limitations of the Law.*

Q. *Is not then the King above the Laws?*
A. No; for the Intention of Government being the Security of the Lives, Liberties, and Properties of the Members of the Community, they never can be supported by the Law of Nature, to give an *arbitrary Power* over their Persons and Estates. The *King* can have no Power but what is given him by *Law*; even the *supreme,* or *legislative Power* is bound, by the Rules of Equity, to govern by *Laws* enacted, and published in due Form; for what is not *legal* is *arbitrary.*

Q. *Why do Those, who endeavour to destroy the Authority and Independance of any of the Branches of the Legislature, subvert the Constitution?*
A. By the fundamental Laws of the Constitution

stitution, the free and impartial Consent of each of the three Members is necessary to the Being of a Law; therefore if the Consent of any of the Three is omitted, or obtained by Terror or Corruption, the Legislature is violated; and instead of Three there may be really one Branch of the Legislature.

Can'st Thou illustrate This by any Example?
The royal Authority, and That of the of Peers were both destroyed by the but of Commons, in the late civil War; the very Form of Government was annihilated.

Q. May not the Form of Government be kept, and yet the Constitution destroyed?
A. Yes. At Rome, there was a Senate, Consuls, and Tribunes of the People; as one might say King, Lords and Commons; yet the the Emperors were always despotick.

Q. How fell that great People into Slavery?
A. By Faction, Corruption, and standing Armies.

Q. But did ever any Parliament of this Nation give up the Liberty of the People?
A. Yes. A pack'd Parliament, in Richard II.'s Time, established by a Law the King's arbitrary Power, with Leave to name a Commission with Parliamentary Authority. Parliaments in Henry VIII's Time were Slaves to his Passions, and One gave the King a legislative Authority. There are many Instances of Parliaments making dangerous Steps towards the Destruction of Liberty.

Q. Who were the English Monarchs, most indulgent to the Liberties of the People?
A. The great King Alfred, who declar'd that the English Nation was as free as the Thoughts of Man; Edward I. Edward III. and Henry. V. who would not let his People swear to him till he had an Opportunity of swearing to them, at his Coronation. And Q. Elizabeth, who declar'd it by Law High Treason, during her Life, and a Praemunire afterwards, to deny the Power of Parliament in limiting and binding the Inheritance of the Crown.

Q. When were those Maxims of hereditary indefeazable Right and Prerogative, superior to Law, introduced?
A. In the Time of James I. who, by endeavouring to establish them, laid the Foundation of all the Miseries, which have since happened to his Family; and it is the greatest Security to the present Branch of it, that such Doctrines are by the present Establishment quite exploded.

Q. What do'st thou learn from those Histories?
A. That a King of this Realm, in the full Possession of the Affections of his People, is greater than any arbitrary Prince; and that the Nation can never be effectually undone but by a wicked Parliament; and lastly, to be thankful to God that under our present most gracious King, our Constitution is preserved entire, tho' many Circumstances call loudly for Vigilance.

Q. What are Those?
A. Such as have been the Fore-runners and Causes of the Loss of Liberty in other Countries; Decay of Virtue and publick Spirit, Luxury and Extravagance in Expence, Venality and Corruption, in private and publick Affairs.

Q. How is there a Decay of publick Spirit, when there's such a Desire to serve the Publick?
A. If a Desire to live upon the Publick be a publick Spirit, there is enough of it at this Time when Extravagance makes People crave more, and the Administration of a publick Revenue (perhaps treble what it was before the Revolution) enables the Crown to give more than formerly.

Q. What do'st thou fear from This?
A. That such as serve the Crown for Reward may in Time sacrifice the Interest of the Country to their Wants; that Greediness of publick Money may produce a slavish Complaisance, as long as the Crown can pay; and Mutiny, when it cannot.

Q. What woud'st thou do for thy Country?
A. I would die to procure its Prosperity; and I would rather that my Posterity were cut off, than be Slaves; but as Providence at present requires none of these Sacrifices, I content myself to discharge the ordinary Duties of my Station.

Q. What are the Duties of your Station?
A. To endeavour, as far as I am able, to preserve the publick Tranquility; to give my Vote for the Candidate whom I judge most worthy to serve his Country; for if on any partial Motive I should give my Vote for one unworthy, I should think myself justly chargeable with his Guilt.

Q. Thou hast perhaps but one Vote of 500, and the Member perhaps one of 500 more; then your Share of the Guilt is but small?
A. As He, who assists at a Murder, is guilty of Murder, so He, who acts the lowest Part in the enslaving his Country, is guilty of a greater Crime.

Q. Is enslaving one's Country a greater Crime than Murder?
A. Yes; inasmuch as the Murder of human Nature is a greater Crime than the Murder of a human Creature.

Q. Why is enslaving Mankind murdering human Nature?
A. Because Mankind in Slavery and Freedom is a different Sort of Creature; for Proof of This I have read what the Greeks were of old, and what they are now.

Q. What is become of the Heroes, Philosophers, Orators, and free Citizens of Greece?
A. They are now Slaves to the great Turk.

Q. The Scipio's and Cato's of Rome?
A. They sing now on the English Stage.

Q. Does not the Tranquillity, occasioned by absolute Monarchy, make the Country thrive?
A. Peace and Plenty are not the genuine Fruits of absolute Monarchy; for absolute Monarchies are more subject to Convulsions than free Governments, and Slavery turneth the fruitful Plains into a Desart; whereas Liberty, like the Dew from Heaven, fresheneth the barren Mountains. Though I have but one Vote, many Unites make a Number, and

and if *every Elector* should reason after the same Manner, that he has but *one*; what must become of the whole? A *Law* of great Consequence, and the Election of the *Member*, who voteth for *that Law*, may be both carried by *one Vote*. Great and Important Service for the Liberties of their Country have been done by *ordinary Men*. The Institution of the Tribunes of *Rome*, or the whole Power of the Commons, was owing to a Word spoke in Season by a *common Man*.

Q. *Is it not Lawful to take a Bribe from a Person otherwise worthy to serve his Country?*

A. No more than for a *Judge* to take a Bribe for a *righteous Sentence;* nor is it any more lawful to *corrupt*, than to *commit Evil that Good may come of it. Corruption* converts a good Action into Wickedness. Bribery of all Sorts is contrary to the Law of God; it involves in it the Sin of Perjury, and is besides the greatest Folly and Madness.

Q. *How is it contrary to the Law of God?*

A. The Law of God saith expresly, *Thou shalt not wrest Judgment; Thou shalt not take a Gift.* If it is a Sin in a *Judge*, it is much more in a *Lawgiver*, or an *Elector*; because the Mischiefs occasioned by the *first* reach only to Individuals; That of the *last* may affect whole Nations, and even the Generations to come. The Psalmist, describing the Wicked, saith, *his right Hand is full of Bribes.* The Prophet, describing the Righteous, tells us, *he shaketh his Hands from holding a Bribe. Samuel*, justifying his Innocence, appeals to the People, *of whose Hands have I taken a Bribe?* Then as to divine Vengeance, holy *Job* tells us, *that God shall destroy the Tabernacle of Bribery. Achan* and *Gehazi* were punished by God. Therefore He, that taketh a Bribe, may justly expect what is threatned in holy Writ; *He shall not prosper in his Way, neither shall his Substance continue; his Silver and Gold shall not be able to deliver him in the Day of the Wrath of the Lord.*

Q. *Why is He, that taketh a Bribe, guilty of Perjury?*

A. Because on a late act he is obliged to take the following Oath.

I A. B. *do swear (or being one of the People called Quakers, do solemnly affirm) I have not received, or had by my Self, or any Person whatsoever in Trust for me, or for my Use and Benefit, directly or indirectly, any Sum or Sums of Money, Office, Place or Employment, Gift or Reward, or any Promise or Security for any Money, Office, Employment or Gift, in order to give my Vote at this Election; and that I have not before been polled at this Election.*

Q. *What thinkest thou of Those, who are bribed by Gluttony and Drunkenness?*

A. That they are viler than *Esau*, who sold his Birth-right for a *Mess of Porridge.*

Q. *Why is taking a Bribe Folly or Madness?*

A. Because I must refund Ten-fold in *Taxes* of what I take in *Election;* and the Member who bought me has a fair Pretence to sell me.

Q. *What wilt thou say then to the Candidate, that offers thee a Bribe?*

A. *Thy Money perish with Thee! As Thou art now purchasing thy Seat in Parliament, I have just Reason to suspect that thou resolvest to sell thy Vote. What thou offerest, and what thou promisest may be the Price of the Liberties of my Country. I will not only reject thy Bribe with Disdain, but will vote against Thee.*

Q. *Is not the Justice of a King sufficient Security for the Liberty of a People?*

A. The People ought to have more Security for all that is valuable in the World than the Will of a *mortal and fallible Man.* A King of *Britain* may make as many Peers, and such as he pleaseth; therefore the last and best Security for our Liberties is a *H. of Commons genuine and independant.*

Q. *What meaneth a genuine H. of Commons?*

A. One, that is the true Issue of the People, and no Bastard.

Q. *How is a Bastard H. of Commons produced?*

A. When the People by *Terror, Corruption* or other indirect Means, chuse such as they otherwise would not chuse; when such as are fairly chosen, are not returned; when such as are returned, are turn'd out by partial Votes in controverted Elections, and others not fairly chosen set in their Places.

Q. *How may a H. of Commons be dependant?*

A. When the *Freedom of Voting* is destroy'd by Threatning, Promise, Punishments, and Rewards; by the open Forces of the Government, or the Insults of the Populace; but above all by private Influence.

Q. *Can a King have a more faithful Council than a* House of Commons, *which speaketh the Sense of the People?*

A. None; for They will not only give him impartial Council, but powerfully an chearfully assist him to execute what they advise.

Q. *What are the Marks of a Person, worthy to serve his Country in Parliament?*

A. The Marks of a *good Ruler* given in Scripture will serve for a *Parliament-man; Such as rule over you shall be Men of Truth, hating Covetousness; They shall not take a Gift; They shall not be afraid of the Face of a Man,* Deut. xvi. therefore I conclude, that the Marks of a *good Parliament-man* are Riches with Frugality; Integrity; Courage; being well-affected to the Constitution; Knowledge of the State of the Country; being prudently frugal of the Money, careful of the Trade, and zealous for the Liberties of the People; having stuck to the Interests of his Country in perilous Times, and being assiduous in Attendance.

Q. *Who is most likely to take a Bribe?*

A. He who *offereth one.*

Q. *Who to be frugal of the People's Money?*

A. He, who puts none of it in his *Pocket.*

Q. *Tom seem by This to be averse from chusing such as accept Places, and Gratuities from the* Crown; *Tour Reason for this Partiality?*

A. I am far from thinking that a Man may not serve his *King* and his *Country* faithfully at the same Time. Nay, their Interests are inseparable

parable. Mr. *Such an one*, my Lord's Steward, is a very honest Man; and yet, if I had any Affairs to settle with my Lord, I would chuse my *Neighbour* for a Referee rather than my *Lord's Steward*.

Q. *Why is* Frugality of the People's Money *so necessary at this Time?*

A. Because they have run out much, and are still much in Debt. My Father and I have paid our Share of *one hundred Millions*, and I have heard there are near *Fifty more to pay*. I grudge not this prodigious Expence, as far as it has been the necessary Price of *Liberty*; but, as it would grieve me much to see this Blessing ravish'd from me, which has cost me so dear; so on the other Hand I think it expedient to save, now the Government is settled.

Q. *Who are most careful of our Trade?*

A. Such as are willing to keep it from all vexatious Interruptions by *Inspections, entering into Houses, Seizures, Suits*, and the *Oppression of Tax-gatherers*, as much as possible; and to take off burthensome *Duties*.

Q. *As you have a Freehold, would you not be willing to be excus'd from paying 2s.* in the Pound?

A. No doubt but every *landed Man* would be glad to be free from paying *Two Shillings in the Pound*; but, at the same Time, I would not raise, *by another Tax*, two Shillings in the Pound, *nor* one Shilling in the Pound *for a Perpetuity*; for *Parliaments* who have no more to give, may be disappointed in the Redress of their *Grievances*. Besides, I would not be deluded by an Impossibility; for if my Tenant has any *new Tax* laid upon him, I am afraid he will not pay me so much Rent; so that the *new Tax* must still affect *Land*. Then it is impossible to raise by *Excises* what shall be equivalent to *two Shillings in the Pound*, without the Ruin of *Trade*; for the *Excises*, settled already, generally speaking, raise double the Duty upon the *People*, of what they bring in to the Government.

Q. *How can'st thou prove That?*

A. By Experience of *several Excises*, as of *Leather, Candles, Soap, &c.* Whatever is bro't into the Publick by *those Excises* is raised double upon the *People*; therefore if a *Million of Money*, or what is equivalent to *two Shillings in the Pound*, were levy'd by *Excise*, it would be *two Millions* upon the excis'd Commodities, which must destroy all Trade.

Q. *Why is a* Knowledge of the State of the Country a *necessary Qualification for a Parliament-man?*

A. Because there are many Corporations, that never saw their Members.

Q. *Is then a Writ of Parliament only a* Conge d'Elire *for a Bishop, where the King nominates?*

A. God forbid! The *Crown* is never to meddle in an *Election*.

Q. *Why is* assiduous Attendance *so necessary?*

A. Because if *Representatives* do not attend, I may have a Law impos'd upon Me, to which I had no Opportunity to Assent.

Q. *Then hast prudently and justly resolved to promote the publick Tranquillity, What are the Advantages then propos'd from That?*

A. All the Advantages resulting from political Society depend upon the *publick Tranquility*. Besides, by publick Tranquility, *Armies*, which are a Mark of Distrust of the Affection of the People, may be disbanded.

Q. *Do'st not thou love* Armies *in time of Peace?*

A. *Armies* have overturn'd the Liberties of most Countries, and all, who are well-affected to *Liberty*, ever hated them; because they are subject to an *implicit Obedience to their Officers*, and to a *Law of their own*; because they are so many lusty Men taken from *Work*, and maintain'd at an extravagant Expence upon the *Labour of the rest*; because they are many ways burthensome to the People in their *Quarters*, even under the best Discipline, especially in *dear Counties*; because there are so many Preferments in the Hands of *destroying Ministers*; and lastly, because the *King* will never be deny'd an *Army* as great as he pleaseth, when it is *necessary*.

Fog's Journal Sept. 22. Nº 255.

IN a former Paper, (see p. 366-7-8.) *Fog* gave an Account of a Progress made by Sir *Sydrophel* and his Man *Whaccum*. In this he entertains us with two Speeches, one he puts into the Mouth of Sir *Sydrophel*, the other into *Whaccum's*, both full of quackish Drollery, and intended to expose certain Characters, of Note. The chief of what is *new* in it, is where Sir *Sydrophel* says, *My Friends, I own I have been a little scar'd by the thing I most despised, that is Justice, and no Wonder, for several whom I took to be my Friends begin to forsake me, but I shall learn by it how to treat Persons hereafter.* Experto crede Roberto. *Cartouch always enter'd a new Man with a Murder, to prevent his impeaching, and had these People been well dipp'd in Mud with us, they would not have deserted. I have try'd the force of Money to get new Men, but can't brag much of Success, having gain'd but one, whom if a Man had found in the Streets, he'd hardly think worth picking up.* —— *If Bribery loses its Force, Heaven help the Righteous.* But we cannot inlarge here, having Subjects of more Importance.

Universal Spectator, Sept. 22. Nº 259.

An Example for young Ladies.

MR *Stonecastle*, at the Request of *Sophronia*, whose only Sister has discover'd a Design of marrying a *Serving Man*, gives a Lecture on the Folly of young Ladies, who, by this Means often ruin themselves, and disgrace their Families; of which he gives an Instance.

Lindamira, a young Lady, with her
Fortune

Fortune in her Hands, married her Father's Footman; enamour'd with her *Adonis,* she laugh'd at the *Remonstrances* of her *Friends,* and the *Witticisms* of her *Enemies*; the *Honey-moon* was not half run out, before he began to exert the *Authority* of a *Husband*; affronted her before Company; would suffer no *Man* to see her, and would have commenc'd Amours with all the *Ladies* that did: Her Female Acquaintance disdaining her Husband's Impudence forsook her; and when she had been long abus'd by her *Husband,* entirely abandon'd by her Friends, She broke her *Heart* with *Grief* and *Shame.*

Grubstreet Journal, Sept. 27. N° 198.

THE Initial Entertainment is entitled Part of Mr JOHN GABRIEL's *State of the Nation.* Chap. XIV. *A Dissertation upon a Pin's Head.* We have already given several Specimens of this Writer's Wit and Humour, (see p. 997, 1067, Vol. II. and 27 Vol. III.)

§ Dear Mr BAVIUS,
Battersea, Sept. 5. 1733.

YOUR publishing my Abilities some Months ago, in cutting People for the Simples, has brought me so much Business, that I was obliged to learn my Daughter *Penelope* to cut; by whose Assistance we have heaped up a comfortable Sum of Money; and I know no better way to requite your Kindness than by offering you my Daughter in Marriage, with a Fortune of fifteen-under a pound, to be paid you on the Wedding Day.

I must beg your Assistance to acquaint two female Correspondents, *Julia* and *Fidelia,* that I pity their Case——*Julia's* Husband, because she proves fruitful, lies in the Garret; not considering that Children will be born some times, whethether they are got or no.—— *Fidelia's* Coxcomb teizes her to Death, because, she is not with Child: Whereas she assures me she does every thing an honest Woman should to bring it to pass; but he is such an eternal Smoaker, that he dries himself up, and takes so many Whets in a Morning, that he spoils his Appetite for a Dinner; and stays out so late of a Night; that she is generally asleep when he comes to Bed; and he so boozy, that he hardly knows a Hawk from a Hand-saw——Yet this is the Man that finds Fault with his Wife, because she is not——as I told you before. Now, both these Men must be cut for the Simples, or they are utterly ruined.

URSULA MAMBRINO.

Free Briton, Sept. 27. N° 202.

MR *Walsingham* vindicates the *Dissenting Teachers* from an Aspersion thrown on them in a Paragraph of News in *Fog's Journal* Sept. 1. where 'tis asserted "they will never be *thoroughly Satisfy'd,* till they get into Possession of ALL the *Cathedrals and Churches of this* as well as of our *neighbouring* Kingdom (*Ireland*".)

This *charitable Paragraph* is the more remarkable, as this *very Writer,* a few weeks before, *testified* his *great Satisfaction* of the *Dissenters* Behaviour, and that *High Church* had taken both *Quakers* and *Presbyterians* into its Bosom, as worthy of its *affectionate* Care. (See p. 316 H)

Let the *Dissenters* compare these several Declarations from the *same Party,* and consider, how far *such Men* who *sollicit their Votes* to get into Parliament, are fit to be trusted.

London Journal. Sept. 22. N° 743.

I Know (continues Osborne *in this third Address to the Dissenters*) nothing can induce you to act contrary to your *Obligations* as *Englishmen* and *Protestants*; yet I have been jealous of *some of you* left *Resentment* against Persons might have carried them to Actions detrimental to their *true Interest,* which consists in *adhering closely* to the *Court Whigs* against all their Enemies:

The Gentlemen in the *Opposition,* indeed, put it all upon the Conduct of *One Gentleman,* and make, very *unjustly* his *whole Conduct* rest upon *one Action.* But should this be a Reason with the *Dissenters* to join *Tories* and *Jacobites,* and break the *Whig Interest?*

I own, with the *Craftsman,* that the *Gentleman* did vote against the *Repeal.* I *then* thought him wrong in doing it, and I think so *now.* What then? Is any Man free from Error? Who did the reputed *Patron* of the *Craftsman* vote with at that Time? Was He *out* of, or *in* Power? Was He for or against the Repeal? *Let him who is without Sin cast the first Stone.* Do these *Writers* pretend to talk against the *Gentleman* for being against the Repeal, when in the same Paper they declare, "They don't mention the Repeal of the Test, with a Design it should *ever be repealed*; but only to expose the Insolence of those who plead a Sort of Title to the Favour of the *Dissenters.*"

Which

What *Cowards* and *Slaves* are these Men to the *Tories?* What *blundering Reasoners*, to induce you to join them, against a *Gentleman*, who hath not yet obliged you with the Repeal of the *Test*, by *declaring*, They think *it ought never to be repealed*. As to the *Gentleman* you are desired to hate, I never knew *One* in publick Life, more a *Whig out of Power*; or, a *Minister* more a *Whig in Power* than himself: No, not the Minister who *repealed* the *Occasional and Schism Acts*; for they dar'd not do it till they were *driven*, near 300 *Whig* Members sent for Secretary *Craggs* to the *Bedford Head*, and told him *they would have them repealed.* So that if he has *err'd* at any Time towards you, it may be forgot; especially when you consider, he has been a *Friend to the Dissenters* thro' the Course of his Life; and has bestowed more *Places of Honour and Profit* upon them, than *some Church Whigs* will allow to fall to their Share. He is also *disposed* to repeal the *Test*, and will do it as soon as the *general Interest* will permit. There are not the same *political, publick, or national Reasons* for repealing it *here* as in *Ireland*, the Ministry therefore, intend to do that first, as in that Kingdom there are 8 or 9 *Papists* to one *Protestant*. His Majesty, therefore, 'tis said, has given *Instructions* to the Lord-Lieutenant to promote the *Repeal of the Test* in that Kingdom; and may be assured, that when good Policy allows it, the same *Justice* will be done you in *England*. However that may happen, Let us remember, that voting with the Court Whigs, is not voting *for a single Man*, as is given out to deceive you, but to keep up the *Whig Interest*, 'tis voting for our *Country* and *Liberties*, against *Persons* who stand ready to *devour* us, and to put an *End* to that Happiness which nothing can put an End to, *but a Division among our selves.*

To conclude: Our great Security and Felicity, as *Englishmen* and *Protestants*, depend upon our *prudent and just Behaviour* at the next Election; I doubt not yours, nor *the Success* of the Day.

F. OSBORNE.

The **Craftsman**, Sept. 29. No. 378.

MR *D'anvers*, in answer to Mr *Walsingham's* incoherent Justification of his Patron in relation to his Conduct towards the *Dissenters* (See p. 474.) says, he has made Enquiries, and proved from a Deduction of his Behaviour towards them, that he hath no more Right to their Favour than even *Those*, who first projected and passed the *Schism Act* against them. At the same time I acknowledged, says *D'anvers*, he spoke and voted against the *Schism Bill*.

My Assertion was, *That his Patron opposed the Repeal of the* Schism Act, without entering into the *Motives of his Conduct*, (See p. 426 B) and he engaged to convict me of Falshood in that Assertion; but instead of That, we are told, that he did not oppose the Bill meerly on Account of the *Schism Act*; but as a complicated Bill, and then gives a Detail of the Proceedings of Parliament in Queen *Anne's* Reign, *concerning the Rise of the* Schism Bill. But what is all this to the Purpose?

It is plain, at least, from Mr *W.'s* own way of Reasoning, that his *Patron* was against the Repeal of the *Occasional Conformity Act*; and therefore let the *Dissenters* consider how far they can depend on seeing the *Test Acts* repealed by the *very Man*, who thought the *Bill*, already passed in their Favour, *contained more than it ought*, (See p. 475. H)

That the *Dissenters* themselves had formerly the same Opinion of *this Gentleman's* Conduct, with Relation to the Repeal of the *Schism Act*, appears from a Pamphlet publish'd about that time, entitled a *Letter from some* Protestant *Dissenting Laymen, in Behalf of the whole Body, to their Friends in the* British *Parliament* &c. The Authors, after acknowledging the Services of Mr *W—le* in opposing the *Schism Act*, when first brought into Parliament, go on to the *Protest* of several Lords against it. Some of whom are hinted at as having forgot the Force of their own Reasoning. And then proceed thus, *It is very strange, that those very Persons, who in the late Reign so warmly opposed the passing of penal Laws against Protestant Dissenters, should now shew an utter Aversion to* REPEALING THEM? *especially since we are not conscious of any Provocation on our Part, that can excuse their renouncing their old Friendship. To have spared their Eloquence, when they found it was like to go for nothing, would have been a Crime somewhat pardonable; but what Apology can be made for Men, who threaten to open their Mouths against a Cause, which they but of late Years espoused with the greatest seeming Earnestness? or how account for the Sincerity of their former Zeal*

Zeal? This is exactly agreeable to what I formerly quoted from the *Character of an Independant Whig.* (See p. 426. C)

They go on: *One of the most prevailing Arguments we may suppose is, Their insufferable Ambition and Avarice could not be satisfied, without engrossing to themselves the whole Trust and Power of the Nation. This made them, when they had the Reins of the Administration in their own Hands, for keeping all Things upon the same narrow Bottom as formerly; lest, if there was any Relaxation of Terms and* Penalties, *there should be too many sharers in the Benefits, which make Men cry aloud for those Distinctions, which enrich, and aggrandize* one Party of Protestants, *and disable all others from serving either themselves or their Country.* Now their *Pride* has driven them out of the Ministry, they are furiously bent upon *Revenge* to clog and over-power it.

Here *D'anvers* puts the ministerial Advocates in mind, that *Ambition, Avarice, Disappointment and Revenge* were as strongly charged on their *Patron,* when a *Country Gentleman,* even by the *Dissenters,* as they can be against any Gentlemen in Opposition to him.

It is likewise insinuated in *this Pamphlet,* that Bishop HOADLEY was obliged to the *same Gentleman and his Adherents* for the Favour of setting the *Convocation* on his Back, to deter the *Ministry* from relieving the *Dissenters;* upon which *our Authors* make this Observation.

"This mean Malice of justifying their *former Neglect of us by directly opposing our Interest,* ought to be so far from deterring truly great Men from attempting to relieve us, that it should animate Them with just Resentment against THOSE, who would make their most laudable Actions unpopular, and tye up their Hands by the noisy, ill-grounded Clamours of the *Church's Danger.* Bring but *this Business* once into the House, and leave their *own Shame* to keep Them silent at least. Even the *Men,* whose Side They now strengthen, should they openly oppose *this Affair,* will with Contempt hear every Speech, that contradicts their *Declarations,* when it was thought necessary to oppose THEM, and court Us; and doubt not that their *own Fears* will keep Them from voting against all their *former Arguing.*

Mr *W's* Apology for his Patron is, That he acted in Conjunction with the late D. of *Devonshire* and E. *Cowper.*

It is true indeed, the late D. of *Devonshire* generally concurred with this *Gentleman's* Measures, whether in, or out of Power. It it likewise true, that the late E. *Cowper* opposed the *Bill* under Consideration; for it contained not only a Repeal of the *Conformity* and *Schism Acts,* but likewise of the *Sacramental Test.* He declared; *He would readily give his Vote for repealing the* Schism Act, nor objected to the Repeal of the *Conformity Act;* whereas it does not appear, that Mr *W's Patron* made any such Discrimination; but warmly opposed the *Bill in general,* Besides, E. *Cowper* seems improperly introduced as this Gentleman's *Compurgator,* whose Measures he opposed to his dying Day.

Mr *W.* tells us, Mr *P——y himself spoke and voted in the same manner.* But where does Mr *W.* find this? In all the Accounts published of the principal Speakers both *for* and *against* the *Repeal,* amongst the *latter* the Names of Mr *Horatio W——le* and Mr *Robert W——le* are particularly mentioned; Mr *P——y's* not at all. I hope you did not receive your Information from the *same Person,* who gave you an Account of Mr *P——y's tampering with* a Juryman *about two Years ago in the* Exchequer *Coffee-house;* which you promised to prove by undoubted Evidence, but have not yet made your Words good tho' often defy'd to do it.

This is all I shall say to *Walsingham* who is so utterly abandon'd to all Sense of Shame, that He will not scruple *to assert any Thing, even the* MOST NOTORIOUS FALSHOODS, *in order to serve a present Purpose.* I shall therefore leave Him to wallow in that Mire, for which he was designed by Nature, and in which only He seems to take any Delight.

I cannot conclude without acknowledging, that though Mrs *Osborne* is certainly a very silly, prattling, old Gentlewoman, yet she seems to have some Regard for *Veracity,* and very fairly gives up her *Patron,* as to the *Repeal of the* SCHISM ACT. I shall therefore, in my next Paper, make some Observations on what she hath advanc'd upon this Argument, with Relation to the *Dissenters.*

London *Journal.* Sept. 29, No. 744.

A Judicious writer observes, that Q. *Elizabeth* never *tugged* with the People, nor the People with her, about *Prerogative* and *Liberty;* but the *Stuarts* did, and their Reigns were *unhappy* and *ignominious.*

We live in a Reign quite different, in which the Prince never struggled with the People for any *Prerogative* or *Power* ; yet the People are *warmly struggling* with him for what they call *Liberty*. His Majesty seems perfectly satisfied with the *legal Rights* of the Crown ; but there are certain *factious Leaders* of the People, who endeavour to *wrest some of them* out of his Hands: But the *People*, who are not *interested* in their Pursuits, desire nothing more than to be governed, as they are, by *Laws of their own making*.

The *Pretence* of the Opposition is *Liberty* ; But surely in vain is the Net spread to catch you ; for you are a *wise* and *honest* People,

The Game they are playing, is to *deprive* the King of all *real Power*. For Instance, they are always declaring against *Places in the King's Gift*, which they seem endeavouring to put into the Power of Parliament, or a COMMITTEE OF SAFETY: for they say, we cannot have *our Constitution* preserved, while the *King* can dispose of Places. But if the King had not *many* and *great Places* in his Disposal, the *Monarchy of England* could not stand ; the *Balance* would be destroy'd, and be all on the *Common's* Side, and all *Power* would be in them.

A *House of Commons* may save us against King and Lords ; a *House of Lords* may save us (as to their *immortal Honour* they did in the *Close* of a late Reign) against the Prince and Commons ; and the *King and Lords* may save us against the *Commons*: For the *Commons* may turn *Tyrants*, and subvert the Constitution.

When the *House of Commons*, in 1641. obtain'd of the King to pass an Act, that they should not be dissolved without their *own Consent*, the *Constitution* was then *dissolved*: And Ld *Dorset*, who met the King next Day in the Park, call'd him very properly, *Fellow Subject* ; for he was no longer *King*, there being two *Co-equal* and *Co-ordinate Powers* in the Kingdom.

The King may be deprived of so much of his *real Power*, as not to be able to make use of his *Negative* Voice ; which would have been the Case of K. *Wm.* had he been without *Dependencies* and *Places* in his Gift : And, had that been the Case, most of the *House of Commons* in his Reign, would have sent him from whence he came ; *restored* the *abdicated King*, and so *finished our Slavery* beyond Redemption.

Our Security consists in the *Three Powers* being able to *refuse* and to *oblige*, as the Reason of Things require. And tho'

this may sometimes cause little *Contentions* and *Struggles* between the several Powers ; yet better be content with those Difficulties, than be in the Hands of any *Single Power* upon Earth.

The *Faction* is likewise angry at the *Riot Act* ; and so may *Highwaymen* for being *restrained* by Law from robbing, and may say, They are nail'd down to *passive Obedience* too, and can't *rob*, but they must do it at the Peril of being *hang'd*. Suppose this *Riot-Act* had existed before the *Revolution* ; does Mr *D'anvers* think it would have hindred the bringing it about? Or, that those *brave honest* Men, who did not fear an Army of 30,000 Troops on *Hounslow-Heath* or *Salisbury-Plain* would have been afraid of a Constable reading a Proclamation?

The *Universal Spectator,* Sept. 29 No. 260

PHilogynes, a profess'd Admirer of the *Fair Sex*, bestows high Encomiums on the Ladies, and recommends an Essay written in their *Defence*, by *J. Bland*, Physician, in which the *Doctor* has prov'd to *Demonstration*, that their *Reason* and their *Passions* are dealt out by *Providence* in a more *exquisite Proportion* and *Mixture* than the Colours of *Red* and *White* on their *Cheeks* ; that their *Affections* rise and fall with Degrees of *Softness* far beyond the *Motion* of their *own Breasts* ; and *that* the most *beautiful Shape* bears no *Analogy* to the *Regularity* of their *Judgment*.

By way of Contraste to This, the Spectator inserts a Letter, signed G. R. which exposes several little *Foibles* in the *Fair*, which, as they are very common, prove that Sex is not all *Perfection*.

The *Weekly Miscellany* of this Date has some further Strictures against the celebrated Mr *Gordon*, and besides something curious, under the *Literary Article*, in Defence of Mr *Buckley's* Edition of THUANUS, a pretty Poem on the Death of a *Parson's only Cow*, which being long, we cannot insert this Month.

FOG gives us a Discourse, chiefly extracted from the Writings of M. *Barbeyrac*, designed to shew, that all things are not just, which are lawful ; and that the Laws want mending ; a Subject he has often treated of before, which therefore we shall entirely omit.

We have postponed also some other Pieces that don't claim an immediate Regard, to enlarge upon those which do.

Weekly Miscellany, Sept. 22. No. 41.
Remarks on Mr Gordon's *Translation of*
Tacitus.

IN giving an Account of his Work, Mr
Gordon complains of *Coldness* and want
of *Force* in our English *Language*; under
this and *other Difficulties*, he has, he says,
attempted a Translation that should represent not only the *Sense* but the *Spirit*,
and Eloquence, and Turns of Tacitus, by
*drawing the English Idiom as near as
possible to that of the Latin,—by leaving
the beaten Road, dropping Particles, trans-
posing Words, and beginning a Sentence
where it is usual to end it.* For Example, When *Tacitus* says *Bellum ei Tempe-
state nullum*, Mr *Gordon* will not translate,
There was then no War abroad, but, *War
at that time there was none.* Domi res
tranquillæ, he will not render, *All things
were quiet at Home*—but, *in profound
Tranquillity were Affairs at Rome.* What
an easy thing is *Eloquence,* if it is only
ringing the Changes upon Words, and beginning a Sentence at the *wrong End!*
The *Latin* Order of placing Words gives,
indeed, a Majesty and Solemnity to poetical Compositions; and even in *Prose*,
it has its Beauties, when *judiciously* and
sparingly used. But to be perpetually *ecchoing* back the Latin Order (as Mr *Gordon* does) is a Sneer upon the Original,
as an affected, servile Imitation is nauſeous and disgustful.

Mr *Gordon* owns, that *this manner of
Writing would be strange, and even ridiculous, in plain or familiar Subjects,* but
adds, that *where the Subject is high and
solemn, there must be a Conformity of
Stile.* How this way of writing agrees
with Historical Narrations, appears in
Milton's English History, the Stile of
which, Mr *Gordon* complains, is harsh
and *uncouth.* However, *Milton* made a-
mends for this by a certain Justness, Accuracy, and Manliness in his Periods,
which is not to be found in Mr *Gordon*,
who has blended the *Stiffness* of the *Pedant* with the *Negligence* or *Foppery* of
French Writers. If this was a Fault in
Milton as an *Author*, it must be equally
culpable in a *Translator*, and *worse*, as it
is an Injury to the Original. An Author
of Sense will treat familiar Subjects in a
familiar way; from which the more a
Translator departs, the less he expresses
of the Author's *Spirit* and *Genius.* This
is the Case of *Tacitus.* His Stile is short
and nervous, not lofty and solemn; un-

(*Gent. Mag.* Vol. 3. No. xxxiii.)

less in his Speeches, which are more a-
dapted to move the Passions, than represent the Facts. One Instance will suffice
to shew how thorough a *Bigot* Mr *Gordon* is to *his own way.* It is a short Account of the Empress *Julia,* given by
Tacitus, Lib. 1. Cap. 53. and translated
by Mr *Gordon,* Vol. 1. P. 40.

Daily Courant, Sept. 19. against
the *Craftsman,* 8. (see p. 469.) says, it is
no wonder *D'anvers* quarrels with the
Riot Act, and other Laws made in the
late Rebellion, to secure the Peace of the
Nation; since some of the Authors of
that Paper were engaged therein. As
for the *Army,* a noble Ld, whom he hath
extoll'd much of late, was last Session of
Opinion it ought rather to be augmented than reduced.

Daily Courant, Sept. 25. turns the Tables upon the *Craftsman,* in relation to his
allegorical Account of the *Game of Chess*; and
tells us, a certain bold Player, (Ld *B—e*)
once play'd for no less than his *Life* and *Fortune,* and lost it by losing his *Queen,* yet has the
Vanity to engage the best Player in *England.*

*Several Printed Papers have been trans-
mitted to us, containing Queries and Addresses to the Freeholders of certain Counties on the Contest already begun for Members of Parliament. They are wrote with
a good deal of Spirit, and it might be expected we should give some Extracts from
them; but as they have been sufficiently
publish'd in the Counties they relate to, and
turn mostly on the Conduct of the Candidates,
or their Party, in Parliament, with Regard to Proceedings which have been well
argued in the Debates, and so often canvass'd in other political Parts of our Book,
we have the less Occasion to enlarge on
those Subjects; especially since we have
given such a long Extract from the Free-
holder's Political Catechism.—Voting for
bringing in the* Excise-Bill *continues the
general and chief Objection to one Set of
Candidates, who on the other hand as in
p. 464, 465, recriminate, and defend that
Scheme in the best manner they can: But
we observe, Sir R—tt S—eb—y C—tt—n,
Bart, Candidate for C—shire, excuses his
voting for bringing in the Tobacco Bill,
by pleading he did it, that the Merit of
the Scheme might be consider'd thoroughly in Parliament, to which his Conduct
the Freeholders ought not in Reason to
object, especially as he voted against the
Army and Salt Bill, the only Points which
appear'd to him to affect their Interests.*

The

The CONTEST.

A London Eclogue, *in Imitation of the seventh Pastoral of Virgil.*

Facundi calices quem non fecere disertum. Hor.

BEneath a *Tun*, whose vast capacious Sides,
Glitt'ring with Gold the *drunken God* be-
 strides,
Beneath this *Tun* two *jolly Song sters* lay,
And with a Genial Bowl chas'd *Care* away:
Both Sons of *London,* both alike inspir'd
With Rival Arts, and Thirst of Glory fir'd:
Resolv'd before an *Umpire* to contest,
Who could the *longest* sing, and sing the *best:*
Tom Piper, Warbling Charmer of the Street,
Next to the *Tun* as *Umpire* claim'd his Seat.
Thither, by Chance or Fortune led astray,
Unknowing where I rov'd, I took my Way:
My Way *of them* I ask'd;—but with a Smile
Piper reply'd, — Pray, Sir, sit down a while;
Be free from *Care*, as you are free from *Harm,*
And tho' our Hut is *homely,* it is *warm:*
Stay 'till the Crowd from out the *Streets* are gone,
Then reel *Majestik* home, for all the Street's
 your *own:*
But lest unhappy you again should *stray,*
Jack with his *friendly Torch* shall lead the Way.
What could I do? — Nor *Sue* nor *Phillis* nigh
To guard my Pockets with observing Eye:
What cou'd I do? — Silence the Swains invoke,
In short I risk'd my *Safety* for a *Joke.*
To sing alternately the *Rivals* chose,
Chauntclear these *Rymes* rehears'd, and *Rancus*
 those.

Chauntclear.

(*a*) *Ægidian Nymphs,* in Cells or Garrets hear:
Inspire my *Theme,* and make my Music *clear:*
Next *Warbletini* let me be profess'd,
For *you'll* allow that he can sing the best:
But if my *wild Ambition* soars too high,
Aiming to grasp at *Immortality:*
For ever I resign my tuneful Task,
And hang my *String of Ballads* on the Cask.

Rancus.

(*b*) *Hockleian Tenths,* inspire my rising Mind,
With *Wreaths* of *Juniper* my Temples bind:
Tho' *Warbletini* may deny me Praise,
My *Wreath's* as honour'd as if made of *Bays:*
This *Chaplet* shall protect me from his Tongue,
Lest by some secret Charm it marr my Song.

C.] This Silken *Handkerchief* which here I wear,
(My first Reward for singing at the Fair)
I offer, *Warbletini,* to thy Shrine,
To speed my Song, and make my Notes divine:
Each Nymph shall *Warbletini* then adore,
Admire thy *tuneful Lays,* and own thy *vocal*
 Pow'r.

(*c*) *R.*] O *Stokes* renown'd, this *Holland Shirt*
 I've on,
(At Country Fair by dint of Valour won)
Accept; for as from *Thee* I *learnt* that Art,
'Tis but the Tribute of a grateful Heart:
But should *succeeding Honours* crown the *Fight,*
Succeeding Songs shall crown the Day and Night:

(*a*) A Poetical Epithet for St *Giles's.* (*b*) Of Hockley
in the Hole. (*c*) A *Sutton* Prize Fighter.

While you in *Triumph* pass, each Nymph I'll
 charm,
With Tales of *conquer'd Chiefs* their Souls alarm
'Till they in *Raptures* lost, shall bless thy
 conqu'ring Arm.

C.] O fair (*d*) *Hoppæa* with thy *tripping Feet,*
Neat as a *Milkmaid,* as a *Milkmaid sweet;*
Come with thy charming Mein, and graceful Art,
Come to thy *Chauntclear,* and rejoice his Heart;
Come when fatigu'd, coroding Cares abound,
And make my *midnight Hours* with *Jollitry* go
 round.

R.] O *Cynderaxa,* may I seem to you
Loathsome and hateful as a *Toupee Beau,*
Who with short quick-fetch'd Steps trips fast
 along,
And as he *paces* murmurs out a *Song.*
Such may I be, if that when you're not near,
An *Hour* seems not a *Day,* a *Day* a *Year.*

C.] *Te sacred Liquors,* moving easy sleep,
Te Hogsheads which those *sacred Liquors* keep,
Fend me from *Cold:* The Summer Warmth is
 o'er,   [Shore.
And sharp bleak Winds come whistling on the

R.] When tir'd with Dirt, and wet with Rain
 and Mire,
This Hospitable Shop affords a Fire:
Me Wind nor Weather can no more affright,
Than (*e*) *Divers* fear the *Dusk,* or *Thieves* the
 Night.

C.] Our Bowls with Floods of *Juniper* are
 crown'd,
Berries distill'd lie, scatter'd o'r the ground,
And smiling *Bounty* strows her Gifts around:
But should poor *Filch* at the *next Sessions* die,
Tuns might unheeded flow till they were *dry.*

R.] Tho' *hoarse* my *Voice,* tho' *spent* my little *store,*
Tho' *Gin* deny'd her *all-solacing* Pow'r:
Shou'd but my *Chloe* once recross the *Main,*
And bless my solitary Haunts again;
No *Care,* no Want my Quiet should destroy,
But all around me wear the *Face* of *Joy.*

C.] *Majestic* stalks the *Dutchess* in *Brocade,*
Neat Dimety adorns the *rural Maid;*
The *jolly Hostess* in her *Sattin* flares,
And *Drury Nymph* in *Velvet* shows her *Airs.*
Clean, tho' not *gay,* tho' not *new* all her *own,*
My *Phillis* charms in a plain *Linnen-Gown;*
And while my *Phillis* will her *Linnen* wear,
No *Dimety* shall please, no *Sattin* flare,
Nor *Velvet* nor *Brocade* with *Linnen* shall
 compare.

R.] Songs on *Excise* near *Change* meet most
 Reward,
And *loving Ditties* best suit *Paul's Church-yard:*
But shou'd my *Chloe,* e'er to ease my Pain,
Revisit this forsaken Clime again:
To her those *Songs* shall yield which bring *Reward,*
And those soft Ditties *prais'd* in *Paul's Church-*
 yard.

These were their *Rymes,* which I at leisure pen'd,
When bold rough *Rancus* did in vain contend;
From *Street* to *Street* now *Chauntclear* charms
 the Town,
And with *unrival'd Ditty* charms *alone.*

(*d*) This Name seems taken from Petit *Assemblies*
or Hops. (*e*) Pickpockets.

To a certain LADY *intolerable* PERT.

CÆLIA's the prettiest, sprightliest thing,
　Still frolicksome and gay ;
She's sure to blame whate'er you do,
　To laugh whate'er you say.

If for some Time you gravely talk,
　Her Hints will say 'tis dull ;
If loosely, quick she takes her Fan,
　And smartly raps your Scull.

Then if you fly 'tis Cowardice,
　To fear a Female's Hand ;
But if you turn, and romp, still worse,
　That Female to withstand.

She'll say ten thousand crossing Things,
　Poor STREPHON to provoke ;
And cry, though still he vows and swears,
　Yes, Sir, you Men can joke.

Yet hope not, my mistaken Fair,
　To wound us with those Darts ;
Their Points soon kindling into Fire,
　Not pierce, but melt our Hearts.

DAMON *and* DELIA.

DAMON.

TELL me, my *Delia*, tell me why
　My kindest, fondest looks you fly.
What means this cloud upon your brow ?
Have I offended, tell me how ?
Some change has happen'd in your heart,
Some rival there has stole a part ;
Reason these fears may disapprove,
But yet I fear, because I love.

DELIA.

First tell me, *Damon*, why to-day
At *Belvidera's* feet you lay ?
Why with such warmth her charms you prais'd
And every trifling beauty rais'd,
As if you meant to let me see
Your flattery is not all for me ;
Alas ! too well your Sex I know,
Nor was so weak to think you true.

Damon.] Unkind, my falshood, to upbraid
When your own orders I obey'd .
You bid me try by this deceit,
The notice of the world to cheat,
And hide beneath another name,
The secret of our mutual flame.

Delia.] *Damon*, your *Prudence* I confess,
But let me wish it had been less.
Too well the lover's part you play'd,
With too much art your court you made ;
Had it been only art, your *eyes*
Wou'd not have join'd in the disguise.

Damon.] Ah cease thus idly to complain,
And rack thy tender breast in vain ;
While thus at fancy'd wrongs you grieve,
To me a real pain you give.

Delia.] Tho' well I might your truth distrust,
My foolish heart believes you just.
Reason this faith may disapprove,
But I believe, because I love.

EPIGRAM ON a Lady, who despised DRYDEN's
Fables, and the Comedy of the *Drummer* ;
while she praised HAYWOOD's *Novels* and
the Farce called *The Devil of a Wife.*

I Tell of a Lady, (her first name is KITTY),
　Who never was wise, nor will ever be witty ;
Yet a critic, a a wit, in her voice, in her thought ;
As a wit she can scold, as a critic find fault.
As true she can spell (for deep learning her guft is)
As a young tonpce lord, or an old country justice.
To her DRYDEN's Fables are stuff of no use ;
HAYWOOD's Novels have charms——they're so
　charmingly loose !
For ADDISON's Drummer, her wit never spares it ;
Like her neighbour's good name, all to pieces she tears it
Tho' the poor drumming Devil to her has no merit ;
Yet the Devil of a Wife is a Devil of spirit.
Like to like! she's a wit, she's the Farce to the life ;
For the wit of a woman is——the Devil of a wife.

The Happy LOVER's *Invocation to* Night.

NIGHT ! to lovers joys a friend,
　Haste, and thy Assistance lend ;
Hasten, goddess, lock up day,
Bring the willing Nymph away ;
She comes, so kind, so killing fair,
'Tis more than mortal man can bear ;
Her wanton look, her thin attire,
Her ev'ry motion fans my fire ;
She gives a loose to love and me,
She suffers all she does not see,
O night ! how much I owe to thee !

A Dialogue between SLY *and* LOVETT.
At FIELDING's Booth at *Bartholomew* Fair.

S. 　SWEET, if you love me, smiling turn,
　　　Smiling turn, smiling turn :
Sweet, &c.
　Ah! Let me take a thousand slips
　From those dear balmy ruby lips,
　　And gently slip into thy——
　Smiling turn, smiling turn,
　　And let me slip into thy favour.
L. *Pray now give o'er, you court in vain,*
　Pray give o'er, pray give o'er :
　　Pray now, &c.
　And yet so warm was ev'ry kiss,
　An earnest of such future bliss,
　　I fear at last he'll——
　Pray be gone——pray now stay ;
　　I fear at last he'll gain my favour.
S. *Thus let me press thee close, my dear,*
　Close, my dear, close my dear :
　　Thus let me, &c.
L. *Fie, now you make me blush,, I sweat ;*
　Fie for shame ; fie for shame :
　　Fie now, &c.
S. *Ah! do not frown upon me now,*
L. *I feel I'm growing kind, I vow.*
S. *Since you this kind embrace allow.*
L. *O dear, he has so mov'd me now.*
S. *O let me slip into thy——*
L. *I fear he'll slip into my——*
S. *Kiss, my dear.*
L. *Fie for shame.*
S. 　{ *And let me slip into thy favour.* } together
L. 　{ *I fear he'll slip into my favour.* }

The MODERN GOLIAH: Or HERO of HEROES.
A PANEGYRIC, humbly addreſs'd to the
venerable and worthy ſet of *Free-thinkers.*

SING the Hero in ſtrains ſo ſublime, O my muſe,
  That my patrons the ſong may attentive peruſe;
The Hero, who, fir'd with a generous diſdain,
Of a mind that's enſlaved, bravely ſhakes off the chain:
So elate are his thoughts, and ſo high his deſires,
He abhors the low hopes, which CHRIST's goſpel
    inſpires;
Tea ſo high, that he ſcorns to have ought in his whole
Compoſition ſo abject and mean as a ſoul;
And himſelf, with his friends, always greatly ſuggeſts
The glory of living and dying like beaſts:
To which lofty conceits he does proſelytes win
By the wonderful powerful of a ſneer and a grin:
And when theſe allies fail him, calls in to's relief
The aid of rhetorical mutton and beef;
The diſputants ſlyly engages to dine,
When his thoughts to each gueſt appear noble
    and fine,
—For what can reſiſt a perſuaſive ſurloin?
Through mazes they wander, and often in vain,
Who endeavour to come at the heart by the brain;
Whereas he to that place, cunning fox! has in truth,
Always found the way eaſier by far from the mouth.
When in logical forms, mens aſſent we demand,
Some won't be convinc'd, and ſome can't underſtand;
But doctrines bid fair for engaging all hearts,
When prov'd by ſyllogiſtical chickens and tarts.
Thus to conqueſts we ſee they've but ſlender pretence,
Who truſt ſuch dull weapons as reaſon and ſenſe:
But on him, oh! what triumph, what victory waits,
Who is aided by advocate diſhes and plates!
And whoſe punch-bowl too is ſuch a notable elf,
That it reaſons and argues, as well as—himſelf!
I ſhould now, to conclude my detail of his merit,
Chant forth his moſt wonderful courage and ſpirit,
Who in war with his maker dares fearleſs engage,
And undauntedly ſneers at omnipotent rage;
Who adventures (ſtout heroe!) to call God a liar,
And ſmiles at the thoughts of unquenchable fire;
Who mocks at ſuch fools as with fears are poſſeſs'd,
And thinks to be damn'd, a moſt excellent jeſt.
And whereas it on ſearching the ſcriptures appears,
That Chriſtians are ſtyl'd there God's children and
    heirs;
He gallantly chooſes for ever to die,
Before he'll commence a relation ſo nigh
(Oh! ſtinging diſhonour!) unto the moſt High.
And ſince benefits conferr'd, tho' exalting the givers,
Denote imperfection and want in receivers;
He ſcorns, ſince the donor eſteems it a favour,
T' accept the mean preſent of living for ever.
And tho' kingdoms and crowns t' engage him unite,
And glory, and honour, and bliſs do invite;
He a conſtancy firm and wiſhaken will boaſt,
And prefers his old friend and acquaintance, the duſt.
But here I reſign, and the ſubject diſmiſs,
Unable to celebrate merit like this:
Such inverted heroics ſuit ill with my pen,
And the taſk is more proper for devils than men.

The Author of the Weekly Miſcellany, who frequently
attacks the Freethinkers and Infidels, quotes from the Layman's Faith a beautiful Paſſage ſomewhat to the Purpoſe of the foregoing Lines, but we choſe not to inſert
'em both.

The deſpairing LOVER.

AS a clear ſilent ſtream crept penſive along,
  And the winds murmur'd ſolemn the willows
    among,
On the green turf complaining a ſwain lay reclin'd,
And wept to the river, and ſigh'd to the wind.

In vain, cry'd he, nature has waken'd the ſpring;
In vain bloom the violets, the nightingales ſing;
To a heart full of ſorrow no beauties appear,
Each zephyr a ſigh, and each dew-drop's a tear.)

In vain my Zelinda has graces to move
The faireſt to envy, the wiſeſt to love.
Her preſence no longer gives joy to my eye,
And without her to live, is more pain than to die.

O that ſlumber its pinions would over me ſpread!
And paint but her image in dreams in her ſtead:
The beautiful viſion would ſoften my pain—
But ſleep's a relief I ſolicit in vain.——

The wretch that, like me, is heart wounded with
    care,
Is deluded with hope, and undone by deſpair;
His pangs, ever-waking deny him repoſe,
And the moments but vary, to vary his woes.

CUPID defeated at BATH.

LOve told his mother t'other day,
  I'th rooms he'd ſpend an hour,
See what they do, hear what they ſay,
  And try his utmoſt power.

He chang'd his form, he hid his wings,
  Clapt on a ſmart Toupee,
And was adorn'd with all thoſe things
  A ſpritely beau ſhould be.

On Celia firſt he fix'd his eyes,
  She ſhun'd his am'rous Arts,
Impatient from the God ſhe flies
  To Wiltſhire's ace of hearts.

Fair Cloe next the youth addreſt,
  With eloquence and ſkill
But ſhe her high diſdain expreſt,
  He could not play Quadrille.

Poems to Daphne he repeats,
  Tranſlated out of Maro ;
But wiſely ſhe prefers thoſe cheats
  That deal to dupes at Faro.

Repuls'd by thoſe, he talk'd to more,
  Yet talk'd alas in vain ;
From ten years old to full threeſcore,
  Their ſole purſuit was gain.

The god enrag'd at their contempt
  Reſum'd his native air,
Diſplay'd his wings, his bow unbent,)
  And thus beſpoke the fair. ,

Adieu, he cry'd, ye giddy fair;
  I will no longer ſtay;
Thoſe hearts deſerve from me no care
  That are uſurpt by play.

Hymen and I give up the field;
  Avarice now reigns alone;
Since cards and dice ſuch joys can yield,
  Marriage and love are gone.

                                    The

The NYMPHS of the THAMES.
A BALLAD.

FULL *of Dreams of bright Beauties, and fond*
　　to explore
new World of such Charms as I'd ne'er seen before;
travell'd thro' Italy, Germany, France,
And I think my Curiosity led me a Dance.

On the Banks of the Seine, *I was pleas'd to survey,*
such Crowds of fair Nymphs, and all merry and gay,
but then they were merry and gay to Extreams,
And no Nymphs could I find like the Nymphs of the
　　Thames.

From the Seine *to the* Loire, *from the* Loire
　to the Rhone,
till in hopes of Success, I have eagerly flown;
And on each there was shewn me of Beauties great
　　Store.　　[*no more.*
Which, if shewn on the Thames, *had been Beauties*

The Alps *next I crost, so tremendous and high*
For Beauty will lead us o'er wet, and o'er dry)
I pursue my Enquiries, and see if perchance
Fair Italy *had what I found not in* France.

Then I travers'd each Mountain, each River, each
　　Plain,
But my Labour, alas! was all Labour in vain:
O Tiber *! O* Po*! why so fam'd are your Streams,*
Since no Nymphs you can boast, like the Nymphs of
　the Thames?

Not Venice, *so proud of her Masks and her Fair,*
Can for Beauties, bright Beauties, with London
　compare;
And, tho' Sea-born, Love's Goddess herself would agree,
That our Nymphs on the Thames *outshine those on*
　the Sea.

But of Italy's *Merit and Fame, to say true,*
And give (as 'tis fit) every Country its due,
Here each Nymph like a Syren, *with Music inflames;*
But what's a slight Song, to the Charms of the Thames?

As for Germany, *there I was struck with Surprize,*
What the Belles want in Brightness, they make up in
　Size;
And if Beauties they were to be measur'd like Wine,
For a Quart *on the* Thames, *you've a* Tun *on*
　the Rhine.

And thus having finish'd my whimsical Round,
Convinc'd that I sought what could no where be found,
I of roving repent, and accuse my vain Dreams,
That kept me so long from the Nymphs of the Thames.

Now ye Youths of Great-Britain on wand'ring so
　keen,
To feed your fond Fancies with Beauties unseen;
Believe what I say, you'll be baulk'd in your Aims
If you seek more such Nymphs, as the Nymphs on the
　　Thames.

But if you should argue my Voyage too small,
And say my Experience proves nothing at all;
Go enquire of the Sun, and he'll tell you his Beams,
Ne'er have shone on such Nymphs, as the Nymphs
　on the Thames.

First RIDDLE *in our last, p.* 435. *answer'd*

A TOP well scourg'd with leathern string,
　　Is said to sleep, stand, run and sing,
Why not as well to dance a Jigg
Like any School-boys WHIRLIGIG?

Second RIDDLE, *ibid. answer'd.*

A S in soft whisper with my love
　　I rudely once was told,
We were as great as HAND AND GLOVE,
　She blush'd, but cou'd not scold;
Don't mind the clown, said I, my dear,
　He envies me the bliss;
'Cause from you napping I U PAIR
　Just got by stolen Kiss.

In Praise of VIRTUE.

V Irtue, thou ornament of human life,
　　That crowns the Virgin, and adorns the
Wife,
From thy blest treasure of contentments flow
All the true blessings we enjoy below;
Those sweet delights, which in thy bosom dwell,
Rise up in springs, and into rivers swell;
Which know no Ebb, or Storm, but free from
　noise
Flow calmly in a constant tide of Joys;
Thou bring'st contentment to the meanest birth,
And givest us a taste of Heav'n on Earth:
From whence, thro' crystal innocence, we see
A pleasing prospect of eternity,
Where Angels, to receive the virtuous, wait,
And bid them welcome to a happier state.

The HAPPY PAIR.

W HO says, my *Lord* and *Lady* disagree?
　　A pair more like in *all things* cannot be.
My *Lord* indeed will *damn* the marriage chain;
My *Lady* wishes it *unloos'd* again.

Ever with Rakes, my *Lady* likes his room.
He swears his *Boy* is not his *real Son*;
My *Lady* thinks it is not *all* his own.

He'll have a *sep'rate bed,* —— 'tis her desire,
Sheets warm'd, bed made, the *smiling pair retire:*
The *cause,* tho' *hidden,* yet the *same* their *want,*
He sends for *Miss,* and *she* for her *Gallant.*

If *Union* then makes *blest'd* the *marriage Life,*
The *same* the *husband,* and the *same* the *wife;*
If in *two* breasts *one* mind gives *joy sincere,*
What *two* more *happy* than this *comely pair.*

The VI. ODE of ANACREON.

W Ith rosy garlands round our temples twin'd
　　Choice wine we drink, and laugh with
mirth refin'd
While dancing to the lyre, some nimble fair
The verdant thyrsus brandishes in air,
Round which in curls the rattling ivy plays;　5
And every step her well-turn'd legs displays.
A beauteous youth, from whose perfumed head
Locks bright as gold in wanton curls are spread:
Through well-pair'd pipes, which sweetest
　breath inspires,
Pours softest sounds in consort to the lyre's.　10
The God of love adorn'd with golden hair,
With comely BACCHUS, and with VENUS fair,
With merry COMUS in the banquet join,
Which youth restores in age's last decline.

　　　　　　　　　　D. B.

The following STANZAS *are taken from a Poem now in Manuscript, entitled an* Epithalamium, *on the Nuptials of his Serene Highness* WILLIAM *Prince of* ORANGE *with her R. H.* ANNE, *Princess Royal of* Great Britain, *to be published on a proper Occasion.*

'TIS done; her princely heart she yields,
    A conquest worth an empire's crown!
Or triumphs gain'd in bloody fields!
    Or all ambition calls renown!

Her virtues, eminently bright,
    To sweet perfection early grew;
Goodness and majesty unite,
    And all her Father greatly shew.

Behold the amiable dame!
    What radiant glories round her shine!
Such virgin EVE to ADAM came;
    And such to GEORGE, was CAROLINE,

Form'd by her royal mother's care
    Her charms incessantly improv'd;
And now in blooming Lustre are,
    By all admir'd, rever'd, and lov'd.

Imperial graces take their place,
    And strike with reverential awe;
Her mind and form contend to raise
    A consort worthy a NASSAU.

O happy youth! Illustrious prince!
    What envy'd bliss thy fate awaits!
Thy just pretensions GEORGE befriends;
    And ANNA's love thy joy compleats.

On Mr. WHALEY of Pembroke-Hall, Cambridge, being elected Master of Peter-House.

GROWN Slaves by Bribery and Venal Gold,
    Some Fool to Liberty this Maxim hold,
' *Virtue in* Britain *must neglected die,*
' For they can ne'er succeed who cannot buy.
    Britons, should Gold debauch your free-born
      Will,
Taught by your Granta's Sons, be Britons still:
Learn from a *private College* whom to trust,
The *Wise*, the *Good*, the *Faithful*, and the *Just*;
Of Granta's Sons th' *impartial* Choice regard,
And learn *distinguish'd* Virtue to reward.

To Sir GIMCRACK NODDY.

SIR Gimcrack round his Hall hangs all Things
    odd,
An embalm'd Pismire, and a Straw-stuff'd Cod,
Alike to Things *antique* his Taste inclines,
Old Roman Shields, maim'd Heads, and rusty Coins;
But if the *oldest*, *oddest* Thing in Life
To these you'd hang, Sir Gimcrack — hang your
    Wife.

To Mrs PRITCHARD, Appearing on the Stage.

WHAT admiration fills my mind
    To see and hear thee, lovely fair!
Thy actions free, and unconfin'd,
    Thy voice attracts th'attentive ear.

Why hast thou been obscur'd so long;
    Thy person fitted for the stage:
Nor hast till now, with jocund song
    Began to charm the wond'rous age.

Reason and sense,' thy action grace;
    Nature with wit has strongly join'd,
To add to thy enchanting face
    The brighter beauties of the mind.
How wilt thou on some nobler stage
    Thy rival actresses outshine!
While they exert their puny rage,
    To hear the praises justly thine.   R. S.

EJACULATION, proper for the TIME.

WISE men suffer, good men grieve;
    Knaves invent, and fools believe:
Help O lord! send aid unto us;
Or fools and Knaves will quite undo us.

PLAISTOW. A POEM.
By J. D. Esq;

THE nymphs of Plaistow fields begin my Song,
    To rural themes the softest notes belong.
Bright Delia's eyes, or Chloe's charming air,
Belinda's shape or Sylvia lovely fair
I sing no more; do thou my voice inspire,
Who Pope inflam'd'st with such poetick fire:
When he sung Windsor forest's cool retreat,
At once a monarch's and the muse's seat.
O could I chant like him, the country swains
Should leave their bleating flocks upon the plains,
And ravish'd listen to my rural strains.
Then should my PLAISTOW Phœnix park ou shine,
And strength and beauty flow thro' every line;
But he no more his lyre seraphic strings,
No more He in harmonious numbers sings,
But now retir'd from worldly cares doth dwell,
Amid'st those pleasures he describ'd so well,
And which advent'rous I attempt to tell.
Assist ye gods that haunt the shady woods,
And help ye Naiads of the silver floods;
Be instant all, who bless the farmer's care,
And crown with plenty each succeeding year.
Thy meadows, PLAISTOW, and thy fleecy Care,
Thy yellow harvest, and thy healthy air,
Invite my Lays. Attend ye sylvan maids,
Lay by your work and seek the cooling shades,
Arcadia's fields, or Candia's lovely plains,
Or Tyber's meads describ'd in softest strains,
Can't equal thee in any thing but song,
'Tis from their Poets they exist so long,
And were my heart inspir'd with equal flame,
Our village justly shou'd excell their fame.
What tho' our hills no azure summits crown,
With bearded grain our fertile plains abound.
Houses thick interspers'd and trees appear,
Whose lofty tops ascend the ambient air.
A chequer'd Land-skip each parterre displays,
Admitting all the genial Sun's bright rays.
Here flowers rise, in gayest dress the Rose,
Opening each morn, doth sweet perfumes disclose,
With white the Snowdrop, Hyacinth with blue,
Jonquil with yellow, Iris varied hue
Kind nature decks, Why should I move? the field,
Unask'd, a thousand different beauties yield.
The Greeks advance their old Arcadia's Fame,
The Reign of Faunus, and their lovely Dame.
Saturnian days the Romans Latian Meads
Praise; and he flocks which fertile Mantua feeds,
While Greeks Arcadia, Latins Mantua Praise,
PLAISTOW shall shine tho' in less tuneful Lays.

nona here her richest blessings pours,
d from each tree descend th' empurpl'd show'rs;
id Ceres here repays the farmer's toils
th plenteous harvest every furrow smiles;
there his flocks to flowry herbage leads,
'd while they're feeding, tunes his seven-fold reeds.
When youth with sprightly vigour warms the blood,
d purer spirits swell the purple flood,
th' ardent courser give the loosened reins,
d hast impatient to the dusty plains.
from the Post with equal speed they bound;
fleet as wind they trace the measur'd Ground;
to the Goal in view they urge the steed,
d thirst of Glory animates their speed.
up in the horses side the rowel lies,
purple fluid all the meadow dies;
wish'd for prize rewards the victor's pains,
ilst shouts loud eccho round the neighb'ring plains.
With sultry heat when fiery Sirius glows,
d thro' the shade the gentle Zephyr blows,
youth in troops the shady wood beset,
use a fleet Buck, or spread the waving net;
death devote, he quits his native bounds,
ift fly the steeds, and close pursue the hounds;
ide o're th' extended fields his course he takes,
ups o're the banks and plunges thro' the lakes,
n at his heels he bears the opening hounds,
his shrill horn the weary huntsman sounds,
d, from the levell'd tube, the flying buck be
  wounds.
he whizzing lead arrests him as he flies,
falls; his nerves unbrace, he struggling lies,
rt beats his breath, and death invades his eyes.
r yet doth Winter want its Country sport;
to the whit'ned fields the birds resort;
unwearied Fowler wakes at early dawn,
leathern buskins treads the dewy lawn,
w o're the barren heath intent he roves,
r seeks the pheasant in the leafless groves,
m o're his head the clam'rous Plovers fly,
w flocks of fieldfares cloud the dusky sky,
his unerring hand his gun he takes,
he frozen air a short-liv'd thunder breaks,
leaden death suspends their airy flight,
fluttering they fall, and seek the realms of night.
Now to the hoary fields the Youth repair
ith well train'd beagles hunt the circling hare,
thro' the lanes the subtile Fox they chace
ernd sworn foe to all our cackling race.
In spring when Flora with fair flowers is crown'd,
nd genial vapours breath along the ground,
patient fisher seeks the purling brook,
alls out his rod, then baits his barbed hook;
fe to the shallow bank, fixes his beat,
en views the bending rod and dancing float,
w fertile streams produce a various race,
he Carp with golden scale, and shining Dace,
he silver Eel, and Perch with scarlet fins,
he healing Tench, and Trouts with freckl'd skins,
wise Gudgeons search the well-known store for food,
and Pikes relyn tyrants o're the scaly brood.
Happy the man, who breaths the country air,
unvex'd by anxious strife and free from care;
he seeks the murmuring streams and cooling shades,
he mossy fountains and the open glades,
njoys beyond the reach of cruel hate,
ts easy fortune, tho' a small estate;

Who knows to use the gifts that heaven bestows,
And none but wicked men accounts his foes;
Wrongs not his conscience for a private end,
Sincere his promise is to serve his friend;
Blest in the chaste embraces of a Wife,
To share the pleasures, and the cares of life;
No dreams affrighting discompose his rest,
Wish sweet delight each rising morn is blest;
Who to his neighbour hopes nor wishes harm,
His whole endeavour's to improve his farm.
Free from the trouble of the rich and great,
No grand attendance at his table wait,
He owns no gilded rooms, nor beds of state.
Content with plain but cleanly furniture,
He keeps no porter waiting at his door
To admit the rich, and drive away the poor.
Frugally liberal, merciful, and kind,
His friends a hearty welcome always find,
Each day with wholesome food his table's crown'd,
And health and honest joy throughout abound,
With pleasure he surveys his native fields,
And waving harvest which each furrow yields;
Sometime he wand'ring in a serious mood,
Attends the duty of the wise and good.
His greatest care's how best his life to mend,
Revere his maker and regard his end.
Or nature's secrets deep employ his care,
The weight and force elastick of the air.
He seeks what cause gives rattling thunder birth,
And whence cool show'rs refresh the fruitful earth,
Why its vast womb is rent by earthquakes dire,
And why Volcanos spout out liquid fire,
Now takes his glass to view the motes that play
In each sun beam (a nation of a day)
Or seeks for healing herbs that can give ease,
To groaning mortals, and remove disease.
With wine and oyl new spirits to impart,
And drive all sadness from the sinking heart.
The scope of all his study is to find
Somewhat to please or benefit mankind.
A life like this philosophers admire;
Grant I, like them, one day may so retire.

[To be finish'd in our next.]

VIRGIL's TEMPEST *Imitated*.
By Mr MORRICE.

THE rushing storm from every quarter pours,
  The cordage rattles, and the Sailor roars;
Cover'd with foam the mounting billows roll.
And bell'wing thunder shakes the distant pole.
Heav'n and the day are snatch'd from human eyes
And flashing fires illuminate the skies;
Night shrouds the deep, dire dissolution near,
And all things big with instant fate appear.

Foe, Sept. 15. has a remarkable Poem, occasion'd by
the Bishops of Ireland endeavouring for an Act to divide
Church Livings: But it was first printed in our Magazine for June 1732, p. 821. This we think necessary to
mention, lest those who are lately added to the Number
of our Readers, should think we omitted it thro' Partiality
In like manner the excellent Birth Day Hymn by a Gentleman (viz. of the North) which we inserted in April last
p. 207, has been this Month reprinted in some of the Lon-
d n, and most of the Country Papers. And we could
instance in many other original Productions, inserted in
this Book, and afterwards copy'd from it.
We must refer to another Opportunity the Verses we
have been favour'd with from several Hands.
We pity the Case of Mr R. S. A Bashful Lover rarely
meets with Success; and we imagine the Publ x at as
of his Lines will do him no Service.

THE
Monthly Intelligencer.
SEPTEMBER, 1733.

Saturday, 1.

ON the Garden of Mrs *Stephens* at *Epsom*, an Aloe blow'd, itsHeight above the Tub 21 Feet and a Half; the Circumference 7 Feet 4 Inches; its Circumference at the Points of the Leaves 31 Feet; the Stem 19 and a half high, and out of it proceed 39 Branches or Sconces, many of them 2 Feet 6 Inches long; some of them containing 196 or 198 Pods, bearing yellow Flowers; the Liquid in the Pods as sweet as Honey.

Sunday, 2.

Capt. *Clarke*, in his Passage from *Dublin* to *Chester*, met with a Cloud of Flying Insects, of various Sorts, which stuck about his Rigging and Vessel in a surprizing manner.

Monday, 3.

At *Carlton* in *Yorkshire*, some Workmen digging a Well, about 18 Feet under Ground discover'd a Sepulcher 8 Feet in length and 5 broad, having in it a Set of large human Bones, white as Ivory, and a Helmet standing over the Head in a Nich. Some Saxon Characters appear'd on the Wall, and the Date 992, which was 74 Years before *Wm* the Conqueror.

In several Parts of *Kent*, the Farmers, notwithstanding the low Prices of all Sorts of Grain, were obliged to raise the Wages of their Labourers, and yet were distressed for want of Hands to get in their Harvest; which is attributed to the great Numbers who employ themselves in Smuggling along the Coast.

Wednesday, 5.

Their Majesties and the Royal Family hunting a Stag in *Surry*, he pass'd the River Thames, and took into some strong Inclosures near *Staines* in *Middlesex*, belonging to one *Richd Violet*, who clapt up a Chain, and refused the Sportsmen Admittance, telling the Noblemen, who expostulated with him, *he was King in his own Grounds.* Some of the Courtiers were for violent Measures; but their Majesties being inform'd of it, order'd the Farmer some Gold, and then he took down his Chain, and the Stag was soon after kill'd.

Receipts for the first Payment of 1*l.* upon every Ticket subscribed for in the Charitable Corporation Lottery, was deliver'd at the Bank.

Friday, 7.

Ended the General Goal Delivery for the City and County of *Bristol*, when the following Persons receiv'd Sentence of Death, viz. *Wm Russel*, and *James Jeans*, (who have since been hang'd) for stealing 22 Pieces of Lawn, Ribbons, &c. and *John Philips* for stealing Pork and other Meat, and likewise a Mare.—— After Business was ended at the Bar, the Grand Jury complimented the Hon. *John Scrope* their Recorder, on the Services he had done that City in Parliament, and invited him to stand as Candidate at the ensuing Election. They likewise gave the same Invitation to Sir *Abraham Elton*; They Both thank'd them in a handsome Manner, and accepted the Offer.

Tuesday, 11.

The Widows of 16 Navy Officers, whose Husbands died on or since the 30th of *August* 1732, were admitted by the Court of Assistants, to the Charity established for their Relief.

Wednesday 12.

Embarked on board the *Savannah*, 132 Persons for the new Colony of *Georgia*.

About the Beginning of this Month his Majesty presented the Pr. of *Orange*, with one of the finest Sets of Horses in *Europe*.

Saturday, 15.

The Sessions ended at the *Old Bailey*, when, of 110 Prisoners that were tried, the 10 following receiv'd Sentence of Death, viz. *John Bromley*, for robbing his Master a Turner in *Newgate-street*, of Money and Gold Rings to the value of

6ool. Anne Soames, for robbing her Miſtreſs, of 34 Guineas, 4 Gold Rings, &c. —— *Richd Lamb,* for the Murder of his Wife; *John Cannon,* for raviſhing *Mary Foſſey,* an Infant of 9 Years of Age; *Joſeph Blunt,* for the Murder of *Robert Adair* his Corporal, by ſhooting him in the Barracks in the Tower; *Edw. More,* for robbing Mr *George Polley,* of 3 Guineas, 3 Moidores, a 36s. Piece, and a Silver Watch; *John Pierſon,* for Horſe-ſtealing; and *George Richardſon, Laurence Grace,* and *John Smithſon,* for robbing *John Gordon,* in *Lincolns-Inn-fields.* 1 burnt in the Hand; and 41 caſt for Tranſportation. When the Trials were over, the Grand Jury preſented 4 noted Solicitors for infamous Practices, in fomenting and carrying on Proſecutions againſt innocent Perſons for the Sake of Rewards, &c. whereupon the Court return'd Thanks to the Grand Jury, and aſſur'd them that the Offenders ſhould be rigorouſly proſecuted.

Monday, 17.

The D. of *Dorſet,* Lord Lieut. of *Ireland,* (accompanied by his Dutcheſs and Family) arrived there from *England,* to meet the Parliament of that Kingdom.

Tueſday, 18.

At a Court of Ld Mayor and Aldermen at *Guildhall,* 'twas reſolv'd to appoint a new Ordinary of *Newgate* within a Month; and to encourage ſome able Divine to execute that important Office as it ought, they determin'd to add one Freedom a Year (valued at 25l.) to that already enjoy'd by the Ordinary of *Newgate* over and above the Salary of 40l. *per Ann.* and Perquiſites, with a Houſe to live in, &c.

Thurſday, 20.

Was the firſt Meeting of the Commiſſioners appointed by his Majeſty's moſt Honourable Privy Council, to inſpect and ſettle the Fees of the Officers and Clerks of the ſeveral Courts of Judicature, when they appointed Mr *Sharp* of the *Temple,* to be their Secretary.

Was held a General Court of the Bank of *England,* when a Dividend of 2 and three quarters *per Cent.* on their Stock, for Intereſt and Profits, was agreed upon, for the half Year ending at *Michaelmas* next, the Warrants for which to be deliver'd on the 19th of *October.*

Mr *de Loſs,* Envoy Extraordinary from the Elector of *Saxony,* had his firſt private Audience of their Majeſties and the Prince of *Wales.*

(*Gent. Mag.* Vol 3. No. xxxiii.)

Monday, 24.

Baron *Stork* arrived here in the Character of Envoy Extraordinary from the D. *Holſtein Gottorp,* to negotiate a Marriage between that Prince and her Royal Highneſs the Princeſs *Amelia.* His Highneſs is about 33 Years of Age. His Mother was *Sophia,* favourite Siſter to *Charles* XII. late King of *Sweden,* and to the preſent Queen; to which Kingdom his Highneſs will probably ſucceed after the Death of their preſent Majeſties. He was a great Favourite at the *Ruſſian* Court in the Reigns of *Peter* the Great and *Katherine;* and marry'd in 1725 the Princeſs *Anne,* Siſter of the late *Peter* II. Emperor of *Ruſſia,* but ſhe died 3 Years after, leaving one Son.

Friday, 28.

At a Court of Huſtings held at *Guildhall, Robert Weſtley,* and *Daniel Lambert,* Eſqs. were ſworn into the Office of Sheriffs of this City, and County of *Middleſex;* Mr *Timms* of *Wood-ſtreet,* and Mr *Webber* of *Coopers Hall,* are appointed Under-Sheriffs.

Saturday, 29.

At a Court of Huſtings Sir *Wm Billers,* Kt, being next the Chair, was elected Ld Mayor of this City for the Year enſuing, in the room of the Rt Hon. *John Barber,* Eſq; the preſent Ld Mayor, who addreſſed the Citizens in the following manner,

GENTLEMEN,

I Beg Leave, to take this Opportunity, before I reſign my Office, to return you my hearty Thanks, not only for the Favours I myſelf received, but alſo for your Readineſs to concurr with me upon all Occaſions where the Trade and Welfare of this City were concern'd; the great ſhare which you, and every honeſt Citizen had, in oppoſing *a late Attempt againſt Both,* will ever be remember'd to your Honour; and I ſincerely congratulate you on the happy Effects which viſibly appear'd from your Conduct.

Whenever this renew'd City exerts herſelf in a proper Manner, her Intereſt will have a great Influence in all Places, and can ſeldom fail of being crown'd with Succeſs; more eſpecially when ſhe is ſo wiſe as to lay aſide all Names of Diſtinction: and when all Ranks and Degrees of People unite, as one Man, to the Support of the Common Cauſe. As an Union, ſo univerſal, was attended with ſuch glorious Conſequences, it ought to be the earneſt Endeavour of all true Lovers of their Country, to preſerve that Union inviolable; for then we ſhall have no Cauſe to fear that any *paſt Attempts will be*

Q o o   *revived*

ceived, or any new ones made, to our Prejudice.

As you, Gentlemen, are my proper Judges,
to you I submit my past Behaviour ; and, if
I am so happy as to merit your Approbation,
I shall esteem it an Ample Reward, and be
proud to dedicate my self in any other Capacity to the Service of you, my Fellow Citizens.

Sir William Billers *thank'd the Citizens
for the Honour they had done him, in chusing him to that high Office, promised to
administer Justice impartially, and to
assert their Rights and Privileges on all
Occasions.*

Sunday, 30.

At the Anniversary Meeting of the Sons
of the Clergy this Month, at *Newcastle
upon Tyne,* 257*l.* was collected ; and at
Gloucester Cathedral, 70*l.* for putting out
Orphans of poor Clergymen.

The Pr. of *Orange*'s Departure from
Holland was put off for a Month.

MARRIAGES.

THE E. of *Chesterfield,* married to
Melosina de *Schulemburgh,* Countess of *Walsingham* in *Norfolk,* and Baroness of *Aldborough,* (both Royal Titles) conferr'd on her by Letters Patent,
dated *April* 10, 1722. Her Portion is said
to be 50,000*l.* down, and 3000*l. per Ann.*
payable out of the Civil List Revenue in
Ireland, during her Life. Soon after they
were married the Pr. of *Wales* sent his
Compliment to them thereupon.

Mr *Stacey,* Son to Mr *Stacey,* Master
Builder of the King's Yard at *Deptford,*—
to a Daughter of *John London,* of *Newington,* Esq; formerly Representative for
Wilton in *Wiltshire.*

Edward Spencer, Esq;—to Miss *Elizabeth Tims,* with 10,000*l.* Fortune.

Mr *Burton,* of *Coleman-street,*Merchant,
—to Miss *Herne,* with 40,000*l.* Fortune.

Capt. *Mudge* of *Rotherhith,* an old Commander in the *West India* Trade,—to Miss
Hopton of *Poplar,* with 5000*l.* Fortune.

Ogilvie, Esq;—to Miss *Gray,* a
Fortune of 10,000*l.*

John Sinclair, of *Cheshunt,* Esq;—to
Miss *Colby* of *St Albans,* a 4000*l.* Fortune.

Thomas Ferne, Esq;—to Miss *Vane* of
Lincolnshire.

Theobalds, of *Watling-street,*—to
Miss *Loughton* of *Hackney.*

Mr *John Montier,* a Broker in *Tower
Royal,*—to a *French* Lady, with a Fortune of 5000*l.*

Capt. *Whitcombe,* late arrived from
New-England,—to Miss *Betty Wadmough*
of *Finch Lane.*

The Revd Mr *Blomberg,* of *Fulham*
—to a Daughter of the Dean of *Durham.*

Mr *Joseph Thompson,*Attorney of *Gray's
Inn,*—to Miss *Floyer,* of *Red Lyon Square,*
with a Fortune of 16,000*l.*

Dr *Howley,* a Physician,—to Miss *Ann.
Polton,* of *Finsbury.*

Tho. Osborne, of *Lambeth,* Esq;—to Miss
Jane Hutchins, a Fortune of 6000*l.*

Capt. *Scarlet,*—to the Daughter of the
late Col. *Gower,* a Fortune of 2500*l.*

Richd Baylis, Esq; a Common Council
Man of *Bread-str.* Ward,—to Miss *Ryin.*

The Revd Mr *Geo. Neale,* Minister of
Ottley in *Yorkshire,*—to a Daughter of Dr
Bland, Dean of *Durham.*

Hesketh, of *Meals, Lancashire,*
Esq; — to Miss *Fleetwood,* Heiress of
Ross Hall in that County.

The Revd Mr *Burgomter,* Minister of
the Lutheran Church at St *James's,* — to
the Daughter of the late Revd Mr *Dooty,*
Minister of the said Church.

DEATHS.

Aug. 29. MRS *Mary Malton,* at *Reading* in *Berks,* a Maiden La-
dy, Aged 105, reputed worth 10,000*l.*

30. *John Lewis,* at *Barkhamstead, Hart-
fordsh.* Esq; formerly Com. of a Man of War.

31. *Sam. Palmer,* Esq; in *Southwark,* Distiller, and formerly High Sheriff for *Surry.*

Rob. Jennings, Esq; of *Hammersmith.*

Mr *Charles Mason,* at *Acton,* formerly a
West-India Merchant.

Sept. 1. Mr *Hartoff,* eldest Son of *Baron
Hartoff,* his Majesty's Principal Minister for
the Affairs of *Hanover.*

The Revd Mr *Arnold,* Minister of St
James's in *Bristol.*

Langdale, Esq; at *Buscomb, Wiltshire.*

2. *John Billingsley,* Esq; at *Park Place,* reputed worth 30,000*l.* and 700*l. per Ann.*

3. The Revd Mr *Lewis Debordes,* Vicar
of *East-Ham,* in *Essex,* and Chaplain to the
D. of *Dorset.*

4. *Geo. Stapleton,* Esq; in the Commission
of the Peace for *Middlesex.*

5. The Wife of Mr *Primatt,* an eminent
Chymist in *Aldersgate-street,* in Childbed.

John Robinson, Esq; in the Commission of
the Peace for *Middlesex,* Chief Burgess of
Westminster, and one of the Commissioners of
Sewers, reputed worth 50,000*l.*

The Relict of Mr *Woodward,* late Banker in *Exchange-alley.*

6. The Revd Mr *Beverly,* A. M. Rector
of *Fifield,* and *Willingham Doe,* both in *Essex.*

William Sikes, Esq; in the Commission of
the Peace for *Hertfordshire.*

7. Mr *Thomas Sandbridge,* an Usher in the
Court of *Exchequer.*

Solomon

Solomon Price, Esq; formerly in the Commission of the Peace for *Middlesex.*

John Wallingford, Esq; at *Cheshunt, Hertfordshire,* Wine Merchant.

The Wife of *Wm Huxley,* Esq; Brother to *Geo. Huxley,* Esq; Member of Parliament and Commissary Gen. of all his Majesty's Forces.

8. Mrs *Martha Cunningham,* at *Colchester,* a Maiden Gentlewoman. She left 10,000l. to *James Cunningham,* Esq; her Brother, an Advocate in *Scotland;* 50l. and a Year's Wages to an old Servant Maid.

Sir *James Conier,* at *Hollyport* near *Windsor,* an Irish Gentleman.

9. *John Agar,* Esq; a Justice of Peace for *Westminster.*

Mr *Jn Simpson,* at *Mile-End,* Hop-Mercht.

Thomas Marwood, Esq; formerly an *East-India* Merchant.

10. Mr *Trust,* at *Claybill* near *Endfield,* aged 112. He was a Soldier in *Oliver Cromwell's* Army.

John Kynaston, Esq; who lately petition'd for the Barony of *Powys.* He was Representative in several Parliaments for *Shropshire;* by his Death an Estate of 8000l. *per Ann.* fell to his Son *Corbet Kynaston,* Esq;

The Lady of the Ld *Digby,* at *Sherborne,* in *Dorsetshire.*

Cox, Esq; at *Clapham, Surry.*

Mr *Walker,* at *Paddington,* Dry Salter.

Richards, Esq; in *New Palace Yard, Westminster,* reputed worth 80000l.

11. *James Bradley,* Esq; formerly a *Virginia* Merchant, and one of the Directors of the *Royal Exchange* Assurance Company.

Major *Wright,* of the first Regiment of Foot Guards.

Thomas Thornton, Esq; at *Petersham, Surry.*

John Brownlow, Esq; at *Stalnes,* in *Middlesex,* formerly Merchant of this City, and in the Commission of the Peace.

Mr *Caleb Colton,* Postmaster at *Oxford.*

Tracey Pauncefort, Esq; Nephew to the Solicitor General to the Pr. of *Wales.*

Joseph Pickering, Esq; at *Roehampton, Surry.*

Mr *Belton,* a Coal Merchant, drowned by falling from the Side of a Ship.

12. *John Hagger,* Commander of one of her Majesty's Ships in the late War with *France.*

Mr *John Willis,* Master of the Ballast Office, a Place of about 300l. *per Ann.* in the Gift of the Elder Brothers of *Trinity House.*

The Lady *Eliz. Fitz-Maurice,* aged 83.

Joseph Saunders, Esq; of *Somersetshire.*

Henry Hinckley, Esq; in the Commission of the Peace for *Staffordshire.*

13. *John Jackson,* Esq; at *Hammersmith,* Turkey Merchant.

Edward Collins, Esq; in the Commission of the Peace for *Northamptonshire,* and formerly an Officer of the *Green Cloth.*

Mr *Tho. Haughton,* an Alderman of *Derby.* ———Among other Legacies, he left 30l. *per Annum,* to the Parish of St *Werburg,* where he liv'd, to put out poor Children Apprentices, *&c.*

Mr *Martin,* Merchant of this City.

14. *George Cooke,* Esq; at *Doncaster,* in *Yorkshire,* possess'd of 5000l. *per Ann.*

15. *East,* Esq; in the Commission of the Peace for *Middlesex,* and formerly a *Hamburgh* Merchant.

Mr *John Phillips,* in *Oxford Square,* a Master Builder.

16. *Geo. Petersfield,* Esq; at *Little Chelsea.*

The Lady of Sir *John Smith,* Bt, present High Sheriff for *Somersetshire.*

William Sanderson, Esq; Son of the late Sir *Wm Sanderson.*

Horatio Little, Esq; in the Commission of the Peace for *Surry.*

Morley, Esq; in *Bloomsbury,* a Gentleman of *South Wales.*

17. *John Bentley,* Esq; at *Staines,* in *Middlesex,* possess'd of 300l. *per Ann.*

Mr *Tho. Maynard,* Ironmonger at *Queenhithe, London.*

Jacob Ward, Esq; at *Hollyport,* by *Windsor.*

18. One of the new-born Twins of Sir *John Heathcote,* Bt.

Philip Hodgkins, Esq; at *Petersham,* in *Surry,* worth 500l. *per Ann.* which devolves to his only Daughter, 16 Years of Age.

The Wife of the Revd Dr *Harcourt,* Vice Dean of *Bristol.*

19. *Cannon,* Esq; formerly a *Spanish* Merchant, found dead in his Chambers in *Gray's-Inn.*

George Dowse, Esq; formerly in the Commission of the Peace for *Middlesex.*

Mr *Wm Garbert,* at *Plaistow,* formerly one of the Directors of the S. Sea Company.

20. Capt. *Philip Wentworth,* a Commander in the Royal Navy.

Rev. Mr *Smith,* Vicar of *Helmerton, Wilts.*

Lady *Anne,* Wife of Ld *Charles Cavendish,* and fourth Daughter of the D. of *Kent.*

22. Mr *Miller,* Sadler to their Royal Highnesses the Princesses.

23. Mr *Man,* Father of *Robert Man,* Esq; at *Wandsworth,* reputed worth 20,000l.

The Revd Mr *Vincent,* Rector of *Warnford, Hampshire.*

24. *Gilbert Urwin,* Esq; many Years one of the Attornies of the *Marshalsea* Court, reputed worth 15,000l.

25. The Lady of Sir *George Downing,* Bt. Knight of the *Bath,* and Representative for *Dunwich:* Sir *George* when under fourteen, Married her, but they never cohabited; She was the Daughter of Sir *Wm Forrester.*

John Radcliffe Smith, Esq; one of the Governors of *Bartholomew, Bridewel,* and *Beth-*

kbem Hofpitals, and Nephew to the famous Dr *Radcliffe*; on whofe Eftate he receiv'd a Rent Charge of 500*l. per Ann.* which devolves to the Univerfity of *Oxford.*

Charles Houghton, Efq; in the Commiffion of the Peace for *Suffolk.*

27. *Tho. Hamingway,* Efq; Barrifter at Law. The eldeft Son of *Charles Talbot,* Efq; Sollicitor General. He intended to have ftood Candidate for the County of *Glamorgan* at the next Election.

James Chambers, Efq; formerly Banker in *Fleet-ftreet,* and in 1730. fined for Sheriff; remarkable for his Generofity and good Nature, having in his Life-time given near 30,000*l.* to his Nephews and Nieces (himfelf being a Batchelor) and by his Will bequeathed feveral thoufand Pounds more to his furviving Relations, befides handfome Legacies to charitable Ufes; among which is 50*l.* to the Charity Children of St *Dunftan's in the Weft.* He left Mr *Abraham Chambers,* Banker in *Fleet-ftreet,* his fole Executor, and Refiduary Legatee, to whom devolves all his real, and the Bulk of his perfonal Eftate.

Mrs *Edwards,* at *Kenfington,* related to the Ld *Anne Hamilton.*

A Woman and her Son in *Grub-ftreet,* ficken'd after eating a Supper of Mufhroons, in which, 'twas fuppos'd, were fome Toad-ftools, and dy'd; the Father and two Daughters, who were feized with a violent Vomiting, recover'd.

Mr *Player,* an *Englifh* Gentleman who had own'd himfelf a Proteftant, was found dead laft Month in a Wood near *Montdidier* in *France,* with his Sword on, Watch, and Purfe of Money in his Pockets.

Ecclefiaftical Preferments *conferr'd on the following Reverend Gentlemen.*

Matthew Bell, M. A. prefented to the Rectory of *Geftingthorpe, Effex.*

Pearce, M. A. — to the Rectory of *Hodent, Shropfhire.*

Mr *Jofeph Harris,* — to the Rectory of *Shaddingfield, Suffolk.*

Mr *Thomas Manning,* — to the Vicarage of *Sperfhot, Hampfhire.*

Thompfon, M. A. — to the Rect. of *Cold Kerby* in *Torkfhire.*

Mr *John Tracey,* — to the Vicarage of *Rufhall, Norfolk.*

Mr *Dubordieu,* — to the Living of *Sabridgeworth, Hertfordfhire.*

Burton, B. D. Fellow of *Corpus Chrifti* College, *Oxon,* made Fellow of *Eaton* College, in the room of the faid Dr *Richardfon.*

Mr *Still,* made Chaplain to the Firft Reg. of Foot Guards, in the room of Dr *Herbert,* who died in his Paffage from *Georgia.*

Dr *White,* Fellow of *Merton* College,

Oxon, fucceeds Archdeacon *Hunt* in his Canonry of *Wells.*

Mr *Stevens,* Rector of *Malden* in *Surry,* and formerly Chaplain to the Factory of *Oporto,* and Proctor of the Univerfity of *Oxford,* collated to a Prebendary of *Winchefter,* vacant by the Removal of Dr *Barton,* to the Canonry of *Chr. Ch. Oxford.*

Charles North, A. M. chofen Minifter of the New Church of St *John's, Southwark.*

Mr *Collins,* — to the Rect. of *Coltbert,* in the County of *Flint.*

Thomas Coney, D. D. elected Rector for the City of *Bath.*

A Difpenfation *is pafs'd to enable,* *Samuel Drake,* B. D. to hold the Vic. of *Holme* in *Spalding Moore, Torkfh.* with the Rect. of *Freeton* in the faid County.

John Harris, M. A. Chaplain to the Ld *Arundel,* to hold the Rectory of *Lifton, Devonfhire,* with the Rectory of *Cheriton-fitzpain,* in the faid County.

PROMOTIONS.

Brig. Gen. *Charles Churchill* preferr'd to the command of Lieut. General *Evans's* Reg. of Dragoons; And

Lieut Gen. *Evans,* to the Command of the Queen's own Royal Reg. of Horfe.

Mifs *Margaret Williams* Daughter to a Gentleman of that Name in *Herefordfhire,* appointed Maid of Honour to her Majefty, in the Room of Mifs *Mary Fitzwilliams,* now Countefs of *Pembroke.*

The Earl of *Balcarres,* — Colonel of a Company in the E. of *Stair's* Reg. of Dragoons.

The Hon. *Wm. Herbert,* Brother to the E. of *Pembroke,* fecond Brigadier in the firft Troop of the Life Guards, appointed Major of the faid Troop, in the Room of Major *Wright* deceafed.

The eldeft Daughter of *Auguftus Schutz,* Efq; Privy Purfe to his Majefty, appointed firft Maid of Honour; and Mrs *Swinton,* Mrs *Charles,* and Mifs *Dive,* — Dreffers to the Princefs Royal.

Mr *Simpfon,* elected Treafurer of the Stationer's Company in the Room of his Father deceafed.

Jacob Elton Efq; chofe Mayor of *Briftol.* *George Proctor,* Efq; appointed Steward of the Lordfhips, Manors, &c. of *Windfor* and *Windfor Caftle,* in the room of *Jobs Owen* Efq; decd.

Capt. *Carpenter,* a Relation to the Ld *Carpenter,* made Captain Lieutenant of Sir *Charles Wills's* Reg. of Foot Guards in the room of Col *Lafcelles,* promoted to a Company in the faid Reg.

Mr Ald. *Morgan,* chofe Mayor of *Bath.*

WARSAW, *Sept.* 12. Upon Advice that the *Ruffians* haften'd their March towards this City, the Primate and his Adherents refolved no longer to defer the Election of a King. —Every Thing being concerted, it commenced this Day towards Noon; and the Suffrages being taken, were found to be in favour of K. *Stanislaus*, who being come hither by Land, appeared; and was received with great Acclamations. Whereupon the Primate inftantly proclaimed him King, with all the ufual Formalities, and *Te Deum* was fung in the great Church. But many of the Palatinates who had left the Field, protefted againft the Election, and retired to Prince *Wiefnowiski*, Governor of *Lithuania*, at *Praage*, where their Camp was foon augmented to 10,000 Men, againft whom the following Oath was refolved on in the Dyet of Election.

I'T tends to the eternal Shame and Difhonour of the Polish Nation, that there fhould be Polanders, or Men fo call'd, of the Ecclefiaftical as well as Temporal Order, who, with a prepens'd Defign, and Rafhnefs unheard of, have call'd in foreign Troops, in order to difturb a free Election, to endanger their Country's Safety as well at home as abroad, and to involve it once more in thofe Calamities, from which it is not yet fully recover'd. And as fuch Men are real Monfters, degenerated from the Humane Species into cruel Vipers, devouring their own Mother; fo this Mother, namely, the Republick, from henceforth difowns them; fhe rejects them from any Benefit of her Parentage, and feparates them from among thofe who have been brought up in the State of Liberty, as Men unworthy of fo ineftimable a Bleffing. She cuts them off from the Body of the Nation, as rotten Members, infefted with the Fire of infernal Rage. She declares them illegitimate Children, having no Claim to the Inheritance of their common Mother, becaufe they have dar'd to lift up their unnatural Hands againft her. She looks upon them pro Hoftibus Patriæ & Capitibus invindicabilibus, fince they have prefum'd fo far as to introduce the Enemy (Hoftiles Copias) into the Country, and have thereby immerg'd it in a Deluge of Tears. Actuated therefore by thefe Reafons, I oblige my felf to rife up in Arms againft fuch Perfons, Refeize their Eftates, and annex them to the Revenues of the Royal Treafury for augmenting the Army: I moreover engage myfelf to lay their Dwellings in a Heap, and thereby build up a Monument that fhall bear the Characters of fo detefted a Treafon to lateft Pofterity; nor will I ever confent that any Amnefty be granted to their Perfons. In Teftimony whereof I fubfcribe this prefent Oath, &c.

Warfaw 16. The King and Senate fent a Deputation to the Opponents at *Praage*, to invite them to an Accommodation, but without effect; whereupon 'twas refolved to attack them in their Camp: This they were inform'd of, and retreated to a Neighouring Wood, but the Troops came up with the Rear, feiz'd the Baggage, and kill'd near 200 of them.

Warfaw, Sept. 19. The King fwore folemnly to the *Pacta Conventa*.

Warfaw, Sept. 20. M. *Poniatowski* refigned to the King his Poft of Regimentary of the Crown, with which his Majefty invefted M *Potoski*, Palatine of *Kiow*, Brother to the Primate.

Warfaw Sept. 22. The Van of the *Ruffian* Troops being advanced near this City, the King, Primate, and moft of his Party retir'd towards *Dantzick*

From *Conftantinople*, That the *Turks* and *Perfians* had come to a decifive Battle, which lafted between 8 and 9 Hours, and that the latter were defeated with the lofs of 30,000 Men. The Governor of *Bagdat* on the news of this Victory, iffued out upon the *Perfians* his Befiegers, and obliged them to retreat.

From *Dantzick*, That they heard that *Staniflaus* and the Primate of *Poland*, were affaffinated near *Warfaw*. But the Truth of this Report was much doubted.

From *Vienna*, that the Polifh Election was conducted very irregularly, and is confequently void. According to one of the Articles of the Confederacy in the previous Diet of Convocation, no Perfon fhould be proclaimed King without the unanimous Confent of the Electors; but feveral entire Palatinates never enter'd the Camp of Election. Many others protefted and withdrew; and a confiderable Party declar'd againft King *Staniflaus*, even at the Moment when the Primate was collecting the Suffrages. There was indeed an Attempt made in the Camp to reduce all to one mind, by affaffinating the No's, and about ten of the firft Negatives were knock'd o'th' Head accordingly: But this Method of taking the Poll, inftead of intimidating the Voters, urg'd them to be defperate, and the Executioners found they fhould have more Work upon their Hands than they were at firft aware of. The Opponents being join'd by the *Ruffians*, declar'd for the Elector of *Saxony*.

From *Geneva*, that a Body of *French* Troops have poffeffed themfelves of the City and Caftle of *Chambery*, the Metropolis of the Dutchy of *Savoy*.

Course of Exchange.	STOCKS	Monthly BILL of Mortality, from Aug. 28, to Sept. 25.
Amsterdam 35 4	S. Sea Trading Stock 80	Christned { Males 628 } { Females 602 } 1230
Ditto at Sight 34 1	—Bonds 1 *l.* 10*s*	
Hamburgh— 35 5	—Annuities 105	Buried { Males 1019 } { Femal. 1033 } 2052
Rotterdam— 35 5	—Ditto new 104	
Antwerp — 35 5	—dit. 3 *per* C. 97	Died under 2 Years old --- 962
Madrid —— 42¼	Bank 143	Between 2 and 5 ---- 158
Bilboa —— 41½	New Cir. 3*l.* 5	Between 5 and 10 ---- 42
Cadiz —— 42½	India 151	Between 10 and 20 ---- 65
Venice —— 49¼	—Bonds 3 *l.* 14 *s.*	Between 20 and 30 ---- 124
Leghorn — 50½	Ditto at 3 *per* C. 2 *l.*	Between 30 and 40 ---- 193
Genoa —— 53¼	Million Bank 116	Between 40 and 50 ---- 159
Paris —— 31¼	African 27	Between 50 and 60 ---- 120
Bourdeaux -- 31¼	Royal Ass. 102	Between 60 and 70 ---- 132
Oporto—— 5 4½	London Ass. 13	Between 70 and 80 ---- 61
Lisbon—— 5 5½ *a* ¼	Eng. Cop. 1 *l.* 16	Between 80 and 90 ---- 28
Dublin—— 11¼	Welch ditto 1 *l.*	Between 90 and 100 --- 8
	Lottery Tickets, for the Receipts 4*s.* Discount.	2052

Price of Grain at *Bear-Key, per* Qr.		Buried.	Weekly Burials
Wheat 22 *s.* to 26 *s.*	P. Malt 20*s.* to 23*s.*	Within the walls, 182	*Aug.* 4 --- 514
Rye 12 *s.* to 16 *s.*	B. Malt 16 *s.* to 18 *s.*	Without the walls, 613	11 --- 540
Barley 13 *s.* to 15*s.* 6*d*	Tares 20 *s.* to 22 *s.*	In Mid and Surry, 846	18 --- 503
Oats 10 *s.* to 15*s.*	H. Pease 16*s.* to 19*s.*	City and Sub of West 411	25 --- 495
Pease 21 *s.* to 23*s.*	H. Beans 21 *s.* to 23*s.*	2052	2052

Prices of Goods, &c. in *London.* Hay about 1*l.* 16*s.* to 2 *l.* a Load.

Coals in the Pool 24*s.* to 26*s.*
Old Hops per Hun. 2*l.* 10*s.* to 4*l.*
New Hops 5 *l.* to 6*l.*
Rape Seed 10*l.* to 11*l.* per Last
Lead the Fodder 19Hun. 1 half on board, 14*l.* to 16*l.* 00 *s.*
Tin in Blocks 4*l.* 00 *s*
Ditto in Bars 4*l.* 02 *s.* exclusive of 3 *s.* per Hun. Duty.
Copper Eng. best 5*l.* 15 *s.* per C.
Ditto ord. 4*l.* 16 *s.* to 5*l.* per C.
Ditto Barbary 70*l.* to 80*l.*
Iron of Bilboa 14*l.* 10 *s.* per Tun
Dit. of Sweden 15*l.* 10 *s.* per Tun
Town Tallow 30 *s.* to 32*s.* per C.
Country Tallow 28 *s.* 32*s.*
Salt 4 *s.* to 4 *s.* 6 *d.*

Grocery Wares.
Raisins of the Sun 28*s.* 0*d.* per C.
Ditto Malaga Frailes 19*s.*
Ditto Smirna new 20*s.*
Ditto Alicant, 18 *s.*
Ditto Lipra new 19*s.*
Ditto Belvedera 20
Currants new 45*s.*
Prunes French 18*s.*
Figs 20*s.*
Sugar Powd. best 59*s.* per C.

Ditto second sort 46*s.* to 50*s.* per C.
Loaf Sugar double refine 8*d.* Half-penny a 9*d.* per lb.
Ditto single refin. 56 *s.* to 64 *s.* per C.
Cinamon 7 *s.* 8 *d.* per *lb.*
Cloves 9 *s.* 1 *d.*
Mace 15 *s.* 0 *d.* per *lb.*
Nutmegs 8 *s.* 7 *d.* per *lb.*
Sugar Candy white 14 *d.* to 18 *d.*
Ditto brown 7 *d.* per *lb.*
Pepper for Home consf. 17 *d.*
Ditto for exportation 13 *d.* Farth.
Tea Bohea fine 10 *s.* to 11*s.* per *lb.*
Ditto ordinary 7 *s.* to 9*s.* per *lb.*
Ditto Congo 10*s.* to 14*s.* per *lb.*
ditto Pekoe 9*s.* a 14*s.* per *lb.*
ditto Green fine 8*s.* to 12*s.* per *lb.*
ditto Imperial 10*s.* to 16 *s.* per *lb.*
ditto Hyson 24 *s.* to 28 *s.*

Drugs by the lb.
Balsam Peru 14 *s.* to 15*s.*
Cardamoms 3 *s.* 3 *d.*
Camphire refin'd 19 *s.*
Crabs Eyes 2 *s.* 5 *d.*
Jallap 3*s.*
Manna 20 *d.* a 33 *d.*
Mastick white 4*s.* 0*d.*

Opium 11 *s.* 00 *d.*
Quicksilver 4 *s.* 3 *d.*
Rhubarb fine 25 *s.* a 30 *s.*
Sarsaparilla 3 *s.* 0 *d.*
Saffron Eng. 28*s.* 00 *d.*
Wormseeds 3 *s.* 5 *d.*
Balsam Capaivo 2 *s.* 9 *d.*
Balsam of Gillead 18 *s.* 00 *d.*
Hipecacuana 7 *s.*
Ambergreace per oz. 12 *s.*
Cochineal 18 *s.* 3 *d.* per *lb.*

Wine, Brandy, and Rum.
Oporto red, per Pipe 36*l.*
ditto white 24 *l.*
Lisbon red 30*l.*
ditto white, 26 *l.*
Sherry 26 *l.*
Canary new 30*l.*
ditto old 36 *l.*
Florence 3 *l.* per Chest
French red 30*l.* a 40 *l.*
ditto white 20 *l.*
Mountain malaga old 24*l.*
ditto new 20 to 24*l.*
Brandy French per Gal. 7 *s.*
Rum of Jamaica 7 *s.*
ditto Leew. Islands 6*s.* 4*d.*
Spirits Eng. 26*l.* per Tun.

A REGISTER *of* BOOKS *publish'd in* SEPTEMBER, 1733.

1. A New Account of *Poland* and *Lithuania*. Describing their Government, Palatinates, &c. The 2d. Edition with an Appendix. Printed for *J. Pemberton*, pr. 2 s. 6 d.

2. Some Observations on the Translation and Abridgment of Dr *Boerhaave's* Chymistry; wherein that learned Professor is vindicated from the unjust Representations and weak Criticisms of his Abridger. By *J. Rogers*, M. D. Printed for *J. Swaie*, pr. 1 s.

3. The English Clerk's Instructor, in the Practice of the Courts of King's Bench and Common Pleas. Vol. II. by *Daniel Reading* Attorney at Law. Printed for *A. Bettesworth*, pr. 5 s.

4. The Man-midwife Unmasqued: Or Dr *D——* indicted for a Rape; shewing how the Bill was brought in *Ignoramus*. Printed for *J. Dormer*, pr. 6 d.

5. A new Crop of Blockheads: or, the poetical Harvest-Home. A Court Ballad. Printed for *J. Dormer*, pr. 6 d.

6. *Robin* and *Will*: or, The Millers of *Arlington*. A new Ballad. Printed for *W. Webb*, pr. 6 d.

7. Dying in the Faith, open'd and improv'd. A Sermon. Occasion'd by the Death of the late Mrs *Mary Coope*. Preach'd at *Peckham*, *July* 8 1733. By *Thomas Hadfield*, M. D.

8. Liturgia: Seu Liber precum Communium & Administrationis Sacramentorum, aliorumque Rituum & Ceremoniarum in Ecclesiâ Anglicanâ receptus, &c. Editio quinta, Prioribus longe emendatior. Impensis *J. J.* & *P. Knapton*.

9. The Apprentice's Vade Mecum: Or, Young Man's Pocket Companion. In 3 Parts. Printed for *J. Roberts*, pr. 1 s.

10. The Freeholder's Political Catechism. Printed for *J. Roberts*, pr. 4 d.

11. The Landed Interest consider'd: Being serious Advice to Gentlemen, Yeomen, Farmers, and others concern'd in the ensuing Elections. By a Yeoman of Kent. Printed for *J. Roberts*, pr. 6 d.

12. Mother *Osborn's* Letter to the Protestant Dissenters, faithfully render'd into English Metre, from the *London Journal*, *Sept.* 8, 1733. By Mother *Bench*, Sister to the said Mother *Osborne*. Printed for *J. Roberts*, pr. 6 d.

13. A Defence of the most essential Articles of Christian Belief, against the Cavils of Modern Atheists and Infidels, particularly of the late Mr *C—ll—ins*, and the late *Matthew* Tindal, Doctor of Laws. In a Letter to a Friend. price 1 s.

14. The Life of *Joseph Addison*, Esq; with a Critical Account of all his Writings, extracted from No. III. and IV. of the *General Dictionary*. To which is prefix'd the Life of Dean *Addison* his Father. Printed for N. *Prevost*. pr. 1 s. 6 d.

15. Two Chronological Dissertations of the true Years of the Birth and Death of Christ. Printed for *J. Wilcox*.

16. A New Edition of the Last Will and Testament of that famous Christian Freethinker *Matthew Tyndall* L. L. D. (by appointment of the Executor and Legatee) pr. 6 d. *Note*, Eustace Budgel, *Esq; as the Dr's Principal Executor, declares it is not by his* Appointment, *and takes Occasion to caution the Publick, that as he is desired by the said Will to Publish a new and correct Edition of all Dr* Tyndall's *Works, he will set his Name thereto, to prevent any Imposition.*

17. A Political Lecture; occasioned by a late Political Catechism; addressed to the Freeholders. Printed for T. *Cooper*, pr. 4 d.

18. Poems on several Occasions. By the Rev. Mr *Fitzgerald* of Westminster School. Sold by *Benjamin Barker*.

19. Bellus Homo et Academicus. Recitarunt in Theatro Sheldoniano apud Comitia Oxoniensia, 1733; *Ludovicus Langton*, et *Tho. Baker*, Coll. Div. Magd. Commensales. Accedit Oratio *Petri Francisci Conrayer*, S.T.P. habita in iisdem Comitiis, Quint. Id. Julii Prostant venales apud *J. Wilford*, pr. 1 s.

20. The Beau and the Academick, A Dialogue in Imitation of *Bellus Homo & Academicus*, Printed for *J. Roberts*, pr. 6 d.

21. The Proceedings in the Old Bailey for the City of London and County of Middlesex from the 12th to the 15th of *Sept.* 1733. Printed for *J. Wilford*, pr. 6 d.

22. A Letter to the Freeholders, &c. of *Great Britain*, concerning their Duty before and after the Election of their Representatives. With the Characters of several Statesmen and political Writers. Printed for *J. Roberts*, pr. 6d.

23. Christianity shewn to be prov'd and supported by a sufficient Evidence, and all extraordinary Evidence to be unnecessary and improper. A Sermon preach'd at the Visitation of the Bishop of *Lincoln* at *Bedford*, *June* 25, 1733. By *Lewis Monoux*. Printed for T. *Osborne*.

24. A Word to the Freeholders and Burgesses of *Great Britain*. Being seasonable and serious Remarks upon the inconsistent Conduct of certain Boroughs, in sending Instructions to their Representatives, to oppose the Excise Bill, and Re-electing them after their being rewarded with Places for voting for the same. price 1 s.

25. Kick him Jenny. A Tale. pr. 6 d.

26. Christianity older than the Creation or the Gospel the same with natural Religion. By *George Johnston*. Printed for *J. Noon*. pr. 1 s.

27. A Letter to the *Craftsman*, on the Game of Chess: Printed for *J. Peele* pr. 6 d.

28. Of the Duties of the People towards their

their Minifters. A Sermon at the Ordination of Mr *Daniel Stevens*, in *White-ftreet, Southwark*, May 30, 1733. By *Peter Goodwin*. Printed for *R Hett*. pr. 1 s.

29. An Effay on the Improvement of Midwifery, chiefly with regard to the Operation. To which are added 50 felect Cafes. By *Edmond Chapman*, Surgeon. Printed for Meff. *Betteſworth* and *Hitch*.

30. An Effay on Hunting. By a Country Squire. Printed for *J. Roberts*.

31. The Prefent State of Popery in *England*. Printed for *A. Dodd*, pr. 6 d.

ADVERTISEMENTS.

Mr JOHN CLARKE, *known to the Learned by his various Writings, is Removed from the Town of Hull to the City of Gloucefter.*

Juſt Publiſh'd.
The THIRD EDITION, of
An Introduction to Natural Philosophy; or Philoſophical Lectures read in the Univerfity of *Oxford, Anno Domini 1700.*

To which are added,

The Demonftrations of Monfieur Huygens's Theorems concerning Centrifugal Force and Circular Motion.

By John Keill, M. D. Savilian Profeffor of Aftronomy, F. R. S. tranflated from the laft Edition of the Latin.

Printed for John Osborne and Thomas Longman, at the Ship in Pater nofter Row.

Where may be had,

I. Sir Ifaac Newton's Algebra in Englifh.
II. His Syftem of the World in Latin, 4to.
III. Gravefande's Mathematical Elements of Natural Philoſophy, in 2 vols 8vo.
IV. His Effay on Perfpective.
V. The Religious Philoſopher, or the right Uſe of Contemplating the Works of the Creator in 3 vols. 8vo.
VI. An Analytick Treatiſe of Conic fections and their Uſe. By the Marquis de l'Hofpital, 4to.

October, 2. 1733.

This Day is Publiſh'd.
CONTINUED down to the laft SESSION of PARLIAMENT incluſive, Neceffary to be conſulted by every ENGLISHMAN at this Juncture,

AN Exact and Compleat Collection of all the Laws relating to Elections of Members to ſerve in the Houfe of Commons, digeſted under the Heads of the Electors, the Elected, and the Returning Officers, whereby may be ſeen at one view the care of the Legiſlature for preſerving the freedom of Elections.

To which is added an Alphabetical Index referring to the ſeveral Sections. Printed for Cæfar Ward at the Ship between the Temple Gates in Fleetftreet, and ſold by Meff. Ward and Chandler at Scarbrough. price Bound two Shillings.

The RECEIPT *for preparing*
SIR JOHN HEWETT's FAMILY POWDER, ſo famous for Its Succeſs in Curing of all Sorts of FITS In grown Perſons or Children, of both Sexes, (as has been experienced during the many years it hath been given a way in a Charitable manner,) is now for a more univerſal Good communicated to his Nephew Tyrrel Hewett, Apothecary in Potton, Bedfordfhire, where all Ladies, and Gentlewomen, &c. inclined to keep by them ſo uſeful a Medicine for the charitable Affiftance of the Afflicted, either in their own Family or Neighbourhood, may be furniſh'd. In a ſhort time Places will be appointed to ſerve the Public with it in different Parts of the Kingdom, particularly at London and Weftminfter; mean while any Perſon may have a fufficient Quantity ſent for from POTTON, or a more particular Account of Its Virtues ſent to them to any Part of England, on ſignifying ſuch their Deſire to the Printer hereof at St John's Gate.

Juſt Publiſh'd,
For the Uſe of Families, (beautifully printed in two Volumes 8vo.) adorned with 34 Copper Plates, engraven by Mr STURT,
DUPIN's EVANGELICAL HISTORY: Or the Records of the SON of GOD, and their Veracity, demonftrated in the Life and Acts of our Bleffed Lord and Saviour Jeſus Chrift, and his holy Apoſtles. Wherein the Life of our Bleffed Jeſus is related in all its Circumftances according to the Order of Time. His Parables, Miracles, and Sufferings ſet in a juft Light and defended from all Oppofitions of wicked and defigning Men.

Printed for R. Ware, at the Bible and Sun in Amen Corner, near Pater-Nofter-Row. Price 8 s.

Where may be had juft publiſhed

1. An Hiftorical Narration of the whole Bible. In two Parts, The firft treating of the old Taftament, with the various Hiftorics of the Lives and Travels of our Bleffed Saviour and his Apoftles. With a Summary of the the Matter, Doctrine, Scope and Divine Authority of all the Canonical Epiftles, and an Explanation of ſeveral chief Heads in the myfterious Book of St John's Revelation. By J. Hammond, D. D. and curiouſly adorned with Cuts, engrav'd by John Sturt, Price 4 s. 6 d.

2. The large HOUSE BIBLES, Folio, with fix Maps of Geography and a brief Concordance for the more eaſy finding out of the Places therein contained, by J. DOWNHAME, B. D.

Bound in Calf Leather——1 l. 8 s. per Book.
And with Mr. Sturt's Cuts, at——2 l. 3 s. ditto.
On a fine Paper with Cuts——3 l. 3 s.

3. A curious FIELD's BIBLE, Folio with fine Cuts, in two Vols. Bound in Turkey Leather. Price 20 l.

4. One an Imperial Paper, Three Volumes, with fine Cuts. Price 30 l.

Likewife the greateft Variety of all Sorts of Bibles and Common Prayers, in ſeveral curious Bindings, with or without Cuts, by Wholeſale or Retale.

Juſt Publiſh'd.
No XIV. Vol. I. No XIV. Vol. IV.
THE CEREMONIES and Religious CUSTOMS of the various NATIONS of the known WORLD; faithfully tranflated from the French Original, and illuftrated with about 173 Folio Copper Plates, all beautifully defign'd by Mr Bernard Picart; together with an Addition of ſeveral curious Head-Pieces, and Tail-Pieces, and initial Letters, not only new defign'd, but adapted to the various Topicks, to which they are applied, and executed here in England, by the beft Hands.

Propoſals at large, with beautiful Specimens, are to be ſeen at the Print-ſellers and Engravers, where Subſcriptions are taken in, viz. Claude Dubois, at the Golden Head in Charles-ſtreet, Covent-Garden; T. Bowles, in St Paul's Church-Yard; P. Overton near St Dunſtan's Church; T. Glaſs, Royal-Exchange-Stairs; J. Bowles, at the Black-Horſe in Cornhill; J. Regnier, in Newport-ſtreet, J. Hulton, at the Bottom of the Hay-Market; P. Fourdriner, Charing-Croſs; J. King, in the Poultry; Mrs Berbeck in Weftminfter Hall; J. Clark, Gray's Inn, and Mrs Sympſon in the Strand; alſo by J. Abree in Canterbury, and W. Dicey in Northampton.

N. B. The Explanations of the Prints will be curiouſly engraved in Englifh and French, on the Bottom of each Plate, to render the ſame more generally uſeful; and the Publick may be affured, that no Pains or Expence ſhall be wanting to make the whole, in all Reſpects, as compleat as poffible, and we freely ſubmit the Execution to their Cenſure or Approbation.

Lately Publiſh'd.
FOURTEEN SERMONS Preach'd on ſeveral Occaſions. By WILLIAM REEVES, M. A. late Vicar of St MARY's in READING, Author of the Apologies, in 2 Vols. 8o. Among which is contain'd that Remarkable ONE Preach'd at the Time of an Election for Members of Parliament for that Place; on Matthew XXVII. 3. 4. entitled, The Fatal Conſequences of Bribery, exemplified in Judas. Now Recommended as ſeaſonable to be read by all Perſons concern'd in the enfuing Election, as a proper Antidote and Preſervative againſt being drawn into thoſe fatal Snares of Bribery and Corruption. Printed, and Sold by S. Birt, at the Bible and Ball in Ave-Mary-Lane.

The Gentleman's *Magazine*

LondGazette
Londō Jour.
Fog's Journ.
Applebee's ::
Read's :: ::
Craftsman :
H. Spectator
Grubstreet J
W.ly Register
Free - Briton
Hyp - Doctor
Daily Court
Daily - Post
Dai. Courant
Da. Post-boy
D. Advertiser
Evening Post
St James's Eb.
Whitehall Eb
Lōdon Eb Eg
Flying - Post
Weekly Mif-
rellany.
General Eve-
ning Post

St John's Gate.

Book - Neb
Dublin i ::
Edinburgh
Bristol :::
Norwich a
Exeter : ::
Worcester
Northampt
Gloucester:
Stamford :
Nottingham
Bury Journ
Chester ditt
Derby ditto
Ipswich do
Reading do.
Leeds Merc
Newcastle
Canterbury
Birmingham
Manchester
Boston ::: e
Jamaica, &c
Barbados : :

Or, MONTHLY INTELLIGENCER.

For OCTOBER, 1733.

CONTAINING,

more in Quantity, and greater Variety, than any Book of the kind and Price.

By *SYLVANUS URBAN*, Gent.

LONDON: Printed for the Author, and sold at St *John's Gate*: By F. *Jefferies*, in *Ludgate-street*; all other Booksellers; and by the Persons who serve Gentlemen with the News-Papers. *Of whom may be had* Compleat Sets, *or any* single Number. A few on Royal Paper.

CONTENTS.

It's deſired that all Letters to the Author of the GENTLEMAN's MAGAZINE
may be directed to St JOHN's GATE, near Weſt Smithfield, in which Caſe
they will always come to hand ſooner than otherwiſe.

PROCEEDINGS *and* DEBATES *in laſt* Seſſion of Parliament.

DEBATE *on the* ARMY *continued.*

FTER the D---ke of A---le had ſpoke as mentioned in our laſt (ſee p. 460.) the L---d B---ſt roſe up and ſpoke to the Effect as follows, *viz.*

The Noble Duke, *My Lords,* who ſpoke laſt, has ſpoke ſo fully in favour of a Standing Army, that if it were poſſible to convince me that a Standing Army is conſiſtent with the Liberties of any Country, that Noble Duke would have done it; I ſhould even be afraid to riſe up to offer any thing in anſwer to what he has ſo well ſaid upon that Subject, if it were not, that I think myſelf under a Neceſſity of giving your Lordſhips ſome Reaſon for my voting as I ſhall do in the important Queſtion now before us.--I was glad, *My Lords,* to hear that Noble Duke allow, that the Militia of the Kingdom might be put upon ſuch a Footing as to be uſeful for our Defence, becauſe I think it the only Defence, next to our Fleet, which we can with any Safety truſt to; and as there is no Man more capable than he, for putting us in a way of making our Militia uſeful, I wiſh he would give us his Thoughts upon that Subject; I am ſure there is nothing he can offer but what will be well received and readily agreed to. As to the Expence of keeping our Militia under a proper Diſcipline, I do not think that it is of any Conſideration in the preſent Queſtion, if it ſhould amount to a great deal more than what we now pay for maintaining our Regular Army, it would be an Argument of no Weight with me againſt the Scheme; for I am ſure if the Expence were greater, our Power would be rendered in Proportion much more extenſive, and our Liberties much more ſecure.--If, *My Lords,* the Militia were to be put upon ſuch a Footing as to be really uſeful for the Defence of the Country, it is not to be ſuppoſed, that the People would grumble at any Charge or Inconvenience they were put to upon ſuch reaſonable Account. The many Loads they have quietly ſubmitted to of late Years, ſhew us, that they are not apt to grumble, when they are convinced of the reaſon of the Thing;

but at preſent they know, that the Militia are of no publick Uſe, that the drawing (See Vol. I. p. 208.) them out to Exerciſe tends to no End but that of putting Money in the Pockets of the Officers, and therefore they grumble.--Though the Militia of the Kingdom be under the Command of the King, though their Officers be all named by the King, yet under ſuch a Military Force, our Liberties muſt be ſafe: The Militia of the Kingdom are the People of the Kingdom, and it is impoſſible to make uſe of the People for oppreſſing the Liberties of the People; but a Standing Army of Regular Forces ſoon begin to look upon themſelves as a Body Separate and Diſtinct from the People; and if the People in general neglect the Uſe of Arms, and truſt entirely to ſuch a Military Force for their Defence, the King, who has the abſolute Command over them, may eaſily fall upon Ways and Means to make uſe of them for oppreſſing the Liberties of the People; by granting particular Favours to ſuch a Military Force, and by preſerving the Affections of a few Men bred up to Arms and Military Diſcipline, he may do whatever he pleaſes with the Multitude who have neither Arms in their Hands, nor any Knowledge how to uſe them, if they had. What the Noble Duke ſaid as to Auxiliaries is moſt certainly true; thoſe who truſt entirely to Auxiliaries for their Defence, muſt always be Slaves to thoſe in whom they put their Truſt; It is, *My Lords,* for this very Reaſon that I am againſt a Standing Army; for it holds equally true of a Standing Army of our own Subjects, as of an Army of Foreign Auxiliaries; whoever truſts his Defence to any thing but himſelf, muſt be a Slave to that in which he puts his Truſt; and whenever People put their whole Truſt in a Standing Army, even of their own Subjects, will ſoon come to be as great Slaves as the People who put their Truſt in an Army of Foreign Troops; the Maſters may be different, but the Slavery is the ſame, and will be equally grievous.--I believe it never was ſaid, that a Standing Army is the only Method by which an Arbitrary Power may be eſtabliſhed; but I am ſure that it can never be long ſupported without a Standing Army. By a Political and Cunning Adminiſtration the People may be cheated out of their Liberties;

berties; by some specious Pretence or another they may be induced to give up all those Barriers which are the Defence and the Protection of their Liberties and Privileges, but the Fraud will at last be discovered, and as soon as it is, People will resume their ancient Privileges, if there be no new sort of Power established for protecting the Arbitrary Government against any such Resumption, which Power can never consist in any thing else but a Standing Army of some kind or other.——A Standing Army must therefore, *My Lords*, be of dangerous Consequence to the Liberties of every Country. In some free Countries there may be at least a Shew of Reason for their submitting to such a Danger, but in this Country there cannot be so much as a Shew of Reason; we have a Fleet superior to that of any of our Neighbours, and we know how difficult it is for any of our Neighbours to invade us with a considerable Force; such Designs must always be discovered long before they can be ready for Execution; and as long as we preserve a superior Fleet, we shall always have it in our power to prevent the Execution of any such Design; but granting that they should by any strange Fatality or Negligence, escape our Fleets at Sea, yet still we should have time to prepare for their Reception; if our Militia be always kept in good Order, and under a proper Discipline, they will be sufficient for our Defence against any Power that can be brought against us, as long as the King is possessed of the Affections of the People in general; and those he can never lose so readily as by despising the People, and trusting entirely to his Standing Army.——As for those small Invasions which the noble Duke was pleased to mention, what though they had landed? What would have been the Consequence? I hope it is not to be imagined, notwithstanding the contemptible State to which our Militia has been by Neglect reduced, that this Country is to be conquered by six or seven thousand Men. Even the late K. *Wm*. though he had escaped the *English* Fleet, where it is supposed he had a good many Friends, though he had double that Number of Men, and though he got all his Troops safely and without Opposition landed upon the *English* Shore, yet, upon his seeing so few come in to join him upon his first Landing, he was very near going off again. It is not an easy matter to bring about a Revolution against an established Government; but it is still much more difficult to come in as Conquerors, and pretend to subdue such a powerful and populous Country as this is. And if the great K. *Wm*, who came to relieve us from Slavery and Oppression, who brought along with him so great an Army and so powerful a Fleet, was so doubtful of Success upon his first landing, what have we to fear from any small Invasion? Surely from such the Nation can never have

any thing to fear, whatever such a Government as that of K. *James's* was, may have to fear from such small Invasions encouraged, called in, and supported by the Generality of our People at home. This is a Case which I hope never will again happen; it is a Case against which we are not to provide, and for these Reasons I shall be for agreeing to the Reduction proposed.——As to our Armies not being obliged to obey any illegal Orders, I do not know, *My Lords*, whether it be so or not; but in my Opinion the noble Duke has given us a good Hint for an Amendment to the Bill; this Word. *Legal*, ought certainly to be put in, and then in case of any Disobedience to such Orders, a Council of War would certainly have it in their Power to examine first into the Legality of the Orders given, as to which there may be some Doubt as the Bill stands at present; it may be at least alledged, that as the Bill now stands, the Council of War would be obliged to pass Sentence against the Soldiers for Mutiny, whatever they might do with the Officer who gave the illegal Orders.

L—d C——t.] So many Lords have spoke so well in favour of the Reduction proposed, and have so fully answered all the Objections made against it, that I should not have given your Lordships any Trouble on the present Occasion, if it had not been that I now find, that not only a Standing Army, but an Army of the full Number we have at present on foot, seems to be made a Part of our Constitution: The old Pretence of continuing the same Number of Regular Forces for one Year longer, seems now to be laid aside: His Majesty in his Speech from the Throne told us that the Publick Tranquillity was now so fully established, that he had no other Reason for calling us together but only for the ordinary Dispatch of the Publick Business; and must this be looked on as a Part of the ordinary Business of the Year? Must the continuing of a Standing Army of 18,000 Men in time of Peace be a Part of that Business which is yearly to pass of course in Parliament? It has been a long Time continued from Year to Year, but if it once comes to be an Affair which is yearly to pass of Course, wherein will it differ from those Standing Armies by which the Liberties of other Countries have been undone?——A Standing Army alone may not perhaps be sufficient for bringing so great a Misfortune upon a People; there must be other Causes concurring; but it may be averred, that in all Countries where Arbitrary Power and Abject Slavery have been introduced, the fatal Change in the Constitution has been owing to a numerous Standing Army, a great Number of Officers of the Revenue, and a Prostitute Clergy; and even these three concurring together, must require some time before they can get the Better of the Liberties of a brave People: The Army

Army muſt be ſo long kept up, and modelled in ſuch a manner, as to be entirely dependent on the Crown; it is not to be ſuppoſed, that the Officers and Soldiers of an Army raiſed from among a free People can be immediately diveſted of all thoſe Notions of Liberty with which they were endowed when they firſt liſted in the Army; but if they have a brave and cunning Commander, this may be done in a few Years, the Generality of them may be ſoon made regardleſs of every thing but the Will and Pleaſure of him who can prefer them to a ſuperior Command: A large Revenue, and many Officers cannot be at once eſtabliſhed upon a free People, this muſt be done by ſlow Degrees, and requires many plauſible Pretences: And it is to be hoped that the Honour and Virtue of the Clergy would ſtand ſome little Shock, they could not at once be brought to that Degree of Proſtitution which is neceſſary for the Eſtabliſhment of Arbitrary Power.--- At preſent, we may depend upon his Majeſty; we are convinced that he will not attempt to encroach upon the Liberties of his People; we may likewiſe depend on it, that our preſent Army would not ſupport any ſuch Meaſures, were they to be attempted; his Majeſty has been ſo good as to employ Men as Officers in the Army, whoſe Honour and Integrity we may depend on, but we are not ſure of having always a King ſo wiſe and good, or an Army of ſo much Virtue and Honour; and under the beſt of Kings we ought to provide againſt the worſt. --- I do not ſay, that we are now in any immediate Danger of loſing our Liberties, but we are getting into that Way by which the Liberties of every Country hath been undone; we are eſtabliſhing the Cuſtom of keeping up a ſtanding Army in time of Peace; we are every Year increaſing the Number of Officers of the Revenue; what will the Conſequence be? I tremble to think of it! We are not indeed under any Danger while his preſent Majeſty lives to reign over us: But will not every ſucceeding King ſay, why will you treat me worſe than my Predeceſſor? Why will you refuſe to grant me that Number of Regular Forces, or that Revenue which in the ſame Circumſtances you granted to my Father? And we well know, how complaiſant Parliaments generally are in the Beginning of a Reign; they are generally more apt to increaſe both the Revenue and the Army of the Crown than they are to diminiſh either; and if an ambitious Prince ſhould ſucceed to the Crown, ſupported by ſuch a numerous Standing Army as what is now propoſed, ſo long kept up as to have formed themſelves into a different Body from the People to whom they belong, and with ſuch a Crowd of Officers of the Revenue as we have at preſent, all depending upon him and removable at his Pleaſure, what may he not do? --- I am ſurprized to hear

it ſaid, that Standing Armies have had no Hand in the Overturning the Liberties of the ſeveral Countries of *Europe*. It is true that the moſt numerous Army can be of no dangerous Conſequence to the Liberties of any Country, as long as it depends upon a great many Heads; an Army can never be of dangerous Conſequence, till it comes to be entirely dependent upon one Man, as it generally does when it is long kept up, more eſpecially if any one Man comes to get the whole Power into his own Hands both of paying the Army, and of naming and preferring the ſeveral Officers employed therein. *Julius Caſar* had too long a Head not to be ſenſible of this, and therefore he procured himſelf to be ſent into *Gaul*; there he continued for ſeveral Years at the Head of numerous conquering Armies, and having got into his own Hands both the Power of paying and preferring in his Army, he ſoon managed it ſo as to make them entirely obedient to him; then he commanded them to march againſt, and with them he conquered his Country. If there had been no Standing Armies of either Side, the Conſequence could not have been the ſame; though a Civil War had broke out, the Armies newly raiſed by each Side muſt have had a Dependance upon a great many Chiefs, and which ever Side had got the Victory, the Chiefs would have taken Care of the Liberties of their Country; they would have ſettled them upon the antient Foundation, or upon a better, if any better could be contrived.--- In *Spain* it was likewiſe by ſuch an Army that their Liberties were deſtroyed. The Inquiſition, it is true, was ſet up much about the ſame Time, and in all Countries an Inquiſition of ſome kind or another generally accompanies Arbitrary Power; there may be Courts of Inquiſition with regard to Civil Affairs as well as Religious, and all Inquiſitions are at firſt eſtabliſhed upon ſome plauſible Pretence: The Baniſhing of the *Moors* and *Jews* out of his Kingdoms, was the Pretence made uſe of by *Ferdinand*, then King of *Spain*, but the Extending of his own Power was the latent and the chief Reaſon: The Inquiſition was not, however, the chief cauſe of the Loſs of the *Spaniſh* Liberties, it was only a Conſequence; for before the ſetting up thereof, he had got the abſolute Command of a great Army, which had been kept up for ſeveral Years under Pretence of their War with *Portugal*, whoſe then King laid Pretenſions to the Crown of *Spain*; and by keeping his Country in continual Wars, he found Pretences to keep up a great Standing Army, with which it is true, he conquered and baniſhed the *Moors*, but he therewith likewiſe conquered the Liberties of his Country; and the Chains of the People were ſoon riveted by a Prieſt, a Cardinal Prime Miniſter, who compleated the cruel Work which *Ferdinand* by his Ar-

my

my had so successfully begun.—In *France* too, *My Lords*, it was by Standing Armies chiefly that their Liberties were undone, it was not indeed, by Armies modelled as they have them at present, but it was by altering the antient Military Force of the Kingdom that their Liberties were destroyed; it was by their King's taking the army *à sa Solde*, as they call it; for anciently the Military Force of that Kingdom depended chiefly upon the Nobility or great Princes; their Armies were composed of the Troops sent to the General Rendezvous by the several Princes of the Kingdom, who generally paid their respective Troops; or if at any Time they had them maintained at the Publick Charge, yet each Prince retained in his own Hands the Naming and Preferring the Officers employed in his Troops, and therefore no one Man could procure to himself an absolute Command over the Armies of that Kingdom; but at last this laudable Custom was laid aside, the King got into his own Hands the whole Power of raising and paying the Armies to be employed for the Defence of the Kingdom; and though for some time after he had no Money for that purpose but what was given him by the States of *France*, yet we may really look upon this Change as the Beginning of the *French* Slavery. However for a long time after this, the Kings of *France* could never prevail with their States to provide him with Money for continually keeping up a numerous Standing Army; their Armies were raised only when they had Occasion for them, and as soon as the Danger was over their Armies were dismissed; and yet, they had for some Part of that time a Pretender to their Crown; our *Edward* the IIId then claimed to be King of *France*, and he, *My Lords*, was a very terrible Pretender; yet even by that imminent Danger they were then exposed to, they could not be induced to keep up a Standing Army; they never had any thing but Militia, or Troops raised as Occasion required, and with these they at last banished the *English* quite out of their Kingdom.— But as soon as the Kings of *France* got thus free of an Enemy within the Bowels of their Kingdom, they thereafter took Occasion of every foreign War that happened to encroach a little further upon the Liberties of their Subjects, to multiply Taxes and Tax-Gatherers upon them, and to get the Armies of the Kingdom more and more under their Command: In all which they succeeded beyond Expectation, by a most stupid Indolence that then reigned among the Nobility of *France*; and yet that Nation still retained some Remains of Liberty, till a Priest, Cardinal *Richlieu* by Name, gave their Liberties the last Stab.—— He indeed was a great Minister , and a great Politician, though he oppressed the Subject at home, yet he not only supported

but raised the Grandeur of the Nation abroad ; he committed no Blunders in his Administration, nor did he submit to any foreign Power in the Treaties or Negotiations he had with them; and we may remember that in his Political Testament, he left it as a Maxim, " that the King ought never to part with any Tax he has once got established, even though he has no use for the Money; because by giving up the Tax he loses the Officers that are employed in the collecting thereof."—This great Prime Minister was succeeded by another, a foreign Priest, who had all his bad Qualities but none of his good; so that by his Misconduct *France* was soon involved in a Civil War; and it is said that one of the greatest Men of *France* at that time, and one of the greatest Generals of the Age he lived in, told the Queen Regent, that she had a Fellow at the Head of her Affairs, who, for his Crimes deserved to be tugging at the Oar in one of her Gallies. But the Arbitrary Power of the King of *France* had by his Predecessor been so firmly established, that it could not be shaken even by the many Blunders he was guilty of ; the Nation however was not yet rendered so tame, but that it was a long while before they would quietly submit to that Cardinal's Administration; and we must allow that even but lately there has a noble Spirit of Liberty broke forth in that Country, such a Spirit as might probably reinstate the People in the full Enjoyment of their former Liberties and Privileges, if it were not for the great Standing Army now kept up in that Country.—In *Denmark*, it was their Nobles that were the Occasion of the Loss of their Liberties; they had for some time thrown the whole Weight and Charge of the Government off of themselves, and had laid it on the Necks of the Commons ; the whole Expence of the Publick they had for some time raised by Taxes which fell chiefly upon the poor People, and to which they contributed but a Trifle; and the Commons being quite tired out with these Oppressions and unjust Exactions, resolved at last to put the whole Power into the Hands of their Sovereign; so that whilst the Nobles were sitting and contriving Ways and Means how to load the poor Tradesmen and Manufacturers with such Taxes as did not much affect them, they were sent for to the Castle, and there were obliged to join in that Deed by which an absolute Power was put into the Hands of the King, who could not make a worse use of it than they had done: This was the Method by which Arbitrary Power was established in *Denmark*, but it has ever since been supported only by a Standing Army.—In *Sweden*, their Liberties were not only destroyed but they were again restored by their Army; in this last Change, that Country had the good Luck to be most singularly happy, but how was that most

strange

ſtrange and extraordinary Turn of their Affairs brought about? I have ſome Reaſon to know it, becauſe I was in that Kingdom when it happened. The late King of *Sweden* is well known to have been the Darling both of his Nobles and Commons; he was ſo much the Darling of the whole *Swediſh* Nation, that almoſt every Man in it was at all times ready to ſacrifice both his Life and his Fortune in his Service, and therefore he had no Occaſion to model his Army for any bad Purpoſe; he had employed none as Officers in his Army, but the Nobility and Quality of the Kingdom, or ſuch whoſe Merit and Services fully entitled them to whatever Preferment they were honoured with by him. His Prime Miniſter however got at laſt too great an Aſcendant over him; Baron *Gortz* I mean, who was a Man of no high Birth, nor any ſuper-eminent Qualities; yet by his Cunning he got ſuch a Power over his Maſter, that nothing was done without him, no Poſt Civil or Military was beſtowed but according to his Direction, the Men of the beſt Quality in the Kingdom, the greateſt Generals in the Army, were obliged to ſubmit and to ſue to him even for that which they were juſtly entitled to; if they ſhewed him the leaſt Neglect, they immediately loſt all Intereſt about the King; if any one of them diſobliged the firſt Miniſter, he might perhaps be allowed to keep his Poſt in the Army, he was made uſe of when they had Occaſion for his venturing his Life for them, but from the Moment he diſobliged the King's ·Prime Miniſter, he loſt his Intereſt with reſpect to the Army, he could not ſo much as make a Subaltern Officer; on the contrary his Recommendation was a ſure Bar to any Man's Preferment.——The Nobility, the Generals, all the chief Men in the Army were ſenſible of this Slavery they lay under, and were reſolved to free themſelves therefrom if poſſible; but their Government was then abſolute, there was no way of coming at Relief, but by making their King ſenſible of the Diſcredit that accrued to him, by allowing himſelf to be ſo much under the Management of any one Man: They knew their King to be a Man of Judgment and Penetration, and therefore a great Number of them reſolved at laſt upon venturing to preſent a Memorial to him upon that Head. This Memorial, was actually drawn up and ſigned, and was ready to have been preſented when that brave King was killed by a Random Shot from *Frede-rickſtadt* which he was then beſieging.—If the King had lived to have received this Memorial, we cannot judge what might have been the Conſequence; notwithſtanding of its being ſigned by ſo many of the Nobility and chief Commanders; notwithſtanding of the King's Judgment and Penetration, his Affection for his Miniſter might have got the Better of the Reſpect he owed to ſuch

a Number of his Nobility and Generals; and if ſo, as he was a moſt abſolute Prince, the Memorial would have been deemed to be a ſeditious and a treaſonable Libel, and ſome of them would certainly have paid with their Heads for their Preſumption; but the King's Death rid them of this Danger, and the Prime Miniſter who had done ſo many ill Things, was immediately ſeized, tried, condemned and executed under the Gallows.——By this Piece, of publick Juſtice, the Nobles and the Generals of the Army, whom he had principally offended, were ſatisfied, they did not deſire to purſue their Vengeance further than in the Grave; but the Clergy of that Kingdom, thoſe Men who but a few Weeks before were his moſt humble Slaves, thoſe Men who would have deified him, if the Chriſtian Religion had not ſtood in their Way, they had a Mind to ſhew a ſuperior Degree of Zeal, they petitioned in a Body that his Corps might be buried under the Gallows.——By the King's Death the ſlaviſh Dependance of the Army was at an End; there was then no one Man who could pretend to any abſolute Sway over the Army, and as it was generally commanded by the Nobles of the Kingdom, they had it freſh in their Memories what Inconveniences both they and the whole Nation had been ſubjected to by the abſolute and uncontroulable Will of their former King; as there was no one of them that could have any Hopes of ſucceeding to his Arbitrary Power, therefore they all reſolved to put born the Government of the Kingdom, and the Command of the Army, upon a new and a very different Footing. As to the Government of the Kingdom, they eſtabliſhed a limited Monarchy, and finding that they muſt neceſſarily keep up a Standing Army to defend their large Frontiers, they therefore reſolved, in order that the Army might not be entirely dependent on the Crown, that for the future the Officers thereof ſhould have their ſeveral Commiſſions *Quam diu ſe bene geſſerit*. Which Regulation a Nobleman of that Country told me, they took from the Regulation we have in *England* with reſpect to our Judges. It is a wiſe and a neceſſary Regulation, a Regulation that ought in every Country to prevail, where-ever a Standing Army makes a Part of their Conſtitution: In all ſuch Countries the Officers Commiſſions ought certainly to be *Quam diu ſe bene geſſerit*, and Preferments ought to go in Courſe according to Seniority, ſome few Caſes excepted; for it is hard that a Gentleman who has nothing but his Commiſſion to depend on for his daily Bread, ſhould be obliged either to forfeit his Commiſſion or his Hopes of Preferment in the Army, or otherwiſe to do what he knows to be inconſiſtent with the Laws and Liberties of his Country.——I hope that a Standing Army will never come to be a

Part

; Part of our Constitution; but if ever it does, I will say, that without such a Regulation as I have mentioned, we shall then have nothing to depend on for the Preservation of our Liberties, but the Honour of the Army, the Integrity of the Clergy, and the Vigilance of the Lords.——From what I have said it is apparent that a numerous Standing Army must always be of dangerous Consequence to the Constitution of this Country; and I leave it to every Man to judge, whether we ought to expose our Constitution to such a Danger, for the pretended Apprehensions of any Insurrection at home, or of any Invasion from abroad? As to Insurrections at home, we are in no Danger of any such as long as his Majesty reigns in the Hearts and Affections of the Generality of his Subjects; and as to Invasions from abroad, I think the little Success the many designed Invasions mentioned by the noble Duke has met with, is an unanswerable Argument for shewing us that we ought not to be under great Apprehensions of any such in time to come; and that we ought not to subject ourselves to any thing that may be in the least dangerous to our Constitution, for the sake of a Danger which Experience has shewn to be so very inconsiderable.——If we should ever be threatned with a formidable Invasion, we should have Time to increase our Army to any Number we pleased, we should even have Time to discipline that Army before we could be attacked by any great Force, and thereby we should be in a Condition to defend ourselves at Land, if our Enemies should have the good Luck to escape our Fleets at Sea: And as to any small and unforeseen Invasions, if ever any such should be intended against us, they may probably meet with the same Fate that the former have done; but if they should meet with better Luck, if they should come safe to Land, they could not bring above five or six thousand Men, our Fleets would prevent their being reinforced, and surely an Army of 12,000 Men in Great Britain, and another of equal Number in Ireland, would be sufficient to give a good Account of any such contemptible Invaders.——It is not now proposed to disband our Army entirely; nor to throw out the Bill now before us; we are for keeping up as great a Number as may be necessary for preserving the Peace and Quiet of the Kingdom; but we are against keeping up such a Number as may be dangerous to our Constitution. Though the Lords who were last Year for a Reduction, voted against the passing of the then Mutiny Bill, 'tis not from thence to be concluded, that they were against any Mutiny Bill, or any Number of Regular Forces; they were against the whole Bill as it then stood, but if that Bill had been thrown out, another might have been brought in according to their Liking, and that new Bill would then have been unanimously agreed to,

E—l of I---ay.] *Whatever some Lords may be pleased to say about an Army continued from Year to Year by Parliament, there is certainly a very great Difference, My Lords, between such an Army, and an Army continued at the sole Pleasure of the Crown. It has, I think, been granted on all Hands, that while our Army is commanded by such Officers as it is at present, while Men of Fortune and Figure have the command of the Army, our Liberties are secure; but it is said that these Officers may be turned out, this Army may be so modelled and garbled as to be made fit for any bad Purpose: This, My Lords, I shall easily grant might be done, if our Army were to be established for any Number of Years; if it were to be continued at the sole Pleasure of the Crown, an ambitious Prince might be able to model it so as to make it subservient to his arbitrary Views; but while it is continued only from Year to Year by Parliament, this is impossible to be done. It is no easy matter to model an Army so as to make it fit for such Purposes; we know how difficult it is to know the private Sentiments of Men's Hearts; in such Cases Men often conceal their real Inclinations under the Cloak of a feigned Zeal for the direct contrary Opinion, which would make it very difficult for a Government that had any Designs against the Liberties of the People, to know what Officers were to be turned out, or who were proper to be continued, or to be put in the Room of those turned out. It would be impossible to accomplish this in a Year's time, and if any such Practices were begun, if any Steps should be made towards modelling the Army for a bad Purpose, the Parliament at their next Meeting would most certainly take notice of it, and would apply a proper Remedy, before it could be possible for any Prince or Administration to make the Wound incurable; and therefore I must still be of Opinion that our Army, while it is continued from Year to Year by Parliament, cannot be of the least ill Consequence to our Constitution, were it much more numerous than what is now proposed.——On the other Hand, My Lords, the Danger of reducing any Part of our Army is very great: We know that such Reductions have often been attended with designed Invasions or Insurrections against the Government; this is a Danger we know by Experience, and therefore in common Prudence we ought not to come into any Measure by which our Country may be again exposed to such a Danger. It is probable that none of those Invasions lately intended against us would have been successful, though they had got safe ashore; I hope no such ever will; but every one of them, if they had landed, would have thrown the Nation into terrible Convulsions. Is then, the Peace and Quiet of our Country of no Consideration? Shall we expose our Country to frequent Alarms and Confusions, for the sake of avoiding an imaginary Danger, a Fear which can have no Foundation, as long as our Army is continued only from Year to Year by Parliament?——We know that there is a Party in the Nation disaffected to the Government, there always will, I am afraid, be such a Party; and* they, or at least, a great many of them, will always join any Invasion that can be made upon us: Even out of Charity to them we ought not to afford them any Hopes of Success, by disbanding a Part of our Army; while they have no Hopes of Success they may grumble a little in private, but they will never venture to rebell openly against the Government, and while they continue in a peaceable State they may live easily as Subjects, they will at least preserve their Lives and Estates from being forfeited by the Law; whereas if we reduce our Army, it will encourage Foreigners to invade us, it will encourage the Disaffected to rebell against the Government; the Nation will never be free from Alarms, and we must be every now and then executing, or at least forfeiting some of our Countrymen, perhaps some of our Relations.

E—l of B—l.] My Lords, I have often heard the present Argument debated in Parliament; I was one of those who were the Cause of the Army's being reduced so low after the Peace of Ryswick; perhaps I repented of what I did at that time, because of the Turn that the Affairs of Europe took soon after: But I am fully convinced, I never shall have Occasion to repent of being for the Reduction now proposed. I cannot but say, that the Question now before us puts me in Mind of what happened to a Farm House of mine. The Wall of the House upon one Side had failed, and the House had sunk a little; some Workmen persuaded me, that they could raise it up, and repair the Wall without pulling the House down, and to work they went; but in planting Posts and other Engines to raise up that Side which had sunk, they raised the House so high on that Side, that they tumbled it quite over.

At last the Question was put upon the E—l of O—d's Motion for the Instruction to the Committee, which upon a Division was carried in the Negative. And the Bill was passed, whereupon a Protest was entered, (see Vol. II. p. 815) by the following Lords, viz.

Bruce,	Masham,	Gower,
Montjoy,	Strafford,	Northampton,
Bathurst,	Litchfield,	Oxford and
Foley,	Bristol,	Mortimer
Berkshire,	Coventry,	

In our Magazine for August (See p. 401, 2, 3, 4.) we gave an Account of the Resolutions the House of Commons had come to in relation to the Sugar Colony Affairs, and of a Bill's having been ordered to be brought in pursuant to those Resolutions: That Bill was accordingly brought in, and on the 8th Day of March, Sir J—n B—d opened to the House a Petition of Richard Partridge, Agent for the Colony of Rhode Island, and Providence Plantations in America, against the said Bill, and moved for Leave to bring it up; in which he was seconded by Mr A—n P—y; whereupon there ensued a Debate, in which the following Gentlemen spoke in Substance, or to the Effect as follows, viz.

On Petitions.

Sir W——m Y——ge] Sir, The Petition which the Hon. Member over the Way has now in his Hand, is, I find, a Petition praying for Leave to be heard against a Bill now depending in this House, by which some certain Duties are to be laid on several Commodities mentioned in the Bill. I believe, it has been the constant Usage of this House for many Years, to receive no Petitions against Duties to be laid on; but as there are none who understand better than you, the Practice of the House in such Cases, therefore I shall in this submit entirely to your Determination, and hope you will give us your Opinion thereupon. However, I must take Notice of another Thing which I observe in the Petition; they therein tell us, that as to the Bill now depending before us, they apprehend it to be against their Charter. This, I must say, is something very extraordinary, and in my Opinion looks mighty like aiming at an Independency, and disclaiming the Authority and Jurisdiction of this House, as if this House had not a Power to tax them, or to make any Laws for the Regulating of the Affairs of their Colony; therefore if there were no other Reason for our not receiving their Petition, I should on this single Account be against giving Leave to bring it up.

L—d T—l.] Sir, I cannot agree with the Honourable Member who spoke last, for I shall never give my Vote for rejecting a Petition before I know what is in it; and this I cannot know 'till I hear it read. The Question now before us; is not Whether the Desire of the Petition shall be granted or no? After the Petition is brought up and read to the House, we may then judge whether the Desire thereof be reasonable or no, and may accordingly grant or refuse it, but the refusing to have the Petition brought up and read to the House, seems really to be a Determining the Desire of the Petition to be unreasonable, before we know what it is; and therefore, I shall be for having it brought up.

T——t W——e Esq;] Sir, I stand up to speak to Order and to the Method of Proceeding in this House; it has been a Custom always observed in this House, not to receive any Petitions against those Bills which were brought in for the laying on of any new Duties; I do not indeed say but I am sure they are very rare, and never happened but upon some very extraordinary Occasions; for if we were to receive all such Petitions, there would be such Multitudes of them against every such Bill, that the Nation might be undone for want of an immediate Supply for the Publick Use, while we were sitting to hear frivolous Petitions against those Bills brought in for granting that Supply. The Honourable Gentleman near me took Notice of the Petitioners pretending, that the Bill now before us is against their Charter; I hope, they have no Charter which debarrs this House from taxing them as well as any of the other Subjects of this Nation; I am sure they can have no such Charter; but if it were possible, if they really had such a Charter, they could not say that the Bill now before us were any Infringe-

Infringement of it, because the 'Tax to be thereby laid on, is no Tax upon them, it is a Tax which is to be laid upon the *French* only; and shall this House receive any Petitions, or hear any Reasons that can be offered, for not taxing the *French*, more especially when the Tax to be laid upon them, will most evidently tend to the Encouragement of our own Sugar Colonies? I hope no such Petition will ever so much as be allowed to be brought up or presented to this House.

Sir J....n B......d.] Sir, the Petitioners do not pretend to say that the Bill now depending is against their Charter, nor did I say any such Thing when I opened the Petition to this House, at least if I did, I am sure I did Injustice to the Petition, for the Words of it are, *That they humbly conceive, that the Bill now depending, if passed into a Law, would be highly prejudicial to their Charter.* But, I am really surprized at the Method of Reasoning made use of by the two Honourable Gentlemen who have appeared against the bringing up of this Petition: One of them says, that the Petitioners are aiming at an Independency, and are disowning the Authority of this House. This, in the present Case, seems a very odd Assertion; is not their applying by Petition to this House, as direct an Acknowledgment of the Authority of this House, as can be made by Men? The other Gentleman says, that the Bill now before us is a Bill for Taxing the *French* only; this seems to be as odd an Assertion as the other: Does the Gentleman imagine that the Tax paid in this Island upon *French* Wine, is a Tax upon the *French*? Does not every Body know, that the whole of it is paid by the Consumers here? It is so far from being a Tax upon the *French*, that they have considerably raised the Price of their Wines since the high Duties were laid on them here. As to the Matter of Form, I do not pretend to be a great Master of it; but since I have had the Honour to sit in Parliament, I remember that several Petitions have been received against Duties to be laid on: However, granting that it were a constant and perpetual Rule not to receive Petitions against such Duties, yet certainly that Rule could relate only to those Duties which were to be laid on for raising Money for the Current Service of the Publick, it could not be presumed to relate to those Duties which were to be laid on for the Regulation of Trade only; and this last is the Case now before us, the Duties to be laid on by this Bill are so far from being Duties for the Supply of the Government, that I do not believe that even those Gentlemen who appear so fond of the Duties to be laid on by it, so much as to expect or wish that any Money shall be thereby raised for the Use of the Publick; the Bill is not intended for any such End; it is rather in the Nature of a Prohibition, and it was never pretended that no Petitions were ever to be received against a Bill for prohibiting any sort of Commerce. It may be this House has sometimes refused to receive Petitions from some Parts of *Britain* against Duties to be laid on; but this can be no Reason why the Petition I have now in my Hand, should be rejected : The People in every Part of *Great Britain* have a Representative in this House, who is to take Care of their Particular Interest, as well as of the General Interest of the Nation; and they may, by means of their Representatives in the House, offer what Reasons they think proper against any Duties to be laid on; but the People who are Petitioners in this Petition, have no particular Representatives in this House, and therefore they have no other way of applying or of offering their Reasons to this House, but in the way of being heard at the Bar of the House by their Agent here in *England*; therefore if that general Rule of not receiving Petitions against Duties to be laid on, be ever to be receded from, the Case now before us ought to be an Exception to the general Rule.

J--n C---t Esq;] Sir, I apprehend it has always been the Custom of this House, I am sure it has been the Custom ever since the Revolution, to refuse receiving Petitions against Duties to be laid on, and that without any Distinction whether the Duties were to be laid on for raising Money, or for the Regulation of Trade: As our Colonies are all a Part of the People of *Great Britain*, they are generally represented in this House, as well as the rest of the People are; and in all the Resolutions of this House, a due Regard will certainly be had to the particular Interest of every one of them, in so far as it is consistent with the general Interest of the Whole; for which reason I can see no Occasion for making an Exception as to them; and therefore I cannot but be of the same Opinion with those Gentlemen who are for refusing their Consent to the bringing up of this Bill. As for the Duties on Wine mentioned by the Honourable Gentleman who spoke last, tho' they are paid by the Consumers here, yet they may be looked on as a Tax upon the *French*, for if it were not for those Duties, a much greater Quantity of their Wines would be consumed here than there is at present, and consequently they would thereby draw a much larger Sum of Money out of this Nation than they now do; and as to the Advance of the original Price of their Wines, there are a great many other Causes it may be owing to, but it never can be owing to the Diminution of the Quantity consumed.

W---m P---y Esq;] I do not pretend, Sir, to be a Master of Form, but I believe there may be many Precedents found for justifying the House in receiving the Petition now offered to us. I very well know, how great a Master you are of the Forms and Methods of Proceeding in this House, and therefore I shall

shall always be as ready as any Gentleman in the House to submit to your Opinion when any such Question arises; but I cannot think, that any of your Friends would desire you to give your Opinion thus upon a Surprize, in a Matter which seems to be so contested, nor do I believe that you would be ready to comply with any such unreasonable Desire; if you should once give your Opinion in any such Dispute, I should be afraid afterwards to inspect the Journals of the House, lest they should be found to contradict the Opinion you had given. But if we are to search for Precedents, I am sure that as to the present Case, there will be no Occasion for going any further back than the Revolution: Before that Time I believe we can find few or no Precedents any way relating to the Question now in Hand, because Parliaments were not then so frequent, and Taxes very rare. Let any Gentleman but look into the Statute Books lying upon our Table he will there see to what a vast Bulk, to what a Number of Volumes our Statutes relating to Taxes have swelled since the Revolution, and how this, how few the Volumes are that contain all the Statutes relating to Taxes that ever were made before that time. It is monstrous, it is even frightful to look into the Indexes, where for several Columns together we see nothing but Taxes, Taxes, Taxes! It is true, when Gentlemen reflect on the many Blessings we thereby enjoy, when they consider the many Advantages we reaped by the Revolution, they will think that we could not pay too dear for so happy a Turn in our Affairs.—As to the Question now before us, I cannot see why it should be so much debated, I cannot see why the Receiving of this Petition should be so much opposed, unless it be that the Rejecting of this Petition is to be made use of as a Precedent for receiving no Petitions against a certain Scheme which we expect soon to be laid before us: This, I am afraid, is really the Case; for then Gentlemen, who are but little conversant in the Journals of the House, may quote a Precedent of but few days standing for not receiving any Petitions that may be offered against that Scheme; I do not indeed know whether there will be any such Petitions; but if I may judge by the Spirit which has already appeared in the Nation, I can make no doubt but that Petitions will be sent up from all Parts of the Country against that Scheme.

Sir *T—s A—n*] Sir, as to the Point of Form which is now the Subject of Debate, I cannot venture to give my Opinion thereon; but I am surprized that the Hon. Gentleman should have any Apprehensions of our refusing to receive any Petitions that may be offered against the Scheme he hinted at: For whatever Objection there may be against the House's receiving any Petitions that are offered against Duties to be laid on, there cannot surely be any Objection against our receiving Petitions that may be offered against

a new and a dangerous Method of collecting Duties already laid on.

S—l S—ys Esq;] Sir, since Gentlemen seem so much to differ as to the Point of Form, I shall move that a Committee may be appointed to search Precedents in relation to the receiving or not receiving Petitions against the imposing of Duties; for as some Gentlemen have affirmed it to have been the constant Usage of this House ever since the Revolution, to reject all such Petitions, I must take the Liberty to affirm the Fact to have been otherwise, and it is so far otherwise, that if my Motion be agreed to, I believe, more Precedents will be found for receiving, than for rejecting of such Petitions.

This Motion was seconded by *G—ge H—te* Esq; and thereupon Sir *J—n B—d* desired to withdraw the Motion he had made, but that being opposed, and some Debates arising as to that Point, Mr *S—r* acquainted the House of its being their constant Rule, that when any Motion is once made and seconded, the Question, if insisted on, must be put upon the Motion; it could not be withdrawn without leave of the House, whereupon the previous Question was moved for, and of Course put, which was carried in the Affirmative 140 to 112. Then the Question was put for bringing up the Petition, which passed in the *Negative*; and lastly, the Question was put for searching Precedents, which likewise passed in the *Negative*. Besides the above-mentioned Speakers, Sir *W—m W—m* and *P—p G—n* Esq; spoke for bringing up the Petition; and Mr *C—r* of the *E—r*, and *C....l B....n* spoke against it.

On the BRANDY ACT.

March the 9th. The House of Commons went into a Committee to consider of Methods for encouraging the Manufacture and Export of home-made Spirits, when *H....te W....le* Esq; spoke to the Effect as follows, *viz.*

Sir, as we are now in a Committee for encouraging home-made Spirits, it may not be improper for us to take into our Consideration that the Duties payable on *French* Brandies and other Foreign Spirits: As the Laws now stand, the Duties payable upon *French* Brandies amount in the whole to about 6 s. and 5 d. per Gallon, which has always been looked on rather as a Prohibition than as a Duty to be fairly and honestly paid either by the Importer or Consumer; and indeed it has in Fact been always found to be so, for few or none have ever paid that Duty; those Brandies have always been smuggled and stole in upon us notwithstanding all the Methods we could ever take to prevent it; or they have made Use of an Artifice to evade the Laws, which is this; as the Laws stand at present, the Duties payable on *Flemish* Brandies amount in the whole but to 4 s. per Gallon, and as it is not possible to distinguish *Flemish* Brandies from *French* Brandies, therefore

fore great Quantities of *French* Brandies were carried firſt to *Rotterdam*, and from thence imported upon us as *Flemiſh* Brandies; after that they were carried to *Oſtend*, and from thence imported as *Flemiſh*; and now for ſome Years paſt, they have been carried to *Dunkirk*, and from thence brought to the ſeveral Ports of *Britain*, and entered as *Flemiſh* Brandies.——As this Practice is an Evaſion of the Laws in being, it ought certainly to be remedied, and the Manner how, will be the proper Queſtion now to be conſidered: If the Duties now payable upon *French* Brandies ſhould be laid on all Foreign Spirits, it would not only encourage the Smuggling and running Trade, but it would be a Prejudice to our Diſtilling Trade, for our Diſtillers are under a Neceſſity of mixing up a certain Proportion of *French* Brandy with our *Engliſh* Spirits, in order to make them fit for uſe either at home or abroad; and therefore if ſuch a Duty can be thought of to be laid upon all Foreign Spirits, as will prevent their being ſold in this Country ſo cheap, as to interfere with the Conſumption of our home-made Spirits, and yet not diſable us from importing honeſtly and fairly as much as our Diſtillers may have Occaſion for in the Manufacture of our home-made Spirits, I hope Gentlemen will readily come into ſuch a Propoſition.——In order to make ſuch a Propoſition to this Houſe, I have for ſome time conſidered the Caſe, I have talked with ſome of the moſt noted Diſtillers in Town about it, and I have made all the Enquiries I thought proper for attaining to a full Information as to this Particular; and from the whole I believe that a Duty of 5 s. *per* Gallon upon all Foreign Brandies is the moſt proper Medium to be fixed on.

This Propoſition was not much oppoſed; only ſome Gentlemen ſeemed to think, that 5 s. 6 d. would have been a more proper Medium; and upon this Occaſion S——l S——s Eſq; ſpoke to the following Effect.

Sir, I am glad to hear from the Hon. Gentleman over the Way, that all Mixtures are not to be looked on as publick Frauds; for it ſeems the mixing of French Brandy with Engliſh Spirits is not only no publick Fraud, but a Mixture which ought to be encouraged, as being uſeful and neceſſary in the Diſtilling Trade; yet with reſpect to the Publick, I cannot conceive how the mixing of Engliſh Cyder with Portugal Wine can be conſidered as a greater Fraud than the mixing of French Brandy with Engliſh Spirits.——I muſt likewiſe take notice that the ſame Gentleman ſeems to admit, that the Laws of the Cuſtoms and Exciſe when united and joined together, are found to be ineffectual for collecting the Duties payable upon the Commodities he mentioned, or for the preventing the Smuggling and Running of them into this Kingdom; and therefore I hope, I ſhall not hereafter hear any Propoſition, either from that Gentleman or any of his Friends, for laying any other Duties under the ſame Circumſtances, more eſpecially ſince the uni-

ting of the Laws of the Cuſtoms and Exciſe is well known to be in all Caſes, an Union, which is moſt grievous and moſt burthenſome to the Subject.

On DUNKIRK.

Some Gentlemen having upon this Occaſion mentioned Dunkirk as a Port, Sir W——m W——m ſtood up and ſaid, That he was ſurprized to hear it ſo much as mentioned as a Port; that it was againſt the Honour of the Engliſh Nation to acknowledge it as ſuch, or to admit that it ſhould ever be made uſe of as ſuch. This, ſays he, is not now the proper Subject of our Conſideration, but I hope that this Houſe will at ſome other time reſolve itſelf into a Committee to conſider of this Affair.

Whereupon Mr C——r of the E——r ſtood up and ſaid, That he hoped Gentlemen would not be diverted from what was then the proper Subject of their Conſideration; that Dunkirk's being mentioned as a Port muſt neceſſarily raiſe the juſt Indignation of every Engliſhman; that no Engliſhman ever did, or ever could admit is as a Port. And, ſays he, whatever Terms Gentlemen may inadvertently make uſe of, yet I hope no Pretence will ever be from thence taken to infringe thoſe Rights which this Nation is by a moſt ſolemn Treaty juſtly entitled to.

After the above-mentioned Gentlemen and ſeveral others had ſpoke, the Committee reſolved that it was their Opinion, That the Act paſſed in the ſecond Year of his preſent Majeſty (entitled, An Act for laying a Duty upon Compound Waters or Spirits, and for licenſing the Retailers thereof) had been a Diſcouragement to the diſtilling of Spirits from Corn in Great Britain, a Drawback or Allowance of 6 L. 8 s. per Ton, ought to be paid and allowed on the Exportation thereof; and that the Duties payable upon Brandy and Spirits imported, except from his Majeſty's Plantations in America, ſhould from and after 24th of June then next, ceaſe and determine, and that in Lieu thereof there ſhould be granted to his Majeſty a Duty of five Shillings per Gallon, on all Brandy and Spirits imported from Foreign Ports, except ſuch as ſhall be of the Growth and Manufacture of his Majeſty's Plantations in America; which Reſolutions were on the 12th of March agreed to by the Houſe, and a Bill ordered to be brought in purſuant to them.

Mr C——r of the E——r having on Wedneſday the 7th Day of March, moved, that the Houſe might upon that Day ſeven-night reſolve itſelf into a Committee of the whole Houſe, to conſider of the moſt proper Methods for the better Security and Improvement of the Duties and Revenues already charged upon and payable from Tobacco and Wines; and the ſame having been ordered accordingly, the Houſe did upon Wedneſday the 14th of March reſolve itſelf into the ſaid Committee, according to the ſaid Order, the many Accounts, Returns, and other Papers which the Houſe had before called for, being firſt referred to the ſaid Committee, and the Commiſſioners of the Cuſtoms and of the Exciſe being attending purſuant to an Order of the preceding Day.

[To be continued.]

The

The Free-Briton, Oct. 4. No. 203.

*Of Good Nature in Political Contests; by
a Gentleman of a Neighbouring Kingdom.*

GOOD Nature, says a
celebrated noble Au-
thor, *is a Quality so
peculiar to the Eng-
lish Nation, that no o-
ther Language hath a
Word to express it.* How-
ever that be, this is
certain, that the two most comprehensive
Languages we know, have no Word of
equal Import. Neither the *Philanthropy*
of the *Greeks,* nor the *Humanity* of the
Romans can raise in us such a lively and
amiable Picture, as that beautiful Expression *Good Nature.*

Perhaps we pay our Country too great
a Compliment in endeavouring to engross
a Character, which either is, or ought
to be common to the whole Species.
However it must be allow'd, that our
natural Genius and Temper does, in this
respect, greatly surpass that of most Nations round us. This appears both from
the Complexion of our Laws, and the
whole Thread of our History, in which
we find but few Instances of that Ravage
and Barbarity, of which the Records of
all other Kingdoms in the Universe are full.

In private Life *Good Nature* is acknowledged a Quality absolutely necessary to
finish a Character truly amiable, manly,
and divine. We chuse it in a Friend, or
a Companion, preferably to superior Wit
and Understanding. Among Enemies it
has been celebrated with the loudest Encomiums in all Ages. *Alexander's* Treatment of the unfortunate Family of *Darius,*
and the Behaviour of our illustrious *Black
Prince* to his Captive *John* of *France,* are
Instances of Good Nature, that will always shine in History.

But 'tis a Question with some, whether this worthy Quality ought to mingle
in our Endeavours to serve the Publick;
or whether the Exercise of it is justifia-
ble, towards those who are engaged in
Measures dangerous to the Interests of our
Country. As to barefaced Usurpation, or
Tyranny, there's scarce room for the
Question. Here Tenderness to Individuals
would be Cruelty to Multitudes. But as
there may arise Contests of a dubious
Nature, there may be room to exercise
the highest Degree of publick Spirit,
which is nothing else but Good Nature
widely diffused.

(*Gent. Mag. Vol. III. N° xxxiv.*)

Demosthenes and *Eschines* were Rivals
for Fame and Power. Their Contest
drew the Attention of all *Greece;* and
Demosthenes at length got the Victory;
Eschines was banished by the Suffrages of
two thirds of his Countrymen. But his
Adversary had Good Nature, and knowing his Poverty, follow'd him out of the
City with a Present of a considerable Sum
of Money to support him in his Exile.
This drew from *Eschines* that fine Exclamation, *How can I chuse but regret to
leave a City, where one finds Enemies
more generous than Friends are to be met
with elsewhere?* and not long after he
publickly acknowledg'd the superior Merit
of his Rival, with regard to that very
Oration which occasion'd his Banishment.

Cicero imitated *Demosthenes* in his E-
loquence, and excell'd him in his Good
Nature. He was engaged in Opposition,
with most of the great Men his Co-tem-
poraries. With what Decency does he
every where speak of all the Men of
Distinction in *Rome,* except only *Catiline*
and *Anthony,* who were not only notorious Enemies to their Country, but profligate in their private Morals. Tho' a
declared Enemy to *Cæsar,* yet he never
detracts from his good Qualities; on the
contrary, he celebrates all those Accomplishments which have given him that
Figure he makes in History. Even those
noble Patriots, who imbru'd their Hands
in the Blood of *Cæsar,* were too generous
to tarnish his Fame.

Our own History affords us Instances to
the same Purpose. In the Reign of K.
Charles I. the E. of *Strafford* had enter'd
into a formal Conspiracy to enslave his
Country. The Friends of Liberty prosecuted him to his Attainder, but none
of them with Contempt, and scarcely
any of them with ill Language; and
most of them expressed the utmost E-
steem of his Person, and Reverence of
his Parts. It was a Game left to the Patriots of the Present Age to run down
those as *Fools* and *Blunderers,* who have
triumphed over all their Enemies. They
seem to pay themselves the same Kind
of Compliment, with which the Marshal
de Tallard aggravated his Misfortune at
the Battle of *Hochstedt. Tout Grace,* said
he to the D. of *Marlborough, has defeated the finest Troops in the World.* The
victorious General more justly observ'd
that the Marshal had not the good Manners to *except those Troops that had the
Honour to beat them.* But what must he
have

Q q q

have faid, had the Marſhal call'd them *Scoundrels, Runaways,* and *Cowards.*

The E. of *Shaftsbury,* in the Reign of K. *Charles* II. had offended all Parties in their Turns, and broke with every Adminiſtration; yet his Opponents, when the Torrent run higheſt againſt him, celebrated his Abilities, both as a Judge, and a Stateſman.

The Uſe of ſuch Examples is obvious. The Complexion of the Temper, and Manners of a whole People hath been, and will be in the Tincture of thoſe Qualities, which are predominant in their Leaders and great Men, who, if they throw off all Regard to Decency, Good Nature, and Generoſity, what can this produce amongſt the People, but perpetual Noiſe and Clamour?

No Doubt, but the Actions of our Governors ought to be freely canvaſſed and cenſured. But then Honeſty, and good Policy require this ſhould be done without mixing perſonal Animoſity with Zeal for the Publick. There is a Difference betwixt Accuſation and Calumny. In the one Caſe, Proofs are requir'd; but in the other a Man is condemned unheard and without due Proofs.

To apply this. We live in a Government ſettled and conducted upon the Principles of Liberty, and publick Good; yet no Government, nor Miniſters in any Age, have been treated with ſo much Abuſe and ill-Nature as the preſent. Their Enemies, both within Doors, and without, have been called upon to bring forth their Charge againſt them and reduce it to Particulars; but inſtead of this, they have gone on in their old Track of calling ill Names, and forging ill Deſigns. They are therefore juſtly chargeable not only with Ill-Nature, Perverſeneſs, and Diſhoneſty, but accountable for all the fatal Effects, which a Spirit of Faction and Sedition is capable of raiſing.

Among other impudent Calumnies, it is ſometimes inſinuated, that the Adminiſtration have made Gentlemen of the largeſt Fortunes and worthieſt Characters dependant by Means of Power and Employment. But with how ill a Grace is this ſaid? For when any good Laws, paſſed under this Adminiſtration, have been inſiſted on, as an Argument in Favour of the Miniſtry, the other Party cry out, the Miniſtry had no hand in thoſe Laws, but were enacted in direct Oppoſition to them. As if Men could be ſo weak as to let Things paſs againſt them in an Aſſembly where they poſſeſs a Power, unlimited, and uncontroulable.

Grubſtreet Journal. Oct. 4. N° 197.
Of Inoculation.

Mr Bavius,

THE Doctrines of the Bow-ſtring, and of inoculating in the Small-pox, are both of Mahometan Original, and can never ſuit a freeborn Engliſh Conſtitution. As to Inoculation, if it be ſaid, that many of the Learned, the Noble, and the Wiſe are for it, I anſwer, many are againſt it too. But if all ſuch were for it; if it be not lawful, that would not juſtify the Practice; and till the Advocates for this ſort of Manſlaughter can produce ſome Text of Scripture, to warrant our giving ourſelves a Diſtemper we might never have, or not till a more proper Seaſon, they do nothing.——Would theſe Gentlemen, if the Plague was amongſt us, inoculate for that? The ſame Reaſon holds good in both.

Did none inoculated ever die? Or if an Inoculation from a good diſtinct ſort, always produced its like, and not an ugly confluent Kind, as is commonly the Caſe; or if with the Small-pox, no other Diſtemper was inoculated, (as the Grandpox, Leproſy, the Evil, &c.) which cannot be avoided, if the Patient, from whom the pocky *Virus* was taken, was infected therewith, and which has been communicated to the Patient inoculated, then, indeed, ſome thing might be pleaded for the Practice. But how many Lives have been loſt this way, let the mourning, inconſolable Parents declare, who have drank of this bitter Cup! 'Tis true, the Intention conſtitutes the Act of Murder: But if Lives, loſt by Innoculation, be no Manſlaughter (be the Intention never ſo innocent) I am at a loſs what Name to give it.

It is commonly boaſted, that very few that are inoculated die. But if only one has died, yet that one had not died, if he had not been inoculated; and who muſt be charged with the Loſs of that one Life? But .the Reaſon why ſo few die that are inoculated, is, becauſe they are of the Young, the Healthy, and the Rich, whoſe Bodies are prepared for the Operation, and have all the Help, that Art and Affluence can give. But the greateſt Part of thoſe who die of it the natural way, are either aged or diſeaſed, or poor, or want Neceſſaries, have bad Nurſes, no Phyſician, improper Medicines, or are
obſtinate

obftinate and ungovernable. Let our In-
oculators try their Skill on fuch as thefe,
and compare the Numbers that die either way.

But if they will take the Almighty's
Work out of his Hands, inftead of inoculating the Patient, let him be had into
a Chamber, where a young Perfon has a
good Sort: Tho' this feems unjuftifiable,
and not to be done without hazarding a
Life, over which we have no Power,
and without any Regard to Providence ;
for it is one Thing to truft Providence,
and another to tempt it. DEMOCRITUS.

To this paper *Bavius* fubjoins a fhort
Hiftory of Inoculation pretended to be
written by the famous M. *Voltaire*, as
follows.

The Circaffians *being poor, and having
beautiful Daughters, furnifh the Seraglios
of the Turkifh Sultan, of the Perfian So-
phy, and of thofe who are wealthy enough
to purchafe and maintain fuch precious
merchandize. Thefe Maidens are very
honourably and virtuoufly inftructed to
fondle and carefs Men, and repeat their
Leffon to their Mothers, in the fame manner as little Girls among us repeat their
Catechifm. Now it often happened, that
after a Father and Mother had taken the
utmoft Care of the Education of their Children, they were fruftrated of all their
Hopes in an inftant. The Small-pox getting into a Family fo deformed their
Daughters that the unhappy Parents were
compleatly ruin'd. The Circaffians obferv'd
that fcarce one of a 1000 was ever attack'd by a Small-pox of a * violent Kind.
In order therefore to preferve the Life and
Beauty of their Children, they gave them
the Diftemper by inoculating in the Body
of a Child, a Puftle of the moft favourable fort. The Turks adopted this Cuftom.
And in the Reign of K. George I. the
Lady Wortley Montague, being with her
Hufband, who was Ambaffador at the
Port, inoculated her Infant of which fhe
was deliver'd at Conftantinople, which
had the moft happy Effect. At her Return, fhe communicated the Experiment
to the Princefs of Wales, who immediately caus'd an Experiment to be made on
four Criminals fentenc'd to Die. By which
being affur'd of its Ufefulnefs, caus'd her
own Children to be inoculated. A great
part of the Kingdom follow'd her Exam-*

ple ; *and fince that Time,* † 10,000 *Children, at leaft, of Perfons of Condition owe
in this manner their Lives to her Majefty,
and the Lady* Wortley Montague ; *and as
many of the fair Sex are oblig'd to them
for their Beauty.*

London Journal, Oct. 6. No. 745.

SUch is the Malignity and Inveteracy
of the *Faction,* that if we lived in
the Reigns of the worft Tyrants, we
could not make louder or more general
Complaints of *Slavery* and *arbitrary Power* ; yet our *Rights* and *Properties* are *facredly* and *inviolably* maintained.

The Cry of thefe *Malignants* is a *Coalition of Parties !* and a *Country Intereft !*
I have now full in my View, fays *Osborne,*
a harden'd thorough *Jacobite,* known to
have been with the *Pretender,* and that
lives by the King's Mercy, who, on a
late remarkable Occafion, gravely affumed the Air of a *Patriot,* infolently arraign'd the Court of *Defigns* to deftroy
Trade and *Liberty,* begg'd the People
would chufe a Man of his *untainted Honour* and *publick Virtues* to reprefent
them, and then exhorted to a *Coalition
of Parties,* on Purpofe to *fubvert* the Government ; for that *infamous Speech-mak-
er* could have no other Intention.

In a Speech faid to be made at *Bedford,*
Sir *Jeremy Sambrooke,* is complimented
at the Expence of the *Honour* of the Government ; for that by his *virtuous Vote*
againft the *Tobacco* Scheme, he preferved
the very Being of Parliaments ; they
might as properly have added, *the very
Being of the Univerfe.*

Is it not monftrous to hear Men talk of
a *Country Intereft* againft the Court, when
there is no Intereft of the *Court* againft
the *Country* ; when the *Laws* are made
the *ftanding Meafures* of the King's Government and the People's Obedience ?
Yet fo abandon'd to all Virtue are thefe
Malecontents grown, that they are continually *infinuating,* " That tho' we have
the *Form* of Liberty, yet we have loft
the *Subftance* ; that we are in the State
of old *Rome* under the Emperors, who
were always *defpotick* and always *Tyrannical :* And then add, the worft of all
Governments is Tyranny fanctified by
the

---

* *Bavius* obferves, it was only this *violent
King* that kills or disfigures Perfons ; and
fince it happen'd to fcarce one in a 1000, what
Occafion was there to practice Inoculation ?

† This Account of 20,000 or 15,000 Children at leaft, inoculated in *England,* 10,000
of whom were *Children of Perfons of Condition,* and *as many* of them are now beautiful
young Ladies, was till now a great Secret to
the World.

the *Appearance* of Law. " Who doubts this? But when this is convey'd in *Political Catechisms*, (see p. 477.) and *Weekly Libels*, on purpose to infuse into the Minds of the People, *That such is the deplorable State of Things in* England; then the Authors are guilty of the most compleat Wickedness human Nature is capable of. For, in the Reign of those Emperors, when the *Names* and *Forms* of Consuls, Senates and Tribunes existed, what Wickedness did they not commit under the *Forms* of Law and Magistracy? but *here* Equity and Justice are supported by the *Reality* of Law, and the *Senate* and *Tribunes* of the People, or *Lords* and *Commons*, have *real* and *substantial Powers*, and where the *King himself* hath no Power *without them*; nor any Power against the *Meanest* of his Subjects, till *that Subject* hath invaded the Rights of his Fellow-Subjects; then judge what we ought to *compare* these Men to, who *compare* this Government with the *Tyrannical* Government under the *Roman* Emperors, where they possessed no *real Liberty*, and where they knew no such Thing as *Property*.

By these Remarks the Friends of the Government may see, to what vile Purposes this Noise of a *Coalition of Parties* and a *Country Interest* are made subservient; no less vile, than *Overturning* the Government.

Others, indeed, may not intend to carry Things so far; but let them look back, and they will find, they have carried Things already much farther than was *at first* intended: And God only knows, how far they will be carried, if *Occasions and Circumstances* drive them. The *Malecontent Whigs*, already say; There's no Difference between a *Whig* and a *Tory*, a *Whig* and a *Jacobite*. And in a little Time they may say there's no Difference in *Governments*, nor in *Kings*; that our *Government* differs only in *Name and Form* from that in *Turkey*; that the *Revolution* was a Piece of *political Phrenzy*, &c.

But what has been done by the *King*, or the *Ministry*, or by *that Minister* against whom all this Clamour is rais'd, to deserve this Usage? But *Innocence* is no Protection against Rage and Malice. A *French* Historian observes, That few Ministers ever serv'd a Prince so faithfully, as *Mons. de Rony* his great Master *Henry* IV. or, with greater Regard to *the Interest* of the *Publick*; yet *his Credit with*

the King, and two or three great *Employments*, serv'd for the Ground of several *Conspiracies*; and he sometimes found it a *hard Task* to stand: He was often thought *guilty*, even when he was most *innocent*: He was sure to disoblige some even by obliging others; several thought themselves at least as well qualified as he for his Place: Thus even his *Excellencies* created him Enemies , for *Causa periculi, non crimen ullum, sed Gloria viri*.

As much may be as *justly* said of the *Minister* whom 'tis *the Faction* to abuse; the *Reasons* and *Motives* of Scandal are exactly the same *now* as then, i. e. *personal*. For, even *the late Scheme, the Occasion* of creating him so many Enemies, was certainly design'd for a *publick Benefit*, and that his Enemies know: Whether he was *mistaken*, is not to the Purpose: The Thing was *designed well*, and therefore the People, when they are *cool* enough to *think*, will have no Prejudices remaining against him; and will distinguish *the true Interest* of the Nation from the *little Views* or *particular Interests* of particular Men; who, to gratify their *Ambition*, have thrown the Nation into a Flame; which, if not quenched by the *good Sense* and *Honesty* of the People, may produce such Consequences as an *Englishman* would tremble to name.

. F. *Osborne*.

Fog's Journal. Oct. 6. N° 257.
Of Places, Pensions, and Bribery.

Mr FOG,

THAT a poor Man indebted to his severe Landlord 10 *l.* and unable to pay such a Sum, should be enticed by 5 *l.* to give his Vote to a wheedling Candidate, may be expected. He reflects, if Men adorn'd with high Titles, possessed of vast Riches, in every thing obey the Directions of a first Minister, ought not I, a poor unhappy Man, imitate such illustrious Examples? Weak Reasons will prevail, when put in the Scale with Interest, and to disswade the Generality of Men from pursuing it were vain. Even the Laws to prevent Bribery and Corruption in the Election of Members to serve in Parliament, have hitherto prov'd so insufficient, that Gentlemen of the largest Fortunes and most reputable Characters, have thought it necessary frequently to offer Bills to incapacitate an exorbitant Number of the House of Commons, from possessing Places or Pensions dependant on the good Will of

a

a principal Minister, as the best means to preserve our Constitution.

Such Bills have often passed the House of Commons; and some People cannot comprehend, why the Lords Temporal should oppose a Bill, which intrenches not on their Privilege of monopolising Offices, nor why the Right Rev. Fathers of the Church, should so unanimously concur in rejecting a Bill, which in no wise prevents the most *antient* and *Christian* Practice of Translations; and are more amazed, when they observe these Bills seem to be approv'd by some Directors in the Lower House, and yet by their Authority and Influence are rejected in the Upper. The Conclusion they draw from such Practice is, that the Lords are not chosen by their Fellow-Subjects, and so run no Hazard of forfeiting their Seats in Parliament; and that whoever of the Commons should oppose it, he might expect the same Resentment in a future Election, as it is pretty apparent they will, who have, or may vote for the Extension of Excise Laws, or the Continuance of an Army in Times of Peace, which in all Countries has been the Overthrow of Liberty.

But as some self-interested Man of moderate Estate may shuffle himself into the House of Commons, wholly on the Prospect of increasing his Fortune, I shall confine my Address to such only. That there are Employments attended with a large share of Power and of great Profit, by *certain Ways and Means,* I am convinc'd; however, not numerous, and which, probably, will be reserved for the Kindred, or for the *Minions* of the *Minion.* It may happen, indeed, that some will be disposed of to those, who, tho' they hate and are hated, yet, to share the Plunder of the Publick, will labour to prop him in his unwieldy Grandeur, and forward his Schemes however wild and pernicious. But, indeed, most of those great Offices, are not only few, but so far from being profitable, that they are really an Incumbrance to a generous Spirit, by the Attendance they require; an Affliction to the Avaricious, by compelling him to a more sumptuous and expensive Manner of Living. If the Accounts of the State of *England* inform us rightly, the Salary of the Lord President is 2000 *l. per Ann.* of the Lord Privy Seal, 1500; of the Master General of the Ordnance, 1500. The Wages and Board-wages of the Lord Steward amount to 1460; of the Lord Chamber-

A

B

C

D

E

F

G

H

lain to 1200; of the Treasurer of the Houshold to 1076; of the Comproller to 1092; of the Captain of the Band of Pensioners; of the Captain of the Yeomen of the Guard; of the Lords of the Bedchamber, to each 1000 *l. per Ann.* These are generally Men of high Birth and great Estates; and to imagine their Salaries are enlarged, when we are so loaded with Debts and Taxes, would be saucily accusing the present Management of the Minister; and to intimate that these noble Lords make more of their Employments than their Salaries, were a Derogation to their Honour; then let any one judge, how likely these Stations are to enrich them.

But allowing they were more profitable, it's plain few can arrive at that Eminence; and therefore let the Country Gentleman and Merchant consider, what they propose to themselves, by toiling, drinking, meanly flattering, lavishly bribing, to be return'd a Representative in Parliament.

Suppose a Man of 1000 *l.* or 1500 *l.* a Year; how many such vainly aim at increasing their Riches by basely submitting to the Dictates of an insolent Minister? How few of those who succeed, think themselves fully rewarded for their *Prostitution* with an Office of 6 or 700 *l.* If secur'd with a Pension, half the Sum will suffice; because that being conceal'd he can pretend it is Principle, not Interest sways him.

When the Employment is obtained, let him consider the Waste of Time he has been at, the slavish Attendance, obsequious Behaviour, fulsome Flattery, fallacious Hopes, real Fears, the Expence of his Election, and then let him count his Gains; and whether a prudent Oeconomy of his Affairs, and living at Home frugally, yet hospitably, would not have kept more Money in his Purse than his Employment has put into it.

It may be objected, that Gentlemen of moderate Fortunes, and who seek not Preferment, are however obliged to an Attendance in Parliament, and are at a great Expence by living in *London.* It is allow'd. The Purport of this Letter is not to extol those worthy Men who deserve so well of their Country; but to desire that pernicious Creature, who is wholly devoted to Self-Interest, to consider, that the Man in Office is under much greater Expences, than the real Patriot. So that all Things consider'd, he is far from bettering his Fortune.   The

The **Craftsman**, Oct. 6. No. 379.

The true Interest of the DISSENTERS *consider'd.*

IN the last *Craftsman* (see p. 483. G) Mr *D'anvers* acknowledged Mrs *Osborne* had some Regard to Veracity, by giving up her *Patron*, as to the *Repeal of the* SCHISM ACT; and it's obvious she has given up her Brother *Walfingham*. However, she hath prevaricated a little for the Service of her Cause.

She begins her Paper of *Sept.* 15. (see p. 472. G) with asserting *that* WHIGS, *and* TORIES, JACOBITES *and* PAPISTS, *are the same Men they used to be; and have the same general Principles, Views, and Designs.*

As to *Jacobites* and *Papists* perhaps it may be so; but both *Whigs* and *Tories* are so far from being the *same Men they used to be,* that by their *Practices* they seem to have changed *Principles* by Consent. Nothing is more demonstrable than that the *Court-Whigs* are the same kind of Creatures with the *Court-Tories* before the *Revolution*; and that the Body of the *present Tories* have adopted the Spirit of the *old Whigs*; and by acting in Conjunction with the *independent Whigs* of our Times, who adhere to their antient Principles, have, in a great Measure, abolish'd those *Silly Appellations*, and made COURT and COUNTRY the only prevailing Distinction amongst us. It is therefore pleasant to hear *Osborne* tell the *Dissenters, that we have liv'd to see the glorious Day when* Court *and* Country *Interest are one.*—That would be a *glorious Day indeed!* But what we may almost despair of seeing; because there's scarce an Instance in History of any Reign in which the *Prince* or his Ministers, have not had some private View or Interest inconsistent with the general Welfare. Therefore the People are sufficiently happy, when *Men in Power* confine their particular Views within reasonable Bounds.

To convince the *Dissenters the* Tories *are the same Men they used to be,* they are presented with some Passages from a Pamphlet, entitled, the *Loyal Revolutional Tory,* which *Osborne* supposes *was wrote under the Direction of that* Body of Men; but it is visible at first View, it was written either by a *Court Tory*, or by some *Creature in Power*, who assum'd that Character to cajole the *Tories* over to their Party. It has been even suggested that the World has been obliged for it

to the same *reverend Champion,* who formerly pleaded for the *Dependency of the* House of Commons *on the* Crown. However, says *D'anvers,* I am glad to hear there are such Men as *loyal Revolutional Tories*; and hope *Attachment to a Minister,* or doing the *Drudgery of a Court*, are not the only Criterions, by which we are to judge of them.

It having been affirmed *that the* Church Whigs *and* Revolutional Tories are the Means, *of which the* Jacobites *and* Dissenters *are the* Extremes, Mrs *Osborne* cries out, *See how you are* coupled!—*Coupling of Extremes* is certainly a Discovery far beyond *squaring the Circle.*—A Line or two after, she calls the *Jacobites* the *New Allies* of the *Dissenters*, with the same Propriety, as if she should say the Guelphs were the Allies of the *Gibelines.*

Instead of making any Reflections on this *Time-serving Pamphlet, D'anvers* shews the Sense of the *Dissenters* themselves upon this Subject, from a Tract published last Winter entitled, *The Interest of the* Protestant Dissenters *consider'd*; whence he quotes the following Passages.

Another political Rule, adapted more especially for the smaller, and weaker Parties, is This; *not to attach Themselves immovably to the Service of* ANY OTHER PARTY; *but to preserve their Independency, and to have always in View the keeping a* DUE BALLANCE *among the other and greater Parties*; for the *Friendships among Parties are like the Alliances among States,* which are no longer preserved than while *one* stands in need of the *other's Help*; and when *one Party* becomes so strong, as not to want the Assistance of their *lesser Allies,* They will not treat Them any longer with the Regard, that is due to *Friends.* 'Tis dangerous therefore for the *smaller Party* to aid their Friends so much, as till their Friends want their Help no longer; as likewise *it is* sometimes advisable to forbear aiding Them, that they may be put upon observing the Use They are of to them, and thence be induced to make suitable Returns. It is a Mistake of the *Dissenters*, to imagine that the Dislike of the *Tories* towards them is meerly on Account of their *tender Consciences,* 'tis *because the* Dissenters *are always a* dead Weight *against Them at the* ELECTIONS.

I will here add one Thing; that This seems to be the most seasonable Time, if it be ever possible, to moderate the Dislike, that the *Tories* have of the *Dissenters*, since

since the Dispute and Controversy of this Age is not, as formerly, about *Rites* and *Ceremonies*. All That is ceas'd, out of Date, and esteem'd trifling. But now the Controversy on Foot is about the Foundations and Truth of *Christianity* itself; in which the *Dissenting Writers*, greatly to their Honour, stand amongst the ablest and fairest Champions.

The *real Friends of the Dissenters*, tho' they be few in *Number*, yet are They not inconsiderable in *Weight*; but are not found among *Parties*, meerly as a *Party*, and very seldom among *Ministers of State*; but are to be found among *such Gentlemen, as have unto good Parts and Knowledge join'd a Freedom of Thought and free Enquiry into Matters of Religion*. These are Friends to the *Dissenters*, not from any Similitude of having the *same Scruples* with Them; but from considering Them as a Party engaged in Interest to be for LIBERTY.

Another Writer, (in a Letter to SAMUEL HOLDEN, *Esq;)* on this Subject, expresses the same Sentiment in the following Terms.

" Most Men in the Kingdom are so far improved in their Judgments, as to believe that *Heaven* is not so entailed upon any particular Opinion in Religion, as to sacrifice the *Liberties of their Country* in Defence of them. The State of Things in the Nation is greatly alter'd from what it was *forty Years ago*. The *Dissenters* have neither that Rigidness among Them as formerly, nor the *Low-Churchmen* that ill-Will to Them, as *Neighbours* and *Englishmen.*"

But pray, *Madam*, are the *Tories* the only Persons in Opposition to your *Patron*? You know that the Body of the *Country Whigs* in general, with many of the *greatest and richest Peers* in the Kingdom at the Head of them, have shook off *his Supremacy*, and listed themselves in the Cause of the People. Why therefore may not the *Dissenters* take the same Side, if they please, and join their old Allies the Church-Whigs, without any Imputation of leaguing with *Jacobites*, or Danger of breaking the *Whig Interest*? No, say you, *the Church Whigs and Dissenters together are not equal in Number to the* Jacobites *and* Tories; *and have always been forced to supply what they wanted in* natural Strength *with great Art.* (See p. 472. F) If this is the Case, the *present Government* stands upon a weaker and worse Foundation than I apprehend it. By *great Art* you must mean *Force*, or *Corruption*, or *Both*. A Government, thus supported, cannot surely be denominated a *free Government*, which consists in ruling a People by their *own Consent*.

The *Universal Spectator*, Oct. 6. No. 262.

Of a *deceitful* Countenance.

THE Features of the Face and Gesture of the Body are esteemed the Interpreters of the *Mind* and the silent Language of the *Heart*: If so, they are guilty of *Immorality* who put on a Look *foreign* to their *Mind*, and carry a *Lie* on their *Countenance*. This Mr *Stonecastle* illustrates by the following Letters.

SIR,

I Know no Vice more prevalent, or more dangerous, yet less satiriz'd than the *Dissimulation* of the *Features* of the Face. I have seen so much *Treachery*, *Villany*, and *Falshood* conceal'd in a *Smile*; so much *Irreligion*, *Knavery* and *Atheism* disguis'd in a Pair of *canting Eyes*; so much *Sensuality*, *Immodesty* and *rank Lust* in a pretty *innocent* Face, that I'm almost bro't to judge by Contraries, in Regard to the *outward Aspect* of Mankind. The *Physiognomists* pretend to judge the *Temper* and Habits of the *Mind*, by the Lines in the *Face*; but what *Physiognomist* could form any Judgment from a *modern Countenance*, which is varying its Lines contrary to *Rule*? which is pleas'd, tho' it frowns, and designs *Ruin*, tho' it appears Smiling? Nor is this Species of *Vice* confin'd to any Degree of Men; but is equally to be seen at the *Circles* of the *Great*, the *Levees* of the *Gown*, and the *Cabals* on the *Exchange*. There are some such Masters of this *Art* of *Dissimulation*, that you cannot but believe them, till you have been *once* deceiv'd; they act by *Rule*, and improve by *Habit*; they attest a *Lie* with such Singularity of *Innocence* in their *Face*; they *hug*, nay, *kiss* them they *despise*, with such *Transports of Friendship*, that, till you knew their *Hypocrisy*, it would be Injustice, not to *believe* them.

'Tis needless to mention how *hurtful* to *Society* this *Vice* must be, when it tends to destroy all the noble Sentiments of *Friendship* and *Honesty*. The Means therefore to put a Stop to it in common Life, would be to expose such a *Hypocrite*, and treat him as an *Enemy* to *Mankind*. At Court, indeed, it is improv'd into a *Science*, and is the Ruin of many. The *Followers* of a *Court* would disguise this *Vice* into a
. sort

fort of *Commendation*, by calling it the *Art of Address:* But whatever Name may be given to an *alluring Grin*, where you bate; a *consenting Nod*, to what you never intend to *perform*, in a *Court Phrase*, in *common Honesty*, it's nothing but 'the *base Artifice* of a *mean Lie*.

W. HEARTFREE.

§ *'Squire Stonecastle,*

I AM of the antient and distinguish'd Family of the *Cyphers:* Sir *Arthur Cypher* came into *England*—no Matter when; but his *Descendants* have been very eminent in this Nation, and some or other of our Family have adorn'd most *Professions:* For some secret Policy, which I cannot account for, all my present Relations disown their *Family Name*, and my being any Kin to them; they say I'm a very *insignificant Fellow*, and of *no Account*; nor have they chang'd their *Name* only, but by a *fashionable Artifice* have vary'd their *unmeaning sheepish Family Face* into an *Aspect of Wisdom* and *Importance:* As the House of *Austria* was famous for the *Lip*, another for the *Eagle Eye*, a third for the *Roman Nose*, ours was distinguish'd by the *Simplicity* of the *whole Face*; but however they *disguise* their *Features*, their Actions betray them; therefore whatever *Lord* puts on a *busy Face* when he has *nothing* in Reality to *do*; whatever *Member* at *Westminster* would seem of *Importance* to his *Country*, tho' in the *House* he says only *Tea* or *Nay*; whatever *Reverend*, or *Right Reverend* looks *wise* in his *Chariot*, and is *dull* in his *Pulpit*, are all different *Cyphers* in *Court*, *Senate*, and *Church*; and whatever Airs they may give themselves, are of no more *Consequence* to the *World* than *their* discarded Cousin, and *your* insignificant Correspondent,

Jemmy Cypher.

Free Britton, Oct. 8, 9. Nº 204, 5.
The Craftsman *convicted of* Falshood *and* G
Prevarication. Part I.

THE Question with the *Protestant Dissenters* is, Whether the present *Ministers*, and the *Great Person* at the Head of it, or the late Ld B——ke, Sir W——m W—ndh—m, &c. are the best Friends to our *Religious Liberties?* The *Craftsman* puts them on a Level, and affirms that the *Great Person* in Power *voted against the Repeal of the Schism Bill*, which the *Craftsman's* Patrons, B—l—ng—ke and W—ndh—m, first ob-

tained as a Law (See p. 482.) This *Walsingham* denied (See p. 474.) and here more amply enlarges on the same Point; and asks, that supposing the *Honourable Gentleman*, the late E. C——wt—r and D. of D—v—nsh——re had erred in Judgment when they oppos'd the *Repeal* of the Occasional Conformity *Act*, whether that will *level* them with B—ngb—ke and Sir Wm W—ndh—m? or prove them to be of the same *persecuting Habit?* or that they have acted thro' the whole *Tenor of their Lives*, with Relation to the *Protestant Dissenters*, as Ld B—ngb—ke and his *Pupil* have constantly acted?

Such a *Series of Actions* and Measures, as made every *Parochial Pulpit* the *Stage of Invective* against all the *Protestant Dissenters*, in every Parish of the Kingdom; as caused the *National Clergy* to assemble in *Convocation*, meerly to denounce the *Curse of God*, and inspire civil Rage against all who differ'd from Orthodox Authority; as inflamed the Outrage of the Multitude, so far as to *pull down the religious Houses of Worship*, and to threaten the very *Dwellings of the Dissenters*; levying War and raising Rebellion within the Capital of the Kingdom, and not ending in Lawless Rage, were carried into *Parliament*, which *enacted Persecution by Law*; which destroy'd the *Fundamentals of the Revolution*, and its greatest Blessing, our *religious Liberties*, which were so far retrenched that the *Protestant Dissenters* were deprived of the *Education* of their own *Children* thro' *England* and *Ireland.* Such were the *Prostitutions* of the most *Sacred Name* in Heaven, and such the *Perversion of Civil Power*, by which Ld B—ngb—ke and Sir W——m W—ndh—m distinguished themselves, in all those Parliaments and Councils where they had Credit to carry on publick Mischief.

But will any Man charge such a Spirit, or such Proceedings, upon any of those *Whigs* who oppos'd, in 1718, a Bill which perplexed and complicated *the Repeal of the Schism Act*, by adding it to the *Repeal of the Ocasional Conformity Act?* Or charge the *Great Person* now in Authority with any such violent Measures?

Who supported, or oppos'd the *Quakers* Petition to Parliament to have their *Affirmation* explained? Did not the *Honourable Gentleman* obtain that Law in their Favour? Did not Sir W——m W—ndh—m, and *all the Tories*, oppose it in every Step of its Progress?

At

At the laſt *general Election*, Mr *B—rn—d* then a *Candidate* for *London*, was reported to be of *perſecuting Principles*; and it was averred by a Perſon of *unqueſtion'd Integrity*, that *he* had been *openly an Advocate* for Dr *Sacheverel*. Did not the *Craftſman* then excuſe him on Account of the *Heats* and *Miſtakes* of the Times? Did he not plead even the *Diſtance of Time*, and complain of it as *an Hardſhip* that a Gentleman's *Character* ſhould be *cenſur'd*, and *his whole Life determin'd by one Inſtance?* Yet does the *Craftſman* think it *juſt Uſage* of a *Great Miniſter*, to miſrepreſent *one Fact* which happen'd 15 or 16 Years ſince, and from thence make an Inference againſt the *whole Tenor of the Honourable Gentleman's Life?*

The *Craftſman*, to confound the Reader cites a Parcel of *mouldy Libels*, written to abuſe the *Honourable Gentleman* now in Power, to ſerve or court the *then ſtanding Adminiſtration:* But what can they prove? Nothing, but that ſome Perſons, a great while ſince, as others do at this Time, thought fit by *Libels* and *Invectives*, to enflame the *Proteſtant Diſſenters* againſt the *Honourable Gentleman now in Power*. I do not now wonder, ſays *W.* that a *Gentleman*, who is engaged in the Defence of this Miniſtry ſhould think, that the *Honourable Gentleman* proceeded as he is charged to have done; which *imagined Proceeding* he blames, as, he ſays, he then did (ſee p. 473 A) I can account for *his* Miſapprehenſion, not only as I know the *Diſtance* at which he then lived from the *Scene of publick Buſineſs*; but as I ſee, by the *Craftſman's* Citations from the *Pamphlets of thoſe Times*, what Arts were uſed to propagate *falſe Reports* of *Parliamentary Meaſures*, thro' the *ſeveral Counties* of this Kingdom.

But that the *Honourable Gentleman* did not oppoſe the *Repeal of the Schiſm Act*, or the *Act* for ſtrengthening the *Proteſtant Intereſt*, than as before mentioned, is well known to *thoſe Members* who were *Witneſſes* of the Debates in the *Houſe of Commons*. Nay, the *Craftſman* himſelf *authenticates* the main of what I have aſſerted; for, he ſays, E. *C—p—r diſtinguiſhed* in this Caſe, and ſaid *he would readily give* his *Vote for repealing the* Schiſm Act; but can't find that the *Honourable Gentleman* made ſuch a *Diſcrimination*. (ſee p. 483 A) Now, I am informed, that the *Gentleman* did make ſuch a *Diſcrimination*, and I appeal to

the Memory of *all the Members now living*. But, let the *Craftſman* produce the Record wherein 'tis ſaid, the *Earl diſtinguiſhed* in this Caſe, and I will ſhew the *Honourable Gentleman's* Diſcrimination enter'd on that *very Roll*. I could mention *Perſons* of as great and *deſerved Weight and Integrity* as ever ſat in Parliament, who can atteſt, that, when the *Honourable Gentleman* roſe up to ſpeak, on that Occaſion, be begun in theſe Words; *I ſhall ſpeak to the Bill, and I ſhall ſpeak as a Whig.* The Import and *Drift* of *which Words* muſt evince that he ſpoke altogether concerning the *Seaſon and Circumſtances* of the Affair, ſpeaking *as a Whig*, by *diſtinguiſhing* as E. *C—p—r* did, and *very willing to give his Vote for the Repeal of the* Schiſm *Bill in any Act ſingly* by itſelf.

Part II.

The *Craftſman* is ſo ſenſible of the *Weight* which the *Names of theſe noble Lords* muſt have in this Argument, that he objects to their being *named at all*. How idle and unjuſt is this Pretence? He cenſures that Oppoſition in the moſt odious Terms; yet pretends *he reflects on none* but the *Gentleman* now in Power. This *Gentleman's Voice* was but one in the Oppoſition; and, is *he by himſelf* to bear the Cenſure thrown upon it? Or does not that Cenſure *extend to all concerned in it?* Can the *Great Perſon* be thus arraigned, when Ld *C—p—r* and D. of *D—nſh—re*, who concerted the Meaſure *charged upon him*, are acquitted? And is it not more *conſiſtent*, more *honeſt in me*, to maintain that he is *guiltleſs of all ſuch* Oppoſition to the Intereſt of the *Diſſenters*, becauſe he *governed himſelf by* the Opinions and *Examples of thoſe excellent Men*, who were incapable of acting to the *Diſſenters Prejudice?*

To this the *Craftſman* hath nothing to reply, but that he thinks Ld *C—p—r* ought not to be this *Gentleman's Compurgator*, becauſe his Lordſhip *often differ'd* with him; and the D. of *D—nſh—re* is objected to, *becauſe he* always agreed *with him.*

So that the *Craftſman* is brought to Confeſſion, that the *Honourable Gentleman's* Oppoſition ſtands *juſtified* by the *Example* of that *illuſtrious Peer*, whom he acquits of all *Byaſs, Partiality, and Prejudice on his ſide?*

Does the *Craftſman* likewiſe declare, that the late D. of *D—nſh—re agreed in Opinion with the Honourable Gentleman*, *not only when he was in, but out of Power?* It is a *Testimony* to the Worth and Abilities of the *Honourable Person,* which not only his Friends must *rejoice in,* but his worst *Enemies* ENVY, and will raise a nobler *Monument to his Fame* than Titles, or Power, or Fortune. Such Evidences of the *Honourable Person's* Integrity expose that *Writer* to Scorn, who pretends to impeach it from *Scraps of anonymous Libels,* published almost 20 Years since; and from those *idle, imperfect* Accounts of *Debates in the H. of C—m—s,* found in the *Historical Register,* the Compiler of which lived and died a *Papist.* How incredible it is, that he or others could know the Debate in 1718, from any thing but *vulgar Report,* or his own *Invention,* may be judged from the *great Number of Members* then in the House, and the Impossibility that *Strangers* could be allowed to attend those Debates. 447 Members divided on the Bill for *Repealing the Schism and Occasional Conformity Act,* not including the *Speaker* and *Tellers;* of whom Sir W—m ?——ge, was a *Teller* For *the Bill.*

One Libel is mention'd by the *Craftsman,* which *insinuates,* that the *Gentlemen* procur'd the *Attack in Convocation* upon Bishop H—dl—y, for *writing in Defence of Liberty of Conscience, and against* the penal *Laws* extended to protestant *Dissenters* (see p. 483 E)—But, will any Man say, that the *Honourable Person* had the least Influence or *Credit with the* Convocation of *those Times,* or Disposition to forward *their* Proceedings? I can tell him who were their Favourites, Counsellors, and Leaders; and believe the *Craftsman* is acquainted with the Heads of that *pious Cabal;* but I defy him to shew, that the *Honourable Gentleman* did ever enter into the Cabals or *Conferences* of Sir W——m W—ndb—m, or any *other Tories* of their *Alliance.* Now, what Credit can be given to a *Writer* of such *notorious* PROFLIGACY, that he *himself,* even in the *Craftsman,* did expressly vilify this *Rev. Prelate?* These are *his Words,* " That the Bishop *had render'd* not only *his* Orthodoxy, *but even his* CHRISTIANITY suspected, *by his Writings* for Liberty of Conscience.'' If there can be a clearer Conviction of *Baseness, Insincerity,* and *abandon'd Principles* in any Person, I will own *then,* that the *Craftsman* may find somebody *second* to himself in the *Want* of moral *Honesty.* And can *such a Man as* this

pretend to advise the *Protestant Dissenters;* can he ask their *Credit for himself* and their *Votes for* his Party, after having so *infamously vilified* a BISHOP who defended THEM, and *aspersing him* as one who had made himself *suspicious,* even as a CHRISTIAN, by defending *them,* and *all our religious Liberties?*

Consistently with this *Course of* Deceit and *Hypocrisy* he raises a Clamour in *one Paper* against the *Ministers,* as having *maltreated the Dissenters;* and in the next, (see p. 477.) propagates a Tract called the *Freeholders Political Catechism,* but purposely strikes out *what relates to the* Toleration of *Protestant Dissenters,* and *Liberty of Conscience.'* For in p. 4. of the *Political Catechism* it is *honestly* said, *Neither in the State of Nature nor in the State of Civil Society, hath any Man an absolute Power over another Man's Mind or Conscience; from whence it follows, that, in the first of those States, no Man could give the Magistrate a Power, which he had not to give; and that, in the second of those States, the Exercise of that Power is impossible: Compulsion without Conviction making a Man a Hypocrite that is a Criminal, but can never secure the publick Peace.*

It was maintained, That Mr P——y was *one of those Members* who appeared in 1718 against the *Junction of two Appeals* in one Bill, (See p. 475 C) therefore if those Gentlemen *erred concerning the Dissenters,* still it will not give Mr P——y or his *Cabal* the *Preference; because* HE *committed the same Errors.* Now what says the *Craftsman* to this? First he trifles with his *doughty Records,* the *Historical Register,* and says he never met with Mr P——y's Name there, as one *who voted* against *the Bill;* which equally proves, that instead of 202 *Votes* in the *Negative,* which appear *on the Journal* of the House, there were but 20, because scarce so many *Names* are to be found in the *Craftsman's* foolish Records.——Again, he asks me, *Whether* Mr P——y *was not then in the Country?* &c. He might as well ask me, *Whether Mr P. was not then at* Church? It is highly probable *he could not be absent* from so *full a House of* Commons, debating a *Matter of so great* Concern. And have been informed by *Members who then sat there,* that HE *was among them,* and *divided against the Bill.* If this be not true, why hath not the *Craftsman* denied it? He who knows Mr P. and all *his Affairs*

fairs so perfectly, as to tell us *what hap-pen'd at Midnight*, in *his* and neighb'ring *Families*, upon *Alarms of Fire*; he who knows *what past* even in the *King's Closet*, when Mr *P.* had the Honour to be *admitted there*, and not only published suchP R I V A T E C O N V E R S A T I O N, as did happen with him in Confidence, but such as *never did happen at all*, (See Vol. I. p. 258) Surely this *well informed Writer* doth, or *may know*, and *ought to declare*, whether Mr *P.* did, or did not *vote against this Bill*.

The *Free Briton.* Oct. 11. No. 206.
Address to the Freeholders and Electors.

GENTLEMEN,

THere cannot be a Matter of greater Importance to you all, than the Election of *Persons proper to represent you.* From that Moment, when the *Writs of Election* issue, till the Returns are made, the Publick is suspended, and its Being at Stake. The Laws of Liberty, and the Fences of Property, are no longer to be relied on, than whilst the *supreme Legislative Power* is able and *willing* to assert them. The frequent Conventions of *Parliament enable* your Representatives, yearly, to assert your Rights and Immunities; but unless you chuse *such Representatives*, as have *Judgment to discern*, and *Wisdom to support* your *true and natural Interests*, such Conventions would be *worse than none*, and your Constitution destroy'd by your own *mistaken* Elections.

You are a *free People*, because your *Kings* and Magistrates are equally bounded by your *own Laws*, in the same Degree with the *meanest of yourselves*. You are supported in this State of Freedom, by having a *Protestant* Royal *Family* to govern you, whose *Title to the Crown* arises from those very *Laws which declare* your *Rights and Liberties*. But under no other Power upon Earth can you either *enjoy Liberty*, or *elect Parliaments*. Before the *Revolution* of 1688 ensured a *Protestant Succession* to you, the most grievous *Interruptions*, both of *Liberty* and *Parliaments*, were beheld and lamented by you.

But then consider, that this *Protestant Succession*, which took its Rise from the *Power of Parliament*, may date its Fall from the *Elections of Parliament Men*. And if you chuse such Members as offer themselves, without *sincere and unquestionable Resolutions* to maintain the *Pro-*

testant *Succession*, and the Blessings it procured, you will find the *Foundations of publick Happiness* will be shaken, when they have lost the *natural Aid* of an *Affectionate Parliament*. It is now in your Power to chuse *faithful Friends* to the *Protestant Succession* to be your *Representatives*. But if you chuse *Men who were* never *its Friends, that*, which is now *in your Power to strengthen*, will scarcely *then* be in your Power to *save*.

Consider, the *Protestant Succession* hath more than once been in Danger from *mistaken Elections*. The Vote of the *House of Commons*, in 1702, which determined the Law that made it *High Treason* to oppose this *Succession*, was carried but by *one Voice*; and had *that* been wanting, the *Succession* must have wanted *that Security* in a Season when the *Enemies* of Liberty desired no *greater Encouragement*, than *Impunity*, to overthrow the *British Constitution. What hath been may be*; unless you prevent it by your *careful* Attention to the *Characters, Temper*, and *Spirit* of those whom you are to chuse: And the most *essential Security* of our Liberties may *want Voices* on its Side, in the *next House of Commons, if you want* just *Distinction* in the *next Elections.*

Be not deluded with false and unmeaning Distinctions *between the* King *and* his *Ministers*; for it is *his* Authority that they administer, and *the Crown* cannot exercise any Power *but by its Officers*, who will always be opposed, as well by the *King's Enemies* as by their own. Be watchful, that this *Pretence* of opposing *Ministers* do not become the *Cloak of Disaffection*, or *Want of Affection* to the *King*; and be attentive to the Characters and *Conduct of those* who oppose the *Service of the Publick* in every Thing, under the Cover of differing with *none but those who are trusted in that Service*. It is a *safer* and more *successful Way* of opposing an *established Government*, by Dissembling the Motives of such Opposition, as it is more safe to *undermine* than to *fight against Stone-Walls*; and the strongest Men may be in their Habits of *Disaffection*, the more powerful Necessity will there be for *Deceit.* No Man the most of all *hates the Prince on the Throne*, or *his Title*, will find it so easy to ensnare his Subjects by *arraigning his Authority*, as by *vilifying his Administration.* Many of those, who now pretend to oppose the *Ministers only*, were once as violent against the *Throne itself*, and avowed their

Hatred

Hatred to the Protestant Succession: They thought it the *Season* to declare themselves, and they did *declare themselves in Arms.* When it grew dangerous to question the *King's Title,* and they found the Sceptre strong enough to crush *Rebellion,* they still found it *safe* to distress the *King's Service;* and, by giving Opposition *new Names,* made that, which before was detected as *Treason,* be asserted as *publick Virtue.* In Truth, they have found the Convenience of the Disguise.

If you find then any *such Candidates* as are remarkably distinguish'd *by their Opposition* to *all the Measures of* his Majesty's *Administration,* Fear them, and *Try Them.* Consider, that if any Men, who apply for your Votes, should be *Patriots in Pretence,* and *Jacobites in their* real *Meaning,* they are more terrible than those who would raise even an *Army* for the *Pretender's Service;* they are actually *raising A House of Commons* for the *Pretender's Service;* a Project big both with *Fleets* and *Armies* to destroy *our Liberties.* Are there no *Jacobites* who will endeavour to get into Parliament? Doubtless there are *many.* But will there be even *one* who will own his *Jacobitism* to you? And if he *disguise* it, will it not be by the *old Distinction* between the *King* and his *Ministers.*

How many Persons are still remaining of that Party, which *invited the Pretender to* invade *these Kingdoms,* during his late Majesty's Reign? How many of these Persons will be desirous of *your Voices,* to chuse them Members of the ensuing Parliament? And can you *trust* them with the *Custody of* those *very Liberties,* which so many of them ventured their *Lives and Fortunes to destroy?* Suppose they should tell you, they are now become *different* Men; will you therefore *trust them?* ask them, how the *Difference* appears? Is it to be found in the *Distinction* between opposing *the King's Title and his Government;* or in the Difference between *their Attempts* at that Time *to dethrone him, and their Endeavours* ever since *to distress him?* Judge of *their* Allegiance *to the King,* by their *Acts of* Kindness, *or Service to the King;* and if they have *always* stood in *Opposition to his Measures,* will you chuse them as the *fittest* Persons to *support* him *in War,* or to *preserve* him *in Peace?*

As the *King on the Throne,* and his *Royal Family* are the *only* Princes in the World, who can govern you comfortably

with your *Liberties,* consider *their Title to the Crown* as the *Title to your own Estates.* And which of you all would make those Persons *Trustees* or *Guardians of your Children's Fortunes,* who had already endeavoured *to dispossess* you *of that very Inheritance?* Men who have once exerted *their utmost Endeavours* to *Ruin* you, are hardly fit to be *trusted* with *full Powers to ruin you.* They may indeed *magnify* their *Affection for you* in the present Season; but if, after having attempted to make you *Slaves* and *Beggars* by Violence, they talk in this Strain, that you may *receive them into Confidence,* there is abundant Reason to believe, that they are now labouring to *ruin you by Fraud,* in the very same Manner as they would once have *destroyed you by Force.*

The *Craftsman,* Oct. 13. N° 580.

Continu'd from p. 519.

MRS *Osborne* farther endeavours to terrify the *Dissenters,* by telling them *They cannot lead the* Tories, *but must ingloriously follow them.*— Now, I, *says D'anvers,* can see no Occasion for either *leading,* or *following,* in this Case. Why may not Men of all Denominations act in Conjunction, when they see their joint Interest in Danger, as they did against the late *Excise Scheme,* without any Dispute about *Superiority,* or *Dependence?* We are so far from advising the *Dissenters* to throw themselves into a Body under the Direction of *any Party,* that we only desire them to preserve their *Independency,* and to act in Concert with their Countrymen, as they shall see Occasion, at this great *Crisis;* and leave it to the Consideration of the *Dissenters,* whether it is more for the publick Interest, or their own particular Views, to join the *Court* or *Country Party.*

But they have been ask'd what Advantage they can propose to themselves, by voting for the COUNTRY PARTY; since even the anti-ministerial Writers *have declared they are resolved to preserve a Neutrality between the* CHURCH *and the* DISSENTERS. This is a little unfairly quoted. What I said, on that Subject, may be seen in my Preface to the Volumes of the *Craftsman.* But Mrs *Osborne's* Comment upon it is extraordinary. She addresses them thus; *What Cowards and Slaves are these Men to the* Tories! &c. (see p. 402. A) I thought a Declaration of *Neutrality,* especially towards the *weaker Party,* was rather a Mark of *Friend-*
ship

Dip rather than *Hostility*. Where did I declare, *the Test Act ought never to be repealed?* — Indeed, *Mother*, you should leave such dirty Work to your Brother *Walsingham*, who is retain'd to assert *Falshoods*, and abuse *Persons*, when *Argument* is against him. I always mentioned the *Dissenters* in the most affectionate Terms, as *Fellow-Protestants*, and *Fellow-Subjects*, without any invidious Distinctions between *Churchmen* and *Them*.

As to the *Repeal of the* TEST ACTS, you know it's a Point much disputed by the *Church Whigs*, both of the *Court* and *Country Party*, as well as the *Tories*; but I defy you to prove I ever endeavour'd to obstruct it, either by my Writings or Discourse. I did not, indeed, like yourself, (see Vol. II. p. 1115.) obtrude my own private Judgment on the Publick, in so nice a Case; or give the *Dissenters* any Promises I could not make good; for tho' you call me the Mouth of the *Independent Whigs*, I have not their Consciences under my Girdle, as your *Patron* may possibly have those of the *Dependent Whigs*. But this I will venture to say, that if the *Dissenters* would conciliate the Minds of all Men towards them, they cannot take a more effectual Method, than by proving themselves hearty Friends to our *civil Liberties*, and acting independently, without Regard to *former Disputes* and *Animosities*. Likewise, every *Country Gentleman*, *Whig* or *Tory*, will, probably, be as grateful to the *Dissenters* for their Interest, as any *Courtier* whatsoever; tho' they do not reproach them with their former Services, nor insolently demand their Votes in Return. Neither have they instructed any of their *Advocates* to tell the *Dissenters* that they are their ONLY FRIENDS, and that if they don't act just as they bid them, they are ungrateful, and ought to be persecuted. Yet this is the Language towards them from *the other side*; even from *Dame Osborne* herself (see p. 472, H)

But Mrs *Osborne* being conscious she has gone a little too far, she endeavours to pacify them in her next Paper, with the good Tidings, *that his Majesty has actually given Instructions to the Lord Lieutenant of* Ireland *to promote and encourage the Repeal of the Test Act in that Kingdom,* (see p. 482 D) from whence she concludes *that her Patron is dipos'd to repeal it in* England, *as soon as he thinks the general Interest will permit him*. I have heard, indeed, he gave some *leading Dissenters in Town* such a Promise, and

I mention'd it as a new Expédient to keep them in a Dependence, (see p. 426 G) However I will not dispute this Point with Mrs *Osborne*, who hath her Intelligence from the Fountain-Head; but refer the *Dissenters* to the *Lord Lieutenant's Speech to the Parliament of* Ireland for the Truth of her Information, (see Occurrences *Oct.* 4.)

Mrs *Osborne* proposes, in the same Paper (see p. 462) to put this Argument about the *Dissenters* on the Character of her *Patron*, as a Friend to *Liberty in general*.—*Shew me the Man*, says she, *that ever made a more moderate or temperate Use of his Power. He never advised the making of* one *Law, that should lessen our Liberties; nor exercised* one *Act of Power upon the bitterest and most implacable of his Enemies.*—A noble Panegyrick, indeed! His *moderate Acquisitions* are a sufficient Proof of the *first Article*; the late *Excise Bill* will sufficiently purge him of the Imputation in the *second*; and his exceeding Lenity towards *Gentlemen, Booksellers*, and *Printers*, suspected of writing Papers against his Administration, amply justify his Conduct with Regard to the *third*.

Leaving him therefore in full Possession of those Praises, which so justly belong to him, I shall conclude with a short Address to our *Protestant Dissenters* of all Denominations.

Gentlemen,

IT hath, I think, been proved that a *certain honourable Gentleman* hath not such a peculiar Title to your Favour, as his *Advocates* pretend. I believe that you are likewise convinced that *no particular Bodies of Men* have that Dislike to you at present, they formerly had. You cannot help observing that the Cry of the *Church* hath been long out of Date, and all Virulence of Parties, on that Account, almost lost in a general Contention for *Liberty*. The Dispute of this Age is not about *Persons*, but *Things*; nor should I have troubled you so much about the Conduct of the *honourable Gentleman*, in your Affairs, if his *Advocates* had not made it necessary by their foolish Encomiums and ridiculous Claims. But even *Persons* are not beneath your Consideration, as far as they relate to *publick Affairs*, and the general Interest of the Nation is affected by Them. Consider, *Gentlemen*, that though We have been in Peace for these *twenty Years*, We still continue under

der the Preffure of an *immenfe Debt*, loaded with *burthenfome Taxes*, terrify'd with a *large, ftanding Army*, and almoft overwhelmed with *Luxury* and *Corruption*. This is the State of our *domeftick Affairs* ; and I am afraid you will find, upon Enquiry, that our *Affairs abroad* are not in a much better Situation. The Face of *Europe* is again clouded over ; and I wifh the Storm, which hath been long gathering, may not foon burft upon us, notwithftanding all our late flattering Promifes of Serenity and fine Weather. Our only Hopes of Relief depend on a *free* and *uncorrupt Parliament*, which it will foon be very much in your Power to obtain for us. You would therefore do well to reflect, to *whom* thefe Diftreffes have been principally owing, and whether it will be prudent to truft Them a-gain. You have been told, *Gentlemen*, by one of the *minifterial Writers* (I think Mrs *Osborne* Herfelf) that We are already advanced to the very Banks of the RUBICON. This alas! is too true, and if We proceed any farther, our *Liberties* are gone ; perhaps, for ever. I am therefore inclined to hope, that you will make the Prefervation of our *Conftitution* your firft Care, and confider any *particular Eafe to your felves* only as a fecondary Point. Thus will you approve your felves *good Englifhmen*, and really deferve all the Indulgence from the Legiflature, which you can reafonably defire. Thus will you intitle your felves to the good Wifhes of the prefent Age, and the Bleffings of all Pofterity.

Weekly Mifcellany, Oct. 13. N° 44.
Remarks on Mr Chubb's *Notions*.

MR HOOKER,

THE Medium us'd by Mr *Chub* to prove his darling Propofition, *viz. That Reafon either is, or ought to be, a fufficient Guide in all Matters of Religion*, is as follows: " Man in his natural State devoid of Revelation, is fuppos'd to be an accountable Creature: If fo, he has a juft, and equitable Claim upon his Maker for Capacities fufficient to enable to. him, to difcharge his Account: Confequently, fince thofe are the Capacities of *unaffifted* Reafon, Reafon *alone* either is, or ought to be, a *fufficient* Guide in all Matters of Religion". This is his Argument. But before we can determine any thing of its Conclufivenefs, it's neceffary to ftate the Meaning of its Terms. The firft of them, *viz.* The Suppofition

of Man's being accountable, will admit of three different Conftructions: 1. It may mean, that Man is *equally* accountable in fuch a State, as under the Guidance of Revelation. 2. That he is *more fo* ; or, 3. That he is *lefs fo*.

If he fays, that Man is equally accountable in his natural State, as under the Direction of Revelation, it follows, that unaffifted Reafon can make Man as knowing and able, as the Light of divine Revelation in fuch a State ; *i. e.* That every Man can difcover by his bare Reafon, every Truth that even God himfelf can teach ; which is the higheft Arrogance and Pride that can be imagin'd.

But fhould he mean, that Man is more accountable in fuch a State, than under the Guidance of Revelation, the fame Objection, but ftrengthen'd, occurs ; *viz.* That he fuppofes, what every Man's Knowledge and Experience muft convince him is falfe. And Mr *Chub*'s Reafoning muft imply, That Man is equally, or more accountable in a State devoid of Revelation, than he would under its Affiftance. But thefe Conftructions being chargeable with fuch Abfurdities, it follows, that his Meaning fhould be, That Man is lefs accountable in a State deftitute of Revelation, than under its divine Influence : Therefore has Faculties equal to his Account : Therefore has lefs Faculties: Therefore has lefs Reafon : Therefore has lefs Power to diftinguifh Right and Wrong, Truth and Error : Therefore, fince the Religion of a rational Creature (for to fuch the relative Terms of Right and Wrong muft refer) confifts in the Obfervance of what is Right, in avoiding what is Wrong, the next juft Conclufion muft be, that he has lefs Power to difcover what is the Religion of fuch a Creature. Therefore unaffifted Reafon cannot be fo fufficient a Guide in Matters of Religion, as he could be fupplied with from Revelation.

But let us fuppofe, with him, that Man in his imaginary natural State, is an accountable Creature, without fixing the Degree, and attend to the Juftnefs of his Conclufion. Thus

Man is an accountable Creature ; therefore he has a Claim upon his Maker for Capacities fufficient to enable him to difcharge his Account : Therefore fince they are (*ex Hypothefi*) the Capacities of unaffifted Reafon, unaffifted Reafon is, or ought to be a fufficient Guide in all Matters of Religion. From whence thefe

Ab-

Abſurdities will follow——What may be ſaid of Man in general, may be ſaid of every individual Man. Therefore every individual Man, in a State devoid of Re-velation, is accountable: Therefore every individual Man has, or ought to have **A** Faculties ſufficient to enable him to diſ-charge his Account: Therefore the Rea-ſon of every Man is a ſufficient Guide in all Matters of Religion: Therefore the ſmalleſt Degree of Reaſon is as ſuf-ficient, for all the Purpoſes of Religion, as the greateſt: But the only End and **B** Purpoſe of Religion in a rational Crea-ture, is, that it tends to advance his Na-ture to the greateſt Perfections; that is, to the neareſt Similitude or Likeneſs to his Maker, and, conſequently, to his greateſt Happineſs; therefore the ſmalleſt Degree of Reaſon, will make a Man as **C** perfect, as like his Maker, as happy as the greateſt. Which is juſt as abſurd as to ſay, That the ſame Power that can acquaint him with ſome Part of his Ma-ker's Will, muſt for that very Reaſon be able to acquaint him with, and enable him to fulfill his whole Will. Had Mr **D** *Chub*, when he drew this Conſequence, meant only, that it is ſufficient to acquit him before his Maker, who placed him in ſuch a State, and cannot require more than is given him, there would have been no Diſpute; no Chriſtian of common Senſe would have oppoſed him. But **E** barely to acquit a Man before his Maker, can never amount to the ſame, as making him ſo perfect, as that he muſt needs appear amiable in his Sight; yet this is what the Riligion of a rational Creature may effect; and therefore what a ſuffici-ent Guide in it muſt be ſufficient for ef-fecting. God's Juſtice is clear, as to every **F** Individual, if he has it in his Power not to ſuffer more Evil than he enjoys Good by his Exiſtence. All beyond is to be eſteemed Favours, which ceaſe to be ſo, when they can be challenged.

PHILALETHES. **G**

London Journal, Oct. 13, N° 746.
Of Whigs and Tories.

THE *Diſſenters* ſo thoroughly under-ſtand their *Duty* and *Intereſt*; and are ſo *firmly reſolved* to perform the one and purſue the other that they need no **H** Aſſiſtance or Advice. I am allow'd, ſays *Oſborne*, to ſay upon the *beſt Authorities,* and know it to be true from my own Converſation, and divers Letters from ſeveral Parts of the Kingdom, that they

believe the preſent *Court Whigs* to be as good *Whigs*, if not better, than any of the *boaſted Independent Whigs*, and that they are *determin'd* to vote in their In-tereſt, againſt the *late Combination* of *Jacobites* , *Tories*, and *Malecontent Whigs.*

Mr *D'anvers*, in his late Paper (See p. 518.) hath ſaid nothing to the Purpoſe, but contented himſelf with throwing out *low Scurrilities* and *puerile Witticiſms*; ſuch as *coupling Extremes*, and *Squaring Circles*: As tho' it was any *Impropriety,* when an Author had, thro' his whole Book, joined *Jacobites* and *Diſſenters*, as Deſtroyers of the Church; to ſay he *coupled* them together.

In my Letters to the *Diſſenters*, I laid down ſeveral *Propoſitions*, as carrying their own Evidence (See p. 470, 1, 2, 451) And what Anſwer does the *Craftſman* return to all that is there ſaid? Why, That the *Whigs* and *Tories* are ſo far from being the *ſame Men* they uſed to be, that they ſeem to have *changed Principles* by Con-ſent (See p. 527.) The *very Man* who affirms this, without *one Fact* to ſupport it, calls himſelf a *Whig*, yet is become *an ignominious* Slave to *Tories*, and pays Homage to *Jacobites* and *Papiſts*. He ſays, PERHAPS *they be the ſame*. He is not ſure; he hopes better Things. He is more Civil to theſe *great Friends* of his, than to call THEIR KING a *Pretender*; nobody, ſays he, can be a *Jacobite*, with-out being for THE PERSON who gives *Name* to the Party. He would have ſaid, The ROYAL PERSON, or the UN-FORTUNATE ROYAL PERSON. He *ſeems* to *wiſh* he could have ſaid; but *durſt* not go ſo far yet.

What a Writer is this, to pretend to gain over the *Diſſenters*, who has not only ſtruck up a Solemn League and Covenant with *Tories*, but is ſervilely pay-ing his Court to *Jacobites* and *Papiſts*! and who never yet *dared* to ſay, that he or his Party of *Independent Whigs* were in Opinion, or would be in *Practice*, for the *Repeal of the Teſt.*

But let us examine his grand Propoſi-tion, That the *Court Whigs* of this Age are exactly the ſame *kind* of *Creatures* with the *Court Tories* before the *Revolu-tion*, and *vice verſa.*

By their *Fruits* we ſhall *know* them. The '*Court Tories* before the *Revolution*, triumph'd over all the *Laws of England*; they were always for *Arbitrary Power* and *Tyranny* in Church and State; ſet up *Prerogative* above Law; made *Proclama-tions,*

tions, Law ; and declared, that the *Royal Will*, in impoſing Taxes, without Conſent of Parliament, binds the *Subjects Conſcience* on pain of *eternal Damnation*. By the Advice of theſe *Court Tories*, many of the beſt Quality and Condition, were committed to Priſon, with unheard of Circumſtances, for *refuſing* to pay Money demanded *without* and *againſt Law*. Supplemental *Acts of State* were made by *Court Tories*, to ſupply what they call'd *Defects of Law* : Kings themſelves, taught by *Court Tories*, told their Parliament, That they were a *Generation of Vipers* ; that they *exiſted ſolely* by their Favour, and were TO BE, OR NOT TO BE, *at their* Pleaſure.

Theſe *Counſellors* were all *Tories*, tho' the Name was not given till after the *Reſtoration* ; when, indeed, for ſome Time, they kept a little within *Forms* of Law ; but ſoon grew ſo wicked, that *no Forms* could be found to *ſcreen* their Actions : Then they ſet up thoſe *infamous* Tools Bp *Parker* and L'*Eſtrange*, to cry up *Prerogative*, to write down the *Laws* and to make a *total Subverſion* of the Conſtitution, by teaching the Doctrines of Abſolute *Paſſive Obedience* and *Nonreſiſtance* to the King's Will and Pleaſure : They got *Oaths* to be made and impoſed, " That the Subjects ſhould not reſiſt the King, nor any *commiſſion'd* by him, on ANY PRETENCE whatever" : And after a thouſand Rogueries and Tricks of State, as the King's *buying* his Subjects at home and *ſelling* himſelf to Princes Abroad ; *Murders* on a *Civil* Account ; Whippings, Fines, Impriſonment, Dungeons, &c. on a *Religious* Account ; and finiſh'd their own *Wickedneſs*, and our *Deſtruction*, by adviſing the King, *That he might break thro' or* DISPENSE *with all the Laws of* England.

How ſay you, Mr *D'anvers* ? Are theſe *Facts*, or not ? I leave *you* to draw the *Parallel*, and maintain your Aſſertion, That the preſent *Court Whigs* are the ſame *Kind of Creatures*, as theſe *Court Tories* before the *Revolution*.

As for the other Part of his *Affirmation*, " That the *Tories* are turn'd *Whigs*" ; how ſhall we know this ? For by their *laſt Actions in Power*, in the Cloſe of the Queen's Reign, they appear'd *the ſame* as of old ; and ever ſince they have been *out of Power*, they have ſhewn the ſame *Spite* and *Enmity* to the *Revolution*, and the *preſent Royal Family*, as the *Whigs* uſed to ſay they had in their Hearts. They were in *Plots* and *Rebellion* againſt

the *firſt Prince* of the *Hanover* Family, and have ever ſince choſen ſuch Men to *repreſent them* in Parliament, as have conſtantly oppoſed the Preſent Royal Family, and *their Country* too ; and have choſen SOME, whom all the World knows to be THOROUGH AND COMPLETE JACOBITES

They *pretend now*, indeed, they are for *Liberty*, and for our *Civil and Religious Rights* ; juſt as the *Royaliſts*, in *Cromwel*'s Time, were *Republicans*, with whom they fell in, on Purpoſe to *diſtreſs Oliver*, and bring about a *Reſtoration*. Thus ; Who talk'd more in K. *Wm*'s Time, for *publick Good* and for *Liberty and Property*, than the *Tories* ? yet, when they came *into Power*, fell to the ſame dreadful Work of *Tyranny* in Church and State, and introducing a *Pretender*. This they learnt of the *Cavaliers* ; who, as Bp *Burnet* informs us, " were all zealous *Commonwealths-Men*, according to the Directions ſent them from thoſe about the King ; yet, at the Reſtoration they ſhook off *the Diſguiſe*, and return'd to their *old Principles* for a high Prerogative and abſolute Power "

The *Univerſal Spectator*, Oct. 13. No. 261.

IT is a natural Foible in old Men to praiſe the Faſhions and Cuſtoms of a former Age. A Contraſte to this, and equally ridiculous, is the Humour of young Men in valuing themſelves above their Predeceſſors, and thinking nothing bears a true Stamp of Wiſdom, Wit, or Gallantry, but what is of modern Production. An Inſtance of theſe two Foibles, ſays Mr *Stonecaſtle*, we have in our little Society. Sir *Jaſper Truby*, who is regular in his way of living, and a true *Engliſhman*, recommends *Sage Tea* in a Morning, and *Beef* and *Pudding* at Noon. *Harry Careleſs* ſmiles at the Knight's Taſte, and will keep to his *Chocolate* and *Fricaſſes*. Sir *Jaſper* would think it as immoral to break into his Laws of dining at 12, and going to Bed at 11, as to offend againſt any of the Laws of the Land ; *Harry* thinks it as regular to dine at 5, and to go to Bed when he has nothing to do up. The other Evening our Diſcourſe turn'd on the Diverſions of Mankind, and how far they were neceſſary, by unbending our Mind after Buſineſs or Study, to give us a new Vigour to return to them. Here Sir *Jaſper* expatiated in Praiſe of the Diverſions in Uſe of his Time, and declaimed on the Degeneracy of the modern Amuſements ; particularly on the Folly of
ſome

some Cits, who neglect their Shops of Business to follow the Recreations in Vogue.

Harry Careless as much commended the Diversions in Fashion; such as those of the *Mall*, *Assemblees* of the Ladies, a Game at *Quadrille*, &c.——— Mr *True-wit*, to put a Stop to the Dispute, determined it thus: *Recreation*, says he, signifies a Relief from *Study* or *Business*; but when it grows a *Business* itself, it loses its Essence and Nature: A wise Man would use those Diversions which were innocent, and by keeping a *Medium*, he would keep his Humour unruffled, and be not only easy to himself, but agreeable to others. As for *private Recreations*, which distinguish the Humours of particular Persons; every Age produces such as would be a Shame for any *Thing* which bears the Title of *Man* to follow. I'll give two Instances,

Sir *Harry Wildblood*, a Man of the last Age, and one of the Club of *Scowerers*, to recreate himself from the Fatigue of Idleness, began his Morning in a Gaming-House. Tir'd with that he adjourn'd to the Ordinary; and when from the Bottle he had got Spirits enough, he tripp'd to the Playhouse; and thence returned to the Bottle, by which having regain'd his Vivacity, about Midnight scour'd the Streets, broke a Woman of the Town's Windows, beat a Bully, ran a Watchman thro', and then reel'd off, either to the *Round-house* or his *Lodgings*.

Opposite is the Character of the modern Mr *Sprucely*, a Gentleman of a good Estate, and about 30: He lives at Home with his *Mamma*, and *recreates* himself with raising *Paste*, *Candying* and making *Jellies*; *Dressing a Head*, *Quilting* or *Flourishing*: He presents the Ladies with his *Pincushions*, and *Paper Trees* of his own *Cutting* out. When tir'd at Home, he dresses like a *Male Kind*, appears in the *Side-Box*; laughs very loud, and disturbs every Body near him.

Fog's Journal. October 13. No. 258.

Extract of a Pamphlet, entitled, *A Word of Advice to Freeholders*, &c.

THE Author, after having animadverted on the Folly of those Boroughs, which [...] the same Representatives [...] have loudly declared them[...] [...] tells the following Story, [...] is known but [...] [...]nths before th[...] [...] A. Bp *Sha*[...] [...] in the C[...] [...] III.

thus address'd him,——"My Lord, I am sorry to say, that the Measures which the Ministry are pursuing at present are by no Means such as I approve,—they seem to be going very unwarrantable Lengths,—I have hitherto join'd with them, while I thought they had their Country's Interest, and the Welfare of the Church at Heart; but whatever they, or your Lordship may imagine, I am no Pretender's Man, no *Jacobite* nor ever shall be one; but will oppose that Interest to the utmost of my Power.—To be plain, I suspect there is some Design to bring in the Pretender—they shall never have my Concurrence therein,—Wherefore, if your Lordship will join Forces with me, I have still some Interest in the House, particularly with those of my own Order—We will form a Party strong enough to break all their Measures."

Is your Grace in earnest? said the Marquis, I am, reply'd the Arch-Bishop gravely—Let me beg Leave then to tell your Grace a short Story, rejoin'd the Marquis with equal Gravity—I had a Present made me of a fine Bitch, which in due Time produc'd a Litter of Whelps, and pleasing my self with the Fancy that they would prove excellent in their kind, I went every Day to see them; but when the ninth Day came, the Time that all Puppies used to see, these Whelps continued still blind; I tried them the 10th, 11th, and 12th Day, and still they continued the same. Wherefore having no Hopes of them I order'd 'em to be thrown into the Horsepond—Would your Grace believe it? Just as they were sinking their Eyes opened—Which said, he walk'd away, and left the A. Bp to apply the Story.

I doubt not, says the Author, but some will laugh at this Story, and think 'it no way concerns us. But let us turn the Tables, and substitute the Words—Arbitrary Power—Governing without Parliaments—and General Excise, instead of the words Pretender, and Jacobites, and see how it will run then. (See p. 531 E)

But, perhaps, some *Wiseacre*, some State-Dunce, will ask, what Analogy there is between bringing in the Pretender, and bringing in the Excise; and whether I think the one would have been as dangerous to the Constitution as the other. I answer, that Popery considered abstractedly as a Religion, without affecting our civil Concerns, is a meer Bugbear to frighten Fools with—that it is possible for a Nation to be free, not only if the

A s s   Prince

Prince be a *Papiſt*, but if he be a *Maho-metan*; and that the People may be Slaves, even tho' the Prince be a *Proteſtant*.

Our Anceſtors were to all Intents and Purpoſes a free People before the Refor-mation; and *Magna Charta*, with our moſt valuable Privileges, were obtained when our Sovereigns were *Roman Catho-licks*; and the *Swedes* under *Charles XII.* were, and the *Danes* are as much Slaves, as the *French* under *Lewis XIV.* or their preſent Monarch. (*See Occur. Oct. 22.*)

The Free Britton, Oct. 18. No. 207.
An Addreſs to the Proteſtant Diſſenters;
and Fog's Argument in behalf of the
Pretender thoroughly anſwer'd.

THE falſe Aſſertion, *That the Mini-ſtry had* broken their *Faith with the Proteſtant Diſſenters*, hath been al-ready confuted; and the *Craftſman*, by offering nothing in Defence of a Fact, which none but himſelf had advanced, hath *pinned* the moſt notorious FALSHOOD on *himſelf*, that ever was coined to ſupport a *ſilly Invective*.

To you, the *Proteſtant Diſſenters*, this *Solemn Appeal* is made. If you ſee the *diſaffected Whigs*, refuſing to explain them-ſelves in this Affair, or to engage their Votes in Your Favour, or to give even a *frail Promiſe*, not to vote againſt You, Have you not the greateſt Reaſon to believe, that they are too cloſely uni-ted with your *natural Enemies* the *Tories*, and with the *High Church Faction*; and that whenever your Indulgence ſhall be the Queſtion in Parliament, they will be then under the ſame Influence to *vote a-gainſt you*, as reſtrains them now *from promiſing to Vote for you*?

See what different Conſequences will attend your Votes in Favour of *this Admi-niſtration*, and in Favour of *their Oppo-ſers*. The *Court-Whigs* MAY repeal the *Teſts*, and WILL, if you give them *ſuf-ficient* Strength; the *Tories*, you know NEVER WILL; and the *Patriot Whigs*, the more they ſucceed in their Oppoſition to the Miniſtry, and raiſe the *Power of the Tories*, the more will ſuch *Whigs* render it impoſſible even for *themſelves* to do you any Service.

Look back to the late *Diviſions* of the peſent *Houſe of Commons*. In 500 Mem-bers, you would find 300 *for the Court*, and 200 *againſt it*; of theſe 200, near 120 are *profeſſed Tories*, and about 80 *diſſatiſ-fied Whigs*. And if theſe *oppoſing Whigs* were to *vote in your Favour*, the Court

by ſuch a Reinforcement would have a Majority of 260, to *repeal or explain the Teſts.* And if, in the Parliament to be cho-ſen, the *Ballance of Parties* ſhould *not be al-tered* at all from what it is at preſent, ſtill the Court would have a Majority of 100 *Votes* to ſupport *you*, even tho' the *Patri-ot-Whigs* ſhould openly join *their* Tory *Confederates* againſt *you*.

Judge of theſe Men, their Spirit and Diſcretion, by thoſe whom they recom-mend to your Favour, or point out to your Diſlike. You may find in *one Crafts-man*, a Vindication of a certain *dignified Jacobite* in the *City of London*; in another a Declaration againſt the preſent SP..E..R of *the Houſe of Commons*: Are you then convinced that the ſaid *Jacobite* is become a *Whig*; or that the Honourable A——N ON——w, Eſq; is a *Tory*? yet the *mo-deſt Craftſman* aſſures you, on his Veraci-ty, the *Tories* are now become *Whigs*, and the *Whigs* are become *Tories* : Will you, the *Proteſtant Diſſenters*, truſt *your Toleration* on the Credit of this Aſſurance?

If in the Election for a neighbouring Country, my Voice ſhould be given for the *Honourable Perſon* juſt mentioned, there is this to be ſaid in his Favour, that he is deſcended from a *Great* and *Honourable* Fa-mily, and *not from the* Dreggs *of the Popu-lace* : That he hath always been ſincerely attached to the preſent Conſtitution, and zealous for the Support of that *Royal Fa-mily*, on whoſe *Proteſtant Succeſſion* our Liberties depend: That he hath ſerved his his Country, during many Years in Parli-ament, with untainted Integrity; and hath filled the *Chair of that Houſe*, wherein he ſits, with the greateſt Impartiality : That, with a *Diſintereſtedneſs* worthy of himſelf, he hath ſought no Advancement but what he might accept with *Honour* and with *Independency* : That having ow-ed his Promotion to that high Office which he ſuſtains, altogether to the *Weight of his Character*, and to the *unanimous Voice* of that great *Aſſembly*, he refuſed to accept of ſuch Favours from the Crown, as were in any Degree *leſs Independent* : And that when the *Queen* was pleaſed to appoint him her Majeſty's *Chancellor*, though he thought it an Honour to be in her Majeſ-ty's Service; yet he declined the *Salary of the Office*; that he might not not take any Advantage inconſiſtent with the In-tention of the Law, which reſtrains the *Members of that Houſe* from accepting *Employments of Profit* under the Crown; however clear and certain it is, that the Houſhold

Houshould of the *Queen*, or any other Branch of the *Royal Family*, is not comprized within the literal Prohibition.

If too there should be *any Person* in the World, who hath in every Part of his Life, been a most *avowed Jacobite*; who owed *his Rise* to his having been a *low Emissary* of the PRETENDER'S *Faction*; and hath distinguished his Zeal for that Cause by a *Journey to Rome*, with *Remittances of Money* for supporting an *Invasion* from Abroad *against his Native Country*; if such a Person hath *prostituted his Conscience to Oaths* contrary to his *Engagements*, and hath infamously made *such Oaths* subservient to the vile Purpose of obtaining *Trusts under* that happy Constitution, which by *such Trusts* he might sooner destroy: I should be glad to know, whether *such a Man is a Whig*; and by what stupendous Means *he* became converted to *Whig-Principles*?

You see they have laid it down as the CREED OF PATRIOTISM, that none are now *more fit* to preserve the Constitution, than those who formerly laboured to *introduce the* PRETENDER; and that none are *more fit* to support the *Toleration of Protestant Dissenters*, than those who always employed their Power in *persecuting* against them.

To Principles of this Sort you may reasonably add the *Doctrine* laid down in *Fog's Journal of Saturday last*, (see p. 529.) The Writer does not attempt to *dissemble* his *real* Attachments, even his *Attachments* to the *Pretender*.

He proposes it as a Question, *How far bringing in the* Pretender *would be dangerous to our Constitution*; He answers it in an extraordinary Manner, and in *explicit Terms*. (see p. 529, 530.)

Consider what a *Position* is here laid down in a *Weekly Journal*, and circulated through the Kingdom as *Advice to the Freeholders in all Elections*: An Argument asserting, That *it is not dangerous to bring in the Pretender*; that the Pretence of *his Religion* being Popery, is a mere *Bugbear to frighten Fools with*, and that we might continue *free under him*, not only *as he is a Papist*, but even if he were a *Mahometan*.

Did you ever observe in any Reign a more *open Declaration* against the *Prince on the Throne*? And is not this a Doctrine which is most clearly an Offence against the *Statute* of the 4th of Queen *Anne*, Chap. 8. which declares it to be *High Treason* to affirm in writing, *That the Pretender hath*

any Right to the Crown? Against the Tenor of which Law here is a *Writer* affirming, That *the Pretender may, without Danger to the Liberties of the People, be* brought *as King into this free Nation*.

Though every *Englishman* and *Protestant* must have the warmest Indignation against this *infamous* and *abandoned Writer*, who thus maintains *the Safety of such an Expedient as bringing in the Pretender*: Though the *traiterous Libel* deserves no Answer, I will, notwithstanding, tell him, that when he talks of *considering* Popery *abstractedly* as a Religion without affecting our *Civil Concerns*; or, if it may be considered *abstractedly* as a *Religion*, POPERY is of itself that *Slavery of Mind and Conscience*, which induces Submission to the *worst* and most *absolute* Civil *Tyranny*: So that this Assertion will to every *Protestant*, nay, to every *sensible Man* in the World, appear so far from being true, that the *Roman Catholick Religion* is, on the contrary, the *never-failing* Engine *to make Slaves with*.

But I deny, that this *meer Possibility* of our being *free under the* Pretender, *as a* Papist, amounts to *a bare Probability*; for the *Religion of the Prince* will be ever imposed with the highest Hand, 'till it become the *Religion of the State*. What Condition were our *Liberties* in under *James* II. as a *Papist*? Of what Security shall we have; that the *Pretender* will not tread in the Steps of that *Saint* and *Martyr* his *imagined Father*? And whether, having found his *Asylum* in the Bosom of the *Roman Catholick Church*, he will not think it a *Debt of Honour*, as well as the *highest Duty of his Religion*, that he compel *us all to come in*, and be the same *senseless Bigots* as himself?

Hath he ever renounced *any one Claim of Power*, which *James* II. advanced, to the Destruction of our free Constitution? Hath he ever engaged even to *tolerate* our *Religion* as a *Church*, much less to suffer *Dissenting Sects* among us? Will *he* bring *no Swarms of Ecclesiastical Locusts* to devour us, nor *Popish Counsellors* to betray and *sacrifice* the whole Protestant *Interest*, and *Liberties* of *Europe*?

How then is it *possible*, that we can be a *free Nation*, if the *Pretender*, who is a *Papist*, shall be our KING?

The *infamous Writer* says, That *Magna Charta* was granted by a *Roman* Catholick *Sovereign*; and that we were *free* before the *Reformation*. I admit, that we
extorted

extorted *Declarations of our Rights* from several *Popish Princes*; but were far from owing those Concessions to the *Operation of Popery* on *their Consciences*. And that we were free *in some Respects* before the *Reformation* is true; but *Reformation* itself freed us from the *worst* of all *Slavery*, the basest *Vassalage* to *Popish Monks* and *Ecclesiasticks*. So that how the *Liberties of this Country*, as they are now enjoyed, can be so lightly valued, as to have that *poor Pittance of Freedom*, which was allowed us *before the Reformation*, mentioned in Comparison, as if they were equal in Degree with each other, can only be accounted for by that *undisguised Jacobitism* which reigns in *this Writer*, and leads him to perswade us, That our *Civil Liberties* have not been *the better* from the *Protestant Religion*, to the End that we may imagine they will be *never the worse* from the *Reign of a* Popish Pretender.

It is fitting that, in the Conclusion of this Paper, *You*, the *Protestant Dissenters*, should be put in mind of the Equity of such a Faction, who plead with such *Zeal*, that we may with all *Safety receive a* Papist *for our King*; yet will not allow, that a *Protestant Dissenter* should be *suffered to exercise* even the *smallest Employment*.

Grubstreet Journal, Oct. 18. N° 199.

For master secretary Bavis, *Esq; at the sine of the Pig-Alles, in Grub-street Lundun.*

Thick present, with care:

Taunton Dean, the seventh day of October, one thousand seven hundred, and three and thirty.

If your worship pleaseth,

CHE wou'd beg your diversion vor saying, what 'cham going to conuorme, vor your worship conzarning. But virst and voremost, 'che must zay one thing (and that's not two) and that is, as touching your *Jurnal*, that comes here onze a week: it is zo witty, and zo huge clever, that aul the tawne liketh it, and zay, that zartainly your worship must be vastly learned; and when 'che readeth it to my wife Joane, we both laff till we are welly ready to bepiz aur zelues vor joy. But that iz not what 'che writeth about to your worship, only that, by the by; ant that to make zort o' my story, 'che must conrorm ye, that my spouze and she have gotten betwixt uz one only zon, who is kalled Nathan, and who commeth twenty three next graïs: and thof 'che zayeth it, he is az sprunny a buoy of his age as onny iz in the tawne of *Taunton Deane*, or vive miles round it. Now az he iz my

only cheeld, 'che have broft'n up a schollard: and 'che thoft vor to zend in to the versity at *Kambridge*, and make a doctor of visick of'n; but only 'che thoft, he had too much learning vor that; vor he has gon thro' *In speach, Qui, quæ, quod, Di, da and dum*, and all those kind of things, and has lately learn'd, *Asi in per centum*, and *Property que marrowbus*, and *Quos Janus*; and his measter zayeth, he can learn'n no varder. Besides al this, he can write, so as vor many people to read it; and can rigger, and cast counts main well; he understands distraction, and part of the multiplication table, so var as vour times vour, and zeven times two, which you'll zay iz a vilthy deal to learn, in zix weeks time. The buoy has partz, and a woundy memory; vor last zabbath day, a stranger preach'd to aur chorch, and took his text out of the gozpell of *Bell and the dragon*, and zaid a deale about *Genesiz* and the *Revelations*, and about Belznazzer ('che thinks his name waz) King of *Babbloon*, and zaid several things about circumcision, and Zimon Magus, and Lott's *wife* and *Jerico*, and *Jeruzalem*; and 'che heard Mr Wimaleton, and Mr. Peppercorn zay, that they never heard zuch a braave zarmond in al their borne dayes. Vor my own part, che din't much understond zarmondz, but 'che believeth, 'twaz a speciall good one, vor it mad the old women cry: but what 'che bringeth the story vor, iz, that Nathan took the bedz, and tailes of it, in his memory, and repeated a good deal of it extumpere, that evening at the dog and duck, ('che believeth) to ten volk, that were smoaking and drinking there.

Now may hap, Zir, what does ael this magnify? Why, if you will have patience, 'che will tell ye; Nathan knoweth his own accomplishmentz, that he has learning, and aul that; and has had his nativity cast in the coffee grounds by a wise woman, that telleth vortunes, and che zayeth, Nathan is boarn to great varment, if he goeth to Lundun. Zo now nothing runneth in his head, but Lundun, Lundun; and ov all things, he hankereth after being a secretary; the cheeld hath a proud stomach (he taketh avter his mother vor that) and aymeth at great things. He hath now an offer to be secretary to a brick-kilner, (vor as he is known to have wit at will, and to be a schollard, every body is vor katching at'n) but nothing will zarve hiz turn but to Lundun he will go; or if we wou't let'n do that, he voweth most bitterly, that he will go to zea. Now you muzt know, that him is my wives doating piece, and she feareth if he should go to zea, that him wou'd be a kaptain, and zo be kill'd az dead az a doare naile. And whereaz 'cham convorm'd, that your wor- *ship*

ſhip is ſoone to be wedded, and keep a coach, and to joine with Mrs Mambrino to cut ſimpletons, wherevore and therevore, in order to make my ſon NATHAN a ſecretary, ſhe deſireth yaur worſhip to take 'a 'prentice: and now the ſecret is out, and e'en let it goo.

If you'l tak'n, no money ſhall peart uz, and our JOANE will ſend you a couple ov rabbitz, and a new milk cheeze againſt yaur wedding day. 'Che doth knaw, that with a little matter ov ſhowing, in a little time, the buoy wou'd ov his own ſelfe, be able to write *Jurnalz,* as vaſt as hops: therevore if you'l tak'n, zay zo, by the next poaſt. 'Che be a' mon ov zome ſubſtance, 'che keepeth nine kowcz, and a boare; and our JOANE maketh butter and cheeze and eggs, and chickibirdz, and gooſychickz, and thicky kind ov things. Moreover and likewiſe, 'che liveth in my owne; payeth ſcott and lott, hath been twize conſtable, ant 'cham now church-wardens over the high-wai: and beſidez aul thick, 'che have two hundred good ſhillings iħ a bag, in my hutch, and do owe no mon a vour penny piece; nor do care one zingle ſixpence vor my loard mare to be my unkle; but ſhault be huge glad, if you wou'd make my zon NATHAN a zecretary. The buoy reſeaz this zarviz to you, and zo doth my wife, and my own zelf beſidez. The boy's vingerz itch to be wit you; but uz ſhall expeſt that you will bind'n zecretary at hall, that he mty be a yreeman to Lundun. And he zayeth, that him believeth, that him can help ye ro the cutting ov a hundred and vifty ſimple people in thiz tawne, beſidez what may be in the pariſhez about uz. No more at prezant, but 'cham vary wondervully and wid aul mine heart and zoule, Sir,

yaur zarvant, ant zo forth,
ROGER WHISTLEWELL.

'Che vargott to tell ye, (and 'che was to blame vor it) that beſidez the buoy'z latine, him underſtandz ſomething ov 'lozofy, and can tell (within an haure or two) what 'tis a clock by the almanzck; ant zayeth, that if him had but *Littletonz dickzionary* and *Eſops fables* with cutts, him believeth that him could vind out the longitude, vor him iz, az ſharp ommoſt, as a new-ground hatchet; and zo witty, that uz feareth him will not live.

DEMOCRITUS.   R. W.

Fog's Journal, Oct. 20. N° 259.
Of the Uncertainty of Hiſtory.

Mr FOG,

WHEN I firſt began to read, the celebrated Names of antient Philoſophers engaged my Attention; but I quickly diſcover'd they were not only contradictory to one another, but their Tenets, relating to the Supreme Being

the Formation of the Univerſe, and the Origin of Man, were idle and abſurd, and their moral Inſtitutions and Inſtructions infinitely inferior to what is deliver'd in the Holy Scriptures. So that I found that Reflection of *Cicero* truly grounded, *Nihil tam abſurdum, quod non dixerit aliquis Philoſophorum.*

Upon this Diſappointment, I apply'd myſelf to Hiſtory; in which I found Matters of Fact not only variouſly related by the ſeveral Authors of different Nations, but by thoſe of the ſame Country. I concluded therefore, that the beſt Method to diſcover Truth, was to take Notice of the Characters of the Actors: But here I found Authors diſagree as much as in Facts; I found the ſame Man repreſented Religious, Intrepid, Invincible, Magnificent, Virtuous, an Aſſerter and Reſtorer of Liberty: By others of equal Credit, declared void of Religion, of doubtful Courage, conſtantly overcome in War, of a narrow four Temper, addicted to ſhameful Vices, and a very Slave to Ambition. In Proof of this I ſhall only touch on a few Examples.

Livy gives the Character of *Hannibal* as notorious for Avarice, Perfidy, and Cruelty; yet the ſame Author relates many of his Actions which ſeem to reſult from Generoſity, Juſtice, and Humanity. The *French* are far from being a barbarous or cruel Nation; yet their Behaviour in *Germany* during the late Wars, was ſuch that ſome of the Inhabitants ſmart for it to this Day. And for the *German* Troops, it is apparent how they behaved in all Countries and all Ages. A certain noble Commander has lately publickly declared, they make no Diſtinction between Friend and Foe (See Vol. II. p. 936.) —— I cannot believe *Terentius Varro* was ſo arrant a Scoundrel as repreſented. When the Overthrow at *Canne* was attributed to his Ignorance, Cowardice, and Obſtinacy, the Senate met him in their Formalities, and returned him Thanks for not deſpairing of the Safety of the Commonwealth. This was a good political Bravado. But after ſuch Proofs of Miſbehaviour and Weakneſs, that they ſhou'd truſt him with their Armies and Government of Provinces, argues, either that the Senate had leſs Virtue and Judgment than they are repreſented to have, or that *Varro* had more. This is almoſt as incredible, as if a Man in this free Country ſhould be ſaid to have involv'd and

per-

Perplex'd the State with needlefs, contradictory Treaties, under pretext of defending our Liberties, fhould affect to be thought an Encourager of Trade, yet project and perfift in wild Schemes to deftroy it; fhould thro' Indignation be hang'd in Effigies in fome Towns, and yet without any Alteration of Conduct, or Contrition for paft Mifcarriages, that this Man fhould continue in O——, and in thofe very Towns fhould, with his Abettors, be welcomed, carefs'd and flatter'd; I cannot imagine Things fo incongruous fhould ever happen.

I am at a lofs to reconcile many of the Actions to the Character of *Tiberius* as defcribed by *Tacitus*, who gives Inftances of as great Prudence, Bravery, Contempt of Flattery, Generofity and Magnificence in *Tiberius*, as can be fhewn in moft Princes, which feem as inconfiftent with the Multitude of Vices *Tacitus* imputes to him, as it would be to affirm a General was victorious and glorious, and confummate in the Art of War, yet allow, he has often been a tame Spectator of Towns being taken, when his Troops have not been inferior to the Enemy; that he has been forced to raife a Siege by an Army not a third part fo numerous as his own; and that he fcarce ever fhew'd his Face in a Field of Battle but he quitted it, with his Back to it.

The laft Example I fhall Produce is that of *William* Count of *Naffau*, firft Prince of *Orange* of that Family. Great is the Character given him by a certain Author (ever remember'd at *Glenco*). intitled, *A Panegyrick on William the Firft Prince of Orange, occafion'd by his laft dying Words.* The Author obferves it was reported, that the Prince's laft Words were, *Lord have Mercy upon me!* which he judges were beneath the Prince's Character; and affirms they were, *Lord have Mercy on the People!* Notwithftanding this Affertion, Card. *Bentivoglio* relates, that he died, without being able to utter one Word; which feems more probable, confidering he was fhot thro' the Head. Card. *Bentivoglio* likewife fays, this Prince came a Youth from Germany into *Flanders* in the Service of the Emperor *Charles* V. by whofe Favour, rather than Proximity of Blood, he was declared Heir to the Houfe of *Chalon*; *And from a plain and poor Count of* Naffau *he became very rich, and inherited the Principality of Orange in France.* It is certain, his Right to this little Principality was con-

troverted by the Duke of *Longeville* and the Count *de la Chambre*, who obtain'd feveral Decrees againft him. The Cardinal fays, the Pr. of *Orange* was in great Efteem among the *Flemings*; "That he was poffefs'd of many excellent Qualities, Strength of Body, Firmnefs of Mind, fluent in Speech, and ready in Council; his Induftry and Vigilance were wonderful. But thefe Virtues were overbalanced by much greater Vices; there was no Truth in him, no good Nature, no Modefty; his Religion was only in Appearance; of a turbulent Difpofition, and exceffively ambitious; nor ever was there one, who better knew to delude the People, or under a Pretence of publick Good to conceal his private Defigns."
PHILOLETHES.

The Craftfman. Oct. 22. No. 381

Mr D'anvers,

WE have been continually told by Dame *Osborne* and her Brethren of the Quill, that it is factions and feditious to complain of Grievances, *whilft we enjoy all the Liberty human Nature is capable of*; and are fubject only *to Laws of our own making*; that is, made by our *own Reprefentatives freely chofen to Parliament*. Now, fuppofe a Parliament fhould be call'd, in which one fifth Part of the Boroughs fhould *take a Recommendation from the Treafury*, and chufe Perfons meerly under that Influence, I would know whether fuch Perfons fo elected can be properly called *Reprefentatives of the People*; or whether they are not rather *Commiffioners from the Treafury*; whether Laws made by the Force of *their Votes* are made by the Confent of the *People*; I fhould look upon *fuch Members* in the fame Light as my Lords the *Bifhops*, who are elected by a *Congé d'elire from the Crown*, and like *them*, they ought to be placed on feparate Benches, apart from the honeft *Country Gentlemen*.

I believe my Suppofition, that *one fifth Part of the Boroughs may hereafter fall under the Influence of the* TREASURY, will not be thought unreafonable; when it is confidered what a prodigious Multitude of *Officers* our Debts and Taxes have created within 40 or 50 Years paft; befides the vaft Power, which the *Crown* enjoy'd before, by the Difpofition of Preferments, *ecclefiaftical, civil* and *military*, the Nomination of all the *Sheriffs in England*, excepting only the County of *Middlefex*, and other Appendages to the
Sove-

overeignty of these Kingdoms. All our *Port-Boroughs* swarm with *these Officers* of one Kind or other; none of our *Inland Corporations* are quite free from their influence at present; and if a *late Scheme* had succeeded, They would have been in the same Condition with the Port-Boroughs. Indeed, several Regulations have been made as to this Affair, since the *Revolution*; but it is well known what Effect They have had. All Persons in the *Receipt of the Revenue* are disabled from *sitting in Parliament*; They are likewise restrain'd from meddling in the *Election of others*; but not from *voting Themselves* (tho' a Clause to that Purpose was offered in the late Bill, for reviving the *Salt Duty*) and every Body knows that They often do *meddle in Elections* with too much Success, notwithstanding all the Precautions of the Legislature to the contrary. I could never comprehend the Reason of this Distinction between the *Receipt* and *Issues of the Revenue*; for tho' Persons employed in the *Collection of Taxes* may be very oppressive to the People under their Jurisdiction; yet the *Distribution of publick Money* certainly puts it as much in the Power of Men intrusted with it to get Themselves chosen to Parliament by unwarrantable Methods; and *several late Instances* are sufficient to convince us by what Tenure all Persons in Office hold their Places; especially, if They happen to have a Seat in either House of Parliament.

But I shall confine my self to the Power of the Admiralty, which is the Influence chiefly prevalent in the maritime County where I live; and as it may affect too many Boroughs at the next Election, I am surprized that an Evil of this Kind should be so universally known, and so often publickly practised, without any Attempt to put a Stop to it. The Number of *Dockmen* and *Cinque-Port Officers* is as regularly computed at our *County Election*, as a Gentleman reckons his own Tenants; and what is still worse, many of our Boroughs are totally governed by this mischievous Dependence. Hence We frequently see *little, low Creatures above* sent down and forced upon *such Electors*, in Prejudice to the *neighbouring Gentlemen*, whom They love and honour. They have Places in the *Cinque Ports*, or they work in the *Docks*, and are therefore look'd on as the Properties of the *Admiralty*. The *Candidate* comes to Them with a Letter from thence, and it is well

known that They must either pay Obedience to it, or forfeit their Bread. By these Means, such a Fellow as *Walsingham*, or any other *dirty Tool of Power*, may be dragg'd into Parliament, and preferred to a Gentleman of the best Family, Character and Interest in the Neighbourhood. The *Navy* is doubtless the natural Strength of *England*; a Strength unattended with that Jealousy, which must ever be entertain'd of a *Land-Force*. But when That, which was intended to protect our Liberties from all *foreign Enemies*, shall become the Means of weakening those Liberties *at home*; Gentlemen may, with Reason, grow out of Humour, and even the best-affected will pay the *Land and Malt-Tax* with no great Alacrity. This is a Practice like that forbidden in the *Jewish* Law; *to seeth the Kid in the Milk of the Dam*; because it was deem'd unnatural to use That to the Destruction of the Creature, which was intended for its Preservation.

I am persuaded Nobody will say, it is not an Abuse of Power, for an *Officer of the Admiralty* openly to send his Recommendation to a *Port Borough*, attended with an Injunction to every Person, who belongs in any Degree to the *Navy*, to vote agreeably to it, on the Penalty of losing his Post by a contrary Behaviour. I have often thought that *these menacing Letters to Electors* are as bad as the *Incendiary Letters*, by which Persons are threatned with being murdered, or having their Houses burnt, unless they leave such a Sum of Money, as these modest Gentlemen are pleas'd to demand of them, at a particular Place. Death is justly made the Penalty of the Law to *these Offenders*; yet hath the Law provided no adequate Punishment for *Offenders of this Kind*.

By Votes of the *House of Commons*, renewed the Beginning of every Session, it is declared a Breach of Privilege *for any* Peer to intermeddle in *Elections*; and tho' it may be found impracticable to restrain Men entirely from using that Interest, which arises from *their own Estates*, on such Occasions; it cannot surely be so difficult to restrain Men in Possession of *great Offices*, from oppressing their *Inferiors*. If some Stop be not put to such open Invasions on the Rights of our Countrymen, We may expect in a little Time, to find the Qualifications requisite to the Officers, or Workers in the *Dock-Yards*, to be how many Votes They have, either as *Freeholders*, or *Freemen in Corporations*; not how able in in their *Business*, or honest in their *Characters*; and it may become the Practice of a *designing Minister* to extend this Demand so far, as not to suffer even a *Waterman* to be retain'd by the Royal Family, without producing Proof of his Capacity to do some Mischief to his Country, by having a *Vote* ready for Order.

When the Parliament annually provides for the Support of the *Navy*, it can never be their Intention to load their Fellow-Subjects, with *Taxes*, in Order to maintain some Thousands of Men, hired and banded together to overturn the Rights of several Boroughs in the maritime Counties. The Parliament must certainly make such Provision with no other View than the Defence of the Kingdom, and the Protection of Commerce. They intrust the King with the Management of the *Fleet*, with the Appointment of *Officers*, and Disposition of the *Money* granted for that Service; in full Confidence that his Majesty will order it in the best Manner, will appoint the ablest and most honest Officers, and manage the People's Money with the greatest OEconomy. How grosly then do those *Men* abuse his Majesty's Trust, when They employ their Power to corrupt the Elections of all the neighbouring Boroughs? Can it be endured by any Gentleman, who suffers Distress, and contributes to their Grandeur, to hear his Neighbours excusing Themselves to Him in the following Manner * *Sir, I would*

* This Speech a Writer in the *Daily Courant* of the 24th, *mutatis mutandis*, puts in the Mouth of some *Tenants* expostulating with a Friend asking their Votes; that they could not give them, because if they did, Mr *Steward* threatned to turn them out of their *Farms*, having Authority from Mr *Landlord* to do so. Says, he could give the *Craftsman* a List of Country Gentlemen, chosen by such Methods; and mentions the Hon. *Wm Pult---y*, Esq; as having purchas'd his Borough of *Heydon*, in *Yorkshire*, where *all*, or most of the *Electors* are his *Tenants*; by which Means he secures his own Election, and that of *another Member*, who may be said to be a *Commissioner* from Mr *Landlord*. Then adds, Is not the Influence of Mr *Landlord*, as destructive to *Freedom* in Elections, as that of Mr *Commissioner*? and ought not *Tenants* to keep Memorandums of Menaces, *&c*? At last ridicules Mr *D'anvers*'s Blunder in talking of Favours and Kindnesses which wou'd have influenc'd an uninfluenc'd Elector. The *Craftsman* must mean, he would have Influence on one side, and none on the other.

most heartily *vote for you, and serve you to the utmost of my Power. I desire and have Reason to do so, on Account of the many Favours and Kindnesses, which I have received from you; but Mr. Commissioner threatens to turn me out of my Employment, if I act according to my Conscience, and says, He hath Authority from the great Men above to let us all know it.——These Gentlemen would do well to remember that, in the last Session, an Act was passed to prevent Bribery and Corruption in Elections,* with a very strict Oath and severe Penalties. They ought therefore to consider, whether influencing the Electors, by threatning Them with the Loss of the *Places*, which they now enjoy, is not as great an Offence against the Spirit of *that Law*, as even giving *Places*, or *Money*, or *Promises* of either, for the same Purpose; with this Aggravation, that They are guilty, at the same Time, of Injustice and Misdemeanor in their Office; whereas private Gentlemen, who may endeavour to gain Seats in Parliament by the same Methods, give their own Money, and offend only against *that Act.*

But when I reflect on the Industry of the Agent for a *certain Gentleman*, in every Part of the Kingdom; and all the Arts of *Fraud* and *Force* employ'd to support the Power of *that Gentleman*; I can little expect that what you, or I, or any Man can say, will have much Weight; though I have the Pleasure to tell you that in the *County*, where I live, there seems to be a Spirit growing up even amongst those *Men*, who are thus slavishly treated. Let me therefore desire Them to consider, that they are to put Themselves, at the next Election, into the Hands of Men, who may encourage Trade, secure their *Liberties* and *Properties*, lessen the *national Debt*, and consequently lower their *Taxes*; or who may, if They please, give them up to the Will of a *Minister*, to be tormented and devour'd by *Excisemen*. If They are hard press'd with Menaces by *Letters*, or *Messages*, let Them make Memorandums of the *Messages*, the *Persons*, the *Times*, and *Places*; so that if, at last, They should happen to suffer for following the Honest Dictates of their own Hearts, They may be arm'd with Materials to petition the *Parliament*, which will assuredly do them Justice on their cruel *Oppressors*, Abusers of the *Royal Trust*, and Contemners of the *Authority of Parliament*. I am SIR, &c.

Weekly Essays in OCTOBER, 1733.   537

THis is another Differtation upon Infidelity, and continued from p. 473. as that from p. 230. Here the Author affigns two other Caufes of its Increafe, *viz.* the Extravagancies of *Party-Zeal*, and the *Profanation* of the *Sunday.* Thefe we but juft mention, becaufe, our principal Defign being Variety, we would not burthen our Readers with too frequent Effays on the fame Subject.

THE Point Mr *Stonecaftle* undertakes to prove is, That the Study of *Sciences* and the Search after *Knowledge* are no farther commendable than as they may prove of *Ufe* to *Mankind*, and *beneficial* to the *Poffeffor* of them. This he makes appear from the Character of a *meer Academick*, who was lately an accidental Vifitant at their Club.

MR *Osborne* defends himfelf againft the *Craftsman's* Charge of Threatning the *Diffenters.* That if they don't act juft as the *Miniftry*, or the Minifter bid them, they are a Parcel of *ungrateful Fellows, and ought to be perfecuted, even by the* Minifter *himfelf*, (fee p.525G.) This *Osborne* does by quoting feveral Paragraphs from his own Paper, (fee p. 472.) to prove that he could not poffibly mean the prefent Miniftry, or Minifter ; for he is fuppofed to be *gone* before this happens, and a Change made in Favour of the *Tories*, by the *Diffenters* joining the *Oppofition.*

But it feems Mr *D'anvers* did not think it proper, like myfelf, fays *Osborne*, *to obtrude his private Judgment upon the Publick*, (fee p.525 C.) What *a wonderful modeft Man* is he grown! He, who hath been obtruding his *private Judgment* upon the Publick thefe 7 Years paft, in Matters which he *could not poffibly judge a-bout* ; is now fo humble, as not to give his Judgment in a *Point of Liberty*, about which *every Man* can judge.! Are not, therefore, thefe *Independent Whigs* as *Dependent* as the moft dependent Whigs ? Are they not fo afraid of the *Tories*, nay, even of *Jacobites* and *Papifts*, that they dare not fpeak their Sentiments in *Effential Points* of Whiggifm ?

As to thefe *Independent Whigs*, from what I have obferved of all *their Leaders, when in Power* ; and from the paffionate and revengeful, envious and ambitious, perfonal, not *national Part* they

(Gent. Mag. Vol. III. Nº xxxiv.)

have acted *out of Power*, I think they are not fo good Men as the *prefent Dependent Whigs* in Power: And I am firmly of Opinion, that there's not a Man of Senfe in *England*, who believes thefe *Independent Whigs* have any other Motives for their Oppofition, but to *diftrefs* the Miniftry and get in their Places ; and that if they fucceeded, they would not reform *One thing* they have complained of.

A LETTER from a DISSENTER, To Mr OSBORNE.

SIR,

THE great Conteft among the *Weekly Writers* being, *Whether the prefent* Miniftry, *or their Oppofers are beft intitled to the* Votes *and* Interefts *of the* Diffenters *at the next Election?* has naturally led me, and many Hundreds more, to confider what fuch extraordinary *Proceedings as thefe can mean* ; for we are not confcious, that any Behaviour of ours can give the leaft Ground *of Hope to the* Malecontents, *that we will be* by-afs'd *in that Duty we owe to our King and Country. We ftand in Need of no Man's Advice : We do not want to be told who thofe Gentlemen were, that voted for or againft the* Schifm Bill, *nor what Part has been fince acted by any particular Gentleman now in the Adminiftration, in relation to the Repeal of the Teft-Act. We cannot think, that the Mifconduct of any Minifter of State towards us, ought to make us lefs careful of the* Common Caufe, *and induce us to join with the* known Enemies *of our happy Conftitution* ; On the contrary, as we abhor the Thoughts of being any ways inftrumental in bringing about the Defigns of* Jacobites *and* Tories ; *fo likewife do we deteft the giving Encouragement, by any Example of ours, towards promoting the Views of thofe* Whigs, *who have fo long wickedly laboured to create a Mifunderftanding between his Majefty and his People.*

We are too fenfible of the great Benefits we enjoy under his Majefty's moft mild and juft Government, and the happy Profpect of tranfmitting to pofterity the fame ineftimable Bleffings *by virtue of his* Royal Iffue, *ever to be wanting in our Duty : And we do hereby affure all the World, that no Confideration whatever fhall be able to divert us from the Refolution we have taken, to choofe fuch Men, and fuch only, whofe Wifdom, Moderation, and* publick Virtue, *have left us no room to doubt of their fincere Endeavours for pro-*

T t t   *moting*

moting the Publick Good, which 'tis impossible should be the Intention of those who endeavour to recommend themselves to their Country, by distinguishing the Interest of the Country, from that of the King; than which nothing can more effectually contribute to the weakening and undermining, if not destroying, Both.

I do solemnly assure you, Sir, that the Ministry need not be in the least doubt of the Assistance of the Dissenters; I know this to be true, by Accounts from several Parts of the Kingdom: And within this Month, I have met several Hundreds of the most Eminent of them; from whom I am fully convinced, that notwithstanding all the vile Arts which have been used to work the People up to a Disaffection, the Opposition will find, at the next Election, the greatest Disappointment they ever met with in their Lives. Yours, &c.

Free Briton. Oct. 25. No 208.

MR *Walsingham* replies to the *Craftsman's* Proposal of a Method of conciliating the Minds of all Men to the Dissenters, (see p. 525.) That to make Dupes of the Dissenters, they are treated as Men with whom all sorts of Persons are not yet reconciled; they must, therefore, forget all former Disputes and Animosities; their Oppressions and Oppressors: They must, by their own Votes, bring those Tories into Parliament, who promoted so many Acts of Parliament to enslave and destroy them. Hard Terms, that they must submit to the infamous Drudgery of voting against their Friends, and of voting for their worst Enemies, the Tories.

The Dissenters are told, that the Repeal or Explanation of the Tests is a disputed Point; that many Court and Country Whigs are against it; and that therefore he (the Craftsman) does not chuse to give his Opinion in the Matter (see p. 525 B) The Truth is, the Tories are against it; and therefore neither the dissatisfied Whigs, who are leagued with them, dare undertake to vote for it; nor the Craftsman, to explain himself upon it.

The Craftsman, in the same Paragraph, challenges his Adversaries to shew, where he hath declared against the Repeal of the Tests.] Walsingham thinks he declares it in this very Passage: For he declares, that many of the Country Whigs, or Whigs of his Faction, dispute it. This is an open Declaration, that, whenever the Dissenters shall apply to Parliament for the Repeal, many of the Patriot Party will dis-

pute it with them. As to the Court Whigs being of the like Sentiments, I dare affirm, that the Dissenters know it to be true, that, whenever the Administration shall propose this Relief to the Dissenters, the Court Whigs will not appear in greater Numbers, Spirit, and Chearfulness, than they will appear in Support of this Proposition.

Grubstreet Journal. Oct. 25. No 200.

THE Society, according to their annual Custom, on the Expiration of the Lord Mayor's Office, have prefix'd to this Journal an hierogiyphical Representation of a Barber's Shop, in which several Figures are plac'd in different Attitudes, according to the Whim of the Projector; which Mr Bavius calls the Art of Trimming. Several Interpretations of it are given by the Members of the Society; which being unfinish'd, we refer to our next.

The Craftsman. Oct. 27. No. 382.
On Parties Civil and Ecclesiastical.

THIS Dissertation, by Way of Letter to Mr D anvers, runs in the following Terms.

Sir, To CORRUPT and to DIVIDE are the wicked Expedients, by which some Ministers in all Ages have affected to govern. There is however a Difference between these two Expedients, to the Advantage of the latter, and by Consequence between the Characters of those who practice them. A Bribe in the Hand of the most blundering Coxcomb, will prevail as much as in the Hand of a Man of Sense. H—e may govern as triumphantly by this Expedient as the great Knight his Brother, and the great Knight as Burleigh himself. But every Character cannot attempt the other Expedient of Dividing, or keeping up Divisions, with equal Success; there is need of Cunning and Experience, a System of Sedition and Fraud; against which our Countrymen should be on their Guard, especially at this Juncture, when so much Artifice is used to maintain, and, if possible, to create new Divisions. The Nation is now not only brought into an Uniformity of Opinion concerning the present Administration, but we are grown into an Unanimity about Principles of Government, which the most Sanguine could scarce have expected without Extravagance. Certain Associations of Ideas were made so familiar to us, about half a Century ago,

and

and became so habitual that we should not have been able, even a few Years since to break them.

The Power and Majesty of the People, *an* original Contract, *the Authority and Independency of* Parliament, *Liberty, Exclusion, Abdication, Deposition,* were Ideas, then, associated to the Idea of a *Whig,* and supposed inconsistent with the Idea of a *Tory.*——*Divine hereditary, indefeizable Right, lineal Succession, passive Obedience, Prerogative, Non-Resistance, Slavery,* nay *Popery,* were associated in many Minds to the Idea of a *Tory,* and deemed inconsistent with the Idea of a *Whig.*

But now, *these Associations* are broken, *new Combinations* force themselves upon us. The Bulk of *both Parties* are united on Principles of *Liberty,* in Opposition to an obscure Remnant of *One Party,* who disown those Principles, and a mercenary Detachment from the *other,* who betray them,

There has been no Complaint so general, as that about *national Divisions,* and the Spirit of *Party,* which inspires Animosity and breeds Rancour. It is Time, therefore for all good Men to join their Efforts to heal our *National Divisions,* and to change the narrow Spirit of Party into a diffusive Spirit of publick Benevolence as an Encouragement to which it may be proper to consider the *Advances* already made to a *National Union.*

Let us begin with the present Temper of the Members of the Church of *England* towards the *Dissenters,* who are now free from the Terror of persecuting Laws, and those designed to hinder the Propagation of their Principles, and shut the Door of all publick Preferments, are repealed, and even those who have been reputed their Enemies, and who have acted as such, acknowledge their Error, and from the Frankness of *These,* if I was a *Dissenter,* I should sooner entertain Hopes of future Favour, than from the double Dealing of *Those,* who lean on the *Dissenters,* when they are *out of Power,* and who esteem them a Load upon them, when they are *in it.* We are in the true and only Road, which can possibly lead to a Reconciliation among Protestants, and an Abolition of all their trifling *Differences.* This must be obtained by mutual *goodWill*; not by *Force. Force* indeed may support a Rivalship, and erect even *Counter-Establishments*; but by the same means our antient Disputes will be revived; the *Church* will be thought really in Danger;

and religious Feuds will once more disturb the Peace of the State. It's certain our *religious* and *Civil Contests* have mutually and almost alternately, fomented each other. The best way therefore to compose their Differences on the former, is to improve the growing Union between them on the latter.——In our political Divisions of *Whig* and *Tory,* the *Dissenters* have adhered to the *former,* and they want no Apology for doing so. But if in Truth there be neither *Whig* nor *Tory,* but a *Court* and *Country Party* in Being; if the political Principles which the Dissenters formerly avowed, are pursued on *one Side*; and those which they have opposed, and others equivalent to them in their Effects, are pursued on the *other*; can the *Dissenters* hesitate about the Option they are to make? What would be said, should they make their Option to stand by the *M——y*? What must be the Consequence of their standing by the *Nation* in Opposition to *Him,* is easy to tell, and impossible to deny. They will prove, in this Case, that the *Spirit of Liberty* animates and Conscience alone determines their Conduct. They, who could never brook a *Regal,* will have the Merit of saving their Country from the Danger of *ministerial Tyranny.*

As to the great national Division of *Whig* and *Tory,* whoever assents to the Principal Articles of your *civil Faith,* (see p. 339.) will scarce be a *Heretick.* But the Principles of the *Court Party,* as avowed in their Writings, are more dangerous to *Liberty,* tho' not so openly levell'd against it, than even any of Those, which *some of these Men* value themselves for having opposed.

In short, the *Revolution* is looked upon by all as a *new Æra*; but the *Settlement* then made is looked upon by the whole *Country Party* as a *new Magna Charta,* from whence *new Interests, new Principles of Government, new Measures of Submission,* and *new Obligations* arise. From thence we must date both *King* and *People.* On this Foundation all the *reasonable, independent Whigs and Tories* unite. They could unite on this alone; for the *Whigs* always profess'd the Principles which paved the Way to the *Revolution*; and whatever the *Tories* may have professed, they acted upon the same Principles, or none, when they brought about that great Event, in Concert with the rest of the Nation. To this *Magna Charta* and *these Principles* let us adhere inviolably,

in

in Opposition to *Those*, who *difown* them, and to *Those* who *betray* them. On this it will depend whether *They*, who oppose the Progrefs of *Corruption* fhall prevail; or *They*, who nourifh and propagate it. Whether *They* fhall prevail, who conftantly infift againft the Continuance of a *Standing Army, in Times of Peace*; or *They*, who plead for it. Whether *They* fhall prevail, who endeavour to conceal the *Frauds*, that are practiced, and to fcreen the *Fraudulent*, at the Rifque of publick *Credit*, as well as to monopolize in the Hands of a *few* the whole wealth of the *Nation*; or *They*, who do their utmoft to bring the *former* to Light, and the *latter* to Punifhment at a Time, when *glaring* Fraud, or ftrong Symptoms of *Fraud*, appear in fo many parts of publick Management. Whether *They* fhall prevail, who would maintain the Dignity of *Great Britain*; or *They*, who are eager, on every Occafion, to proftitute her *Dignity*, to pawn her *Purfe*, and to facrifice her *Commerce*, by intangling her not only too much with the *other great Powers of Europe*, from whom fhe may fometimes want reciprocal Engagements; but even with *thofe diminutive Powers*, from whom it would be ridiculous to expect any.

Fog's Journal Oɛt. 27. No. 260.

Contains a Century, or a Lift of 100 Names of Members of the Houfe of Commons of the Rump Parliament; fhewing which are Officers of the Army contrary to the *Self-denying Ordinance*: together with fuch Sums of Money, Offices and Lands, as they gave to themfelves, for Service done, and to be done, againft the *King* and *Kingdom*. This Lift the Writer recommends to the Perufal and Animadverfion of the Author of the *Remarks on a late printed Lift*; and obferves, that if ever we fhould fee a Parliament like this, confifting of Placemen, Military Officers and Penfioners, the certain Confequence muft be, that the People muft be loaded with Taxes to fill their Pockets, and he kept in Poverty and Slavery to make them great.

London Journal. Oɛt. 27. No 748

IF the *Craftfman* could have prov'd, that the *Diffenters*, by voting againft the Court, would obtain a Parliament of *Independent Whigs*, who would have kept themfelves independent, and never have accepted a Place; and that thefe *Whigs* would have done for them what the *Court*

Whigs have left undone, he would have faid fomething to gain the *Diffenters*: But all the Argument has been on t'other Side.

The *political Rule* recommended in a Pamphlet quoted by the *Craftfman* (See p. 518.) " for the weaker Parties, not to attach themfelves *immoveably* to any other Parties; but always to keep a *due Ballance*" is nothing to the *prefent purpofe*; for the State of the Kingdom is fuch, that a *Ballance* between Parties cannot be preferved, without the *clofe Union* of *Church Whigs* and *Diffenters*, againft Tories, and their Auxiliaries of *Nonjurors*, *Jacobites*, and *Papifts*. As to what I afferted " That the *Whigs* were forced to fupply with *great Art*, what they wanted in *natural Strength*," I did not mean thereby *Force* or *Fraud*, as the *Craftfman* affirms, but fuch *Arts* as *Trading Whigs* ufe in Cities and great Towns, that is, of employing fuch *Journeymen* and *Dependents* of all Kinds who have *Votes*, and *other Methods* of the fame Nature, and thefe are *laudable* and *juft* Arts: But, with all thefe Arts they have been but juft able to beat the Enemies of the Conftitution. If, therefore, the *Diffenters* fhould *revolt*, the *Ballance* would be entirely deftroy'd.

That thofe who *think freely* are *thorough* Friends to the *Diffenters*, (See p. 519 B) is true; but where are they to be found? *Chiefly*, if not *only*, among the *Whigs*.

Tho' it be alfo true, that there are *more Men* in *England*, who *think freely*, than in former Times; yet thefe are but few, and thofe chiefly in Cities and great Towns. The People are not *Latitudinarians* they are juft the *fame* they ufed to be: The *Tories* examine nothing, and are *the fame Bigots* as in Days of old: If they had Power, they would fhew all *Freethinkers*, *Latitudinarians*, and *Diffenters* too, that they did not much regard the *Tendernefs* of their Confciences; but would call them whimfical, infolent, proud Fellows, who ought to be punifh'd as *Difturbers* of the Publick Peace.

Univerfal Spectator. Oɛt. 27. No 264.

MR *Stonecaftle* rallies the cringing Behaviour, and the ceremonious Politenefs in fafhion at the Levees of the Great; from whence he defcends to the Carriage of our young Mafters, and takes notice of their fafhionable Implement the *Long Stick*: But as in this particular he falls in with the *Auditor*, we need only refer to p. 74, and 76.

PRIZE VERSES No. X.

To the QUEEN *on her* GROTTO.

HAil matchless Queen! whose worth each
　　deed displays,
Not less in giving, than deserving praise;
At whose command the willing stones advance,
Too rude for art, too regular for chance;
Grac'd with those Busts, whose living worthies
　　stood
Foremost amongst the wise, the great, and good.

By *Boyle* enlighten'd sciences takes new charms,
Solves all our doubts, and ignorance disarms;
The works of nature, that in embryo lay,
Dawn into life, and in a flood of day
Newton's great genius to the world convey;
The harden'd sinner, touch'd with *Clark*'s advice,
Melts into tears, and softens into sighs
Nature in thee, O *Wollaston*, clearly shines,
What truth she shews, what doctrine she enjoins;
In *Lock* the force of reason cheers the sight,
Unveil'd from clouds and bursting into light.

While thus, great Queen, you consecrate each
　　head,
Encourage learning, and its followers lead,
Smile on the living, and revere the dead,
Tho' their examples may success less prove,
Yet your example cannot fail to move;
Hope wings our flight, with pleasure we proceed,
And smile at last to find that hope succeed;
Feel emulation rising in its kind,
And blush to want those art, that grac'd their
　　mind.
Oh! could my lines but equal my desire,
Then would I sing with more than mortal fire,
Sing, how you eternize each sacred name,
Reward their virtues, their deserts proclaim,
The first in merit, as the first in fame.
The ecchoing Grotto should resound my lays,
The building's beauty, and the builder's praise.

PRIZE VERSES No. XI.

On her MAJESTY *and the* BUSTOES *in the royal* GROTTO.

ONce more, ye *Muses*, to your sacred hill
　　I come with unassur'd and trembling feet'
Fearful of sharp rebuke, presuming thus
To touch the strings of MILTON's hallow'd lyre.
Yet let the mighty theme, let CAROLINE,
Whose graces blaze like the meridian sun,
Excuse the bold attempt: BRITANNIA smiles
To see the grateful song with various art,
But equal zeal, employ her tuneful sons.
As a firm rock amid surrounding floods
Defeats the furious tide's impetuous force,
Whose marshall'd waves in endless ranks advance;
(A force to sight invincible) yet fail
In the fierce onset, and in foam expire:
Such CAROLINA's pious zeal appear'd,
In the great tryal found victorious:
In vain ambition all his musters pow'rs,
Presenting crowns, and thrones, and boundless
　　empire;
A female virtue triumphs o'er the foe

Who had his thousands crush'd: what eye that
　　sees.
This Heroine seated on the *British* throne,
But turns in silent ravishment to heav'n,
Convinc'd that providence presides below.
But stop, too vent'rous muse, nor vainly try
To blazon all her worth; too arduous task!
In narrower limits fly, and seek the groves
Of RICHMOND, long for royal names renown'd;
But now consign'd to everlasting fame
By CAROLINA's contemplative CELL:
Divine retreat! the surest, best relief
For all the cares, the tumults, and fatigue,
Of regal state. Hither at chosen hours,
The royal Hermit takes her lonely way,
Indulging thoughts which lift the raptur'd soul
Above mortality; her solemn Busts
Of sages (greater than proud *Greece* can boast,
Or antient ROME, or those of modern date
Innumerable, that blindly follow these)
Sublimest themes suggest—The wood'rous form
Of human knowledge from the birth of thought,
Working by slow gradations to the height
Of mathematick certainty—The rules
Of universal moral duty, taught
By nature's book immutable—The light
Of revelation that dispels the mists,
Th' infectious mists, which sin and folly breathe,
Perplexing the strait path to endless peace.
Thus musing, o'er aware she soars intranc'd
Among etherial worlds, with large survey
Contemplating the mighty maker's works:
Unnumber'd systems, in unmeasur'd space
Rolling, the motions on their orbs impos'd
By wisdom infinite: the seats perhaps
Thro' which the transmigrating soul shall pass
To vision beatifick: here my muse
Stop thy bold flight, and join the royal saint
In elevated praise to the great source
Of all existence; join thy vows with hers
To cultivate the virtues which prepare
For an eternal life of perfect bliss.

An ejaculation on the PRIZE-VERSES.

OThat her majesty for this same metre,
　　Wou'd please to make each poet a BEEF-
　　eater!
For know, however grand the verse, the writer,
Is commonly some indigent SHEEP-biter.

The FRANK LOVER.

NOT Chloe, that I'm more sincere,
　　Or am less apt to rove,
That I a heart so constant bear,
　　So faithful in its Love.
I'faith my Chloe, like the rest,
　　From fair to fair I'd range,
But that it's more my Interest
　　Still to love on than change.
All charms which others recommend,
　　In thee alone I find;
Beauty and temper kindly blend,
　　The handsome and the kind.
Then why should I inconstant prove?
　　Why other nymphs pursue?
When here I have *all* I cou'd love,
　　'Tis prudence to be *True*.

A RIDDLE

THou tyrant, whom I will not name,
   Whom Heav'n and Hell alike diſclaim;
Abhorr'd and ſhunn'd for wholſom ends
By Angels, Jeſuits, Brutes, and Fiends;
What terms to curſe thee ſhall I find,
Thou plague peculiar to mankind?
Oh may my verſe excel in ſpite
The willeſt, wittieſt imps of night!
Then lend me for a while your rage,
Ye Maidens old, and Matrons ſage,
So may my vein ſatyrick ſeem
As vile and hateful as my theme.

   Eternal foe to ſoft deſires,
Enflamer of forbidden fires;
Thou bane of freedom, eaſe and mirth;
Thou Pre-damnation upon Earth;
Which makes the tender ſex endure
Repeated deaths without a cure;
Thou ſerpent with a harmleſs face;
Thou lawful ſcourge of human race;
Thou Scorpion, whom the Angels fly;
Monſter, whom birds and beaſts defy;
Whom ſubtle *Romiſh* Prieſts eſchew,
And Satan (let him have his due)
Was never ſo confirm'd a dunce,
To riſque perdition more than once;
That wretch (if ſuch a wretch there be)
Who hopes for happineſs in thee,
With vain purſuit may ſearch as well,
For truth in whores, or eaſe in hell.

To an Infant expiring the ſecond day of its Birth. Written by its Mother, in Imitation of NAMBY PAMBY.

TEnder ſoftneſs, infant mild,
   Perfect, pureſt, brighteſt child;
Tranſient luſtre, beauteous clay,
Smiling wonder of a day:
E're the laſt convulſive ſtart
Bends thy *unreſiſting* heart:
E'er the long enduring ſwoon
Weighs thy precious eye-lids down,
Oh regard a mother's moan,
Anguiſh deeper than thy own!
Faireſt eyes, whoſe dawning light
Late with rapture bleſt my ſight,
E're your orbs extinguiſh'd be,
Bend their trembling beams on me:
Drooping ſweetneſs, verdant flow'r
Blooming, with'ring in an hour;
E're thy gentle breaſt ſuſtains
Lateſt, fierceſt, vital pains,
Hear a ſuppliant! Let me be
Partner in thy Deſtiny.

The Christian and the Tindaliſt.

A Convert of *Tindal's* a *prieſt* to confute,
   And ſneer at the *parſon*, begins a diſpute:
From *Tindal* he proves that the writings of *Moſes*
Are the *cant* of a *knave*, and at beſt but *ſuppoſes*;

That the doctrines of *Chriſt* were mere *trifling ſtuff*,
That there was *without them* religion enough,
That all *perſons* were *cheats*, their *religion* a *lie*.
—To whom with a *ſmile* the *meek prieſt* made reply,
If *Chriſt* we obey, tho' *needleſs* his *rules*,
What *harm* will it prove?
Tind.—————It will prove you all *fools*.
Chr. But ſhou'd they be *needful*—ſhould *they* g:in
               (us *ſalvation*—)
Tind. That never can be, I'll prove by *quotation*—
Chr.—————— But *ſhou'd* they?——
Tind.—Why—then we expect muſt damnation.
Chr. With all your *deep learning*, pray who is moſt
                (*wiſe*,
We, who *follow* Chriſt's doctrine, or you who
               (*deſpiſe*;
Since this, Sir, as *fact*, is allow'd by *your croſs*;
We're *ſafe*, tho' it's *falſe*, you're *damn'd* if it's
               (*true*.

To an Old-bigotted TINDALIST.

IN *youth* by *nature* folly's path you trod,
   In *age* by *will*, a rebel to your *God*;
Thus ever *wrong*, thy *day of life* has been,
A *morn* of *folly*, and an eve of *ſin*:
Why then, *vain hoary wretch*, to *reaſon* loſt,
Doſt thou thy *reaſon* and thy *wiſdom* boaſt?
The *pow'rs* of *Dullneſs* ſtrong in thee are met,
To riſe in darkneſs, and in darkneſs ſet.

A Paraphraſe on the 90th PSALM.

BLeſs'd *king of kings*, with what paternal love
   Haſt thou for ever guarded human kind?
E're ſwelling mountains rais'd their tow'ring
     heads,
When Nature lay conceal'd in dark abyſs;
Even beyond the utmoſt ſtretch of time
Thou wer't the ſame tremendous great *Jehovah*.
At thy beheſt to native duſt we turn,
Till thou art pleas'd to bid us re-aſſume
Our priſtine form; when ev'ry ſep'rate atom
Trembling, ſhall re-unite at thy command:
For thou, *Jehova*, know'ſt no bounds of time;
Ages to ages join'd, with thee but ſeem
A day, a flitting hour of midnight watch:
And when with wrath divine thou pour'ſt thy
     vengeance,
Like irreſiſtleſs floods thou bear'ſt away
The ſons of men to death's cold icy boſom,
Where, as a mimic dream they end in nothing:
Or like the ſhort-liv'd Flowers of the Field,
Scarce to their morning bloom and verdant pride
They riſe, before their day of glory's gone,
And wither'd by an ev'ning blaſt, they die.
O *God*, when with thy miniſters of wrath
Thou'rt circled, who not ſhudders and adores!
For all the ſecret mazes of our hearts,
Our embryo crimes and ſins, but yet in thought
Are manifeſt to thee as Mid-day ſun:
And ſhould we call thy juſt avenging hand,
To nought we dwindle like a paſſing ſhade,

And rolls of years are but a winter's tale
Trifling, and yet untold. ———
But if by heaven's indulgency we live
To sev'nty Years, the stated age of man ;
Or if by strength superior we have past
The ruffling storms of winters full fourscore,
Each *day* will then bring on an *age* of pain,
Till with our nerves unbent we stagger to the
    Grave.   [head,
  What son of earth *God's* wrath can compre-
Or judge his anger equal to its weight!
Guide then great *God* each moment of our life,
And fix our erring feet in *wisdom's* track :
O give us *mercy*, and with *mercy peace* ;
So shall our souls be glad, and we with joy
Shall journey blithsome through the stage of life;
Eternal sov'reign of the heav'ns and earth,
May'st thou still guide us thro' this *vale of tears*,
Prosper our deeds, when *virtue* is our aim,
Inspire our *thoughts*, when *thou* art in our mind.

To MISS, &c.

SUch charming lines, and from a hand so fair,
  How shall I strive to praise, or how forbear!
Such heav'nly sense with so much beauty joya'd!
An angel-form! and a seraphic mind!
Transported with variety of charms,
Th'inviting theme my glowing bosom warms :
But when I would my fair's perfections write,
With awful fear I view the distant height,
Confess my weakness, and correct my flight.

So the fond nymph with silent rapture hears
Her lover's sighs, and sees his tender tears ;
Pleas'd with his passion ; willing, yet afraid ;
By nature yielding, by her doubts dismay'd ;
With anxious pain suspends the promis'd joy,
Yet to her lover seems unkind, and coy.
Forgive me then, my kind, my lovely maid,
If, by such doubts and fears as these delay'd,
I left too long my debt of thanks unpay'd.

Here you, perhaps, expect I should relate,
The various pleasures of a rural state ;
Describe the fragrant bow'rs and painted plains,
The sweet retreats of happy nymphs and swains :
Who feel no wants, nor no misfortune prove,
None but the sweet anxieties of love.
Delightful vision! but, alas! my dear,
Arcadian pleasures are not every where :
Virtue is fled from earth ; and we can trace
No golden age, but in the muse's glass ;
The world itself declines, a ruin'd pile !
And guilt and folly shoot in every soil.

Thus, you the niceness of a court condemn :
But we may curse the contrary extream,.
'Tis true, affected beaus infest the town :
But what's a beau revers'd ? --a country clown.

You hate your forward sparks, your man of fire :
But, o ! the dullness of a landed squire !
Who courts by proxy, and whose compliment
Is a long rent-roll, and large settlement.
But, bury'd in the arms of such a slave,
What's an estate, but a more spacious grave ?

You fly from clouds, impertinence, and noise ?
We pine for chat, in company rejoyce ;
Pleas'd if, by chance, we hear a human voice.

Such is the world's great scene : what you pursue
We have, yet slight, and fondly envy you.
Few are content with what the Gods bestow ;
But seeking pleasure meet a real woe.

Happy the nymph, who free from vain desires,
With wise delight within herself retires,
Tastes the calm pleasures of a quiet mind,
Approv'd by all, yet careless of mankind ;
Blest with each grace, that we perfection call,.
Approves their worth, and yet disdains them all :
All, but the charms of virtuous innocence,
Her joy, her hope, her portion, her defence.
Happy'st of mortals! only happier he,
Whom heav'n shall bless with such a nymph as
  thee.

N. B. We have received four very good Pieces from Dublin, in praise of their late active Lord Mayor, Humphry
French, Esq; who used very frequently to visit the Markets,
Bakers-Shops, Prisons, &c. in Person ; but not having
room for more than one, we prefer the following, as it
touches with a masterly hand the subject of Elections, now
the chief topick of this Kingdom.

An ODE, address'd to the Citizens of *Dublin*; on Occasion of their late worthy Lord Mayor, HUMPHRY FRENCH, Esq; standing a Candidate to represent that City in Parliament.

HOW long must ye be deaf and blind?
    Hear, citizens, these lines, or read 'em.
For what were parliaments design'd,
    But to support the nation's freedom ;
If such the weight, the charge be such,
    What choice of Members should be them ?
How upright should they be, how much
    Above the race of vulgar men ?
Tou say, "One man's authority
    " Is but a trifle among members,
  "Nor does it matter whether he
    "Says ay or no, or wakes or slumbers.
  "One man among a crowd is lost,
    "And multitudes must still prevail:
But then consider to your cost,
    A grain may sometimes turn the scale.
Behold your wretched country's fate,
    Alas how wan and pale is waxes!
How arts and trade decay apace!
    And would you yet augment her taxes?
Who hath not heard her plaintive sounds?
    Unhappy isle, of hope bereft!
Preserve at least, to bind her wounds,
    The rag of liberty, that's left.
However faction may conspire,
    To bribe the freedom of your voice ;
Let virtue bid, and what bids higher,
    If reason must determine choice?
All sects and parties should accord,
    However opposite in thinking,
To save their country, as on board
    All hands to save the ship from sinking.

                  Urge

Urge not your promises to me,
Ierne now your voices, craves;
Lo! GEORGE and nature make you free,
Then why should choice confirm you slaves?

The Drapier be your Guide in this,
Which he can have no private view in,
The patriot will not vote amiss,
Who sav'd you more than once from ruin.

Tho' hedg'd by pow'r, constrain'd to dwell
With poverty beneath a cottage,
The man of virtue will not sell
His birth-right for a Mess of Pottage.

Is there a sage and ample mind,
Whose breast with innocence is arm'd;
Whose sense by virtue is refin'd,
Whose virtue by religion warm'd?

Whose soul, by prejudice unmov'd,
No frauds nor vices can connive at;
Who acts as reason hath approv'd,
And makes the publick good his private?

Who in a vile corrupted age
The sword of justice bravely draws,
Restrains the giddy rabble's Rage,
And animates the dying laws?

Whose conduct, faithful to his trust,
All precedents so far exceeds,
His successors, however just,
Can only imitate his deeds;

In words, which Athens well might hear,
While Marlay prais'd him from the bench,
Who would not wish to lend an ear?
Who would not glory to be FRENCH?

* *Not Rome could boast in all her pride*
  " *One juster to the publick cause,*
  " *Tho' deathless Tully was her Guide,*
  " *Tho' Cato sanctified her Laws.*

For laws and liberty he fights,
Enlist your selves beneath his banners;
Who better can defend your rights
Than he, who has reform'd your manners?

Ierne's fame shall reach the skies,
And faction sink beneath her embers,
While she beholds her senate rise,
Compos'd of such heroic members.

§ *Thus the great mother, richly crown'd,*
Thro' Phrygian towns triumphant rode,
Beheld her hundred sons around,
With joy beheld each son a god.

* These Lines allude to a passage in the Lord
  Chief Baron's Speech.
§ —— *Qualis Berecynthia Mater &c.*   Virgil

The HERMIT, or Father Philip's GEESE.

A BALLAD; *To the tune of*
As Thomas *and* Harry, *one* Midsummer-day.

How irresistless are the Darts of Love!
How piercing female Charms! when Mahomet
Had long been hamm'ring, in his lonely cell,
Some dull insipid tedious paradise,
A brisk *Arabian* girl came tripping by,
Passing, at him she cast a sidelong glance,
And look'd behind in hopes to be pursu'd;

He took the hint, embrac'd the flying fair,
And, having found his heav'n he fix'd it there.
                                   DRYDEN.

Young Anna and Philip, a kind loving pair,
   Brisk, airy, and pleasant, and affable were,
Young Anna was brighter than Sol's piercing ray,
And sweeter her breath than the breezes in May:
And Philip was jolly, proportion'd each limb,
He liv'd but in her, and she liv'd but in him.
But alas! as no pleasure is permanent here,
She brought forth a son, and was snatch'd from her dear.

Poor Philip bewail'd his sad wretched state,
The loss of his nymph, and now curses his fate:
The boy from the world determines to take,
And live like two hermits for poor Anna's sake.
All women seem'd odious, since Anna was dead,
And the world but a forest, or dismal wild glade,
Where rapine, and perj'ry, and interest reign'd,
And honour and justice were greatly disdain'd.

He goes to a wood, where no human track
Could be seen on the ground, with the boy on his back,
And there he hides from him a hundred odd things,
As luxury, pride, self-love, pomp of kings;
Of passions, and darts, and Cupid and fires;
Nor mention'd a woman, nor ought of desires.
To the growth of his years, apt rules did enroll,
Which always were tending to good of his soul.

The youth being now at least five years old,
Father Philip to him the birds and beasts told;
The name of the plants, the fruits, and the flowers,
Their uses and virtues, their beauties and powers;
And amidst these discourses which boys pleasant call,
He mingled the threats of chimeras, and all
That of death and the de'il, damnation and hell,
Which are the first lessons to children we tell.

But now ten years passed, his conduct he unfolds,
And if ah hereafter the riddle unfolds;
Yet naught of fair woman he ever brought in,
As if such fine creatures there never had been.
The stars he described, the moon, and the sun,
And how in their orbs they gradually run;
He mention'd the Author of earth, sea and air,
But nothing of woman wou'd Philip declare.

But at length well stricken in years being grown,
And scarce able to trudge to the neighbouring town,
Well knowing that nature must one day decline,
And submit to all conqu'ring death's meagre shrine;
But how soon it might be his fate did not know;
Alas! what shou'd then his poor tender son do?
For wolves have no pity, nor feel pious qualms,
And lions and tygers ne'er knew to give alms.

Therefore Philip thought it wou'd be the best way
His son to the village to carry one day;
That when he departed this sad hated life,
So full of all ills, since the loss of his wife,
That the youth for himself might be able to shift,
And on the world's mercy not be run adrift:
For poor is the mortal who trusts on the same,
He must live without comfort, and die without fame.

But 'ere he wou'd venture on this hated train,
The youth first his twentieth year did attain;
That come, to the town the boy led by his sire
Thro' boggs, and thro' lanes of dirt and of mire;
He stares all around, and not one thing he knew,
But alas! is amaz'd at such wonders to view,

squires what's that, what's t'other, and this,
nd the Father strait tells him whatever it is.
But Phillis approaching in a purple gay vest,
'e ask'd, pray what's that, sir, so charmingly drest?
is a goose, reply'd Philip, pray son hold your peace
'er skin's more like down of swans than of geese;
'Tis a delicate fowl! (full of joy, cries the youth) ·
et us carry one home our sorrows to sooth;
warrant it sings well:——a brood let us raise;
n the wood where we live they may all of 'em graze.

Cantilena Cantabrigiensis.

FUgit atas & facessis;
  Forma decor deflorescit:
'alix calix, & amores
'rocul abigant marores:
Da basia, Chloe, vinum puer,
Dies it, præsenti fruar:
Nulla, nulla sit formido,
Quamvis cacus sit Cupido,
Per maandros & amores,
Palpat viam ad marores.
Fugit atas & facessit,
Forma decor deflorescit,
Da basia, Chloe, vinum puer,
Dies it, præsenti fruar.

The LATIN imitated

TIME impatient flits away,
  Charms of beauty soon decay:
Love and wine, true foes to grief,
For those sorrows bring relief:
Kiss, then Chloe, kiss, my lass;
Fill, my boy, the sparkling glass:
We'll the present hour employ,
And secure the flitting joy;
Fear not, fear not Cupid blind,
Tho' he's wanton, he is kind;
Fear not then his pointed dart,
Which gives pleasure with the smart;
Tho' thro' mazes he will rove,
Yet he smooths the way to love;
Then tho' time shou'd flit away,
Then tho' beauty should decay,
Kiss me, Chloe, ——kiss again
For we will not live in vain;
We'll not think what time may bring,
But of life enjoy the spring:
While we thus our time improve,
We shall live an age to love.

VERSES sent by a young lady, lately married,
  to a quondam lover, inclosing a green
  ribbon noozed.

DEAR D,
IN BETTY lost, consider what you lose,
  And for the BRIDAL knot accept this nooze;
The healing ribbon, dextrously apply'd,
Will make you bear the loss of such a bride.

ON the foregoing

THIS lady's fine gift apparently shews,
  That her quondam lover has scaped one nooze;
Then let him t'other, 'tho' stiffen, restore
Her spouse may it want, when HONY-MOON'S o'er.

Old COLIN *and* Young COLIN.

OLD COLIN a Man of Note was employ'd,
  K. Wm some Miles on his Progess to guide;
The Coach turning o'er in a sad dirty Place,
COLIN, threatned, scour'd off in pitiful Case——
Young COLIN soon after a Ramble made,
And spent all the Money he'd taken in Trade;
But for an Excuse this Story he sobb'd,
On his Creditors all, that oh! he was robb'd.
Old COLIN suspecting the Case was not so,
Must needs to a strict Examining go; [Place.
Doubt you it? says the Son, I can shew you the
'Twas just where you left his Majesty's Grace.

The IMPOLITICK MAIDEN.

PHILLIS, young innocent, and fair,
  But too little vers'd in love,
Thus with a gay coquetting Air
My sighs and passions doth reprove.

' Damon, now once your heart is lost,
  ' You may urge but urge in vain;
As I would numerous conquests boast,
  ' Hearts I'd have and not the Men.

In vain your boast, my thoughtless fair,
  Vain is all your little cheat;
Wou'd you the fame of Victors share:
  Make your conquests quite compleat.

Ah, Phillis, learn a wiser Art,
  Nor half Victories thus pursue;
But as you've deign'd to take my heart,
  Kindly take my body too.

Occasion'd by a Lady's reading the Translation of SAPPHO's hymn to VENUS.

WHen Delia reads such soft and tender lines,
  And to just thoughts pathetick accent
joins
I stand transported, and with wonder praise
The sweet, enchanting, and harmonious lays;
But if to her I cast a wishful eye,
My bosom feels seraphic ecstasy;
Her lovely shape, her graceful air and mien,
And downy bosom, dangerous to be seen;
Her beauteous face, her all observing eye,
And hands that with the fairest lillies vie;
Her Charms innumerable, all conspire
To waken love, and kindle soft desire.
O son of Venus, gentle Boy, avert
The arrows thus you level at my heart;
Or if to me no pity you will show,
With equal wishes let her bosom glow;
Inspire with tenderest thought her virtuous mind;
And thus let love with love be paid in kind.

On the Marriage of her R. Highness the
  PRINCESS ROYAL with his Highness the
  Prince of ORANGE

Moribus, ingenio, formàque, atate, bonísque
  Estis, et herum nobilitate pares.
Nobiliore tamen, majus si terra tulisset,
  Censeo te dignam conjuge, tegue viro.

U u u

PLAISTOW, a Poem, continued from p. 491.

I Now would sing who spend their fleeting fames.
Retir'd from noise, in PLAISTOW's verdant
   lanes;
With Co——'s name adorn the shining page,
Co—r as much rever'd for wealth as age.
In homely piety, and homely fare,
He, parsimonious, spends the rolling year.
No shining fires are in his kitchen seen,
But, like his parlour, 'tis delightful, clean.
No cates there charm the smell, allure the eye,
But, happy abstinence! is all the cry.
No dark'ning smoak pollutes his chimneys fair,
Which, white as snow, lift high their heads in air,
And prove what blest'd Frugality is there.
To learned D——r next devote a line,
In whom good breeding, and complacence join,
And round whose Feet the suppliant muses twine.
Bright Flavia's bloom, and Cygnus' innocence;
Julietta's shape, and Teraminta's sense;
These are the village talk, these I rehearse,
Proud of a theme that dignifies my verse.
When Laura speaks, or to her spinnet sings
Inchanting sounds rise from the voice and strings;
The heav'nly Accents sweetly wake desire,
Soft charm the soul, and raise the strongest fire.
Rauſtina next, my best and greatest care;
What praise is due, thou fairest of the fair?
In virtues pleasing paths you strictly walk,
And daily act what others only talk.
At church a constant member you are known,
And spread'ſt thy bright example thro' the town;
A sense of shame upbraids the people's mind,
And makes them blush at being left behind.
At home when you domestick cares attend,
You act the mistress like the kindest friend.
For every object you have still to spare,
To feed the hungry, and to cloath the bare.
The sick and maim'd in you find sure Relief,
A healing balm you have for ev'ry grief,
But me; and that, O cruel to endure!
The wounds your self inflict, admit no cure.
. To worthy Speerman sure a verse is due,
And these that follow are address'd to you.
Your sweet retreat did first my Soul inspire
With sacred raptures of poetick fire.
Thy loss of Sight propitious heav'n supplies,
And wisdom gave, when it eclips'd your eyes;
Bless'd you with greatest good in human life,
A prudent, virtuous, and obliging wife,
The humble muse, confin'd to rural lays,
Can't raise a flight sufficient for your praise;
That they must sing whose skill can best commend
The kind companion and as firm a friend;
Enough that I, without a sordid view,
Admire those virtues which I can't pursue.
. I now attempt to paint the neighb'ring fields
Of which your house so bright a prospect yields.
What pleasure hence to view a verdant plain,
And russet heath, which purple flowrets stain?
See Epping's lofty woods before me rise,
Survey the forests with admiring eyes.
See Castlemain's delightful sylvan scenes,
His verdant alleys and surrounding greens;
See Wanstead bid among a tuft of trees,
And Woodford's shady groves that ever please.

Here shady walks the barren wastes adorn,
There springing oaks, and there the bearded corn.
Wrapt with the prospect could the muse but raise
Her flowing Numbers equal to thy praise,
And sing the various kinds of game you breed,
Windsor would envy what it can't exceed.
Now see, where London's lofty towers rise;
See spiral wreaths of smoak obscure the skies;
Of sumptuous buildings a continued pile,
The wealth and glory of the British Isle.
See various Domes for various uses made,
Some law, religion some, and some for trade.
While thus retir'd and pleas'd I Lay me down
Far from the noise and hurry of the town,
I learn its reigning follies to despise,
To slight its pleasures, and abhor its vice.
Now this way looking view her marshy scene;
See snowy flocks that browse the tufted green.
See swiftly gliding thro' the flowry plain
Thames roll his billows to the stormy main;
Safe in her ports see ships at anchor ride,
And waving reeds that crown her verdant side.
Majestic on her bank, * a fabrick stands,
Whose busy dome the neighb'ring shore commands,
NASSAU; who gain'd for us immortal fame,
Improv'd the plan, a glory to his name.
Here when chill blood glides slowly thro' the vein,
Sweet peace and ease reward the sailors pains;
No more the ratling din of war they hear,
No more loud cannon thunder in their ear;
The noise of winds aloft and viewing sails
Are lost in sweeter notes and softer gales.
From sea retir'd they view the past delight
Of spoils and trophies in a naval fight;
What wonders each has for his country done,
Relate what ships they took, what towns they won;
How at Gibraltar, Alicant, Mahon,
They fought to pull the haughty Spaniards down;
How Rook at Vigo, o'er the French prevail'd;
How Bing in order from the Baltick sail'd;
How Wager since he plough'd the watry plain
To bar the Czarian fleet, and frighten Spain;
How brave Sir Cloudesly, by untimely haſt
On Scilla's dreadful rocks was furious cast;
How many more by Tempest on the main,
Are since fast link'd in death's eternal chain,
They tell, and wrapp'd in pleasure hear
Of cares and dangers that were once their fear.
Thus the lone traveller, when cold and night
O'ertake his weary steps, bereav'd of light,
Plods pensive on, till the rejoicing sound
Of Heylock barking from a neighbouring town,
New vigour adds; his lagging steps he mends,
And joyful to the noise his Ear he lends,
Till at the Inn arriv'd, with pipe and pot
In merry Tale the rugged way's forgot.
No more the muse presumes, as yet too young,
To sweeter lyres she leaves the blooming song;
Reduce thy flight, content with the small praise,
That thou here first has wak'd the rural lays.

* Greenwich Hospital.

N. B. We shall take the first Opportunity to oblige *Cleophilus*, (whose Papers have been mislaid) and our Correspondents, who may think themselves neglected.

THE
Monthly Intelligencer.
OCTOBER, 1733.

Monday. 1.

Thomas How, Efq; was sworn Lord Mayor of *Dublin* for the Year enfuing, in the Room of *Humphry French*, Efq; who had the higheft Encomiums given him by Chief-Baron *Marlay*, (*See p. 544*) for his fteady Execution of Juftice, the preceding Year. The Guild of Merchants, the Coopers, and feveral other Corporations prefented him with his Freedom in Gold and Silver Boxes, as a Teftimony of their Gratitude. A certain Author gives him this Character.—*He hath fhewn more Virtue, more Activity, more Skill in one Tear's Government of the City, than a hundred Tears can equal, he hath endeavour'd with great Succefs to banifh Frauds, Corruptions, and all other Abufes.—A Dozen fuch Men in Power would be able to reform a Kingdom.*

Friday. 5.

The D. of *Dorfet*, Ld Lieut. of *Ireland*, met the Parliament, and made the following Speech;

To which both Houfes return'd their moft dutiful and loyal Addreffes of Thanks.

My Lords and Gentlemen,

IT is with the greateft Satisfaction I return to meet a Parliament, ready on all Occafions to give frefh Proofs of their Zeal and Affection to his Majefty's Perfon and Government; and have the Commands of a moft gracious Sovereign to give you the ftrongeft Affurances of his tender Regard and Concern for your Happinefs. And to recommend to you the Confideration of whatever may beft contribute to the Welfare of this Kingdom.

In fo happy a Situation I may with Reafon expect, that all your Proceedings will be carried on with Temper and Unanimity: And that this Seffion will end to the Advantage of the Nation, and to the mutual Satisfaction of his Majefty, and all his faithful Subjects.

The Linnen Manufacture is fo beneficial to this Kingdom, and fo capable of being further extended, that it fhould be your conftant Endeavour to improve and enlarge that moft valuable Branch of Trade, which well deferves, and will amply reward, all the Care and Attention you can poffibly beftow upon it.

Gentlemen of the Houfe of Commons,

I have directed the proper Officers to prepare the feveral Accounts and Eftimates, in order to be laid before you. And I have nothing from his Majefty to ask, but fuch neceffary Supplies as may fupport the Eftablifhment, and provide for the National Debt, in fuch manner as may be moft expedient, and leaft burthenfome to his Subjects.

As a frugal Management of the Revenue hath been the principal Object of my Adminiftration; fo it will be my greateft Pleafure, if thofe Publick Services can be effectually provided for, with Honour to his Majefty, and with Security and Eafe to his People, without raifing new Taxes, or encreafing the National Debt. And this I perfuade myfelf can only be effected by finding out fome Means to prevent the great Diminution of the Revenue, by the fraudulent Importation of Goods.

I muft therefore recommend to you, the preparing fuch Heads of a Bill, as may be moft likely to attain that defirable End.

My Lords and Gentlemen,

The Treaty of Marriage concluded between the Princefs Royal and the Pr. of O-*range*, muft be agreeable to all his Majefty's good Subjects, and particularly to thofe of this Kingdom. The great Share they had in the ineftimable Advantages procured to us by the ever-glorious K. *William* the third, cannot fail of making them participate

Cipate largely of the Joy, which is ſo univerſal upon this happy Occaſion.

As the eminent Virtues and Accompliſhments of her Royal Highneſs, could not
but make an Alliance with her, earneſtly A
ſought for; ſo his Majeſty ſolicitous for
the future, as well as preſent Good of his
People, could not give a more endearing
Proof of his Reſolution to perpetuate their
Happineſs, than by yielding to the Inſtances of that Houſe,—which hath ſo gloriouſly diſtinguiſhed itſelf in the Cauſe of B
Liberty, and the Proteſtant Religion.

You are now in Poſſeſſion of thoſe invaluable Bleſſings, under the mild Government of a moſt gracious King, who e-
ſteems it his chief Glory to protect us in
the full Enjoyment of all our Civil and
Religious Rights.

An inviolable Attachment to his Royal
Perſon and Family, and a firm Union a-
mong all Proteſtants, who have one common Intereſt, and the ſame common Enemy, will be the ſureſt Means (under God)
of ſecuring theſe Bleſſings to our lateſt
Poſterity.

Saturday, 6.

The 8 following Malafactors were executed at *Tyburn*, viz. *William Robinſon*,
for a Street Robbery; *Richard Lamb* for
the Murder of his Wife; *John Cannon*,
for raviſhing *Mary Foſſet*; *Jonas Peirſon*,
for Horſe-ſtealing; *Lawrence Grace*, *John* E
Smithſon and *George Richardſon*, for robbing one *Gordon* in *Lincolns-Inn-Fields*;
and *Joſeph Blunt*, for the Murder of his
Corporal *Robert Adair*; (ſee p. 492.) *John*
Bromley, *Anne Soames*, and *Edward Dore*,
were reprieved.

Tueſday, 9.

Both Houſes of Parliament met and
were prorogued to the 15th of *November*.

Friday, 12.

The Seſſions ended at the *Old Bailey*,
when the following Criminals receiv'd
Sentence of Death, *viz.* *Francis Cotchet*,
a Fiſhmonger, for robbing Mrs *Banks* and
Mrs *Clifton*, of a Gold Watch, Agate Snuff
Box, and ſome Silver, by *Buckingham* G
Wall, in the Way to *Chelſea*; *John Brown*
and *Margaret Berry*, for Coining; *John*
Butler, *Joſeph Cox*, and *John Weedon*, for
the Highway; *Dorothy Carter*, for ſtealing from *John Connieri* 3 pieces of Lace;
and *Thomas Whitby*, for a Street Robbery. H
Margaret Berry, pleaded her Belly, and
was found quick with Child; 6 were burnt
in the Hand; 22 caſt for Tranſportation.
The Jury intimated to the Court that they
believ'd Mr *Cotchet*, was a Lunatick; and

the Court replied, they were of the ſame
Opinion. This they concluded, not only
from his Behaviour on his Trial, but from
the Extravagance of the Robbery itſelf,
which he committed in a very publick
manner, and afterwards rode full ſpeed
thro' the Streets, with 100 People after
him; from whom eſcaping he was taken
at night in his own Shop, by a Coachman
that knew him.

Saturday, 13.

A Hind hunted on *Sunbury* Common,
croſs'd the *Thames* three Times, run the
ſame Ground over again, and affording
excellent Diverſion, his Majeſty ordered
her Life to be ſpar'd, and a Silver Collar
to be put about her Neck

Tueſday, 16.

Dr *Hare*, Biſhop of *Chicheſter*, conſecrated the new Church in *Old-Street*, by
the Name of St *Luke*.

The Duke of *Devonſhire's* fine Houſe
in *Piccadilly*, was almoſt burnt to the
Ground in the Day time, the Fire breaking out at 8 o'Clock in the Morning,
while the Workmen employ'd to make
ſome Alterations, were at Breakfaſt.

Thurſday, 18.

The Contract of Marriage between the
Prince of *Orange* and the Princeſs Royal
was ſigned at *Hampton Court* on the Part
of his Majeſty

Monday, 22.

Came on before the Maſter of the Rolls,
a Cauſe between *John Hopkins*, Eſq; Couſin and Heir at Law of *John Hopkins*
Eſq; late of *Broad-ſtreet*, deceaſed, and his
ſix Daughters Plaintiffs, (*See our* Magazine
for July 1732. p. 832.) againſt Sir *Richard*
Hopkins, *John Rudge*, Eſq; and *James*
Hopkins, Eſq; deceaſed, and other Defendants, relating to the real and perſonal E-
ſtate of the ſaid *John Hopkins*, which a-
mounted to near 300,000 *l.* His Honour
was pleaſed to Order and Decree, that the
whole Real Eſtate ſhould deſcend to the
Heir at Law, until ſome Perſon, now unborn, ſhall be born, and attain to the Age
of 21 Years, and that he ſhould enjoy the
Poſſeſſion and Profits thereof until that
Time to his own Uſe and Benefit.

The Princeſs Royal enter'd the 25th
Year of her Age, and was complemented
on the ſame by a vaſt Concourſe of Nobility,

The Publiſhers of *Fog's* Journal of the
13th and of a Pamphlet there quoted (*See*
p. 529, 530.) were taken into Cuſtody
of a Meſſenger; but were admitted to
Bail,

Thurſ

Thursday 25.

A Court of Common Council was held at *Guildhall*, when the Lord Mayor delivered a Paper, containing the Methods used (when he and Sir *John Williams* were Sheriffs) in recovering such Effects, within the Liberties of the City as belonged to Col. *Chartres*, which Proceedings were order'd to be recorded. The Court granted the Petition of *Michael Hillersden*, Esq; praying a Remittance of 200 *l.* part of the Fine he lately paid to be excused from serving the Office of Sheriff; it appearing he had offer'd his Fine before he was elected. The Business of the Court being over Mr *Bosworth*, a Common Council Man of the Ward of *Farringdon without* address'd himself to the Lord Mayor in the following Terms.

My Lord Mayor,

WE should be much wanting to ourselves, should we slip this Opportunity of declaring the grateful sense we have of your worthy Administration; an Administration which has diffused a general and well-grounded Joy throughout the Kingdom: Yet just and reasonable as that Joy was, it had been turn'd into Mourning, and interpreted as highly Criminal, had not your Lordship exerted yourself in its Defence. I could gladly pursue the Subject, but am sensible personal Praise is ever disagreeable to great and generous Minds; and therefore I shall not give you, *my Lord*, the pain of hearing, what other Englishmen listen to with pleasure, but now content myself with moving that the Thanks of this Court be given your Lordship—which was agreed to.—Whereupon his Lordship thus express'd himself;

Gentlemen,

YOur Thanks are the best and greatest Reward to one entirely devoted to your Service: If I have in any Degree been instrumental to assert your Liberties, I shall always consider it much more as an Instance of my Felicity than my Merit.

Tuesday, 30.

His Majesty enter'd the 50th Year of his Age; but was pleased to defer the Celebration of that Day at Court till her Royal Highness's Nuptials.

Wednesday. 31.

The King's Barges fell down the River to meet the Prince of *Orange*.

BIRTHS.

THE Lady of *Wm Fowlis*, Esq; Daughter to the Ld Visc. *Downe*, deliver'd of a Daughter.

The Lady of Sir *William Humble* of *Thorp-Underwood*, *Northamptonshire*, Bart, deliver'd of a Son.

The Lady of Sir *John Shelley*, Bart and Sister of the D. of *Newcastle*, delivered of a Son and a Daughter.

The late Governour *Lowther's* Lady deliver'd of a Daughter.

MARRIAGES.

SIR *James Elphingston*, of *Logie*, Bar. Married to the Daughter of Mr *Rattray* of *Craighall*.

Jacob Wright, of *Grosvenor-street*, Esq; —to a Daughter of Mr *Pearsehouse* of *New Bond Street*.

Mr Serjeant *Birch*,—to Miss *Tashmaker* of *Edmonton*, with 14,000*l.* Fortune.

James Wanchop, of *Edmonston* Esq;—to a Daughter of Sir *John Inglis*, of *Cramond*, Bart. both of *Scotland*.

Philip Palmer, Esq; Brother to Sir *Cha. Palmer*, Bart.—to Miss *Thompson* of *Ludgate-Hill*.

Mr *Shelley* a Portugal Merchant,—to Miss *Maria Anna L'Eglise*, Daughter to a *French* Wine Merchant, and Sister to his Brother's Wife.

The Revd Mr *Thomas Robinson*,—to the only Daughter of *John Standish*, of *Broxborn*, in *Hertfordshire*, Esq;

Mr *John Harvey*, Linnen Draper in *Cornhill*,—to Miss *Froboch*, of *Ipswich*, with a Fortune of 8000*l.*

Henry Middleton, Esq; of *Middleton-hall* in *Carmarthenshire*,—to Mrs *Eliz. Price.*

The Hon. and Rev. *Francis Hamilton*, Son to the E. of *Abercon* ———to the Second Daughter of *James Forth*, Esq; at *Dublin.*

Wm Robinson, of *Wrexham*, *Denbighsh.* Esq;—to his first Cousin, one of the Daughters of the late *Robinson Lytton* of *Nebworth*, *Hertfordshire*, Esq;

Mr *Jeremiah Apsley*, Goldsmith in the *Strand*,—to Mrs *Arabella Fuller.*

DEATHS.

Sept. 27. THomas *Arundel*, Esq; at *Stoke Park*, in *Northamptonsh.* who leaving no Issue, his Estate devolves on his Widow, eldest Daughter of *Peter Wentworth*, Esq; Brother to the E. of *Strafford.*

James Laydeman, Esq; at *Edmonton*, in the Commission of the Peace.

28. *Charles Howard*, Earl of *Suffolk*. He married *Henrietta*, Sister to *John* Ld *Hobart*, Knt of the *Bath*, by whom he had Issue *Henry* Ld *Walden*, his Successor.

29. The Relict of Sir *Peter Eaton.*

Capt. *Hunter*, late Comm. of an India Man.

30. Major *John Cornforth*, aged 98.

Capt.

Capt. *Eberson*, formerly Commander of the *Nassau* Man of War.

2. *Jn Knight*, Esq; at *Gosfield-Hall*, *Essex*, Representative for *Sudbury*, *Suffolk*.

Mr *Webb*, one of the City Bridge Masters.

Rodney Fane, Esq; Counsellor at Law, and in the Commission of the Peace for *Middlesex*, reputed worth 25,000 l.

The Revd Mr *Peters*, Rector of *Barnford*, in *Durham*.

The Revd Mr *Abraham Franks*, D. D. Rector of *West Dean*, in *Wilts*.

Withers, Esq; at *Manedrow*, *Hants*.

Edw. Reynolds, Esq; of *New-house Grange*, *Leicestershire*.

John Avery, Esq; an *East India* Merchant.

5. Mr *Bennet*, 50 Years House-keeper and Head Door-keeper to the Admiralty Office, reputed worth 25,000 l.

Capt. *Lancaster*, the oldest Officer in Gen. *Evan*'s Reg. of Horse.

7. The Revd Mr *Hodges*, M. A. Minister of *Shipton Moyne*, near *Tadbury*, *Gloucestershire*.

The Lady *Margaret*, Spouse to *John Campbel*, Esq; and Daughter to the late E. *Loudon*.

9. Mr *Moreland*, Head Master of St *Paul's* School, aged 80.

10. Capt. *John Vernon*, Commander of the *Namure*, a 2d Rate, in the late War.

Sir *John Stonhouse*, Bar. Knight of the Shire for *Berks*.

Alexander Elphington, Esq; at *Leith*, Son to the Lord *Balmerino*.

Sir *Wm Douglas*, of *Killhead*, Bart.

Mr *Reason*, Master of New *Tunbridge Wells*.

11. Mr *Musquet*, formerly a *Portugueze* Merchant, at *Edmonton*.

13. Mr *Samuel Gale*, Steward of St *Thomas's Hospital*, *Southwark*.

The Wife of *Henry Villiers*, Esq; Gentleman Usher to the Princess Royal, and Governor of *Tinmouth Castle*.

The Wife of *Philip Gybbon*, Esq; Representative for *Rye* in *Sussex*.

14. *Jacob Martin*, Esq; at *Petersham*, *Surry*.

15. *Geo. Lawrence*, Esq; in *Leicester-fields*.

16. The Wife of ⸻ *Trevor*, Esq; a near Relation to the late Ld *Trevor*.

17. Capt. *Broome*, of *Westminster*, a great Dealer in Pictures.

Rev. Mr *Fell*, Rector of *Benshon*, *Cornw*.

Rev. Dr *Stamper*, a Prebendary of St *Paul's*.

Mr *Pope*, a Messenger to the *H.* of *Commons*.

Sir *Edw. Betenson*, Bt. at *Chisleburst*, *Kent*.

Nicholas Hammond, of *Swafham*, *Norfolk*, Esq. By his Death an Estate of 400 l. per *Ann*. goes to the 2d Son of *Anth. Hammond*, Esq; Brother-in-Law to Sir *Robert Walpole*. Likewise 15,000 l. to the erecting and endowing a Charity School in *Swafham*.

18. *Joseph Skinner*, at *Moseley*, *Kent*, Esq;

20. *Miles Philipson*, Esq; Counf. at Law.

John Lynch, Esq; in the Commission of the Peace for *Kent*.

21. Sir *Wm Drake*, Bart of an antient Family in *Devonshire*.

22. *James Corten*, Esq; formerly a Linnen Draper in *Freet-street*, reputed worth 12,000 l.

Robert Lewt, Esq; at *Sherbourn*, *Hants*.

24. *Joseph Shaw*, Esq; at *Lambeth*, Author of a Book entitled, *The Practical Justice of the Peace*.

Jn Medlicott, Esq; formerly Wine Merch[t].

Mr *Holmes*, Rent-gatherer and Town-Steward to the E. of *Burlington*.

The jun. Dutchess of *Marlborough*, Wife of the E. of *Godolphin*. Leaving no Issue Male the Title of D. of *Marlborough* descends to the E. of *Sunderland*. By her Death an Estate of 5000 l. per *Ann*. came to the E. of *Godolphin*.

24. *Francis Molineux*, Esq; one of the Verduters of *Sherwood* Forest, eldest Son of Sir *Franbis Molineux*, Bart of *Treverset*, *Nortinghamshire*.

Sir *John Stapylton*, of *Myton Yorkshire*, by a fall from his Horse.

26. *Henry Hure*, Esq; Collector of the Customs of *King's-Lyn*, *Norfolk*.

Nathaniel Manlove, Esq; one of the Governors of *Bethlehem*, *Bridewel*, and *Christ Hospitals*.

27. *Samuel Reads*, Esq; at *Hackney*, reputed worth 80,000 l.

29. The Rev. Mr *Serle*, one of the Officiates of St *George's Bloomsbury*.

PROMOTIONS.

THE D. of *Athol*, elected one of the 16 Peers of *Scotland*, to sit in the Parliament of *Great Britain*, in the room of the E. of *Sutherland* deceased.

The E. of *Pembroke* and *Montgomery*, appointed Ld Lieut. of the County of *Wilts*.

Thomas Rigg, Esq; late Sheriff of *Bucks*, —one of the Commissioners of the Revenue in *Ireland*, in the room of his Father-in-Law, *Thomas Medlicott*, Esq;

Lieut. *Carr*,—Capt. Lieut. in the King's own Royal Reg. of Horse.

Mr *Dowdy*, Messenger of the Navy-Office,—Inner Door-keeper to the Lords of the Admiralty, in the room of Mr *Bennet*, decd. And

Mr *Wyat*—Messenger of the Navy Office.

Charles Howard, Esq;—Deputy Clerk of the Patents, in the room of *John Tench*, Esq; decd.

Capt. *Driver*, Exempt,—Major of the First Troop of Guards, in the room of Major *Wright*.

Capt. *Herbert*,—Exempt in his room; and Capt. *Elways*,—Sub Brig. in Capt. *Herbert*'s room.

Mr *Rambouillet*,—Gentleman Usher; Mr *Poyntz*, Nephew to *Stephen Poyntz*, Esq;

Efq; and the Son of Major *Derby*, of the Foot Guards, — Pages of Honour to the Princefs Royal after her Marriage.

Capt. *Robert Frazer*, — Major in Col. *Harrifon*'s Reg. in the room of Major *Howe*, decd.

Maurice Bockland, Efq; Reprefentative for *Yarmouth* iu the *Ifle* of *Wight*, — to the Command of a Troop in his Majefty's own Royal Reg. of Horfe, in the room of Capt. *Lancafter*, deceafed.

Cha. Harrifon, Efq; chofen Bailiff of the Corporation of *Seaford, Suffex*.

Mr *Balling*, appointed a Sealer in Chancery, in the room of Mr *Symonds*.

Mr *Willis*, who built the Pay Office, and Commiffary'sOffice at *Whitehall*, — Mafter Carpenter of *Weftminfter-Abbey*, in the room of Mr *Norris*, who has refign'd.

Dr *Peters*, one of the late Dr *Radcliff*'s Travelling Phificians, appointed Phifician Extraordinary to the King.

The Ld *Southwell* of Ireland, — Mafter of the Horfe to the Princefs Royal.

Robert Ravenhill, Efq; — Mayor of the City of *Hereford*.

Henry Boyle, Efq; chofen Speaker of the Houfe of Commons in *Ireland*.

Sir *Philip Tork*, Knt. Attorney General made Ld Ch. Juftice of the *King's Bench* with an Addition of 2000 *l. per Ann.* Salary to him and his Succeffors.

Capt. *Bembow*, — Lieutenant in the E. of *Pembrook*'s Royal Reg. of Horfe.

The Lady of the Ld *Herbert* of *Cherbury* — Lady of the Bedchamber to the Princefs Royal.

Ecclefiaftical Preferments *conferr'd on the following Reverend Gentlemen.*

MR *Thomas Frampton*, prefented to the Vic. of *Helmerfton*, in *Wilts*.

Francis Clarke, L. L. D. — to the Living of *Benfleet*, in *Effex*.

John Brice, A. M. — to the Rectory of *Willingate-Doe, Effex*.

Mr *James Bentham*, — to the Vicarage of *Stapleton, Cambridgefhire*.

Dr *Long*, chofen Mafter of *Pembrokehall, Cambridge*, Dr *Hawkins* refigning.

Mr *Thomas Woodford*, Minifter of *Alhallows LondonWall*, inftalled one of the Prebendaries of *Salifbury*.

Mr *Jackfon*, of *Coventry* — a Prebendary of the Church of *Litchfield*.

Mr *Moody*, appointed Chaplain to the Lord Mayor.

A Difpenfation is pafs'd to enable,

Caleb Parfett, M. A. Chaplain to the Lady *Ramney*, to hold the Rectory of *Caxton, Kent*, together with the Vicarage of *Shane* in the fame County.

Jofua Harrifon, M. A. Chaplain to the E. of *Pembroke*, to hold the Rectory of *Blunfden St Andrew, Wilts*, together with the Vic. of *Sharton St Margarets* in the County aforefaid.

A LIST *of the Commiffioners appointed to furvey the Offices of the Courts of Juftice in* England *and* Wales, *and to enquire into their Fees*, &c. (fee p. 379.)

Court of King's-Bench.

Sir Richd Hopkins	Tho. Hufey, Efq;
Sir John Barnard	Wm Wynne, Efq;
Sir Henry Hankey	Wm Cowper, Efq;
Alderman Kendal;	Rob. Hucks, Efq;
John Marfh, Efq;	John Lawton, Efq;
BeverfhamFilmer,Efq;	Tho. Crofs, Efq;

Court of Common-Pleas.

Sir John Chefhire	Alderman Alfop
Sir John Darnel	Alderman Salter
John Buyoes, Efq;	Sir Thomas Croofs
Wm Hawkins, Serjeants at Law.	Sir Wm Wynne
	Juftice Blackerby
Sir John Eyles	John Ellis, Efq;
Sir John Thompfon	

Court of Exchequer.

Sir Edwd Bellamy	Henry Hoar, Efq;
Sir Richd Brocas	Tho. De Veil, Efq;
Alderman Parfons	Tho. Abney, Efq;
Alderman Godfchall	Henry Stevens, Efq;
Sir Tho. Clarges Bt.	Wm Bunbury, Efq;
John Bride, Efq;	Wm Guidot, Efq;

Ecclefiaftical Courts.

Sir John Lade, Bt.	John Andrews L L. D.
Sir John Williams	StephenCottrel LL. D.
Sir John Tafh	George Lee, *Doctors*
Sir Wm Ogborne	*of Law.*
Sir Jofeph Eyles	Thomas Maylin, Efq;
Ald. Champion.	Thomas Lnwes, Efq;
Wm Strahan, L L. D.	

BANKRUPTS.

Robert Smith, of Great Oulmow, Effex, Cha pman
Archibald and Wm Downey, Steyniog, Suffex, Chapman
James Daws, of White Walton, Berks, Chapman
Geo. Pepper of St Martin's in the Fields, Mid. Chapman
John Franks, of Loughborough, Leicefterfhire, Mercer
Richard King, of Wilton, Wilts, Malifter
William Davis, of Bradford, Wilts, Clothier
Thomas Afhburner, of London, Merchant
Richard Quane, of London Merchant
Andrew Lavington, of St Leonard, Devon. and
Richard Paule, of Exon, Merchants and Partners
John Beavis, of Covent Garden, Middlefex, Mercer.
Reginald Thomas, of Morva, Cornwal Tinman.
Jofeph Brookfbank, of Eland, Yorkfhire, Merchant.
Edmund Cock, Junr. of Eaeter, Merchant.
Thomas Cox, Tooley Street Southwark Grocer.
Jofhua Robinfon, of Thames-Street, London- Victualler.
Henry Reftall, of the Strand, Victualler.
James Graham, of the fame, Merchant.
Jonathan Newfon, of Farnham Suffolk, Grocer.
William Hart, St Jame's, Weftminfter, Merchant.
Richard Owen, of London, Salefman.
Mary Savage, Grofvenor Street, Middlefex, Milliner.
Thomas Toompfon, of Waltham Abby, Effex, Draper

Towards the End of the Month.

Course of Exchange.	STOCKS	Monthly BILL of Mortality, from Sept. 25. to Oct. 23.
Amsterdam 35 4	S. Sea Trading Stock 73	Christned { Males 626 } 1255
Ditto at Sight 34 1	—Bonds at Par	{ Females 629 }
Hamburgh— 35 5	—Annuities 101	Buried { Males 942 } 1876
Rotterdam— 35 5	—Ditto new 100	{ Femal. 934 }
Antwerp — 35 5	—dit. 3 per C. 92	Died under 2 Years old — 761
Madrid — 42 ¼	Bank 132	Between 2 and 5 —— 159
Bilboa — 41 ½	New Cir. 1 l.	Between 5 and 10 —— 69
Cadiz — 42 ¼	India 140	Between 10 and 20 —— 41
Venice — 49 ¼	—Bonds 12 s. Pre.	Between 20 and 30 —— 121
Leghorn — 50 ½	at 3 per C. 8 s. Disc.	Between 30 and 40 —— 172
Genoa — 53 ¼	Million Bank 115	Between 40 and 50 —— 193
Paris — 31 ⅞	African 25	Between 50 and 60 —— 140
Bourdeaux -- 31 ½	Royal Ass. 91	Between 60 and 70 —— 124
Oporto— 5 4 ½	London Ass. 12	Between 70 and 80 —— 56
Lisbon — 5 5 ½ d ¼	Eng. Cop. 1 l. 15	Between 80 and 90 —— 34
Dublin— 11 ¼	Welch ditto 17 s.	Between 90 and 100 —— 6

Lottery Tickets, for the Receipts 4 s. Discount.   1876

Price of Grain at *Bear-Key, per* Qr.		Buried.	Weekly Burials
Wheat 22 s. to 26 s.	P. Malt 18 s. to 21 s.	Within the walls, 163	Oct. 2 — 482
Rye 12 s. to 16 s.	B. Malt 16 s. to 20 s.	Without the walls, 603	9 — 421
Barley 13 s. to 18 s. 6 d	Tares 20 s. to 22 s.	In Mid and Surry, 754	16 — 525
Oats 10 s. to 15 s.	H. Pease 16 s. to 18 s.	City and Sub of West 356	23 — 448
Pease 20 s. to 22 s.	H. Beans 18 s. to 20 s.	1876	1876

Prices of Goods, &c. in *London*. Hay about 1 l. 16 s. to 2 l. a Load.

Coals in the Pool 24 s. to 26 s.
Old Hops per Hun. 2 l. 10 s. to 4 l.
New Hops 5 l. to 6 l.
Rape Seed 10 l. to 11 l. per Last
Lead the Fodder 19 Hun. 1 half
on board, 14 l. to 16 l. 00 s.
Tin in Blocks 4 l. 00 s.
Ditto in Bars 4 l. 02 s. exclusive
of 3 s. per Hun. Duty.
Copper Eng. best 9 l. 15 s. per C.
Ditto ord. 4 l. 16 s. to 5 l. per C.
Ditto Barbary 7 o l. to 80 l.
Iron of Bilboa 14 l. 10 s. per Tun
Dit. of Sweden 15 l. 10 s. per Tun
Town Tallow 30 s. to 32 s. per C.
Country Tallow 28 s. 32 s.
Salt 4 s. to 4 s. 6 d.

Grocery Wares.
Raisins of the Sun 28 s. 0 d. per C.
Ditto Malaga Frailes 19 s.
Ditto Smirna new 20 s.
Ditto Alicant, 18 s.
Ditto Lipra new 19 s.
Ditto Belvedera 20
Currants new 45 s.
Prunes French 18 s.
Figs 20 s.
Sugar Powd. best 59 s. per C.

Ditto second sort 46 s. to 50 s. per C.
Loaf Sugar double refine 8 d. Half-
penny a 9 d. per lb.
Ditto single refin. 56 s. to 64 s.
per C.
Cinamon 7 s. 8 d. per lb.
Cloves 9 s. 1 d.
Mace 15 s. 0 d. per lb.
Nutmegs 8 s. 7 d. per lb.
Sugar Candy white 14 d. to 18 d.
Ditto brown 7 d. per lb.
Ditto for exportation 13 d. Farth.
Tea Bohea fine 10 s. to 11 s. per lb.
Ditto ordinary 7 s. to 9 s. per lb.
Ditto Congo 10 s. to 14 s. per lb.
ditto Pekoe 9 s. a 14 s. per lb.
ditto Green fine 8 s. to 12 s. per lb.
ditto Imperial 10 s. to 16 s. per lb.
ditto Hyson 24 s. to 28 s.

Drugs by the lb.
Balsam Peru 14 s. to 15 s.
Cardamoms 3 s. 3 d.
Camphire refin'd 19 s.
Crabs Eyes 2 s. 5 d.
Jallop 3 s.
Manna 20 d. a 33 d.
Mastich white 4 s. 0 d.

Opium 11 s. 00 d.
Quicksilver 4 s. 3 d.
Rhubarb fine 25 s. a 30 s.
Sarsaparilla 3 s. 0 d.
Saffron Eng. 18 s. 00 d.
Wormseeds 3 s. 5 d.
Balsam Capaiva 2 s. 9 d.
Balsam of Gillead 18 s. 00 d.
Hipecacuanha 7 s.
Ambergreece per oz. 12 s.
Cochineal 18 s. 3 d. per lb.

Wine, Brandy, and Rum.
Oporto red, per Pipe 36 l.
ditto white 24 l.
Lisbon red 30 l.
ditto white 26 l.
Sherry 26 l.
Canary new 30 l.
ditto old 36 l.
Florence 3 l. per Chest
French red 30 l. a 40 l.
ditto white 30 l.
Mountain malaga old 24 l.
ditto new 20 to 24 l.
Brandy French per Gal. 7 s.
Rum of Jamaica 7 s.
ditto Leew. Islands 6 s. 4 d.
Spirits Eng. 26 l. per Tun.

The King of France's *Manifesto on Occasion of his Declaring War against the Emperor.*

THE King has given, since his Accession to the Crown, so many shining Proofs of his Moderation and Love for his Country, that an Imputation may even lie against him for having urg'd it to an Excess. But notwithstanding he has constantly preferr'd the Quiet and Welfare of his People to any Ambition of extending the Limits of his Empire, Moderation has its Bounds as well as other Virtues; and *Europe* might have still enjoy'd a profound Peace, if the Enemies of *France* had not forc'd his Majesty to take up Arms in Defence of the Dignity of his Crown, the Glory of the *French* Nation, and the Honour and Liberty of *Poland.*

Since the Throne of *Poland* has been vacant, the King has paid a tender Regard to the Polish Liberties; he has exacted nothing from a People free and Arbiters of their own Fate. The Republick herself implor'd his Succour; she doubled her Importunity, as her Dangers increas'd, and as she saw herself environ'd with hostile Armies; she implor'd an Asylum in the Justice and Power of his Majesty; an Asylum always open to Powers threaten'd with Oppression. The King, after the Example of his Ancestors, has assur'd *Poland* of his Protection. He declar'd it to the respective Powers, in Terms the most inoffensive, and with a Moderation suiting the Dignity of great Princes; nay, he acquainted the Court of *Vienna,* upon the earliest Occasion, with the sole Expedient that could possible prevent Disorders in *Europe,* and all the Steps he has since taken, are so many illustrious Monuments of his Care for the Preservation of the publick Tranquillity.

But a Conduct so prudent has not hinder'd the Court of *Vienna* from thundering against a Prince born in the Bosom of *Poland,* and allied to his Majesty by the nearest Ties. That Court, encouraged by some former Measures tending to the Advancement of its private Views, has surpriz'd all Mankind in answering his Majesty's Declaration with Terms the most galling, and such as ought to be unknown to Princes whose Scepters render them equal. The King has not exceeded the Limits that Wisdom and Decency prescribe him: he has not appear'd eager to take the Revenge that a Personal Insult upon his Honour requir'd; and if his Preparations seem'd to declare a Resentment, he suspended the Effects of it as long as it was possible, without wounding the Dignity of his Crown, and the Honour of his Blood.

Is it to be doubted, whether the Personal Interest of the Emperor has not determin'd his Conduct, and influenc'd the Engagements he enter'd into, to dispose of a Crown distinct from the Empire, even before it was become vacant? He then pretended equally to exclude *Stanislaus,* because of his Ties to *France;* and the Elector of *Saxony,* because he seem'd at that time to have Interests opposite to those of the House of *Austria.* — The Death of King *Augustus* gave Field for new Projects; the Elector hasten'd into the Views of the Emperor, and from that Moment ceas'd to deserve the Exclusion which that Prince and the Czarina had given him. This Exclusion has been taken off, a new Treaty has been concluded to raise the Elector of *Saxony* to the Throne of *Poland,* and several Armies hover'd upon the Borders of *Poland* to frighten her into a Compliance.

The *Poles* thought it most necessary to their Liberty, to exclude any Foreign Prince from setting up as a Candidate to their Crown. This Exclusion was agreed upon in the Diet of Convocation, and seem'd of so essential a Nature, that it was confirm'd by a solemn Oath. The Court of *Vienna* has labour'd incessantly to break down this new Barrier; there has been nothing left unattempted to procure an Absolution of this Oath: as if the Interests and unlimited Projects of the House of *Austria,* were of sufficient Importance to destroy an Engagement consecrated by a solemn Act of Religion.

The Emperor redoubled his Efforts, he declar'd, That he would never permit that *Stanislaus* should re-ascend the Throne of *Poland,* either under pretext of his first Election, or in any other manner whatever. His Ministers at *Warsaw* acted in the closest Concert with those of *Saxony* and *Muscovy;* they even triumph'd in their Union; they exhibited it to publick Notice at *Warsaw* with all possible Pomp. But indeed, all their Declarations have been in the same Stile, alike Insults upon the King of *Poland,* and alike Orders to the Republick. The secret Intrigues, the open Menaces, the most unjust Suspicions, the March of Troops, all, all were mutually agreed between them, and alike the Effect of the good Intelligence that reign'd between 'em. The Ministers of *Saxony* and *Muscovy,* at the time of the Election, retir'd to the Imperialists; and to set their Union and Sameness beyond all Question, the Emperor's Minister join'd with the Minister of *Muscovy,* to notify publickly to the Primate the Entry of the *Muscovites* into *Poland,* and to insult the several Orders of the Republick then assembled, with a View of the Chains they had prepar'd for them.

With what Face could the Court of *Vienna* hope to impose upon *Europe,* and how flatter herself with a Shelter from the Storm, by only deferring to march her Troops into *Poland,* when 'tis known that she alone had instigated the *Muscovites* to make an Irruption? She promis'd herself, that the Arms of the *Muscovites* would be sufficient to intimidate and enslave the *Poles;* and thought is enough to have the *Imperial* and *Saxon* Troops upon the Frontiers, ready at hand

to

to second the Violence of the others.

By all these Marks, 'tis impossible to mistake the Aggressor. The Treaties by which the Emperor has endeavoured to dispose of the Crown of *Poland*, as if he was the absolute Master of the Republick, and its Rights and Liberties; the Exclusion that he has pretended to give, without either Authority or Power, to a Prince whose Virtues render him worthy of the Throne; the Promises made the Elector of *Saxony* as a Recompence for his tractable Disposition; the March of the Imperial Troops in Concert with those of *Saxony* and *Muscovy*; the Hostilities which the *Muscovites* committed during the time of the Election, to secure by Force of Arms the Success of the Emperor's Projects; this Hostility approv'd, and even declar'd by his Minister, indicates a Conduct which will remain a lasting Evidence, that this Prince is the sole Author of the War; that he has compell'd the King to take up Arms by the Outrage done his Majesty; and by the Violences he has made use of, by himself or his Approbation, against the Republick of *Poland*.

If all these Efforts prove at last ineffectual to disturb the Election, the King and Kingdom of *Poland*, is only indebted to him, to whom appertains the Disposition of Crowns; and who hath in his Care, as well the Hearts of the People, as those of Kings. The Courage of the *Poles* set them free from that Slavery in which the Court of *Vienna* would have involv'd them; the King has therefore only to take Satisfaction of the Emperor for his Opposition to the Re-accession of the King of *Poland*; for his injurious Declarations distributed throughout all *Europe* by the Enemies he has stir'd up against *France* and *Poland*, who desir'd nothing more than the Enjoyment of Peace and Liberty; for the Councils he gave the Court of *Russia*; for the Hopes he dealt to that of *Saxony*; and in short, for all his latter Efforts to support his first Designs.

In vain does the Court of *Vienna* hope to conceal her Intrigues from the Eyes of *Europe*; her pernicious Councils, her ill-intentioned Principles, her indecent Expressions, her Projects form'd against the *Polish* Liberty, is every where conspicuous.

The illustrious Prince, against whom the Emperor bestirs himself in such a manner, is the same, in whom the greatest Part of the Sovereigns of *Europe*, and particularly the late Emperor *Joseph*, acknowledg'd the sacred Character of Royalty. But, the Alliance which King *Stanislaus* has contracted with the King, has chang'd these Dispositions, and the Language of the Court of *Vienna*. This Prince became from that Moment, according to the Language of the Allies, a Citizen proscrib'd by his Country; and the Change would indeed have been surprizing, had not the Scheme which the

Emperor has form'd, to insult his Majesty in the Person of this Prince, who is most dear to him; and the Project of rendering himself the Distributer of Crowns, been conspicuous from its very Birth and Original.

The Republick of *Poland* has no Prerogative more valuable than that of the Disposal of her Throne, the most glorious Attribute of her Liberty, and for the Preservation of which she has never been sparing of her Blood. Upon this made the Emperor his Attempt. He neither fear'd to point out the Prince whom he would exclude, nor him whom he would raise to the Crown. He has undertaken to pronounce without Authority, upon what has pass'd in the Bosom of the Republick, in relation to the first Election of a King of *Poland*; he has taken upon him, in the Character of a Sovereign Law-giver, to decide what Laws ought to subsist in *Poland*, and to inspect the Foundation of her Liberties, in order the better to subvert them. The sole Artifice he has us'd towards her, is to disguise his Designs under the Appearance of a treacherous Protection, and under the Cover of a pretended Treaty, which a Tumult of Arms precipitately gave Birth to, and which the Republick, when return'd to herself, thought it culpable to comply with.

The Emperor and the *Czarina* have always explain'd themselves to the Republick, in Terms proper towards a tributary Kingdom, or a Nation subdu'd: Their Threats were immediately follow'd by the March of their Troops to the Frontiers; the *Muscovite* Army at length enter'd *Poland*, in order to fulfil her Engagements, with the Emperor, even during the time of the Election, in Expedition, and with Intent, to drown with the Noise of Arms, both the Voice of the Laws and the Suffrages of the Republick.

The *Polish* Nation nevertheless, deliberated upon the Election of her King with the Calmness, which the Justice of her Cause could alone inspire, in the midst of so many Dangers. The Wishes of the Republick were compleat upon the Return of the King of *Poland*, his Presence cemented their Inclinations, the Field of Election rang with one Voice in his Favour, and this Deliberation was consummated with an Unanimity to which the Archives of *Poland* can furnish no Parallel.

'Tis this Unanimity which ought to impose an eternal Silence upon her Enemies, since the Voice of the People is therein discover'd to be the Voice of God; and 'tis this Unanimity which the *Poles* are determin'd to support to the last Extremity. Violence has done its worst, it can no more. The *Muscovite* Army, at the Instigation of the Allies, advances towards *Warsaw*; the Troops of the Emperor and those of the Elector of *Saxony*, are ready to take the same Steps, in case the Arms of the *Muscovites* shall not be ufficient to enslave a free People, who claim their Privileges by an incontestable Right, and demand by the same Right the glorious Use of their Liberty.

The Courts of *Vienna* and *Russia* ought to drop the august Title of Protectors of *Poland*; for that Title does not empower them to open or shut the Avenues which lead to a vacant Throne: It is not in trampling upon the Rights of a Nation that the Name of Protector is acquir'd, but in defending it against such as would oppress it. Of this his Majesty's Conduct might exhibit an Example to the Emperor; nor does he fear to challenge the Republick herself, or all *Europe*, to be his Judges. For how much soever the King might wish the Re-accession of a Prince whom *France* receiv'd in his Misfortunes, and whom the most sacred Ties have since united to him, yet he has exacted nothing of the *Poles*, being convinc'd that it belongs to none but the *Polish* Nation to recall a Prince whom Misfortunes have a long time estrang'd from its Bosom. His Majesty's Letter to the Primate of the 6th of *July*, breathes nothing but Peace and Justice: *Europe* may peruse therein the Uprightness of his Majesty's Intentions; she may see there how far the King is from inspiring the King of *Poland* with Sentiments separate from the Interest of the Republick; and may discover, that however anxious he has been for the Re-establishment of that Prince, 'tis only to join with him in the Observance of those Treaties which regard the Republick, and to contribute at the same time to the Glory and Happiness of *Poland*, and the Tranquillity of the North.

'Tis then with no ambitious or self-interested Views that the King has Recourse to Arms; content to possess a flourishing Kingdom, and to reign over a dutiful People, his Majesty seeks not to extend the Bounds of his Dominion. In vain does the Emperor, in order to draw the Empire into his Projects, strive to alarm them with Designs which are falsely imputed to his Majesty. The Emperor has brought upon himself a War, which he has render'd unavoidable by the Violence offer'd his Majesty, in a particular that ought to be held the most sacred amongst Sovereigns; and his Majesty is determin'd to wipe off the foul Blemishes cast upon him, and to light up the Honour of *France* in its brightest Lustre. For, from Motives so just the *French* Troops shall receive a double Ardour. They are already eager to revenge their King, and to prevent his illustrious Allies from being overwhelm'd by the Forces which the Emperor has caus'd to be pour'd in upon them. 'Tis to God to give Victory to our Arms; the King calls upon him with Confidence, and is bold to hope, that his Successes will answer up to his Moderation, his Patience, and the Purity of his Sentiments,

Declaration of the most Christian King, to the Electors and Princes of the Emperor.

ALTHO' the Memorial containing the Motives which induced the King's Resolutions at this Conjuncture, may have sufficiently demonstrated to all *Europe*, the Purity of his Majesty's Intentions; nevertheless, whilst his Troops are passing the *Rhine*, he would more particularly present to the Empire his Sentiments, and the Principles he acts upon. He desires to preserve Peace with the *Germanick* Body, and is intirely dispos'd to observe with it all the subsisting Treaties so long as his Majesty may look upon it as a Friend. If his Majesty in attacking the Fort of *Kehl*, endeavours to secure to himself the Passes of the *Rhine*, 'tis not with any ill Intention against the *Germanick* Body, to whom he has evidenc'd upon many Occasions, how dear its Interests are to him. He will offer no Violence to any of its Members; nay, he proposes by gaining a Passage over the *Rhine*, to be in a Condition to succour such of the Princes of *Germany*, as the Emperor would compel to be subservient to his private Views, and the Execution of his Projects. He has given Orders to his Generals, that the Estates of those Princes who stand neuter, and furnish no Succour against him, shall be created with all kind of Regard and Tenderness. His Majesty, well satisfy'd with the Bounds of his Dominion, and far from desiring to extend them by the Success of his Arms, does not hesitate to declare solemnly, that he has no Views of making Conquests, nor to gain any new Footings, which may expose the Security of the *Germanick* Territory. He is solely intent upon pursuing his just Resentment for the many Injuries the Emperor has done him in the Face of all *Europe*. He will omit nothing that may more and more convince the Princes of *Germany*, how ardently he desires to preserve with them that good Intelligence which is so necessary, and so agreeable between the Guaranty of the Treaties of *Westphalia*, and the Members of the *Germanick* Body.

From *Warsaw*, That the Elector of *Saxony* was chosen King of *Poland* the 5th instant at 4 in the Afternoon, at *Grokow*, by K. *Stanislaus*'s Opponents. About the same Time 30,000 *Muscovites* pass'd the *Vistula*, and made themselves Masters of this City.

From *Paris*, That a Treaty is concluded between *France*, *Spain*, and the K. of *Sardinia*; by Virtue of which those Powers were to join their Forces to attack the Emperor of *Germany* in *Italy* and *Sicily*, and That the K. of *Sardinia* was to be Generalissimo of these Forces, and the Marshal *de Villars* to have the chief Command under him. That the French Army having past the *Rhine*, had taken Fort *Kehl* after 10 Days stout Resistance.

A REGISTER of BOOKS publish'd in OCTOBER, 1733.

THE Natural, Experimental, and Medicinal History of the Mineral Waters of *Derbyshire, Lincolnshire,* and *Yorkshire,* particularly those of *Scarborough.* By *Thomas Short,* M. D. of *Sheffield.* Sold by *F. Gyles.*

2. New Standard Tables, wherein Bullion Gold and Silver of any Fineness, and at any Standard Price, are valued at Sight to the 1000th Part of a Penny. By Mr *R. Hayes.* Printed for *W. Meadows.*

3. A Serious and useful Scheme to make an Hospital for Incurables of universal Benefit to all his Majesty's Subjects; occasion'd by a Report that the Estate of *Richard Norton,* Esq; was to be appointed by Parliament for such an Endowment. To which is added, a Petition of the Footmen in and about *Dublin.* By a celebrated Author in *Ireland.* Printed for *J. Roberts,* pr. 6 *d.*

4. The certain Futurity of Free Actions no Contradiction; or, God's Knowledge of all Events not inconsistent with human Liberty. Printed for *J. Noon,* pr. 4 *d.*

5. A Short Account of the Hurricane, that pass'd thro' the English Leeward Charibbee Islands, on Saturday, *June* 30th 1733. Sold by *J Brotherton.* price 6 *d.*

6. An Enquiry into the Nature of the Human Soul, wherein the Immortality of the Soul is evinced from the Principles of Reason and Philosophy. Sold by *G. Strahan.*

7. The History of *Poland* during the Reign of *Augustus* II. which contains the great Dispute between that Prince, and the Princes of *Conti* and *Sobieski* for the Crown; with the other important Transactions of his Life, &c. Translated from the *French* of the Abbe *de Parthenay,* by *John Stacie,* Esq; Printed for *W. Lewis,* and *F. Cogan.*

8. The Importance of the Doctrine of the Holy Trinity asserted, in Reply to some late Pamphlets. By *Daniel Waterland,* D.D.

9. A Specimen of a New Translation of the Book of Psalms; with Critical Observations upon several obscure Passages in it. Sold by *J. Batley.* pr. 1 *s.*

10. The Duty of Parents and Masters of Families, with regard to the Good Education and sober Demeanor of their Children and Servants. Printed for *C. Rivington,* pr. 1 *s.*

11. A Copy of the Will of Dr *Matthew Tindal,* with an Account of what passed concerning the same, between Mr *Lucy Price,* Eustace *Budgel,* Esq; and Mr *Nicholas Tindal.* Printed for *T. Cooper,* pr. 4 *d.*

12. The Rise and Fall of the late projected Excise, impartially consider'd. Printed for *J. Peele,* pr. 1 *s.*

13. Some Observations upon a Paper, entitled, the List. That is, of those who voted for and against the Excise Bill. Printed for *J. Peele,* pr. 6 *d.*

14. Motives for the Resolution of his most Christian Majesty, with his Declaration to the Electors and Princes of the Empire; containing the Reasons for the present Measures of the Court of *France,* in *French* and *English.* Printed for *F. Cogan,* pr. 6 *d.* See p. 553, 4, 5.

15. Some Reasons for continuing the present Parliament. Printed for *T. Bowman,* price 6 *d.*

16. Parish Law; or, a Guide to Justices of the Peace, Ministers, Churchwardens, Overseers, Constables, &c. By *Joseph Shaw,* Esq; Printed for *F. Cogan.*

17. * A System of *English* Ecclesiastical Law extracted from the Codex Juris Ecclesiastici Anglicani of the Rt Revd. the Lord Bp of *London*; for the Use of Young Students in the Universities, who are designed for holy Orders. By *Richard Grey,* D. D. the 2d Edition. Printed for *C. King.*

18. A Letter to the Freeholders, &c. of Great Britain, concerning their Duty before and after the Election of their Representatives; with the Characters of several Statesmen and political Writers. Printed for *J. Roberts,* pr. 6 *d.*

19. The Mock Lawyer. A Ballad Opera. Written by Mr *Phillips.* Sold by *T. Astley,* price 1 *s.*

20. The Livery Rake, and Country Lass. An Opera. Printed for *J. Watts.*

21. The Finish'd Rake: Or, Gallantry in Perfection: Being the genuine and entertaining Adventures of a Young Gentleman of Fortune. Printed for *A. Dodd,* pr. 1 *s.*

22. A Paraphrase and Notes on St *Paul's* Epistle to *Titus.* In Imitation of Mr *Locke's* Manner. To which is added an Essay concerning the abolishing the Ceremonial Law, &c. Printed for *R. Ford,* pr. 2 *s.* 6 *d.*

23. The Happy Marriage. In Imitation of Virgil's Tityrus. With other Poems. Printed for *J. Duke,* pr. 6 *d.*

24. Erasmi Colloquia Selecta Decem: Or, Ten Select Colloquies of Erasmus. By *N. Bailey.* Printed for *J. Brotherton.*

25. Of the Duties of the People towards their Ministers. A Sermon preach'd at the Ordination of Mr *Daniel Stevens,* in White street, *Southwark,* May 30, 1733. By *Peter Goodwin,* pr. 1 *s.*

26. Phædri Augusti Cæsaris Liberti. Fabularum Æsopiarum, Liber Quinque. Cum Versione Anglica, in qua Verbum de Verbo, quantum fieri licuit, exprimitur, Notis, quoq; & Indice. Or, the 5 Books of Æsopian Fables of Phædrus Augustus Cæsar's Freedman; with an English Translation as literal as possible, Notes, and an Index. By the Rev. Mr. *Edmund Wayes.* Printed for Mess. *Bettesworth* and *Hitch,* price 1 *s.*

The Remainder in our next.

The Gentleman's Magazine:

London Gazette
Lond. Jour.
Fog's Journ.
App ebee's ::
Read's : : ::
Craftsman :
U. Spectator
Grubstreet J
W. ly Register
Free - Briton
Daily Court
Daily :: Post
Dai. Journal
Da. Post-boy
D. Advertiser
St James's Eb.
Whitehall Eb
Lodon Eb Eſg
Weekly Miſc
Corncutter's J.
Gen. Eb. Poſt
What d'ye call't J

St John's Gate.

York - News
Dublin 6 :::
Edinburgh 2
Briſtol :::: :
Norwich 2:
Exeter 2 :::
Worceſter ::
Northampton
Glouceſter ::
Stamford ::
Nottingham
Bury Journ.
Cheſter ditto
Derby ditto
Ipſwich do.
Reading do.
Leeds Merc
Newcaſtle C
Canterbury
Boſton ::: ¶
Jamaica, &c.
Barbados : :

Or, Monthly Intelligencer

For NOVEMBER, 1733.

CONTAINING,

more in Quantity, and greater Variety, than any Book of the Kind and Price.

I. Proceedings and Debates in Parliament continued, *viz.* The firſt Grand Debate on the Exciſe Scheme, for improving the Revenue on Tobacco, open'd with the Motion and Speech of Sir R——t W——le, and continued by Mr A——n P——y, Sir P——l M——n, Mr A——y G——l, W——m P——y, Eſq; Sir W——m W——m, and Sir J——n H——d C——n; with an exact Liſt of Thoſe who voted on either Side of the Queſtion moved for, and the Reſolutions thereupon.

II. A View of the Weekly Eſſays, humourous, moral, and religious.

III. Of the Political Diſſertations and Diſputes.

IV. A ſelect Collection of Poetry; *viz. Staniſlaus*; the *Happy Nuptials*; on

an Election at *Grantham*; *ad Declarandum*, to Lord *Gower*; on Dr *Swift's* Effigy, done by *Vertue*; the Sigh; Laureat Sentenc'd; a Leaf for his Garland; Nuptial Song; the cheating Uncle; Ld H——y to Mr *Poyntz*; Politick Cit; a Remonſtrance from the Clouds; The Parſon's Cow; a Riddle, Epigrams, &c.

V. Domeſtic Occurences, Births, Marriages, Deaths, Promotions Civil and Eccleſiaſtical, &c.

VI. Prices of Goods, and Stocks; Bill of Mortality, &c.

VII. Foreign Affairs.

VIII. Books and Pamphlets.

IX. A Table of Contents.

By SYLVANUS URBAN, Gent.

LONDON: Printed, and ſold at St *John's Gate*: By F. *Jefferies*, in *Ludgate-ſtreet*, all other Bookſellers; and by the Perſons who ſerve Gentlemen with the Newſpapers. All the Numbers wanted are in the Preſs, and will ſpeedily be publiſh'd.
   A few are done on Royal Paper, of which Compleat Sets may be had.

CONTENTS.

THE
Gentleman's Magazine:
NOVEMBER, 1733.

PROCEEDINGS *and* **DEBATES** *in* last Session of Parliament.

DEBATE *on the* Excise Scheme *March* 14, *in a* Committee *of the* House *of* Commons. Mr C---r *of the* E---r, to this Effect:

SIR,

AS I had the Honour to move for the House's resolving itself into this Committee, I think it incumbent on me to open to you what was then intended to be proposed as the Subject of your Consideration. We are now in a Committee for considering of the most proper Methods for the better Security and Improvement of the Duties and Revenues already charged on, and payable from Tobacco and Wines: This can be done in no Way so proper or effectual, as that of preventing for the future those Frauds by which the publick Revenues have been so much injured in Times passed. I know, who ever attempts to remedy Frauds, attempts a Thing, very disagreeable to all those who have been guilty of them, or who expect a Benefit by such in Time to come. This, *Sir,* I am fully sensible of, and from this have sprung all those Clamours raised without Doors against what I am now to propose. The Smugglers, fraudulent Dealers, and those who have for many Years been enriching themselves by cheating their Country, foresaw, that if the Scheme I am now to propose took Effect, their profitable Trade would be at an End; this gave them the Alarm, and from them I am persuaded it is, all those Clamours have originally proceeded. ——In this 'tis certain they have been most strenuously assisted and supported by another Set of People, who, from Motives much worse, and of much more dangerous Consequence to their Country, are fond of improving every Opportunity for stirring up the People, to Mutiny and Sedition. But, *Sir,* notwithstanding all the Clamours such wicked and deceitful Men have been able to raise, as the Scheme I have to propose will be a great Improvement to the publick Revenue, an Improvement of a or 300,000 l

per Ann, perhaps more, and as it will likewise be of great Advantage to the fair Trader, I thought it my Duty, not only as being in the Station I am in; but also as a Member in this House, to lay it before you; for no such Clamours shall ever deter me from doing what I think is my Duty, or from proposing any thing I am convinced will be of such signal Benefit to the Revenue and to the Trade of my Country.—— It has been most industriously spread abroad, that the Scheme I am now to propose, was a Scheme for a General Excise, but I aver no such Scheme ever entered my Head, nor, for what I know, the Head of any Man I am aquainted with: My Thoughts were always confined solely to those two Branches of the Revenue arising from the Duty, on Wine and Tobacco; and it was repeated Advices I had of the notorious Frauds committed in these two Branches, and the Clamours even of some of the Merchants themselves that made me turn my Thoughts particularly towards considering those two Branches In order to find out, if possible, some Remedy for the growing Evil; what I am now going to propose will, I believe, if agreed to, be an effectual Remedy; but If I now fail in, it will be the last Attempt of this Kind I shall ever make, I believe the last that will ever be made, either by me or any that shall succeed me in the Station I am now in.——At present, *Sir,* I shall lay before you only the Case as it now stands with Respect to the Tobacco-trade, and the Revenue arising therefrom; it will be necessary first to consider the condition of our Planters of Tobacco in *America*; if we can give any Credit to what they themselves say we must conclude they are reduced almost to a State of Dispair, by the many Frauds committed in that Trade, the heavy Duties the Importers of Tobacco are obliged to pay upon Importation, and the ill Usage they have met with from their Factors and Correspondents in *England,* who, from being their Servants, are become their Lords and Masters. These poor People have sent Home many Representations of the bad State of their Affairs, and have lately sent over a Gentiman with a Remonſtrance ſetting forth their Grievances, and praying for ſome ſpeedy Relief: This they may obtain by Means of the Scheme I intend to propoſe, and I believe it is from this Scheme only that they can expect any Relief.——Next, we are to conſider the State of the Tobacco-trade, with Regard to the fair Trader; the Man who deals fairly with the Publick, as well as with private Men, who honeſtly pays, all thoſe Duties the Publick is juſtly entitled to, finds himſelf foreſtalled almoſt in every Market within the Iſland, by the Smuggler and fradulent Dealer; and even as to our foreign Trade in Tobacco, thoſe who have no Regard to Honour, to Religion, or the Welfare of their Country, but are every Day contriving to cheat the Publick by Perjuries and falſe Entries, are the greateſt Gainers; and it will always be ſo, unleſs we can fall upon ſome Way of putting it out of their Power to carry on any on any ſuch Frauds for the future.—— Laſtly, Sir, we ought to conſider the great Loſs ſuſtained by the Publick, by means of the Frauds committed in the Tobacco-trade, and the Addition that muſt certainly be made to the publick Revenue, if thoſe Frauds can be prevented. By this Addition we may be enabled to relieve the Nation from ſome of thoſe Taxes which it has laboured under ſo many Years; whereas, as the Caſe now ſtands the honeſt Part of the Nation are charged with Taxes which they would be free from, if the fraudulent Dealers and Smugglers could be obliged to pay that is juſtly due by them to the Publick. This, Sir, will, I am convinced, be the Effect of the Scheme I am to propoſe; whoever therefore views it in its proper Light, muſt ſee the Planters, the fair Traders and the Publick ranged upon one Side in Favour of it, and none but the unfair Traders and the Tobacco-factors upon the other.—I ſhall beg Leave to mention to you, Sir, ſome of thoſe Frauds which have come to my Knowledge. The Evidence I have had of them is to me very convincing. But in ſuch Caſes Gentlemen ought always to conſider what Evidence it is impoſſible to bring, what Evidence it is by the Nature of the thing unreaſonable to expect.

Then he gave a moſt exact Account of the ſeveral Frauds practiſed of late Years in the Tobacco-trade, from which he made Calculations of the Loſs the Publick thereby ſuſtained, particularly that of getting the Tobacco weighed at an under Weight upon Importation, and upon Exportation at a Weight much above what it ought to be.

A particular Inſtance of this Fraud, (*ſays he*) we came lately to the Knowledge of by mere Accident: One *Midford*, who had been a conſiderable Tobacco-merchant, happened to fail, he owed a large Sum of Money upon Bond to the Crown, whereupon

an Extent was iſſued out immediately againſt him, and thereby the Government got Poſſeſſion of all his Books, by which the Fraud he had been guilty of was diſcover'd; for it appeared as may be ſeen by one of his Books I have in my Hand, that on the Column where the falſe Quantities had been entered at the Importation, by Colluſion between him and the Officer, by which he paid or bonded the Duty payable on Importation, a Slip of Paper had been ſo artfully paſted on, that it could not be diſcover'd, and upon this Slip of Paper were written the real Quantities which were entered, becauſe he was obliged to produce the ſame Book when that Tobacco was entered for Exportation; but then on Exportation the Tobacco was entered according to the Quantities marked on this ſlip of Paper by which he got a Drawback, or his Bonds to near double the Value of what he had actually paid Duty for on Importation. Yet, Sir, this *Midford* was as honeſt a Man, and as fair a Trader as any in *London*; I mean, that before theſe Frauds came to be diſcovered, he was always reckoned as honeſt a Man and as fair a Trader as any in *London*, or in any other Part of the Nation.

After this he mentioned the ſeveral Frauds following, viz. That of Re-landing the Tobacco after it was ſhipped off for Exportation ; of Socking Tobacco, which was a Cant-word uſed for ſtealing and ſmuggling it out of the Ships after their Arrival in the River, before they were unloaded at the Cuſtom-houſe. That of Stripping the Leaves from the Stalks, and afterwards ſplitting and preſſing the Stalks by an Engine contrived for that Purpoſe, and then exporting them. That of giving Bonds for Duty payable on Importation, whereby the Government had loſt ſeveral large Sums by the Failure of Payments of ſuch Bonds. That of the rich Moneyed Men making Prompt-payments, by which the Publick was obliged to allow them Ten per Cent. Diſcount as to the Duties, and by entering the Tobacco ſoon after for Exportation, they drew back the whole Duties, ſo that the Government actually loſt Ten per Cent. upon all the Tobacco ſo entered.

Theſe Frauds, Sir, (*ſays he*) are notoriouſly known; and as the Laws of the Cuſtoms have been found ineffectual for preventing them it is propoſed to add the Laws of Exciſe, and by Means of both it is probable, I may ſay certain, all ſuch Frauds will be prevented. *Here he gave an Account of the ſeveral Acts of Parliament for laying Duties on Tobacco; then he went on.* By all which, Sir, it appears that the Duties now payable upon Tobacco on Importation, amount to 6d. and one third Part of a Penny, *per* Pound Weight, all which muſt be paid down in ready Money on importation, which the Allowance of ten *per Cent.* on prompt-payment, or otherways muſt be Bonds given with Sureties for the Payment thereof, which is of

us

ten a great Lofs to the Publick, and it is always a great Inconvenience to the Merchant-importer; whereas by what I am to propofe the whole Duties to be paid for the future will amount to no more than 4*d.* 3 Farthings *per* Pound-weight, and not to be paid till the Tobacco comes to be fold for Home-confumption; fo that if the Merchant exports his Tobacco, he will be quite free from all Payment of Duty, or giving Bond therefore, or finding proper Sureties for joining with him in fuch Bonds; he will have nothing to do but to re-load his Tobacco on board a Ship for Exportation, without being at the Trouble to attend for having his Bonds cancelled, or for taking out Debentures for the Drawbacks; all which I conceive, *Sir*, muft be a great Eafe to the fair Trader; and to every fuch Trader the preventing of Frauds muft be a great Advantage, becaufe it will put all the Tobacco-traders in *Britain* upon the fame Footing, which is but juft and equal.---Now, *Sir*, to make this Eafe effectual to the fair Trader, by preventing as much as poffible any Frauds in Time to come, I propofe, to join the Laws of Excife to thofe of the Cuftoms, and to leave the one Penny, or rather three Farthings *per* Pound, called the further Subfidy, to be ftill charged at the Cuftom-houfe on Importation of any Tobacco, which three Farthings fhall be payable to his Majefty's Civil Lift as heretofore; and I propofe that all Tobacco for the future, after being weighed at the Cuftom-houfe, and charged with the faid 3 Farthings *per* Pound, fhall be lodged in a Warehoufe to be appointed by the Commiffioners of the Excife for that Purpofe, of which Warehoufe the Merchant-importer fhall have one Lock and Key, and the Warehoufe-keeper to be appointed by the faid Commiffioners fhall have another, in order that the Tobacco may lie fafe in that Warehoufe till the Merchant finds a Market for it, either for Exportation or for Home-confumption: That if his Market be for Exportation, he may apply to his Warehoufe-keeper and take out as much for that Purpofe as he has Occafion for, which when weighed at the Cuftom-houfe fhall be difcharged of the 3 Farthings *per* Pound with which it was charged on Importation; fo that the Merchant may then export it without further Trouble: But if his Market be for Home confumption, he fhall then pay the 3 Farthings charged upon it at the Cuftom-houfe on Importation, and then calling his Warehoufe-keeper may deliver it to the Buyer, on paying an Inland-duty of 4*d. per* Pound-weight, to the proper Officer appointed to receive the fame.---- And whereas, *Sir*, all the Penalties and Forfeitures due by the Laws now in Being for Collecting the Duties on Tobacco, which is not given to the Informers, now belong to the Crown, I propofe that all fuch fhall for the future belong

(*Gent Mag.* Vol. III. No. xxxv.)

long to the Publick, and be applicable to the fame Ufes to which the faid Duties fhall be made applicable by Parliament; and for that Purpofe I have his Majefty's Commands to acquaint this Houfe, that he, out of his great Regard for the publick Good, with Pleafure confents that they fhall be fo applied, a Condefcenfion in his Majefty, that I hope every Gentleman is fully fenfible of, and will freely acknowledge.---I know, *Sir,* there has been this Objection made, againft what I now propofe: That many Retailers will be fubjected to being tried in a Multitude of Cafes by the Commiffioners of Excife, from whom there is no Appeal, but to Commiffioners of Appeal, or to Juftices of Peace in the Country, all named by the King and removable at Pleafure, from whom the Appellants cannot expect to meet with any Juftice or Redrefs. I am far from thinking there is any Ground for this Complaint, but in Order to obviate any Objection of this Nature, I propofe that all Appeals in this, as well as in all other Cafes relating to the Excife, fhall for the future be heard and determined by two or three of the Judges to be named by his Majefty, out of the twelve Judges belonging to *Weft-minfter-hall*; and that in the Country all Appeals from the firft Sentence of his Majefty's Juftices of the Peace, fhall be to the Judge of Affize upon the next Circuit, who fhall in all Cafes proceed to hear and determine fuch Appeals in the moft fummary Way, without the Formality of Proceedings in Courts of Law or Equity. From fuch Judges, and from fuch a Manner of Proceeding, every Man muft expect to meet with the utmoft Difpatch, and with the moft impartial Juftice.---- This is the Scheme which has been reprefented in fuch a dreadful and terrible Light: That many headed Monfter, which was to devour the People, and to commit fuch Ravages over the whole Nation. How juftly it has been reprefented in fuch a Light, I fhall leave to this Committee, and to the whole World without Doors to judge. I have faid, I will fay it again, that whatever Apprehenfions and Terrors People may have been brought under from a falfe and malicious Reprefentation of what they neither did nor could poffibly know or underftand, I am firmly perfwaded, when they do come to know and fully to underftand the Scheme which I have now had the Honour to propofe to you, they will view it in another Light; and that if it has the good Fortune to be approved of by Parliament, and comes to take Effect, the People will foon feel the happy Confequences thereof, and will no longer think thofe People their Friends who have fo grofsly impofed on their Underftandings. ---I look upon it as a moft innocent Scheme; I am convinced it can be hurtful to none but Smugglers and unfair Traders; I am certain it will be of great Benefit and Advantage to the publick Revenue; and if I had thought otherwise of it, I never would have ventured to have proposed it in this Place; therefore I shall now beg leave to move, that it may be resolved, That it is the Opinion of this Committee, that the Subsidy and additional Duty upon Tobacco of the *British* Plantations, granted by an Act of the 12th of K. *Charles* II. and the Impost thereon, granted by an Act of the first of K. *James* II. and also the one third Subsidy thereon, granted by an Act of 2d of Q. *Anne*, (amounting in the whole to 5 Pence and one third Part of a Penny *per* Pound) for several Terms of Years in the said respective Acts mentioned, and which have since been continued and made perpetual, subject to Redemption by Parliament, shall, from and after the 24th Day of *June* 1733, cease and determine.

Upon this Speech and Motion ensued the grand Debate, in which the following Gentlemen spoke in Substance, or to the Effect as follows, viz.

Mr A—n P—y) Sir, The Hon. Gentleman has taken up a great deal of the Time of the Committee, in stating a great Number and Variety of Facts, and in drawing Conclusions, upon the Supposition that every one of those Facts was exactly as he has been pleased to represent them to us. This, I cannot D entirely agree with; for, if all those Facts were exactly as he has represented them, and if all the Computations he has made upon that Supposition were just, that Quantity of Tobacco, the Duties of which the Publick is thereby supposed to be entirely defrauded of, would amount to a much greater Quantity of Tobacco Yearly than grows in the whole E Country from which we fetch that Commodity. I did not expect to have heard such a long Detail of Facts, or so many particular Computations. I do not think it at all necessary on the present Occasion; I expected the Gentleman would have taken a much more general and a more just Method. I thought he would have F stated to us the Quantity of Tobacco Yearly imported, the Quantity Yearly exported, (See p. 133 G) and would have given us the best Proofs that could be found for justifying his Computations in that respect, because from thence every Man might have easily seen what Quantity remained for home Consumption, and what Sum of Money that would have G Yearly brought in, if the Duties had been all regularly paid; and upon comparing that with what those Duties have really amounted to for some Years past, we might have been able to have made some guess of the Value of the Frauds that have been committed, and of the H Advantage that may accrue to the Publick, supposing that all Frauds were to have been by his Scheme prevented in time to come.--This is the proper, the only Way of coming at any certain Knowledge in the Affair before us, but I am afraid, if we consider it in this Way, we

should find the Scheme now proposed to us of no such mighty Advantage to the publick Revenue as has been represented, even · supposing all Frauds be thereby entirely prevented; and considering that no Method of Collection, no A Pains or Penalties, can be supposed effectual for preventing every Fraud that may in time to come be invented and set on foot; we should have found no great Temptation for agreeing to any Scheme by which the Liberties of our Country may be brought into the least Danger, for the sake of any Advantage that we could B suppose would have thereby accrued to the publick Revenue. That there are Frauds committed in the Tobacco-trade, I make no Doubt; there are too many in that as well as in every other Branch of the publick Revenue : But upon a fair State of the Case, I am sure they cannot amount to near that Value which the Hon. Gentleman has been pleased to mention; C and therefore I shall beg leave to examine a little the particular Frauds and Calculations mentioned by him.

Here he examined all the Frauds that had been mentioned, and all the Computations that had been made; more particularly as to the Bonds he said, It has been pretended that the Publick has sustain'd, and are still in D Danger of sustaining great Losses by the Method of granting Bonds for the Duties payable on Tobacco : This I had before heard hinted at by the hon. Gentleman, and therefore I have lately had a Meeting with several of the Merchants in *London*, trading in Tobacco : We have examin'd that Affair, and I can now tell that Gentleman, that I have E it in Commission from them to propose, that if the Government will give us a Discount but of 20,000 *l*. we will secure the Payment of all the Bonds they are now possessed of, which are not become desperate by the Bondsmen being already gone off.---As to that Fraud called Sucking, it has been already discover'd, and F I hope prevented. (See P. 351 H) But then it was the Merchants that discover'd it, and complained of it to the Commissioners of the Customs, and assisted the Officers of the Customs in putting an effectual Stop thereto. This I must know, because I had the Honour to go at the Head of several Merchants trading in Tobacco to the Commissioners of the Customs, to request that we might be allowed to give a Gratuity to one of their Officers, who had been most instrumental in the detecting and preventing that Fraud, and accordingly I paid that Officer a very handsome Sum of Money, which we all thought his Diligence and Integrity well deserved. --- As to the Frauds committed at the Weighing of the Tobacco either on Importation or Exportation, I am afraid they are too frequent, but as the Tobacco is always weighed upon the publick Custom-house Keys, where Custom-house

Officers

Officers fwarm like Bees before a Bee-hive, and as there muft be two or three Officers of the Cuftoms, attending and over-looking the weighing of every Caſk of Tobacco, we cannot fuppofe that thefe Frauds were ever fo enormous as they are reprefented to be. Whatever Frauds are committed in that Way muft be either by the Neglect or the Collufion of the Officers, and I cannot fee how the Scheme now propofed to us will make the Officers either of the Cuftoms or the Excife more diligent in their Duty, or more faithful than they were heretofore. As to the re-landing of Tobacco after it has been entered for Exportation, it was never pretended that that was practifed at the Port of *London*, nor that any great Quantities of fuch Tobacco were ever confumed in *London*. That is a Practice that may perhaps have been frequent in the Northern Parts of the Ifland, and in fome diftant Creeks and Corners of the Coaft, and while there is fuch a vaft Difproportion between the prime Coft and the Duties on Tobacco, I may prophefy that in fuch remote Places this will always be a Practice: It could not be prevented by ten times the Number of Officers we have, even tho' we had a much more numerous Army, to fupport them than we have at prefent. And as for the Stripping, Cutting, and Preffing the Stalks, and the Engine invented for that Purpofe, it is no Fraud, nor a late Difcovery; it is a bufinefs that has been honeftly and publickly carried on for many Years; that has improved our Tobacco-trade, and is as common and as well known as the Bufinefs of a Woollen or a Linnen-Draper.----Permit me now, to take fome Notice of the Tobacco-planters, and of the Hardfhips they are laid under by their Tobacco-factors, who are, it feems, now become their Lords and Mafters. I am fure none of them ever thought of Complaining till they were put upon it by Letters and by Applications from hence. There are Hardfhips in all Trades, which Men muft neceffarily fubmit to, or give up their Bufinefs; but every Man that underftands the Tobacco-trade muft fee, that the Hardfhips the Factors labour under, are by much the moft numerous and the moft grievous; and if this Scheme fhould take Effect, they will become fo grievous, that no Man would be able to continue in the Trade, by which the Planters would be utterly undone, and the Trade quite loft to this Nation; for it will be impoffible for them to manage their Plantations, or to fend their Produce to *Britain*, without having fome confiderable Merchants fettled here, to fend Ships to fetch the fame from *America*, to receive and difpofe of it after it is landed here, and to fupply them with ready Money till their Tobacco can be brought to a proper Market. As to the Remonftrance mentioned by the hon. Gentleman, to have been lately fent over by

the Tobacco-planters, it was obtained by Letters fent from hence, and I believe many of thofe who joined in it, now heartily repent of what they have done; it was drawn up in the Form of a Petition to this Houfe, and was defigned to have been prefented, but it feems the Promoters of it have thought better of the Matter: However, that it was obtained in the unfair Manner I have reprefented, I am now ready to prove.---This then being the Cafe, as the Scheme now propofed cannot be fuppofed to be of any great Benefit to the publick Revenue, as it will be fo far from being an Advantage to the fair Trader, or to the honeft Planter, that it may probably ruin both, and entirely deftroy our Tobacco-trade; tho' I and all honeft Men, (and I defy that hon. Gentleman, I defy the whole World to reproach me with one unfair Practice, in the whole Courfe of my Life) I fay tho' I and all honeft Men wifh from our Hearts, that Frauds may be prevented in this as well as in every other Branch of the publick Revenue, yet I cannot give my Affent to a Propofition that may be of fo dangerous Confequence; a Propofition which I look upon to be inconfiftent with our Conftitution; I am convinced it would prove to be a moft fatal Stroke to the Liberties of my Country, which will I doubt not be made plainly appear by other Gentlemen, of much greater Abilities than mine; and to every Man who has a Regard for his Country, or for the People he reprefents, this laft muft be a fufficient Reafon for being againft it, even tho' it were, other ways, the moft beneficial Scheme that had ever been propofed.---But fince I look upon my being a Member of this Houfe, as the greateft Glory of my Life, and that Day on which I was chofe one of the Reprefentatives of the City of *London*, as the moft aufpicious Day of my whole Life, I cannot tamely fit ftill and hear the whole Body of the Merchants of that great City reprefented by that hon. Gentleman as a Pack of Rogues, Smugglers, and unfair Traders. It is a Treatment they no way deferve, and fuch a Treatment as I am fure they never will forget, I believe they never will forgive. (See p. 175 E)

Sir *P---l M---n*,] Sir, when I firft heard of this Scheme, I was in the Country, and there I muft fay it had been reprefented in fuch a Light, as created a general Diflike to it, and raifed great Apprehenfions in the Minds of moft People. It was reprefented as a Scheme for introducing a general Excife; fuch a Scheme, I own, I would not allow myfelf to think was contrived or approved of by any Gentleman in the Adminiftration. I did imagine that all thofe in the Adminiftration, were very well convinced that a general Excife was what the People of *England* would never quietly fubmit to, and therefore I would not allow myfelf to believe, any of them would ever countenance a Scheme which had the least Tendency that Way : But now after having heard it opened, and fully explained, I cannot but think it is a wide Step towards establishing a general Excise upon the People of this Nation, and therefore I must be excused in giving my Dissent to it.——In so far as it relates to Trade, with which it certainly has a very close Connection, I shall leave to be explained by others who are more conversant in those Affairs than I am ; and as to how far it may be a Remedy for Frauds I will not take upon me to say ; but there is another Concern, which I shall always, while I have the Honour to sit in this House, have a particular Eye to, and that is, Sir, the Liberty of my Country. The Danger this Scheme seems to threaten to the Liberty of many of my Fellow-Subjects, is alone of sufficient Force to make me give my Negative to the Question moved for. Let Gentlemen but cast their Eyes back on the several Laws that have been made since the Revolution, they will find, that there has been already more Power vested in the Crown than may be thought altogether consistent with the Constitution of a free Country, and therefore I hope this House will never think of adding to that Power.——The Laws of Excise, Sir, have always been look'd on as most grievous to the Subject: All those already subjected to such Laws, are, in my Opinion, in so far depriv'd of their Liberty; and since by this Scheme, a great many more of his Majesty's faithful Subjects are to be subjected to those arbitrary Laws, let the Advantages accruing to the Publick from it, be never so great, or so many, they will be purchased too dear at the Expence of the Liberty of the meanest of his Majesty's Subjects; for even the meanest Man in the Nation, has as natural and as good a Right to his Liberty, as the greatest Man in this or in any other Kingdom.——Our neighbouring Nations in *Europe*, were all once free ; the People of every one of them had once as many Liberties and Privileges to boast of, as we have now, but at present they are most of them reduc'd to a State of Slavery ; they have no Liberty, no Property, no Law, nor any Thing they can depend on. Let us examine their Histories, let us enquire into the Methods, by which they were depriv'd of their Liberties. and we shall find a very near Resemblance between those Methods and the Scheme now propos'd to us. Almost in every Country in the World, the Liberties of the People have been destroyed under Pretence of preserving, or of rescuing the People from some great Evil, to which it was pretended they were exposed. This is the very Case now before us; in order to enable the Crown to prevent some little Frauds pretended to have been committed in the antient Method of collecting the pub-

lick Revenue, it is proposed to us to put such a Power in the Hands of the Crown, as may enable some future Prince to enslave the whole Nation. This is really the Light in which this Scheme appears to me, but to the hon. Gentleman who proposed it. I am perswaded, it appears in a quite different Light, otherwise I am certain he would never have proposed it to this Committee: However, since the Generality of the Nation have already shewn a great Dislike to it ; I therefore hope the hon. Gentleman may be prevailed on to delay it till another Session of Parliament. In such a Delay there can be no Danger, no great Loss to the Publick, especially, since the Money to be thereby raised, is not so much as proposed to be apply'd to the current Services of this present Year. If it be delay'd till another Session of Parliament, Gentlemen will then have Time to consider it fully, and to consult with their Constituents about it ; by that Time it may possibly appear in a quite different Light, both to me and to many other Gentlemen without Doors as well as within ; and then if upon Examination it appears to be as good a Thing as some Gentlemen now seem to believe, it will without doubt be approved of by the Generality of those without, as well as by the Majority of those within.——But I hope those Gentlemen who have now so good an Opinion of the Scheme will not think of thrusting it down People's Throats, when they see that the Generality of the Nation have a quite different Opinion of it ; such an Attempt might produce Consequences, I tremble to think of ; and this is another Motive which is of great Weight with me. I have, Sir, the Honour to know his Majesty, his Royal Person I have formerly had the Honour to approach, and I know him to be a Prince of so much Goodness, that, were this Scheme represented in this Light to him, he never would approve of it ; to him it will always be a sufficient Reason against any Proposition, that the Generality of his People have shewn their Dislike to it. I love his Majesty, I have a sincere and a dutiful Respect for him and all his royal Family, and therefore I shall always be afraid of any Thing that may alienate the Affections of any of his Majesty's faithful Subjects, which I believe would be the certain Consequence of the present Establishment of this Scheme; therefore if the Question be now pushed, I shall most heartily give my Negative to it.

Mr A---y G---l.] Sir, After the hon. Gentleman had opened to the Committee in a Manner so full and so clear, a Scheme which had met with so unfair and so ungenerous a Treatment, before those who treated it so could know any thing about it, I little expected that the hon. Gentleman who spoke last, or any Gentleman in this Committee, could have taken it in the Light they now do. In my Opinion, the Debate is now put upon

upon a Footing very different from what it ought to be; what can the Affair now before us have to do with our Constitution? There is nothing, there can be nothing supposed to be in the Proposition made by my hon. Friend, that can in the least tend towards incroaching on our Constitution, or towards affecting the Liberty of the Subject. The only Consideration at present before us is, whether we shall allow those gross Frauds and Abuses formerly committed in the Tobacco-trade to be still carried on with Impunity, or if we shall accept of a Remedy, which by effectually preventing these Frauds for the future, will considerably improve the publick Revenue, will be of great Advantage to the fair Trader, and of singular Use and Benefit to the whole Nation?---This, Sir, is the plain Question now before us, and if it be consider'd in its proper Light, without confounding it with other Matters with which it has no Manner of Relation, I am sure it cannot admit of any Debate. The hon. Gentleman in opening this Affair to us, made it so manifest, that there have been great Frauds committed in that Branch of Trade, and that the preventing of those Frauds wou'd be a great Improvement to the publick Revenue, and what he advanced upon that Head, has not been opposed or contradicted: And this House has been upon all Occasions so very careful of the publick Revenues, so ready to agree to any Measures for preventing Abuses in the collecting of them, that I cannot help thinking that the Dislike which appears against the Remedy now proposed, must proceed from some other Motives than Gentlemen are willing to own. ---- It is certain that by the Frauds and Abuses that are committed in this Branch of the Revenue, not only the Publick is cheated of what is due to them, but likewise every private Consumer is most grosly imposed on; for he pays the same Price as if the Duties had actually been paid. He pays a high Price for what he consumes, but then he has this for his Comfort, that he thinks a great Part of that high Price goes towards the pub'ick Good of his Country, but in all fraudulent Trade he is imposed on; the high Price he pays goes every Farthing of it into the Pocket of the fraudulent Dealer. This then being plainly the Case, I should think that the Gentlemen, who are to oppose this Scheme, should endeavour to shew us, that no such Frauds as are pretended, have been committed, or are so inconsiderable that they are not worth minding, or that what is now proposed would be no sort of Remedy for them; but upon the present Question, to talk of our Constitution, seems really to me to be a sort of Insinuation, as if Frauds in the Collecting of the publick Revenue, were become a Part of our Constitution, and that whoever attempts to Remedy them must attempt something against our Consti-

tution: And as to the Liberty of the Subject it is not possible for me to find out any Liberty that can be struck at by the Scheme now before us, but the Liberty of Smuggling; for as to National Liberty, as to that Liberty which has always been, and I hope always will be the Glory of the People of these Kingdoms, it is certain, that our publick Revenues are its greatest Security; How then can that Scheme be said to tend towards the destroying of Liberty, which so evidently tends towards the Improvement of that upon which our Liberty manifestly depends? --- As to the raising of Clamours and Disaffection among his Majesty's faithful Subjects, there can be no Reason for apprehending any such Thing from the Scheme now proposed to us: Whatever Clamours may have been unjustly raised by ill-designing Men against the Scheme before it was known, will certainly all evanish as soon as it comes to be publickly known, that there never was any Thing intended by the Scheme, but only to enable the Publick to receive those Duties they are already by Law entitled to, and to prevent the fair Trader's being undone by Rogues and Smugglers; so that one strong Argument with me for agreeing to the Scheme is that by carrying it into Execution, and thereby shewing to every Man what it really is, those ill-grounded Clamours, which have been raised by the Enemies of the Government, may be allay'd, and may be made appear to be at least as groundless as they were at first malicious. Besides, as one of the chief Things intended by this Scheme is the Relief of the Landed-Interest, it must contribute towards establishing his Majesty and his Government in the Hearts and Affections of all the Landed-Gentlemen in *England*, when they see themselves so considerably relieved as to a Tax which they have been charged with for a great many Years, and that without loading them or any of their Fellow Subjects with any new Tax whatever, or obliging one honest Man in the Kingdom to contribute a Farthing to the Publick Charge more than he did before. This must secure to his Majesty the Affections of all honest Men, and it will greatly improve our Character among our Foreign Neighbours; for when they see that the Government may be supported in Times of Peace, without the Assistance of that Imposition which is yearly raised upon the Landholders of *Great-Britain*, they will be careful of giving us any Disturbance, they will all see that we have a Fund in Reserve, ready at all Times and sufficient for supporting a most heavy and expensive War. As to the Severity of the Laws of Excise, I am surpriz'd to hear Gentlemen talk so much of it as they do. They talk of those Laws, as if there were something in them most singularly severe, when it is well known that the Laws of the Customs are in many Cases as

severe

severe as those of the Excise, and the Powers granted by the former are in most Cases as extensive as the Powers granted by the latter: An Officer of the Customs has in many Cases a Power of entering the House of any Subject in *Britain*: This is a Power absolutely necessary, and will as long as we have any Duties to be levied: It is a Power they have had for many Years, and yet it never has been, I hope it never will be abused; if ever it should, the Parliament would without doubt severely chastise that Officer that committed such an Abuse, or those Commissioners who dar'd to encourage it. In this therefore the Laws of the Excise are no more severe than the Laws of the Customs, and in most other Cases we shall find them pretty much the same with respect to Severity; for which Reason I could not but be surpriz'd to hear the hon. Gentleman who spoke last say, that he thought all those who were subject to the Laws of Excise were downright Slaves, and entirely depriv'd of their Liberty: I believe that most of those People, who are now subject to the Laws of Excise, look upon themselves to enjoy as much Liberty, as any other of his Majesty's Subjects. ——One of the great Complaints against this Scheme is that it will greatly encrease the Number of Excise-Officers; a new Army of Excisemen it is said must be raised for the Execution of this Scheme, and this may be of dangerous Consequence to our Liberties. But how little Weight there is in this Argument I leave to every Gentleman to judge: The whole Number proposed to be added is not above 126 Officers, besides Warehouse-keepers; but granting that there were to be 150, is this Nation to be enslaved by 150 little Excisemen? In this there is really something so ridiculous, that I am almost ashamed to mention it. —— Another Objection is, that thereby a great many People will be subjected to be tried by the Commissioners of Excise, or by Commissioners of Appeal, who are entirely dependent on the Crown, and removable at Pleasure; but this Objection is I think entirely removed by making the Appeal to three Judges in *Westminster-hall*, who are all Judges for Life, and are consequently entirely independent on the Crown. To this the Gentlemen answer, that even before those Judges, the Subject is not to be tried by a Jury, and this is loudly complained of, as if the subjecting of *Englishmen* to any Tryal but that by a Jury were a great Innovation, and a dangerous Encroachment upon our Constitution. I own, that by the Great Charter, by one of the fundamental Articles of our Constitution, every *Englishman* is to be tried by his Peers; but has not the Wisdom of the Nation found it necessary to admit of many Exceptions to this general Rule; we have several of our most eminent Courts, which are in every Method of their Proceeding an Exception to this Rule; in

the Court of Chancery we have no Trials by Juries; in the High Court of Admiralty we have no Trials by Juries; and in many particular Cases it is order'd that the Affair shall be tried in the most summary Way without any Jury: In all these Cases the Wisdom of the Nation found it necessary to depart from the general Rule established by the *Great Charter*, and therefore they alter'd the Method of Trial; why should not the Legislature now do the same? Is not their Power the same? And if they see good Reason for it in the present Case, ought not they to do it? Whatever is done by the Wisdom of Parliament becomes a Part of our Constitution; and whatever new Method of Trial is thereby introduced becomes from thenceforth as much a Part of our Constitution as ever the old one was. —— If ever there was a Reason in any Case for altering the antient Method of Tryal by Jury, I am sure there is with Regard to Trials concerning the Revenue: Every Gentleman the least conversant in the Courts of *Westminster-hall*, well-knows the Partiality of Juries in favour of those who are sued by the Crown for any Frauds in the Publick Revenue: I could give many Instances of it; but I shall mention only one.

Here he informed the House of the Case.

The Defendant, *Sir*, in this Case was one of the most notorious Smugglers in the whole Country, he had often been tried for such Practices, and though he had always before escaped, yet it was thought impossible he should then get off; the Evidence against him was so very full and clear, that I believe there was not a Man in the Court, except those on the Jury, who were not fully convinced of the Truth of the Evidence given against him; yet the Gentlemen of the Jury thought fit to bring in a Verdict in his Favour: So that really, *Sir*, the Crown can never pretend to prevent Smogling or unfair Trading, as long as the Trials are to be for the most Part by Juries, and where it becomes necessary, to alter that Method of Trial, the altering it in that new Case can no more be said to be an Innovation or an Incroachment on our Constitution, than the altering of it formerly in another Case was. —— In short, I have as great a Value for the Liberty of my Fellow-Subjects as any Gentleman in this House; I shall always be ready to appear for the Liberties of my Country, whenever I see them in any Manner attacked; but as Liberty does not at all enter into the present Question, I shall be very ready to give my Assent to the Motion made by the hon. Gentleman.

Sir P――l M――n] *I rise up, Sir, only to explain myself as to one Particular in which the hon. and learn'd Gentleman over the way, for whom I have a very great Respect, seems to have mistaken me, or rather indeed has misrepresented what I said. For I did not say, that those who are now subject to the Laws of Excise are downright*

right Slaves, or that they are totally deprived of their Liberty. I should be sorry if any such Thing could be said of any Man that has the least Pretence to call himself a Subject of Great Britain; but I said that those who are subjected to the Laws of Excise, are in so far as they are subjected to such Laws, deprived of their Liberty: They are deprived of a Part of their Liberty, and therefore cannot be said to be as free as any other of his Majesty's Subjects. This Sir, is still my Opinion, and if those who are so unfortunate as to be subject to the Laws of Excise were to be asked the Question, Whether they think themselves as free in all Cases as those who are subject to no such Laws? I believe there is not one of them but would answer, No.

Sir J——n B——rd.] I find, Sir that the Hon. Gentleman who opened this Scheme to the Committee, and the hon. and learned Gentleman who spoke last, make great Complaints of some People's having maliciously misrepresented their Scheme, before those malicious Persons knew what it was. For my Part, I happen to be of a very different Way of Thinking; for tho' I am far from thinking that the Scheme, as now opened to us, is the very same with what it was when first formed, yet even as it is now opened, it is such a Scheme in my Opinion as cannot, even by Malice itself, be represented to be worse than it really is. Now it appears to me to be a Scheme that will be attended with all those bad Consequences apprehended from it before it was known; and I plainly foresee it will produce none of those good Effects Gentlemen have been pleased to entertain us with the Hopes of. They have indeed gilded the Pill a little, but the Composition within is still the same; and if the People of *England* be obliged to swallow it, they will find it as bitter a Pill as ever was swallowed by them since they were a People.--- The learned Gentleman was pleased to say, that he was of Opinion that the Opposition to this wicked Scheme, (for so I must call it) proceeded from other Motives than Gentlemen are willing to own; I don't know what Motives he can mean; but I believe those Gentlemen who propose this Scheme, have some Secret Views which it would neither be convenient or safe for them to own in this Place. For as to any Reasons or Views which may be openly avowed for the proposing of this Scheme, I know of none but that of preventing the Frauds that may be committed in that Branch of the Revenue now under our Consideration; and that this Scheme will not answer that Purpose, has I think been made plainly appear by my worthy Brother near me; but granting that this Scheme should answer such a Purpose, if the Laws now in being duely executed are sufficient for answering that Purpose, what Necessity is there for applying this new, this desperate Remedy, a Remedy which is certain-

ly much worse than the Disease? Before I proceed any further, I shall desire the Commissioners of the Customs, may be called in.

The Commissioners were accordingly called in, and being asked by Sir, J——n, What they thought the Value of the Frauds committed in the Tobacco-Trade might amount to on Year with another? Their Answer in effect was, that they had never made any Computation; but one of them said, that by a Computation he had made only for the satisfying his own private Curiosity, he believed the Frauds come to their Knowledge might amount to 30 or 40,000l. per Annum, one Year with another. Then Sir J——n put the following Question to them, Whether or no it was their Opinion, that if the Officers of the Customs performed their Duty diligently and faithfully, it would not effectually prevent all, or most of the Frauds that could be committed in the Tobacco-Trade ? To which they answered, that it was their Opinion it would. Then he asked them, Whether or no it was their Opinion, that if the Commissioners of the Customs had the same Power over their Officers, that the Commissioners of Excise have over their's, it would contribute a great Deal towards making them more exact, and more faithful in the Discharge of their Duty, than they now are? And their Answer was, That they believed it would. After this, the Commissioners being withdrawn, Sir J——n went on to the Effect as follows, viz.

I now, Sir, leave it to every Gentleman to consider, what real Pretence can be formed for introducing such a dangerous Scheme, as has been proposed to us. The only Pretence I have yet heard made use of is, the Preventing of Frauds, by which, say they, the fair Trader will be encouraged, and the Revenue encreased; but now you see, that it is the Opinion even of the Commissioners of the Customs, that, by a due Execution of the Laws in Being, all, or most of those Frauds may be effectually prevented; and I am sure if they can be prevented by the Laws in Being, the preventing of them by that Method will contribute much more to the Increase of the publick Revenue, and to the Encouragement of the fair Trader, than the preventing of them by Means of the dangerous Scheme now proposed to us. I now leave it to the whole World to judge, who are they that have secret Motives which they are not willing to own, which they dare not own: Whether it be those who are the Proposers and Promoters of this Scheme, or those who are the Opposers of it? —— The learned Gentleman seemed to be surprized how our Constitution, or the Liberties of our Country came into the present Debate; he said, he thought they had no Manner of Concern in the present Question. I am sorry, Sir, to differ from a Gentleman, who by his Profession ought,

ought, and certainly does underſtand the Nature of our Conſtitution, as well as any Man in *England* ; but I am of Opinion, that the Conſtitution of our Government, and the Liberty of the Subject was never more nearly concerned in any Queſtion, than in the preſent ; they are both ſo deeply concerned, that their Preſervation or total Overthrow depends entirely on the Succeſs of this Scheme now under our Conſideration : If the Scheme ſucceeds, they muſt tumble of Courſe ; if the Scheme is defeated, they may be preſerved : I hope they will be preſerved till Time ſhall be no more ; but I muſt ſay, that the learned Gentleman, and every Gentleman who appears as an Advocate for the Scheme now propoſed to us, is much in the right to keep, if they can, the Conſtitution and the Liberties of their Country out of the Debate; it is from thence that the principal Arguments are to be form'd againſt their Scheme, as muſt appear unanſwerable to every Man who has a Regard for either ---- The Gentleman tells us, there are but 120, or 150 Exciſe-Officers, beſides Warehouſe-keepers, to be added by the Scheme now before us, and this additional Number, they ſeem to make a Ridicule of; but conſidering the Swarms of Tax-gathers we have already eſtabliſhed, this ſmall Number (as they call it) is no trivial Matter ; and I would be glad to know from thoſe Gentlemen, what Number of Warehouſe-keepers may be neceſſary ? I hope they will allow that a Warehouſe-keeper, appointed, and paid by the Treaſury, is an Officer of the Revenue, as much as any other Officer ; and if the Number there muſt be of them be added to the other, I believe we may find the Number of Revenue-Officers, to be added by this Scheme, muſt be very conſiderable. ----
As for the new Method of Appeal propoſed, I can ſee no Advantage, that it will be of to any unfortunate Man that may have occaſion therefor. In all Caſes the Charge and the Trouble of attending muſt be very great, and the Event very precarious ; but in moſt Caſes, where poor Retailers may have Occaſion to be concern'd, the Charge and the Trouble of Attendance muſt be much greater than the Subject can bear, ſo that all ſuch People muſt ſubmit to the Determination of the Commiſſioners of Exciſe. The Judges of *Weſtminſter-Hall* are, 'tis true, for Life, but they are all named by the Crown ; I ſhall ſay nothing of the preſent Judges, who ſo worthily fill the Benches of *Weſtminſter-Hall* ; but if they ſhould die, and if the Crown ſhould be reſolved to uſe that Power the Parment had put into their hands, in order to oppreſs the Subject, they will always find Judges fit for their Purpoſe ; Judges are ſubject to the ſame Frailties that other Men are, and the Crown has always Plenty of Baits

wherewithal to tempt them. A Judge may be made a Lord Chief Juſtice, a Lord Chief Juſtice may be made a Lord Chancellor, and every one may have a Son, a Brother, or a Couſin to be provided for. The Crown has many Ways to win over even a Judge, more eſpecially when he is to adminiſter Juſtice in a ſummary Way, and without the uſual Forms of Proceeding in Courts of Law and Equity. For by this new Method of Appeal, which has been ſo much bragg'd of, Care has been taken that the ſubject ſhall not be reſtor'd to their ancient Birth-right, that is, to a Trial by a Jury : No, this I find is moſt carefully avoided, and yet I think it muſt be allow'd that it is the inherent Right of every *Engliſhman* to be tried by his Peers. I am not ſo much acquainted with Law as to give an Account of the ſeveral Caſes in which this Method of Trial hath been ſet aſide, or the Reaſons for ſo doing ; but I will venture to ſay, that wherever that Method of Trial has been ſet aſide, whether the ſame was done by the Wiſdom of the Nation, or otherwiſe, ſuch Alteration was an Innovation, and was a dangerous Encroachment upon the original Charter of our Conſtitution. ----As to the pretended Partiality of Juries, ſo much complain'd of by the learned Gentleman, it is of no Weight with me : I cannot ſee how that hon. Gentleman, can pretend to know what Reaſons a Jury may have for giving their Verdict. No Gentleman has a Right to be believ'd upon his ſingle Say-ſo, againſt a Verdict given by 12 honeſt Men upon Oath. If there have been ſo many Verdicts given againſt the Crown, as that learned Gentleman ſeems to inſinuate, it is to me a ſtrong Proof that Proſecutions have been ſet on Foot againſt the Subject upon the Evidence of Witneſſes, whoſe Credibility or Veracity have not been very much to be depended on ; which is ſo far from being an Argument for altering the Method of Trial by Jury, that it is a very ſtrong Argument for the Continuance of that Method. But, as it is now very late, and as I ſhall probably have another Opportunity of giving my Sentiments more fully on the Affair now before us, I ſhall trouble you no further at preſent, but only to declare, that now, after hearing this Scheme open'd to us, I diſlike it as much as ever I did any Repreſentation of it, that ever I heard of, and therefore I ſhall give my Negative to the Queſtion propoſed.
M----r *of the* R---lls.] Sir, as the Affair, which is at preſent the Subject of our Conſideration, has been much talk'd of, and very variouſly repreſented without Doors; and as it has been for ſome Months the Subject of Converſation amongſt People of all Ranks and Qualities, I was reſolved to ſuſpend entirely paſſing any Judgment in Relation to it,

till

till I should hear it fully opened, and laid before this House. There were indeed, such Clamours raised without Doors, and it was represented in so many hideous Shapes, that I cannot say but that I really came this Morning to the House prejudiced rather against, than in Favour of any such Project; but still I came, as I always do, altogether undetermin'd, and resolved not to determine myself till I was fully informed by other Gentlemen, in the Course of the Debate, of all those Facts which ought to be known before any Determination can be made in an Affair of so great Importance. - - - - I had before heard, that by this Scheme the Landed-Gentlemen were to be eased of a Part of the Land-Tax; that the Publick Revenue was to be greatly improv'd; and that the Planters in *America*, and our fair Traders at Home, were to be greatly encouraged; but all these Considerations would have had no Weight with me, if I had found, that so many of my Fellow-Subjects were thereby to have been subjected to the grievous Laws of Excise without any Alleviation or Alteration. I must own, that the Severity of the Laws of Excise has been long justly complained of; but at the same Time I must say, that the many Frauds committed in that Branch of the publick, Revenue now under our Consideration, are most heavy and grievous, and what I cannot think of seeing the Nation suffer any longer under, without applying some proper Remedy; and since by the Proposition now made to us, there is not only an effectual Remedy against all those Frauds, but likewise a Method proposed, by which the Edge of the Laws of Excise is to be blunted; and that Severity taken quite off, which hitherto always afforded just Ground of Complaint; therefore I cannot hesitate one Moment as to giving my Assent to what is now proposed.--- This Consideration, Sir, is of the greater Weight with me, and must be so with every honest Man, that by what is now proposed, the Laws of Excise are to be rectified not only in the Case now before us, but in every other Case; the whole Body of those Laws are to be reform'd and rectify'd in such a Manner as to remove the greatest Objection, with me indeed the only Objection, could ever be made against the Extension of them; and if this Proposition be now rejected, it is not easy to know when we shall have such an Opportunity of reforming those Laws, which have been so long thought so grievous. With me it hath always been a Principle to hearken to any reasonable Scheme for suppressing of those Frauds, which are committed against the Publick; I look upon the Persons guilty of such Frauds as the greatest of Criminals, and if they have any Character, if they observe any Decency in private Life, I take it

Gent. Mag. Vol. III. No. xxxiv.

to be only because they have no Opportunity to do otherwise; for that Man must have a very whimsical Conscience, who cheats the Publick, and yet would scruple to cheat a private Man, if he had the same Opportunity. — Whatever Resolutions we may come to in this Committee, there will probably be a Bill or Bills order'd to be brought in, pursuant to them; and if in the Course of the Debate any real Difficulties be started, if any reasonable Objections be made, without doubt all proper Care will be taken, in the forming such Bill or Bills, to obviate all the Difficulties and Objections, that shall or may occur; and therefore I can find no manner of Difficulty in giving my Assent to the Question proposed.

G--ge H--te, Esq;] Other Gentlemen have, Sir, already fully explain'd the great Inconveniencies, which must be brought on the Trade of this Nation by the Scheme now proposed to us; thence arises a very strong Objection against it: But the greatest of all arises from the Danger to which this Scheme will most certainly expose the Liberties of our Country: Those Liberties for which our Ancestors have so often ventur'd their Lives and Fortunes, those Liberties which have cost this Nation so much Blood and Treasure seem already to be greatly retrenched: I am sorry to say it; but what is now in Dispute, seems to me to be the last Branch of Liberty we have to contend for; we have already establish'd a standing Army, and have made it in a Manner, a Part of our Constitution; we have already subjected great Numbers of the People of this Nation to the arbitrary Laws of Excise, and this Scheme is so wide a Step towards subjecting all the rest of the People of *England* to those arbitrary Laws, that it will be impossible for us to prevent the fatal Consequences of it. ---- We are told that his Majesty is a good and a wise Prince; we all believe him to be so: But, I hope, no Man will pretend to draw any Argument from thence for our surrendering those Liberties and Privileges, which have been handed down to us by our Ancestors: We have indeed nothing to fear from his present Majesty; he never will make a bad Use of that Power which we have put into his Hands; but if we once grant to the Crown too great an Extent of Power, we cannot recal that Grant, when we have a Mind; and tho' his Majesty should never make a bad Use of it, some of his Successors may: The being governed by a wise and a good King, does not make the People a free People: The *Romans*, Sir, were as great Slaves under the few good Emperors they had to reign over them, as they were under the most cruel of their Tyrants. After the People have once given up their Liberties, their Governors have all the same Power

Z z z   of

of oppreffing them, tho' they may not perhaps all make the fame wicked Ufe of it ;
but a Slave who has the good-fortune to meet
with a good-natur'd and a human Mafter, is
no lefs a Slave than he that meets with a
cruel one. Our Liberties are too valuable,
and have been purchafed at too high a Price,
to be fported with, or wantonly given up even
to the beft of Kings : We have before now
had fome good, fome wife and gracious Sovereigns to reign over us ; but we find that under them our Anceftors were as jealous of their
Liberties, as they were under the worft of
our Kings : It is to be hoped, that we have
ftill the fame Value for our Liberties; if we
have, we certainly will ufe all peaceable Methods to preferve and fecure them ; and if
fuch Methods fhould prove ineffectual, I hope
there is no *Englifhman* but has Spirit enough
to ufe thofe Methods for the Prefervation of
our Liberties, which were ufed by our Anceftors in Defence of theirs, and for tranfmitting
them down to us in that glorious Condition,
in which we found them. There are fome
ftill alive who bravely ventur'd their Lives
and Fortunes in Defence of the Liberties of
their Country; there are many whofe Fathers were embark'd in the fame glorious
Caufe. Let it never be faid, that the Sons of
fuch Men wantonly gave up thofe Liberties
for which their Fathers had rifk'd fo much;
and that for the poor Pretence of fuppreffing
a few Frauds in the collecting of the Publick
Revenues, which might eafily have been fup-
preffed without entering into any fuch dangerous Meafures. This is all I fhall trouble
you with at prefent, but fo much I thought
was incumbent upon me to fay, in order to
enter my Proteft againft the Queftion now
before us.

W---m P---y, Efq;] Sir, the Honourable
Gentleman who opened this Affair to us, took
up fo much of the Time of the Committee,
and it is now fo very late, that I am almoft
afraid of giving you any Trouble at prefent ;
but, I hope, confidering the Importance of the
Subject, Gentlemen will excufe me, and
allow me to take fome Notice of what has
been faid by the Hon. Gentleman who introduced the Debate, and the hon, and learned
Gentleman who fpoke laft but one. As to
the Frauds, which the Hon. Gentleman
dwelt fo long upon, and which the hon. and
learned Gentleman was pleafed to call heavy
and grievous, I believe every Gentleman in
the Committee is convinced that there are
fuch Frauds ; that they are moft heavy and
grievous ; but I do not believe, that it is but
of late that the Hon. Gentleman has come
to the Knowledge of them ; nor that the
Frauds, relating to Wine and Tobacco are
the only Frauds he has heard complained of ;
there is hardly a Gentleman in the Kingdom

but has heard of Frauds in almoft every Branch
of the Public Revenue ; even that Hon. Gentleman muft have heard many Years ago of
the Frauds committed in the Tobacco and
Wine-Trade ; why then, was there no Remedy fooner propofed ? How could that Gentleman fee the Publick Revenue, for which
he expreffes fuch a tender Concern, fuffer fo
long by thofe Frauds, without propofing fome
Expedient for preventing them : The Expedient now propofed is certainly no fuch new or
extraordinary Thing ; it might, I dare fay, it has
often been thought of before this Time ; but
it feems it was never thought proper to propofe it before now ; at leaft it was never till
now thought neceffary, and yet it cannot be
faid, but that the Frauds both in Wine and
Tobacco were as great formerly, as they are
at this prefent Time.——The Hon. Gentleman has been pleafed to tell us, that his
Thoughts are entirely confined to the two
Articles of Wine and Tobacco ; and that nothing elfe was ever defigned by him, or any
of his Acquaintance, to be fubjected to the
Laws of Excife : Whatever his Thoughts
may have been in Time paft, he muft excufe me, if I fay, that I do not believe they
will be fo much confined in Time to come.
Are there not Frauds committed in every
Branch of the Publick Revenue ? Will not
that Hon. Gentleman think himfelf as much
bound in Duty to lay thofe Frauds before this
Houfe, and propofe a Remedy for them, as
he now thinks himfelf bound to expofe, and
to offer a Remedy for preventing the Frauds
in Wine and Tobacco ? And if the Remedy
now propofed be deemed by Parliament the
moft proper and moft effectual, for preventing
the Frauds in Wine and Tobacco, will not
that be made ufe of as an Argument for applying the fame Remedy as to the Frauds in
every other Branch of the Publick Revenue ?
So that from the Gentleman's own Way of
arguing as to the Cafe which he has been
pleafed now to lay before us, one may fee
a moft evident Defign of a much further Extenfion of the Laws of Excife ; one may clearly fee a Defign of fubjecting every Branch of
the Public Revenue to thofe arbitrary Laws ;
only the Gentleman has a Mind, it feems, to
be a little cunning, and to do it by Piece-
meal.——Whatever Opinion the hon.
and learned Gentleman may have of the Propofition made by his hon, Friend, it is plain
it breathes nothing but the Principles of the
moft arbitrary and tyrannical Governments
eftablifh'd in *Europe:* The enlarging the
Power of the Crown ; the increafing the
Number of Dependents on the Crown ; the
rendering the Happinefs of the Subject precarious and uncertain, and depending in a manner entirely on the good Will of a prime Minifter, or of thofe employ'd under him, are
the

he certain Consequences of the Scheme now proposed to us: They are the certain Consequences of all Schemes for extending the Laws of Excise, and are probably the principal Views of all those who set up such Projects. Let Gentlemen but read the Political Testaments of *Richlieu* and *Luvois*, those Legacies which were left by the Authors to their Master, for instructing him in the Principles of arbitrary Government; and they will see that the Author of this Scheme, whoever he be, must be very well versed in them; how well it agrees with the Principles there laid down for the establishing and supporting of arbitrary Power. It is for this Reason that the *English* Nation has always been so averse to Excise-Projects of all kinds; the very Word Excise has always been odious to the People of *England*. It is true there has been an Excise established by Parliament; but it was at first given us a Purchase for the Court of Wards and Liveries; and tho' that Court was most justly looked on, as one of our greatest Grievances, yet the Purchase has always been reckoned too dear; and that Parliament which gave the Excise has been branded with the infamous Name of a Pensionary Parliament. Even the great K. *William*, notwithstanding all he had done for the People of *England*, his being most generally beloved and esteemed by his Subjects, yet he had like to have suffered by a Notion's prevailing among the People, that some new Excises were to have been established. It was publickly said, that we had got a *Dutch* King; and that therefore we were to be saddled with *Dutch* Excises: That Wise King was so sensible of the Danger he might be exposed to by the prevailing of such a Notion, that he thought it necessary to disavow any such Intention by a publick Declaration.— I most readily believe, Sir, that the hon. and learned Gentleman over the Way comes at all Times to this House undetermined as to any Point to be brought before us: I believe he always comes resolved to be determined by what shall be offered in the Course of the Debate; but I am very much at a Loss to find out what in the present Debate has determined him to be of the Opinion he now seems to be of: He has indeed told us, that the Reformation proposed as to the Laws of Excise, is what very much weighs with him; he says, that the Laws of Excise are to be blunted; that their Edge is to be taken off, by what is now proposed. In this, I must confess my Short-sightedness, I can see no Reformation in what is proposed; what I look on as most grievous in the Laws of Excise, is to continue the same as before; Are not the Officers to have the same oppressive and vexatious Powers continued to them? Are not the Commissioners to have the same dispensing Power with Regard to Fines and Forfeitures? Are Trials by Jury to be restored to the Subject? No, Sir: all these Grievances are to remain: The Power and Influence of the Crown is still to be as great as it was before, only there are by this Scheme many thousands more to be subjected to it; the Method of Appeal is indeed to be a little altered, but I am afraid the Alteration will not be much for the better; the Expence will be much greater, and the Redress as precarious as ever it was before: How then are the Laws of Excise to be blunted? Where is this Reformation so much boasted of, and on which that hon. and learned Gentleman seems solely to ground his Opinions? But it seems he expects, that when this Proposition comes the length of a Bill, many fine things are to be done, many more things than we have ever as yet heard of; If it should come the length of a Bill, which I am in great Hopes it never will, he may very probably find himself disappointed; and if that should be the Case, I doubt not but he will be of a different Opinion.—Gentlemen have said, that there are no Complaints made of the Laws of Excise, or of the Oppressions of the Excise Officers; but, I believe, there is not a Gentleman in this House, who cannot give some Instances even within his own Knowledge, of most cruel Oppressions committed by some of those Officers; I am sure there is no Gentleman who has ever acted in the Country as a Justice of Peace, but can give hundreds of such Instances. The People have complained so often, and so long, of the Severity of those Laws, and the Vexations of those Officers, that they are now weary of complaining. To what purpose should they complain, since they see there has never as yet been any Provision made for their Redress? Their Complaints have been hitherto disregarded, even by those who are in some Manner bound to take Notice of them. The hon. Gentleman was pleased to dwell upon the Generosity of the Crown in giving up the Fines, Forfeitures, and Seizures to the Publick; but in my Opinion it will be but a poor Equivalent for the many Oppressions, which the People will be exposed to by this Scheme. I must say, that the hon. Gentleman has himself been of late mighty bountiful and generous in his Offers to the Publick. He has been so gracious as to ask us, Will you have a Land-tax of two Shillings in the Pound, or a Land-tax but of one, or will you have no Land-tax at all? Will you have your Debts paid? Will you have them soon paid? Tell me but what you want; let me but know how you can be made easy, and it shall be done for you. These, Sir, are most generous Offers, but there is something so very extraordinary, something so farcical in them, that really I can hardly mention them without laughing; It puts me in Mind of the Story of sir *Epicure Mammon*, in the *Alchymist*. He was gulled out of his Money by fine Promises; he was promised the Philosopher's Stone, by which he was to get Mountains of Gold, and every thing else he could desire; but all

ended

ended at last in *some little thing for curing the Itch.*—— I wish the Gentlemen who appear so zealous for this Scheme, would have some little Regard to their Constituents. It is well known, that it was the Custom among our Ancestors, when any new Device was proposed, to desire Time to have a Conference with their Countries: I beg Leave to read a Passage or two on this Subject from my Lord Coke. That great Lawyer, in the 4th Part of his Institutes, Page 14, says, " It " is also the Law and Custom of the Parlia- " ment, that when any new Device is mo- " ved on the King's Behalf in Parliament, " for his Aid, or the like, the Commons " may answer, that they tendered the King's " Estate, and are ready to aid the same, on- " ly in this new Device they dare not a- " gree without Conference with their Coun- " tries ; whereby it appeareth, that such " Conference is warrantable by the Law " and Custom of Parliament. " And again, in Page 34. he tells us, " At the Parliament " holden in 9 Edw. III. When a Motion " was made for a Subsidy of a new kind, " the Commons answered, that they would " have Conference with those of their seve- " ral Countries and Places, who had put " them in Trust, before they treated of any " such Matter. " If such a Conference was ever necessary upon any Occasion, it is surely necessary before we agree to the Device now offered to us ; a Device, which in my Opi- nion, strikes at the very Root of our Liber- ties ; a downright Plan for Arbitrary Power, and in this I am not singular; for there seems to be many Gentlemen of the same Opinion within Doors, as well as without ; therefore I must think that it is necessary, it is in- cumbent upon every Gentleman in this House, at least to desire to have a Conference with his Constituents before he agrees to any such Device: This, Sir, would have been ne- cessary, if we had been entirely ignorant of the Sentiments of our several Countries ; but indeed in the present Case such a Con- ference seems unnecessary : We already know the Sentiments of our Constituents, in Re- lation to the Device now offered to us: The whole Nation has already, in the most open Manner, declared their Dislike to it ; and therefore I hope the Gentlemen of this Committee will reject it with Scorn.

Sir W——m W——m.] Sir, *Tho' it be now very late, yet I must beg Leave to offer my Sentiments on the Question in Debate ; for it is a Question of such Importance, that I should not think I discharged the Duty I owe to my Country without declaring in the most open and publick Manner my Dislike and Abhorrence of the Scheme which has been now opened to us. The Scheme has in my Opinion been no way misrepresented. It is fraught with all those Evils which were ever attributed to it, and must apparently strike at the very Fundamentals of our Constitution. The Collecting of any Duties by the Laws of Excise has, in all Ages, and in all Countries,*

been looked on as the most grievous and most op- pressive Method of Collecting of Taxes, and if one Method of raising an Excise can be more oppressive than another, it must be granted, that the Method now proposed to us, of raising this new Excise, must of all Methods be the most op- pressive, and the most vexatious to the People : In all Countries Excises of every kind are look'd on as Badges of Slavery, and tho' the Eng- lish Nation be now unfortunately subjected to some of them, yet I hope they will never consent to any new Excises, or to any new Extension of the Laws of Excise, let the Pretences for so doing be ever so specious.——But in the present Case, pray, Sir, let us consider, what are the great Advantages proposed for persuading us to consent to the subjecting of so many of his Ma- jesty's faithful Subjects to be plagued and har- rassed by the Officers of Excise? The suppressing of Frauds and the Advantages that will ac- crue therefrom to the Publick and to the fair Trader, is, by what I can find, the only Pretence now made use of ; and yet those Frauds even aggravated as they were by the hon. Gentleman who proposed this Scheme to us, do amount to but a meer Trifle ; so that the Improvement to be made as to the publick Revenue will be but very inconsiderable, if any at all, after deduct- ing the additional Charges of Management, which the Publick will become liable to by the great Increase of Officers : This Pretence there- fore, even when set in the strongest Light, can be no sufficient Argument for prevailing on us to expose our Constitution to the least Danger, or to subject any of our fellow Countrymen to great Hardships ; but this Pretence is still more frivolous since it has been made appear to us, that those Frauds are not at all so considerable as they have been represented ; that all Sorts of Frauds cannot be prevented even by the Scheme now pro- posed, and that many of those Frauds that have been lately committed, might be prevented by the Laws now in Being, if Care was taken to have proper Officers, and to make those Officers diligent and faithful. I grant indeed, that the Power and Influence of the Crown will be greatly in- creased and improved by this Scheme ; that great Numbers of the People of this Nation will there- by be rendered most submissive and obedient to those that shall hereafter be employed by the Crown ; and if this be a Motive for agreeing to this Scheme, I must allow that it is a strong one ; I believe indeed that it is the only real one that any Gentleman can have for giving his Con- sent ; but with me, it is the strongest for giving my Negative to the Question now before us, be- cause I think it absolutely inconsistent with our Constitution.——'Tis true, an Ease to the Landed- interest has upon this, as well as upon some o- ther late Occasions of the like Nature, been thrown out, as a Bait for some Gentlemen ; but I hope the Landed-gentlemen are not to be caught by such Baits ; the Hook appears so plain, that it may be discovered by any Man of common Sense ; however I must say, that the Method of Argu- ing is unfair, the Design is wicked, for it is an Endeavour to set the Landed interest in a man-wer at war with the Trading-interest of the Nation; it is endeavouring to destroy that Harmony which always ought to subsist among the People of the same Nation, and which if once destroyed would certainly end in the Ruin and Destruction of the whole. But every Landed-gentleman in England will do well to consider what Value their Lands would be of, if for the sake of a small and immediate Ease to themselves, they should be induced to oppress and destroy the Trade of their Country; and whoever considers this, will despise all such Projects, and reject them with that Contempt which they deserve: This is one Reason for the Landed-gentlemen not to accept of the pretended Ease now offer'd to them; but there is another strong Reason against it: This House of Commons is mostly composed of Gentlemen of the best Families and greatest Properties perhaps in the Nation, they have generally a great Family-interest in the several Counties, Cities, and Boroughs they represent; if this Scheme should take Effect, that Interest will soon be destroyed; and surely no Man will agree to a Scheme which must inevitably destroy the natural Interest the great Families have, and always ought to have, in their respective Counties, and transfer the Whole to the Crown: If this Scheme should once be established, the Power and Influence of the Crown will be so great in all Parts of the Nation, that no Man can depend upon the natural Interest he has in his Country for being a Member of this House; he must in all future Times for such a Favour depend entirely upon the Crown, and this I hope there is no Gentleman in this House would chuse to submit to. —Q. Elizabeth was so far from endeavouring to divide or throw Discord among her Subjects, that she wisely never gave herself up to any one Minister, or to any one Party; she always preserved a Harmony among all her Subjects, and kept a friendly Correspondence with all Parts and all Parties in the Kingdom; she even kept up a constant personal Correspondence with some of the principal Men in every County, by which she had always a thorough Knowledge of the several Sentiments as well as Circumstances of all her Subjects, and most prudently adapted all her Measures to what she found to be the Sentiments of the Generality of the Nation; more particularly she took Care to avoid every Thing that appeared to be disagreeable to the People: To this wise Politick, it is owing, that her Reign makes such a glorious Figure in our English History; that she reigned with more Popularity than any Prince since her Time, except her royal Successor Queen Anne: Thus she reigned absolutely, but so as I could wish every Prince in England to do; she reigned absolutely over the Hearts and Affections of her Subjects, and thereby had both their Persons and their Purses always at Command.—We are ask'd why do you complain of this Scheme? here is no new Tax to be imposed; only a new Method of raising those Taxes which are already due by Law: But this Nation has once already been more grievously oppressed by a new Method of Raising and Collecting that Money that was before due by Law, than they ever

were by any new Tax. I have already mentioned the Reign of Q. Elizabeth; let us but look a little further back: Empson and Dudley, those two noted Ways and Means-Men, those two wicked Ministers knowing the Avarice of their Master, concluded that no Schemes would be more agreeable to him than those which would fill his Coffers by draining the Purses of his Subjects; and this they did, without imposing any new Taxes, they laid no new or illegal Burdens on the People, they did it by a severe and rigorous Execution of the Laws that had before been enacted. But what was their Fate? They had the Misfortune to out-live their Master, and his Son, as soon as he came to the Throne, took off both their Heads. In this he did justly, tho' he did it against Law; they had done nothing contrary to Law, they had only put the Laws severely in Execution, and what they did was in Obedience to the Commands of the King his Father; yet that could be no Excuse for them, their Manner of Executing those Laws was so grievous and oppressive upon the Subjects, that nothing less than their Lives could be admitted of as a sufficient Atonement to the People; and certainly, that Oppression which is committed under the Sanction of the Laws, or of the Royal Authority, must always be deemed to be the most heinously criminal, and ought to be the most severely punished.——There never was in any Reign a Scheme or Project attempted so much to the Dislike and Dissatisfaction of the People in general; the whole Nation has already so openly declared their Aversion to the Scheme now offered to us, that I am surprised to see it insisted on; the very proposing of such a Scheme to a House of Commons, after so many Remonstrances against it, I must think most audacious; it is in a manner flying in the Face of the whole People of England: And since they have already declared against it, God forbid that we, who are their Representatives, should declare for it.

Mr C——r of the Ex——r. Sir, As I was obliged when I opened the Affair now before us, to take up a great deal of your Time, I then imagined I should not have been obliged to have given you any farther Trouble; but when such Things are thrown out, which in my Opinion are quite foreign to the Debate; when the ancient Histories not only of this Country but of other Countries, are ransacked for Characters of wicked Ministers, in order to adapt them to the present Times, and to draw Parallels between them and some modern Characters, to which they bear no other Resemblance but only that they were Ministers, it is impossible for one to sit still. Of late Years, I have dealt but little in the Study of History, but I have a very good Prompter by me, (meaning Mr A——y G——l) and by his means I can recollect, that the Case of Empson and Dudley mentioned by the hon. Gentleman who spoke last, was so very different from any Thing that can possibly be presumed from the Scheme now before us, that I wonder how it was possible to lug them into the Debate. The Case as to them was, that they had by Virtue of old and obsolete Laws most unjustly extorted

great

great Sums of Money from People, who, as was pretended, had become liable to great Penalties, by having been guilty of Breaches of thoſe Laws, which for many Years before had gone entirely into Diſuſe. I muſt ſay, and I hope moſt of thoſe that hear me, think, that It is very unjuſt and A unfair to draw any Parallel between the Characters of thoſe two Miniſters and mine, which was I ſuppoſe what the hon. Gentleman meant to do, when he brought that Piece of Hiſtory into the Debate. If I ever endeavour'd to raiſe Money from the People, or from any Man whatever by oppreſſive or illegal Means, if my Character ſhould ever come to be in any reſpect like B theirs, I ſhall deſerve their Fate: But while I know myſelf to be innocent, I ſhall depend upon the Protection of the Laws of my Country; as long as they can protect me I am ſafe, and if that Protection ſhould fail, I am prepared to ſubmit to the worſt that can happen. I know that my political and miniſterial Life has by ſome Gentlemen been long wiſhed at an End, C But they may ask their own diſappointed Hearts, how vain their Wiſhes have been; and as for my natural Life, I have lived long enough to learn to be as eaſy about parting with it as any Man can well be.——As to thoſe Clamours which have been raiſed without Doors, and which are now ſo much inſiſted on, it is well known by whom, and by what Methods they were raiſed, D and it is no difficult Matter to gueſs with what Views; but I am very far from taking them to be the Senſe of the Nation, or believing that the Sentiments of the Generality of the People were thereby expreſſed. The moſt part of the People concerned in thoſe Clamours, did not ſpeak their own Sentiments, they were play'd by others like ſo many Puppets; it was not the Puppets that ſpoke, it was thoſe behind the Curtain that play'd E them, and made them ſpeak whatever they had a mind.——There is now a moſt extraordinary Concourſe of People at our Door? I hope it will not be ſaid that all thoſe People came there of themſelves naturally, and without any Inſtigation from others; for to my certain Knowledge ſome very odd Methods were uſed to bring ſuch Multitudes hither; circular Letters were ſent by F the Beadles in a moſt publick and unprecedented Manner, round almoſt every Ward in the City, ſummoning them upon their Peril to come down this Day to the Houſe of Commons: This I am certain of, becauſe I have now one of thoſe Letters in my Pocket, ſigned by a Deputy of G one of the greateſt Wards in the City of London, and ſent by the Beadle to one of the Inhabitants of that Ward, and I know that ſuch Letters were ſent in the ſame Manner about to every Liveryman and Tradeſman in that Ward. By the ſame ſort of unwarrantable Methods have the Clamours been raiſed almoſt in every other Part of the Nation.—— Gentlemen may ſay what H they pleaſe of the Multitudes now at our Door, and in all the Avenues leading to this Houſe, they may call them a modeſt Multitude, if they will, but whatever Temper they were in when they came hither, it may be very much altered now, after having waited ſo long at our Door: It may be a very eaſy Matter for ſome deſigning

ſeditious Perſon to raiſe a Tumult and Diſorder among them, and when Tumults are once begun no Man knows where they may end; he is a greater Man than any I know in the Nation that could with the ſame Eaſe appeaſe them; for this Reaſon I muſt think that it was neither prudent nor regular to uſe any Methods for bringing ſuch Multitudes to this Place, under any Pretence whatever. Gentlemen may give them what Name they think fit, it may be ſaid that they came hither as humble Supplicants, but I know whom the Law calls ſturdy Beggars, and thoſe who brought them hither could not be certain but they might have behaved in the ſame Manner.

Sir J——n B——rd then got up to ſpeak, but there being ſome Diſorder in the Committee, and the Queſtion loudly called for, Sir, J——n H——dd C——n got up and ſpoke thus, To Order, Sir, I hope you will call Gentlemen, to Order; there is now a Gentleman up who ſpeaks as well as any Gentleman in this Houſe, and who deſerves Attention as much as any Gentleman that ever ſpoke in this Houſe: Beſides, he is one of the Repreſentatives of the greateſt and the richeſt City in Europe, a City which is greatly intereſted in this Debate, and therefore he muſt be heard, and I deſire, Sir, that you will call to Order, that the Committee may ſhew him at leaſt that Reſpect that is due to every Member.

The Committee being called to Order, Sir J——n B——rd went on in Subſtance as follows. Sir, I know of no irregular Methods that were uſed to call People from the City to your Door; it is certain that any Set of Gentlemen or Merchants may lawfully deſire their Friends; they may even write Letters, and they may ſend thoſe Letters by whom they pleaſe, to deſire the Merchants of Figure and Character to come down to the Court of Requeſts and to our Lobby in order to ſollicit their Friends and Acquaintances againſt any Scheme or Project which they think may be prejudicial to them. This is the undoubted Right of the Subject and what has been always practiſed on all Occaſions. The hon. Gentleman talks of ſturdy Beggars, I do not know what ſort of People may be now at our Door, but I believe they are the ſame that were there when I came laſt into the Houſe, and then, Sir, I can aſſure you I ſaw none but ſuch as deſerve the Name of ſturdy Beggars as little as the hon. Gentleman himſelf, or any Gentleman. The City of London was ſufficiently appriſed of what we were this Day to be about, and had a right Notion of the Scheme which has been now opened to us; they were ſo generally and zealouſly bent againſt it, that whatever Methods may have been uſed to call them hither, it would have been impoſſible to have found any legal Methods to have prevented their coming.

Several other Gentlemen ſpoke for and againſt H the Scheme; at laſt the Queſtion was put upon the Motion made by Mr C——r of the E——r, whereupon they came to a Diviſion; and as this Affair will probably make a great Figure in the Hiſtory of our preſent Times we ſhall give our Readers the moſt correct Liſt we could procure of thoſe who voted on each Side of the Queſtion.

For *the* QUESTION *(with the* Teller*)* 266.

Note. Those mark'd p voted For e Against the Hessian Troops 1730, lt b. Knight of the Bath, n New Member; the Figure shews how many Parliaments they have sat in.

† These were order'd to bring in the Bill.
✻ These afterwards voted against the Bill.

Tho. Winnington, for *Droitwich, Worc.* Commissioner of the Admiralty, *Teller.*

ALSTON Sir Rowland p 2 Bedfordshire
Andrews Townsend n p Hindon, Wilts *Deputy Paymaster of the Forces.*
Anstruther Sir John p 5 Fifeshire, *Master of the King's Works* in Scotland.
Anstruther Philip p !3 Anstruther, *Col. of a Regiment, since made Deputy Gov. of Minorca.*
Areskine Charles p 2 Shire of Dumfries, *his Majesty's Solicitor General for Scotland.*
Arundel Rich. p 3 Knaresborough Yorkshire, *Surveyor General of his Majesty's Works.*
Ashburnham Sir William p 3 Hastings Sussex, *Chamberlain of the Exchequer, and a Commissioner of Alienation.*
Ashe Edward p 9 Heytsbury Wilts, *Commissioner of Trade and Plantations.*
Austen Sir Robert n New Romney Kent
Bacon Waller p 5 Norwich, *Commissary of the Musters and Stores of Minorca.*
Bacon Sir Edmund p 2 Thetford Norfolk, *who hath a Grant of Crown Lands at Chatham, and a Brother in the Customs*
Baker Hercules p 2 Hythe Kent, *a Captain in the Navy*
Bateman Wm Ld Visc. n e 2 Leominster, lt b.
Beauclerk Lord Vere p 2 Windsor, *Commissioner of the Navy, and Capt. in the same*
Bennet Thomas n Nottinghamshire
Berkeley Hon. Henry p 3 Gloucestershire, *Col. of the 2d Troop of Grenadier Guards*
Bladen Thomas n p Steyning Sussex, *Nephew of*
Bladen Martin p 3 Stockbridge Hants, *Commissioner of Trade, and for settling Commerce*
Bond John n 2 Corfe-castle Dorsetshire
Bradshaigh Sir Roger p 10 Wigan Lancashire
Bridgman Sir Orlando p 3 Blechingly Surrey, *Commissioner of Trade and Plantations*
Bristow Robert p 6 Winchelsea Sussex, *Clerk to the Board of Green-cloth*
Britiffe Robert, 3 Norwich
Brodie Alexander p 3 Shire of Elgin, *Lord Lyon King at Arms in* Scotland
Bromley Henry n Cambridgeshire
Brooksbank Stamp p p Colchester, *Bank Direct.*
Brudenel Hon. James p 4 Andover Hants, *Commissioner of Trade and Plantations, since made Groom of the Bed-chamber*
Burchet Josiah p 5 Sandwich Port, *Sec. to the Admiralty*
Burton William n Rutland
Butler James n p Sussex
Byng Hon. Robert n p Plymouth Devonshire, *Commissioner of the Navy*

Campbell John p 3 Pembrokeshire
Campbell John jun p 4 Dumbartonsh. *Groom of the Bedchamber to the King.*
Campbell Daniel p 3 Glasgow; *one Son a Com. of the Cust. another Receiver Gen. in Scotland.*
Campbell James n Shire of Air, *Colonel of a Regiment, and Groom of the Bedchamber*
Campbell Sir James p 5 for Argyleshire
Campbell Peter 2 Burgh of Elgin, *Officer of the Houshold, since made Lt. Gov. of Portsmouth.*
Carey Walter p 2 Clifton, Dartmouth, &c. *Clerk of his Majesty's Privy Council, Secretary to the Lord Lieutenant of Ireland*
Carre William 2 Newcastle upon Tine
Carnarvon (Marquis of) lt b. n p Hereford, *Ld of the Bedchamber to the Prince*
✻ Cavendish Lord Charles p 2 Westminster, *Brother to the Ld Steward*
✻ Cavendish Ld James e 8 Derby, *his Uncle, and Uncle to the Lord Steward*
Chamberlayne George n Buckinghamshire
Cholmondeley Hon. James n Bossiney, Cornw. *Major of Horse-Guards, Gov. of Chester Cast.*
Churchill Brig. Charles n 3 Castle-rising. Norf. *Groom of the Bedchamber to the King, Colonel of a Regiment of Dragoons, Gov. of Plymouth*
✻ Clark Sir Thomas 5 Hertford
Clayton Sir Wm e 3 Bletchingly, Surrey
† Clayton William p 3 Westminster, *one of the Commissioners of the Treasury*
Clifton Sir Robt lt b. n p Retford Nottinghamsh.
Clutterbuck Thomas p 2 Leskard, Cornw. *a Commissioner of the Admiralty*
Cokburne John p 7 Shire of Haddington
Conduit John a Whitchurch, Southamptonshire *Master of his Majesty's Mint*
Cope Sir John 7 Southampton County
Cope John p 2 Leskard, Cornwall, *Col. of a Reg.*
Copleston Thomas p 3 Kellington, Cornwall, *who has a Place in Ireland*
Corbet William n p Montgomery. Flintshire
Cornwallis Hon. Stephen p n Eye, Suffolk, *Colonel of a Regiment of Foot*
Cornwallis Hon. John n p Eye Suffolk, *Equerry to the Prince*
Cotton Sir Robert Salisbury, n Cheshire *Custos Rotulorum for Denbigh County*
Cracherode Anthony n p Lestwithiel, Cornw. *joint Solicitor to the Treasury*
Croft Sir Archer p 3 Boralston, Devonshire, *Commissioner of Trade and Plantations*
Crosse John n p Wotton-Basset, Wilts
Crowle George p 2 Kingston upon Hull, *a Commissioner for Victualling the Navy*
Cunningham Henry, for the Shire of Stirling *Commissary of the Musters in Scotland*
Danvers Joseph 2 Bramber, Sussex
Darcy Sir Conyers p 3 Richmond, Yorkshire *Comptroller of the King's Houshold*
Docminique Paul p 7 Gatton. Surrey, *Commissioner of Trade and Plantations.*

† Dodding-

† Doddington George p 6 for Bridgwater Som. *Commiſſioner of the Treaſury*, &c.

Douglas Robert *n* Orkney and Zetland, *an Officer in the Army*

Downing Sir George *ht b*. 4 Dunwich, Suffolk

Drummond John *n p* Burgh of Perth, *Commiſſioner of Commerce, an Eaſt-India Director*

Duckett Col. William *n p* Caln, Wilts, *Major to the 2d Troop of Grenadier Guards*

Dunbar Patrick *n p* Bute and Caithneſs

Duncombe Anthony p 3 New Sarum

Earle Gyles p 3 Malmesbury, Wilts, *Clerk of the Green-cloth*

Earle William Rawlinſon, *n* ditto, *his Son, ſince made Clerk of the Deliveries of the Ordnance, and Secretary to the Maſter General of the ſame*

Edgcombe Richard *p* 8 Plympton, Devon, *Vice Treaſurer and Paymaſter of Ireland, &c.*

Edwards Samuel p 2 Wenlock, Salop, *Under-Teller of the Exchequer*

Eliot Richard 2 St Germans, Cornw. *Auditor General to the Prince of Wales*

Erskine Thomas *n p* Burgh of Stirling, Capt. *in a Regiment*

Evans Richard *n p* Queenborough, Kent, *Dep. Gov. of Sheerneſs, and Capt. of Dragoons*

Evelyn John *n p* Helſton, Cornwall, *Groom of the Bedchamber to the Prince of Wales*

Eversfield Charles p 6 Horſham, Suſſex

Eyles Francis *n p* Devizes, *Capt. in the Army.*

Fane Hon. John 4 Buckingham, *Col. of the 1ſt Troop of Grenadier Guards, ſince made Baron Catherlogh in Ireland, and Col. of the firſt Troop of Life Guards*

Fane Francis *n p* Taunton, Somerſetſhire *Solicitor-General to the Prince*

Farrington Thomas p 2 St Michael, Cornwall *Receiver of the Land Revenues in Wales.*

Finch Hon. Henry p 2 Malton, Yorkſhire

Fitzroy Charles *n* Thetford, Norf. *Cornet of Horſe, and Maſter of the Tennis Courts.*

Fitzwilliam Viſc. p 2 Fowey, Cornwall.

Forbes Duncan 2 Fortroſe, Inverneſs, &c. *Lord Advocate for Scotland*

Forteſcue Wm *n p* Newport, Hants, *Secretary to the Chancellor of the Exchequer*

Fox Stephen *c* 2 Shaftsbury, Dorſetſhire.

Frankland Sir Thomas p 6 Thirsk, Yorkſh. *a Commiſſioner of the Admiralty*

Gage Sir William *ht b*. p 2 Seaford, Suſſex

Gallway Ld Viſc. *n* Clithero, Lancaſhire

Gibſon Thomas p 2 Marlborough, Wilts. *Scrivener to Sir Robert Walpole*

Glenorchy Ld Viſc. *n p* Saltaſh, Cornwall *Ambaſſador to the Court of Denmark .*

Gough Sir Henry *n* Torneſs, Devonſhire

Gould Nathanael *n p* Wareham, Dorſetſhire

Gould John *n p* Shoreham, Suſſex

Grant Sir James p 2 Shire of Inverneſs

Gregory George p 4 Boroughbridge, Yorkſh. *Store Keeper of his Majeſty's Ordnance*

Griffith John p 3 Carnarvon County, *Lieut. in the Army*

Grimſton William Ld Viſc p 4 St Albans

Hales Sir Thomas p 3 Canterbury, *Father of*

Hales Thomas p 2 Camelford, Cornwall, *one of the Clerks of the Green-cloth*

Hamilton Alexander *n p* Shire of Linlithgow, *Secretary to the Prince of Wales for Scotland*

Hamilton Ld Archibald *p* 3 Lanerkſhire, *Commiſſioner of the Admiralty*

Hamilton John *n* Wendover, Bucks

Handaſyd Roger 2 Huntingdon, *Col. of a Regt.*

Harbord Harbord *n* Norfolk

Harris John *n p* Helſton, Cornwall

Harriſon George p 2 Hertford

Heathcote Sir John *n* Bodmin, Cornwall

Hedges John p 2 Boſſiney, Cornwall, *Treaſurer and Receiver General to the Prince of W.*

Henley Henry Holt 2 Lyme, Dorſetſh. *Clerk of the Pipe in the Exchequer*

Herbert Henry Arthur 2 Ludlow, Salop

Herbert Hon. Robt Sawyer, for Wilton Wilt. *Commiſſioner of the Revenue in Ireland*

Hervey John Ld p 2 St Edmund's Bury, Suff. *Vice Chamberlain of the King's Houſhold, and ſince called up to the Houſe of Lords*

Hinxman Joſeph *n p* Chriſtchurch, Southam. *Woodward of New Foreſt in that County*

Hoghton Sir Henry p 4 Preſton, Lancaſhire

Hope Thomas *n* Maidſtone, Kent

Hoſte James *n p* Bramber, Suff. *Couſin to Sir R.W.*

Hotham Sir Charles p 2 Beverly, Yorkſh. *Col. of a Regiment, and Groom of the Bedchamber*

Howard Charles *n p* Carliſle, Cumberland. *Lieut. Gov. of the ſame, and Col. in the Foot Guards*

Howarth Sir Humph. p 2 Radnorſhire

Hucks William p 4 Willingford, Berks, *Brewer to his Majeſty's Houſhold*

Hucks Robert p 2 Abingdon, ditto, *his Son*

Huxley George p 2 Newport, Hants, *Commiſſary General of the Muſters*

Jekyll Sir Joſeph *c* 30 Rygate, Surrey, *Maſter of the Rolls*

Jennings Sir John p 4 Rocheſter, *Commander in Chief of his Majeſty's Fleet, Governor of Greenwich Hoſpital, &c.*

Ingoldeſby Thomas *n* Aylesbury, Bucks

Ingram Henry p 2 Horſham, Suſſex, *Commiſſary of the Stores at Gibraltar*

Jewkes John, *n* Bridport, Dorſet

Kelſal Henry p 3 *n* St Michael, Cornwall, *one of the chief Clerks of the Treaſury*

Knight John p 5 Sudbury, Suffolk

Knollys Henry p 2 St Ives, Cornwall

Lane Sir Richard *n p* Worceſter, *whoſe Son is Commiſſioner of Hawkers and Pedlars*

Laroche John *c* 2 Bodmin, Cornwall

Leathes Carteret *n p* Sudbury, Suffolk

Lehcup Iſaac 2 Grampound, Cornwall, *Brother-in-law to Haratio Walpole*

Lewis Thomas of Hants 5 New Sarum

Lewis Tho. p 3 Radnor, *a Brother in the Com.*

Liddel George *n p* Berwick

Lisburne Ld Viſc. *n* Cardiganſhire

Lloyd Richard *n* Cardigan

Lloyd Philip 2 Chriſtchurch, Hampſhire, *Capt. in her Majeſty's Regiment of Dragoons*

Lockyer Charles *n p* Ilcheſter, Som. *Gentleman of the Privy Chamber to his Majeſty*

Longueville Charles p 3 Eaſtlow, Cornwall, *Auditor to the Queen*

Lowther Sir William *c* Pontefract, Yorkſh.

Lowther Hon. Anthony 3 Westmoreland, *Commissioner of the Revenue in Ireland.*

Lumley Hon. John *for* Arundel, Sussex

Lyttelton Sir Thomas *p* 3 Worcestershire, *Commissioner of Admiralty*

Malpas Ld Visc. *p* 2 Windsor, *Master of the Horse to the Prince, now Earl of* Cholmondeley.

Manners Ld William *p* 3 Leicestershire, *Lord of Bedchamber to the King*

Martin Thomas *n p* Wilton, Wilts

Medlycott Thomas *n* 2 Milbourn-Port, Som. *Commissioner of the Revenue in Ireland*

Meredith Sir Roger *n c* Kent, *an Officer of Dover Castle*

Micklethwait Ld *p* 3 Kingston on Hull

Middleton Col. John *p* 4 Aberdeen, Montrose, *a Col. of the Foot*

Mill Sir Richard *n p* Midhurst Sussex

Monson George *n p* Great Grimsby, Linc.

Montagu Hon. Col. Edward 2 Northampton, *Col. of a Regiment, and Governor of Hull*

Mordaunt John *n p* Pontefract, Yorkshire, *Col. in the Guards*

More Robert *n p* Bishops-castle, Salop

Morgan Thomas 2 Town of Brecon

Morton Mathew Ducie *p* 2 Tregony Cornw.

Murray John *p* 2 Selkirk, Peebles, &c.

Munro Sir Robert *p* 5 Kirkwall, Train, &c. *His Brother Capt. of an Independent Comp.*

Munro John, *n* for the Shire of Ross.

Nasmith Sir James, Bart. *n* Shire of Peebles

Neale John 3 Coventry, *Husband to one of the Queen's Bedchamber Women.*

Nicoll Sir Cha. Gounter *k b. n p* Peterborough

Norton Thomas *n p* Edmonds-Bury, Suffolk, *Deputy Governor of Chelsea Hospital*

Offley Crew 3 Bewdley, Worcestershire, *Gentleman of his Majesty's Privy Chamber*

Onslow Arthur [Speaker] 3 Surrey, *Chancellor to the Queen*

Onslow Richard *n p* Guilford, *Adjutant General of the Forces, and Lieutenant Colonel of the first Troop of Grenadier Guards*

Orlebar John *n p* Bedford

Owen William *n* 2 Pembroke Town

† Oxenden Sir George 6 *p* 3 Sandwich, Kent, *one of the Commissioners of the Treasury.*

Papillon David *p* 3 Rumney Kent

Parsons Henry *p* 2 Malden, Essex, *Commissioner for Victualling the Navy and Purveyor of Chelsea Hospital*

Pearse Thomas *p* 2 Weymouth, Dorsetshire, *a Commissioner of the Navy*

Peirse Henry 2 Northallerton, Yorkshire

Pelham Hon. Henry *p* 3 Sussex, *Paymaster of the Forces.*

Pelham Thomas *p* 6 Lewes, Sussex, *Commissioner of Trade and Plantations.*

Pelham Thomas, of Stanmore, *n* ditto, *Secretary to the Embassy in France.*

Pelham James *p* 2 Newark, Notts. *Secretary to the Prince, and to the Ld Chamberlain.*

Pelham Thomas jun. *p* Hastings, Sussex

Percival Ld Visc. *p* Harwich, Essex, *since created E. of Egmont in the Kingdom of Ireland.*

Piers William *n p* Wells, Somerseth. *a Coll.*

Pitt Thomas *n* *p* Oakhampton, Devon.

Pitt John 3 Camelford, Cornwall, *Col. in the 1st Regiment of Foot Guards*

Polhill David *p* 3 Rochester, *Keeper of the Records in the Tower*

Powlett Ld Harry *p* 3 Southamptonshire *since made Commissioner of the Admiralty*

Powlett William *n p* Lymington, Southamp.

Powlet Norton sen. *p.* 3 Petersfield, Hants

Powlet Norton jun. *n c* Winchester

Powlett Cha. Armand *p* Newton, Hants, *Lieut. Col. of Grenadier Guards, since made Deputy-Gover. of the Isle of Wight.*

Price Uvedale *n c* Weobly, Herefordshire

Pulteney Henry 2 Heydon, Yorkshire, *Col. in the Guards, and Equerry to the King, since made 2d Major in the 2d Reg. of Foot Guards*

Purvis George *n* Aldborough; Suffolk, *Captain in the Navy*

Ramsden John *n* Apulby, Westmoreland

Reade Sir Thomas *p* 4 Cricklade, Wilts. *one of the Clerks of the Greencloth*

Reade George *p* 2 Tewksbury, Glouc. *Maj. in the Guards, since made Col. of a Reg. late Ld Albemarle's, at Gibraltar*

Rich Sir Robert 3 St Ives, Cornwall, *Col. of a Regiment of Dragoons, and Groom of the Bedchamber to the King, since made Coll. of the first Troop of Grenadier Guards.*

Ryder Dudley *n* St Germans, Cornw.

Roberts Gabriel *p* Chippenham, Wilts.

Robinson Sir Thomas *n* Thirsk, Yorkshire.

Rutherford James *n* Selkirkshire, *since made Commissary of Peebles.*

St Quintin Math. Chitty *n p* Old Sarum

Saunders Sir George *n p* Queenborough, *Commissioner of the Navy, and Rear Admiral.*

† Scrope Hon. John *p* 2 Bristol, *joint Secretary to the Treasury with* Edward Walpole.

Scot James, for Kincardinsh. *Lieut. Col. of the 3d Regiment of Foot Guards.*

Selwyn John *p* 2 Whitchurch, Hants. *Treasurer to the Queen, and Groom of the Bedchamber.*

Shannon Lord Visc. 5 Grinstead, Sussex, *Col. of the 4th Troop of Horse Guards.*

Schaw Sir John 2 Renfrewshire, *Commiss. for preventing the Import. of Irish Meal into Scot.*

Shelley Sir John *n p* Arundel, Sussex, *whose Brother* Charles Shelley *was just about the Time made Auditor of the Revenues within the Counties of Lincoln, Derby, &c. and also Auditor of Writs of Covenant and Entry in the Alienation Office.*

Sinclair James *p* 2 Dysart, Kirkaldie, &c. *Major to the 3d Regiment of Foot Guards, since made Lieut. Gov. of Berwick and Holy Island, and Col. of a Regiment of Foot.*

Sloper William *p* 2 Great Bedwin, Wilts. *Dep. Cofferer of his Majesty's Houshold.*

Smelt Leonard 4 *p* Northallerton, Yorkshire, *Clerk of the Ordnance.*

Speke George 2 Taunton Somersetshire.

Stanhope Charles *p* 3 Aldborough, Yorkshire, *Brother to the Ld Harrington, Sec. of State.*

Stuart William 4 Air, Irwin, &c. *Carpmaster of the Customs.*

Sutherland William *n p* Sutherlandshire, *now E. of Sutherland.*

Sutton Gen. Richard *p* 6 Newark, Nott. *Col. of a Reg. and fince made Gov. of* Guernfey Ifland
†Talbot Charles *p* 3 Durham, *Solicitor General.*
Thompfon William *n* Scarborough Yorkfhire, *Commiffioner for Victualling the Navy*
Thompfon Richard *n* Reading, Berks
Thornhill Sir James *p* 2 Melcomb, Dorfet, *his Majefty's Serjeant Painter*
Tilfon Chriftopher *n p* Cricklade, Wilts, *one of the chief Clerks of the Treafury*
Towers Chriftopher 2 Lancafter, *and*
Towers Thomas *n p* Wareham, Dorfetfh. *his Brother; Reverfionary Auditors of the Impreft.*
Townfhend Hon. Hor. *p* 2 Heytsbury, Wilts
Townfhend Hon. Tho. *p* 2 Cambridge Univ. *Teller of the Exchequer*
Treby George *p* 6 Clifton, Dartmouth, *&c. Mafter of his Majefty's Houfehold*
Trenchard George *p* 4 Pool, Dorfetfhire
Tuffnel Samuel *n* 2 Colchefter, *Commiffioner for fettling Commerce.*
†Turner Sir Charles, Lynn, Norfolk, *one of the Tellers of the Exchequer*
Tylney *Earl n* Effex
*Tyrconnel Ld Vifc. *n* Grantham, Lincolnfh.
Tyrrel James *p* 2 Boroughbridge, Yorkfhire, *Col. of a Reg. of Foot, fince made Col. of Drag.*
Vincent Henry *n p* Guilford
Wade 'Gen. George *p* 3 Bath, *Col. of a Reg. fince appointed Gov. of* Fort William &c.
Wager Sir Charles *p* 5 Portfmouth, Hants. *Firft Commiffioner of the Admiralty*
Walker Thomas *n* Weftlow, Cornw. *Surveyor General of the Majefty's Land Revenues.*
Walpole Sir Robert *p* 9 Lynn Norf, *Chancellor and Under-Treafurer of the Exchequer*
†Walpole Horatio, *p* 7 Yarmouth, Norfolk, *Auditor of the Plantation Accounts, and Cofferer.*

†Walpole Edward *n* Leftwithiel, Cornwall, *Son of Sir Robert* Walpole, *joint Secretary to the Treafury, and Collector inwards of the Cuftoms.*
Walter Peter *p* 2 Winchelfea, Suffex, *Clerk of the Peace for the County of Middlefex*
Wardour William *n c* Calne, Wilts
Wentworth Sir William *n* Malton, Yorkfhire
White ‡ John *n* Retford, Nottinghamfh.
Whitworth Francis *p* 2 Minehead, Somerfe. *Surveyor of all his Majefty's Woods*
Willes John *p* 2 Weftlow, Cornwall, *chief Juftice of* Chefter
Williams Sir Nicholas *p* 2 Carmarthenfhire
Williams Hugh *p* 2 Anglefea
Wills Sir Charles *p* 3 Totnes, Devonfhire *Lieutenant General of the Ordnance, and Col. of the firft Regiment of Foot Guards*
Windham Thomas *n* Pool, Dorfetfhire
Wollafton William *n* Ipfwich Suffolk
Wynn Thomas *p* 4 Carnarvon, *one of the Clerks of the Green Cloth*
†Yonge Sir William *bt b.* 3 Honiton, Devon. *one of the Lords of the Treafury*
† York Sir Philipp 3 Seaford, Suffex, *Attorney Gen. fince made L. Ch. Juftice of the King's Bench.*
*Yorke John *c* 3 Richmond, Yorkfhire

Sir *T. Prendergaft* (not being then returned) and *F. Knollys* did not appear 'till the Report, when the former voted for the *Excife*, and the latter againft it.

N. B. On the Report Ld *Tyrconnel* declared he was convinc'd the Bill was not a good one and Voted againft it.

‡ The *Political State* and moft other Lifts have it *Thomas*, who is dead.

See the Variations from thefe Lifts on the Queftion for repealing the Septennial Act, Vol. IV. p. 181.

AGAINST *the* QUESTION (*with the* Teller) 205.

Samuel Sandys, *for* Worcefter, Teller.
ABDY Sir Robert *n c* Effex
Aiflabie William *c* 2 Rippon Yorkfh.
Alington Marm. *n* Agmondefham
Annefley Franc. *c* 6 Weftbury Wilts
Aftley Sir John *n c* Salop Town
Afton Sir Thomas *n c* Liverpool Lancafh.
Bacon Thomas *c* 4 Cambridge
Bacon Sir Edmund *n c* Norfolk
Bagot Sir Walter Wagftaff *c* 2 Staffordfhire
Banks John *g* Corf-caftle Dorfetfhire
Banks Jofeph *n c* Peterborough Northamptonfh.
Barnard Sir John *c* 2 LONDON
Barrington Sir John *n p* Newtoun Hants
Bathurft Peter *n c* Cirencefter
Bathurft Benjamin *c* 4 Gloucefter
Belfield John *n c* Exeter
Berkeley Hon. George *c* 3 Dover
Bevan Arthur *n* Carmarthen
Bold Peter *n c* Wigan Lancafhire
Bofcawen Hugh *n c* Truro Cornw.
Bowes George *n* Durham County
Bowles William *n p* Bridport Dorfetfh.
Bramfton Thomas *n c* Maldon Effex

Broke Philip *n* Ipfwich Suffolk
Bromley William *c* 2 Warwick
Browne John *n c* Dorchefter
Bulkeley Lord Vifc. *n* Beaumaris, Anglefey
Burrard Paul *p* 7 ‖ Yarmouth, Ifle of Wight
Burrel Peter *p* 2 Haflemere, Surrey
Cæfar Charles *c* 6 Hertfordfhire
Carew Sir William *c* 5 Cornwall
Cartwright Thomas 10 Northamptonfhire
Cafwall Sir George *p* 3 Leominfter, Herefordfh.
Chafin George 4 Dorfetfhire
Charlton St John *c* 2 Bridgenorth, Salop
Chetwynd Lord Vifc. *c* 8 Staffordfhire
Chetwynd John *c* 3 Stockbridge Hants
Child Sir Francis *c* 2 Middlefex
Childe William Lacon *n c* Salop County
Cholmondeley Charles *c* 4 Chefhire
Clarke Godfrey 5 Derbyfhire
Cocks James 5 Rygate, Surrey
Coffin Richard *p* 2 Birnftable, Devonfh.
Compton George *n* 2 Northampton
Cornbury Ld Vifc. *n* Oxford Univerfity
Cornewall Velters *c* 2 Herefordfhire
Cotton Sir John Hynde *c* 6 Cambridge Town

Courtenay Sir William 9 Devonshire
Crisp Thomas *n p* Ilchester, Somerset
Curzon Sir Nathanael *c* 2 Derbyshire
Dalrymple Col. John *n p* Burgh of Wigtoun
Dalrymple Sir James 3 Burgh of Haddington
Dalrymple Hon. Col. Wm *p* 2 Shire of Wigtoun
Davers Sir Jermyn *c* 2 Suffolk
Devereux Hon. Price *c* 3 Montgomeryshire
Digby Hon. Edward *c* 2 Warwickshire
Drax Henry *n p* 2 Lyme, Dorsetshire
Drewe Francis *c* 4 Exeter
Dundass Robert *c* 2 Shire of Edinburgh
Elton Sir Abraham *c* 2 Bristol
Eyles Sir John *p* 4 LONDON
Eyles Sir Joseph *p* 2 Southwark
Fazakerley Nicholas *n* Preston, Lancashire
Fenwick Nicholas *n* Newcastle upon Tine
Finch Hon. John *c* 2 Higham Ferrers, Northa.
Finch Hon. John *c* 2 Maidstone, Kent
Foley Edward *n* Droitwich, Worcestershire
Fortescue Hon. Theoph. *n c* Barnstaple, Devon
Fuller John *n* Plimpton, Devon
Furnese Henry *p* 3 Dover
Gage Lord Visc. *p* 2 Tewksbury, Gloucester
Gay Robert *n* 2 Bath
Gower Baptist Leveson *n c* Newcastle Staff.
Gower Hon. Wm Leveson *c* 3 Staffordshire
Grosvenor Sir Robert *c n* Chester
Guidott William *c* 4 Andover, Hants
Gybbon Philip *c* 6 Rye, Sussex
Hall Charles *n c* Lincoln
Hanbury John *c* 5 Monmouthshire
Harley Edward *n c* Herefordshire
Harrison Thomas *n p* Old Sarum
Harvey Michael *c* 2 Milbourn-Port, Somers,
Hawkins Philip *n c* Grampound
Heathcote William *c* 2 Southamton
Heathcote George *n c* Hindon, Wilts.
Hedworth John 5 Durham County
Henley Anthony *n* 2 Southampton
Hoby Sir Thomas *n* Marlow, Bucks
Holland Rogers *n p* Chippenham, Wilts
Hope Sir John Bruce *n* Kinross and Clackmanan
Howe John *c* 3 Wiltshire
Howard Henry Ld Walden *n c* Boralston, Devon
Hylton John *n* Carlisle, Cumberland
Inwen Thomas *n* Southwark
Inchiquin Earl of *c* 2 Tamworth, Stafford
Ilham Sir Justin *n* Northamptonshire
Kemp Sir Robert *n* Suffolk
Kemp Robert *n* Orford, Suffolk
Keyt Sir William 2 Warwick
Lawson Gilfrid *c* 2 Cumberland
Lawson Sir Wilfrid *c* 3 Cockermouth, Cumb.
Lee Sir Thomas *c* 4 Bucks
Lee George *n* Brackley, Northamptonshire
Leigh Hon. Charles *n* 3 Bedfordshire
Levins William *n* Nottinghamshire
Lewen George *n c* Wallingford, Bucks
Limerick Ld Visc. *n c* Wendover, Bucks
Lisle Edward *n c* Marlborough, Wilts
Lister Thomas *c* 7 Clithero, Lancashire

Lloyd Salisbury *n p* Flint Town
Lowther Sir James *n* 7 Cumberland
* Lowther Sir Thomas 2 Lancaster
Lutterel Alexander *n c* Minehead, Somersetshire
Lutwyche Thomas *c* 3 Agmondesham, Bucks
Lyster Richard *n c* Salop County
Mackenzie Sir George *n* Cromarty and Nairn
Mansel Hon. Bussy *c* 2 Cardiff, Glamorganshire
Master Thomas *c* 5 Cirencester, Gloucestershire
Master Legh *n.c* Newton, Lancashire
Meadows Sidney *c* 2 Truro, Cornwall
Merril John *n* 2 St Albans
Methuen Hon. Sir Paul 5 Brackley, Northamp.
Middleton Sir William 2 Northumberland
Milner Sir William *p* 2 Yorkshire
Monoux Sir Humph. *n* Tavistock, Devonshire
Morpeth Ld Visc. 3 Morpeth, Northumberland
Morice Sir William *n* Newport, Cornwall
Mostyn Sir Roger 4 Flintshire
Mountrarth Earl of 2 Castle-rising, Norfolk
Newland William *c* 5 Gatton, Surrey
Newton Sir Michael 2 'Grantham, Linc.
Nightingale Joseph Gascoign *n c* Stafford
Noel Hon. Thomas *n c* Rutland
Noel Sir Slobery *n c* Leicestershire, *since dead*
Norris Sir John *p* 6 Portsmouth, Hants
Northmore William *n c* 5 Oakhampton, Dev.
Ongley Samuel *n c* Shoreham, Sussex
Packer Winchcomb *n* Berkshire
Packington Sir Herbert *n c* Worcestershire
Palmer Thomas 3 Bridgewater, Somerset
Parsons Humphrey *c* 2 LONDON
Pelham Charles 2 Beverly, Yorkshire
Perrot Henry *c* 3 Oxfordshire
Perry Micajah *n* LONDON
Peyto William *c* 3 Warwickshire
Philips Erasmus *c* 2 Haverford-west, Pemb.
Plumer Richard *c* 2 Litchfield Stafford
Plumer Walter *c* 4 Apulby, Westmoreland
Plumtre John *p* 6 Bishops-castle, Salop
Pottenger Richard *n p* Reading
Powlett Ld Nassau *p* 5 Lymington, Southam.
Pulteney William 7 Heydon, Yorkshire
Rashleigh Jonathan *n c* Fowey, Cornwall
Reynell Richard *c* 7 Ashburton, Devonshire
Rolle Henry *n* Devonshire
Rowney Thomas *c* 2 Oxford City
Rushout Sir John *c* 5 Evesham, Worcestershire
Sambrooke John *c* 2 Wenlock, Salop
Sambroke Sir Jer. Vanacker, Bart *n* Bedford
St Aubin Sir John *c* 2 Cornwall
St John Hon. John *n c* Wotton-Basset
Saunderson Sir Thomas *c* 2 Lincolnshire
Scawen Thomas *c* 2 Surrey
Scot James *p* Kincardineshire
Sebright Sir Thomas *c* 3 Hertfordshire
Seymour Francis *n* Bedwin, Wilts
Shafto John *n* Durham City
Shepheard Samuel *c* 3 Cambridgeshire
Shippen William *c* 6 Newton Lancashire
Shirley Hon. Robert *n c* Stamford, Lincolnshire

Shuttle;

* *On the Report of the Bill declar'd be bad alter'd his Opinion and voted for it.*

Shuttleworth Richard *c* 7 Lancashire	Vernon Sir Charles, Bart *n* Chipping-wicomb
Slingsby Sir Henry *c* 3 Knaresborough, York	Vernon George Venables *n* Litchfield, Stafford
Somerset Ld Bharles Noel *n* Monmouthshire	Vernon Edward *c* 2 Penryn, Cornwall
Spencer Hon. John *n* Woodstock, Oxford	Vyner Robert *c* 3 Lincolnshire
Stanhope Hon. John *n* || Nottingham	Walcot John *n c* Salop County
Stanhope Sir John William 2 Bucks	Waller Edmond *c* 2 Great Marlow Bucks
Stanhope Charles *n* Derby	Waller Harry *c* 2 Chipping-wicomb, Bucks
Stanley Sir Edw. *n c* Lancashire	Ward John *n c* Newcastle, Staffordshire
Stapleton Sir William *n c* Oxfordshire	Warren Borlace *n* 2 Nottingham
Talbot John Ivory *c* 3 Wilts	Williams Sir John *n* Alborough, Suffolk
Taylor Joseph *n c* Petersfield, Hants.	Willoughby Hon. Thomas 3 Tamworth
Townshend Hon. Wm *p* 2 Yarmouth Norfolk	Winford Thomas *n c* Herefordshire
Tremayne Arthur *n c* Launceston, Cornwall	Wyndham Thomas *n* 3 Dunwick Suffolk
Turner Cholmley *n c* 3 Yorkshire	Wortley-Montagu Edward *c* 5 Huntington
Vane Lord Visc. *n c* Steyning, Suffex	Wrighte George *n c* Leicester
Vane Hon. Henry *c* 2 St. Maws, Cornwall	Wyndham ir William *c* 4 Somersetshire
Vaughan Wm Gwyn *c* 3 Brecon County	Wynn Watkin Williams 3 Denbighshire

On the Call of the House, several Defaulters were excused on Account of Illness or extraordinary Avocations; but the Excuse of *Francis Knollys* not being allow'd, he was order'd to be taken into Custody of the Serjeant at Arms; but being discharged appeared on the Report, and voted against the Bill, as will be seen by the following List of Absenters.

A B S E N T and did not Vote on the Q U E S T I O N.

Aston William *at* Bath	Drummond John *of Meginch*	Lumley James	Sterr Arthur
Aiflabie William		Myddelton Rob. *Sick*	*Stiles Benjamin Haskins
Arscott Arthur	Dutton Sir John	Morgan Maurice *Sick*	Stonhouse Sir John
Bailie George	East William	Nelthorpe James	Strickland Sir Wm
Beauclerck Ld Wm *Sick*	Edwards Thomas	*Noel William, *on the Circuit*	Thompson Edward *in* Ireland
*Beaumont Sir George	*Ellys Sir Rich. *Sick*		
Bertie Hon. James	Eyre Giles	Norris Capt. at Bath	Trelawney Sir John
Bigg John	Finch Hon. Edward	Oglethorpe James	Trotman Samuel
*Bishopp Sir Cecil	Finch William	Oughton Sir Adolphus	*Tucker Edward
Boone Charles	Forbes Sir Arthur	Page John	Tuckfield Roger
*Bootle Thomas, *on the Circuit*	Furnese Sir Robt. *Sick*	Palmerston Lord	Tyrwhit Sir John
	*Gifford John	Parker Long Sir Philip	Vaughan Richard
Bridges George	Glanville William	Piggot Robert	Verney John
*Bunbury Sir Charles	Goddard John	*HeydellEdm Moreton	*Weaver Jonn
Campbel John *Edinb.*	Hardres Sir William	Pole Sir William	Webb Borlace at Bath
Chapple Sir William	Herbert Thomas	Robinson Thomas	Wilson Daniel
Chauncy Toby *sick*	Herbert Richard	*Rudge Edward	
*Clarke George	Heron Patrick	*Rudge John	
*Colerane Lord	*Horner Thomas	Sabine Joseph	
Cornwall Captain	Hughes Edward	Savile Sir George	
*Coryton Sir John	*Jenison Ralph	Selwin Charles	
*Desbouverie Sir Edw.	Jessop William *Circuit*		
Doddington George *sen.*	Keymys Sir Charles		
Douglas Archibald	Keymys Edward		
Douglas William	King John		
Drake Sir Francis	Knight Bulstrode		
Duff William	*Knollys Francis		

Absent	87
For the Question	266
Against it	205
All the Members	558

N.B. *Those marked thus* * *voted afterwards against the Bill, as did Sir Thomas Prendergast and Sir Edward Dering, chose in the Room of Ld Wm Beauclerk, and Sir Robt Furnese deceased; but Ld Wallingford who was chose in the Room of* Toby Chauncy, *Esq; was absent.*

After the Question had been thus carried in the Affirmative, the following Resolutions were proposed and agreed to without any Division, *viz.*

1st, That in Lieu of the Duties, mentioned in the first Resolution so to be determined, there should be granted to his Majesty an Inland-Duty of 4 *d. per* Pound upon all Tobacco imported from the *British* Plantations, to be paid before the taking the same out of the Warehouse.

2d, That the Inland-duties, to be raised and levied upon Tobacco, should be appropriated and applied to the same Uses and Purposes, as the former Duties upon Tobacco, to be determined, were appropriated and applied.

3d, That all Fines, Penalties, Forfeitures, and Seizures, to arise by the said Duties, should be applied to the Use of the Publick, except so much thereof as should be allowed to the Informers or Prosecutors.

Thus the Excise-scheme triumphed for this first Day in the House of Commons, but the Debate had lasted so long, that it was near Two o' Clock on *Thursday* Morning before the House rose, and therefore they adjourned till next Day, being *Friday* the 16th of *March*, on which Day they ordered the Report to be received;

See how many Voters for and against the Excise *were rechose,* Vol. IV. p. 200, &c.

Weekly Miscellany, Oct. 27. and Nov. 3.

On the Heathens Notions *of a future State, with Regard to modern Infidels.*

THE Idea and Expecta-
tion of a Life to come
having been propaga-
ted thro' all Ages and
into every Corner of
the World, there is no
room to doubt of its
Divine Original, the
Light of Nature not suggesting such a
Thing in a certain or general way. This
Principle is the Spring of Virtue and heroic Actions; it was so among the ancient *Greeks*, who have given us such in-
chantingDescriptions of the *Elysian Fields*,
and made the virtuous and vicious Pursuits of Life attend the Manes of the Deceased, or Pleasures and Punishments suitable to their former Behaviour, with the
Propriety even of *Christian Theology*.

Now, whatever *Infidels* may pretend,
that a future State is discoverable and
establish'd by *Natural Deduction* and *un-
assisted Reason*, the contrary is manifest
on the most cogent Evidence of primitive Story. Let me instance in Arts and
Sciences. Will they pretend they could
have found out the Use of them, had they
not been handed down to us? If they
think they could, let them recover the
celebrated Inventions of the Antients
which are now lost.

The *Immortality of the Soul* was a
Doctrine the *Philosophers* could not establish by their Reason. Yet *Zoroaster* and
Pliny say, *Democritus* believ'd the Resurrection of the Dead. *Socrates* also and
Aristotle testify'd their Expectations of
a further Revelation from some great Instructor to make known the Will of Heaven; and the *Sybilline* Oracles account
for the Notion of a great King to come,
about the time of the *Messiah.*

From the Examples of these and other
enlighten'd *Heathens*, the Author argues
against the Wickedness of the Declaimers against the *Christian* Religion, since
the Purity of its Doctrines, adapted, beyond all the boasted Plans of Morality,
to the Peace and Happiness of Mankind,
ought to make 'em silent, whatever Want
they might otherwise have of Conviction.

Grubstreet Journal, Nov. 1. No. 201.

THE Figures in the last Journal, (see
p. 538. B) design'd to represent a'
Barber's Shop, are 1. A Person in the
Chair. 2. A Barber shaving him. 3. Behind the Chair one smoaking a Pipe of
Tobacco. 4. Another holding a Bason,
and a Scroll of Writing. 5. Before the
Chair, one holding several Razors. 6. A-
nother a Tankard. 7,-8. Two Figures
seeming of different Sexes, combing and
tying a Wig on a Block. 9. One Bare-
headed, wearing a Scarf or Ribbond of
some Order. 10. A Clergyman with a
Purse in one Hand, the other extended
towards the last mention'd Figure.

The Members of the *Grubstreet* Society gave several Explanations, but as
Mr *Baxius* did not allow any to have
guess'd right, we shall but just mention 'em.

Dr *Quibus* apprehended the Interpre-
tation to be very difficult, and, tho' the
Drapery was modern, that he could see
Mr *Walsingham's Spirit of Antiquity sublimely expressed in every Stroke*, like *Alexander* engraved by his *Praxiteles*, (see
p. 420 G, p. 469. A)

Gyles Blunderbuss, Esq; thought the
Wig on the Block represented the Will of
Dr *Tyndal* bequeathing 210ol. to *Eustace
Budgell*, Esq; *that his great Talents might
serve his Country*. The Figure like a Fe-
male, to signify the Hon. Mrs *Prise* who
wrote the Will, and the other at the
block, the Hon. Mr *Curl* who publish'd it.
Fig. 10—to be the Revd Mr *Tyndal*; and
Fig. 9—to be *Eustace Budgell*, Esq; become a great Man on the expected Change
of the Ministry, and comforting Mr *Tyndal*
under the Disappointment of his Uncle's
Will, with his Promise of providing for
him and his Family. Lastly, That the
Figure in the Chair represented the same
Gentleman; and the Figures about it, some
Sturdy Beggars, (see p. 556) taking care
to have his Head shaved close before they
give an Answer to his Application to them
for chusing him a Member of Parliament.

Mr *Iolitivo*, thought the Wig on the
Block represented the Crown of *Poland*,
which the *Czarina* and the Emperor were
preparing for the Elector of *Saxony*. And
that the Person in the Chair was *Stanislaus*,
whom the King of *France* and his Allies
were trimming up for Royalty.

Mr *Pamphletero* was partly of the same
Opinion, and that the Cardinal Primate
was signify'd by the Clergyman.

Mr *Spondee* imagin'd the *Operator* sig-
nified some Minist.r of State in a late
Reign assisted by 4 Members in great
Posts, shaving the People by Taxes and
Impositions; Fig. 9—to be a Military
Officer,

Officer, reprefenting a Standing Army, approved and bleffed by the Ecclefiaftical Part of our Conftitution; the Figure in partly a feminine Drefs, intimates that many of the fair Sex, are great Lovers of a Standing Army in general, and a military Officers in particular.

Mr *Dactyl* took it for a Reprefentation of the Tranfactions of the *South-Sea* Company in 1720. The Barber is old *Knight* the Cafhier, who, with the Affiftance of the Directors, fhaved all Orders and Degrees of their Superfluities.

Mr *Poppy* thought it a Reprefentation of the Charitable Corporation,

Mr *Quidnunc* fancied, it typified an Flection at a Country Borough; the Barber, fome Lawyer, who undertakes to be Manager on either Side, that will give the largeft Fees. The whole Groupe of Figures feem to be drinking their new Member's Health. The Gentleman without the Wig ftands for the Candidates who voted for the Excife, who may probably be diftinguifhed by a Red Ribbond. The Peruke on the Block may reprefent the Writ of Election, which the returning Officer, in conjunction with fome intriguing Female, is preparing to fend back in Form. The lower part of her Habit is well fuited to a Lady of her Character, who always wears the Breeches. The Clergyman may ftand for the Minifter of the Parifh, who is in the fame Intereft, in hopes of a better Living.

A Letter from *H. W.* follows, who fuppofes the Cut to reprefent Mr *Bavius's* Shop, which, fince his Marriage with Mrs *Penelope Manibrino*, of *Batterfea*, he hath fet up for himfelf; *H. W.* adapts the Figures to Mr *Walfingham*, Mrs *Osborne*, the *Orator Pufferus*, fome Perfon of Diftinction, and a *Sturdy Begger* whiffing Tobacco at him in Difdain; the reft are Mr *Bavius* and his Affiftants ready to cut them for the Simples. But Mr *Bavius* fays this Explication is erroneous, and built on a falfe Foundation, his Marriage.

London Journal, Nov. 3. No. 749.

MR *Osborne* having cited feveral Paffages from the laft *Craftfman* wherein Mr *D'anvers* fpeaks of the Temper and good Will of the *Tories*, &c. towards the Diffenters, (fee p. 530, F) cries our, How *miraculoufly* happy are the *Diffenters* ! Not an Enemy among the *Papifts, Nonjurors, Jacobites,* or *Tories* ! None, but among the *Court Whigs* ! But let not the Authors of the *Craftfman* trouble

their Heads about the Church of *England* or *Diffenters*; for they will find *Both* againft them; they are refolv'd to fupport the Conftitution againft that *deteftable Coalition*, call'd a *national Union*, of pretended *Whigs*, and *real Jacobites*. How can *High Church* or *Tories* (whom the *Craftfman* perfwades the *Diffenters* to join) boaft of Favours done to the *Diffenters* ? Don't all Men know, that every Law made in *Favour*, or rather Juftice to the *Diffenters*, is entirely owing to the *Whigs*, nay, to fome of the prefent *Court Whigs* ? And were not thofe very *wicked Laws*, which *Court Whigs* repealed, made by *High Church* or *Tories* ? Yes, but it feems they *repent* and *acknowledge* their Error. But how can the *Diffenters* truft them? They always *repent* when out of *Power*, and *fin in Power*; thus they did in K. *William's* Reign; thus they *repented* and *mourned* when all good Men rejoiced, during *the glorious Part* of Q. *Anne's* Reign; but in the *Clofe* of it they finned with a high Hand indeed, when they made that moft *infamous Law* TO ROB THE PARENTS OF THEIR OWN CHILDREN: Some of thofe Law-makers are now alive; fome *now in the Houfe*; and others, 'tis faid, Writers of thofe very *Craftfmen* relating to the *Diffenters*.

Thofe very *Tories* not only *juftified* the *Schifm Act*; but *one* of them, Mr *Str—g—ys*, told a *Diffenter*, in the *Court of Requefts*, " That they had *no Right to their Children*; for they were *the Children of the Publick*. " He *bravely* replied, " Thofe Words are not fit to be fpoke by a *Reprefentative* of the People ! " You talk, Sir, faid the *Tory Member*, " We'll fhortly make you more humble; " which was, by depriving them of their *Votes*, as well as *Children*.

As foon as the *Hanover* Succeffion took Place, thefe very *penitent Tories* began a *Rebellion* againft the beft Government, and the beft Prince in the World. Ever fince, God be thank'd, they have been *out of Power*; and to get into it, the *Diffenters* are to take *their Words* againft *all their Actions* when in Power.

The *Craftfman*, after cajoling the *Diffenters*, falls to *Threatning*, and tells them, that if they don't *vote Right*, but fupport a *Rivalfhip*, they muft expect, that our *antient Difputes* will be revived, &c. (fee p. 539, H) But how can thefe dreadful Things happen if the *Tories* are *converted* ?

The *Diffenters*, they allow, did *right* in adhering *heretofore* to the *Whigs*: And why

hy are they not to do so now? Becaufe
as *Divifion of Parties* fubfifts no longer,
ic *Tories* are Whigs, and the *Whigs* To-
es: They may as well fay a *Mahometan*
a Chriftian, and a Chriftian, a *Jew*.

Fog's Journal Nov. 3. No. 261.

*Then Divifions are fpirited up by a Mini-
ftry, it is time for the People to look to
their Liberties.*

~ *Atherine* of *Medicis* carefs'd the poor
~ *Hugonots* whom she hated, till they
began to be looked upon as the Tools of
her Tyranny; when she had fo render'd
them odious, she facrific'd 'em to gain
over the *Roman* Catholicks; but all the
while was affiduoufly deftroying the Liberties of both.

'Tis hop'd the like will never be attempted here; yet 'tis a little furprizing
to fee Pamphlets and Papers difpers'd all
over the Country, the Tendency of which
is to fet the People at Variance with each
other; and to perfuade the *Diffenters* to
oppofe the general Bent of the Nation.
There is fomething fo abfurd in thefe
and Mr *Ofborne's* Addreffes to them, that
one would think there's but little Danger
of their fucceeding. But what are the
Diffenters to expect in Return? — only
that they will be fo good as to render
themfelves odious to their fellow Subjects, and all becaufe a certain Gentleman
is frighten'd out of his Wits, and dreads
a free P——.

The glorious Emulation which appears
in thefe Pamphlets is, which of them
fhall excel in Falfhood and Abfurdity;
one endeavours to fet the Landed and
Trading People together by the Ears,
for the Man, to ferve whom all thefe
Things are done, is in great Diftrefs for
fome publick Difturbance. His Emiffaries
have been round the Country almoft begging for Riots. We have heard of the
Feats of *fweet* Mr *W. T.* the Letter writer, (fee p. 298, A) in *Devonf.* and a *little*
Gentleman in *Cornwal*, who is taken Notice of for his worthy Pains in fecuring
the Returning Officers of certain Boroughs.

As to the Diffenters, I fuppofe, fays
Fog, a certain Gentleman thinks to ufe
them as his Cloak, to put it on in foul
Weather, and throw it off when 'tis
over; and there feems a thick Cloud gathering, which will require all his Sur-
touts, therefore he is fervilely making
his Court to thofe he fometimes oppofed,
and always neglected: But he thinks he
may without Danger drop the Diffenters;
for, as they muft, by complying with his

Meafures, render themfelves obnoxious
to the Body of the People, he may ufe
them ill, on purpofe to make Friends on
the other Side.

It's faid, the Preachers of fome Diffenting Congregations are in Penfion; it
is pretty fure, that fome who pretend to
be Diffenters and are Directors of Companies, have bragg'd they could head the
Reft; if fo, they are bargain'd for already, and fold like Sheep; however, they
are not oblig'd to ftand by fuch iniquitous
Contracts; they may now remove thofe
little Prejudices which have made their
Neighbours fometimes look * cold upon
them, by acting in the fame generous
manner they lately did in another Affair,
and oppofing every Man who wou'd be a
kind of Tyrant over his Fellow-Subjects.

The **Craftfman,** Nov. 3. No. 383.

Hiftory of Parties continued.

THE Writer of this Difcourfe obferves to Mr *D'anvers*, that nothing will enforce more ftrongly the Ex-
hortation to an *Union of Parties*, fo happily begun, than a fhort Hiftory of *To-
rifm* and *Whiggifm*, from their Cradle to
their Grave.

As your Papers, fays he, have from
the firft been confecrated to the Information of the People of *Britain*, and have
this Merit, that they never fpeak to the
Paffions without appealing to the Reafon
of Mankind; I fhall, therefore, advance
nothing but what Reafon and Truth con-
fpire to dictate. As for the *Drummers
and Trumpeters of Faction*, who are hir'd
to drown the Voice of both, they fhall
not provoke me to break a moft contemptuous Silence. The Subject is too folemn:
They may prophane it, by writing on it:
Far be it from me to be guilty of the
fame Crime by anfwering them. † But to
the Hiftory:

---

* "If I was a Diffenter, I fhould not fo much
regard their looking *cold*, as their looking *bot*.
Are not thefe doughty Politicians? ----to afk
the Diff nters to oppofe thofe Men who have
no *Coldnefs* towards them, no *Shynefs*, *Diftruft*, or *Prejudice* againft them! who declare
that they ought to be relieved from that
Badge of Slavery, the *Teft Act*;—in order to
place their Regard on thofe who own a Coldnefs, and who will make no fuch Declarations? —*Courant, Nov. 7.*

† The Writers againft this Author obferve,
that the Reafon why he will not anfwer them,
is, becaufe both Fact and Argument are a-
gainft him. *See Courant, Nov. 6. and 19.
London Journal, Nov. 17.*

Q. *Elizabeth* defign'd, and the Nation called K. *James* to the Throne, tho' the whole *Scottifh* Iffue had been excluded by the Will of *Henry* VIII. authorized indeed by an *Aft of Parliament*, yet little regarded by Parliament or People. As foon as he was crown'd, an *Aft of Recognition* paffed, declaring his *indubitable Right* to the Crown, &c. This is the *Æra of Hereditary Right*, and of fuch abfurd Notions of the facred *Prerogative* of *Kings*, as had never been heard of, till *that anointed Pedant* broach'd them.——Opinions very different from thofe had crept about even in the Reign of *Elizabeth*; but received fuch Advantages by the Exceffes of *Hierarchical* and *Monarchical Power*, which K. *James* and *Charles* I. exercifed, as to occafion all the Miferies which followed. *Phrenfy* provoked *Phrenfy*; and it hath coft us a *Century* to lofe and recover our *Wits*.

If our Grievances under K. *Charles* I. had been redreffed by a fober Parliamentary Reformation of the State; or if the Civil War happening, a new Government had been eftablifhed on Principles of the Conftitution, not of *Faftion*; of Liberty, not of Licentioufnefs, as there was on the Abdication of K. *James* II. the abfurd and Slavifh Doftrines mentioned would have been exploded. But the Spirit of the Father's Reign was maintained in that of his Son, the *fame Minifters* being continued, which occafion'd the Civil War, the King's Death, and the Exile of his Family. The Exile of thefe Princes having reconciled them to the Religion of *Rome*, and to the Politicks of *foreign Nations*, that fuch *Principles* as would fhock the common Senfe of a *Hottentot*, fhould come in Vogue again at the *Reftoration*, will not appear ftrange, when we confider the Excefs of Joy which many felt, and many feign'd; the Adulation of many to acquire new Merit, and by many to atone for paft Demerit; it is rather a Wonder that our Liberties were not quite given up. That we faved them we owe to thofe great and good Men, *Clarendon* and *Southampton*, who, far from managing *Parliaments* into *fcandalous Jobbs* for the *Crown*, broke the *Army*, ftinted the *Revenue*, and threw the King on the *Affeftions of his People*.

Another Reafon for making a Settlement at the Reftoration on fuch high Principles of Monarchy, was to balance the *Nonconformifts*; it might be thought prudent thro' Dread of relapfing into the Miferies the Nation had juft efcaped, to throw the Bent of Power too far the contrary Way. It was the fame in the Ecclefiaftical Settlement: The Church and the King having been joined in all the Contefts, its *Interefts* and *Refentments* came into the Aid of the Secular: Great Lenity was fhewn at the Reftoration in *looking backwards*, and unexampled, * unimitated Mercy to particular Men, not without Applaufe. This Conduct would have gone far towards reftoring the Nation to its *primitive Temper*; to its *old good Manners*, and *good Humour*, (Expreffions of Lord *Clarendon*, which I never read without being * moved) if great Severity had not been exercifed foon after, in *looking forwards*, and great Rigour ufed to large Bodies of Men; but not juftly, there being a wide Difference between *moral* and *party* Juftice; nor *Politicly*, becaufe it contradicted the foregoing quieting Meafures: It alarmed all the Sects a-new, damped the Spirit of Reconciliation, confirmed an Implacability to the Church, and imprudently drove the *Presbyterians*, who had been piqued againft the other Sectaries, into their antient Confederacies: However, they who had ufed greater (according to Bp *Burnet*) could not complain of thefe Violencies with any very good Grace. The Securing themfelves againft thofe who had ruined them once, was a plaufible Reafon for the *Church Party*. As to the *Promife* and *Declaration* fent from *Breda*, the King feemed difcharged from them on the Refufal of Parliament to confirm them. And the Merit I pleaded by the *Presbyterians* on Account of their Share in the Reftoration, though it was confiderable, could avail but little. The

* A Writer in the *Courant*, *Nov.* 6. fuppofes Vifc. *Bolingbroke*, the Author of this *Craftfman*; upon which he enquires, whether he ever gave the leaft Return of *Applaufe* for the *unexampled* and *unimitated* Mercy extended to him? And then adds,——What a tender compaffionate Nature muft he be compofed of? How hardly can he refrain from Tears, when he fpeaks of *Forgivenefs*, of *unexampled* and *unimitated* Mercy! Doubtlefs he had read *Clarendon* before he became a *Secretary of State*. Yet after all this *Softening* about him, when the *Catalans* fued to him for Mercy, he could turn his Back upon them; and inftead of Mercy, fhew them nothing but *Cruelty unexampled* and *unimitated*.

† *See* Presbyterians Plea of Merit, impartially examin'd. Price Six-pence.

Fruits

Fruits of their Repentance came late, and not 'till they had been wormed out of Power by another Sect. Thus when the legal Constitution of the Church was restored, the *Dissenters* were rigorously treated, in their Turn, without *any Distinction*. I believe this Severity was not in the first Design of the *Ministers*, but was brought on by the Influence of *Popery*. The Artifice of the *Popish* Faction, during the whole Reign of *Charles* II. distressed the *best* Ministers, and encouraged the *worst* to play the *Church* and *Dissenters* against each other, to make them Bubbles to the Common Enemy: To effect this, it is probable that some *Leaders* among the *latter* were encouraged by the *private* Applications of the *Court*. (See *p.* 583 A) For,

Though the 2,000 Ministers, who went out of their Churches on one Day, were far from having one consistent Scheme; tho' many of them must have lost their Benefices, even if they had comply'd with the *Act of Uniformity*, because they were Intruders, and in actual Possession of Benefices legally belonging to others; yet, by uniting in the Point of *Nonconformity*, they appeared as *one Body*, and in some Sense were so.————On which Account,

The King, being addressed, declared himself ready to dispense with several *Things* in the *Uniformity Act* in their Favour; and some Attempts were made, but happily prevented by Parliament; and at last the Dissenters saw they were only to be made Tools to advance the *Prerogative* above Law, and the Toleration of *Popery* against it.

Thus the Parties after the Restoration preserved too near a Resemblance to those before the War. The Dissenters had lost their Power, indeed, but they had Numbers, Property, and Industry.————They did not inflame Matters into a Civil War as before, but without them the Zeal against *Popery* could not have run into a factious Fury, which towards the End of this Reign so raised the Fears of falling again under *Presbyterian* or *Republican Power*, as to drown the Fear of *Popery* and a *Popish* Successor; so as to transport Clergy and Laity into an Avowal of Principles that must have made us Slaves or Papists, had not the very Men who avow'd such Principles, saved themselves and us in direct Opposition to them.

The FREE BRITONS, Nov. 1, 8, & 22. are *Extracts* from a *Pamphlet* on the Excise Scheme, *of which we have already treated very largely.*

The Universal Spectator, Nov. 3, & 10.

The Temple of Love.

THO' Love is a *natural* and noble Passion when well *regulated*, yet nothing gives a more just Occasion for *Raillery* than that soft Seducer, when it fills the Head with *Romantick* Notions, and *imaginary* Happiness. When the *Severity* of a *Philosopher* dissolves into *Effeminacy*; when a *Statesman* gives up his Reason to this Passion, what a ridiculous Scene must it afford? *Harry Careless*, says Mr. *Stonecastle*, diverted the *Club* the other Night with a Satire on this Foible, under the Disguise of a Dream.

I thought myself in the Temple of Love, where sat on a Christal Throne, *Beauty*, the Goddess of the Place.———— Among the vast Company that fill'd the Dome, 'twas not unpleasant to observe a reputed *Woman hater* caressing an *Orange Wench*; a Politician ogling an *Actress*; a *young Parson* addressing a rich *old Woman*. In another Part of the Temple, *Emperors*, *Beaus*, *Generals*, and *Mercers Apprentices*; *Queens*, *Milkmaids*, *Dutchesses*, and *Abigails* were walking together with *folded Arms*, and *jealous Looks*. The Maids practising Airs before their *Glasses*; the old *Maids*, some breaking their *Looking-Glasses*, some at their *last Prayers*, others boasting *former Offers*, and their *Virtue* in refusing them: The *Widows* pursuing the Men; the *Beaus*, with their *Essence* and *Orangeries*, completing before a Peer-Glass.

From hence I went into the Apartment of Marriage; here a *cold Indifference* appear'd in the Aspect of most; those who seem'd mighty *fond* in the Temple of *Love*, here express'd a hearty *Contempt* of one another. Some Ladies were dying with the *Vapours*, occasion'd by Denials their Husbands gave them; one whisper'd her Spouse, she must see the *Ceremony* of the *Nuptials* of the *Princess Royal*; the Gentleman with a Smile replied, he knew not how to get a *Ticket*; down she fell in a *Fit*————Another who had a Ticket wanted a Pair of *Diamond Ear-rings*, which being denied, down she fell. In short, there were not a few of the *Citizens Wives* full of their *Pouts*, *Vapours*, and such *Politick Airs*. Leaving this Scene I enter'd another Part, where every one wore in their Looks the Marks of *Pleasure* and *Joy*: But what chiefly commanded my *Attention* was a Royal Pair seated on a Throne: The *Smiles* and *Content* in *their* Looks set an Example to *others* to *love* like *them*. In the Midſt of this *pleaſing View* the Doors flew open, and *Hymen* and *Love* led in a *blooming Bridegroom* and a *Fair Bride* : They were conducted towards the *Throne*, and plac'd by it ; *Virtue* and *Honour*, *Conſtancy* and *Truth* attended in their *Train* ; *Admiration* and *Pleaſure* ſtood confeſs'd in every one's Face, and in the *Eaſtaſy* of their *Hearts* cried out, *Thus may* Anne *and* Naſſau *ever live*.——The Raptures of my *Soul*, and that *joyful Sound* wak'd me, but *leſſen'd* not my *Pleaſure*, when I conſider'd that *imaginary* Proſpect would ſoon be a real one to the Subjects of *Great-Britain*. *See* Vol. IV. p. 360.

Weekly Miſcellany, Nov. 10. No. 48.

BRitannicus, in a Letter to Mr *Hooker*, gives an Extract from a Piece publiſh'd in 1708, entitled, *The Sentiments of a Church of England Man with reſpect to Religion and Government*. The Author's Deſign is to vindicate the Clergy from that Contempt which is generally thrown upon them by the Laity, particularly the *Whigs*, who, he ſays, might have maintain'd a Majority among the Clergy, and at the Univerſities, if they had not too much encouraged the Intemperance of Speech, and Virulence of Pen, in the moſt profligate of their Party ; reproaching them with Arbitrary and Jacobite Principles ; tho' at the ſame time it could not be forgot, that the Oppoſition made to the Uſurpations of K. *James* II. proceeded chiefly from the Clergy and the Univerſities, whereas the Diſſenters univerſally complied, and ſome of them took † Poſts in the Army raiſed againſt the Prince of *Orange*. However, though the Clergy may be chargeable with ſome Vices, we have no better Materials to compound the Prieſthood of than the Maſs of Mankind ; therefore the Church of England-Man cannot think *Ambition* or *Love of Power* more juſtly objected to them than to other Men, becauſe that would be to make Religion itſelf, or at leaſt the beſt Conſtitution of Government, anſwerable for the Depravities of human Nature.

We are unhappily divided, ſays *Britannicus* in his Remarks on the above-cited Paſſages, into Parties, acting zealouſly in Oppoſition to one another. I ſhall not vindicate or condemn the Conduct of the Clergy who have adhered to the Meaſures of either, it is more perti-

nent to obſerve the Unreaſonableneſs and Injuſtice, in *any* Party, to carry their Reſentment to the *whole Body* of the Clergy, out of Diſguſt at the Conduct of a *Part of* them ; and of the great *Folly*, as well as *Wickedneſs*, of ſuffering thoſe Reſentments to affect their *Faith*.

The Craftſman, Nov. 10. No. 384.

The Hiſtory of Parties continued.

THE Nation began to be indiſpoſed to the *Court* ſoon after the *Reſtoration*. The Sale of *Dunkirk* helped to ruin a great and good *Miniſter* ; — Who knows how ſoon the Re-eſtabliſhment of the ſame *Part* may be laid in Form to the Charge of * *two Men*, ſtrictly and undeniably anſwerable for it ; who ſtagger already under the Weight of ſo many other Juſt Imputations?

The *firſt Dutch War*, which was raſhly undertaken, and ended ignominiouſly for the Nation, augmented the publick Indiſpoſition. Nay, Misfortunes, (ſuch as the *Plague*, and the *Burning of London*) as well as *Miſmanagement*, had this Effect. But We muſt place at the Head of all a *Jealouſy of Popery*, which heated the Minds of Men to ſuch a Degree, that it ſeems almoſt wonderful, the *Plague* was not imputed to the *Papiſts* as peremptorily as the *Fire*.

The Death of Lord *Southampton*, and Baniſhment of Lord *Clarendon* made Room for new Cauſes of Diſſatisfaction ; *Thoſe two noble Lords* had ſtood in the Breach againſt *Popery* and foreign *Politicks* ; *They were* true Proteſtants, *and* honeſt Engliſhmen. *Whilſt they were in Place, our Laws, Religion, and Liberties were in Safety. When They were removed*, England *felt the ill Effects of the Change*.

K. *Charles*, rather the *Duke* and *Pope's Faction*, were now at Liberty to form new Schemes againſt the Religion and Liberty of *England* without Reſerve.

As to the *Parliament*, both *Houſes* were full of Zeal for the *preſent Government*,

---

† See the *Preſbyterians* Plea of *Merit*, p. 12, 13, 14, 15.

* Had the glorious Adminiſtration which this Writer (B——le) was ſo eminent a Branch of, deſign'd that *Dunkirk* Harbour ſhould never be re-eſtabliſhed, why did not they ſtipulate for keeping it in the Hands of the *Engliſh*? —— Now the *French* are Maſters of it, how is it poſſible to prevent their eſtabliſhing it, if they ſet heartily about it? But he is laying his own Crimes to two Gentlemen, who oppoſed every Step of their infamous Peace. *Courant*, Nov. 13.

and

and of Refentments against the *late Ufurpa-*
tions. There was but *one Party* in Parliament ; and no *other Party* could raife its
Head in the Nation. This might have
been the Cafe probably as long as King
Charles fat on the Throne, if the *Court* had
been a little honefter, or a little wifer.
No Parliament ever did more to gain
their Prince than This. they feem'd,
for feveral Years, to have nothing fo much
at Heart as fecuring his *Government*, advancing his *Prerogative*, and filling his
Coffers. The *Grants* They made Him
were Inftances of Profufion in thofe Days;
when 1,200,000 *l. a Tear for the* CIVIL
LIST, *the* FLEET, *the* GUARDS, *and*
GARRISONS, *and all the ordinary Ex-*
pences of the Government was thought an
exorbitant Sum ; how little a Figure foever it would make in * our Times, when
two Thirds of that Sum, at leaft, are appropriated to the Ufe of the *civil Lift*
fingly. But all This was to no Purpofe ;
a *foreign Interest* prevail'd ; a *Cabal* govern'd ; and fometimes the *Cabal,* and
fometimes a *Prime-Minifter,* had more
Credit with the *King* than the whole Body
of his People. When the *Parliament*
faw They could not gain Him over to
his own and their common Intereft by
gentle Methods; They turn'd Themfelves
to fuch as were rough, but agreeable to
Law and the Cuftom of Parliament, as
well as proportionable to the Greatnefs
of the Exigence. That they loft their
Temper, on fome particular Occafions,
muft not be deny'd. They were Men,
and therefore frail ; but their Frailties
of this Kind, proceeded from their Love
of their Country. They were tranfported,
when they found that their *Religion*
and *Liberty* were conftantly in Danger
from the Intrigues of a *Popifh Faction* ;
and they would have been fo tranfported, no Doubt, if *Liberty* alone had been
attack'd by a *Proteftant Faction.* Then
it was, that this *High-Church Parliament*
grew favourable to *Proteftant Diffenters,*
and ready to make that juft Diftinction,
fo long delay'd, between *Them* and *Popifh*
Recufants, that the *whole Proteftant In-*
terest might unite in the common Caufe.

* The Author of the Courant, *Nov.* 13.
fays, this Infinuation is dropt to create
Uneafinefs in his Majefty's Subjects, and yet
is nothing but empty Clamour ;—for the Sum
of 700,000 *l.* was granted to Queen *Anne,* who
had no Child ; and to his prefent Majefty only
800,000 *l.* tho' he has fuch a numerous Royal
Iffue, the Glory and Security of the Nation.

Then it was, that this *Prerogative Par-*
liament defy'd *Prerogative,* in Defence of
their *own Privileges,* and of the *Liberties*
of their Country. Then it was, that this
paffive Obedience and Non-Refiftance Par-
liament went the utmoft Lengths of *Re-*
fiftance, in a *Parliamentary Way* ; and
the neceffary Confequence of the Steps
They made, *in this Way,* muft have
been *Refiftance in another,* if the *King*
had not dropt his *Minifters,* retracted
his *Pretenfions,* redreffed *fome,* and given
Expectation of redreffing *other Grievances.*
In fine, this *Penfioner Parliament,* as it
hath been ftyl'd, with *fome Corruption* in
the Houfe, and an *Army* fometimes at
the Door of it, disbanded the *Army* in
England, and protefted againft the *Mili-*
tia fettled in *Scotland* by Act of Parliament, and appointed to march *for any*
Service, wherein the King's Honour, Au-
thority, and Greatnefs was concern'd, in
Obedience to the Orders of the Privy Coun-
cil. They not only did their utmoft to
fecure their Country againft immediate
Danger, but projected to fecure it againft
remote Danger, by an Exclufion of the
Duke of *York,* who had declar'd himfelf
a *Papift,* from the Crown, after They
had endeavour'd ftrenuoufly, but in vain,
to prevent his entailing *Popery* more eafily upon us by his Marriage with a *Popifh*
Princefs.

When I reflect on thefe Particulars,
and a great many others, which might
be mentioned to the Honour of *this Par-*
liament, I cannot hear it called the *Pen-*
fioner Parliament, as it were by Way
of Eminence, without a Degree of honeft Indignation ; efpecially in the *Age,*
in which we live, and by fome of *Thofe*
who affect the moft to beftow upon it
this ignominious Appellation. *Penfions*
indeed, to the Amount of *feven or eight*
Thoufand-Pounds were difcover'd to have
been given to fome Members of the *Houfe*
of Commons. But then this Expedient of
corrupting Parliaments began under the
Adminiftration of that boifterous, over
bearing Minifter, CLIFFORD. When
the *Court* was in the Intereft of the
People, the Expedient of *Bribery* was
neither wanted, nor practifed. When
the *Court* was in *another Intereft,* the
Practice of *Bribing the Reprefentatives*
of the People commenced. Should a *Par-*
liament act in Compliance with a *Court*
againft the Senfe and Intereft of the *Na-*
tion, Mankind would be ready to pronounce very juftly that *fuch a Parliament*
was under the *corrupt Influence of the*
Court

Court. But in the Cafe now before us, We have a very comfortable Example of a *Court,* wicked enough to ftand in need of *Corruption,* and to employ it; and of a *Parliament* virtuous enough to refift the Force of *this Expedient*; Nei- A ther *Places* nor *Penfions* could hinder *Courtiers* in this Parliament from voting on many fignal Occafions, againft the *Court*; Nay, this *Penfioner Parliament,* if it muft be ftill called fo, gave one Proof of *Independency,* befides That of contriving a *Teft,* in 1675, *to purge their* B *Members on Oath from all Sufpicion of corrupt Influence;* which ought to wipe off this Stain from the moft Corrupt. They drove *one of their Paymafters* out of Court, and impeached the *other* in the Fullnefs of his Power; even at a Time, when the *King* was forced to make, on C Account of *Penfions* privately negotiated from *France,* the Caufe of the *Crown* and the Caufe of the *Minifter* one.

But if fome fevere Cenfor fhould infift that *more Penfions* would have made *more Penfioners;* that *much Money* and *little Prerogative* is more dangerous to *Liberty* than *much Prerogative* and *little* D *Money*; and that the *worft and weakeft Minifter* King *Charles* ever had might have been abfolute in *this very Parliament,* if *fuch a Minifter* had been able to inlift, with Places, Penfions, and occafional Bribes, not a *flender Majority,* which the Detection of a Few might at E any Time defeat, but fuch a *bulky Majority,* as might impofe on itfelf; if any one, fhould infift that *fuch a Minifter,* with *fuch a Purfe,* would have ftood his Ground in the *Parliament* I fpeak of, with how much Contempt and Indignation foever He might have been every F where treated by the People; I fhall not prefume to affert the contrary. It might have been fo. Our Safety was owing as much, perhaps, to the *Poverty of the Court,* as to the *Virtue of the Parliament*; We might have loft our *Liberties.* But G then I would obferve, if this be true, the Prefervation of our *Religion* and *Liberty,* at that Time, was owing, *firft,* that King *Charles* fquandered on his *Pleafures* what He might have employed to *corrupt this* Parliament; *fecondly,* that the *Minifters,* in that Reign, fingering no H Money but the *Revenue, ordinary and extraordinary,* had no Opportunity to filch in the Pockets of every private Man, and to bribe the Bubbles with their own Money; as might be done now, when *Funding* hath been fo long in

Fafhion, and the *greateft Minifter* had the Means of Being the *greateft Stock-jobber,* did not the eminent Integrity of the *Minifter,* and the approved Virtue of the *Age* fecure us from any fuch Danger.

Fog's Journal. Nov. 10. No. 262.

Of Falfe Ambition.

IT's pleafant to obferve what prepofterous Methods fome Men take, only for the little Ambition of being remarkable.——I have heard a Story, fays Fog, of a Student of *Oxford,* who happen'd to be *pluck'd, i. e.* was not able to pafs thro' the Exercifes for his Degrees. Soon after, Sir *R. Steel's* Patent, as Director of *Drury lane* Theatre, was fuperfeded by the prefent D. of *N——le,* then Lord Chamberlain; upon which our *Oxonian* writes a Treatife to prove, it was lawful for Sir *Richard* to kill the *Duke.* This being told at Court, the Gentleman was brought from *Oxford* in Cuftody of a Meffenger. Maugre all this, he got into Holy Orders, and out of the fame Fondnefs of Glory, being admitted into the Pulpit of a great Cathedral, he roars out for *unlimited Paffive Obedience*; which to do in thefe Times, fhews, that had he lived in the Days of *Hugh Peters,* he would have join'd in the Cry of *Bind your Kings in Chains,* &c. but it comes naturally enough from a Defender of Murder.

His Motive, no doubt, was a Defire of rifing in the World.——A good Deanery has a thoufand pretty Conveniencies belonging to it, and is a Step to a good Bifhoprick. Suppofe the Gentleman in Poffeffion of a *Welfh* Bifhoprick, firft, let him refolve never to refide there, nor fee it once in feven Years.——Many Excufes may be made—As it is too far off, the Air not good, or he muft attend at Court.——As to the Cure of Souls, they may go to the D—: But let him take an exact and holy Account of the Revenues, and be as religioufly careful to have them duly collected, as if his Salvation depended on it; for it is a great Sin to fuffer the Church to be wronged. — If he has Sons, let him procure Employments for them; if Daughters, let him marry them, and inftead of Portions, get Profits for the Husband; then let him extol Penfions as heavenly Gifts, and Bribery as *Jure Divino.*

A Clergyman touched with a violent Zeal for Preferment, feldom lofes his Time in ftudying the Doctrine of Chrift.
He

He frequents the Levees of Men in Power; there he humbly defires to know
what are the Principles in Vogue. It is
not what St *Matthew* or St *Mark* taught,
but what St *W*— teaches, that is the Rule
of his Faith.

In fome Countries the People are apt
to be tumultuous, when they think themfelves oppreffed by the Minifters. A-
bout four Years fince, the Prime Vifier
at *Conftantinople* was feiz'd by the Populace, who tied his Legs to the Tail of a
Mule, and dragged him thro' the City.—
I thank God, our People are addicted to
no fuch Violences, and yet, if one was to
judge by the ignominious Treatment they
had received for feveral Months paft, from
the Mercenaries of a certain Perfon, one
would think they * muft have committed
greater Barbarities than the Vizier fuffered at *Conftantinople*; yet they offered
no Infults on a late Occafion to any Man.
I am heartily glad, adds *Fog*, they had
fo much Forbearance.—What fhould we
fay, if after all this Lenity and Mildnefs
of Behaviour, we fhould fee a Fellow
mount a Pulpit; and, like a Dragoon,
hector thefe peaceable People for prefuming to petition, to write, or to fpeak
what they apprehended to be an Oppreffion? If he fhould happen to be fuch a
Perfon, as before defcribed, I fhould only
fay, *the Champion is worthy of the Caufe.*

London Journal. Nov. 10. N° 750.

THE Gentleman who writes upon
Parties in the *Craftfman*, having
been himfelf *for* and *againft* the Conftitution, for and againft the *lawful*, and
pretended King of *England*; of all *Principles*, and of all *Parties*, and having *betrayed all* hath given fuch flagrant Proofs
of his *Indifference* to all Principles and
Actions, that he feems the propereft Man
to write for a *Coalition of all Parties*,

* One would think it fomeunequalled Oppreffion, fome *fhocking* Cruelty, that has been
exercifed *towards thefe undifcerning People*, to
induce any Man to fpirit them up to a Violation of the Laws, and confequently of the
Conftitution, in the moft inhuman Manner:
But this is the Writer, who recommended a
Pamphlet that declared it to be but a *Piece of
Juftice* to ruin the *City* of *Norwich*; becaufe
they cannot agree with a Party of Men in
their perfonal Hatred. This is he, who cannot brook the Act for preventing Riots. This
is he who maintains, a Nation may be free,
not only if the Prince be a Papift, but even
a *Mahometan, Courant, Nov.* 19.

however different in their Views. But a
juft Man will always *diftinguifh* Things
by their *natural* and *effential* Differences:
he will not call a *Jacobite*, a Friend to
the prefent Government; nor *Whigs
Tories*, nor *Tories Whigs*.

To *divide* the *Whigs*, who are the only
fure Friends to our Civil and Religious
Liberties, and by whofe *clofe Union only* the
Ends of the Revolution can be carried
on, is the greateft *National Crime* a Man
can be guilty of; but this is the conftant
labour'd *Defign* of this *Grand Impoftor*,
who cannot carry his Point but by *Deceiving*. In his laft Difcourfe he has given
us an Account of the *Rife* and *Progrefs*
of *Parties, Ecclefiaftical* and *Civil*; but
'twould have been as much to the Purpofe
had he given us an Account of the Rife
and Progrefs of the *feveral Sects* of the
Mahometan Religion. The *Point* in Debate is, Whether the *Diffenters* fhould
leave the *Court Whigs*, and join *Jacobites,
Tories*, and *Male-content Whigs?* or whether there ought to be *an Union of all*
Parties againft the Court, or Miniftry?
For, fuppofe it true, that the *two grand
Parties* of *Whig* and *Tory* rofe politically,
and hated one another from Views of *Intereft* and *Power*; yet it does not follow,
that they don't *hate thoroughly*, that the
Parties don't now *exift*, or that they have
not *now*, very *contrary Views* and *Defigns*.

But 'tis not true that thefe Parties rofe
politically: Falfe Policy, indeed, might
put the *Tories* upon *perfecuting* the *Whigs*
and the Church upon *perfecuting* the *Diffenters*; they were *made* before they
were *perfecuted*, and rofe, like other
Divifions of Men, from *Differences in
Nature, Education*, &c. The *Puritans*,
in Q. *Elizabeth's* Time, did not rife
from Power employ'd againft them, but
Power was employ'd againft 'em; becaufe
they were *rifen* and grown into a Sect
or Party. There ever will be different
Sentiments about Religion and Politicks,
which *Differences* ought carefully to be
diftinguifh'd; efpecially when there are
Principles, call'd *Religious*, for *perfecuting* others, and *Principles* of *Politicks* a-
gainft a *legal* and *juft Government*;
which hath been our Cafe not only before, but ever fince the Revolution.

The Gentleman, who labours fo hard
for a *Coalition of Parties*, hath not given
one *Reafon*, why the *Whigs* fhould *divide*,
nor why the *Diffenters* fhould leave the
Court Whigs. He exhorts them, indeed,
to an *Union of Parties*, in Support of the
Conftitution; taking it for granted that
the

the *Conſtitution* is in Danger, but when called on for Proof of it, wiſely ſays, "Nothing ſhall provoke him to break a moſt contemptuous Silence". (See p. 583 E)

Free Briton, Nov. 15. No. 211.

A Vindication of the firſt Prince of Orange.

THE Enemies to his Majeſty's Title and Government are as remarkable for their Inhumanity, as for their Diſaffection. This *Characteriſtick of Jacobiſm* hath been claim'd by their Leaders and Writers, thro' a long Succeſſion of Years. They confirmed it to themſelves by the barbarous *Aſſaſſination Plot*, projected againſt the Life of K. *William* III. They cheriſhed ſo baſe a *Thirſt of his Blood*, that they conſecrated a *Horſe* for breaking *his Neck*, and daily pledged *the Health of a Beaſt* that accidentally haſten'd his Period.

The ſame *Baſeneſs of Spite*, and *Violence of Outrage* hath conſtantly appeared in this Faction againſt the Friends of our Liberty. On the Death of the late E. of *Godolphin*, they indulged the *pooreſt Jeſts*. When Prince EUGENE *of Savoy* came hither on the Part of his Imperial Majeſty, to ſave the *Common Cauſe of Europe* from the *treacherous Negotiations* of a Tory *Miniſtry*, neither the Luſtre of his own Character, nor the Grandeur of that Auguſt Court from whence he came, could obtain him Reſpect, or *common Decency*, from that Faction which feared his Succeſs; and ſo ſcandalouſly low was their Malice, that the Daily Papers were employ'd to inſult the Aſhes of *his Mother*.

It is with the ſame *Characteriſtical Spirit* of *Jacobitiſm*, the Author of Fog's *Journal* his libell'd the Houſe of *Orange* from its firſt *Founders* to the *lateſt of the Line*. (See p. 534. E) This Libel immediately followed the Royal Directions to bring over that Prince whom his Majeſty had deſtin'd to marry his eldeſt Daughter, with the *higheſt Approbation* of his *Parliament*, and the *warmeſt Acknowledgments* of *all his People*. The Faction thought it neceſſary, when this Alliance was firſt propoſed in Publick, to appear by their *principal Leader* againſt it; that it might not be concluded from any Reſolutions *within Doors*, or from any Rejoicings *without*, that the Spirit of *Jacobitiſm* was wholly extinguiſhed. What the worthy Gentleman ſaid on that Occaſion, tho' none thought fit to add any Thing after he had ſpoken, was meant and underſtood as the *Proteſt of the Party*.

It had been a Departure from their War againſt Humanity, as well as againſt the Prince on the *Throne*, had they not uſhered the Prince of *Orange* into the Kingdom with baſe unmanly Invectives againſt his *brave* Anceſtors; for this *End an abuſive Journal* is ſent all over the Kingdom, aſperſing the Memory of WILLIAM *the Firſt Prince of Orange*. It was Cauſe of Quarrel at all Times, in the Opinion of an *accompliſhed Jacobite*, that this Great Man had been the *Deliverer* of the *Dutch* from the Yoke of abſolute Power: It was ſtill a greater Provocation that he was the Anceſtor of our own *Deliverer* K. *William* III. If any Thing more could inflame their Rage againſt this long-loſt Prince *William* I. *of Orange*, a Marriage of his preſent Heir, to his preſent Majeſty's *eldeſt Daughter* muſt be the Incentive; and hath produced the Effect.

To this baſe Purpoſe the moſt corrupt Hiſtorians of the *Spaniſh Faction*, who palliate the Duke of *Alva's* Tyranny in the *Low Countries*, are revived.

All agree, ſays Bp *Burnet*, that William I. Prince of Orange, *was one of the greateſt Men in Story, who after many Attempts for the Recovery of the Liberty of the Provinces, was in the Concluſion ſucceſsful, and formed that Republick*. But, according to Fog, we are to draw our Ideas of *William* I. Prince of *Orange*, from Card. *Bentivoglio*, a Colleague of the Aſſaſſin, an avow'd *Enemy of the Reformation*, and *all popular Liberty*, who, however, with a Reſemblance of Impartiality gives us ſome *Truths*, ſome *Praiſes* of that Prince, which are beyond the Power of the moſt *outrageous Enemy* to deny. (See p. 534 A)

But not to reſt on Bp *Burnet*, againſt whom the *Jacobite Faction* will always retain a Hatred implacable as their Revenge againſt the *Prince of Orange*; I ſhall appeal to a Writer, who, as he lived without an Enemy, hath made every Reader his Friend; and is the only one in our Language, who hath wrote with univerſal Reputation on the Hiſtory or Affairs of the *United Provinces*, I mean Sir *William Temple*. His Words are,

The Spaniſh *and* Italian *Writers content themſelves to attribute the Cauſes of the* Dutch *Revolutions to the Change of Religion, to the native Stubborneſs of the People, and to the* Ambition *of the* Prince *of* Orange: *But Religion, without Mixtures of Ambition and Intereſt, works no ſuch violent Effects; it produces rather the Example*.

ample of constant Sufferings, than of desperate Actions. The Nature of the People cannot change of a sudden, any more than the Climate which infuses it. ———— *And the Ambition of one Man could neither design nor atchieve so great an Adventure, had it not been seconded with universal Discontent, nor could that have been raised to so great a height without so many Circumstances as fell in from the Course of the Spanish Councils to kindle and ferment it. Tho' it had been hard to head such a Body, and give it so strong a Principle of Life and so regular Motions, without the Accident of so great a Governor in the Provinces, as Prince WILLIAM of Orange; a Man of equal Abilities in Council and in Arms; cautious and resolute, affable and severe; supple to Occasions, and yet constant to his Ends; of mighty Revenues, and Dependence in the Provinces; of great Credit and Alliances in Germany; esteemed and honoured abroad; but at home infinitely loved and trusted by the People, who thought him affectionate to their Country, sincere in his Professions and Designs, able and willing to defend their Liberties,* and *unlikely to invade them by any Ambition of his own. (See Temple, V. I. p. 21.)*

This is that *Prince of Orange* from whom the *illustrious Person*, whose Extraction deserves the Marriage of the *Princess Royal*, derives his Title with a Character worthy of his Descent.

As there was no more than *one Man* in the *whole Representative* Body of this Nation, who opposed this Marriage, it may be charitable to believe there was no more than *one Man* in the collective Body capable of this profane and *outrageous Insult* on the *Ashes of this Prince's Ancestors*. If it should happen, that the *only Opposer of the Marriage* should be the *only Author of such Abuse*, the Reproaches he must expect from every *freeborn Englishman*, will then *only fall where* they have *always* been deserved.

Grubstreet Journal, Nov. 15. No. 203.

Mr Bavius,

IT is now no Secret, that you are upon your Marriage to Mrs PENELOPE

* The *Daily-Courant*, Oct. 20, in Answer to *Fog*, gives a like Character of this Great Prince from the celebrated *Grotius*, who says, his Dying Prayer to God was, ———— *Have Mercy on the People*; that he had a vast Soul equal to the most exalted Condition; and that the Ancestors of his Family of *Nassau* in *Germany*, had formerly been Competitors for the Empire with the House of *Austria*.

MAMBRINO, the *Battersea* Heiress, a young Lady of great Beauty and Merit, with an ample Fortune, as all the young Ladies are, which the News papers have married of late Years: If it be your Destiny to marry this Lady; suffer me, as one that wishes you well, to give you a Word of Advice, how to order your Conduct towards her.

First, let her have her Way, in every thing you yourself like. Secondly, if before Marriage, she absolutely refuseth any Settlement, and forbids you to buy her a Gold Watch, or Diamond Necklace, do not transgress her Commands. If after Marriage, she refuseth going to Masquerades, Balls, Plays, Operas, or Assemblies; do not contradict her. If it be her Pleasure to wear all her old Cloaths over again for seven Years together, buy no new ones in all that time. If she chuseth to keep at home, and neither receive, nor pay Visits, and to drink Water-Gruel, instead of Tea, and Burgundy; readily comply with her. If she loves Brandy; buy an Anchor of it at a time, set it by her Bed's-side, in which put a neat brass Cock, and by it, set a handsome flint Glass, that holds a Quartern, and let her drink her fill: You cannot imagine how this will gain her Affection. If she is inclin'd to fast twice a Week, and to go to Church twice a Day; encourage her pious Intentions. If she is quiet and affable; never trouble yourself to ask her for an ugly crooked Word. If she delights in her Needle, and loves Work; do not discourage her; but let her eat Gold, if she will earn it, and never quarrel with her, for letting you live at peace. If she loves Red-Herrings with Goosberry Tarts, or Mustard with Apple Pye, gratify her Inclination. If she is Sick, and to save Charges, will have no Doctor, comply with her therein: And if she can advance herself, at any time, by changing this Life for a better; be not her Hinderance. — Do thus, and be happy. I am, dear Sir, Yours, &c.

DEMOCRITUS.

Weekly Miscellany. Nov. 17, and 24.

A Writer in these Papers communicates his Remarks on a Piece of Mr *Chubb*'s entitled, *Short Reflections on the Ground and Extent of Authority, and Liberty, with respect to civil Government*, the Design of which is to prove, that *Governors*, as *Governors*, have no Right to interpose at all in Matters of Religion, the

the Consequence of which is, that human Laws are sufficient of and by themselves, *i. e.* abstracted from the Influence of a religious Sense, to procure all the Comforts, which Government, however modified, is capable of giving. The Falsity of which this Writer endeavours to shew from the Difficulty there is in making Laws exact, and equal to the Nature and Extent of Mens Crimes: But especially as nothing but the Sense of a Being, who will make every Creature accountable for the good or bad Use of its Talents, can be a sufficient Motive to act with a disinterested View to the Good of the Community. The urging in answer to this, the Sacredness of Oaths, is frivolous; because all Oaths and the Security founded thereon, necessarily presuppose the Being of a God and another World: Take but away this Belief, the Obligations cease, and Government loses its best Support.

I might here inquire, what Influence the firm Belief of a God, and a Retribution to come, will naturally have upon the Conduct of Men; but I am of Opinion it will be allowed me, that such a Belief will strongly dispose Mankind to the Pursuit of Virtue, and consequently promote the common Felicity; — therefore, tho' Mr *Chubb's* Notion be ever so true, *that the End and Purpose of Association, is not Mens Relation to, and Dependency on God, or the Good or Evil they may receive from him; but only their Relation to, and Dependency on, and the Good or Evil they may receive from each other;* Yet it will never follow from thence, that *Religion or worshipping God, is a Matter with which Society is not concerned, or interested in; that is, that Society is not benefited or damaged by Mens worshipping or not worshipping:* For History informs us, that the more or less *Religious* any Nation was, the more or less happy, and the greater or less Degrees of Conveniencies it constantly abounded with: And accordingly Governors have a Right as Guardians of human Happiness, to tie Men to the Observance of Religion. Hence it was thought reasonable to make the many good Laws we have for that Purpose; but the great Misfortune is, they are not duly executed.

The *Craftsman.* Nov 17. N° 385.

History of Parties continued. (See p. 598.)

TULLY has a Passage extremely applicable to the mischievous, but transitory, Prevalence of those Principles of Government, which K. *James* I. imported into this Country, *viz. Opinionum Commenta delet Dies, Naturæ Judicia confirmat.—Groundless Opinions are destroyed, but rational Judgments, are confirmed by Time.* The Authority of a *Sect,* much more of a *State,* is able to inspire, and Habit to confirm the most *absurd Opinions.* Passion, or Interest, can create *Zeal;* but nothing can give Stability and durable Uniformity to *Error.* There are Cases, where Reason, freed from Constraint, or rouzed by Necessity, acts in some Sort the Part of *Instinct.* We are impell'd by *one,* before we have Time to form an *Opinion.* We are determin'd by the *other* against our *Opinion;* *i. e.* before we can be said properly to have *changed* it. But observe the Perverseness of Man. When this happens, instead of acknowledging the *victorious Truth,* which determin'd him to act, and instead of condemning the *erroneous Opinion,* against which he acted, he is too often apt to endeavour, peevishly and pedantically, to reconcile his *Actions* to his *Error.*

The absurd Opinions about the *Right, Power,* and *Prerogative of Kings* were so little able to withstand Opposition, that few of King *Charles* I's Adherents were determin'd by them. When the *same Opinions* reviv'd at the *Restoration,* the Parliament who had authorised and imposed them, soon acted in direct Opposition to them. When the same Opinions revived again at the End of the same Reign, with a greater Appearance of national Concurrence, they revived but to be exploded. King *Charles* made Use of them to check the Ferment rais'd against his Government; but did not seem to expect they would be long in Force. His *wiser Brother* depended much on them; but his Dependance was vain. They were then wearing out apace; and they wore out the faster for the extravagant Use made of them. Thus these ridiculous Principles were twice revived, and twice destroy'd in less than 30 Years from the *Restoration.*

The *second Revival of these Principles* happen'd soon after the Dissolution of the *long Parliament;* and there we must place the Birth of *Whig* and *Tory,* the spurious Offspring of *Roundhead* and *Cavalier;* tho' these Parties were not mature 'till about 2 Years afterwards: The Dissolution of *this Parliament* was desir'd by *some* with factious Views; by *others* on this honest and true Maxim, that a STANDING PARLIAMENT, or the SAME PAR-

ARLIAMENT LONG CONTINUED, *changes the very Nature of our Constitu-* *on in the fundamental Article, on which* *be Preservation of our whole Liberty de-* *mds.* But the chief Motive which in-uc'd the King to dissolve them was, They attack'd his *Family,* and even him-lf, in the Heats which the Discovery nd Prosecution of the *Popish Plot* occa-on'd. The Attacks on the *Queen,* his *Brother,* and the Prosecution of the E. of Danby, provok'd and embarrass'd him. The Earl was turned out; but the In-tention of this Attack, according to *Ra-in,* was to shew, *that the King, as well* *as his* Brother, *was at the Head of a* *Conspiracy to destroy the Government, and* *the Protestant Religion.* It is certain, that if the E. of *Danby's* Impeachment had been tried, he must have justify'd himself by shewing, that the secret Ne-gotiations with *France,* particularly that for *Money,* were the King's, not his.

Now whatever were the King's Hopes, the next Parliament trod in the Steps of this. How, indeed, could it be other-wise, when the Temper of the *People* determin'd the Character of the *Parlia-ment?* And no *illegal Influence on Elec-tions* was practiced?

One Point, indeed, this Parliament took extremely to Heart, and which was not open to any that follow'd; that was the *Conduct of the* King *in foreign Affairs,* during the War between *France* and *Hol-land.* The Motives to that War, on the Part of the *Aggressor,* were a Spirit of Conquest, and barefac'd Usurpation. The Interest *We* had in it was plain and im-mediate. The Security, and once the very Existence, of the *Dutch Common-wealth* depended on the Event of it. No Wonder then, if the Conduct of the *King,* who join'd openly with *France,* furnish'd ample Matter to the publick Discontent, and help'd to increase the ill Humours of succeeding Parliaments in relation to those *two other Points,* the Prosecution of Persons involved in the *Popish Plot* and the Exclusion of the Duke of *York.* 'Tis surprizing, that a Man should expect to be trusted with a *Crown,* because he was born a *Prince,* in a Country where he could not be trusted by Law, and ought not in Reason, with a *Constable's Staff,* if a private Person. *Henry* IV. of *France,* tho' his Title was hereditary on a better Establishment than any Prince of the House of *Stuarts* to the Crown of *England;* and tho' he was possess'd of

all the personal Qualifications that could endear a Prince to his Subjects, yet he had not been King, had he not been of the *Religion of that Nation.* How then could it be expected, that a Protestant and free People should be less animated by *Religion* and *Liberty both,* than their Neighbours had been by *Religion alone?* Yet there is Reason to wish, that the Prosecution on the Account of the *Popish Plot,* and * more on Account of *another,* set up as a Retaliation for *This,* could be erazed out of the Records of History, and that greater Temper had been join'd to the same Zeal for *Religion* and *Liber-ty.* Men were made to believe that a King, who had given up so many *Mini-sters,* would give up his *Brother* at last; But they were fatally deceiv'd, by the Intrigues of *two opposite Cabals,* that of the Duke of *York,* and that of the Duke of *Monmouth;* which last was for an *ab-solute Exclusion,* and not even that, un-less the Bill passed without any Mention of the Duke's Daughters as next in Suc-cession; with which, says Bp *Burnet,* the Pr. of *Orange* was willing to comply, on the Faith of Assurances he had from hence. It may be observ'd, that the Prince could have no Reason for consenting that his *Wife's Pretensions to the Crown* should not be confirmed by an *Act,* which ex-cluded her *Father,* except the Necessity of uniting different private Interests in the publick Measure of excluding the D. of *York.* If this was his Reason, it proves that a *Spirit of Faction* ran thro' the Pro-ceedings of those, who promoted the *Bill of Exclusion;* and when *Faction* was oppos'd to *Faction,* no wonder if That of the Court prevailed. The pushing the *Exclusion* gave the King an Opportunity of breaking the *Country Party;* of di-viding the Nation into *Whig* and *Tory;* of governing without *Parliaments;* and of leaving the Throne to his *Brother,* with a more absolute Power establish'd than any Prince of his Family had enjoyed.

As soon as the Court had got a plausi-ble Pretence of objecting a *Spirit of Fac-tion* to Those in the *Opposition,* the Strength of the *Opposition* was broken, because the

---

* A Writer in the *Courant, Nov.* 21. ob-serves, No *Protestant* would with more that the Blood of Lord *Russel,* Col. *Sydney, &c.* spilt on Account of the *Rye-House-Plot,* trumpt up against 'em by the *Papists,* should be eraz'd out of our Records, than that spilt on Ac-count of the *Popish Plot.*

national Union was dissolved. A *Country Party* must be authorized by the Voice of the Country. A *Party*, formed on the Principles of *common Interest*, will prevail as long as the *Constitution* subsists; and whenever *such a Party* finds it difficult to prevail, our *Constitution* is in Danger; and when they find it impossible, our *Constitution* must be alter'd. On the other Hand, when the Interests of *particular Sets of Men* prevail, the Essence of a *Country Party* is annihilated, and the Appearance of it will soon be lost.

Such a Dissolution of a *Country Party* was brought about at the Period we are now come to; which with the Division of the Nation into *Whig* and *Tory*, brought us into extreme Danger; this re-united the Nation, and a *Coalition of Parties* saved the whole. Let us hope that this Scene of tragical Folly, the Struggle of Parties, is over, to the Disappointment of *Those*, who are conscious of *past Iniquity*, or who meditate *future Mischief*. There are no others, who wish and endeavour to prolong it.

Fog's Journal. Nov. 17. No 263.

MR Fog publishes a Paper, printed several Months since in *Ireland*, chiefly in Praise of a Gentleman whose Character we gave from the said Paper, in our last, See p. 547 A, also ODE p. 543.

London Journal, Nov. 17. No. 751.

On the Revolution and the H. of Orange.

THIS being the Month in which WM Prince of ORANGE landed in *England* to *rescue* our Liberties, and the Month in which another WM Prince of ORANGE is arrived to solemnize a Marriage which *enlarges* the Prospect of our *Security*, and *strengthens* the *Protestant Interest*; and it being the Nature of Man to *extenuate* their Blessings, and *aggravate* their Evils, one of the best Offices we can do is to put them in mind of what they *enjoy*, and lead them to the Fountain whence they derive their Enjoyment.

Publick Good, general Happiness, and the *Prosperity* of the PEOPLE, were the *Motives* of Resistance at the REVOLUTION; but these were not always the *Motives* of Resistance, nor of all the *Civil Wars*, which, of old, infested this Kingdom. The *Barons Wars* with the King were only a Contention who should be the Tyrants of the People. The Wars between the Houses of *York* and *Lancaster* was only a Struggle among the *Great*

Men, which Family should be King. The *Motives* and *Actions* which produced the *Civil Wars* in K. *Charles* I's Reign, were indeed, of another Nature; the Opp[os]tion which the Parliament in 1640, ma[d] to the *illegal* and *tyrannical* Act[s] the Court, were *highly* reasonable, [mili]tary, and glorious; but *Faction* and [pri]vate Views soon crept in amongst the[m] and, after the *Self denying Ordinance* [wa] pass'd, and *Essex*, and other worthy G[en]tlemen turn'd out of the Army, the [re] Good of the Nation was forgot, and P[ow]er only regarded: So that not having V[ir]tue enough to make a *right Use* of th[at] Power, when they *conquer'd* the K[ing] the Nobility, and the Church, they ov[er] turn'd the Constitution too.

The *Restoration*, indeed, brought us [a]gain to our *ancient Form* of Governm[ent] yet *Prerogative* was not sufficiently [re]strain'd; the *constant Design* of th[e] whole Reign, after the first 8 or 10 Year[s] was to introduce *Popery and arbitra[ry] Power*, tho' *covertly*; but in the ne[xt] 'twas *openly avow'd* and profess'd, an[d] *Regal Power* set up to *dispense* with [all] *the Laws of England*.

Thus was an End put to our Constituti[on]; and our Chains were fasten'd upon [us] beyond all Possibility of removing them, had not the *Prince of* ORANGE came t[o] our Deliverance. To this glorious PRINCE, we owe a *Country* of *Laws*, *equal* Liberty, and the Blessings of the present Ro[yal] Family; a *Family* distinguish'd by *Virtues* unknown to sovereign Power. A higher Proof of *national Virtue* cannot be shewn, than his *Majesty's* giving the PRINCESS ROYAL in Marriage to the *Prince of* ORANGE. For, by this Act, in which there can be no *self-interested* Views, the King *enlarges* our Prospect of *Protestant Heirs* to the Crown of *Great Britain*; he shews his *Justice* and Gratitude to the House of *Orange*, and his Respect to the Prince now in *England*, a Prince of great Politeness, Honesty, and Generosity.

Grub-street Journal, Nov. 22. No. 204.

WE are presented with a State of the Controversy between Mr *Tindal* and Mr *Budgell*, relating to the Will of the late Dr *Tindal*, with Mr *Baron's* Notes thereupon.

On the Part of Mr *Tindal* 'tis affirm'd, that his Uncle had lately made a Will, appointing him his sole Heir, according to his settled Intention, known for many Years, and according to what me Lost[s] himſelf had told him about five Weeks ɔre his Death; that Mr *T.* was told the Woman of the Houſe, in *Cold Bath 'ds*, whither the Dr had been removed n his Chambers in *Gray's-Inn*, by the ſuaſions of Mr *Budgell*, that his Uncle A writ for him, but the Letter had not a ſent to the *Poſt-houſe*; that Mrs e and Mr *B.* had been continually h him, during his Sickneſs, and that *B.* was concerned in the Dr's Will. n Anſwer to this, the Vindicators of B *B.* ſay, The late Dr *Tindal* was no at Admirer of *Parſons*; his Nephew, vever had made ſuch *ſtrong (a) Profeſ- s* to him on *ſome certain Points*, that was once going to have left him his *ks* to publiſh. The Dr had a leſs O- ion (*b*) ſome Time before his Death, h of his Nephew s *Sincerity* and *Abili-* ——The Dr had a (*c*) Right to give *Money* to whom he pleaſed. If he ſly regarded *Perſonal Merit*, the World ſt judge whether he has been miſtaken the Choice of his *Heir.* (*d*) But if Mr *T.* tends a Right to his Uncle's *Money* on- as a *Relation*, the Dr had ſeveral *other lations* full as *near* as *himſelf*; ſo that haps he has already *more* than his Share. The Circumſtances attending the Dr's ath, according to Mr *B.* were, That : Dr being taken with a violent Fit of : *Stone, Aug. 6.* he told Mr *B. he would ike his Will immediately*; (*e*) but would t have it done by an *Attorney*, becauſe, he had reſolved to be extremely kind Mr *B.* he was afraid a Man of that ofeſſion might make his Court to Sir *bert Walpole*, by acquainting him with : Contents of his *Will*; and the Dr's n Hand, when he was in full Health, F is hardly *legible.* He dictated every ord of his Will, and afterwards read it er 5 or 6 Times himſelf. The Wit- ſſes (*f*) were, the Lady of the Houſe ere he lodged, and a young Man then ing with Mr *B.* but whoſe Father kept : *Globe Tavern* in *Fleet-ſtreet*, and left G n 500 *l.* The Doctor ſealed up the *ll* with his own Seal, and on the Out- e wrote, *In this Paper is contain'd my Will.* MATT. TINDAL.

(*a*) If theſe *Points* and *Profeſſions* were in- ſiſtent with the ſolemn Declarations and bſcriptions of every Clergyman when or- ned, it would end the Controverſy, by taking ɔy all Credit from the Aſſertions of Mr *T.* (*b*) Tho' the Doctor might change his O- nion concerning his *Nephew's Sincerity*, a tle before his Death, he could not ſo well ɛn entertain a Different one of his *Abili-*

ties, with which he muſt have been ac- quainted many Years.

(*c*) Tho' this may be true, yet 'tis thought, he would have acted more agreeable, not on- ly to the revealed Law, but even to his be- loved Law of Nature, had he permitted his *near Relations* to partake of his *Generoſity.*

(*d*) The Doctor, almoſt fourſcore, (who is ſaid to have been inveigled to lend almoſt all he was worth on very ſlender Security) was not perhaps a better Judge of *perſonal Merit* than moſt other *great Men* are at that Age; and till the World is ſatisfy'd that the Doctor m ade *this Choice of his Heir*, it cannot *judge*, *whether he has been miſtaken or not in the Choice.*

(*e*) The Dr effectually ſecured it from all *Male-practices*, by avoiding all *Male-Attor- neys*, and wiſely employ'd one of the female Sex, who having been the Wife of an eminent Judge, was well acquainted with the Law.

(*f*) One Witneſs lets Lodgings; the other is Mr *B.'s* Footman, tho' ſo rhetorically ſet off.

Univerſal Spectator, Nov. 24, No. 268.

Of Free-thinking.

THO' nothing is *nobler* in itſelf, yet nothing has been more corrupted than the *favourite* Doctrine of *Free think- ing*; that Term which ſhould diſtinguiſh the *Philoſopher* and the *Chriſtian*, from the *Fool* and the *Bigot*, is become Syno- nimous for the *Libertine* and the *Atheiſt.* To think *freely*, according to Mr *Addi- ſon*, is not to *think at random*; but our *Freedom of Thought* ought to be under proper *Regulations.* It was that laudable Spirit which firſt inſpired this Nation to break off from the Tyrannic Superſtition of the Church of *Rome*: Yet, as it is now managed, it will not be a Preſervative a- gainſt a *falſe Religion*; but an Introduc- tion to *none at all.* This Mr *Stonecaſtle* exemplifies in the following Letter :

S I R,

I Am the Wife of a *Tradeſman*, with whom, the firſt ten Years of our Mar- riage, I lived in all the Pleaſure that *Eaſe, Content*, and *Love* could give. My Husband was *ſober* without *Moroſeneſs*, and *gay* with *Virtue*; in the *Oeconomy* of his Family regular, and behaving like an *honeſt* Man, and a *good* Chriſtian, with reſpect both to his *Servants* and *Children.* But alas! having lately made himſelf one of a *Weekly Aſſembly* of Neighbours, who meet to diſpute upon *Morality* and *Religion*, his *Behaviour* is quite *altered*, the *Morals* of his *Servants* and *Children* unregarded, and frequenting the *Church* ridicul'd : He talks againſt *Religion*, and ſhocks me with his *Blaſ- phemy*

phemy and *Infidelity.* —— Hence commenc'd his ill *Usage* of me, —at home he is continually dogged, sullen, and outrageous. I soon found he had lost his *Principles of Honesty* with his *Principles of Religion*, for amidst his railing against *Priestcraft* he would assert the Lawfulness of having as many *Wives* as he pleas'd, and he now looks on me only as the *Clog of Life*, But tho' he is so *haughty* a *Tyrant* over his *Wife*, and so bold a *Champion* in the Cause of *Irreligion*, he is in himself a *contemptible Coward:* If his *Head* does but *ake*, he is in the utmost *Confusion*; he is *alarm'd* at the *fear of Death*; a *Doctor* is sent for, he *groans*, he *sighs*, he *despairs*; and tho' so imperious over me his *Wife*, he is *hen-peck'd* by a *Harlot.* The other Day she came into his Compting-House, and demanded 200 l. to be paid her directly; on his hesitating, *What,* cries she in a Rage, *you ungrateful Monster, have I been so civil to you? and do you, who are worth so many Thousands, deny me such a Trifle!* —This *haughty Husband* was so aw'd, that he *bought his Peace*, and immediately paid her what she required. —— By *this* Man's Example, you may convince some *honest City-zens*, that by gaining a *free Way of thinking* they may, without the greatest Care, lose their *Love* to their *Wives*, their *Care* to their *Children*, and *Humanity* and *Morality* to *all Mankind.*

SOPHONISBA.

The *Craftsman* Nov. 24. No. 385.

Mr *D'anvers,*

IF 'twas ever necessary to shew *Britons* their real Interest, 'tis now, when the most *mercenary Writers* are employ'd to calumniate Gentlemen in the Interest of their Country; and their Writings sent to *Coffee-Houses* and *Inns*, unrequested and Duty-free. On the other Hand, all Papers wrote for Liberty, and against the *Enemies of our Constitution* are forbid, and no Clerk of the Post-Office dare transmit them to his Correspondents in the Country. An Opposer of an *Odious Projector* is represented as a *Jacobite*, or a *Republican*; and he, who has disdained to join in bringing in an *Excise*, is immediately *a Friend to the Pretender.* *Popery* and *Jacobitism* ought to be treated with the utmost Abhorrence. But should *they* be treated with less, who, assuming another Title, act upon the *Principles of both?* If a Man is to be enslaved, it matters little what religious Sentiments the

Author of his Misery professes. Card. [?] sey was a *Papist*, and *another Gentle[?]* now living may be a good *Protesta* but I am sure *Wolsey* could not have bro[?] ed a worse Scheme than *he* has lately i[?]

As for *Jacobitism*, it is almost [?] out; and if the *Papists* are increased is because our *Churchmen* are more i[?] on *Civil* than *religious Matters*. W[?] certain Fraternity of *venerable Sages* i[?] their whole Time in writing *minist[?] Pamphlets* and *Letters* to the *Free-[?]* it's no wonder that the industrious Pr[?] of *Rome* should gain more Converts to [?] *Church*, than the others do to the S[?]

Some late Proceedings have convi[?] all *Englishmen*, that they ought to b[?] prehensive of *other People* besides *Pa[?]* and *Jacobites*; and to guard against [?] *Gentlemen* who seem so conscious of [?] Impressions that their late Conduct [?] made upon the People, that they have tained a whole Army of *mercenary [?] vocates* to intercede for them. But [?] the *ministerial Grubs* I am best plea[?] with the *Couranteers.* There is somet[?] very diverting in their Writings; [?] put themselves in a great Passion, bea[?] no Body will answer them.———[?] it is a little cruel in you to treat th[?] with such Contempt; should the G[?] Man discard them, because they are [?] taken Notice of, you may be justly ch[?] ged with robbing them of their Bread[?]

I shall now proceed to shew the *Fr[?] holders* and *Electors* their true Interest [?] the ensuing Election.

First, it is demonstrable that our R[?] presentatives ought to be Persons super[?] to the sordid Views of *Self-Interest*, oth[?] wise they may be induced to make a T[?] fick of their *Trust.* The Persons least [?] be suspected of *Corruption* are those [?] enjoy a considerable Share of Propert[?] The indigent Man is under a thous[?] Temptations to be dishonest: For th[?] Reason, it has always been a principal A[?] of *wicked Ministers* to render Elect[?] as expensive * as possible, to deter Coun[?]

---

* The *Courant*, Nov. 27. lays to this A[?] sertion,—That it is as well known as [?] Thing can be, that the *Male-contents* v[?] themselves on the Magnificence of their E[?] tertainments, and have begun to make t[?] all over the *Kingdom*; and instances in [?] jacent *Borough*, where have been given [?] ral extravagantly expensive *Feasts*; and [?] the *Craftsman* has the *Politeness* and *As[?] rance* to pass a severe Sentence on the Elec[?] tors who partake of their *splendid* Trea[?]

Gent[?]

Gentlemen, and so procure their own Creatures to be returned ; or if that Stratagem fail, the *Gentlemen of the Country* may be so oppressed with Debts they have contracted in serving their Fellow-Subjects, that they must be obliged to betray their Interests to save themselves and Families from Ruin. This wicked Scheme was formerly thought so fatal in its influence, that the Legislature was forced to enact a Law to prevent it, *viz. The late Act against Bribery and Corruption. Direct Bribery*, I hope, is thereby prevented ; but, if *expensive Treats* are expected from the Candidates, the fatal Inconveniencies before mentioned still remain.— The Crime of an indigent Wretch, who sells his Voice for a Sum of Money will admit of some Alleviation ; but he who meanly prostitutes his Conscience for a *Drinking-Bout*, is without Excuse.

I fear there are others, besides Persons of mean Fortune, who ought to be suspected ; and it was once the Opinion of *King, Lords,* and *Commons*, that no Man, who had a *Place* or *Pension from the Crown*, should sit among the *Representatives of the Commons* of England. It is difficult for a Man to serve two Masters, and to preserve a due *Medium* between his Gratitude to his *King*, and Duty to his *Country*.

These Considerations relate principally to *New Candidates*. The Gentlemen who have served before, and make Application again, will be judged by their former Conduct, and meet with a suitable Reception. Those who have executed their Office with Baseness and Treachery, will be treated with Contempt. It's evident, that the Liberties of *Englishmen* now depend upon the approaching Crisis. One false Step may be irretrievable.

Few *Free-States* have lost their Liberties by *foreign Conquest*, in proportion to those, who have been enslaved by the Bribery of their *Magistrates*, and the Corruption of the *People*. *Rome* was enslav'd by the *Venality of the People*. But I hope that will never be our Case ; at least the present Spirit of the People gives a better Prospect. 'Tis credibly reported, that a few Persons at TAUNTON, who had it in their Power to turn the Election of a *Mayor*, lately refused a sum of 2000 *l.* for their Votes, upon that Occasion ; and we have had some Instances of the like Nature at ROCHESTER and other Places. If the Electors in general would follow their Example, they would not only purge themselves from the Imputation of *Cor-*

ruption, but prove the glorious Instruments of preserving our Constitution in its full Vigour.   *Yours, &c.*

Fog's Journal, Nov. 24. No. 264.

ALL Political Writers, and among them *Machiavel*, who lived about the 15th Century, agree, that the Government of *France* was as wisely contrived for making the People happy, as that of any Nation in the World : But the Power of their Parliaments, says *Fog*, is lost by the gradual Encroachments of the Royal Prerogative. Standing Armies, and numerous Excises have broke the Spirit of the common People, and impoverish'd the midling Gentry ; and the vast Increase of Civil and Military Employments, have brought such Numbers of Families to be dependant on the Court, that when the People are oppress'd they know not where to apply for Relief.

It may be ask'd, if *France* be in such a Condition of Servitude, how comes it, that being quite exhausted by a long War, we now see her in so flourishing a Condition ? — 'Tis answer'd, that an arbitrary Government, wisely and honestly administer'd, may produce such a good Effect. But had they been harrass'd with as many Troops in Peace as in War—had they been burthen'd to pay useless Employments and viler Pensioners—had neither their Debts nor Taxes been lessen'd after a Peace of 20 Years—had their Subjects been plunder'd by Foreigners, for want of Protection—had their Treasures been squander'd in buying Alliances of no Strength to their Interests, they must have bow'd their Necks to the Yoak.

Here *Fog* gives Minutes from the Histories of several of the *French* Kings from the Foundation of their Monarchy, and by observations on the Conduct of several of their Ministers, attempts to shew how the Prerogative has gradually gain'd Ground on the Liberties of the People. But the principal Cause of their Slavery he ascribes to their Princes delegating too much Power to their Ministers ; by Means whereof, some of them, particularly *Pepin* and *Hugh Capet*, dethron'd their Masters, and reign'd in their Rooms.

Tho' this had happen'd so often, yet nobody suspected Card. *Mazarine* of such a Design ; his low Genius seem'd cut out for little Tricks and Expedients, for filling his own Pockets, for making foolish Treaties abroad, and for finding out foolish Reasons for fleecing the People at
Home

Home. In a Word; he was one of the worst Ministers *France* ever saw, one who was extoll'd by his Mercenaries and Creatures, for that silly and knavish Quality call'd Cunning, which never suffer'd him to do one good Thing to gain the Affections of the People to the Court, nor one wise Thing to keep them quiet and obedient, so that he alone was the Cause of the Civil War which tore the Country to pieces in his Time.

London Journal. Nov. 24. No. 752.

THE Writer *on Parties* in the *Craftsman* is so well skill'd in *History* and *Human Nature*, that, had he not a *bad Cause*, his Abridgments, Anecdotes, and Remarks, would be of admirable Advantage; but at present his *great Abilities* serve only to aggravate his *Crime*.

His Intent is to *overturn* every Thing that stands in his Way to Power, not excepting the Government itself. It is therefore proper, for the People's sake, to separate the *Truth* which he hath so artfully mix'd with *Falshood*.

His main Point is to make a *Coalition of Parties*, or a *National Union* against the Court: To this tends all his Art. The Business of the last *Craftsman* is to shew, that the *Jacobites* and *Tories* have entirely lost their Principles. His Text is from *Tully*, "That *groundless* Opinions are *destroyed*, but rational Judgments *confirm'd by Time*." But this is not *always*, nor *generally* true, as our Author himself in the next Paragraph allows, (see p. 592.)—Opinions, which at their *Rise* were look'd upon as *ridiculous*, have by *Time*, been *consecrated*, and grown into such *dreadful-steady* Articles of Faith, as to make Men *burn* and *damn* others, and *suffer Martyrdom* themselves. Rational Judgments are made but by *few*, for tho' LIBERTY has shewn its Head these 40 or 50 Years, scarce one in a Thousand *dares* think for himself, abstract from the Principles in which he was bred.

As to what our Author asserts, " that the absurd Opinions of *Divine Right, Power* and *Prerogative*, were so little able to take *Root*, that few of those who were for K. *Charles* I. were *determin'd* by them"; 'tis answer'd, The Authority of a *few Men of Sense*, weighs nothing against this Truth, that *these* were the *Opinions* of the *Generality* of those who fought for the King. His affirming that *these* Opinions were *revived* and *destroy'd*, is an Argument against himself: For, how shall we know that they are *dead*

or won't *revive*, when 'tis the miraculous Nature of those *High Church* Notions to *die* and *rise again* ?—The Truth is, the *Tories* had *thoroughly imbib'd* these Notions about Divine *Hereditary Right* ; but when their *Interest* or *Passions* lay another way, they *acted* against them ; as *other Sinners do*, and as one of their own Authors confess'd, *Nature would rebel against* Principle. Thus in K. *James* II's Reign, the Men, who had for near 30 Years past taught the Doctrine of absolute Passive Obedience upon Pain of eternal Damnation, *yet oppos'd* King *James*, and invited over the Prince of *Orange* ; not because their Principles were *destroy'd* or alter'd, but because the Introduction of *Popery* would have entirely *destroy'd them*. They did not *design* to dethrone him; some of the Bishops, put in the *Tower* for not obeying the King against Law, even the A. Bp of *Canterbury* himself, held their Principles of *Jure Divino Hereditary Right* so fast, that when *the Settlement* of the Crown was made upon the Prince of *Orange*, they turn'd Nonjurors, and perverted a great Part of the Nation.

So it is with regard to *Religion* ; tho' Men act every Day against their Principles, yet they *believe* them so firmly, that they would *burn* a Man who did *not*.

'Tis true, the Danger the Nation was in from *Popery* and *Arbitrary Power* in K. *James*'s Reign, caus'd a *National Union*, and a *Coalition of Parties* ; yet as soon as the Danger was over, the *Jacobites* and *Tories* resumed their old Principles, and invented the Distinction of Kings *de Jure* and *de Facto* ; and those who sought Preferment, talk'd of a *Right* by *Conquest* ; but none of 'em came into the true *Whiggish* Notion of a *Right* by *Consent* of the *People* constituting the Prince of *Orange* Lawful King of *England*. Our Author, indeed, says they are chang'd. The only way to know this, is (but God forbid it should ever be tried!) to *trust them with* Power. Nothing else will satisfy a reasonable Man, that they do not put on *the Form* of *Whigs* to conceal their *true* Notions, and *real Views*.

N. B. *When we have an Opportunity we shall give some Specimens of the* Coccutter's and What-do you call it Journals; *also of the* Free-mason, *which succeeds the* Hyp-Doctor *laid down; and pay all the Regard we can to the* Auditor, *which on the 28th* Instant *was revived* The

The HAPPY NUPTIALS. *By Mr* Carey.

GERON. DAPHNIS.

Ger. HOW comes it, *Daphnis*, that our
nymphs and ſwains
With more than uſual joy, and gladſome ſtrains,
Thus wildly wanton frolick in exceſs,
Unknowing how their tranſports to expreſs ?

Daph. Can any *Briton* ask?—but thou art old,
And to life's gaieties entirely cold,
Or thou had'ſt known, that from the *Belgic* ſhore,
A Royal Stranger late is wafted o'er ;
Never was *Adiou* with a nobler grac'd,
In whom the Gods have ev'ry virtue plac'd.

Ger. You ſpeak his praiſes like the voice of fame;
But has this miracle of men no name?

Daph. Of anceſtors heroic, race divine,
Illuſtrious branch of the *Naſſovian* line ;
WILLIAM his name, from mighty WM ſprung,
Of whoſe immortal deeds great PRIOR ſung.

Ger. No wonder then, that univerſal bliſs
Succeeds th' arrival of a prince like this ;
NASSAU! the very name does joy inſpire,
And renovates my ſoul with youthful fire:
What inſtinct from the kindred Gods above
Induc'd his bleſs'd arrival ?

Daph. —— powerful love:
Fir'd with the fame of royal ANNA's charms,
What could with-hold her from his longing arms?
Seaſons and ſeas in vain his way oppoſe,
For ſuch a bride who would not life expoſe ?
In whom all virtues, all perfections join,
A form angelic, and a ſoul divine:
To grace whoſe nuptials nature's ſelf looks gay,
And night illumin'd, brightens into day :
Ev'n winter now becomes another ſpring,
In honour to the DAUGHTER of our King.
Quite loſt in joy, behold the gladſome throng,
All haſte to hail them in a rural ſong:
See, in what pompous pleaſure they advance,
And to *Sicilian* meaſures nimbly dance;
Young *Lycidas*, the choiriſt, tunes his lays
In j yful epithalmicks to their praiſe
The *Chorus* aids him with exulting voice,
While heav'n applauds our tranſports, and their
choice.

AIR I. *Lycidas.*

Thrice welcome, royal ſtranger,
To greet thee, ſee all Nature ſmile;
Whom *Neptune*, free from danger,
Has wafted to our iſle.

II. [*Ch. Thrice welcome, &c.*
By ANNA's charms invited,
NASSAU defies the ſtormy ſea ;
In ANNA's charms delighted,
What God ſo bleſs'd as he !

III. [*Ch. Thrice welcome, &c.*
May ev'ry joy attend 'em,
No end their ſweet endearments know,
And bounteous heav'n befriend 'em
With all it can beſtow
[*Ch. May ev'ry joy, &c.*

STANISLAUS: Or, *Inſtructions to a Painter.*

HAIL Majeſty reviv'd! whoſe glorious rays,
With force improv'd the northen world
emblaze

Firm keep thy ſeat, or *Poland* is undone,
And lend no more the chariot of the ſun.
Thy well try'd virtue the weak muſe wou'd ſing,
Which ſhall ſhe moſt admire the *man* or *king*!
But ſince thy chaſter ears ſuch ſtrains refuſe,
The painter's licence ſhall relieve the muſe.

Dandridge, with various lights the ſcene refine;
Let antient heroes in one form combine :
Thy draughts expreſſive are ſo full deſign'd,
That thy creative pow'r preſents the mind:
So ſtrong the vivid paſſions can enforce,
Thy pictures breathe, thy images diſcourſe.
In *Staniſlaus* let *Rome* her beams conſpire,
Th' *Auguſtan* mildneſs with the *Julian* fire:
(Mankind's delight!) again *Veſpaſian* lives,
And *Trajan* his judicious air revives.
Paint how his firſt addreſs Swede's monarch
fires,
How each prolifick genius each inſpires!
While for his friend the patriot asks a crown,
And ſhews his merit he diſplays his own:
The lover's agent thus ſo nobly pleads,
That he himſelf the prize of beauty weds.
Election ; nobleſt teſt of ſterling worth,
Thou ſureſt call to bring a genius forth :
Were but the nation to thy maxims juſt,
None would the tyrant or the drone entruſt.
No faint drawn image of a ruſty line,
Wou'd plead to paſſive fools his right divine.
Each ſuitor let the varied canvas ſhew,
And the whole man in light and ſhade review,
In *Staniſlaus* is found no ſhade to truth,
All his demerit is imputed *youth* (*a*)
His regal worth 'gainſt numbers would prevail,
Tho' nicely weigh'd in Heav'ns impartial ſcale,
O *Rome!* what monſtrous Scenes thy tale
affords !
When *King* and *Villain* were promiſcuous words,
Thy *Neros* and *Domitians* all are good,
When flies or fiddles can divert from blood.,
In vain the ſons of glorious ſcience ſhine,
In vain aſpires the human ſoul divine,
Succeſſion abſolute, that *Hydra* dire,
Damps ev'ry rational ambitious fire ;
One fiend deſtroy'd the pregant monſter's found
To ſhoot a ſpawn unnumber'd thro' the wound.
Cold *Europe's* baſer ſchemes have long confeſſ,
The golden leſſons of the glowing eaſt.
There wit and ſolid wiſdom ſign'd the *plan*,
And ſpoke the great *Confucius* more than *man*.
There godlike *kings* their ſilly race diſown,
Their genius found unequal to a crown.
Merit alone is heard ;—none pleads from blood,
And the ſole ſanction is the publick good,
From eldeſt time this ſyſtem ſtands entire,
With that the well-built fabrick will expire,
And yield to nought but JOVE's all-ſearching
fire.
The muſe perhaps has wander'd here to far,
She now returns to her bright northern ſtar.
Artiſt proceed, and ſhew the aſtoniſh'd eye,
In ambuſh where the dark aſſaſſins lye : (*b*)

(*a*) The Primate, who made ſome Objections to ſeveral,
could ſay nothing againſt Staniſlaus, but that he was t
Young to be made a King.   oo
(*b*) King Staniſlaus knowing where ſome Villains lay
in wait to aſſaſſinate him, went boldly up to them, and
flinging them a Purſe of Gold, bid them go and be honeſt Men for the future.

Prodigious virtue proves the *sole defence,*
Intrepid and *presumptuous innocence!*
Here charge the piece with dangers not his own,
Chains with his friend(s) are nobler than a crown,
The royal partners dignify *distress,*
The kings are greater, tho' the warriors less.
His *polish* manners and his well-turn'd mind,
To friendship's laws the barbarous *Turk* resin'd.
In exile the brave soul preserves her state;
All soils are native to the truly great.

Draw, how fatigu'd, the sacred head reclines
In *Dioclesian's* grand retirement shines,
The mind in her own place; the passions even,
Can render ev'ry situation heav'n.

Fir'd with his fame in this sublime recess,
To view the king let distant nations press;
By instinct *Britons* should engage his eye,
And share his smiles as sons of liberty.
Here paint in strongest lines th' instructive scene,
Where the fire forms the daughter and the queen,
Genteel yet solid ; what *Ulysses* was,
In judgment and address is *Stanislaus,*
The father's dictates charm the daughter's ear,
And leave indelible impressions there ;
What easy dignity! what grace serene!
The parent genius shines thro' all her mien.

Now paint with nicest strokes the crown
resign'd;
The chastest image of the noblest mind,
The genius of fair liberty draws near.
T' inform with patriot-strains the monarch's ear,
Who, but the first-rate spirit of human kind,
Had, (arm'd with Power) his sacred rights
declin'd! (*d*)

Obsequious majesty, sublimes the scene;
Conscious, not vain ; reluctant, yet serene :
Alternate strokes, in contrast, should evince,
How grand the noble, and how meek the prince.
Here set the canvas shew the vacant throne,
Once more by merit and by choice his own :
Here crowds salute the native and the king,
Thro' all the exulting land loud *Io's* ring,
While here the senate's venerable band.
In tears ambiguous their lov'd prince demand ;
Tears which by turns, a double tribute pay,
For sorrows past, and this triumphant day:
In sweet confusion all proclaim his cause,
And infants learn to lisp a *Stanislaus.*

Thy Merit and thy righteous cause combin'd
Demand the joint assistance of mankind ;
The *Gaul* puissant, and the gallant *Swede,*
In gen'rous leagues with thee consent to bleed,
The *Turk* and *Tartar,* foes to liberty,
In brave resentment are ally'd to thee.
May *Britain's* monarch make thy cause his own,
To thy magnetic soul and unison.
" War's genius and the mortal instruments
In council meditate profound events.
Rous'd by thy wrongs, see famine, fire and sword
Impatient wait to catch th' alarming word.

---

(1) Alluding to his Confinement with the King of
Sweden after the Action at Bender.
(*d*) Stanislaus, tho' advised to insist upon his former
Right, as having been elected and crowned already, absolutely refused to do so, and sent his Resignation in
Form, to the Diet, that they might elect whom they
pleased for their King.

Thy foes, unconscious of the flow-pac'd hour,
In rebel-triumph brave th' impending pow'r.
But *freedom* claims a sanction from above,
The cause of *freedom,* is the cause of *Jove.*
When the storm wakes at his imperial nod,
They'll shrink at thunder, and confess the *God.*

Upon King STANISLAUS'S *Election.*

Translated from the French of M. Voltaire.

TO the fierce off-spring of the north a king
Competriot heroes meet to give by voice,
Russia and *German* eagles mount on wing,
POLAND to menace, and o'er-rule her choice.
Virtue from *France,* her country, and her throne,
On *Warsaw's* crouded plains descending shone,
Mars guides her steps ; *Vienna* shakes dismay'd,
Poland the goddess on her knees ador'd.
For *Mars,* and me, O people born. she said.
Still from my hands receive your destin'd lord;
That moment, *Stanislaus,* led by *Fame,*
Arriv'd, appeared, elected, king became.

On Mr LANGLEY's *being chosen* Alderman *of* Grantham, Oct. 19. 1733.

*Tu civem patremque geras, tu consule cunctis,
Nec tibi, nec tua te moveant, sed publica vota.*

HAil, sacred town ! to honour's laws devote,
May characters of gold preserve thy vote !
Th' important choice does all around proclaim
Thy care for trade, for liberty, and fame.
May *Pope's* unbounded and unrival'd wit
Record thy praise, and the brave deed transmit
In his sweet verse; may all *Britannia* see
The glories they must reap which copy thee!
Speak out, my muse! let glorious truths be told,
Grantham withstood the sov'reign charms of
gold,
And bravely scorn'd to have our freedom sold!
In vain for thee, the tempting coin was spread,
In vain for thee, the golden baits were laid,
In vain thy (*a*) HEROES! shall oppos'd be,
Corrupting gold can never influence thee!
Honour's thy creed, a general good's thy aim;
Thy country's interest, and thy own's the same.

MARTIAL, Ep. 39. Lib. 1.   *Ad* DECIANUM.

*SI quis erit raros inter numerandus amicos,
Qualis prisca fides, famaeq; novit anus:
Si quis Cecropia madidus, Latiaeque Minerva
Artibus, et vera simplicitate bonus:
Si quis erit recti custos imitator honesti,
Et nihil arcanum qui roget ore deos:
Si quis erit magna subnixus robore mentis
Dispeream, si non hic Decianus erit.*

To the Rt. Hon. the Lord G—w—n.

IF ever man to many was a friend,
Such as you've heard old beldame fame com-
mend ;
If ever man to manly arts inclin'd,
Was by those arts accomplish'd and resin'd;
If there exist a man sincerely just,
True to his God, and faithful to his trust;
If ever man a noble courage bore,
You can't mistake him, if you think on G—w—l.

(*a*) Ld Tyrconnel and Sir Michael Newton.

A RIDDLE. *See it answer'd,* Vol. III. p. 709.

AT firſt you diſcern I of parents have
plenty,   (near twenty,
For their marks in my face counts thrice ten and
Tho' their features all vary, I unlike am to none,
Nor when ſev'rally askt will e'en one me diſown;
In allegiance with all on their ſubſtance I thrive,
Tho' when I'm firſt born, ſcarce a tenth is alive.
They're each day to be ſeen in all paths of the
'— town,   (known,
By a hoarſe or ſhrill voice their approach is well
But I never ſtir out, above once in a moon.
There's retinue is ſlender, for at moſt they've but
four,
But I'm always attended by pages threeſcore ;
Some in politicks deep who are always at jarrs;
Theſe give high words for peace, thoſe are hum-
bly for wars!
But I never promote either former or latter,
Tho' by *multiply'd* feuds I grow ſo much the fatter;
So they ſwell the account, it is all one to *Sawney*,
Whether they be diſtinguiſh'd by *Orange* or *Tawney*
Some *pompous* appear to the praiſe of their owner,
For they're cloath'd at court, and called pages of
honour;   (rear,
And for thoſe my attendants, who bring up the
They're known by the ſcarves or the favours
they wear ;
Yet for all this parade, I'm cloath'd with a rag,
And for my much chatt'ring, my friends call me
MAG.

On G. Faulkner's *Promiſing to have the Dean of
St* PATRICK's *Effigy done by Mr* Vertue, *pre-
fix'd to the beautiful and compleat Edition of his
Works in 4 Vols. 8vo. which he is printing at
Dublin, by Subſcription raiſed in Great Britain
and Ireland.*

IN a little dark room at the back of the ſhop,
Where poets and criticks have din'd on a
chop,
Poor *Faulkner* ſat muſing alone thus of late!
' Two volumes are done—it is time for the plate,
' Yes, time to be ſure—but on whom ſhall I call,
' To expreſs the great *Swift* in a compaſs ſo ſmall?
' Faith *Virtue* ſhall do it—I'm pleaſ'd at the
thought
' Be the coſt what it will, the copper is bought.
APOLLO o'er heard (who, as ſome people gueſs,
Had a hand in the work and corrected the preſs)
And pleaſ'd he reply'd, Honeſt *George* you are
right.
' The thought was my own, howſoe'er you came
by't ;
' For tho' both the wit and the ſtile is my gift,
' 'Tis *Virtue* alone can *deſign* us a *Swift*.

The LAUREAT *Sentenc'd*.

WHat different effects does the LAUREL
produce!   (juice,
In its Bough there is honour, † But Death in its
Since C—b—r has brought its honour ſo low,
He ſhould taſt of the juice, for abuſing the bough.
† (See Vol. I. p. 264.)

The SIGN. *Or a Prayer to the Wind*.

FLY thou gentle whiſtling wind,
Bear this ſigh, and if thou find

Where my cruel fair doth reſt,
Caſt it into her ſwowy breaſt ;
For inflam'd by my deſire,
It may ſet her heart on fire.
The ſweet kiſſes thou ſhalt gain
Will reward thee for thy pain:
Boldly light upon her lip,
There ſuck balm : thence take a trip,
To her boſom laſtly fall
Down and wander over all :
Range about thoſe iv'ry hills,
From whoſe ev'ry part diſtills
Ambroſial dew, there ſpices grow,
And ſweet ſtreams of nectar flow ;
There perfume thyſelf and bring
All her ſweets upon the wing :
As thou returneſt by thy pow'r
Change ev'ry weed into a flow'r,
Turn each thiſtle to a vine,
Make each bramble, Eglantine.
For ſo rich a booty made,
Do but this, and I am paid:
As thou can'ſt with pow'rful blaſt,
Heat a-pace, and cool as faſt ;
As thou canſt raiſe an hidden flame,
And as ſoon deſtroy the ſame ;
So for pity, either ſtir
Up the fire of love in her,
That alike both flames may ſhine ;
Or elſe quite extinguiſh mine.

By a young Gentleman *robb'd of his
Miſtreſs by an old* Uncle.

CHLOE and *Lydia* ſtill by turns,
Horace his muſe and love incroach'd,
For am'rous wars he eager burns;
Till age (the death of love) approach'd.
When luſtres ten his ſtrength abates,
And feeble ſcarce his ſword can wield,
To *Venus* wiſely dedicates,
His Arms, vectes, and his ſhield
But *Hugh*, whom bloomy *Evans* charms,
Prepares to make her yield,
At eighty buckles on his arms,
But vainly takes the field.
Ceaſe then, old *Hugh*, at years fourſcore,
A virgin to engage ;
Vanquiſh'd at firſt, attempt no more
Unequal war to wage.

A NUPTIAL SONG; *from* Theocritus.

IN *Sparta* once when MENELAUS led,
The bluſhing HELEN to the bridal bed ;
A frolick quire of virgins blithe and gay,
Fair as the birth of ſpring and mild as may
Their hair inwreath'd with each rich-tinctur'd
flow'r)
To the ſoft cittern danc'd before the bow'r ;
And while their feet in wanton meaſures play
The ſoft aſſembly ſung this nuptial lay.
Hail prince, whom CYTHEREA wafted o'er
With happy omens from thy native ſhore.
Oh! may her altars blaze who gives thy love
The radiant daughter of the Cretan JOVE.

D d d d

Oh! may the offspring from that soft caress,
In miniature the mother's charms express;
Ake her all gay, all blooming may he be,
He a new CUPID, as a VENUS she.

We come, a beauteous train, who us'd to sport
On smooth Eurota's banks, our cool resort;
Where, bath'd with od'rous oils each shining lass,
Would dress her beauties in his natural glass.
Tho' each as bright as morn, as evening fair,
Our forms their lustre lose, when HELEN's near:
For she superiour charms with sprightlier grace,
And HARMONY with skill has form'd her face;
Nor does a softer blush AURORA deck,
Or tinge with lovelier hue her ruddy cheek.

When o'er the web her curious fingers rove,
Who can behold her, and forbear to love?
With such gay art the mingling colours joyn'd,
Express each soft idea of her mind.
No tender nymph of all the virgin quire,
So sweet can tune the voice, or touch the lyre.
She's perfect all and nature joins with art,
To charm each eye, and ravish ev'ry heart.

For thee, sweet bride, we thro' the valleys stray,
But sigh to find that HELEN is away:
A hundred nymphs, in beauty fresh and fair,
There cull the choicest flow'rs to bind thy hair;
Where fragrant hyacinths their forms disclose,
The maiden lilly, and the silken rose.
Then, while perfumes around their odours breathe
We on the mirtle hang the various wreath:
And, grief diverting with our rural play,
Deep on the bark inscribe this tender lay:
' Fair youths and smiling maids, bow low to me,
' For I was VENUS once, now HELEN's tree;
Hail wedded pair; and may you still receive,
Each sweet that you can wish, or HYMEN give;
May VENUS, and her son, for ever nigh,
With lighted torch your mutual flames supply.
Blest pair, in sweet embraces lye reclin'd,
Your souls united, as your bodies joyn'd;
There sleep till morn;----but at the prime of day
Awake, again to hear the bridal lay.

Rejoice O HYMEN: for 'till now thy care,
Ne'er join'd a prince so gay, a nymph so fair.

To a POLITICK CIT.

TO bring thee custom Dick, thy wife is made
To flaunt it in thy shop in gay brocade;
And on each heedless passenger to try
The am'rous Efforts of her asking eye:
By this you'll get no custom, silly else,
For thy dear spouse will get it all herself.

A new Leaf for the Laureat's GARLAND.

THou miscreant murd'rer of a poet's name!
Scape-goat of infamy,—disguis'd in fame,
Why, when thy sov'reign's virtues feel thy spite,
Dost thou forget to do his patience right?
What mercy, e'er could more extensive be,
Than his—who, tho' he reads, can pardon, thee!
Above all greatness shines his fix'd disdain
Of glory—which he bids thee live to stain!
A thousand kings have felt the force of wit,—
A thousand paid, to have their praises writ,—
But, never -before so marr'd with fame,
To bribe a rhyming devil to blast his name!

From Lord H—Y, to Mr. POYNTZ, with Dr SECKER's Sermon on Education.

WHile Secker's rules in this discourse I view
How quick each Maxim turns my
thoughts on you!
Who in each Art of education skill'd,
Severe in precept, yet in manner mild;
Canst form the man, and yet not shock the
child!
You by persuasion to instruction join'd,
Know without force to cultivate the mind;
And to rough tasks communicating ease,
E'en to the taught can make the teacher please;
While to a Court adapting ev'ry rule,
Without enervating the strictest School:
At once may strengthen and adorn the Heart,
With Spartan virtue and Athenian Art:
Nor vain thy toils, nor fruitless are thy cares,
For, see! thy royal charge in rip'ning Years,
The second hope of our Augustan Age,
Like lov'd Marcellus ev'ry Heart engage:
But to his Years Heav'n grant a longer date,
Nor with Marcellus virtue give his fate!
Long may he live the glory of our isle,
And each Minerva on his fort ne smile:
Let this in senate her assistance yield,
Let that direct and guard him in the field;
In peace and war still useful to the state,
In council prudent and in action great:
Then ev'ry rule throughout this theory shewn,
Shall by thy practise in this youth be known;
And the world find by one example taught,
How well on Poyntz's conduct Secker wrote.

An Answer from the CLOUDS to a Poem entitled, a new Simile for the Ladies. (See Vol. II. p. 922.)

PResumptuous bard! how cou'd you dare
A Woman with a Cloud compare?
Strange pride and insolence you show,
Inferior mortals there below.
And, is our thunder in your ears
So frequent, or so loud as theirs?
Alas our thunder soon goes out,
And only makes you more devout.
Then, is not female clatter worse,
That drives you, not to pray, but curse?
We hardly thunder thrice a year!
The bolt discharg'd, the sky grows clear:
But, ev'ry sublunary dowdy,
The more she scolds, the more she's cloudy.
Some criticks may object, perhaps,
That clouds are blam'd for giving Claps;
But what, alas! are Claps Ætherial,
Compar'd for mischief, to Venereal!
Can Clouds give bubo's, ulcers, blotches,
Or from your noses dig out notches?
We leave the body sweet and sound;
We kill, 'tis true, but never wound;
You know a Cloudy sky bespeaks
Fair weather, when the morning breaks;
But women in a Cloudy plight,
Foretell a storm to last till night.
A Cloud, in proper seasons pours
His blessings down in fruitful show'rs
But woman was by fate design'd
To pour down curses on mankind.

When * *Syrius* o'er the welkin rages,
Our kindly help his fire aſſwages;
But woman is a curſt inflamer,
No pariſh ducking-ſtool can tame her.
To kindle ſtrife dame-nature taught her:
Like fire-works, ſhe can burn in water.

For ſickleneſs how durſt you blame us ?
Who for our conſtancy are famous.
You'll ſee a *Cloud* in gentle weather
Keep the ſame face an hour together ;
While women, if it could be reckon'd,
Change ev'ry feature, ev'ry ſecond.
Obſerve our figure in a morning ;
Of foul or fair we give you warning;
But, can you gueſs from woman's air,
One minute, whether foul or fair ?

Go read in antient books enroll'd,
What honours we puſſeſs'd of old!
To diſappoint *Ixion*' rape.
JOVE dreſs'd a *Cloud* in *Juno*'s ſhape:
Which when he had enjoy'd he ſwore
No goddeſs could have pleas'd him more;
No diff'rence could he find between
His *Cloud*, and JOVE's imperial queen:
His *Cloud* produc'd a race of *Centaurs*,
Fam'd for a thouſand bold adventures,
From us deſcended *ab origine*;
By learned authors call'd, *Nubigena*.
But ſay, what earthly Nymphs do you know,
So beautiful to paſs for *Juno* ?

Before *Æneas* durſt aſpire
To court her majeſty of *Tyre*,
His mother begg'd of us to dreſs him
That *Dido* might the more careſs him ;
A coat we gave him, dy'd in grain ;
A flaxen wig, and *Clouded* cane,
(The wig was powder'd round with ſleet,
Which fell in *Clouds* beneath his feet)
With which he made a tearing ſhow:
And *Dido* quickly ſmoak'd the beau.

Among your females make enquiries;
What nymph on earth's ſo fair as *Iris* ?
What heav'nly beauty ſo endow'd ?
And yet her father is a *Cloud*,
We dreſs'd her in a gold brocade
Befitting *Juno*' favourite maid.

'Tis known, that *Socrates* the wiſe,
Ador'd us *Clouds* as deities ;
To us he made his daily pray'rs,
As *Ariſtophanes* declares ;
From *Jupiter* took all dominion,
And dy'd defending his opinion.
By his authority; 'tis plain,
You worſhip other gods in vain,
And from your own experience know,
We govern all things here below.
You follow where we pleaſe to guide;
O'er all your paſſions we preſide ;
Can raiſe you up, or ſink you down,
As we think fit to ſmile or frown :
And juſt as we diſpoſe your brain,
Are witty, dull, rejoice, complain.

Compare us then to female race!
We, to whom all the gods give place!
Who better challenge your allegiance,
Becauſe we dwell in higher regions,

* *The Dog-Star.*

You find the gods in *Homer* dwell
In ſeas, and ſtreams, or low as hell,
Ev'n *Jove* and *Mercury* his pimp,
No higher climb than mount *Olymp*,
Who makes you think, the *Clouds* he pierces,
(He pierce the *Clouds* ! He kiſs their ar—es:)
While we, o'er *Tenariffa* plac't,
Are loftier by a mile at leaſt,
And when *Apollo* ſtruts on *Pindus*,
We ſee him from our kitchen windows ;
Or to *Parnaſſus* looking down,
Can p--ſs upon his lawrel crown.

Fate never form'd the gods to fly;
In vehicles they mount the ſky.
When JOVE would ſome fair nymphs inveigle,
He comes full gallop on his eagle.
Tho' *Venus* be as light as air,
She muſt have doves to draw her chair.
Apollo ſtirs not out of doors
Without his lacker'd coach and four,
And jealous *Juno*, ever ſnarling,
Is drawn by peacocks in her berling :
But, we can fly were-e're we pleaſe,
O'er cities, rivers, hills and ſeas ;
From eaſt and weſt, the world we roam,
And, in all climates are at home ;
With care provide you as we go,
With ſun-ſhine, rain, and hail, or ſnow,
You, when it rains like fools believe,
JOVE p--es on you through a ſieve:
An idle tale, 'tis no ſuch matter ;
We only dip a ſpunge in water :
Then ſqueeze it cloſe between our thumbs,
And ſhake it well, and down it comes;
As you ſhall to your ſorrow know;
We'll watch your ſteps where-e'er you go ;
And ſince we find, you walk a-foot,
We'll ſoundly ſoule your Frize ſurtout.

'Tis but by our peculiar grace,
That *Phoebus* ever ſhows his face ;
For when we pleaſe we open wide
Our curtains blue from ſide to ſide :
And then, how ſaucily he ſhows
His brazen face, and fiery noſe ;
And gives himſelf a haughty air,
As if he made the weather fair.

'Tis ſung, where-ever *Celia* treads
The vi'lets ope their purple heads ;
The roſes blows, the cowſlip ſprings,
'Tis ſung, but we know better things,
'Tis true ; A woman on her mettle,
Will often p--ſs upon a nettle;
But though we own, ſhe makes it wetter ;
The nettle never thrives the better :
While we by ſoft poliſick ſhow'rs,
Can ev'ry ſpring produce you flow'rs.

Your poets, *Chloe*'s beauty height'ning,
Compare her radiant eyes to light'ning ;
And yet I hope, 'twill be allow'd,
That light'ning comes but from a cloud.

But gods, like us, have too much ſence
At poets flights to take offence,
Nor can hyperboles demean us ;
Each drab has been compar'd to *Venus* :
We own your verſes are melodious ;
But ſome compariſons are odious.

Advice to the Roman Youth: From *Petronius's*
Artis severa si quis amat effectus, &c.

Whoe'er with gen'rous ardour burns to know
    The honours which from erudition flow,
To temperance must a strict observance pay,
And all her laws religiously obey,
He ne'er must on the smiles of sov'reigns wait,
Nor the luxurious tables of the great:
Ne'er in the joys of wine indulge his soul,
Nor drown his genius in the circling bowl,
Nor taint the blossoms of his early age,
With the infectious softness of the stage.
But wheresoe'er the muse his youth embowers,
Or whether in Tritonia's lofty towers,
Or where the Spartan tills the laughing plain,
Or warbling Syrens chant the heav'nly strain:
Let poesy his happy soul engage,
And *Homer's* fountain drench his bloom of age.
Next when Socratic draughts have fir'd each vein
Let his bold hand indulge a freer rein.

And dauntless shake the mighty spear and shield
Which great *Demosthenes* was us'd to weild.
Nor must you fail, suffus'd with Grecian lambe,
To taste the flow of Roman eloquence.
Sometimes the buskin'd muse your fame may
And sound a sweet vicissitude of praise: [raise,
Or with th' historic page, prolong the feast,
While rising empires furnish the repast:
Or bid unconquer'd *Tully's* thunders roll,
When arts like those have dignify'd your soul,
Pierian streams shall ev'ry vein extend,
And from your tongue all Helicon descend.

From CATULLUS.

Odi et amo, quare id faciam fortasse requiris.
Nescio: sed fieri sentio et excrucior.

I Love yet hate, how can that be?
    Some forward Spark may say.
Why faith! I can't the reason see,
    But feel it ev'ry Day.

A Letter from a young Parson to an old one on the Death of his favourite Cow.

Tu semper urges flebilibus modis
Raptam Juvencam, nec tibi Vespere
Surgente decedunt Amores,
    Nec rapidum fugiente Solem.   HOR.

You, with incessant wails deplore,
That gentle MULLY is no more;
Evening and morn bring no relief,
No milking to assuage your grief.

This moment, brother, I receiv'd
    The news, at which I'm much a-
griev'd,
That she your favourite of late,
Dear MULLY has resign'd to fate,
MULLY, from whose indulgent side
You were so lavishly supply'd,
With what might decently afford
A dish successive on the board.

When Pudding enters all are pleas'd,
Their bowels seem already eas'd;
And if the Butter richly now,
Glibly the luscious morsels go.

Happy's the table then partakes
Of tender custards, frail cheese-cakes,
Or syllabub, by artists beat
To an obliging empty cheat.
Too like the kisses of the fair,
So light, you almost nothing share,
So tempting, that you can't forbear.

The dinner with perfuming cheese
Is nobly crown'd—now each of these,
All understanding housewives know,
Their essence to a dairy owe.

A thousand pleasures, inter meals,
The monarch of a dairy feels:
With purest cream now softens tea,
Now calls for posset drink, and whey;
Commands variety of good,
Either for physick, or for food.
With friendly visits always pleas'd,
He unprovided can't be seiz'd:
A hearty welcome ne'er refus'd,
Nor gives instead of that Excuse,
If, when the day declines, by hap
Some unexpected guests should rap,
And tarry, till the heifer roam
For Susan, to unload her stores,
His open soul, dispos'd to treat
With dainties exquisitely sweet.
A portion small of gen'rous wines
With grated spice and sugar joins,
Then summons due to stream upon't
Milk smoking from the native font:
Forthwith ambrosial curds arise,
Beneath while flowing Nectar lies.

They lade or suck (there's little odds)
Immortal Medley, fit for Gods.
    I might, in counting Blessings tire,
    All which in MULLY now expire.
But here imprudently I dwell,
On what you recollect too well,
Not suffer'd, by your gratefull mind
To lie in this account behind.
Severe's your fate must be allowed!
Stupid the mortal is, that wou'd
Be unconcern'd in such a case;
Yet that you gently screw your face,
Nor take this over much to heart,
Resistless reasons I'll impart.
Consider, willingly, or no,
You must endure th'uneasy blow.
Then why disconsolately grieve,
At what no conduct can retrieve?
Then lodge this truth within your breast,
All things are order'd for the best.
Misfortunes from the stars are sent
In kindness, more than punishment.
You say, you had not valued half
So much the loss but from a calf
Up the fond simpleton you brought
And sucking with your finger taught:
That long acquaintance with each
feature,
Had much endear'd you to the creature:
This makes the affirmation plain,
Which I endeavou'd to maintain,
That you too warmly lov'd the brute,
And often stole a sly salute:
Pretending, with a cunning fetch,
The flavour of her breath to catch.
If so, the fates have this design'd,
To raise and elevate your mind,
This world's uncertainty to show,
And warn you from concerns below.

This, or whatever be the reason,
Assure yourself, she dy'd in season.
Beside, had I this loss sustain'd,
I had with justice, more complain'd,
Who have, except my MULLY, little
For conversation, or for vittle.
But tho' you are of her bereft,
Unnumber'd blessings still are left.
The charms of an engaging spouse;
And plenty, smiling round your house:
Your tulips in the spring appear,
And children blooming all the year.
Then comfort up a fleeting life,
Since MULLY's gone e'en kiss your
wife. [wife,
This, your affliction to relieve,
Is what advice a friend can give.

If deaf to admonition, still
Your Thoughts lie brooding o'er the Ill,
Rather than endless you repine
Your fav'rite lost, I'll lend you mine:
Who, tho' her usual bounties, now
She's near her time, refuse to flow,
(See keeping in a leathern bottle
Her liquor for the groaning twat'ling)
And will your expectations bilk,
If much they hanker after milk;
Yet in your company as good,
As when a virgin she was woo'd,
And with her sister, in my eye,
She might for wit and beauty vie.
You'll hardly one in thousands find
More suited to relieve your mind.
'Twill probably assist your case,
Oft to survey her comely face.
And when her rival lowings ring,
It may some consolation bring.
Such kindly visit she shall pay
While this vexation wears away.
But if her young one's troublesome,
When she's deliver'd, send them home,
And should you, when (or quickly after)
I lend my J. wel, spare your daughter
In harmless waggery and play
Engag'd, we'd cheat the sultry day,
And banish sorrow far away.
And in this sweet exchange, tho' short
I'll pawn my gown and cassock for't,
The lovely Patty shan't be hurt.
The smiling charge I'll safe resign
Again when MULLY shall be mine.
Should MULLY's issue prove a Nancy,
And, with her looks attract your fancy,
Return the mother home for food,
Keep Nan, in Patty's place for good.
Thrice happy both when thus supply'd,
You, with a heifer; I, a bride.

If, neighbour, you shall be requir'd
To dignify the brute expir'd,
And rear some monumental stones,
Where dying, she bequeath'd her bones,
Which near the crib we may suppose,
The work let this Inscription close.

The EPITAPH.

Here, wheresoe oft was strok'd and fed,
    All that remains of MULLY's laid
Enclos'd within this narrow bound,
That rang'd the whole Enclosure round,
Her fate, with sorrow is deplor'd.
Who gave us pleasure, when she roar'd.
Her welcome plaints kept me alive,
O! cou'd she now by mine revive!

THE
Monthly Intelligencer.

NOVEMBER, 1733.

Wednesday 7.

ABOUT twelve o'Clock *William Charles Henry Friso*, Prince of *Orange*, Heir to K. *William* III. arrived off *Woolwich* on board the *Fubb's* Yacht from *Holland*, being attended from thence by the Hon. *Horatio Walpole* Esq; in that Yacht, and a great Retinue of Foreign Gentlemen in two other Yachts: To Sir *Charles Hardy*, Capt. of the *Fubbs*; his Highness gave a Diamond Ring, and to the Sailors 100 Guineas: To the Sailors of the Second Yacht 40; and to those of the 3d 30 Guineas. His Highness being there met by the *Dutch* Ambassador, and all the King's Barges, was received by Sir *Clement Cotterel* into one of them, and proceeded to *Tower-Wharf*, where Ld *Lovelace* and the King's Coaches waited for him. His Highness proceeded directly through the City, the Streets being crouded with People, expressing their Joy on his Arrival with loud Acclamations, till he came to *Somerset-House*, where he was received by the Dukes of *Montagu* and *Devonshire*. Soon after, he was congratulated on the Part of their Majesties and the Royal Family by several Noblemen deputed for that purpose.

A Gentleman in *Holland* has attempted the Character of this Prince in *French*; which is to the following Effect : *His Highness inherits the Estates of K.Will.III. and the other Heroes from whom he is descended. —— But why do I say he inherits their Estates, when he is also possess'd of their Virtues? Virtues easier to be admir'd than imitated.—— This is no proper Place for a Panegyrick, none but a Homer can celebrate the Gods, none but an* Apelles *can paint an Alexander. It would even be below his Merit to represent him possess'd of all the Qualifications necessary to form one born to Power; to mention a graceful Air, an Engaging Deportment, a Wit e-*

(Gent. Mag. Vol. III. No. xxxv.)

qually lively and penetrating, fine and delicate; a just Discernment, a solid Judgement, a happy Disposition, which ranks him among those who find in their Inclinations no Obstructions to Virtue : Generous Sentiments, a Heart obliging, courteous, compassionate; though of high Station, yet without Pomp; Great without Pride; Polite without Affectation : True, Just, Sincere, Loved by those who know him, ador'd by those who have Access to him. But I will not fully his Character by weakly attempting it, my Pencil is unequal to the Task. The inimitable Author of an excellent Piece would not have sought Minerva *in the Person of* Mentor *for the forming of his Hero, had he known that such a Prince would by his Descent, Application, and by the Education afforded him by his illustrious Mother, have been in Fact what he had fram'd to himself in his* Telemachus, *only in Imagination.*

Thursday 8.

The Ld Chancellor, the Foreign Ambassadors, and great Numbers of the Nobility, waited on the *Pr. of Orange*, to congratulate him on his safe Arrival in *England*. His Highness returned their Compliments in a very polite and agreeable Way : distinguishing the E. of *Chesterfield*, whom he had frequently convers'd with in *Holland*. —— His Highness has 25 Servants in Livery, which is exceeding rich; but his whole Retinue, with the Officers of his Houshold, and Gentlemen of Rank who attend him, is about 80 Persons.—In the Evening his Highness waited on their Majesties and the Royal Family, who received him in the most tender and affectionate manner, and afterwards he supped with them.

Friday, 9.

Mr *Paul Chamberlayne*, Author of a Pamphlet, entitled, *A Word to the Freeholders*, was taken into Custody; and being examin'd, was order'd to give Bail in a Recognizance of 200 *l.* and two Sureties .00 *l.* each.

Saturu

Saturday 10

Sir *Matthew Decker*, Bt. and about 70 *Dutch* and *Hamburgh* Merchants, went in a Body to congratulate the Prince of *Orange*, and to invite him to their Church. A

Sunday, 11.

His Highness was at the *Dutch* Church in *Austin Friars*, where finding himself seiz'd with a feverish Indisposition, he presently withdrew, leaving 25 Guineas to the Poor's Box, and return'd to *Somerset-house*; on which Account the Royal Nuptials, appointed to be celebrated the next Day, were put off. *See Vol.* iv. p. 160. B

Monday 12

This Evening being appointed for celebrating the Nuptials between her Royal Highness the Prince of *Orange*, was observed in the distant Parts of the Kingdom, where they had no Advice of its being put off, with Illuminations, Fireworks, and all other Tokens of Joy suitable to such an Occasion. C

A Cause was tried in the Court of *King's Bench*, on an Ejectment upon a Lease brought by the Comedians late of *Drury-Lane*, now acting in the *Haymarket* under the Authority of the Master of the Revels, against the Patentees of *Drury-lane* Theatre, which went in Favour of the former; it appearing that they took the Lease of the two Trustees appointed by the 36 Sharers of *Drury-Lane* House, with the Consent of 27 of those Sharers. E

Thursday 15.

The Parliament met, and were further prorogued to the 17th of *January* next.

Thursday 20.

Mr *Harper*, one of the Comedians in the *Haymarket* Company, who had been committed to *Bridewel* by Sir *Tho. Clarges*, upon the Act made against common Strollers, was brought by *Habeas Corpus* to the Court of *King's Bench*, where it was agreed he should be discharged out of *Bridewel*, upon his own Recognizance. G

Wednesday 21.

Came on a Hearing in the Arches Court of *Canterbury* between a noble Lord and a Gentlewoman, who stiled herself Baroness of —— otherwise ——; when the Judge of the Court decreed that for the future, the Cause be set out by the Stile of *Anne Mead*; but on a Motion of his Lordship's Proctor, the Cause was referr'd to a Court of Delegates. *See* Vol. IV. p. 352.

Thursday 29.

Being appointed for *Peter* Ld *King*, Baron of *Ockham*, Lord High Chancellor of *Great Britain*, to resign his Office and his Lordship being so ill of a Fever that he could not go to Court, about 10 in the Morning, the Ld *Harrington* went by the King's Command with a Letter under his Majesty's Sign Manual, directed to the Lord Chancellor, requiring his Lordship to deliver up the Great Seal; and about 3 in the Afternoon he sent it to the King by two Gentlemen commission'd for that Purpose. After which a General Council was held, and his Majesty declar'd *Charles Talbot*, Esq; Solicitor General, to be Lord High Chancellor of *Great Britain*.

A Cause was tried in the Court of Exchequer at *Westminster*, on an Information against Capt *Tobias Jewers*, of the *Chandois* Sloop, trading to *Rotterdam*, for making a false Entry at the Customhouse; but it appearing that the Goods charged to be omitted in his Bill of Entry, were clandestinely brought into and concealed in the Vessel, without his Knowledge, and against his Order, a Verdict was given for the Defendant.

Friday, 31.

Baron *Starcke*, Envoy Extraordinary from the Duke of *Holstein Gottorp*, has begun to negociate a Marriage between his Master, and the Princess *Amelia*.

The *British* Exportation of Corn was so great about this Time, that the Freight rose from 25 to 45 s. *per* Ton; and the Price of Wheat in some Places to 4 s. *per* Bushel.

Ten Ships of War are fitting out.

Our Letters from *Dublin* say, the Bill for repealing the TEST was expected to be brought into the House of Commons before the End of this Month, and that some smart Pamphlets had been publish'd on both Sides.

Boston, Sept. 17. The Church Wardens of *Christ-Church* received his Majesty's Present of Plate for the Communion-Table, Weight 187 Ounces, with Bibles, and other rich Furniture, obtained by the Interest of Governor *Belcher*.

From *Jamaica*, That the Negroes were in Rebellion, and had killed several white People; but had been driven into the Mountains by a Body of Sailors sent against them, after a sharp Fight; wherein were killed 40 of the former, and 11 of the latter. *See* Vol. IV. p. 277.

BIRTHS

BIRTHS.

THE Lady of Sir *Charles Gounter Nicol* delivered of a Daughter, about eleven Hours after her Husband's Death.

The Countess of *Albemarle* of a Daughter.

Mrs *Vansittart*, Sister to the Lord *Gower's* Lady, of a Son.

The Wife of *Thomas Clutterbuck*, Esq; Representative for *Leskard* in *Cornwal*, and one of the Lords of the *Admiralty*, of a Daughter.

The Wife of *Isaac Garnier*, Esq; Apothecary General to the Army, delivered of a Daughter.

MARRIAGES.

THE Lord *Gower*, married to the Relict of Sir *Henry Atkins*, Bart, and Daughter of the late Sir *John Stonhouse*, Bar.

Dudley Ryder, Esq; Member for St *Germans* *Cornwal* : : to Miss *Newnham* of *Stretham*.

Hon. *Piercy Widdrington*, Esq; : : to the Dutchess Dowager of *Norfolk*.

Valentine, Esq; Page of the Presence to her Majesty, : : to Miss *Sarah Ladenam*.

Mr *Lilley*, Apothecary in *Cheapside*, : : to Mrs *Hammond*, a Widow of 10,000 *l.* Fortune.

Tullet, Esq; : : to Miss *Lacy* of *King-street*, *Westminster*.

The Son of Brig. Gen. *Warren*, : : to Mrs *Humphreys*, a Widow of 30,000 *l.* Fortune.

Robert Thornton, Esq; a Director of the Bank, : : to the Sister of *Charles Newby*, Esq;

The Son of Sir *Cane James*, Bart : : to a young Lady of *Cambridge*.

DEATHS.

Oct. 19. SIR *Thomas Mollyneux*, Bart, State Physician of *Ireland*.

27. *John Chetwode*, L. L. D. of *Cambridge*.

28. The Rev. Mr *Tho. Davis*, alias *Pewry*, Rector of *Little H. Eingsbury*, *Essex*.

Rev. Mr *Fordham*, Minister of *Shafham*, *Flintshire*.

Major *John Webb*, Gov. of *Upnor Castle*.

31. *Tho. Lassells*, Esq; at *Stoke Newington*.

Nov. 2. *John Blacks*, Esq; at *Brompton*.

3. Col. *Groves*, an experienced Officer.

The Widow of the Rev. Mr *Paul Lorrain*, formerly Ordinary of *Newgate*.

6. Sir *Tho. Miller*, Bart, near *Chichester*. He is succeeded in his Estate and Honour by his Son, now Sir *John Miller*. He was Representative of *Chichester* in the two last, as his Father and Grand-father were in several former Parliaments.

7. *John Hanks*, Esq; at *Epsom*.

Dame *Mary Coote*, Daughter of the E. of *Bellamont* of *Ireland*, and Sister to Ld *Coote*.

8. Sir *James Ash*, Bart. at *Twickenham*. He left 4000 *l.* per Ann. and 10,000 *l.* in Cash to *Joseph Windham*, Esq; who married his eldest Daughter: His youngest, Relict of *Tho. Jobber*, Esq; died 8 Days before him.

Mr *Wigmore*, Wine-Merchant at *Rottersea*.

9. The Countess of *Plymouth* in *Hanover-Square*. She was Daughter to *Tho. Lewis*, Esq; of *Soberton* in *Hampshire*.

David Boyle, Earl of *Glasgow*. He was one of the Commissioners for the Treaty of Union, several Times High Commissioner to the General Assemblies of the Church of *Scotland*; and in 1708, was made Lord Register. His Son and Heir, *John* Earl of *Glasgow* succeeded him.

11. *Thomas Whiston*, in the Isle of *Ely*, Esq;

John Spelman, Esq; in *Andover-street*.

12. *James Stuart*, Esq; 2d Son of the Ld *Gairlis*, at *Dalkeith*, *Scotland*.

13. The Lady Visc. *Windsor*, Wife of Ld *Montjoy* Visc. *Windsor*.

Mr *Dixon*, a Merchant.

Mrs *Lucas*, Oyster-Purveyor to his Majesty.

15. *Tho. Hornsby*, Esq; at *Old Windsor*.

Philip Morean, Esq; at *Knightsbridge*, possessed of an Estate of near 50,000 *l.* the Bulk of which devolves to his only Son *James Philip Morean*, Esq; He left 3000 *l.* to his Daughter, the Widow of Col. *Hubert*; 3000 *l.* to his Grandson, *Alex. Hubert*; 1000 *l.* to *Christ's Hosp.* and 300 *l.* to the Poor of *Knightsbridge*.

The Lady *Tyrawley*, Mother, to Ld *Tyrawley*, Envoy Extraord. to *Portugal*.

The Lady of Sir *Henry Parker*, Bart. at *Honington*, *Warwickshire*.

Glover, Esq; at *Bath*.

16. Rev. Dr *Littleton*, Fellow of *Eaton-College*, and Rector of *Maple-Durham*, *Birks*.

17. The Relict of *Nicholas Corsellis*, Esq; formerly Representative for *Colchester*.

22. *Samuel Beachcroft*, Esq; a Nephew of the late Sir *Robert Beachcroft*, Alderman of *London*.

18. *Tho. Mackland*, Esq; at *Dover*.

Edw. Hanbury, Esq; Son of *John Hanbury* of *Pont-y-Pool*, *Monmouthsh.* Esq; by a Fall from his Chaise.

19. The Wife of Mr *Caer*, an Upholsterer in the *Hay-market*, and Daughter of the late Sir *George Hampson*, Bart.

The Rev. Mr *Cooper*, Rector of St *Christopher's* behind the *Royal Exchange*.

20. The Dutchess of *Ormond*, 2d Wife of the late D. of *Ormond*, and Daughter of *Henry* D. of *Beaufort*, a Lady of singular Charity, Piety, and Integrity, aged 68.

Mr *Durlem*, *Hamburgh* Merchant.

Peter Lepipre, Esq; in *Bartlet's* Buildings.

22. Mr *Samuel Longley*, Coal Merchant, worth 20,000 *l.*

The Wife of *John Barlow*, of *Colby* in *Pembrokeshire*, Esq; eldest Daughter to the late Ld Visc. *Harcourt*.

Mrs *White* in *Ormond-street*, reputed worth upwards of 30,000 *l.*

23. *Thomas Maynard*, of *Worcestershire*, Esq;

24. Sir *Charles Gounter Nicol*, Kt of the *Bath*, and Representative for *Peterborough*.

27. Capt.

27. Capt *John Waters*, aged 94. He was in all the Wars with the D. of *Marlborough*, and loft a Leg by a Cannon Ball.

29. Mr *Vanbretton*, a *Dutch* Merchant.

Ecclesiastical Preferments Conferr'd on the following Rev. Gentlemen.

MR *Peter Maurice*, Dean of *Bangor* made D. D.   And

Mr *Baron*, Dean of *Norwich*, made D. D. both by the A. Bp of *Canterbury*.

Mr *Gibbon*, Curate of St *Christophers*, chosen Lecturer of that Parish.

Mr *Crump*, chosen Head Master of St *Paul's* School.

Mr *Hildrop*, of *Marlborough*, presented to the Rectory of *Maulden, Bedfordshire*.

Mr *Tho. Tatham*, to the Rectory of *Myreton, Essex*.

Mr *W. Paxton*, to the Rectory of *Tolverton, Norfolk*.

Winch Holsworth, D. D. to the Rectory of *Gatton, Surry*.

Mr *Wade*, to the Vicarage of *East-ham, Essex*.

Mr *Samuel Collins*, to the Vicarage of *Walthamstow, Essex*.

A Dispensation pass'd to enable *William Owen*, M. A. to hold the Rectory of *Allington, Wilts*, together with the Rectory of *Bighton, Hants*.

Mr *Gregory*, M. A. collated to a Prebendary in the Collegiate Church of *Southwell*.

Mr *Cronk* chosen Preacher of *Lincoln's-Inn*.

Mr *Buttonshaw* presented to the Vicarage of *Brookland*, who with Mr *Robert Jenkins* B. A. are made Minor Canons of the Church of *Canterbury*, in the room of Mr *D'Evereux* and Mr *Gostling*, deceased.

Mr *Tho. Richards*, M. A. presented to the Rectory of *Ladchurch, Pembrokeshire*.

Mr *Jonathan Daddow*—to the Living of St *Justin Rowland, Cornwall*.

PROMOTIONS.

LORD Chief Justice *Yorke*, created a Peer of *Great-Britain*, by the Title of Baron *Hardwick*, in the County of *Gloucest*.

Charles Talbot, Esq; Sollicitor-General, appointed Lord High Chancellor of *Great-Britain*.

Earl *Cholmondeley*, made Lord Lieut. of *Cheshire, Montgomery, Flint, Merioneth, Carnarvon* and *Anglesea*.

Mr *Tho. Read*, made Surveyor of Houses in *Berks*.

Mr *James Ralph*, for *Cambridgeshire*.

Capt *Towns* appointed Commander of the *Shoreham* Man of War of 20 Guns.

Capt *Berkley*, Major of Lord *Tyrawly's* Reg. of Foot.

Maj. *Galfe*, made Gov. of *Upnor Castle*, in the room of Maj. *Webb*.

Richard Bendysh, Esq; Captain of a Company in Gen. *Sabine's Welsh* Fusileers.

Mr *John Hardesty*, Clerk of the Stores at *Gibraltar*, in the room of Mr *Maberly*.

Robert Auchmuty, made Judge of the Vice-Admiralty;

William Shirly, Esq; Advocate: and *Benj. Pemberton*, Esq; Clerk of the Navy-Office in *New-England*.

John and *James Collier*, Gent. made jointly Usher and Crier of the Court of *King's-Bench*, in the room of the late *Richard* and *William Cobinge*.

John Turner, Esq; a Commissioner of the Stamp-Duties, made Collector of the Customs at *Lynn Regis*, in the room of Mr *Har*, dec. which first Place he has resigned.

John Collier, Esq; :: Surveyor Gen. of the Riding Officers of the Customs in *Kent*.

Mr *Elphiston*, : : Crier of the Sittings of the King's Bench in *London* and *Middlesex*.

Hon. Mr *Herbert*, : : Capt. of the *Diamond* Man of War of 40 Guns.

John Sinclair, Esq; Brother-in-Law to the E. of *Caithness*, made one of the ordinary Lords of Session in *Scotland*, in the room of Sir *William Calderwood*, dec, by the Title of Lord *Murchil*.

The E. of *Strathmore*, :: Capt. of a Comp. in Brig. *Barrel's* Reg. at *Minorca*.

Mr *Summerfield*, : : Lieut. in Col. *Fielding's* Reg. of Foot.

Capt *Richard Kennish*, on Half-Pay, made Capt. of a Reg. of Foot on the *Irish* Estab.

Lord *Howard*, Heir apparent to the E. of *Effingham*, :: Cornet in *Pearce's* Horse.

Capt. *Mann* :: Commander of the *Oxford* Man of War, in the room of Capt. *Cobham*, who has resign'd; and Capt. *Martin* is made Commander of the *Sunderland* in his room.

BANKRUPTS.

ANNE Tanner, Abergavenny, Monmouth Mercer.

Arthur Pearson of Elton, Huntindon, Woolcomber.

David Thomson of Cowlane, London Joyner.

Alex. Bancroft, of St Giles's Middlx Weaver.

Charles Roberton of Exchange-Alley, London Coffee-man.

Anne Heale, } of Uxbridge, Middx, Distiller.
Joseph Heale, }

John Reynaldson, Jun. of Layburne, Yorkshire, Worsted-Maker.

Benjamin Turvile, of St Martins in the Fields, Middlesex, Hosier.

John Edwards of Leuminster, Herefordshire Sadler.

James Fitzgerald of St Clements Danes, Midd. Nichaller.

Tho. Jenepe of St Edmunds, Suffolk, Grocer.

Rich. Smith of Newberry, Berks, Bargemaster.

Francis Rudston, } of Newcastle upon Tyne
John Read, } Merchants.

FROM *Madrid*, That Mr *Keene*, in an Audience he had of their Catholick Majesties, pressed the Acceptance of an Accommodation which the King of *Great-Britain* had proposed for putting an End to all Differences. The King answer'd, "That he was infinitely obliged to the K. of *England* for the great Pains he had taken, and should always gratefully remember them; but was concerned to say, he could not at present give his Britannick Majesty the Satisfaction he desir'd, the *Emperor's* Resolution being come too late.

The K. of *Sardinia*, amongst other Motives which induced him, in Conjunction with *France*, to declare War against the Emperor, alledges his Ties of Blood and Friendship to the *French* King; the Insult upon K. *Stanislaus*; many Acts of Injustice done by the Imperial Court, as well to himself, as to his late Father, K. *Victor Amadeus*; by Delays in fulfilling Treaties made in his Behalf, by spiriting up Opposition, and Contests of every Kind against him, and by supporting the unjust Pretensions of the State of *Milan* to certain Lands contiguous to his Estates, designing, as appears, from the general Tendency of the Maxims of that Court, as soon as an Occasion should offer, to dethrone him without Relief. Having mentioned these and other Motives his Majesty promises an inviolable Union with the August *Germannick* Body, among whom he ranks himself.

From *Italy*, That the Citadel of *Milan* is blocked up; that the *French* and *Savoyards* have invaded *Fizzighitoni*, a strong Town in the *Milanese*; *Lodi, Pavia, Vigevano, Cremona*, and the City of *Milan* are already in their Possession; the *Germans* not having Strength enough to maintain them. *Novara* and *Tortona* are blocked up.

The Viceroy of *Naples* is making all necessary Dispositions for the Defence of that Kingdom.----The Court of *Rome* are perplexed about the Double Elections in *Poland* and seem determin'd to disoblige neither Party.---The *Venetians* are resolv'd to observe a strict Neutrality.

From the *Hague*, Nov. 13. That the Marquis *de Fenelon*, and the Deputies of the States Signed the Act of Neutrality for the *Austrian Netherlands*, which the Marquis sent directly to *Paris* to be ratifi'd. That their High-mightinesses have put an End to their Guardianship, declared the Prince of *Orange* of Age, and ordain'd that he shall be put into immediate Possession of his Domains, as well as the King of *Prussia*, pursuant to the Treaty of Partition between his Majesty and his Highness.

The Emperor's Answer to the *French* King's Manifesto (See p. 553.) being very long we can only give the Purport of it, viz. One can hardly imagine a more frivolous Motive, than than which the Crown of *France* borrows of the *Polish* Election, openly to break the Peace, and commit Hostilities against the Emperor and his Estates in *Italy*; and to persuade the K. of *Sardinia*, treacherously to conclude an offensive and defensive Alliance with that Crown against his Imperial Majesty, at the very Time he was taking the Oaths of Fidelity for the Fiefs he possesses dependant of the Emperor, who had undertaken nothing against either of those Powers. The Entrance of the *Russian* Troops into *Poland* was the Plea *France* made Use of to threaten, that tho' his Imperial Majesty's Troops should not enter *Poland*, she would nevertheless declare War against him, because he was in good Intelligence with the *Czarina*, and, because her Majesty will not recall her Troops and give up her Right of Guarantee to the *Acts* of the Dyet 1717, whereby *Stanislaus* was proscrib'd and declar'd for ever ineligible. His Imperial Majesty after observing, that he had not caused one Single Soldier to enter *Poland* to this Day, nor taken the least Step which might draw upon him the Reproach of Hostilities; and, on the contrary, how the Constitution of *Poland* had been violated by *France* and the Primate, leaves it to the Princes of the Empire to consider whether *France* has not been the Aggressor; and so relies on the Assistance of the Holy Empire, his Faithful Allies, the Justice of his Cause, and the Divine Protection.

From *Germany*, That the Campaign being at an End on the *Rhine*, the *French* Army was retired into Winter Quarters; and that the Electors of *Bavaria* and *Cologn*, had declared for a Neutrality.

The Method of proceeding in the new Court of Record at Savannah in Georgia, when any of the People die there without Friends:

JULY 28. it was presented, that *Joshua Overend*, a Free-holder of that Town, died the 28th of *June*, leaving no Relation there to take Care of his Estate and Effects: A Jury of Freeholders was thereupon impannell'd and sworn; and upon a full hearing of Witnesses found that he died possessed of a House, Garden, and fifty Acres of Land, not cultivated, and and that he had no Children; and that the said House, Garden, and one Moiety of the Land legally descended to *Mary Overend*, his Wife, then in *England*; and that the Remaining Moiety of the said Land immediately descended to his next Heir Male; also the House and the other Moiety of Land, after the Death of the said *Mary Overend*. A Cow, Calf, and Steer of the Deceased was sold for 4 l. 2 s. Sterling, the Remainder of which Sum after a Debt of 37 s. 8 d. paid, was order'd to be transmitted to the said *Mary Overend* in *England*, together with some other Effects; and the Proceedings herein had.

Towards the End of the Month.

Course of Exchange.	STOCKS.	Monthly BILL of Mortality, from Oct. 23. to Nov. 27.
Amsterdam — 35 8	S. Sea Trading Stock	
Ditto at Sight 34 1	72 ¼	Christned { Males 793 } 1536 { Females 743 }
Hamburgh — 35 5	——Annu. 101	
Rotterdam -35 10	——Ditto new 100	Buried { Males 1171 } 1387 { Females 1216 }
Antwerp ——36 5	Dit. 3 per C. 92	
Madrid —— 40	——Bonds 5s. Disc.	Died under 2 Years old —— 883
Bilboa —— 40	Bank 130	Between 2 and 5 —— 235
Cadiz —— 40 ¼	New Circulation 1 L	Between 5 and 10 —— 95
Venice —— 49 ¾	India 136	Between 10 and 20 —— 64
Leghorn —— 50 ¼	——Bonds 4s. Pre.	Between 20 and 30 —— 171
Genoa —— 53 ¼	at 3 per Ct. 2s. Disc.	Between 30 and 40 —— 241
Paris —— 30	Mil. Bank 112	Between 40 and 50 —— 241
Bourdeaux —— 31 ¾	African 25	Between 50 and 60 —— 203
Oporto —— 53 ¼	Royal Ass. 90	Between 60 and 70 —— 109
Lisbon - - -53 ¼ a ½	Lon. ditto 11 ½	Between 70 and 80 —— 84
Dublin - - - 12 ¼	Eng. Copp. 1 l. 15 s.	Between 80 and 90 —— 51
	Welsh ditto 17 s.	Between 90 and 100 —— 9

Lo. Tickets 3 s. 6 d. disc.

Price of Grain at *Bear-Key,* per Qr.		Buried.	Weekly	
Wheat 22 s. to 26 s. 0 d.	P. Malt 19 s. to 22 s.	Within the walls. 226	Oct. 30	507
Rye 12 s. to 16 s. 0 d.	B. Malt 18 s. to 20 s.	Without the walls. 701	Nov. 6	447
Barley 13 s. to 16 s. 6 d.	Tares 18 s. to 20 s.	In Mid and Surry. 974	13	446
Oats 10 s. to 15 s. 0 d.	H. Pease 16 s. to 18 s.	City and Sub of West 486	20	429
Pease 18 s. to 22 s.	H. Beans 20 s. to 22 s.	2387	27	478
				2387

Prices of Goods, &c. in *London.*   Hay 38 to 40 s. a Load.

Coals per Chaldron 24 s. to 25 s.	Figs 18 s.	Mastick white 4 s. 6 d.
Old Hops per Flam. 50 s. to 4 l.	Sugar Powder best 59 s. per C.	Opium 10 s. 06 d.
New Hops 3 l. 10 s.	Ditto second sort 49 per C.	Quicksilver 4 s. 4 d.
Rape Seed 10 l. to 11 l. 00 s.	Loaf Sugar double refine 09 d.	Rhubarb 18 s. a 20 s.
Lead the Fodder 19 Ham. 2 half	for. per lb.	Sarsaparilla 3 s. 0 d.
on board, 14 l. 10 s.	Ditto single refin. 60 s. to 70 s.	Saffron Eng. 2⁶ s. 00 d.
Tin in Blocks 3 l. 18 s.	per C.	Wormseeds 4 s. 6 d.
Ditto in Bars 4 l. 02 s. exclusive	Cinnamon 7 s. 9 d.	Balsam Caprou 2 s. 10 d.
of 3 s. per Hun. Duty.	Cloves 9 s. 1 d.	Balsam of Gillead 14 s. 00 l.
Copper Eng. best 5 L. 05 s. per C.	Mace 16 s. 6 d. per lb.	Hypecacuana 5 s. 6 d.
Ditto ordinary 5 l. 16 s. per C.	Nutmegs 8 s. 7 d. per lb.	Ambergreece per oz. 14 s. 00 l.
Ditto Barbary 85 l. to 95 l. 00 s.	Sugar Candy white 12 d. to 17 d.	
per C.	Ditto brown 6 d. Halfpenny per lb.	Wine, Brandy, and Rum.
Iron of Bilboa 14 L. 20 s. per Tun.	Pepper for Home consump. 14 d.	Oporto red, per T. 32 L. a 34 l.
Dit of Sweden 15 L. 10 s. per Tun	Ditto for exportation 10 d. halfpenny	ditto white 40 l.
Tallow 36 s. per C. or 5 d. s. per.	Tea Bohea fine 12 s. to 14 s. per lb.	Lisbon red 36 l.
p. lb.	Ditto ordinary 10 s. per lb.	ditto white 36 L.
Country Tallow 2 L. 27 s. 0 d.	Ditto Congo 12 s to 16 s. per lb.	Sherry 27 l.
Cochineal 17 s. 9 d. per lb.	ditto Pekoe 18 s. per lb.	Canary new 26 l.
	ditto Green fine 12 s to 15 s. per lb.	ditto old 36 L.
Grocery Wares.	ditto Imperial 14 s. per lb.	Florence 3 l.
Raisins of the Sun 27 s. 0 d. per C.	ditto Hyson 35 s. to 00 s.	French red 36 L. a 50 l.
Ditto Malaga Frails new none		ditto white 20 l.
Ditto Smirna new 17 s.	Drugs by the lb.	Mountain malaga old 30 l.
Ditto Alicant 15 s.	Balsam Peru 16 s.	ditto new 24 l.
Ditto Lipra new 16 s.	Cardamoms 3 s. 4 d.	Brandy Fr. per Gal. 6 s. to 6 s. 6 d.
Ditto Belvedera 17 s.	Camphire refin'd 23 s.	Rum of Jem. 6 s. to 7 s. 6 d.
Currants 37 s.	Crabs Eyes 22 s.	ditto Leew. Islands 6 s. to 10.
Ditto new none.	Jallap 3 s. 9 d.	
Prunes French 17 s.	Manna 2 s. 4 d. 2 s. 6 d.	

A REGISTER of BOOKS publish'd in NOVEMBER, 1733.

THE Presbyterians Plea of Merit; in Order to take off the Test, (in Ireland,) impartially Examined. With an Account of the State of Popery in that Kingdom, and of the Origin and Principles of the Dissenters in General. To which is added, An Ode to Humphry French, Esq; Late Lord Mayor of Dublin. Sold by A. Dodd, price 6 d.

2. A Letter to the Hon. Sir Hans Sloan, Bart. in Vindication of the Characters of those Greek Writers in Physick that flourish'd after Galen, but particularly that of Alexander Trallian; containing an Account of the Birth-place, Age, Stile, Method, Practice, &c. of that excellent Author. By E. Milward, M. D. Printed for A. Bettesworth, price bound 5 s. sew'd 4 s.

3. Philosophical Transactions, No 426, for the Months of November and December 1732, continued and published by Cromwell Mortimer, M. D. R. S. S. pr. 1s. 6d.

4. De sacra vernacula Epistola. Per Edm. Massey, M. A. Printed for L. Gilliver, pr. 1 s. 6 d.

5. The Apprentice's faithful Monitor, directing him in the several Branches of his Duty to God, his Master, and himself. Price 1 s. 6 d. bound;

6. The Oration, spoke at Joyner's-Hall in Thames-street on Monday Sept. 24, pursuant to the Will of Mrs Jane Hive, who departed this Life Aug. 19, 1733. Proving 1. The Plurality of Worlds. 2. That this Earth is the Hell. 3. That the Souls of Men are the Apostate Angels. And 4thly. That the Fire which will punish those who shall be confined to this Globe after the Day of Judgment will be immaterial. With large Notes confirming the Hypothesis, and refuting Dr Lupton's Opinion of the Eternity of Hell Torments. By her Son and Executor. Printed for T. Cooper pr. 1s.

7. A Vindication of Eustace Budgell, Esq; from some Aspersions thrown upon him in a late Pamphlet, entitled, A Copy of the Will of Dr Matthew Tindal, with an Account of what pass'd concerning the same, between Mrs Lucy Price, Eustace Budgell, Esq; and Mr Nicholas Tindal, price 3 d.

8. A Proposal to his Highness the Prince of Orange.

9. A Letter to Mr Curll, Bookseller, from the Rev. Mr Tindal, with Mr Curll's Answer. The 3 last are printed for E. Curll, price 1 s. 6 d.

10. The Theatre turn'd upside down; or, the Mutineers. A Dialogue, occasion'd by a Phamphlet, call'd the Theatric Squabble. Sold by A. Dodd, price 6d.

11. A Letter to the Chessman, on the Game of Chess; Occasion'd by his Paper of the 15th of Sept. 1733. Printed for J. Peele, price 6d.

12. The remarkable Speech of Stanislaus, on his remounting the Throne of Poland, to the Primate and Electors, containing many curious Observations on the present Posture of Affairs in Europe. The Primate's congratulatory Answer, in behalf of himself and the Senators. To which is added, an authentick Account of the Motives inducing his most Christian Majesty to declare War against the Emperor of Germany, with his Majesty's Declaration of War faithfully translated from the original Copies. Printed for E. Nutt, pr. 6d.

13. A political Conversation, which lately happened between a Couple of staunch Patriots, and a Revolter to the Court Interest. Publish'd for the Benefit of the People. Printed for T. Cooper, price 6d.

14. A Discourse on the Wickedness and Danger of fomented Divisions in a State. Printed for J. Roberts price 6d.

15. The Landed Interest consider'd: Being serious Advice to Gentlemen, Yeomen, Farmers and others concern'd in the ensuing Election. By a Yeoman of Kent. Printed for J. Roberts, price 6 d.

16. A Letter of Advice to the Rev. Mr Scurlock, occasion'd by his extraordinary Sermon, preach'd the 7th of October at St Paul's. By a sturdy Beggar, Citizen and Merchant of London. Sold at the Pamphlet Shops, price 6 d.

17. A Letter to the Protestant Dissenters of all Denominations, on the present Situation of Affairs. Printed for R. Hett, price 3 d.

18. Serious Reflections on the present Condition of Great Britain. In an Address to the Electors of Members to represent them in the next Parliament, from some of their Friends in the Cities of London and Westminster. Printed for J. Roberts, price 6 d.

19. The Crisis; or, Briton's Advocate: Being a full Answer to the Observations on a Paper, entitled, The List, &c. Printed for J. Torchy, price 1 s.

20. A Pastoral Poem. Printed for W. Mears, pr. 6d.

21. The Art of Scribbling. Address'd to all the Scribblers of the Age. By Scriblerus Maximus. Printed for A. Dodd, price 1 s.

22. The Muse in Distress. A Poem. Occasion'd by the present State of Poetry. Printed for T. Cooper, pr. 1s.

23. The Insufficiency of Reason, and Necessity of Revelation, to assure Men of the Pardon of Sin. A Sermon preach'd at the triennial Visitation of the Right Rev. Father in God Richard Ld Bp of Lincoln, held at Melton-Mowbray in Leicestershire, August 2, 1733. By Christopher Clarkson, D. D. Cambridge, printed for C. Crownfield.

24. A Sermon preached before the Right Hon. the Lord Mayor, &c. the 30th of September, 1733. Being the Day of Election of a Lord Mayor for the Year ensuing. By Matthew Pilkington, A. M. Chaplain to the Lord Mayor. Printed for B. Motte, price 6d.

25. A Sermon, preach'd before the Trustees for establishing the Colony of Georgia in America, and before the Associates of the late Rev. Dr Thomas Bray for converting the Negroes in the British Plantations, and for other good Purposes, at their anniversary Meeting in the Parish Church of St Mary le Bow, on Thursday, March 15 1732. By John Burton, B. D. Fellow of Corpus Christi, Oxon, and Eaton Colleges.

26. A Discourse concerning the Universality and Order of the Resurrection: Being a Sequel to that wherein the Personal Identity is asserted. By Henry Felton, D. D. Printed for B. Motte, price 6d.

27. A Caution against speaking Evil of our Governors and of one another. As it was deliver'd in a Sermon preach'd at St Paul's Cathedral, on Sunday the 7th of October, 1733. By David Scurlock, M. A. Vicar of Pottern, Wilts. To which is prefix'd the Preacher's Advertisement to the Publick, shewing his Reasons for publishing the same. Printed for J. Roberts, pr. 6d.

28. A Funeral Sermon on Occasion of the Death of John Archer, who died Sept. 23, 1733. Preach'd at Tunbridge Wells. Sept. 30. By Ben. Mills. Printed for R. Ford, price 6d.

29. A Specimen of a new Translation of the Book of Psalms; with critical Observations upon several Obscure Passages in. By a Gentleman of Wadham College, Oxford. Sold by J. Bailey, price 1s.

30. The Importance of the Doctrine of the holy Trinity asserted; in Reply to some late Pamphlets. By Daniel Waterland, D. D. Chaplain in Ordinary to his Majesty. Printed for W. Innys, price 6s. 6d.

31. The Book of the Opera of Opera's: Or Tom Thumb the Great. Sold by J. Roberts, price 6d.

32. An Epistle to a Lady who desired the Author to make Verses on her, in the Heroic Stile. Printed for J. Wilford, price 1s.

33. An Essay on Faction. A Poem. Printed for J. Peel price 1s.

34. The Impertinent: Or, A Visit to the Court, A Satire. Printed for J. Wilford.

35. The Union. A Poem. Humbly inscrib'd to her Royal Highness the Princess Anne. Printed for J. Roberts, price 6d.

36. The Gods in Debate; or, No Bribe like Beauty A new Ballad on the Prince of Orange's Arrival. Printed for J. Roberts, price 6d.

37. A Poem on the intended Nuptials of Anne Princess Royal of Great Britain, with his Highness William Prince of Orange. Printed for J. Jackson, price 6d.

38. Marriage at last! Or, the Fortunate Prince. A new Opera. Sold by the Booksellers, price 1s.

39. The Royal Marriage. Prince Lemuel's Lesson of Chastity, Temperance, &c. By O. D. Printed for P. Meighan, price 4s.

40. The Procession Order for the Marriage of her Royal Highness Anne, Princess Royal of Great Britain with his Highness William Prince of Orange. Sold by J. Dormer, price 6d.

41. The Parioniad. A Satire. Inscrib'd to Mr Pope. Printed for C. Corbett, price 1s.

42. The Court Legacy. A New Ballad Opera of Three Acts. As it is acted at the Utopian Palace. By the Author of the Atalantis. Sold by J. Dormer pr. 1s 6d.

43. A Poetical Description of the Life, Pranks, and Practice of that noted Actress Valida, and her Confident Grimaria. Printed for S. Slow, price 6d.

44. The Lady's Decoy: Or, the Man-midwife's Defence. Printed for S Slow, price 6d.

45. Memoirs of the Life of Barton Booth, Esq; with his Character. To which are added several Poetical Pieces

Pieces written by himself, &c. Printed for J. Watts price 1s. 6d.

46. Historiæ Puerilis: Or, a Collection of little Histories, &c. By Robert. Wharton. Printed for Tho. Wotton, price 1s.

47. A Treatise of the Education and Learning proper for the different Capacities of Youth, founded on the Principles of Natural Philosophy. Extracted from the Examen de ingenios of the famous Spaniard Dr John Stuarres. Printed for C. Rivington.

48. The Lives of the Princes of the Illustrious House of Orange, continued down to the present Time. Collected from the best Authorities and Manuscripts. In 2 Vols. Printed for W. Mears, price 3s.

49. The Jurisdiction of the Chancery as a Court of Equity research'd; and the traditional Obscurity of its Commencement clear'd. With a short Essay on the Judicature of the Lords in Parliament, upon Appeals from Courts of Equity. Printed for Joel Stephens, price 1s.

50. A Supplement to the first Edition of the Attorney's Pocket Companion. Printed for R. Gosling, pr. 1s. 6d.

51. Some seasonable Reflections on the imminent Danger to which the Liberties of Europe are exposed by the exorbitant Power of the House of Bourbon, and the Necessity of giving immediate assistance to the House of Austria and the Empire. Printed for W. Mears, price 1s.

25. The Koran, commonly called the Alcoran of Mohammed. Translated into English immediately from the Original Arabic, with Explanatory Notes, &c. By George Sale, Gent. Printed for J. Wilcox, pr. 1l.

52. The Court Kalendar. Sold by J. Watson, pr. 6d.

54. A Letter from a Livery Man in London, to a Freeholder in the Country. Printed for J. Roberts.

55. Do you know what you are about? Or, a Protestant Alarm to Great Britain; Proving our late Theatric Squabble to be a Type of the present Contest for the Crown of Coland; and that the Division between Handel and Senesino has more in it than we imagine. Also that the latter is no Eunuch, but a Jesuit in Disguise. Printed for J. Roberts, price 6d.

56. An Expostulatory Address to the Protestant Dissenters, on their present Conduct. Printed for J. Roberts price 6d.

57. Remarks upon a Pamphlet, called the Report of the Committee, &c. of the Parish of St Botolph without Aldersgate. Printed for J. Wilford, pr. 6d.

58. The fatal Consequence of Bribery, exemplify'd in Judas: A Sermon preach'd at St Mary's in Reading, on the Occasion of the Election of Members of Parliament. By Wm Reeves, A. M. Printed for J. Wilford, price 6d.

59. The Respect due to the Church of God. A Sermon preach'd the 11th of October, 1735. at the Consecration of St George's Chapel at Tiverton by the Bp of Exon. By George Parker, Prebendary of St Peter's in Exeter. Printed for S. Birt, price 6d.

60. A Second Essay upon the Nature, Manner, and End of the Christian Revelation. By Christopher Robinson. A. M. Printed for J. Pemberton, pr. 1s.

61. The Thoughts of an Impartial Man upon the present Temper of the Nation; offer'd to the Consideration of the Freeholders of Great Britain. Printed for J. Roberts, price 6d.

62. The Court Parrot. Printed for J. Dormer, pr. 6d.

63. Credendits in Chancery: Being a Collection of Cases argued and adjudged in the High Court Chancery from the Year 1689, to 1722. Printed for Mess. Bettesworth and C Hitch. price 1l. 5s.

64. A Treatise concerning the State of Departed Souls, before, at and after the Resurrection. Translated into English by Mr Dennis, price 5s.

65. The Faith and Duties of Christians, a Treatise in eight Chapters. Translated into English by Mr Dennis, price 4s.

66. De Statu Mortuorum & Resurgentium Tractatus, Adjicitur Appendix de Futura Judæorum Restauratione, price 6s.

67. Archæologiæ Philosophicæ sive Doctrina Antiqua de Rerum Originibus. Libri Duo. Editio Secunda. Accedunt eiusdem Epistolæ Duæ de Archæologiis Philosophicis, price 6s.

68, i.e Fide & Officiis Christianorum. Liber Posthumus. Editio Secunda, price 4s.

The five last written by the learned Dr Thomas Burnet, late Master of the Charter House. And sold by Mess. Bettesworth and C. Hitch, in Pater noster Row.

69. The Danger of Strife, a Sermon preached at the Chapel Royal at St James's, Jan. 30, 1726-7. Printed for J. Roberts, price 6d.

Lond.Gazette
Londŏ Jour.
Fog's Journ.
Applebee's ::
Read's :: ::
Craftsman :
D. Spectato;
Grubstreet J
W.ly Register
Free-Briton
Free-mason
Daily Court
Daily-Post
Dai.Courtnal
Da.Post-boy
D.Advertiser
St James's Ev.
Whitehall Ev.
Lŏdon Eveťg
Flying-Post
Weekly Misc
Corncutter's J.
Gen.Ev.Post
What d'ye call't
Auditą :: ::

St JOHN's GATE.

York 2 News
Dublin 6 :::
Edinburgh 2
Bristol ; : : :
Norwich 2 :
Exeter 2 : : :
Worcester ; :
Northampton
Gloucester ::
Stamford : :
Nottingham
Bury Journ.
Chester ditto
Derby ditto
Ipswich bo.
Reading bo.
Leeds Merc
Newcastle C
Canterbury
Birmingham
Manchester
Boston ::: ¶
Jamaica, &c.
Barbados ; :

Or, MONTHLY INTELLIGENCER.

For DECEMBER, 1733.

CONTAINING,

more in Quantity, and greater Variety, than any Book of the Kind and Price.

I. Proceedings and Debates in Parliament continued, *viz.* The Grand Debate on the Excise Scheme, concluded; Speeches by Sir *J—n B—r—d*, Sir *T—n R—b—n*, Sir *T—s A—n*, *Wm P—y*, Esq; *W—r P—r*, Esq; &c. *London* Petition and Debate thereon, Bill dropt; *Nottingham*, *Coventry*, and Druggists Petition; Bills for regulating Stock jobbing, and Proceedings of Ecclesiastical Courts, Motion concerning Receivers of the Land Tax, Orders about Tumults, &c.

II. A View of the Weekly Essays, humorous, moral, and religious, from the *Spectator*, *Grubstreet*, *Miscellany* &c.

III. Of the Political Dissertations and Disputes, from the *Craftsman*, *Fog*, *Free-Briton*, *London Journal*, &c.

IV. A select Collection of Poetry, *viz. Chloe* Singing; Fees on both Sides; Mr *Dennis* to Mr *Thomson*; *Coventry* Assembly; *Bury* Glories; *Chloe's* Picture; *Cupid* turn'd Thief; Satire on Mr *P—e* by Ld *H—y*, On the Players giving Mr *Dennis* a Benefit; On the same; Dr *Tindal* canoniz'd or murder'd; on the Lord Chancellor *Talbot's* Promotion; Advice to the Laureat.

V. Domestic Occurrences, Births, Marriages, Deaths, Promotions Civil and Ecclesiastical, &c.

VI. Prices of Goods, and Stocks; Bill of Mortality, &c. Monthly and Yearly.

VII. Foreign Affairs.

VIII. Books and Pamphlets, publish'd.

IX. A Table of Contents.

By *SYLVANUS URBAN*, Gent.

LONDON: Printed, and sold at St *John's Gate*: By F. *Jefferies*, in *Ludgate-street*, all othe Booksellers; and by the Persons who serve Gentlemen with the Newspapers. *Of whom may be had any of the Numbers*, except for the Year 1731. which are reprinting some of them the Fifth time. A few are done on Royal Paper, of which Compleat Sets may be had.

CONTENTS.

THE
Gentleman's Magazine:
DECEMBER, 1733.

A View of the PROCEEDINGS *and* DEBATES *in last* Session *of*
Parliament, *continued from p. 580.*

continued from p. 580.

DEBATE. Friday, March 16.
In altering the Duties on Tobacco to EXCISE.

SIR *Cha. Turner* having reported to theHouse the Resolutions the Committee had come to in Relation to the Duties on Tobacco (See p. 580.) the Serjeant at Arms, according to order, summon'd the Members to attend the Service of the House, and eing returned, the first Resolution (See p. 60 A B) was read and the Question being roposed for agreeing with the Committee herein, a Debate ensued, in Substance as ollows:

Sir *J---n B----rd*, Tho' the Resolutions, ir, which have been now read were agreed by a Majority of those present in the Committee, yet I make no Doubt, but now, Gentlemen have had Time to consider that Affair seriously, many will be of a different opinion. For my own Part, the more I consider that Scheme on which these Resolutions are founded, the more Objections I ad to it, the less I find in those Arguments which were offered in Support of it. One f the chief Ends proposed by this Scheme is the preventing of those Frauds which ave formerly been committed in the Tobacco-trade; but, if we particularly examine hose Frauds, we shall find, that every one f them may either be prevented by the aws already in Being, or they are such as annot be effectually prevented by any Thing n the Scheme proposed.—The Fraud comitted at Weighing of Tobacco at the Custom-house, and likewise that of exporting ne Sort for another, is altogether owing, as as been already observed, to a Neglect of Duty in the Officers, and not to any Defect n the Laws: As to the Frauds of running r re-landing Tobacco after it has been entered for Exportation, and received the raw-backs, which are those by which the ublick has, and always will suffer the most, here is nothing in the Scheme that can any way contribute to the preventing them; for it is not the Manner of collecting of Duties, but the Amount of the Duties, which occasions Smuggling or Running in all Countries and in all Branches of Trade; and since the Duties on Tobacco are by this Scheme to be very near as high, as they were before, we may expect, there will be as much Smuggling as there was formerly; where the Temptation is great, there will be a great many that will run the Risque, be it ever so great.—As for the Warehouses proposed, if there be any Thing in that Part of the Scheme, which may be of Use against Smuggling, it is not to this Scheme that the Proposition owns its Birth; it is what the Merchants themselves have long ago desired; and for that Purpose I drew up some Time ago a Clause to have been offered to this House, which I shewed to the hon. Gentleman on the Floor, and at that Time the Affair would have been pushed, but there arose some Disputes among the Merchants themselves, which occasioned its being deferred: That Part of the Scheme therefore I shall find no Fault with, I believe no Merchants will, but then we would have it without the Laws of Excise; for this Reason the hon. Gentleman cries out against he Merchants as unreasonable; he says they formerly desired to have Warehouses, and now refuse to accept of them. But do not Gentlemen see where the Difference lies? The Merchants desire to have Warehouses without an Excise, and the hon. Gentleman will not it seems favour us with the one without loading us with the other. —As to what the Civil List may get by this Scheme, it will depend entirely upon the Effect the Scheme may have in relation to the Preventing of Frauds; but it is certain, if the publick Revenue get any Thing by the Scheme, the Civil List will get in Proportion, or rather more; for, that Part of the Duty which goes towards the Civil List is still to be payable on Importation at the Custom-house, and to be drawn back on Exportation, as before: Now it is manifest, this will be a great Advantage to the
Civil

Civil List, and often a great Inconvenience to the Merchant; for once in every six Weeks that Money will be carried to the Exchequer, and when once it is lodged there, I believe it will there remain; it will never be sent back to the Custom-house, to answer any Occasion there may be for it at that Place; so that when the Merchant comes to export a Quantity of Tobacco, and to call for his Draw-back, if the Commissioners have none of that Civil List Money in their Hands, they cannot apply the Produce of any other Branch of the publick Revenue to that Use; and therefore the Merchant must wait for his Draw-back till some new Tobacco's be imported; by which Means the Crown may often have the Use of that Money, which should have been applied to the Payment of the Merchant, perhaps for near a Twelve-month at a Time; and the Lying-out of that Money for so long a Time may often happen to be of dangerous Consequence to the Merchant's Credit.——The hon. Gentleman talked of making *London* a free Port, I wish, with all my Heart he would do so; it is certainly what every Merchant wishes to see done, and what would greatly contribute to the Increase and Encouragement of the Trade of this Nation; but how such a Pretence can be set up in Favour of the Scheme now before us, I cannot comprehend: For it appears evident to me, that by this Scheme the Port of *London*, and all the other Ports of the Kingdom, will be so far from being made free, that at every one of them the Merchant will be subjected to more Trouble and Expence, both upon Importation and Exportation, than ever he was before. 'Tis true that, upon the Importation of Tobacco, the Merchant was formerly obliged to pay down the whole Duties, or to give his Bond with sufficient Sureties for them, but this was never any Hardship, because, if he had ready Money, he advanced it for the prompt Payment of the Duties, and he had an Allowance for so doing, which was but a reasonable Allowance, considering how long he was sometimes obliged to keep his Tobacco on his Hands, before he met with a Market, and how many Months Credit he was often after that obliged to give to the Buyer; and if he had not ready Money at Command, he could formerly give his Bond for the whole Duties with two sufficient Sureties, which a Man of tolerable Credit could always easily find; whereas by this Scheme, every Merchant importer of Tobacco must pay some Part of the Duties at the Entry, which to a poor Man is a new Hardship, and to a rich Man a greater Hardship than the Payment of the whole, considering that he is to have no Allowance for prompt Payment.——I am surprised that Brewers make no Complaints on Account of their being subjected to the Laws of Excise; I never conversed with any of them who did not complain of it

as a very great Grievance, and could not give very substantial Reasons for their Complaints. There are many Ways by which the Officers of Excise may be vexatious to the Brewer, but there is one which is generally practised all over the Kingdom, and that is, obliging the Brewers to shew them their Books as often as they have a Mind, by which Means they not only pry into all the Mysteries of their Trade, but likewise into their Circumstances. Can any Gentleman look upon this as no Grievance? Is it not a Hardship upon any Man to have the Secrets of his Trade exposed to every little Fellow the Commissioners of Excise shall put in Authority over him? But is it not still a greater Hardship to be obliged to discover his Circumstances to one who is an utter Stranger to him, perhaps to one who is his most implacable Enemy?——The hon. Gentleman, I find, values himself much on the small Increase of Excise-Officers to be made by his Scheme, but he seems to forget the Warehouse-keepers, who are all to be named by the Crown, and paid by the Publick, consequently they are certainly to be called Officers of the Revenue: They will be as expensive to the Publick, and as great Slaves to the Administration, as any other Sort of Officers whatever. As there are a great Number of Tobacco-warehouses in *Britain*, there must be a great Number employed to attend those Warehouses as often as there shall be Occasion for them, otherwise it will be impossible for the Merchant to manage or dispose of the Goods he has there lodged; of Warehouse-keepers will be much more from whence I conclude, that the Number than double the Number of the other new Officers to be added by this Scheme.——Gentlemen seem to think it will be no Inconvenience to the Merchant to be debarred all Access to his Goods, but at those Hours when the Warehouse-keeper is to be obliged to attend him. Those who argue at this rate, know but little of the various Accidents that happen in Trade; but this is not the only Inconvenience that even the Merchant is to be exposed to by this Scheme; he must, for every Quantity of Tobacco he sells, make a Journey, or send a Messenger to the Permit-office for a Permit, which must necessarily put him to a great deal of Trouble, and Expence; and therefore, that the Merchant may be as much eased as possible, I hope that as soon as those publick Warehouses are all appointed, there will be two little Lodges like Centry-boxes, built somewhere adjoining to each Warehouse, one for the Warehouse-keeper, and the other for the Officer who is to grant the Permits.——It has been said, that Liberty has nothing to do in the Question before us, but, in my Opinion, if it is not deeply concerned in this Question, it never can be concerned in any that can come before this House: Is not every Man's House looked on as his Asylum? Is then the giving a Power to any little paltry Excise-man to enter People's Houses at all Times of the Day and Night no Encroachment upon the Liberty of those People? If it is not an Encroachment upon a Man's Liberty, it certainly is a very direct one upon his Property, and of Consequence it will be found to be an Encroachment upon his Liberty; for can any Man be said to be free, who must be the humble Slave of his Excise-man, otherwise he must expect no Quiet or Comfort within his own Dwelling-house? The most blameless Conduct cannot secure him against Vexation; and no Man can be said to be free, who cannot depend upon his Innocence for his Protection: An Officer, invested with such Power, may fall upon twenty Ways to vex the most innocent Man upon Earth: One of my Acquaintance, who has the Misfortune to be subject to the Laws of Excise already in Being, was, for a considerable Time together, regularly visited by his Excise-man at the Hour the Family went to Dinner, and if they civilly asked the Gentleman to call at any other Time, his Answer was, *No, Sir, I'm in a Hurry, I have a great deal of other Business to attend besides yours; I must immediately visit such a Place, if you will not allow me I must go, and I know what to do.* By this rude Behaviour the whole Family was disturbed, and one of them was always obliged to get up from Dinner, in order to go and let him visit such Places in the House as he had a Mind.——These are the Fellows, who, by this fine Scheme, are to be put into every Man's House that is a Dealer in either of the two Commodities of Tobacco or Wine: These are the Lord *Danes*, who are to be by Law appointed to lord it over every such Dealer and his whole Family: We know what was the Fate of the Lord *Danes* we had formerly in *England*, and I shall be very little surprised if these new ones meet with the same Fate. In short, Gentlemen may dress up this Scheme in what Shape they please, but to one, who considers it coolly and impartially as I have done, it must appear in its true Colours. I am convinced that it will produce nothing but the most mischievous Consequences, not only to those who are to be immediately affected by it, but likewise to the Liberties and Properties of the Nation in general, and therefore I am entirely against agreeing to the Resolution of the Committee.

H--io W--le spoke next for agreeing with the Committee; T--s Br--st--n Esq; spoke against it; L--d H---y for it.

Sir T--s R---n.] As I had not an Opportunity in the Committee of giving my Opinion in this Question, I hope I shall be indulged the Liberty of doing it now, since I find the Whole is to be canvassed over again. I will take up as little of your Time, as possible, in making a few Observations on the Scheme itself as it now appears to

us, and on what has fell from some Gentlemen in the Course of this Debate.—Sir, I cannot help expressing my Surprise, to hear so often repeated the cruel Usage the *English* Merchants have met with of late: For God's sake let all that has been said in this House, during the Time this Affair has been upon the Anvil, be impartially canvassed, and 'twill come out to be against the unfair Dealers in Wine and Tobacco, and against them only; Why should Gentlemen therefore apply it to Merchants in general? Give me Leave to say, those who make such Application, pin the Question upon the whole Body of Merchants, and not those Gentlemen who think the Method proposed of Collecting this Revenue, will secure to the Publick what they have an undoubted Right to. All that has been said on this Head, and what we are now endeavouring to do by this Bill, is calculated to affect those Men only, whose Artifice and Cunning have hitherto evaded the Customs.——Surely, no Gentleman who appears for this Scheme, would for his own sake countenance it, if he imagined the Success would either affect our Trade, or the Body of the *English* Merchants immediately concerned in the Exportation of our own Manufactures, or by way of Return for them in the Importation of foreign Productions useful and necessary to us; for it is to our Trade and our Merchants that the real Causes of the Wealth and Prosperity of this Nation are principally to be ascribed. But this Scheme is not intended to affect, nor will I think in any Shape reach these Men, which when they come impartially to consider, they must be sensible of; and then they will be able to judge, whether they have been alarmed at the Approach of real or only at the Noise of imaginary Dangers.—I am very sorry to hear so often urged that these Restrictions proposed only for the preventing of Frauds will be a Discouragement to Trade in general; for the natural Conclusion from thence would seem to be, that Frauds and Trade were inseparable: A Stranger in the Gallery, who was to hear our Debates, would naturally imagine a Continuance of, or a Connivance at Frauds was in this Country a necessary Encouragement to Trade.—Sir, as this Bill appears to me to be attended with certain Advantages to the Tobacco-trade, and as I should be glad to be set right, if I am mistaken; I beg Leave to ask a few Questions of those who are conversant in Trade: Whether high Duties on Goods imported are not a great Weight on every Branch of Trade so loaded; as it not only obliges the Merchant to keep a double Stock in ready Money, but of course confines that Trade to a very narrow Circle of Dealers, and surely it can never be the Interest of a trading Nation to encourage Monopolies: Then I must ask, whether, as the Law now stands, the Tobacco-trade has not this Hard-

ship

ſhip attending it? If it be ſo, I would ask, whether this Clog is not entirely removed by this Scheme; no Duty being to be paid at Importation, nor any Money demanded till the Factor has made his Bargain with the Retailer, who is to pay the whole Duty? — Is it not another allowed Maxim in Trade, that one of the greateſt Temptations to Frauds are large Draw-backs on Goods exported, nay, the very Parent of Frauds in this Commodity? If this be a Fact, is not this Motive to Frauds entirely removed, there being by this Scheme no Temptation whatever to Frauds on this Head; for by this Scheme as now amended, there is no Part of the Duty to be paid at Importation, there is not a Farthing of the Duty ever to be paid for the Tobacco which ſhall hereafter be re-exported; ſo that the hon. Gentleman . who ſpoke firſt in this Debate, and who always ſpeaks ſo well, and with ſo much Weight in this Houſe, has in this Particular miſtaken the Scheme now before us. -- Has not, the Method of bonding the Duties, till very lately at leaſt, been univerſally allowed to be often fatal to both the Planters and Factors, and as often detrimental to the Publick? Is not this Hardſhip quite obviated by this Scheme? -- Were not the Charges in the Bills of Sale from the Factor to his Planter a very great Hardſhip on the latter? According to all thoſe I have ſeen, they never amounted to leſs than a5 *per.Cent,* often to much more, on the whole neat Produce returned to the Planter for his Tobacco. I beg I may not be thought to accuſe the Factor of taking an extravagant Gain on this Head; but what we are now contending to remove, is the Pretence for and the Foundation of theſe Charges, which have been ſo greatly detrimental to that Trade; and ſo great a Hardſhip on your *Virginia* and *Maryland* Planters, who now ſend you a Merchandize that proves ſo to this Nation, by the great Quantities re-exported to foreign Markets, a very beneficial Branch of your Commerce; and if ſomething be not now done in their Behalf, I am told from very good Hands, we ſhall run the Riſk of loſing this Staple of Tobacco: Then 'twill be too, late to conſider what Methods are beſt for collecting the Duties on it; and therefore were there no other Motive for this Bill, this Conſideration alone would weigh greatly with me, to make a Trial at leaſt of the Method now propoſed for giving a Relief to ſo conſiderable a Part of your *American* Colonies. -- As the Law now ſtands, Four Pence three Farthings neat Money at leaſt is paid on each Pound-weight of Tobacco immediately on Importation, tho' the Importer takes the Advantages of of all the Diſcounts on prompt-Payment, otherways the Duty comes higher; -but by this Scheme the whole Duty will be at the higheſt but four Pence three Farthings *per* Pound weight, and will not be demanded

till the Tobacco is taken out of the Warehouſe for Home-conſumption, and therefore may ſometimes not be paid till eighteen Months, or two Years after the Landing of the Tobacco: Let therefore who will advance the Money, this further Credit given by the Publick, for the Payment of the Duty, muſt be a certain Benefit to this Trade; and thus, by poſtponing the Payment of the Duties till ſo much nearer the Time of Conſumption, the Dealers in Tobacco will be enabled and ought to afford it to the Conſumer on more reaſonable Terms. -- If then this Scheme be found to be no real Detriment to the fair Merchant, and a certain Benefit to the Planters, I believe in another Particular it will be a demonſtrable Advantage to the Publick, I mean an Improvement of the Revenue: But what appears to me pretty extraordinary, is, to hear that Improvement urged as one of the chief Objections againſt the whole Scheme, becauſe the Civil Liſt Revenue will alſo of courſe receive ſome Increaſe. Whatever Appearance of Weight there might have been in this before the Scheme was known, yet now it appears that the Crown in Return gives up to the Publick all Forfeitures and Seizures, this Objection can be but of little Weight: But ſurely this could never have been thought a ſufficient Objection for the Legiſlature to refuſe a Remedy againſt the known Frauds practiſed in the Collection of the publick Revenue, becauſe 'twould have prevented thoſe practiſed againſt the Crown; eſpecially when even this Improvement of the King's Income is no more than what was in Effect granted by the Parliament, when they appropriated the Produce of thoſe Duties to his Majeſty for Life. -- But ſince it is ſaid that this Alteration in the Method of collecting the Duty on Tobacco will be ſuch an Augmentation to the Revenue, though no new Tax be laid on, nor an Addition made to any one now in Being, it may be asked, From whence this Augmentation will ariſe? To this the bare Enumeration of the ſeveral Frauds at preſent practiſed in the Collection of this Duty would be a ſufficient Anſwer, eſpecially if we conſider the large Sum, which the Frauds diſcovered yearly amount to, and that it cannot be ſuppoſed, one fifth Part of the Frauds which are really committed, have ever come to the Knowledge of the Publick, or of thoſe entruſted with the Collecting of this Duty; but as the hon. Gentleman, who opened this Affair in the Committee, has ſo fully and ſo demonſtrably ſhewn the Particulars of theſe unlawful Tranſactions, and as there are in this Houſe ſo many Gentlemen thoroughly acquainted with the Courſe of the publick Revenues, who can ſpeak more minutely to the Nature of theſe Frauds than I am capable of doing, I ſhall not enter into a Detail of them, only take Notice, that there have been ſome Inſtances where a triple Fraud

has

has been committed in the Difpofal of the fame individual Parcel of Tobacco; he indeed who practifes this Method muft be very adroit in the Bufinefs of Smuggling, but it is certain it has been practifed; the unfair Trader has contrived to receive the full Duty twice from the Publick, without having ever paid it once: He has received from the Government the Draw-back on a Quantity of Tobacco which he found Means to import without paying any Duty; and by again running the fame Tobacco from *Holland* in fmall Parcels, he has a fecond Time received the Draw-backs from the Confumers, by felling it to them as if the Duties had been honeftly paid; and the Difficulty to prevent thefe kind of Frauds, as there is but one Check in the Cuftoms, is almoft infurmountable; fince in fome Cafes the unfair Dealer in Tobacco may very well afford to give fuch Bribes to the Cuftomhoufe Officer, as will even more than compenfate to him the Lofs of his Place, if he fhould be difcovered. -- So that in this Light the Parties in this Conteft are the Publick, the Planter, and the fair Trader on one Side, and the unfair Dealer only on the other. It is a Duty the Nation pays, the Planter and the fair Trader feel the Inconvenience of it, but the Benefit is intercepted by the fraudulent Dealers; and in this View your landed Confumers of Tobacco have doubly paid the Duty; they have paid it once by buying the Tobacco at an advanced Price, as if the Duty had been paid by the Seller, and again by a future Call upon them by the Legiflature to make good the Deficiency occafioned by the Frauds of the Sellers; fo that by this Method of Taxation a Duty has been laid on one Subject, which another has by Artifice not only prevented coming into the publick Purfe, but has converted towards the enriching of himfelf. -- But there is another Reafon, which will have the greateft Weight with me for coming into this Propofition, and that is, becaufe I think that in its Confequences the Land-holders of *Great Britain* will find a confiderable Relief. I have always heard the Land-tax complained of as the moft unequal and moft grievous of our Taxes; unequal, as it is only paid by a Part of thofe who poffefs Property in *Great Britain*; and fo great a Difproportion is there in this Particular, that I believe the Money arifing by this Tax is paid only by five out of fix of thofe who poffefs the Riches of this Nation; and it has hitherto been the more grievous, as there was no Profpect that any one of this Generation would have been relieved from the Burthen of it. From the Land-holders alone 64 Millions and a half have been raifed fince the Revolution, an Eftate of 1000l a Year fully feffed fince that Time has paid 6450l. which Sum amounts to near one fixth Part of the whole Produce of fuch an Eftate in that Time, which bears no Manner of Proportion to

what has been paid by any other Set of Men, towards defraying the Charges of the Government fince that Time. This has always been moft juftly reputed a Grievance upon the Land-holders, yet now when a Scheme is offered, which, as it appears to me, would be a certain Relief to the Landed-intereft, a new Language, a new Opinion has ftarted up, and prevails at leaft without Doors, that the Lands of *Great Britain* fhould ftill continue to carry that Burthen, which till very lately all Mankind were unanimous they ought to be relieved from. -- If fome Gentlemen may think there can be any material Weight thrown into the Scale of the Crown by the Addition of a few Excife-Officers, let them on the other fide reflect on the Relief given by this Scheme to the Land-holders of *Great Britain*, who always have been, and ever muft be in Time of Neceffity, the real and folid Support of the Liberties of the Nation. -- And as the Landed-intereft muft be allowed to be our principal Strength, all Attempts to invade our Liberties muft prove unfuccefsful, while the Gentlemen of landed Eftates fhall continue refolute, and retain fufficient Force to oppofe any arbitrary Defigns: Any Thing therefore that tends to put them upon a better Footing, and to encreafe their Subftance, ftrengthens our Conftitution in the moft effential Part; for this Reafon, when the Eafe that will be given to the Land-holders is impartially confidered, the Addition of a few Excife-men, with Salaries of 40 or 50l. a Year each, will not have that Weight in this Day's Debate, which at firft Sight it might feem to carry with it. -- I have mentioned the Advantages which will naturally arife to the publick Revenue, to the fair Trader, to the induftrious Planter, and to the Land-holder by this Scheme; and I think there is another Benefit attending it, which Gentlemen do not feem to give fufficient Attention to, I mean the Reformation that will be made on this Occafion in the Laws of Excife; for tho' the Extenfion of them, as they now ftand, might have been thought by fome a ftrong Objection to this Scheme, however beneficial in other Refpects it might prove to the Publick, yet I think the Weight of this Objection is greatly removed, when we confider, that the Alteration now propofed, will take away many of thofe Powers which might in Time to come have been abufed to the Oppreffion of the Subject. One of the moft material Objections I ever heard ftarted was, the Want of a proper Appeal from the Determination of the Commiffioners of Excife; but this I think is entirely obviated by the allowing of an Appeal to three Judges chofen from the different Courts in *Weftminfter-hall*, or from the Juftices of Peace to the Judges of Affize in their refpective Circuits, who are to determine in a fummary Way, without either Delay or any confiderable Expence

to

to the Parties concerned; for whatever Influence the Nomination of these Officers by the Crown might have on their Actions, or however regardless their Power being uncontrollable might make them in their Determinations, this Check must prevent the Execution of their Intentions, were they inclined to abuse their Power in Favour of the Crown; it will certainly make them more deliberate in giving Judgment, when they shall reflect, that their Judgments are liable to be canvassed in a superior Court, where no Favour, no Interest can screen an ill Action; the Judges to whom the Appeal must be made have their Offices for Life, and therefore cannot reasonably be supposed to be biassed so as to countenance any unlawful Steps of the Commissioners, let them be the Favourites of any Minister whatever, or let the Party oppressed be ever so obnoxious to an Administration. --- There is also another Benefit that will attend the Success of this Scheme, which is the Repeal of an Act made the 11th Year of the late King, which obliges People to accuse themselves: As this is certainly a very great Grievance, the Repeal must be a very agreeable Relief to those subject to it. I hope therefore, if this Question passes, when the Blanks in the Bill come to be filled up in the Committee, those Gentlemen who think that there are any unnecessary Clauses in the Laws of Excise, will take this favourable Opportunity to have those Laws reviewed, and by the Addition of proper Clauses to the Bill now to be brought in, to extend the Regulations of them in Behalf of the Subject, as far as may not leave the Duties under the Management of the Commissioners open to gross Frauds. --- This Scheme therefore, as it is intended to be a Review of the Excise Laws, and an Amendment of the Rigour of those Parts of them, where less Severity would secure the Duty to the Publick, appears in this Light as much in favour of the Subject, as of the Revenue; and when it comes to be rightly apprehended, and the Benefits attending it are felt and diffused through the whole Nation, I believe it will soon take a more favourable Turn among the People; the ill Impressions of it that may now be industriously spread Abroad, I should think would soon subside and be forgot. --- I shall only add, that since upon the Examination of the particular Merits of this Scheme, the Advantages proposed by it, appear to me to be certain, and of such a Nature, as not only to increase the Publick Revenue, without any new Tax on the Subject, or an Addition to any one now in Being, and advance the Interest of our Trade and Plantations; but also at the same Time to raise the Value of the Lands of *Great Britain*, I shall therefore readily give my Assent to it.

᷈ A᷈᷈ spoke next against it,

and among other Things took Notice, That it was his Misfortune to know too much of the Influence that the Officers of the Customs and Excise had at Elections; for at his own Election, there were many of the Voters were so free and open, as to come to him and tell him, they would vote for him rather than any other, but that those Officers had threaten'd to ruin them if they did; and others told him, that they had Promises either for themselves or their Sons to be made Officers in the Customs or Excise by his Antagonist; and as their Bread depended upon getting those Promises fulfilled, which they could not expect, if they did not vote against him, therefore they hoped he would excuse them.᷈᷈᷈ Thus, Sir, *says he*, I know the Evil of this illegal Influence by Experience, and therefore I shall always be against any Measure that may tend to encrease it, as this Scheme most evidently will; for, I hope, I shall always disdain to owe the Honour of representing my Country in Parliament to any Administration whatever; I hope I shall always depend upon the free Votes of my Fellow-Subjects, and for that reason I must be against what I think will destroy that Freedom, upon which only I am resolved always to depend.

After him the L᷈᷈d G᷈᷈᷈᷈᷈y spoke for agreeing, L᷈᷈d M᷈᷈᷈᷈th against it. W᷈m C᷈᷈᷈n, Esq; one of the L᷈᷈ds of the T᷈᷈y for it. And then

W᷈᷈ P᷈᷈y, Esq;] Sir, I must say, that the recommending the Care of the publick Revenue to this House, the recommending to us a Scheme which he thinks may tend to the increasing of it, are Doctrines which come very properly from the Hon. Gentleman that spoke last, who for several Years has had the fingering of the publick Money, as he himself was pleased to express it: But I hope those Gentlemen will consider that they and their Posterity are not all to enjoy the same Posts they enjoy at present; they may perhaps expect that they themselves are all in for Life, but they cannot imagine that their Posts are to go by way of Inheritance to their Heirs; and therefore I hope, that for th sake at least of their Posterity, they will consider a little the Power and Influence this Scheme will give to the Crown, and such a Consideration must certainly be of same Weight in the present Debate even with those Gentlemen. --- The Liberties of this Country depend upon the Freedom of our Elections for Members of Parliament; our Parliaments, especially the Representatives of the People in Parliament assembled, are design'd for, and generally have been a Check upon those who were employ'd in the executive Part of our Government; but if it shall ever come to be in their Power to have such an Influence over most of the Elections in the Kingdom, as to get any person chosen they please to recommend amend, they will then always have a Majority of their own Creatures in every House of Commons, and from such Representatives what can the People expect? Will such a House of Commons ever be any Check upon those in Power, or find Fault with the Conduct of the most rapacious, the most tyrannical Ministers, that may hereafter be employed by the Crown. — It is well known, that every one of the publick Offices have already so many Boroughs which they look on as their Properties; some may be called Treasury Boroughs; others Admiralty Boroughs; in short, Sir, it may be said, that almost the whole Towns upon the Sea-Coast, are already seia'd on by the Officers of the Crown: In most of them they have so great an Influence, that none can be chosen Members of Parliament, but such as they are pleased to recommend. But as the Customs are confined to our Sea-ports, this Scheme seems to be contrived to extend the Laws of Excise, and thereby the Influence of the Crown over all the Inland Towns and Corporations in *England*. — This seems plainly the chief Design of the Scheme now under our Consideration; and if it succeeds (which God forbid) our future Ministers of State will be very much obliged to the Gentlemen who projected it: the Election of a House of Commons, will be an easy Task for whoever shall be prime Minister under any of our future Kings; he may sit at Home, and issue forth his Orders to most of the Counties and Boroughs in *Great Britain*, to chuse such Persons for their Representatives in Parliament, as he shall please to think most proper for his Purpose: Most of the chief Clerks of the Treasury, and other great Offices, are already Members of this House; they deserve it, they are Gentlemen, and Men of Figure and Fortune in their Country; but if this Scheme takes Place, we may in a little Time see all the little under Clerks of the Treasury, and other Offices, Members of this House; we may see them trudging down to this House in the Morning, in order to give their Votes for imposing Taxes upon their Fellow Subjects, and in the Afternoon attending behind the Chair of a Chancellor of the Exchequer, a Secretary of State, or other chief Minister; Nay, some of us may live to see a vain over-grown Minister of State driving along the Streets with six Members of Parliament behind his Coach. — These Sir, must be the fatal Consequences of the Scheme now under our Consideration; and therefore I must think that every Man who has a just regard to the Constitution of his Country, or to the Liberties and Properties of those that have put their Trust in him, is in Duty bound to give his Negative to the present Question. — Gentlemen may indulge themselves in the vain Conceit, that by this

Scheme all Manner of Frauds in the Tobacco-Trade will be prevented for the future; but the Thing is in its own Nature impossible; when the Duties amount to five or six times the prime Cost of the Commodity on which they are laid, it will be impossible to prevent Frauds; and therefore the Increase of the publick Revenue by this Scheme is so far from being certain, that it is altogether precarious; and unless it be thereby greatly increased, the Land-holders can expect no Relief: But granting that the Benefits expected by this Scheme were certain, it is as certain, that our Constitution will be thereby destroy'd; and are we to make a Sacrifice of our Constitution, for the poor Consideration of adding 4 or 500,000 l. a Year, to the publick Revenue? That Increase may soon be dissipated by an Administration under no Fears of being called to an Account by Parliament, and then they will be obliged to come upon the Land-holders for Money to answer the necessary Services of the Publick. There never was in any Country a Scheme set up for introducing arbitrary Power, but what was supported by some specious Pretences: The preventing of Mobs, Insurrections, Invasions, Frauds, or the like, have in all Countries been made the Pretences for introducing arbitrary Power; but in such an Assembly as this, where the Principles of Liberty so much prevail, where there are so many Gentlemen of good Sense and Penetration, I hope no such Pretence will ever be of any Weight. To me it appears indisputable, that this Scheme is absolutely inconsistent with a free Election of Members of Parliament, and of Consequence it must be inconsistent with our Constitution; therefore tho' the Advantages to be reaped therefrom were greater, and much more certain than they are, I should be most heartily against it, and for that Reason I must give my Negative to the present Question.

Mr C----t of the E---t *spoke next. Then* W----m P----y, *Esq; spoke again. And after him.*

W----r P---r, Esq; stood up, and among other things took Notice of some Gentlemens having said, that no Body had opposed the subjecting of Coffee, Tea, and Chocolate to the Laws of Excise, but the hon. Gentleman under the Gallery (meaning Sir *J*--*n B*---*rd*.) But, *says he*, I must put those Gentlemen in Mind, that I had then the Honour to be a Member of this House, and I thank God I did oppose that Excise-Scheme as well as I shall do this, and every such Scheme that shall ever be offered to this House, while I have the Honour of sitting in it. I know how grievous and oppressive the Laws of Excise are to my Fellow Subject; and therefore I think I cannot answer to my Country, if I do not to the utmost of my Power oppose every

every Scheme that shall be offered for the Extension of those vexatious and arbitrary Laws.

H—m—y P—s Esq; *spoke next against agreeing to the Resolution.* M—n B—n Esq; *spoke for it.* Sir J—n H—d C—n *against it.* Sir W—m Y—ge *for it.* Sir W—m C—y, and G—ge B—t, Esq; *against it.* J—n N—le Esq; and Sir W—m L—r *for it.* And G—d L—n, Esq; Sir G—ge C—ll, and H—y W—t, Esq; *against it.*

At last the Question was put upon the 1st. Resolution, which on a Division was carried in the Affirmative, 249 against 189.

The Question was then severally put upon the two next Resolutions, which were agreed to without any Division; and the last Resolution being read a 2d time, Mr. Chancellor of the Exchequer acquainted the House, *That his Majesty gave his Consent, that the House might do as they should think fit, in relation to the said Fines, Penalties, Forfeitures, and Seizures.* Whereupon the Question was put, and agreed to without any Division.

Then it was ordered, that a Bill should be brought in, pursuant to the said Resolutions, and that Sir *Charles Turner,* Mr Chancellor of the Exchequer, Mr Attorney General, Mr Sollicitor General, Mr Doddington, Mr Clayton, Sir *William Younge,* Sir *George Oxenden,* Mr Scrope, and Mr *Edward Walpole,* should prepare and bring in the same.

This famous Bill, (*See* p. 301-2. *and* p. 309, 310.) was accordingly brought in the 4th of *April,* and read a first Time; after which Mr *Chancellor of the Exchequer* by his Majesty's Command, acquainted the House, that his Majesty consented to their making such Alterations as they should think fit, for the publick Service, in relation to the Subsidy on Tobacco then payable on Account of his Majesty's Civil List. It was next objected, that some Parts of the said Bill were not within the Resolutions of the House, pursuant to which the said Bill had been ordered to be brought in; and therefore moved that the Bill should be withdrawn, which passed in the Negative, 232 against 176: Then a Motion was made for adjourning, which also passed in the Negative: At last it was resolved that the Bill should be read a second time, and order'd that it should be read a second Time on that Day se'nnight, 236 against 200. *April* 5. a Motion was made for the printing such a Number of Copies of the said Bill, as should be sufficient for the Use of the Members of the House; but on the Question's being put, it was carried in the Negative, 128 against 112.

As this Bill very much concerned the Trade and Commerce of this Nation, the Lord Mayor of the City of *London* procured a Copy of it soon after it was brought into the House of Commons, and laid it before the Common Council, where it was resolv'd to petition the House against it, and a Peti-

tion being immediately drawn up and agreed to, the same was presented to the House on the 10th of *April,* and is as follows:

To the Honourable the Commons of Great Britain *in Parliament assembled,*

The Humble Petition of the Lord Mayor, Aldermen, and Commons of the City of *London,* in Common Council assembled,

Sheweth,

That your Petitioners observe, in the Votes of this Honourable House, that a Bill has been brought in, pursuant to the Resolutions of the 16th of March, *for repealing several Subsidies and an Impost now payable on Tobacco of the* British *Plantations, and for granting an Inland Duty in lieu thereof.*

That they presume therefore in all Humility, by a respectful Application to this House, to express, as they have already done, in some Measure, by their Instructions to their Members, the universal Sense of the City of London, *concerning any farther Extension of the Laws of Excise.*

That the Burthen of Taxes already imposed on every Branch of Trade, however chearfully born, is severely felt; but that your Petitioners apprehend this Burthen will grow too heavy to be born, if it be increased by such vexations and oppressive Methods of levying and collecting the Duties, as they are assured, by melancholy Experience, that the Nature of all Excises must necessarily produce.

That the Merchants, Tradesmen, and Manufacturers of this Kingdom, have supported themselves under the Pressure of the Excise-Laws, now in force, by the comfortable and reasonable Expectation, that Laws which nothing but publick Necessity could be a Motive to enact, would be repealed in favour of the Trade of the Nation, and of the Liberty of the Subject, whenever that Motive should be removed; as your Petitioners presume it effectually is, by an undisturbed Tranquillity at home, and a general Peace so firmly established abroad.

That if this Expectation be entirely taken away, if the Excise-Laws, instead of being repealed, are extended to other Species of Merchandize not yet excised, and a Door opened for extending them to all, your Petitioners cannot in Justice to themselves, to the Merchants, Tradesmen, and Manufacturers of the whole Kingdom, and to the general Interest of their Country, conceal their Apprehension that the most fatal Blow, which ever was given, will be given on this Occasion to the Trade and Navigation of Great Britain; *that that great Spring from which the Wealth and Prosperity of the Publick flows, will be obstructed, the Mercantile Part of the Nation will become not only less able to trade to advantage, but unwilling to trade at all; for no Person who can enjoy all the Privileges of a* British *Subject out of Trade, even with a small Fortune, will voluntarily renounce some of the most valuable of those Privileges, by subjecting himself to the Laws of Excise.*

That

That your Petitioners are able to shew that these their Apprehensions are founded both in Experience, and in Reason; and therefore your Petitioners must humbly pray, that this honourable House will be pleased to hear them by their Counsel against the said Bill.

The presenting of this Petition brought the Excise Scheme again on the Carpet. The City of *London* has always enjoy'd this Privilege, that any Petition from them is presented to the House by their Sheriffs, and is brought up by the Clerk of the House and read at the Table, without asking the Leave of the House for that Purpose; whereas all other Petitions must be presented by a Member of the House, and cannot be by him brought up or read at the Table by the Clerk, till Leave be first asked of, and granted by the House. Accordingly this Petition was brought up, and read at the Table; and as soon as it was read, Sir *J---n B---rd* got up, and in a Speech full of that Strength of Reason and Perspicuity of Expression, which he is so much Master of, he shewed how much the City and Citizens of *London*, as well as all the other Trading Part of the Nation, were to be affected by the Bill for altering the Method of raising the Duties payable upon Tobacco, and how just Reason they had to insist upon being heard by their Counsel against it, and concluded with a Motion for granting them Leave to be heard by their Counsel, if they thought fit.

In Opposition to this Motion, it was insisted on, *That it had always been the Practice of that House, never to receive any Petitions, and much less to admit Counsel to be heard against any Bill for imposing of Taxes upon the Subject; for that if any such Thing were to be admitted of, it would be impossible ever to pass any such Bill, because that there would be so many different Petitions presented against it by those who were to be subject thereto, that it would be impossible to hear Counsel separately upon every such Petition, within the usual Time of the Continuance of one Session of Parliament: And that in refusing to admit Counsel to be heard, there could be no Inconvenience, because every Man, and every Body of Men, had their Representatives in that House, if any particular Hardship was to be put upon them.*

To this it was reply'd, *That the House had never pretended to any general Custom of refusing Petitions, except against those Bills which were called Money Bills, such Bills as were brought in for raising Money for the current Service of the Year; and that even as to them there were many Precedents where the House had admitted the Parties whom they thought to have a real Interest therein, to be heard by their Counsel against the passing of such Bills: That the admitting of Counsel even in such Cases could never prevent the passing of such Bills, because the House could always order all Parties petitioning to be heard at one Time, and could give such Directions, that it would never take up many Days to hear every thing that could be objected by every one of the Parties petitioning: That though every Part of the Nation had their Representatives in that House, yet it was well known, that speaking in Publick was a Talent that every Man was not endowed with, from whence it might happen, that the particular Persons, or Part of the Nation, which was then to be aggrieved by what was passing in the House, might not have any such Members as were proper to lay their Case fully and clearly before the House; and that therefore, even as to Money-Bills, it was proper to admit Parties to be heard against them, when it appeared that they were very particularly interested therein. --- But as to the Case then before them, there was not the least Pretence for refusing the Desire of the Petition, because the Bill against which it was presented, was no Money-Bill; it was granted by the Advocates for the Bill; it was even insisted on, as the greatest Argument for it, that there was no new Duties to be imposed; it was a Bill only for altering the Method of collecting the Taxes already imposed; and therefore it could not be pretended that there was any Practice, or Custom of the House for refusing to admit Parties interested to be heard against such a Bill: That if there had been such a Custom introduced it ought not to be observed, especially when such a considerable Body as the Lord Mayor, Aldermen, and Common Council of the City of London, come with a humble Petition to be heard against a Bill, which they thought would not only be highly injurious to them in particular, but destructive of the Trade and Commerce of the whole Nation.*

In this Debate there were many Precedents brought by Mr *S---yt*, Mr *G---b---n*, and Mr *B---tle*, where the House had received Petitions, and admitted Counsel to be heard against Money-Bills; and there were likewise Precedents brought by Sir *W---m T---ge* and Mr *W---on*, where the same had been refused, the reading of which took up a great Part of the Day.

The Principal Speakers for granting the Desire of the Petition, were,

Sir *J---n B---d*,	Sir *W---m W---m*,
S---l S---y, Esq;	*W---r P---r*, Esq;
P---p G---n, Esq;	*G---ge H---es*, Esq;
T---s B---le Esq;	*T---s W---m*, Esq;
W---m P---y Esq;	

And the Principal Speakers against it, were,

Mr *C--r* of the *E--r*,	Mr *A---y G---l*,
H---e W---le Esq;	Sir *W---m T---ge*,
T---s W---n Esq;	Hon. *H--y P--m* Esq;
Mr *S---r G---l*.	

Upon the Question's being put for allowing the Petitioners to be heard by their Counsel against the Bill, there was a Division, and the Question was carried in the Negative, 214 against 197.

But it was ordered that the Petition lie on the Table, until the Bill be read a 2d time.

April 11. A Petition of the Mayor, Aldermen, and Common Council of the Town and County of *Nottingham*, (in Council assembled)

ſembled) in Behalf of themſelves, and the reſt of the Merchants and Tradeſmen dealing in Tobacco in the ſaid Town, was preſented to the Houſe, and read; alledging, that the Bill depending in the Houſe for repealing ſeveral Subſidies, and an Impoſt then payable on Tobacco, &c. would be highly prejudicial to them, and encroach on their Liberties and Properties, and expreſſing their Apprehenſion that the ſaid Bill, if paſſed into a Law, would ſubject them to great Oppreſſions and Inconveniences; by the Officers frequently entering their Houſes, and taking Account of their Stocks, which ſuch Officers might diſcover to any others; by being obliged to ſeek for, and ſend Permits with their Goods, and the Hardſhips thereof with reſpect to time; by not being allowed the valuable Liberty of redreſſing their Grievances by a Jury; and by the great Trouble, Charge, and Loſs of Time in weighing their Tobacco at any Time required by the Officer, and the Prejudice to their Goods in uncaſking and breaking them; and therefore beſeeching the Houſe to conſider and favour their Petition, and prevent the paſſing a Law, which would be any ways deſtructive of the Trade, or dangerous to the Liberties of the Petitioners, which Petition was ordered to lie upon the Table.

Immediately after which, a Petition of the principal Inhabitants, and Traders of the ancient and loyal City of *Coventry*, in Behalf of themſelves and the reſt of their Fellow-Citizens, was preſented to the Houſe and read; expreſſing the Apprehenſion of the Petitioners, that the Bill, depending in that Houſe, for repealing ſeveral Subſidies and an Impoſt then payable on Tobacco, &c. would be prejudicial to the Trade of the Nation in general, and of the ſaid City in particular, and alſo injurious to the Liberties of their Fellow-Subjects; and therefore praying the Houſe to take the Premiſes into Conſideration, and give the Petitioners ſuch Relief therein, as to the Houſe ſhould ſeem meet. Which Petition was likewiſe ordered to lie upon the Table.

The Order of the Day being then read for the ſecond Reading of the ſaid Bill, the Serjeant at Arms attending the Houſe, was of Courſe ordered to go with the Mace into *Weſtminſter-Hall*, and the Courts there, and into the Court of Requeſts, and the Places adjacent, and ſummon the Members there to attend the Service of the Houſe; and he being returned, inſtead of reading the Bill a ſecond time, a Motion was made by Mr. C---y of the E----y, that the Bill ſhould be read a ſecond Time upon the 12th of *June* then next. Tho' by this Motion it evidently appeared that the Bill was to be dropt, yet ſome of the Gentlemen who had from the beginning appeared ſtrenuouſly againſt the whole Scheme, were not ſatiſfy'd with letting it drop in ſo eaſy a Manner, and therefore t were for having it rejected;

but this Propoſition did not come the length of a Motion, or a Queſtion; ſo that the firſt Motion was agreed to without Oppoſition; and upon the *Friday* after, which was the Day appointed for the Houſe to reſolve itſelf into a Committe of the whole Houſe, to conſider further of the moſt proper Methods for the better Security and Improvement of the Duties and Revenues then charged upon, and made payable from Tobacco and Wines, it was reſolved, that the Houſe would upon the 14th of *June* then next reſolve itſelf into the ſaid Committee, 118 againſt 76: So that that Part of the Scheme relating to the Duties on Wine was never laid before the Houſe.

There having been great Crowds of People about the Houſe on the 11th of *April*, and ſome of them having behaved in a tumultuous Manner, the next Day Complaint was made to the Houſe by ſeveral Members who had voted in favour of the Scheme, that a tumultuous Crowd of People had been aſſembled together the Night before and ſeveral Days during the Seſſion, in the Court of Requeſts, and other Avenues to that Houſe; and that they themſelves and ſeveral other Members of the Houſe had been laſt Night, in their Return from the Houſe, menaced, inſulted, and aſſaulted, by a tumultuous Crowd of People in the Paſſages to that Houſe; whereupon it was reſolved and declared, *Nem. Con.* 1ſt, *That the aſſaulting, inſulting, or menacing any Member of that Houſe in his coming to, or going from the Houſe, or upon the Account of his Behaviour in Parliament was an high Infringement of the Privilege of that Houſe, a moſt outragious and dangerous Violation of the Rights of Parliament, and an high Crime and Miſdemeanor.* 2dly, *That the aſſembling and coming of any Number of Perſons in a riotous, tumultuous, and diſorderly Manner to that Houſe, in order either to hinder or promote the paſſing of any Bill or other Matter depending before the Houſe, was an high Infringement of the Privilege of that Houſe, was deſtructive of the Freedom and Conſtitution of Parliament, and an high Crime and Miſdemeanor.* 3dly, *That the inciting and encouraging any Number of Perſons to come in a riotous, tumultuous, and diſorderly Manner to that Houſe, in order either to hinder or promote the paſſing of any Bill or other Matter depending before the Houſe, was an high Infringement of the Privilege of that Houſe, deſtructive of the Freedom and Conſtitution of Parliament, and an high Crime and Miſdemeanor.*

Then it was ordered, 1ſt, *That the Members for the City of* London, *ſhould ſignify the ſaid Reſolutions and Declarations to the Lord Mayor of* London. 2dly, *That the Members for the County of* Middleſex, *ſhould ſignify the ſaid Reſolutions and Declarations to the Sheriff of* Middleſex. 3dly, *That the Members for* Weſtminſter *ſhould ſignify them to the High-Bailif of* Weſtminſter. Which Orders were accordingly ſignified by their reſpective Members, who

who next Day reported their having done so to the House.

March 21. His Majesty gave the Royal Assent to several Bills. See p. 155 B.

April 2. The Order of the Day for the House to resolve itself into a Committee of the whole House to consider further of the Bill for granting an Aid to his Majesty, by a Land-Tax to be raised in *Great Britain*, for the Service of the Year 1733. being read, a Motion was made, that it should be an Instruction to the said Committee, that they should be impowered to receive a Clause to enable and direct the several Commissioners to be appointed in the said Bill, for putting the same in Execution, to nominate and appoint a Receiver or Receivers-General for each County, Riding, City, Borough, Cinque-Port, Town, or Place respectively, within *England, Wales,* and *Berwick,* for which they were appointed Commissioners, and to make the said respective Counties, Ridings, Cities, Boroughs, Cinque-Ports, Towns, or Places, for which they were appointed Commissioners, answerable for any Deficiency, that might happen by such Receiver or Receivers. In favour of this Motion it was urged, that the Commissioners in each County, &c. were much better Judges of the Persons proper to be appointed Receivers in the several Counties, &c. than the Gentlemen employed in the Administration; that they were also better Judges of the Persons offered as Sureties for such Receivers; and that it would be a great Advantage to the Publick, which had often suffered by the Insolvency of such Receivers, and the Insufficiency of the Security that had been given for them: But some Gentlemen opposing this Motion, upon putting the Question, it passed in the Negative.

Next Day an ingrossed Bill to render more effectual an Act made in the ninth Year of the Reign of her late Majesty Q. *Anne,* intitled, *An Act for securing the Freedom of Parliaments by the further qualifying the Members to sit in the House of Commons,* was read the 3d Time; which Bill was much the same with what had passed several times through that House; but upon the Question's being put, it passed in the Negative.

April 9. Sir *Nathaniel Curzon* presented to the House the following Bill, which was received, and read the first time, and ordered to be read a second time. And was to this Effect:

A BILL for the better Regulating the Proceedings of Ecclesiastical Courts.

FOR *the better regulating the Proceedings of Ecclesiastical Courts within that Part of* Great Britain, *called* England, Dominion *of* Wales, *and Town of* Berwick *upon* Tweed, *Be it Enacted, &c. That from and after the Day of   no Suits or Prosecutions, filed pro Salute Animæ, or pro Reformatione Morum, or for any criminal Mat-*

ter, shall be commenced in any Ecclesiastical Court, either by Inquisition, or Denunciation, against any Person whatsoever, but by Accusation only, at or upon the Information or Promotion of some Person, who shall, at the Time of exhibiting such Information, enter into Bond to the Register of the Court, in which such Information shall be exhibited, in the Sum of   with or more Surety or Sureties, in the Sum of   who shall severally justify themselves by Oath, in open Court, (which Oath the said Courts are hereby impowered to administer gratis) to be respectively worth the said Sums in the said Bonds mentioned, over and above their just Debts; which Bonds shall be conditioned to prosecute such Suit or Information with Effect, and to pay   Costs to the Defendant or Party accused, in Case such Defendant shall not be found guilty; or if the Suit or Prosecution be abated or discontinued for the Space of

And the said Register is hereby required, immediately on the Acquittal of the Defendant, or such Discontinuance of Prosecution, to assign the said Bond to the said Defendant, by endorsing the same; and attesting it under his Hand and Seal, in the Presence of   or more credible Witnesses, in the same Manner as Bail-Bonds, given to Sheriffs in Suits in the Temporal Courts, are now by Law assignable; upon which Bond the said Defendant may bring any Action or Suit in his or her own Name, in any of his Majesty's Courts of Record at Westminster, (in which Suit the said Assignment shall be full Evidence of his or her Acquittal, or Discontinuance of the Suit) and shall recover thereon, against the said Informer and Sureties, Costs of Suit in the said Ecclesiastical Court.

And it is hereby further Enacted, That no Citation or other Process, shall issue, to cite any Person to appear to any Articles, Information, Libel, or Accusation, for any Criminal Cause, till the Informer or Promoter shall have given such Security, as aforesaid: And the Person making out any Citation, shall indorse it with the Name and Place of Abode of the Informer and Sureties; and any Officer of any Ecclesiastical Court, making out or issuing any Citation against any Person, before such Surety given, or neglecting to indorse the Name and Place of Abode of such Informer and Surety as aforesaid, shall   And every Person serving any Citation in any Criminal Cause, not indorsed as aforesaid, shall

And all Proceedings in any Criminal Cause, without such Security taken as aforesaid, are hereby declared to be

And every Proctor, Apparitor, or other Ecclesiastical Officer, being Informer or Promoter, or Exhibiting any Articles, Information, or Libel in his own Name, in any criminal Cause, in any Ecclesiastical Court, shall be deemed a   and shall

And be it further Enacted, That in all Suits and Prosecutions, filed pro Salute Animæ, or pro Reformatione Morum, or for any other criminal Cause, if the Party accused shall at any time before Judgment suggest, (without Oath) that

GGGg   *that*

that he or she is not guilty of the Crime laid to his or her Charge, it shall and may be lawful to and for any of his Majesty's Courts of Record, (who now have Power to grant Prohibitions) to grant a Prohibition to any Ecclesiastical Court, where such Prosecution is depending; the Judge or Judges whereof immediately upon Receipt of such Writ of Prohibition, are hereby required to certify, under the Seal of the Court, the original Libel, Articles, or Information against such Person, and return the same, together with the Bond entered into by the Informer and his Surety as aforesaid, into the Court, from which the Prohibition issued, who are hereby impowered, on the Defendant's pleading not guilty to the said Libel, Articles, or Information, to try the same by a Jury of twelve Men of the County, where the Offence is said to be committed, as Indictments removed by Certiorari from inferior Courts are tried: And if the Person accused on such Trial shall be convicted, the said Court, out of which the Prohibition issued, is hereby directed to grant a Writ of Consultation, and send back the said original Libel to the Ecclesiastical Court, out of which the Cause was removed, that the said Ecclesiastical Court may proceed to inflict such Ecclesiastical Censures, as they may do by Law: But if the Person accused shall be acquitted on such Trial, then it shall be lawful for such Court, granting the Prohibition as aforesaid; to allow the Defendant Costs in both Courts, and to enforce the Payment of the said Costs, by Attachment against the Informer and Sureties, as in Cases of Costs in other Actions; and all Proceedings in such criminal causes, contrary to such Writ of Prohibition, sued forth, and delivered to the Judge of any Ecclesiastical court, shall be

And be it farther Enacted, That upon Proof that a Citation, or other Process to appear in the said Ecclesiastical Courts, hath been personally served, on the Defendant in such Suit, or left with the Wife or Servant of such Defendant, at his or her Dwelling-house, or usual place of Abode, if the Defendant so served shall not appear, by him or herself, or by his or her Proctor or Attorney, at the Time and Place appointed by that Citation, a second Citation indorsed as aforesaid, shall issue, which being proved on Oath to be served in like Manner, and the Defendant neglecting to appear, as before, the Judge of the Ecclesiastical Court, out of which such Citation or Process shall have issued, shall certify the same under his Hand and Seal, upon which Certificate it shall be lawful for the High-court of Chancery to issue a Writ of Contumacy, to compel the Defendant or Defendant to appear at the Return of the Writ in the said Ecclesiastical Courts, either personally, or by his or her Proctor or Attorney, which if the Defendant shall refuse or neglect to do, a second Writ of Contumacy shall issue, and so from time to time, until the Defendant or Defendants, shall personally, or by his or their Proctor or Attorney, appear in the said Ecclesiastical Court, upon which Writ of Contumacy, the Sheriffs shall return issues, and proceed, in every Respect, as they

now do on Process of Distress issuing out of any of the Courts at Westminster, against privileged Persons or Corporations.

And be it further Enacted, That no Money hereafter to be paid by any Offender in any Criminal Cause, as Commutation of Penance, or in Lieu of, or to excuse the Offender from any kind of Penance, shall be paid to or received by any Person whatsoever, except to the Overseers of the Poor, where such Offence shall have been committed; which Money being received by the Overseers, is hereby directed to be distributed by them amongst the Poor of the Parish, where such Offence was committed, in such Manner as shall be directed by Justices of the Peace residing in or near such Parish; and every Person (other than such Overseer) receiving any such Money for Commutation of Penance, and every Person paying any such Money for Commutation of Penance to any Person (except the said Overseers) and every such Overseer refusing or neglecting, for the Space of Days to distribute the said Money, according to such Direction of the said Justices as aforesaid, shall

And it is hereby further Enacted, That all Prosecutions shall be commenced in the said Courts, within the Space of after the Offence committed, and that no Person shall be prosecuted twice for the same Offence.

And it is hereby further Enacted, That no Person who shall be excommunicated after shall incur by such Excommunication any legal Disability whatsoever; but every Person excommunicated shall enjoy all Privileges and Benefits of the Law, in as full and ample a Manner, as if they had never been excommunicated; any Law, Usage, or Custom to the contrary notwithstanding.

And it is hereby further enacted, That no Judge, Officer, or any other Person belonging to any Ecclesiastical Court, shall ex officio, make out or issue, or cause to be made out or issued any Summons or other Process to oblige any Person to prove any Will, or to take out Letters of Administration, unless some Legatee, Creditor, Relation of the Deceased, or Person concerned in Interest in the Estate of the Deceased shall apply to the said Court for the same; and every Judge, Officer, or other Person belonging to any such Court, making out, or issuing, or causing or suffering to be made out, or issued, any such Citation, Summons, or Process, contrary to the Intent and Meaning of this Act, or neglecting, or refusing to cite the Executors, or next of Kin of any deceased Person, upon Application of any Legatee, Creditor, or such Relation, as aforesaid, shall

This BILL, after several Alterations and Amendments made to it, was dropt; yet as some such Law seems to be necessary, it is thought that the Affair will be re-assumed.

April 19, 24, & 25. The House proceeded to chuse a Committee by Ballot, to enquire into Frauds in the Customs, an Account of which, and of the Enquiry the said Committee made, we gave p. 350, 351, 352. See their Names, and the Number of Votes each List had, p. 316.

April

April 20. A Petition of the Druggists, and Grocers, China-men, and others dealing in Coffee, &c. was presented to the House and read; setting forth, that by an Act passed in the tenth Year of King *George the First*, intitled, *An Act for repealing certain Duties therein mentioned, payable upon Coffee, &c. imported, and for granting certain Inland Duties in Lieu thereof.* &c. the Petitioners were made to hope, that the Duties arising from the said Commodities would be better secured, and the Interest of the fair Trader better supported; but that the Petitioners had found themselves, from fatal Experience, subjected to Laws most oppressive and injurious to Trade; were deprived of the Privileges of Juries, and subjected to the judicial Determination of Commissioners, and to the Inquisition and Inspection of Persons unknown to them, who entered their Houses at Pleasure, and to whom they were made accountable for all their Dealings; and after having paid Duty for their Goods, had not Liberty to sell the same without Permits from the Officers of Excise, expressing the Names and Places of Abode of the respective Buyers and Sellers to the great Damage of the Petitioners, and the exposing the Extent and Circumstances of their Trade to the said Officers, and to whomsoever they thought fit to communicate the same; and were subject to severe Forfeitures for Errors or Neglect of Entries in their Books, which were absolutely unavoidable; and were moreover, by a Clause in an Act of the 11th of King *George the First*, liable to be examined upon (*See p.* 133 D 620 C.) Oath touching the Entries in their Books, and in Case of Neglect or Refusal were subjected to heavy Fines; that by these Grievances the Petitioners, as they conceived, were in a worse Condition than any of his Majesty's Subjects, and that the clandestine Importation of Tea was never at a greater Height than at that present Time, to the Prejudice of the Revenue, and the Ruin of the fair Traders, who only were subject to those oppressive Laws; and therefore praying that the House would give them such Relief, as to their great Wisdom should seem meet.

Upon this Petition a Motion was made, and the Question put, that the Petition should be referred to a Committee of the whole House; but it passed in the Negative, 250 against 150.

April 27. A Motion was made, that the Directors of the *South-Sea* Company should lay before the House an Account of what Sums of Money, *South-Sea* Stock, and *South-Sea* Annuities had been received from the Trustees for raising Money on the Estates of the late Directors of the *South-Sea* Company and others, distinguishing the Time of such Receipts, and the Application thereof, with all the Orders and Directions of the general Courts of the said Company, relating to the Disposition thereof. But upon putting the Question, it pass'd in the Negative.

April 30. The ingrossed Bill to prevent the infamous Practice of Stock-jobbing, was (according to Order) read the third Time. Of which the following is a Copy, *viz.*

WHEREAS *great Inconveniencies have arisen, and do daily arise, by the wicked, pernicious, and destructive Practice of Stock-Jobbing, whereby many of his Majesty's Subjects have been and are diverted from pursuing and exercising their Lawful Trades and Vocations, to the utter Ruin of themselves and Families, to the great Discouragement of Industry, and to the manifest Detriment of Trade and Commerce; For Remedy whereof;*

Be it Enacted, That all Contracts and Agreements whatsoever which shall from and after the be made between any Person or Persons whatsoever, for delivering, assigning, transferring, receiving, putting, or refusing any publick or joint Stock, or other publick Securities whatsoever, or any Part, Share, or Interest therein, and shall not be expresly stipulated, and agreed to be performed within the Space of from the making thereof; and also all Wagers and Contracts in the Nature of Wagers, relating to the then present or future Price or Value of any such Stock or Securities aforesaid, shall be to all Intents and Purposes whatsoever; and all Premiums, Sum or Sums of Money whatsoever, which shall be paid or delivered, upon all Contracts or Agreements not expresly stipulated, or agreed to be performed within from the making thereof, shall be restored to the Person who shall pay or deliver the same, who shall be at Liberty within from and after the making such Contract or Agreement, or laying any such Wager, to sue for and recover the same from the Person to whom the same is or shall be paid, or delivered with

And it shall be sufficient therein for the Plaintiff to alledge, That the Defendant is indebted to the Plaintiff, or has received to the Plaintiff's Use the Money or Premium so paid or received, whereby the Plaintiff's Action accrued to him, according to the Form of this Statute, without setting forth the special Matter; and in Case the Person or Persons, who shall pay or deliver such Money or Premium, as aforesaid, shall not within the Time aforesaid really and. bona fide. without Covin or Collusion, sue, and with Effect prosecute for the Money or Premium so by him or them paid, given, or delivered, as aforesaid, then it shall be law'ul to and for any other Person or Persons whatsoever, within Months next after the making such Contract as aforesaid, by any such against any such Person or Persons, who shall receive or take the same.

And, for the better Discovery of the Monies or Premiums, which shall be given, paid, or delivered. and to be sued for or recovered, as aforesaid. it is hereby further Enacted, That all and every the Person or Persons, who by

Virtue

Virtue of this present Act shall or may be liable to be sued for the same, shall be obliged and compelled to answer upon Oath such Bill, as shall be preferred against him or them for discovering any such Contract or Wager, and the Sum of Money or Premium so given, paid, or delivered, as aforesaid.

And be it further Enacted, That all and every Person or Persons whatsoever, who shall enter into, or execute any such Contract, not expresly stipulated or agreed to be performed within ___ after the making thereof, as aforesaid; or shall lay any such Wager, as aforesaid, except such Person or Persons who shall actually and bona fide, without Covin or Collusion sue, and with Effect prosecute for the Recovery of the Money or Premium, paid by him, her, or them, as aforesaid, and also except such Person or Persons, who shall discover, and actually and bona fide, without Covin or Collusion, repay such Monies or Premiums, as he, she, or they shall have received, as aforesaid; and also all and every Broker, Agent, Scrivener, or other Person, negotiating, transacting, or writing any such Contract, Bargain, or Agreement, not to be performed within ___ after the making thereof as aforesaid, shall

And, for preventing the evil Practice of compounding, or making up Differences for Stocks, or other Securities, bought, sold, or at any Time hereafter to be agreed so to be, Be it further Enacted, That no Money or other Consideration whatsoever, shall from and after the ___ be voluntarily given, or received, for the compounding or making up any Difference for the not delivering, transferring, or receiving any publick or joint Stock, or other publick Securities, or for the not performing of any Contract or Agreement so stipulated and agreed to be performed, but that every such Contract and Agreement shall be specifically performed and executed on all Sides, and the Stock or Security thereby agreed to be assigned, transferred, or delivered, shall be actually so done, and the Money or other Consideration agreed to be given and paid for the same, shall also be really given and paid; and every Person who shall from and after the ___ voluntarily compound, make up, pay, take, or receive such Difference, Money, or other Consideration whatsoever, for the not delivering, transferring, assigning, having, or receiving such Stock or other Security so to be agreed to be delivered, as aforesaid, shall

And whereas it is a frequent and mischievous Practice for Persons to sell and dispose of Stock or other Securities, of which they are not possessed, Be it therefore further Enacted, That all Contracts whatsoever, which shall from and after the said ___ be made or entered into for the buying, selling, or transferring of any publick or joint Stock or Stocks, or other publick Securities, whereof the Person or Persons contracting or agreeing, or on whose Behalf the Contract or Agreement shall be made to sell, assign, or transfer the same, shall not, at the Time of making such Contract or Agreement, be actually possessed of, or entitled unto, in his, her, or their own Right Name or Names, shall be null and void to all Intents and Purposes whatsoever; and every Person contracting or agreeing, or on whose Behalf, and with whose Consent, any Contract or Agreement shall be made, to sell, assign, or transfer any publick or joint Stock, &c. whereof such Person or Persons shall not at the Time of making such Contract be actually possessed of or entitled unto, shall

And every Broker who shall negotiate such Contract, and shall know, that the Person on whose Behalf such Agreement shall be made, is not possessed of, or entitled unto, the Stock or Security, concerning which such Contract shall be made, shall for every such Offence

And be it further Enacted, That from and after the said ___ all and every Broker or Brokers, or other Person or Persons, who shall negotiate or act as a Broker in the buying, selling, or otherwise disposing of any of the said publick or joint Stocks or other publick Securities, shall respectively keep a Book or Register, which shall be called The Brokers Book, in which said Book he and they shall fairly, justly, and truly enter all Contracts Agreements and Bargains, that he or they shall from Time to Time make between any Person or Persons whatsoever, on the Day of making such Contract or Agreement, together with the Names of the principal Parties, as well Buyers as Sellers, and also the Day of making such Contract or Agreement, and shall produce such Book or Register, when thereunto lawfully required; and in case such Broker or Brokers, or any other who shall negotiate or act as a Broker, in relation to any the Matters aforesaid, shall not keep such Book or Register, as aforesaid, or shall omit to enter therein fairly, justly, and truly any such Contract, as aforesaid, shall for every such Offence or Omission

Provided always, that nothing in this Act contained shall extend to any Contracts or Agreements for the Purchase or Sale of any Stock Annuities, or other publick Securities, to be made with the Privity of the Accomptant-General of the Court of Chancery, in Pursuance of any Decree or Order of the said Court; but that all such Contracts and Agreements may be made and performed in the same Manner, as they might have been, if this Act had never been made.

Provided always, and be it further Enacted, That this present Act shall continue and be in Force from the ___ for the Term of ___ and from thence to the End of the then next Session of Parliament, and no longer.

N. B. On passing the foregoing Bill ensu'd a DEBATE; an Account of which, together with the OTHER PROCEEDINGS concluding the SESSION of PARLIAMENT 1733; we shall insert in the SUPPLEMENT to this our VOL. III. to be published some Time in the ensuing Month of January, with proper Indexes to the whole, too copious to be comprized in this Number.

Grubſtreet Journal, Nov. 29. No. 205.

Of Quackery.

Mr *Bavius*,

IT is evident, that we grow (*a*) too populous, not only in this City, but all over the Kingdom; and that all Arts are proportionably improved, but too many of the Artiſts can hardly ſubſiſt. And how ſhould it be otherwiſe when ſo many Quacks ſwarm in every Place, whoſe Bills invite People to their Deſtruction ? In the mean Time, the (*b*) regular Surgeon whoſe Subſiſtence depends moſtly on Venereal Patients, can ſcarce get his Bread, whilſt theſe ignorant Raſcals impoſe upon the Publick, ruin the Credulous, and live in Plenty.

It is a hard Caſe, that a (*c*) Gentleman ſhall educate his Son in all proper Learning, at a very great Expence, and then a Barber, Farrier, Sow-Gelder, &c. ſhall have the Liberty to practiſe, and often get more Buſineſs, by pure Dint of (*d*) Impudence.

Another Parcel of (*e*) bold Upſtarts are the Barbers, that let People Blood, to whoſe Fear it is more owing, than to their Knowledge, that more Miſchief is not done. Surely then, they ſhould be prohibited from the Operation ; and 'tis hoped that this Parliament, which has done ſo many great and memorable things, will make an (*f*) Act to encourage Men of Skill, and to ſuppreſs all Quacks not regularly educated and rightly qualified to practiſe.   ÆSCULAPIUS.

Mr *Bavius's* Remarks.

(*a*) *If we grow too populous, a good Number ſhould be conſtantly deſtroy'd; and if Quacks are continually employ'd in deſtroying ſupernumerary Perſons, they are performing a neceſſary Work.*

(*b*) *If ſome new Method could be found of propagating the* Venereal Diſeaſe, *it would both contribute to the Subſiſtence of the regular Surgeons, and promote the neceſſary Work of thinning too populous a Nation ; but ſome regular Surgeons think, that Quacks rather increaſe than hinder their Buſineſs.*

(*c*) *Why does he not ſave this great Expence, and put his Son to a Barber, a Farrier, or a Sow-gelder ?*

(*d*) *What is there to be done without it ? Does it not ſupply the want of otherTalents?*

(*e*) *If* Miſchief *be prevented, is it of a-*

ny Conſequence, whether it be by Knowledge, or by Fear ? And if they did more of what is here called Miſchief, they would make the Buſineſs of a regular Surgeon more, and the Number of too numerous a People leſs.

(*f*) *Such an Act would tend very much to the Detriment of our Society, as well as to the Revenue of the Crown, as it will diſcourage many of our Members from writing Books of Phyſick and Surgery, and the Number of Advertiſements, which at preſent are a great Support to our Papers, would be thereby greatly diminiſhed.*

The free Briton. Nov. 29. No. 213.

OnFranking News-Papers in the Poſt-office.

THE *Craftſman* tells us, that, *if ever, it is now neceſſary to open the Eyes of the People,* and complains, 1.That the *worſt Writers* have been employ'd, to expoſe the Deſigns and Practices of his Patrons. 2. That their Writings have been publickly diſtributed. 3. That the *Poſt-Houſe* conveys theſe Writings into the Country. 4. That his *Papers,* and *thoſe of his Party,* are not ſuffer'd to be diſſeminated by the Clerks of the Poſt-Office. 5. That he and the *Members of his Cabal* are charged with advancing *the Intereſt of the Pretender. (See p.* 596.H)

In anſwer to this Charge, (ſays *Walſingham*) If we are the *worſt Writers,* what Hurt have we done you, or can we do you ? And if you are, as you ſtile yourſelves, *Gentlemen in the true Intereſt of your Country,* what Falſehoods can you be afraid of ? Or what Aſſertions can wound Characters of ſuch diſtinguiſhed Merit ?

I beg Leave to offer in my own Defence, and a *modeſt Man* may inſiſt, that he cannot in *every Senſe* be the *worſt Writer,* whilſt the Government of his Country is defamed every Week by a *Nonjuring Prieſt,* a *Scotch Jeſuit,* and a *mendicant Oxonian,* under the Inſtruction of one who was *Secretary of State to the Pretender,* with this *Similitude of Morals* between the *Patron* and his *Pupil,* that as the one hath *betray'd* all Parties, the other hath *libell'd* all.

As to the Charge of *Calumny, Falſehoods,* and *Impudent Aſſertions* of which they complain, as they have Advantages from the Trade, it ſeems unconſcionable in them to make it a *Monopoly.*

This their *Trade of Abuſe,* 'tis thought, has conſiderably declined, ſince *particular Writings* obtained againſt them. A

few

few Years fince, the *Craftsman* boafted, that the Publick received by his Stamps, 1000 *l. per Ann.* Are not thefe Gentlemen very unreafonable ? If your Writings fpread and fell with fuch Advantage, why do you repine that your Adverfaries, who have not Succefs of this Kind, fhould be aided by a different Method of Circulation ? Are you afraid they fhould be read ? Or is the Subject of Invective exhaufted fo far, that you are forced to employ it on this weighty Complaint, that the *Clerks of the Roads* are not allowed to be *Hawkers of Libels* againft the Government *by franking* them ?

One of the *low Implements of Scandal,* who thought it a profitable *Craft,* to improve the Sale of a *News-paper,* by larding it with abufive Paragraphs, *perfonally reflecting* in the coarfeft Manner on the greateft Characters, fell under this Misfortune at the *Poft-office* ; and advertifes his Calamity in the alarming Stile of *A late Attempt on the Liberty of the* Prefs *at the* Poft office, *&c.*

As in this Kingdom any Writings againft the Government may be publifhed if Perfons will run the Rifque : fo the *Poft-office* will circulate them on paying the *ordinary Poftage.* But that the *Clerks of this Office,* who hold their Privilege of *Franking,* meerly by favour from the Government, fhould themfelves propagate Poftage free, Writings which *vilify* that very Government, is fuch a monftrous Abfurdity, as a reafonable Man would be afham'd of falling into.

I never knew, that the Clerks of the Roads had received fuch Directions, but am glad they underftand their Duty fo well. Let the Authors of the *Craftfman* apply this Cafe to themfelves. Some of them, 'tis faid, are *Members of the Houfe of Commons.* Suppofe one of them fhould truft a *Servant* with a *Frank,* and fuch Servant fhould therein convey a Letter into the Country, folliciting Votes or Intereft againft his Re-election, would he not *turn him out of Doors* the Inftant of his Detection ? Such a Cafe happened about 6 or 7 Years fince, to one of the *warmeft Patriots* in the *Craftfman's Cabal,* and was accordingly refented. Again ; would any of thefe Gentlemen *frank* any *Papers* or *Pamphlets,* wrote againft thefe *excellent Patriots* ? Shall then the *Government,* or *Adminiftration,* be required to exempt even *Invectives againft the Adminiftration,* from the *ordinary Rates of Poftage* ? A Practice that would diminifh the King's Civil Lift Revenue.

In *Weftminfter-Hall,* 'tis Law, that whoever conveys a Libel by the Poft, is guilty of *publifhing that Libel.* If a Clerk in the Poft-Office had *franked that Libel,* the *Hague-Letter,* in the *Craftfman,* would not fuch Clerk have been guilty of the fame Crime of which the *Craftfman's* own Publifher was convicted ; with this Aggravation, that he had *betray'd his Truft* ?

Not many Months fince fome *Coffee-Houfes about the Exchange* were compelled to exclude certain *Papers on the fide of the Adminiftration.* How did the *Craftfman* triumph in the Succefs of this *low Jobb* ? Yet if an *Evening-Poft* is denied *Pranking* at the Poft-Office, or the Proprietors of a Daily Paper change their Printer, it is thought *An Attempt upon the Liberty of the Prefs.*

In fhort, it is left to the Publick to judge, whether a Minifter or *Servant of the Crown* could reconcile it to his Oaths and Obligations, or could juftify himfelf to his Sovereign, if Papers, tending to *alienate the Affections of the People,* were fuffered to be frank'd by *Clerks in Office.*

The **Craftsman** Dec. 1. N° 386.

Of Difcernment of Spirits.

NOTHING is more ufeful or neceffary, in the Conduct of publick Affairs, than a juft *Difcernment of Spirits.* This is that fuperior Talent, which abounds fo happily in our *Minifters of State,* and is rarely found in thofe of *other Countries.* By this they difcover the moft fecret Difpofitions of *other Courts,* and thereby prevent their Defigns. By this they watch over the Publick Tranquillity *at Home,* and forefee what Effect every Step they take will have on the Sentiments and Temper of the People.

A Want of this juft *Difcernment of Spirits* defeated the Defigns of thofe, who fo vigoroufly profecuted the *Popifh-Plot,* and the *Exclufion of the D. of York* : For the greateft Genius is unfit to *difcern the Spirit of others,* when he hath once *overheated his own.* All Men are fallible, and liable to Error ; but fome deliberately and fupercilioufly proceed from Blunder to Blunder, in one perpetual Maze of confufed, incoherent, unmeaning Schemes of Bufinefs. The *Exclufionifts,* tho' not of this Clafs, yet hoped, they fhould frighten or force the King into a Compliance with them, *(See p.* 593 C) not confidering, that the Methods they took were equally proper to frighten and force a great

part

part of the Nation from them, by reason of the particular Circumstances at that Time. This gave the *Court* an Opportunity of growing up into a *Party* (*See* p. 953 F) to divide the People with them.

If we compare the Conduct of the long Parliament in 1674 and 1675, with the Attempts made during the Administration of the *Cabal*, (*See* p. 587 D) with the Secret of the *Second Dutch War*, and other Practices of the *Court*, then come to Light; with the State of *Scotland*, (*See* p. 587 C) then subdued under a *real Tyranny*; and with that of *Ireland*, where at best the *Act of Settlement* was but ill observed; it will not appear that the *House of Commons* were immoderate tho' warm, nor factious tho' vigorous; yet old Resentments, Jealousies, and Fears began to revive; and an Apprehension of falling back under the Influence of *Presbyterian*, and *Republican Principles* (*See* p. 585 G) began to shew itself in the House of Lords and in the Nation. This indeed, had no immediate Consequence; because the *Popish-Plot* broke out soon afterwards, and made the *Church* and *Dissenters* run into one (*See* p. 587 G) as they had begun to do before; and the sole Division of *Parties* was that of *Court* and *Country*; which, by an Alarm given to the Church, soon gave way to *two new Parties*.

These *new Parties* were not raised whilst the *long Parliament* sate, because 'twas generally thought, that however angry the *King* and *Parliament* might be with each other, a few popular Steps made on *one Side*, and a little Money granted on the *other*, would soften Matters between them. As much, therefore, as People might think the Parliament exceeded their Bounds, yet 'twas difficult to perswade them, that a *Parliament*, like this, would destroy a *Constitution* they had settled and supported; or draw the Sword against a *Prince*, to whom they had borne so much Affection, (*See* p. 587 A) But in the following *Parliament*, 'twas otherwise; as will appear from the Authorities of *Burnet* and *Rapin*.

In 1676, before the Exclusion of the D. of *York* was in Agitation, the chief Opposers of the *Court* were very industrious to procure a Dissolution of the *long Parliament*, and negotiated it with the *Duke*, who concurred in a Vote for an Address to dissolve it; and they undertook that *a new Parliament should be more inclinable to grant the Papists a Toleration, than they would ever find*

this. The *Papists* were in Earnest for this Measure; *as it would divide the King and his People*. The *Protestants* came into it upon very different *Views*. (*See* p. 592 H) They, who were resolved to carry the *Exclusion*, and who foresaw the Difficulties of it, might not think *this Parliament* so proper as another to engage and persist in such Measures? So far they judg'd better than the King, who came into the *Dissolution* upon different Motives. (*See* p. 593 A) But as to the Consequence of engaging a *new Parliament* in such strong Measures, the Event shew'd the King judg'd better than They.

The *Dissenters*, who had been long persecuted by the Parliament, and banter'd and abused by the *Court*, took Advantage of the Horrour of the *Popish Plot*; and were very active and successful in the Elections of the new *Parliament*. *Rapin* asserts that many of the new Members were *Presbyterians*. The Leaders for the *Exclusion* look'd on this Turn as an Advantage; and it might have been so, had it been improv'd with Moderation: *Rapin* owns, that *Complaisance for the Presbyterians was carried, perhaps, too far, in the Bill for the Comprehension of Protestant Dissenters*. Bp *Burnet* says more plainly, *many began to declare openly in Favour of the* Non-Conformists; *upon* This *the* Non-Conformists *behaved very indecently; they fell severely on the Body of the Clergy; and made the Bishops and Clergy apprehend that a* Rebellion, *and the pulling the Church to pieces, was design'd*. This no Doubt, gave an Alarm to the *Clergy*, and set them *to make Parallels between the late and present Times*; and to infuse the Fears and Passions, which agitated them, into the Nation, the *Bishop* says, with much *Indecency*. But Men frighten'd out of their Wits, will be apt to be *indecent*; and *Indecency* begets *Indecency*.

At the same Time, that these Jealousies of a Design to destroy the *Church* prevailed, others likewise prevailed of a Design to alter the *Government of the State* — *The* King *came to think Himself* (says Bp *Burnet*,) *levell'd at* (See p. 593 B) And *Rapin* says, *Things seemed to be in the same Course as in the Year* 1640. But whatever those who knew themselves irreconcilable with the *King* as well as the *Duke*, and some Republicans might intend, the *Party* who promoted the *Exclusion*, had not the least Intention to destroy, but to preserve, by that very Measure, the *Constitution in Church and State*. When the Resolution was once

taken

taken of rejecting all Limitations, on the Belief, fo artfully propagated, that the *King* would yield, (*See p.* 593 C) if the Parliament perfifted, the neceffary Confequence of the King's adhering inflexibly to his *Brother*, were Thofe *Fulmina Parliamentaria*, harfh Votes, angry Proceedings, Addreffes no better than Remonftrances, Affociations, Pretenfions to the Power of *Difpenfing with the Execution of Laws*; that very Prerogative they had fo juftly refufed to the Crown, and many more. . All thefe would have been Blafts of Wind, if the King had yielded; and they were pufh'd upon that very Confidence by the Bulk of the *Party.* Some few might be defirous that the King would not yield, in Hopes to bring Things into a State of Confufion: But it would be hard, if *Parties* were to be characterized from the Particular Views or paft Conduct of fome amongft them. *Whig* and *Tory* were now formed into Parties; yet they were not now, nor at any time, what they believed one another, nor what their Enemies reprefented them. The *Whigs* were not *Roundheads*, nor the *Tories, Cavaliers.* The *Whigs* were not *Diffenters*, nor *Republicans*, tho' they favour'd them; nor had the *Tories* any Difpofition to become *Slaves* or *Papifts*, tho' they abetted an exorbitant Power in the *Crown*, and fupported the Pretenfions of a *Popifh Succeffor* to it.

Fog's Journal. Dec. 1, 8. No. 265, 6.

Of Governing according to Law.

CArd. *Richlieu* fo difguis'd all his Defigns, that fome fpecious prefent Good always appear'd, while the Mifchief that lurk'd in them lay deep from Sight; infomuch that the Parliament of *Paris* was deceiv'd into the paffing many Edicts calculated to extend the Prerogative. Some fancy the Cardinal form'd his Scheme of Power only to laft his own life; and that he did not therefore undermine the Foundation of Liberty, by endeavouring to fubdue that Parliament by Corruption; but did that by Art and Addrefs which a very Blunderer might have brought about by fquandering away the Treafure of the Kingdom, to gain over a Majority of that Affembly, which was to exift in Form only.

Machiavel fays, that thofe who would deftroy the Liberties of a free People, muft fuffer Things to retain their ufual Forms, becaufe the People will be fo deceived by thefe Forms, that they will not fee their Liberties are going, till they feel the Change by the Severities of Arbitrary Power. This was the Method taken by *Auguftus*, as it's related by the Tranflator of *Tacitus.* That Monfter. *Tiberius* too, purfued the fame Policy. *Pompeius Macer* the Pretor ask'd him whether a certain Perfon, who was fuppos'd to have written againft him, fhould be tried by the Laws againft Treafon? *Tiberius* anfwer'd, *by all Means the Laws muft have their Courfe, and be duly executed.* By which the Pretor underftood the Man muft be condemned. *Sejanus*, the Favourite, play'd the Tyrant with the fame nice Regard to the Laws; and what is more remarkable, after he fell into Difgrace, he was put to Death, his Daughter ravifh'd by the common Hangman, and his whole Race extirpated likewife according to a Law of the Senate.

Card. *De. Retz* remarks how much Mankind are abufed by that ridiculous Pretence of governing according to Law; whereas the Law itfelf becomes the moft intolerable of all Grievances, when adminifter'd by felf-interefted, corrupt, and ambitious Men. The *Roman* Law againft Treafon included all thofe who betray'd the Army abroad, or rais'd Infurrections at home, fuch as corruptly and faithlefly adminifter'd a publick Office, and debafed the Majefty of the *Roman* People. —Thefe were ouvert Acts which moft of the Minifters were guilty of. Yet this Law was made inftrumental in defending them in their worft Practices.

He obferves further with how much Infolence the Mercenaries of Card. *Mazarine* reproached the Gentry and common People for their oppofing a Minifter, who never acted any thing contrary to Law. This, fays he, will ever be the Cant; but Men of Senfe will difcern, that fuch Mercenaries cannot mean the ancient Laws, but certain new Laws which their Patrons have caufed to be made on purpofe to tie the Hands of the People, and to make themfelves above Controul.

I have feen, fays Fog, fome Pamphlets written in thofe Times both for and againft the Cardinal. Thofe for him were probably wrote by his Direction, and the Writers paid out of the publick Money; for I fuppofe he was in the Condition of another Perfon, no Man ferv'd him for Affection. Their Method likewife of juftifying him, was much the fame as practifed in later Times—they never attempted to defend any one Meafure that occafion'd the Clamour againft him iim (*See p.* 288 F 516 H) but run into per-onal Invectives against thofe that oppo-ed him, afferting that nothing made them iis Enemies, but becaufe they were not ratified with Places and Employments. Thus the *Mazarinians* diftinguifh'd heir Oppofers by the difcontented *Fatti-*n, the Malecontents, and fometimes the file Incendiaries; it will be therefore >roper to fhew of what this Faction con-ifted. They were the greateft Part of he antient Nobility, who reckon'd it >eneath their Dignity to ferve under fo bafe a Fellow; others who refign'd their Employments, rather than join in his de-ftructive Meafures; the whole Body of the Gentry, who faw the Deftruction of :heir antient Freedom by the Introducti-on of new Laws, and the Pretence of acting according to Law; — of Mer-chants and Men of Trade; and the whole Mafs of the common People, who had dearly paid for his Blunders; fo that this little difaffected Faction might confift uf about 19 Million and a half of Souls.

They who fupported his Greatnefs, were fuch, as inheriting great Wealth from the fuccefsful Knavery of their Fa-thers, wanted Titles, and the Diftinction of ftrutting with a Bit of Ribbon tied to their Tails; a few mean fpirited Nobles; a few profligate Prelates, who would have ferv'd the Devil to gratify their Avarice; fuch as had enrich'd themfelves by pub-lick Frauds and Cheats upon the People; and a Rabble of Cuftomhoufe Officers, Excifemen, and Informers, to which may be added, all thofe that deferv'd hanging.

Card. *Richlieu* was a skilful Phyfician, and therefore none of his Medicines ever caus'd any Convulfions in the State; but *Mazarine* the Quack went on opening of Veins, without giving the Body poli-tick Time to recruit. The Confequence of which was, a Kind of Lethargy feiz'd the whole Nation. The Nobility feem'd content that they were fuffer'd to fleep quietly, and wafte their Days in Luxury; the common People had been fo harrafs'd with Taxes and Excifes, that they almoft lay down under the Burthen; and the very Spirit of the Parliament of *Paris* feem'd to be broken. But an Accident happen'd that rous'd the whole Nation. About the Year 1647 the Cardinal drefs'd up an Edict call'd *the Edict of the Tarif*, by which an *Excife* was to be rais'd up-on all the Goods that enter'd *Paris*. This he got regifter'd in the *Court of Aids*, a Court appointed to redrefs the Complaints of private Perfons injur'd by Tax-gatherers;

however, the Cardinal provided himfelf with a Chancellor and Judges, who gave it as their Opinion that the *Court of Aids* had a Right to verify Edicts. Juft as the Minifters were putting the Edict in Execution, the Parliament took the Alarm; the Cardinal, to pacify them and gain Time, laid it before them to be examined; they found it fo abominable, that they publifh'd a Manifefto, forbid-ding all the Subjects to pay a Farthing to be demanded by Virtue of the faid Edict, condemning it as Arbitrary, Op-prefifve, and Illegal. This caus'd a ge-neral Joy, and the People dream'd of no-thing but recovering their antient Liber-ties. But how could this be done fo long as the Court itfelf was a Slave to the Minifter? No Good could be expected, unlefs they could chace this Beaft of Prey out of the Kingdom.

Things being come to this Pafs, the Court fent him away; or rather he re-treated only to quiet the prefent Uproar; tho' the Parliament receiv'd the moft folemn Affurances he fhould never return. In fine, he was twice fent away, and as often return'd.

London Journal, Dec. 1. N° 753.

THE Authors of the *Craftfman* may fee, by their late *memorable Defeat* about the *Diffenters*, the hard Fate of thofe Men, who are obliged to *affume* Principles, yet are obliged to *act* againft them. They pretend to be *Whigs*; yet to carry on their Defign of over-turning the Miniftry, are forced to the fhameful Drudgery of *Sacrificing the Whig-Intereft*, by exhorting the *Whigs* and *Diffenters* to join *Jacobites* and *Tories*; and to fay, a-gainft the *Evidence* of their own Senfes, that *Tories* are turned *Whigs*, and *Whigs Tories*; and that they write in Defence of *Liberty*, againft the *Enemies* of the *Conftitution*, when they know there is no Enemy to the Conftitution, but among their own Adherents. The moft *impu-dent* of all their Affertions, is, what they affirm of the *Neceffity* and *Importance* of a *Country Intereft* at this Time; when there is not the *leaft Reafon* to believe, that any Intereft is carried on at *Court* a-gainft the *Country*.

Had we lived under the Reigns of the *Stuarts*, which the *Craftfman* hath been lately defcribing, it would have been highly reafonable to have afferted the *Country Intereft*, becaufe there was a *Court Intereft* in direct Oppofition to the *Good* of the *Country*; then there were Defigns

on

on Foot to introduce *Popery* and *arbitrary Power*, then we had *Murders in Form of Law*, *reasons against the Constitution*, *Suspensions of Law, surrendering and betraying of Charters*, *Perversions of the whole Course of Justice, by wicked Judges and infamous Juries, backed by a more infamous Court*, till the *Constitution* was destroy'd, by setting up a *Regal Power to dispense with all the Laws of* England *at Pleasure*; while the Interest of *Great-Britain*, and of all *Europe*, was basely sacrificed to *Lewis* XIV. for *Pensions*, and little mercenary Self-Views. Then the *Whigs* made a noble Stand, supported a *Country Interest*, and exhorted their Fellow-Subjects to *defend* their Liberties. But what was *wise then*, is *Cant* and *Folly now*. 'Tis our Happiness that our Government is perfectly legal; and that our *Laws* are the Security of our *Liberties* and *Properties*; that not *one* unnecessary *Tax* has been laid; nor the *least Sign* of an *Intention* in his *Majesty* towards arbitrary Power, nor one *Step* taken in favour of it. All the *Noblemen* and *Gentlemen* about the Court have always been, and still are *Patrons of Liberty*, and *strenuous Defenders* of our Constitution. To talk, therefore, of a *Country Interest* against the *Court*, is to talk of a Country Interest against itself; as a *national Union* against the *Court*, would be a *National Union* against a *national Good*: For the *Court* is the greatest *National Good* we ever enjoy'd; and the Ministry have behaved so well, that it would shew great Ignorance in human Nature ever to expect *better Englishmen* in their room.

Hence it follows, that this Noise of a *Country Interest* could not spring from the *People*. For what are their *Grievances*? Don't they flow in Wealth? Had they ever a better Trade? Were ever such Quantities of Commodities *manufactur'd* at home, and sent *abroad*, as at present? Are not their *Properties* as secure as 'tis possible any Thing can be made? Are not their *Liberties* so extensive, that every Man *says* and *does* what he will? Witness the infamous Libels published every Week against the Court and Ministry. To set up a *Country Interest* therefore, at such a Time is a Crime of the highest Nature; and a more *infamous* Work, than that of those *infamous Tools*, *L'Estrange* and *Bp Parker*; for they only endeavoured to support a *bad Government*, but these labour to destroy a *good one*; and to steal away the *Affections* of the People from

the Government, by *Misrepresentations*, *Falshood*, and *impudent Assertions*, which naturally tend to Rebellion and Civil War. The *Craftsman* calls the *Act of Settlement* our *New Magna Charta*; and affirms, that *That Act is broke thro'* (See p. 415) The Inference from which is, That the People are absolved from their Allegiance, and may *justly* take Arms when they please.

P. S. *In Answer to the* Craftsman's *Story of* 2,000 l. *being refused on an Election at* Taunton, Osborne *tells us of* 10,000 l. *offered by an* Anti-Courtier, *being refused at another Borough.*

Universal Spectator, Dec. 1. No. 262.

Of Charity.

THE Topick at our last Club, says Mr *Stonecastle* was *Curiosity*, a Passion peculiar to rational Beings, is powerful in both Sexes, and in *all Degrees* of Mankind. We discover it in new-born Infants; and *Solon*, as he lay dying, had the *Curiosity* to ask what his Friends *whispered about*.

Mr *Worthy* observed, there are two *different* Degrees of *Curiosity*, the one *useful*, the other *ridiculous*: The first should be the Passion of a *wise Man*, the other only the Foible of a *Woman*. *Useful* Curiosity excites an earnest Desire of *Knowledge*, and the Discovery of Things of Service to our Country and Fellow-Creatures. From this *Principle* all Arts and Sciences took their Rise. It was that excited the Genius of Sir *Isaac Newton* to resolve those Mysteries in Philosophy, which before were thought too perplexed for the Wit of Man to unravel. *Tully* observes, a Wise Man cannot resist the Temptations of Curiosity. When the *Syrens*, says he, would have retarded the Voyage of *Ulysses*, *Homer* makes them not tempt him by the *Sweetness* of their *Voice*, and the *Harmony* of their *Notes*; but by their Promise of *discovering hidden Things*.

Sir *Jasper Truby* observed of *ridiculous Curiosity*, that it keeps all *useful* Knowledge out of the Mind, and is as strong as the other: It will warmly engage Men even to their Ruin in impertinent Enquiries. There's Mr *Staytape*, *Haberdasher of Small-wares*, to support the Character of a curious Man, is in all Places but those where he should be, and talking of all Subjects but those that concern him; he is listening about the great Stair Case at St *James's*, or haranguing with the Cavaliers at the *Horse-Guard Bench*

Bench, on the Affairs of *Italy* and *Po-land*, when he should be busy in his Shop.

Curiosity, says *Harry Carelefs*, is no where more prevalent than in the *Female Sex*, and their Defire generally turns on Things, which, if known, would give them the greatest Uneasiness: The continual Resort of Ladies to the late *Deaf* and *Dumb Campbel*, is an evident Proof of it. The *good-natur'd Flavia* has been *fcolding* her Chambermaid, *Rattling off* her Footman, and *Flouncing* at her *Lovers*, ever since she visited an *Adept* in *Hand-Alley*, who told her she was to marry a *tallifh* Gentleman; and Mr *Dapper*, the Perfon she likes, will not answer the *Defcription*. Madam *Prudely* has been put in the *Vapours* by the fame *Noftradamus*, because he could not by his *Art*, facrifice half a Dozen *Female Charafters*, and let her into fome *private Scandal*.

Mr *Stonecaftle* concludes with a Letter from a Student at *Cambridge*, who, led by his Curiofity, has gone into every kind of Study, that he heard commended, 'till he fell into the Acquaintance of a *German Mountebank*, who in teaching him the Art of *Tranfmutation of Metals*, had *tranfmuted* all his *Gold* and *Silver* into *bafe vulgar Copper*.

Weekly Miscellany, Dec. 1. No. 51.

MR. *Hooker* vindicates the *Miscellany* from the Reflections made upon it, by *Frank Square*, whose firft Objection to it, is *Confufion of Thought*, and *Want of Method*. But, *fays* Mr *Hooker*, it was not the *Defign* of, nor is it poffible for a *Miscellany* to obferve *one continued Chain of Argumentation*. The Scheme of the *Miscellany* was to check the Growth and Licentioufnefs of certain infidel Writers.

Another Miftake of Mr *Square* is, that he thinks the Defign of the *Miscellany* is to *convert Infidels*. But all that can be expected of this kind, is, to prevent the *Perverfion* of wavering and unfettled Believers.

Mr *Square* likewife objects, that we treat Infidels too *indifcriminately*, fince they agree no more among *themfelves* than with *us*. However, *fays* Mr Hooker, they are agreed in denying the Truth of *Chriftianity*; and fo far they are to be looked upon, as *common* Enemies.

Out of a *religious* Concern for *well-meaning* Infidels, Mr *Square* exhorts me to judge *charitably* of their *Intentions* and *Motives*. Now I apprehend it a fair way to judge of Mens *Defigns* by their *Prin-ciples*, where the Tendency of them is obvious. If a Man can propofe any poffible *Good* by propagating Infidelity, I'll think of them as well as he would have me; but till then, I muft think them a Set of Men, who from *Vanity*, or *malicious Wickednefs*, labour to fubvert Society.

My Correfpondent is likewife offended at fome *few* Attempts to be witty. But as it is difficult to be *truly* and *difcreetly* witty, no Wonder if fuch as have any Share of Modefty and Prudence, are cautious how they venture upon fuch a hazardous Undertaking. Tho' in the Plan of our Paper *inoffenfive Wit* and *Humour* was made an Article; yet this was not intended, ftrictly, as a *Promiffory Note*; but an *Invitation* to others to fend in Contributions.

The Univerfal Spectator, Dec. 8. No. 270.

On Theatric Entertainments.

THERE are no Entertainments in *themfelves* more *innocent*, or to the Publick more *inftruftive*, than thofe of the *Theatre*; *Grotefque*, *Pantomime*, and *Harlequin Productions* excepted. The noble Force of *Tragedy* excites in us an Ambition to be virtuous; and *Comedy* humoroufly lafhes our *Vices*, and with Satire drives away our *Follies*. *Comedy* carries with it fuch a Vein of Mirth mixed with Morality, that it's no Wonder we chufe to read *Tragedy*, but to have *Comedy* exhibited to our *View*; yet he who only ftudies to raife a Laugh, tho' he meets with Succefs, will in the Judgement of Men of Senfe, be efteemed but a wretched Poet. It is not the fmart Jeft, the odd *Drollery*, or the lively *Repartee* that diftinguifh the *Farce*, but the *natural View of Life*, the *Manners*, *Vices*, *Singularity*, and *Humours of Mankind*, pleafantly reprefented, which are worthy to be called the Entertainments of *Comedy*. Of all our Comic Writers *Ben. Johnfon* is reckon'd the moft judicious, who exhibits *Nature* of the moft beautiful Kind, as he not only excites Men to be *good*, but would make *good* Men *better*.

This Mr *Stonecaftle* illuftrates by fome Obfervations, which Sir *Jafper Truby* lately made at the Reprefentation of *Volpone*, or the *Fox*, and the feveral Incidents of that Play, in the unravelling of which the Knight difcovered a peculiar Satisfaction in the Punifhment which the Poet had allotted to Covetoufnefs, and in the Succefs of *Virtue*.

The

The Craftsman, Dec. 8. N° 387.

Of Publick Hatred and Applause. With Remarks from the Courant, *Dec.* 12.

MOnſ. *de la Rochefoucault* is cenſur'd for aſcribing all human Action to the ſingle Motive of *Self-Love* ; and thereby weakening the Duties of Religion and Morality. However that be, I believe one may affirm, that *it* hath a great ſhare in the Determination of the Will ; and, indeed, it would be too much to require of frail Man to purſue Virtue ſeparately from Hopes or Fears, pleaſing Conſciouſneſs or Remorſe, Fame or Infamy.

These complicated Causes are so far from altering the Effect, or leſſening the Merit of virtuous Actions, that they maniſeſt the Excellency of Virtue, by ſhewing us how many different Motives concur to invite us to every good Action, whilſt only ſome one Paſſion precipitates us into each bad one. (*a*)

Of theſe conſpiring Motives, the Opinion of Mankind ſeems the ſtrongeſt. There is hardly a Man, who takes any Step, whether in publick or private Life, but firſt conſiders What will my Acquaintance, Friends, Enemies, and the World ſay of it? and then heightens it to the Degree of Luſtre he wants to acquire, or ſeeks for Palliatives to prevent the Cenſure he apprehends.

Many have been the good Effects of the Deſire of *publick Praiſe*, and the Fear of *publick Obloquy*. Let the *Stoick* call this Sentiment a Weakneſs, it is ſurely an happy Failing, and produces the beſt Effects. As, on the contrary, an Inſenſibility of *Infamy* is a Proof of the Perfection of Wickedneſs.

Nemo repente fuit turpiſſimus is a true Obſervation ; to which we may add, that no Man is at once willing to be thought ſo. Neither Men nor Women ſlight Reputation till they have loſt it. It is then they enjoy, tho' againſt their Will, the Sweets of their infamous Liberty, and give a Looſe to their profligate Words and Actions.

I cannot conceive a greater, publick Peſt than a (*a*) Perſon, who hath ſet all Decency and Shame at Defiance. The wickedeſt Man, while he retains ſome Regard for the general Opinion, tacitly confeſſes the Blackneſs of his Crimes by his Endeavours to conceal them ; whereas the *Wretch* who prides himſelf in the Notoriety of his Infamy, deſtroys or infects all who approach him. He is exaſperated by the *publick Hatred* ; and, thus grown deſperate with Society, his own Preſervation muſt depend upon corrupting others to be like him, or by Force ſubduing thoſe he cannot corrupt.

How terrible muſt *ſuch a Creature* be, in every Branch of Society, either in a natural or civil Capacity? He is equally the Curſe of a Village, or the Scourge of an Empire.

Oderint modo timeant, was the Saying of one of the Tyrants of Antiquity ; it is the Principle (*a*) of them all ; and has juſtly proved the Ruin of many. What can be expected from (*b*) *a Prince*, hated by his Subjects, but Violence and Oppreſſion, Rage and Reſentment? Poor and precarious is the Comfort he would draw from their *Fears*. Thoſe *Fears*, ſooner or later, will ſubſide ; but their *Hatred* never ; and the Fate of a Nation, in ſuch Circumſtances, cannot be long in Suſpence. It muſt ſoon be decided, either by enſlaving the People, or by the overthrow of the Prince.

Card. *de Retz*, ſpeaking of an *unpopular Queen*, who ſupported a *deteſted firſt Miniſter*, ſays, He could never make her comprehend, what was meant by the *Publick* ; and her Adminiſtration, during the long *Minority of the King*, was one continued Scene of domeſtick Troubles ; occaſion'd by the alternate Starts of female Rage and Fear. She lov'd her *Miniſter*, only becauſe ſhe knew he was as much hated as herſelf, and that his Refuge was only her ; and the Miniſter accepted her Favour upon thoſe Terms ; and knowing he could not be ſafe, whilſt there was any Freedom in a Country which he had oppreſs'd and plunder'd, he gave the laſt mortal Blow to the long torrur'd Liberties of *France*.

If we may credit that authentick Piece, *the Enquiry*, the Duke *de Ripperda* was

---

(*a*) *This and ſeveral other Paſſages in this* Craftſman (*which the* Courant *hints was wrote by Mr* Sh———n) *are a lively Reſemblance of the Author, and his reſtleſs and* audacious *Spirit, who has been heard to ſay publickly—*They *are all of them Tyrants and Uſurpers.*

(*b*) *Can this* Creature *flatter himſelf that this Scurrility can injure one of the beſt and wiſeſt Princes that ever fill'd the* Britiſh *Throne? What has he done to fear or deſerve the Hatred of his Subjects? Was ever greater Clemency or Forgiveneſs in any Reign, than in ſuffering ſuch Writers to go on with Impunity?*

nuch in the fame Condition when Prime Minifter of *Spain.* — *The* King's *Minifters n* Spain, *faid he, and the whole* Spanifh Nation *are bitter againft me ; but I* augh at *all That. The* Queen *will pro-eĉ me. I have done her fuch Service hat fhe can't abandon me* — Yet he foon 'ell a Sacrifice to the Refentments of the 'eople ; for the Queen had good fenfe :nough to difcover that fhe could not >roteĉ him any longer, without bringing he King's Affairs into the utmoft Dif-refs, and perhaps ruining her Family.

A *firft Minifter, univerfally hated,* is :ertainly a Being inconfiftent with the Liberties of any Country. The Nation s his Enemy, and the Law of *Self-De- ence* tells him he muft weaken or ruin t. — The Cafe is ftill worfe, when he 1ot only deferves, but boafts of the *ge-neral Hatred* ; when he urges it to his *Prince* as a meritorious Claim to his Fa-/our ; and avows it to the *People,* as a ult Caufe for his Refentment and Re-/enge ; and is heard to fay publickly, *I c) have no other Refuge ; I know I am lefperate ; but Thofe, who made me fo ball repent of it.* — It is then Time for :he People to be upon their Guard.

It may be objeĉed that *publick Hatred* may fall upon an *innocent Man.* This I abfolutely deny, and challenge any Body to give me an (d) Inftance where

(c) *How much better does this Speech fuit this Writer himfelf ? Who has no o-ther Refuge, but in heightening his* Faĉion *to that Degree of* Luftre, *as to appear n open* Rebellion.

(d) *What does he think of Ld* Chancellor Clarendon ? *Will he deny that he was an* honeft Minifter, *or that* publick Hatred *unjuftly fell upon him ? Even the* Crafifl-man *gives him that great* Charaĉer (See p. 586 E) *and fays he fell a Sacrifice to the Malice of his Enemies.* — *According to* Rapin *and other Hiftorians, the fame low arts of* Lies *and* Scurrility, *Drollery and* Ridicule *were ufed to raife an* univerfal Hatred *againft him, as are fince repeated againft a certain honourable Perfon.* — *When the Chancellor was coming, fays* Rapin, *fome Lords would fay to the King* Here comes your Schoolmafter. *The* D. *if* Buckingham *ufed to walk in a ftately manner with a Pair of* Bellows *before him, to mimick the* Chancellor *with the* Purfe, *whilft* Col. Titus *carried a Fire-*Shovel *on his fhoulders for a* Mace. *And fo the Nation came to be pleafed with, tho' they afterwards fuffer'd for, the Sacrifice of this noble Lord.*

univerfal Hatred or *univerfal Applaufe* ever center'd in one Man, who did not deferve a great Share of *one,* or the *other.* However, let us imagine an *honeft, un-corrupt Minifter* unjuftly hated by the whole Nation. Would he ftruggle with the *publick Averfion ?* Surely not ; but more fenfible of *Calumny,* than of Danger, would withdraw from the Exalted Station which, very probably, had turned *Envy* into *Hatred.* He would reprefent to his *Prince* the Impoffibility of carrying on right Meafures thro' his Means, and the Injuftice, and Danger, of attempting wrong ones to fupport him. He would fcorn the Affiftance of *Power* to fcreen his Aĉions from publick En-quiry ; he would more willingly be ex-ecuted in *Reality,* than hang'd in *Effigy.* Such were the Sentiments of *Tully* in his Oration againft (e) *Catiline,* where, in reafoning upon the Heinoufnefs of his Crime he advifes him to withdraw him-felf from *Rome,* where he was fo ge-nerally hated, and his Prefence detefted.

(e) *Is not the Cafe of* Catiline *and this* Writer *exaĉly the fame ? Or rather, does not his* Infolence *exceed that of* Cati-line ? *Did* Catiline *continue in* Rome *af-ter making fuch a Declaration to the* Senate, *as this Man makes to his Prince?* — My Fears of you, Sir, may and will, fooner or later, fubfide, but my *Hatred* never. *Would he aĉ even as honeft a Part as* Catiline, *he would abandon his Country he had confpir'd to ruin, and go over to that pretended Prince, who, 'tis fuppofed, is not one of his Tyrants of* An-tiquity, *but one educated and inftruĉed in all the* merciful *and* forgiving *Tenets and Doĉrines of* Modern Rome.

London Journal, Dec. 8. No. 754.

Remarks of on the Review of the Excife Scheme.

THE Author of the *Review* gives it for a Reafon, why the *Tea-Aĉ* paffed fo eafily in 1725. *That the People were not at that Time apprehenfive of the Nature, Confequences, and Progrefs of Excifes, i. e.* After an *Experience* of above fixty Years, and extended to a Multitude of Traders and Dealers, they were not difcovered to be oppreffive, nor dangerous to *Liberty,* till propofed by Sir R. W. Tho' the *skilfulleft Writers* had re-commended this Method of raifing Taxes ; and the *ableft Minifters,* fince the *Revo-lution,* of all Denominations and Parties, praĉifed it preferably to any other ; yet

Sir *R. W.* could not make use of it, but from a *blundering* Head, and a *wicked* Heart!

The Author affirms, *That Excises are* Poll-Taxes *upon the Consumers, raised without Distinction, at an* immoderate *and* unnecessary *Expence*: Yet the Earls of *Godolphin* and *Oxford*, who had seen several Trials of a *Poll-Tax*, chose rather to establish *New Excises*, than to have Recourse to it. Above half that formidable Catalogue of Excises this Writer mentions, were added during the short Administration of the last of these Ministers; and some of the loudest *Declaimers* against Excises at present, and then in Employment, not only *suffer'd*, but *concurred in rivetting* (as our Author has it) *those galling Fetters on the Legs of the* British *Nation*. And tho' the E. of *Oxford* was suspected of Designs against Publick Liberty; yet his Opposers never had *Malice* or *Madness* enough to suggest that he was effecting them by *introducing* Excises.

He also affirms, *Excises are Inventions of Cruelty, an Abridgment of English Liberty,* and an Infringement of *Magna Charta* itself; and adds, where the People are deprived of their Rights, either by the executive or *legislative* Power, (as he affirms they are in this *Case*) having no Appeal on Earth, they have Liberty to appeal to Heaven; that is, *All Traders* under the Laws of *Excise, have a Right to rebel!* Such a publick calling the People to Arms, not to oppose *new Taxes*, but to *abolish* those which were established before the greatest Part of them were born; and some of them adjudged to be the *legal Inheritance of the Crown; is an Attempt* above the *Correction of a Writer.*

After this, no wonder he should assert, *That the Projector himself knew the Increase of* Half a Million by an Excise *on* Wine *and* Tobacco, *to be a meer Chimera; and that by the most rigorous Collection of the Duty upon* Tobacco, *it could not be proved there was a Possibility of raising an additional Sum of* 30000l. per Ann. *and that chiefly upon* N. Britain.

'Tis answer'd; the Duty on *Tobacco*, as given in the *Craftsman* [See p. 406 H] is about 200,000 *l. per Ann.* but when that Duty was *more vigorously* collected, the *Impost Duty alone* amounted by a Medium of 3 Years, from 1686 to 1688, both inclusive, to upwards of 150,000 *l. per Ann.* and the *Impost* being not half the *present Duty*, only nine Nineteenths,

it follows, if the Consumption of *Tobacco* be not lessened in the Kingdom, that the Duty should now produce above 320000*l.* in *England*; and if the Consumption in *Scotland* be 1 fourth of the Whole, the Produce there would be 100,000 *l.* a Year more. So that it appears evident, that by another Method of collecting this Duty, there would have been *an Addition* of above 200,000 *l. per Ann.*

As to *Wine*, if Mr *Houghton on Trade* was well informed, there had been before the Revolution, 30,000 Tuns imported into *London* in a Year, which is 1 third more than at present; tho' from the vast Increase of *Wealth* and *Expence* in the Town, one would conclude, there is rather an Increase than an Abatement in the Consumption of Wine. But should it be only the same, the Duty of it, added to that gained by another Method of collecting the Duty on Tobacco, amounts to near 500,000 *l.* which, says the *Reviewer, was the utmost of the Projector's Romantick Calculation.*

The *Adulteration* of Wine is too notorious to be denied, therefore he only cavils about the *Degree* of it; but says, the *Scheme* was calculated for *increasing* the Consumption of a *Foreign* Commodity, which *must inevitably* turn the Ballance of Trade against us; yet owns, we could not export our own Manufactures, without taking *Foreign Commodities* in exchange for them. This is true; the more we import from any Nation, the *more Goods they take from us.* Does not our Trade with *Portugal*, compared with what it was sixty Years ago, *prove* we may *increase* the Consumption of the Commodities of a foreign Country to ten Times as much, without *inevitably* turning the Ballance of Trade against us?

But, says he, Had the Scheme answer'd *its End, whatever* additional Sum is *raised upon any Commodity, either by a* new Tax, *or a more rigorous Collection of an old one, the Price of it will be* augmented *above double, to the* Augmentation *of the Revenue.*] But if he consults Dr *Davenant*, he will find, that the Excise on Beer and Ale only, was increased by the *Method of Collection*, from 1683, to 1689, above 150,753 *l. per Ann.* without augmenting the Price of the Commodity. That it has *sometimes* happened, *That the Duty has been sunk in the Price of the Commodity:* And it appears by the Book of Rates, that the Value of a Pound of Tobacco was *formerly* 20 d. whereas now, when

when the *Duty* is 6 Times as much as then, Tobacco, as bought from the Merchant, is about 7 *d.* or 8 *d. per Pound.*

But this Author's *own Discovery* in the Affair of *Tea*, is a Confutation of himself: For, as he states it, the Crown gains *above double the original Value* of the *Tea*, with a *sufficient Profit to the Trader*, yet it's sold for 1 *Third* of the Price it was sold at 50 Years ago, when the Duty was much less.

But, it seems, the Land would not have been eased by this *Scheme*; for, says he, it has been proved by *unanswerable Authority*, that *all Taxes* in this *Kingdom*, must *ultimately affect Land.*

I answer, This is a Matter not to be proved by *Authority*, but by *Reason* and *Experience*; and if the *Reviewer* will so prove, that the *Lands* of *England* are affected by the *Excise* upon *Cards, Dice, Wrought Plate, Coffee, Tea, Chocolate,* &c. *Erit mihi magnus Apollo.*

But have any of those *unanswerable Authors* denied, that a *Tax directly upon Land* affects it to a vastly greater Degree? Or, if they have, will they not be refuted by the *Feeling* and *Experience* of every Free-holder in *England*, on whom the Pressure of a *Land-Tax* of 4 *s.* in the Pound, is felt in a very different Manner from that of the *Excise* on *Beer* and *Malt*, which yet raise as much to the Publick.

Weekly Miscellany, Dec. 8. No. 52.

IS an Extract of a Book lately published, entituled, *The Apprentice's Vade Mecum*; the Author of which commenting on that Part of the Indenture, which prohibits a young Man the *haunting* of Playhouses has kept a proper Medium between the Disputants, who contend for the *Lawfulness* and *Unlawfulness* of the *Stage*. He is of Opinion, that under proper Regulations the *Stage* might be made subservient to excellent Purposes, and be a useful Second to the *Pulpit* itself: Even as it is conducted, it's a tolerable Diversion to such as know not how to pass their Time, and who perhaps would spend it much worse in Drinking, Gaming, &c. But for a young *Tradesman*, or much more an *Apprentice*, to make this his favourite Diversion, and to *haunt* a Playhouse, who can bestow his Time much more to the Advantage of his Business, which will probably suffer by it, must be of pernicious Consequence in several Respects: As, 1. All our modern Plays are calculated for Persons in *upper Life*,

and the Moral and Instruction lies so deep and hidden, as seldom to fall within the Sphere of those in *low* Life. 2. The Loss of Time and Expence of Money. 3. The great Resort of lewd Women to those Places. 4. Most of our modern best Plays are so far from being *intended* for Instructions to a Man of Business, that such Persons are generally made the Dupes and Fools of the Hero of it. To make a Cuckold of a rich Tradesman is a masterly Part of the Plot; and such Persons are always introduced under the most contemptible Characters. All manner of Cheats, Frauds, and Villainies, committed against such, are incouraged and inculcated upon an Audience; the genteeler Part of which are too ready to take the Hint, as the Men of Trade every Day find to their Cost: Its Followers are infinitely of more Consequence, and deserve more to be incouraged, than any other Degree or Rank of People in it. Can it then be prudent, or even decent, for a Tradesman to encourage by his Presence, or support by the Effects of his Industry, Diversions so abusive of the Profession by which he lives, and by which not only these Catterpillars themselves, but the whole Nation, is supported? 5. The great Depravity of Writers in general. A good Dramatick Writer is a Character this Age knows nothing of. Genteel Comedy has long left the Stage, as well as the nobler Tragic Muse; and all our Heroes and Heroines of the Drama have been fetched from *Newgate* and *Bridewell*. The celebrated *Congreve's Niky, Horner*, and others, were detestable Characters; but then there was so much Wit mingled with the Immorality, as made it pass when we could get no better. But now the horrid Pantomime, and wicked Dumb Shew, the infamous Harlequin-Mimickry, introduced only to shew how to cozen, cheat, deceive, and cuckold; together with the wretched Group of Rogues formed from the Characters of *Shepherd, Jonathan Wild, Blueskin*, and others, remarkable for their superlative Wickedness, are exhibited, not for the sake of Poetical Justice in their Execution, but to divert the Audience by their *Tricks* and *Escapes*. 6. Frequent visiting a Playhouse too much detaches the Mind from Business, and fills it with light and airy Amusements.

·The Increase of Playhouses, and the Encouragement they meet with, are sad Instances of the Luxury of the present Age. There was a Time, when publick

Spec-

Spectacles, Shews, Drolls, and Farces were exhibited to good Purpoſes. Every Trading Town or populous City had its annual Fair, which brought to it from adjacent Villages a great Reſort of People, who had been labouring for Months be- A fore harder than uſual, to ſave ſomething to ſpend at that Time ; and to purchaſe Fairings for thoſe they beſt affected ; whereby vaſt Quantities of Manufactures were diſpoſed of. It was then that *Bartholomew* and *Southwark* Faits were the only Times that induſtrious Citizens indulged themſelves in that ſort of Diverſion. But now we are grown more *polite*, forſooth ; our Young Men aſpire to the Taſte of their Betters, and they are bleſſed with a Set of Authors who have wrote down to theirs.

There's but one Inſtance, where the Stage has condeſcended to make itſelf uſeful to the City Youth ; and that is the Play of *George Barnwell*, which our young City Gentry may be allowed to ſee once a Year, on Condition not to deſire to go oftner, till another Play of an equally good Moral and Deſign was acted.

Playhouſes therefore, muſt be of pernicious Conſequence, when ſet up in the City, or in thoſe Confines of it, where People of Induſtry generally inhabit. Nor will the Minds of young Women (or young Ladies as they are now to be called) be leſs tainted than thoſe of young Men, with the Vanities of the Stage, and the frequent Scenes of the pretty Gentlemen, introduced with a View to debauch their Morals, and triumph over their Innocence. This muſt be a ſtrange School for the Daughters of ſober Citizens, who ought to have nothing in View, but what would become a Life of Buſineſs and Induſtry. Inſtead of which, to have planted among them an Infamous Troop of wretched Strollers, and a collected String of abandon'd Harlots, impudently propagating to an *under-bred* and *unwary* Audience, Fornication, Adultery, Rapes, and Murders, by heighten'd Action, muſt have fatal Effects on the Morals both of G Men and Women ſo circumſtanced. And, 'tis hoped, this in Time will be duly conſider'd (notwithſtanding the Civil Power, and City Magiſtracy have been braved and inſulted) and that effectual Care will be taken to remove them from a Quarter ſo improper for ſuch Diverſions.

The Free Britton, Dec. 13. No. 215.

THE *London Evening-Poſt* of November 27. inſerted an Account of the Death of Sir *Charles Gounter Nicoll*, and a Commentary on his Character in theſe Terms : *He was bleſſed with an ample Fortune, which he enjoy'd in a Manner that rendered him in* early Years *of Life,* a truly valuable Husband, *and* a Friend. —— *He could not, however, be called a Friend to his Country ;* for *he exchanged his Principles for a* Red Ribband, *and* voted for *the* Excise.

When the *untimely* Stroke of Fate hath ſnatched from the World a Perſon of great *Diſtinction*, and of *greater Integrity*, whoſe Life was valuable to his Friends, whoſe *ample Fortunes* were leſs than his *generous Benevolence*, who endeared himſelf to Mankind in every Action, and was loſt to his Friends, his Family, and his *beloved Conſort*, in the Vigour of his Youth. To make this *terrible* Accident ſerve as the Subject of *Spleen* and *Malice* ; to aggravate the Sorrows of his Friends and Relations, by *mangling* his *Character*, and *butchering his Memory*, while his Corpſe lies breathleſs before them, is an *(a)* Act of ſuch *monſtrous Cruelty*, and *Immorality*, that no Reſentment can be too ſevere, nor Words expreſs the juſt Deteſtation of ſo enormous a Crime.

The *ſcandalous Author* of this Defamation thruſt himſelf into the *Strife of Parties*, and endeavoured to advance the Profits of an *Evening-Poſt* by making it the Means of *enflaming our Paſſions*, and of encreaſing our *Diviſions* ; but having met ſuch Checks as were highly *juſt* and *warrantable (See* p. 630) now attempts to ſignilize himſelf by his *Inhumanity to the Dead*.

If this be the Method of promoting

(a) The Authors of the London Evening-Poſt *of* Decem. 15. *aſſure the Publick, that this was inadvertently inſerted in their Paper in the Abſence of the Printer ; and as it may be thought to carry an indecent Reflection upon a Gentleman, who is dead, are ſorry they ſhould be thus impoſed upon : But think* Mr Walſingham's *manner of treating this Affair, turns it into Ridicule ; ſince it cannot be forgot in how cruel a manner he diſturbed the Aſhes of the late* Daniel Pulteney, Eſq; *by putting a Heap of ſcandalous Ribbaldry in his Mouth ; and when he was handſomely rebuked by the* Craftſman, *inſtead of making any Apology for it, redoubled the Inſult, and ridiculed all Regard for the* Aſhes of the Dead. See Vol. I. p. 392, 430.

a *Country Interest*; and rendering a Court *unpopular*; far be it from me to envy the Success of such abandon'd Men.

As to the *late Scheme of Excise*, as it has been long since given up to the Dislike of the People, I shall never recommend it; and I know, that those whose Sentiments are of far greater Importance than mine, are determined *never to revive it in any Shape*, or on any Occasion: But, at the same Time, I am as sensible that *others* of the *best Intentions to Mankind*, and of the *greatest Integrity*, from *honest Convictions*, gave their Votes in Favour of it. And to suppose on any Question, that many on *both Sides* had not *honest Views*, would be such Want of Charity and Candour, as I should be ashamed of, were I even defending *Christianity* itself against *Turks*, *Jews*, or *Infidels*.

This Falshood is not only of the most impudent Species, but a *Scandal of the highest Nature*; a base Imputation on the *King*, and the *honourable Person*.

To colour this *wicked Aspersion*, there is not so much as the idle Pretence, that the *Vote* was given, and the *Ribband* received in Recompence; for the *honourable Gentleman* was deservedly made *Knight of the Bath* long before the Excise was attempted or opened: And how this could influence *his Vote* is inconceivable. I see not only *Red*, but *Green* and *Blue Ribbands* on both Sides the Question.

Grubstreet Journal. Dec. 13. No. 207.

Of Politeness.

Mr BAVIUS,

AGREEABLE to the Education I had under my Father in the Country, I have, since I come to Town, constantly frequented the Church. I live with an Uncle at the polite End of the Town, where, my Parents us'd often to tell me, I might meet with daily Opportunities to improve myself. My present Request to you is, that you will explain the Word *polite*, and how am I to understand it in order to my Improvement. — We poor Innocents in the Country were taught to hold, that nothing could be *polite* that was not decent. A chearful Countenance we always thought decent and becoming and therefore not unpolite. But in this our great Parish Church, where we abound with Lords, Ladies, and other great Folks, near three parts in four demonstrate their *Politeness*, by the Sour-

(Gent. Mag. Vol. III. N° xxxvi.)

ness of their Countenance; and their Decency, in their Loquaciousness during divine Service. Look when you will you will find Heads and Tongues in a continual Motion. Pews are not able to part them: For I have seen venerable Ladies, of Quality too, whisper distinguishably loud over a Pew, in the Middle of the Church. The young ones are equally polite, tho' in a different way. They enter with Countenances somewhat more than chearful; and tho' the Fan is immediately clapt before the Face, it is, for the most Part taken away before they can have utter'd the shortest Response in the Litany. But that may proceed from their vast Zeal to pay their Addresses to their numerous Acquaintance in the Congregation. But another Piece of politeness more surpriz'd me—Last Sunday, so soon as the Organ began, I took Notice that a certain Gentleman pretty near the upper End of the Church who had several Sundays before directed his Eyes towards my Pew lean'd over his Desk, and whisper'd to a small Attendant, who went out directly, and quickly return'd with a Spying Glass, so soon as he got it he levell'd it at your humble Servant. Now, I don't think myself a Monster, neither had I, as the Moon is said to have, spots in my Face; and therefore I appeal to you for the Decency or *Politeness* of his Behaviour. Be pleased also to distinguish, which, if any of these, are any Part of the *Politenesses*, by which I am to improve myself.   *Martha Meanwell.*

The Craftsman. Dec. 15. No. 388.

Of Publick, Ridicule and Contempt; Continued from p. 637.

THE late Ld *Shaftsbury* asserts, that *Ridicule* is the surest Test of † *Truth* and *real Worth*; because it will never

† Dr *Clarke*, says a Writer in the *Daily Courant*, Dec. 19. asserts, that "Banter is not capable of being answered by Reason; not, because it has any Strength in it; but because it runs out of all the Bounds of Reason and good Sense, by extravagantly joining together such Images, as have not in themselves any Manner of Similitude or Connection; by which Means all things are alike easy to be render'd ridiculous, by being represented only in an absurd Dress. Christianity has suffer'd from no one thing so much as from *Ridicule* and *Buffoonery*. So far is it from being true that *Ridicule is the surest Test of Truth and real Worth* &c. that it is evidently false both as to Religion and Politicks. (See p. 637.)

hold where it is not juſt; and, inſtead of wounding the *Object*, recoils upon the *Author*. Wit and Humour can only diſcover and diſplay *Ridicule*, but cannot create it. If the Cloaths don't fit, the *Taylor*, not the *Wearer*, is blamed.

Contempt and *Ridicule* are near a-kin, with this Difference only, that a Man may be very *contemptible*, without being *ridiculous*, but cannot be very *ridiculous*, without being *contemptible*; *Contempt* ariſing from a Privation of good Qualities; *Ridicule* from an Affectation of 'em. Thus a *Fellow of eminent Incapacity and illiberal Manners*, who pretends to Buſineſs, or Politeneſs, riſes from a Solid Object of *Contempt*, into a ſhining one of *Ridicule*.

The greater the Diſtance between the *real* and the *affected Qualifications*, the ſtronger is the Contraſt, and the higher the *Ridicule*. The *Aſs in the Lyon's Skin* was much more ridiculous than if he only aſſum'd the Kindred Appearance of an *Horſe*. This will ever be the Caſe of *Thoſe*, who, being form'd by Nature for the *meaneſt Functions of Life* abſurdly aim, and ſome times unaccountably arrive at the *greateſt*. The Oddities of a *Beau, Coxcomb, Pedant, Bully*, only furniſh Laughter to private Circles; but the impenetrable Head, and porterly Manners of a *Stateſman* and a *Courtier* are glaring Objects of national and univerſal Mirth.

Some People are born ſo much below the reſt of their Species, that it's *ridiculous* and even *preſumptuous* in them to imitate the Actions of the common Run of Mankind. I once knew a Man, ſays this Writer, ſo form'd by Nature for *Dirt* and *ill Manners*, that they almoſt became him; and he grew *ridiculous* by putting on *Civility* and *clean Linnen*.

Dr South remarks, *that many a Man hath run his Head unſucceſsfully againſt a Pulpit, who might have done his Country good Service at a* Plough-Tail. This Obſervation holds equally good in the *State*.

Let us ſuppoſe Men, born with Talents below the Vulgar, and thoſe puzzled and perplexed, not improved by a laborious Application, advanc'd to high Stations only by Birth, or ſome whimſical Concurrence of Circumſtances; rather bewilder'd in the Mazes, than engaged in the Diſpatch of Buſineſs; wallowing in Papers of which they neither comprehend the Subſtance, nor underſtand the Language; whoſe bodily Hurry would in

vain compenſate the Sluggiſhneſs of their Minds; whoſe Eloquence is only a Profuſion of miſplaced and unconnected Words; and whoſe . Politeneſs conſiſts in the Vehemence of a ruſtick and ungentleman-ly Addreſs;—when *ſuch People* pretend to the Conduct of Affairs, the Diginity of Employments, or the good Breeding of a Court, their *high* Poſts are a ſort of *political Pillory* to them, which invites Paſſengers to club their Lump of Dirt at *Heads*, ſo ridiculouſly expoſed.

This is not the worſt. They are not only the Cauſe of *national Mirth*, but of *national Misfortune* too. The Adminiſtration ſinks into *Contempt*; grows uſeleſs at beſt, commonly dangerous. Men who can miſtake themſelves ſo groſsly, are capable of miſtaking every Thing. Where they mean to ſtrike *Terror*, they create *Mirth*. *Harmleſs Squadrons* convey their Threats, and *ſilent Cannons* proclaim their Glory. *Miſtaken Intereſts* are the Baſis of their Negotiations, and *inevitable War* the neceſſary and immediate Conſequence of their *Treaties of Peace*.

An Adminiſtration, in ſuch ſhameful Circumſtances, cannot ſubſiſt long; eſpecially if *ſome Members* of it join the *publick Hatred* to the *publick Contempt* acquired by *others*. It muſt then inevitably and immediately yield to the ſeldom-united Attacks of *national Ridicule* and *national Odium*.

There is always a ſtrange Awkwardneſs in a Government ſo circumſtantiated. One ſees a lazy, reluctant Co-operation in all the ſubordinate Parts of it. *Some* diſcover the Conſciouſneſs of their Shame by a ſilent Diſcontent and a ſurly Concurrence. *Others* hope to leſſen it, by a frank Confeſſion, and pleading their Neceſſities like *Debtors*, who ſkulk within the *Verge of a Court*; but all impatiently wait to be relieved from their *opprobious*, or *ridiculous Servitude*.

To conclude, This is not our Caſe. Our Adminiſtration is ſo admirably conſtituted, that like a choice Piece of Moſaick, it preſents you all together with the Perfect Images of *Popularity* and *Dignity*; and I hope it may be ſaid, without the leaſt ſuſpicion of Adulation, that our *preſent Miniſtry is without a Precedent*.

Fog's Journal, Dec. 15. No. 267.
Againſt continuing the preſent Parliament.

ABOUT a Month ago, ſays a Writer who ſigns himſelf *L.D.* a Pamphlet was publiſhed, entitled, *Some Reaſons*

'ons *for continuing the present Parliament.*
As wretched a *Performance* as it is, yet
has it received the same Honours with
other *Pieces* published in Defence of the
great *Projector*, and been dispersed in the
Country by *Postmasters* and *Excisemen.*
Here he gives an Abstract of it, and the
Reasons the Author offers for the Continuance of the present *Parliament*, but in
Fog's usual drolling Manner; whereby
the Writer's Arguments are made to turn
against himself, and then proceeds: This
Work, I dare say, has not made a single
Convert in the whole Kingdom, notwithstanding the Industry with which it has
been propagated. Nor has the Author
urged half so much as the Subject would
have fairly admitted. I could furnish
him with fitter Materials than any he has
used for a *Panegyrick* on the present
House of Commons. I don't mean that
signal Proof of Loyalty in supplying the
Deficiencies of the Civil List, with
115,000 *l.* nor their Tenderness of the
landed Interest, by a *Revival of the Salt
Duty*: In short, I do not mean any thing
they *have done*, but a certain Matter,
which they have *not done.* They *have
not*, they *would not* pass the late famous
Excise-Bill. And this negative Merit is
sufficient to entitle them to universal
Esteem. But tho' I wish that the glorious 204, and 204 more of the same Spirit and Principles, may have Seats in *Parliament* next Winter, yet I should no
longer consider 'em as Patriots, if they
were to take Possession of St *Stephen's*
Chapel, by their own Authority. *Stale
and standing Parliaments* (as a famous
Author observes) *tho' they should not be
corrupted by Pensions and Places, and
turning out of Places, yet will stagnate,
and be like a Country Pond, which is over-
grown with Ducks Meat.*

But after all our *Pamphleteer* has said,
I am under no Apprehensions of a Design to continue the present Parliament;
nor that the *able Statesman*, who, according to the London *Journ.* Courants, Free.
Britons, &c. is so happy in the Affections of the People, and so easy in his
present Situation, can need such an ex-
traodinary Support, as our Author would
perswade him to make use of. Besides,
he has always shewn himself so sincere a
Friend to the People, that tho' his great
Merits should hereafter be unhappily distressed, yet he will never add any new
Weight to the Prerogative, to relieve
the Exigency of his own Affairs. But
as some future Minister may found his

whole Power in Corruption, and finding
himself universally detested, may endeavour his own Preservation by the Subversion of our Liberties; we therefore
ought to be on our Guard, and to continue, as we now are, firmly united. As
long as the present glorious *Coalition* subsists, we cannot be hurt by foreign or domestick Enemies. However we may be
alarm'd by the Clamour of our *Adversaries*; yet we need not fear, that our
trading Cities will fall to the Ground, because a Company of *embroidered Slaves,*
or a String of *party-colour'd Priests*, may
be commanded to walk round them, and
blow their Rams Horns.   L. D.

London Journal, Dec. 15. N° 755.

*Of the People's Right of Petitioning and
Instructing Members of Parliament.*

THE Pamphlet entitled, the *Review
of the Excise Scheme* being published
with a manifest Tendency to excite Rebellion, I thought it a Matter of such
Consequence, says an anonymous Writer
in this Journal, as to deserve a Particular
Consideration; especially what he advances about the *People's Right of Petitioning* and *Instructing* their Members.
The *Considerer*, it seems, is highly in-
cens'd at this Practice, and calls these
Seasonable Applications, *positive Commands, and authoritative Instructions,*
&c. whereas the Author of the *Review*
cannot recollect, that the Word *Command
or Injunction,* or any Word *synonimous*
or *equivalent*, was made use of in any
Part of the Instructions last Winter.—
The Stile of the *Kentish Petition* was,
*We most humbly implore this honourable
House to have Regard to the Voice of the
People?* Yet, the House voted it *scandalous, insolent, and seditious, tending to
destroy the Constitution of Parliaments,
and the established Government of the
Realm.* And the Instructions of the City
of *London* (See *p.* 98.) and Borough of
Southwark, our Author confesses to be
in an *authoritative Stile*, and to direct
their Members how to behave in the
momentous Affair of Peace and War.
As to the Point of *petitioning* and *Instructing*, the *Reviewer* says, " As Parliaments
have often run contrary to the *Sense* and
Interest of the People, in such a Case
what is to be done? And asks, whether
the Members of the *House of Commons*
are the People's *Representatives*, or not?
And, whether, unlike all other *Deputies*
and *Trustees*, they are *absolutely independent*

pendent of their *Principals* and *Constituents?*" The *Reviewer* may take his Answer from the celebrated *Algernon Sidney*, who says,—" The *Powers* of every County, City, and Borough of *England* are *regulated* by the *general Law* to which they have all *consented*; and, by which they are all made Members of one *political Body.* This obliges them to proceed with their *Delegates* in a manner *different* from what is used in the *United Netherlands*, or in *Switzerland*; amongst those, every Province, City, or Canton, making a distinct Body, *Independent* from any other, and *exercising Sovereign Power* within itself, looks upon the rest as *Allies*, to whom they are bound only by such Acts as *they themselves* have made; and, when any *new Things*, not comprehended in them, happent to arise, they oblige their *Delegates* to give them an Account of it, and *retain* the Power of *Determining* those Matters to *themselves.* 'Tis not so amongst us: *every County* does not make a *distinct Body*, having, in itself, a *Sovereign Power*, but is a Member of that *Great Body* which comprehends the *whole Nation.* 'Tis not therefore for *Kent* or *Sussex*, *Lewes* or *Maidstone*, but for the *whole Nation*, that the Members chosen for *those Places*, are sent to serve in Parliament; and tho' it be fit for them, as *Friends* or *Neighbours* (as far as may be) to hearken to the Opinion of the Electors for the Information of their Judgments, and to the End that what they shall say shall be of more weight, when every one is known not to speak his own Thoughts only, but those of a great Number of Men; yet they are not *strictly* and *properly obliged to give an Account of their Actions to any*, unless the *whole Body* of the Nation for which they serve, could be assembled. This being impracticable, the *only Punishment* to which they are subject, if they betray their Trust, is *Scorn, Infamy, Hatred*, and *an Assurance* of being *rejected* when they shall again seek the same Honour." —

The *Reviewer* hopes this Point (*Petitioning* and *Instructing* Members, &c.) will be *fully established.* Let us examine then what *Instances* or *Authorities* he produces for it. The first is in the Parliament of *Edward* III, when a Motion was made for a *Subsidy* of a *new Kind*, the Commons answer'd, They would have Conference with their several Counties and Places, before they treated of any such Matter. But is there any thing

more in this than what Mr *Sidney* recommends, *i.e.* To hearken to the Opinion of their Electors? And the same Answer will serve equally to his other Instance of the 13th of the same Reign, when the King wanted Aid of the Commons to pay a Debt of 30,000 *l.* To which the Commons answer'd " they durst not agree without further Conference with their Counties." From both which Instances it appears, not that the People applied to their Representatives, with *Petitions* and *authoritative Instructions*, but that their Representatives applied to them of their own *mere Will and Motion.* The Expression of *not daring to do it* without Conference, signifies no more, than it would for a Father to say, *he dared not* dispose of his Estate without consulting a Son, deserving well of him.

If we come down to *Long Parliaments* " we find, says the *Reviewer*, the same Right exerted upon several Occasions; and in the Reign of K. *Charles* II. we meet with several Addresses of this Kind."] But were the many Addresses of this Kind made expedient by *the Length* of that Parliament, to which they were directed? or a *short one* that met in *October* in 1680? This Observation is only to remark the constant Deviation of this Author from Truth, when 'tis against him. Several Counties, Cities, and Corporations might indeed return their respective Members Thanks for their past Services, and for asserting their undoubted *Right of Petitioning.* But was this *Right* such as we are now contesting? The *Reviewer* knows, that it was no more than a Right to *Petition* the King for the *Calling and Sitting of Parliaments:* The traducing *such Petitioning* it is, that the Votes of the House declared a *Betraying* the *Liberties* of the Nation.

But, says the *Reviewer*, " They not only returned their Representatives Thanks for their glorious Conduct, but requested them not to consent to any Money Bill, till *all their Grievances* were redressed; and even Promising to stand by them *with their Lives and Fortunes.*" And these Things, says he, were written for our Instruction.

But were any of these Addresses presented while the Parliament was sitting, or after *the Prorogation* of it? If the Latter, no Wonder they pass'd without Censure; otherwise, 'tis hardly imaginable a House of Commons, so vigorous in asserting the Rights of the *Subject*, would so meanly *betray their own.*

[Universal

Univerfal Spectator, Dec. 15. No. 271.

A Husband's Curtain Lecture.

Mr SPECTATOR,

I BEG your Affiftance in putting an End
to a Difpute between an ill bred
Wretch of a Husband a Philofopher, and
a polite modern Wife extremely fond of
Dice and a Pack of Cards. Yefterday
Morning I had but juft awak'd, when he
faluted me with a *Curtain Lecture*, a
Right which has been, Time out of
Mind, folely vefted in our Sex. " My
Dear, faid he in an authoritative Tone,
I am much amaz'd at your Proceeding!
Is it poffible Common Senfe can be made
confiftent with your Conduct! You ruin
my Fortune, hazard your Virtue, deftroy
your Beauty, and impair your Health;
you difregard me your Husband, neglect
your Children, mifpend your Time, and
make no Provifion for Eternity." Now,
as I had quietly condefcended to be the
Perfon Lecter'd, inftead of the Perfon
Lecturing, I did the Duty of my Place,
and heard him out with great Patience
and a profound Silence. When he had
done, " My Dear, faid I, fince you have
difputed my Right and Title to Common
Senfe, let me ask you, what Demonftration you have given of your own? Is it
poffible your great Wifdom can imagine,
that a dull Repetition of a tedious Story
is ever the Way to render it agreeable?
Your mufty Doctrines and dry Precepts
would found well enough from a grave
old Gentleman in a Pulpit, and might
ferve for Rules of Conduct were we confin'd to live always in a Church: But
how ridiculous would they be in the
Drawing-Room or Opera-Houfe? All
Perfons are not in Love with the fame
Things, nor are the fame Actions proper
for all Places. You may fall in Raptures
at a Sermon, or tranfcribe all the Rules
in the *Whole Duty of Man* for your own
Conduct; but the *Duty of a fine Woman*
is to be learnt at the Drawing-Room,
the Park, the Play, or the Mafquerade;
Places which, as you never appear in,
you know not the Charms of. But thus
Abfurdities muft ever happen, People
will judge in Things they are Strangers
to. I am refolv'd however to do the Duty of a good Wife; and fhall convince
you, that I have too tender a Regard for
your Reputation, to let this Morning's
Behaviour of yours be publifh'd to the
World, or whifper'd at Madam Spadille's
Affembly." This I fpoke out of pure
Good Nature: For you and I, Mr Spec,

know very well, how ill it will found
at half the Tea-Tables in Town, that
the wife and learned Mr *Spendthrift*
quarrel'd with his Lady, for the heinous
Crime of keeping the beft Company, and
the intolerable Extravagance of only
lofing one Year's Income at a Sitting.
My Spoufe however was fo ungrateful
as to tell me, " He thought it almoft
fcandalous to have a good Character a-
mong fuch People; and that the Difgrace
of being ill fpoken of at thofe Places,
was a fhame he fhould always glory in."
I confefs I was for fome Time ftruck
dumb with Aftonifhment, to find him
fuch an abandon'd *Tramontane*. He perceiving there was no Hopes of an Accommodation, ask'd me if I would refer
this important Point to your Determination? I agreed; and accordingly defire
you to inform us, whether you think
Fortune, Reputation, Beauty, Health,
Husband, Children, Body, or any Thing,
are to be compar'd to a *Nick* at *Hazard*,
and a *Sans prendre Mattadore Volte* at
enchanting *Quadrille*?

Martha Spendthrift.

The **Daily Courant**, Dec. 17.

A Diffenter, in order to perfuade his
Brethren not to join the *Tories* at
the next Election, gives a long Catalogue
fumm'd up in about 30 Queries of oppreffive Acts, and violent Proceedings of
the *Tories* againft the Diffenters; moft
of which we have touch'd on before
from the *London Journal.* (See p. 582 D)
If it be ask'd what have the *Whigs* done
to entitle themfelves to our Favour? why,
fays he, the Reverfe of all this; and
concludes, I differ from our pretended
Friend the *Craftfman,* who defires,
that all the hard Ufage that the Proteftants have met with, might be eraz'd
out of our Hiftory. (See p. 593 B) On the
contrary, I would never have it forgot,
but hope it will be tranfmitted down in
its proper Colours to lateft Pofterity, *not
to revenge it,* but that we, and they who
are to come after us, may be upon our
Guard to prevent the like Treatment.

The **Daily Courant**, Dec. 18.

WE are told in our publick Prints,
*That at the Horfe Races at Shrewf-
bury, there was the greateft Appearance
ever known on the like Occafion, of Gentlemen entirely devoted to the true Intereft
of their Country, and who are neither a-
fhamed nor afraid to profefs fuch Principles
as become free-born Englifhmen.*] Had
they

they explained what they meant by the *true Interest of their Country*, and the *Principles they are not asham'd of*, we should know whether they become *free-born Englishmen or not*; however, by their own Acknowledgment, they are opposite to the *Principles* of those who set on foot the *Horse-Race*, whom they call *Gentlemen of a contrary way of thinking and acting*; yet such as were always hearty Friends to K. *George* and his Government; and in 1715, by a Royal Commission, at their own Expence raised and maintain'd a Regiment in Defence of our Establishment; when those, who then called themselves Friends *to the true Interests of their Country*, were engaged in *a very different way of thinking and acting.* These new Patrons of Liberty and Property, will surely be *afraid to act on* such Principles, tho' not *asham'd to profess them.*

They also tell us, that *the great Concourse was not more remarkable, than the real Order and Decency observed by People of all Ranks; and that there was no other Cry heard, than what* (say they) *is the universal Voice of the People throughout the Kingdom, No Excise, Liberty and Property.*

The great Concourse was, indeed, very remarkable, considering the Time, the Midst of the Harvest, and the *Occasion* a *Horse Race*; above two Thirds of the Number being Farmers and Tenants, would gladly have been excused, but come they must, and *No Excise, Liberty and Property* was the Cry they eccho'd to their Leaders; but this was not the only Cry, nor is it the *universal Voice of the People.* All faithful Subjects abhor the Cry; and thankfully acknowledge the many great Blessings they enjoy under his Majesty's Government, by which *Liberty* and *Property* are secured to us and our Posterity.

But why is *no Excise* tacked to *Liberty* and *Property*? Why, to express *their Gratitude at the Sight of those worthy Patriots, who have ever opposed any Invasion of them, by an Extension of the Excise-Scheme.* If this Reasoning be good, every Addition to the Excise from the Days of K. *Charles* was an Invasion of Liberty and Property; and these *worthy Patriots* have not *ever* opposed such Invasion, but have voted for the Extension of *Excise Laws* in several Instances. How comes it to be more dangerous now than formerly? Really it is not; if we consider that by this Scheme, two Thirds more than what is now paid would be raised, without increasing the Price to the Buyer, or requiring of the Seller more than what he was before to pay.

The Circular Letter Writer of *Chester* assures us, that popular Discontents, not founded in Reason, will soon subside: He and his Friends will soon find this true; for they are hardly able to raise by their Arguments and Ale, even from their own Dependants, a faint Huzza! upon the Credit of their *No Excise.*

Let them not deceive themselves; we know who is at the Head of this pretended Patriotism, a wretched Politician. as he owns himself, in a Letter to Mr *Prior. Dear Matt,* says *Bolingbroke, hide the Nakedness of thy Country; we are as wretchedPoliticians, as theFrench arePoets*

Free Briton, Dec. 20. No. 216.

Against the Craftsman, Dec. 8.

INfinitely abusive is this *Craftsman* with Relation to a *Great Person* in his Majesty's Service; but the Invective will wound no Man but the *Author* of it, to whose Character it may most of it be apply'd. This *Great Minister* hath had the Fate of all Ministers, and his elevated *Station may perhaps have turned Envy into Hatred.* (See p. 637 B) But as a *private Man*, he hath hardly had an Enemy, and as a publick Minister hath had *more personal* Friends, than any Man in Power was ever blest with before him. And if among any Part of the People his *Measures* or his Person have not been approved, it must have been owing to'their Ignorance of both.

The *Craftsman* insists that " publick *Odium* is an Evidence of *Guilt*; that the *unanimous Consent* of Mankind hath always been admitted as an *unquestionable* Proof of the most *awful Truth*, and can never be totally or in any *great Degree* groundless." This is no more true, than *universal Consent* is a Proof of the *Truth* of *Popery* and *Mahometanism.*

I am so far from finding the *popular Odium* to lie against the Administration, or against the *Great Person* at the Head of it, that, however divided we may have been on any *particular Points*, there are *few People* in *England* who wish † B—*ke*

---

† Walsingham *had in the beginning of this Paper given this Person's Character at large in publick and private Life; which we omitted here having in many Places touched on the Same.* See p. 584 G. 406 B. 547 F.

in

the Place of Sir R—t W—le, as there re that a *Popish Pretender* should fit n the Throne of this Kingdom. *Power* nd *Favour* will always be *invidious*, or can a Minister, who hath possessed em 13 Years, escape the common Share f *Obloquy and Ill-Usage*. But he hath he Blessing of a *Competitor*, who, without either Power or Favour, is *universally odious*, tho' it is near 20 Years since he ath been the Dread or Envy of any Man. As to what the *Craftsman* says of a *rince* hated by the People, an unpopular *ueen*, and a *first Minister* hated as a cing inconsistent with the Liberties of ny Country, *W.* answers, That when the *Minister* is not only struck at, but the *King, Queen,* and the *whole Royal Family* are alike *Objects of Abuse*, there is en less Reason to fear the Success of at Mischief and Malice, which disappoints itself, by discovering the Extent f its *infamous* Views: And a *Minister*, *hose* Enemies *speak to the Throne in his Language*, will never be sorry, that ey are *his Enemies*; but will know, hat *they* and he must *hate* each other ith the same *Constancy*, as he preserves is *faithful Duty*, or they persist in their *vicked Views* and Designs.

Universal Spectator, Dec. 22. No. 272.

The Town Gentleman.

I Am a young Fellow of a good Family, and Heir to a good Fortune, nt up by my Father to one of the *Inns f Court* for *Education*. The early Impressions of *Virtue* he instill'd into me, aade him think he might trust me with n extraordinary Allowance, and enjoin'd e, so to accomplish myself in *polite ompany*, that I might keep up the redit of my *Family*. But to my Surize I found that the *Town Language* vas very different from the *Ideas* I had orm'd of *polite Company* and *Men of igure*, who, I was soon instructed, were hose with a *glaring Equipage*, a well ancied *Dress* and *Trimming*, a *genteel ortune*, or even a *genteel Appearance*; hat their *Polite Company*, were such as ad a *Taste* for the *Entertainments* of the own, the *Assemblies, Operas, Plays, Masquerade, Quadrille,* and *Hazard*; ncluding those who had a *humorous 'alent* of laughing at every Thing that s *serious*, or pedantically bore the Appearance of *Learning*. As I found myelf generally deceiv'd in my Acquain-

tance, I began to forbear their Company. They perceiv'd my *Reservedness*, and a-greed to laugh me out of it, and endeavour'd to seduce me from my *Manners* and *Morals*, as the only Method to attach me to *Politeness*. I am now the common *Mark* of their *Raillery*, and Topick of their *Wit*; they sneer at my *Sobriety* as *unbecoming* a *Gentleman*, and my *Deference* to *Religion* as an *unfashionable Foible*. Tho' I have arm'd myself with as much *Philosophy* as I was Master of, yet their repeated *sarcastical Witticisms* have given me some Uneasiness.

R. G.

Mr *Stonecastle*, in his Remarks on the foregoing Letter, says, Nothing has more extinguish'd the Virtuous Principles in the Minds of young Gentlemen, than their Incapacity of bearing a *Jest*. The bashful Youth, not having Philosophy enough to disregard repeated Raillery, or the Imputation of *Scandal*, becomes *fashionably vicious*, rather than be esteem'd *unpolitely innocent*. The Calumny and Satire of an immoral Man should be look'd on as an Honour to ourselves, and which all good and wise Men will esteem so. Thus thought *Socrates*, when in the publick Theatre he receiv'd the *universal Hiss* of his *Fellow Citizens*. The *Constancy* he then shew'd should be an Example to those who would be thought *wife*, or at least *prudent*; for no Commendation is so free from Flattery as the Detestation of a *wicked Man*.

Fog's Journal, Dec. 22. No. 268.

Mr Fog,

I T's our Misfortune, that the same malignant Party that lately deprived us of the Benefit of the new Excise, being possessed with the same lying Spirit, have industriously spread divers Rumours of Wars in *Europe*, to the great Discredit of the many wise Treaties made by our Ministers, the Disturbance of the Quiet of many of his Majesty's good People, and a Loss of above twelve Millions of their Estates in the Funds. Therefore I thought it proper to remove those Fears by recommending a Piece published upon the Subject of the Peace of *Seville*, entitled, *The natural Probability of a lasting Peace in Europe,* &c. 1732. in which the Author bestows many Encomiums on the happy Situation at that Time of Affairs both at Home and Abroad, and presages a long Tranquillity to this Nation and to the

the reſt of *Europe*; happily effected by the Management of the *Engliſh* Miniſtry.

If any Man is ſo mad to prefer the Credit of a Parcel of lying News-papers to this miniſterial Declaration, let him periſh in his Folly. Upon the Faith of this Prediction I bought *India* Stock at 196, and will not part with a Groat of it, till it riſe again by the Diſſipation of theſe falſe Reports. Becauſe, if we add the Veracity of the Miniſters of a certain Nation to their Judgment, this Prediction muſt ſtill appear to be the more relied on; nor has their Induſtry been leſs than their Sagacity; they have bound *Europe* to Peace by Multitudes of Treaties, as by ſo many Cords of Love, that if one ſhould give way, another might hold. Did they not ſtrengthen the Treaty of *Utrecht* by that of *Hanover*, to ſupport the languiſhing State of F——, againſt the exorbitant Power of *A——a*? When the Treaty of *Hanover* gave Way, was it not fortified by that of *Seville*; if that of *Seville* ſhould fail, that of *Hanover* muſt hold; and if all ſhould prove too weak, I don't queſtion but they have a new one ready twiſted to ſupply the Place of all the reſt. Nor have they been leſs careful to compoſe Differences among their Neighbours. Who reconciled *France* and *Spain*; and behold the comfortable Fruits of their Labour, *Europe* having nothing to fear from the formidable Conjunction of *Spain*, and the Houſe of *Auſtria*? Has not B—— behaved herſelf peaceably to all her Neighbours? Has ſhe not *taken patiently the ſpoiling of her Goods?* Her coſtly Fleets and Armies have never terrified her Neighbours. Her capital Ships have ſerved as Tenders to the *Sp*— Navy to increaſe the Pomp of D—— C—— Entry into *Italy*. And what Return has ſhe demanded or accepted, except a Picture ſet with Diamonds to the Admiral? From all which 'tis plain, that the Prediction of our *Engliſh Machiavel* muſt be true; and tho' ſome may aſſert, there is at preſent War on the Continent, I defy any Man to ſhew there has been any Battle, or even an Army or Encampment on the contrary ſide: For War without Reſiſtance I take to be a Contradiction.

The **Craftſman,** Dec. 22; No. 389.

On Parties; continued from p. 632.

IF *Charles* II. could have been prevailed upon to ſacrifice the chimerical di-

vine Right of his *Brother* to the real Intereſt and Right of his *People*, it would have made him ample amends in future Eaſe and Quiet, and the Nation in future Security. But he reſolved not to do it, and the Meaſures taken to force him, enabled him to reſiſt. The *oppoſite Spirit* ſpent itſelf in Blood and Violence. The *Spirit for him* roſe viſibly in the Nation. And he ſaw the Time approaching when he might appeal to his *People* againſt his *Parliament*. This Time was come, when Men were once convinced that a *Country Party* prevail'd no longer, but that *Faction* had taken its Place. Many Appearances ſerved to propagate this Opinion; particularly the almoſt avowed Pretenſions of the D. of *Monmouth,* carried on even in Defiance of the moſt ſolemn Declaration made by the King, *That be bad never married his Mother.*

Some of the worthieſt and warmeſt Men for the *Excluſion,* complained from the firſt, of the private Intereſts and factious Intrigues amongſt them. *I muſt confeſs,* (ſays a *conſiderable Man,* who laid down his Life for the Cauſe afterwards) *I do not know three Men of a Mind. Some look who is fitteſt to ſucceed. They are for the moſt part divided between the Prince of* Orange, *and the D. of* Monmouth. *The firſt hath plainly the moſt plauſible Title. The ſtrongeſt Reaſons for* Monmouth *are, that whoever is oppoſed to* York *will have a good Party; and all* Scotland *certainly favours him, and is ready to take Arms.*

Here aroſe another Motive for the Diviſion and Animoſity of Parties. The *Tories,* apprehended that the *oppoſite Party* might ſucceed in ſetting up a *King of their own Nomination.* A Notion then entertain'd by many, *that the worſe Title a Man had, the better King he was likely to make,* did not perſwade them. They had ſuffered under the *Tyranny of a Party;* and they fear'd a *Party-King.* Thus the D. of *York* gain'd Adherents, not by Affection to him, but by an Averſion to *Monmouth,* which increaſ'd among the *Tories* (thro' Jealouſy, ſays Bp *Burnet*) in Proportion as his Popularity increaſed among the *Whigs.*

I ſay nothing of the Apprehenſions on one Side, and the Expectations of the other, from *Scotland*; becauſe, tho' there was from the Beginning a Concert between thoſe who were oppreſſed by the *Court* there, and thoſe who oppoſed it here; yet the ſeditious Spirit, that occaſion'd theſe Apprehenſions and Expectations

:ations, was roufed and exafperated by the Inhumanity of the D. of *Lauderdale*, who, though a *Presbyterian* himfelf, was he Butcher of that *Party* ; pufh'd the warmeft of them into unjuftifiable Ex- :effes ; revived their filly Zeal for the *Covenant* ; and wrought up their Enthu- iafm to *Affaffination* and *Rebellion*. This was the Fault of the *Court*, and could not be imputed to the *Whigs*. The Violence of the *Conventiclers* was founded high to palliate the Severities exercifed in the Government of *that Kingdom*. But the reafonable Men of all Parties thought then, as they always will, that it is the Duty of thofe who govern, to difcern *the Spirit of the People*, and to confider their *Paffions, Weakneffes*, and *Prejudices* ; they who punifh what they might prevent, are more culpable than the *Offenders*.

As the *two Parties* were form'd, fo was their Divifion maintained, by mutual Jea- oufies and Fears. The moft improbable; Reports, carried about in Whifpers, were enough to raife a *Terror* in *one Party*, or he *other*. Thefe were improved by fre- quent Repetition, to raife the Alarm and Hatred of *Parties* to the higheft Pitch. He that endeavoured to lay the Ferment was called a *Trimmer* ; and he, who was a common Friend was treated as a com- mon Enemy. Some who voted *for the Bill of Exclufion*, were not heartily for it; and thofe who voted againft it, and declar'd for *Limitations* concurred in the End; though, they differed in the *Means*, with- thofe who promoted the *Bill* ; yet they were marked out as *Favourers of Popery*, and *Enemies to their Country*. Thus, in the *other* Party, Men, who had no other View but to fecure their *Religion* and *Li- berty*, and to force the *Court* into reafon- able Compliances, were ftigmatiz'd as *Fanaticks* and *Republicans*. And thus it is at prefent, when any Man, who de- clares againft a *certain Perfon*, againft whom the Voice of the Nation hath al- ready declared, or complains of Things fo notorious, that no Body can deny them, is followed with the Cry of *Jacobitifm* or *Republicanifm*. But there's a great Dif- ference between the *two Cafes*. The *prefent Cry* being void of *Pretence*, is without *Effect*. It is heard in *few Places*, and believ'd only in *one*.

When the Nation was thus divided, the *oppofite Principles*, advanced by the two Parties, were carried higher, as they grew more inflamed, the Meafures they purfued to get the better of each other

were equally dangerous. The Meeting of the Parliament at *Oxford* had a Kind of hoftile Appearance ; and as foon as *Parliaments were laid afide*, which hap- pened on the fudden Diffolution of this, the Appearance grew worfe. No Secu- rity having been obtain'd, by *Parliamen- tary Methods*, againft the Dangers of a *Popifh Succeffor, Methods* of *another Kind*, fuch as extreme Neceffity fuggefted, were thought on, and happily purfued, when *this Succeffion* had taken Place, and jufti- fied all that had been faid againft it ; when the Nation was ripe for *Refiftance*, and the Prince of *Orange* ready and able to fupport fo great an Enterprize. But the Attempts which were wife at *one Time*, would have been defperate at the *other* ; and the Meafures, which produced a *Re- volution*, in the Reign of K. *James*, would have produced, in the Reign of K. *Charles*, a *civil War* of uncertain Event at beft ; What was projected in 1670, would have been effected ; and the Religion and Li- berty of *Great-Britain* would have been deftroy'd by Confequence. 'Tis hard to fay how far the Hands of Party had gone into Meafures for employing *Force*. Per- haps little more had paffed than rafh Difcourfe about dangerous and indigefted Schemes : But the *Court*, who wanted a *Plot* to confirm and increafe their *Party*, took the firft Opportunity of having one, furnifhed by the imprudent but honeft Zeal of *fome* ; and by the Villainy and Madnefs of *others* ; and they profecuted it fo feverely, with the Help of *forward Sheriffs, willing Juries, bold Witneffes*, and *mercenary Judges*, that it anfwered all their Ends. The Defign of affaffinat- ing the *King* and the *Duke* was certain- ly confined to a few defperate Villains ; *but too many had heard of it from them, who were both fo foolifh and fo wicked, as not to difcover them*, fays *Burnet*.

As this *Event* difpirited and broke *one Party*, fo it ftrengthen'd and united the *other*. The *Tories* were now con- firmed in their Prejudices againft the *Whigs*, and run headlong into all the Meafures taken for *enlarging the King's Authority*, and *fecuring the Crown to the* D. of York. The Principles of *divine hereditary Right, Paffive Obedience*, and *Non-Refiftance*, were revived and pro- pagated with greater Zeal than ever, e- ven by learned and reverend Bodies of *Men*, who little thought that in 5 Years Time, that is, in 1688, they fhould act conformably to fome of the very *Propo- fitions*,

K k k k

sitions, which at this Time they declared *false*, *seditions*, and *impious*.

In short, the *Guelphs* and *Gibelines* were never more animated against each other, than the *Tories* and *Whigs* at this Time; and in such a national Temper, considerable Steps were made towards the Destruction of our Constitution. One of those Steps, which *Rapin* gravely enumerates, would make one smile, *viz. The King, in order to make his People feel the Slavery he had newly imposed upon them, affected to review his* Troops, *which amounted, by the Return of the Garrison of* Tangier, *to* 4000 *Men.* † The *Whigs* were then so averse to *standing Armies*, that they thought even those Troops, called *Guards*, unlawful. But the *Tories*, who had shewn their Dislike of *standing Armies* in the *long Parliament*, might think it however no unreasonable Thing, when *Insurrections* and Designs of *Assassinations* were so lately come to Light, that a Number of *regular Troops*, tho' five Times less than we have since seen kept up in the Midst of the most secure Tranquillity, should be wink'd at, *till these Distempers* were over.

But that which laid the Ax to the Root of our Liberties was, by giving the Crown *such an Influence over Election of Members to serve in Parliament*, as could not fail to destroy that *Independency*, by which alone the Freedom of our Government is supported. The Proceedings by *Quo Warranto*, and other Methods, to force or persuade Corporations to surrender their old *Charters*, and accept *new ones*, were violent, arbitrary, and scandalous. But still it was the *Consequence* that terrify'd

† *The* Craftsman *misquotes this Passage to make Room for a Sneer at* Rapin, *whose Words are,* "*To make the People in some Measure fully sensible of their new Slavery, the* King *affected to muster his Forces, which, with one Regiment of Foot, and one Troop of Horse*—raised *by himself, with the Murmurs of Numbers of his Subjects* — *now amounted to* 4000 *well armed and disciplin'd Men.*" *It was not the Number, but the King's raising Troops himself, that the* Whigs *were averse to, and thought unlawful; and which the* Tories, *running headlong to enlarge the King's Authority, did not think unreasonable. What Forces we have since kept up have been by Parliamentary Authority, and found necessary from Experience.*

Daily Cour. Dec. 26.

those who had not sold themselves to the *Court*, nor lost all Regard for their *Country*, more than the *Means* employed upon that Occasion. It was reasonable for the *Friends of Liberty* to expect that Men who had been injured, should seek Relief on the first Opportunity. But if they had been *corrupted*, and the Practice of *selling Elections* had been established, the Friends of Liberty would have thought the Case more desperate and provoking. It is certainly less dangerous to struggle with a *great Prince* who stands on *Prerogative*, than with a *weak* but *profligate Minister*, if he hath the Means of *Corruption* in his Power. But it was *Prerogative*, not *Money*, that had like to have destroy'd our *Liberties* then. Government was not then carried on by *Undertakers*, to whom so much *Power* was entrusted for Return of so much *Money*.

Garbling Corporations to strengthen their *Party*, in favour of the *Crown*, hath been objected to these *Tories*; but if some who reproach them therewith, have since shared in the more dangerous Practice of *corrupting* Corporations; such Men have Fronts of Brass, and deserve all the Indignation due to Iniquity aggravated by Impudence.

In short, the Conduct of both Parties were liable to Blame: The *Tories* acted on the most abject *Principles of Submission to the King*, and for the Succession of a Prince whose Bigotry rendered him unfit to rule a *Protestant*, *free People.* —— The *Whigs* maintain'd the *Power of Parliament to limit the Succession to the Crown*, and avowed the *Principle of Resistance*; in which they had *Law*, *Example*, and *Reason* for them. But then the Fury of *Faction* was for doing that without *Parliament*, which could be only done *by it*; and their Leaders acted in an extravagant *Spirit of Licence*, rather than a *Spirit of Liberty*.

London Journal. Dec 22. No. 756.

ALgernon Sidney, of immortal Memory, who suffer'd for Writings he never publish'd, containing a Doctrine to which the whole *Nation* hath since borne Testimony, alledges it in his Speech at his Execution, for an undeniable Proof of the Innocence of his Writings, *That nothing of particular Application unto Time, Place, or Person, could be found in them*; as he observes had ever been done by those who endeavoured to raise Insurrections. Particular *Application* is, indeed,

indeed, the Characteriſtick of an Incendiary; for thus Propoſitions of *general Truth* may become *treaſonable*; and ſuch a Writer as the Author of the *Review* may quote Blaſphemy from the Bible.

There could not be a greater Indignity offered to the Memory of Mr *Locke*, than to apply the Paſſages this Writer quotes from him, to the Affair of *Exciſes*: For Mr *Locke* lived when they were firſt introduced, and ſaw them extended to vaſt Multitude of Traders; yet he never diſcovered, that theſe were *wicked Schemes*, and was ſo far from thinking the *Exciſe-Laws* an *Infringement* of the Conſtitution, that he was for many Years a *Commiſſioner of Appeals*, without any Suſpicion of ſerving the Purpoſes of *arbitrary Power*; unleſs he can be ſuppoſed to reſemble a Friend of the *Reviewer's*, the forwardeſt Inſtrument of *Power* in Employment, and the buſieſt Tool of *Faction* in Diſgrace.

A Writer, form'd by reading Mr *Locke*, would have been reſtrain'd by *Truth, Duty,* and *Decency*, from anſwering this Queſtion, *If this Nation was not in every Inſtance govern'd by Law? That it would be hard to prove that Tiberius ever broke any Law in his Publick Acts, nor needed, when he had a Senate, that made and paſſed Sentences by Law, according to his Pleaſure* —— and think himſelf excuſed by adding, *This is not our Caſe at preſent.* As if he imagined his Readers below a *Playhouſe Audience*, who never want to be inſtructed what *Anthony* is doing, tho' he adds, Brutus *is an honourable Man.*

A Writer who had imbibed from Mr *Locke, true Principles of Liberty,* would have been as careful not to *violate* that of another, as to preſerve his own, much leſs would he reproach the King's Judgment in the Choice of his Miniſters. As to what is ſaid of the Miniſter's being of a mean and abject Spirit, and in Fear of his Perſon, the *Reviewer* contradicts himſelf, and aſſures us, "That the *Diſlike* and *Reſentment* of the *Populace*, were ſo far from *altering* his Purpoſe, that they ſeemed to *add new Vigour* to him"; and I have been told by a *noble Perſon*, and one not *partial* to him, who was in the Houſe the Day the Bill was drop'd, *when there was a ſtrong Probability, nay almoſt a Certainty, that the Bill would be thrown out in ſuch a Manner as might have the worſt Conſequence to him*; He then appeared, without any Confuſion of *Guilt* or *Fear*; and in the hardeſt Conjuncture, that perhaps ever a *great Miniſter* was expoſed to, preſerved his Wits enough, even by the *Confeſſion of the Reviewer*, to expatiate *very largely on the Advantages of it*, and to furniſh him with the *moſt lively Expedient* with regard to it. And if from his *Obſervation* of the *general Reſentment* of thoſe *without Doors*, and his *particular Knowledge* of the Sentiments of ſome within, he could not be without *ſome Apprehenſions*; yet he made it appear, he had too much *Spirit* to ſink under his Fears, and too much *Wiſdom* to give his Enemies any Encouragement by *diſcovering them.*

§ *Fog* having aſſerted (*See* p. 643 A) that a Pamphlet, entitled, *Reaſons for continuing the preſent Parliament*, was wrote in Defence of a great *Projector*, and had been diſperſed in the Country by *Poſtmaſters*, and *Exciſemen*, *Oſborne* anſwers, I have enquired at the *Poſt-Office*, and the *Comptroller* aſſures me, *There never was one of theſe Pamphlets at the Office*; that *he never ſent one of 'em away, nor was ever ask'd to ſend them away*; and that the Piece was wrote by the moſt bitter Enemy to the Miniſtry, who are ready to ſubmit their Conduct; therefore do not fear a new Parliament.

Weekly Miſcellany. Dec. 22. & 29.

Remarks on the Hiſtory of the Puritans.

IN the Preface to this Hiſtory Mr *Neal* tells us, that *the Controverſy that gave Riſe to the* Separation *began in* K. Edward VI's *Reign, on Occaſion of Biſhop Hooper's refuſing to be conſecrated in the* Popiſh Habits. This Reflection is to poſſeſs the Reader, the *Habits* uſed by the *Biſhops* and *Prieſts* of the Church of England are *Popiſh Veſtments*. But the Matter of Fact is thus: In the *Roman Pontifical* the Epiſcopal Habit mentioned is, *Sandals*, an *Amict*, *Alb*, *Surcingle*, a *Stole Pectoral Croſs*, a *Tunicle*, *Dalmatic*, *Gloves*, a *Planet*, a *Mitre* gilt on the Edges, a *Pontifical Ring*, *Paſtoral Ring*, *Paſtoral Staff*, *Maniple*, and *Pluvial*. All theſe Veſtments are order'd to be ſolemnly bleſſed or conſecrated, by being croſſed, or ſprinkled with Holy-Water, and a Prayer ſaid over them for the Deſcent of the Holy Ghoſt upon them, to impart to them a myſtick Virtue, and ſecret Power.

But now, the Liturgy and Communion Office, and *Form of Ordaining Biſhops* having being reform'd, no Habits were retain'd, but a *plain Surplice* and *Cope*, and even theſe not to be bleſſed or conſecrated.

Gg

On *May* 15. 1550, Dr *Hooper* was consecrated Bp of *Gloucester* in a *Surplice* and *Cope* as Habits of Distinction only. As for the long Scarlet Chimere worn over the Linnen Rochet, and the Square Cap; he scrupled the Wearing them, as they were not requir'd by this Order, and only an Academical Habit worn by Doctors of Divinity. In this Form was inserted the Oath of Supremacy, enacted 28 *Hen.* VIII. which concluded thus; *So help me God, all Saints, and the Holy Evangelists.* This *Hooper* scrupled as offending the third Commandment, and as an Argument of Impiety, and of false Belief in swearing by any Creatures.

Mr *N——* adds, that *the Habits retained by the reform'd Ordinal, were the* known Badges of Popery, and *he is afraid that* at this Day *many both of the* Clergy *and* Common People *are too inclinable to apprehend, that the* Administration of the *Priests receive their Validity, from the* consecrated Vestments.

Had Mr *N——* ever seen a Priest dressed in his Mass-Habit, he could never think a *plain Surplice* or *Rochet*, a Badge of *Popery*. 'Tis as plain there are no *Vestments consecrated* in the Church of *England*; nor is there any special Worthiness attributed to them.

Mr *N——* further observes, that the Queen (*Elizabeth*) *having conceived a strong Aversion to the* Puritans——*erected a new Tribunal called the* Court of High Commission. This seems contrary to Fact; even according to Mr *N——* himself, who informs us, that the first High Commission *was given out about* Midsummer 1559, when no such Distinction as *Puritans* was amongst us, nor did they appear as a Party till 5 Years after. Very different Accounts from this of Mr *N——* are also given by *Rapin* and *Stillingfleet.*

Mr *N——* should likewise have distinguish'd between the Orthodox, peaceable Puritans, and the erroneous and factious Ones, as Bp *Andrews* has done in his Account of them to Card. *Bellarmine.*

A *Puritan*, says Mr *N.* was *a Man of severe Morals, a Calvinist in Doctrine, and a Nonconformist to the Ceremonies and Discipline of the Church*, and refers to Dr. *Fuller* for this Character; but that Writer is so far from confirming it, that he divides them into *two* Ranks, the *mild* and *moderate*, and the *fierce* and *fiery*; and gives Instances in the Behaviour of some of the latter sort, who were guilty of Clamour and Evil-speaking and Disrespect to the Queen and her Ministers.

Grubstreet Journal, Dec. 27. No. 209.

On *Christmas Pye.*

Mr Bavius,

IT's natural to delight in talking of that one loves; you will therefore the less wonder at my sending you an Essay on Christmas Pye; tho' indeed, it falls properly under Female Oeconomy.

I need not say any thing of its grateful Flavour, which is so well known; but it seems surprizing there should be such a thing as a Fricasee, or Ragout in the Kingdom; and that we should be so foolishly fond of Fashions, as to imitate the Cookery of a fantastical Nation, whose natural Scarcity of Provisions puts them upon tossing up the little they have an hundred Ways.

In the Crust may be observed the Regularity of the Figures into which it is usually raised; which seem to owe their Original to the martial Genius of our Nation. The Rules of military Architecture are observed, and each of them would serve for the Model of a Fortification. It might have been antiently the Amusement of our Heroic *British* Ladies, while their Spouses and Lovers were engaging their Enemies abroad, to describe in Paste the Draughts of the Towns and Castles besieged, to have the Pleasure of storming them in Effigy.

That this Dish is most in Vogue at this Time of Year, some think is owing to the Barrenness of the Season, and the Scarcity of Fruit and Milk, to make Tarts, Custards, and other Desserts, this being a Compound that furnishes a Dessert itself.

But I rather think it bears a religious kind of Relation to the Festivity from which it takes its Name. Our Tables are always set out with this Dish just at the Time, and probable for the same Reason, that our Windows are adorned with Ivy. I am the more confirm'd in this Opinion, from the Zealous Opposition it meets with from the Quakers, who distinguish their Feasts by an heretical Sort of Pudding, known by their Name, and inveigh against Christmas Pye, as an Invention of the Scarlet Whore of *Babylon*, an Hodge-Podge of Superstition, Popery, the Devil and all his Works.

Another Sort of People who deserve Reproof are those who indulge themselves in this excellent Food, but would cut out the Clergy from having any Share in it, under Pretence that a sweet Tooth and liquorish Palate, are inconsistent with the Sanctity anûity of their Charaûer. Againſt ſuch he famous *Bickerſtaff* roſe up, and with becoming Zeal defended the Chaplains f Noblemen in particular, and the Cler-y in general. *The Chriſtmas-Pye*, ſays 1e, *is in its own Nature, a kind of con-ecrated Cake, and a Badge of Diſtinc-ion ; and yet 'tis often forbidden to the Druid of the Family. Strange! that a Sirloin of Beef, whether boiled or roaſted, when entire, is expoſed to his utmoſt De-wredations and Inciſions ; but if minced into ſmall Pieces, and toſſed up with Plumbs and Sugar, changes its Property, and forſooth, is Meat for his Maſter.*

This muſt be allow'd unfair Treatment. But if in the Compoſition the Neat's Tongue be uſed inſtead of the Sirloin, and if that Part of our Bodies receives a greater Proportion of the Nutriment, which anſwers to that Part of the Crea-ture whereof we eat, then this Sort of Food is the propereſt in the World for the Clergy, as it muſt be a Strengthner of the great Inſtrument of Speech, the Vo-lubility of whoſe Motion is of the grea-teſt Conſequence both to themſelves and the Publick ; but when improved with Plumbs, &c. it muſt ſweeten the Speech into the moſt perſwaſive Eloquence.

Now, if the Ladies think I have inva-ded their Province, they may take their Revenge of me, and bring my Diſſerta-tion nearer to its Subjeû, by putting it under the next Chriſtmas-Pye they make.

PHILO-CLERICUS.

The **Free Briton**, Dec. 27. No. 217.

THE *Writer* of the *Craftſman* ſup-poſes (See p. 637 A) that an *honeſt uncorrupt* Miniſter *unjuſtly* hated would withdraw from his publick Station, and chuſe to be the *Viûim* even of *publick Injuſtice*, rather than live the Objeû of *groundleſs Reproach*.] This is ſuch an abſurd and illogical Inference, that I be-lieve no Man would inſiſt that a Miniſter ought to *withdraw from his Duty*, on Account of *unreaſonable Clamour*, but one who actually *withdrew from his Trial*, on Account of too *juſt* an Im-peachment. An *honeſt* Miniſter who is *hated only* becauſe he is *envied*, muſt know, that it would be no Service to his Sovereign, to *withdraw* from his Councils while he can be of any Ad-vantage to them. Much leſs could he think of *reſigning* in Favour of *thoſe* who are far from *deſerving* the Charac-ters of *honeſt* Men. Nor can ſuch a Mi-niſter be hated long, by any formidable

Part of the People, if he perſiſt in his Duty, and prove as *firm* as he hath al-ways been *juſt*.

From the preſent Miniſtry *no Damage* to the People is to be feared. Under any new Miniſters *all muſt be uncertain*. But if *B——ke* is to be the *Miniſter*, which is the ſole Tendency of all the *Calumny* publiſhed againſt the *honourable Perſon* at preſent in that Station, what *Crimes muſt we cancel?* But how much more *reaſonable* will it be to reſt content with the preſent *Adminiſtration*, to forget our late *unhappy Diviſions*, and to embrace and adhere to thoſe, by whom in Reality we have never been injured?

The **Craftſman**, Dec. 29. N° 391.

Continued from p. 650.

Every *clumſy, buſy, bungling Child of Fortune* may govern ſafely by *corrupting a People*, but every Charaûer is not fit to do it by *dividing* them.

THO' the Deſigns of K. *Charles* II. were neither deeply laid, nor deep-ly fixed in his own Mind ; yet in gene-ral they were founded on *bad Principles*, and directed to *bad Ends*. He deſired indeed to be eaſy, and to make his Peo-ple ſo ; but on Conditions inconſiſtent with good Government. We have ſeen how the *Whigs* weaken'd their *own Party* and gave Strength and Provocation to the *other*. But there were other Advantages, without which theſe Diviſions could neither have been fomented nor ſupport-ed. Theſe Advantages aroſe chiefly from the Charaûer and Conduû of the *King*.

The *Engliſh* Nation was not then *cor-rupted*. Parties there were ; ſome run in-to ſeditious Praûices, others into the vileſt Submiſſion, but ſtill the *Spirit of Liberty* remained in many. We were then properly *Freemen*, becauſe not only the *Laws* aſſerting our Rights were maintain-ed and improved ; but alſo *private Inde-pendency* which can alone ſupport *Publick Liberty*. Such a People, as we then were, could neither be *bought* nor *driven* ; and I think K. *Charles* could not have *divid-ed* and *led* them, if he had wanted any of the Qualities he poſſeſſed, or had held another Conduû. Sir *William Temple* ſays, *He had not a Grain of Pride, or Vanity in his whole Compoſition*; but was the moſt affable, beſt bred Man alive. He treated his Subjeûs like *Noblemen*, like *Gentlemen*, like *Freemen*, not like *Vaſſals*, or *Boors*. Whatever Notion he had of *hereditary Right*, he owned his Obligation for the Crown to his *People*, as much

much as if he had stood at the greatest Distance in the Lineal Succession, and been called to it from the low State, in which he was before, by the free Gift and Choice of the Nation. His Professions were plausible, and his whole Behaviour engaging; so that he won upon the Hearts, even whilst he lost the good Opinion of his Subjects. Further, he observed the Temper of his People, and complied with it. He gave up to the Murmurs of his People, not one *or two such Ministers* as may be found almost behind every Desk, but several *great* and *able Men*, nay *whole Cabals of such*, who had Merit with Him, tho' they had none with the *Nation*. He started often out of the true Interest of the People, but their Voice almost as often reclaimed him. He made the *first Dutch War*, but he made the *Triple Alliance* too. He engaged with *France* in the War of 1672, but he made a separate Peace with *Holland*. True, indeed, neither his *Parliament* nor *People*, could prevail on him to enter in earnest into the War against *France*. But there was then no mutual Confidence between him and his Parliament. And in *home Affairs*, besides his frequent Concessions, he passed the *Test* and *Habeas Corpus Bills*, and many others for the publick Benefit; and scarce any *popular Act* stopped at the Throne, except That about the *Militia*, which he apprehended an Encroachment on the *Prerogative*, and one another in Favour of the *Dissenters*, which was contrived, meanly enough, to be stolen off the Table in the *House of Lords*.

What has been said will be sufficient to shew, how King *Charles* was enabled to *divide a Nation* so united and heated as this Nation was, on the Discovery of the *Popish Plot*, to oppose so resolutely the *Exclusion of his Brother*, and yet to attach so numerous a Party to *himself*, nay to his *Brother*; to lay aside Parliaments for several Years; and not only to stand his Ground, but to gain Ground at the same Time. Another thing is, he not only prepared for the Storm, but acquir'd Strength in the midst of it. He would gladly have kept the *Popish Plot* out of Parliament, but when it was once there, he put on the Appearances of great Zeal for the Prosecution of it. These Appearances help'd him to screen his *Brother*, as the ill Success of the *Exclusion Bill* in the *House of Lords*, where it was rejected by 63 against 30, helped to screen himself from the Violence of the *House*

of *Commons*. But that which gave him the principal Advantage was, his declaring in a *Speech* to his Parliament his Readiness to pass any Bills to make his People safe in the Reign of his *Successor*, *so they tended not to impeach the Right of Succession, nor the Descent of the Crown in the true Line*. Tho' he persisted in this Declaration, and refused what his *Parliament* press'd on him in the *Manner* and on the *Principle* they pressed it; yet his *Refusal* was follow'd by *Expedients*; which varied the *Manner*, and yet might have been managed so as to produce the *Effect*. Numbers avowed the *Principle*; and the *Tests* made many Persons think *Religion* safe; as the *King's Offers* made them think is was no Fault of his, if it was not made safer.

The *Council* had prepared *some Expedients*; and the *Limitations*, and other *Provisions* against a *Popish Successor*, proposed directly from the Throne by the *Chancellor*, in 1679, went a great way towards binding the Hands of *such a Successor*, and lodging the Power, taken from him, in the *Parliament*. But the Scheme of *Expedients* debated in the *Oxford* Parliament, was a real Exclusion from every Thing but the Title of *King*. The *first Article* banish'd the D. of *York*, during his Life, 500 Miles from *England*, *Scotland*, and *Ireland*; and the *tenth* excluded him *ipso facto*, if he came into any of these Kingdoms; and that the Sovereignty should vest forthwith in the *Regent*; that is, in the Princess of *Orange*. This Scheme, however liable to many Difficulties and Inconveniencies, was at this Time, the utmost that could be hoped for. But the Leaders of the *Whig* Party were resolved, says Bp *Burnet*, *to let all lie in Confusion, rather than to hearken to any Thing, besides the Exclusion*. The *Tory* Party grew as obstinate, and as furious, on their Side; and thus the Nation was deliver'd over, on the Death of K. *Charles*, to *the Folly and Madness of his Brother*, which however cured the *Folly* and *Madness of Party*. The common Danger approach'd, *Whig* and *Tory* felt Impressions of it alike, and both purged themselves, on that great Occasion, of the Imputation laid to their Charge by their *Adversaries*; that the real Distinction of the *two Parties* expired at this Æra; and though their Ghosts continued to haunt and divide us many Years afterwards, yet there neither is, nor can be any Division of *Parties* at this Time, reconcilable with common Sense

Senfe, and common Honefty, under the *prefent Conftitution*; except *Churchmen* and *Diffenters*; *Court* and *Country*.

The Behaviour and Conduct of King *James* II. would be fufficient to fhew, that as ftrong Prejudices are the Parents, fo a weak Underftanding is the Nurfe of Bigotry and Injuftice, and Violence and Cruelty its Offspring. He was above 50 when he came to the Throne. He had great *Experience*, efpecially of the Temper of the Nation, and the Impoffibility to attempt introducing *Popery*, without hazarding his Crown. But his *Experience* profited him not: He believed he could play Parties againft each other better than his Brother. He paffed for a fincere Man, and fpoke always with great Emphafis of the *Word of a King*; yet never was the meaneft Word fo fcandaloufly broken as his in the Debate in 1678, about the *Teft*; when he got a Provifoe put in for excufing himfelf. Bp *Burnet* affirms, that fpeaking with *great Earneftnefs, and with Tears in his Eyes, be folemnly profeffed, that whatever his Religion might be, it fhould only be a private Thing between God and his own Soul; and that no Effect of it fhould ever appear in the Government.*

At his Acceffion to the Throne, in Council firft, and after that, in *full Parliament*, he made the ftrongeft Declarations in Favour of the Conftitution in Church and State, and took the moft folemn Engagements to defend and fupport it. But *Bigotry* broke thro' all.— On the Complaifance of the Parliament, and the ill Succefs of the D. of *Monmouth*, and the E. of *Argyle*, he determined to pull off the Mask. *This Parliament*, according to Bp *Burnet*, *were neither Men of Parts nor Eftates.* 'Tis true, the Circumftances were fuch as might puzzle the Heads of the wifeft Men. They had more to lofe than Dr *Burnet*; and therefore proceeded deliberately: It's Impoffible to believe that their Confidence in the *King's Word* was fuch as they affected. But, like drowning Men, they caught at a Straw. And *Monmouth's* and *Argyle's* Expeditions were fo far from affording the Nation any Opportunity of mending their Condition, that they proved favourable in fome Refpects to the Defigns of K. *James*. They gave him the Pretence, which he feiz'd, of raifing, and keeping up a *ftanding Army*. But in the Event, they forwarded our Deliverance, by precipitating his Attempts a-

gainft our *Religion* and *Liberty*. The fame Day that the Invafion in *Scotland* was communicated to the *Parliament* here, the *Commons* voted him that great Revenue, which they gave him for Life. After thefe *Invafions* were over, they voted a Supply to maintain the *additional Forces*. They offered to pafs a Law for indemnifying his *Popifh* Officers from the Penalty they had incurred; and to capacitate *fuch others* as he fhould name in a Lift to be given to the Houfe; But would neither give him the whole fupply of 1200,000 *l.* which he asked, nor fanctify the Practice of keeping up a *ftanding Army in Time of Peace.* They would neither repeal the *Teft* and *Penal Laws*; nor fubmit to his *difpenfing* or *fufpending*, which was in Effect a *repealing Power.* Wherefore he quarrelled with them; loft the 700,000 *l.* they had voted rather than fuffer them to fit any longer; and never met them more.

Things haften'd to a Decifion. The King's Defigns were openly avowed, and defperately purfued. The Church of *England* oppofed them with Vigour. The *Diffenters* were cajoled by the Court, and became Abbettors of his Ufurpations. The *Revolution* foon followed. Many of the moft diftinguifh'd *Tories* were engaged in it. The *Whigs* were zealous in the fame Caufe, and they both coalited, but the latter did not fuffer the former to have any Influence in their Councils. The Caufe of *Liberty*, was no longer made the Caufe of a *Party*, and pufh'd in fuch a Manner, as *one Party* alone approved.

The *Revolution* was defign'd to reftore and fecure our whole Conftitution. Had the Leaven of Republicanifm in the *Whig* Party prevailed; or the *Tory* Party continued to be influenced by Popifh Councils, tho' averfe to Popery, the Coalition of Parties had been broken; but the Revolution was a Fire that purged off the Drofs of both Parties.

Fog's Journal. Dec. 29. contains a Paper of Advice to the Citizens of *Dublin*, recommending their late moft worthy Lord Mayor; whom accordingly they chofe, to be their Reprefentative. But we can't fee *Fog's* Defign in reprinting thefe ftale Irifh Papers, unlefs it be to draw a Parallel between that eminent Magiftrate, and one of this City, who fignaliz'd himfelf on a particular Occafion, and from thence to point him out to his Fellow Citizens as a proper Perfon to reprefent them in Parliament.

CHLOE

CHLOE SINGING: *Made at School.*

CEASE, charmer, cease, for pity urge no
　　more
The conquest that your eyes have gain'd before.
Thus doubly arm'd: Who can withstand the
　　flame?
Your face resistless, and your tongue the same.
If from your fatal beauty we wou'd fly;
Pursu'd, and taken by this charm, we dye.
Oh! then suppress th' attractive powerful noise,
And think we die by lift'ning to your voice.
Think that the magic of your song does leave
The wound incurable your eyes did give.
But still, fair Syren! still your art employ
For sure the pain is ballanc'd by the joy:
With pleasure to the dying you destroy.
No more with guarded ears the charm I'll fly,
Since 'tis by an extatick fate I die:
Since I partake of what th' immortals do,
Who rapt'rous sing, and beauteous look like you.

The WISE LAWYER: *or Fees on Both*
Sides strict Justice.

OLD counsellor *Double* well vers'd in the *Laws*,
Can never consent to lose *client* or *cause*;
Hence oft the wise *sage* we at *Westminster* see
On *each side* retain'd, and on *each side* take *fee*,
Yet say not too *rashly*, he forfeits his *truth*,
To *neither* he's *false* when he pleases 'em *both*.
While *one* he will *charm* by his *strenuous bawl*,
He'll gain *t'other's* cause by not *speaking at all.*

To Mr THOMSON *on his generous Concern*
for Mr DENNIS's *last Benefit.*

WHile I reflect thee o'er, methinks, I find
Thy various SEASONS, in their author's
　　mind!
Spring, in thy flow'ry *fancy*, spreads her hues;
And, like thy soft compassion, sheds her dews.
Summer's hot strength in thy *expression* glows;
And o'er thy page a *beamy* ripeness throws.
Autumn's rich *fruits* th' instructed reader gains,
Who tastes the meaning *purpose* of thy strains.
Winter—but *that* no 'semblance takes from thee!
That hoary season's type was drawn from ME
Shatter'd by time's bleak storms, I with 'ring lay,
Leafless, and whitening, in a cold decay.
Yet shall my propless *Ivy*,—pale and bent,
Bless the short sunshine, which thy pity lent.
　　　　　　　　　　　　　　　　J. D.

I'm glad to find my brother's grateful lay,
*Like medlar fruit, delicious in decay.　*Bavius.

The Beauties of COVENTRY *Assembly.*

VENus has left th' *Idalian* groves;
COVENTRIA is her court.
Come hither all ye little loves;
No more on *Ida* sport:
With rosy garlands crown'd appear,
A thousand graces wait you here.

In *Paphos* yet was never seen
Of nymphs so bright a train;
Nor ever yet did beauty's queen,
So irresistless reign.

CUPID no more of PSYCHE boast:
A fairer PSYCHE is the toast.

Who sees the blushing morn arise,
From dear MARIA's cheek;
And in full lustre from her eyes,
The sun triumphant break;
But owns (tho' envy will tee-hee)
Perfection in epitome?

Ah dear MARIA! had kind heav'n,
Which form'd that lovely face,
Indulgent to our bliss, but giv'n,
A little taller grace;
No Polly then, with Brobd'nag charms,
Should fright a conquest from thy arms.

But POLLY, tho' thou'st fairly won,
Thou canst not keep the field.
See, POLLY is herself undone!
And those who vanquish'd, yield.
Ye white-glov'd rabble stand aside:
JENNY, may VENUS be thy guide!

Each Belle with indignation glows,
And for soft triumph arms;
But JENNY's modest looks disclose,
Her heart feels no alarms.
All see the arrows fly around,
But only she who gives the wound.

Strange kind of fates are these which still
Upon perfection wait!
To cure, it either wants the will,
Or knows it's pow'r too late.
O COLIN! happy had it been,
Hadst thou been blind, or she but seen?

But if thou wilt, my friend, receive
Probatum est of eyes;
Thy fond, thy useless passion leave,
And take a friend's advice.
See, where the fair POTENTIA walks!
Ah listen!——It's an angel talks.

Or see, where sweetest NANCY trips,
Flush'd in full bloom of charms;
Joy revels on those rosy lips;
Ah! take her to thy arms.
One kiss will stifle all thy pain,
And give thee all thy peace again.

But whither wanderest thou my muse?
You've overlook'd a grace.
DORINDA, dearest maid, excuse
The unbecoming place.
Your merit should have first been nam'd;
But be the muse, not poet blam'd.

Nor must BOMBVERA, lovely fair,
Deny her timely aid;
Nor her soft locks of ebon hair,
To spin the muse's thread.

Whilst ev'ry treach'rous blush reveals,
That worth so fondly she conceals.

Nor thee, ESSONIA, shall my song,
Whilst I have pow'r to praise,
Forget to warble from my tongue,
In all-respectful lays:
But when there's beauty to excess,
Unequal words but make it less.

Ah me! why this unbidden sigh?
I tremble, and I fear;
And why this sudden flush of joy?
Ah me! FLORELLIA's here.
What heavenly elegance of mien!
It must be she, or beauty's queen.

No, beauty's queen could never give
Such extasy of bliss;
Tor e'er did happy MARS receive,
A pleasure like to this:
ch raptures from FLORELIA's eyes
ust come, or virtue in disguise.
faint beneath the dear extream.
Of transports too sincere,
Ah! CUPID, fan the scorching flame;
Or grant thy vot'ry's pray'r:
or ever let the angel stay,
r waft me hence to heav'n away.

The GLORIES of BURY.

THO' pompous structures, BURY's antient
boast,
re now in Heaps of cumbrous ruins lost;
Iles that in Ages past *Canutus* rear'd
'hen *Edmund's* Ghost, as Legends say, he fear'd,
ho' now the traveller views with wond'ring
    eyes
There broken walls in craggy fragments rise,
.n Abbey's Grandeur, and a Prince's Court
'rgrown with Ivy, mouldring into Dirt;
et let 'em not these dreary scenes bemoan,
ut tell the modern glories of the town.
Henry's Guilt in Tow're destroy'd appear,
'he greater Name of *Edward* we revere,
Le, virtuous Prince, for Love of Learning prais'd,
ere for her Sons a noble Building rais'd,
Vhere em'lous Youths are gradually inur'd
'o tread **.** paths by rising Pleasures lur'd;
Iere their young Souls first catch the gen'rous
    Flame,
'o reach at Greatness by a virtuous Fame.
ome brighter Genii have by (a) *Leeds's* Art,
Acquir'd what *Rome,* what *Athens* could impart.
Iere first instructed, now the Realm they grace,
Iigh in their merit, as advanc'd in place;
uch I would mention with respectful awe,
Lights of our church, or guardians of our law,
Iere *Bristol's* earl was bred, illustrious Peer!
fonour unstain'd, mankind in him revere,
'o liberty a sure, a steady friend,
If all his actions this the noble end.

Two (b) prelates here began their learned search,
ly worth distinguish'd! Fathers of the church!
Vho, while their sov'reign's gracious smiles they
    share,
Adorn those mitres they are call'd to wear.
Here first that great, that (c) venerable sage
mbib'd rare science in his greener age:
Vho on the aweful bench now foremost deals
strict justice round with equitable scales.
If in *Rome's* capitol the list'ning throng,
Vith deep attention heard a *Tully's* tongue;
Thus in the seat of judgment *Reynolds* charms,
Virtue protects, and guilty souls alarms;
low vast his talents, how sincere his heart,
Let those who hear, let those who feel impart:
should fair *Astræa*, in his room decree,
such would her orders, such her sentence be
As he would form, and we rejoice to see.

An *Hanmer* too went hence, none more admir'd
In sciences of public life --- tho' now retir'd;
But no retirement can a genius shroud,
It darts like light'ning thro' the blackest cloud.

Tho' *Hervey's* bloom our *Bury* must not claim,
His riper worth reflects a brighter fame;
Thrice has he been our corporation's choice,
To senates sent by an *united Voice*;   (cause,
Where strenuous he maintain'd his country's
And, like another *Tully,* gain'd applause.
His eloquence soon struck a *Walpole's* ear,
Statesman judicious, penetrating, clear,
Whose eagle eyes can see, whose candour own
Virtues so rare, and merit in its dawn.
Forgive, my Lord, these feint efforts of praise
In my rough numbers, and unpolish'd lays.
Had I your genius, or your sterling wit!
O could I write such lines as you have writ!
I'd strike the trembling lyre, nor fear to sing
How godlike *George,* our father, and our king,
The just reward of services allows,
And the patrician coronet bestows.
Fain wou'd my muse employ her vent'rous wing,
But dreads what Poets of rash *Icarus* sing.

As high distinction ne'er can me entice
To cringe to folly, or to flatter vice,
My honest lays flow only from esteem,
Tho' far, --- too far unequal to my theme.

Next beauty calls --- still a more arduous part
Too great for mine --- worthy the highest art,
Now is the (d) season when the sprightly fair
In shining crowds to *Bury* town repair.
He, who professes skill in female charms,
Whose heart each amiable beauty warms,
Whose pencil too can every brightness trace,
Alone must draw the glories of the place.
To (e) *Ickworth,* lovely maid, first let him pay
Due homage. --- Her 'tis freedom to obey,
Her sprightly graces each beholder wound,
While she, unconscious, spreads her triumphs
    round.
Peculiar sweetness charming (f) *Smith* displays,
We're lost in raptures, while we wond'ring gaze,
(g) Both, in each feature happily disclose
In fairest light the stem from which they rose.
Celestial deities of old thus shew'd
How *Berecynthia* was in them renew'd.
Th' enchanting aspect of (h) *Cornwallis* tells
How much good-nature in her bosom dwells;
A copious fancy, mem'ry, reas'ning strong,
The boast of men, not less to her belong.
Who sees her *Virgin Sister* but admires
A group of *Cupids* kindling dangerous fires?
Or whom will not that lustre still surprize
Which emanates so quick, from *Townshend's* eyes?
In *Devers,* he'll observe, is blended seen
With rural innocence the courtly mien:
How *Cytherea* and *Minerva* strove
To *Chester* which should most indulgent prove!
Well may we then that charmer's pow'r confess,
Whom rival goddesses were proud to bless,

(a) Near 50 Years Head Schoolmaster in Bury.
(b) St David's and Norwich.   (c) Ld Chief
Baron Reynolds.
    (*Gent. Mag.* Vol. III. No. xxxvi.)

(d) The Fair-day.   (e) Lady Anne Hervey
(f) Lady Louisa.   (g) Daughters of the Countess of Bristol.   Lady Cornwallis.

Each glance of *Monk* our painter will employ,
For she is form'd to give unbounded Joy;
Another of that name be here will meet,
With virtue, lovely, and in temper sweet.

Fanquier's complexion can't his notice scape;
Nor the exactness of bright *Affleck's* Shape;
Within her sister's tresses sleek as jett,
That wanton urchin *Cupid* weaves his net.

Dalston from northern climes has deign'd once
To visit *Bury*, and our bliss restore; [more
Once more we view the dimpled maid, who roves
In morning walks, thro' *Sanham's* plains and [groves;
And while she passes o'er the groves and plains
By nymphs is envy'd,—languish'd for by swains.

Here's *Lambert* too, whose absence *Ipswich* mourns,
Its glory half extinct, till she returns;
Her form majestick, noble in her Air;
We can't but love—yet, while we love—despair.

Here dancing sprightly *Wollaston* inspires;
Here *Stiles* infuses various soft desires;
More than our eyes are pleas'd; a *Syren's* tongue.
Charms in her voice, and holds th' attentive
  throng.

Wou'd perfect symmetry the Critic trace,
'Tis in each *Bacon's*, and in *Barker's* face.
Young *Barnadiston* justly may command
The nicest touches of a master hand;
And if he chuses further still to range,
Not less the bloom of *Capel* or *L'Estrange*.
Let him shew how humility and ease
Make *Goaday's* conversation always please;
Or, when the cheeks of modest *Coleman* flush,
How fine's the tincture of each rosy blush.
Let him relate how *Spencely*, and how *Hayes*,
By conduct strict, esteem deserve and raise.
Medcalf, how winning gay; let him reveal,
Turner how chearful, *Eldred* how genteel!
How oft *Degrey* has thrown unerring darts!
How numbers here to *Lee* resign their hearts;
If health's retriev'd while in deep seas she laves,
No wonder 'tis — for *Venus* sprung from waves.
Thus far with transport — but we must lament
That of the *Fitzroy* face none *Easton* sent,
Since in the dawn of *Caroline* all see
What her meridian blaze will shortly be,
And may presage what conquests she will gain,
Like her who flourish'd in great *Nassau's* reign;
Like her majestick; none with her could vie,
Who led the stars in (k) *Granville's* galaxy.
Delightful *Alston*, and engaging *Seame*,
By cruel fate were both detain'd at home
How amiable they, cou'd I rehearse!—
Such gems would radiate, and preserve my verse.

These are feint sketches of an artless hand;
A thousand more perfections round me stand;
Beyond my utmost reach:—Let him whose muse
Sublimest heights can reach, the subject chuse;
A full reward from beauty's smiles he'd find,
And never-fading bays his temples bind.

(*l*) *Lady Caroline D. of Grafton's eldest Daughter.* (*k*) *See the Progress of Beauty by Lord Landsdown.*

On CHLOE's Picture.

WHen *Chloe's* picture was to *Chloe* shown,
Adorn'd with charms and beauty not her own
Where *Hogarth*, pitying nature, kindly made
Such lips, such eyes, as *Chloe* never had:
Ye gods, she cries in ecstacy of heart,
How near can nature be expres'd by art!
Well—it is wond'rous like!!—Nay, let me die
The very pouting lip,—the killing eye!
—Blunt and severe as *Manly* in the play,
Downright replies,—like, madam, do you say?
The picture bears this likewise, it is true;
The canvas painted is, and so are you.

CUPID turn'd THIEF. A TALE.

In Imitation of the 20th Idyllion of Theocritus

CUpid the errant'st knave alive,
Stole from *Mamma* to rob a hive,
As soon as he his prize had took,
With merry laugh his sides he shook;
The honey-comb in frolick vein
He suck'd—then laugh'd—then suck'd again—
—But pleasure oft is mix'd with woe,
And grief will after blisses flow.
A bee enrag'd, the thief to brand,
Fix'd his keen sting upon his hand;
Strait he began to stamp and roar—
—His finger throb'd—he stamp'd the more,
And like a little trooper swore. }
When he found nothing cou'd assuage
The fortune of its burning rage;
All-swell'd his eyes, all-smear'd his cheeks,
With tears which trickled down in streaks;
Blubb'ring he to his *Mamma* run,
Cry'd—*Mam*—*Mamma*—you've lost your son:
Held his swell'd finger up to move her,
And sobbing told his story over:
But 'mid his sobbings wou'd complain,
That such a thing, so small, so vain, }
Shou'd have the pow'r to give such pain.
Venus soft smiling at his tale,
His finger buss'd, and all was well:
Then added: ' You Sir—you your self
' Are like that *Bee*, a tiny Elf,
' A little busy flutt'ring thing,
' Unhap'ly arm'd with pointed sting;
' And tho' you such an *Irchin* are,
' Can give a wound which none can bear.

Advice to the LAUREAT, on the approaching Royal Nuptials.

LET C——n add new beauties to his muse,
And dress her feet in orange-colour'd shoes.
May he excite as much surprizing mirth
On day of *Marriage*, as on days of *Birth*.
Or rather, having lavish'd all his store
On birth-day sonnet, and in numbers poor,
His fancy on the stoop, and drain'd of verse,
Let him his huge harmonious sack-but pierce
Make bridal-possets, and supply the lack
Of luscious ode with matrimonial sack.

Memoriæ sacrum, D. M. T. B. B. & L. P.

GReat TINDAL's gone, *the Lord knows how,*
  ot whither: [him thither.
To heaven we hope. 'Tis faid BUDGE fends
To vend his wit.—How fo? -- The *Bee* by this
Will prove *The* DOCTOR's *Apotheofis.*
Thus canoniz'd by BUDGE, fure all men muft
Confefs, *he dy'd like* SOCRATES *the juft;*
Fair LUCIA this attefts, -- fhe faw him rife,
By *G* - - *d!* by *Bees* tranfported to the fkies.
  The fact, the phyz, the name, in gold fhall
   fhine;
Th' Athenians thus ftamp'd SOCRATES *divine.*
The oath and emblem's juft: Rome's fenate
   thus,
Made Gods of CÆSAR and of ROMULUS.

. The BEE Sharply attacks Mr *Ruffel* as author of the *Grubftreet Journal,* upon a Charge
that the above Verfes *roundly affert that Mr*
Budgell *actually* murder'd Dr *Tindal;* and that
they can mean nothing lefs, *Socrates, Romulus,
and Cæfar,* to whom they allude, having been
all *murder'd* ---- The *Grubftreet Journal* replies, that the Words *Badge fends him thither*
can intend nothing but Mr *B.*'s Canonifing his
great and *Godlike* Friend; that Mr *B.* himfelf
had compar'd the Dr to *Socrates* in his *Contagi-
ons* dying; therefore would not imagine the
Verfes contain a Charge of murder, unlefs his
Brain be turn'd. Then gives the following
Epigram:

   E P I G R A M *on the foregoing.*

BELLUS, purfu'd for frolics in the dark,
  His hunters having almoft caught the fpark,
In hopes to ftop them fhort from running further,
Cries out, Watch fwatch! Oh! murther! murther!
  murther!

On the Free Gift of a Benefit to Mr DENNIS.
  by the Players in the Haymarket.

UNask'd, though pitying Players grant
  Kind charity to worth in want;
So cheap will Lawyers plead its caufe,
Or priefts deferve the like applaufe?
Never, while riches blind their eyes,
And fupercede all nature's ties;
Never, till truth and reafon reign,
And true religion live again.

On the foregoing. By Mævius, *in the* Grub. J.

PRiefts few, or none, on plays in judgment fit,
  But *Lawyers* in abundance crowd the pit.
Why then on thefe are harfh reflections thrown,
Who fill your pockets, emptying their own?
When *charity* you gave *to worth in want,*
Theirs was the coin, and yours the boafting cant.

On the Right Hon. Mr Talbot's *being made
  Lord High Chancellor.*

SEE ELOQUENCE afcends with gen'ral choice,
  How great the fanction of the publick voice!
TALBOT, the ftudies of Humanity
Are fpecify'd with grace fupreme in thee:
The lovely violence of thy courtly founds, -
Charms while it ftrikes, and pleafes while it
  wounds:

All ears thy mufick's fweet oppreffion feel,
Sublime, perfpicuous, nervous and genteel.
How ftrong that charm! That voice how ex-
  quifite!   . .
Whofe effence *reafon!* and whofe drefs *is wit;*
  SOMERS in thee revives his learned ftore,
COOPER the gentleman and orator,
HARCOURT unravels intricate deceits,
His equal condefcenfions KING repeats.
  Such TALBOT is -- a CANDOUR of his own,
Of thefe united graces is the *Crown:*
This point of time paft Eloquence renews;.
And if we credit the prophetic mufe,
TALBOT's decrees, fhall guide all future SEALS;
And this great *Æra* fix their laft APPEALS.

A Satire on P——Es *by Ld* H——Y.

GUiltlefs of thought, each blockhead may com-
  pofe
This nothing-meaning verfe, as faft as profe,
And P—E with juftice of Such lines may fay,
His Lordfhip fpins a thoufand in a day.
Such P—E himfelf might write, who ne'er cou'd
  think:
He who at *crambo* plays with pen and ink;
And is call'd poet, 'caufe in rhyme he wrote
What DACIER conftrued, and what HOMER
  thought;
But in reality this jingler's claim,   .
Or to an author's, or a poet's name,
A judge of writing would no more admit,
Than each dull *Dictionary*'s claim to wit;
That nothing gives you at its own expence,
But a few modern words for ancient fence.
'Tis thus, whene'er P—PE writes, he's forc'd
  to go
And *beg a little fenfe,* as fchool-boys do.
  " For all cannot invent, who can tranflate;
No more than thofe who cloath us can create.
When we fee CELIA fhining in brocade,
Who thinks 'tis HINCHLIF all that beauty made?
And P—PE, in his beft works, we only find
The gaudy HINCHLIF of fome beauteous mind.
To bid his genius work without that aid, ⎫
Would be as much miftaking of his trade, ⎬
As 'twould to bid your *batter* make a *head.* ⎭
Since this mechanic's, like the other's pains,
Are all for daeffing other people's brains.
But had he not to his eternal fhame, ⎫
By trying to deferve a fat'rift's name, ⎬
Prov'd he can ne'er invent but to defame; ⎭
Had not his *Tafte* and *Riches* lately fhown, ⎫
When he would talk of genius to the town, ⎬
How ill he chufes, if he trufts his own. ⎭
Had he, in modern language, only wrote,
Thofe rules which HORACE, and which VIDA
  taught;
On GARTH or BOILEAU's model built his fame,
Or fold BROOME's labours printed with P—PE's
  name:
Had he ne'er aim'd at any work befide,
In glory then he might have liv'd and dy'd;
And ever been, tho' not with genius fir'd,
By *fchool-boys* quoted, and by *girls* admir'd.
    *Epiftle from a Nobleman to a
    Dr of Divinity*

A *moft proper Reply* is threatned to the above
Satire unlefs it be fpeedily retracted.

Monthly Intelligencer.

DECEMBER, 1733.

Saturday, December 1.

A S a Ballot at the Hand-in-Hand Fire-Office on Snow-Hill, 475 against 151, whereby agreeable to their Conftitution, it was determined, that any Infurer may be capable of being elected a Director ——— The Defign of the Queftion was to confine this Office to thofe only who had 1000 l. Infurance in their own Names.

A Caufe was tried in the Court of Common Pleas, Weftminfter, between Mr Shaw, an Apothecary, of Peckham, Plaintiff, and Mr Richardfon, a Youth upon Liking, in order to be his Apprentice, Defendant, for criminal Converfation with the Plaintiff's Wife, which not being fufficiently proved, the Jury gave a Verdict for the Defendant.

Tuefday, 4.

In the Court of King's-Bench, Weftminfter, William Refit was tried on an Indictment for extorting from William Cole, Victualler, 14 d. as a Servant or Agent to Thomas Robe and Charles Peter, Efqs, Clerks of the Market of his Majefty's Houfhold. The Defendant claimed 14 d. as a Fee due to the Clerk of the Market, for fealing or marking 14 Pewter Pots; but not being able to prove it by living Witneffes, as the Court enjoin'd him to do, the Jury gave a Verdict for the King.

Likewife a Caufe between fome Mafter Shoemakers, and one that is free of the Company of Cordwainers, who calls himfelf a Leather-Cutter, for his felling of Leather not being red tann'd, duly fearched, fealed, and regifter'd according to Statute; and a Verdict was given for the Plaintiffs.

Thurfday, 6.

A Caufe was tried in the Court of Common Pleas, Weftminfter, between Mr Cornifh Plaintiff, and Mr Burleigh,

Defendant, for Affault and Battery, and falfe Imprifonment, the Plaintiff having been taken up and accufed of robbing the Defendant of upwards of 30 l. of which the Plaintiff was prov'd innocent; and a Verdict was given in his Favour, and 40 l. Damage.

Friday, 7.

A Caufe was tried in the Court of Common-Pleas, between the Company of Gun-makers of London, Plaintiffs; and a Foreigner, Defendant; for following the Bufinefs of a Gun-maker, not being regularly bred to it. The Defendant's Council finding the Proof ftrong againft him, propofed that he fhould undertake by Rule of Court, not to make or fell any Fire-Arms for the future, which was agreed to.

Saturday, 8.

The Seffions ending at the Old-Baily, Sentence of Death paffed upon John Baxter, John Rook, John Collington, John Curphoy, and John Freelove, for the Highway; Elizabeth Rann, for breaking open a Cheft; William Johnfon (a Deer Stealer) for the Murder of James Taaman, by fhooting him through the Head with a Piftol as he was attempting to take him: William Brown, and Jofeph Whitlock, for breaking open and robbing the Houfe of Col. Des Romaines at Paddington, of Goods, Money, Rings. and Plate to the Value of 161 l. John Anderfon, James Baker, alias Stick-in-the-Mud, and Francis Ogilby, for breaking open and robbing the Houfe of Thomas Rayner, a Silver-Smith; Elizabeth Wright, and Mary her Daughter, for Counterfeiting the current Coin of the Kingdom. Thirty-fix were caft for Transportation, and 29 acquitted. Elizabeth Wright pleaded her Belly, but was found not quick with Child. She confeffed fhe had practifed Coining for 8 Years paft. Boddenham, a Watchmaker, was tried and convicted of receiving Part of the Plate ftolen from Col. Des Romaines, and fen-

ntenced to be tranſported for 14 Years.
—— The Sheriffs of *London* ordered
o *l.* to be paid immediately to the Wi-
ow of *Henry Tadman.*

Monday, 10.

A Cauſe was heard before Dr *Betteſ-*
vorth, in *Doctor's Commons,* between
Mark Freaker Eſq; and others, who were
appointed by Parliament to propound the
laſt Will and Codicils of Col. *Richard*
Norton, deceaſed (who, by his ſaid Will,
made the Parliaments his Executors in
Truſt) Plaintiffs; and Dr *Chichley* and
others, the Deceaſed's nearest Relations,
Defendants; when the Judge pronounced
for the Validity of the ſaid Will and
Codicils. Accordingly Mr *Freckar, &c.*
were ſworn Administrators; but order'd
to give 1000 *l.* Security each.

Tueſday, 11.

The Prince of *Orange,* being indiffe-
rently well recovered from a tedious Indiſpoſition, with which he was ſeiz'd the
11th of *November* laſt (See p. 606) removed to *Kenſington* Palace in Hopes, by
a Change of Air, and a gentle Exerciſe
in riding out, to perfect his Recovery:
His Highneſs, during his Illneſs, was attended by Sir *Hans Sloane,* Dr *Hollings,*
and Dr *Teiſſier.*

Wedneſday, 19.

Thirteen Malefactors were executed
at *Tyburn,* viz. *John Baxter, John Rook,*
John Collington, and *John Beach,* the laſt
declar'd himſelf innocent at the Tree, for
the Highway; *Thomas Whitby,* for a
Street Robbery; *Wm Johnſon,* (for the
Murder of *William Taaman,* and for Deer
Stealing; *William Brown,* and *Joſeph*
Whitlock, for robbing Col. *Des Romaine*
at *Paddington; John Anderſon, James*
Baker, and *Francis Ogleby,* for Burglary;
John Brown and *Elizabeth Wright,* for
Coining, who were drawn in a Sledge;
Brown being hang'd, was ſlaſh'd a-croſs
the Body; and *Wright* was chain'd to a
Stake, firſt ſtrangled, and then burnt.

Friday, 21.

The Common-Council was choſen for
the City of *London,* with very little Variation from the laſt.

Tueſday, 25.

Dr *Gilbert* preach'd before their Majeſties, in the Chapel Royal at St *James's*
the Prince of *Wales,* and the three Eldeſt Princeſſes received the Sacrament
from the Hands of the Bp of *London,*
as did the Prince of *Orange,* the Dutch
Ambaſſador, and about Twenty of his
Highneſs's Domeſticks, in his private A-

partment at *Kenſington,* from the Hands
of Dr *Boulton,* Miniſter of the *Dutch*
Church in *Auſtin-Friars,* being attended
by two Elders, and two Deacons.

Wedneſday 26.

The *South-Sea Company's* annual Ship,
the *Royal Caroline* arrived in the *Downes*
in 52 Days from *La Vera Crux.* Her
Cargo conſiſts of

750000 Pieces of Eight
900 Bags of Cochineal, Value 150,000 *l.*
700 Serons of Indigo —— 26,000 *l.*
With other Particulars: In all to the Value of about 400,000 *l.* Sterling. Upon
this the Trading Stock roſe 5 *per Cent.*

Friday, 28.

The Prince of *Orange,* attended by
Ld *Hervey,* and Sir *Clement Cottrel,* went
in one of the King's Coaches from *Ken-*
ſington to St *James's.* His Highneſs was
with their Majeſties near two Hours, and
dined in her Royal Highneſs's Apartment
with the Prince of *Wales,* the Princeſs
Royal, the Princeſſes *Amelia* and *Caroline,*
and about 7 return'd to *Kenſington.*

Monday, 31.

The *Eaſt-India Company* have reſolv'd
to ſend two Commiſſaries to *China* to
enquire into the Affairs between Mr *Naiſh*
and that Company; and that the Law-
Suit between them be ſuſpended till the
Report of their Negotiation.

Angria, the famous Pyrate, who in-
feſted the *Indian* Seas has made a Truce
with the *Engliſh,* and ſent the Gov. of
Bombay 63 *Engliſh* Priſoners.

The Middle of this Month was very
ſtormy; great Damages were done at Sea
and Land. The new Steeple of St *Mi-*
chael's at *Southampton* was ſhatter'd by
Thunder and Lightning.

The Quantities of Corn exported from
the Port of *London,* from *Chriſtmus* 1732,
to 1733, were

236870 Quarters of Wheat,
5700 Quaters of Barley, and other Grain.
The Royal Nuptials are deferr'd, till the
Pr. of *Orange's* Return from *Bath,* which
Place he deſigned to reach this Week.

BIRTHS.

THE Dutcheſs of *Leeds,* Wife of
the E. of *Portmore,* delivered of a
Daughter.

27. The Wife of *Auguſtus Schutz,*
Eſq; —— of a Daughter.

The Wife of *Charles Caſar,* Eſq; jun.——
of a Daughter.

The Wife of *Thomas Lawly,* Eſq; of
Stockwell, Surrey, —— of a Son and Heir.

MAR.

MARRIAGES.

WILLIAM *Davies*, Esq; Commander of his Majesty's Ship *Edinburgh*, married to the Daughter of Mr *Best* a Brewer at *Chatham*, with a Fortune of 10,000 *l.*

Hugh Barlow, of *Lowpeni*, *Pembrokeshire* —— to Miss *Skirm*, a Fortune of 400 *l. per Ann.* and 14,000 *l.* in Cash.

Counsellor *Reynolds*, eldest Son to the Bp of *London* —— to the youngest Daughter of the Ld *Haversham*.

Mr *Watson*, Distiller in *Wallbrooke* —— to a Daughter of —— *Sutton*, Esq; late of *Kensington*.

Thomas Bradshaw, of *Chiswick*, Esq; 90 Years of Age —— to a young Gentlewoman not 20.

Jacob Hudson, of *Knightsbridge*, Esq; to the Daughter of *Samuel Bowlin*, of *Westminster*, Esq;

George Knapp, of *Hertfordshire*, Esq; —— to Miss *Norris*, of *Santon-Square*.

The Ld Visc. *Duncannon*, of *Ireland* —— to the Lady *Tullamore*, of 2000 *l.* a-Year Estate, and 10,000 *l.* in Ready-Money.

Joseph Fellows, of *Sudbury*, *Middlesex*, Esq; —— to Miss *St Quintin*, of *Duke-Street*, *Westminster*, a Fortune of 4000 *l.*

The Rev. Mr *Brotherton* —— to Miss *Anne Chandler*, Daughter to the Bp of *Durham.*

Sir *Philip Hobsworth* —— to Miss *Fitzgerald*, of *Hamton-Town.*

George Langdel, of *Staines*, Esq; —— to the only Daughter and Heiress of *John Ingram*, Esq; of the same Place.

George Graham, Esq; —— to Miss *Montgomerie*, Neice to the E. of *Eglinton*, a *Scots* Peer.

Charles Newland, Esq; of *Grantham*, *Lincolnshire* —— to Miss *Jane Olden*, of the same Place.

Mr *John Forbill*, an Attorney at *Chichester*, —— to Miss *Norman*, of the same Place, a Fortune of 10,000 *l.*

Edward Eliston, Esq; —— to Miss *Gibbon* of *Sutney.*

DEATHS.

DR *Houston*, a famous Botanist, who was sent over by the Trustees for *Georgia* to collect the most useful Plants in *America*, for that Colony, died in *Jamaica* in *August* last.

Nov. 23. *John Meller*, Esq; at *Erbig* in *Denbighshire*, late a Master in Chancery. He left the Bulk of his Estate in Lands and Money to upwards of 100,000 *l.* to his his two Sisters, the one a Widow, and the other married to Major *Roberts*.

28. Col. *Pennyfaiber*, Accomptant General of *Ireland.*

30. Capt *Thomas Bowler*, formerly Commander of his Majesty's Ship *Kea*, well known for his gallant Behaviour in the Streights under Adm. *Hopson.*

Dec. 1. Mr *Stephen Smith*, an East *India* Merchant, in *Grosvenor-street.*

Thomas Hornbey, Esq; in the Commission of the Peace for *Middlesex.*

2. Mr *Lessett*, a Surgeon in *Cheapside.*

Robert Boothby, Esq; at *Chigwel*, Essex.

3. The Wife of Mr *Anthony Loubin*, a *French* Merchant.

4. *John Collier*, Esq; formerly a Wine Merchant.

Mr *Peck*, a 30,000*l.* Turkey Merchant.

Relict of Monf. *Touloufe*, Embroiderer to the late Q. *Anne*, who left the Bulk of his Estate to the *French* Chapel in the *Savoy*, only reserving an Annuity of 100 *l. per Ann.* to his Widow, which he also order'd to be applied after her Demife to the same Use.

Nich. Bennet, Esq; of the CofferersOffice.

5. The Wife of *Joseph Skinner*, Esq; First Clerk of the Board of Green Cloth.

Sir *Samuel Clark*, Sheriff for this City in 1713. He left handsome Legacies to *Bartholomew* and *Bethlehem* Hospitals.

Capt. *Dillington*, at *Roehampton*, *Surry.*

Mr *Fitzgerald*, one of the Clerks of the House of Lords.

The Rev. Mr *Hore*, Curate of St *Mildred* in the Poultry.

7. *Evan Seys*, Esq; of *Boverton* in *Glamorganshire.*

Mr *Joseph Graves*, Merchant, in *New Broad-street.*

Mr *Waddell*, Plumber and Undertaker of Buildings, reputed worth upwards of 20,000 *l.*

8. The only Son of *William Jones*, Esq; of *Bedford-street*, *Covent Garden.*

John Suckling, Esq; Lieut. Colonel in Ld *Kerr's* Regiment.

Mr *Tuffnell*, Master-Builder and Bricklayer to the Company of New River Waterworks, reputed worth 30,000 *l.*

9. *Thomas Tufton*, Esq; fifth Son to Col *Sackville Tufton.*

Th. *Griffin*, of *Stonyhurst*, *Lancash* Esq;

10 Miss *Hamilton*, Niece to the E. of *Abercorn.*

Sackville Stewart, Esq; Nephew to Sir *James Stewart*, of *Goostrees*, *Scotland*.

11. *Linthwait Farrant*, Esq; Deputy Register Assumed of the Prerogative Court of *Canterbury.*

The Wife of *Henry Ladyton*, Esq; in *Berwick-street.*

Robert Neile, Esq; a noted Clothier of Wilshire, at Gerard's Inn, reputed worth 5,000 l.

Mrs Jane Ash, Sister to the late Sir James Ash Bar.

12. John Casley, Esq; Wine Merchant. George Talbot, E. of Shrewsbury, Baron Talbot in England, and E. of Wexford and Waterford in Ireland; descended from Richard Talbot, who in the Reign of William the Conqueror was the Senior Earl of this Kingdom. He married the Daughter of the Ld Visc. Fitzwilliams of Ireland, by whom he had one Son, and one Daughter; George, now Lord Talbot, a Minor, and Lady Barbara.

Sir Nathaniel Loyd, Doctor of Laws, and one of the King's Advocates.

13. Capt. Butler, a military Officer.

Dr Brailsford, Dean of Wells.

Capt Daniel, an Old Officer in the Army, at Shrewsbury.

14. Mr De Cuney, Silversmith in Spurret Leicester Fields.

James Blake, Esq; in the Commission of the Peace for Surry.

William Lawton, Esq; one of the assistant Clerks of the Treasury.

15. Mrs Ann Tench, a near Relation of Sir Fisher Tench.

The Relict of the late Sir William Capel at her House at St Albans.

Mr John Wharton, a Clerk in the Victualling Office on Tower Hill.

The only Son of John Phillips of Tilgetty Pembrokeshire, Esq;

16. Thomas Hutchins, Esq; Inner Clerk of the Ordnance.

Joseph Alston, Esq; Brother to the Lady of Dr Hare, Bp of Chichester.

Mrs Mary Huckel, Widow. Her Jointure of 400 l. per Ann devolves to her Brother, James Williams, of Walton upon Thames, Esq;

Sir Edward Lovet Pearce, Surveyor General of the Fortifications in Ireland, and Member of Parliament there.

17. James Edwards, Esq; at Croydon, in the Commission of the Peace for Surry.

Mr John Eden, late Secretary of the Chelsea Waterworks, died lately in his way from Jamaica to Buenos Ayres, where he was one of the Factors of the the South Sea Company.

The Wife of Morley, Esq; in Child-bed, at her House in Golden Square.

Miss Henrietta Blackford, a rich Heiress.

18. Mrs Hall, near Lewes in Sussex, aged 102.

The Rev. Dr Peake, Rector of Bridge Casterton in Rutlandshire.

19. Thomas Moore, Esq; Register of the Diocese of Rochester, and Auditor and Librarian to the Dean and Chapter of Westminster. He was Secretary to Bp Spratt, and instrumental in saving that Prelate's Life, and the Lives of A. Bp Sancroft, the late D. of Marlborough, and several others of great Note, by detecting the Falshood of Blackhead and Young's Evidence against them, as being concerned in a pretended Assassination Plot, in the Reign of K. William.

Barton Brace, of Meckleham in Surry, Esq.

21. The Wife of Powlet St John, Esq; and sole Heiress of Sir John Rushout Bar.

Mrs Eyre, a near Relation to the Ld Chief Justice Eyre.

Mrs Sherman, one of the Nurses to the late D. of Gloucester, for which Q. Anne gave her a House in St James's Park, and 100 Guineas a Year during her Life.

Capt. Shrimpton, at his House in Great Marlborough-street. He left 15,000 l. to Charles Stanhope, of Holleyborn in Kent, Esq; 1,000 l. to Mr Edwards, his Servant, to his Houskeeper 30 l. in Money, and a Freehold House of 25 l. per Ann. to his Cook, 12 l. a Year for her Life; and 5 l. and a Year's Wages to all the rest of his Servants.

Capt. Coleston, of the first Regiment of Foot Guards.

Tho. Burrell, Esq; at Hampstead.

Dr Harris, Professor of modern History and Languages in the University of Cambridge.

22. The Rt Rev. Elias Sydal, D.D. Bp of Gloucester. He was first promoted to the See of St Davids in 1730, in the room of Dr Chandler, and from thence in 1731, translated to that of Gloucester, in the Room of Dr Wilcox.

23. The Relict of the late Sir John Mordaunt. She requested by her Will, that her Corpse might remain untouch'd 3 Days and 3 Nights, she having always been apprehensive of dying in a Trance.

Dr John Innes, Professor of Medicine at the University of Edinburgh, and Physician to Heriots Hospital.

24. Mrs South, a Maiden Gentlewoman Sister to the late Rev. Dr South.

25. Richard Whitbed, Esq; at Norman's Court in Hampshire, which has lineally descended in that Family ever since the Conquest. He was Cousin and Heir at Law to the late Richard Norton, Esq; whose real Estate he died possess'd of, in Opposition to his remarkable Will. (See p. 57.) Being unmarried he left the Bulk

of his Eſtates to his Nephew *Francis Thiſtlethwayte*, Eſq; and to his. Heirs Male, whom he enjoyned to take the Name of *Whithed.*

27. *George Perſhouſe*, Eſq; of *Great Ormond-ſtreet*, with a Fit of an Apoplexy.

Lindſey, Eſq; ſuddenly in his Chair, at a Coffee-houſe in *Red Lyon-ſtreet Clerkenwel.*

The Rev. Mr *Ford*, Vicar of *Prieſtly Hereforſhire.*

The Wife of *George Vernon*, Eſq; in Child-bed, at *Newnham Paddock, Warwickſhire.*

28. *Joſeph Jeffries*, Eſq; Counſellor at Law.

PROMOTIONS.

JOHN *Cuffe*, Eſq; created a Peer of *Ireland*, by the Style and Title of Baron of *Deſſart* in the County of *Kilkenny.*

The Rt. Hon. *Charles Talbot*, Eſq; — Lord Chancellor, created a Baron of *Great Britain*, by the Name, Stile, and Title of Lord *Talbot*, Baron of *Henſol* in the County of *Glamorgan.* His Lordſhip appointed the following Officers;

Mr *Toung*, Purſebearer.

Mr *Woodford*, Secretary of the Petitions.

Mr *Howells*, —— of the Bankrupcy.

Mr *Le Heup*, —— of the Preſentations.

Mr *Perkins*, —— of the Lunaticks.

M. *Capper*, —— of the Injunctions.

Mr *Roew* — of the Commiſſion of *Peace.*

Mr *Heberington*, —— of the *Fines.*

Mr *Cunnington*; Gentlemen of the
Mr *Blackburn*; Chamber.

Mr *Arrowſmith*,
Mr *Smith*, Uſhers of the Court.
Mr *Clottle*

William Groves, Eſq; —— Clerk of the Preſentations.

John Verney, Eſq; made Chief-Juſtice of *Cheſter*, in the room of *John Willes*, Eſq;

Mr *Applebury*, —— one of the Surveyors of the *London Brewery* in the Exciſe.

John Willes, Eſq; —— Attorney-General in the Room of *Charles Talbot*, Eſq; now Ld Chancellor.

Dudley Ryder, Eſq; —Sollicitor-General.

Capt. *Thomas Lynn*, on Half-pay, appointed to the Command of a Company in Gen. *Pocock's* Reg. of Foot.

Capt. *Hattaway Fleming*, on the Half-Pay —— to a Company of Invalids.

Capt. Lieut. *Bell*, made Captain of Grenadiers in Col. *Harriſon's* Reg.

Thomas Guiſe, Eſq; —— Captain of a Company of Invalids.

Thomas Elton, Eſq; —— a Commiſſioner of the Stamp-Duty.

John Brookesby, Eſq; —— a Land Surveyor in the Port of *London.*

Eccleſiaſtical Preferments, conferred on the following Reverend Gentlemen.

MR. *Watſon*, made a Prebendary of *Hereford.*

Mr *Hughes*, M. A. —— Prebendary in the Collegiate Church of *Brecknock.*

Mr *Willis*, A. M. choſen Lecturer of *St Michael, Woodſtreet.*

John Wolrig, M. A. preſented to the Vicarage of *Broad-Hempſton, Devonſhire.*

Mr *Smith*, Chaplain to the Ld *Digby* — to the Rectory of *Woodborough, Wilts.*

Mr *John Howel* —— to the Rectory of *Robenſton, Pembrokeſhire.*

Mr *Sneyd* —— to the Rectory of *Eſſingham, Eſſex.*

Mr *Lewis Palmer* —— to the Rectory of *Carlton-Curlew, Leiceſterſhire.*

Mr *John Edwards*, L. L. D. —— to the Rectory of *Rudbaxton, Pembrokeſhire.*

Mr *Zephaniah Peirſe*, M. A. ——to the Rectory of *Horndon, Eſſex.*

Mr *Turner* —— to the Rectory of *Stevenage, Hertfordſhire.*

Mr *Sinclair*, M. A. —— to the Rectory of *Branford*, in the County of *Durban.*

Mr *William Goldwin*, Rector of *St Nicholas, Briſtol*, elected Fellow of *Eaton-College*, in the room of Dr *Lyttelton*, dec.

Dr *Lynch*, made Dean of *Canterbury*, in the room of Dr *Sydal.*

Diſpenſations paſſed to enable,

William Aſpkin, M. A. Chaplain to the E. of *Uxbridge*, to hold the Vicarage of *Horley* and *Hornton, Oxfordſhire*, together with the Rect. of *Barithorp, Glouceſterſ.*

Mr *Degge*, M. A. Rector of *Backleon*, to hold the ſaid Living, together with the Vicarage of *Fowey*, both in *Cornwall.*

STOCKS Dec. 29.	Monthly BILL of Mortality, from Oct. 23. to Nov. 27.		The Yearly Bill, from Dec. 12. to Dec. 11.	
S. Sea Trading Stock 81 ¾	Chriſtned { Males 600 Females 631 } 1231		Mal. 8811 Fem. 8654 } 17465	
—Bonds 1s. Prem. —Annulties 102	Buried { Males 826 Femal. 850 } 1676		Mal. 14372 Fem. 14861 } 29233	
—Ditto new 102	Died under 2 Years old --- 668		——11738	
—dit. 3 per C. 92	Between 2 and 5 ---- 159		—— 2409	
Bank 137	Between 5 and 10 ---- 53		—— 957	
New Cir. 2l. 10s.	Between 10 and 20 ---- 39		—— 754	
India 141	Between 20 and 30 ---- 96		—— 1857	
—Bonds 22s. Pre.	Between 30 and 40 ---- 166		—— 2564	
it 3 per C. 5s. Prem.	Between 40 and 50 ---- 171		—— 2685	
Million Bank 109	Between 50 and 60 ---- 131		—— 2196	
African 25	Between 60 and 70 ---- 110		—— 1871	
Royal Aſſ. 95	Between 70 and 80 --- 50		—— 1188	
London Aſſ. 11 ¼	Between 80 and 90 --- 28		—— 804	
Eng. Cop. 1 l. 15	Between 90 and 100 ---- 4		—— 198	
Welch ditto 17s.	Between 100 and 106 ---- 1		—— 11	
Lot. Tickets 4 l. 2 s.	112 —— 0		—— 1	
		1676	Total 29233	
	Caſualties in the Year paſt 459		Increaſ. 5875	

Buried in the 97 Pariſhes within the Walls ——— 2610
In the Pariſhes of St *Andrew Holbourn,* and St *Martin's* in the *Fields* 3300

Price of Grain at *Bear-Key, per* Qr.		Buried.	Weekly Burials
Wheat 23 s. to 31 s.	P. Malt 19s. to 21s.	Within the walls, 153	Dec. 4 --- 434
Rye 12 s. to 19 s.	B. Malt 16 s. to 20 s.	Without the walls, 459	11 — 394
Barley 16 s. to 18s. 6d	Tares 19 s. to 21s.	In Mid and Surry, 706	18 — 492
Oats 15 s. to 18 s.	H. Peaſe 16s. to 18s.	City and Sub of Weſt 358	25 --- 356
Peaſe 20 s. to 22s.	H. Beans 20 s. to 22s.	1676	1676

Prices of Goods, &c. in *London.* Hay about 1 l. 16s. to 2 l. a Load.

Coals in the Pool 24s. to 26 s.	Ditto ſecond ſort 46s. to 50s. per C.	Opium 09 s. 00 d.
Old Hops per Hun. 2l. 10s. to 4l.	Leaf Sugar double refine 8 d. Half-	Quickſilver 4 s.
New Hops 5 l. 10s.	penny a 9d. per lb.	Rhubarb fine 18 s. a 24 s.
Rape Seed 11l. to 12l. per Laſt	Ditto ſingle refin. 56 s. to 64 s.	Sarſaparilla 3 s. 00 d.
Lead the Fodder 19Hun, 1 half	per C.	Saffron Eng. 22s. 06 d.
on board, 14l. to 14l. 10 s.	Cinamon 7 s. 8 d. per lb.	Wormſeeds none
Tin in Blocks 3l. 18 s	Cloves 9 s. 1 d.	Balſam Copaiva 2 s. 9d.
Ditto in Bars 4l. 00 s. excluſive	Mace 15 s. 0 d. per lb.	Balſam of Gillead 20 s. 00 d.
of 3 s. per Hun. Duty.	Nutmegs 8 s. 7 d. per lb.	Hipocacuana 5 s. 6d.
Copper Eng. beſt 5l. 05 s. per C.	Sugar Candy white 14 d. to 18 d.	Ambergreece per oz. 08 s.
Ditto ord. 4l. 16 s. to 5l. per C.	Ditto brown 6 d. per lb.	Cochineal 19 s. 6d. per lb.
Ditto Barbary 85 l. to 95 l.	Pepper for Home conf. 16 d.	Wine, Brandy, and Rum.
Iron of Bilboa 15 l. 05 s. per Tun	Ditto for exportation 12 d. Farth.	Oporto red, per Pipe 34 l.
Dit. of Sweden 16l. 10 s. per Tun	Tea Bohea fine 10 s. to 12s. per lb.	ditto white none
Town Tallow 30 s. to 31s. per C.	Ditto ordinary 9 s. to 10s. per lb.	Liſbon red 37 l.
Country Tallow 29 s. 30s.	Ditto Congo 10 s. to 14 s. per lb.	ditto white, 38 l.
Salt 4 s. to 4 s. 6 d.	ditto Pekoe 14 s. 16 a s. per lb.	Sherry 26 l.
Grocery Wares.	ditto Green fine 9 s. to 12s. per lb.	Canary new 28 l.
Raiſins of the Sun 32s. 0d. per C.	ditto Imperial 10 s. to 13 s. per lb.	ditto old 34 l.
Ditto Malaga Fraitts 28 s	ditto Hyſon 25 s. to 30 s.	Florence 9 l. per Cheſt
Ditto Smirna new 22s.	Drugs by the lb.	French red 30 l. a 40 l.
Ditto Alicant, 20 s.	Balſam Peru 14 s. to 15s.	ditto white 20 l.
Ditto Lipra new 22s.	Cardamoms 3 s. 6 d.	Mountain malaga old 24 l.
Ditto Belvedera 22	Camphire refin'd 14 s.	ditto new 22 to 21 l.
Currants new 44 s.	Crabs Eyes 1 s. 8 d.	Brandy French per Gal. 7 s.
Prunes French none	Jallap 22 s. 6 d.	Rum of Jamaica 7 s.
Figs 20 s.	Manna 03 s. a 04 s.	ditto Leew. Iſlands 6 s. 4 d.
Sugar P. md. beſt 59 s. per C.	Maſtick white 4 s. 0 d. (4M)	Spirits Eng. 26 l. per Tun.

FROM *Constantinople,* That the chief Mufti had been ftrangled for being fufpected of favouring the *German* Intereft; that the Grand Vizier, and Kirler Aga, the only Perfons that engrofs the Sultan, are known to be faft Friends to the *French* Court; but that as the *Turkiſh* Army had been routed by the *Perſians*; the Grand Seignior would not be at leifure to efpoufe one or other of the Interefts which diftract the Kingdom of *Poland.*

From *Vienna,* That the Emperor had refufed to accept the Neutrality for the *Auſtrian Netherlands,* and that Count *Daun,* on his Arrival from his Government of the *Milaneſe,* was not fuffer'd to come to Court, but arrefted for Male-Adminiſtration, and fuffering that Country to be fo eafily taken by the Enemy. The Imperial Forces are faid to be in all 143,000 Men; of which three Armies are to be form'd, and to act, next Spring, offenfively in *Italy,* on the *Rhine* and the *Moſella.*——The *French* would refine their Hoftilities in *Germany,* and the actual taking of Fort Kehl, to be only a Quarrel with the Emperor, not the Empire. But his Imperial Majefty omits nothing to gain the Germanick Body to his Intereft; and that the Elector of *Bavaria's* Miniſters had receiv'd in the Name of their Mafter the Inveftiture of his Eftates.—— A report obtains that the Emprefs is with Child; and 'tis to be wiſh'd, for the Intereft of *Europe,* She may have a Prince.

From *Italy,* That the Fortreffes of *Lecco, Frezzo,* and *Fuentes* had fubmitted to the Allies without fcarce a Blow; *Pizzighitone* is reduc'd; the Caftle of *Milan* befieg'd in Form and near taken; *Mantua* block'd up; fo that in all probability the *Milaneſe* will be foon entirely in the Poffeffion of the *French* and *Sardinians*; nothing can excufe the Imperial Court, and their Governor-General for leaving thus defencelefs the tenable Places of that Dutchy, unlefs it was the Security they had on the Faith and Honour of a neighbouring Potentate, whom they had lately fo much oblig'd. The Imperialifts are refolv'd to have an Army here in the Spring, to be commanded by Prince *Eugene,* to give the Confederates Battle, and thereby if poffible to drive them out of *Italy.*

From *Legborn,* That the Grand Duke of *Tuſcany* had declar'd for an exact Neutrality, not only as Grand Duke, but likewife as Guardian and Adminiftrator of the Dutchies of *Parma* and *Placentia,* for Don *Carlos.* And that the K. of *Spain,* by an Exprefs, had affur'd the Merchants, that that Port fhould enjoy an exact Neutrality and Freedom in the prefent War. Don *Carlos* being made Generaliffimo of all the *Spaniſh* Forces had declar'd himſelf of Age.

From *Paris,* That the Queen is with Child; the King is determin'd to head his Army in Perfon on the *Rhine*; and 35 Ships of the Line are fitting out at different Ports. The Parliament having made Remonftrances againft fome pecuniary Edicts lately iffued by his Majefty, he caufed them to be alter'd, conformable to their Reprefentations, and then they regifter'd them.

From *Lisbon,* by way of *Paris,* That the Emperor having defired of the K. of *Portugal,* his Brother-in-law, a Loan of 18 Millions of Florins, was anfwer'd, that the King wonder'd his Imperial Majefty fhould defire it, fince he promifed to raife his Brother Don *Emanuel* to the Throne of *Poland,* but fo far from taking the leaft Notice of that Pr. had endeavour'd to procure that Crown for the Elector of *Saxony.*

From the *Hague,* That the Emperor had defired the States General to lend him 12 Millions of Florins, upon a Mortgage of the Auftrian Netherlands; but they begg'd to be excufed.

From *Genoa,* That 18,000 *Spaniſh* Foot, and 1500 Horfe were landed at *Vado,* about ten Leagues from that City; another Body at *La Spezie*; and another at *Legborn.* Thofe landed at the *Vado* and *La Spezie* are to join the Confederacies; and the laft, 'tis faid, are to make a Defcent in *Sicily.*

From *Madrid,* That his Catholick Majefty had publifhed a Manifefto or Declaration of War, the Motives to which turn on the following Heads, viz. The Injury done to his Nephew the K. of *France* in the Perfon of K. *Staniſlaus*; his Imperial Majefty's Behaviour in relation to Don *Carlos,* in trumping up the Dutchefs of *Parma's* pretended Pregnancy; other Artifices ufed to procraftinate the ferene Infant's taking Poffeffion of his Territories in *Italy*; Difficulties in admitting the *Spaniards* there; the ill Grace with which the Emperor fuffer'd it at laft; the Decrees fince iffued againft the Great D. of *Tuſcany* and Don *Carlos*; the one for receiving the Homage as Great Prince of that Dutchy, and the other for permitting it; and the Refufal of a Difpenfation of Age to the Infant Duke: And concludes with profeffing his Obligations to his *Britannick* Majefty, and his Refolution to maintain a ftrict Union between their two Crowns.

From *Petersburgh,* That Orders were given for raifing 50,000 new Troops from among the Peafant Vaffals, by taking one out of every 102 fit to bear Arms, purfuant to a Computation, by which it appears, that the Number of Peafants in *Ruſſia* are upwards of 50 Millions, from each of whom a Capitation or Pole-Tax is annually levy'd equal to 3s. 4d. Sterling.

A REGISTER of BOOKS publish'd in DECEMBER, 1733.

A Review of the Facts objected to the first Volumn of the History of the Puritans. By Dan. Neal. M. A. Printed for R. Hett. Pr. 1 s. (See p. 651.)

2. Tit for Tat, or Vice versa. Printed for W. Rayner. Price 6 d.

3. An Answer to a Paper entitled, Motives of the French King's Resolutions. Printed for J. Brindley. Price 1 s. 6 d.

4. An Enquiry into the Original of Moral Virtue. By Arch. Campbel, S. T, P. Printed for J. Oswald.

5. Necessity of a new Parliament asserted; being an Answer to some Reasons for continuing the present. Printed for S. Clarke. Price 6 d. (See p. 642.)

6. A Review of the late Excise Scheme, in Answer to the Rise and Fall of the late projected Excise impartially consider'd. Printed by H. Haines. Price 1 s. (See p. 637.)

7. The Statutes at large concerning the Provision for the Poor. Printed for R. Gosling. Price 1 s. 6 d.

7. Timon in Love; or, the Innocent Theft. A Comedy. Printed for J. Watts, Price 1 s. 6 d.

8. Duplicata Ratio Musices: Or, the Double Harmony of an Algebraical Music hitherto unknown. By Quirin Van Bladkenburgh. Sold by J. Brotherton. Price 5 s.

9. An Oration, in which an Enquiry is made whether the Stage is, or can be made a School for forming the Mind to Virtue. Spoke in the Jesuit's College at Paris. By Charles Poree. Translated by J. Lockman. Printed for C. Davis. Price 1 s. 6 d.

10. An Address to the Whigs, and particularly to the Dissenters, on the present Posture of Affairs. By a Freeholder. Printed for J. Noon.

11. Self-Possession the Happiness only of a true Christian. Printed for R. Hett. Pr. 1 s.

12. The Proceedings at the Old Baily. Dec. 5, 6, 7, 8. Price 1 s.

13. An Epistle to Eustace Budgell, Esq; occasioned by the Death of the late Dr Tindal. Printed for J Hughes. Price 1 s.

14. The Conduct of the Emperor and Muscovites compared with that of France since the Treaty of Utrecht. By Mr John Bruce. Printed for Thomas Perkins. Pr 6 d.

15. A Prospect of Poetry, By James Dalacourt, A. B. Printed for J. Roberts.

16. Liberty and Property: Or, a Defence of the Citizens of London, &c. Sold by Harper. Price 1 s.

17. The History of Pego the Great. Printed for T. Cooper. Price 6 d.

18. The Pike. A Tale. Sold by J. Penn Price 6 d.

19. Oysters. A Poem. Sold by the Booksellers. Price 6 d.

20. A State of the South Sea Stock, from its Original in 1711, to Christmas 1733. Printed for T. Hatchett. Price 6 d.

21. The Downfal of Bribery, or the Honest Men of Taunton. A Ballad Opera. By Mark Freeman. Price 1 s.

22. On Rural Felicity: In an Epistle to a Friend. Printed for J. Wilford. Pr. 1 s.

23. On Poetry: A Rhapsody. Sold by J. Huggonson. Price 1 s.

24. True Christianity: From the first speaking of Children, untill they come to the Holy Communion. By The. Colebatch. Printed for L. Gilliver. Price 2 s. 6 d.

25. A Vindication of the Protestant Dissenters from the Aspersions in a Pamphlet, entitled, The Presbyterian's Plea of Merit, &c. Sold by A. Dodd. Pr 1 s.

26. The Wisdon and Goodness of God in the Vegetable Creation, confider'd in a Sermon at the Church of St Leonard Shoreditch, on Whitson Tuesday, 1733. By John Dinne, D. D. Printed for J. Pemberton. Pr. 6 d.

27. Englishmen's Eyes open'd; being the Excise Controversy set in a true Light. Printed for J. Wilford. Price 1 s.

28. Geneva; A Poem in Blank Verse, Occasion'd by the late Act of Parliament for allowing Liquors Compound of English Spirits. Written in Imitation of Philips's Splendid Shilling, with a Dedication to all the Gin Drinkers in Great Britain and Ireland. By Stephen Buck, of Stocks Market, Price 6 d.

December 29. 1733.

This Day is Publish'd, Nᵒ 30.

(Adorn'd with a Curious Copper Plate of that bold Pyrate Capt. AVERY, of

THE LIVES and ADVENTURES of the moſt famous Highwaymen, Murderers, Pyrates, &c. By Capt. CHARLES JOHNSON. Two ſheets of this work is publiſh'd every Week for two pence; and Eight Sheets will be every Month Stitch'd in Blue Paper for thoſe who don't chuſe to be troubled with weekly Subſcriptions, at the Price of Eight Pence, except when Cuts, which will be only one Half-penny more; and the whole will be adorn'd with Prints of the moſt remarkable ſtories, curiouſly Engraved on Copper.

Note If any of our Subſcribers are neglected, and will pleaſe to ſend to J. Janeway by the Penny-Poſt, the Poſtage ſhall be allowed, and particular Care ſhall be taken for the Future.

N. B. As the Deſign of publiſhing Books in this manner Weekly, is to lighten the Expence of them, in ſuch ſort that it may hardly be felt, by laying out only Twopence (or Two pence Half-penny with Cuts) at a Time; any Perſon, who is willing to encourage this Work, may commence a Subſcriber whenever he thinks fit, and have the firſt Number deliver'd to him by the following Perſons, or any of the News Carriers, and ſo on every Week, without being obliged to take all that have been already publiſh'd together, viz. J. Janeway, Printer, in White Friars, near Fleetſtreet; Mr. Wyatt, Copper-Plate Printer, near the Vine-Tavern in Long-Acre; Mr Dickenſon, Printſeller in the Strand; Mr Shropſhire in New-Bond-Street; Mr Orpe, Bookſeller, near the Ram-Tavern, Tooley Street; Mr Lye, Printſeller, near the India-houſe, Leadenhall-Street; Mr Clare, over-againſt St. Andrew's Church, Holborn; Mr Bell, in Long's Court, Leiceſter-Fields; Mr Phillimore, at the Three Compaſſes in Creed-Lane, near St. Paul's; Mr Heſter, under White-Friars Gate; Mr Pool, Bookbinder, at the Lamb in Houndſdich; Mr Dean, in Spicer-Street, Spittle-Fields; Mr Kent, in George-Court, Princeſs Street, Leiceſter-Fields; Mr Amey, near the George-Tavern, Charing-Croſs; and by the Pamphlet-Sellers in Town and Country; where Propoſals are given Gratis.

Where may be had,

PROPOSALS for printing by Subſcription the Hiſtory of the Inquiſitions of the Kingdoms of Spain, Portugal, &c. Illuſtrated, with copper Plates which will be given gratis to Subſcribers only. This Book will contain about Eighty Sheets, in one Volume in Quarto, beautifully and correctly printed on a good Letter and Paper, and will be delivered to the Subſcribers, ſtitch'd in Blue Paper, four Sheets every Fortnight, at their own Houſes, or any other Place they ſhall appoint, for Sixpence each Number, by any of the above named Perſons, and the firſt

Number will be publiſh'd on Saturday the 16th of February next adorned with a curious Frontiſpiece of the Inquiſition Houſe at Granada.

CAſes in Midwifry: Written by the late Mr William Gifford Surgeon and Man midwife. Revis'd and Publiſh'd by Edward Hody M. D and F. R. S.

Printed for Lawton Gilliver, at the Homer's head againſt St Dunſtans Church, Fleetſtreet.

Where likewiſe may be had

The Art of Nurſing: or the Method of Bringing up young Children according to the Rules of Phiſick for the Preſervation of Health and the Prolonging Life. The Second Edition. To which is prefixed, an Arcana, with its Dimenſions uſed abroad to prevent the Overlaying of Children.

THE Preſent State of the Republick of Letters for the Month of December. 1733. which finiſhes the 12th Vol. with an Index to the ſame. Printed for W. Innys and R. Manby at the Weſt End of St Paul's.

N. B. This Work is publiſhed Monthly, and deſigned chiefly for the Uſe of ſuch Gentlemen as live in the Country, and have not an Opportunity of ſeeing the new Books that are publiſhed; it contains not only an Account of what New Books are printed, as well as printing, both at home and abroad, but Extracts from the moſt curious of them, together with ſeveral Diſſertations on various Subjects.

Books lately Printed for T. Worral at Judge Coke's Head, againſt St Dunſtants Church in Fleet-ſtreet.

I. THE Apprentice's Faithful Monitor: Directing him in the ſeveral Branches of his Duty to God, his Maſter and Himſelf, and ſhewing the fatal Conſequences of his Neglect thereof with regard both to his Temporal and Eternal Happineſs. Pr. 1s. 6d. bound, or 15s per Dozen.

II. Friendſhip in Death: in Twenty Letters from the Dead to the Living; the third Edition Pr. 1s.

III. Letters Moral and Entertaining in Proſe and Verſe in 3 parts, by the Same Author, the 3d. Edit. Pr. 5s. 6d. Stitch't.

IIII. Dr Young's true Eſtimate of Human Life in which the Paſſions are conſider'd in a New Light: Pr. 1s. the 4th. Edition.

V! Dr Lupton's Twelve Sermons on Several Occaſions; With his Effigies prefix'd, curiouſly Engraven by Mr Vertue Pr. 5s.

VI. Advice from a Mother to her Son and Daughter, by the celebrated Matchioneſs de Lambert. Pr. 2s. neatly bound.

VII. The Married Philoſopher; a Comedy as Acted at the Theatre Royal in Covent-Garden. Wrote by John Kelly, Eſq; Pr. 1s. 6d.

SUPPLEMENT

TO THE

Gentleman's Magazine:

For the YEAR 1733.

The Proceedings *in last* Session *of* Parliament, *Concluded.*

Debate *on the* Bill *to prevent the infamous Practice of* Stock-jobbing. *See* p. 627.

THIS Bill met with little Opposition till the 3d Reading, *April* 30. when the Question being put, Mr *Gl—s* spoke **A** in Substance as follows:

Sir, in my Opinion, a very great Hardship is to be put by this Bill upon the Proprietors of the publick funds. As the law own stands, a Gentleman may sell his estate, a Merchant or Tradesman his goods, every man may dispose of his property by a **B** bargain for time, or in whatever manner he pleases: but by this Bill the creditors of the publick, those who have put their trust in the publick faith, are to be laid under a particular restraint; which they were no way subject to when they lent their **C** money: from henceforth they must not dispose of their property, but in the particular manner by this Bill prescrib'd —— I am as great an enemy to Stock-jobbing as any Gentleman in this House, and for preventing that pernicious practice, shall be glad to join in any measures not destructive **D** of publick credit, or injurious to private persons, with respect to the free use of their property; but, as I think the measures proposed by this Bill will certainly be destructive of the one, and injurious to the other, I cannot let it pass without taking the liberty of objecting against it.— 'Tis in all cases a great hardship put upon **E** people, to subject them to penalties which may often by meer ignorance be incurr'd; but in this case the hardship is the greater, because there are many proprietors of the

publick funds, particularly women, who cannot be presum'd to be readers of Acts of Parliament : they put an entire confidence in their Brokers, and if the Broker happens to neglect some of the forms prescribed, the most innocent persons may be brought under great penalties. Nay, if this Bill passes into a Law, it will always be in the power of two or three Brokers to subject those that employ them to the severe penalties to be enacted by this Bill; for if two Brokers should combine together, and enter in their books a bargain for time, as made between two of their correspondents, they might easily get a third person to combine with 'em, and to inform against the presumed buyer and seller, the Brokers books sworn to by the Brokers whom they usually employ'd would be a strong proof against them; and thus innocent men might be brought to suffer severely for an agreement which had never enter'd into their heads. —— It often happens, Sir, that a Gentleman who foresees that he shall have use for his money in 3 or 4 months time, is well satisfied with the price his stock bears, but cares not to sell it for ready money, because he does not know what to do with his money in the mean time: but as the law now stands, he may take the advantage of the current price of stock, he may sell it out at that price, to be deliver'd only when he knows he shall have occasion for the money; this he acquaints his Broker of, who may probably find out a man who likes the then current price and expects money to be thrown into his hands in 3 or 4 months, which he resolves to employ in that fund : in this case the

buying

buying and selling for time is convenient for both, and it's not to be question'd but many are encouraged to become purchasers of Stock on this very account; therefore the forbidding of any such agreement for the future, will not only prove an inconvenience to many now possessed of Stock, but will prevent people's becoming purchasers, and consequently prejudice publick credit. — The chief support of the credit of our publick funds is owing to the ready access people have at all times to their money there lodg'd; but this ready access will, by this Bill, be made very precarious to all those who shall hereafter be obliged to sell at once all the property they have in any particular fund; for if the purchaser should fail to comply with his agreement, the seller cannot on the transfer-day compound the difference with him, and sell out his Stock to another, in order to raise the money he has immediate use for: no, he must sue the man he sells to, and for that end he must make a transfer of his Stock, which transfer must stand upon the books during the suit; he cannot, in the mean time, sell his Stock to another; for if he does, he will not be able to shew at the Tryal, that he had made a specifical performance on his part, and consequently he will be nonsuited, and obliged to pay costs. This, Sir, will be a most intolerable grievance upon all the proprietors of our publick funds, and will make many of them resolve to turn their money to some other use. —— I must be of opinion, that the making a Law to prevent mens coming to an amicable composition of any difference that may be between them, seems to me something extraordinary. This will be such a discouragement, that no man, I believe, will chuse to become a purchaser of any of our funds, when he knows that he cannot afterwards sell out his Stock, without exposing himself to the danger of being involved in a law-suit, to which he is by law expressly prohibited to put an end by an amicable agreement. And if a purchaser should by any disappointment, be disabled to comply with the purchase he had made, but was willing to pay down, in ready money, the difference, which might not, perhaps, amount to five pounds, it would be very hard to oblige him to stand out a law-suit to the very last, which would cost him, at least, treble that money.—That of obliging a man to answer upon oath, in a case where great penalties may be incurred, seems likewise to me to be a

very new and extraordinary clause; it is no way consonant to the spirit of our laws, to oblige any man to accuse himself, and as it lays a foundation for every person that pleases to be so malicious, to bring a Bill in Chancery against any man, who is, or ever was possess'd of any of our publick funds, it will be a great discouragement to any man's becoming a purchaser, or continuing to be a proprietor of those funds, and will of course tend to the destruction of publick credit.——Another hardship, is, that no man, for the future, can employ a Merchant to buy or sell Stock for him; for if a Merchant should be employ'd, and should charge commission for his trouble, he would incur some of the penalties of this Bill, unless he kept a regular book, and fairly entered therein all such transactions. —— All these are hardships which I think the creditors of the publick ought not to be subjected to; and therefore, I cannot give my consent to the passing of this Bill. I would sooner have taken notice of these things, but there happen'd to be such a noise in the House both upon the 2d reading of this Bill, and likewise when it was in the Committee, that I could not expect to be heard, and therefore I did not then rise to say any thing against it.

· W——m B——les, Esq; *spoke also against the Bill's passing, and then*

Sir G——ge C——ll.] Sir, it is evident that this Bill will be extremely inconvenient to all the proprietors or dealers in any of our publick securities: The words of it are so general, that I do not know, but that even Navy-Bills, and contracts for furnishing the Navy with provisions, will be comprehended; and, if they are, the usual way of dealing in such affairs will be entirely prevented, which may be of dangerous consequence to the Nation; for it is well known, that those who contract for furnishing the Navy with provisions, seldom or never have as much money of their own as is sufficient for making good the contracts they enter into. It is usual for a man who has not, perhaps, 10,000 *l.* of his own, to contract for furnishing the Navy with 40,000 *l.* worth of provisions; and in such cases the method always hitherto observed, is, for the Contractor, as soon as he has made such contract, to go to some money'd man, who furnishes him with what money he stands in need of, upon his becoming bound for the money advanced with interest from the date, and obliging himself to deliver Navy-Bills, at the price then agreed on, equal

equal to the principal money then advanced, and the interest that shall in the mean time grow due.——These Bills I look on as publick Securities, because they are generally every year provided for by Parliament, and therefore I take them to be within the general words of this Bill; and as all such Bills vary a great deal in their price, insomuch that I have known them at 45 *per Cent.* Discount, it will for the future be impossible for those who contract for furnishing the Navy with provisions to enter into any such agreement with any money'd man whatever; consequently no man can hereafter contract for furnishing the Navy with more provisions than he can purchase with his own money, which will of course make the providing for the Navy much more difficult than heretofore.——This is one very great inconvenience, which must arise from this Bill, but there are so many others, that in my opinion, the title of the Bill ought to be altered and instead of calling it a Bill for preventing the scandalous practice of Stock-jobbing, it ought to be called a Bill for the destroying of publick credit.

Sir *J—n B—rd.*] I did not offer to rise up sooner, because, as we are now on the 3d reading of this Bill, against which few or no objections were made in any part of its progress thro' this House, I was willing to hear all the objections that were to be made against it. I am indeed surprized to hear any Gentleman say, there was such a noise in the House that he could not be heard: It is true, when a Bill is a passing, which is thought to be a Bill of course, but few Gentlemen give great attention to it, and many fall a talking with one another, which must of course occasion some little noise in the House; but upon any such occasion, whoever inclines to speak to the Bill in hand, may rise up and call to the Chair, whose duty it is to order silence, and then the house will become attentive to the Gentleman who is to speak.——I wish, Sir, that the Gentlemen had made their objections to this Bill, when it was before the Committee, for then it might have been made to their own liking, if it be possible to make any such Bill to their Liking. When any Bill is brought into this House, it's usual for all Gentlemen who have a mind that some Bill of that nature should pass, to make the objections, either upon the 2d reading, or upon its being committed, that such amendments may be then made

to the Bill, as may obviate all the objections that can be reasonably made against it: but when Gentlemen have no mind any Bill of that nature should pass, they reserve all their objections to the very last, in order to throw out the Bill on its 3d reading: for this reason I must have some suspicion, that those Gentlemen, who now begin to make their objections against this Bill, have no mind that any such Bill should pass as would effectually put an end to the practice of Stock-jobbing.——I find it is granted on all hands, that the practice of Stock-jobbing is pernicious to trade, and ought to be remedied if possible: By the Bill now before us, we propose to remedy this Evil. Now, in all such cases, it is certain no remedy can be proposed, but will be attended with some inconveniences; therefore we are to consider whether the inconveniencies remedied by the Law proposed, are more considerable than those that may be occasion'd thereby? If we judge that the first are the most considerable, we are surely to pass the Bill: If we judge that the last are the most considerable, we are to throw out the Bill, and rather continue under an evil than subject ourselves to a greater. By this rule let the Bill now before us be tried.——The many bad consequences of Stock-jobbing are well known, and that it is high time to put an end to that infamous practice, I hope most Gentlemen in this House are convinced of. It is a Lottery, or rather a Gaming-house publickly set up in the middle of the city of *London*, by which the heads of our Merchants and Tradesmen are turned from getting a livelihood by the honest means of industry and frugality, and are inticed to become Gamesters by the hopes of getting an estate at once. It is not only a Lottery, but one of the very worst sort, because it is always in the power of the principal managers to bestow the benefit Tickets as they have a mind. It is but lately, since by the Arts of Stock-jobbing, the *East-India* Stock was run up to 200 *per Cent.* and in a little time after, it tumbled down again below 153. Several Millions were lost and won by this single jobb, many poor men undone; so bare-faced were some at that time, in the infamous practice of Stock-jobbing, that after that Stock began to fall they sold it cheaper for time, than for ready money, which no man would have done, unless he had been made acquainted with the Secret which came afterwards to be unfolded, but was then known

to

to a very few.——We know how apt mankind are in their own natures to become Gameſters, but in this game of Stock-jobbing, our Merchants, Tradeſmen, and Shopkeepers are prompted not only by their own inclinations, but alſo by ſome of their acquaintance, who have taken up the trade of Brokers in *Exchange-Alley*. It is natural for men to endeavour to make the moſt of their buſineſs; and as there are ſuch a number of Brokers, we may believe ſome of them do endeavour to perſuade thoſe of their acquaintance to become Stock-jobbers. The Broker comes perhaps to the Merchant, and talks to him of the many Fatigues and Dangers, the great trouble and ſmall Profits that are in his way of trade; and after having done all he can to put him out of conceit with his Buſineſs, which is often too eaſily effectuated, he propoſes to dig for him in the rich Mine of *Exchange-Alley*, and to get more for him in a day than he could get by his trade in a Twelvemonth. Thus the Merchant is perſuaded, he engages, he goes on for ſome time, but never knows what he is a doing 'till he is quite undone: His juſt Creditors are ſurpriz'd, and ſay *This man had a good ſtock to begin with, he has had a good Trade for ſeveral Years; he never lived extravagantly, what is become of his Effects and Money?* They enquire into his Affairs, and at laſt perhaps find out, that the whole was gam'd away by his Broker in *Exchange-Alley*.

This may increaſe Publick Credit for a Time, but I am ſure it is a great Diſcouragement to Trade, which is the chief, the only ſolid Support of Publick credit; and it is the Ruin of all private Credit, it deſtroys that mutual Faith among Merchants, by which only our Trade can be made to flouriſh. This is a domeſtiak Evil, which, tho' fatal in its Conſequences, yet does not perhaps immediately draw any money out of the nation; but there is a foreign evil attending the game of Stock-jobbing, by which the nation may be plundered of great Sums at once. It is by the means of ſtock-jobbing always in the power of every foreign court to raiſe contributions upon this nation whenever they pleaſe: They need do no more but ſend over and order a great deal of ſtock to be ſold out at the current price for time, then raiſe an alarm of the *Pretender*, or ſome ſuch alarm, by which they may make all our publick funds fall, and ſo purchaſe in ſtock perhaps 20 *per Cent.*

cheaper than they ſold, in order to perform their part of the contracts they had before made for time. Thus, they may make a harveſt of the fall of our publick funds, and as they know beſt when the alarm will blow over, they may make a new harveſt of their Riſe.——Theſe are but a few of the many inconveniences that ariſe by Stock-jobbing. Give me leave now, Sir, to examine thoſe Inconveniences, which 'tis pretended will be occaſioned by paſſing this Bill into a Law: As to the real and honeſt creditors of the publick, I have as great a regard for that faith which ought to be preſerved towards them as any Gentleman whatever; I ſhall never be for doing any thing, that may leſſen their ſecurity as to the payment either of their principal, or intereſt, and I wiſh that every Gentleman in this houſe were of the ſame mind. But can it be ſaid, that the making ſuch regulation as the publick good requires for the transferring of their property from one to another, is any impeachment of the publick faith? The preventing of Stock-jobbing is ſo far from being a breach of publick faith, that I am ſure it is what all the honeſt creditors of the publick deſire: And as there is nothing in the Bill that can be a hardſhip upon any fair purchaſer, or ſeller, it will be ſo far from being deſtructive to publick credit, that it will rather increaſe it, becauſe it will make the value of every man's property in the publick funds more certain and invariable; for all thoſe who have no other aim but to receive their dividends punctually, and to have their principal money ſecure, chuſe to be in that fund which is ſubject to the feweſt and leaſt mutations; and this is the reaſon that we always ſee the annuity funds bear a higher price in proportion than any of our trading ſtocks.——To ſay, that no penalty ought to be inflicted on a practice that is found to be inconſiſtent with the publick good, becauſe perſons ignorant of the law may thereby ſuffer, ſeems to me, to be a very odd pretence. I hope Gentlemen will in all other caſes be as careful of inflicting penalties upon the ſubject: It is indeed what ought never to be done but in caſe of the utmoſt Neceſſity; but where the Advancement of the publick good, or the ſecurity of private property can be come at in no other way, it muſt be done, and every man is obliged to know the law, or to apply himſelf to thoſe that do. In the preſent caſe no man can by ignorance ſubject him.

himself to the penalties proposed in this Bill, without some dishonest intent, for I am convinced, that no man ever did, or ever will either buy or sell stock for time, unless he knows more, or at least thinks he knows more about that stock than the man to whom he sells, or from whom he buys; which intention is certainly not very fair, tho', when it is not extended too far, it may be necessary to overlook it in the way of commerce.——This leads me to consider the pretended conveniences of bargains in stock for time. Suppose a Gentleman finds he must sell out his stock three months hence, suppose another expects money in 3 months time, which he intends to lay out on the purchase of stock, I believe neither the one will purchase, nor the other sell 'till that time comes, unless he knows, or thinks he knows some secret relating to that stock which other people are not aware of; for if he that is to sell expects no variation in the value of his property, why should he sell 'till he has occasion for his money? But granting that he is so much satisfied with the then current price, that he resolves to sell at that very time, may he not sell for ready money, and lodge it in the bank 'till he has occasion for it, as to the buyer, I am sure no wise man will venture to purchase stock 'till he has the money at command, unless he does it in expectation that the stock will rise, which is downright gaming, and what is intended by this Bill to be prevented.———As to a man's being obliged to answer upon oath to any Bill filed against him, it can be no hardship, because, whoever does so answer, and fairly discovers the Agreement made, is free from all penalties; he becomes liable to nothing but to return the money which he received; and as the law now stands, whoever receives money to another's use, is obliged to answer upon oath, and will be obliged to return the money he confesses so to have received.——To pretend that by this Bill men may be subjected to great penalties by the perjury and conspiracy of two or three brokers, is another Objection for which there is no foundation; for against perjuries and conspiracies there can be no guard but that of a fair tryal by an honest jury; and it would be almost impossible for 3 Rogues to concert their story so, but that the conspiracy would be discovered by examining them apart, and cross-questioning each, in the manner usual at all tryals; so that this too is nothing but an imaginary evil,

and is as strong an objection against every penal law, that ever was or ever can be enacted, as it is against the Bill now before us.—There is nothing in this Bill, that can oblige any man to go to law, contrary to his inclinations, or prevent his making up any difference there may be between him and another; for tho' the buyer of the stock may not be able to pay for the stock he had bought, because of some disappointment he has in the mean time met with, yet it is not to be presumed, that he will not be able to pay the difference in ready money; and if he can pay that in ready money at the books, cannot he immediately sell out the stock to another at the then current price, and thereby raise the rest of the money, which he may order to be delivered to the man who sold to him? May not every bargain be thus specifically performed, if the parties are inclined so to do? In this the only inconvenience is, that there must be a double transfer, which is performed with so little trouble or expence, that I hope, it will be no way regarded in the present debate. It may be supposed, if this Bill passes into a law, there will be few or no purchasers, but such as are able to perform at the time they purchase, therefore, the other objection, of the seller's being obliged to keep his stock till the end of a tedious law-suit, is of no weight, as there will be no room for law-suits on that head.——I am really surprised, to hear Gentlemen talk of their being by this Bill prevented from employing a Merchant or friend to buy or sell stock for them, such Gentlemen do not, it seems, know, that commission and brokerage are two different articles: If a Merchant is employed to buy or sell stock for another, he may either do it himself, or he may imploy a broker; if he employs a broker, be charges both brokerage and commission, and if he does it himself he charges only commission: In neither case does he act as a broker, nor will he be obliged to keep any book for that purpose.—I have now gone thro' all the material objections I have heard made against this Bill. I hope, I have shewn that there is no weight in any of them; that all the inconveniences which are pretended to arise from this Bill, are imaginary; and yet very real inconveniences arise from the infamous practice of Stock-jobbing; We ought to consider that no bad custom ever crept into any Nation, but what some people got by; and, let it be as per-

pernicious as it will, we may preſume that thoſe who get by it, will endeavour to raiſe objections againſt every effectual remedy that can be offered; but as no Gentleman in this houſe can be any way concerned in the gettings by Stock-jobbing, ſo, I hope, they will not allow themſelves to be miſled by frivolous objections ſtarted without doors by thoſe who are.

S—y B——k,] Eſq; Sir, I make no doubt but there was a great deal of money loſt and won by the late ſudden riſe and fall of *Eaſt-India* ſtock, and I am perſuaded that a great many of thoſe who became purchaſers upon the riſe, were ſuch as never intended to hold the ſtock for the ſake of the dividend, but bought only with a view of making an advantage by ſelling it out again at an advanced price: This, 'tis true, is a ſort of gaming, but ſuch a ſort as cannot be entirely prevented even by the Bill before us; in ſuch a caſe no great benefit can be expected by the Bill, and in many caſes it will certainly be attended with great inconveniences. I ſhall mention only two; firſt that of the long annuities: It often happens that in the ſale of ſuch publick ſecurities, the ſeller muſt deduce his title in the ſame manner as if he were to ſell a land eſtate; ſo that it will be impoſſible for him to compleat the Conveyance in ten days, which is the time limited in this Bill, and therefore I am of opinion, that the ſale of ſuch annuities will, in many caſes, become impracticable if this Bill ſhould paſs into a law.—It is certain, that all merchants may ſell goods they deal in to be delivered at any time the contracters ſhall agree on: I know that in the *Ruſſia* trade it is uſual for the Merchants to enter into contracts to deliver hemp at a certain price, at a certain future time, tho', perhaps, at the time of making the contract, the hemp is not ſo much as purchaſed or contracted for in *Ruſſia*, and I can ſee no reaſon why the proprietors of our publick funds ſhould not enjoy the ſame privilege.—The other inconvenience is, the diſappointments ſome of the publick creditors may meet with in the ſale of their properties, which will certainly be much aggravated by this Bill: Suppoſe a man enters into an agreement for the purchaſe of a land eſtate, and covenants to pay the price againſt ſuch a day under a great penalty; for enabling him to perform his agreement he ſells out 10,000 l. of his ſtock, to be delivered ſome few days before that

day on which he is, by his covenant, obliged to pay for his eſtate: Suppoſe the purchaſer of the ſtock does not come to accept of the ſtock, or to pay the price; as the law *now* ſtands, the ſeller of the ſtock may make a tender of his ſtock at the books, and may ſell it out next transfer day at the riſk of the buyer, by which he is enabled to pay for his eſtate, and he may recover from the purchaſer of his ſtock what he loſt by his not accepting and paying for the ſtock according to agreement: But if this Bill paſſes into a law, the ſeller of ſtock muſt, I preſume, keep his ſtock 'till the end of the law-ſuit between him and the buyer, in order that he may be always ready to make a ſpecifical performance; by which means, if he has no other fund for raiſing ready money, he muſt ſubject himſelf to the penalty of his covenant as to the purchaſe of the eſtate. As theſe are inconveniences which may often occur, I think it is hard to ſubject the proprietors of the publick funds to them; therefore I ſhall be againſt the Bill's paſſing in the form it is at preſent.

Mr C—r of the E——r.] Sir, I wiſh the objections now ſtarted againſt paſſing this Bill had been mentioned either upon the ſecond reading, or in the Committee: I do really think that the Bill might have been drawn up, as to ſome Parts of it, with more perſpicuity, ſo as to have intirely obviated the objections now made to it; but as moſt of the objections now made are founded upon miſtakes, as to the meaning and intention of the Bill, I am therefore of opinion, that they ought not to be of weight enough to prevent its paſſing.—As to what the hon. Gentleman was pleaſed to mention about navy-contracts, I can't think they come any way under the preſent caſe. The navy always contracted to pay ready money to all thoſe who agree to furniſh them with any ſtores or proviſions, and after a man has entered into ſuch a contract, he may certainly ſell, or aſſign any intereſt he has therein to another, notwithſtanding the Bill before us. Upon ſuch contracts the money is indeed generally paid by navy-bills, but that cannot hinder the private contracter to raiſe money upon his contract after what manner he pleaſes; he may even oblige himſelf to deliver navy-bills at ſuch a price; for, before they are iſſued they ſurely cannot be deemed to be publick ſecurities; and if, upon delivering the ſtores and proviſions, the navy ſhould actually pay ready money to the private

con-

contracter, can it be so much as pretended, that he would be then obliged to deliver navy-bills to the person from whom he had borrowed money upon his contract with the navy? Would not, the repayment of the money borrowed with interest be a full performance of his Engagement with the lender? Navy-bills, indeed, after they are once issued, do certainly become publick securities, and are to be bought and sold in the manner prescribed by this Bill, which can no way injure publick credit.—As to the objection against compounding, or voluntarily receiving any difference money, I cannot think, that the law, as to the performance on the seller's part, is any way altered by this Bill. He is not by this Bill obliged to keep the stock sold, in his possession, any longer than he was before; he may certainly perform upon his part by a tender of the stock, he may then sell out his stock, and bring his action against the buyer for not performing his part of the contract, upon which action he will recover the difference by way of damages. —Indeed, that objection relating to the long annuities has something more in it, and therefore, I wish it had been provided against; but it is a case that will happen but seldom, and the difficulty may be, by proper management and dispatch, in all cases surmounted; therefore I do not think it sufficient for throwing out the Bill; for the practice of Stock-jobbing has been so prejudicial to this nation, that no trivial objection ought to take place against a Bill by which, I think, that practice will be prevented for the future. —I have long wished for some such Bill: Every one knows, that even the administration has been sometimes distressed by the practices of Stock-jobbers: they have correspondents settled at all the courts of *Europe*, and upon all occasions of moment have their expresses, who being paid better make much greater dispatch than the Government expresses.—I must say, that the late practices in the *East-India* stock, were really something surprising; there might perhaps be some, who upon its rise bought only with a view of selling out again at an advanced price; but I am persuaded others bought even at the highest price with an honest intention, of holding the stock they bought, and taking their dividends as they should become due. The price of that stock, and of every other stock, must always be according to the value of money at the time, and the dividend made, or that may probably be

made upon the stock: At that time our 4 *per Cents.* were selling at a *Premium* even our 3 *per Cents.* were selling at very near *Par*, and therefore we must conclude according to the value of money at that time, an annuity of 4 *per Cent.* was worth 100 *l.* principal money. That company had divided 8 *per cent.* for many years, had but just before paid 200,000 *l.* to the Government for a prolongation of their term; and at the same time declared they were able to do all this, and likewise to pay off 4 or 500,000 *l.* of their bonds, out of the profits of their trade: From all which those who were not in the deepest secrets of their affairs, had very good reason to conclude, that they would have been able to have continued the same dividend for many years; therefore 100 *l. East-India* stock was a cheap purchase when bought, even for 200 *l.* The resolution was soon after taken for diminishing their dividend, and that was as natural a reason for the fall of their stock, as their former declarations had been for its rise. What were the motives for this management I shall not pretend to determine; but I am afraid, the game of Stock-jobbing is often the cause of managements in that, and all other publick funds: If we destroy the cause, the effects must cease, and of consequence the price of all publick stocks will become more certain, which will, I am sure, make them more valuable to all honest purchasers. The fluctuating of the price can be no advantage to any but brokers, and to those who have a mind to make indirect advantages by Stock-jobbing: Those practices will, I think, be prevented by this bill, consequently it will tend to the improvement of publick credit, therefore I shall be for its passing.

L—d H—y,] I cannot agree with my friend over the way. I must be of opinion, that if this Bill passes, no seller can sue for any difference upon the Stock sold, nor can he recover damages, which I take to be the same with difference, unless he has the Stock in his possession the whole time of the suit: by this Bill every bargain is to be specifically performed, therefore the seller, as I take it, must sue only for a specifical performance, which he can't do unless he is, at all times, during the continuance of the suit, in a condition and ready to perform specifically upon his part, for which end he must always have of that Stock which he has sold, at least as much as he is obliged to deliver to the buyer; therefore, if a Man has sold all the share he has in any publick fund, in order to

enable

enable him to perform his part of an A-
greement about something else, if the
buyer does not come to take the Stock,
and pay the price, the seller must subject
himself to the penalty of his other Agreement, or give up all pretences for recovering any thing from the buyer of his Stock,
either by way of difference or damages.
This will be a great hardship upon all
Stockholders, and as they will, by this
Bill, be subjected to a great many other
Inconveniencies, and to several heavy penalties, I shall be against its passing.

Sir W—mT—ge.] Sir, in the case now before us, I take it to be of no consequence,
whether or no the seller can recover either difference or damages, and therefore,
whether or no they be in effect the same
is no material question. I am very well
convinced, that no circumstances can ever
lay a Man under the necessity of selling or
buying for time; no Man can so much as
have an inclination that way, unless he be
endowed with the spirit of gaming, or unless he knows a secret by which he thinks
he can make an unjust advantage of the
person he sells to, or purchases from; therefore, I look upon the putting a final end
to this practice to be one of the principal
aims of this Bill, to which, I have not
heard one material objection offered; as
I was one of those appointed to bring it
in, I can say, that all possible care was taken to make the words as plain, and the
terms as easy as were consistent with putting an effectual end to the evils against
which the Bill was originally proposed.
However, as the Bill is to go to another
place, I do not know but some few words
may be added or altered, in order to obviate, as much as possible, all objections
that have been or may be made to it.

Sir J—n B—rd,] Sir, it is very certain
that long annuities are included in this
Bill; they must not be bought or sold hereafter but according to the manner prescribed by it. But I am certain, that can be
no objection to its passing; for no wise,
no honest Man, will presume to sell any
thing till he has made his title to it as
clear as the nature of the thing can admit
of; therefore I think, no possessor of a
long annuity will presume to sell 'till after
he has deduced his title, and made it clear,
in which case all such bargains may be specifically performed within ten days after
the making; but if any accidental delay
should in the mean time happen, the parties may, by mutual consent, put off the
specifical performance for what time they
please; nothing in this Bill can prevent

such a mutual Indulgence. I did not before take notice of the objection made,
that this Bill, if it passes, may be the occasion of the bringing many suits in equity against the possessors of our publick
funds. This, I must say, I am surprised
at; what guard has any Man, as the law
now stands, against *Chancery* suits? May
not any Man now bring a Bill in equity a-
gainst me, and set forth, that I owe him
a large sum of money, tho' I never had
any dealings with him in my life? Such a
Bill may certainly be brought, but what
would be the fate of it? it would be dif-
missed with costs. This is my dependence,
I know I have never done any thing that
may render me liable to the having of
such a Bill brought against me, therefore
I depend on it that no such Bill will be
brought. And would it not be the same
if the Bill now before us should pass? Is
it to be supposed, that any Man would
subject himself to the immediate expence
of 10 or 12l. and the danger of being o-
bliged to pay 20 or 30 more, unless he
had very strong proofs against the Man
whom he made defendant to his Bill?
This is really putting cases almost impossible, in order from thence to raise objections against a Bill, for the remedy of
what is by every Gentleman in this house
acknowledged a most insufferable evil.

W—m Gl—le, Esq;] Sir, I must observe,
that the possessor of a long annuity, who
has a mind to sell, may think his title as
clear as the sun at noon-day, and yet when
he comes to shew it to the purchaser, he
may find several objections: In such case
it must be laid before the purchaser's council; he must examine all the title-deeds,
and a conveyance must be drawn up and
settled by council, both for the seller and
buyer, and this will be admitted, I believe,
not to be practicable in ten days, so that
I must still be of opinion, the sale of such
publick Securities will, by this Bill, be
made very dangerous and difficult, if not
altogether impossible. As to Bills in equity it is certain, no Man will ever file such
a Bill unless he expects some discovery by
the defendant's answer. As the law now
stands, no Man can expect any discovery
from a Man with whom he never had any
transactions: but by the Bill now before us,
every man will have some encouragement
to expect a discovery of something he
may make an advantage of by the defendant's answer, if such defendant ever was
a dealer in any of our publick funds; because, if he ever made a contract contrary
to the terms of this Bill, he will be obliged

ged to discover it by his answer, and tho' he may be thereby discharged from the penalty, yet the other party contracting with him is not ; so that the person who files the Bill may thereby make an advantage, either by recovering the money received by the defendant upon an unlawful contract, or by grounding an information upon that answer for recovering a penalty from the other party concerned in such unlawful contract or composition ; therefore, I think, it is evident, that if this Bill passes, the proprietors of the publick funds will be more liable to have Bills in equity preferred against them, than any other persons in the kingdom are. I shall conclude with taking notice of one case where people are often obliged to sell before they can be ready to deliver, that is, in the case of executors and trustees, where the trust-stock must generally be sold by a Bill in Chancery. According to the practice now observed, they must sell before they bring their Bill, because the purchaser is always made a party to the suit ; and a *Chancery* suit cannot be begun and ended, and the bargain specifically performed in ten days.

T—s B—tle, Esq;] Sir, I rise up only to rectify some mistakes that I find gentlemen seem to be in. According to the present practice, no Man that sells stock is obliged to keep it after the day on which he contracted to deliver it : If the buyer do not come on that day to accept the stock, and pay the price he agreed to give for it, the seller makes publication at the books for him to accept, and pay for the stock then ready to be deliver'd according to contract : An actual transfer is made upon the books, and stands 'till the shutting up of the books for that day ; if the buyer do not come to accept of, and pay for the stock so transferred, the transfer is then cancelled, and upon next transfer-day the seller may sell his stock to whom he pleases at the current price, and if he sells it at a loss, he has an action for breach of covenant against the buyer, upon which action he always recovers the difference by way of damages : The publication and transfer made at the books upon the day agreed on proved duly in court, is always taken for a specifical performance on the part of the seller ; the buyer has no title at any time after that day to demand a new specifical performance. This is the present practice in all such cases, and there is nothing in the Bill now before us which can alter it ; therefore I must conclude, that as to this case, no Stockholder can be brought under any hardship by the Bill

before us. With respect to the long annuities, why may not they be sold as land-estates generally are ? When the seller finds out one who is willing to purchase, the first thing he does is to satisfy him about the title, before they so much as talk about the price. If this method be observed with respect to the sale of long annuities, it cannot be said, but that the agreement may be specifically performed by both parties within ten days after making the same. As to the sale of stock vested in executors or trustees, there is no necessity of selling it before the Bill in Chancery be filed, or before a decree passes for that purpose : It may be suggested in the Bill, that such a Man is willing to purchase ; and he may be made a party to the suit, as well as if he had actually become a purchaser ; the effect would be the same, and he would get his costs in the one case as well as in the other. And as to Stock-holders being exposed to the danger of having Bills in Chancery filed against them, there is nothing in it ; no fair dealer in Stocks can ever be exposed to such danger, for whoever files such a Bill must set forth the unlawful contract particularly. We are not to imagine, that, from any clause in this Bill, a Man will be allowed to bring a Bill in equity, and suggest generally that the defendant has made some unlawful contract in Stocks ; no, the plaintiff must certainly set forth the particular contract of which he prays a discovery ; and this he cannot do, unless there has not only been some unlawful contract, but such unlawful contract as he has had information of ; and if upon the issue of the cause his information appears groundless, he may expect to pay all costs ; so that no Man can have reason to be afraid of any such Bill being filed against him, unless he has actually made some unlawful contract ; and that no such Man should rest in security is the very design of this Bill. In short, Sir, from all the objections and cases that have been put, I can see nothing but imaginary difficulties ; and as the Bill now before us will, in my opinion, put an end to many real evils, of the most dangerous consequence, therefore I shall with all my heart be for its passing this house, and hope it will be passed into a law.

J—ph D—rs, Esq; spoke next against the Bill ; and then the question was put for its passing, which on a division was carried in the affirmative, 55 against 49. It was accordingly sent up to the House of Lords, where it met with so many amendments, that upon its return, it was entirely dropt.

May 10. *The House of Commons having (according to Order) reſolved itſelf into a Committee of the whole Houſe, to conſider of methods for the relief of ſuch of the Sufferers in the Charitable Corporation, as were Objects of Compaſſion.*

L—d T—l *roſe up, and after a ſhort but moving ſpeech in favour of thoſe poor Sufferers, made a Motion for the Houſe to come to a Reſolution, That the relief to be given to ſuch of the Sufferers in the Charitable Corporation, as were Objects of Compaſſion, ſhould be by way of Lottery, not exceeding one Million.*

S—l S—ys, *Eſq; ſpoke next, and ſaid, that he was of opinion, that by the Order of the Houſe for going into that Committee, they had no power to come to any* C *ſuch Reſolution ; in ſupport of which he gave ſeveral reaſons, and was anſwered by Sir W——m Y——ge. After him*

G—es E—le *Eſq; ſpoke to this Effect,* Sir, I am very much for giving all the relief we can to ſuch as are Objects of Charity, but I am as much againſt doing D it by way of Lottery ; for by ſuch a method, in order to relieve thoſe who have been cheated and undone, we ſhall give a handle by which a much greater number of weak people may be undone.

T—s P—r *Eſq;*] Tho' I always was, Sir, and always ſhall be againſt all Lotteries, yet I ſhall be glad to ſee thoſe poor E unhappy people relieved, and I hope ſome effectual methods may be taken for operating that relief ; but do not let us think of giving it, by ſetting up what has been always deemed a publick Nuiſance: I believe it will be better to grant a ſum of money to the Crown for the relief of F thoſe of the Sufferers who are really objects of compaſſion ; but, whatever relief is to be granted, I think it ought to be very much confined ; for as to all thoſe who ſhall appear to have been Gameſters in that Stock, they no more merit the compaſſion of the publick, than thoſe who G are undone at a Gaming-table. I doubt much if any of the *Men* who became adventurers in that Corporation deſerve much compaſſion ; I am afraid moſt of them purchaſed, either with a View of making an unjuſt profit by the advanced price of the ſhares, or with a View to have a higher Intereſt for their money H than they were by law entitled to ; in either caſe they are almoſt as fraudulent as the Managers ; for he that cheats, or extorts from a man 1 s. is as much guilty of fraud, as he that cheats him of 1000 l. Indeed, as to the Ladies, a great many

of them may have been innocently drawn in, and their caſe is really to be pitied ; they only are the proper Objects of Compaſſion, and therefore I hope whatever relief is to be given, will be confined to the Fair Sex only.

L—d T—l.] I have, Sir, as great a regard for the Fair Sex, as the Gentleman who ſpoke laſt, and with him, I think they are really the greateſt Objects of our Compaſſion ; but, Sir, let us conſider, many of thoſe Gentlemen, who have been undone, have wives and daughters, whom I cannot but look upon to be at leaſt as great Objects of Compaſſion, as any of thoſe Ladies who have been undone by their own act and deed.

Sir C—s W—r] In my opinion, Sir, the only means we can think of, for relieving theſe unhappy Sufferers is to make a Lottery for their benefit ; but that a Lottery of a Million will be too large ; I believe one of 500,000 l. may be ſufficient ; and therefore I ſhall ſecond the Motion to the amount of that ſum.

M—r of the R—ls.] Sir, before we think of granting any money to the Crown, or in any other way, for the relief of thoſe Sufferers, we ought to conſider, whether or no we have Power to grant away the publick money for relief of private perſons, I muſt really be of opinion that we have not ; we are to diſpoſe of the publick money for publick uſes : 'Tis true, we have ſometimes granted money to the King for the rewarding of private Perſons, but ſuch Grants have always been made for ſome Services, render'd by thoſe perſons to the publick ; therefore the money granted was really for the uſe of the publick. Even the raiſing of money by Lottery, is raiſing money upon the people, and if any part of it is granted away to private perſons, I muſt look upon it to be a converting the publick money to private uſes, which I think we have no power to do ; and upon that Account, as well as the many inconveniences that attend Lotteries,I muſt be againſt the Motion.

T—s W——n, *Eſq;*] Sir, I have always had a great regard for the opinion of the hon. and learned Gentleman who ſpoke laſt ; but I hope he will excuſe me, if I ſay, I do not think the objections he has now made againſt the propoſition in hand, are near ſo ſtrong as thoſe uſually made by him. As to granting money for the relief in queſtion, I do not know what power we may have, but there are ſeveral inſtances where we have granted even a publick Tax for the relief of private rate perſons. Every Gentleman in this Houſe may remember the caſe of the Suitors in Chancery, whoſe money had been loſt by the miſ-conduct of the late Lord Chancellor and the then Maſters in Chancery: This houſe laid a Tax upon the Law, which I take to be a Tax upon the People, becauſe the whole is paid by the Clients in that Court, and not by the Lawyers; and the money to ariſe by this Tax was appropriated towards making good the Loſs which the Suitors in that Court had ſuſtained. Another Inſtance of the ſame nature is that Tax which was granted for relief of the Orphans within the City of *London*; and I believe ſeveral other inſtances could be given, if we were to examine the Journals of this Houſe.——However, I do not take this to be the queſtion now before us; for I cannot imagine how it can be thought, that the granting a Lottery is either a Tax or an Impoſition upon the publick. By granting a Lottery we do not oblige any man to pay towards it, no man is to be forced to become an adventurer; it is really not ſo much a grant of money, as it is a repeal in ſo far of an Act of Parliament lately made againſt private Lotteries; for if it were not for that ſtatute, the Charitable Corporation could of themſelves ſet up ſuch a Lottery as is now propoſed: and as the making of that Law was occaſion'd by the many frauds that were committed by the means of private Lotteries, and the downright bites that were often put upon people under that name, the cauſe entirely ceaſes with reſpect to the Lottery now propoſed, from which no fraud or bite can be ſo much as ſuſpected.

Sir *W—m W—m.*] Sir, I am afraid we are beginning at the wrong end. We are now in a Committee to conſider of ways and means for relieving ſuch of the Sufferers in the Charitable Corporation as ſhall be deemed objects of Compaſſion, and we are now going to reſolve upon a certain ſum to be appropriated for it, before we know any thing about the ſufferers; whether there be any, or how many of them may be objects of Compaſſion; or what ſum will be neceſſary for giving them a proper relief? All theſe queſtions ought I think to be reſolved, before we proceed to grant any ſum for that purpoſe, I am firmly of opinion, we have no power to lay on any publick impoſition for the relief of private perſons; and to give a relief by way of Lottery, is to eſtabliſh by Law a new deceit, for the relief of

thoſe who have ſuffered by an old one. As to our power to relieve private perſons by publick Taxes, the inſtances mention'd by the hon. Gentleman who ſpoke laſt, are not at all to the preſent caſe. The ſuitors in Chancery were in a very different ſituation from thoſe we are now about to relieve. The court of Chancery is one of the publick courts of the kingdom, and conſequently is the ſame with the Publick; whatever money was put into the cuſtody of that Court, was put into the cuſtody of the publick, and if any of it was purloined by thoſe Officers who are appointed by the publick, there is no queſtion but that the publick is obliged to make it good: beſides, thoſe who had their money in that Court did not voluntarily put it there: they were all obliged, contrary to their inclination, to leave it in that Court; they could not get it out again without an order of Court for that purpoſe; nor enquire in what manner it was diſpoſed of: Whereas, with reſpect to the Sufferers in the Charitable Corporation, they have no Pretence of having truſted the publick with their money; they voluntarily put it there; they might have taken it out when they would, or have inquired into the management of it; ſo that what they have loſt is entirely owing to their own act and deed, or at leaſt to their own neglect; they have nothing but compaſſion to plead for any relief from the publick, and I am afraid, if we conſider the publick aright, and the loads it already labours under, we muſt conclude it is not in a proper condition for granting ſuch large Charities. That other inſtance relating to the Tax for relieving the Orphans of *London*, is ſtill leſs to the preſent caſe; it is a local Tax, it extends no further than that City, and it was moſt reaſonable, that the Citizens of *London* ſhould be obliged to make good the loſs. —— As to Lotteries, the hon. Gentleman miſtakes, if he imagines the Frauds committed in private Lotteries was the only reaſon for prohibiting by an expreſs Law the ſetting up of any ſuch. Every Lottery, publick or private, is a publick nuiſance, becauſe it makes many poor unthinking people ruin themſelves by venturing more money in that way than their circumſtances can admit of; and as all Lotteries are a ſort of gaming tables, they give great encouragement to idleneſs and extravagance, by buoying up weak people with the Hopes of getting riches without induſtry and frugality, the only way of getting riches that ought to

be

be encouraged by a wiſe people ; therefore the reaſon of the law does not ceaſe with reſpect of the Lottery now propoſed, but will, I believe, grow more ſtrong againſt it, than againſt any publick Lottery that ever was propoſed ; for conſidering the expences of management, it is certain that the Corporation, or the ſufferers therein can make little by a Lottery, unleſs it be made ſo diſadvantageous to the Adventurers, that none but a Madman will put money into it, and if ſuch a Lottery ſhould fill, it would be a powerful argument againſt this and every ſuch Lottery that can be propoſed ; for it is really granting a licence by act of Parliament to cheat people out of their money, which is a ſort of project for raiſing money this Houſe will never, I hope, agree to in any caſe whatever.

L—d H——y.] In my opinion, no poſſible relief can be given to thoſe unfortunate people, but what muſt be attended with ſome inconveniences. I am in general as much againſt encouraging lotteries as any Gentleman in this Houſe ; but where no real fraud is committed I cannot think a Lottery is a thing of ſo bad conſequence, where the money thereby raiſed is duly apply'd, and no underhand dealings allowed to be put in practice, which, to be ſure will be taken care of in the preſent caſe, it cannot be attended with many inconveniences ; and as a Lottery is the only method I have yet heard mention'd, or can think of, for giving relief to thoſe objects of compaſſion we have now under our conſideration, I have ſo much pity on them, that I think the few inconveniences that can attend ſuch a ſmall Lottery as that of 500,000 l. ought in the preſent caſe to be overlook'd. —— Upon the petition of this Corporation we have all had two things under our conſideration. The firſt was that of doing Juſtice by puniſhing the Guilty : in this we have gone on as we ought to do in all ſuch caſes ; we have proceeded with the utmoſt caution ; becauſe, if we had been rigorous in that point, we might readily have deviated into ſeverity, which in all caſes ought to be carefully avoided ; but as to giving relief to the unfortunate Sufferers, the point now before us, there is no need of ſo great caution : If in this we ſhould go a little too far, it is erring upon the ſafe Side ; the greateſt fault we can be guilty of, is that of ſhewing too much compaſſion for thoſe innocent Perſons, who have by the frauds of others become proper objects of it.—— It cannot, I think, be ſaid,

we are beginning at the wrong end, by voting for a 500,000 l. Lottery, before we know the number of the ſufferers that are objects of compaſſion, or the ſum that will be wanted for giving them a proper relief ; becauſe, we are not now to ſettle the ſcheme of the lottery ; before that is ſettled, there will be time to inquire what ſum will be neceſſary for giving ſuch relief. According thereto the Lottery may be made more or leſs advantageous for the adventurers : if 100,000 l. ſhould be found neceſſary, there muſt be a fifth part of the money contributed by the adventurers ſunk for the uſe of the ſufferers ; and, if it ſhould be found, that half that ſum will be ſufficient, then it will not be neceſſary to ſink above a tenth part. Whatever is ſunk by the adventurers, is not to be look'd on as thrown away, but as ſo much money given by them for a charitable uſe ; and the raiſing of this charity by Lottery is propoſed only as an inducement for ſome people to contribute towards a charitable uſe, who would not perhaps other wiſe contribute to the moſt charitable uſe that can be imagined.

M—r of the R—ls again.] I am Sir, convinced, and it is generally allowed, that a Lottery is in itſelf a bad thing, and, I think it is likewiſe allowed, that there is no reaſon for our coming into ſuch a meaſure at preſent, but only the neceſſity we are under, and becauſe no other means of relief can be thought of. No ſort of Lottery can be ſet up, but what muſt expoſe multitudes of people to be undone, and it is impoſſible to prevent ſeveral fraudulent practices which are always ſet up under the ſanction of every publick Lottery. If then a Lottery be in itſelf a bad thing, ſurely the leſs we have of it the better ; why ſhould we vote for a Lottery of 500,000 l. if one of 150,000 l. will do the buſineſs ? This conſideration alone makes it, in my opinion, neceſſary firſt to conſider who are Objects of Compaſſion, and what ſum will be ſufficient to relieve 'em.

G—ge H—te, Eſq;] Sir, I muſt confeſs what is now propoſed ſeems to be a new method of raiſing Charity, but I hope the charitable diſpoſition of the people of this nation is not ſo much decay'd, as to make it neceſſary to trick them into the giving of Charity, when they are fully convinced, that the uſe for which the money is raiſed, is really charitable. In ſuch caſes I have never as yet obſerved the people backward in contributions ; I am, indeed, afraid the objects of charity now under conſideration would not meet

with

with any great relief from the people; who generally think, that thoſe who are undone by any ſort of gaming or ſtock-jobbing, are not proper objects of charity. Thoſe who are ruin'd by ſhipwrecks, fire, or ſuch accidents, are certainly much greater Objects of Charity, and more entitled to a parliamentary relief, than thoſe who ever were, or can be undone by the miſmanagement of any publick Stock; becauſe every proprietor may look into the affairs of the company, and may prevent the miſmanagement, if he is but tolerably careful of his own intereſt; yet we have never ſeen any of the former claim a relief from Parliament. —— I muſt obſerve, what we are now about may come to a very bad precedent; it will make all proprietors of publick funds leſs careful of their managers; ſo that I am afraid, we may have many applications of the ſame nature. There is now a company under our conſideration, which will likewiſe, I believe, ſtand in need of the ſame ſort of relief; and I do not know, but that in 9 or 10 years, another great company may find themſelves under a neceſſity of applying for ſomething of the ſame nature, eſpecially if they ſhould go on with their preſent ſcheme of diminiſhingt ſo conſiderably their trading capital, and loading it with all the debts they now owe. For theſe reaſons, as well as a great many others, I cannot but be againſt the motion now in hand.

The following Gentlemen ſpoke likewiſe for the Lottery, viz. J—n C——is, *Eſq;* F—s W—th, *Eſq;* and J—n N—le, *Eſq; Then a Motion was made for the Chairman's leaving the Chair, which was ſeconded by* W—t P—r *Eſq; whereupon the Queſtion was put, but on a diviſion, was carried in the Negative* 85 *to* 61: *Then the Committee went on, and came to ſeveral Reſolutions, which being reported on the* 8th *of* May, *were agreed to, and the Houſe ordered a Bill to be brought in, which accordingly was brought in, and paſſed into a Law, for a Lottery. See the Scheme, p.* 268.

Mr Chancellor of the Exchequer *then acquainted the Houſe, That he had a Meſſage from his Majeſty to the Houſe, ſign'd by his Majeſty; and he delivered the ſame to the Speaker, which he read as follows:*

GEORGE, R.

HIS *Majeſty having received from the prince of* Orange *propoſals for a treaty of marriage between the princeſs royal and the ſaid prince, and his Ma-* *jeſty having been pleaſed favourably to accept the inſtances made by the prince, his highneſs has ſent over a miniſter, inſtructed and authorized with full powers to treat of and conclude the articles of marriage: His Majeſty has therefore thought it proper to communicate this important affair to this houſe; and as he makes no doubt but this marriage will be to the general ſatisfaction of all his good ſubjects, he promiſes himſelf the concurrence and aſſiſtance of this houſe, in enabling him to give ſuch a portion to his eldeſt daughter, as ſhall be ſuitable to the preſent occaſion, and may contribute towards ſupporting with honour and dignity an alliance, that will tend ſo much to the further ſecurity of the proteſtant ſucceſſion to the crown of theſe realms, and to the proteſtant intereſt in* Europe.

Whereupon the houſe immediately reſolved upon an addreſs to his Majeſty, for which ſee p. 260, and his Majeſty's anſwer p. 265.

May 9. The houſe having reſolved itſelf into a committee of the whole houſe to take his Majeſty's moſt gracious anſwer into conſideration, and come to the following reſolution, *viz. That out of the money then remaining in the receipt of the exchequer ariſen by ſale of the lands in the iſland of* St Chriſtopher's, *his Majeſty be enabled to apply the ſum of* 80,000l. *for the marriage portion of the princeſs royal:* It was next day reported and agreed to by the houſe, and it was ordered, that it ſhould be an inſtruction to the Gentlemen, who were appointed to prepare and bring in a Bill, purſuant to the reſolution of the houſe of the 26th day of *February* laſt for raiſing the ſupply granted to his Majeſty (See p. 447 E) that they ſhould prepare and inſert a clauſe therein purſuant to this reſolution.

May 10. A very extraordinary affair happened in the houſe, and of conſequence they came thereupon to a very extraordinary reſolution: The affair was this, A memorial of the council, and repreſentatives of the province of the *Maſſachuſets*-Bay, was preſented to the houſe, and read, ſetting forth, *The difficulties and diſtreſſes they labour'd under, ariſing from a royal inſtruction given to the then preſent Governor of the ſaid province in relation to the iſſuing and diſpoſing of the publick monry of the ſaid province, and moving the houſe to allow their agent to be heard by council upon that affair; repreſenting alſo the difficulties they were under from a royal inſtruction given, as aforeſaid, reſtraining the emiſſion of bills of credit; and praying the houſe to take their caſe into conſideration, and become interceſſors for them with his Majeſty, that he would be graciouſly pleaſed to withdraw the ſaid inſtructions, as contrary to their charter, and tending in their own nature to diſtreſs, if not ruin them.*

The houſe not only thought it unneceſſary to inquire into this affair, but after ſome little debate came to the following remarkable reſolution, *viz.*

Reſolved, *That the complaint, contain-* B *ed in this memorial and petition, is frivolous and groundleſs, an high inſult upon his Majeſty's Government, and tending to ſhake off the dependency of the ſaid colony upon this kingdom, to which by law and right they are and ought to be ſubject.*

Ordered, *That the Petition be rejected.* C

This reſolution ſeems entirely to diſcourage complaints to parliament from our colonies in the *Weſt-Indies*; and the following, further to check the petitioners in particular. The petition thus rejected, a moſt juſt complaint was made to the houſe by C—l B——n, of the proceedings of D the houſe of repreſentatives of the ſaid province of *Maſſachuſets-Bay,* againſt *Jeremiah Dunbar,* Eſq; and the cenſure paſt upon him by the ſaid repreſentatives in *December* and *January* laſt, for giving evidence in the year 1730, before a committee of the houſe, to whom a bill then depending in the houſe for the better ſecuring and encouraging the trade of his Majeſty's ſugar-colonies in *America* was committed; and a paper printed at *Boſton* in *New-England,* intitled, *votes of the houſe of repreſentatives,* being offered to the houſe, was brought up, and ſeveral paragraphs were read, in which the a- F forementioned proceedings againſt, and cenſure paſt upon, the ſaid *Jeremiah Dunbar,* were contained: Whereupon it was

Reſolved, Nemine Contradicente, *That the preſuming to call any perſon to account, or to paſs a cenſure upon him, for evidence given by ſuch perſon before that* G *houſe, or any committee thereof, was an audacious proceeding, and an high violation of the privileges of that houſe; and*

Ordered, *That a committee be appointed to enquire, who were the authors and abettors of the ſaid proceedings againſt* Jeremiah Dunbar Eſq;

A Committee was appointed accordingly, with power to ſend for perſons, papers, and records: *But we do not hear that this committee ever made or are likely to make any report, for the Delinquents, were at ſuch a diſtance that they could hardly*

have had a return if they had begun their enquiry the very firſt day of the ſeſſion, and we believe a committee appointed in one ſeſſion, cannot well make A *a report in any following ſeſſion, nor can the houſe found any reſolution or orders upon enquiries made, or examinations taken by any committee of a former ſeſſion, or even by the houſe itſelf, without an act of parliament for that purpoſe.*

May 17. His Majeſty came to the houſe of peers, and gave the royal aſſent to ſeveral bills, (See p. 267.)

SOUTH-SEA Affair in the H. of Lords.

May 3. *The lords were going upon the ſugar-colony Bill, but before the houſe reſolved itſelf into a committee, L—d B—ſt ſtood up and ſpoke to the following effect, viz.*

My Lords, I have a ſmall motion to make and therefore take this opportunity before your lordſhips enter upon the buſineſs of the day. I do not know, but that ſomething relating to the *S. Sea* Company may ſpeedily come before your lordſhips, and as in ſuch caſes we ought always to be well prepared, and fully inſtructed by having all proper papers laid before us, therefore, I will take the liberty to move to your lordſhips, *that the directors of the* South-Sea *company may be ordered to lay before this houſe, an account how the produce of the forfeited eſtates of the directors of that company in the year 1720, has* E *been diſpoſed of, and all the orders made in the general courts of that company relating to the diſpoſal thereof.* — This account, my Lords, I now move for, that the preſent directors of that company may have time to prepare it, that ſo the buſineſs of the houſe may not be retarded, if on any emergency we ſhould have occaſion for it. In looking over the papers upon our table, I find there is an account lying there of the total amount of thoſe forfeited eſtates; which account was laid before this houſe in purſuance of a clauſe in an act of parliament, by the truſtees appointed by the ſame act of parliament for collecting thoſe eſtates for the benefit of the company; and accordingly, after the moſt of thoſe eſtates were collected, the truſtees were ordered by other acts to deliver over the produce of the ſaid eſtates to the directors of that company. H This account therefore being already upon our table as a charge againſt the truſtees, and the directors of that company, and as we have as yet ſeen no account of diſcharge in relation to that money, I think it is neceſſary, it is even incumbent upon

your

your lordſhips to call for the ſame, in order that you may ſee, and that the reſt of the nation may by your means be ſatisfied, that the terms of the act of parliament have been punctually complied with.

This motion was ſeconded by the Earl of C——ld, *and the* L——d D——r, *(who then ſat as ſpeaker of the houſe in the abſence of the lord chancellor,) having repeated the motion in order to put the queſtion upon it, the* D—ke *of* N——le *ſpoke in ſubſtance as follows, viz.*

D—ke of N——le.] My Lords, I did not well hear this motion when it was firſt made by the noble Lord, but now that I have heard it repeated, I muſt ſay that I cannot find out any reaſon your lordſhips have for calling for the account now moved for, at leaſt at this time: There is at preſent nothing before us relating to that company, nor do I know of any thing that is to be laid before us; there is not, I am ſure, any Lord in this houſe that can know of any bill to be brought before us any way relating to the affair of that company, at leaſt no Lord can know of ſuch a bill in a way proper for grounding ſuch a motion upon. If there really be any ſuch bill, it is, I think, time enough to call for ſuch an account when the bill is actually brought before us; the pretence made uſe of for moving at this time for ſuch an account, I can ſee no ground for, becauſe if any ſuch bill be brought before us, the directors of that company will have time enough to prepare and bring in the account between the firſt and ſecond reading of the bill; therefore, my Lords, 'till I ſee ſome ſuch bill brought into this houſe, I ſhall be againſt making any ſuch order as is now moved for.

L——d B——ſt.] When I made this motion, my Lords, I hardly expected it would have been oppoſed, but ſince I find it is like to be ſo, I muſt beg leave to give my reaſons for it more at large. As to the account I have moved for, I think your Lordſhips have not only good reaſon, but it is your duty to call for it, whether there be any bill relating to that company to come before us or no. I told you, that I was the other day ſo far in my duty as to be looking over and conſidering the papers upon our table, which is a duty I have, I muſt confeſs, too often neglected; among thoſe papers I found an account of a very large ſum of money received by the truſtees out of the eſtates of the directors of the *South-Sea* company in the year 1720: Upon ſeeing that

account I began to examine a little further into that affair, and I found that that account was laid before us in purſuance of the directions given by an act paſſed in the year 1721, by which thoſe truſtees were appointed to give a particular account in writing to the king, and to either houſe of parliament of the effects of their proceedings: And by two acts ſince the bringing in of that account I find, that the truſtees are directed to to deliver over to the directors of the *South-Sea* company the produce of thoſe eſtates, to be by them diſtributed among the proprietors according to the directions of thoſe acts.—I hope there is no Lord in this houſe who imagines that we are in any caſe to ſee only one ſide of an account; are we to ſee people charge themſelves with the receipt of two or three Millions of money in truſt for the proprietors of the *South-Sea* company, and to take no care or concern further about it? Surely the very nature of the thing requires, that we ſhould ſee them diſcharge themſelves honeſtly and fairly of that money, which they have, by an account now upon our table, charged themſelves with.—This we have not only a title, but we are in duty bound to enquire into: We have a right to enquire into the management and diſpoſal of all publick monies, and are at preſent the more obliged to exerciſe this right, becauſe of the many enormous frauds lately diſcovered in the management of the affairs of ſuch companies. I do remember, my Lords, that a noble Lord, for whom I have always had a very great eſteem; ſaid laſt year, in this houſe, moſt juſtly and moſt emphatically, that if we did not take care to put a ſtop to ſuch enormous abuſes, our credit would entirely ſink among our neighbours abroad; foreigners would look upon the whole nation to be a perfect den of Thieves. Even as to the company now under our conſideration, there have been many and loud complaints of frauds and abuſes in the management of their affairs; which publick complaints, if there were no other reaſon, ought to be an inducement for us to enquire into their management. Upon enquiry I hope theſe complaints will appear to be groundleſs; but it is certain that the people cannot be ſatisfied without making a narrow ſcrutiny, at leaſt into that part of their affairs, which the motion I have now made relates to. We cannot, my Lords, diſcharge our duty to our country without making ſuch an enquiry;

quiry; therefore the motion, I hope, will be agreed to; for if it fhould not, I dread the confequences; the putting a negative upon fuch a queftion would certainly injure the publick credit of the nation among foreigners; it might probably be the caufe of their drawing all their money out of our funds at once, which would give fuch a fhock both to the trade and the credit of this nation that I tremble to think of it.

E—l of Sc——gh.] My Lords, I am much obliged to the noble Lord who fpoke laft, for the good opinion he has expreffed of me. I remember well, that laft feffion I faid, upon a remarkable occafion, that foreigners would look upon us as a den of thieves, if proper care were not taken to fee the affairs of our publick companies more honeftly managed than they have been for fome time: I am ftill of the fame opinion, and as I think there is no more effectual way of making the managers of fuch companies honeft, than that of frequent parliamentary enquiries into their conduct, therefore I have always been for encouraging fuch enquiries, and I fhall never be againft a propofition for any fuch, when it is reafonably offered by any lord in this houfe: In the prefent cafe, the noble lord, who made the motion, has not only a great deal of reafon for what he propofes, but it is abfolutely neceffary for us to agree to it; for tho' there were no complaints made againft the late management of that company's affairs, yet the difpofal of that money, which is now moved to be enquired into, feems to have been fo directly put under our care, that we cannot in honour fhun making an exact enquiry into it; and if there is any reafon for delaying the enquiry, it certainly ought to come from the truftees, or from the directors of that company, it cannot come properly from any Lord in this houfe; when fuch excufe comes to be made to us, we may then judge, whether it is a good one or not; but that can be no reafon for our delaying to order the account now moved for to be laid before us.

E—l of I—ay,] It has always been my opinion, that when any unexpected motion is made by any Lord in this houfe, it ought not to be immediately debated or agreed to, the debate ought to be adjourned, and a day appointed for taking the motion into confideration, that thereby every Lord may have an opportunity of being fully apprifed of the queftion a-

bout which he is to give his opinion; for when long and complicated motions, fuch as we are now on, are made to the houfe, it is impoffible to underftand all the parts of them, and to confider fully the confequences with which they may be attended, without having fome little time allowed for that purpofe. For my own part, I never fhall be againft enquiries when there appears any foundation for the making of fuch: It is certain that the enquiring ftrictly into the management of affairs of any kind, is the only way of making the managers diligent and faithful in the difcharge of their duty; but as the making of no enquiry might be attended with very bad confequences, fo the making of too frequent or groundlefs enquiries might be attended with full as bad, if not worfe: too frequent or groundlefs enquiries into the management of our publick funds would make people's properties in fuch funds fo precarious, and would keep them always in fo fluctuating a condition, that no man would like to have any property or fhare in them; therefore, for preferving publick credit both at home and abroad, a medium ought to be obferved. We are not whenever it fhall pleafe any Lord in this houfe, to move for an enquiry into the affairs of any of our publick companies, to agree immediately with the motion: We ought firft to examine whether there be any grounds for fuch an enquiry, and what may be the confequences of it, and after the moft mature deliberation to agree with the motion or difagree as we fee caufe. Shall we, my Lords, without any caufe or reafon for fo doing, except that of its being moved for, give the managers and fervants of a publick company the trouble, and put them to the expence of attending for months together at this houfe; of bringing their books of account, their vouchers and other papers before us, and thereby put a full ftop to the bufinefs of that company for perhaps a quarter of a year at a time: fuch a piece of complaifance is not to be expected by any Lord in this houfe; inftead of fupporting, it would moft certainly ruin all manner of publick credit whatfoever. As to the enquiry now moved for, I do not know, but that it may be neceffary; I do not know but that there may be very fufficient reafons for our calling immediately for fuch an account, but I cannot fo quickly determine myfelf either one way or the other: It is an affair that has fo long lain over, and at the fame time it is an affair of fuch confequence,

that

hat I do not think any of your Lordſhips ought to determine yourſelves off-hand. All thoſe who have not before conſidered his queſtion ought to have ſome time allowed them for that purpoſe, and therefore, my Lords, I ſhall move, that the debate upon the motion now made, may be adjourned only 'till to-morrow: This is ſo ſhort a delay, that I hope none of your Lordſhips will be againſt it.

E—l of C——ld.] *My Lords, if the motion now made to us, had been for an enquiry into the affairs of the South-Sea company; or if the queſtion were complicated, ſome time might be neceſſary to conſider of it; but, the motion is not for any ſuch enquiry; it is no complicated queſtion, it is as plain, as ſimple a queſtion as ever came before this houſe. We have had ſeveral years ago an account laid before us, by which ſome Gentlemen have charged themſelves with the receipt of a very large ſum of money for the publick uſe; thoſe Gentlemen have ſince been directed by Act of Parliament to apply that money to the proper uſe, and the queſtion now before us is only, that thoſe Gentlemen may bring in their account of diſcharge. The noble Lord who made the motion did not, at firſt, ſo much as mention the enquiry, and that account when it comes in will, I hope, be ſo full, ſo plain, and ſo ſatisfactory, as to prevent an enquiry, if any ſuch thing were really deſigned; but ſince we have had the account of charge laid before us, it is ſurely incumbent upon us to call for the account of diſcharge. It is, my Lords, our duty, and ſhall we require time to conſider whether or no we ought to do our duty? I hope no Lord in this houſe will inſiſt upon having ſo much as one hour to conſider of ſuch a queſtion. The calling for that account has already been too long delayed; the affair has lain dormant too long, and therefore, I hope, your Lordſhips will not want any time to conſider whether or no we are now to do that which ought to have been done ſome time ago.*

D—e of N——le.] My Lords, I muſt beg leave to think, that the very argument which the noble Lord who ſpoke laſt has made uſe of for our not taking time to conſider of this queſtion, is a ſtrong argument for our taking ſome time to conſider of it. It is now 10 or 12 years ſince that affair happened which the preſent queſtion relates to, and no enquiry having been made into it in all that time. Is, in my opinion, a very good reaſon for not agreeing now to enter upon ſuch an enquiry without taking ſome time to refreſh

our memories, and to conſider of what we are going about. The noble Lords may call the motion now made to us by what name they pleaſe, they may call it a motion for an enquiry or not, as they think proper; but the calling for an account is certainly the beginning, at leaſt, of an enquiry: When that account comes in, it is to be ſuppoſed, that your Lordſhips will then enquire, at leaſt, into that affair which the account relates to. If there were no other reaſon, I ſhould be for delaying it, at leaſt, 'till to-morrow, out of regard to the Lords who now happen not to be preſent: A queſtion of ſuch conſequence ought not to be agreed to without giving every Lord, at leaſt, an opportunity of being preſent, and of giving his opinion upon it. There is at preſent no neceſſity for our being ſo ſpeedy in our determination. There may, perhaps, be ſome complaints againſt the management of that company's affairs; but there are none laid, as yet, before us. Neither the company nor any of the proprietors have come to us with any complaint, and ſurely we are not to proceed upon general ſurmiſes: Our proceedings ought always to be founded upon good information, and upon complaints from thoſe who are ſome way or another intereſted in what they complain of. Therefore, as a delay of 24 hours can be attended with no bad conſequence, but upon the contrary will evince to the world, that in all affairs we proceed with the utmoſt caution and deliberation, I ſhall be for adjourning the debate 'till to-morrow, according to the motion of the noble Lord for that purpoſe.

L—d C——t.] *My Lords, the noble Duke ſeems to miſtake the affair now before us; he ſeems to think that it has for a long time lain over, without ever having been moved in, or enquired after by your Lordſhips, and that therefore, we ought not now ſo much as begin to enquire into it without the moſt deliberate and ſerious conſideration; but, I muſt beg leave to ſhew, that the affair has not lain over ſo long as that noble Duke imagines. It is very far from having lain over 10 or 12 years, as may appear from the Acts of Parliament made relating thereto. I muſt deſire the 58th and 59th ſections of the Act of the 7th of his late Majeſty, intitled, An Act for raiſing money upon the eſtates of the late directors——to be read, (which being read, his Lordſhip went on to the effect as follows, viz.) Now, my Lords, by a miſtake in that act, the produce of thoſe forfeited eſtates was to be appropriated to*

the

the uſe of the South-Sea company, for increaſing their capital Stock, which could not poſſibly be done; for as their Stock can conſiſt of nothing but the debt due to them by the publick, their Stock could not be increaſed without increaſing the debt of the publick, and conſequently the annuity due to them from the publick; which could not have been done unleſs the whole produce of thoſe eſtates had been paid into the publick by way of a new loan, and this was no way the intention of that Act. In the 13th of his late Majeſty the truſtees appointed by that Act, brought into this houſe an account of the produce of the eſtates and effects of the ſaid late directors, as by the ſaid Act they were directed to do, and the ſaid miſtake having been then diſcovered, a new Act was then made for amending the former; but even that new Act was found not to be ſufficient, and therefore a new application was made to Parliament for an explanation of that Act, which laſt application was made only in the firſt year of his preſent Majeſty, and conſequently but 4 years ago; and after that matter was thus fully explained by Parliament, it was neceſſary to allow the directors ſome time to apply the ſaid produce according to the directions of the ſeveral laws made for that purpoſe. I hope they have by this time applied it accordingly; but it appears that the affair is ſo far from having lain over, or from having been neglected by your Lordſhips, that I do not ſee how we could have called for this account ſooner. This affair therefore, cannot but be freſh in every Ld's memory, and the motion now made ſeems to me to be a motion of courſe; for by the Act of the 7th of the late King, the truſtees were directed to lay before your Lordſhips an account of the produce of thoſe forfeited eſtates; they accordingly did ſo; but, I hope, my Lords, it is not to be imagined that your Lordſhips are to go no further: Are not you in conſequence to ſee that this produce has been duely and regularly applied, and actually diſtributed among the proprietors of that company, according to the directions of the Acts of the 13th of his late Majeſty, and the firſt of his preſent Majeſty? The thing is in itſelf ſo clear, that I wonder to hear any Lord ask for time to conſider of it. Are we to ask for time to conſider whether we ſhall do that which was certainly intended by thoſe laws we ſhould do? It is no enquiry into the affairs of the South-Sea company; it is only calling for an account of diſcharge, to anſwer that account of charge which is now upon our table. In matters of importance

and intricacy I ſhall always be for proceeding with deliberation, and for taking time to conſider before we come to any reſolution; but, to deliberate upon, and to take time to conſider about an affair which all the world muſt ſee is an affair of courſe, is inconſiſtent with the honour and dignity of this houſe, therefore I ſhall be againſt taking any time to conſider of this motion, or adjourning the debate for that purpoſe.

E—l of I—ay.] I now find that thoſe Lords, who at preſent ſeem to be of the other ſide of the queſtion, have conſidered this affair before this motion was made: They have mentioned ſeveral laws relating to it, and ſeem to be ſo well acquainted with the ſeveral clauſes of them, that I muſt beg leave to think, that they have lately had this affair under their conſideration. Now, my Lords, as I have not lately conſidered any of thoſe laws, as I never have conſidered them with a view to the queſtion before us, I deſire only til to-morrow to look over them, that I may be upon an equal footing with their Lordſhips. I have a very great regard for their opinion, and it is very probable that I ſhall to-morrow be of the ſame with 'em; but in all matters of importance every Ld ought to examine by himſelf the affair about which he is to give his opinion, and after he has fully ſatisfied himſelf, he ought then to vote for that which appears to him to be right: This is the method, which I ſhall always obſerve; and when any thing comes before this houſe, that I am not fully ſatisfied about, I ſhall never be aſhamed to ask ſome ſhort delay, that I may have time to examine the affair to the bottom, before I give my opinion either on one ſide or the other. As I have ſaid, I ſhall never be againſt enquiries of this nature, when I can ſee but the leaſt ground for them at the time they are propoſed; but if ſuch enquiries be precipitatly gone into, I do not know where they may end, or what fatal conſequences may be thereby produced. There are in this nation, ſeveral other companies, beſides the *South-Sea* company; it is well known that the *Eaſt-India* company has been, for theſe 20 years, repreſented by ſome as a bankrupt company, yet I believe they always have been, and are ſtill in very good circumſtances. There have likewiſe been great complaints, and many inſinuations thrown out againſt the management of the Bank: Surely we are not, upon every ſuggeſtion within doors, or upon every groundleſs clamour without doors, to expoſe the trade of any one of our

our great companies to the whole world. Such a proceeding might expose both the trade and the credit of every one of our companies to innumerable difficulties and dangers. In all trading companies, as well as in the trade of private men, there are some transactions which, tho' exactly honest and just, ought not to be exposed to publick view, because strangers might thereby be let into the mysteries of their trade, by which they would be enabled to undermine them, and to disappoint even their best-concerted projects; for which reason, I shall always be of opinion, that no such enquiry ought to be set on foot, without some more solid foundation than that of an idle clamour: No such enquiry ought ever to be resolved on by this house without the most mature deliberation.

L—d C——t.] My Lords, *what is now moved for is no enquiry; it has already been so fully explained, that it cannot in any sense be taken to be an enquiry. If an enquiry had been moved for, I should have asked for no time to consider, whether or no I ought to have agreed to it. The complaints against the late management of that company's affairs have been so loud and general, that I think we are, in justice to the nation, in justice even to the Gentlemen who have been concerned in the management of them, obliged to enquire into it: If upon such enquiry it comes out, as I hope it will, that their affairs have been honestly and carefully managed, it will be a vindication of the characters of those Gentlemen; and if the contrary should appear, the sooner we go into that enquiry, the more speedy justice will be done to the injured, and many evil consequences may be prevented. Why should we shew such a tenderness, and such a concern for the characters of some Gentlemen? Why should we be so cautious of making an enquiry into their management? I must think that we thereby do them no great honour; it betokens a jealousy, that the enquiry will explain and confirm what has been so generally surmised. The late clamours against the management of that company's affairs are no idle clamours: They seem to be better founded than I could wish. Do not we all know, is it not publickly known, that the proprietors of that company have had lately above six per cent. of their capital annihilated for the payment of a part only of their debts? Could it have been imagined, that company had had so much debt, more than their money and effects in trade could have answered? It can hardly be thought, that*

this debt has been all contracted since the year 1721; and if it was contracted before that time, it was a crime to conceal it from Parliament; for if it had then been known, the Parliament would certainly have expresly ordered the produce of the directors estates, as well as the Stock then undisposed of, to have been applied towards payment of the debts of the company, instead of ordering them to be divided among the proprietors. This was the only proper way of applying both, if the company was in debt at that time: And if the debt has been all contracted since, the publick is entitled, and we have reason, to enquire how it came to be so. The debts of every one of our companies ought to be publickly known. Do not we know that their debt is by law a mortgage upon their Stock, and the concealing of that debt is a fraud upon every ignorant person who becomes a purchaser after the contracting of their debt? It is as much a fraud as it would be to sell a mortgaged estate without acquainting the purchaser that there was such a mortgage upon it. ——— As to the East-India Company, I wish an enquiry had been made by us into their Affairs when they last applied to this House for a prolongation of their Term; but I hope an enquiry was made by those concerned in the Administration; it was their duty to do so before they agreed to the bargain then made with that Company; if they did not, I shall always look upon such neglect as a very high crime; I can see no evil consequence of letting the general circumstances of a Company be publickly known; as to the East-India Company, it would have prevented some very odd Practices made use of: The Directors, or perhaps some few of the Directors, were probably the only persons for half a Year together in the secret of that Company's not being in a condition to continue their former dividend; such a secret was sufficient to enable any man, or small number of men to plunder their Fellow subjects, and make to themselves what estates they had a mind. We know there were but a few Men in this secret, and that at a Time when the world generally believed, when methods were taken to make all mankind believe, that Company was in the most flourishing state, and able to continue their dividend of 8 per Cent. for many years. By these methods, my Lords, that Stock was run up to a very high price, we saw how it fell down again almost 50 per Cent. in three months time, by which management we may.

may believe that millions were loft and won; we may judge who were the winners; they perhaps were but few in number; but we may certainly conclude, that many innocent perfons were thereby undone. And while fuch practices are fo publickly carried on, fhall we fit in this houfe and fee them pafs unpunifhed? But my Lords, this is not the queftion before us: The queftion is, whether or no we fhall call for an account of difcharge as to a particular affair, in order to anfwer the account of charge, fome years ago laid upon our table in purfuance of an Act of Parliament: Surely this is a queftion that requires no time to confider of, therefore I fhall be againft adjourning the debate.

L—d V——t F——th.] I am, my Lords, inclined to be for adjourning the debate 'till to-morrow, but when I tell your Lordfhips my reafon, I hope you will not think that I am againft any enquiry into the affairs of the *South-Sea* company; for I am fo much convinced of the neceffity and benefit of fuch enquiries, and of the propriety of the motion now made that, I hope, no Lord in this houfe will, after due confideration, be againft it; therefore I wifh it were adjourn'd 'till to-morrow in order that it may then be unanimoufly agreed to.

The E—l of W——ca, and the E—l of Str——d fpoke againft adjourning and for the motion. At laft the queftion for adjourning the debate 'till next day was put, and paffed in the negative 35 againft 31; after which the queftion was put, to agree to the motion or not, and carried in the affirmative without any divifion.

Order'd, That the directors of the *South-Sea* company do lay the faid account, &c. before the houfe.

The Lords who voted on each fide of this momentous queftion, were as follow:

Againft adjourning, confequently for the motion.

Dukes of Bolton Bridgewater Kent Montrofe St. Albans. *Marquifs of* Tweedale. *Earls of* Berkfhire Buchan Chefterfield Coventry Fitzwalter Ker Macclesfield Marchmont Northampton Pomfret Rothes Scarborough Shaftsbury Stair Strafford Thanet Warrington. *Vifcounts* Cobham Falmouth Tadcafter. *Barons* Bathurft Bruce Carteret Clinton Cornwallis Foley Gower Haverfham. *Bifhop of* Lincoln.

For adjourning, confequently againft the motion.

Dukes of Ancafter Devonfhire New-

caftle Rutland. *Earls of* Albemarle Afhburnham Cowper Craufurd Dunmore Hallifax Jerfey Ilay Morton Selkirk Wilmington. *Vifcounts* Lonfdale Torrington. *Barons* Abergavenny Byron Delawar Harrington Hobart Lovel Lynn Walpole. *Bifhop of* London and five more.

The account was accordingly brought in, and ordered to be taken into confideration the 24th of *May.*

DEBATE *on the account of the difpofal of the S. S. directors forfeited eftates.*

May 24. The order of the day being read, L—d B——ft ftood up, but the D—ke of N——le ftanding up about the fame time the L—d C——r pointed to the D—ke, and L—d B——ft not offering to fit down, L—d C——t ftood up, and faid, if there was any difpute which Lord was to fpeak, the L—d C——t was not to determine the queftion, but the opinion of the houfe was to be asked upon it; as for his part he was fure the noble Lord by him was up fome time before the noble Duke.

L—d B——ft faid, My Lords, I defire to fpeak to order. When any Lord makes a motion on which follows any order or refolution of this houfe, and a day is appointed for taking that order or refolution into confideration, it has always been the cuftom of this houfe, out of complaifance to the Lord who made the motion, to hear him firft, becaufe it is to be expected that he has fomething to fay, or fome farther motion to make in confequence, or in explanation of the motion he had before made; therefore as I had the honour to move for the account you are now to take under your confideration, I think I have a title to be firft heard, tho' I had not been firft up.

The D—ke of N——le fitting down, L—d B——ft went on to the effect as follows: *I had, my Lords, the honour to move for the account now before us, and your Lordfhips were fo good as to comply with my defire. The intention of my motion was, that your Lordfhips might fee that the produce of the directors eftates in the year 1720 had been regularly and fairly applied, according to the directions of the feveral laws for that purpofe made; and from the account brought in, and now under our confideration, I think, it moft plainly appears, that not fo much as one fhilling of that money has been fo applied. To me it appears from that account that the large fum of money arifing from thefe*

for.

forfeited eſtates had been all diſtributed among the proprietors by way of dividend, even before the application was made to parliament in the 13th year of his late Majeſty's reign for directions how to apply it; therefore, my Lords, I muſt take the liberty to move to your Lordſhips, that it may be reſolved, That the diſpoſing of any of that money by way of dividend, and without any order of a general court for that purpoſe, was a violation of the act of parliament made for directing the diſpoſal thereof, and a manifeſt injuſtice done to the proprietors of that ſtock.

D—ke of N——le.] My Lords, it is my opinion that a narrow ſcrutiny into the affair now before us is abſolutely neceſſary: This I am now ſo firmly perſuaded of, eſpecially ſince the bringing in the account now under our conſideration, that no man can be more heartily inclined to enter into ſuch ſcrutiny than I am; but this account, which the preſent directors have laid before us is ſo confuſed, and ſo obſcure, that, to me, it is altogether unintelligible: I believe there is not a Lord in this houſe who will ſay that he thoroughly underſtands it; therefore, I do not think that it can be a proper foundation for the motion the noble Lord has been pleaſed to make, or for any other motion. An enquiry into the diſpoſal of the produce of the forfeited eſtates of the directors in the year 1720, is certainly very proper, but then, for the honour and diginity of this houſe, we ought not to proceed upon any ſuch enquiry 'till we have all proper materials before us; therefore, I hope your Lordſhips will agree with me in the motion I am to make before you proceed any further in this affair. — The preſent directors of that company have indeed given us an account, but it is ſo imperfect and ſo indiſtinct, that it cannot be looked on as any ſort of compliance with your Lordſhips late order. What may have been their reaſons for giving us ſuch an account I ſhall not determine, but if it was either to conceal the crimes of the guilty, or to load the innocent with jealouſies and ſuſpicions, I hope, in either caſe, your Lordſhips will inforce your own orders, and oblige them to clear up what appears to be obſcure in the account they have already given in. It is incumbent upon us, my Lords, always to ſee our orders punctually obeyed, but eſpecially when they relate to the diſcovering of thoſe that are unjuſtly ſuſpected of crimes: This ſurely is the next ſtep your Lord-

ſhips ought to take in this affair, and therefore I ſhall move, That the preſent directors of that company may be ordered to lay before this houſe a further and more diſtinct account how that money has been diſpoſed of.

E—l of C——ld.] I am glad, my Lords, to ſee the effect the bringing in of this account, obſcure as it is, has produced. I find that ſome Lords, who at firſt ſeemed to want no information in this affair, who at firſt appeared to be againſt any ſuch enquiry, are now for making a thorough enquiry into that whole affair, and are for having a full information of every particular circumſtance relating to the diſpoſal of that money. I am of the ſame opinion, and therefore I look upon the motion made by the noble duke to be a very proper motion: I ſhall moſt heartily join with him in that motion; but then I think it is time enough to come to that motion after the motion made by the noble Lord is agreed to; the noble Duke's motion ought to be the concluding motion of this day. The account laid before us is, it is true, obſcure and indiſtinct, but let us make as much of it as we can before we aſk for any further account. Even this obſcure account is ſufficient to raiſe a ſuſpicion in every Lord of this houſe, that the produce of thoſe directors eſtates has not been diſpoſed of according to the directions of the act of parliament made for that purpoſe, therefore I muſt think, we have from thence ſufficient ground for the reſolution firſt moved for. We may then examine this account a little further, and at laſt we may come to the motion made by the noble Duke, and give ſuch particular orders and directions relating to the ſeveral articles which we want to have cleared up, that the preſent directors may know how, and will be neceſſarily obliged to lay a clear and diſtinct account of that whole affair before us, if any ſuch can be had. I ſhall therefore be for the motion made by the noble Lord, and at laſt I will join with the noble Duke in the motion he has made.

E—l of S——gh.] My Lords, as to the motion made by the noble Duke, I ſhall join in it with all my heart, as ſoon as I think it proper for us to come to ſuch a motion. I do not doubt but the noble Duke who made the motion is moſt zealous in the affair now before us; his grace has declared ſo, therefore I make no doubt of it, becauſe I am fully convinced of the honour and integrity of that noble Duke; he never did profeſs any thing but
what

what were his real fentiments, and I am perfuaded the motion he has made proceeds from a fincere and ardent defire of coming at the bottom of the affair now before us. I am always forry when I differ in the leaft from him; but in the prefent cafe my opinion happens to be different; I do not think that what he propofes ought to be the firft ftep we are next to take in the affair before us, and tho' I may, and fhall always be ready to change my opinion upon a better information; yet my opinion, while it is my opinion, I will not give up even to him for whom I have the greateft regard and efteem.—As we have, my Lords, already an account before us, I think we ought to examine it before we order any farther account to be laid before us. If there is any thing obfcure, in this account the Gentleman who figns it is attending at the door, and if your Lordfhips call him in, and examine him, he may perhaps be able to explain all or moft of the articles that appear to be obfcure, and if, at laft, there fhall remain an obfcurity in the account before you, your Lordfhips may then make a new order for the directors to bring in a farther, a more clear and diftinct account: You will then, and not 'till then, be able to give fuch particular orders, as to the feveral articles that remain obfcure, as cannot be mifunderftood by the directors. We have, my Lords, by our former order called for an account how that money was difpofed of, and if we fhould only renew that order without adding fome new and particular directions, the fecond account may, and probably will be more obfcure than the firft; therefore, that we may be able to give fuch particular direction as may be eafily underftood by the directors, I muft move for calling in Mr *De Golz*, and examining him as to the feveral articles of this account.

The D—ke of N——le thanked the noble Lord who fpoke laft for the good opinion he had expreffed of him. That noble Lord, *fays he,* cannot have a better opinion of me than I have of him: There is no man more fully convinced of that noble Lord's Honour and Sincerity than I am, becaufe there is no man, I believe, knows him better. *His Grace added a little to the Queftion in hand, and then*

L—d C——t ftood up, and fpoke to this effect: My Lords, I fhall readily join with the noble Duke's Motion, as foon as it is proper for this Houfe to go upon it. The account now before us is, indeed, a very

imperfect and indiftinct account; whether this be the effect of neglect or defign, I fhall not determine; but I muft fay, my Lords, wherever I fee an obfcurity in accounts I am apt to fufpect fome indirect practices; however, notwithftanding the obfcurity of the account now under our confideration as to fome other parts, it is not obfcure as to that part to which the motion made by the noble Lord refers. It has not been fo much as denied by any Lord, but that the difpofing of that money by way of dividend among the proprietors, without orders from a general Court, was a violation of the Act of Parliament, and a manifeft injuftice done to the Company: And it is plain that in the account now before us, there does not appear any order for the difpofal of that money: There appears to us nothing but an order for the Truftees to deliver that money over to the Directors, therefore we ought now to declare our opinion as to this matter, that the prefent Directors, in making a new account, may be fufficiently inftructed as to that article, and directed to report clearly to us, whether or no there was any order of a general court for the difpofal of that money. If there was any proper order for that purpofe, our coming to a refolution, according to the noble Lord's motion, can affect no man; and if there never was any fuch order, thofe who difpofed of that money otherwife, do deferve, and, I hope, will meet with a much higher cenfure. ——— For the honour and dignity of this Houfe, we ought, my Lords, immediately to come to fome ftrong refolutions in the affair before us; the giving in fuch an account feems to be a trifling with this Houfe, and if your Lordfhips now refufe, or even delay doing any thing further in this affair till you have a new account, it will be thought to be a throwing of cold water upon the enquiry before us. Your Lordfhips may declare what you pleafe as to your willingnefs to enter upon an Enquiry into this affair; but the putting it off without coming to any refolution till you have a new account from the Directors, will without doors be looked on as a waving of the Enquiry propofed, and this opinion will the more readily, and more generally prevail, becaufe this new account can hardly be expected to be brought in during this Seffion of Parliament. ——— By the account before us it appears, that upwards of 2,000,000 *l.* was delivered by the Truftees to the Directors of that Company

pany in the year 1729, and that it was never brought to the Company's account till the year 1732. For God's sake, my Lords, what became of that great sum, during that long interval, the very interest of it amounts to above 100,000 *l.* which is a sum that Company itself would certainly have looked after, if they had not been either negligent of their own affairs, or under an influence to which I shall not give the name it deserves; but whatever may be the case, as to the Company, we ought to consider the widows, and the fatherless infants who have no vote at their general courts, and for the sake of those we ought to enquire what became of this money for so considerable a time: As to this and all the other articles of this account, the Gentleman who signs it, and who is now attending at our door, can without doubt fully inform us; and therefore I shall join with the noble Lord by me in the motion he has made for having him called in and examined.

E—l of [—ay] My Lords, since your Lordships seem to be all of opinion, that the account laid before us by the present Directors of the South-Sea Company, *in pursuance of our late order, is a very indistinct account, I think the first thing you ought to do, is to see your order as fully complied with as possible. The Directors were ordered to lay before you all the orders of general Courts made for directing the disposal of that money, and I find they have given us no account of any such order; but of one only which (for what I know) may be all the orders they have to shew; but if there is any other order relating to the disposal of that money, it ought to be laid before us; and if there is none other, we ought certainly to be assured of it in a proper way, before we proceed further in this affair: Till we have from the Directors all the information we can possibly get, it will be irregular to come to any resolution, or to call any witness to be examined at the bar; and in every affair that comes before this House, I hope your Lordships will always be careful of doing nothing but what is regular and just, without any regard to what may be said without doors. —From the Account before us, it appears, indeed, that the money paid by the Trustees to the Directors in the year* 1729, *was not brought to the Company's account, till the year* 1732; *and I do not know but Mr* De Golz, *who signs this Account, and is now attending at your Door, may*

be able to inform you what became of that money in the Interim. But it is not from Mr De Golz that we want an Account; it is from the Directors of that Company, that we ought to be informed of all these matters; and after the Directors have told us, that they can give us no farther information, we may then examine them, their servants, and whatever witnesses we think proper, at the Bar of this House, as to the truth of the several articles of the Accounts given in by the Directors, and likewise as to the clearing up and explaining such articles as may at last remain obscure.——As to any Lord's having at first appeared against calling for the Account, I do not know that any Lord did appear against it: When the first Motion was made relating to this Affair, it appeared to be of such consequence, that several Lords desired some time to consider of it, but it is not from thence to be inferred, they were against calling for any such Account: Their asking for such a short time as till next day, was a proof of their not being against it; and if they had got that time, they would, I believe, have been as much for it as those Lords who had considered of the affair before the motion was made. The event, my Lords, shews, they were in the right in asking for some time to consider it, for if the affair had been better considered at first, our order would perhaps have been made more particular, and then the return to it would, in all probability, have been so distinct and clear, that we might have proceeded without loss of time; but as the case now stands, I think it would be very irregular to proceed to the making of resolutions, or to examine witnesses till we have the matter further cleared up; therefore I shall be for putting the previous Question as to the motion made by the noble Lord, and if that passes in the negative, as I hope it will, I shall be for agreeing with the motion made by the noble Duke.*

DEBATE *about* ORDER.

Besides the Lords already mentioned, the D—ke of M——se, M—s of T——le, E—l of W——ea, and E—l of M——nt spoke for calling in Mr De Golz; and the E—l of Ch——y, L—d D——r, L—d L——l, L—d K—g, and the B—p of B——r spoke against it.

The previous Question was then going to be put as to L—d B——ft's Motion; but L—d C——t got up, and spoke to Order; That as Mr De Golz was attending at the door by virtue of their Lordships

ships order, and a noble Lord having moved for calling him in, be thought, that according to the Rules of Proceeding in that House, the Question to be first put was, Whether or no Mr De Golz should be called in? That it was certainly proper he should be examined before they proceeded even to make an order for bringing in a further account; as they would thereby be enabled to give much more particular and distinct directions how that further account should be framed, than they could otherwise do; for if they went upon issuing out a new order before they examined that Gentleman, the same thing might happen, which a noble Lord seemed to think had before happened by their making the first order in that Affair without taking time to consider of it: The Directors might not understand their second order; And thus, said his Lordship, we shall have a second Return, as indistinct and obscure as the first.

In this Question as to order, L—d C—s's opinion was supported by the E—l of W——a and L—d B——ft; and was opposed by the D—ke of N——le, the E—l of I—y, and L—d D——r.

Then the E—l of S——d said, That for avoiding the dispute about order, he would be for putting the previous question as to the motion made by the noble Lord, and thereupon he would give his Negative, as he would likewise do upon the previous question as to the motion made by the noble Duke, in order to come at the motion made for calling in Mr De Golz, which he would certainly agree to.

M—s of T——le. My Lords, I am of the same opinion with the noble Lord who spoke last: What his Lordship has proposed is a most proper method for avoiding all disputes about order; and as I am for calling in Mr De Golz, and examining him before every thing else; therefore, if you put the previous question as to the first Motion, I hope it will pass in the negative; then we may regularly put the previous Question as to the motion made by the noble Duke; to which I shall give my negative, and I hope all the Lords who are for having Mr De Golz called in and examined, will do the same, that so it may likewise pass in the negative; we come next to the third motion, that for calling in Mr De Golz, to which I shall most heartily give my affirmative.

Hereupon the previous question was put as to the motion made by L—d B——ft, and passed in the negative without any division. Then the previous

question was put as to the motion made by the D—ke of N——le, upon which the House divided.

The Lords who voted in this remarkable question, were as follow, *viz.*

Against the previous Question, consequently for calling in Mr De Golz.

Duke of Somerset.
† of St. Albans.
* Duke of Bolton
Duke of Bedford
* Duke of Montrose.
Duke of Kent
† D. of Greenwich, (Argyle) *since made Col. of the King's own Reg. of horse Guards, Visc. Tadcaster, (Earl in the room of the D. of Bolton*
† Duke of Manchester
Duke of Bridgwater
Marquis of Tweedale
Earl of Northampton
Earl of Denbigh
Earl of Berkshire
Earl of Winchelsea
* Earl of Chesterfield
Earl of Thanet
E. of Sunderland, *now D. of Marlborough.*
Earl of Shaftsbury
Earl of Litchfield
Earl of Gainsborough
† Earl of Scarborough
Earl of Coventry
† Earl of Rothes
Earl of Buchan
* Earl of Marchmont
Earl of Strafford
* Earl of Stair
Earl of Fitzwalter
Earl of Oxford
Earl of Harborough
Earl of Macclesfield
† Earl of Pomfret
Earl of Ker
Thomond)
* Viscount Cobham
† Viscount Falmouth.
* Lord Clinton
Lord Bruce
Lord Craven
Lord Carteret
Lord Weston, (*Earl of Arran*)
Lord Haversham
Lord Gower
Lord Masham
Lord Foley
Lord Bathurst
† Lord Cornwallis
Bishop of Lincoln

Present 48
Proxies 27
75

* Thus marked since removed from their Places.
† Having Posts, continued in them.

For the previous Question, consequently against the then calling in of Mr De Golz.

Lord Chancellor (King)
Lord President (Wilmington)
Lord Privy Seal (Lonsdale)
Lord Steward (Devonshire)
Lord Chamberlain (Grafton)
Duke of Montagu, *Master of the great Wardrobe, since made Gov. of the Isle of Wight*
Duke of Ancaster
Duke of Newcastle, *Secretary of State*
Duke of Chandos
Duke of Dorset, *Lord Lieutenant of Ireland*
Earl of Pembroke, *Capt. of the third Troop of Guards, and Lord of the Bed-chamber*
Earl of Warwick
Earl of Clarendon
Earl of Albemarle, *Capt. of a Troop of Guards, and Lord of the Bed-chamber*
Earl of Jersey, *since mad. Lord of the Bed-Chamber to the Prince*
Earl of Godolphin, *Groom of the Stole*
Earl

Earl of Cholmondeley, *Maſter of the Horſe to the Prince*
Earl of Craufurd, *Capt. of Dragoons*
Earl of Morton, *Vice-Admiral of Scotland*
Earl of Selkirk, *Lord of the Bed-chamber, ſince made Clerk Regiſter of Scotland, in the room of the E. of* Marchmont.
Earl of Dunmore, *Col. of a Reg. of Guards*
Earl of Orkney, *Col. of a Reg. and Governor of* Virginia *and* Edinburgh Caſtle.
Earl of Ilay, *Lord Juſticiary and Privy Seal of* Scotland
Earl of Tankerville, *Lord of the Bed-chamber, and ſince made Maſter of the Buck-Hounds.*
Earl of Halifax, *Auditor of the Exchequer*
Earl Cowper, *Lord of the Bed-chamber*
Earl of Aſhburnham, *Lord of the Bed-chamber.*
Earl of Effingham, *Col. of a Regiment, and Deputy Earl Marſhal*
Viſc. Lymington, *Lord Juſtice in Eyre, ſince made Warden of* New Foreſt, *and Ld Lieut. of* Hants
Viſc. Torrington, *Treaſurer of the Navy*
Lord Harrington, *Secretary of State*
Lord Abergavenny
Lord Delawar, *Treaſurer of the Houſhold*
Lord Lovelace
Lord Byron
Lord Lynn, *Maſter of the Jewel-Office*
Lord Cadogan, *Colonel of a Regiment*
Lord Walpole, *Clerk of the Pells*
Lord Monſon, *ſince made Capt. of the Band of Gentlemen Penſioners.*
Lord Lovel, *ſince made a Commiſſioner of the Poſt-Office.*

BISHOP	BISHOP
of London	of Oxford
of Wincheſter	of Briſtol
of Salisbury	of Norwich
of St David's	of Litchfield & Coventry
of Bangor	of Ely
of Durham	of Rocheſter
of Exeter	of St Aſaph
of Chicheſter	of Landaff
of Bath and Wells	

Preſent 57
Proxies (of whom ſix were *Biſhops*) 18
                                        75

☞ By the above Liſts, there was a Majority of 22 LAY LORDS for calling in of Mr *De Golz,* tho' in the whole the Votes were equal.

By the method of proceeding in the Houſe of Lords, nothing can be reſolved on unleſs a majority be for it : Thus in the preſent caſe, the previous queſtion being, Whether the queſtion ſhould be then put upon the motion made by the D—ke of N—le, for the S. S. Directors to bring in a further Account ? and there being exactly as many *againſt* putting the Queſtion as *for* it, therefore the previous queſtion was carried in the negative.
Then the E—l of S—gh renewed his

(*Supplement to Vol. III.*)

motion for calling in Mr *De Golz* : whereupon the D—ke of N——le got up and moved, that the previous queſtion might likewiſe be put as to that motion. Here
The E—l of S—d roſe up, and ſpoke to this Effect : — For God's ſake, my Lords, do not let us put a previous queſtion as to this motion. Mr *De Golz* was ordered to attend this day : What was he ordered to attend for ? Surely it was to be examined in caſe we found any difficulty in the Account now under our conſideration, and every Lord that has ſpoke in this debate confeſſes that he finds difficulty in it, and allows it to be very confuſed and obſcure. It will really look very odd, to refuſe examining that Gentleman as to what appears difficult or obſcure in the account before you, ſince he is attending for that purpoſe by virtue of an Order of the Houſe. We may pretend what we pleaſe, but no man will think we are in earneſt in what we are now about, if the calling in and examining of this Gentleman ſhould be put off. —
Several other Lords ſpoke to the ſame purpoſe, on which the D—ke dropped his motion ; tho' if the previous queſtion had been put, and every Lord had voted and given his Proxies as in the former diviſion, it is certain there would have been an equality, conſequently the calling in or examining of Mr *De Golz* would have been put off at leaſt for that day. The motion as to the previous queſtion being thus dropped, the queſtion was put for calling in Mr *De Golz,* which was carried without any diviſion. He was accordingly examined, but did not give any great ſatisfaction as to the clearing up of the account. After he was withdrawn L—d B——ſt renewed his motion, whereupon the
E—l of S——gh roſe up, and ſpoke in ſubſtance as follows :— My Lords, I muſt be of opinion, that as this motion tends towards the charging of ſome Gentlemen with very groſs miſmanagement, and with acting contrary to an expreſs Act of Parliament, we ought to proceed with the utmoſt caution : And as I really think that we have not, as yet, ſufficient ground for ſupporting ſuch a reſolution, I cannot now agree to it. Our coming immediately to ſuch a reſolution can do no manner of ſervice either to the publick or to any private perſon, and it may do harm to ſome Gentlemen, who, for what we can pretend to know, are innocent ; but that we may ſearch this affair to the bottom, that we may have all the inſight

Q q q q   into

into it that is poſſible, and that we may diſcover and puniſh the guilty, if any there be, I will now join with the noble Duke in the motion he made; and I hope in forming that Order yourLordſhips will give ſuch directions as may not only enable but oblige the Directors of that company to give us a full, clear, and diſtinct account of that whole affair, if any ſuch account can be had. When that account comes in, or when we are told no ſuch account can be had, we may then conſider the motion made by the noble Lord, and may come to that reſolution, or to ſuch other reſolutions as we ſhall then think proper.

D—e of Ar—le.] My Lords, in all enquiries of this nature we ought to proceed with zeal, but not with fury. I hope I am as zealous for enquiring thoroughly into the matter now before us as any of your Lordſhips ought to be. For this reaſon I was for poſtponing the motion made by the noble Duke, in order to have Mr *De Golz* examined: I did indeed expect he would have explained to your Lordſhips moſt of the articles of the account before us, which appear to be obſcure and unintelligible; but I find I am diſappointed : I believe your Lordſhips have received no great ſatisfaction from him ; for to me he ſeemed to be ignorant almoſt of every thing ; he could not ſo much as give a clear and diſtinct anſwer to any one Queſtion that was put to him, which, I muſt ſay, is to me very ſurprizing: I did think it almoſt impoſſible that a man who had been ſo long in ſuch a high poſt in that Company's ſervice, could be ſo ignorant of their affairs as this man appears to be. However my Lords, notwithſtanding the little ſucceſs we have met with in the examination of this Gentleman, I hope we ſhall fall upon ways and means for bringing this matter to light; but till we have ſome further information about it, I do not think we have a foundation for the reſolution which the noble Lord has been pleaſed to move for : Our proceeding ſo haſtily to ſuch a reſolution would really be a going on with fury, inſtead of going on with that juſt zeal which we ought to ſhew upon all ſuch occaſions, and I am perſuaded, if this affair were to be left to the ſingle determination of the noble Lord who made the motion, he would not, upon re-conſidering the caſe, come to ſuch a determination as he has now moved for, without enquiring farther into the matter ; therefore I hope the noble Lord will for the preſent wave

his motion, that the ſame may be again revived, after we have got a more full and diſtinct information about this affair.

Hereupon L—d B——ſt agreed to wave his motion for that time, and afterwards the Houſe ordered the preſent Directors, and alſo the laſt Directors of the S. S. Company to attend to be examined, and likewiſe the late Inſpectors of that Company's accounts.

Debate *on the Manner of providing a Marriage Portion for the Princeſs Royal.*

May 30. The Bill for granting to his Majeſty a certain ſum out of the ſinking Fund for the ſervice of the year 1733. and for the farther application of the ſame Fund ; and for enabling his Majeſty, out of the money ariſen by the ſale of lands in *St Chriſtophers*, to pay 80,000 *l.* as a Marriage-portion for the Princeſs Royal, &c. was read a ſecond time in the Houſe of Lords, and upon the Motion's being made for committing it, the

E—l of W——ea ſtood up and ſpoke to this effect : —— I do not riſe up, my Lords, to oppoſe the Bill now before us, but I ſtand up to take notice of the ſtrange method of huddling ſo many things together ; and particularly I cannot but take notice of that part of it by which 80,000 *l.* is granted as a portion for the Princeſs Royal. It is ſo unbecoming a thing to ſee that grant made in ſuch a hotch-potch Bill, a Bill which really ſeems to be the ſweepings of the other houſe, that I cannot let it paſs without teſtifying my diſlike. After his Majeſty had been moſt graciouſly pleaſed to communicate to both houſes of Parliament the intended marriage of that Princeſs, after both houſes had preſented to his Majeſty moſt dutiful and loyal addreſſes thereupon, I think, the leaſt that ought to have been done, was to have provided a marriage-portion for that Princeſs in a particular Bill by itſelf; that it might have ſtood upon our records as a teſtimony of the reſpect and duty of the nation towards the Royal Family now upon the throne. I have ſo great an eſteem for his Majeſty and his Family, and ſuch a particular regard for that illuſtrious Princeſs, that I am ſorry to ſee her name ſo much as mentioned in ſuch a riff-raff Bill as this is. —— But beſides this indignity to the Royal Family, the ſending up a Bill with ſo many different things tacked together, is a ſort of indignity to this houſe. It is a breach of one of your ſtanding orders, and is a laying of us under a neceſſity of agreeing

ing to every Item in a Bill, or of putting a negative upon every one of them: In fhort, to me it really feems to be a defign to make ufe of one particular article in the Bill in order to cram all the reft down our throats. Upon both thefe accounts I could not help taking notice of this moft extraordinary Bill, but fince it cannot now be remedy'd, I am fo fond of enabling his Majefty to provide a fufficient marriage-portion for the Princefs Royal, I am fo ready to join in any Meafures for providing for the current fervice of the year, that, rather than difappoint either, I will now pafs over thofe informalities, I will not oppofe this Bill, but I hope care will be taken hereafter not to fend up any more fuch Bills to this Houfe.

E—l of C——ld.] I do not either rife up, my Lords, to oppefe the Bill before us, but I think it is incumbent upon me to declare, that it is, in my opinion, a moft indecent thing to provide for the Princefs Royal of *England* in fuch a manner: it is moft difrefpectful to the Royal Family, to provide a marriage-portion for fo illuftrious a branch of it in fuch a Bill of *Items*. Here is *imprimis* 500,000 l. for the fervice of the year. *Item* 10,000 l. by way of charity for thofe diftreffed perfons who are to tranfport themfelves to the colony of *Georgia*. *Item* fo much by way of charity for repairing an old Church. *Item* for repairing a Dormitory. And *Item* 80,000 l. as a marriage-portion for the Princefs Royal of *England*. How incongruous is it, my Lords, for fuch a provifion to come in by way of *Item* among fo many and fuch *Items* for charitable ufes! In duty to the Family of which that Royal Princefs is defcended, out of that regard and efteem which we ought to have for her, and fhe fo much deferves, not only from us but from the whole world, her marriage-portion ought to have been provided for in a particular Bill by itfelf; no foreign matters ought to have been mix'd with it. Your Lordfhips were fo careful in that refpect, that when you were about drawing up an Addrefs of thanks to his Majefty for communicating to this Houfe the intended marriage of the Princefs Royal, you would not receive a few words offer'd by way of compliment to the States General, which might very properly have come in, becaufe you were refolv'd to put nothing into that Addrefs any way foreign to the intended marriage.——As I am refolved not to oppofe this Bill, I fhall not fay any thing to the method of racking made ufe of on this occafion; nor fhall I now object againft

the means made ufe of for providing for the current Service of the year; but both ought certainly to be taken notice of, and I hope your Lordfhips will, on this occafion, come to fome Refolutions that may tend to prevent the like practices for the future.

D—e of N————le.] My Lords, I am fo far from thinking it indecent or difrefpectful to provide for the Princefs [R. by this Bill, that I think it the only way fuch a Provifion could have been made. It could not well have been done by a particular Bill, becaufe the Marriage is not as yet fully concluded; and a particular Bill was lefs neceffary, becaufe the provifion is to be made without laying any new burden on the people: it is to be made out of what did not originally belong to the publick, but to his Majefty. The money arifing by the fale of the lands in *Nevis* and *St Chriftophers* the publick had no right to, till his Majefty was fo good to give it up, for the ufe of the publick.

E—l of I——ay] My Lords, I muft fay that the two noble Lords who fpoke firft on this fubject, have been pleafed to give the Bill before us fome very extraordinary epithets, which in my opinion it no way deferves. There is in this Bill nothing of an extraordinary nature; furely your Ldfhips would not have a particular Bill fent up for every fmall fum that is granted for the current fervice of the year. Your Lordfhips know it is not ufual: it has always been the cuftom of Parliament to provide for feveral particular fervices by one Bill. As to the marriage-portion of the Princefs Royal, I have as great a regard for that moft deferving Princefs, and as great a refpect for the royal family of which fhe is defcended, as any Lord in this houfe; but I really fee no difference in the providing for her marriage portion by a particular Bill, for that purpofe, or by a claufe in fome other Bill. It will ftand equally upon all our records in the one way as in the other; and the duty and refpect which the nation owes to his majefty and his illuftrious Family will be fhewn as much and teftified as ftrongly, by the claufe in this Bill, as if there had been a particular Bill brought in and paffed for that purpofe only.—As to the orders of this houfe there is nothing in this Bill that is againft any of them; the order which now feems to be referred to is, I prefume, that by which it is ordered that nothing of a foreign nature fhall be tacked to any money Bill: This, is the only order I can think of which has any manner of relation to the queftion in hand, and I am am fure there is nothing in this Bill contrary to that order: There is nothing of a foreign nature, there is nothing in it but what relates to the granting of money, and therefore there is nothing in it that can in any way be faid to look like tacking. Since the noble Lords had no mind to oppofe the Bill, I muft think that they might have let alone faying any thing upon this head 'till after the Bill had been ordered to be committed: Then, if they had any motion to make relating to any irregularities in this Bill, they might have fpoke to it; but it is not ufual for any Lord to fpeak againft a Bill, unlefs it be with a defign to oppofe its paffing in the form it is in.

After this the Bill was ordered to be committed, and then enfued the

DEBATE *on the Sinking Fund.* See p. 447.

L—d B——ß ftood up and fpoke in fubftance —— My Lords, I did not before give your Lordfhips any trouble, becaufe I had not a mind to oppofe this Bill which we have now fordered to be committed; for tho' I was of opinion, and I find I am not fingular, that the fending up fuch a Bill was both irregular and contrary to the orders of this houfe, yet I thought it was neceffary to pafs it, not only becaufe of the defire I had to fee all the current fervices of the year provided for, but likewife becaufe of the great regard I had for that branch of the Royal Family provided for by this Bill; tho', I fhould have been glad to have feen that Royal Princefs provided for by a particular Bill for that purpofe only: for whenever a grant is to be made by Parliament in favour of any particular perfon, the doing of it by a claufe may perhaps, have the fame effect, but the doing of it by a Bill certainly fhews a greater regard for the perfon to whom the grant is made. There is indeed a method by which one houfe of Parliament may be made to fhew a very extraordinary regard to any particular thing provided for only by a claufe in a Bill; this method has perhaps been practifed, tho' I fhall not fay, my Lords, it has in this cafe; it is when either houfe of Parliament has a Bill before them which they fufpect may be thrown out in the other houfe, therefore, to carry it thro' the other Houfe, they add a claufe in favour of fome thing, or fome perfon which they know the other houfe will fhew a great regard to; in fuch cafe, if that other houfe do pafs fuch a Bill for

the fake of that claufe, it is certainly fhewing a very extraordinary regard to the perfon in favour of whom that claufe was thus purpofely introduced. If I admit bad company into my houfe for the fake of one particular man who happens to be among them, I certainly fhew him a greater regard than if I admitted him fingle and alone, but he is little obliged to thofe who put him upon the office of gaining admittance for fuch troublefome attendants. — However, I fhall infift no longer upon this part of the Bill, my principal defign is to take notice of the manner in which the current fervice of the year is provided for by this Bill; It is a very extraordinary method, a method I fhall never approve of; I have always looked on the Sinking Fund as a moft facred pledge for fecuring the payment of the debts of the nation, and for relieving the people from thofe many taxes and burthens they groan under. Now, I find, that by this Bill, that facred fund is to be robbed of 500,000 l. at one ftroke. There have been feveral large fums formerly ftolen from that fund; but, I believe it was never before plundered of fo large a fum at once, or in fo direct and open a manner as by this Bill is to be introduced. Therefore, I hope, your Lordfhips will come to fome Refolution for preventing any fuch practices for the future: It is now, my Lords, really become neceffary for us to fignify to the other houfe our opinion, That the Sinking-Fund ought never to be applied to any other purpofe than that for which it was originally defigned; and I think, the beft way of fignifying fuch opinion, is, by having a Refolution to that purpofe entered upon the journals of this houfe; for which reafon I fhall take the liberty to move for a refolution in thefe or in fome fuch terms, *That it is the opinion of this houfe, that the Sinking-Fund ought always for the future to be applied to the redeeming thofe taxes which are moft prejudicial to the trade, moft burthenfome on the manufactures, and moft oppreffive upon the poor of this nation.*

L—d C——t.] My Lords, I muft upon this occafion declare it to be my opinion, that the creditors of the publick have, in a manner, a right to that facred Fund, called the Sinking-Fund; it is in its own nature a fecurity to them; firft, for the payment of the intereft coming yearly due to them, and next for the payment of their principal fums. The whole people of *England* have a right to have it

It duly applied; because it is by such application only that we can get free of those many and grievous taxes which lie so heavy upon the poor, and are such a clog to the trade and manufactures of this nation; therefore the applying that Fund to any other use is a robbing the publick creditors of their right, it is doing an injustice to the whole people of *England.*—The present circumstances of this nation are, in some manner deplorable. By the many taxes we now pay the necessaries and conveniences of life are rendered so dear, that it is impossible for our tradesmen or manufacturers to live so cheap, or to sell the produce of their labour at so small a price as our neighbours do; from hence it is, that our neighbours are every day encroaching upon us, and our trade is daily decaying. If a journeyman in any manufacture whatever, can live better in *France* or *Germany* on a fix-pence a day than he can live in *England* on a shilling, we may depend on it that most of our tradesmen will at last find the way thither, if they are not prevented either by our own good politicks, or by some very bad politick among our neighbours; and if a master tradesman can get the same work done in *France* for sixpence, which would cost him a shilling in *England*, he certainly can undersell the *English* tradesman in all the foreign markets of the world. The only method therefore, my Lords, to preserve our trade is to take off those taxes which now lie so heavy upon the poor tradesmen and labourers, and this the whole people of *England* know can be done no other way but by a due application of the Sinking Fund. How shocking then must it be to the whole nation to see that Fund plundered of so large a sum at once? The whole nation must from hence conclud, that they must for ever groan under those taxes and burthens which they now find almost insupportable, and which must soon become absolutely so, by the decay of our trade and our manufactures.—This Fund, my Lords, has been clandestinely defrauded of several small sums at different times, which indeed together amount to a pretty large sum; but by the Bill which we have now ordered to be committed, it is to be openly and avowedly plundered of 500,000 *l.* at once. After such a direct misapplication of that fund, can any publick creditor depend upon his being ever paid his principal sum? or think himself secure even of that yearly interest or annuity which is due

to him? By this Bill he sees one half of the Sinking-Fund applied to the current service of the year; in a time of the most profound peace and tranquillity. How then can he be certain but that the whole Sinking-Fund may be next year applied to the same purposes? He must then see himself deprived of all hopes of ever receiving his principal sum; and if the funds now appropriated to the payment of the yearly interest, or annuities growing due to the publick creditors should hereafter prove deficient, where could they have recourse for the payment even of those annuities? The Sinking-Fund being otherwise applied, their annuities, or at least some part of them, must remain unpaid, and, at last perhaps, the whole might cease. Such a suspicion may, even by this misapplication, arise among the creditors of the publick; and if such should arise, it would be the most terrible shock that ever happened to the publick credit of this nation. To prevent therefore any such suspicion, it will be absolutely necessary for your Lordships to come to some resolution for quieting the minds of the people, and for assuring them that no such misapplication shall for the future be admitted of; the passing of the Bill now before us makes our coming to such Resolution the more necessary, and therefore I am for agreeing with the motion made by the noble Lord who spoke last.

D—ke of N———le.] I wonder, my Lords, to hear it affirmed by any Lord in this House, That the publick creditors have any manner of right in the Sinking-fund: They certainly have no right to any part of it: They have a right only to receive their yearly interest when it becomes due; for the payment of which there are other funds appropriated, and therefore as long as they are regularly paid their interest they have nothing to fear or complain of. It is well known that the Sinking-fund was from its very first original subject to be disposed of by Parliament, and the Parliament has it still in their power to apply it to the paying off a part of the publick debt, or to what other publick use they shall think most proper; in this year there is as much of it applied towards the paying off the publick debts as is either necessary or convenient. —— By this very Bill there is a Million to be applied towards the paying off a part of the publick debts of the nation, which is more than the Creditors of the publick either want or desire. The Circumstances

ſtances of this nation are now ſo happy, and the publick Credit ſo well eſtabliſh'd, that none of the publick Creditors deſire to have their Money : On the contrary, we ſee thoſe Funds bear the higheſt price, and are the moſt ſought after, which are expected to be the longeſt in being paid. In ſuch Circumſtances we have an opportunity to look about us, and to apply a part of that fund where we find it is moſt wanted : This is what is propoſed by this Bill ; it muſt be granted, that the landed Gentlemen have of all others borne for many years the greateſt ſhare of the publick Charge, they ought therefore to be the firſt relieved ; and for this reaſon 500,000 *l.* part of the Sinking-fund, is to be applied to the current ſervice of the year, in order to relieve them of a part of that Burthen they have long labour'd under. Since then by this Bill the landed Gentlemen are to be relieved, and the ſervice of the year provided for without contracting any new debt, or laying any new burthen upon the people, it muſt be allowed to be a publick Benefit—That part of the ſinking-fund which in eaſe of the landed Gentlemen is by this Bill to be applied to the current ſervice of the year, is not, my Lords, to be called a half of the ſinking-fund, becauſe it is not to be taken out of the produce of that fund for one year ; it is what has ariſen from the Surpluſſes of that fund for ſeveral years, over and above the Million, which for ſome time has been yearly applied to the payment of the publick debts : And ſince none of the publick Creditors either wanted or deſired their money, I muſt think that theſe ſurpluſſes could not have been applied better than to the relief of thoſe who have been for many years the moſt grievouſly taxed. This is the true deſign of the Bill, which we have ordered to be committed. It is a good deſign, it is ſuch a deſign as can give no man an alarm ; it can raiſe no jealouſies or fears, and therefore I cannot think that there is any occaſion for your Lordſhips to come to ſuch a reſolution as the noble Lord has been pleaſed to move for.

E—l of I—ay.] I am really ſurprized, my Lords, to hear ſuch expreſſions made uſe of in this houſe, as ſome Lords have taken the liberty to uſe. Robbing, Stealing, Plundering, Defrauding, Miſapplying, are ſuch terms as are not uſual in any polite converſation, and much leſs ought they to be made uſe of in any debate in this houſe ; but when I reflect upon what they are applied to, I cannot but think they are ſtill more irregular. It has been ſaid, that the Sinking-fund has been plundered and robbed ; I would gladly know, my Lords, by whom this ſacred fund has been ſo uſed ?—To the beſt of my knowledge, there has never yet been 1 *s.* of it applied to any uſe but by virtue of an Act of Parliament for that purpoſe ; and if it be ſaid that it has been plundered and robbed by Act of Parliament, who are to be called the plunderers and robbers? Why the King, the Lords, and the Commons. Can this be ſaid to be decent? Theſe are terms very far from being proper upon any occaſion in this houſe, and ſurely they are moſt improperly applied to the Parliament's diſpoſing of that fund, which by its firſt Inſtitution was, and ever ſince has continued to be entirely at the diſpoſal of Parliament. The Sinking-fund is to be appropriated to the payment of the publick debts from year to year by authority of Parliament ; but if the Parliament ſhall think proper to diſpoſe of any part of it, or even the whole in any one year to ſome other uſe, they certainly may ; the diſpoſing of it in ſuch a manner is neither plundering, or miſapplying.——For my own part I muſt beg leave to ſay, I do not know what the noble Lord means by the Reſolution he propoſes. The Sinking fund is in its own nature to be applied yearly to the payment of the publick debts, unleſs the Parliament ſhall, in any one year, think the applying of it to ſome other uſe will be more beneficial to the nation : And I hope your Lordſhips do not mean by ſuch a Reſolution to tie up this houſe, in all future Seſſions, not to apply that fund to the uſe which ſhall then be deemed moſt for the benefit of the nation : Even as Act of Parliament could not have ſuch an effect : Are your Lordſhips to make a Reſolution which is to be held more ſacred, and more unalterable, than an Act of Parliament? Are we to reſolve not to truſt ourſelves for the future with the management, or the diſpoſal of this money? In ſhort, my Lords, ſuch a Reſolution is, in my opinion, quite unneceſſary, and if agreed to, could be of no manner of uſe.——As for the paying off the publick debts, and relieving the nation from the taxes it now pays, I am as much for it as any Lord in this houſe ; but if it were poſſible to pay off all our debts in one year, it would not be prudent to do ſo : The debts are to be paid off gradually ; there would be great dis-

ger in paying off too many at once : By ſuch a glut of money coming to be thrown at once into the hands of private Men, the Intereſt of money·in this nation would be run down lower than the circumſtances of *Europe*·could at that time admit of ; the certain conſequence of which would be, that·vaſt ſums of money would at once be carried out of the nation, in order to place it at an Intereſt ſomewhere elſe; this would drain us of all our ready money, which of conſequence would put an end even to our paper-credit, and thereby the Intereſt of money would in a little time be raiſed higher than would ·be conſiſtent either with the trade or the credit of the nation.——I ſhould be glad to ſee this nation free of moſt of the taxes now charged upon it ; but I cannot believe thoſe taxes are ſo burthenſome upon our trade, or our manufactures in ſuch decay as ſome Lords have been pleaſed to repreſent; I believe both our trade and our manufactures are at preſent in as good and as thriving a condition as they ever were: Our People, 'tis true, pay taxes, but I would gladly know where there is a People that pay none: I believe there is not now a country in *Europe* where the taxes are leſs burthenſome to the People, than they are in this, nor is there a country in the world, where an induſtrious tradeſman may live more happily ; and therefore we need not be much afraid that any induſtrious and frugal tradeſman will leave us. The fact I take to be otherwiſe ; I believe there are many more foreign tradeſmen come yearly to ſettle in *England*, than there are of our natives who go to ſettle in any foreign parts.—— If it be laid down as a maxim, that every application of the Sinking Fund to any other uſe beſides that of paying off the publick debt, is to be look'd on as a miſapplication, then certainly the applying it towards the redeeming of any of our taxes muſt be deemed to be a miſapplication ; and therefore I hope thoſe Lords, who inſiſt ſo much upon its being 'a fund ſacred to the payment of our debts only, will be againſt the reſolution propos'd.

L—d C—t.] My Lords, if we inquire into the riſe of the Sinking fund, we may eaſily find that the publick creditors have ·not only ſome ſort of right, but a moſt juſt claim to that fund. The fund, which is now called the Sinking fund, aroſe from the diminution of the Intereſt payable to the creditors of the publick : They had formerly, at leaſt moſt part of them had, an intereſt of ſix *per Cent.* or above ; and

while that Intereſt continued, the whole ſinking fund was actually appropriated to the payment of the yearly Intereſt due to them ; but then, there was no fund eſtabliſhed for the payment of their principal money ; this made all thoſe who had a concern for the publick uneaſy ; and without doubt there were many of the publick creditors who were not quite eaſy under ſuch circumſtances; therefore they have all conſented by degrees to the reducing of their Intereſt to four *per Cent.* Thus have they given up one third part of their yearly Intereſt, to ſecure the payment of their principal money : and for this reaſon they have not only an Intereſt in the ſinking fund, but a right to claim that it may never be applied to any thing but the gradual payment of the principal money due to them.——I am ſurpriſed, my Lords, to hear it ſaid they have a right only to their yearly Intereſt. Have not they a right to come and demand their principal money whenever they pleaſe ? 'Tis true, they do not now want their money, there are none of them come at preſent to demand their money of the publick ; but from whence does this proceed ? Does it not proceed from their being, by means of this very fund, ſecure, not only as to the regular payment of their yearly Intereſt, but likewiſe that their principal money will be all paid at laſt ? From hence it is that all publick ſecurities ſell at leaſt at par, and therefore, if any publick creditor ſtands in need of his money, he has no occaſion to come and demand it of the Government, becauſe he may every day ſell his ſecurity in *Exchange-Alley* at the full value ; but if the Sinking fund ſhould be taken away, they would be rendered leſs ſecure of the regular payment of their Intereſt, and they muſt deſpair of ever having their principal ; they could not then ſell their publick ſecurities for the full value, or perhaps for any value, and conſequently they would not only have a right, but they would certainly come and demand payment of their principal money from the publick.—But, granting that the publick creditors neither do, nor ever will demand payment of their principal money, is that any reaſon for the publick never to think of paying them ? If a Man has a mortgage upon my eſtate, and does not deſire it to be paid off, becauſe he has a higher Intereſt, more regular payments, and a better ſecurity from me than he can find any where elſe ; ſurely that can be no reaſon for my delaying to pay him off,

off: On the contrary, it is one of the beſt reaſons can be given for my paying him off as ſoon as poſſible.—The publick meaſures now ſeem to be much changed from what they were a few years ago; it was then thought that the taxes moſt grievous to the poor, were the moſt proper to be firſt redeemed. This meaſure ſeemed then to be ſo much the favourite of the Government, that his Majeſty from **A** the Throne recommended to us the relieving of the labourers and manufacturers from thoſe taxes that lay moſt heavy upon them; and in purſuance of his Majeſty's moſt gracious Speech, the tax which was juſtly deemed to be the moſt grievous upon them, was in that Seſſion of Parliament taken off. But, this ſalutary meaſure was all of a ſudden quite altered; what the poor labourers and manufacturers had done to merit our Indignation I do not know, but they were entirely forgot, the whole cry was for relieving the landed Intereſt; Nay, ſo far did this new meaſure prevail, that that very tax which had been taken off as the moſt grievous on the poor, was again laid on for the pretended relief of **D** the landed Gentlemen, I ſay, the pretended relief; for it was but a pretended relief; as all thoſe reliefs will for ever prove to be, which are given by ſubſtituting a tax upon the neceſſaries or the conveniences of life to the whole, or to any part of the land-tax. It is certain that the **E** landed Intereſt ſuffer much more by the many taxes we now pay than they ever can do by a land-tax, were it to be double the higheſt that was ever heard of in this nation. There is not a guinea that a landed Gentleman pays out of his pocket for the neceſſaries or conveniences of **F** life, but at leaſt 8 ſhillings of it go towards the payment of thoſe taxes to which theſe things are ſubjected; and this every landed Gentleman in *England* muſt pay to thoſe with whom he deals, beſides the land-tax which he pays directly to the publick. If then a landed Gentleman who ſpends the income of his Eſtate yearly, were free of all thoſe other **G** taxes, if he could have as many of the neceſſaries and conveniences of life for 13 ſhillings as he now has for a Guinea, could he not then eaſily pay even 4 ſhillings in the pound land-tax, in caſe the ſame ſhould be found neceſſary for the **H** ſafety of his country?—To pretend, my Lords, that applying a part of the ſinking-fund to the current ſervice of the year, is a providing for that ſervice without

contracting any new debt, or laying any new tax upon the people, is a mere impoſition upon the publick. What is neceſſary for the current ſervice ought always to be raiſed within the year; the contrary method tends to the ruin both of the trade and credit of the nation: it is a temporary expedient which muſt always be attended with fatal conſequences, and looks as if an adminiſtration were ſuſpicious of their intereſt in Parliament, or were afraid of aſking from the people what by their meaſures they had made **B** neceſſary for the current ſervice of the year. Tho' the landed Gentlemen be eaſed a little, tho' no new tax be laid on, yet it cannot be ſaid that the current ſervice of the year is provided for without running the nation in debt. The applying towards the ſervice of the year, that money which ought to have been applied **C** towards the payment of an old debt, is the ſame thing with contracting a new debt.—But, this is not the only miſchief, we are not only putting off the payment of old debts, but we are every year running into new. Why might not theſe ſurpluſſes, as they are called, have been applied towards the payment of a part of the Navy debt lately contracted? Do not the accounts upon our table ſhew us what a large ſum is lately become due to the Navy? There is now above a million due upon that ſingle article, which muſt ſome day be provided for by Parliament. Some temporary expedients may be found out for putting off that proviſion for a little time; but ſuch expedients are always ruinous; the longer ſuch a neceſſary proviſion is put off, the greater handle is given to Uſurers and Extortioners to make unjuſt advantages of the poor Officers and Sailors belonging to the Navy, and the more heavy it will fall upon the nation at laſt; either the Sinking-fund muſt be at laſt applied to the paying it off, or the people muſt be charged with ſome new tax for that purpoſe: I do not know but there may be deſigns of making that debt a pretence for continuing one of the moſt pernicious taxes that was ever laid on the poor of this nation.—To pretend that there is a danger in paying off too much of the publick debt at once really ſeems to me to be ſomething very extraordinary. Our Sinking-fund is not ſo great, nor can it ever be ſo great as to give the leaſt foundation for ſuch fears; if it were moſt exactly and moſt religiouſly applied to that purpoſe for which it was originally deſigned, there would be no danger of
people's

people's carrying their money out of this nation. There are but few countries where there is any great credit either publick or private, and in all those where either the one or the other abounds, the Intereft of money is rather lower than it is in this country; fo that if the Intereft of money in this nation were run down a good deal lower than it is, we fhould be put upon a par with fome of our neighbours; and when people faw that our publick faith was in every circumftance exactly obferved, they would be fo fond of continuing their money in this country, that they would accept of a lower Intereft here than they could have in other countries, efpecially in thofe where the fecurity has always been very much fufpected.—The noble Lord who fpoke laft feems to miftake the Refolution propofed. The applying of the Sinking-fund towards redeeming taxes is the fame, with applying it towards reducing the publick debts; for as our moft grievous taxes are pledged to the creditors of the publick, thofe debts for which they are pledged muft be paid off before the taxes can be redeemed: fo that the Refolution moved for is fomething more ftrong than if it had been in general words, *that the Sinking-fund ought always to be applied towards the reducing of the publick debts*; for thefe general words plainly appear to be included in the Refolution, and farther, that it ought firft to be applied towards the paying off thofe debts for which the taxes moft prejudicial to our trade and manufactures, are mortgag'd; for till thofe debts are paid off, we cannot abolifh thofe taxes; but the debts being once paid off, and thofe taxes thereby redeemed, it will then, and not till then, be in the power of Parliament to confider whether or no the tax ought to be abolifh'd. The refolution therefore, as moved for, is a moft proper refolution, and can't be put in better or ftronger terms than the Lord who made the motion has put it. Such a refolution is, my Lords, become abfolutely neceffary; it is fhewing to the other houfe what is the opinion of this; it is fhewing to the whole nation, that the finking Fund is for the future to be deemed facred; it is not tying up this houfe to any thing but what we ought to be tied up to. Tho' a private man be abfolute mafter of his own affairs, yet every private man lays down to himfelf fome general rules, from which he never departs without fome very urgent neceffity. In this Houfe we do the fame:

(Supplement to Vol. LII.*)*

Howmany ftanding orders have we made? I hope it will not be faid that all our ftanding orders are ufelefs, becaufe we may depart from them, or alter them when we have a mind. If this Refolution be agreed to, it is certainly to be underftood in the fame fenfe as all our ftanding orders are; it is never to be departed from but in cafes of the utmoft neceffity.

E—l of S——gh.] My Lords, I am very well convinced that the Sinking-Fund ought never to be applied to any thing but that for which it was eftablifhed, and for which it was originally intended; and I hope, that your Lordfhips are not only now, but always will be of the fame opinion; I hope, that that facred Fund will never for the future be applied to any ufe but that of difcharging the publick debts, except in cafes of the utmoft Extremity. This is my way of thinking, yet I cannot agree to our coming to fuch a refolution as the noble Lord has been pleafed to propofe. Surely we do not mean, we cannot pretend to tie up the hands of the Legiflature fo, as that they muft never touch that Fund, even in the times of greateft danger and neceffity. If there fhould arife a wicked and unnatural Rebellion in the country; if the nation fhould be invaded, and 30 or 40000 foreign troops landed in our Dominions, are we to tie ourfelves up, fo that the Sinking-Fund is not even in fuch a cafe to be touched? Many other cafes may happen, in which it might be more for the benefit of the nation to apply a part of that fund to fome other ufe, than to apply the whole to the payment of the publick debts.——We do not know what inconveniences may be occafioned by our having fuch a Refolution entered upon the Journals of our Houfe: There is one terrible confequence which now occurs to me, and which (in my opinion) may very probably arife from our coming to fuch a Refolution. It may very naturally be the caufe of a difference between the two Houfes of Parliament, which would be of the moft dangerous confequence to our conftitution: The other houfe may look upon it as a directing of them in what they are to do, with refpect to the application of that Fund: Or, if the other Houfe fhould not take it amifs, yet, if they fhould up, on any future Emergency, which they thought preffing, apply a part of that fund otherwife than to the payment of the national Debt, your Lordfhips might perhaps think yourfelves in honour bound up ty such a Resolution, so as not to agree with them in such application: This would naturally raise a contest between the two Houses which would put a full stop to all publick business of the nation; and who can tell the consequence of such a Contest, or how long it might last? — This, my Lords, is one inconvenience which immediately occurred to me, and other Lords may, I believe, foresee a great many more. As that Fund is in its own nature sacred to discharging the Debts of the nation, I hope that without coming to such a Resolution, your Lordships will never agree to the applying of it in any other Way except in cases of the greatest necessity. Such a resolution I must therefore think quite unnecessary, and as I think it may be attended with dangerous consequences, I cannot agree to it.

L—d B——ft.] My Lords, the noble Ld who spoke last has made me think of an amendment to the resolution I proposed; and as I am always fond of having that noble Lord's Approbation, I shall, therefore, propose that the Resolution may be to this effect: *That it is the Opinion of this Honse, that the Sinking-fund ought for the future to be applied, in time of peace and publick tranquillity, to the redeeming of those Taxes which are most prejudicial to the Trade, most burthensome on the Manufactures, and most oppressive upon the Poor of this nation.*

L—d S——gh.] Besides the case of an Invasion or Rebellion, there are many other cases which may happen; and I believe I gave several other reasons for my being against coming to the resolution proposed; therefore, tho' I am very much obliged to the noble Lord for the honour he does me, yet I cannot agree to the resolution even as now amended.

The M——s of T——le, the E—l of W——ea, and the E—l of S——d spoke also in favour of this resolution: However, at last, upon putting the question it was carried in the negative without any division.

June 1. The House of Lords went upon the Examination of the Directors of the S. Sea Company. The present Directors of that Company were first called in and examined; after them the late Inspectors of the Company's accounts, and lastly the former set of Directors were examined. Then

L—d B——ft moved for this Resolution, viz. *That it appeared to that Honse, that on the 5th of December, 1729, the general Court of the South-Sea Company then held, resolved, That the then present Directors should be the Trustees for the Company, with relation to the produce of the forfeited Estates of the Directors and others in the year 1720, vested in the Company by an Act of the 7th of King George I. and that the then Trustees should surrender, and deliver over to the said Directors, the said produce, and all the books of accounts, papers, and writings relating thereto; In pursuance of the Act, passed in the then last Session of Parliament*

ment: *And that that was the only order or direction of any general Court of the said Company relating to the disposal of the produce of the said estates.* Upon this the

E—l of I——ay stood up and said, That he would not oppose the motion in general, but he thought they could not positively affirm that that was the only order or direction of any general Court relating to the disposal of that money; and therefore he would propose an amendment to the latter part of the noble Lord's motion, which was, that it should run thus: *And that it did not appear to them that there was any other order or direction of any general Court of the said Company relating to the disposal of the said Estates.* Which Amendment was approved of by L—d B——ft, and then his motion, thus amended, was agreed to by the House without any opposition.

Then the E—l of W——ea moved for the House to resolve, *That the disposing of the forfeited estates of those who were the Directors of the South-Sea Company in the Year 1720, without any order or direction of a general Court for that purpose, was contrary to Law.* Adding that he hoped he had no occasion to say much in support of this motion, because the words of the Act of Parliament were so plain and express, that it was a certain consequence of the Resolution they had just then come to.

The Lord Chancellor offering to put the question upon this motion, the

D—ke of D——re stood up, and spoke to this effect: — I cannot, my Lords, agree to this motion, because I think it is anticipating the judgment of this House in an affair which may perhaps come before us as a Court of Judicature. 'Tis true, there does not appear to us to have been any other order or direction of any general Court of that Company for the disposal of those forfeited estates, except that which is mentioned in our former resolution; but still there may be other orders: and granting that there never was any other order, yet we ought not I think to pass judgment even upon that order, without having all proper parties before us, and the case fully debated and considered. As the resolution proposed is a sort of decree or determination as to a point in which private men are certainly concerned, we ought not to pass it till the parties concerned are properly before us, and are fully heard as to what they may have to say against it, for which reason I cannot agree to the resolution proposed.

The B—p of B——r and another B—p spoke next against this resolution, and the B——p of B——r particularly took notice, that he could not agree to the resolution, because he thought it would be in some manner a giving of directions to the Courts below; how they were to determine, in case that affair should ever come before them.

L—d C——rt.] My Lords, the words of the Act of Parliament are so plain and express

preſs and the Reſolution moved for by the noble Lord is ſo exactly agreeable to thoſe words, that I am really ſurprized to hear any Lord ſignify the leaſt ſcruple as to a-greeing with the Motion. The words of the Law are, That the produce of thoſe for-feited Eſtates ſhall be diſpoſed of by the orders and directions of the general Courts of that company, *and not otherwiſe:* The words of the Reſolution are, That the ha-ving diſpoſed of that produce otherwiſe is contrary to Law, Can any thing be more evident? There may be orders of the gene-ral Courts of that Company relating to the diſpoſal of this Money which your Lord-ſhips have not ſeen, but can the poſſibility of there being any ſuch be an argument a-gainſt agreeing to this Reſolution? We do not by the reſolution propoſed affirm, that there never was any orders of a general court for directing the diſpoſal of that money: we affirm no fact: We only declare our opi-nion in a point of Law, which to me is as clear and as evident, as any Demonſtra-tion I ever met with. —Suppoſe that this affair does come before ſome of the inferior Courts, and that it does then appear that there were other orders of the general Courts of that Company for directing the diſpoſal of this money, beſides that lying before your Lordſhips, the Reſolution now moved for could not in ſuch a caſe be any direction to thoſe Courts; they would certainly be at as full liberty as if no ſuch reſolution had ever been made; and if it ſhould appear before any of the Courts below, that no other or-der was ever made by any general Court of that Company for directing the diſpoſal of this money, could any Court determine o-therwiſe than according to the Act of Par-liament? My Lords, the caſe is ſo plain, the words of the Law are ſo very expreſs, that I cannot think there is any occaſion for hear-ing the point debated; and therefore I ſhall agree to the Reſolution.

E—l of I—ay.] My Lords, tho' there were really no other order or direction of any general court of the *South-Sea* company relating to the diſpoſal of the money in queſ-tion, beſides that which has been laid before your Lordſhips, I do not know but that it may be pretended, that even the order which your Lordſhips have ſeen was a ſufficient authority for the diſpoſal of that money; I: was certainly a ſufficient authority for the truſtees to deliver the produce of thoſe eſ-tates to the directors of that company, and when in purſuance of that order it was de-livered into the hands of the directors; I do not know but that it may be ſaid, that the terms of the act of Parliament were then complied with, and that the directors might thereafter diſpoſe of it in that way which they thought moſt beneficial for the company, as they do of ſome other parts of that com-pany's property, without any particular or-der of a general court for that purpoſe; Thi

is a queſtion which I ſhall not pretend now to determine; I ſhall not ſo much as offer any arguments either of one ſide or the other, but from thence I conclude, that even the order which we have ſeen deſerves ſome fur-ther conſideration, before we come to any ſuch Reſolution as is now propoſed; for af-ter your Lordſhips have ſeen and conſidered that order, your coming to ſuch a Reſoluti-on is certainly a determination, that the order you have ſeen and conſidered, is no proper or legal order for the diſpoſal of that money. The courts below will certainly look upon it as ſuch; and even tho' they ſhould be of opinion, that that order was a ſufficient au-thority for the diſpoſing of that money, and that no future order was requiſite, yet they would be loath to give a judgment ſo con-trary to what appeared to have been the judg-ment of this houſe.---The point now before us cannot be ſaid to be an indiſputable point, and therefore I muſt think that your Lord-ſhips coming to ſuch a Reſolution is a de-termining of a queſtion in diſpute, and a making a ſort of decree againſt the Gentle-men who were at that time in the manage-ment of that company's affairs, before they have been heard either by themſelves or their council upon a queſtion in which both their honour and intereſt are ſo nearly concerned: This is a method of proceeding which, I hope, this houſe will never come into, or in-to any Reſolution which may affect either the character or eſtate of any private man, without firſt giving him an opportunity to be heard againſt it.—We ought, my Lords, to conſider that we are a court of equity, and tho' it ſhould appear that the money ariſing from thoſe forfeited eſtates had been diſpoſed of without ſuch an authority as was neceſſary in the ſtrict terms of law, yet if it has been diſpoſed of in the beſt manner for the benefit of the company, the then directors ought in equity to ſtand acq itted. they ought not to be loaded with any thing like a ſentence of ſo auguſt an aſſem ly a-gainſt them; and therefore, it is really my opinion that you ought not to come to ſuch a Reſolution as now moved for, 'till the affair comes properly before you, and all parties are heard what they have to ſay either in law or equity in their own behalf, there-fore I muſt move for the previous queſtion.

E—l of S—gh.] My Lords, as to the or-der of the general court of the *South-Sea* company, which has been laid before your Lordſhips, ſurely it cannot be looked on ei-ther in law or equity as an order directing how the money in queſtion was to be diſpo-ſed of, nor can it ever be perſumed that it will be the opinion of any court, or of any man, that an order directing only who ſhould be the truſtees of the company as to that money, was an order for directing to what uſes it ought to be applied; therefore, if that point were to be expreſsly determined, it could not be of any bad conſequence in any

C c c *a*

case whatever; but by the Resolution proposed, even that question, if it must be called a question, is not to be expressly determined: We are now, to determine nothing but a point of law, which to me appears so plain that I cannot hesitate one moment in giving my opinion. The words of the act of Parliament are so very express, that there can be no doubt of its being contrary to law, to dispose of that money, without any order or direction of a general court for that purpose; and I am sure it is as plain, that the delivering of that money by the trustees to the directors is not such a disposal of the money as is intended by that act.---If it shall afterwards appear, that the produce of those forfeited estates was disposed of according to the directions of general courts, the resolution, or, if your Lordships please, the determination now proposed can affect no man, and if there never was any other order or direction of a general court for that purpose besides what we have seen, our Resolution can affect none but those who without all question are guilty at least of an error, for which they certainly deserve to be censured.---I do consider, my Lords, that this house is a court of equity, but the Resolution moved for has relation only to a point of law, it has no manner of relation to equity, nor can any man be thereby debarred from having relief in equity, either before your Lordships, or before any of the courts of equity below; and therefore, if those Gentlemen should hereafter come to shew, that tho' they neglected the due forms of law, they did nevertheless dispose of that money in such a manner as was most for the benefit of the company, I should not think myself any way restrained by this resolution from giving them all the relief in equity that their case can deserve. Therefore I shall make no scruple of agreeing to a Resolution which I think just, and absolutely necessary, because it will oblige those who are concerned to be at pains to clear up, if they can, an affair which is certainly as yet very obscure, and which your Lordships are in honour obliged to see fully cleared up, if it be possible.

The E---l of C---ld spoke also for the Resolution, and the D. of N---le against it. The previous question was then put, and upon a division there were of Lords present 45 contents, and 57 not contents; and of proxies 25 contents, and 18 not contents; so that it was carried against the Resolution by a Majority of five.

DEBATE on a motion for a committee of enquiry, to examine into the Affairs of the S. S. Company.

June 2. L--d B--st stood up and spoke in substance as follows;----My Lords, notwithstanding all the pains your Lordships have been at in your enquiries as to the disposal of the produce of the forfeited estates of those who were directors of the South-Sea company in the year 1720, I cannot say that I have met with any satisfaction as to that affair; and I believe no other Lord has. It appears that the accounts of that company have been kept in so confused and irregular a manner, that there is no coming at the knowledge of any one particular, without a thorough enquiry into the whole. From what already appears to your Lordships, I believe, you will be all of opinion, that such a general and exact enquiry is now become absolutely necessary; because we are, in my opinion, obliged in honour to see the affair relating to the disposal of those estates fully cleared up; by the very first act of Parliament relating to this affair, the trustees were directed to give a particular account, in writing, to the King and to either house of Parliament, of the effects of their proceedings. To what end, my Lords, were the trustees directed to give such an account? The intention certainly was, that the King, the Lords and the Commons should, as guardians see that money fairly collected, and honestly disposed of for the benefit of the proprietors of that company, according to the directions of this or any future act of Parliament for regulating the disposal of that money. This house therefore is in honour obliged to see that it was honestly disposed of. In such a case are we to satisfy ourselves with being told, that tho' the terms of the act of Parliament were not strictly complied with, yet the money was equitably disposed of for the benefit of the proprietors; especially when this equitable disposal comes out at last to be, a disposal of it towards payment of debts, as to which no man can tell how or when they were contracted? I must observe, that it looks much the more suspicious, because such a large debt was paid off without any orders of a general court for so doing; if directions had been asked for, it may at least be presumed that the general court would in their turn have asked, how such a large debt came to be contracted?----Therefore, my Lords, as a general enquiry into that company's affairs is become absolutely necessary, and as it cannot be supposed that we shall have time this session, or even during any one whole session of Parliament, to go through such a general enquiry, I shall take the liberty to move, That a committee may be appointed to examine into the management of the affairs of the South-Sea company ever since the year 1720, and for that purpose to sit during the recess of Parliament at such places and times as they shall appoint, and that they may have power to send for persons, papers and records.---- The appointing such a committee is, my Lords, a method that in former cases has been practised by both houses; and if the other house thinks proper they may likewise appoint a committee of their house, to sit in conjunction with the committee to be appointed by your Lordships, to the end that both houses may against next session of Parliament be made fully acquainted with all the

pro-

proceedings and transactions in the management of that company's affairs. By this method, if there has been any mismanagement, as seems apparent, your Lordships will be able fully to discover who have been the authors of it, you will be able to distinguish between the guilty and the innocent: The characters of the latter will thereby be vindicated from those jealousies and suspicions they now labour under, and upon the guilty, I hope, your Lordships will inflict such penalties as may prevent all such practices for the future. This committee which I now move for ought, I think, to be chosen by ballot, and may consist of any number your Lordships shall please to appoint; seven will, I believe, be sufficient, and therefore I shall move for that number.

L—d C—t.] My Lords, I shall readily agree with this motion, because I think we have met with so little satisfaction as to the particular affair we have enquired into, that it is incumbent upon us, we are for the honour and dignity of this house, and in duty to our country bound to proceed further, and to make a general enquiry into the whole management of that company's affairs, ever since the year 1720. The creditors of the publick ought always to be under the special care of the publick; and as this house has joined with the other parts of the legislature in vesting almost the whole debts of the nation in the three great companies of *East-India, Bank,* and *South-Sea,* your Lordships are, I think, in honour obliged to take care that the creditors of the publick shall not be cheated by those, whom they may from time to time chuse to be directors of their affairs.---This, my Lords, ought always to be our care, but more especially when some very odd pieces of management appear even at the bar of our own house. If the books of the *South-Sea* company had been kept in a distinct and regular manner, it would have been easy for your Lordships to have had all the satisfaction that could have been desired, either with respect to the general state of that company's affairs, or with respect to any particular branch of their business; but from the enquiry we have already made it appears, that the books of that company have been kept in a very confused and irregular manner; altogether unintelligible to those who are strangers to the management of their affairs, and cannot, we find, be explained even by those who are the book-keepers and servants of the company. From hence, I think there is great cause to suspect some lurking frauds, and that their books were kept in this manner with design to conceal some practices which the managers durst not expose to publick view.---This consideration alone is sufficient, in my opinion, to engage your Lordships to enter into a general enquiry as to the affairs of that company; and since it appears that such an enquiry must take up a very long time, and will require

an exact scrutiny into many volumes of books of account, I think the only effectual way of carrying on such an enquiry will be, to appoint a committee for that purpose, to sit during the recess of Parliament, in order that they may have time to prepare matters, and to put the accounts of that company into as distinct and clear a method as is possible between this and next session of Parliament; for which reason I am for agreeing with the motion made by the noble Lord near me.

D—ke of N—le.] My Lords, I shall always be ready to join in any measure which I think proper and consistent with our constitution, for enquiring into the management of any publick affair, when such enquiry becomes necessary; but as to the appointing such a committee as is now proposed, I must think it is neither proper nor consistent with our constitution. I even doubt, if such a committee can be appointed any other way, than by an act of Parliament; for if this house should assume a power of appointing such a committee, it would be giving in some measure a perpetual Being to this house; it would be putting it out of his Majesty's power to prorogue the house; for if we did not sit as a house, we might be always sitting as a committee; we might delegate what power we pleased to such committees, we might make them of what number we pleased; we might even order, that every Lord that came should have a Vote. If such a committee should be appointed, it would not be easy, to confine it to any particular affair recommended to them by the house; they might find pretences to enquire into any other affair they pleased, as being some way connected with that into which they had been appointed to enquire; thus they might extend their enquiries into all the publick affairs of the nation, and into all the business of the administration. A committee of both houses sitting during the recess of Parliament, with power to send for persons, papers, and records, and without any restraint upon that power, would be a most terrible thing, and might be turned to the oppression of many of his Majesty's best subjects. -- But granting, that the appointing of such a committee, in the manner now proposed, is consistent with our constitution, yet, it is a very extraordinary method of proceeding, and therefore ought never to be practised but in matters of the greatest consequence, and as such require the utmost dispatch, neither of which can be so much as pretended with respect to the affair in hand. It is so far otherwise, that, in my opinion, there has nothing of a fraud appeared in the late management of the *South-Sea* company's affairs, from any enquiries we have made. It has, my Lords, been made appear at your bar, that the produce of the late directors estates was all applied to the benefit of the proprietors, by paying off the company's debts; and if such application was made without the di-

directions of a general court, it was only a miſtake as to form, it was only neglecting to have that expreſs approbation, which the directors might have had from any general court of that company; and as that was a publick tranſaction, and well known to all the proprietors, their never having found fault with it in any general court of that company, held ſince that time, is, in my opinion, a tacit approbation of what was then done.——But if it had actually appeared to us, that there had been frauds committed, if any of your Lordſhips are ſuſpicious of ſuch a thing, you may, at the beginning of next ſeſſion of Parliament, enter upon ſuch an enquiry, and may certainly finiſh it before the end of the ſeſſion: In the mean time, neither the affair itſelf, nor the company, nor any private perſon, can ſuffer by the delay: It is not ſo much as ſuſpected, that any Gentleman, concerned in the late management of that company's affairs, will withdraw; and the books of the company, and all the papers neceſſary for ſuch an enquiry, muſt remain in the ſtate they are now in: It is not to be ſuppoſed, any of them will be altered, or deſtroyed, becauſe the affairs of that company are now under the management of a quite different ſet of Gentlemen, who will certainly never permit any thing to be done, to thoſe that may involve them in the guilt of other men.——In ſhort, my Lords, whatever ſtate the company's affairs may be in, as there does not appear to us any complaint among the proprietors of that company, ſince no application has been made to us by them, I can ſee no neceſſity for our entering upon it immediately; and, for that end, to make ſuch an encroachment upon our conſtitution, as would be made by appointing a committee in the manner propoſed; therefore I cannot agree to it.

E——l of C————ld.] My Lords, the appointing ſuch a Committee, is no way inconſiſtent with our Conſtitution, but has been frequently practiſed, and is often neceſſary for preparing things to be laid before the next Seſſion of Parliament. From ſuch a Committee nothing is to be dreaded by any but thoſe who have been guilty of Crimes, and under a juſt and prudent Adminiſtration, Criminals ought never to be left at eaſe; it ought always to be the Lot of the guilty to be under continual fears and apprehenſions; it is what they always will be, whether we appoint ſuch a Committee or no. It will be impoſſible for this Houſe, or any Committee we ſhall appoint, to examine ſo many voluminous books of accounts, or to extract any Thing that may be clear and ſatisfactory, out of ſuch a heap of confuſion, during ſuch a ſhort time as that of the uſual continuance of one Seſſion of Parliament.——As to there being no Application from the Proprietors, it is of no manner of ſignification in the preſent caſe: It is well known, that there are loud complaints againſt the late management of that Company's affairs, and from what we have ſeen and heard at our own Bar, it appears, that theſe Complaints are not altogether groundleſs. Our having had no application from the Proprietors of that Company, made to us, is ſo far from being an argument againſt our entering upon an enquiry, that it is a ſtrong argument for it: Conſidering what we hear without doors, and have ſeen within doors, the want of ſuch an application ought to be a convincing proof, that moſt of thoſe who uſually compoſe the general Courts of that Company, are under an influence which prevents their looking into their own affairs: But conſider, my Lords, that among the Proprietors, there are many widows and orphans, many who cannot appear at general Courts, or look into the management of their own affairs; theſe are properly under your care, and I hope your Lordſhips will never think any time ill ſpent, in doing what may prevent the entire ruin of the widow, and the fatherleſs.——The Proprietors of publick ſtocks never come to either Houſe of Parliament to complain, till their affairs are paſt redreſs; as long as they can ſell their property at any price, they are afraid of applying for redreſs, left the current price of their property ſhould thereby be diminiſhed; therefore they never come to complain as long as there is any thing left. Then indeed, they reſolve upon applying to parliament, and, upon ſuch occaſions, we generally find, that women and children are the greateſt Sufferers.——To conclude, as neither your Lordſhips nor the publick have received any ſatisfaction from the enquiry hitherto made, it is become neceſſary for us to appoint ſuch a Committee as has been moved for, becauſe if this Seſſion ſhould break up without proceeding any further than we have yet done, it will be believed, that the whole affair is at an end; from thence there may be conjectures made derogatory both to the honour and dignity of this Houſe; and therefore I am for agreeing with the motion.

The E——l of S————d declared for the motion, but ſaid, as the laſt Committee of that nature had conſiſted of 12 Lords, therefore he would propoſe that the motion ſhould be for appointing a Committee of 12; which L——d B————ſt approved of.

Beſides the Lords before-mentioned, the B——p of L——n ſpoke for the motion, and the E——l of I——ay, the E——l of W——th, the L——d V——t F——th, and the B——p of B——r againſt it; at laſt the queſtion being put, it was carried in the negative without any diviſion; upon which there was a proteſt, which ſee p. 295.

After this nothing extraordinary happened in either Houſe of Parliament, and upon *Wedneſday* the 11th of *June*, his Majeſty came to the houſe of Peers, and gave the Royal Aſſent to ſeveral Bills. See p. 322.

Then

Then his Majesty made a most gracious speech to both Houses of Parliament. See p. 324.

And after that the Lord Chancellor, by his Majesty's Command, prorogued them to *Thursday* the 26th of *July* next. From thence they were prorogued to *October* 9, from thence to *November* 25, and from thence to *January* 17, when they sat to do business.

N. B. *If any material omission or mistake has been made in our account of these proceedings or speeches we shall be very ready to amend it on notice given.*

The Reader is desir'd to correct the following and what other errors may have escap'd us in the Hurry we are oblig'd to be in at the Conclusion of every Month.

PAge 47. column 1. line 29. for *Sheffield* read *Chesterfield.* p. 102. col. 1. l. 43. for *Relict* r. *Wife,* p. 111. col. 2. at the end of line 23. dele *who.* p. 472. col. 1. l. 45. for *February* r. *September.* p. 487. col. 2. for *Fieding* r. *Fielding.* 5 lines farther for *Slips* r. *Sips.* p. 658. col. 2. for *likewise* r. *likeness* 18. lines farther for *forture* r. *torture.* p. 659. col. 2. for *guileless* r. *guiltless.* p. 662. col. 1. l. 11. for *Bp* of London r. *Bp* of Lincoln. p. 663. col. 1. l. 9. instead of *Richard Talbot, who in the Reign of William the Conqueror was the Senior Earl of this Kingdom* r. *Richard Talbot, Esq; who lived in the Reign of William the Conqueror.* *Note,* The Earldom of *Shrewsbury* is the Senior Earldom in the Kingdom.

The following POEMS *are inserted to make some variety, and to oblige such of our readers in particular, who, we are sensible, don't much relish political affairs.*

The RIDDLE *in No.* 35. *for* NOV. p. 601. *answer'd. By* J. B.

THy parents, the journals, we num'rous confess,
And tedious, and noisy, and apt to increase:
We thank thee for saving our time and expence,
By purging the language, and keeping the sense ;
Thy progress is monthly, and monthly thy name;
And parties to thee we perceive are the same.
Whether stitch'd in blue paper, or bound for his highness,
In spite of thy mystical pages and shyness,
We know thee full well by thy *Gentleman's* mien ;
And thy sirname—in short—is, at length, MAGAZINE.

The following piece is taken from the second Edition of a collection of Poems on several Occasions, written by Mr Bancks, *and first publish'd last Winter by Subscription.*

On FALLING in LOVE.

WHO can describe, in numbers fit,
All the new pangs by lovers found,
When undesigning first they meet,
Give and receive the destin'd wound ?

Who can ? yet since this friendly lay
Damon demands, O muse rehearse
What govern'd fancy bids thee say——
May *Phœbus* aid the flowing verse !

Love wears a thousand diff'rent forms,
He wins the heart a thousand ways:
Now like a deity he storms;
Now in disguise the soul betrays.

As varied in the anguish felt,
When *two* begin to grow *the same :*
With stifled heat some inly melt;
While some confess, and urge their flame.

Yet would the GOD to nature bend,
His boundless sway could law restrain;
Thus might I paint him to my friend,
Thus state the measures of his reign.

Two chosen names, on fate's long roll,
In the same character he reads:
Remarks the frame of either soul,
And, unobserv'd, in both proceeds.

Occasion, bound by firm compact,
The place, the time, the cause contrives:
Brings them together, to transact
Some common business of their lives.

Expects my *Damon* I should tell
Of love's activity and force ?
The light'ning I could paint as well,
That pierces all things in it's course!

It enters——in the breast it stays——
(Believe it done as soon as thought !)
About the heart it kindling plays——
It takes——by all the soul 'tis caught.

The generous youth, the first on fire,
Looks kinder things than others speak ;
And sighs, and broken words conspire,
In vain, his mighty thoughts to break.

IIe

He views the nymph, while o'er her
   cheeks
The red and white alternate flow;
'Till, sympathetic, (what he seeks)
Her soul like his begins to glow.

Disorder'd now, the boy perceives,
And, eager, fans the kindled fire:
'Till her heart pants, her bosom heaves;
And the whole maid is one desire!

Now both submit, love only sways—
They talk, they toy, they burn, they gaze,
Send forth, and mix incessant rays;
'Till all their souls unite and blaze.

But O the raptures that succeed,
And bless the flame divinely pure!
Strong as the sun, themselves they feed,
And, like his beams, they still endure!

*Verses designed to be printed under Capt.
Gulliver's head in* Faulkner's *new Dublin edition of Dr* Swift's *works.*

HEre, learn from moral truth, and wit
   refin'd,
How vice and folly have debas'd mankind,
Strong sense, and humour arm in virtue's
   cause;
Thus her great vot'ry vindicates her laws:
While bold and free the glowing colours
   strike;
Blame not the painter, if the picture's like.

The following humorous Fable from Dublin
*comes opportunely for a place in this
supplement. Our correspondent assures
us it is generally attributed to the person in the world most admir'd for his
witty performances, but that one Mr
B——, fancying himself to be disadvantageously treated therein, had demanded
a promise of the supposed author to disown it, in a letter to the said Mr B——,
which was agreed to, on condition that
Mr B—— should make the letter publick.*

On the Words, BROTHER PROTESTANTS,
and FELLOW CHRISTIANS.

AN inundation, says the fable,
   O'erflow'd a farmer's barn and stable;
Whole ricks of hay and stacks of corn
Were down the sudden current borne,
While things of heterogeneous kind
Together float with tyde and wind:
The generous wheat forgot his pride,
And sail'd with litter side by side,
Uniting all, to shew their amity,
As in a general calamity;
A ball of new-dropt horse's dung,
Mingling with apples in the throng,
Said to the pippin plump and prim,
See, brothers! how *we* apples *swim.*

Thus *Lamb,* renown'd for cutting corns,
An offer'd fee from *Ratcliff* scorns;
Not for the world! *we doctors, brother,*
Must take no fees from one another.
Thus to a dean some curate sloven
Subscribes, dear sir, *your brother loving.*
Thus all the footmen, shoeboys, porters,
About saint *James's* cry *we courtiers!*
Thus *H—ce* in the house will prate,
Sir——*we ministers of state.*
Thus at the bar the booby B——,
Tho' half a crown out-pays his sweat's
   worth,
Who knows in law nor text nor margent,
Calls *Singleton* his brother sergeant:
And thus *fanatick saints,* tho' neither in
Doctrine or discipline our brethren,
Are *brother protestants* and *christians,*
As much as *Hebrews* and *Philistians.*
But in no other sense than nature
Hath made a rat our fellow creature,
Lice from your body suck their food,—
But is a louse your flesh and blood?
Tho' born of human filth and sweat, it
May be said man did beget it;
But maggots in your nose and chin
As well may claim you for their kin.
Yet criticks may object, why not?
Since lice are brethren to a *Sc—t.*
Which made our swarm of sects determine
* Employments for their brother vermin.
But be they *Irish, English, Scottish,*
What protestant can be so sottish,
While o'er the church these clouds are
   gathering,
To call a swarm of lice their brethren?
As *Moses* by divine advice
In *Egypt* turn'd the dust to lice,
And as our sects by all descriptions,
Have hearts more harden'd than *Egyptians;*
As from the trodden dust they spring,
And turn'd to lice infest the King;
For pity's sake it would be just,
A rod should turn them back to dust.
Let folks in high or holy stations
Be proud of owning such relations,
Let courtiers hug them to their bosom,
As if they were afraid to lose 'em;
While I with humble *Job* had rather
Say to corruption, thou'rt my father:
For he that has so little wit
To nourish vermin, may be bit.

* Alluding to what is advanc'd in *The
Presbyterians Plea of merit for taking
off the Test in Ireland impartially examin'd.*

INDEX

INDEX *to the Poetical* ESSAYS.

We return Thanks to our kind Correfpondents for
the Share they have contributed to this Poetical
Collection.